ENCYCLOPAEDIA

OF

MEDICAL ASTROLOGY

By

HOWARD LESLIE CORNELL, M.D., LL.D.

(Honorary Professor of Medical Astrology at the First National
University of Naturopathy and Allied Sciences, Newark, N. J.)

Author Of
"Astrology and the Diagnosis of Disease", 1918
A Bound Volume of His
"Magazine Articles on Medical and Biblical Astrology", 1924

Member Of
The New York Psychical Research Society; National Geographic Society;
The British Institute of Medical Astrology and Metaphysical Science;
Permanent Member of the National Eclectic Medical Association.

Formerly
National Secretary of the National Astrological Society of the United States,
and of the American Astrological Society.

Published By
THE CORNELL PUBLISHING COMPANY
3108 Humboldt Street
Los Angeles, California, U. S. A.
1933

LONDON
L. N. Fowler & Co.
7, Imperial Arcade, Ludgate Circus, E. C. 4

Astrologically Yours,

H. L. Cornell, M. D., D. A.

Volume 2

LETTER OF INTRODUCTION

FIRST NATIONAL UNIVERSITY OF NATUROPATHY

AND

ALLIED SCIENCES

143 ROSEVILLE AVENUE
NEWARK, N. J.

COMBINING
N. J. COLLEGE OF OSTEOPATHY
MECCA COLLEGE OF CHIROPRACTIC
U. S. SCHOOL OF NATUROPATHY
U. S. SCHOOL OF PHYSIOTHERAPY

February 3, 1933

COURSES
PROFESSIONAL AND POST GRADUATE
3 YEARS OF 9 MONTHS EACH
4 YEARS OF 7 MONTHS EACH
4 YEARS OF 9 MONTHS EACH

TO WHOM IT MAY CONCERN:

I have examined the preliminary sheets of the work on Medical Astrology by Doctor H.L. Cornell, and this work will be a monument to Doctor Cornell, and to Astro-Science.

It is a Work that should be in every Astrologian's Library for study and reference. As soon as this book is off the Press, the First National University of Naturopathy will make it one of the standard Textbooks for the Chair in Astro-Pathological Diagnosis.

We have known Doctor Cornell for many years, and have given him our highest Honors. He has spent the best years of his life in research study along the lines of Medical Astrology, and also used this knowledge to practical advantage in his many years of Practice as a Physician. This Encyclopaedia is the only book of its kind ever attempted in the history of the World, as far as we know, and it gathers together the knowledge along the lines of Medical Astrology in a way that students can get at it, as subjects are all arranged alphabetically.

We trust the book will be well-received, and appreciated by the Astrological and Scientific World, and by Healers of all Schools who are interested in Astrology as an aid in Pathological Diagnosis, Prognosis, and in the etiological factors in knowing more about the Philosophy of Disease, and the Planetary Causes of Disease.

Respectfully,

F.W. Collins, M.D., A.M., Dean

Frederick W. Collins, M.D.,A.M.,Dean
FIRST NATIONAL UNIVERSITY OF
NATUROPATHY AND ALLIED SCIENCES.

ABBREVIATIONS AND SYMBOLS USED IN THIS BOOK

ABBREVIATIONS—

affl.—afflicted, afflicting.
apply.—applying, apply.
A.P.—(See Vertebrae).
Asc.—Ascendant.
asp.—aspect.
asps.—aspects.
AT.—(See Vertebrae).
AX.—(See Vertebrae).
B.—birth.
Card.—Cardinal.
Chap.—Chapter.
Coc.—Coccyx.
C.P.—(See Vertebrae).
d.—days.
Dec.—Decanate, Declination.
Decan.—Decanate.
decumb.—decumbiture.
decr.—decrease, decreasing.
deg.—degree, degrees.
Desc.—Descendant.
Dir.—Direction, Directed.
E.—East, Equinox.
Eq., Equi.—Equinox.
espec.—especially.
Fem.—Feminine, Female.
Fig.—Figure.
gd.—good.
H.—House.
Horo.—Horoscope.
Hor'y Q.—Horary Questions.
H.P.—(See Vertebrae).
incr.—increasing, increase.
infl.—influenced, influence.
ill-dig.—Ill-dignified.
1001 N.N.—1001 Notable Nativities.
K.P.—(See Vertebrae).

ABBREVIATIONS—

Lat.—Latitude.
Long.—Longitude.
I.C.P.—(See Vertebrae).
Li.P.—(See Vertebrae).
L.P.P.—(See Vertebrae).
Lu.P.—(See Vertebrae).
m.—months.
M.C.—The Midheaven.
M.C.P.—(See Vertebrae).
Mut.—Mutable.
N.—North.
N.N.—Notable Nativities.
No.—Number.
occi.—occidental.
ori.—oriental.
Per.—Periodic.
P.P.—(See Vertebrae).
Pr., Prog.—Progressed, Progression.
Q.—Question, Questions.
R—Retrograde.
Rev.—Revolution.
S.—South.
Sac.—Sacrum.
Sec.—Section.
sepr.—separating.
Sig.—Significator.
Sigs.—Significators.
Spl.P.—(See Vertebrae).
S.P.—(See Vertebrae).
Subs.—Subluxations.
Tr., tr.—Transit.
U.P.P.—(See Vertebrae).
V.—Vertebra, Vertebrae.
W.—West.
well-dig.—well-dignified.
y.—years.

ASPECTS—

⊻—Semi-Sextile—30°.
∠—Semi-Square—45°.
✶—Sextile—60°.
□—Square—90°.
△—Trine—120°.
⊡—Sesquiquadrate—135°.
8—Opposition—180°.
P.—Parallel.
☌—Conjunction.

SIGNS OF THE ZODIAC—

♈—Aries.
♉—Taurus.
♊—Gemini.
♋—Cancer.
♌—Leo.
♍—Virgo.
♎—Libra.
♏—Scorpio.
♐—Sagittarius.
♑—Capricorn.
♒—Aquarius.
♓—Pisces.

PLANETS—

☉—Sun.
☽—Moon.
♆—Neptune.
♅—Uranus.
♄—Saturn.
♃—Jupiter.
♂—Mars.
♀—Venus.
☿—Mercury.

OTHER SYMBOLS—

⊕—Part of Fortune.
R—Retrograde.
☊—Ascending Node.
　　Dragon's Head.
☋—Descending Node.
　　Dragon's Tail.
°—Degrees.
'—Minutes.
"—Seconds.
×—Multiplied By.
+—Plus.

THE CHART OF BIRTH

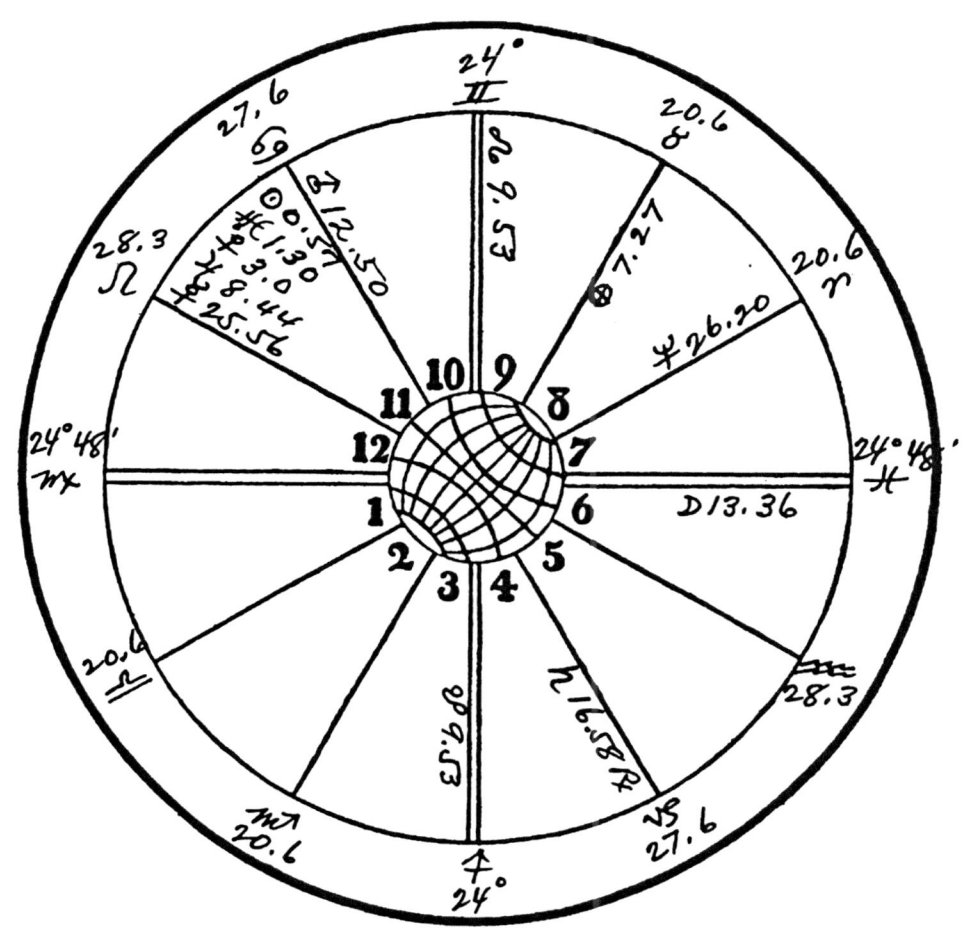

H. L. CORNELL, A.M., M.D., Ph.D.

Born July 23, 1872, 9:27 A.M.
Hartsville, Bucks County, Pennsylvania
75° W. L., 40° 12′ N. Lat.

FOREWORD

For some years in my study of Astrology as a Physician and Surgeon, and in an effort to get at the Planetary Causes of disease, I searched through the Textbooks of Astrology to find something about the disease I was treating, but my efforts were often in vain. There are many fine things said in the Textbooks along the lines of Medical Astrology, but such statements are often made at random, and in obscure places, and are not indexed. To be sure, there are classified lists of the Planets in Signs, and the diseases they cause, but in making a study of any one disease, it is almost impossible to find in the regular Textbooks and Manuals of Astrology all that has been said about this disease, and its planetary causes, and this knowledge could only be obtained by a systematic search through my entire Astrological Library. Being so inconvenienced myself, and with a desire to get the knowledge along the lines of Medical Astrology into classified shape, about fifteen years ago I conceived the idea of making this Encyclopaedia, and of arranging the Disease Subjects alphabetically, and of gathering up the material on each subject from all the Astrological books of my Library. This has been a momentous and tedious task. To begin with, I opened up a Ledger Account for each disease subject, and began a systematic digest of my entire Library, and in reading, line by line, would post the thoughts into the Ledger under each disease subject as I would come to them. By keeping up this practice for some years I eventually had two large Ledgers filled with material. Then came the task of arranging, classifying, disentangling, and writing up these ledger Articles into readable form, as each Article was posted in as read, and like a jungled mass, and without form. It took me four years to go thru this and finish the first writing entirely in English. Then, in 1928 the idea came to me that I should retype and rearrange the entire book, and type it on an Astronomical Typewriter, and use the Symbols for the Planets, Signs, and Aspects. In this second writing it was necessary to rearrange the subjects, and place many Articles under a different letter. The system of Synonyms and cross references in the book has taken a great deal of time, and to see to it that such references were in harmony. To shorten the manuscript I have used many abbreviations, and a list of these abbreviations you can find in the front of this book.

When this mass of material was straightened out, arranged, classified, and the various influences causing a disease were gotten together and studied, it has been an interesting study to note the fundamental influence and nature of the various Planets, and how these influences were in the minds of the various Writers, from the time of Ptolemy, and on down thru the Centuries until the present time, and with these facts and data before me, it has become an easy matter for me to see what influences were missing, and which have never been listed or tabulated in any book, as far as I have been able to discover, and to fill these in, and to do my part in helping to develop the Science of Medical Astrology, and get the knowledge along this line into such shape that students can get at it quickly, and by merely turning to a subject in the alphabetical arrangement. Also in this Encyclopaedia I have given attention to the Higher and Spiritual side of Astrology, to Esoteric Astrology, and have tried to arouse the readers to an inner consciousness of their Higher Powers, to rule their stars, and not be a slave to the various planetary aspects and influences which operated over them at birth, or may be manifesting themselves along thru life.

The fundamental purpose of this Encyclopaedia is to give the planetary influences which cause the various diseases, afflictions, events, accidents, and injuries of life, and to gather such knowledge under subjects, and arrange them alphabetically. I am not attempting to repeat the Classifications to be found in the various Textbooks of Astrology, and the student is asked to use this volume in connection with his other books. Also this book does not attempt to go into the Elements of Astrology, or to be a Textbook of such Elements, although many Articles do deal with these Elements, and especially as they are related to Medical Astrology, and the Diagnosis of Disease by Astrology. The student, in order to use this Encyclopaedia intelligently, should first be a student of Astrology, and to know the Elements and Fundamentals of Astrology and Astronomy, and be familiar with the Signs and Symbols of Astronomy. Also this book is not intended to be a Treatise on the various Systems of Healing, or Schools of Treatment, but to give the planetary causes and philosophy of disease, and to allow each student to use his own methods of treatment. I honor and respect all Schools of Healing, and recognize that there is good in all, but it would be impossible in a book of this kind to go into the merits of the different Schools. The Theory of Chiropractic is closely related to Astrology, due to the planetary rulerships over the Spine and Vertebrae, and I have attempted to give and list, under various diseases, the Subluxations caused by the planetary influences. It is also my desire to have students in the various Schools of Healing, and when they are studying a certain disease, to consult this Encyclopaedia on the subject in hand, and note the planetary influences which cause such disease, and to understand the philosophy of the case, and not to be satisfied merely with the treatment of the ailment. In Ancient Times all Physicians and Healers were required to know Astrology, and its relation to disease, and to the individual afflicted, as by a study of his Star Map of Birth, and the adverse Directions which might be operating over him, and such applicants for Medical, or Healing Licenses, were not allowed to become full-fledged Physicians until they could pass a satisfactory examination in Astrology. But, for various reasons, the knowledge of Astrology became more or less suppressed during the Middle Ages, but is now being revived again, and coming into its own, and is being more and more recognized as a true and Ancient Science. Physicians and Healers should lay aside their prejudices, and investigate Astrology, prove it by observation, and when they do, I feel sure they will give it its rightful place in their Schools and Colleges of Healing, and in their daily practices among their patients. In my own practice I found Astrology of inestimable value in diagnosing my cases, and to quickly determine the seat of the disease in the patient, how long they have been sick and ailing, and to form a reasonably accurate prognosis.

In this book, the Form and Shape of the body, and the planetary influences along the lines of Form, Shape, Height, Weight, Complexion, Hair, etc., are given. Also there are many Articles along the lines of Conduct, Habits, Morals, Temperament, etc. Also the prominent Fixed Stars, and their influences, are listed. Under each subject the sub-heads are arranged alphabetically for quick reference, and the student can very quickly get at the knowledge he is seeking, on any subject, as far as they are listed and recorded in this book.

One very great difficulty I have encountered in building up this Encyclopaedia has been to determine what subjects should go in, and what should be left out, and especially along the lines of Mental Traits. The Mind and Body are so closely related, and there are so many Mental Traits which are Pathological, and practically amount to a diseased Mind, that I have listed in this volume a great number of the less desirable Mental Traits, and also for a study in contrasts, some of the more desirable ones. During my years of study in the preparation of this volume I have gathered enough material for a separate Encyclopaedia, to be known as "The Encyclopaedia of Psychological Astrology", and hope soon to begin to assemble this book, and leave it to the World as the sister book to this present volume.

In the Fall of 1918, after many years of active Practice in Medical work in this Country, and in India, I gave up the Practice of Medicine, moved my family to Los Angeles, and have lived here ever since, and given my whole time to Astrology, Writing, and in the preparation of Star Maps, Horoscopes, and Astrological Health Readings for people over the World. When this Encyclopaedia is out, circulated, and established, it is my plan to make a World Lecture Tour, and speak before the various Healing Centers and Schools in the U. S. A., and other Nations, and to make an effort to have the various Faculties make Medical Astrology one of the required studies for their students who are aspiring to be Healers. I plan to have this Encyclopaedia in the prominent Public Libraries in the large Cities over the World, and also in the Occult, Metaphysical, Astrological, and Healing Centers, and where students can have access to it. I am giving this book to the World as a labor of love, and trust it will prove of great help to you and be a fitting monument to my life work.

H. L. CORNELL, M.D.

Los Angeles, Calif.
March 21st, 1933.

INTRODUCTION TO SECOND EDITION

The results which this book will produce on the readers and students will, of course, depend largely upon the attitude of mind and mental advancement in which they approach the subject with which it deals.

Many students approach metaphysical phenomena with ingrained disinclination, to accept facts and conclusions which interfere with their preconceived opinions and dogmatic, **youth-instilled** beliefs.

Readers of this category will be necessarily incapable of comprehending the **message** and helpful advice contained in the following pages.

Those who are ready, cosmically speaking, to study this subject with an open, unbiased and unprejudged mind will find, perhaps, that whilst they can accept factors stated, they cannot reconcile themselves to PROGRESS—progress in thought, progress in the application thereof, no matter how sane they may appear to them.

The exposition as portrayed by Dr. Cornell in his treatise of something new, that has been suppressed for the past century, is but the beginning of a NEW ERA in the field of the Healing Arts; whatever conclusions or repercussions may arise therefrom are but a step FORWARD in the RIGHT DIRECTION.

A science whose significance is so far reaching and whose influence on the entire field in the Healing Arts will be revolutionary, to say the least, is bound to have repercussions from the old, obsolete and, by demonstration, impractical methods belonging to the past.

But, we must not overlook the fact, that with all our so-called advancements of standards of living, we still have with us a daily floating hospital population of close to 2,500,000 sick and ailing people in these United States. What is the cause? Too many 'Doctors' or not enough? Maybe not the right kind that know how to CURE disease or to alleviate suffering? Something surely IS wrong! Maybe, after all, the ancients knew more about relieving pain and suffering when they used common sense remedies, such as herbs, teas, poultices, made from various roots, plants and foliage.

Everything in this world was created for a well-defined and special purpose, including the stars, which were the first LINK between Man and the Heavens. The ancients knew well how to interpret the influence of these stars, especially that of the planets, upon ALL things terrestrial, including our health.

One of the most ancient and most reliable writers on this subject, Ptolemy, in his Quadripartite on the influence of the Stars, makes special reference to the stellar influence regarding localities north or south of the equator. Nicholas Culpepper, in his treatise on English Herbs (edition of 1695) allocates not less than 369 herbs to the various planets and their correlation to the Healing Arts. L. D. Broughton, M.D., in his work on this subject (Elements of Astrology) brings out very potent and convincing factors that the stars were made for something other than for professional 'Star-gazers' to look at.

An eminent Viennese medico, Dr. Friedr. Feerhov, as late as 1914, blazed the trail in Europe by publishing an astro-medical treatise, setting forth the close relationship between physical manifestation and metaphysical influence, between chemistry and biochemistry and alchemical allocation of human types.

At that time his 'findings and observations' were ridiculed by whom? By such who **"Were down on something on which they were not up on!"** It is the same today, albeit in a lesser way. After all, whenever I hear 'people' talking against something they do not know anything about, I am reminded of Shakespeare's lines in Julius Caesar, act I, scene III: "And that which would appear offence in us, His countenance, like richest alchemy, will change to VIRTUE and to WORTHINESS."

All good things take time! Ever since the beginning of the Aquarian age new systems within the healing arts have been proposed and expounded. Yet, the attacks made against all and everyone by the old, intrenched and well organized medical oligarchy (serum trusts and patent medicine vendors) have wrought havoc within the ranks of progressive exponents. Yet, with all the opposition, the 'old' must give way to the 'young' and the same holds good in medicine.

Disease is caused by retention of septic matter within the body; cure can be effected only by elimination of such septic retentions. The homeopathic and naturopathic systems have done more good than all the allopaths together.

I am well aware of the consequences of this statement, but, having graduated from both schools I know whereof I speak. Anyone, who is sceptically inclined, is advised to read: "Devils, Drugs and Doctors." (Howard W. Haggard, M.D., 1929.)

At the present time, there is a revolutionary trend within the ranks of the orthodox practitioners against the dictum of the medical trust. Yet, with all their wrangling they are not able to diminish the present day, ever-increasing 2,500,000 daily floating hospital population in the United States. Something is wrong somewhere. But the guilty parties are too stubborn to admit defeat from within. It will come from without.

The natural methods of healing, when well understood and judiciously applied, bring results. They fail only when suffocated herbs are used; this latter happens quite often lately, more so since the universal use of transparent water-proof wrapping material which excludes all oxygen not only from foods, but also from therapeutics. No wonder cancer has increased by leaps and bounds since the initiation of this oxygen-excluding wrapping material.

But, we are not interested in 'health-destroying' agencies; the point is to introduce something that WILL alleviate human suffering, and Dr. Cornell's book is one link in the long chain of Real Healing.

It might not be amiss to mention that Dr. Cornell, in his later years of life, became a loyal follower of the great genius, Emanuel Swedenborg, who, albeit not having been a licentiate of any orthodox school, laid the foundation of naturopathic principles.

Undoubtedly, Dr. Cornell gleaned many valuable pointers from Swedenborg's doctrines.

Dr. Cornell, whom, unfortunately I met too late and lost too soon, has built himself an everlasting monument; the future generation will honor him alongside the great souls, such as Pasteur, Koch, Lavoisier, Roentgen, Florence Nightingale, Lord Lister, for his contribution to mankind.

R. I. P.

HENRY J. GORDON, M. D., A. M., N. D., PH. D. *h. c.*

Los Angeles, California
Easter, 1939

LUMBAR—The Lumbar Region—Lumbar Vertebrae—The Lumbar Region is ruled by ♎. The Lumbar Vertebrae are under the structural rulership of ♎. The bones and nerves of this region are ruled by ♎. For influences concerning the Lumbar Ganglia, and also the Lumbar branches of the Solar Plexus, see Ductless Glands (see Ductless); "Basal Ganglia", "Lumbar Ganglia", under Ganglion.

Circulation In — Obstruction of — ♄ affl. in ♐; ♄ in ♐, ☌, □ or ☍ ♃ or ♀; Subs at PP, UPP, LPP.

Cold and Chill In—Organic Weakness In—♄ affl. in ♎.

Diseases Of—♎ diseases, and afflictions in ♎.

Fifth Lumbar Nerve—Obstruction of —♄ in ♐ in □ or ☍ ♃.

Neuralgia In — ♅, ♂, or ☿ affl. in ♎; Subs at PP, and LPP.

Organic Weakness In — (See "Cold" in this section).

Pain In—♂ in ♎ in the 6th H., or affl. the ☽ or Asc. (See "Neuralgia" in this section).

Vertebrae—(See "Lumbar" under Vertebrae).

Weakest Part—Lumbar Region Weakest Part—The ☉ or ♃ affl. in ♎, or ♎ on the Asc.

LUMINOUS — Luminous Gas In the Spinal Canal—(See Ether; "Canal" under Spine).

LUMPISH APPEARANCE—In Hor'y Q. ♄ Sig. in ♉. (See Corpulent, Fat, Fleshy, Plump, Short, Stout).

LUMPS — Lump — Lumpy — Generally caused by the afflictions of ♄ and ♂, and in the parts ruled by the Signs containing these planets at B. Also caused by ♃ or ♀, due to disturbed circulation in a part. (See Abscesses, Boils, Bruises, Cysts, Deposits, Enlargements; "Hardening" under Faeces; "Lump" under Feet; Growths, Hurts, Injuries, Stone, Swellings, Tumors, Wart, Wen, etc.).

LUNACY — Insanity — The subject of Lunacy is more fully considered under the subject of Insanity, and the influences given here are supplemental to those in that Article. Lunacy is a disease of the ☽, and is called Lunacy after Luna, Lunar, the ☽, and lunacy patients are more affected, agitated, restless, or raving at the time of the Full ☽. (See "Full Moon" under Moon). If ♃ or ♀ are ori. or angular, and have any configuration with the ☽, it is curable. If the ☽ is with ♃ it can be cured by medicine. If the ☽ is with ♀ it will cure itself. If the Benefics be cadent or occidental, and the malefics oriental, the disorder will be incurable. Other influences causing Lunacy are ♂ in evil asp. the ☽ at the Full, or ♄ at a change in ♐ or ♓; ♂ afflicting the ☽ and ☿, and the ☽ in □ or ☍ ☿, causes violent lunacy. Epilepsy and Insanity are very closely associated. (See Epilepsy, Insanity). Case—Child Born of a Mad Mother In a Lunatic Asylum—See "Mad Mother", No. 074; "Obsession", No. 130, in 1001 N.N.

LUNAR — From the Latin word Luna, the Moon.

Lunar Activities Depleted This is so at the time of the New ☽, the First Quarter, at the Full, and at the Last Quarter. (See Eclipses; Decrease, Full Moon, New Moon, Quarters, under Moon).

Lunar Diseases — (See "Lunar Diseases" under Moon).

Lunar Eclipses — (See Eclipses; Full Moon, New Moon, under Moon).

Lunar Epoch—(See Prenatal Epoch).

Lunar Functions—(See "Action" of the Moon", and the various paragraphs under Moon).

Lunar Horas—(See Horas).

Lunar Power Weakened — (See "Lunar Activities" in this section).

Semi-Lunar—(See Ganglion).

Solar-Lunar Activities—(See Solar).

LUNATICS—(See Insanity, Lunacy).

LUNATIONS—These are a New or Full ☽ which coincide with, or immediately precede, a dangerous accident or severe illness, and are important influences to study in connection with an illness, or the nature and immediate cause of an accident, hurt, or injury. When a Lunation falls on the place of one of the malefics in the radical map, trouble, anxiety, or illness are apt to result, and especially if there is an adverse primary direction operating over the nativity at the same time. (See Directions; "Threatened", "Time", under Disease; Eclipses, Insanity; Full Moon, New Moon, under Moon).

Periodic Lunation—(See Periodic).

LUNGS — Organs of Respiration — Respiratory System — Pulmonary — Bronchial — Pleura, etc. — The Lungs are ruled principally by ☿ and the ♊ sign, the 3rd and 4th Houses, and are influenced, or afflicted by all the common signs, and by the four cadent houses, when such are occupied by planets at B. The common signs, as ♊, ♍, ♐, and ♓, all affect the lungs, and rule them by their internal government. The upper lobes of the lungs are ruled by ♊, are under the internal rulership of ♊, and the lower lobes are ruled by the ♋ sign. Jupiter also rules the lungs, and in the Astral Body ♃ has direct relation to the lungs. The Bronchial Tubes are especially ruled by ♊. (See Bronchial). The Chest Cavity as a whole, and as a receptacle, is ruled by the ☽. (See Chest Trunk). The Arteries of the lungs are ruled by ♃, and ♀ rules the veins. The Pleura, the lung coverings, are ruled by ♃ and the ♋ sign, and also influenced by afflictions in ♊, and other common signs. The ♉, ♊, and ♋ signs rule the Respiratory System, and afflictions in any of these signs tend to affect the organs of Respiration. The 3rd Dorsal Vertebra, Lu.P., is the Lung Place in the Spine. (See Breath, Pleura, Pulmonary, Throat). The Tidal Air in the lungs is ruled by the ☽.

Absorbent Vessels—Of the Lungs Affected—(See Absorption).

Acute Disorders—(See "Acute" under Bronchial, Phthisis; "Pleurisy" under Pleura; Pneumonia, Psittacosis).

Afflictions In — (See "Pulmonary Affections", and the various paragraphs in this section).

Air—(a) Air Cells of the Lungs—☿ in ♉, ♊, or ♋ rules and affects the air cells, the breath, windpipe, and nerves of the Lungs and Respiratory System. (See "Air Cells" under Cells). (b) Tidal Air—Of the Lungs, ruled by the ☽. (See Tidal).

All Diseases In—Signified by the 4th H.

Altitude — The Lungs as Affected by Altitude—(See Altitude).

Anaemia — As a Cause of Lung Disorders—(See Anaemia).

Angina—(See Angina).

Apoplexy Of—Pulmonary Apoplexy—(See "Pulmonary" under Apoplexy).

Asthma—Phthisic—(See Asthma).

Blood In Lungs—Poor Circulation of —♄ or ☋ ☌ ♃ in ♊ tends to poor circulation of the arterial blood in the lungs, and ♄ or ☋ ☌ ♀ in ♊, poor circulation of the venous blood. (See "Poor Circulation" under Circulation; Congestion). Jupiter afflicted in ♉, ♊, or ♋ tends to Pleurisy and Blood Impurities of the Respiratory System. (See "Impure Blood" under Impure).

Breath — Breathing — Disorders of — (See the various paragraphs under Breath).

Bronchial Affections—(See Bronchial).

Capacity—Good Lung Capacity—Good Lung Expansion—Full Chest—♃ well-aspected in the Asc. (See Chest).

Capillaries—Of the Lungs—(a) Contracted and Spasmodic Action of—♅ in ♊. (See Oxygenation). (b) Obstruction of—Afflictions in ♊; ♄ affl. in ♊; afflictions of ♄ to ♃ or ♀ in ♊; the prog. ☽ ☌ ♄ in ♊ in the radix; a New ☽ in ♊ ☌ ♄ in ♊; a New ☽ afflicting the ♊ sign, and malefics in □ or ☍ to ♊. (See Capillaries, Obstruction). (c) Oxygenation — Capillary Oxygenation Disturbed—♅ affl. in ♊. (See Oxygenation). (d) Restricted—Spasmodic Contraction of—♅ in ♊. (See Oxygenation).

Cases of Lung Trouble — Birth Data, etc.—See Fig. 4A, 4B, 4C, 6A, 9C, 19C, in the book "Astro-Diagnosis" by the Heindels; Fig. 16, 25, 26, 35, in the book, "Message of the Stars" by the Heindels. Also see Chap. XIII in Daath's Medical Astrology.

Catarrh Of — The ☽ affl. in ♊. (See "Catarrh" under Bronchial; Catarrh).

Cells—Air Cells of Lungs—(See "Air" in this section).

Chest—Colds In—Congested and Feverish—(See Colds, Congestion, Feverish, in this section).

Chronic Disorders In — (See Asthma; "Chronic" under Bronchial; Consumption, Phthisis, Pleurisy, Tuberculosis).

Circulation In — Poor Circulation — (See "Blood" in this section).

Colds On Chest—Cold In—♅ in ♊; ♅, ♆, or ♄ in ♓ and afflicting the ☉ or ☽; the ☽ affl. in ♓; ♄ or ♂ affl. in ♊ or ♐. (See "Bronchitis" under Bronchial; "Tightness" under Chest; Cold, Colds, Cough, Expectoration, Pleurisy, Pneumonia).

Congestion of Lungs — Pulmonary Congestion—The ☽ in ♊, ☌, or ☍ ♄; ♄ affl. in ♉, ♊, or ♋; ♄ ☌ ♃ or ♀ in ♊; ♃ or ♀ affl. in ♊; ♂ affl. in ♊, congested and feverish; many planets in lung signs and affl. by ♄; the afflicted bodies in ♒, as ♒ rules largely over the circulation. (See Asthma; "Congestion" under Bronchial; Consumption; Blood, Pulmonitis, in this section). Case of Congestion—See Chap. XIII in Daath's Medical Astrology.

Consumption Of — Pulmonary Consumption—(See Consumption, Phthisis, Tuberculosis, Wasting). Case — See Daath, Chap. XIII.

Convulsive Movements — Spasmodic Lung Cough—♅ in ♊. (See "Convulsive" under Cough).

Cough — Lung Cough — Hard, Dry, Spasmodic Lung Cough—♅ in ♊. (See "Cough" under Bronchial; "Lung Cough" under Cough; "Spasmodic" in this section).

Crystallization — Hardening — Of the Lung—♄ affl. in ♊. (See Consumption, Crystallization, Hardening).

Death — From Lung Disease — Death by Inflammation of the Lungs—♃ affl. the hyleg by dir., and ♃ much afflicted at B. and holding the dominion of death; ♃ shows; afflictions in common signs, and espec. in ♊; ♄ in the 8th H., and affl. the hyleg, and ♄ in ♊. (See "Death" under Bronchial, Consumption).

Defect—Some Defect In the Lungs—Born under ♃. (See Defects; "Structural" in this section).

Deficient Respiration—Due To Tight Lacing and Indiscretions In Dress—♀ affl. in ♉, ♊, or ♋. (See "Indiscretions" under Dress).

Diseased Lungs—Disordered Lungs—Trouble In the Lungs—The ☉ ☌ ♄ in ♓; ♄ affl. in ♊ in the 6th H.; ♊ on the Asc. at B., and containing malefics; common signs on the angles, and espec. ♊, ♐, and ♓; Subs at Lu.P. (See "Cases", "Pulmonary Affections", and the various paragraphs in this section).

Dress — The Lungs Disturbed by Improper Dress—(See "Deficient" in this section).

Dropsy — Of the Chest — Hydrothorax —(See "Dropsy" under Chest).

Dry Lung Cough — (See "Cough" in this section).

Dust Inhalation — (See "Pneumoconiosis" in this section).

Dyspnoea—(See "Labored Breathing" under Breath; Dyspnoea).

Expansion Good — (See "Capacity" in this section).

Expectoration — Great Expectoration —(See Expectoration, Mucus, Phlegm).

Feverish and Congested—♂ affl. in ♊; the ☽ in ♉ and affl. by ♄, due to obstructions near the lungs, and caused by plethora from high living. (See "Fever" under Heart; "Lung Fever" in this section).

Fibrosis In—♄ affl. in ♊. (See "Fibrosis" under Fiber).

Gas Poisoning—Death By—(See "Poisoning" under Gas).

Gemini—Diseases of the Gemini Sign —(See Gemini, Third House).

Haematosis — Pulmonary Haematosis —Disturbances of — (See Haematopoiesis).

Haemoptysis — The Expectoration of Blood—(See Haemoptysis).

Hard Lung Cough — (See "Cough" in this section).

Hardening—Of the Lungs—♄ or ☋ in ♊. (See Consumption, Hardening).

Hemorrhage — In the Lungs — The ☉ or ♆ in ♊ ☍ ♂; ♄ or ♂ in ♊, and afflicted; the prog. ☽ ☌ ♄ in ♊, the capillaries obstructed; Subs at Lu.P. (See "Hemorrhage" under Bronchial; "Vicarious" under Menses; "Capillary" in this section).

Hydrothorax — (See "Dropsy" under Chest).

Hyperaemia — Of the Lungs — The ☉ affl. in ♉, ♊, or ♋. (See Hyperaemia).

Impaired Breathing—(See Breath, Deficient, in this section).

Impurities — Blood Impurities In — (See "Blood" in this section).

Inefficiency — Pulmonary Inefficiency —(See "Lungs" under Inefficiency).

Inflammation — Of the Lungs — Pulmonitis—(See "Pulmonitis" in this section).

Inhalation of Dust — Lung Disorders From—(See "Pneumoconiosis" in this section).

Innervation — Pulmonary Innervation —(See Innervation).

Interlobar Pleurisy — (See "Pleurisy" under Pleura).

Irritations — (See Congestion, Cough, Dust, Inflammation, Obstructions, and the various paragraphs in this section).

Lacing—Bad Effects from Tight Lacing — (See "Deficient Respiration" in this section).

Left Lung—The Lower Lobes of are disturbed by afflictions in ♋. (See "Lobes" in this section).

Lobes — Of the Lungs — The upper lobes of the lungs are ruled by ♊, and the lower lobes by ♋, and the lobes are affected by afflictions in these signs. The upper lobes are more affected by Subs at Lu.P. (3D), and the lower lobes by Subs at Li.P. (4D).

Lung Cough — (See "Cough" in this section).

Lung Disease — (See "Pulmonary Affections", and the various paragraphs in this section).

Lung Fever—Croupous Pneumonia— (See Croup; "Croupous Pneumonia" under Pneumonia; "Feverish and Congested" in this section).

Lungs Weak—Lungs Weakest Part— (See Weak, Weakest, in this section).

Motion — Spasmodic Motion of the Lungs—(See Cough, Spasmodic, in this section).

Mucus In—Phlegm—(See "Bronchitis" under Bronchial; Consumption, Cough, Mucus, Phlegm, Tuberculosis).

Nerves Of — The Nerves Affected — (See "Air Cells" in this section).

Obstructions In—(a) In Bronchials— (See "Obstruction" under Bronchial). (b) Capillary — (See "Capillaries" in this section). (c) In Lungs—The ☽ or ♄ affl. in ♊; ♃ affl. in ♍; ♊ ascending at the Vernal Equi., and ☿ afflicted, Countries and Peoples under ♊ will suffer thru corrupt air, obstructions of the lungs and bronchial tubes, and by high winds. (See "Corrupt Air" under Air; "Irritations" in this section). (d) Near the Lungs, and with Fever Resulting — (See "Feverish" in this section). (e) In Windpipe—The Trachea Obstructed with Phlegm — (See "Breast" under Phlegm; Trachea).

Oedema—Of the Lungs—The ☽ affl. in ♉, ♊, or ♋; Subs at Lu.P., and KP. (See "Catarrh" under Bronchial; Oedema).

Oppressed — The Lungs Oppressed — The ☽ in ♉ or ♊, ☌, or ill-asp. ♄ (or ☿ if he be of the nature of ♄) at the beginning of an illness or at decumb., and also causes obstructions. (See Congestion, Dyspnoea, Feverish, Inflammation, Obstructions, Pain, and the various paragraphs in this section).

Organic Defects — (See "Defect" in this section).

Osmosis In — Morbid Osmosis — (See Osmosis).

Over-Activity—The ☽ in ♐, and coming to the ☍ ♃ in ♊, tends to over-activity of the lungs, stomach and nerves; the ☉ in ♐. (See Over-Activity).

Oxygenation — Disturbances of—(See Oxygen; "Capillaries" in this section).

Pain In — (See Angina; "Bronchitis" under Bronchial; "Pains" under Chest; Dyspnoea, Pleurisy, Pneumonia; "Pulmonitis" in this section).

Parenchyma—The Pulmonary Parenchyma Affected—(See Parenchyma).

Paroxysmal Dyspnoea—With Oppression—(See Asthma, Breath, Dyspnoea).

Phlegm — Phlegm and Mucus In the Lungs—(See "Bronchitis" under Bronchial; Mucous, Phlegm).

Phthisic—(See Asthma).

Phthisis — Wasting — Consumption— (See Consumption, Phthisis, Tuberculosis, Wasting).

Pleura — The Serous Membrane Enveloping the Lungs — Disorders of — Pleurisy, etc.—(See Pleura).

Plexus — Pulmonary Plexus — (See "Middle Cervical" under Ganglion).

Pneumoconiosis—The Lungs Diseased from Inhalation of Dust — ♅ or ♄ afflicted in ♊; Subs at Lu.P.

Pneumogastric Nerve—(See Pneumogastric).

Pneumonia—(See "Pneumonia" under Bronchial; Pneumonia).

Poisoning — Gas Poison — (See "Gas" in this section).

Poor Circulation — (See Blood, Congestion, Obstructions, in this section).

Prevalent — Lung Diseases Prevalent —(See "Public Health Bad" under Public).

Pulmonary Affections—Lung Trouble—Diseased Lungs—Liable to Lung Diseases—The Lungs Afflicted—Pulmonary Complaints, etc.—The ☉, ☽, ♄, ♃, or ☿ in ♓ and afflicted; the ☉ or ☽ in the 6th H. in common signs, and afflicted by malefics; the ☉ affl. in ♊ or ♐; the ☉ in ♍ and affl. by ♃; the ☉ prog. to the □ or ☍ the ♊ sign, and afflicting any planets in ♊ at B., and also at the same time a malefic in the 6th H. by transit; the ☽ in the 6th H. in common signs and afflicted; the ☽ hyleg in ♊ or ♐, and afflicted, and espec. with females; the ☽ in ♐ in ☍ to ♃ in ♊; the ☽ afflicted in ♓; ♅ ☌ ☽ in ♊ or ♐; ♄ affl. in ♊, ♐, or ♓; ♄ in ♊, angular, and direct in motion at a Vernal Ingress, tends to a great prevalence of lung disorders; a ♃ disease; ♃ in the 6th H. at B. in common signs, and affl. by the ☉ or ☽; ♃ affl. in ♊ or ♓; ♃ in ♊ in ☍ to the ☽ in ♐; ♂ in ♊ in the 6th H., and afflicted; ♂ in an angle and occi. of the ☉, and ori. of the ☽; ♂ promittor in ♓, and ☌ or ill-asp. the ☉; ♀ affl. in ♊ or ♐; ♀ in ♐ and affl. the ☽ or Asc.; ♀ affl. in ♐ in the 6th H.; ☿ affl. in ♎; ☿ in the 6th H. in common signs, and afflicted; the Asc. to the ☌ ♃ by dir., and ♃ afflicted at B.; airy signs on the Asc. and afflicted by malefics; ♊, ♐, or ♓ on cusp the 6th H.; many planets (a Stellium) in the 3rd H.; planets in ♊ in ☍ to planets in ♐; afflictions in common signs, and espec. in ♊; the malefics, or afflicting planets, in flexed or common signs; ♐ on the Asc.; afflictions in ♊, ♋, ♐, ♑, ♒, and ♓; a ♉, ♊, ♋, ♐, and ♓ disease; Subs at Lu.P., Li.P., and KP. Lung diseases and affections depend largely upon the peripheral sympathetic nerves and circulation, ruled by ♑, and upon the abdominal organs ruled by ♍. Thus chill of the skin, causing internal congestions and bowel disorders, are usually at the beginning, and the preliminary causes of lung disturbances. By keeping the bowels in proper order, and the surface of the body at an even temperature, many lung disorders and congestions can be prevented. (See Centripetal, Colds, Congestions; the various paragraphs in this section).

Pulmonitis—Inflammation of the Lungs—Pain In the Lungs—Congestion—The ☉ in ♊ or ♐, and to the ☌ or ill-asps. ♂ by dir.; the ☉ or ♂ in ♊ or ♐ at B., or by dir., and espec. if the ☉ or ☽ are afflicted by ♄ or ♂ at B.; the ☉ or ♂ afflicted in ♉, ♊, or ♋; a ♃ disease; ♃ shows death by inflammation of the lungs when much afflicted at B., and afflicting the hyleg by dir.; caused by ♃ when the dominion of death is vested in him; ♂ affl. in ♉, ♊, or ♋; ♂ affl. in ♊ or ♐, and espec. with ♂ in the 6th H. in these signs; ♂ in ♐ and affl. the ☽ or Asc.; a disease of the ♋ sign and afflictions in ♋; the ☽ in ♋ at B., and the tr. of ♂ over the radical ☽ if the ☽ is afflicted at B., and espec. if the constitution is weak; Subs at Lu.P. (See "Bronchitis" under Bronchial; "Pleurisy" under Pleura; Pneumonia).

Rapid Breathing—Rapid Dyspnoea—(See Breathing, Dyspnoea).

Residence—Lung Trouble Benefitted By—(See Altitude).

Respiratory Troubles—(See Breath).

Restricted Capillaries—(See "Capillaries" in this section).

Right Lung—Disorders In Lobes of—(See "Lobes" in this section; Left, Right).

Sclerosis—Hardening, Induration, and Thickening of the Connective Tissue of the Lungs—(See "Hardening" in this section; Sclerosis).

Spasmodic Affections—Of the Lungs—♅ affl. in ♊; ♅ in ♊ or ♐, ☌ the ☉ or ☽. (See Capillaries, Convulsive, Cough, in this section; "Spasmodic" under Breathing; Spasmodic).

Stenosis—Pulmonary Stenosis—Constriction—♄ affl. in ♊. (See "Capillaries" in this section; Constrictions, Stenosis).

Structural Defects—The ☉ in ♊ and afflicted. (See "Defect" in this section).

Suffocation—A Feeling of—(See Angina; "Labored" under Breath; Dyspnoea; Suffocation).

Tidal Air—Of the Lungs—Ruled by the ☽. (See Tidal).

Tight Lacing—Lungs and Breathing Affected By—(See "Deficient Respiration" in this section).

Tightness—Of the Chest—(See "Tightness" under Chest).

Tissues—Wasting of—♆ affl. in ♉, ♊, or ♋, and also to Consumption. (See Wasting).

Trachea—Obstructed—(See "Breast" under Phlegm; Trachea).

Trouble—Lung Trouble—(See "Pulmonary Affections", and the various paragraphs in this section).

Trunk—(See Chest, Thorax, Trunk).

Tuberculosis—(See Consumption, Phthisis, Tuberculosis, Wasting).

Ulceration—Of the Lungs—♄ in ♋ when ♄ is the afflictor in the disease; the ☽ in ♉, ☌, or ill-asp. ♄ (or ☿ when of the nature of ♄) at the beginning of the disease, or at decumbiture (Hor'y). (See Ulcers).

Upper Lobes—(See "Lobes" in this section).

Wasting—Of the Tissues—(See "Tissues" in this section).

Weak Lungs—Lungs the Weakest Part—Weak Chest and Lungs—The ☉ in the 6th H. in a cardinal sign and afflicted, weak chest; the ☽ affl. in ♓, weak lungs; ♄ ☌ or ill-asp. the ☉ in mutable signs; ♄ affl. in ♊; ♄ ☌ ♂ in ♊; ♄ in the 6th H. at B., in common signs, and affl. by the ☉ or ☽; ♄ affl. in ♓; ♃ affl. in ♊ if the native be dark in complexion; ♂ ☌ ☋ in ♊; ♂ in the 6th H. in common signs; ☿ affl. in ♊ in the 6th H.; ☿ ruler of the Asc., and in the 6th H. in ♐ or ♓, and afflicted; ☿ in ♓, ☌, or ill-asp. any of the malefics as promittors, sometimes a little lung weakness; ♊ on cusp the 6th H., and afflicted, and with malefics in ♊ in the 6th. (See Consumption, Phthisis, Pulmonary, Tuberculosis, and the various paragraphs in this section).

Windpipe Obstructed—(See "Trachea" in this section).

Winds — Easterly Winds Which Produce Bronchitis—(See "Winds" under Bronchial).

LUPUS—A Chronic Tuberculous Skin Disease—Caused by ♄; ♄ affl. in ♎ or ♑; ♄ rising and affl. the ☉ or ☽. Red color, the color of ♂, and the remedies of ♂, are good in the treatment of Lupus, as ♂ opposes, and tends to remedy and alleviate the diseases of ♄; Subs at MCP (4C), and KP. (See Red, Skin, Tuberculosis). Case of Lupus—See "Lupus", No. 363, in 1001 N.N.

LUST—Lustful—Inordinate Lust—Salacious—Wanton—Libidinous, etc.—The ☉ to the ill-asps. ♀ by dir.; the ☽ decr. and sepr. from ♂ and applying to ♀, disgrace thru wantonness; the ☽ to the ill-asps. ♀ by dir., and ♀ badly afflicted at B.; ♂ ☌ or afflicting ♀; ♂ Sig. □ or ☍ ♀; ♂ to the ☌ or ill-asp. ♀ by dir.; ♀ in ♏ and affl. by ♂; ♀ in ♏ ☌ the ☽ or ♂, unbridled or violent lust; ♀ afflicted by □ and ☍ aspects tends to turn love to lust, and espec. when afflicted by malefics; ♀ ruler of the horoscope and afflicted by malefics; ♀ in a feminine sign alone, and in ☌, □, or ☍ ♂; ♀ affl. at B., and to the ☌ or ill-asp. the Asc.; ♀ and ♂ both in masculine signs tends to make females more lustful; Fixed Stars of the nature of the ☽ and ♂ ascending at B. tend to wantonness. (See Amorous, Amours, Debauched, Degenerate, Depraved, Deviations, Disgrace, Effeminate, Excesses, Impotent, Infamous, Lascivious, Lewd, Licentious; "Adulterous" under Love Affairs; Low; "Loose Morals" under Morals;; Nymphomania, Obscene, Passion, Perversions, Pleasure, Scandal, Sex, Shameless, Virile, Wanton).

Females Lustful — (See Effeminate; "Males Nearly Impotent" under Impotent; Nymphomania, Shameless, Virile).

Health Injured—By Inordinate Lust—♂, ♅, or ♆ in the 5th H. and afflicted; ♂ ☌ or ill-asp. ♀; ♀ afflicting the Asc. at B.; ♀ in the 5th H. and afflicted by malefics; lord of the 6th in the 5th H.; lord of the 10th in the 5th H., by pleasure, or too much indulgence in improper living. (See Amorous, Harlots; "High Living" under High; "Health Injured" under Men; "Health Suffers" under Opposite Sex; "Passional Excesses" under Passion; Venereal, Venery).

Lusty Bones—(See "Healthy Bones" under Bones).

Men Lustful — (See Effeminate; "Licentious" under Men; Virile; the various references in this section).

LUXATIONS—(See Dislocations).

LUXURIANT — Luxuriant Hair — (See "Abundance" under Hair). The ♈ sign is Luxuriant. (See Aries).

LUXURIES — Luxury — Extravagance—Lavish—

Fond of Luxuries — Luxuriant Living —The ☉ afflicted in ♎ or ♓; the ☉ affl. in ♉, fond of luxuries in food, indulgence in rich foods; the ☽ Sig. ☌ ♀; the ☽ to the □ or ☍ ♃ by dir.; ♄ in ♎; ♄ Sig. in ♎, prodigal of expense (Hor'y); ♃ afflicted in ♉; ♂ affl. in ♎, a luxurious disposition; ♀ afflicted at B.; ♀ in aspect with ☿, fond of luxury; ♀ affl. in the 6th H., and ill-health from. (See Amusements, Appetites, Comforts, Conduct, Diet, Dress, Drink, Eating, Epicureans, Expense Extravagance, Feasting, Food; "Free Living" under Free; Gluttony, Habits; "High Living" under High; Ornaments, Pleasure, Prodigal, Riches, Sports, etc.).

Health Undermined — By Luxuries — (See Extravagance; "Undermined" under Health).

LYING—Liars—(See Liars).

LYMPH — Lymphatics — The Lymphatic System — Lymphatic Glands — Absorbent Glands — The Lymph is ruled by the ☽, and the ♒ and ♓ signs. Under the internal rule of ♓. The watery signs are lymphatic, and especially ♓. Venus is also lymphatic. The lymph is carried principally by the Thoracic Duct, ruled by ♋. The ☉ and ☽ acting thru the ♒ sign, and thru the Sanguineous System, affect the Lymphatic System, the nutrition of the tissues, the legs and ankles, and give way to the Splenic Diathesis. The ☽ in her last Quarter acts especially on the lymph. The ☽ in ♉, ♊, and ♋ rules and affects the absorbent and lymphatic vessels of the throat, lungs, and respiratory system. (See Absorption).

Circulation—The Circulation Is Impeded—♄ ☌, □, or ☍ ☽.

Deficiency In — ♄ or ♆ ☌ ☽; ♆ ☌ ☽, and in □ or ☍ ♃. Case—See Fig. 18A in the book, "Astro-Diagnosis", by the Heindels.

Diseases Of—Disorders of—The ☉ afflicted in watery signs; ☽ diseases, and afflictions to the ☽; the ☽ ☌ or ill-asp. ♄ or ♆ at B., and by dir.; many afflictions in watery signs at B.; ♓ on the Asc., and afflicted. (See "Diseases Of" under Glands).

Disturbed—The Lymphatics Disturbed —♂ ☌ ☽ in ♍.

Exudation — Lymph Exudation — Occurs in Eczema. (See Eczema).

Functions Of — The ☽ well-aspected in ♋ or ♓, the lymphatic and absorbent vessels are regular in their functions, and the ☽ afflicted tends to disturbed functions.

Impeded Circulation — (See "Circulation" in this section).

Inflamed—The Lymphatic Glands Inflamed, and with Fever—♂ ☌ ☽ in ♍.

Lacteals—Disorders of—♄ affl. in ♍. (See Chyle).

Leukemia—Lymphatic Leukemia—♄ affl. in ♍. (See Leukocytes).

Lungs — Lymphatic Vessels of Disordered—The ☽ affl. in ♉, ♊, ♋.

Obstructed—Impeded—(See "Circulation" in this section).

Respiratory System — Lymphatics of Disordered—☽ affl. in ♉, ♊, ♋. (See Absorption).

Signs — The Lymphatic Signs are ♋, ♏, ♓, the watery signs. (See "Signs" under Water).

Swelling—In Lymphatic Glands In the Groin—(See Bubo).

Temperament — The Lymphatic Temperament—Indolent Temperament—Ruled and given by the ☽. Also ruled by the water signs and ♀. Also ♆ is strongly associated with this Temperament, and adds his influence to the ☽, ♀, and the watery signs. This is a temperament of thinking and feeling rather than action. There is a lack of brisk vascular action in this temperament. Lethargy of the Pituitary Body is also given by this temperament. Serous discharges are also characteristic of this temperament. Also a lack of tone is given by the lymphatic temperament. This is also called the Phlegmatic Temperament, and is classed as cold and moist. (See Anaemia, Dropsy, Dull, Lassitude, Lethargy; "Cold and Moist Body" under Moisture; Pale; "Temperament" under Phlegmatic; Pituitary; "Blood" under Red; Serous; "Lymphatic" under Temperament; Tone, etc.).

Throat — Lymphatic Vessels of Affected—☽ affl. in ♉, ♊, ♋. (See Throat).

Vesicles—(See Vesicles).

LYNCHING — Lynched — Death By— ♄ afflicting the hyleg, and in signs of human form. (See "Common People" under Common; Hanging; "Human Signs" under Human; Mobs, Riots).

M

MACHINERY—Inventions—Ruled by ♅.

Accidents By—Danger By—Hurts or Injury by In the Employment—Danger of Death By—♅ afflicted at B., and by dir.; the ☉ ruler of the 9th or 10th H. at B., and the ☉ to the ☌ or ill-asp. ♅ by dir.; the ☉ to the □ or ☍ ♅ or ♂ by dir.; the ☉ directed to Praesepe or The Cratch; the ☽ to the ☌ or ill-asp. ♅ by dir. (See Electricity; "Accidents" under Employment).

Death By—In the Employment—(See "Death" under Employment; "Accidents" in this section).

Head—Hurts or Injuries To the Head by Machinery—♅ in the 1st H., and afflicted. (See "Accidents" under Head).

MADNESS — Mad — Mania — Rabid — Insane—Raving—Fury, etc. This subject is also considered under the subjects of Delirium, Frenzy, Fury, Insanity, Mania, Raving, etc. See these subjects.

Cases of Madness—Became Mad—See "Mexico", No. 824; "Mad Mother", No. 074 in 1001 N.N.

Death by Madness—Death by Fury—Accident or Injury By—☿ afflicting the hyleg, the Giver of Life, by dir.; ☿ affl. by ♂ at B., and holding the dominion of death.

Distempers—Mad and Sudden Distempers—Caused by ♂. (See Fulminating; "Sudden Distempers" under Head; Noisome; "Diseases" under Sudden).

Mad Acts—Mad and Brutish—♂ afflicted in ♈. (See Anger; "Brain Storms" under Brain; Brutish, Cruel, Excitable, Feelings, Fierce, Frenzy, Fury, Ravings, Savage; "High Temper" under Temper).

Mad Dog Bites—(See Hydrophobia).

Mad Mother—(See "Cases" in this section).

Mad with Pain — (See "Mad" under Pain).

Madness Plague—♂ affl. in ♊ or ♍, and ♂ ☌ or evil asp. the Asc. by dir.

Madness Threatened — Tendency to Madness or Mania—Causes of Madness—♂ afflictions tend to Madness and Mania, and also afflictions to ☿, and espec. ♂ afflicting ☿, the mental ruler; ♂ afflicting the ☉, and espec. ♂ □ ☉; ♂ □ ☿; ♂ ☌ the Asc. by dir.; the ☉ affl. in ♌ when the ☉ is the afflictor in the disease; the ☉ hyleg and the ☉ to the □ or ☍ ♂ by dir.; the ☽ to the ill-asps. ☿ and ☿ greatly afflicted at B.; a disease of the ☽, and espec. if afflicted by malefics, and the malefics strong and dominant; the ☽ hyleg, and affl. by ♄, or by ♂ and ☿, threatens madness and death; the ☽ to the □ or ☍ ♂ or ☿ by dir.; ♆ affl. in the 12th H. (see Hallucinations, Obsessions); ♅ in the 6th H., and affl. by the ☽ or ☿; ♄ and ♂ in angles, elevated above ♅, the ☽ or ☿, and if ♅, ☿, the ☽ and Asc. be unconnected with each other by good aspects, but are afflicted by ♄ and ♂, and with no assistance from the benefics; ♃ Sig. ☌ ☉, and the ☉ ill-dignified, and espec. if the ☽ and ☿ be afflicted; a ☿ disease; caused by ☿ when the dominion of death is vested in him, and ☿ affl. by ♂; ☿ affl. at B., and the ☽ to the ill-asps. ☿ by dir.; ☿ in the 8th H., and afflicted at a Solar Ingress of the ☉ into ♈, and ☿ afflicting the ☽ or planet ascending; ☿ □ or ☍ ♄, and with ♂ also afflicting ☿; ☿ and ♂ □ or ☍ ♄; ☿ ☌ ♂, and affl. by the ☽, ♅, or ♄; fixed stars of the nature of ☿ denote death by madness; the phantasies are often prejudiced when ☿ is weak, afflicted and unfortunate at B., and under evil directions. (See "Prejudiced" under Fancies). Also caused by Subs at AT and AX. The Asc. to the □ or ☍ ♀ or ☿ by dir. (See Anger, Anguish; "Delirium Tremens" under Delirium; Drink, Enthusiasm, Epilepsy, Fears, Frenzy, Fury, Insanity, Irrational, Mania, Melancholy, Noisome, Raving, Suicide, Worry, etc.).

MAGIC—Magical Powers—Ruled largely by ♅ and the ♏ sign, and also the 8th and 12th H. are usually involved.

Black Magic—♆ affl. by ♂ gives tendency to, and espec. where the 8th or 12th H. are involved in the configuration, or the 8th and 12th signs, as ♏ and ♓; the 13° ♓ on the Asc. (See "Black Magic", "Faith Healers", under Healers; "Low Grade" under Psychic; Science, Spirit Controls, Witchcraft).

Ceremonial Magic — Ritual — Presided over by ♃, and is also ascribed to the 6th H. (See "Ritual" under Religion).

White Magic—Ruled by the same influences as govern Black Magic, only with the good aspect of ♂ to ♆, and fortunate influences in the 8th and 12th H., or in ♏ and ♓. (See "Treatment" under Hypnotism; Magnetism, Necromancy).

MAGISTRATES—(See Judges, Law).

MAGNESIA PHOSPHATE—Ruled by the ♌ sign. This Salt supplies the Nerve Sheaths. (See "Salts" under Zodiac).

MAGNETISM—Magnetic—The ♏ sign tends to give much magnetic and attractive power, and for this reason also attracts disease and infectious complaints. (See Contagious, External, Infections). Magnetism is strongly allied with Electricity, and ruled by ♅. (See Electric, Electricity; "Native Country" under Native). Terrestrial Magnetism is ruled by ♅. (See "Operations" under Nature; Uranus). In disease the magnetic influences are stronger at night due to the ☽ influences, and hence diseases are usually more raging at night, and espec. with acute fevers. (See "Diseases" under Night). During the daytime the electric forces of the ☉ tends to diminish the fevers, and ease the disease. Also ♄ is cold and magnetic. (See Saturn).

Animal Magnetism—Under the rule of ♂ and ♅. (See Animal).

Aura—The Magnetic Aura—(See Aura).

Body—Magnetic Body—♃ well-aspected in the 12th H.

Healers—Magnetic Healers—The ♏ influence strong and prominent at B.; ♏ on the Asc.; the ☉ well-asp. in ♏; ♆ ☌ ♀ and in ✱ or △ ☿; ♃ in ✱ or △ ☽; ♂ in the 12th H., free from affliction, in his exalted sign ♑, or in ♌ or ♐; the 24° ♓ on the Asc. (See "Magnetic Healers" under Healers; Hypnotism, Incompatibility, Magic, Mesmerism; "Curing" under Nature; Psychic, Scorpio).

Iron—Magnetized Iron—(See Lodestones).

Man—A Magnetic Man—Case—See "Magnetic Man", No. 849 in 1001 N.N.

Nature—Magnetic Nature—Born under the strong influence of ♅; the ☽ to the ✱ or △ ♅ by primary or secondary dir., the magnetic power is increased; ♅ in 6th H., and well-asp. by ♆ and ☿; ♂ in good asp. the ☉; the 24° ♓ on the Asc.

Negative Signs—The negative signs are divided into two parts, called Horas, which are alternately magnetic, and magneto-electric. (See Horas; "Signs" under Negative, Positive).

Planets—The Magnetic Planets—(See "Negative Planets" under Negative).

Signs—Magnetic Signs—♏ is classed as the principal magnetic sign. The feminine, or negative signs, are considered magnetic. (See "Negative" in this section; "Attracts Disease" under Attracts; "Signs" under Feminine, Negative; Scorpio).

MAIMED—Maiming—Mayhem—

Maiming of the Body—♄ to the ☌ or ill-asp. ♂ by dir.; ♄ casting an evil asp. to ♃ or ♀, and ♂ in □ or ☍ ☿ at the same time; ♂ □ or ☍ the ☉ at B., and by dir. (See Mutilated).

Males Born Maimed—Crippled from Birth—Defective In the Private Members—♀ in an angle, with ♄ and ♂ ascending after ♀, and configurated with the ☉ and ☿, the ☉, ☽, and ♀ being in masculine signs, and the ☽ in her decrease,—then males are born maimed, crippled, or injured in their private members, especially under ♈, ♌, ♏, ♑, or ♒, and females will remain childless and unprolific. (See "Crippled" under Birth; Congenital).

Males Maimed by Castration—Violent Castration—(See "Violent Castration" under Testes). See Eunuchs.

MAINTENANCE—Of Life—(See "Maintenance" under Life).

MAJESTIC—Majestic Carriage—(See "Majestic" under Gait).

MAJOR—

Major Bodily Disorders—(See Chronic, Constitutional, Consumptions, Invalids, Lingering, Malignant, Morbid, Organic, Serious, Severe, Structural, Tedious, Wastings, etc.).

Major Planets—Superior Planets—♆, ♅, ♄, ♃ and ♂. Diseases ruled by these planets are of greater consequence, and more severe in their effects, and espec. when they also hold the dominion of death. (See Severe). The diseases of ♀ and ☿, the minor planets, are less serious unless they hold power at B., hold the dominion of death, or greatly afflict the hyleg both at birth and by direction. (See Perihelion).

Major Subluxations—Of the Vertebrae—(See Subluxations, Vertebrae).

MAJORITY—Majorities of the Planets In a Nativity, and Their Effects—In the diagnosis, prognosis, and consideration of disease, the majorities of the planets in Signs, Houses, Rising, Setting, Elevated or Below the Horizon, Retrograde, etc., should be taken into account. Many planets, or a Stellium, in one sign or house, tend to greater afflictions of the parts of the body ruled by such sign and house. The majority of the planets in the positive signs gives greater will-power, and the ability to overcome disease, obstacles and the limitations of life. (See Positive, Negative). The ☉, and a majority of the planets rising at B. usually give greater vitality and resistance to disease, while a majority setting at B. tend to weaken the physical powers, and give less power to overcome obstacles and make life come your way, as the planets when setting are weaker, and deprived of much of their power, unless greatly dignified by sign, house, and aspect. The majority of planets in fiery signs tend to increased vitality, whereas a majority below the Earth at B. tend to weaken the constitution, and espec. when the majority is in the 6th H., and below the western horizon at B. A study along these lines will help you in judging the map along the lines of health and disease, and to better analyze the case. Life also tends to be longer when the majority of the planets are rising and elevated, and in fiery signs, regardless of many other evil influences of the map. (See "Signs" under Air, Cardinal, Earth, Fire, Fixed, Mutable, Water; Cure, Diagnosis, Elevated, Life, Prognosis, Recuperation, Resistance, Rising, Setting, Stellium, Vitality, Will, etc.).

MAL—Sickness—(See Disease, Ill-Health, Sickness).

Mal-Adjustment—(See Saint Vitus Dance).

Mal-Assimilation—(See Assimilation, Digestion; "Malnutrition" under Nutrition).

Petit and Grand Mal—(See Epilepsy).

MALACIA—Malacosis—Malacoma—A Morbid Softening of the Tissues—A ♀ and ♓ disease; ♀ affl. in ♓. (See Softening).

Malacia—A Depraved Appetite—(See "Abnormal", "Depraved", under Appetite).

MALADIES—Malaena—(See Disease, Ill-Health, Sickness).

Exhibition of Maladies—(See Exhibition).

MALAISE—A Feeling of Uneasiness and Discomfort—(See Discomfort, Restlessness).

General Malaise—Attacks of Malaise Arising from Plethora—♄, ♅, or ♆ in ♏, and affl. the ☉ or ☽, general malaise; ♄ affl. in the 6th H. (See Aches, Debility, Discomfort, Dull, Lassitude, Listless, Plethora, Weak).

MALARIA—Ague—Intermittent Fever—♂ affl. in ♌, ♍, ♐, or ♑. (See Ague, Intermittent, Miasma, Moonlight, Noxious, Quartan, Remittent, Spleen, etc.).

MALE—Males—Masculine—The ☉ is the strong ruler in a male nativity, and also ♂ rules the male sex generally, and the ☽ and ♀ rule females. Afflictions to the ☉ tend to cause disease and affliction to the male, and afflictions to the ☽ or ♀ to the female. The ☉ is considered hyleg in a male nativity, and the ☽ hyleg in a female, unless they are greatly out of dignity and afflicted, when one of the Benefics, or the Asc., may be taken as hyleg. The following subjects have to do with Males, Masculine. Also see Brother, Father, Husband, Men, Son, Uncle.

Accidents to Males—Hurts—Injuries—Wounds—Danger of—Malefics to the ☌ or ill-asp. the ☉. (See "Hurts" under Brother; "Accidents" under Father, Husband).

Afflictions To—(See the various paragraphs in this section).

Appearance—Women Masculine In Appearance—Masculine Women—(See Deviations, Effeminate; "Coarse" under Voice).

Bad Health For—(See Disease, Ill-Health, Short Life, in this section).

Barrenness—In the Male—(See Barren; "Anchorite" under Husband; Impotent).

Births—Male Births—A Male Child Is Promised—In male nativities the 5th H. is male, and the 4th H. female, and the conditions of these houses will show the predominance of sex, and which gives the greater promise of fruitfulness, and the opposite houses show detriments, etc. Planets which promise children, when posited in the 10th, 11th, 4th or 5th H., in male signs, or in aspect to the ☉, promise male children. Mars in ⚹ or △ asp. the Asc. by dir., birth of a male child is promised. If the ☉, ☽, or Asc., or planets in aspect with them, or with the Asc., be in masculine signs, or are masculine by being oriental, the child conceived will be a male if such conditions exist at conception. Jupiter in ⚹ or △ the ☉ by dir., if ♃ is strong and well-dig. at B., promises a male child. Mercury is masculine or feminine as he is aspected. He is also masculine when ori. of the ☉, and feminine when occidental. If the dispositor of the ☽, and the lord of the hour be angular, and ♃ in the 7th H., the mother has quickened and the child will be a male, and if ♐ or ♓ be in the 7th H. under these conditions the child is a female (Hor'y). If the 1st or 5th, their lords, the ☽ and the planet to which she applies, be all or most of them, in masculine signs, or in aspect with masculine planets or stars of a masculine nature, the child will be a male, and vice versa. (Hor'y). For Cases of three males conceived, two males and one female, one male and two females, see Triplets; for two males, see Twins. (See "First-Born Child" under Children; "Birth of a Female" under Female; Predetermination, Son).

Brain—In the male, ruled by the ☉. (See Brain).

Brother—(See the various paragraphs under Brother).

Children—Male Children Born or Conceived—(See "Births" in this section).

Colors—Orange and Red, colors of the ☉ and ♂, are the predominant masculine colors.

Conceived—Male Child Conceived—(See "Births" in this section; Conception).

Constitution—(a) Strong Constitution—The ☉ in a strong sign and house, free from afflictions, and well-asp. by ♃. (See "Strong" under Constitution). (b) Weak Constitution—(See "Sickly", "Unhealthy", under Children; "Death" under Infancy; "Low" under Vitality; "Weak Body" under Weak).

Crippled—Born Crippled or Maimed—(See Crippled; "Males Born Maimed" under Maimed).

Danger to Males—Afflictions to the ☉ at B., or by dir.; born at time of eclipse of the ☉, may die at B. (See Eclipse. Also note the various paragraphs in this section).

Death of a Male—In the Family—The ☉ directed to Cor Scorpio; the ☉ badly afflicted by malefics at B., and by dir.; born at time of an eclipse of the ☉, may die soon after birth. (See "Death" under Brother, Father, Husband; "First-born" under Children; Eclipses; "Male" under Infancy, etc.).

Debility In—(See Impotent; "Ill-Health", "Weak", in this section).

Degrees—Masculine Degrees of the Zodiac—♈ 8, 15, 30; ♉ 11, 21, 30; ♊ 16, 26; ♋ 2, 10, 23, 30; ♌ 5, 15, 30; ♍ 12, 30; ♎ 5, 20, 30; ♏ 4, 17, 30; ♐ 2, 12, 30; ♑ 11, 30; ♒ 5, 21, 27; ♓ 10, 23, 30. If the ascendant or its lord be in one of these degrees the native will be more masculine in appearance even tho a female. (See "Appearance" in this section; Predetermination).

Disease In the Male—In a male horoscope afflictions to the ☉ tend to cause disease, or an earlier death, and the ☉ also in a weak sign or house, and much afflicted by malefics; the ☉ hyleg and much afflicted tends to give a weaker constitution, and more subject to disease and ill-health all thru life; ♄ affl. the ☉ at B., and by dir. The ☉ is general Significator of health in the male, and the ☽ in the female. In an adult nativity the ☉ rules the male, and the ☽ the female. (See "Ill-Health" in this section).

Effeminate—Males Effeminate — (See Effeminate).

Eyes—In the Male—(See Eyes; "Eyes" under Left, Right).

Father—(See the various paragraphs under Father).

Females—(a) Injury to Males By—(See Grief, Health, Injured, Treachery, Women, under Men). (b) Masculine Women—(See Appearance, Degrees, in this section).

First Child—In a Male Nativity—(See "First-Born" under Children).

Fruitfulness — In the Male — (See Fruitful; "Fruitful" under Husband).

Genitals—In the Male—(See Genitals).

Good Health—For Males—The Health Strengthened—Men More Robust—The ☉ strong at B., and well-aspected; the ☉ well-aspected by the ☽ and ♂; the ☉ in a fiery sign, better prospect of good health and long life; ♂ in good asp. to the ☉, as ♂ always augments the ☉; ♂ in a female sign and ♀ in a masculine sign, and both oriental. (See "Constitution" in this section; "Good Health" under Health; "Body" under Strong; "Good" under Vitality).

Grandfather—(See Grandparents).

Health—The ☉ is the Sig. of health with males, and the ☉ weak and ill-dig. at B., and afflicted, tends to impair the health, and espec. under evil directions to the ☉. (See Good Health, Ill-Health, and the various paragraphs in this section).

Heart Disease—In the Male—The ☉ affl. in ♌; afflictions to the ☉, as the ☉ rules the heart in the male. (See Heart).

Hermaphrodites—(See this subject).

Horoscope—The ☉ has great influence in a male horoscope, and to judge of the prospects of a male in health, and other matters, study the position, aspects, sign and house position of the ☉ at B., and also the directions to the ☉ after birth, and when they culminate. (See Horoscope).

Houses—The Masculine Houses—The odd numbers, as the 1st, 3rd, 5th Houses, etc., as these houses corres-

pond to the masculine and positive signs, as ♈, ♊, ♌, etc. (See "Masculine" under Houses).

Hurts To—(See "Accidents" in this section).

Husband—(See the various paragraphs under Husband).

Hyleg—In the Male Nativity—The ☉, as a rule, unless the ☉ is weak and badly afflicted at B. (See Hyleg).

Ill-Health—For Males—The ☉ rules the health in males. The ☉ affl. at B., as by ♄; the ☉ ☌, □, ☍ or P. ♄; the ☉ hyleg at B., and much afflicted; the ☉ in the 6th or 12th H. at B., and affl. by malefics, unless the laws of health and hygiene are observed, and the vital powers conserved; the ☉ ☌ ♄ in ♋ or ♑ in the 1st H.; the adverse aspects of the ☉ to any of the malefics by dir., and espec. among the aged, feeble, and those of frail constitution; the prog. ☉ to the □ or ☍ the Asc.; the prog. ☉ to the ☌ or ill-asp. ♄; the afflicting planet a malefic, and elevated above the ☉, and the health will be worse than it would be if the ☉ was elevated above the malefic; the ☉ affl. in ♓, and with ♓ or ♋ on the Asc. at B. The health will not tend to be exceptionally bad if ♂ is in favorable asp. to the ☉, even tho ♄ afflict the ☉, as the good asp. of ♂ tends to augment the animal heat. (See "Disease", and the various paragraphs in this section; "Sickly Children" under Children; Eclipses; "Bad Health", "Periods of Ill-Health", under Health; "Low" under Vitality; "Weak Body" under Weak).

Impotency In—(See Barren; "Unfruitful" under Husband; Impotent).

Infant—Death of a Male Infant—(See Eclipses; "Death" under Infancy).

Injuries To—(See Accidents, Females, in this section).

Left Eye—In Male—Hurts To—Afflictions to the ☽ at B., and by dir., as the ☽ rules the left eye of a male, and the ☉ the right eye. (See "Eyes" under Left).

Length of Life—For Males—The ☉ is usually taken as hyleg and Giver of Life in a male nativity, and the length of life may be forecasted according to the sign, house, and strength of the ☉ at B., and the aspects to him, whether good or bad, etc. (See Long Life, Short Life, and the various paragraphs in this section; "Death" under Childhood, Children, Infancy, Middle Life, Old Age, Youth; "Early Death" under Early, etc.).

Long Life—For Males—Prospect of—The ☉ in a fiery sign at B., and favorably aspected by benefics; the ☉ strong at B., and not much afflicted; the ☉ hyleg, strong, and well-aspected. (See "Long Life" under Life; "Good" under Vitality; "Good Health" in this section).

Maimed — Males Born Maimed — (See Maimed).

Male Births — (See "Births" in this section).

Male Organ — Penis — Disorders of — (See Genitals, Penis, Urethra, Venereal).

Marriage Of—(See Fiance, Husband, Marriage, Marriage Partner, Wife).

Masculine—(a) Masculine Degrees of the Zodiac—(See "Degrees" in this section). (b) Masculine Houses—(See "Houses" in this section). (c) Masculine Planets—(See "Masculine" under Planets). (d) Masculine Signs—(See "Masculine" under Signs). (e) Masculine Women—(See Appearance, Degrees, in this section).

Men—(See the various paragraphs under Men).

Mixture of Sex—(See Hermaphrodites).

One Male Conceived—(See "Births" in this section; "Single Births" under Children; Conception; "Birth" under Son). For two males, or three males conceived, or born, see Twins, Triplets).

Organ—The Male Sex Organ—(See "Male Organ" in this section).

Penis—(See "Male Organ" in this section).

Planets—Masculine Planets—(See "Masculine" under Planets).

Predominate—Males Predominate In the Family—(See "Female Children" under Children; "Births" in this section).

Quadrants—The Male Quadrants In the Star Map of Birth—(See Quadrants).

Recuperation—Augmented or Slow for Males—(See "Males" under Recuperation).

Relatives—(See "Male Relations" under Relations).

Right Eye—Of a Male—Ruled by the ☉, and the ☉ to the ☌ or ill-asp. a malefic by dir. tends to hurts, injuries, or blindness in the right eye, and espec. if the ☉ is badly afflicted at B., or with Nebulous Stars. The ☉ afflicted at B., and to the ☌ or ill-asp. the Asc. by dir. tends espec. to hurts to the right eye. (See Blindness; "Eyes" under Left, Right; "Left Eye" in this section).

Robust—Males Robust—(See "Good Health" in this section; Impotent, Robust, Ruddy; "Good" under Vitality).

Scrotum—(See Scrotum).

Sex—(a) Mixture of Sex In—(See Hermaphrodites). (b) Male Sex Organ—(See "Male Organ" in this section).

Sharp Illnesses In—Severe But Soon Over—The ☉ in a fiery sign at B. (See Severe, Sharp).

Short Life—For Males—Note especially the aspects to the ☉ at B., and by dir. A train of primary directions culminating soon after birth, and espec. where the ☉ is badly afflicted, or in childhood, tend to early death of males. The ☉ hyleg at B., and afflicted by directions soon after birth, tends to death. (See "Death" under Childhood, Children, Infancy, Youth; "Early Death" under Early; Eclipses; "Short Life" under Life).

Significator—In Hor'y Q. the ☉ is taken as the Sig. in dealing with males, and espec. in health matters.

Signs—Masculine Signs of the Zodiac—(See "Masculine" under Signs).

Sons—(See "First-Born" under Children; Son; "Births" in this section).

Sterility In—(See "Barrenness" in this section).

Strength and Vigor—Males Have—(See Constitution, Good Health, Long Life, Robust, in this section).

Strong Constitution—(See "Constitution" in this section).

Sun—The ☉ is the Sig. of health in male nativities. (See Sun).

Testes—(See Testes).

Three Males Born—(See Triplets).

Triplets—Three Males—Two Males and One Female—One Male and One Female—One Male and Two Females—(See Triplets).

Twins—Two Males—One Male and One Female—(See Twins).

Two Males Born—(See Twins).

Uncles—(See Uncles).

Venereal Diseases—(See Venereal).

Vigor and Strength—For Males—(See "Strength" in this section).

Virile Members—Excessive Virile Members—(See Virile).

Vitality In—(a) Good Vitality—The ☉ well-asp. in a fiery sign. (See "Good Health" in this section). (b) Weak Vitality—The ☉ in a water sign, and espec. in ♋ or ♓, afflicted, and with one of these signs on the Asc. at B.; the ☉ ☌ ♄ in the 6th H. (See "Sickly" under Children; "Low" under Vitality; "Weak Body" under Weak).

Voice—The Voice Masculine and Rough In Women—(See Appearance, Degrees, in this section).

Weak Constitution—(See Constitution, Vitality, in this section).

Wife—(See the various paragraphs under Wife).

Women—Males Injured By—Masculine Women—(See Appearance, Females, in this section).

Wounds To—(See "Accidents" in this section).

Zodiac—Masculine Signs of—(See "Masculine" under Signs).

MALEFICS—The Malefics—The Infortunes—♆, ♅, ♄, and ♂ are called the malefic planets. Also ☋ (Cauda) is considered malefic, and of the nature of ♄. Saturn tends to give excess of cold in the system, and ♂ excess of heat, and are malevolent in this regard, and espec. in health matters. However, ♄ is said to exert a good influence by his favorable aspects, but is very evil by his adverse aspects, and tends to afflict any sign he is in at B., or after by dir. or tr., and to afflict the part of the body ruled by such sign. The places occupied by the malefics at B. are always considered points of affliction, or weakness, in the body, or in the mind if a mental sign is so occupied, or the mental rulers afflicted by malefics. The signs and houses occupied by the malefics at B. indicate the weak parts of the constitution. The malefics afflict by their ☌,

P., □, and ☍ aspects, but their good aspects, as the ⚹ and △, tend to assist in health matters for the time, and to give more peace of mind. The more angular, oriental, or elevated a malefic may be at B., or elevated above the ☉, ☽, or benefics, the more evil are their effects, and to make disease more tenacious, severe, or incurable. A malefic elevated above the Lights denotes misfortune, sickness, or death, and when Anareta tends to a violent death if the map is a violent one. Any of the malefic planets may become the Anareta, or the killing planet. These matters, and the nature of the influence of each of the malefics, is discussed under these planets. The malefics are stronger when in the positive, or Solar Horas of the Signs. (See Horas). In Perigee or Zodiacal Parallel ♃ lessens the evil of a malefic, but ♃ when in ☌ ♄ or ♂ increases their evil when of the same, or near Latitude, but less so when of widely different Latitude. (See Anareta, Angles, Benefics, Elevated, Evils, Incurable, Malevolent, Malignant, Mars, Neptune, Oriental, Saturn, Severe, Uranus, etc.).

MALEVOLENT—Evil—An Evil Disposition Toward Others—Malicious—The ☉ or ♂ Significators in □ or ☍ ♄; the ☽ afflicted in ♏; the ☽ in ♏ and affl. by ♄ or ♂; the ☽ Sig. in ♏; the ☽ or ☿ Significators □ or ☍ ♂; the Full ☽ sepr. from ♂ and applying to ☿ in a nocturnal geniture; ♄ as Sig. denotes a malicious person; the influence of ♄ strong at B.; ♄ Sig. □ or ☍ ☿; caused by the evil aspects of ♄; ♄ ☌ or ill-asp. ♂, and espec. in angles; in Hor'y Q. ♄ Sig. in ♎ or ♓; ♂ in evil aspect to ♄; ♂ Sig. □ or ☍ ♄. (See Cruel, Evil, Malice; "Mean-Spirited" under Mean; Mischief, Revengeful, Treachery, Vicious).

MALFORMATIONS — An Abnormal Shape or Structure—Deformities—Irregularities In Form, Whether Congenital or Acquired—

Acquired Malformations — Some malformations are acquired after birth, and may be the result of disease and various afflictions. They may be caused by the hindrances, retentions, excess deposits, stoppages, and suppressions of the ♄ afflictions. Also ♂ can cause them by an accident, violence, or an excess of heat to a part, as in Ankylosis, the melting of a part, and result in a deformity and abnormality in shape. This subject is largely dealt with in the Articles on Deformities, and also listed under Saturn Diseases, Mars Diseases, etc. The planet ♆ also causes malformations thru wasting of the tissues. (See the Diseases listed under Neptune, Wasting). The following is a list of some of the Acquired Malformations, and abnormalities of shape, due to conditions arising after birth. See these subjects in the alphabetical arrangement — Ankylosis (see Ankylosis, Joints); Atrophy; Contractions; Fractures (the result of); Gout (from Mineral Deposits); Kidney (Floating); Joints (Ankylosis, and Enlarged Joints); Lameness; Paralysis; Rheumatism (from Deposits of Minerals, Wastes, Urea); Rickets; Swellings; Twistings; Wastings; Wry Neck (see Neck), etc. For subjects not listed here, look in the alphabetical arrangement for the subject you have in mind.

Congenital Malformations — And Deformities — If malformations exist at B. they are caused by prenatal conditions and afflictions during the period of gestation, and the prenatal map for the time of conception, and for each month during pregnancy, should be studied to trace the causes of malformations which exist at B. The following are some of the influences which have been observed to exist at B. in congenital malformations—the ☉ or ☽ in ♉, ☌ a malefic; the ☉ ☍ ☽ in angles, and □ ♄ or ♂, with no help from benefics, with benefics in a weak sign, or below the Western Horizon at B.; ♄ □ ♆; ♂ ☌ or ill-asp. ♄ at B., and espec. in angles, and affl. the ☉, ☽, Asc., or hyleg. Congenital Malformations are legion, and too numerous to mention and list here in this Article, but you will find them in the alphabetical arrangement. Consult the Articles which deal with the parts and organs of the body, and the defects, malformations, and irregularities of such parts, or organs, will be found listed in such Articles, and giving both the congenital and acquired malformations. Also see the Articles on Deformities, Extremities, Limbs, Members, Organs, Parts. The following are some of the more prominent congenital malformations, and also the more obscure ones, and which are listed here that they may not be overlooked. See the following subjects in the alphabetical arrangement — Abdomen (Prominent, Rickets); Abnormalities; Arms (Forearm Missing); Barrenness; Beastly Form (see Beasts); Birth (Born Blind, Deaf, Dumb—Paralyzed from Birth—See the paragraphs under Birth); Blind from Birth (see Birth, Blindness); Breastbone (Pigeon-Breasted); Chest (Hollow); Cloaca; Club Feet (see Feet); Conception; Crooked Body (see Crooked); Congenital; Contortions; Contractions; Crippled; Cyclops; Deafness — Deaf and Dumb — (see Dumb, Hearing); Defects; Deformities; Diminished; Distortions; Dogs — Resembles Dogs—(see "Dogs" under Children); Dwarfed; Enlargements; Eunuchs; Excrescences; Extremities; Eyes—Born Blind—Crossed Eyes—(see Eyes); Feet (Club Feet); Foetus; Forearms (Missing); Frog Child (see Forearm); Generative System; Genitals; Gestation; Growth; Harelip (see Lips); Hearing (Deaf and Dumb); Heart (see "Partition", "Right Side", under Heart); Hermaphrodites; Humpback (see Spine); Hydrocephalus; Idiocy; Ill-Formed; Incomplete; Inhuman; Limbs; Maimed; Members; Misshaped; Monsters; Mutes; Organs; Paralysis — From Birth (see Distortions, Excrescences); Parts; Prenatal Epoch; Rectum (see Cloaca); Sex Organs (see Hermaphrodites, Virile); Siamese Twins (see "United" under Twins); Undersized; Undeveloped; Urethra; Virile, Void Of, etc. For a better understanding of the prenatal conditions which tend to congenital malformations, the student should make a thorough study of the book, "The Prenatal Epoch", by Mr. E. H. Bailey, Editor of the British Journal of Astrology, at 10 and 11 Red Lion Court, Fleet St., London, E.C.4, England. (See the Article on Prenatal Epoch in this book).

MALICE—Malicious—Revengeful—Signified by ♄; a ♄ characteristic; ♄ to the ☌ ☋ by dir. (See Cruel, Malevolent, Revengeful, Treachery, Vicious). Malice is also one of the low forms of the ♂ action, and espec. when acting thru his night sign ♏. Also people born under ♆ and ♅, and afflicted by the evil aspects of these planets, tend to malice. The Mercurial Temperament also when afflicted tends to petty malice and vindictiveness. (See Ambushes, Aversions, Enemies, Enmity, Feuds, Hate, Jealousy, Mischief, Murderous, Plots, etc.).

Malice Aforethought—♄ Sig. in ♓.

Malicious Eyes — (See "Leering" under Eyes).

Malice of Fortune—(See "Malice" under Fortune).

MALIGNANT—Virulent—Fatal—Poisonous—The malefic planets ♄ and ♂ are quite malignant at times by their afflictions. Mars is more malignant in day nativities, and ♄ in night ones. (See Day, Night, Noxious, Poisonous). Jupiter in ☌ ♄ increases the malignancy of ♄, and ♃ in close ☌ with ♂ increases the malignancy of ♂ except where ♂ differs widely in Latitude.

Air — Malignant Air — (See "Malignant" under Air).

Chronic Diseases — Malignant Forms —The ☽ in a fixed sign at B., and afflicted, and applying to ♄ in a Solar Revolution. (See "Death By" under Chronic; "Fatal Illness" under Fatal).

Diseases — Malignant Diseases — Caused by the hyleg much afflicted at B., and by dir., and espec. if affl. by ♄; ♃ Sig. □ or ☍ ♂. (See Carcinoma, Chronic; "Constitutional Diseases" under Constitution; Decay, Gangrene, Influenza, Latent, Morbid, Mortification, Organic, Structural, Wastings, etc.).

Fevers — Malignant Fevers — Danger of Death From—♃ Sig. □ or ☍ ♂. (See "Low", "Pernicious", under Fever).

Gangrene—Malignant Gangrene with Pus—(See "Gangrene" under Pus).

Growths — (See "Malignant", "Non-Malignant", under Growths).

Influenza — (See "Malignant" under Influenza).

Scars—Malignant Scars—(See Scarlatina).

Tumors — Malignant Tumor — (See Carcinoma; "Malignant" under Tumors).

Vesicle — A Malignant Vesicle — (See Carbuncle).

MALNUTRITION—(See Nutrition).

MAMMARY—The Mammae—Mammary Glands — The Breasts — (See Breasts, Glands, Lacteals, Milk, Secretions).

MAN—

Hand of Man — Death by Human Means, as by Accident, Assassination, or in War—Death by Human Hands—The afflicting planets in human signs, and espec. ♂, as in ♊, ♍, ♒, and the 1st half of ♐; the ☽ in an airy sign and to the ☌ or ill-asp. ♂ by dir. (See Ambushes, Assassination, Assaults, Duels, Enemies, Events, Gunshot, Hand of Man; "Human Signs" under Human; Judges, Killed, Murdered, Plots, Poison, Stabs, Sword, Treachery, War, etc.). Violent death by human hands is apt to result when the ☉ or ☽ are in human signs, in angles, in □ or ☍ ♂ from angles, and espec. in the 10th or 4th H.

Life of Man—(See "Man" under Life).

Odors from Man—(See Odors).

MANDIBLE—(See Jaws).

MANE OF LEO—A Nebulous Cluster—The ☉ or ☽ with at B., or by dir. tend to blindness, and the loss of one eye. (See "One Eye" under Blindness; **Eyes).**

MANGLED — Torn— Mutilated—The afflictions of ♅ tend to cause accidents with machinery in the employment, and whereby the native may be mangled, torn, mutilated, or killed. Also ♅ is the cause of many Railroad accidents, explosions, sudden and unexpected events, injuries, etc. (See Accidents; "Wild Animals" under Animals; Beasts, Employment, Explosions, Lacerations, Machinery, Maimed, Mutilated, Railroads, Uranus).

MANHOOD — The Age of Manhood or Womanhood — (See Adults, Husband, Marriage, Men, Middle Life, Old Age, Puberty, Wife, Women, etc.).

MANIA—Maniacal—Madness—Frenzy—Fury — Phrenitic—An Insane Person—Furious Madness — Toxic Psychosis—Delirium, etc.—Mania is usually caused by afflictions to ☿, the mental ruler, and espec. when afflicted by ♂ or ♆. The ♆ influence tends to Obsessions, Evil Spirit Controls, Delirium Tremens, Demoniacal Demonstrations, etc., and espec. when ♆ is afflicted in the 12th H. at B., and by dir.; ♆ □ or ☍ ♅ at B., danger of obsessions, abnormal fears, dreads, etc.; ♆ in ♈ at B., and greatly afflicted by the other malefics at B., and by dir., and espec. if ♆ is in the 6th, 8th, or 12th H.; afflictions at a Solar Ingress of the ☉ into ♈, the brain sign, and ☿ afflicting the ☽ at the same time, or the planet ascending, tends to outbursts, or a return of maniacal attacks, and espec. if Mania is indicated in the radix. (See Fury, Insanity, Madness; the various paragraphs in this section). See the following subjects in the alphabetical arrangement when only listed here—

Acute Mania — ☿ afflicted by ♂ at B., and by dir.

Alcoholic Mania—(See "Delirium Tremens" under Delirium).

All Forms Of — Caused by ♆ and his afflictions, and are ♆ diseases. (See Neptune).

Anarchists — The ♆ and ♅ influences and afflictions tend to make Anarchists, and a mania for certain lines of destructive action. (See Anarchists).

Aversions; Blues—The Blues—Melancholy—(See Blues, Depression, Despondency, Melancholy).

Brainstorms—(See Brain).

Cases of Mania—(See Religious, Sexual, in this section).

Chaotic Religious Mania — (See "Religious" in this section).

Confusion—The Mind Confused—Ideas Confused—(See Confusion).

Dangerous Maniacs—♂ afflicting ☿ at B., and by dir., and ☿ weak and otherwise afflicted at B., and in no relation to the ☽ or Asc. (See "Dangerous" under Insanity; "Violent" in this section).

Death From — (See "Death" under Madness).

Delirium—Mania with Delirium—(See Delirium Tremens, Wild Delirium, under Delirium).

Delusions; Dementia; Demoniacs;

Deranged—Mentally Deranged—(See Insanity; "Derangement" under Mental).

Deviations — Of the Mental Faculties —(See Deviations).

Dipsomania — An Uncontrollable Desire for Strong Drink — (See Dipsomania).

Ego Mania—(See Ego).

Emotions—Extreme Disturbances of —(See Emotions, Feelings).

Enthusiasm—The Fury of—(See Enthusiasm).

Epileptic Mania—(See Epilepsy).

Erotic Mania—Morbid Sex Desires—♆ afflicted in the 5th H.; ♆ affl. in ♏; the ☽ or ♀ affl. by ♄. (See Amorous; "Morbid" under Imagination; Nymphomania; "Passional Excesses" under Passion; Perversions; Unsavory).

Excitement—Extreme Mental Excitement—(See Excitable).

Fanatical—Irrational Zeal—(See Fanatical).

Fancies — Turbulent Fancies — (See Fancies).

Fears; Feelings — (See Anger, Emotions, Feelings).

Fits of Mania—♆ afflicted, and espec. by ♅ and ♂ at B., and by dir. (See "Fits of Fury" under Fury).

Fixed Ideas — (See Anxiety; "Fixed Ideas" under Ideas).

Frenzy; Fury; Hallucinations;

Hereditary Mania—Latent—Inherent —Is usually caused by the severe afflictions or ♆ or ♂ to ☿ at time of conception, and the Prenatal Epoch map should be studied. (See Heredity).

High Temper — (See "High" under Temper).

·**Homicidal Mania**—(See Homicide).

Ideas—Fixed Ideas—(See Ideas).

Illusions; Imaginations — Disordered Imagination — (See the various paragraphs under Imagination).

Inherent Mania — (See "Hereditary" in this section).

Insanity — (See Dangerous, Outrageous, Violent, under Insanity).

Intoxication Mania From — (See "Strong Intoxicants" under Intoxication).

Irrational; Kleptomania—Morbid Desire to Steal—(See Kleptomaniac).

Latent Mania — (See "Hereditary" in this section).

Lunatics—(See Insanity, Lunacy).

Madness; Mentally Deranged — (See "Deranged" in this section).

Mind Disorders of (See "Derangement" under Mental; "Diseased Mind" under Mind. Also note the various paragraphs in this section).

Moisture of Brain — Causing Fury or Mania—(See "Brain" under Moisture).

Monomania—Insanity on One Subject —☿ in a fixed sign, and affl. by the ☽ and ♂; many afflictions in fixed signs, causing Mania, and with fixed signs also on the angles. (See Delusions; "Fixed Signs" under Fixed; Hallucinations; "Fixed Ideas" under Ideas).

Morbid Mind — (See "Morbid" under Mind; "Compulsions" under Morbid).

Morphomania—(See Narcotics).

Murderous — A Mania to Murder and Kill—(See Murder).

Neurotic Mania—Mania of a Neurotic Character — ♆ afflicted by ♂. (See "Highly Neurotic" under Nerves).

Noisome Diseases — With Loud and Maniacal Demonstrations — (See Noisome).

Notions—Chaotic Notions—(See Chaotic; Notions).

Nymphomania; Obsessions; Paranoia —Insanity with Delusions—(See Paranoia).

Persecution — Delusions of, and Bordering on Mania—(See Paranoia).

Perversions—(See Perversions).

Phantasies; Phrenitic Man — (See "Wild Delirium" under Delirium).

Phrenzies—(See Frenzy).

Prenatal Epoch—Often Explains the Causes of Mania, as Inherent Mania— (See Prenatal).

Prevalence—Of Mania—Of a Neurotic Nature — (See "Neurotic" in this section).

Psychic Disturbances—(See Psychic).

Puerperal Mania—(See Puerperal).

Pyromania—(See Incendiarism).

Ravings; Religious Mania — Chaotic Religious Mania—Caused by ♆; ♆ in the 9th H., and afflicting ☿; ☿ ☌ or Par. ♄, and afflicted by the □ or ☍ ♂, and with ☿ in a weak sign, as in ♓; ☿ or the ☽ afflicted by ♆. (See Ecstasy, Exaltation, Excitable, Fanatical, Frenzy, under Religion). Cases of Religious Mania — See "Marriage" No. 834; "Mentally Defective", No. 408, in 1001 N.N.

Return of Mania—(See the Introduction to this Article).

Sex Mania — (See "Licentious" under Men; Nymphomania).

Spirit Controls — Demoniacal Obsessions—(See Demoniac, Spirit Controls).

Suicidal Mania—(See Suicide).

Temper—(See Cruel; "High Temper" under Temper).

Terrors—Strange Terrors—(See Demoniac, Hallucinations, Imaginations, Obsessions, Spirit Controls; "Terrors" under Strange; Visions).

Transitory Mania—Of Short Duration—☿ weak at B., afflicted by ♂, disconnected with the ☽ or Asc., and with ☿ afflicted by the evil transit of ♂, or by an adverse secondary dir. of the ☽. (See Transient).

Treatment of Mania — The blue color is soothing to Maniacs, and violent Maniacs when confined in a blue room, with the walls and all colorings blue, are soon calmed. A suggestive treatment under Hypnosis is also often successful, and reaches the subconscious mind, removing the disturbing influences there, or the obsessing spirit, if it is such, is driven out. See the account in Matt. 8:28-32.

Typhomania—The Delirium of Typhus Fever—(See Typhus).

Violent Mania — Violent Maniacs — Caused by the afflictions of ♂ to ☿, and where ☿ is weak at B., and otherwise afflicted by malefics, and espec. when ☿ is disconnected with the ☽ or Asc. at B., and where the radical map shows a tendency to Insanity, Epilepsy, or Madness. (See Frenzy, Fury; "Violent" under Insanity; Madness).

MANKIND — Humanity — The Human Race—The ☽, and planets in signs of human form, tend to affect mankind for good or ill, and to bring disease, suffering, and sorrow upon human beings. At a Solar Eclipse, when the Zodiacal Constellations, and those of the ruled Fixed Stars out of the Zodiac, are in signs of human form, the effects fall upon the human race, for good or evil, according to the signs occupied. For influences and afflictions which tend to affect Mankind in general, or a part of Humanity, according to location, etc., see Air, Atmosphere, Birthrate, Blizzards, Calamity, Casualties, Catastrophies, Cholera, Climate, Cold, Common People, Countries, Crime, Crops, Disasters, Drought, Earth, Earthquakes, Eclipses, Endemic, Epidemics, Events, Evils, Famine, Fevers (see "Prevalance" under Fever); Fire (see "Great Fires" under Fire); Floods, Fruit; Great (Death of the Great—see Great); Grief, Hail, Heat (see "Extreme Heat" under Heat); Human, Humanity, Influenza, Kingdoms, Kings, Miseries, Misfortune, Mortality, Mourning, Nations, Nobles, Pandemics, Perigee, Perihelion, Pestilence, Pests, Plague, Prevalent, Princes, Public, Rain, Robberies, Rulers, Sea, Ships, Snow, Sorrow, Storms, Summer, Vermin, Volcanoes, War, Water, Weather, Winds, Winter, etc.

Lower Order of Mankind—Always In Trouble With — Receives Many Injuries From—The ☽ Sig. □ or ☍ ♄. (See "Low Company" under Low).

MANNER—Manners—The Manners are ruled by the ☽ and the Asc., or chiefly influenced by them. See the following subjects in the alphabetical arrangement when only listed here—

Abrupt—In Manner—♅ ascending at B., or with the chief Sig. of the nativity; a prominent and afflicted ♅; fixed sign influences tend to terse and sudden expression. (See Cruel, Eccentric, Fierce; "High Temper" under Temper).

Accomplished Manners — Accomplished Mind—♃ Sig. in ♐; ♀ Sig. ☌ or good asp. ☿, or vice versa, a refined and accomplished mind and manner. (See Genteel; "Great Ability" under Great; "Popular" under Reputation).

Action—(See the various paragraphs under Action, Conduct, Movement, Walk, etc.).

Address — (See "Manly" in this section; Appearance, Speech).

Agreeable — The ☽ on the Meridian, or coming to, and well-aspected by ♀. (See Accomplished, Obliging, in this section).

Amiable — Even Temper — Good Disposition—The airy signs produce, and with the ☉ or ☽ well-aspected in them, or with an airy sign on the Asc.; the airy signs are known as the Sweet Signs, and tend to give a sweet, kind, and affable disposition when well occupied and aspected at B.; the ☽ Sig. ☌ or good asp. ♀, or vice versa; the ☽ sepr. from ♀ and apply. to ♃; ♃ in the Asc.; ♃ ☌ ♀ in the Asc.; ♃ well-asp. in ♉, ♒, or ♓; ♃ in the M.C., and ♀ in the Asc., and in good asp. to each other, and if the ☉ and ☽ are free from ♄ affliction; ♃ Sig. in ♈; ♄ Sig. in ♒; ♄ in ♐ or ♒, affable, courteous and obliging; ♀ having chief dominion over the mind and disposition; ♀ in ♉, ♍, ♎, ♐, or ♒; ♀ Sig. in ♒, very courteous and affable; ♀ Sig. ✶ or △ ♃; ♀ in good asp. with ☿. (See "Many Friends" under Friends; Mild; "Popular" under Reputation; Agreeable, Genteel, Pleasing, and the various paragraphs in this section).

Blunt—(See "Abrupt" in this section).

Breezy—Brisk—Animated—Sprightly—A ♌ characteristic if ♃ is also well-placed and aspected; ♃ strong at B., or born under a ♃ sign, as ♐ or ♓. (See Brisk).

Brisk — (See Brisk; "Breezy" in this section).

Coarse — In Manner — Rough — (See Coarse, Gross, Rough, Unrefined).

Coldness—Of Manner—♄ influence; ♄ strong at B., and espec. acting thru the negative signs; lack of planets in the fiery signs; planets obscurely placed, out of dignity, and espec. in the mutable, watery and earthy signs. These influences tend to reserve. (See Indifferent, Recluse, Reserved, Secretive).

Commanding — (See Commanding, Proud).

Conduct—(See the various paragraphs under Conduct).

Courteous — (See Amiable, Genteel, Obliging, in this section).

Cross—(See Abrupt, Gruff, in this section; Anger; "High Strung" under High; Irascible; Irritable; "High Temper" under Temper; Vicious).

Death — Manner of Death — (See the various paragraphs under Death).

Disagreeable—The ☉ Sig. in ♏; the ☉ Sig. ☌ ♄; ♄ Sig. □ or ☍ the ☉, or ☌ ☿; ♃ Sig. in ♊ near Aldebaran; ♂ Sig. in ♋, unamiable; ☿ Sig. in ♑. (See Abrupt, Coldness, Cross, Gruff, Ill-Mannered, Rough, in this section).

Disposition; Dreamy; Elegant — Refined and Engaging In Manner— The ☽ in an angle, or in ♉ or ♎ at B.; ☿ Sig. ⚹ or △ ♀; ♂ ascending at B., and free from the rays of other planets. (See Agreeable, Amiable, Obliging, in this section).

Engaging—(See Amiable, Elegant, in this section).

Evil—(See "Manners" under Evil).

Excellent—(See "Elegant" in this section).

Excitable—(See Excitable; "Cross" in this section).

Explosive—(See "Abrupt" in this section; Anger; "Manner" under Explosive; Fierce; "High Temper" under Temper).

Fascinating — (See Agreeable, Amiable, Elegant, Obliging, in this section; Beautiful, Complexion, Countenance, Expression, Eyes, Face, Glances, Hair, Look, etc.).

Fierce—♂ people. (See Anger, Cruel, Fierce, Vicious, Violent).

Forceful — (See Active, Energetic, Forceful, Quick).

Genteel—(See Genteel; Amiable, Elegant, in this section).

Good Manners — (See Accomplished, Agreeable, Elegant, Genteel, Obliging, in this section).

Graceful Manner — (See Graceful; "Good" in this section).

Gross Manners—(See Gross; "Coarse" in this section).

Gruff—Cross—Rude—Surly—In Hor'y Q. ♄ Sig. in ♌. (See "Cross" in this section; Rough).

Habits—(See the various paragraphs under Habits).

Haughty—(See Breezy, Proud, in this section).

Highly Accomplished — ☿ Sig. in ♎. (See "Accomplished" in this section).

Ill-Mannered—The ☽ Sig. ☌ ♄. (See "Disagreeable" in this section).

Indifferent Manner — (See Apathy, Dull, Indifferent, Inert, Lassitude).

Jerky and Nervous — (See Jerky; "Nervous" in this section).

Jumps Forward — (See "Skippish" in this section).

Life — Manner of Life — (See Active, Ambition, Careless, Companions, Conduct, Criminal, Drink, Dull, Dishonest, Extravagant, Gamblers, Gluttonous, Habits, Happy, Honest, Idle, Immodest, Improvident, Inactive, Indulgent, Intemperate, Lazy, Low, Miserable, Miserly, Men, Morals, Neglectful, Poverty, Prodigal, Reckless, Riches, Riotous, Shameless, Social Relations, Thieves, Women, Wretched, etc. Also look in the alphabetical arrangement for the subject you have in mind).

Mad and Fierce—(See "Fierce" in this section; "Angry Look" under Look; "High Temper" under Temper).

Manly and Sober — In Address and Manner—♃ in the Asc.; ♃ ruler and well-aspected; born under ♃, sober and commanding. (See Commanding, Grave, Serious).

Meek; Mild; Modest—Retiring—(See Bashfulness, Immodest, Meek, Modesty, Reserved. Retiring, Shy).

Nervous Manner—♄ in the 1st H; ♄ ruler and afflicted at B. (See Jerky, Nerves, Restlessness).

Obliging — Polite—Courteous—Agreeable — Decorous — Excellent Manners, etc.—The ☉ influence tends to great decorum outwardly, and also the ☊ influence; the ☉ Sig. in ♊, affable, courteous and kind; ♄ well-asp. in ♒, courteous; ♃ in the Asc.; ♃ Sig. in ♈, ♊, or ♐; ♃ in ♎, obliging; ♃ in ♐, courteous; the ☽ Sig. in ♒, affable, courteous and inoffensive (see Harmless); ♀ Sig. in ♉, ♊, or ♐; ♀ Sig. in ♒, affable and courteous; ♀ Sig. ☌ ☿; ☊ gives a courteous and free disposition. (See Accomplished, Agreeable, Amiable, Elegant, Genteel, in this section).

Pleasing; Polite—(See "Obliging" in this section).

Profane; Proud—(See "Breezy" in this section; Proud).

Quarrelsome—(See Quarrels).

Refined—(See "Elegant" in this section; "Elegant Mind" under Elegant; Refined).

Reserved—(See Meek, Modest, in this section).

Retiring—(See "Modest" in this section; Grave, Melancholic, Prudery, Quiet, Recluse, Retiring; "Secretive under Secret; Serious, Shy).

Rough — (See Coarse, Brutish, Pity, Rough; Disagreeable, Gruff, Ill-Mannered, Violent, in this section).

Rude — (See Disagreeable, Gruff, Rough, in this section).

Skippish Manner — Jumps Forward When Speaking—(See "Nodding" under Head; Skippish).

Sober and Manly — (See "Manly" in this section; Sober).

Speech — Manner of Speaking — (See Speech).

Stately—(See Commanding).

Stiff In Manner—(See Coldness, Disagreeable, Reserved, Retiring, in this section).

Surly—(See "Gruff" in this section).

Taciturn—Silent—Reserved—Not Inclined to Converse—♄ influence. (See Melancholic, Reserved, Retiring, Secretive, Serious).

Temperament—(See Temper, Temperament).

Unpleasant Manner—(See Coarse, Disagreeable, Gruff, Violent, in this section).

Unrefined—(See Coarse, Disagreeable, Gruff, Ill-Mannered, Rough, Violent, in this section; Unrefined).

Untidy; Violent—In Manner—Rough—Rude—Disagreeable—Repulsive, etc.—♅ ascending at B., or with the chief Sig. of the map; ♂ in the Asc. or M.C., and affl. by ♄; ♂ in ♈ or ♍ in the Asc. or M.C., and afflicted; the ♍ influence strong at B.; the ☉ or ☽ in ♍ and affl. by ♂. (See Anger, Brutish, Cruel, Pity, Vicious, Violent).

Walk—Manner of—(See Gait, Stooping, Walk). Also for other study see such subjects as Appearance, Countenance, Expression, Gestures, Glances, Expression, Eyes, Face, Look, Motion, Movement, Quick, Slow, etc.

MANSLAUGHTER—Danger of Committing—The ☽ to the ☌ Caput Algol. (See "Fratricide" under Father; Homicide, Murder).

MANUBRIUM—(See Sternum).

MANY—

Many Calamities—(See Calamities).

Many Children—(See Children).

Many Complications—In Disease—(See Complications; "Complications" under Disease).

Many Dangers—Subject To—(See "Many Dangers" under Dangers; Perils).

Many Diseases—(See Diseases).

Many Enemies—(See Enemies; "Hated by Others" under Hate).

Many Friends—(See Friends).

Many Long Illnesses—(See "Many Illnesses" under Ill-Health; "Long Illnesses" under Long).

Many Sicknesses—(See Sickness).

MAP—The Star Map of Birth—The Nativity—Geniture—The Radix—Chart of Birth—The Figure of the Heavens for the actual Moment of Birth, at the time of the first cry, when the magnetism of the Universe is breathed into the lungs, shows the stamp which is put upon the native, and the tendencies of temperament he will be apt to follow during his lifetime, the rate of his vibrations, etc. This figure is like a flashlight picture, and the native is really a miniature picture, or photograph, of the Universe for that moment, and as seen from the place of birth, and he will partake of the vibrations, forces, and influences that were operating in the Universe, and the Planetary forces that were reflected and focussed to the place of birth. In Astrology, the moment the child is ushered into the world, or when the cord is cut, are not considered a basis for the map of birth, but the time is taken for the first cry, or breath, when the vibrations of the Universe are indrawn and stamped upon the native. Thus, by a study of the Map of Birth, and the Signs, Houses, and Aspects of the Planets at birth, forecasts can be made about the Health, the Mind, the Diseases liable to, the Temperament, Prospect of Life, the Degree of the Vitality, the best Location for Health, the Shape of the Body, the Physical Constitution, the Complexion, the Financial Prospects, the Business Suitability, whether Positive or Negative, a Leader or Follower, the Religious Propensities, about Friends, Enemies, Marriage, Love Affairs, Travel, Residence, etc., and about every subject that is vital to human life, and in the affairs, fate, destiny, character, success or failure, good health or ill-health of the native, etc. This map, however, does not necessarily show the inner, or real character, but only tendencies, the environment and possible contacts with the outer world, the problems to be worked out during the present life. The real character, the Ego, the Spirit, its nature, present stage of Evolution, etc., are better shown and indicated by the map for the time of Conception, known as the Prenatal Epoch Map, for such map indicates the nature of the incoming Ego, its past, and also much of the fate that is overhanging the native, the causes and effects, the sowing and reaping, the difficulties of life and temperament that must be overcome if the native would advance, and not stand still, or fall behind, or become a straggler in the Universe. Every student should make a deep study of Astrology, the Secret and Esoteric Doctrines, that he may the better understand the plan of life, destiny, why you are here, where you came from, and where you go from here, and these matters are well discussed in the various textbooks and writings of the Occult and Metaphysical Societies of the World, and also in various Religious Organizations. The Map of Birth is said to reveal the secrets of the Soul, and if you do not want these to be known, and your true nature revealed, your weaknesses, as well as your strong points, do not give your birth data to a qualified Astrologer. Every student should make a thorough study of the mathematics of star map work, and be able to erect a map for any time and place on Earth. To learn to make Star Maps, purchase the book, "Casting the Horoscope" by Alan Leo. This book can be purchased from Occult Book Centers, or direct from the "Modern Astrology" Office at 42 Imperial Buildings, Ludgate Circus, London, E. C. 4, England. This Office also sends out a very reliable Correspondence Course of Lessons in Star Map Work, and on Esoteric Astrology, and the writer of this Encyclopaedia took this Course many years ago, and got a good start in Map and Horoscope work. Other Lesson Courses in Star Map work, and Astrology in general, are sent out by "The Church of Light", (formerly "The Brotherhood of Light"), at 818 Union League Bldg., Los Angeles, Calif. Also a Lesson Course is sent out by the Llewellyn College of Astrology, at 8921 National Blvd., Los Angeles. The A. F. Seward & Co., Astrological Publishers and Book Dealers, 3620 Rokeby St., Chicago, Illinois, also send out a Lesson Course in Astrology, and Star Map work. The practicing student also needs a set of Raphael's Ephemeris for the years from 1860 to the present time, so as to have the Planetary Tables at hand to look up the planetary influences at birth among his clients and friends, and from which to make Star Maps of

Birth. The student also needs Dalton's Tables of Houses, to get the Signs and Degrees of the Zodiac on the cusps of the Houses for the various degrees of Latitude over the Earth, and at the birthplaces of people born in the different Nations and Countries of the World, and at any hour of the day or night, whether in the Northern or Southern Hemispheres. With this equipment, and a thorough knowledge of the Elements of Astrology, Physicians and Healers should be able to become very proficient in Medical Astrology, Diagnosis, Prognosis, etc.

For further study along this line see such subjects herein as Aspects, Baptism, Benefics, Birth, Character, Conception, Congenital, Day, Destiny, Diagnosis, Diathesis, Directions, Dominion, Elevated, Evil, Fate, Free Will (see Will); Geocentric, Good, Heredity, Horoscope, Houses, Majority, Malefics, Moment of Birth (see "Moment" under Birth); Natal, Nativity, Negative, Night, Occidental, Oriental, Planets, Positive, Powerful, Prenatal, Prognosis, Radix, Rising, Sensitive, Setting, Signs, Vulnerable, etc. Also look in the alphabtical arrangement for subjects you may have in mind.

MARASMUS—A Wasting or Emaciation —Tabefaction—(See Assimilation, Atrophy, Consumptions, Decay, Degeneration, Emaciation, Lean, Nutrition, Phthisis, Tabes, Thin, Tuberculosis, Wasting, etc.).

MARCASSITE—(See Iron).

MARITIME—Pertaining to the Sea—

Loss of Life—Much Loss of Life Among Maritime People—Much Injury to Sailors—Shipwrecks and Much Loss of Life At Sea, etc.—♄ in ♏, lord of the year at the Vernal Equinox, and occidental; ♄ in S. Lat. in ♓, and lord of the year at the Vernal E. (See "Long Journeys" under Journeys; Navigation, Ocean, Sailors, Sea, Ships, Shipwreck, Travel, Voyages, Water).

Maritime Pursuits—Fond of—♃ in ♋ or ♓; ♃ Sig. ☌ ☽. (See "Fortunate Upon the Seas" under Sea).

MARKAB—A violent star of the 2nd magnitude, in the 5th. Face of ♓, of the nature of ♂ and ♀. Said to threaten a violent death when with the Asc., and to bring great dangers and sufferings to the native when joined with the ☉, ☽, ♂, or the Asc. (See Disgrace; "Females" under Fever, Imprudent; Ruin; "Death by Soldiers" under Soldiers; "Death" under Violent; "Death by Wild Beasts" under Wild). The ☽ when directed to Markab by good aspect is said to give good health. (See "Good Health" under Health).

MARKS—Marked—Marks of—Personal Marks On the Body—Blemishes—Moles —Scars, etc.—Marks, Moles, or some kind of a Blemish, usually are found on those parts of the body ruled by the Signs or Houses containing Planets at B., and especially on the parts ruled by the Asc., Midheaven, or 6th H. Marks may occur on any part of the body, and under the different parts, as Head, Face, Arms, Legs, etc., look for "Blemishes", "Marks", "Moles", "Scars", etc., under these parts, or any part you may have in mind. The influences of the two malefic planets ♄ and ♂ are largely responsible for Marks, Scars, or Blemishes other than Moles, while the ☉ influence away from ♂, and not afflicted by ♂, tends to Moles. Marks tend to be Moles when the part is not afflicted by ♂. The malefics indicate Marks according to their positions. The part ruled by the sign ascending is also subject to Marks, Moles, or a Scar, and also on the part ruled by the sign containing the lord of the Asc., lord of the 6th H., or on the part ruled by the sign on cusp of the 6th. The sign or planet signifying the Mark, when much afflicted, makes the Mark more eminent, obvious, conspicuous, and prominent. The color of Marks is largely determined by the Planets, and the color given by each planet. Thus the ☉ gives a chestnut or olive mark; the ☽ one of a whitish hue, or partly of the color of the planets she aspects; ♄ gives a dark, black, or obscure mark; ♃ a purple of bluish mark; ♂ a red mark, a red mole, or a red birthmark, and a blemish of a reddish color; ♀ gives a yellow or yellowish mark; ☿ one of a pale or lead color. The Mark is on the right side of the body if the sign or planet are masculine, and on the left side if the sign or planet are feminine. If the Significators of the Mark or Mole be above the Earth, or horizon, the Mark is on the forepart of the body, and visible. If the planet be below the horizon, the Mark is inside and invisible, or on the hinder part of the body. The Marks are on the upper, middle, or lower parts of the part ruled, according to whether the first, middle, or last part of a sign ascend, or a planet be in the first, middle, or last part of a sign. (See Left, Lower, Middle, Right, Upper). Saturn in ☌ ♂ in any sign or house tends especially to a mark on the part ruled by such sign or house. Thus ♄ ☌ ♂ in ♈, or in the 1st H., a mark on the head or face; ♄ ☌ ♂ in ♉ or the 2nd H., a mark on the neck, etc. For further examples of the location of Marks or Moles see "Location" under Moles. Peculiar personal Marks are due to the rising of ♄ or ♂. The subject of Marks, Moles and Scars, etc., and their location, kind, color, description, etc., is dealt with very extensively in the books on Horary Astrology, which books are listed in the Article on "Horary Questions" in this book. (See Colors, Horary). The following subjects have to do with Marks, their location, description, causes, etc., which subjects see in the alphabetical arrangement when not considered here.

Accident—The Mark May Be Congenital, or the Result of An Accident—♂ rising in the Asc.

Arms—♄ or ♂ in ♊ or the 3rd H., or ♄ ☌ ♂ in these positions. (See "Moles" under Arms).

Back Part—Of the Body—Marks On—Indicated by planets below the horizon at B.

Birthmarks—(See Moles, Naevus).

Black Marks—Given by ♄.

Blemishes; Bluish Mark—Given by ♃.

Breasts—(See "Marks" under Breast).

Chestnut Color—Given by the ☉.

Chin—(See "Mark" under Chin).

Congenital Marks—(See Birth, Congenital, Naevus; "Accident" in this section).

Conspicuous—The sign or planet signifying the mark being much afflicted. The Sig. of the mark above the Earth at B.

Cuts—(See Lameness, Paralysis, under Cuts).

Dark Marks—Given by ♄.

Defects; Deformities; Dents — ♂ the afflicting planet in a fiery sign tends to a dent or scar.

Expression—A Marked Expression—(See "Difficult" under Expression).

Eyes—A Mark or Scar Near the Eyes —(See Marks, Scars, under Eyes; "Eyes" under Blemishes, Left, Right; "Right Eye" under Scars).

Face—(See Marks, Scars, under Face).

Feet—(See "Marks" under Feet).

Forepart of the Body—Marks On— The Planet or Sign causing the Mark being above the Earth at B.

Foreteeth—(See Teeth).

Front Part—Of the Body—Marks On —(See "Forepart" in this section).

Good Health—Marks of—(See "Good Health" under Health).

Head—(See "Marks" under Head).

Hinder Parts—Marks On—(See "Back Part" in this section).

Horary Questions—The Kind, Location, Color, and Nature of Marks Indicated In — The general influences given in the various paragraphs in this Article also apply to Horary Indications, as many of them are gathered from the Textbooks on Horary Astrology.

Incisors—Marks On — (See "Foreteeth" under Teeth).

Injury—Marks From—Caused usually by ♂, and ♂ rising in the Asc. (See Burns, Cuts, Scars, Stabs, etc.).

Inside — The Marks Inside and Invisible—Given by planets below the horizon at B.

Invisible—Hidden—Inside—(See Back Part, Inside, in this section).

Knees—(See "Scars" under Knees).

Lead Color—Pale and of a Lead Color —Given by ☿.

Left Side—Of the Body—Marks On— The sign or planet causing the mark being feminine. (See "Eyes" in this section).

Location—Of Marks—(See the Introduction, and the various paragraphs in this Article; "Location" under Moles).

Long Life — Marks of — (See "Long Life" under Life).

Lower Parts—Marks On—Caused by the last part of a sign ascending, or a planet in the last few degrees of a sign. In such case the mark is on the lower part of the organ, or part, ruled by such sign. Also malefics in signs which rule the lower parts of the body, as the Legs, Knees, Thighs, Ankles, Feet, etc., cause marks on these parts. (See Lower).

Middle Parts—Of an Organ or Part— Marks On—(See "Organs" under Middle; the Introduction, Lower Parts, Upper Parts, in this Article).

Moles—(See Blemishes, Marks, Moles).

Naevus—Birthmarks—(See Naevus).

Neck—Marks On—Malefics in ♉, the 2nd H., or very low in the Asc. at B. (See "Marks" under Face, Neck).

Obscure—(See "Invisible" in this section).

Obvious—(See "Conspicuous" in this section).

Olive Color—Given by the ☉. Also gives chestnut color.

Pale—Lead Color— ☿ influence.

Parts of Body—Moles On the Various Parts—(See the Introduction, and the various paragraphs in this section).

Peculiar—♄ or ♂ rising tend to peculiar personal marks.

Personal—(See "Peculiar" in this section).

Pitted Degrees—Of the Zodiac—The Asc. or its lord in any of these degrees make the native subject to deep marks, scars, pockmarks, etc. (See Pitted).

Pockmarks—(See "Face" under Smallpox).

Prominent — (See "Conspicuous" in this section).

Purple Marks—Given by ♃.

Rear Parts—Of the Body—Marks On —(See "Back Part" in this section).

Red Marks—And Moles—Given by ♂.

Right Foot — (See "Marks" under Feet).

Right Side—Of the Body—Marks On —The Planet or Sign causing the Mark being Masculine, marks on the right side of the body, or of a member. (See "Left" in this section; Left, Right).

Scars—(See the various paragraphs under Scars).

Shoulders—Marks On—(See "Marks" under Shoulders).

Upper Parts — Of the Body — Upper Parts of an Organ—The 1st face or decanate of a sign rising, or planets in the first part of Signs, marks on the upper part of a part or organ. (See Upper; Arms, Breast, Face, Head, Neck, Shoulders, in this section).

Visible—(See "Conspicuous" in this section).

Whitish Hue—Given by the ☽. (See White).

Wounds—Marks From—Caused by ♂, with ♂ rising, or in the Asc. at B., and by dir.

Yellow Marks—Given by ♀. (See Yellow).

MARRIAGE—The ♎ Sign and the 7th H. rule over Marriage and the Marriage Partner. Marriage affairs are also governed by the ☽. Due to the many paragraphs, or subdivisions, the subject of "Marriage Partner" is made into a separate Article, and just following this one. The following paragraphs have reference to Marriage, the Husband, Wife, their Joys, Happiness, Afflictions, Sorrows, Weaknesses, Health Matters, etc.

Adultery—(See "Adulterous" under Love Affairs).

Antipathy—(See Antipathy, Aversions, Likes, Opposites, Sympathy; "Unhappy" in this section).

Aversion from Marriage—Indifferent to Marriage—The Significators of Marriage in sterile signs, cadent, combust or ℞, as in ♈, ♊, ♌, or ♍; the lord of the 7th H., planets in the 7th, the planet to which the appropriate Luminary first applies, or ♀, the ☽, or lord of the Asc. in a barren sign; the 7° ♍ on the Asc.; ♄ in the 7th H., or in □ or ☍ ♀, tends to, or to delay or deny marriage, or cause separation after marriage. (See Apathy, Bachelors, Celibacy, Deviations; "Free from Passion" under Passion; Perversions, Spinsters).

Bachelors—(See Bachelors; "Aversions" in this section).

Bad Time—For Marriage—(See "Marriage" under Husband).

Barrenness—Sterility—No Promise of Children—(See Barrenness; "Anchorite" under Husband; Impotent; "Unfruitful" under Wife).

Best Time To Marry—The Athenians married at the time of the New ☽, or just after, in the increase and light of the ☽, and the ☽ free from affliction, which was considered the best time. Marry between the New ☽ and her 1st Quarter. The ☽, the Asc., or lord of the Asc. should be in ♊, ♍, ♐, or ♓ at the time of engagement or marriage, for the best results. Let the rulers of the Asc. and 7th H. be in good asp. to each other. Let the ruler of the 10th H., or a benefic in the 10th, be in good asp. with the lord of the Asc., or the ☽. (See the various chapters on Marriage in the Textbooks of Astrology).

Celibacy In—(See Celibacy; "Chaste" under Females; "Anchorite" under Husband).

Children—Death of—Many Children—No Children—Sickness of—Children Not Wanted, etc.—(See Barren, Birth, Children, Fruitful; "Children" under Husband; "Childbirth" under Wife).

Clandestine—Given to Clandestine Love Affairs—(See "Free Love" under Free; "Unfaithful" under Husband; Adulterous, Liaisons, Unconventional, Unfaithful, Unlawful, under Love Affairs; "Clandestine" under Sex; "Untrue" under Wife).

Death—Of the Marriage Partner—Of Fiance or Fiancee—(See "Death" under Fiance, Husband, Marriage Partner, Wife). Case—See "Death on Eve of Marriage", No. 677 in 1001 N.N.

Delayed Marriage—Marriage May Be Denied—Born under ♄; ♄ in the 7th H., or ruler of the 7th; ♄ ☌ ☉ or ♀ in a female nativity, and ♄ ☌ ☽ in a male nativity; ♄ ☌ ♀ in ♑; the ☽ in an Occidental Quarter at B., as between the Nadir and Asc., or between the M.C. and Descendant. These rules are more fully given and elaborated upon in the chapters on Marriage in the various Textbooks and Dictionaries of Astrology. (See Apathy, Aversions, Bachelors, Deviations; "Free From Passion" under Passion).

Denied—Marriage Denied—The ☽ or ♀ affl. by ♄, if ♄ is strong and the Significators of Marriage weak at B.; the ☽ or ♀ in barren signs and afflicted by ♄; the ☽ in the occidental quarters and affl. by the ☉ and ♄; the ☽, ♀, and ruler of the 7th H. in barren signs and affl. by ♄ or ♅. (See the chapter on Marriage in Sepharial's Manual of Astrology, and other Textbooks).

Deviations—(See Apathy, Aversions, Celibacy, Deviations, Perversions).

Divorce—Separation—(See "Unhappy" in this section).

Early Marriage—The ☉, ☽, ♀, and lord of the 7th H. well-aspected, and free from ♄ affliction; no malefic influence over the 7th H.; the ☽ in an oriental quarter at B. Early marriage is before the 28th birthday, and a late marriage after that age, as considered in Astrology. The ☉ ☌ ♀ with females usually leads to a very young marriage, and espec. if ♄ does not afflict these bodies, or the 7th H.

Elderly Person—Marries One Older Than Himself—(See "Older" in this section).

Fiance—Fiancee—Death of—(See Fiance).

Fickle—The Affections Changeable—(See "Fickle" under Love Affairs).

Free Living—Free Love—Free from Passion—(See Free; "Free From" under Passion).

Fruitful Marriage—♃ or ♀ in the 5th or 11th H. in maps of both parents. (See Fruitful; "Fruitful" under Husband, Wife).

Gains by Marriage—♃ Sig. ☌ the ☽ or ♀; the 8th H. fortunate, occupied by a benefic, and free from the affliction of malefics, apt to gain wealth by marriage; the 4th H. free from malefics, lord of the 4th a benefic, or a benefic in the 4th, the home life is more happy and beneficial.

Happy Marriage—Benefics in the 7th H., or lord of the 7th a benefic and free from affliction of malefics; absence of malefic influence over the 7th H.; the ☉, ☽, and ♀ free from the affliction of ♄ and malefics at B.; ♀ well-aspected in ♉, ♎, or ♓, her strong signs.

Husband—(See the various paragraphs under Husband).

Ill-Health—Of the Marriage Partner—(See "Death", "Unhappy", in this section; "Ill-Health" under Husband, Wife; "Sickly" under Marriage Partner).

Incompatibility—(See Antipathy, Unhappy, in this section).

Indifferent—To Marriage—(See "Aversion" in this section).

Late Marriage—(See "Delayed" in this section).

Length of Marriage—The Sig. of marriage coming to the ☌ or ill-asp. a malefic after marriage usually terminates the marriage, either by separation or death of the marriage partner. Thus if ♀ were in the 1° ♎, and ♄ in 10° ♎, the length of the marriage would ordinarily be 10 years, etc. (See the Chapter on "Length of Marriage" in Sepharial's Manual of Astrology).

Liaisons—(See "Clandestine" in this section).

Libra—The Sign of Marriage—(See Libra, Seventh House).

Loose Morals—(See Morals).

Many Marriages—The ☉, ☽, and many planets in the double-bodied signs at B.; the ☽ in ♊, ♐, or ♓, and aspected by several planets from bicorporeal signs, tends to plurality of wives; the ruler of the Asc. in the 7th H. in a double-bodied sign, or in ☌ the ruler of the 7th in such a sign, plurality of marriages. (See Double-Bodied).

Marriage Partner—(See the next Article after this one. Also see Husband, Wife).

Mother Fixation—Tendency to Marry a Woman Older Than Himself, and a Replica of His Mother—Caused by the ♋ sign prominent at B., or the ☽ strongly afflicted by ♄. In a female nativity the ♑ sign strong or prominent, and with the ☉ affl. by ♄, a tendency to marry a man older than herself, or one who resembles her father in mind, temperament, and body.

No Marriage—(See "Denied" in this section).

Not Inclined to Marry—(See "Aversion" in this section).

Nymphomania—Unbridled Passion In Women In the Married Life or Single—(See Nymphomania).

Occult Views On—Born under the strong influence of ♆ or ♅. (See Celibacy; "Anchorite" under Husband; "Vows and Restraints" under Love Affairs; Unconventional; "Platonic" in this section).

Older Than Himself—Marries An Elderly Person—Born under the strong influence of ♄, or who have ♄ as ruler; ♄ affl. the ☉, ☽, or ♀, and where the love nature is grave, sedate, and rather mournful, and not frivolous, joyous, or careless. (See "Mother Fixation" in this section).

Opposites—Marrying Opposites—(See Opposites).

Passion—Excess of—Free From—(See Amorous, Apathy, Aversions, Bachelors; "Free From", "Passional Excesses", under Passion; Spinsters; "Aversions" in this section).

Perversions—(See this subject).

Platonic Unions—♆ in or afflicting the 7th H.; ♆, ♅, or ♄ in the 5th H., or affecting this house or the lord of the 5th; ♆, ♅, or ♄ in the 5th or 7th H., or divided between these houses, and aspecting each other; ♂ afflicting ♀, and espec. where ♆, ♄, or ♅ may also enter into the configuration, giving advanced or occult views as to marriage and sex life. (See Apathy, Celibacy, Co-

habitation; "Chaste" under Females; "Free from Passion" under Passion).

Plurality of Marriages—(See "Many Marriages" in this section).

Quarrels In—Malefics in ♎ or the 7th H.; ♄ or ♂ ☌ ♀; ♀ affl. in ♏. (See Antipathy, Clandestine, Deviations, Fickle, Occult, Unhappy, in this section; "Unfaithful" under Husband, Love Affairs; "Untrue" under Wife).

Restless In—The ☽ afflicted in the 7th H.; many planets in double-bodied signs at B.; ♀ afflicted in ♋ or ♏. (See "Fickle" under Love Affairs; "Many Marriages" in this section).

Second Marriage—The ☽ in ♊, ♋, ♏, ♐, or ♓, and aspected by many planets, and espec. if there is a planet in the 7th H. which does not aspect the ☽; the ☽ in a double-bodied sign, and aspected by several planets from signs of this nature. (See "Many Marriages" in this section).

Separation—Or Divorce—(See "Unhappy" in this section).

Seventh House—The House of Marriage—(See Seventh House).

Several Marriages—(See "Many" in this section).

Sex Disturbances—In Marriage—(See Aversion, Celibacy, Deviations, Passion, Unhappy, and the various paragraphs in this section).

Sickness In—(See "Ill-Health" in this section).

Sorrows In—(See "Unhappy" in this section).

Spinsters—(See Spinsters; "Denied" in this section).

Sympathy In—(See "Happy" in this section).

Time of Marriage—(See Early, Late, in this section. Also see the Chapter on "The Time of Marriage" in Sepharial's Manual of Astrology).

Troubles In—(See "Unhappy", and the various paragraphs in this section).

Unconventional Views—(See "Occult" in this section).

Unfaithful—(See "Clandestine" in this section).

Unfortunate Marriage—(See Antipathy, Clandestine, Unhappy, in this section).

Unhappy Marriage—Unfortunate—Troubles In Marriage—Danger of Separation or Divorce—The ♅ influence and affliction seems to be inimical to a happy marriage, and espec. when in the 7th H. at B., and tends to separation, to make one less conventional, to chafe under vows and restraints, more apt to favor free love, and to have some peculiar views about sex; ♀ afflicted by ♅, and ♀ ☌ ♅, tend to many troubles in marriage, and with possible ill-health resulting therefrom; malefics in the 7th H., or ruling this house. (See Antipathy, Clandestine, Fickle, Quarrels, Restless, in this section; Husband, Incompatible, Marriage Partner, Opposites; "Law Suits" under Public; "Married Women" under Sex; Sympathy, Wife, Widowers, Widows).

Unlikely—Case—See "Marriage Unlikely", Nos. 246 and 278, in 1001 N.N.

Vows—Chafes Under Vows and Restraints—♅ influence; ♅ in the 7th H., or afflicting ♀. (See "Occult" in this section).

Widower; Widows; Wife—(See the various paragraphs under Wife).

Women—Married Women—(See Marriage Partner; "Married Women" under Sex; Wife).

MARRIAGE PARTNER—This subject is also considered under Husband, Wife, and Marriage. The influences in this section may apply to either husband or wife unless qualified.

Accident To—♅ or ♂ afflicted in ♎ or the 7th H.

Death Of—The ☽ in a male nativity applying first to ♃, and then to ♅, or the ☉ in the same way in a female geniture, and espec. if ♅ or ♄ be in the 7th H.; ♅ or ♄ affl. in the 7th H., according to aspects; ♅ in the 7th H. in □ or ☍ ♄ or ♂; ♄ affl. in the 7th H. in a mutable sign; malefics in the 7th H.; lords of the 6th or 8th in the 6th H., and afflicted; lord of the 7th a malefic, and afflicted in the 12th H., does not live to be old. The marriage partner usually dies before the native when he (or she) has ♄ afflicted in the 7th H. in the radix. (See "Death" under Husband, Wife; Early Death, Sudden, Violent, in this section).

Drink—Drunkenness—Marriage-Partner Given to Drink or Drunkenness—(See "Husband", "Marriage Partner", under Drunkenness; "Drink" under Husband, Wife).

Early Death Of—Short Life—The ☉ ☌, □, or ☍ ♄ at B.; ♆, ♅, or ♄ in the 7th H. and afflicted; ♄ in the 7th H. whether afflicted or not; ♄ affl. in ♎; lord of the 8th H. a malefic, and afflicted in the 7th. (See "Early Death" under Early, Husband, Wife).

Fiancee—Death of—(See Fiance).

Husband—(See the various paragraphs under Husband).

Ill-Health Of—(See "Sickly" in this section).

Neurotic—Neurotic Wasting of the Marriage Partner—♆ affl. in the 7th H. (See Wasting).

Relatives Of—Kindred—Ruled by the 9th H., lord of this house, planets occupying the house, and the aspects affecting this house or its lord, show their state and condition, and their attitude toward the native. (See "Relatives" under Husband, Wife).

Self-Indulgent—♃ afflicted in the 7th H. (See Self-Indulgent).

Sex Addict—♂ in ♎, ♏, or ♓ in the 7th H., and espec. ♂ affl. in ♏, or ♂ ☌ ♀ or the ☽ in ♏. (See Amorous, Nymphomania; "Passional Excesses" under Passion).

Short Life—(See "Early Death" in this section).

Sickly—♄ in the 7th H., and espec. if afflicted by the ☉ or ☽; lord of the 7th a malefic, and in the 12th H. and afflicted. (See "Early Death" in this section; "Ill-Health" under Husband, Wife).

Sudden Death Of—♅ or ♂ afflicted in the 7th H.; ♅ affl. in ♎, by accident, or some sudden, strange and mysterious malady; ♂ affl. in ♎, by accident or acute disease. (See "Sudden Death" under Husband, Wife).

Violent Death Of—♂ afflicted in the 7th H. (See "Death" under Violent).

Wasting Disease Of—Neurotic Wasting—(See "Neurotic" in this section).

Which Will Die First—(See "Dies Before Wife" under Husband; "Dies Before Husband" under Wife).

Wife—(See the various paragraphs under Wife).

MARROW—The Fatty Substance in the Cavity of a Long Bone—

Inflammation Of—Osteomyelitis—Caused by ♂, and in the part ruled by the sign containing ♂ at B.; ♂ affl. in ♐ tends to inflammation of the marrow in the femur of the leg. Fracture of the femur may occur when ♄ is ☌ ♅ in ♐, and inflammation of the marrow in the femur result. Also osteomyelitis in the marrow of the bones, and with pus development, may follow an injury caused by ♂ in the part ruled by the sign containing ♂, and when there are also other malefics in the same sign with ♂. Case—A Case of Osteomyelitis—See Fig. 15C in the book "Astro-Diagnosis" by the Heindels. (See "Marrow", "Osteomyelitis", under Bones; Femur).

Osteomyelitis—(See "Inflammation" in this section).

MARS—The Red Planet, and known as "The God of War". In size ♂ is smaller than the Earth. Mars is, perhaps, the most written about Planet in Astrological Literature, and has more to do with human ills than any other planet, and creates more disturbances in human affairs by his afflictions than any other planet. However, ♂ has a good and powerful influence also, and along with the ☉ is constructive, gives energy, heat, and force to the body, as well as courage and stimulus to the mind. For convenience of reference this Article is arranged in three Sections. Section One, about the General Influences of Mars; Section Two, what Mars Rules, and Section Three, the Diseases and Afflictions of Mars.

— SECTION ONE —

GENERAL INFLUENCES OF MARS—Mars is known as "The Lesser Infortune", and ♄ as "The Greater Infortune", and both are considered as malefic planets, and especially by their afflictions. The action of ♂ is more acute and violent, while that of ♄ is more slow and chronic. The following paragraphs, arranged alphabetically, give briefly the various influences of Mars. For his special Qualities see the paragraph "Qualities" in this section.

Action of Mars—The action of ♂ is inflammatory, hot, dry and barren, and corresponds to pungent odors, burning astringents and hot acids. The action of ♂ is centrifugal, from the center out, tending to redden the surface, cause congestions of the surface of the body, being rubefacient in action, and is not circumferential in circles like the ☉, but a violent expulsion along the lines of the radii. Mars is rubefacient, inflaming, and reddening, and brings the blood to the surface. (See Caustic, Centrifugal, Rubefacient). The plus, or tonic action of ♂, tends to exaggerated action. Mars is an energetic, dynamic, positive, inflammatory, acute, excessive, destructive, constructive by bringing fevers to burn up poisons in the system, is generally an antagonistic influence, and one of the most potent forces among the planets. Mars occidental causes dryness only, and when oriental both heat and dryness. Mars is sudden and intense, while ♄ is slow, tardy, and restrained. Together ♄ and ♂ act as heat and cold, acute and chronic. Mars influence may be compared to a fever, very severe for a time, but not lasting. The basic forms of ♂ action are inflammatory, intensive, poignant, and centrifugal. Mars accelerates and intensifies, and tends to hurts or illnesses by excesses. Mars tends to action, and to make people assertive, and to do and say what they think and believe, and he never makes hypocrites as ♄ does. (See "Planets" under Tonic. Also for the various actions of ♂ see the different paragraphs in this Article).

Afflicted—An afflicted ♂ tends to cause excess of heat, eruptions, fevers, inflammations, excessive action, and violence.

Anareta—♂ may become the Anareta, or the Killing Planet. (See Anareta).

Angel of Mars—Samael.

Aries Sign—Ruled by ♂, and also ♏ is the night sign of ♂. (See Aries, Scorpio). Mars is strong in ♈, ♏, ♑. He has his exaltation in ♑ and his fall in ♋.

Author of Strife—♂ is the author of strife, quarrels, and contentions, as well as of War.

Blood—Takes Part In Blood Making —Draws Blood To the Surface—(See Centrifugal, Haematopoiesis, Haemoglobin, Iron).

Burns Up Impurities—By Fevers and Inflammation—(See Constructive, Fever, Inflammation).

Causes—♂ causes hot diseases, such as Measles, Smallpox, Scarlatina, Fevers, Erysipelas, Inflammations, Typhus Fever, Eruptive Diseases, etc. The ☉ or ☽ joined with ♂ at B. cause the same diseases as if ♂ were in the Asc. (See the Diseases of ♂ in Sec. 3 of this Article).

Centrifugal Action—(See "Action" in this section).

Classification Of—♂ is classified as positive, masculine, electric, hot, dry, fiery, barren, inflammatory, heating, active, forceful, accelerating, intensifying, etc. (See "Qualities", and the various paragraphs in this Article).

Cleansing—♂ cleanses the system by bringing fevers to burn up the excess of poisons and wastes. (See Constructive, Fever, Inflammation).

Color—♂ is known as the "Red Planet", and rules red as a color. Also ♂ rules red in the Solar Spectrum. (See Red). Mars produces a fiery red color, the result of intemperate heat and dryness. Also ♂ rules Iron color, and rules Iron, Steel, etc. (See Color, Iron).

Constructive—The ♂ force is very useful and constructive when properly harnessed and controlled, but destructive when allowed to run wild in our natures. Mars is pathologically constructive by bringing inflammation and rapid fevers to burn up and eliminate the wastes and poisons from the system. (See "Cleansing" in this section).

Day—The Influence of Mars In a Day Nativity—(See Day, Night; "Day" in Sec. 3 of this Article).

Denotes—♂ denotes high blood pressure, sharp pains, rapid fevers, external and internal hemorrhages, heat, inflammation, swellings, sores, ruptures, effusion of blood, etc. Mars denotes, or shows death by fevers, burns, injuries, violence, etc. (See "Death" in Sec. 3 of this Article).

Destructive—The ♂ influence, and especially his afflictions, are very destructive and pernicious over the average person who is drifting in life, and uncontrolled, and leads to much strife, to quarrels, contentions, bloodshed, etc. His influence is also constructive in many ways, by making blood, haemoglobin, cleansing the body, and by giving daring, courage, and fortitude to meet the battles of life. (See Action, Cleansing, Constructive, Pernicious, in this section).

Directions of Mars—The Directions of ♂ are more dangerous during the ♂ Period of Life, from the 42nd to 56th years, a 14-year period. (See Directions, Periods).

Diseases Of—(See Sec. 3 of this Article; "Denotes" in this section).

Drugs Of—(See Herbs, Remedies, Typical Drugs, in this section).

Eighth House—The House of ♏ and ♂. (See Eighth House).

Emotional Nature—♂ is King of the Emotional, Sense, and Passional nature. (See Desire, Emotions, Passion).

Exaltation—♂ has his exaltation in the ♑ sign.

Exerts—♂ exerts a quick, hot, positive, electric, heating, and infectious nature.

Fall—♂ has his fall in the ♋ sign.

First House—The House of ♈ and ♂. (See First House).

Focuses Heat—♂ focuses heat and draws an abundance of blood to the part ruled by the sign he is in at B.

Friendly To Nothing—♂ is classed as a violent planet and is said to be friendly to nothing, and ♂ people are usually very blunt, abrupt, quarrelsome, and unfriendly.

Geometrically—Geometrically ♂ is the angle, the acute angle, sharp and piercing.

Glycogen—The ♂ Influence Over Glycogen—(See Glycogen).

Heat—♂ is hot and fiery and produces and focuses heat. (See Fevers; "Animal Heat" under Heat; "Focuses" in this section).

Heat and Dryness—♂ is hot and dry by nature. (See "Heat and Dryness" under Dry).

Herbs Of—(See "Mars Group" under Herbs).

Hot In Nature—♂ is the planet of action, and stirs life into action, is hot in nature and sets everything to boiling. (See Action, Heat, in this section).

Hour of Mars—(See "Hours" under Planets).

Houses of Mars—The 1st and 8th Houses are especially affiliated with ♂, which houses correspond to the ♈ and ♏ signs, the signs ruled by ♂, and ♂ when in these houses is very strong and powerful in health matters, disease, accidents, hurts, etc., according to his aspects, or the afflictions to ♂ at B., and by dir. The house and sign occupied by ♂ at B. are centers of activity, energy, and augmentation. (See Eighth House, First House).

Impurities—♂ burns up the impurities of the system. (See "Constructive" in this section).

Indicates—♂ afflicted indicates involuntary muscular action. (See Afflicted, Tends To, and the various paragraphs in this section).

Influence of Mars—This subject is covered largely by the various paragraphs in this Article. Note especially the adjectives under "Qualities" in this section. Mars is dynamic energy, which is said to be the most salient characteristic of ♂. Mars by reflecting the Solar Forces gives dynamic power, but the dynamic energy of ♂, unless directed and controlled, tends to palpitation, to accelerated motion, and to tear everything into pieces. Mars tends to give an active, hasty, and intensive life, and is just the opposite of the ♄ influence, which tends to delays, hindrances, decay, defects, denuding, stoppages, and to slow down the powers and forces of the native by his afflictions. Mars gives some of our worst faults, as well as some of our best virtues, for without his influences at B. we would tend to be cowards, very timid, weaklings, without courage, bravery, and resolution. (See Action, Constructive, Destructive, Qualities, Zest, and the various paragraphs in this Article).

King Of—(See "Emotional Nature" in this section).

Lesser Infortune—♂ is the Lesser Infortune, and ♄ is called the Greater Infortune, but some Authorities think and say that ♂ should be called the Greater Infortune, for his damage and destructive powers are almost without parallel when he is afflicting the native, and especially in a violent map. (See Action, Destructive, in this section; Malefics).

Life—♂ being the planet of action stirs life into action. The ☉ and ♂ are friendly, and both play their part in giving life, blood, vital force and energy to the system, and also courage, daring, and fortitude to the mind. (See "Fires of Life" under Life).

Malefics—The Malefic Planets are ♆, ♅, ♄, ♂. (See Malefics).

Martial—♂ tends to make people martial, bellicose, belligerent, warlike, and fond of Martial Exploits, and to be a good Soldier. (See War).

Mental Qualities—Given by ♂—Antagonistic, Courageous, Energetic, Impetuous, Quarrelsome, Rash. (See "Qualities" in this section).

Metal Ruled by ♂—Iron and its products, as Steel, Sharp-Edged Tools, Weapons made of Iron and high-tempered Steel. (See Iron, Therapeutics).

Minerals Ruled by ♂—Trap Rocks, Cinnabar.

Motion—♂ quickens, accelerates, and increases motion, movement, and action in body and mind. (See "Accelerated" under Motion).

Night—♂ influence by night, and in Night Nativities—(See Day, Epilepsy, Insanity, Night; "Night" in Sec. 3 of this Article).

Occidental—♂ when occidental produces dryness only. (See Occidental, Oriental; "Action", "Oriental", in this section).

Oriental—♂ when oriental causes both heat and dryness. (See "Action", "Occidental", in this section; Oriental).

Own Worst Enemy—People born under ♂ tend to be quarrelsome, and their own worst enemy. (See "Own Worst Enemy" under Enemies).

Passion—♂ is the King of the Passional Nature. (See Passion).

Pathological Action—Of Mars, and of the ♂ Group of Herbs and Minerals—Pathologically ♂ is Caustic, Vesicant, Eruptive, Febrile, Heating, Inflammatory, Rubefacient. Mars also by his afflictions, or by the action of a ♂ Drug or Remedy, tends to affect, disturb, or change the action of the Cerebro-Spinal and Sympathetic Nervous Systems, the Ductless Glands, the Genito-Urinary and Renal Systems, and Vaso-Dilatation. The pathological action of ♂ is both constructive and destructive. (See Constructive, Destructive, Tonic, in this section).

People—Mars People are usually quick and active, and move about freely. (See "Martial", and the various paragraphs in this section, for the various characteristics of ♂ people).

Period—The Mars Period of Life— (See "Directions" in this section).

Pernicious—♂ is very pernicious and destructive in his influences when following or succeeding the ☉. (See "Destructive" in this section; Pernicious).

Plants and Herbs—(See "Mars Group" under Herbs; Therapeutic, Typical Drugs, in this section).

Predisposes To—Accidents, Anger, Cuts, Excitability, High Fever (see Fever); Foolhardiness, Fractures, Gunshot Wounds, Haste, Hurts, Inflammations, Injuries, Murder, Rashness, Recklessness, Scalds, High Temper (see Temper); Violence, etc. (See these subjects).

Presides Over—Mars presides over the Haematopoiesis, or Blood Making; the Red Blood Corpuscles and the Haemoglobin in the Blood; the Iron in the Food and Blood; the Hepatic Process (see Liver); the Sthenic Process. (See Haematopoiesis, Haemoglobin, Iron, Sthenic).

Principle Of—Anger, Energy, Expansion, Inflammation.

Produces—♂ produces the heat and dryness of the body, fevers, inflammations, accidents, injuries, wounds, rashness, etc.

Professions Ruled By—Vocations of —The Employments of—Chemists, Surgeons, Dentists, Pharmacists, Butchers, Military People, Warriors; Workers with Sharp-edged Tools, Metals and Fire; Hazardous and Dangerous Callings.

Qualities Of—Abrupt, Abusive, Accelerating, Accentuating, Acidy, Action, Active, Acute, Aggravating, Aggressive, Amorous, Anger, Antagonistic, Aphrodisiac, Argumentative, Assertive, Astringent, Augmentative, Barren, Bellicose, Belligerent, Boiling, Bold, Brave, Burning, Caloric-Producing, Caustic, Centrifugal, Choleric, Coalescent, Coarse, Combative, Combustive, Congestive, Constructive, Contagious, Contemptuous, Contentional, Courageous, Cruel, Dangerous, Delusive, Derisive, Destructive, Discordant, Disdainful, Disorderly, Disruptive, Domineering, Drastic, Dry, Dynamic, Electric, Eliminating, Emotional, Energetic, Energizing, Enhancing, Enlarging, Eruptive, Escharotic, Evolutionary, Exaggerating, Excessive, Exciting, Expansive, Explosive, Expulsive, Fearless, Febrile, Festering, Feverish, Fierce, Fiery, Foolhardy, Forceful, Frenzied, Fulminating, Furious, Harmful, Harsh, Hasty, Heating, Hot, Hot-Tempered, Hurtful, Impetuous, Impulsive, Incisive, Infectious, Inflammatory, Injurious, Intemperate, Intensive, Jealous, Kinetic, Lacerating, Lascivious, Life-Giving, Loosening, Lustful, Malefic, Malevolent, Malicious, Malignant, Martial, Masculine, Militant, Mischievous, Mocking, Murderous, Nocturnal, Offensive, Painful, Passionate, Pathological, Penetrating, Pernicious, Poignant, Poisonous, Positive, Pungent, Quarrelsome, Radiating, Rapid, Rash, Reckless, Red, Reddening, Resolute, Resolvent, Revolutionary, Robust, Rough, Rubefacient, Ruddy, Savage, Scornful, Self-Preservative, Sensuous, Severe, Sharp, Stimulant, Sudden, Tonic, Torturing, Turbulent, Uncompromising, Uncontrolled, Unfriendly, Unreasonable, Unruly, Vesicant, Vicious, Violent, Vital, Volcanic, Wanton, Warlike, Warring, Willful, Worrisome, Wounding, Zestful, etc.

Red Planet—♂ is known as the Red Planet, as his color is red as he appears in the sky. He rules the color Red. (See Red).

Remedies Of—(See "Mars Group" under Herbs; "Treatment" under Red; Therapeutic Qualities, Typical Drugs, in this section).

Representative Of—♂ is representative of Courage and Animal Strength.

Represents—♂ represents the Male Sex generally, Doctors, Surgeons, Military Men, and all who use force and energy, and who are positive, assertive, and aggressive.

Ruler—♂ as Ruling Planet tends to give force, energy, boldness, aggressiveness, courage, etc., to the native. (See "Mental Qualities", and the various paragraphs in this section).

Salient Characteristic—Dynamic Energy. (See Dynamic).

Saturn and Mars—These planets act in an opposite manner. Mars is acute, and ♄ chronic; ♂ is accelerating, while ♄ slows up the action and functions of the body. The diseases of ♂ are relieved by the remedies of ♄. Mars is hot and ♄ is cold. Mars is centrifugal, working from the center out, driving blood to the surface, while ♄ is centripetal, chilling the surface, and driving the blood inwards, causing internal congestions. (See "Action", and the various paragraphs in this Article; Saturn).

Scorpio Sign—The Night Sign of ♂. (See Scorpio).

Sense Nature—♂ is King of. (See "Emotional Nature" in this section).

Significator Of—♂ is Sig. of Violence and Murder; of High Fevers and Inflammations; of Acute Diseases; of Quarrels, Disputes, War, etc.

Signs Ruled by Mars—♈ and ♏.

Stars of Mars Nature—Fixed Stars and Nebulous—Aldebaran, Antares, Bull's North Horn, Castor, Cor Leo, Crater, Deneb, Hyades, Hydra's Heart, Markab, Pleiades, Pollux, Regulus, Sirius. (See these subjects. Also see Nebulous; "Mars Group" under Stars).

Strife—♂ is the Author of—(See "Author Of" in this section).

Strong—♂ is strong in ♈, ♏, ♑, and in the Asc. or 10th H. (See "Aries Sign" in this section).

Sun and Mars—These two bodies are sympathetic in nature, both fiery, life-giving, constructive. Mars aids the ☉ in maintaining life, and by bringing fevers and inflammations to burn the refuse and impurities out of the system. In this way ♂ has a constructive influence over the body. Mars transmutes the Solar Forces into passion, anger, and animal spirits, and is ever a dangerous and consuming fire unless controlled by the Will, the Reason, and by Spiritual Attainment. Mars working with the ☉ tends to aggravate and accentuate the ☉ diseases. The aspects of ♂ to the ☉ are necessary to give zest to life, and his bad aspects are better than none at all. (See Sun).

Surgery—♂ the planet of. (See Operations, Surgeons).

Temperament—♂ gives the Choleric Temperament. (See Choleric).

Tends To—Mars influences tend to exaggerated action, violence, disputes, quarrels, destructiveness, bleeding, effusions of blood, cuts, burns, high fevers; short, quick, and violent diseases and affections. (See the various paragraphs in this Article).

Therapeutic Qualities—Aphrodisiac, Caustic, Escharotic, Resolvent, Rubefacient, Stimulant, Tonic, Vesicant. (See these subjects).

Tonic Action Of—The plus, or Tonic Action of ♂, tends to exaggerated action of mind and body. (See Exaggerated, Motion, Tonic).

Typical Drugs Of — Arnica, Arsenic, Bryonia, Cantharides, Capsicum, Cinchona, Iron, Nux Vomica, Quinine, Sarsaparilla, Strychnine, Sulphur, Tonics. (See "Mars Group" under Herbs; "Therapeutic Qualities" in this section).

Vocations Of—(See "Professions" in this section).

War and Quarrels—♂ is the Author and Instigator of. (See Quarrels, War).

Zest—The aspects of ♂ are necessary to give Zest. (See Zest).

— SECTION TWO —

MARS RULES—The different subjects over which Mars rules are here listed alphabetically. See these subjects in the alphabetical arrangement—Accelerated Motion in the Body; Accidents; Acids (Hot Acids); Action and Insistent Action; Adventures; Aggravations; Aggressiveness; Ambitions; Anger; Animal Lust and Passion; Animal Magnetism; Animal Spirits; Animal Strength; Antagonisms; Aries and Scorpio Signs; Arms (Muscles of); Arnica; Arsenic; Assertiveness; Assimilation; Astringents; Augmented Mobility and Sensibility; Barbers; Battle; Bile; Blood Corpuscles (Red); Blood Fibrin; Blood (Hemorrhages of); Blood-Making (Haematopoiesis); Bloodshed; Boldness; Bowels (Muscles of); Bryonia; Burns; Butchers; Cantharides; Capsicum; Centrifugal Action in the Body; Cerebral Ganglia; Cerebral and Genital Poles of Paracelsus; Cerebral Hemisphere (Left); Chemists; Childbirth; Choleric Temperament; Cinchona; Cinnabar; Coction Process in the Body (Combustion, Digestion); Color (Red and Iron Color, Scarlet Red and Shot Crimson); Combativeness (Mental); Combustion (Coction Process); Condiments; Constructive Energy in the Body; Contests; Controversies; Counterirritants; Courage; Criminal Tendencies; Cuts; Dangers and Dangerous Callings; Death by Sharp Fevers, Injury, Violence, etc.; Desire and Insistent Desire; Destructive Energy; Diaphragm; Digestion (Coction Process); Dilator Action (see Vaso); Dissentions; Doctors (Surgeons); Drugs (see "Typical Drugs" in this Article); Dryness of the Body, Earth, and Atmosphere; Ductless Glands; Duels; Dynamic Energy; Ear (Left Ear); Effusion of Blood; Elation and Elevation of Spirits; Elimination of Wastes and Poisons; Emotions; Energy; Enlargements; Eruptions and Eruptive Action; Exaltation and Elation of Spirit; Excesses; Excretion of Urine; External Genitals; External and Internal Humoural Secretions; Face; Fevers; Fibrous Tissue Building; Fire and Fires; Focussed Heat in the Body; Foetus (Growth and Development of Limbs of); Food (Highly Seasoned Food and Condiments); Foolhardiness; Force; Forehead; Forethought (Lack of); Fundament; Gall and Gall Bladder; Ganglia (see "Vaso-Dilator" under Vaso, and the Introduction under Bowels); Generative Organs (External Genitals); Genital and Cerebral Poles of Paracelsus (see Aries, Scorpio); Growth (Increase of); Guns and Gunshot; Haematopoiesis (Blood-Making); Haemoglobin; Head, and Hurts To; Heart (Muscles of); Heat in the Body, and Fevers, and the Heat in the Body Given by Iron and Haemoglobin; Hepatic Process (Adding to or Subtracting from); Herbs of Mars (see "Mars Group" under Herbs); High Death Rate (see Mortality); High Temper (see Temper); Highly Seasoned Food and Condiments; Hot Diseases; Hot-Headedness; Hour of Mars (see "Hours" under Planets); Houses of Mars (see First House, Eighth House); Humoural Secretions (External and Internal); Hurts by Violence; Imagination; Impulses and Impulsiveness; Incisions; Increase of Growth (Enlargements); Inflammations; Injuries; Insistent Action, Desire, and Will; Intemperance; Intemperate Heat and Dryness; Intercostal Muscles; Internal and External Humoural Secretions; Intestinal Ganglia and Plexuses (see the Introduction under Bowels); Iron Metal and Color, and the Iron in Food and the Blood; Jealousies; Kidneys (Pelvis of and the Parts where Stones are Formed); Left Cerebral Hemisphere, and Left Ear; Legs (Muscles of); Life from 42 to 56 Years (see Periods); Liver; Lust; Madness; Magnetism (Animal); Male Relatives; Mental Combativeness; Military People; Mobility (Augmentation of); Motor Nerves; Motor Segment of Spinal Cord; Movement in the Body; Murder; Muscles (Muscular Force and the Muscular System Generally, and the Muscular and Destructive Energy); Naso-Pharynx; Nerves (The Motor Nerves, and the Sympathetic Nervous System); Nose; Operations (Surgical); Organs (External Genitals); Pain (Sharp, Acute and Violent); Palpitations and Accelerated Motion in the Body; Paracelsus (Cerebral and Genital Poles of); Parturition; Passion and Passional Excesses; Pepper (Red); Pharmacists; Pineapple; Plants and Herbs of Mars (see Herbs); Plexuses (see Introduction under Bowels); Poison, Poisoning, and Poison Death; Privates; Prowess; Pungent Odors (see Acids); Quarrels; Quick Action; Quinine; Rashness and Uncontrolled Thinking; Rectum; Red (Red Blood Corpuscles and Increase of, Red Color in the Solar Spectrum, Red Hair); Reins; Relatives (Male); Reproductive Organs; Resolution; Respiratory System (Diaphragm of); Rubefacients; Sarsaparilla; Scalds; Scarlet Color; Scorpio Sign; Secretions (External and Internal Humoural); Sense Nature; Sensibility (Augmentation of); Sensuality; Severe and Violent Diseases; Sex Organs (External, and the Uterus, Vagina); Sharp (Sharp-Edges Tools, Sharp Fevers and Sharp Pains); Signs of Zodiac (Aries and Scorpio); Sinews; Smell (Sense of); Soldiers; Spinal Cord (Motor Segment of); Stabs; Steel; Sthenic Process in the Body; Stimulants; Strife; Strychnine; Sudden Death; Sulphur; Surgeons; Sympathetic Nervous System;

Tar; Taste (Sense of); Temper (High Temper); Tension in the Body; Testicles; Tonics; Trap Rock; Tuesday (Day of the Week); Typical Drugs (see Sec. 1 of this Article); Uncontrolled Thinking; Unfriendliness; Urethra; Urine (Excretion of); Uterus; Vagina; Vaso-Dilator Action of the Cerebral Ganglia; Veins; Viciousness; Violence (Violent Death, Violent Actions, Violent Diseases); Vital Energy; Vitality; War; Warriors; Wastes and Poisons in the Body (Elimination of); Will (Insistent Will and Desire); Witch Hazel; Womb; Wounds; Youth (The Flourishing Time of); Zest.

— SECTION THREE —

MARS DISEASES AND AFFLICTIONS—Here are a few general considerations concerning the action of ♂ in disease, health matters, and his efforts to vitalize, cleanse, and restore the balance to the system. The ☉ and ♂ act together in sympathy in disease, and the diseases of the ☉ are accentuated by ♂. The ☉ joined with ♂ causes the same diseases as when ♂ is in the Asc. The fevers and inflammations caused by ♂ are of a more destructive, quick, burning, and contagious type, while those produced by the ☉ are slower, but severe. Mars by his fevers and inflammations burns up the impurities of the system, and in this regard is constructive. Mars is rubefacient, caustic, centrifugal, and draws or drives the blood to the surface. Mars causes hot diseases, such as Measles, Smallpox, Scarlet Fever, Fevers, Inflammations, Erysipelas, Typhus Fever, etc. Mars is less malignant at night, as his heat is moderated by the moisture of the night. An afflicted ♂ tends to cause heat, eruptions, and excessive action. Also ♂ afflictions indicate involuntary muscular action. Mars diseases tend to be relieved when the Prog. ☽ forms a good aspect to ♀. Mars focusses heat, and draws an abundance of blood to the part ruled by the sign he is in. Mars exerts a quick, hot, positive, electric, heating, and infectious nature. The plus, or tonic action of ♂, tends to exaggerated action of the mind and body. For the Pathological Action of ♂, his Therapeutic Properties, and Typical Drugs of, Remedies of, see these paragraphs in Sec. 1 of this Article. The following are listed as Diseases and Afflictions of Mars, which see in the alphabetical arrangement when not more fully considered here—

Abortion—Death By—(See Abortion).

Abrasions; Absent—♂ Diseases Absent—(See "Nil" in this section).

Accidents; Action—Excessive Action —(See Action, Exaggerated, Rapid).

Acute Diseases—(See Acute).

All Feverish Diseases—And Inflammatory Disorders—(See Fever, Inflammation).

Alteration of Tissues—(See the Introduction under Inflammation).

Amusements—Injury In—Blindness By—(See Amusements, Blindness).

Aneurysm; Angina; Ankylosis;

Artifice—Blindness By—(See Artifice).

Augmentation—(See Augmented).

Battle—Wounds or Death In—(See War).

Bile—Disorders of—(See Bile).

Bladder—Disorders of—Pain In—Stone In—(See Bladder).

Bleeding—Loss of Blood—(See Bleeding; "Loss of Blood" under Blood; Effusions, Hemorrhage).

Blindness—By Amusements, Artifice, Burns, Explosions, Fire, Gunshot, Smallpox—(See Blindness; "Blindness" under these subjects).

Blisters; Blood—The activity of ♂ in the Blood tends to Hemorrhages, Rupture of Blood Vessels, Hemorrhoids, and Excessive Menses. Also ♂ has a centrifugal action on the blood, causing it to rush to the surface, producing congestions and reddening, inflammations, Hyperaemia, etc. Other ♂ disturbances in the Blood, or relating to the Blood, are—Bloody Flux, Corrupt Blood, Determination of Blood to the Head or a Part, Rush of Blood, Flow of Blood, Expectoration of Blood, High Blood Pressure, Hot Blood, Loss of Blood, Shedding of Blood, etc. (See the various paragraphs under Blood).

Blood Vessels—Rupture of—(See Apoplexy, Hemorrhage; "Rupture" under Vessels).

Boils; Bowels—Inflammation and Obstructions In—(See "Muscles" under Bowels; Inflammation, Obstructions).

Brain Fever—(See Brain).

Breakings Out—(See Eruptions).

Breast—Affections and Pains In—(See Breast).

Bruises; Burning Fevers—(See "High" under Fever).

Burns; Bursting Blood Vessels—(See "Rupture" under Vessels).

Calculi—In Kidneys and Bladder—(See Stone).

Carbuncles; Cells—Inflammation of—(See Cells).

Centrifugal Action—(See Centrifugal).

Cerebro-Spinal Disorders—(See "Pathological Action" in Sec. 1 of this Article).

Chickenpox; Childbirth—Dangers, Injury, or Death In—(See Parturition).

Children—Worms In, and Various Diseases of—(See Children, Worms).

Cholera; Choleric Distempers—(See Choleric).

Colliquative Sweats—(See "Night Sweats" under Phthisis).

Congestion of Blood—On the Surface —(See Centrifugal).

Conjunctivitis—(See Conjunctiva).

Constant Fevers—(See "Constant" under Fever).

Consumption—Liable to Consumption —(See "Consumptive" under Consumption).

Contagious Fevers—(See Contagions, Epidemics, Infections).

Corrupt—Corrupt Blood—Corrupt Humours—(See Humours, Impure).

Cough—Dry Cough—(See Cough).

Courses Overflowing—(See Menses).

Crusts—Of Dead Tissue—(See Eschar; "Skin" under Hardening; Sloughing; "Crusts" under Tissues).

Cutaneous Eruptions—(See Eruptions, Skin).

Cuts; Day—The Diseases Caused by ♂ in a Day Nativity—Mars is more malignant by day, due to his increased heat, and augmented by the heat of the ☉, and ♂ is less malignant at night, at his heat is moderated by the coolness and moisture of the night. (See Day, Epilepsy, Insanity, Night).

Dead Tissue — (See "Crusts" in this section).

Death — Mars rules, or causes Death in the following ways. See "Death" under these subjects—Abortion, Accidents, Acute Diseases, Assassination, Battle, Bruises, Burns, Bursting of Blood Vessels (see Vessels); Childbirth (see Parturition); Contagions, Contests, Cuts, Daggers (see Stabs); Dog Bites (see Dogs); Epidemic Diseases; Erysipelas, Excesses, Falls, Fatty Degeneration of the Heart, Fevers, Fire and Fires, Fire Arms, Fractures (Compound); Frenzy, Fury, Gunshot, Hemorrhages, Hot Diseases, Incised Wounds, Infections, Inflammations, Injuries, Lacerations, Loss of Blood, Mad Dog Bites (see Dogs); Madness, Mania, Miscarriage, Mortification, Murder, Operations, Passional Excesses, Ruptures, Scalds, Short and Sudden Illnesses, Smallpox, Spitting of Blood, Stabs, Stone in the Kidney or Bladder, Strangury, Sudden Death, Suicide, Sword, Syphilis, Venery, Violence, Violent Hemorrhage, War, Wounds, etc. (See the various paragraphs under Death).

Degeneration—Fatty Degeneration of the Heart, and Death By—(See Degeneration, Fat, Heart).

Delirium; Depletion—Of the Vitality—(See "Wasted" under Vitality).

Determination of Blood—To the Head or a Part—(See Determination, Flow; "Blood" under Head).

Diabetes; Diaphragm — (See Hernia, Inflammation, under Diaphragm).

Diarrhoea; Diphtheria;

Disfigurements; Distempers—Choleric Distempers, Distempers In the Head, Mad and Sudden Distempers, Venereal Distempers—(See Distempers).

Distentions; Dog Bites—(See Dogs).

Drought; Dry Cough—(See Cough).

Dry and Hot Diseases—(See Fevers; "Dry and Hot Diseases" under Heat).

Dry Sloughing—(See Sloughing).

Dryness—Diseases Concomitant With —Diseases from Excessive Dryness In the Body, or In the Atmosphere—(See Dryness).

Ductless Glands—Disturbed Action of —(See Ductless; "Pathological Action" in Sec. 1 of this Article).

Duels—Injury or Death By—(See Duels).

Dysentery; Dysuria—(See "Strangury" under Urine).

Ear—Left Ear—Pain and Disease In —(See "Left Ear" under Ears).

Effusion of Blood—(See Effusions).

Elation—Undue Exaltation of the Feelings and Emotions—(See "Exaltation" under Emotions).

Enlargements; Enteric Fever—(See "Fever" under Bowels).

Epidemics; Epilepsy — (See "General Causes" under Epilepsy).

Erethism; Eruptions; Erysipelas;

Eschar—(See Eschar, Sloughing).

Exaggerated Action — (See Exaggerated).

Exaltation — Of the Feelings and Emotions—Elation—(See "Exaltation" under Emotions).

Excesses — Hurts or Illness From — Passional Excesses — (See Excesses, Passion, Venery).

Excessive Action—(See Action, Exaggerated; "Hyperkinesia" under Muscles).

Excessive Disorders—(See the various paragraphs under Excess).

Excitation—Unduly Excitable—(See Excitable).

Excoriations; Expansions;

Expectoration of Blood—(See Haemoptysis).

Explosions—Blindness, Death, or Injury By—(See Explosions).

External — External and Internal Hemorrhages—Disorders of the External Genitals — (See Genitals, Hemorrhage).

Eyes — Inflamed — Rheum In — (See Conjunctiva; "Inflamed", "Rheum", under Eyes).

Face — Hurts To — Pockmarked — Smallpox In—Scars On—(See "Hurts", "Scars", under Face; "Face" under Smallpox).

Falls; Famine; Fatty Degeneration—Of the Heart—(See Heart).

Feet — Accidents To — Corrupt Humours In—Excessive Sweats In—Lameness In—(See Feet).

Fevers—All Kinds—Acute—Burning — High — Constant — Habitual — Epidemic—Contagious—Eruptive—Hectic —Rapid — Intermittent—Sharp—Violent—Pestilential—Semitertian—Death By, etc. (See the various paragraphs under Fever).

Fibers — Over-Braced Tonic Fibers — (See Fiber).

Fierce Disorders—And Fevers—(See Fierce, Rapid, Sharp).

Fiery and Hot Diseases—(See Fiery).

Fire — Fires — Blindness, Injury, or Wounds By—(See Blindness, Fire).

Fire Arms—Injury or Death By—(See Gunshot).

Fistula; Flightiness; Fluxes;

Flying Gout—(See Gout).

Focussed Heat — In the Body — (See Fevers, Inflammation; "Focuses Heat" in Sec. 1 of this Article).

Forehead—Hurts To—(See Forehead).

Fractures; Frenzy; Functions—Excessive or Painful—(See Functions).

Fundament—Disorders of—(See Fundament).

Fury; Gall—Gall Bladder—Bile—Disorders of—(See Bile).

Gastric Disorders—(See Gastric).

Generative Organs—Disorders of—(See Generative, Genitals, Privates, Secrets, Sex, Womb, etc.).

Genitals — Disorders of — (See Genitals).

Genito-Urinary System—Disorders of—(See Genito-Urinary).

Gonorrhoea; Gravel; Guns — Gunshot—Injury or Death By—(See Gunshot).

Habitual Fever—(See "Hectic" under Fever).

Haemoptysis; Hands—Lameness In—(See Hands).

Head—Accidents and Hurts To—Rush of Blood To—Violent Pains In—(See Head).

Heart—Disorders of—Fatty Degeneration of—(See Heart).

Heat—Abundant—Excessive Heat In the Body — Focussed Heat In Body — Fevers, etc.—(See Fever, Heat).

Hectic Fever — (See "Hectic" under Fever).

Hemorrhages; Hemorrhoids;

Herbs of Mars—And their Therapeutic Properties—(See "Mars Group" under Herbs). The remedies and herbs of ♄ and ♀ combat and oppose ♂ diseases, as they are soothing and quieting to the quick and fiery diseases of ♂. (See Antipathy, Opposites, Sympathy).

Hernia; Herpes; High Blood Pressure—(See "Pressure" under Blood).

High Death Rate—(See Mortality).

Hips — Humours In — Pains In — (See Hips).

Hot Diseases — Fevers—Hot Body—Hot Eruptions—Hot and Dry Diseases—Hot Urine, etc.—(See Eruptions, Fevers, Heat, Urine).

Hot Liquids — Death or Injury By —(See "Hot Liquids" under Heat; Scalds).

Humours — Choleric — Corrupt Humours In the Feet — Humours In the Hips, Legs and Thighs—(See Humours).

Hurts; Hydrophobia; Hyperaemia;

Hyperkinesia — (See "Excessive Action" in this section).

Hypertrophy; Hysteria;

Ideas—Flightiness of Mind and Ideas—(See Flightiness, Ideas).

Illness—From Excesses, Fevers, Hurts, Unbridled Passion, etc.—(See Excesses, Fevers, Hurts, Passion).

Illnesses — Sharp and Sudden — (See "High Fever" under Fever; Sharp, Sudden).

Imaginations; Immoderate Heat—Illness From—(See "Excessive Heat" under Heat).

Incised Wounds—Danger or Death By (See Cuts, Incised, Operations).

Incrementations; Infections;

Inflammations—Inflammatory Diseases — (See the various paragraphs under Inflammation).

Injuries—(See the various paragraphs under Accidents, Cuts, Hurts, Injuries, Wounds, etc.).

Inner Parts — All Diseases In — (See Reins).

Insanity; Instruments—Wounds By—(See Instruments).

Intemperance; Intermittent Fevers—(See Intermittent).

Internal Hemorrhage — (See Hemorrhage).

Involuntary—Involuntary Muscular Excitement—(See "Involuntary" under Muscles).

Inward Parts—All Diseases In—(See Reins).

Iron or Steel — Injuries, Wounds, or Death By—(See Iron).

Irregularities — (See "Painful Complaints" under Forethought; "Disease or Injury" under Rashness).

Itch; Jaundice; Kidneys—All Diseases In—Stone In—(See Kidneys, Stone).

King's Evil—(See Scrofula).

Knees — Injuries To—Lameness In—Pains, Inflammation, and Swellings In—(See Knees).

Lameness — In the Arms, Hands, Knees, Feet—(See Lameness; "Lameness" under these subjects).

Left Ear—Pain and Disease In—(See "Left Ear" under Ears).

Legs—Humours, Lameness, Pains In—(See Legs).

Lightning—Blindness or Injury By—(See Lightning).

Lithiasis—(See Stone).

Liver—Disorders of—(See Deranged, Inflammation, under Liver).

Loins—Weakness In—(See Loins).

Loss of Blood—And Death By—(See "Loss of Blood" under Blood; Effusions; "Death" under Hemorrhage).

Lues—(See Syphilis).

Lungs — Hemorrhage of — Inflammation of—(See Lungs).

Madness — Mad — Mad Distempers — Mad Dog Bites, etc.—(See Madness).

Malaria; Malignant Diseases—Malignant Scarlatina—(See Malignant).

Mania; Measles; Megrims — In the Head—(See Migraine).

Mens' Genitals — Diseases In and Injury To—(See Genitals).

Menses—Excessive—(See Menses).

Metorrhagia—(See Menses).

Migraine; Miscarriage — Death By —(See Abortion, Miscarriage, Parturition).

Mobility Augmented—(See "Accelerated" under Motion).

Mortification—Death By—(See Mortification).

Motor — Motor Nerves — Motor Segment of the Spinal Cord—Disorders of —(See Motor; "Motor" under Spine).

Mouth — Extreme Heat In — (See Mouth).

Murderous—(See Murder).

Muscles—Disorders of—(See Muscles).

Nasal Disorders—(See Nose).

Naso-Pharynx — Inflammation In — (See Nose).

Neck — Inflammation and Pains In — (See Neck).

Nephritis—(See Kidneys).

Nerves—Nerve Centers—Disorders of — Inflammation and Vascular Excitement of the Nerve Centers — Nervous Irritability, and Abnormal Increase of —Disorders of the Motor Nerves, etc.— (See Centres, Erethism, Nerves; "Motor" in this section).

Night—Night Sweats—The Action of ♂ In Night Nativities and Disease At Night — (See Day, Night; "Night Sweats" under Phthisis; "Day" in this section).

Nil — ♂ diseases are almost entirely absent, and are not epidemic, when ♂ has little power and is not elevated above, or configurated with the ☉ or ☽ at an Eclipse, Equinox, or Solstice, and ♂ neither ℞ nor in perigee. (See Eclipse, Perigee).

Nose—Disorders of—(See Nose).

Obstructions — (See "Bowels" in this section).

Operations — Danger of Death By — (See Operations).

Organs — Enlargement or Inflammation of—(See Enlargement, Inflammation, Organs).

Over-Braced Tonic Fibers — (See Fiber).

Over-Heated Blood—And Diseases From — (See "Over-Heated" under Blood).

Pain — Pains—Painful Complaints—♂ tends to cause acute, sharp, darting, cutting, sudden and severe pains in almost every part of the body, according to the sign he is in at B., his aspects, afflictions by dir., transits, etc. Mars also causes painful complaints due to rashness and want of forethought. (See "Pain" under the various parts and organs of the body, such as under Arms, Bladder, Breasts, Head, Hips, Legs, Neck, Reins, Shoulders, Stomach, Thighs, Throat, etc. See Forethought, Rashness, and note the various paragraphs under Pain).

Palpitations; Part—Determination of Blood to a Part—(See "Determination" in this section).

Parts of Organs—Enlargement or Inflammation of—(See Enlarged, Inflammation, Parts).

Parturition — Childbirth — Fever, Injury, or Death In—(See Parturition).

Passion — Passional Excesses, and Diseases From — (See Amorous, Passion, Venery).

Pathological Action—Of Mars—(See "Pathological" in Sec. 1 of this Article).

Pectoral Affections—(See Breast).

Penis—Ulceration, and Diseases of—(See Genitals, Penis, Urethra, Venereal).

Perityphlitis—(See Caecum).

Pernicious Diseases; Pestilence;

Pharynx — Naso-Pharynx — Disorders of—(See Pharynx).

Phrenzies—(See Frenzy).

Phthisis; Piles—(See Hemorrhoids).

Plague; Pneumonia; Pock-marked;

Poisoning—Death By—(See Poison).

Private Diseases — Private Injury — Private Parts—(See Private).

Privates — Genitals — Disorders In — (See Genitals, Generative, Genito-Urinary, Penis, Private, Reproduction, Sex, Urethra, Vagina, Venereal, Vulva, Womb, etc.).

Process—The Hepatic and Inflammatory Process — (See "Alterations" under Cells; the Introduction under Inflammation, Liver).

Prodigality; Puerperal Fever — (See Parturition, Puerperal).

Pyelitis—(See Kidneys).

Quarrels; Quick Diseases—(See Acute, Quick).

Quinsy—(See Tonsils).

Rapid Fevers — And Diseases — (See Rapid).

Rash Acts—Injury or Death By—(See Anger, Folly, Foolhardy, Forethought, Fury, Rashness, Recklessness, Violent).

Recklessness; Rectum — Disorders of —(See Rectum).

Reddening — (See Caustic, Rubefacient).

Regenerative Organs — Diseases In — Ulcer In — (See Generation, Genitals, Privates, Regeneration, Reproduction, Secrets, Sex Organs, Venereal, Womb).

Reins—Disorders In—(See Reins).

Religious Frenzy—(See Excitable).

Renal Calculi — (See "Stone" under Kidneys).

Respiratory System — Disorders of — (See Breath, Bronchial, Diaphragm, Lungs).

Rheum In Eyes — (See "Rheum" under Eyes).

Rheumatism—(See "Tendency" under Rheumatism).

Ringworm; Rubefacient; Rupture — Hernia, and Death By — Rupture of Blood Vessels—(See Hernia, Rupture, Vessels).

Rush of Blood — To the Head — To a Part—(See Determination).

Scabies; Scalds; Scarlatina;

Scars On Face — (See "Scars" under Face).

Sciatica; Scrofula; Secret Parts—Diseases In—(See Secrets).

Semitertian Fevers — (See Semitertian).

Sensibility Augmented — (See Sensibility).

Sex Organs—Diseases In—Injuries To —(See "Regenerative Organs" in this section; Sex).

Sharp Fevers—Sharp Illnesses—Sharp Pains—Sharp Instruments and Injuries By—(See Sharp).

Shingles—(See Herpes).

Shock—Violent Shock—(See Shock).

Short Illnesses — Short and Sudden and Death By—(See Acute; "High Fevers" under Fever; Rapid, Sharp, Short, Sudden, Swift, Violent).

Signs—Diseases of ♂ in the Signs of the Zodiac — ♂ in each of the signs tends to inflammations, hurts, injuries to the part, parts, or organ ruled by such sign, and also to cause an excessive supply of blood to be drawn to the part at times. (See the list of Diseases under each of the Signs, as "Aries Diseases" under Aries; "Taurus Diseases" under Taurus, etc. For a classified arrangement of the diseases of ♂ in each of the Signs, see the regular Textbooks and Dictionaries of Astrology).

Skin Eruptions — (See Eruptions, Skin).

Sloughing — Dry Slough — Crusts of Dead Tissue—(See Sloughing).

Smallpox—Blindness From—Smallpox In the Face, and Pockmarks — (See "Smallpox" under Blindness; "Face" under Smallpox).

Smell—Disorders of—(See Smell).

Sores—(See Plague, Sores).

Spinal Cord—Disorders of Motor Segment of—(See "Motor" under Spine).

Stabs; Steel and Iron—Hurts, Cuts, Injury or Death By—(See Iron).

Stomach—Disorders of—Ulcer of—Inflammation—(See Gastric, Stomach).

Stone—Stone In the Reins, Kidneys, Bladder—(See Stone).

Strangury—(See Urine).

Sudden Illnesses—Sudden Death— Sudden Distempers—Sudden and Short Illnesses—(See "Short" in this section; Sudden).

Suicide; Sunstroke; Surfeits;

Surgical Incisions—(See Operations).

Sweats—Night Sweats of Phthisis—(See Phthisis).

Swellings; Swift Diseases — (See Swift).

Sword—Injury or Death By—(See Duels, Sword).

Sympathetic Nervous System—Disorders of—(See "Pathological Action" in Sec. 1 of this Article; Sympathetic).

Syncope—(See Fainting).

Syphilis; Temper—(See "High" under Temper).

Temperament—(See Choleric).

Temperature—Increase of—High—(See "High Fever" under Fever).

Tension—In the Body—High Nervous Tension—(See Excitable, Tension).

Tertian Fevers — (See Intermittent, Tertian).

Tetter; Thighs—Humours In—Pains In—Tumors In—(See Thighs).

Thinking — Uncontrolled and Rash Thinking—(See Anger, Rashness, Vicious, Violent).

Throat—Disorders of—Extreme Heat In—Pains In—(See Throat).

Tissue — Alteration of — Hypertrophy of—Crusts of Dead Tissue—(See "Alterations" under Cells; Hypertrophy, Sloughing, Tissues).

Tone—Of the Body—Disturbances of —(See Recuperation, Resistance, Stamina, Tone, Vitality).

Tonsils—Tonsilitis—(See Tonsils).

Tonic—Tonic Action and Disorders of — Tonic Color (Red) — Tonic Fibers Over-Braced — Tonic Medicines — (See "Organs" under Enlarged; Tonic).

Treatment—Of ♂ Diseases—The Herbs and Remedies of ♀ are very favorable, as ♀ opposes ♂, and are used on the principle of Antipathy. Also the Herbs and Remedies of ♂ can be used to combat ♂ diseases, on the principle of Sympathy, as in Homeopathy. Also the Remedies and Herbs of ♄, the cold planet, can often be used to relieve the heat, fever, and congestion of ♂ diseases. The color Blue may be used to soothe and quiet the exciting qualities of ♂ diseases, and especially where the mind is affected. (See Blue; "Mars Group", "Saturn Group", "Venus Group", under Herbs; "Remedies", "Therapeutic Qualities", "Typical Drugs", in Sec. 1 of this Article, and also under Mars, Saturn, Venus).

Tumors In Thighs — (See "Tumors" under Hips).

Tympanies; Typhoid Fever; Typhus;

Ulcers—In Genitals, Vagina, Womb, Secret Parts, Stomach, etc.—(See Ulcer).

Uncontrolled Thinking—Disease or Injury By—(See "Thinking" in this section).

Urethritis—(See Urethra).

Urine—Hot Urine—(See "Scalding" under Urine).

Uterus—Ulcer of—(See Womb).

Vagina—Ulceration of—(See Vagina).

Vascular Excitement—Of Nerve Centers—(See Erethism).

Vaso-Dilatation—(See "Vaso-Dilator Action" under Vaso).

Venereal Diseases—(See Venereal).

Vessels—Rupture of Blood Vessels—(See Vessels).

Violence—Injury or Death By—(See Assassination; "Death" under Injuries; Murdered, Violence).

Violent Disorders—Violent Hemorrhage—Violent Tendencies—(See Fierce, Hemorrhage, Pernicious, Rapid, Severe, Sharp, Violent).

Vital Force—Wasting of—(See "Health Suffers" under Opposite Sex; "Waste" under Vital; "Wasted" under Vitality).

Vitality Wasted—(See "Wasted" under Vitality).

Voluntary Power — Excessive — (See Voluntary).

Vulva — Abscess or Ulceration of — (See Vulva).

Wasting—Of the Vital Forces—(See "Vital" in this section).

Weakness—In Loins—(See Loins).

Womb—Inflammation of—Ulcer of—(See Womb).

Worms—In Children—(See Worms).

Wounds—In Battle—Blindness By—Death By—By Fire, Burns, Scalds, Iron and Steel, Sharp Instruments—Sudden and Spontaneous, etc.—(See the various paragraphs under Accidents, Blows, Cuts, Hurts, Injuries, Instruments, Iron, Violence, Weapons, Wounds, etc.).

Yellow Jaundice—(See Jaundice).

Zoster—Herpes—(See Herpes).

MASCULINE—Male—Pertaining to the Male Sex—Masculine Qualities Masculine Appearance—Masculine Births —Masculine Children—Masculine Degrees—Masculine Houses—Masculine Colors—Masculine Nativity—Masculine Planets—Masculine Sex Organs—Masculine Signs of the Zodiac—Masculine and Coarse Voice In Women, etc.— (See "Masculine", and these various paragraphs under Male.

MASOCHISM—A Form of Sexual Perversion which Delights in Cruel Treatment—♂ ☌ or ill-asp. ♀ at B.; ♂ ☌ ♀ in ♏; a ♂ influence, and with ♂ configurated with ♄ and ♀; ♂ ☌ ♄ and ♀ in ♏; malefics in the sex sign ♏, and especially ♂ afflicted in this sign. (See Cruel, Perversions).

MASSACRE—Danger of Death In Massacre Abroad—(See "Massacre" under Abroad).

MASSAGE—(See Healers).

MASTICATION—The Process of Chewing—

Fast Eater—Does Not Chew the Food Well—(See "Fast Eater" under Eating).

Spasm of Muscles Of—(See Lock-Jaw).

MASTOID—The Mastoid Bone, Process, Cells and Sinuses—

Mastoid Abscess—Mastoiditis—Inflammation of the Mastoid Cells—The Mastoid Cells in the interior of the Mastoid Process, and which are lined with mucous membrane, open on the posterior wall of the middle ear, and are affected by afflictions in ♉, which sign rules the Ears generally. Saturn or ♂ in ♉, and espec. when in the 12th H., and affl. the ☉, ☽, or ☿ tend to Mastoid Abscess. Also afflictions in ♈ or ♎ may cause the trouble, and the extension of Ear Abscess over into the Mastoid Process. The right or left Mastoid Processes are affected according to sex, and whether ♄ or ♂ are the afflictors. Also this trouble is sometimes caused by the Prog. ☽ in ☌ with planets in the radical map, and espec. if in ☌ with ♄, ♂, ♀, or ☿ in this sign. (See Abscesses, Left Ear, Right Ear, under Ears). Case of Mastoiditis—See Fig. 7B in the book, "Astro-Diagnosis" by the Heindels.

Sterno-Mastoid Region—The Sterno-Mastoid Muscle—Disorders of—Afflictions in the latter part of the ♉ sign, or in first few degrees of ♊; Subs at LCP (6, 7C).

MASTURBATION—Self-Abuse—(See "Solitary Vice" under Vice).

MATERIA MEDICA—The Branch of Medical Science Treating of Drugs— Many Drugs, Herbs, Plants, Metals, and Minerals are listed alphabetically in this book, and giving their Planetary Rulership, Action, Therapeutic Value, etc. Look in the alphabetical arrangement for the subject you have in mind. Also under each of the Planets see such subjects as "Drugs", "Herbs", "Metal", "Remedies", "Therapeutic Qualities", "Typical Drugs", "Treatment", "Pathological Qualities", etc. Also see the general subjects of Antipathy, Cure, Drugs, Healers, Herbs, Medicines, Metals, Minerals, Narcotics, Opposites, Pathological, Poisons, Remedies, Salts (see "Salts" under Zodiac); Signs of the Zodiac (under each of the Signs note the Drugs and Herbs each Sign rules); Sympathy, Therapeutics, Treatment.

MATERIALISM—A ♄ influence; ♄ strong at B., ruler, or in the Asc.; ♄ in the 9th H., the house of the Higher Mind and Religion; many planets in earthy signs at B.; earthy signs on the Angles. People born with many planets in the earthy signs tend to be more earth-bound, materialistic, and to have a more slow, plodding, and laborious career, and also to be more given to Melancholy, Despondency, Hypochondria, Mental Depression and Dejection, and to have a greater desire for wealth and the things of this World, and to the possible neglect of their spiritual welfare. Brooding over worldly matters may tend to ill-health, and to weaken the vitality. The negative earth sign people, as ♉, ♍, ♑, tend to Materialism, and to diseases, such as Gout, Rheumatism, Crystallization, Hardening, Suppression of the Functions, Excess Deposit of Wastes and Poisons in the system, which are ♄ diseases, and these diseases usually go with a Materialistic Mind, as the mind is turned downward toward the Earth, and earthly things, in most cases, rather than upward toward the higher and more spiritual Truths, and the Secret Doctrines and Mysteries. The good aspects of, and the higher influences of the planets ♆ and ♅, tend to uplift the native, and away from Materialism. (See Metaphysical, Neptune, Occult, Rationalism, Saturn, Scepticism, Spirituality, Uranus).

MATERNITY—Maternal—Pertaining to the Mother and Motherhood—In these matters the positions and aspects of the ☽ and ♀ are to be considered. The supreme function of maternity depends almost wholly upon the positions and affections of the ☽ and ♀, and the conditions of these two bodies in the horoscope of the mother. The wife may be fruitful, and have a fruitful map of birth, yet may not become a mother unless she also has a fruitful husband, as many men are impotent and sterile from birth. Therefore, if a prospective bride wishes to make sure that she is fruitful, and will have children, she also should know beforehand that her intended husband has a fruitful map, or she may make a mistake, and be sorely disappointed. Also there are women who are fruitful, but who have the malefics ♄ and ♂ in the 5th H., the house of children in their maps, which would indicate unfortunate children, or their early death, and it would be well for a woman to know of these things before she marries, so as to know what to expect, what to prepare for, and how to the better understand her children, and early take them in hand, and give them the proper care and training. Some women, while fruitful, tend to be unfortunate as to children, and make very undesirable mothers.

Aunts and Uncles—Maternal Aunts, Uncles, and Relatives—The mother's relations are ruled by ☿ in your map, and the aspects to, or by ☿, and the position and strength of ☿ at your birth will determine your relation largely to your relatives on your mother's side, and also their condition, illnesses, or possible death. Aunts and Uncles on the mother's side are also ruled by the 6th H. in a male nativity, or on the father's side in a female geniture. The 12th H. rules the opposite conditions. (See Aunts, Brethren; "Aunts", "Relatives", under Father; Relatives, Uncles).

Death of Maternal Relatives—Death of Maternal Aunts and Uncles—Suffering and Illness of—♄ ruler of the 12th H. at B., and ♄ ☌ or ill-asp. the Asc. by dir. (See "Death" under Relations; Sixth House, Twelfth House).

Functional Trouble—In Maternity—The ☽ in the 5th or 6th H. at B., and afflicted; ♀ afflicted in the 6th H. (See Functions).

Instincts—Maternal Instincts—These are strong when the ♋ sign, or the 5th H. are well and favorably occupied and aspected at B. Mars in the 5th H., and well-aspecting the ☽, gives a strong desire for children, but danger of accidents and sickness to them. The maternal instincts are lessened when ♆, ♅, or ♄ occupy the 5th H. at B., and also many planets in the positive and masculine signs at B. (See the influences under "Amativeness", which give a strong desire for children, and to propagate the Race. Also see Barren, Fruitfulness, Instincts).

Maternal Place—In the Map of Birth—The place of ♀ by day, or the ☽ by night, in the map of the mother. (See Conception, Family, Foetus, Moon, Mother, Parturition, Paternal, Pregnancy, Prenatal Epoch, Puerperal, Venus, Wife, etc.).

Maternal Relatives—(See "Aunts and Uncles" in this section).

MATHEMATICAL—A Good Mathematician—Mathematical Prodigy—Lightning Calculator—The ♉ sign is said to give good mathematical ability. Also ♂ is associated with ☿, either by ☌ or ☍. The □, P., or any aspect of ♂ to ☿, tends to make the mind more keen for mathematics. In Hor'y Q. ♂ Sig. ☌ ☿, or in ⚹ or △ ☿, indicate a good mathematician. Mars and ☿ in angles, in aspect, or in houses of mind, the 3rd or 9th H. Some of the greatest Mathematical Geniuses, Lightning Calculators, Chess Players, Mechanical Geniuses, Inventors, etc., and even as Child Prodigies, have ♂ ☌ or ☍ ☿ in the 3rd or 9th H., and also with ♅ lending a good and strong aspect to ☿. Neptune also in good asp. to ☿ at the same time gives a higher, intuitional, inspirational, and spiritual trend to the mind, and capable of great mental and spiritual feats. The greatest Mathematicians are usually Advanced Souls. It is said also that high attainments and gifts in mathematics are indications of a genuine and highly developed spiritual nature, but not necessarily an emotional nature, or religious fervor, which may be mistaken for spiritual power. (See Freaks, Genius; "Great Ability" under Great; Learning, Mechanical; "Quickened" under Mentality; Precocious, Premature, Prodigies, Scientific, Spiritual).

MATRICIDE—(See "Patricide" under Father).

MATRIX—The Womb—(See Womb).

MATTER—Substance—Material Things—The ☽ is typical of Matter, and the ☉ of Spirit. Matter is condensed Ether, or condensation of the etheric and gaseous particles which float in the Ether. During the great Cosmic Nights of the Universe all Matter, Planets, and Bodies in space, are dissolved back into their etheric and gaseous state. It is said that "Matter is Condensed Spirit". No matter is ever lost in the Universe, but merely changes form. The influence of ♄ tends to decay, or resolution of matter into its primary elements and gases, and to bring on the "Death", or separation, of living cells and organisms, such as the human organism. A corpse is much alive as the cells becomes disorganized, their leader, master, and organizer, the Ego, having departed, and each cell struggles for its freedom that it may enter into other organized forms and combinations. (See Ether, Spirit, Substance).

MATURE—Maturation—Maturity—Ripening—Is typified by the full ☽. In the Kakala mature age was dedicated to ♃. (See "Full Moon" under Moon).

Dies Before Maturity—Will Not Live to Maturity—Rarely Lives to Maturity—The ☉ or ☽ in an angle at B., ☌, or ill-asp. a malefic, and with no good aspects from the Benefics; a malefic rising and afflicting the lord of the 8th H.; ruler of the Asc. in the 6th H., and afflicted by lord of the 8th H., and with no assistance from Benefics. For other influences along this line see "Death" under Childhood, Children, Infancy; "Early Death" under Early; "Short Life" under Life; "Dies Before Middle Life" under Middle Life; "Death In Youth", "Early Youth", under Youth).

Rarely Lives to Maturity—(See "Dies Before Maturity" in this section).

Reason — Lack of Mature Reason — (See "Lack Of" under Forethought; Irrational, Irresponsible; "Bad Judgment" under Judgment; "Weak Mind" under Mind; Reason).

Tubercle—Maturation of—(See Tubercle).

Will Live to Maturity—Prospects of Long Life—A strong sign on the Asc. at B., and the ruler well-placed and free from affliction, and at the same time the hyleg free from affliction, the child will live to maturity, have good powers to withstand disease, and to recuperate rapidly from illness. (See Adults; "Good" under Constitution, Health, Recuperation, Resistance, Stamina, Tone, Vitality; Immunity; "Long Life" under Life; "Death" under Middle Life).

Youth—The Time of Adolescence and Maturity—(See Manhood, Puberty, Youth).

MAXILLARY—Pertaining to the Jaws—(See Jaws).

MAYHEM—(See Maimed, Mutilated).

MEAGRE—Thin—Emaciated—Inadequate—Scanty, etc.—♄ and ♑ influence.

Meagre Body—(See Emaciated, Thin).

Meagre Face—(See "Meagre" under Face).

Meagre Hair—The Hair Scanty or Thin—No Hair—(See Baldness; "No Hair", "Scanty", under Hair).

MEALS—Eating—Food—(See Assimilation, Diet, Digestion, Drink, Eating, Epicureans, Feasting, Food, Gluttony, Indigestion, etc.).

MEAN—Medium—Middle—Mean Stature—Mean Actions, etc.—

Mean Abilities—The Mind, Talents, and Abilities More Mediocre—Not Especially Brilliant—(See Dull; "Fails In Examinations" under Examinations; "Lack Of" under Forethought; Idle, Improvident, Indifferent; "Bad" under Judgment; Lassitude, Lethargy; "Shallow" under Mental).

Mean Actions—Hating All Sordid and Mean Actions—♃ in the Asc. at B., and free from the affliction of malefics. (See Honest, Honorable, Humane; "Popular" under Reputation). For the influences which tend to a mean disposition and temper see Anger, Cruel, Hate, Revengeful; "High Temper" under Temper; Vicious, Violent; Mean-Spirited in this section.

Mean Creature—♂ Sig. in ♋, mean, servile, and unfortunate; ☿ Sig. in ♋, a mean little wretch if ☿ is afflicted.

Mean-Spirited—Mean Disposition—The ☽ Sig. ⚹, △, □, or ☍ ♄, mean in actions; the ☽ in ♑ in partile asp. the Asc.; ♃ Sig. ☌ ♄, mean and deceitful disposition; persons devoid of ♂ influence at B.; ☿ Sig. ☌ ♄; ♀ on the Meridian at B., and affl. by ♄. (See Anger, Choleric, Conduct, Cruel, Deceitful, Dishonest, Evil, Hatred, Jealous, Malevolent, Malice, Revengeful, Secretive, Savage; "High Temper" under Temper; Thieving, Vicious, Violent, etc.).

Mean Stature—Middle Stature—Short—The ☉ in ♋ or ♑, a mean and ill-made body; the ☽ in ♑ partile the Asc., a mean, small, weak figure; the ☽ in ♓ partile the Asc., a short, mean stature, but plump or fat; ♄ shortens the body, and the ♄ sign ♑ when strong at B., tends to a medium, mean, or short stature; ♃ in ♑ partile the Asc.; ♂ in ♑ partile Asc.; ♂ in ♓ partile Asc., mean, short, and fleshy body; ♀ in ♉ partile Asc., comely, but with a mean stature; ♀ in ♑ partile Asc., mean, short stature; ☿ in ♈ partile Asc., thin, mean stature; ☿ Sig. in ♏; ☿ in ♏ partile the Asc., mean stature, but well-set and broad-shouldered; ☿ in ♑ partile the Asc., a mean figure, crooked, often bow-legged, and with a thin face; ☿ in ♓ partile Asc., a mean, short stature, and some Writers say this influence gives a short, thin body. The ♉, ♋, and ♓ influences produce small persons, and of mean stature. The ♑ sign gives a short, slender, and ill-formed person, and often corpulent. (See Corpulent, Fat, Fleshy; "Middle Stature" under Middle; "Moderate Stature" under Moderate; "Body" under Short).

MEASLES—Rubeola—Principally a ♂ disease; ♂ exactly rising or setting at B. tends to; ♂ coming to the ☌ or ill-asps. the Asc. early in life causes smallpox, measles, or scarlatina; ♂ in the 1st H.; ♂ affl. in ♑; ♂ afflicted in ♓, and ☌ or ill-asp. the Asc. by dir.; ♂ afflicting the Asc. at B.; ♂ ☌ the Asc. by dir.; the hyleg much afflicted by ♂; the ☉ to the □ or ☍ the ☽ by dir.; the ☉ afflicted in ♋; the ☉ to the ill-asps. the ☽ by dir., and the ☽ affl. by ♂ at B.; attacks occur under the directions of the ☉, ☽, or Asc. to ♂, or to the ☉ or ♃ if either be afflicted by ♂ at B.; the ☉ coming to the ill-asps. the Asc. early in life; the ill-asps. and directions of the ☉ to the hyleg if the ☉ be afflicted by ♂; afflictions to the ☽, and espec. by ♂; the ☽ to the ☌ or ill-asp. ♂ by dir.; a disease of the ☽; the ☽ in ♋ at B., and the transit of ♂ over the ☽ if the ☽ is afflicted, and espec. in children of a weak constitution; the ☽ in ♏, and afflicted by the ☉ or ♂ when taken ill (Hor'y); the ☽ to the □ or ☍ ♀ by dir., with ♀ in a watery sign, and espec. in children; ♄ in ♋, ♏, or ♓, ☌, or ill-asp. the Asc. by dir.; ♃ peregrine in an airy or watery sign in ☌ the Asc. by dir.; ♀ afflicted in a watery sign at B., and the ☽ to the ill-asps. ♀ by dir.; a pustular disease denoted by ♀; an ♈ disease when there are malefics in ♈; a ♌ disease, and afflictions in ♌; the Asc. to the □ or ☍ ♃ by dir., and ♃ afflicted by ♂; the Asc. to the place of ☋ by dir.; Subs at MCP (5C) and CP, KP. (See Chickenpox, Eruptions, Exanthema; "Pustular Diseases" under Pus; Scarlet Fever, Smallpox; "Vascular Tissues" under Vascular).

Blindness from Measles—(See "Measles" under Blindness).

Epidemic of Measles—♂ is supreme in years of Measles and Smallpox Epidemics, and of other Eruptive Diseases, as Chickenpox, Scarlatina, and Scarlet Fever. These Epidemics occur when ♂ is perigee, and the major planets ♄ or ♃ in perihelion. Mars supreme at the Equinoxes and Solstices; ♂ predominating at the ☌ of three or four of the superior planets, and is severe in type, but milder when ♂ is in ☌ or ☍ only one other superior planet, and ♂ holding power; ♂ Lord of the Year in ♈ at the Vernal Equi., and afflicted by ♄. (See Dengue, Epidemics, Perigee, Perihelion, Pestilence, Plague, etc.).

MEAT—

Ill-Digested Meat—Illness From—The ☽ in ♎, ☌, □, or ☍ ♄ (or ☿ if he be of the nature of ♄) at the beginning of an illness or at decumbiture. (See "Meat" under Indigestion).

Meat Eating—One Astrological Authority advises that people who have ♂ in ♈ at B. should avoid meat as food. Meat is somewhat heating, it is said, and does not agree very well with people born with many planets in fiery signs. Also meat contains the passion, vibrations, and poisons of the animal, and with people badly afflicted by ♄ at B., or born under ♄, tends to Gout and Rheumatism, excess of deposits and wastes, and would tend to have better health to live on nuts, vegetables, fruits, fruit juices, etc., and avoid meat. The question of Meat•Eating is a large one, and many Authorities advise the eating of Meat, while others are against it. The Occult Writers in general seem to be against Meat Eating, and the killing of animals for food, and say that it is not right to take the life of animals. The Religions of the Orient are especially strong against taking the life of animals, birds, or even insects. Blood is strongly related to the Astral Plane, and the Occult Masters teach that the eating of the blood of animals tends to violent vibrations in the body, and to increase the passion, and also to incorporate the poisons and wastes of the flesh of the animal into the human body. Dr. Duz, the famous French Medical Astrologer, strongly advocated meat eating. The question of Meat Eating, both from an Occult and Physiological standpoint, and also Vegetarianism, are discussed in the book, "Cosmo-Conception", by Max Heindel, of the Rosicrucian Fellowship. (See Diet, Eating, Food, Fruit, Vegetables).

MECHANICAL—

Mechanical Displacements—(See Displacements).

Mechanical Genius—Mechanical Skill —Is due to the combination of the ♂ and ☿ influences, and ♂ configurated with ☿; ♂ ruler of the horoscope at B.; ♂ Sig. ☌ ☿; ☿ Sig. ✳ or △ ♂. The Fixed Star Rigel also tends to give mechanical ability when culminating or setting at B. (See Genius, Inventive, Mathematical, Prodigies).

MEDDLERS — Triflers — Prattlers — Busy-Body—♃ Sig. in ♋; ☿ ill-dignified at B.

MEDIASTINUM — The Septum of the Thoracic Cavity — Tumor of — (See Chest, Thorax; "Mediastinum" under Tumors).

MEDICAL ASTROLOGY — The Branch of Astrology which has to do with the Planetary Causes of Disease, and also the Planetary Rulership of Herbs, Metals, Minerals, Plants, etc., and their Therapeutic value. In every Nation and Tribe there is a remedy, an Herb or Mineral, for the cure and alleviation of every disease known to such locality, and the Medicine Men of such communities generally know of such Remedies. Every Herb is governed by a Planet, but the highest efficacy of such herbs depends largely upon the time they are gathered, and under the right planetary influence. Medical Astrology deals with the Star Map of Birth from the health standpoint, showing tendencies, weaknesses, the parts of the body most afflicted from birth, the probable degree of vitality, and the times along thru life, under directions, progressions, transits, etc., when accidents, disease and ill-health are apt to come in the life of the ordinary individual, and the time of the duration of such indisposition, when it may begin, and when it will end in the course of Nature, the quality and nature of the disease, and the planetary aspects be more favorable again for normal health, peace of mind, and freedom from worry and anxiety. In Ancient Times, all Physicians were required to be Medical Astrologers, and to know the Planetary Causes of Disease, and the Philosophy of Disease, before they were permitted to Practice upon, or Treat the Sick. This practice should be revived today, and the subject of Medical Astrology taught in every School of Healing, whether it be in Schools which teach the use of Drugs, or in the Drugless Healing Schools. The First National University of Naturopathy, and the Mecca College of Chiropractic, located at 143 Roseville Ave., Newark, N. J., under the able leadership of their Founder and President, Dr. Frederick W. Collins, A.M., M.D., have already established a Chair of Medical Astrology, and other Schools should speedily follow their example. It is my desire to spend the remaining years of my life visiting the various Schools of Healing over the World, to Lecture, and bring before the Faculties the value of Medical Astrology as an aid in Diagnosis and Prognosis, and to have them establish such study in their Curriculums. In my years of Practice as a Physician, I have, by the use of Astrology, been able to very quickly locate the seat of the disease, the cause of the trouble, the time when the patient began to feel uncomfortable, as based upon the birth data of the patient, and this without even touching or examining the patient, and my intense desire to get this knowledge and wisdom before students and Healers in a classified form, is the reason for this Encyclopaedia, as such knowledge is today in a rather scattered and unclassified condition, and not available for the student unless he spends years in going thru a large library of books on Astrology. When once you have discovered the cause of the disease, and understand its philosophy and the relation of the patient to the great Scheme of Nature, the matter of Treatment I leave to you, and according to the System and Methods you may be using. Read the Books, "Astro-Medicine" by Dr. Duz; "Daath's Medical Astrology"; "Elements of Astrology", by Dr. Broughton; "The Textbook of Astrology", by Dr. Pearce. These books are especially strong along the lines of Medical Astrology. Also, Mr. E. H. Bailey, the Editor of the British Journal of Astrology, has issued a course of brief lessons on Medical Astrology to send out as Mail Order Lessons. Also read the book, "The Prenatal Epoch", by Mr. Bailey, which deals with the Prenatal causes of disease, Congenital Defects, the time of Conception, etc. Medical Astrology is one of the very important Branches of Astrology, and should be carefully and scientifically studied by every student.

In this volume see Cure, Drugs, Healers, Herbs, Map, Medicines, Nativity, Prenatal Epoch, Prognosis, Remedies, Surgeons, Therapeutics, Treatment. Also under each of the Planets see "Drugs", "Pathological", "Remedies", "Therapeutic", "Treatment". "Typical Drugs", etc.

MEDICINES—Medicine—Drugs—Remedial Agents—Medicine As a Profession, etc.—Drugs have a local action on the body, and in order to be remedies must operate on the same organs the disease affects, as each organ has an affinity for a certain drug, whether it be a mineral or herb. (See Chap. V in Pearce's Textbook of Astrology). For a list of the Therapeutic Values of the different Medicines see the Article on Drugs. The names of the various Medicines and Remedies mentioned in this Encyclopaedia will not be listed or mentioned in this Article, and for such see the Articles on Herbs, Metals, Minerals, Poisons, etc., and also see the paragraph on "Typical Drugs" under each of the Planets. The names of drugs, and also their Therapeutic Qualities, are listed alphabetically in this book. Look in the alphabetical arrangement for the subject you have in mind.

Best Time to Take Medicine — When the ☽ is in ♒ or ♓, as these signs are moist and have strong absorbing powers; when the ☽ is on the place of ♃ or ♀ at decumbiture; when ♃ or ♀ are in the Asc.; in a ♀ or ☿ hour. (See "Hours" under Planets).

Care In Taking Medicine — The Star Map of Birth should be carefully studied before giving medicines, to know what organs are especially afflicted, and what dangers there are to combat in the use of drugs. Be careful what medicines are taken when the Asc. has come to the place of Cor Leo by direction, as they are more liable to disturb the heart action.

Cooling Medicines—♄ remedies. They should be taken when the Asc. comes to the place of The Ascelli, or Capricornus. Externally, Ice or Snow, ruled by ♄, may be used. (See Refrigerant).

Dealing In Medicines—♀ ruler of the Profession favors dealing in Medicines, Perfumes, Cordials, Wines, etc., and if ♄ gives testimony, to deal in poisons. (See "Make Good Chemists" under Chemists).

Herbs—Herbs Ruled by the Planets—(See Herbs).

Ill-Health—From Taking Medicines—♆ influence strong at B.; ♆ afflicted in the 6th H.; ♆ □ or ☍ ♄. (See Narcotics).

Improper Medicines—Injured By—When the lord of the 6th H. is in the 4th H. at B. The 10th H. signifies the medicine given in sickness. The medicines and their nature, and whether they are proper or not, are shown by the 5th H. and its lord. When the lord of the 8th is in the 6th H., there is danger of the Physician giving the native a wrong medicine by mistake. (See "Injured By" under Healers; "Sickness from Poisoning" under Poison).

Medicines Do Little Good — (See "Worse" under Crises; Fatal; Incurable; Relapses; Worse).

Medicines Ruled by Planets — (See Herbs, Metals, Minerals; "Drugs", "Remedies", "Typical Drugs", under each of the Planets).

Metals—(See Metals, Therapeutics).

Minerals—(See Minerals).

Narcotics — Drug Habit — (See Narcotics).

Ointments; Opening Medicines — Physic — Catharsis — (See Physic; "Bowel Disorders" under Yellow).

Pathological Action—Of Medicines and Herbs of the Planets—(See "Pathological Action" under each of the Planets; Pathological).

Physic—(See "Opening Medicines" in this section).

Poisons—(See Poisons).

Practice of Medicine—Success or Failure In — (See "Failures", "Success", under Healers).

Salts—Zodiac Salts—Tissue Remedies —(See "Salts" under Zodiac).

Sickness — The medicine given in is indicated by the 10th H. (See "Improper Medicines" in this section).

Signature—The Law of Signature In Drugs—(See Signature).

Study — Given to the Study of Medicine and Surgery—(See "Practice of Healing" under Healers; Surgery).

Therapeutic Qualities — Of Drugs — (See Herbs; "Therapeutic Qualities" under each of the Planets).

Tonic Medicines—Ruled by the ☉ and ♂. (See Stimulants, Tonics).

When to Give Medicine — (See "Best Time" in this section).

When Not to Give Medicine — When the ☽ is passing thru a Ruminant Sign, thru a sign symbolic of an animal which chews the cud, as ♈, ♉, or ♑. Medicines taken in a ♄ hour tend to do more harm than good. Do not give when the 1st face of ♊ is on the Asc. Emetics are best given when the ☽ is passing thru a ruminant sign, as vomiting is more easily induced at such times. (For further study, see Antipathy; "Chemical Action" under Chemical; Compatability; "Cure of Disease" under Curable; Drugs, Emetics, Explosions; "Curable" under Fits; Incompatibility, Incurable, Moderation; "Medicines" under Obsessions; Opposites, Remedies, Roots, Ruminant, Sympathy, Treatment).

MEDIUM—

Medium Coeli — The M.C. — The Midheaven — Tenth House — (See Tenth House).

Medium Stature — Medium Height — Middle Stature — ☿ indicates people who are of medium height, and also tall and thin; ♈, ♎, ♍, and ♏ give a medium stature; ♍ on the Asc., medium, slender, and well-made; ♓ on the Asc. (See "Mean Stature" under Mean; "Middle Stature" under Middle; Moderate).

Medium Vitality—(See Vitality).

MEDIUMSHIP — Mediumistic — The influences and aspects of ♆ at B., and by dir., are largely responsible for the powers of Mediumship, for good or evil, and whether it is voluntary or involuntary, under control, or irresponsible).

Cases of Mediumship — Birth Data, etc.—See "Medium", No. 966, and also "Suicide", No. 171, both in 1001 N.N.

Dangers Thru Mediumship—♆ affl. in the 12th H. at B.; ♆ ruler of the horoscope, and afflicted; caused by the evil aspects of ♆; ♆ afflicted in the Asc., 10th, 12th, or 6th H.; ♆ affl. in ♍ or ♓; ♆ □ or ☍ ♅, ♄, or the ☽; ♆ ☌, P., □ or ☍ ♂; ♆ prog. in ☌, P., □ or ☍ ♅, and vice versa; ♆ by transit in ☌ the ☽ or ☿ if ♆ is afflicted at B.; the □ or ☍ aspects of ♆ are especially evil; the ☽ or ☿ afflicted by ♆; the ☽ in ♓ and afflicted by ♆; the prog. ☽ ☌, P., □, or ☍ ♆ if ♆ be afflicted at B.; ♅ in the 6th H., and affl. by ♆; ♅ affl. in ♓; ♓ on the Asc. (See Forebodings, Hypnotism, Obsessions, Spirit Controls).

Genuine Mediumship — (See "Voluntary" in this section).

Involuntary — Irresponsible Mediumship — Intermittent — Not Under Control—Undesirable Phases of, and with Vain Fears and Obsessions—♆ □ or ☍ ♅ at B.; the ill-aspects of ♆ to Antares (see Antares); ♆ afflicted in the 12th H.; ♆ ☌ the Asc., and afflicted. (See Clairvoyance, Fears, Obsessions, Prophetic, Spirit Controls).

Voluntary Mediumship — Under Control—Genuine—Responsible—The good aspects of ♆ to ♅, the ☽ or Asc.; ♆ △ the ☽, ♅, ♄, or ☿; the 4° ♓ on the Asc., Mediumship of a high order. (See Pituitary).

MEDULLA—Bulbar—Medullary—

Bulbar Paralysis — ♄ afflicted in ♉; several planets in ♉ in ☌, and afflicted by the □ and ☍ aspects of other planets; ♉ or ♏ on the Asc., and afflicted. (See Brain; "Cord" under Spine). Case of Bulbar Paralysis—See Case One, in Chap. XIII, of Daath's Medical Astrology.

Kidneys — Medullary Substance of — Ruled by ♀ and ♎. (See the Introduction under Kidneys).

Medulla Oblongata — The Lowest Division of the Brain, and the enlarged portion of the Spinal Column in the Cranium—Is located in the Zone of Taurus, and ruled largely by ♉, and affected by the ♏ sign thru reflex action to ♉. (See Occiput). Is also influenced by the ♌ sign, which sign rules the Spinal Cord. Authorities seem to be uncertain at present as to what Planet rules the Medulla. The ☉ and ☽ acting thru the ♏ sign tend to affect the Medulla. (See "Basal Ganglia" under Ganglion).

Medullary Substance—The Medullary and Cerebral Substance and Juices are augmented at the Full ☽, and suffer diminution at the New ☽. The Brain is also smaller at the New ☽. (See "Full", "New", under Moon).

Medullary Substance Inflamed—Neuromyelitis— ☿ afflicted by malefics at B., and by dir.; afflictions in ♌; ♂ afflicted in ♉ or ♏; ♉ or ♏ on the Asc., and afflicted. (See "Neuritis" under Nerves).

MEDUSA'S HEAD—(See Algol).

MEEK—In Manner—The ☉ Sig. in ♊. (See "Modest" under Manners).

MEERSCHAUM—A Mineral under the rule of ♆. (See "Metals and Minerals" under Neptune).

MEGRIMS — In the Head — (See Migraine).

MELANCHOLY — Melancholia — Melancholic Temperament—Atrabiliary—Vapours — The Nervous Temperament — Saturnine—Black Bile—Blues—Athymia, etc.—The earthy signs ♉, ♍, and ♑ are known as the Melancholic Signs, and people born under these signs are more given to melancholy.

Afflicted with Melancholy—(See Melancholia, Tendency To, in this section).

All Tendencies To—(See "Tendency" in this section).

Appearance—Melancholic Appearance —Sad Appearance—Melancholic Face —Given by ♄, born under ♄, and ♄ rising in the Asc. or M.C., and strong at B.; ♄ ☌ the ☉, ☽, or Asc. at B.; ♄ or ♀ Sig. in ♈; ♄ in ♍; the 2nd face of ♉, or the 5th face of ♒ on the Asc. (See Grave, Pensive, Sad, Serious).

Black Bile—Atrabilarious Attacks— (See "Black Bile" under Bile).

Blood—Melanchoic Blood—The ☽ afflicted in ♍ when the ☽ is the afflicter in the disease.

Blues—Attacks of the Blues—(See "Vapours" in this section).

Bowels—Bowel Disease from Melancholy—☿ afflicted in ♑.

Death by Melancholy—♄ and ☿ denote death by; ♄ occi. at B., and afflicting the hyleg by dir.; ☿ affl. by ♄ at B., and ☿ holding the dominion of death; ☿ afflicting the hyleg, the Giver of Life, by dir.; ☿ in ♑, and afflicted by ♄, ♃, and the ☽, tending to poor judgment, worry, and bad thinking.

Diseases—Melancholic Diseases—Diseases Which Proceed from Melancholy —A Melancholic Disease—Melancholic Distempers—The ☽ ☌ or ill-asp. ♄ (or ☿ if he be of the nature of ♄) at the beginning of an illness, or at decumb. (Hor'y); the ☽ to the ☌ ☋, a melancholic disease proceeding from Phlegm; ♄ to the ill-asps. his own place by tr. or dir.; ♄ afflictions tend to dry and melancholic diseases; ♄ to the ill-asps. the ☉, ☽, Asc., or hyleg by dir.; lords of the 1st or 6th H., or the ☽ in earthy signs, cause melancholy, or melancholic diseases, such as Agues, Consumptions, and all Chronic diseases. (See "Tendency To" in this section).

Disposition — Melancholic Disposition or Temperament—Also called the Nervous Temperament—Born under strong ♄ influence; ♄ ruler at B., and with ♄ in the Asc. or M.C., and afflicting ☿; ♄ Sig. □ or ☍ the ☽; ♄ Sig. in ♑; ♄ in ♍; ♄ promittor in transit over the radical ☽, or in ill-asp. the ☽ by dir.; the ☽ Sig. in ♍; the ☽ Sig. □ or ☍ ♄; ☿ afflicted in ♑; ♉ influence tends to melancholy; the Asc. to the place of

Arcturus. (See Arcturus; "Nervous Temperament" under Temperament; "Tendency", and the various paragraphs in this section).

Dry and Melancholic Distempers—Caused by ♄, and are ♄ diseases; ♄ afflicting the ☉, ☽, Asc., or hyleg by dir. (See "Diseases" in this section).

Face—Melancholic Face—(See "Appearance" in this section).

Fears—(See "Morbid" under Fears).

Fevers—Melancholic Fevers—♄ mixing signification with ♂ in fiery signs at a decumbiture.

Fits of Melancholy—(See "Melancholic Fits" under Fits).

Gout from Melancholy—☿ afflicted in ♑. (See Gout).

Habitual Melancholy—♄ ruler and afflicted; ♑ on the Asc.

Health—Melancholic About the Health—(See Hypochondria).

Imagination—A Melancholic Imagination—(See "Melancholy" under Imagination).

Inclined to Melancholy—(See Disposition, Tendency, in this section).

Joy—Life Robbed of Its Joy—(See Joy).

Little—A Little Melancholic—☿ Sig. ⚹ or △ the ☽, and espec. if ☿ partake of the nature of ♄.

Low Spirits—(See Low).

Melancholia—Vapours—Much Depression of Spirits—Gloominess—(See Disposition, Tendency, in this section; Dejected, Depressed, Despair, Despondency, Gloom, Grave, Hypochondria; "Low Spirits" under Low; Worry, etc.).

Melancholic Temperament—(See "Disposition" in this section).

Much Melancholy—The Patient Is Melancholic—The ☉ or ☽ to the ☌ or ill-asp. ♄ by dir.; the ☽ in ♐, ☌, P., □ or ☍ ♄ (or ☿ if he be of the nature of ♄) at the beginning of an illness, or at decumb. (Hor'y); ♄ Sig. in ♑; ♄ ruler of the year at the Vernal Equi., and affictiong the ☉ or ☽, much melancholy everywhere, sadness, bereavement, and sorrow. (See Prevalent; "Sorrow" under Public).

Nervous Temperament—The Melancholic Temperament—(See "Disposition" in this section).

Patient Is Afflicted—With Melancholy—(See "Much Melancholy" in this section).

Religious Melancholy—(See "Melancholia" under Religion).

Repining—(See Regretful, Repining).

Rheumatism—From Melancholy—☿ affl. in ♑. (See Gout, Rheumatism).

Sadness—Sorrow—Melancholy From—(See "Much Melancholy" in this section; Sadness, Sorrow).

Signs—The Melancholic Signs of the Zodiac—The earthy signs ♉, ♍, ♑.

Temperament—The Melancholic Temperament—(See "Disposition" in this section).

Tendency to Melancholy—The ☉, ☽, or ☿ in ♑, and afflicted; the ☉ hyleg, and to the ☌ or ill-asp. ♄ by dir.; the ☉ or ☽ afflicted in earthy signs; the ☉ or ☽ in the 12th H., and affl. by the ☌, □, or ☍ ♄; the ☉ in ♒ and afflicted by ♄; the ☉ or ☽ to the ☌ ☋; the ☽ afflicted in ♍ or ♑; the ☽ to the ☌ or ill-asp. ♄ by dir.; the ☽ in ♍ in partile asp. the Asc.; the prog. ☽ to the ☌ or P. ♄; the ☽ ☌ ♄ in the Asc., and in an earthy sign; the ☽ and ♀ □ or ☍ ♄; ♆ afflicted in ♑; ♄ ruler of the horoscope; caused by ♄ influence and afflictions; ♄ ☌, P., □ or ☍ the ☉, ☽, or ☿; ♄ in the Asc. or M.C.; ♄ in the 12th H. in ☌ the ☉ or ☽; ♄ affl. in the 1st H., melancholic, and with many sorrows; ♄ in ♉, ♍, or ♑, in partile asp. the Asc.; the afflictions of ♄ to the hyleg and mental ruler denote death by melancholy; ♄ ☌ the Asc. by dir.; ♄ in the 3rd or 9th H., and afflicted; ♄ ruler of the Asc.; ♄ in ♎, ☌, □, or ☍ the Asc. by dir., and ♄ ruler of the 1st H. at B.; signified by ♄ in ♈ when ♄ is the afflicter in the disease; ♄ Sig. in ♑; ♄ afflicted in ♉; ♄ in ♈, ♉, ♍, ♏, or ♑, and affl. the ☉, ☽, ☿, Asc., M.C., or hyleg; ♄ prog. ☌ or ill-asp. ☿, or vice versa; ♄ by tr. ☌ or ill-asp. the ☉, ☽, ♃, ♀, or ☿; ♄ to his own bad aspects by dir.; fixed stars of the nature of ♄ ascending at B.; ♄ in the 12th H.; ♄ in ♌ in bad asp. the ☽; ♄ or ☋ in the Asc. or M.C., and with ♑ on the Asc.; the ♄ sign ♑ on the Asc. or 6th H.; ♃ Sig. ☌ the ☉ and the ☉ ill-dignified; ♃ Sig. ⚹ or △ ♄; ♃ affl. in ♎, due to deficient Adrenal secretion (see Adrenal); ♃ affl. in ♍ or ♑; ♃ in ♒ and affl. by ♄; ♀ affl. by ♄; ♀ affl. in ♑; ☿ in ♓ and affl. by ♄; ☿ in the 6th or 12th H., ☌ or ill-asp. ♄; ☿ affl. in ♌; caused by ☿ when the dominion of death is vested in him; ☿ □ or ☍ ♄ from common signs or ♑; ☿ in the 1st H., and affl. by ♄; fixed stars of the nature of ☿ cause melancholy; afflictions in ♍, and a ♍ disease; Asc. to the ☌ Rigel, Arcturus, Orionis, Deneb, or North Scale; ♉, ♍, ♑, or ♒ on the Asc.; the Asc. to the ☌, □, or ☍ ♄ by dir., and ♄ occi. at B.; lord of the Asc. in the 8th H., and afflicted; a ♎ disease, as this is the exalted sign of ♄; caused by the star Dorsa Leonis, the Lion's Back; the 27° ♊ on the Asc.; the 12° ♋ on the Asc., melancholic and taciturn; the 20° ♍ on the Asc., a melancholic fate; the 30° ♍ on the Asc.; the 2nd, 8th, 13th, or 30° ♎ on the Asc.; the 3rd decan. of ♑ or ♒ on the Asc. Case—Of Melancholy—See Figures 12 and 25 in the book, "Message of the Stars" by the Heindels. (See Death, Diseases, Disposition, and the various paragraphs in this section).

Treatment of Melancholy—Blue, the color of ♀, has a soothing effect upon a melancholic person, and to live and study in a room with blue colorings. (See Blue). The best way to prevent melancholy is to seek Truth, have an understanding of the Universe, its plan, about the Secret Mysteries, to Know Yourself, and how to rule and shape your destiny, and to find your true calling in life, and do your work. This entails study and research along Occult, Mystical, and Metaphysical lines. You must find the God in you, and discover your Higher Self, conquer your lower nature, strike at the source of the evil in your nature and tear it out of your heart, and fight daily the battle against evil, depression, failure, and be optimistic. Advanced and enlightened Souls are not given to melancholia, but know how to conquer the conditions of their environment, rise above, and not be affected by them in an adverse manner. There are many Books, and Systems of Teaching, which will bring you this Light, and these you will find for yourself when you are ready for them. "When the Pupil is ready, the Teacher appears", is an Occult Maxim. Medicines and lines of physical treatment do not cure Melancholy, and if you do not relieve the cause, and get your Understanding broadened and enlightened, you will not make much progress. Keep your Personality, or Lower Mind, under control, and let your Ego, your Spirit, your Higher Mind, which is Divine, rule you. Know first your Star Map of Birth, your tendencies, your weak and strong points, and thus know what the plan of God over you is for the present life, then keep down the evils of your Map, let the good in you predominate, and do the work to which you have been called. (See Character, Destiny, Fate, Horoscope, Map, Nativity, Star Map).

Vapours — Vapors — The Blues — Low Spirits—Hysteria—The ☽ to the ☌ or ill-asp. ♄ by dir. or transit; ♄ in ♈ or ♌; signified by ♄ in ♈ when ♄ is the afflicter in the disease; ♄ to the evil aspects his own place by direction. (See "Tendency" in this section). For further influences, and collateral study along this line see Anguish, Anxiety, Brooding, Chaotic, Delusions, Discontent, Disgrace, Distress, Ennui, Expression, Fears, Fretfulness, Grief, Hallucinations, Helplessness, Hope, Ideas, Illusions, Imaginations, Introspection, Irritable, Look (see "Downward Look" under Look); "Mind Threatened", "No Peace of Mind", under Mind; Miserable, Moods, Morose, Mournful, Negative, Obsessions, Peevish, Pensive; "Quality of the Disease" under Quality; Restless, Reverses, Ruin, Serious, Suicide, Suffering, Stone, Trouble, Unhappy, Worry, Wretched.

MELTING—Of the Tissues—(See Adhesions, Ankylosis; "Heat" under Mars).

MEMBERS—Of the Body—

Brevity Of—A ♍ influence. (See Brevity; "Short Limbs" under Limbs; "Body" under Short).

Conformity—In the Members—(See Beautiful, Comely, Handsome, Harmony, Well-Proportioned).

Disease—The Members, or Parts of the Body Affected by Disease, or Other Affliction—The Member, or Part, apt to be so afflicted is shown by the Sign in which the Significator of the disease is placed. (See "Locating the Disease" under Diagnosis; Organs; "Afflicted Parts" under Parts).

Generation—Members of—Diseases of —(See Generation, Genitals, Privates, Regeneration, Reproduction, Secrets, Sex, etc.).

Long Members—(See "Long" under Arms, Bones, Hands, Legs, Thighs; also see Tall).

Missing Members—(See "Armless" under Arms; "Missing" under Forearm, Legs; "No Hands" under Hands).

Short Members—(See "Brevity" in this section).

Virile Members—(See Strong, Virile).

Weak Members—(See Weak).

MEMBRANES—Membranous—Tunics—

Affected—The planet ♅ in the different signs tends to affect, or rule, the membranes of a part when in the sign ruling such part. Thus ♅ in ♈ rules and affects the membranes of the Brain; ♅ in ♋ rules and affects the membranes of the stomach, etc. (See "Membranes" under the various organs and parts of the body).

Brain—Membranes of—(See "Membranes" under Brain; Meninges).

Deposits—Membranous Deposits—(See Croup).

False Membranes—(See Croup, Diphtheria).

Mucous Membranes—(See Mucous).

Respiratory Membranes—(See Breath, Bronchial, Lungs, Pleura).

Sacs—Membranous Sacs—(See Cysts).

Serous Membranes—(See Serous).

Spinal Cord—Membranes of—(See Spine).

Synovial Membranes—(See Synovial).

Tunics—(See Tunics). For the inflammations and diseases of the membranes of the various parts, and organs of the body, such as of the Bowels, Eyes, Head, Heart, Lungs, Nose, Stomach, Throat, etc., see "Membranes" under the part, or organ, you have in mind. (See Cells, Exudations, Peritoneum, Tissues).

MEMORY—The Retentive Faculty of Mind—Recollection—The Memory is ruled by ♄ and ☿, but principally by ☿. Also ruled by the ☉. A ♄ person has a strong memory for injuries done him, as malice and revenge are ♄ traits. In the Hindu System of Astrology the 1st H. rules the Memory.

All Defects In—☿ diseases and afflictions to ☿.

Amnesia—Loss of Memory for Words —☿ afflicted by ♄ and the ☽, and ☿ in no aspect or relation to the Asc.; ☿ affl. in ♈; ☿ combust, and afflicted by ♄ and the ☽, and also setting in the West, out of dignity, and in a weak sign; Subs at AT. (See Forgetful, Impaired, and the various paragraphs in this section).

Defective Memory—☿ badly afflicted at B., and by dir.; Subs at AT and AX. (See the various paragraphs in this section).

Dual Personality—Many planets in double-bodied signs at B., and such signs also on the angles; ☿ in a double-bodied, or bicorporeal sign, as ♊, ♐, or ♓, and afflicted by ♄ and the ☽. The influence of ♄ is to restrain the mind when afflicting ☿, and to limit the mental faculties, and to cause disturbances of, and an unbalanced mental state. (See Double-Bodied, Dual, Personality).

Forgetfulness — Defective Memory — Poor Memory — ☿ alone having dominion over the mind, and ill-disposed; ☿ Sig. ☌ the ☉, combust; a ☿ disease, and with ☿ weak, ill-dignified, and badly afflicted at B., in □ or ☍ the ☽, and in no aspect with the Asc.; ☿ afflicted in ♓; ☿ affl. in ♏, carelessness and forgetfulness of Nature's requirements, and to be neglectful of the body, as in eating, habits, bowel movements, etc.; the ☽ □ or ☍ ☿, and in no aspect the Asc.; ♆ □ or ☍ ☿; a ♓ disorder, and with ☿ afflicted in ♓, and ♓ produces ailments thru forgetfulness and carelessness. (See Carelessness; "Fails In" under Examinations; "Incapable" under Learning; "Shallow" under Mentality; "Weak Mind" under Mind).

Identity — Loss of — Disorientation — (See Identity).

Impaired Memory — ☿ in mutable signs or cadent houses, and afflicted by malefics; ☿ affl. by the ☽, ♄, and ♃, and in no aspect to the Asc.; the ♓ element strong in the nativity.

Inhibited — The Memory Inhibited — Never Had Any Memory — No Trace of a Memory — ☿ in ♊, ☌ the ☉ or ♂, and in □ the ☽, and ☿ in no aspect to the Asc. and benefics.

Lack of Memory — (See Inhibited, No Memory, Poor, in this section).

Little or No Memory — Case of a Female — This case is written up, with birth data, in Chap. VIII in Daath's Medical Astrology.

Loss of Memory — (See "Amnesia" in this section).

Mindful of An Injury — Never Forgets An Injury — (See Enmity, Hatred, Jealousy, Malice, Revenge, Treachery).

Never Had Any Memory — (See "Inhibited" in this section).

Poor Memory — Forgetful — Defective Memory — (See "Forgetfulness", and the various paragraphs in this section).

Retentive Memory — The ☽ strong at B., dignified and well aspected, and espec. when in good asp. to ☿ and the Asc.; ♃ ☌ or good asp. ☿; ☿ strongly posited and well aspected at B.; the ♒ sign strong at B., and free from malefic afflictions. (See Genius, Intellect; "Good" under Judgment; Learning, Mathematical; "Quickened" under Mentality; "Good Mind" under Mind; Reading, Scholar, Study; "Wonderful" in this section).

Weakened Memory — ☿ weak and afflicted at B., in evil asp. the ☽, and in no relation to the Asc., and also not fortified by benefics; ☿ ☌, P., □, or ☍ ♄; ♆ ☌ or ill-asp. ♄, and also with ☿ out of dignity and afflicted; ♆ □ or ☍ ☿. (See Forgetful, Impaired, in this section).

Wonderful Memory — Case — See "De" (Mr. H. De), No. 266 in 1001 N.N. (See "Retentive" in this section).

Words — Loss of Memory for Words — (See "Amnesia" in this section). For collateral study see Apathy, Chaotic, Confusion, Dull, Idiocy, Imbecile, Insanity; "Clouded Mind", "Weak Mind", under Mind.

MEN — Conditions Which Affect Adult Males — The ☉ rules the male in adult Nativities, and the ☽ and ♀ in the female. Many of the planetary influences affecting adult males are also given under "Male", but for convenience of reference the conditions listed here are especially referred to in the Textbooks of Astrology as having to do with Men. (See the various paragraphs under Father, Husband, Male). See the following subjects in the alphabetical arrangement when not more fully considered here—

Accidents to Men — Or Males — (See "Accidents" under Male).

Addicted to Women — Fond of Females — The ☉ Sig. in ♒, ♑, or ♓; ♄ Sig. ☌ ♀; ♃ Sig. in ♒; ♃ Sig. in ♊ near Oculus Taurus (see Oculus Taurus); ♂ Sig. ☌ ♀; ♂ Sig. in ♉, ♌, ♎, or ♓; ☿ Sig. in ♉, ♏, or ♓. (See Amorous; "Free Love" under Free; "Low Company" under Low; "Loose Morals" under Morals; "Passional Excesses" under Passion; Fascinating, Harlots, Women, in this section).

Apathy Of — Free from Passion — (See Apathy, Bachelors, Celibacy; "Anchorite" under Husband; "Indifferent" under Marriage; "Free from Passion" under Passion).

Bachelors; Baldness;

Barrenness — (See Barren, Impotent).

Beard; Blindness — Hurts to the Eyes — (See Left Eye, Right Eye, under Male).

Brain In — Ruled by the ☉. (See Brain).

Constitution — Strong Constitution — The ☉ in a fiery sign and well-aspected; the ☉ in a strong sign and house, and well-aspected by ♂ and benefics. The ☉ in a weak sign, and afflicted tends to a weak constitution. (See "Good", "Strong", "Weak", under Constitution, and note especially the ☉ influences).

Crippled from Birth — (See "Crippled" under Birth).

Danger to Men — The ☉ afflicted by malefics at B., and by dir.

Death by Hand of Man — (See "Hand of Man" under Man).

Death of Men — Many Deaths Among Men — Great Mortality Among — The ☉ ☌ or ill-asp. ♄ at the Vernal Equinox, and ♄ lord of the year; ♄ passing thru a fixed sign; ♄ in a fixed sign at the Vernal, or a Solar Ingress, and afflicting the lord of the year; ♂ in ♎ at the Vernal, and lord of the year; Comets appearing in ♊. (See "Death" under Father, Husband, Male; "Young Men" under Young).

Debauched; Debility of Men — Men Debilitated — ♆ in the Asc. at B.; ♀ in a masculine sign, and ♂ in a feminine sign at B., and both occidental. (See Debility, Impotent).

Deportment of Men — (See the various subjects listed under Conduct).

Depraved; Desires — The Desires Unnatural, Obscene, and Impure — (See Desires, Lewd, Obscene, Perversions, Shameless, Unnatural, etc.).

Detriment to Men—(See "Danger" and the various paragraphs in this section).

Disease In Men—(See "Disease In" under Male).

Diseases Peculiar to Men—(See Penis, Perversions, Scrotum, Testes, Urethra, Venereal).

Drink; Drunkenness; Effeminate;

Eunuchs; Excellent Men—Death of—(See "The Great" under Great; Kings, Nobles, Princes, Rulers).

Excesses In—(See Eating, Excesess, Gluttony, Intoxication; "Passional Excesses" under Passion; Sports, etc.).

Excessive—Excessive Virile Members—(See Virile).

Eyes—Blindness In—Hurts To—(See "Blindness" in this section; "Males" under Eyes).

Famous Men—Death of—(See Famous, Great; "Excellent" in this section).

Fascinating—To Women—Favorites with Women—Has the Love and Favor of Women—Seeks Female Company—Fond of Women—Successful by the Help of Women, etc.—Men born under the strong influence of ♀; ♀ in the Asc. or M.C., or in ☌ the ☉ or ☽ at B.; ♀ Sig. ☌ ☿; ♀ Sig. ⚹ or △ the ☽; ♀ on the Meridian at B., and well-aspected; the ☉ Sig. ⚹ or △ the ☽; the ☉ ☌ ♀; the ☽ ⚹ or △ ♀; the ☽ Sig. in ♎; the ☽ on the Meridian, or culminating, and well aspected by ♀; ♄ Sig. ☌ ♀; ♃ Sig. ☌ the ☽ or ☿; ♃ Sig. ⚹ or △ ♀; ♂ Sig. in ♎, much beloved by women, but also ruined by them; ♂ Sig. ☌ ☽; ♂ Sig. in ♌, but generally to his prejudice or undoing; ♂ Sig. ⚹ or △ ☽, receives much assistance from females; ♂ Sig. ⚹ or △ ♀, exerts his fascinating influence over females to the utmost. (See "Addicted To" in this section; Love Affairs).

Female Company—Seeks Female Company—(See Addicted, Fascinating, in this section).

Female Friends—Has Many—(See 'Fascinating" in this section).

Females—Grief Thru—Ill-Health Thru Associations With—Injured By—Poisoned By—Treachery By, etc.—(See Grief, Hate, Health, Injured, Poison, Treachery, in this section).

Firmness—Lacking In—(See "Resolution" in this section).

Fruitfulness In—(See Fruitfulness; "Fruitful" under Husband).

Genitals of Men—Diseases and Injuries To—(See Genitals, Penis, Testes, Venereal).

Gonorrhoea—Among Men—(See Gonorrhoea).

Good Health—For Men—The ☉ strong and well aspected at B. (See "Good Health" under Males).

Great Men—Death of—(See Great).

Grief—Thru Women—The ☽ to the ill-aspects her own place by dir.; the ☽ or ♀ to the ☌ ♄, ♅, or ♂ by dir. (See "Females" in this section).

Habits—In Men—(See the various subjects under Conduct, Habits).

Handsome Man—♀ Sig. ⚹ or △ ♂. (See Commanding, Handsome).

Harlots—Liable to Associate With—May Associate with Low Women—♀ ill-dignified at B.; ♀ afflicted by ♂; ♂ Sig. ☌ ♀. (See Harlots, Lewd, Licentiousness; "Low Company" under Low; Lust, Obscene, Passion, Perversions, Sensuality, Shameless, Wanton).

Hated—By a Female—(See "Females" under Hate).

Head—Affections of—(See "Men Suffer" under Head).

Health—Good or Bad Health for Men—(See Constitution, Good Health, Injured, in this section).

Health Injured—Thru Women—Lord of the 6th in the 5th or 7th H. (See "Injured" in this section; Debauchery; "Passional Excesses" under Passion; Venereal, Venery).

Health Not Bad—Not Exceptionally Bad—The ☉ afflicted by both ♄ and ♂, as any aspect of ♂ to the ☉ helps to increase the vitality and resistance. (See "Bad" under Health).

Health Worse—The Health Worse Than Otherwise—An afflicting malefic elevated above the ☉ at B. tends to more ill-health than if the ☉ were elevated above the malefic. (See "Ill-Health" under Males).

Heart—The Heart In Man—Ruled by the ☉. The ☉ afflicted in ♌ tends especially to heart diseases and disturbances in men. (See "Heart Disease" under Male).

Hermaphrodites—In Males—A Mixture of Sex In Males—♂ and ♀ both in masculine signs, apt to cause such manifestations. (See Hermaphrodite; Virile).

Hips—(See "Men" under Hips).

Hurts—To Men—The ☉ afflicted at B., and by dir., by ♅, ♄, or ♂. (See "Accidents" under Male).

Hyleg—In a Male—The ☉ is to be taken as Hyleg when strong, and not badly afflicted. Also ♃ or the Asc. can be taken. (See Hyleg).

Ill-Health—For Men—(See "Ill-Health" under Male; "Public Health Bad" under Public; "Injured", and other paragraphs in this section).

Ill-Health Thru Women—(See "Health Injured", "Injured", in this section; Venereal).

Impotence; Impurity—Among Men—(See Lewd, Licentious; "Loose Morals" under Morals; Obscene, Passion, Perversions, Shameless, etc.).

Infirmities Among—(See "Public Health Bad" under Public).

Injured Thru Women—The Health Injured—Meets with Bodily Injury or Violence By—Lord of the 6th H. in the 5th or 7th H., the health injured; the ☽ to the place of Hydra's Heart (see Hydra's Heart); the ☽ in the 12th H. in ♏ or ♑, and afflicted; ♂ ☌ or ill-asp. the ☽ or ♀ at B., and by dir.; ♂ Sig. in ♌ or ♎; ♀ afflicted in the 1st H.; caused by fixed stars of the nature of ♀. (See Harlots, Jealousy; "Passional Excesses" under Passion; "Poison Death" under Poison; Treachery).

Left Eye—Blindness In, or Injury To—(See "Left Eye" under Male).

Left Side of Body—In Males—Afflictions To—(See "Males" under Left).

Length of Life—(See "Length of Life" under Males).

Licentious—Men Highly Licentious, Obscene, and Lustful—Sex Gratification In Men—If the Luminaries be in feminine signs in a male horoscope, and also ♀ in a female sign and afflicted by ♂, men will tend to be wanton, licentious, soft, and seek connection contrary to nature, but in privacy, and not openly. If ♂ also be in a feminine sign, and afflicting ♀, men will tend to shamelessness and publicity in their sex practices. Mars with ♀ alone and ♄ absent. Mars rules the passions in men, and ♀ in women. Venus in a feminine sign alone and afflicted by ♂. (See Deviations, Exhibitionism, Lasciviousness, Lewd, Licentiousness, Lust, Obscene; "Violence" under Passion; Perversions, Sadism, Scandalous, Sex, Shameless, Sodomy, Unnatural, Wanton, etc.).

Long Life—For Men—The ☉ well-aspected in a fiery sign. (See "Long Life" under Males).

Loved by Females—(See "Fascinating" in this section).

Low Women—May Associate With—(See "Harlots" in this section).

Lustful—(See Lascivious, Lewd, Lust; "Licentious" in this section).

Maimed—(See "Males" under Maimed).

Male In Family—Death of—(See "Death" under Father, Husband, Male, Son).

Male Organ—Disorders of—Injuries To—(See Genitals, Penis).

Manly—Sober—(See Honest; "Manly and Sober" under Manners; Noble, Upright).

Manners—(See Manners).

Marriage—(See Fiance, Husband, Love Affairs, Marriage, Marriage Partner, Wife).

Men—Death at the Hands of Men—(See "Hand of Man" under Man).

Men In Power—(See Great, Kings, Rulers; "Power" in this section).

Middle Life—Men At Middle Life—(See Middle Life).

Mortality Among—(See "Death of Men" in this section; "Just Men" under Mortality).

Neck—The Neck Afflicted with Men—(See "Men" under Neck).

Obscenity—Given To—(See Obscene; "Licentious" in this section).

Opposite Sex—Health Suffers By—Injured By—Little Attraction For—(See "Health", "Injured", in this section; Apathy, Bachelors, Celibacy; "Anchorite" under Husband; "Indifferent" under Marriage; Opposite Sex; "Free from Passion" under Passion).

Passion—In Men—Ruled by ♂. For Excess of Passion in Men, or Lack of, see Amorous, Apathy, Celibacy, Excesses; "Free from Passion", "Passional Excesses", under Passion; "Licentious" in this section).

Penis—Male Organ of Generation—(See Genitals, Penis, Urethra).

Perversions—Sex Perversions—(See Deviations, Indecent, Obscene, Perversions, Shameless).

Poisoned—Death by Poison By the Treachery of Women—(See Poison, Treachery).

Power—Men In Power—(a) Gains Much by Patronage of—♂ Sig. in ⚹ or △ the ☉. (b) Incurs Displeasure of—Often Ruined By—Oppressed By—♄ Sig. □ or ☍ ☉; ♃ or the ☽ Sig. ☌ the ☉. (See Judges, Kings, Princes, Rulers). (c) Death of Men In Power—(See "Death" under Great, Kings, Rulers).

Prostate Trouble—(See Prostate).

Recuperation Slow—Or Rapid—(See "Males" under Recuperation).

Regenerative Organs—Reproductive Organs—Diseases of In Men—(See "Genitals" in this section).

Relatives—Men, or Male Relatives—Conditions Affecting—(See "Relatives" under Male).

Resolution—Firmness—Lack of—The ☉ in ♊; ♂ weak and ill-dignified at B.; born under the strong influence of ♀. (See "Mutable Disposition" under Mutable; Negative).

Right Eye—Blindness In—Hurts To (See "Right Eye" under Male).

Right Side—Of the Body—(See "Left Side" under Left; "Right Side" under Right).

Robust—Men More Robust—(See "Good Health" under Males; Robust).

Ruined by Women—(See "Ruined by Women" under Love Affairs).

Seminal Fluid—Disorders of—(See Semen).

Senility—(See Old Age).

Severe Illnesses—Sharp Illnesses In Men—The ☉ afflicted in fiery signs, but soon over. (See "High Fevers" under Fever; Severe, Sharp).

Sex Gratification—In Men—(See "Licentious" in this section; "Violence" under Passion).

Sex Organs—Diseases of—Injuries To—(See "Genitals" in this section).

Shameless Practices—(See "Licentious, Lustful, Perversions, in this section).

Sharp Illnesses—(See "Severe" in this section; Pernicious, Sharp).

Sober and Manly—(See "Manly and Sober" under Manners; "Manly" in this section).

Sterility In—(See Barrenness).

Stricture of Urethra—(See Urethra).

Strong Constitution—(See "Constitution" in this section, and under Male).

Syphilis; Testicles; Thighs—The Hips and Thighs Affected In Men—(See "Men" under Hips).

Treachery—Suffers Treachery by Women—(See Poison, Tragical, Treachery).

Unnatural Desires—And Practices—(See Desires, Licentious, in this section; Unnatural).

Untimely Death Of—(See "Early Death" under Early; "Death" under Middle Life; Untimely).

Urethra—Disorders of—(See Urethra).

Valiant Men—♂ strong at B., or ruler. (See Bold; "Qualities" under Mars; Warrior).

Varicocele; Venereal Diseases—(See Genitals, Gonorrhoea, Privates, Sex, Syphilis, Venereal).

Violent—In Sex Gratification—Given to Violent Actions—(See Cruel, Sadism; "Shameless Practices" under Shame; Violent).

Virile Members Excessive—(See Hermaphrodite, Virile).

Vitality In—(See "Vitality" under Male; "Good", "Low", under Vitality).

Widowers; Women — Wastes His Money and Substance On—♄ Sig. ✳ or △ ♀. (See Debauched, Dissipation, Expense; "Energies Wasted" under Love Affairs; Opposite Sex, Passion, Prodigal, Venery, etc.). For the various dealings of men with women see in this section,—Addicted To, Fascinating to Women, Females, Grief, Harlots, Hated, Health Injured, Injured Thru Women, Licentious, Marriage, Opposite Sex, Poisoned, Ruined by Women, Treachery, etc.

Worse—The Health Worse—The ☉ afflicted at B., and by dir. (See "Ill-Health" under Males).

Wounds To—(See "Accidents" under Males).

Young Men—Great Mortality Among —(See "Young Men" under Young). For further study along this line see the various paragraphs under Brothers, Father, Females, Grandparents, Husband, Love Affairs, Marriage, Marriage Partner, Son, Uncles, Wife.

MENIDROSIS — Bloody Sweat — (See "Haematidrosis" under Sweat).

MENINGES—Membranes of the Brain —Dura Mater, the Outer Membrane of the Brain and Spinal Cord—(See Brain, Dura Mater; "Cord" under Spine). The Meninges, or Brain Coverings, are ruled by ♅ and the ♋ sign.

Cerebral Meningitis—Inflammation of the Cerebral Meninges—The ☉ or ♅ afflicted in ♈; the ☽ in the 6th H., and much afflicted at B., and by dir., and espec. if ☿ also be afflicted and not in the Asc.; Subs at AT and CP. (See Cerebral).

Cerebro-Spinal Meningitis — (See Brain, Cerebro-Spinal, Dura Mater).

Leptomeningitis—Inflammation of the Pia and Arachnoid Membranes—♅ afflicted in ♈; Subs at AT.

Spinal Meningitis—♅ afflicted in ♌ or ♒; ♌ on the Asc.; a ♌ disease; ♆ ☌ the ☉ and ♄ in ♌, and afflicted by ♅; Subs at AT, AX, CP, and KP. (See Spine). Case of Spinal Meningitis—Birth Data, etc.—See Chap. XIV in Daath's Medical Astrology.

MENKAR—Whale's Jaw—(See Ceti).

MENOPAUSE — The Change of Life — Menses Stopped — (See "Menopause" under Menses).

MENORRHAGIA — (See "Profuse" under Menses).

MENS SANA—(See "Sound Mind" under Mind).

MENSES—The Monthly Flow from the Womb — Menstrues — Periodics — Courses—Catamenia— Feminine Functions, etc.—The Menses are an excrementitious fluid ruled by the ♏ sign. (See Excretion). The Menses begin when the Prog. ☽ reaches the sign and degree opposite to her radical place. This time may be earlier or later in different individuals according to the signs of long or short ascension thru which the ☽ must pass. This is equivalent to the Full ☽, or the 2nd Quarter of the ☽ by progression from her place at the birth of the native. The Change of Life occurs at the progressed Third Quarter of the ☽ from her radical place. (See "Menopause" in this section). The natural female functions are ruled by the ☽. (See Functions, Moon).

Abnormal Menses — (See Imperfect, Irregular, Painful, Profuse, and the various paragraphs in this section).

Absence Of—Arrested—Amenorrhoea —(See Irregular, Never Occur, Suppressed, in this section).

Amenorrhoea — Irregularity or Suppression of the Menses—(See "Absence" in this section).

Change of Life—(See "Menopause" in this section).

Chlorosis—Anaemia In Young Women, and Attended with Menstrual Disturbances—(See Chlorosis).

Courses Overflowing— Copious — (See Flooding, Profuse, in this section).

Delayed—(See "Puberty" in this section).

Deranged Menses — (See "Puberty Weakened", and the various paragraphs in this section).

Difficult and Slow — (See Painful, Slow, in this section).

Disturbances Of — (See "Irregular", and the various paragraphs in this section).

Dysmenorrhoea—(See "Painful" in this section).

Effusion Of — (See Flooding, Hemorrhage, Profuse, in this section).

Excessive—(See Flooding, Hemorrhage, Menorrhagia, Profuse, in this section).

Flooding Hemorrhages—Menorrhagia —Metorrhagia — Excessive Menses—♂ afflicting ♀, and ♀ also afflicting the ☽; ♀ afflicted in ♏: Subs at PP. (See "Profuse" in this section).

Functions—The Menstrual Functions Disordered—The ☽ hyleg in ♏, and afflicted. (See Irregular, Suppressed, and the various paragraphs in this section).

Hastened—Earlier Manifestation of— (See the Introduction, "Puberty" in this section).

Headache—At Time of Periods—(See "Periodic" under Headache).

Hemorrhage—(See Flooding, Profuse, in this section; "Hemorrhage" under Womb).

Immoderate Discharges—(See Flooding, Hemorrhage, Profuse, in this section).

Imperfect Menstruation—The ☉ in ♏ in evil asp. to ♆, ♅, or ♄; the ☉ in ♉, ♌, or ♒, and afflicted by ♄, ♅, or ♆. (See Irregular, Suppressed, in this section).

Incoordination—At Time of Menses—♅ afflicted in ♉ or ♏ at B., and especially at times when ♅ is also afflicted by direction, or afflicting planets in ♉; Subs at PP. (See Incoordination).

Irregular Menses—A ♉ and ♏ disease, and afflictions in these signs; the ☽ or ♀ afflicted by ♄; the ☽ □ or ☍ ♀, and ♄ also afflicting ♀; the ☽ to the ill-asps. ♀ by dir., and ♀ in a water sign at B.; the ☽ or ♀ afflicted in ♏; the Prog. ☽ in the sign and degree in ☍ to her place at B., and afflicted by malefics; ♂ in ♏, ☌, or ill-asp. the ☉; ♀ afflicted by ♄; ♀ in ♒ in the 6th H., and afflicted; ♀ in ♒ and afflicting the ☽ or Asc. (See Painful, Suppressed, in this section; "Irregular" under Functions).

Irritating and Painful — (See "Painful" in this section; "Hour Glass Contraction" under Womb).

Lungs—Menstruation Thru the Lungs —(See "Vicarious" in this section).

Menidrosis — Vicarious Menstruation Thru the Sweat Glands — (See "Menidrosis" under Sweat).

Menopause — The End of the Menstrual Life — The Change of Life In Women — Menstruation begins when the ☽ by progression reaches the sign and degree in ☍ to her radical place, on her first course around after birth of the native, which is usually about the 14th year of life. The Menses stop, and are discontinued, when the ☽ by progression reaches her 3rd Quarter from her radical place, on her second course around thru the 12 Signs. The beginning or ending of the Menses may be earlier or later in life according to the nature of the signs thru which the ☽ passes, whether they be signs of long or short ascension. (See "Ascension" under Long). The Menopause takes place at from the 43rd to 48th years of life.

Menorrhagia — An Excessive Menstrual Flow — Metorrhagia — (See Flooding, Profuse, in this section).

Menstrual Trouble—Deranged Menses —Catamenial Disorders—The ☽ hyleg in ♏, and afflicted; ☽ diseases; the ☽ afflicted at B., and by dir.; the ☽ affl. by ♀; the ☽ to the ill-asp. ♀ by dir.; the ☽ afflicted in ♉ or ♏; ♂ or ☿ afflicted in ♏; ♂ in ♏ in the 6th H., and afflicted; ♂ in ♏ and afflicting the ☽ or Asc.; a ♏ disease; malefics and afflictions in ♉ tend to by reflex action to the ♏ sign. (See Imperfect, Irregular, Profuse, and the various paragraphs in this section).

Never Occur — Entirely Absent — Menses May Never Occur—♀ afflicted by the ☽ and ♄, and ♀ in a sign of ♄. This may also lead to sterility. (See the ♀ influences under Barrenness).

Nose—Menstruation Thru the Nose— (See "Vicarious" in this section).

Obstruction — Of the Menses — (See Painful, Suppressed, in this section; Obstructions).

Overflowing — Of the Courses — (See Flooding, Hemorrhage, Profuse, in this section).

Painful Menstruation—Irritating— Difficult and Slow — Dysmenorrhoea — Painful Catamenial Discharges — The ☉ or ☽ in ♏, ☌, or ill-asp. any of the malefics as promittors; the ☉ in ☍ and afflicted by one or more malefics; the ☽ □ or ☍ ♀, and ♄ also afflicting ♀; the ☽ in a fixed sign, and espec. in ♏, and afflicted by malefics; ♄, ♂, ♀, or ☿ afflicted in ♏; ♂ afflicting ♀ and ♀ evilly aspected by the ☽; ♀ afflicted in ♏, and especially with ♀ in the 6th H., or ♀ afflicting the ☽ or Asc. (See Imperfect, Restricted, Suppressed, in this section).

Profuse Menses — Excessive—Overflowing — Flooding — Menorrhagia — Metorrhagia — Immoderate and Copious Discharges — Menstrual Effusions — Catamenia Profuse and Weakening — The ☉ in ♉, ♌, ♏, or ♒, and afflicted by any of the malefics; afflictions in the fixed signs, and espec. in ♏; the ☽ afflicted in ♏; the ☽ □ or ☍ ♀; the ☽ to the ill-asps. ♀ by dir., and ♀ in a water sign at B.; the ☽ □ or ☍ ♂; ♂ afflicting ♀ and ♀ also afflicting the ☽; ♂ in ♉ or ♏, and afflicting the ☽ or ♀; ♂ ☌ or ill-asp. the ☽; ♂ in ♏, ☌, or ill-asp. the ☉; caused by ♂ as ♂ rules hemorrhages and rupture of blood vessels; ♀ afflicted in ♏; ♀ afflicting the ☽, and espec. when both are in water signs. (See "Women" under Anaemia; Leucorrhoea, Plethora; "Flooding", "Vicarious", in this section).

Puberty Weakened — Ill-Health At Puberty—The Menses Hastened or Delayed — Sensuous Imaginations At Adolescence — Suppressed Menses— Painful Menses—The ☽ afflicted by ♀; afflictions in ♉ or ♏. The removal of the tonsils in childhood (tonsils ruled by ♉) tends to make the puberty period more disturbed, and also increased disturbances later in parturition and childbirth. (See Puberty, Tonsils; Irregular, Menopause, Suppressed, in this section).

Restricted Menses — ♄ afflicted in ♉ or ♏; ♄ ☌ ♆ in ♉. (See "Suppressed" in this section).

Scanty Menses — (See Imperfect, Irregular, Painful, Suppressed, in this section).

Sick with Menses—In Hor'y Maps if the ☽ is in the 6th H., in ill-asp. to ♀ in ♏, it denotes that the patient is sick with Menses if a female.

Slow and Difficult—The ☽ in a fiery sign at B., the female functions are slow and difficult. (See "Fire Signs" under Fire; "Impeded" under Functions).

Stomach — Hemorrhages Thru — (See "Vicarious" in this section).

Suppressed Menses — Amenorrhoea — Arrested Menses — The Menses Obstructed — Suppression of the Catamenia — The influence of ♄ tends to delay, suppress, and hinder the functions of the body, and espec. when afflicting the ☉, ☽, or Asc. The ☉ and ♄ in ♏ when they are the afflictors in the disease; the ☉ or ☽ in ♏, ☌, or ill-asp. ♄, or any of the malefics; the ☉ in ♉, ♌, or ♒, and afflicted by ♄, ♅, or ♆ as promittors; the ☽ in any of the fixed signs, and especially ♏, and afflicted by ♄, ♅, or ♆; the ☽ affl. by ♀; the ☽ or ♀ affl. by ♄; the ☽ □ or ☍ ♀, and ♄ also afflicting ♀; ♄ affl. in ♏; ♀ in the 6th H., and affl. by ♄; ☿ affl. in ♏, and espec. when he is afflicted by ♄, or is of the nature of ♄; many planets in fixed signs at B. (See Imperfect, Irregular, Never Occur, Painful, Restricted, in this section).

Tonsils — Removal of In Childhood Disturbs the Menses at Puberty and In Later Life—(See "Puberty" in this section).

Vicarious — Vicarious Menstruation—The Menses Thru Some Other Passage Than the Womb—Menstrual Effusions—The blood must have an outlet, and when the ♏, or womb sign, is badly afflicted at B., as by ♄ in ♏, the outlet of blood is suppressed thru the womb, and is diverted thru the Nose, Lungs, Stomach, or Sweat Glands. Mars in ♏, and afflicted by ♄ and the ☽, tends to hemorrhage thru the Nose at the time of the period. Afflictions in ♊ tend to hemorrhage thru the lungs at such times. Afflictions in ♋, hemorrhage thru the stomach. Afflictions which cause vicarious menstruation may also cause death by excessive hemorrhages, and espec. if the afflictions come from the 8th H., the house of death. (See "Hemorrhage" under Lungs, Stomach; "Epistaxis" under Nose; Sweat, Vicarious; "Blood" under Vomiting).

Weakened—The Puberty Weakened—(See "Puberty" in this section).

Young Females — Weaknes Incident to Young Females At Adolescence—(See "Females" under Puberty).

MENTAL — Mentally — Mentality — Pertaining to the Mind—This Article, or section, is a part of, and supplementary to the Article on "Mind", but arranged under "Mental" for convenience of reference, as there are so many references in the Textbooks of Astrology as "Mental". For subjects not found in this section see Intellect, Mind, and also look in the alphabetical arrangement for the subject you have in mind. The Cardinal Signs are Mental in Temperament. Mercury has relation to the Mind, and all Mental Diseases. The Mentality is ruled by the Pineal Gland, presided over by ♆.

Abilities—Mental Abilities—Many of these are listed in the Article on Mind, and also in this section. (See Elegant, Examinations, Genius; "Great Abilities" under Great; Learning, Mathematical, Mechanical, Mind, Reading, Scholar, Study, etc. Also look in the alphabetical arrangement for the subject you have in mind).

Abnormal Mental Trouble—♆ afflicted in the 3rd or 9th H., and especially when in □ or ☍ to ♄ or ♂ from these houses. (See Abnormal).

Action — Excessive Mental Action — (See "Over-Active Mind" under Active). For the opposite conditions of Mind see Apathy, Dull, Indifferent, etc.

Activity—Mental Activity—An Active Mind—♂ ☌ ☿ gives, and the capacity for hard mental work unless in ♓; the ☽ to the good asps. ☿ by dir., and ☿ strong at B.; the signs ♊, ♍, and ♐ all tend to great mental activity, and this activity is greatly increased if the ☽ or ☿ be aspected by ♅ or ♂. (See "Active Mind" under Active; Effervescent; "Mental Energy" under Energy; "Quickened" in this section).

Acute Mentality — (See Activity, Quickened, in this section; "Good" under Mind).

Affliction — Mental Affliction — Affliction of Mind—The ☉ to the ill-asps. ☿ by dir., loses interest in studies, and is averse to learning for the time; the ☉ or ☽ to the ☌ or ill-asps. ♄; the ☽ to the ☌ or ill-asps. the ☉ or ♄ by dir., afflicted in mind and body; ♆ afflicted in the 9th H.; ♄ passing over the place of the radical ☽, or ♄ at a Solar Rev. ☌ the ☉ or ☽. (See Anguish, Distress, Disturbances, Infirmities, in this section; "Mental Afflictions" under Affliction; Examinations; "Affliction of Mind", "No Peace of Mind", "Troubled In Mind", and other paragraphs under Mind).

Anguish — Mental Anguish — (See Anguish).

Anxiety — Mental Anxiety — (See Anguish, Anxiety, Cares, Fears, Worry).

Arrested Mental Powers—Retarded—Inhibited — The ☉ or ☽ in the 6th or 12th H., and afflicted by malefics; ♉, ♏, or ♑ on the Asc.; the malefics are usually closely associated; ♅, ♄, or ♂ in ☌ or ☍ in fixed signs; rays, or bodies of malefics, are in or directed upon the 5th, 6th, or 12th Houses, or their cusps, or to the ascending degree; many planets in ♍, and the 6th or 12th H. These same influences may also retard the growth of the body, or cause deformities, dwarfed conditions, hunchback, etc. (See Arrested, Backwardness, Deformities, Dwarfed; "Mind" under Growth; Humpback (see Spine); Idiocy, Imbecility, Insanity; "Weak Mind" under Mind; Childlike, Deficiency, Derangement, Retarded, Weak, Weakened, in this section).

Bad Mental Traits — (See "Undesirable" under Mind).

Blindness—From Mental Exertion, or Too Much Reading and Study — (See "Mental Exertion" under Blindness).

Breakdown Mentally — (See "Brain Fag" under Brain; "Mind" under Exercise; "Over-Exertion" under Exertion; "Mind" under Fatigue; Insanity, Reading, Study, etc.).

Chaotic Mental States—(See Chaotic).

Childlike Mentality—Mental Suppression — Never Grew Up — Case — (See "Mind" under Children).

Clouded Mentality—(See Clouded).

Combative — (See Anger, Choleric, Quarrelsome; "High Temper" under Temper; etc.).

Complaints—Mental Complaints—(See the various paragraphs in this Article, and also under Faculties, Intellect, Mind, Perception, Reason, etc.).

Confusion — Mental Confusion — Clouded Mind — Chaotic — Mixed Ideas, etc. — (See "Mental Chaos" under Chaotic; Clouded, Confusion; "Dreamy Mind" under Dreams; Ideas, Memory; "Absent-Minded" under Mind).

Conservation — Of Mental Powers — (See Conservation).

Craziness — Mental Deficiency — (See "Deficiency" in this section; Insanity, Madness, Mania).

Curable Mental Diseases—(See "Curable" under Brain; Conspicuous, Curable, Epilepsy, Incurable, Insanity).

Death—From Mental Disorders—(See "Death" under Epilepsy, Madness, Melancholy).

Debility — Mental Debility — (See "Mental Debility" under Debility; "Weak Intellect" under Intellect; "Debility" under Mind).

Decanates and Mentality—(See Decanates).

Defects — Mental Defects — (See "Deficiency" in this section; "Foolish Mind" under Foolish; Idiocy, Imbecility, Insanity; "Weak Mind" under Mind).

Deficiency— Mentally Deficient—The Mind Afflicted—The affliction of ♄ to the 3rd H., ♄ in the 3rd, or afflicting the ruler of the 3rd, is usually at the bottom of mental deficiency. Mercury and the ☽ may be strong at the same time, and also the ☉ or Asc. not afflicted. Also the water signs are usually on the 3rd H., or intercepted in this house, and containing malefics. Venus is often afflicted by the □ or ☍ of ♄ or ♂. The Mutable Signs are often involved, and espec. the 22° of the Mutables; ♆ in the 3rd H., and afflicted, tends to; ♄ and ♂ afflicting the cusp of the 3rd H.; the ☉ ruler of the 3rd H., in ♓, and afflicted by ♄. Cases — See Chap. VIII, in Daath's Medical Astrology; also see "Mentally Defective", No. 408, and "Defective Mentally", No. 670, both in 1001 N.N. (See Idiocy, Imbecility, Insanity; "Diseased Mind", "Weak Mind", under Mind; Arrested, Derangement, Unbalanced, in this section).

Demoniac — Mental Obsession — (See Demoniac, Insanity, Obsessions; Spirit Controls).

Depression—Mental Depression—(See Dejected, Depressed; "Low Spirits" under Low; Melancholy, etc.).

Derangement — Mental Derangement — ☿ and the ☽ weak at B., and unconnected with each other or the Asc.; the ☽ hyleg at B., and to the ☌ or ill-asps. ♄ by dir.; ♃ to the ill-asps. ☿ by dir., and ☿ weak and afflicting at B.; ♈ denotes, and afflictions in ♈; cardinal signs on the cusp the 6th H.; the 30° ♍ on the Asc. Temporary mental derangement may be caused by the ☽ being in the 6th H. at B., and much afflicted at B., and by dir., and especially if ☿ also be afflicted, not in the Asc., or connected with the Asc. or ☽. (See Deranged, Epilepsy, Fears, Hallucinations, Hypochondria, Idiocy, Imaginations, Insanity, Madness, Mania; "Diseased Mind" under Mind). Case—See Chap. XIII, in Daath's Medical Astrology.

Desirable Mental Traits — (See "Desirable" under Mind).

Destructive—Mental Destructiveness —(See Destructiveness).

Development — The Mental Development Arrested, Obstructed, Precocious, Premature, etc.—(See Arrested; "Mind" under Growth; Incomplete, Precocious, Premature, Prodigies; "Suppressed" in this section).

Deviations—Deviation of the Mental Faculties—(See Aversions, Deviations).

Disabilities—Mental— ☿ diseases and afflictions to ☿ at B., and by dir. (See "Mental" under Disabilities; Intellect, Mind; the various paragraphs in this section).

Diseases — Mental Diseases — Mental Disorders—Danger of—Causes of—The ☉ afflicted in the 6th H., and with ☿ also weak and afflicted at B.; the ☽ afflicted by ♆; the ☽ afflicted by ☿; the ☽ and ☿ weak and afflicted at B., and unconnected with each other or the Asc.; the ☽ affl. by ♄ at B., and to the ☌ or ill-asp. ♄ by dir.; ♆ in the 3rd or 9th H., and afflicting the ☽ and ☿; ♅ afflicting the 3rd, 6th, 9th, or 12th H.; born under strong and adverse ♄ influence, liable to mental disorders and infirmities; ☿ afflicted at B., and to the ill-asps. the ☽, or the hyleg by periodic revolution, or by dir., often causes mental diseases or Epilepsy; ☿ in the 6th H. in ♊, ♐, or ♓, and afflicted, mental diseases to be feared; ☿ afflicting the ☽, and the ☽ afflicted by the ☌ or ill-asps. the malefics. (See "Mental" under Infirmities; "Diseased Mind" under Mind; the various paragraphs in this Article).

Disorders—Mental Disorders— ☿ has relation to all nervous and mental disorders; ☿ afflicted in ♈; ☿ □ or ☍ the Asc. (See "Diseases", and the various paragraphs in this section, and under Mind).

Distress — Mental Distress — (See Anguish, Anxiety, Despondent; "Hopeless" under Hope; Melancholy; "Tormented In Mind" under Mind; Worry).

Disturbances—Mental Disturbances —(See "Irritations", and the various paragraphs in this section, and under Mind).

Effervescent—Effervescent Mental Activity—(See Effervescent).

Ego—Exaggerated Ego—(See Ego).

Energy—Mental Energy—An Active, Energetic Mind — (See "Active Mind" under Active; "Mental" under Energy; "Quickened" in this section). For the opposite conditions of mind see Apathy, Dull, Idle, Lassitude, Lethargy, etc.

Excessive Mental Action—(See "Over-Active Mind" under Active).

Exertion — Mental Over-Exertion, Blindness, and Other Ills From—(See "Mental Exertion" under Blindness; "Over-Exertion" under Exertion; "Mind" under Fatigue).

Extremes—Goes to Mental Extremes —(See Anger, Choleric, Cruel, Extremes, Fury, Ideals, Madness, Riotous; "High Temper" under Temper; Violent, etc.).

Face — The Mental Type Face — (See Decanates; "Narrow" under Face).

Faculties—The Mental Faculties Endangered—Signs of Danger To—The ☽, ☿, and the Asc. in no relation to each other, and at the same time ☿ be afflicted by the ☌ or ill-asp. the malefics. (For other conditions concerning the Faculties see the various paragraphs under Faculties).

Fantasies — Mental Fantasies — (See "Dreamy Mind" under Dreams).

Feeble Mentality—(See Feeble; "Foolish Mind" under Foolish; Idiocy, Imbecile; "Weak" in this section).

Force — Mental Force — The ♈ sign gives much mental force, and with the ☉ or ♂ in this sign in the Asc. (See "Mind" under Force; "Quickened" in this section).

Forces—Conservation of the Mental Forces—(See Conservation).

Freaks; Genius—Mental Genius—(See Genius).

Good Mental Traits—(See "Desirable" under Mind).

Growth—Mental Growth Accelerated or Retarded—(See "Mind" under Growth; Arrested, Quickened, Retarded, in this section).

Healing — Mental Healing — (See "Psychic Healing" under Healers).

Illusions; Imaginations—(See Imagination).

Imbecile; Impaired Mentality — (See "Diseases" under Mind; "Mental Faculties" under Impairment; Affliction, Arrested, Deficiency, Derangement, in this section).

Impediments—Mental Impediments—(See Impediments).

Incapacity—Profound Mental Incapacity—(See Dementia, Demoniac, Idiocy, Imbecile; "Mental Faculties Impaired" under Impaired; Insanity; "Incapable" under Learning; Incompetency, Shallow, Weak, in this section).

Incompetency—Mental—The ☉ ☌ ☿, combust, and in □ or ☍ ♅ or ♂, lack of judgment and forethought; the ☽ and ☿ weak, and unconnected with each other or the Asc.; ♄ or the ☽ □ or ☍ ☿ at B.; ♃ Sig. □ or ☍ the ☽, mind weak and foolish; ♃ □ or ☍ ☿. (See Foolish, Forethought, Idiocy, Imbecile, Insanity; "Bad" under Judgment; Incapacity, Shallow, Weak, in this section).

Inferior Mentality — (See Arrested, Dwarfed, Examinations, Foolish, Imbecile, Judgment, Learning; "Weak Mind" under Mind; Incapacity, Incompetency, Weak, and the various paragraphs in this section).

Infirmities—Liable to Mental Infirmities—(See "Mental" under Infirmities; "Diseases", and the various paragraphs in this section).

Ingenious Mentality — (See "Ingenious" under Genius).

Inhibited Mentality — (See Arrested, Retarded, Weak, in this section; "Mental" under Inhibitions).

Intellect — (See Faculties, Intellect, Mind, Perception, Reason, Understanding, and also note the various paragraphs in this section).

Inventive Mentality — (See Genius; "Inventive" under Learning; Mathematical).

Irritability—Mental—(See Irritable).

Irritations—Mental Irritations and Disturbances—Mental Indisposition—Affliction of Mind—Troubled In Mind—The Mind Disturbed—The ☉ or ☽ to the ☌ or ill-asps. ♄ by dir., mental troubles and afflictions; the ☉ to the ill-asps. ☿ by dir.; the ☽ to the ill-asps. ♅ or ♄ by dir., the mind is troubled and anxious; the bad asps. of the ☽ by dir. to the ☉, ♄, ♅, or the Asc.; ♆ afflicted in the 9th H., danger of mental trouble; caused by the afflictions of ♅ to the ☉, ☽, or ☿; ♅ by transit ☌ ♂, troubled almost to violence; ♅ by tr. in ☌ the ☽ may tend even to a mild form of Idiocy for the time; ♄ ☌ or ill-asp. the ☉, ☽, ☿, or the Asc. by dir.; ♃ to the ill-asps. ☿ by dir.; ♂ in the Asc. at decumb., or the beginning of an illness; the M.C. to the ☌ or ill-asps. the ☽ by dir., troubled in both mind and body; afflictions to ♀ or the ♎ sign, or to any of the airy signs, generally cause discord, inharmony, a troubled mind, and disturbed emotions. (See "Mental" under Afflictions; Anguish, Anxiety, Dejected, Distress, Emotions, Irrational, Irritable, Idiocy; "No Peace" under Mind; Misery, Trouble, Worry, etc.).

Limitations—Mental Limitations—(See Foolish, Idiocy, Imbecile, Limitations, Twelfth House).

Low Mentality — (See "Low Mentality" under Mind).

Melancholic—(See Melancholy).

Mentality Not So Good—When ☿ rises after the ☉, or is combust, but the mind is brightened when ☿ rises before the ☉. (See "Weakened" in this section).

Moisture of the Brain — Mental Diseases Arising From—(See "Brain" under Moisture).

Morbid Deviations — (See "Morbid" under Mind; Morbid, Unsavory).

Never Grew Up—The Mentality of a Child In An Adult—Case—(See "Mind" under Children).

Obsessions—(See Delirium, Demoniac, Insanity, Mediumship, Obsessions, Spirit Controls).

Over-Exertion—Mental—(See "Exertion" in this section; Reading, Study).

Over-Study — (See "Exertion" in this section; "Brain Fag" under Brain; "Eyestrain" under Eyes; "Mind" under Fatigue; Reading, Study).

Perversions—Mental—(See Delusions, Hallucinations, Illusions; "Morbid" under Imaginations; Perversions, etc.).

Pineal Gland—And the Pituitary Body—As Related to the Mentality—(See Pineal, Pituitary).

Planets—The Mental Planets—♅ and ☿ are termed the Mental Planets. (See Mercury, Uranus).

Poor and Shallow—(See "Shallow" in this section; "Fails In" under Examinations; "Weak" under Mind; "Aversion" under Study).

Powers Retarded—(See Arrested, Inhibited, Retarded, Weak, in this section).

Premature—The Mental Development Premature—(See Genius, Precocious, Premature, Prodigies).

Profound Mentality—Depth of Mind—(See Learning; "Deep and Profound" under Mind; Reading, Scholar, Science, Study; Activity, Quickened, in this section).

Qualities—The Mental Qualities—The Mental Traits—Many of these are considered and listed in this book. Look in the alphabetical arrangement for the subject you have in mind. See the list under Conduct, Expression, Habits, Manners, Mental, Mind, Morals, Temper, Temperament, etc. Especially see the paragraphs, "Desirable Mental Traits", "Undesirable Mental Traits" in the Article on Mind.

Quality—The Mental Quality—(See "Quality of the Mind" under Mind).

Quickened Mentality—Forceful Mentality—Presence of Mind—Quick and Sharp Mind—Forethought—Acuteness of Mind—Good Mental Capacity—Good Mental Energy—Great Discernment, etc.—The ☽ or ♂ to the good aspects ☿ by dir.; the ☽ on the Meridian, or coming to it, and at the same time in ✶ or △ ☿, quick-witted and clever; ☿ rising in the East at B., before the ☉, well-aspected by the ☽, and also in good relation to the Asc.; ☿ rising in ♊, ♍, or ♐, well-aspected by ♃, and espec. in ☌ or P. dec. ♃; ☿ ☌ or good asp. the ☽, and free from the affliction of ♄; ☿ ☌ or any aspect ♂; ☿ Sig. ✶ or △ ♂, presence of mind, and an acute and ready wit; ♆ well-aspected in the 3rd H., the mental faculties are enhanced; ♅ or ♂ well-aspected in ♊ or ♍; ♄ in ♒ and not afflicting the ☉, ☽, ☿, Asc., Hyleg, or M.C.; ♂ well-asp. in ♐ or ♑; ♂ Sig. ✶ or △ ☿, acute and penetrating mind; ♂ to the good asps. ☿ by dir.; the ♎ and ♑ influences strong at B. give an acute mind. (See Comprehension, Discernment, Intellect, Judgment; "Sound Mind", "Strong Mind", under Mind; Perception, Reason, Understanding; "Mental" under Vitality; "Activity" in this section).

Rest—Mental Rest—(See Rest).

Retarded Mentality—☿ badly afflicted during the Prenatal Period, or at birth, or after birth, may tend to retard the mental growth; ☿ afflicted in the 12th H., the house of limitations and restraints; also the ♄ influence tends to retard both mind and body by his afflictions, to limit the Senses, etc., and especially when in the 12th H. at B. Cases of congenital Deafness, Dumbness, Idiocy, Imbecility, Foolish Mind, etc., indicate retarded mentality from some cause from the time of conception, on down to birth, and also influences at B., and after birth, may contribute to the condition. (See Arrested, Childlike Mentality, Inhibited, Limitations, Weak, in this section; Congenital; "Weak Mind" under Mind; Saturn, Thyroid, Twelfth House).

Scattered—The Mental Energies Scattered—(See "Scattered" under Energy).

Shallow Mentality—Mean and Shallow Abilities—Superficial Mind—Narrow-Minded—Contracted Mind—Little Depth of Mind—The ☽ □ or ☍ ☿, but little ability; ♀ Sig. ☌ the ☽, not a very deep mind, and promises more than the native is capable of rendering unless ☿ is strong and well-fortified; ☿ Sig. ☌ and combust the ☉, and with no assistance from benefics, little ability for learning or Science, and has a contracted and superficial mind; ☿ affl. in ♐ or ♓; ☿ afflicted in ♐, has a flow of speech, but of little depth; ☿ affl. in ♎, a shallow mind; ☿ setting in the West, in a weak sign, afflicted by the ☽, following after the ☉, and in no aspect to the Asc., has little power for study or concentration, and tends also to bad judgment, lack of foresight. (See Apathy, Dull, Examinations, Idle, Imbecility, Impairment, Improvident, Judgment, Knowledge; "Void Of" under Learning; "Weak Mind" under Mind; Prejudiced; "Incompetency" in this section).

Signs of Zodiac—The Mental Signs are ♈, ♊, ♍, ♒. The airy signs are called Mental Signs.

Strain—Mental Strain—Danger of—☿ afflicted in ♍, ♐, or ♓, warns against over-study and mental strain; ☿ □ or ☍ ☽; ☿ afflicted in the 6th H.; the ☽ afflicted in an airy sign. (See "Exertion" in this section; Reading, Strain, Study).

Strengthened—The Mental Faculties Strengthened—(See Activity, Quickened, in this section).

Studious Mentality—(See "Good" under Intellect; Knowledge; "Studious" under Learning; "Strong Mind" under Mind; Occult, Reading, Science, Study; "Activity", "Quickened", in this section).

Suffering—Mental Suffering—(See Anguish, Anxiety, Dejected, Depression, Despondency, Discontentment, Disgrace, Distress, Fears, Gloom, Hope; "Low Spirits" under Low; Melancholy; "No Peace" under Mind; Misery, Restlessness, Reverses, Ruin, Sadness, Sorrow, Trouble, Unhappy, Worry, Wretched; the various paragraphs in this Article).

Superficial Mentality—(See "Shallow" in this section; "Light" under Mind).

Suppressed Mentality—(See Arrested, Childlike, Inhibited, Limitations, Retarded, in this section; Idiocy, Imbecile, Suppressons).

Temperament—The Mental Temperament—Born under ☿. (See Decanates; "Nervous Temperament" under Nerves).

Temporary—Temporary Mental Afflictions or Deviations—(See Derangement, Irritations, in this section; "Brain Storms" under Brain; Dementia, Demoniac, Idiocy, Insanity, Temper, Temporary, Violence, etc.).

Troubles—Mental Troubles and Afflictions—(See the various paragraphs and references in this Article, and under Mind).

Turbulent Mentality—(See Anarchists, Anger, Brutish, Choleric, Criminal, Cruel, Emotions, Erratic, Feelings, Fierce, Fighting, Irascible, Irresponsible, Irritable, Jealousy, Murderous, Perverse, Quarrelsome, Rebellious, Revengeful, Riotous; "High Temper" under Temper; Vicious, Violent, etc.).

Unbalanced Mentality—Unbalanced Mind—Diseases of the ☽ and ☿, and by afflictions to these bodies at B., and by dir.; ♆ □ or ☍ ☿, mental unbalance. Brain balance is controlled largely by the secretions of the Thyroid Gland, which gland is ruled by ☿. (See "Derangement" in this section; Coordination, Dementia, Demoniac, Frenzy, Fury, Idiocy, Incoordination, Insanity, Madness, Mania, Paranoia, Thyroid, etc.).

Undesirable Mental Traits—Many of these are listed and considered in this book. Look in the alphabetical arrangement for the subject you have in mind. See "Qualities" in this section. See such subjects as Anger, Cheating, Conduct, Criminal, Debauched, Deceitful, Dishonest, Forgers, Gamblers, Hate, Hypocritical, Infamous, Jealousy, Liars, Love Affairs, Morals, Quarrelsome, Revengeful, Selfish, Sensuous; "High Temper" under Temper; Thieving, Treacherous, Vicious, Violent, etc. (See "Undesirable Mental Traits" under Mind).

Undeveloped—(See Arrested, Inhibited, Limitations, Retarded, Weak, in this section).

Ungovernable—Mentally Undefinable and Ungovernable—♂ influence, and ♂ afflicting the mental rulers. (See "Wild Delirium" under Delirium; Demoniac, Frenzy, Fury; "Outrageous" under Insanity; Irrational, Madness, Mania; "Void of Reason" under Reason).

Unusual Mental Faculties—♆ well-aspected in the 3rd H., or in ♊ and ♍; ♅ strong at B., ascending, rising and elevated; ♅ ☌ the ☉ or ☿ in the 10th H. (See Genius, Intuitions; "Great Learning" under Learning; Mathematical, Prodigies, Scholar; "Scientific Mind" under Science).

Weak Mentality—The ☽ and ☿ in no aspect to each other or the Asc. at B., and afflicted by malefics; the ☽ and ☿ afflicting the Asc.; the ruler of the Asc. in a fixed sign, and afflicting the ☽ and ☿ by □ or ☍ aspect. (See "Weak Mind" under Mind; Arrested, Retarded, in this section).

Weakened Mental Faculties—The ☉ ☌ or P. ☿; ☿ rising after the ☉; ♒ on the 6th H. (See "Mental Faculties" under Impairment; Shallow, Weak, in this section).

Weaknesses—Mental Weaknesses and Disabilities—In judging of mental weaknesses, and the liability to Insanity, Epilepsy, and various other mental afflictions, the positions and aspects of ☿ and the ☽ should be considered, their relation to each other and the Asc.; their aspects to the malefics, etc. The ☽ and ☿ in no aspect or relation to each other or the Asc. tends to result in mental weakness, and inability to understand or comprehend things. The ♋ sign on the Asc. at B., and afflicted, and with other conditions of ☿ and the ☽, as just stated, tend to weakness of both mind and body. (See Weak, Weakened, and the various paragraphs in this section, and under Intellect, Mind).

Weariness—Mental Weariness—Ennui—Lack of Interest In Life—(See Ennui, Lassitude, Lethargy, Weariness).

Well-Balanced Temperament—(See Well-Balanced).

Worry—Mental Worry—(See Anxiety, Dejected, Depressed, Despair, Despondent, Gloom, Hope, Hypochondria; "Low Spirits" under Low; Melancholy, Worry, etc.).

MENTHA—Mint—Peppermint—A Typical Plant and Drug of ♃. (See "Jupiter Group" under Herbs).

MEPHITIC—Mephitic Air—(See "Corrupt Air" under Air; "Winds" under Pestilence).

MERCILESS—(See Cruel, Pity).

Merciful—Kind—Humane—Compassionate—♒ influence; ♃ well-aspected in ♒; ♃ strong and well-aspected at birth. (See Humane, Kind, Noble).

MERCURY—The Planet Mercury—Hermes—Also known as "The Messenger of The Gods." This planet is the principal ruler of the Mind, and is known as the planet of Mind, Reason, Logic, etc. Also ☿ rules the Nerves and Nervous System in general. Mercury well placed and aspected at B. gives a good and well-balanced mind, but when weak and afflicted at B., and by dir., various disorders of the Mind and Reason develop, mental diseases and disturbances, shallowness of mind, poor reasoning powers, bad judgment, madness, insanity, epilepsy, nervous diseases, etc. Mercury is strongest at B. when found in the airy signs, as in ♊, ♎, and ♒, and is also strong in ♍. Mercury rules the two signs ♊ and ♍, and is said to be exalted in ♍ or ♒, to have his detriment in ♐, and fall in ♓. Mercury stirs the vocal cords into action, and rules the air which vibrates them. Also the vibrations which give Sight are originated by ☿. The aspects and position of ☿ sometimes express the Features. Mercury exerts a dry influence when masculine, and moisture when feminine, and is considered a variable, varying, or irregular planet, and partakes largely for the time of the planet, or planets, with which he is in aspect. When with ♄ he becomes like ♄ in influence, and tends to cause the same kind of diseases as does ♄, and so with each planet. Mercury is called the Hermaphrodite planet, owing to his dual nature, as he may be either masculine or feminine, according to the nature of the planet with which he is aspected, or associated for the time, or his position. He is masculine when oriental of the ☉, and feminine when occidental. He is masculine when in a masculine sign, and feminine when in a feminine sign; is masculine when with a masculine planet, and feminine when with a feminine planet; is masculine or feminine according to the number of his aspects with masculine or feminine planets, and the sign he is in, or as he is ori. or occi.; is masculine or feminine, diurnal or nocturnal, good or evil in influence, lucky or unlucky, according to the nature of the planets with which he is aspected. Mercury is considered as being ordinarily a cold planet, cold in influence, cold and dry when masculine, and cold and moist when feminine. He is considered a cold, dry, earthy, and melancholic planet, and is also nervous, impulsive, egotistical, malefic when with malefics, and benefic in influence when with the benefics. Mercury when well-aspected and dignified gives a strong mind and memory, active, and subtle. When afflicted he tends to cause overwork, sleeplessness, insomnia, restlessness, nervous diseases, and is indicative of a lack of spiritual calm. Also when afflicted, ill-dignified, or combust, he tends to produce a mean person, a liar, thief, gambler, swindler, etc. He may also be taken for the Anareta when strongly afflicted at B. He is considered by Max Heindel to be the lower octave of ♆, and by most other Authors as the lower octave of ♅. For convenience of reference this Article is divided into three Sections, as follows: Section One, The Influence of Mercury; Section Two, Mercury Rules, and Section Three, The Diseases and Afflictions of Mercury.

— SECTION ONE —

THE INFLUENCE OF MERCURY— The influences of ☿ have been partly considered in the Introduction to this Article.

Action of Mercury— ☿ action is nervous, excitable, quivering, subtle, and ceaseless motion. Is also variable, varying, and causes an irregular course in disease. (See "Qualities" in this section).

Affinity— ☿ has affinity with the Mind, the Nervous System, the Ears, Tongue, Hearing, Speech.

Anareta— May become Anareta when badly afflicted at B. (See Anareta).

Angel Of— Raphael.

Blind Spot of Retina — Is blind because it does not respond to the vibrations of ☿. (See "Blind Spot" under Retina).

Causes— ☿ causes Nervous Disorders, Mental Disturbances, Various Diseases, those which vary in course and are iregular, and also those which return periodically, as in Mental Diseases. (See the Diseases of ☿ in Sec. 3 of this Article).

Classification— A cold planet, cold and dry when masculine, cold and moist when feminine, a variable planet, earthy, melancholic, nervous, egotistical, malefic with malefics, and benefic when with benefics, etc. (See the Introduction to this Article).

Colors— (See "Color" in Sec. 2 of this Article).

Combust— ☿ when combust, in close ☌ with the ☉ at B., or afflicted and ill-dignified, tends to produce a mean person, liars, thieves, gamblers, swindlers, etc., and also to weaken the mind for hard study, but usually to give good commercial instincts. Our best students usually have ☿ separated from the ☉ by from 15 to 25 degrees.

Convertible— ☿ is a convertible and variable planet, and may be masculine or feminine, benefic or malefic, etc., according to the nature of the sign, position, or planet with which he is associated. (See the Introduction to this Article).

Denotes— ☿ denotes mental worry, restlessness, nervous complaints, sleeplessness, over-worked brain, and irregularities in food. (See "Qualities" in this section; Diseases in Sec. 3 of this Article).

Diathesis— (See Cranium).

Dignified— ☿ when dignified, rising and elevated in the East, in one of his strong signs, and well-aspected, gives a strong mind and memory, good judgment, a happier state of mind, good reasoning powers, etc., and also aids the health. This planet is dignified when in the ♊, ♍, or ♒ signs.

Directions— Of Mercury—The adverse primary directions of ☿ are especially evil from the 4th to 10th years of life, the period when ☿ exerts a strong influence for good or ill over the native. (See Directions, Periods).

Diseases— Of Mercury—(See Sec. 3 of this Article).

Drugs— Of Mercury—(See Herbs, Metal, Plants, Typical Drugs, in this section).

Dry Influence— ☿ exerts a cold and dry influence when masculine. (See the Introduction to this Article).

Ears— ☿ has special affinity with the Ears. (See the Introduction under Ears).

Elementary Qualities— Cold and Dry.

Eyes— The Influence of ☿ over the Eyes and Vision—(See the Introduction under Sight).

Feminine— When ☿ is Feminine—(See Introduction to this Article).

Foetus— The Influence of ☿ in the Development of the Foetus—(See Foetus).

Food Stuffs— ☿ represents Food in a general way. (See Food).

Functions— Of Mercury—The special functions of ☿ are in connection with the Brain, Mind, and Nerves.

Herbs— Mercury Group of Herbs—(See "Mercury Group" under Herbs).

Hour— ☿ Hour—(See "Hours" under Planets).

Ill-Dignified— And Combust—(See "Combust" in this section).

Lower Octave— (See "Octave" in this section).

Masculine— When ☿ is Masculine—(See "Convertible" in this section; Variable).

Memory— The Memory and Mercury—(See "Dignified" in this section; Memory; "Good Mind" under Mind).

Metal of Mercury— Quicksilver—(See Therapeutics).

Mind— The Mind and Mercury—(See the Introduction to this Article; "Dignified", "Ill-Dignified", in this section; Intellect, Mental, Mind).

Moist— ☿ exerts a cold and moist influence when feminine. (See Introduction to this Article).

Octave—☿ is said by most Authorities to be the lower octave of ♄. Max Heindel says ☿ is the lower octave of Ψ, as Ψ rules the Higher, or Spiritual Mind. Read about this subject in the book, "Message of the Stars", by Max Heindel, the Chapter on Neptune.

Physiological Action—Of ☿ Plants and Herbs—Through the Solar Plexus they tend to innervation of the Gastro-Abdominal Region. Thru the Brachial Plexus they tend to Pulmonary Innervation, and Pulmonary Haematosis. They also tend to the Nervous Influx, and Periodicity. The general action of the ☿ Group of Plants is Nervine and Periodic.

Plant Group Of—Plant Remedies of—Bryonia Alba, Horehound, Licorice, May Apple, Mandrake, Parsley, etc. (See "Mercury Group" under Herbs).

Presides Over—☿ especially presides over Cellular Irritation and Periodicity, and also over the Mental Faculties. (See Cells).

Principle Of—Reason—(See Reason).

Quality—In Quality ☿ is relative, subtle, ingenious, witty, persuasive, and restless.

Qualities—The following special Qualities, Influences, and Actions are attributed to ☿—Abstractive, Active, Alterative, Anti-periodic, Benefic, Ceaseless Motion, Cephalic, Changeable, Cholagogue, Cold, Cold and Dry, Cold and Moist, Comprehensive, Connective, Convertible, Coordinating, Corrosive, Critical, Debilitating, Defective, Depressive, Disturbing, Diurnal, Dry, Duel, Earthy, Egotistical, Evil, Excitable, Fanciful, Feminine, Flighty, Gambling, Good, Hurried, Imaginative, Impeding, Impulsive, Incoordinative, Ingenious, Intellectual, Intelligent, Introspective, Irrational, Irregular, Irritable, Irritating, Jerky, Lethargic, Logical, Loquacious, Lucky, Lying, Maddening, Masculine, Melancholic, Moderately Fruitful, Moist, Nervine, Nervous, Neurotic, Nocturnal, Obsessive, Obstructive, Periodic, Persuasive, Quivering, Rational, Reasoning, Reflective, Relative, Restless, Spasmodic, Sterterous, Subtle, Swindling, Thieving, Torpid, Unbalanced, Unlucky, Unreasonable, Variable, Vibratory, Wakeful, Witty, Worrisome, etc. These influences and qualities are very opposing in some cases, as ☿ is a variable planet, masculine, feminine, malefic, benefic, etc., according to his aspects. This is explained in the Introduction to this Article.

Reason—☿ is known as the Planet of Reason, and also Reason is the Principle of ☿. (See Reason).

Remedies Of—(See Herbs, Metal, Plant Group, Therapeutic, Treatment, Typical, in this section).

Represents—☿ represents Food Stuffs in general. Also represents the Mind, Reason, and Mental Endeavor, etc. (See Food, Mental, Mind, Reason).

Signs Ruled By—♊ and ♍. The day sign, or house, of ☿ is ♊, and ♍ his night sign. Also ☿ is strong and exalted in ♍; has his fall, and is weakest in the ♓ sign.

Tall Body—☿ gives. (See Tall).

Temperament—☿ rules the Nervous Temperament. Also called the Mental Temperament. (See "Nervous Temperament" under Temperament).

Therapeutic Qualities—Alterative, Antiperiodic, Cephalic, Cholagogue, Nervine. (See Therapeutics).

Tongue—☿ has special affinity with the Tongue and Speech, and afflictions to ☿ tend to defects of speech, as stammering, tongue-tied, etc. (See Speech, Tongue).

Treatment—Treatment by ☿ Drugs, Herbs, Plants, and the Metal of ☿— These remedies tend to combat the diseases of ♃, as ☿ and ♃ rule opposite signs. (See "Planetary Opposites" under Opposites).

Typical Drugs—Apiol, Avena, Calomel, Mercury, Petroselinum, Podophyllin.

Typical Plants—(See "Mercury Group" under Herbs).

Variable—☿ is a variable and convertible planet according to his aspects, etc. (See "Convertible" in this section).

Vibrations Of—The vibrations which give Sight are originated by ☿. (See the Introduction under Sight).

Well-Dignified—(See "Dignified" in this section).

— SECTION TWO —

MERCURY RULES—See the following subjects in the alphabetical arrangement—Acquaintances; Air (the Air which stirs the Vocal Cords to action); Arms (Nerves of); Azure Color; Bile; Blue (Light Blue Color—Sky Blue Color—Blue in the Solar Spectrum—Bluish Colors); Bowels (Nerves and Nerve Fibers of); Brachial Plexus; Brain as a Whole—Brain Functions and Substance (ruled by the ☽ and ☿); Breath and Air Cells; Bronchial Tubes; Cellular Irritation and Periodicity; Cerebral Hemisphere (Right); Cerebral Nerves; Cerebro-Spinal Nervous System; Chylification; Chylopoiesis (see Chyle); Circulation (Pulmonary); Clothing; Color—Bluish Colors—Azure—Light Blue Color—Sky Blue Color—Blue in the Solar Spectrum—Lemon Color—Shot Lemon—Orange—Violet—Yellow, says H.P.B. in her Secret Doctrine (see Colors); Comprehension; Coordination in the Body, and between the Mind and Body; Dryness (when Masculine); Ears (Hearing); Eustachian Tubes; Excitement of Muscles to Action by Nerve Impulses, which Impulses are carried out by Mars; Faculties (the Mental, Rational and Reasoning Faculties); Fancy (The Fancy, Fancies); Features; Feeling; Feet; Fibers of the Nerves; Fluid (the Invisible Vital Fluid in the Nerves); Food (Food Stuffs); Functions (the Voluntary Nervous Functions); Fundament (the Fundament of the Body); Gall (see Bile); Gamblers; Genito-Urinary Organs (Nerves of); Gland (the Thyroid); Hair; Hands (Nerves of); Hearing; Heart (Nerves of); Hemisphere (Right Cerebral); Herbs (Mercury Group); Imagination; Impulses (Nervous Impulses to Muscular Action—See Excitation); Innervation; Intellect; Intelligence; Intestines (Small); Invisible Vital Fluid (in the Nerves); Irritability; Irritation (Cellular); Journeys by Land; Land Journeys (Short Journeys); Larynx; Legs (Nerves of); Lemon Color (Shot Lemon); Letters (Correspondence and Writings); Liars; Life from 7 to 15 Years of Age; Light Blue and Azure Color; Lips; Limbs; Lungs; Meanness; Memory; Mental Faculties and Forces (along with ♅, ♆, and ☽); Mercury (Quicksilver); Mind; Moisture (when feminine); Mother's Relatives; Motion in the Body; Motor Segment of the Spinal Cord; Mouth; Moving Parts of the Body; Nerves — (Nerve Impulses to Muscular Action — Nerve Tissue Building along with ♅ — The Telegraphic System of the Body—Nervous Influx (♂ adds to or subtracts from)— Nervous System as a Whole, along with ♅ — the Cerebro-Spinal Nervous System — Nerve Fibers Over the Body —The Voluntary Nervous Functions— Sensory Nerves, etc.); Nervous Temperament (along with ♅, ♄, and the Earthy Signs); Optic Nerve; Orange Color; Perception, and all Sense Perception; Periodicity (Cellular); Plexus (Brachial); Pulmonary Circulation and Innervation; Quicksilver; Rational and Reasoning Faculties; Reason; Relatives (of the Mother); Respiration; Right Cerebral Hemisphere; Sense Perceptions; Sensory Nerves; Servants; Short Journeys (Inland, and by Land); Shot Lemon Color; Shoulders; Sickness (from Worry, Nervousness, and Diseases Arising in the Mind); Sight; Sky Blue Color; Small Intestines; Speech (Nerves of); Spine (Motor Segment of the Spinal Cord—Spinal and Cerebral Nervous System); Stomach (Nerves of); Subtleness; Telegraphic System of the Body (Nerves); Texture of the Tissues of the Body; Thieves; Thyroid Gland; Tissue Building (Nerve Tissue Building, along with ♅ — Texture of the Tissues of the Body); Tongue; Touch (Sense of); Trachea; Understanding; Vibration (the Air which Stirs the Vocal Cords to Vibration); Violet Color; Vital Fluid (the Invisible Vital Fuid in the Nerves); Vocal Cords and Vocal Organs; Voluntary Nervous Functions; Wednesday (Day of Week); Windpipe; Writings (Letters and Correspondence); Years of Life (4 to 10, says Daath—7 to 15, general—See Periods); Yellow in the Solar Spectrum (see Colors).

— SECTION THREE —

MERCURY DISEASES — Mercury in the different Signs rules the Nerves in the parts of the body ruled by the sign he is in at birth, and if ☿ is badly afflicted at B., and also by dir., the nerves of such part, or parts, are apt to give more trouble. Thus ☿ in ♈ tends to nerve troubles in the head, headaches, brain-fag, etc. Mercury in ♋, disorders of the nerves of the stomach, etc. Mercury is a convertible planet, and produces diseases of the nature of the planet, or planets, with which he is joined and configurated, and also according to the nature of the sign in which he is posited. Mer-

cury causes, and has relation to nervous and mental disorders which affect the nerve fibres of the various organs and parts of the body. Mercury brings danger of Consumptions, Madness, Fits, when badly afflicted, and according to the afflictions, and the signs from which it occurs. Mercury has special affinity with the Ears and Tongue, and in causing Deafness, and disorders of Speech. Mercury may become Anareta, or the Killing Planet, when strongly afflicted at birth. The following is a classified list of the Diseases and Afflictions of Mercury. See these subjects in the alphabetical arrangement when not more fully considered here—

Accidents—And Death By—Death or Injury by Robbers, or In Exercise and Sports — (See Exercise, Robbers, Sports).

All Nervous Complaints — (See "All Nervous Disorders", and the various paragraphs under Nerves).

Apoplexy; Arms — ☿ afflicted in the signs which rule the Arms, Hands, and Legs, tends to Cramps, Neuralgic Pains, and Paralysis in these parts. Also the ☿ and ♄ afflictions tend to cause Gouty Pains, and Rheumatism in the Arms. (See these subjects under Arms).

Asthma; Back—Pains In—Weakness In—(See Back).

Bile—Gall — Disorders of — Bilious Flatulency—(See Bile).

Blindness — From Eyestrain, Over-Study, and Too Much Reading—(See "Over-Study" under Blindness).

Blood—Disordered Blood—Impure Blood—Wind In the Blood—(See Impure; "Blood" under Wind).

Body — Incoordination Between Mind and Body (See Incoordination).

Bowels—Diseases of—Obstructions In —Pains In—Wind In—(See Bowels).

Brain—All Complaints Caused by Diseases of—Disorders of, and Death By —Diseases of from Over-Work and Over-Study—Brain Fag—Disorders of the Brain Functions and Substance— Incoordination Between the Brain, Mind and Body — Lightness In the Brain—Dizziness—Over-Worked Brain —Violent Brain Storms, etc. — (See Brain).

Breath — Breathing — Disorders and Disturbances of — Rapid Breathing — Shortness of Breath, etc.—(See Breath).

Bronchial Disorders—Bronchitis— (See Bronchial, Lungs).

Calm—Lack of Spiritual Calm—(See Spiritual; the Introduction to this Article).

Cellular Irritation—(See Cells).

Cholera; Cold—(1) Cold and Dry Diseases — (See "Cold and Dry" under Dry); (2) Cold In the Knees and Legs —(See Knees, Legs); (3) Cold In the Stomach—Stomach Offended with Cold —(See "Raw Humours" under Indigestion).

Colds — Colds Caught In the Feet — (See Colds; "Cold Taken" under Feet).

Colic—In the Bowels—Flatulent Colic —Wind Colic—(See Colic).

Consumption; Convulsions; Corrosion—Of the Nervous System — (See Corrosion).

Cough—Coughs—Death by Cough—Dry Cough—(See Cough).

Course of Disease—Variable and Irregular Course—(See Course).

Cramps — In the Arms, Shoulders, Hands, Legs, and Feet—(See "Arms" under Cramps).

Deafness—Deaf and Dumb — (See Hearing, Mutes).

Death By—Mercury Causes Death by Accidents (if Violence Attend); Brain Diseases; Cough; Despair; Dry Habit and All Diseases Proceeding From; Epilepsy; Frenzy; Fury; Grief; Lethargy; Madness; Melancholy; Nervous Diseases; Obstructions; Phrenitis; Phthisis; Robbers (Attacks By); Sports; Stomach Disorders, etc. (See "Death" under these subjects).

Debility—Nervous Diseases Due To—(See Debility; "Debility" under Nerves).

Defects of Memory—(See Memory).

Delirium; Depletion — (See "Depletion" under Nerves).

Depression—(See "Mental" under Depressed).

Despair; Distempers — In Reins and Secret Parts—(See Reins, Secrets).

Distillation—Of Rheum — (See Rheum).

Dizziness; Dry Cough—Dry and Cold Diseases—(See Cough; "Cold and Dry" under Dry).

Dryness — ☿ produces Dryness when masculine. Also tends to Diseases from Superabundance of Dryness, and Immoderate Heat. (See "Dry Habit", "Superabundance", under Dryness).

Dumbness—(See Mutes).

Epilepsy; Excitement—Mental—Neurotic—Reflected — Nervous Diseases Arising From—(See Excitement).

Eyestrain — (See "Eyestrain" under Eyes).

Faculties—Disturbed Mental Faculties — (See "Faculties" under Mental; "Diseases of the Mind" under Mind).

Fag—Fatigue—(See "Brain Fag" under Brain; "Mind" under Fatigue).

Falling Fits—(See Fainting).

Fancy—Disorders of—(See Fancies).

Feet—Colds Caught In the Feet—Diseases of the Feet—Gout In—Pains In—Weakness In—(See Feet).

Fits; Flatulency — Flatulent Colic — Bilious Flatulency—(See Flatulence).

Flightiness; Fluxes; Flying Humours—Flying Pains—(See Flying).

Food—Irregularities In—(See Eating, Food).

Foul Tongue—(See Breath, Tongue).

Frenzy; Fundament — Disorders of — (See Fundament).

Fury; Gall—Diseases of—(See Gall).

Gastro-Abdominal Troubles — (See Gastro).

Giddiness—In the Head—(See Fainting, Vertigo).

Gonorrhoea; Gout—Gouty Pains—Goutish Humours—Gout In the Arms, Shoulders, Hands, Head, Feet, Hips, Thighs, Knees—(See Gout).

Grief—Death By—(See Grief).

Gripings; Habit — Dry Habit and All Diseases Proceeding From, and Death By—(See "Dry Habit" under Dry).

Hands—Diseases In—(See Hands).

Hay Fever; Head—Disorders In—Dizziness In — Gouty Pains In — Humours In—Stoppages In—Pains In—Headaches — Spasms In — Snuffling In Nose—(See Head, Headaches, Nose).

Headaches; Heart—Trembling of—Nerve Troubles of — Neuralgia of — Wind Around—(See Heart).

High Strung — (See "Strung" under High).

Hips—Gout In—Swellings In—(See Hips).

Hoarseness; Humours — In the Head — In the Nose — Flying Humours — Goutish Humours—(See Humours).

Hurried Breathing—(See Breath).

Hyperaesthesia; Imagination—Disorders of—(See Imagination).

Impediments — In Speech — (See Impediments, Inarticulate, Speech, Tongue).

Imperfections — Of the Fancies — Of the Speech, etc.—(See Fancies, Impediments, Imperfections, Mental, Mind, Speech).

Incoordination; Influx—The Nervous Influx — ☿ adds to or subtracts from. (See Innervation; "Influx" under Nerves).

Innervation; Insanity; Insomnia—(See Sleep).

Intellect — (See the various paragraphs under Intellect).

Irregular Diseases — Diseases with a Variable Course — (See Course, Intermittent, Interrupted, Irregular, Remittent, Variable, Various, etc.).

Irregularities — (See "Irregularities" under Food).

Irritation—Cellular Irritation—Sympathetic Irritation—(See Cells, Irritation, Sympathy).

Kidneys—Neuralgia In—Obstructions In—(See Kidneys).

Knees — Cold In — Goutish Humours In—Lameness In—(See Knees).

Lameness—In Knees and Legs—(See Knees, Lameness, Legs).

Legs — Cramps In — Cold In — Lameness In—Humours In—Lameness In—(See Legs).

Lesions—Of the Nervous System—(See Lesions).

Lethargy; Lightness In Brain — (See Dizziness, Fainting, Vertigo).

Liver—(See "Torpid" under Liver).

Locomotor Ataxia; Lunacy; Lungs—Afflicted—Diseases of—(See Lungs).

Madness; Mania; Melancholy;

Memory—All Defects In—(See Memory).

Mental—Various Mental Disorders—(See Mental, Mind).

Mind — Disorders of — (See Comprehension, Intellect, Mental, Mind, Perception, Reason, Understanding, etc.).

Mouth—Diseases of—(See Mouth).

Mutes; Nerves — Nervous System — Disorders of — (See the various paragraphs under Nerves).

Neuralgia; Neurasthenia — (See Nerves).

Neurotic Excitement — (See "Nerves" under Excitement).

Nose—Disorders of—Sniffling—(See "Snuffling" under Head, Nose).

Obsessions; Obstructions—In Bowels, Kidneys, Nerves — Death by Obstructions—(See Obstructions).

Over-Study—Blindness, or Disease From—(See "Eyestrain" under Eyes).

Over-Work — Nervous Debility By — (See "Over-Active Mind" under Active; "Over-Worked" under Brain; "Inordinate" under Exercise; "Eyestrain" under Eyes; "Debility" under Nerves; Reading, Study).

Pains — In the Back — In the Feet — Gouty Pains In the Head, Arms, Shoulders, Knees, Feet — Rheumatic Pains In the Arms and Shoulders— Running and Flying Pains Over the Body—Spasmodic Pains In the Stomach—Neuralgic Pains, etc.—(See these subjects, and the various paragraphs under Pain).

Palpitation—(See Heart).

Paralysis — Of the Nervous System — In the Arms, Hands, Legs—(See Paralysis).

Periodical Diseases — (See Epilepsy, Fainting, Insanity, Periodic, Periodicity, Vertigo, etc.).

Phrenitis — (See "Inflammation" under Brain).

Phthisic — (See Asthma; Consumption).

Phthisis; Psychic Disorders — (See Psychic).

Pulmonary Diseases — (See Lungs, Pulmonary).

Quivering — Of the Body — (See Tremors).

Quotidian Fevers—(See Quotidian).

Rapid Breathing—(See Breath).

Rational Faculties—Disorders of— (See Rational).

Reading—Blindness, Eyestrain, Brain Fag, Mental Fatigue, etc., from Too Much Reading and Study—(See Brain; "Eyestrain" under Eyes; Fatigue, Reading, Study).

Reason—Disorders of—(See Reason).

Reflected Excitement—(See Reflected).

Reflex Action—(See Reflected).

Reins—Affected— Diseases In—Distempers In—(See Reins).

Respiration— Disorders of— Hurried —(See Breath, Bronchial, Lungs).

Restlessness; Retention—Of Urine— (See Urine).

Rheum — Distillation of — (See Rheum).

Rheumatic Pains — In Arms and Shoulders — (See Arms, Rheumatism, Shoulders).

Robbers—Accident, Injury, or Death By—(See Robbers).

Running Pains—(See Flying).

Saliva—Too Much—(See Saliva).

Secret Parts — Distempers In — (See Secrets).

Senitiveness; Shallow Mind — (See "Shallow" under Mental).

Short Breath — Hurried—Rapid—(See Breath).

Shoulders— Diseases In — Rheumatic Pains In—(See Shoulders).

Sickness — Arising from Mental Disturbances and Worries—(See Invalids; "Irritations" under Mental; "Neurasthenia" under Nerves; "Slow" under Recuperation; Trouble, Worry, etc.).

Sight — The Sight Affected — (See "Eyesight" under Eyes).

Signs—Diseases of ☿ in the 12 Signs of the Zodiac—☿ in each sign tends to nervous disorders of the part ruled by the Sign, Pains, Neuralgic conditions when ☿ is afflicted, and also if ☿ partake of the nature of ♄, to suppression, retention, etc. For classified lists of the Diseases of Mercury in the different Signs, see the Textbooks and Dictionaries of Astrology.

Sleeplessness—(See "Insomnia" under Sleep).

Sniffling—In the Head and Nose—(See "Snuffling" under Head).

Spasmodic Pains—In the Stomach and Other Organs and Parts—(See Colic, Gripings; "Gripings" under Stomach).

Spasms — Fits — Convulsions—Spasms In the Head—(See Convulsions, Fits; "Spasms" under Head; Spasmodic).

Speech—Disorders of—Stammering— Tongue-Tied — Impediments In — (See Speech, Tongue).

Spiritual Calm—Lack of—(See "Calm" in this section).

Spittle—Excess of—(See Saliva).

Sports—Accidents, Injuries, or Death By—(See Exercise, Sports).

Stammering—(See Speech).

Stertorous Breathing—Hurried—(See Breath).

Stomach—Cold Stomach—Gripings In —Spasmodic Pains In—Stoppage At— Raw Humours In — (See "Raw Humours" under Indigestion; Belching, Gripings, Obstructions, Pains, Worms, under Stomach).

Stoppage—In the Head, Nose, Stomach, Urine—(See "Obstructions" under Head, Nose, Stomach, Urine).

Storms—Violent Brain Storms—(See "Brain Storms" under Brain).

Strain—Eyestrain—Nervous Diseases Arising from Stress and Strain — (See "Eyestrain" under Eyes; "High Strung" under High; "Nervousness" under Nerves; "Nervous Strain" under Strain).

Study—Eye Trouble, Mental Fatigue, from Over-Study and Too-Much Reading—(See "Eyestrain" under Eyes; "Mind" under Fatigue; Reading, Study).

Stuttering—(See Speech).

Superabundance — Of Dryness — Diseases Arising From — (See "Superabundance" under Dryness).

Suppression—Of Urine—(See Supressions, Urine).

Swellings—In the Hips, Neck, Thighs — (See "Swellings" under these subjects).

Swindlers; Sympathetic Irritation — (See "Irritation" in this section).

Thieves; Thighs—Swellings In—(See "Swellings" under Hips).

Throat—Defects In—(See Throat).

Thyroid Gland — Disorders of — (See Thyroid).

Tongue—Foul Tongue—Tongue-Tied —(See "Foul" under Breath; Tongue; "Impediments" in this section).

Torpid Liver—(See Liver).

Trembling—Of the Heart—Tremors— (See Heart, Tremors).

Unbalanced Mind—(See Frenzy, Fury, Idiocy, Insanity, Madness, Mania; "Unbalanced" under Mind).

Urine —Obstruction of — Suppression of—(See Urine).

Uterus—Diseases of—(See Womb).

Vain Imaginations—(See Imagination).

Variable Diseases — (See Variable; "Irregular" in this section).

Vertigo; Violent Brain Storms — (See Brain).

Vital Fluid—Of the Nerves—Lowered or Exhausted — (See "Neurasthenia" under Nerves).

Vitality — (See "Mental Vitality" under Vitality).

Vocal Disorders — (See Inarticulate, Larynx, Speech, Tongue, Voice).

Voice—Loss of—(See Voice).

Water Brash—(See Belching).

Weakness—In the Back, Legs, Feet— (See "Weakness" under these subjects).

Wind — In the Blood, Bowels — Wind Around Heart — Wind Colic — (See "Wind" under Blood, Bowels, Heart, Colic; also see Wind).

Womb—Disorders of—(See Womb).

Worms — In Bowels — In Stomach — (See Worms).

Worry—Mental Worry—Nervous Diseases Arising From—(See Worry).

MERCY—(See Merciless, Pity).

MERIDIAN— Medium Coeli —The Midheaven — Zenith — Tenth House—The Meridian is the highest point, or place of the ☉ each day at Noon, Sun Time, and the ☉ is very powerful at this time. After passing the Zenith, the ☉ begins to set, and is not as powerful in nativities. (See Elevated, Majority, Rising, Setting, Tenth House).

MERRY DISPOSITION—(See Cheerfulness, Contentment, Happiness, Joy).

MESENTERY— The Peritoneal Attachment of the Small Intestines — Ruled by ♍. The Mesenteric Glands are also ruled by ♍. (See "Small Intestines" under Bowels; "Splanchnic" under Ganglion; Peritoneum).

MESMERISM — A Mesmerizer—The 2nd face of ♓ on the Asc., and ♂ therein. Case—See "Moores", No. 816, in 1001 N.N. (See Healers, Hypnotism, Magnetism, Suggestion). Mesmerism was first put into practice by a man named Frank Mesmer, born in 1733, died in 1815. Mesmerism is now identified with Hypnotism.

MESOCOLON—Meso-Rectum—The Mesentery of the Colon—Ruled by ♏. (See Colon, Mesentery, Rectum).

METABOLISM — A Constructive or Destructive Change in the Intimate Condition of Cells or Tissues.

Cells—The Alteration and Metabolism of Cells—(See Alterations; "Alterations" under Cells; Constructive, Destructive, Metamorphosis, Structural, Transformation).

Digestive Tract — Metabolism of Disturbed — (See "Metabolism" under Digestion).

Tissues—Metabolism In—(See "Alterations" under Cells; the various paragraphs under Tissues). Also for further study see Absorption, Alterations, Assimilation, Catabolism; "Chemistry of the Body" under Chemistry; Crystallization, Decay, Decomposition, Degeneration, Diathesis, Digestion, Disintegration, Dissolution, Emaciation, Energy, Gangrene, Growth, Growths, Hardening, Nutrition, Processes, Putrefaction, Resolution, Secretion, Softening, Solution, Structural, Wasting, etc.

METACARPUS—(See Hands).

METALS—Alloys—The ☉ rules Gold; ☽ rules Silver; ♄ rules Lead; ♃ rules Tin; ♂ Iron; ♀ Copper; ☿ Quicksilver, also called Mercury. These are the seven metals used in treatment. (See "Metal" under each of the Planets. Also see Drugs, Medicines, Minerals, Remedies, Therapeutics).

Dross of Metals—Ruled by ♄.

Work In Metals — As a Business or Vocation—The ☽ rules work in Metals, Silver, Silver Plated Articles, etc.

METAMORPHOSIS—Transformation — Structural Change—Largely the work of the ☽. Venus presides over the Cellular Retrogressive Metamorphosis. The Five Processes, known as the Nervous Influx, the Renal Process, the Hepatic Process, the Thoracic Process, and the Splenic Process, form the basis for all Organic and Structural changes undergone by the Cell, and according to the zones occupied in the Zodiac by the heavenly bodies. (See Cells, Diathesis, Metabolism, Organic, Processes, Structural, Tissues, Transformation).

METAPHYSICS — Fond of — Given to Study of—(See "Metaphysical Healing" under Healers; "Metaphysics" under Learning; Ninth House, Occult; "Metaphysical" under Religion; Science).

METATARSUS — (See "Bones" under Feet).

METEORISM — Gas In the Abdominal Cavity—(See "Abdomen" under Gas).

METHODICAL — (See "Methodical" under Habits).

METHODS — Methods Used In the Attainment of Ends—(See Cheating, Conduct, Deceitful, Dishonest, Gambling, Honest, Liars, Motives, Thieves, Treachery, etc.). Look in the alphabetical arrangement for the subject you have in mind.

METONIC CYCLE — (See this subject under Moon).

METORRHAGIA — (See "Flooding" under Menses).

METRITIS—(See "Inflammation" under Womb).

MIASMA — A Noxious Emanation— Air-Borne Germs — Miasmic Ailments — Moonlight and the night air are especially noxious, and tend to Miasmic Troubles and Diseases. The exhalations of the vegetables at night, the prevalence of carbonic acid, and the chemical action of the Moon's rays, become very deleterious at night. The day time is less evil, as the heat tends to absorb the vapors and exhalations. (See Ague; "Corrupt Air" under Air; Carbon, Day, Germs, Malaria; "Moonlight" under Moon; Night, Noxious, Vapors, Vegetation).

MICROBES—(See Germs, Microzymasis, Virus).

MICROCEPHALUS — A Person with a Small Head—Microcephalic Idiot—(See "Small" under Head; Idiocy).

MICROZYMASIS — Microzyma — Micro-organisms Giving Rise to Disease — Principally the physiological action of the ☽, and the Moon Group of Herbs. (See Fermentation, Germs; "Moon Group" under Herbs; Miasma; "Physiological Action" under Moon; Zymosis).

MICTURITION—Painful and Difficult— (See "Strangury" under Urine).

MIDDLE — Middle Parts of Organs — Medium Stature — Middle Stature — Middling—For Middle Life and its conditions see the next Article after this one.

Above Middle Stature—♃ Sig. ✳ or △ ♄ and ♄ well-dignified; ♈, ♌, ♐, or ♒ on the Asc. (See Giants, Growth, Height, Tall).

Below Middle Stature — (See "Body Diminished" under Diminished; Dwarf; "Arrested" under Growth; "Body" under Short, Small).

Cervical Ganglion — (See "Middle Cervical" under Ganglion).

Complexion — (See "Middling" under Complexion).

Corpulent and Middle-Sized—(See the various influences under Corpulent, Fleshy, and also under "Middle Stature" in this section).

Fleshy and Full—Middle-Sized, Fleshy and Full Body—(See Fleshy).

Fleshy and Middle-Sized—(See Corpulent, Fleshy; "Middle Stature" in this section).

Full—Full, Fleshy, and Middle-Sized —(See Fleshy).

Lean and Middle-Sized—(See "Middle-Sized" under Lean).

Mean Stature — (See "Mean Stature" under Mean; "Medium Stature" under Medium; "Middle Stature" in this section).

Middle Life — (See Article following this one).

Middle Stature—Middle-Sized Body— Mean Stature—Medium Stature— Middling Stature—The ☉ Sig. in ♋, ♑, or ♒; the ☉ Sig. in ♋ or ♑, a mean stature, ill-formed and ill-made body; the ☽

Sig. in ♈, ♉, ♋, ♏, ♑, ♒, or ♓; indicated by ♄; when ♄ forms the body he gives a middle-sized stature; ♄ in the Asc.; ♄ lord of the Asc., and ori., as from the Asc. to the M.C., or from the Desc. to Nadir, gives middle stature; ♄ in ♈, ♉, ♏, ♑, or ♓, partile the Asc.; in Hor'y Q., ♄ Sig. in ♉, ♋, ♏, ♑, ♒, or ♓, indicates one of middle stature; ♃ occidental; ♃ ruler of the Asc., and occi.; ♃ in ♉, ♋, ♒, or ♓, partile the Asc.; ♃ in ♒, partile Asc., compact, corpulent, middle-sized; ♃ in ♏ or ♓, partile Asc., full, fleshy, middle-sized; ♂ ruler of the horoscope; ♂ Sig. in ♈, ♉, ♍, ♑, ♒, or ♓; ♂ in ♈, partile Asc., middle, well-set, and large bones; ♂ ♍, partile Asc., middle, well-proportioned; ♂ in ♏ or ♒, partile Asc., well-set, corpulent, but middling, but with ♂ in ♒ some Authorities say a tall body; ♂ ruler of the Asc., and occi.; ♀ in the Asc., fair, medium, and not usually tall; ♀ Sig. in ♈, ♉, or ♓; ♀ ♈, partile Asc., middle, but slender; ♀ ♓, partile Asc., middle, but rather plump and fleshy; ☿ Sig. in ♈, ♉, ♏, ♑, or ♒; ☿ ♉, partile Asc., middle, corpulent, and well-set; ♈, ♉, ♍, ♎, ♏, ♑, ♒, or ♓ on the Asc. tend to produce middle stature; ♉ on the Asc., middle or short, thick, strong, well-set body; ♍ on Asc., middle, but in no way handsome, says Lilly; ♏ on Asc., middle, strong and corpulent; ♒ on Asc., middle, and rarely tall; ♓ on Asc., middle, fleshy and corpulent, but sometimes pale, sickly and short. (See Corpulent, Fleshy; "Mean Stature" under Mean; "Medium Stature" under Medium).

Moderate In Stature—(See Moderate).

Organs—Middle Parts of Organs—Are shown by the middle parts of Signs, from 10 to 20 degrees, the middle or second decanate, and planets and afflictions in this decanate show Moles, Marks, Scars, Blemishes, or afflictions to the middle parts of organs under the rule of such Signs. (See "Parts of Body" under Accidents; Blemishes, Decanates; "Marks" under Face; "Organs" under Lower; Marks, Moles, Navamsa, Organs, Parts of Body, Scars, Upper, etc.).

Parts — Middle Parts of Body or Organs—(See "Organs" in this section).

Plump — Plump, Fleshy, and Middle-Sized—(See Fleshy, Plump).

Short or Middle-Sized—♉ on Asc. (See "Middle Stature" in this section; "Body" under Short).

Slender —And Middle-Sized —(See "Middle-Sized" in this section; Slender).

Stature—Middle Stature— (See "Middle" in this section).

Strong — Strong, Corpulent and Middle-Sized—♏ on the Asc. at B. The opposite sign ♉ on the Asc. tends to give a middle-sized or short, strong, thick, and well-set body. (See "Middle Stature" in this section; Strong, Thick, Well-Set).

Thick and Middle-Sized—Thick, Middle-Sized, or Short, etc.—♉ on the Asc. (See "Strong" in this section).

Well-Formed—And Middle Size—Corpulent—The ☉ or ☽ in ♒, partile the Asc., well-formed and well-made.

Well-Made—And Middle-Sized—(See "Well-Formed" in this section; Well-Formed, Well-Made, Well-Proportioned, Well-Set).

Well-Proportioned—And Middle-Sized—☽ in ♋ partile Asc., middle, fleshy, well-proportioned; ♂ in ♍ partile the Asc. (See Well-Proportioned).

Well-Set—And Middle-Sized—The ☽ in ♉, partile the Asc., but may also be rather short; ♂ in ♏ partile Asc., but corpulent; ♂ in ♒ partile Asc., middle-sized, corpulent and well-set, but some Authorities say Tall. (See Well-Set).

MIDDLE LIFE—Middle Age—People of Middle Age are described by ♃. The full effects of ♃, for good or ill, are not felt until middle life, and espec. when he is in ♋, or in the 4th H. Mars rules the years of life from 41 to 56. (See Periods).

Corpulent—At Middle Life—The ☽ in ♓ at B.; ♍ on the Asc., and attended with a prominent abdomen; ♎ on the Asc. Stoutness in later years is caused by ♃ in the Asc. at B., and well-aspected, or ♃ in ♋ on the Asc., and afflicted. (See "Prominent" under Abdomen; Corpulent; "Body" under Fat; Stoutness).

Death At Middle Life—Danger of—The ☉ in the 8th H., and afflicted, or afflicting the hyleg.

Death Before Middle Life—Danger of—Dies Young—Death In Youth—Lord of the 10th H. in the 5th, thru feasting and dissipation; the 27° ♐ on the Asc.; the 5° ♒ on Asc.; the 9° ♓ on Asc.; thru dissipation and passional excesses; the 11° ♓ on the Asc. (See Adults; "Early Death" under Early; Maturity; "Death In Youth" under Youth).

Eclipses—Solar Eclipses At Middle Life—The ruling places at a Solar Eclipse occurring in the Midheaven tend to affect middle-aged people for good or ill according to the aspects, and signs occupying such places, etc. (See Eclipses).

Fifty-Six—Dies At 56 Years of Age—Case and Birth Data—See "Thrice Married", No. 108, in 1001 N.N.

Friends Die—At Middle Life or Before—(See "Short Life" under Friends).

Lives to Middle Life—(See "Death At Middle Life" in this section; Adults, Maturity, Old Age).

Pimples At Middle Life—(See Pimples).

Solar Eclipse—At Middle Life—(See "Eclipses" in this section).

MIDGETS—A Small Dwarf—(See Dwarf).

MIDHEAVEN—Medium Coeli (M.C.)—The Meridian—Zenith—Tenth House—(See "Passive Planets" under Passive; Tenth House).

MIDRIFF—(See Diaphragm).

MIDWIVES—A Woman Obstetrician—The ☽ rules and signifies Midwives. The ☽ ruler of the horoscope tends to make successful Midwives, and espec. when the ☽ is in the 10th H., or ruler of the 10th, in a female nativity. (See Nurses, Obstetricians).

MIGRAINE—Megrims—A Paroxysmal Headache, generally unilateral, and may be attended with Visual and Gastric Disturbances—An ♈ disease, and caused by the ☉ or ☽ afflicted in ♈; caused by afflictions to the ☉; a ♂ disease and affliction, and caused by afflictions to ♂; Subs at AT. (See Headache).

MILD—Mild Diseases—Mild Disposition—The influence of ♃ is mild, kindly, and benevolent, and espec. when well-placed and aspected at B., and tends to a mild and good disposition, better health and stronger vitality.

Disease Is Mild—Lord of the 6th H. cadent at B. Also the disease is minimized when the attributes are conflicting, as with the ☉ and ♄ when they are the afflicters in the disease, as these are opposing forces and tend to neutralize the influence of each other. (See Colds, Ephemeral; "Non-Malignant" under Growths; Indisposition, Minor, Opposites, Slight).

Mild Disposition—Quiet—Harmless—Even Temper—People born under the strong and good influence of ♀ tend to be mild and quiet in disposition; ♃ Sig. in ♎; ♀ Sig. in ♒ or ♓; ♎ on the Asc., a mild and even temper, as a rule; the ☉ Sig. ✶ or △ ♃; ♂ rather weak at B., and not badly aspected by malefics; many planets in airy signs. (See Cheerfulness, Contentment, Elegant, Excellent; "Many Friends" under Friends; Genteel, Gentle, Happy, Harmless, Humane, Joyful, Kind; "Amiable", "Obliging", under Manners; Quiet; "Popular" under Reputation).

Mild Epidemics—(See "Mild" under Epidemics).

Mild Fevers—(See "Mild" under Fevers).

Syphilis—Mild Form of—(See Syphilis).

MILITARY LIFE—Danger of Injury or Death In—The ☉ or ☽ to the ☌, or P. Dec. Antares; the ☽ to the ☌ or P. Dec. Aldebaran. (See "Battle" under Abroad; Foreign Lands, Maritime, Officers, Sailors, Ships, Soldiers, War).

Officer Killed—A Military Officer Murdered by His Soldiers—Mutiny—Danger of—The ☽ to the ☌ the South Star in the Lion's Neck. Also at such a time the Officer may become violent, and very intemperate in diet and disposition.

MILK—Milk Glands—Lacteals—Mammary Glands—Lactation—Breasts—Milky, etc.—The Milk is ruled by the ☽, ♀, the ♋ sign, and the 4th H. The ☽ rules the basic fluid in Milk. Jupiter adds the fatty constituents. The ☉ adds Casein, the clotted proteid of Milk, and ♄ adds the Salts. Lactation, Nursing of the Child, is ruled by the ♋ sign.

Caked Breasts—(See Breasts).

Child Could Not Nurse—Death of—Case—(See "Nursing" under Children; "Incapable of Nurture" under Nutrition).

Diseases of Lacteals—Afflictions in ♋; ♄ afflicted in ♋; Subs at Lu.P. (4D), KP.

Dry Breasts—No Milk for Nursing—Scanty Supply of—♄ afflicted in ♋; ♄ in ♋ and afflicting the ☽ or ♀; ♄ affl. in ♋ in the 4th H.

Sympathetic Lactation — Case — (See "Sympathetic Lactation", No. 810, in 1001 N.N.

Urine—Milky Urine—(See Urine). See Breasts, Fluids, Glands, Juices, Secretions.

MIND—The Mind—Intellect—Reason—Understanding—The Mentality, etc.—The planet ☿ is the principal ruler of the Mind. The Mind is ruled by ☿, the ☽ and the Asc., and the relation between these three at B. largely determine the Mentality. The ☽, taken separately from ☿ and the Asc., has only partial rule over the Mind. The Hebrew letter Vau (V) is related to the ♉ sign, and is predominant in Mind and Hearing, and the transformation of Thought into Speech. Thus ♈ (Intellect), and ♉ (Speech) are closely related, and the organ of Coordination is located in ♉. An afflicted ☿ tends to disturbances of the Mind, and to Brain and Nerve Disorders. The 3rd and 9th Houses also rule the Mind, and planets therein tend to show afflictions or benefits to the Mind. Mercury and the ☽ are Significators of Mind, and any evil aspect between them tends to weaken and injure the Mind, and its expression. Uranus and ☿ are called the Mental Planets. This subject of Mind is also largely considered under the subjects of Intellect, Mental, Perception, Reason, and Understanding, in this book, and quite lengthy under "Mental" for convenience of reference, as so many of the references in the Textbooks of Astrology use the word "Mental" in giving the influences about the Mind. (See the various paragraphs under Mental). This Article is divided into two Sections: Section One, General Considerations About the Mind; Section Two, Diseases and Afflictions of the Mind.

— SECTION ONE —

GENERAL CONSIDERATIONS—

Divisions and Sub-Divisions of the Mind—Qualities—Manifestations and Expressions of the Mind, etc. See the following subjects in the alphabetical arrangement—

Abilities—(See "Abilities" under Mental).

Accomplished Mind — (See "Accomplished" under Manners).

Acquired Tendencies—(See Acquired).

Action of the Mind — Action of the Mind Upon the Body—☿, the ruler of the ♍ sign, the sign of health, and also the influences of the 6th H. at B., the house of health, and the house of ☿, indicate the action of the mind upon the body, and especially as related to the causes and origins of disease, as the ☿, ♍, and 6th H. influences connect mind and body, and afflictions to these important centers in the radical map tend to physical disorders arising from a mental cause. (See "Mind" under Action; Mercury, Sixth House, Virgo; "Principle" under Vital).

Active Mind—Acute Mind—(See "Active Mind" under Active; "Mental Energy" under Energy; "Quickened" under Mentality).

Acute Mind — (See "Active" in this section).

Affections—The Affections—(See Affections, Desire, Love Affairs, Marriage).

Afterthought — (See "Lack Of" under Forethought).

Aims — Intentions — Purposes — (See Ambitions, Ideals, Motives, Purposes).

Ambitions; Animal Propensities—(See "Animal Instinct" under Animal; Beastly, Fear, Fierce, Hunger, Instincts, Passion, Savage, Self-Preservation, Violent, Wild, etc.).

Apprehension — (See Comprehension, Discernment, Perception, Senses, Understanding).

Attention—(See "Attention" in Sec. 2 of this Article).

Blushing; Body — Action of the Mind Upon the Body—(See "Action" in this section).

Boyishness; Brain — (See the various paragraphs under Brain, Cerebral)

Brightened — The mind is brightened when ☿ rises before the ☉, and gives forethought, precision, concentration, and better powers of mind. (See "Active" in this section).

Capacity—Of the Mind—Is governed largely by the 3rd and 9th Houses, and planets in these houses at B., as these are the houses of mind. (See Ninth House, Third House).

Ceaseless Motion In—(See Motion).

Cells—Each Cell of the body is a center of Intelligence. (See the various paragraphs under Cells).

Cerebral — Cerebellum — Cerebrum — (See Brain, Cerebral).

Character; Cheerfulness; Choices — (See Discrimination, Forethought, Judgment, Reason, Will, etc.).

Clear and Incisive — ☿ well-aspected in ♊; ♂ a strong ruler at B. (See "Good" under Intellect; "Sound Mind" in this section).

Comprehension; Concentration;

Conduct; Congenital—Innate Mental Tendencies—(See Congenital, Heredity, Nativity, Prenatal).

Conscience — The Inner Voice which approves or disapproves of various lines of action and conduct. The predominating planet, or planets at birth, and the majority influences, as well as the degree of knowledge and spiritual advancement, determine the action of Conscience. Born under ♄, the Conscience approves revenge, secretiveness, greed, covetousness, miserliness, etc. Born under ♃, the native is more kind, honest, and his conscience says to do right, and be religious, etc., and so on with each of the planets, according to their nature.

Consciousness; Contentment;

Coordination; Countenance — Reflection of Mental States In—(See Countenance, Expression, Eyes, Face, Glances, Look).

Cultivation— Of the Mind— ☿ strong at B., and well-aspected, leads to, and makes cultivation, learning, and mental growth easier. (See Learning, Reading, Scholar, Science, Study).

Deep and Profound—Depth of Mind— (See "Active Mind" under Active; "Good" under Intellect; Knowledge, Learning, Scholar, Study; Brightened, Clear, Cultivation, Penetrating, Sound, Strong, in this section).

Deportment— (See Conduct, Habits, Love Affairs, Morals, Passion, Religion, etc.).

Desirable Mental Traits — The More Fortunate Traits of Mind—Admirable Physical Traits—As a contrast to the less desirable traits and characteristics of mind and body, some of the more fortunate qualities, and not of a pathological nature, have been introduced into this book for the study of students. See the following subjects in the alphabetical arrangement— Active Mind, Agile, Ambitions, Animated, Balanced, Beautiful, Brisk, Careful, Cheerfulness, Cleanly, Clear Intellect, Comely, Commanding, Comprehension Good, Concentration (Good Powers of); Constructive, Contented, Courage, Determined, Dexterity, Dimples, Discernment Good, Duty (Faithful In); Elegant Mind, Even Temper (see Temper); Excellent, Faculties Quickened, Fair, Favored Mind, Fine, Forethought (Good Powers of); Fortunate, Friendly, Fruitful, Generous, Genius, Genteel, Gentle, Good, Graceful, Handsome, Harmless, Harmonious, Healers, Health Good, Healthy, Honest, Honorable, Hopeful, Humane, Improved Mind, Independent, Inoffensive, Intuitive, Inventive, Joyful, Judgment Good, Just, Juvenility, Keen, Kind, Knowledge (Acquires Easily); Learning (Fond of); Lively, Lovely, Lucky, Magnetic, Manly, Manners (Good, etc.); Marriage (Happy In); Mathematical, Mechanical, Memory Good, Mentality Good, Mild, Mind Strong, Moderate, Modesty, Morals Good, Motives Good, Musical, Mystical, Natural Abilities, Nature (Active, Good, etc.); Neat, Noble, Normal, Opinions Good, Optimistic, Overcoming, Passion (Free From); Patient, Peaceful, Perception Good, Perfect, Perfection of Mind, Persevering, Philanthropic, Philosophical, Pious, Pity, Pleasant, Poised, Polite, Popular, Practical, Prepossessing, Presence of Mind, Proficient, Prophetic, Prudent, Quick Mind, Quiet, Rescue Work (see Rescue); Responsible, Riches (Acquires); Ruddy, Sagacious, Sanguine Temperament, Scholar, Self-Confident, Self-Controlled, Self-Reliant, Sensible, Sincere, Sober, Sound Mind, Strong Mind, Study (Fond of); Sweet Disposition (see Sweet); Sympathetic, Tastes (Good); Temperate, Thinking (Good); Trustworthy, Truthful, Understanding (Good); Vital Force (Plenty of); Wealthy, Well-Disposed, Well-Favored, Youthful, Zealous, Zest, etc. For subjects which may be overlooked here, look in the alphabetical arrangement. (See "Undesirable Mental Traits" in Sec. 2 of this Article).

Desires; Dexterity; Discernment;

Discretion—(See Balance; "Good" under Judgment; Prudence, etc.).

Discrimination; Disposition — (See Decanates, Disposition, Mental, Temper, Temperament, etc.).

Dull Mind—(See Dull).

Educational Mind — Ruled by the 3rd H. and its conditions. A strong 3rd H. gives a good mind for education and learning, and especially along material and worldly lines. The 9th H. strong and well-aspected at B. gives more desire for Philosophy, Truth, Religion, and the recognition of the Higher Mind.

Ego—The Ego—(See Ego).

Elegant Mind—(See Elegant).

Emotions; Exalted Mind — (See Ecstasy; "Mind" under Exaltation).

Excellent Mind—(See Excellent).

Expression; Faculties—(See the various paragraphs under Faculties).

Fancies; Favored Mind — (See Elegant, Favored).

Fears; Feelings; Fickle-Minded—(See "Fickle" under Love Affairs).

Fixed Mind—(See "Fixed Ideas" under Ideas).

Flexible Mind — (See Changeable, Flexible, Mutable, Negative, Susceptible, Receptive, etc.).

Forethought; Fruitful Mind — (See Fruitful, Inventive).

Ganglion — Note the various paragraphs under Ganglion).

Genius; Good Mind—(See "Good" under Intellect; Active, Deep, Elegant, Excellent, Sound, Strong, in this section).

Great Mind—(See "Great Ability" under Great; "Abilities" in this section).

Habits; Happiness; Harmless;

Harmony Disturbed—(See Harmony).

Healing Powers—(See Healers).

Health of Mind—(See "Active Mind" under Active; Cheerfulness, Contentment, Happy; "Good" under Intellect; "Peace of Mind" in this section).

Hearing; Heredity; Higher Mind— (See Conscience, Educational, Individuality, in this section; Ego, Soul, Spirit).

Honesty; Houses of Mind — The 3rd and 9th H. (See Ninth, Third).

Hypnotism; Ideals; Ideas;

Idiosyncrasies; Imagination;

Impulses; Inclinations—(See Conduct, Desires, Disposition, Habits, Ideals, Morals, Motives, Purposes, Temperament, etc.).

Independent; Individuality;

Infertile Mind — (See "Unfertile" in this section).

Ingenious — (See Genius; "Inventive" under Learning).

Innate—(See "Congenital" in this section).

Instincts; Intellect—(See the various paragraphs under Intellect, Mental, and in this Article).

Intentions—(See Character, Conduct Evil, Good, Motives, Purposes, etc.).

Introspection; Intuition; Jealousy;

Judging the Mind—To judge of the mind, consider the sign on the Asc., planets in the 1st H., or Asc., if any, and the aspects of planets to the Asc. The ☽ and ☿ are chiefly to be considered, and the aspects to them, their relation to each other and to the Asc. Also, before judging of the effect of any planet upon the ☽, ☿, or Asc., note how that planet itself is aspected and affected by other planets, as every planet acts upon every other planet by its aspects, except the ☽ and ☿, which are passive. Any planet in the 3rd or 9th H. has a powerful influence upon the mind for good or evil. Uranus and ☿ are termed the Mental Planets, and their aspects, positions, and influences tend to greatly determine the quality, state, and conditions of the mind. (See "Mental Faculties" under Faculties; "Good", "Weak", under Intellect; "Weaknesses" under Mental; Prenatal Epoch; "Quality", and the various paragraphs in this section).

Judgment—Good or Bad Judgment—(See Judgment).

Light In Mind—Little Mind—Credulous—Narrow-Minded—Easily Convinced—Negative—Vacillating—♃ Sig. ☌ ☉; ☿ weak at B., and often in a watery sign, and espec. in ♓, and afflicted; ♒ on the Asc., and the ☽ remote in a common sign, light, credulous, and inconstant. (See Inconstant, Influenced; "Shallow" under Mentality; Mutable, Negative, Prejudiced, Pretender, Reason, Receptive, Restless, Susceptible, Vacillating; "Weak Mind" in this section).

Likes and Dislikes—(See Likes).

Little Mind—(See "Light" in this section).

Look—Intellectual Look—(See Look).

Lower Mind—Instinctive Mind—Ruled by ♄ and ♑. Also ruled by ♂ and ♀ when these planets are afflicted, or afflicting each other. (See Amorous; "Animal Instincts" under Animal; Appetites, Desires, Drink, Excesses, Gluttony, Passion, Personality, etc.).

Manners; Mathematical; Meditative—(See Grave, Introspection, Reserved, Sad, Serious).

Memory—(See the various paragraphs under Memory).

Mesmerism; Methods; Moods; Morals;

Motion—(See Action, Coordination, Energy, Motion, Motor, Movement, Muscles, Walk, etc).

Motives; Movement; Narrow-Minded (See "Light" in this section).

Natural Abilities—(See Natural).

Normal Mind—(See Normal).

Notions; Novelties—Fond of—(See Novelties).

Opinions; Optimism;

Over-Active Mind—(See "Over-Active" under Active).

Peace of Mind—Contentment—Happiness—Joy—Confident—Not Swayed by Fears or Anxieties—A Calm and Tranquil Mind—The ☉ or ☽ to the ☌ or good aspect ♃ or ♀ by dir.; the ☽ to the ☌ or good asp. ♀ by dir., peace of mind espec. to females; the ☽ at a Solar Rev. well-aspected by the ☉, ♃, or ♀, and passing her own place at B.; the Asc. to the ⚹ or △ the ☉ or ☽ by dir.; lord of the Asc. in the 1st H.; the 14° ♓ on the Asc.; good aspects of planets to ♀ and the ♎ sign; ♎ on the Asc. at B. tends to give poise and balance. (See Balance, Contentment; "Good Fate" under Fate; Gentle, Happy, Harmless; "Good Health" under Health; Joyful; "Mild Disposition" under Mild; Optimistic; "Sanguine Temperament" under Sanguine; Spiritual, etc.).

Pedestrianism; Penetrating Mind—♂ Sig. in ♑; ♂ Sig. ⚹ or △ ☿. (See "Active Mind" under Active; "Quickened" under Mental).

Perception—Acute Perceptive Faculties—(See Perception).

Perfection—Of Mind and Body—Given by the ♒ sign. (See Beautiful, Harmony; "Good Mind" in this section).

Personality; Phantasies;

Pineal Gland—(See Pineal).

Pituitary Body—(See Pituitary).

Planets—The Mental Planets—♅, ☿, and the ☽. The Asc. is also strongly mental, along with the ☽ and ☿. (See "Judging the Mind" in this section).

Plexuses; Positive Mind—(See Individuality, Positive, Powerful, Self-Confidence, Self-Reliant, etc.).

Prejudiced; Prenatal Epoch;

Presence of Mind—(See "Active Mind" under Active; "Good" under Judgment; "Quickened" under Mental).

Pretenses—(See Character, Cheating, Deceitful, Dual, Honest, Hypocritical, Motives, Pretender, Purposes).

Principles; Propensities; Prophetical;

Prudence; Psychic Powers; Purposes;

Quality of the Mind—☿ and the ☽, their sign and house positions, aspects, dignity, etc., tend to determine the quality of the mind. Mercury well-aspected by the ☽, ♄, ♃, and the Asc. tend to give a good quality to the mind, and with ☿ also not combust. Mercury combust, in no aspect, or in evil aspect to the ☽, ♅, ♄, ♃, and the Asc. tends to weaken the quality of the mind, give poor abilities, bad judgment, lack of foresight, and many mental ills. (See Intellect, Mental; "Abilities", and the various paragraphs in this section).

Qualities of the Mind—(See "Qualities" under Mental; the various paragraphs in this section). The Qualities of the Mind are legion. Many of them are listed in this book, both the good and the less desirable ones. Look in the alphabetical arrangement for the subject you have in mind. (See "Desirable" in Sec. 1 of this Article; "Undesirable" in this section).

Quickened—The Mind Quickened—(See "Quickened" under Mental; "Active", "Brightened", in this section).

Rational Mind—Rational Faculties—(See Rational, Reason).

Reason—(See the various paragraphs under Reason).

Refined Mind—(See Elegant).

Religion; Rulers of the Mind—(See the Introduction to this Article).

Satisfaction of Mind—(See Cheerful, Contentment, Fortunate, Happy, Joyful; "Peace of Mind" in this section; "Popular" under Reputation).

Scruples—(See Ideals, Ideas, Love Affairs, Morals, Motives, Purposes, Principles).

Senses; Sentient Faculties—(See Sentient).

Sentiments—(See Emotions, Feelings, Ideals, Ideas, Notions, etc.).

Shallow Mind—(See "Shallow" under Mentality; "Light" in this section).

Sharpened—The Mind Sharpened—(See "Quickened" under Mentality; Active, Brightened, Clear, Penetrating, in this section).

Sight—Vision—(See Sight).

Significators of Mind—The ☽ and ☿.

Signs of Mind—The airy signs ♊, ♎, ♒. Also ♍, the sign of ☿, and ♈, the head and brain sign.

Smell; Solar Plexus—(See "Solar" under Plexus).

Solidarity of Mind—Given by any aspect of ♄ to ☿. (See "Good" in this section).

Soul—The Soul—(See Soul).

Sound Mind—A Sound Mind In a Sound Body—Mens Sana In Corpore Sano—The ☽ and ☿ must be strong, connected with each other, the Asc., or with ♃, ♂, or ♀, and free from affliction. The mutual configurations between the ☽ and ☿ are very desirable. Mercury in the Asc., well-aspected, and in his own signs ♊ or ♍. (See Active, Brightened, Clear, Deep, Good, Quality, Quickened, Strong, in this section).

Speculative Mind—(See Speculative).

Speech—(See the various paragraphs under Speech).

Spirit—The Spirit—(See Spirit).

Spirituality—(See Spiritual).

States of the Mind—Are largely ruled by the aspects to the ☽ and ☿ each day and hour of life. Self-control, knowledge, wisdom, foresight, discrimination, and a highly developed spiritual nature, etc., tend to give more poise, balance, and control under the various conflicts and emotions to which the mind is subject daily under the planetary aspects, transits, and directions. (See Anger, Balance, Despondency, Emotion, Fear, Feelings, Grief, Hope, Joy, Melancholy, Optimism, Sadness, Worry, etc.).

Strong Mind—Good Mind—Powerful Mind—Sound Mind—Good aspects of ♃ to the ☽, ☿, and the Asc. tend to give a strong mind and body, and espec. when ☿ and the ☽ are in good relation to each other, and to the Asc., and both ☿ and the ☽ dignified and strong. (See "Good" under Intellect; "Quickened" under Mentality; "Sound" in this section).

Studious Mind—(See "Studious" under Learning; Reading, Scholar, Science, Study).

Subconscious Mind—(See "Animal Instincts" under Animal; the Introduction under Habits; Hypnotism, Reason, Subconscious).

Superconscious Mind—(See Superconscious).

Superficial Mind—(See "Fails In" under Examinations; "Shallow" under Mentality; Pretender; "Light" in this section).

Susceptibility; Suspicious—(See Fears, Suspicion).

Talented Mind—(See Genius, Inventive, Knowledge, Learning, Mathematical; "Abilities" under Mental; Oratorical, Reading, Scientific, Study, Talents; Elegant, Excellent, Good, in this section).

Taste; Tastes; Telepathy; Temper;

Temperament; Tendencies; Thinking—Thought—(See Thinking).

Thyroid Gland; Understanding;

Unfertile Mind—♄ in the 3rd H., and afflicting the mental rulers. (See "Little Depth" under Learning; "Shallow" under Mentality; "Light" in this section).

Vagaries; Views—(See Anarchists, Ideals, Ideas, Materialism, Notions, Opinions, Reformers, Religion).

Vision—(See Accommodation, Sight).

Visions; Volition;

Well-Balanced Mind—The ☉ in a fiery sign, and the ☽ in a watery sign.

Will; Wisdom; Worry; Young Mind—(See Juvenility). There are many other subjects about the Mind, too numerous to list here. Look in the alphabetical arrangement for the subject you may have in mind.

— SECTION TWO —

DISEASES OF THE MIND—Mental Disorders, Afflictions, and Deviations—Disturbances of the Mind—Mental Excesses or Limitations, etc.—See the following subjects in the alphabetical arrangement when only listed here—

Absent-Minded—Chaotic Mental State—Flightiness—Confusion of Mind—Dreamy Mind—A ♆ affliction; ♆ ☌ ☿; ☿ in a ♃ sign at B., as in ♐ or ♓, or ☿ afflicted by ♃ or ♆; Subs at AT. (See Flightiness).

Activity—Effervescent Mental Activity—(See Effervescent).

Adult—With Mind of a Child—Never Grew Up—Case—(See "Mind" under Children).

Affects the Mind—☿ afflicted at B., and by dir. (See the various paragraphs in this section, and under Mental).

Afflicted In Mind and Body—(See "Mind and Body" in this section).

Affliction of Mind—The ☉ to the ill-asps. ☿ by dir.; the ☉ to the ☌ or ill-asps. ♄ by dir.; the ☽ to the ☌ or ill-asps. the ☉ or ♄ by dir., afflicted in mind and body; ♄ passing over the place of the radical ☽, or at a Solar Rev. ☌ the ☽; planets afflicted in the 3rd or 9th H.; ☿ ☌ or ill-asp. ♄ by dir. (See Anguish, Anxiety, Brooding, Dejected, Depressed, Despondent, Gloom;

"Mental" under Infirmities; "Weak" under Intellect and Mentality; "Diseased Mind", and the various paragraphs in this section).

Alcoholism—(See Alcoholism, Drink; "Delirium Tremens" under Delirium; Intoxication).

Alzheimer's Disease—(See "Atrophy" under Brain).

Analgesia; Anguish; Anxiety; Apathy of Mind—(See Apathy).

Aphasia — (See "Aphasia" under Speech).

Aphonia — (See "Aphonia" under Voice).

Apologetic Attitude—(See "Inferiority Complex" under Inferior).

Apparitions — (See Phenomena, Psychic, Visions).

Appetites — Abnormal — Perverted — (See Appetites, Perversions).

Apprehension Dull—(See Dull).

Arrested Mental Powers — (See "Arrested" under Mental; "Weak Mind" in this section).

Attention — Not Able to Fix the Attention — (See Flightiness; "Absent-Minded" in this section).

Aversions; Backwardness; Balance—Lack of—(See Balance).

Bashfulness; Beside Oneself — (See Excitable, Frenzy, Fury).

Blind Impulses—(See Impulses).

Blindness—From Over-Study—(See "Over-Study" under Blindness).

Blues; Body and Mind Afflicted—(See "Mind and Body" in this section).

Bomb Plotters—(See Anarchists).

Brain — Disorders of — (See Brain, Cerebral).

Breakdown Mentally — (See "Breakdown" under Mental).

Brooding; Capacity of the Mind — Limited Capacity — Suppressed — (See Foolish, Idiocy, Imbecile, Insanity; "Arrested", "Weak Mind", in this section).

Catalepsy; Centered On Disease—The Mind Centered On Disease—The ☉ or ☽ afflicted in ♉ or ♍; the ☉ or ♄ afflicted in ♍; ♉ or ♍ on the Asc. It is said the ♉ people fear disease, and the ♍ people court and nurse it. (See "Afflicted" under Body; Taurus, Virgo; "Mind and Body" in this section).

Chaotic Mind — (See "Mental Chaos" under Chaotic).

Child—Adult Has the Mind of—Never Grew Up—(See "Mind" under Children).

Clairaudience; Clairvoyannce; Claustrophobia; Clogging — Of the Mind—(See Clogging).

Clouded Mind—☿ in the 12th H. at B., combust, or afflicted by ♄ or ♂. (See Chaotic, Confused, Dreamy, Flightiness, Insanity; "Absent-Minded" in this section).

Colds — From Over-Exertion of the Mind—(See "Colds" under Exercise).

Coma; Complaints—Mental Complaints — (See "Complaints" under Mental; the various paragraphs in this section).

Comprehension Dull — (See Comprehension; "Mind" under Dull; "Weak" under Understanding).

Concentration — Inability to Concentrate—(See Concentration).

Conduct—Abnormalities, Excesses, and Perversions In—(See Conduct).

Confusion; Consciousness — Clouding of—Loss of—(See Consciousness).

Conspicuous Mental Diseases — (See Conspicuous).

Contracted Mind — (See Imbecile; "Shallow", "Weak", under Mentality; "Arrested", "Light", "Weak", in this Article).

Control — The Mind Should Be Kept Under Good Control—♅ afflicted in ♒. For Lack of Control over the Mind, see references under Control.

Convulsions; Coordination—Disorders of—(See Coordination, Incoordination).

Cravings; Crazy—(See Frenzy, Fury, Insanity, Madness, Mania).

Cretinism; Criminal Tendencies—(See Criminal).

Cruel; Curable Mental Diseases—(See "Curable" under Mental).

Darkened Mind—A Mind of Darkened Desires—♄ afflicted by ♅. The mind tends to be darkened thru fear when ♄ or ☋ are in the Asc. in ☌ the ☉, ☽, or ☿. (See Desires, Fears).

Darkness—Fear of—(See Darkness).

Deafness—A Mental Limitation—(See Deafness, Limitations, Twelfth House).

Death—(See "Death" under Mental).

Debased In Mind—(See Debased).

Debility—Mental Debility—(See "Debility" under Mental; "Diseased Mind", and the various paragraphs in this section).

Deficient Mentally—(See "Deficiency" under Mental).

Deformed—In Mind and Body—♀ Sig. □ or ☌ ♄. (See "Mind and Body" under Deformities).

Dejected; Delirium; Delusions; Dementia; Demoniac; Depraved; Depression; Depth of Mind — Little Depth of Mind—(See "Fails In" under Examinations; "Shallow" under Mentality; "Light In Mind" in Sec. 1 of this Article).

Derangement — Of the Mind — (See "Derangement" under Mental).

Desires—A Mind of Darkened Desires —(See "Darkened" in this section; Depraved; "Low Desires" under Low; Perversions).

Despondency; Development — Of the Mind—Premature, Precocious, Arrested, Late, or Slow — (See Genius, Idiocy, Incomplete; "Arrested" under Mental; Precocious, Premature, Prodigies; "Weak Mind" in this section).

Deviations; Dipsomania; Directions —The Mind Affected By—(See Directions).

Disabilities—Mental—(See "Disabilities" under Mental; the various paragraphs in this section).

Discomfort; Discord — Inner Discord and Inharmony In Mind and Emotions —Afflictions to the Airy Signs, and to ♎ especially. Also afflictions to ♀. (See "Mind and Emotions" under Emotions).

Disease—The Disease Is More In the Mind Than In the Body—Is of Psychic Origin—Is Chiefly In the Mind—(See "Diseases" under Psychic; "Centered On Disease", "Mind and Body", in this section).

Diseased Mind—Diseases of the body act upon the mind thru the Vital Principle, and diseases of the mind upon the body thru the same medium, which medium is ruled by the ☉. (See "Principle" under Vital). Also caused by the ☉ or ☿ in a common sign, and afflicted by the ☌ or ill-asps. of malefics; the ☽ or ☿ affl. by ♆, unhealthy states of the mind; ♄ afflicted in ♑; ♃ or the ☽ to the ill-asps. ☿ by dir.; the 30° ♍ on the Asc. (See "Action of the Mind", and the various paragraphs in this section; Frenzy, Fury, Insanity, Madness, Mania, Melancholy, etc.).

Dishonesty; Disordered Mind—(See "Diseased", and the various paragraphs in this section, and under Intellect, Mental).

Dispersions; Disspirited; Distempers —Distempered Fancies—Distempers of the Mind — Melancholic Distempers — (See Distempers, Fancies; "Dry and Melancholic" under Melancholy; the various paragraphs in this section, and under Intellect, Mental, Psychic).

Distracted; Distress; Disturbances — (See "Irritations" under Mental; the various paragraphs in this section).

Doubts and Fears — (See Doubts, Fears, Gloomy, Melancholic, Morbid, Reserved, Secretive, Suspicious).

Dreads; Dreams — Dreamy — (See Dreams).

Drink—Craving For—(See Dipsomania, Drink, Drunkenness, Intoxication).

Drowsiness — Stupor — Dull — (See "Drowsiness", "Heaviness", "Stupor", under Sleep).

Dual-Minded—(See Dual).

Dull—(See "Mind" under Dull, Heavy).

Dumb; Dwarfed — In Mind and Body —(See "Mind" under Children; Diminished, Dwarfed, Growth; "Arrested" under Mental).

Eccentric; Ecstasy; Effeminate;

Effervescent — Over-Active Mind— (See "Over-Active Mind" under Active; Effervescent).

Ego—Exaggerated Ego—Ego Mania —(See Ego).

Elation—(See "Exaltation" under Emotions).

Emotions — Disorders of — (See Emotions; "Discord" in this section).

Ennui—(See "Weariness" under Mental).

Enthusiasm—The Fury of—(See Enthusiasm).

Epilepsy; Equilibrium—Loss of— (See Equilibrium).

Erotic; Erratic; Erring; Evil — Evil Qualities of Mind—Mind Disturbed by Evil Thoughts—(See "Thoughts", and the various paragraphs under Evil; "Unclean" in this section).

Exaggerated Ego—(See Ego).

Exaltation — (See "Mind and Body" under Exaltation).

Examinations—Fails In—(See Examinations).

Excitable; Exhibitionism; Extremes —(See "Mental Extremes" under Extremes).

Faculties—Disorders of—(See Faculties).

Fag—(See "Brain Fag" under Brain; "Mind" under Fatigue).

Fainting; Fanatical; Fancies—Disorders of—(See Fancies).

Fear—Fears—Phobias—(See Fear).

Feeble-Minded — (See "Mind" under Feeble; Foolish; "Weak" in this section).

Feelings — Disorders of — (See Feelings, Emotions).

Filthy Mind — (See "Mind" under Filthy).

Fits; Flighty Mind — (See Flightiness).

Folly; Foolhardy; Foolish; Force — Dissipation of Mental Force—(See Effervescent).

Forebodings; Forethought — Lack of —(See Forethought).

Forgetfulness—(See Memory).

Foul Mind—(See "Mind" under Filthy; Lewd, Obscene, Shameless, etc.).

Frantic; Frenzy; Fright; Fury;

Gambling; Gloom; Grief;

Growth of the Mind — Growth Arrested—(See "Arrested" under Mental; "Weak Mind" in this section).

Hallucinations; Hatred; Hauntings;

Headaches—From Much Reading and Study—(See "Ocular" under Headache).

Health of Mind — (See "Health of Mind" in Sec. 1 of this Article).

Heavy Mind—Drowsiness—(See Dull; "Mind" under Heavy; "Drowsiness" under Sleep).

Hebetude—Dulling of the Mind and the Senses—(See Dull, Hebetude).

High Temper — (See "High" under Temper).

Homicidal; Homosexuality; Horrors;

Hyperactivity—Of the Psychic Powers — (See "Over-Active Mind" under Active; Effervescent, Excitable; "Mind" under Hyperactivity; Psychic).

Hyperaesthesia; Hypersensitive;

Hypochondria; Hysteria; Idealism — Extremes of—(See Ideals).

Ideas — Chaotic — Confused — Incoordinated—(See Ideas).

Identity—Loss of— Disorientation — (See Identity).

Idiocy; Idiopathy — Morbid State of Mind — (See Idiopathy; "Mind" under Morbid).

Idle and Dull—(See Dull, Idle).

Illness — From Over-Exertion of the Mind—(See "Exertion" under Mental; Reading, Study).

Illusions; Imaginations; Imbecility;

Impaired Mental Faculties—(See Faculties; "Mental" under Impairment).

Imperfections—All Imperfections of the Intellectual Parts—All Evils of—(See Imperfections; "All Evils" under Intellect; the various paragraphs under Mental, and in this section).

Impractical; Improvident; Impulses—Blind Impulses—Morbid—(See Impulses).

Inactive Mind—(See Inactive).

Incendiarism; Incoherence—Of Ideas—(See Chaotic, Confused, Ideas, Incoherent).

Incompetency—Mental—(See Inability, Incapable; "Incompetency" under Mental).

Incomplete; Incomposed;

Incoordination; Incurable—(See "Mental" under Incurable).

Indifferent—(See "Mind" under Indifferent).

Indisposition; Inefficiency;

Inferior Mentality—Inferiority Complex—(See Inferior; "Inferior" under Mental).

Infirmities—(See "Mental" under Infirmities).

Inharmony—(See Inharmony; "Discord" in this section).

Inhuman and Wild—(See Inhuman).

Injured—The Mind Injured—Caused by an evil aspect between the ☽ and ☿, and also when ☿ and the ☽ are disconnected with each other or the Asc. (See Forethought, Imbecile, Insanity, Judgment; "Weak" under Mental, and in this section).

Injuries—Mindful of—Retains Anger—(See "Mindful" under Injuries).

Inner Discord—(See "Discord" in this section).

Insanity; Insensibility; Insomnia—(See Sleep).

Instability—Of Mind—The ☽ afflicted in the Asc.; ☿ afflicted by ♂; ☿ afflicted in ♒ or ♓ unless ♄ be in good aspect to ☿. (See Instability, Mutable, Negative, Restless, Roaming, Vacillating, Wandering, etc.).

Instincts—Disorders of—(See Instincts).

Intellect—Disorders of—(See the various paragraphs under Intellect, Mental, and in this Article).

Intemperance; Introspection;

Intuitions—Disorders of—(See Intuition).

Involuntary Disorders—Loss of Control—(See Involuntary).

Irrational; Irresponsible; Irritable;

Irritations—(See "Irritations" under Mental).

Jealousy; Judgment—Disorders of—(See Judgment).

Kleptomaniac; Knavish; Knowledge—A Pretender to All Manner of Knowledge—(See Knowledge; "Void Of" under Learning; Pretender).

Lack Of—Mental Deficiencies—(See the various paragraphs under Lack Of).

Languishing; Lapsing—Moral Lapsing—(See Lapsing, Morals).

Lascivious; Lassitude; Laxity;

Learning—Incapable of—(See Learning).

Left-Handed—(See Left, Right).

Lesions—Tending to Affect the Mind, and the Expression of Mind—(See Cortical, Lesions, Paralysis; "Aphasia" under Speech).

Lethargy; Lewd; Liable To—Liable to Mental Disorders and Disturbances—(See the various paragraphs under Intellect, Mental, and in this section).

Liars; Libelers; Licentious;

Light In Mind—(See "Light In Mind" in Sec. 1 of this Article; "Weak Mind" in this section).

Limitations—Upon the Mind—(See Limitations).

Lisping; Listless; Locomotion—Disorders of—(See Gait, Locomotion, Motion, Movement, Walk).

Loneliness; Longings; Loose—Loose Habits—Loose Morals—(See Loose).

Loss Of—Loss of Faculties—Loss of Reason—(See "Loss Of" under Faculties, Reason; also see the various subjects under "Loss Of").

Love Affairs—Abnormalities In—(See Amorous, Excesses, Love Affairs, Marriage, Passion, Perversions).

Low Mentality—Mind of a Low Order—♆ afflicted at B., and especially in the 3rd H.; ☿ □ or ☍ ♆. (See "Low and Base", and the various paragraphs under Low).

Low Morals—(See "Loose Morals" under Morals).

Low Spirits—(See Low).

Lower Mind—Lives Much In—(See Appetites, Conduct, Debauched, Depraved, Habits, Lewd, Love Affairs, Morals, Passion, etc.).

Lowering—Lowering Tendency—(See Dejected, Depressed, Despondent; "Low Spirits" under Low; Melancholy).

Lunacy—(See Insanity, Lunacy).

Lustful; Luxuries—Fond of, and Health Injured By—(See Extravagance; "Rich Food" under Food; Luxuries, etc.).

Madness; Magical Powers—(See Magic).

Malefic Planets—Adverse Influences of Over the Mind—(See Malefics).

Malevolent—(See Evil, Malefic, Malevolent).

Malice; Mania; Masochism;

Materialism; Mean-Spirited—(See Mean).

Mechanical; Mediumship—Dangers Thru—(See Clairvoyance, Mediumship).

Melancholy; Memory—Defects In—(See Memory).

Men—Mental Abnormalities In—(See the various paragraphs under Men).

Mental Disorders—(See the various paragraphs under Faculties, Intellect, Mental, Mind, Perception, Reason, Understanding, and also in this Article).

Merciless; Mercury—Mental Disorders Caused by ☿—(See the various paragraphs under Mercury).

Methods; Mind and Body—Afflicted In—(a) The Disease Is Chiefly In the Mind—Of Psychic Origin—(See "Diseases" under Psychic; "Centered On Disease" in this section). (b) The Disease Is More In the Body Than In the Mind—(See "Afflicted" under Body). (c) The Disease Is In Both Mind and Body—The ☽ to the ☌ or ill-asp. the ☉ or ♄ by dir.; ♀ Sig. □ or ☍ ♄, deformed in body and mind; the M.C. to the ☌ or evil asps. the ☽ by dir., and espec. if the ☽ be afflicted at B.; malefics in the Asc., afflicting the lord of the Asc. or either the ☉ or ☽, both body and mind are diseased. (See "Body" under Disease; "Affliction of Mind" in this section).

Mind Centered Upon Disease—(See "Centered" in this section).

Mind Threatened—The ☉ ☌ ♄ in ♑; ♅ □ or ☍ ☿; ♄ ☌, □, or ☍ ☿; ♂ afflicted in ♈. (See Frenzy, Fury, Insanity, Madness, Mania, Melancholy).

Mind Unsettled—(See Changes; "Inability" under Concentration; Discontentment, Home, Journeys, Location, Removals, Residence, Scattering, Travel, Vagabond, Wanderer; "Light In Mind" in Sec. 1 of this Article; "Instability" in this section).

Mindful of Injuries—(See "Mindful" under Injuries).

Moisture of Brain—Mental Disorders From—(See "Brain" under Moisture).

Monomania—(See Mania).

Moods; Morals—Disorders of—(See Morals).

Morbid Mind—Morbid Deviations—Morbid Imaginations, etc.—(See the various paragraphs under Morbid. Also see Anxiety, Brooding, Dejection, Depressed, Despondency, Deviations, Fears, Hallucinations, Hypochondria, Idiopathy, Imaginations, Insanity, Introspection, Low Spirits (see Low); Nymphomania, Unsavory, Worry).

Moroseness; Muddled—Muddled Condition of Mind—☿ afflicted by H. (See Chaotic, Confused, Eccentric, Erratic, Misunderstood, Peculiar).

Murderous; Mutable—A Mutable, Changeable, Restless, Negative, and Scattering Mind—(See Mutable; "Instability" in this section).

Mute; Mysterious Sayings—Given To—Mysterious States of Mind—(See Catalepsy, Demoniac, Insanity, Mysterious, Trance, Weird).

Nakedness—Wandering In—(See "Outrageous" under Insanity).

Nerves—Mental Disturbances from Disordered Nerves—(See Anguish, Anxiety; "Brain Storms" under Brain; Depression, Despair, Excitable, Gloom; "High Strung" under High; Hope, Hypochondria, Hysterical; "Low Spirits" under Low; Melancholy; "Psychic Storms" under Psychic; Restlessness, Sensitive, Worry, etc.).

Neuroses—Anxiety Neuroses—(See Anxiety).

No Peace of Mind—♆ □ or ☍ ♅ at B., no peace of mind, and full of fears and dreads. (See Discontentment; "Signs of Fear" under Fear).

Noisome Diseases—(See Noisome).

Obscene; Obscure Mind—(See "Mind" under Obscure).

Obsessions; Obstructed Mind—♄ ☌ ☿ in ♈. (See "Mind" under Dull; "Weak" in this section).

Organic Disabilities—Tending to Affect the Mind—Are indicated by the ☽ and Asc., their relation to each other, and afflictions to them. (See Organic).

Out-of-Sorts—(See Irritable).

Outrageous—(See "Outrageous" under Insanity).

Over-Active Mind—(See "Over-Active" under Active).

Over-Exertion of Mind—(See "Mind" under Exercise; "Exertion" under Mental).

Pain—Insensibility To—(See Analgesia, Insensibility).

Paranoia; Passion—Perversions of—(See Passion, Perversions).

Passive Faculties—Deviations of—(See Deviations).

Peculiar—Peculiar Appetites and Tastes—(See Appetites, Eccentric, Peculiar, Tastes).

Peevish; Pensive; Perceptive Powers—Impaired—(See Perception).

Perjury—Given To—(See Perjury).

Persecution—Delusions of—(See Paranoia, Persecution).

Personality—Dual or Triple Personality—(See Personality).

Perverse; Perversions; Pessimistic—(See Doubts, Fears, Mistrustful, Morbid, Suspicious).

Pettifogging—Tricky—(See Deceitful, Dishonest, Pettifogging).

Petulant; Phantasies—(See "Prejudiced" under Fancies).

Phobias—(See Fears).

Phrenitic Man—(See "Wild" under Delirium).

Phrenitis—(See "Inflammation" under Brain; "Wild" under Delirium).

Phrenzies—(See Frenzy).

Physical Condition—Often Tends to Clogging of the Mind—(See Clogging).

Pilfering; Pity—Without Pity or Mercy—(See Pity).

Pleasure—Abnormally Fond of—(See Pleasure).

Plodding; Polluted Mind—(See Polluted).

Poor Mentality—(See "Poor" under Mental; "Weak" in this section).

Practices; Precipitate Actions—Fancies—(See Fancies, Precipitate).

Precocious; Prejudiced—Narrow-Minded—(See "Shallow" under Mentality; Prejudiced).

Premature—(See "Premature Mental Development" under Premature; Prodigies).

Premonitions—(See Forebodings, Premonitions).

Presentiments—(See Forebodings).

Pretender; Pretenses— Bragging—Conceited, etc.—(See "Pretenses" under Pretender).

Pride; Primitive Instincts Strong— (See "Animal Instincts" under Animal).

Principles — Scruples — (See Principles).

Procrastination; Prodigal; Prodigies; Profane; Professions—Declarations—Avowals—(See Professions).

Profligate; Projects—Confusion of— (See Projects).

Promises — Profuse In — (See Promises).

Propensities — Evil — Sensual — (See the references under Propensities).

Proud; Prudence — Excess of — Imprudent—(See Prudence).

Psychic Diseases — (See Psychic; the various paragraphs under Intellect, Mental, and in this section).

Purposes; Pyromania — (See Incendiarism).

Qualities of the Mind — (See "Qualities" under Mental; "Desirable" in Sec. 1 of this Article; "Undesirable" in this section. Also look in the alphabetical arrangement for the subject you have in mind).

Quick-Tempered — (See Choleric; "High Temper" under Temper).

Rambling In Speech—(See Speech).

Rape—An Attacker of Women—(See Rape).

Rash Thinking—(See Rashness).

Rationalism; Rattle-Brained — (See "Rapid" under Speech).

Raving; Reactionary; Reality— The Imagination Runs Away from the Limitations of Reality—(See Ideals; "Imagination Runs Away" under Imagination).

Reason—Disorders of—Void of—(See Reason).

Recklessness; Recluse; Reformers; Religion—Religious Mania—Religious Ecstasy—(See Religion).

Remorse; Renunciation; Reserved; Restlessness; Retarded Mental Powers —(See "Arrested", "Retarded", under Mental; "Obstructed", "Weak", in this section).

Retrospection; Revengeful; Revolutionary; Riotous; Roaming; Robbers; Romantic; Rough; Sadism— (See "Violence" under Passion; Sadism).

Sadness; Sarcasm; Satire; Savage; Scandalmongers; Scattering — Of the Mental Forces—(See Scattering).

Scepticism; Scornful; Scruples; Seclusive; Secretive; Self-Indulgent; Sensational; Sensitive; Sensuous; Serious-Minded—(See Serious).

Severe; Sex Addict — (See Addicts; "Addict" under Sex).

Shallow Mind—(See "Shallow" under Mental; "Light" in Sec. 1 of this Article).

Shameless; Simple-Minded — (See Foolish, Idiocy, Imbecile; "Weak Mind" in this section).

Sleepiness—Drowsiness—(See Sleep).

Sleep-Walking—(See Sleep).

Slow Mental Development — Slow of Speech—(See "Arrested" under Mental; "Slow" under Speech).

Sluggish Mind—(See Dull; "Persons" under Sluggish).

Solitude—Fond of—(See Solitude).

Somnambulism—(See Sleep).

Sorrowful Spirit — (See Grief, Sad, Sorrow).

Speech—Disorders of—(See Speech).

State of Mind — Disorders Arising From — The ☉ afflicted in ♒. (See "State of the Mind" under Disease; "Mind" under Indifferent; "Mind and Body" in this section).

Stopped—Growth of the Mind Stopped —Retarded—Arrested—(See Dwarfed, Growth, Idiocy, Imbecile; "Arrested" under Mental; "Weak" in this section).

Storms—Brain and Psychic Storms— (See "Brain Storms" under Brain; Psychic).

Strain — The Mind Should Be Kept Free from Over-Strain—☿ afflicted in ♓. (See "Strain" under Mental).

Strange Terrors — (See "Terrors" in this section).

Strong Fits—(See Fits).

Studies—Loses Interest In Studies— Fails In Examinations—(See Examinations; "Void Of" under Learning; "Shallow" under Mental; "Light In Mind" in Sec. 1 of this Article).

Stupor—Mental Stupor—(See Apathy; "Brain Fag" under Brain; Dull, Fatigue, Idle, Lassitude, Lethargy; "Drowsiness", "Stupor", under Sleep).

Stuttering — (See "Stammering" under Speech).

Suffering In Mind — (See Anguish, Anxiety; "Hopeless" under Hope; Melancholy; "Irritations" under Mental; Worry; "No Peace of Mind" in this section).

Suggestion—Easily Affected By—(See Suggestion).

Suicidal Mania—(See Suicide).

Superficial Mind — (See "Superficial" in Sec. 1 of this Article).

Supersensitive; Swindler; Tact—Lack of—(See "Bad" under Judgment).

Tastes — Disorders of — Perverted — (See Tastes).

Temper—(See Anger, Choleric; "High" under Temper).

Terrors — Strange Terrors of Mind — (See "Terrors" under Strange).

Thieves; Thinking—Rash and Uncontrolled Thinking—(See Anger, Brutish, Choleric, Cruel, Jealousy, Rashness; "High Temper" under Temper; Uncontrolled, etc.).

Thoughtless — (See Foolhardy, Forethought, Judgment, Rashness, Reckless; "Absent-Minded" in this section).

Threatened—The Mind Threatened— (See "Mind Threatened" in this section).

Thyroid Gland—Disorders of—Relation of To the Mind—(See Thyroid).

Tormented—In Mind—(See Anguish, Anxiety, Dejected, Depressed, Despondency, Disgrace, Gloom, Grief, Melancholy, Misery, Misfortune, Pain, Reverses, Ruin, Scandal, Sorrow, Suffering, Tormented, Worry, Wretched).

Torpid Mind—(See Torpid).

Trance; Treatment — Of Mental Disorders — (See Colors, Cure, Healers, Hypnotism; "Treatment" under Insanity; Mesmerism, Suggestion, Treatment).

Triple Personality—(See Personality).

Trouble—In the Mind—In the Mind and Body — Troubled In Mind — (See "Mental" under Infirmities; "Irritations" under Mental; "Mind and Body", "Tormented", in this section).

Turbulent Mind — (See "Turbulent" under Fancies; Riotous).

Twelfth House — Mental Disorders Caused By—(See Limitations, Twelfth House).

Unbalanced Mind—(See "Unbalanced" under Mental).

Uncanny Feelings—(See Uncanny).

Uncertain—The Mind Uncertain—(See Chaotic, Changeable, Confused, Mutable, Negative, Removals, Restless, Scattering, Vacillating, Worry, etc.).

Unclean Mind — (See Debauched, Depraved, Dissipated, Evil, Lewd, Licentious; "Loose Morals" under Morals; Obscene, Perversions, Shameless, Wanton, Wicked, etc.).

Unconsciousness — (See the subjects and references under Unconsciousness).

Uncontrolled Thinking—(See "Thinking" in this section; Uncontrolled).

Understanding — (See "Weak" under Understanding).

Undesirable Mental Traits—

The following subjects have to do with the Mind, its Afflictions, Deviations, Abnormalities, and Undesirable Traits of Mind. See these subjects in the alphabetical arrangement—Agitation, Agony, Ambition (Of No Ambition); Amorous, Anarchists, Anger, Artifice, Assassins, Astral Body, Asylums, Ataxia, Atony, Atrabile, Austere, Aversions, Awkwardness, Bachelors, Backwardness, Begging, Binding, Bold, Brutish, Careless, Cares (Full of); Celibacy, Cheating, Clumsiness, Coarse, Complaining, Countenance, Critical, Curious, Dangerous, Debauched, Deceitful, Denegerate, Dirty, Disagreeable, Discomposed, Discontentment, Disgraceful, Dishonorable, Dislikes, Disorderly, Disorganized, Disrespectful (see Respect); Disputes, Dissatisfied, Dissipated, Dissolute, Divination, Doleful, Downcast, Drunkenness, Ease (Fond of); Enemy (His Own Worst Enemy); Enmity (Strong In); Environment (Much Affected By); Epicureans; Expense (Prodigal of); Explosive Manner; Extravagant, Fading, Failure, Fate, Fault-finding, Feasting, Ferocious, Fierce, Fiery, Fighting, Forgers, Free Love (see **Free**); Fretfulness, Frivolous, Grave,

Gross, Hard Nature (see Hard); Harmful, Harsh, Hasty, Helplessness, Honour (Loss of); Hope (Lack of); Hurtful, Hypocritical, Ignoble, Ill-Disposed, Illicit Appetites (see Appetites); Immoderate, Immodest, Immoral (see Morals); Impetuous, Improper, Imprudent, Impure Morals (see Morals); Incest, Incompatibility, Inconstant, Indecent, Indigent, Indiscreet, Indisposition, Indolent, Indulgent, Inertia, Infamous, Inflexible, Influenced, Inharmony, Injudicious, Inordinate, Insatiable, Intercourse, Intoxication, Intractable, Introversion, Irascible, Irregular, Joy (No Joy); Lamenting, Lazy, Libidinous, Lugubrious, Materialistic, Mean-Spirited (see **Mean**); Meddlers, Misanthropic, Mischievous, Miserable, Miserly, Mistrustful, Misunderstood, Mockery, Moping, Mournful, Murmuring, Nasty Temper (see Temper); Neglectful, Notoriety, Obstinate, Odd, Offended Easily, Outrageous, Over-Indulgent, Penurious, Perverse, Precipitate, Prejudiced, Prudery, Quarrelsome, Queer, Rakishness, Rapacious, Rebellious, Refractory, Regretful, Repining, Resentful, Resigned, Roving, Salacious, Sanctimonious, Saucy, Scheming, Scolding, Scornful, Seclusive, Sedate, Selfish, Servile, Shrewd, Shy, Slothful, Superstitious, Suspicious, Taciturn, Treacherous, Ugly Disposition, Uncertain, Uncleanly, Uncontrolled, Unhappy, Untidy, Vacillating, Vicious, Wanton, Wicked, Wrangling, Wrathful, etc. (See "Desirable Mental Traits" in Sec. 1 of this Article; "Undesirable" under Mental).

Uneasiness of Mind—(See Uneasiness).

Unfertile Mind — (See "Unfertile" in Sec. 1 of this Article).

Ungovernable—Intractable—Insubordinate—(See Ungovernable).

Unhealthy—Unhealthy State of the Mind—(See "Diseased Mind", and the various paragraphs in this section, and under Mental).

Unmanageable — (See "Outrageous" under Insanity; Ungovernable, Unmanageable).

Unnatural Acts — (See Perversions, Unnatural).

Unreasonable—(See Reason).

Unrefined—A Coarse Body and Mind (See Coarse, Unrefined).

Unreliable—(See Deceitful, Dishonest, Mutable, Unreliable, Vacillating; Light, Shallow, Superficial, in this section).

Unruly—(See Rebellious, Ungovernable, Unmanageable, Unruly).

Unsavory Subjects—The Mind Morbid Upon—(See Unsavory).

Unsettled Mind—And Habits—(See "Unsettled" under Habits; "Instability" in this section).

Unsound Mind—(See "Derangement", "Unbalanced", under Mental; Unsound; "Diseased", and the various paragraphs in this section).

Unstable—Unstable and Weak Mind —Unsteady — (See Chaotic, Confused; "Shallow" under Mentality; Mutable, Negative, Restless, Unsettled, Unstable, Vacillating; Instability, Light, Uncertain, Weak, in this section).

Vagabond; Vagaries—Mind Full of—(See Vagaries).

Vague; Vain Fears—(See Fears).

Vapors—Low Spirits—(See Low, Vapors).

Vehement; Vertigo; Vexations; Vibrations—Mental Vibrations Stopped—(See Vibrations).

Vices; Vile Wretch—(See Vile).

Violent Tendencies—(See Violent).

Virgo Sign—A Sign Ruled by ☿, and the Diseases of ♍ are closely related to the Mind. (See Virgo).

Visions—Visionary Mind—(See Visions).

Vitiated—In Mind and Body—(See Vitiated).

Void Of—Void of Reason—Void of Solid Learning, etc.—(See Learning, Reason, Void Of).

Volition—Loss of—(See Volition, Will).

Voluntary Power—Excessive—(See Voluntary).

Voracious; Vulgar—(See Unrefined).

Wakefulness—(See Sleep).

Wandering Mind—(See Chaotic; "Inability" under Concentration; Dreamy, Wandering, etc.).

Warlike—(See War).

Wayward State of Mind—(See Conduct, Criminal, Debauched, Dissipated, Drink, Drunkenness, Morals, Prodigal, Recklessness, etc.).

Weak Mind—Weak and Unstable—Very Weak Mind—Weak-Minded—The ☉ Sig. ⚹ or △ ♄, and ♄ be weak and ill-dignified at B.; ☿ ill-dig. and ☌ ♄ as Significator. (See Foolish, Idiocy, Imbecile, Intellect; "Weak" under Mental; Prenatal; "Diseased", and the various paragraphs in this section). Case of Weak Mind—Birth Data, etc.—See "Weak Mind", No. 145 in 1001 N.N.

Weakened—The Mental Faculties Weakened—(See "Weakened" under Mental; "Weak" in this section).

Weaknesses—Mental Weaknesses—Tendency To—Observe the positions of the ☽, ☿, and the Asc. These unconnected with each other, and afflicted by ♄ and ♂, tend to mental diseases and weaknesses. (See "Weaknesses" under Mental).

Weariness—Of Mind and Body—(See Weariness).

Weeping—Crying Spells—(See the Introduction under Emotions).

Weird Mind—(See Weird).

Wench; Wife—Mind Unsound In—(See "Mind" under Wife).

Wild Delirium—Wild Nature—(See Delirium, Wild).

Will—Weak Will—(See Will).

Wisdom—Lacking In—(See Wisdom).

Wishes—Thwarted—Perverted, etc.—(See Ambitions, Desires, Hopes, Wishes).

Witchcraft; Women—Mental Disorders of—(See Fainting, Hysteria; "Mad Mother" under Madness; Nymphomania; "Mania" under Puerperal).

Words—Loss of—(See "Aphasia" under Speech).

Worry; Wretched; Wrong-Thinking—Wrong Habits—(See Wrong).

Zeal—Intemperate Zeal—Fanatical—Irrational—(See Anarchists, Erratic; "Mental Extremes" under Extremes; Fanatical, Irrational, Irresponsible, Reformers, Religion, Zeal).

MINERAL—Minerals—Mineral Salts—The Minerals of the body are connected with the Earthy Signs ♉, ♍, ♑. (See "Earth Signs" under Earth). The earthy minerals carried by the blood, which are used to form the bony structures, and also the concretions in soft tissues, are ruled by ♄ and the ♑ sign. Saturn rules the bones, and supplies the minerals to the bones, and an afflicted, weak, and ill-dignified ♄, will tend to weaken his action and influence in this regard, and to cause disorders of the bones. (See Bones).

Blood—The Mineral Salts of the Blood Deficient—The Prog. ☽ in ♍, ☌, □, or ☍ ♄ and other malefics; ♄ afflicted in ♍, thru the obstruction of intestinal digestion and assimilation, and indirectly denying the bones and muscles the necessary minerals for their strength, and often resulting in Rickets or Tetanus. (See Rickets; "Influence Of" under Saturn; Tetanus).

Deposits of Minerals—Excess Mineral Deposits Over the Body, Causing Disease—Caused by ♄ and his afflictions, and tend to such ailments as Stone, Calculus, Sand, Gravel, Gout, Rheumatism, Hardening of the Arteries, Deformities, Contortions, the Retention of Wastes, Suppression of the Functions, and the Retarding of Elimination and the Secretions. Leukocytes, ruled by ♄, form a nucleus for mineral deposits. (See these subjects just mentioned. Also see Chalk, Concretions, Crystallization, Deposits, Hardening, Hyperacidity, Impure, Leukocytes, Lime, Retention, Suppression, Tumors, Urea, Uric Acid, Wastes, etc).

Mineral Waters—(See "Mineral Waters" under Healers).

Planets and Minerals—Each Planet has rule over a Mineral, Minerals or Metal—(See Metals; "Drugs", "Metal", Minerals", "Typical Drugs", under each of the Planets).

Zodiac Mineral Salts—(See "Salts" under Zodiac). See Antipathy; "Cure of Disease" under Cure; Drugs, Herbs, Medicines, Opposites, Remedies, Salts, Sympathy, Treatment.

MINES—Mines and Mining Concerns are ruled by ♄, and great riches are often gained if the native has ♃ at B. in ⚹ or △ ♄, and espec. with ♃ in the 2nd H.

Death In Mines—Danger of Accident, Injury, or Death In Mines—♄ ☌ ♂ in ♉, □, ♌, or ♏ in the 4th H., and upon the lower Meridian; the 19° ♑ upon the Asc. at B.

MINIMIZING—Of the Disease—The disease is weakened, minimized, and largely neutralized, when the attributes of the afflicting planets are conflicting and opposing, as when the ☉ and ♄ are the afflictors, as the ☉ opposes ♄, and are opposites in influence. (See Abatement, Amelioration, Antipathy, Crises; "Minimizing" under Disease; Mild, Minor, Moderation, Opposites, Sympathy).

MINISTERS — Clergymen — Priests — Anxiety To—(See Clergymen).

MINOR—Minor Ailments—Minor Bodily Disorders—The Disease Is Not So Important — Mild Disorders — Minor Ailments are ruled by the ☽. These disorders usually occur from the ☽ being posited in a Tropical or Equinocial Sign, which are the cardial signs. (See Cardinal, Equinoxes, Minimizing, Slight, Tropical). The Benefic Planets in a sign, and also the absence of a malefic from a sign, tend to lessen the diseases to the parts of the body ruled by such signs, and to give minor, mild, and slight disorders to that part, and not as malignant or severe.

Minor Fevers — (See "Slight" under Fevers).

Minor Planets—♀ and ☿. (See Major, Mercury, Venus).

Minor Spasm—(See Twitchings).

Minor Throat Ailments—(See "Minor" under Throat).

Women — Minor Disorders of — (See "Minor" under Women).

MINT—Peppermint—(See Mentha).

MIRTH — Mirthful — Joyful — ♃ and ♀ are the planets of Mirth, Joy, Good Cheer, Happiness, Peace and Contentment, when they are strong and well-aspected at B., and the rulers of the horoscope. The Hebrew letter Qoph (K) is connected with the ♓ sign, the sign of ♃, and is predominant in Mirth. For the value of the Hebrew letters of the alphabet, and their connection with Astrology, every student should read the book, "The Tarot of the Bohemians" by Papus. (See Joy).

MISANTHROPIC — Distrust — Mistrustful—Hatred of Mankind—Suspicious—♄ influence; the ☽ to the ☌ or ill-asp. ♄ by dir., and ♄ weak, ill-dig., and afflicted at B. (See Aversions, Hatred, Miserly, Mistrustful, Penurious, Recluse, Seclusive, Secretive, Selfishness, Suspicious).

MISCARRIAGE — Abortion — Premature Birth — Death by Miscarriage — (See "Death by Miscarriages" under Abortion; "Death" under Hemorrhage; Parturition). Cases of Death by Miscarriage—(See "Cases" under Abortion; "Premature Birth" under Premature). Cases of Miscarriage and Premature Birth are often caused when several of the Moon's librations do not return to, and cross the central line of impulse at the monthly period during gestation, thus causing a lack of equilibrium, and an unbalanced condition of the Foetus. (See Prenatal Epoch).

MISCHANCES — Mishaps — Misfortune — "Bad Luck", etc.—(See Accidents, Danger, Fate; "Malice of Fortune" under Fortune; Injury, Luck, Misfortune, Perils, Unfortunate, Wounds, etc.).

MISCHIEF — Mischievous — Pranks — Evil—Damage—Vexations—Injury, etc. —Mischief is usually the result of ♂ being strong in a nativity, and ♂ aspecting ☿. Mischief mixed with the element of covetousness, envy, malice, or revenge, is associated with ♄.

Active to Do Mischief—Mischievous—Tricky—Artful—The ☽ applying to ♂, or conjoined with him in a nocturnal geniture; ♄ Sig. in ♓, active to do mischief; in Hor'y Q. ♄ Sig. in ♏; ♄ Sig. □ or ☍ ☿; ♂ Sig. in ♓; ♂ strong at B., and afflicting ☿; ♀ Sig. □ or ☍ ♄ or ♂, full of mischief. (See Artifice, Cheating, Deceitful, Dishonest, Enemies, Evil, Forgers, Gamblers, Knavish, Liars, Libelers, Malevolent, Malicious, Pettifogging, Poisoner, Scandalmonger, Thieves, Treachery, Trickery, Vicious, Violent, etc.).

Common People — Mischief To — (See Public).

Danger from Mischief—The ☽ to Castor, Cauda, Lucida, and Caput Algol; the ☽ to the place of Hydra's Heart, and espec. for women; ♅ passing over the place of ♂ at B. by tr., or at a Solar Rev., some sudden and serious mischief to the native; ♂ at a Solar Rev. passing the radical ♅, and espec. if the ☉, ☽, Asc., or M.C. were afflicted by ♅ at B.

Dryness — Mischief and Destruction from Dryness—(See Drouth, Dryness, Famine, Heat, etc.).

Enemies — Mischief By — (See Enemies).

Every One—Mischief to Every One—An eclipse of the ☽ in the 2nd Decan. of ♎, mischief and trouble to every one. (See Prevalent, Public, Trouble).

Fevers — Mischievous Fevers — (See Fever).

Full of Mischief—♀ Sig. ☌, □, or ☍ ♄; ♂ Sig. in ♓ if in terms of ☿. (See "Active" in this section).

Mischief At Hand—The ☽ or lord of the 1st H. in the 6th, 8th, or 12th H., afflicted, combust, ☌, □, or ☍ lords of the 4th, 6th, 8th, or 12th H., slow in motion, out of dignity, and with no assistance from benefics. These influences at B., and the ☽ or lord of the 1st afflicted by dir., tend to bring some calamity, mischief, misfortune, and suffering upon the native. (See Accidents, Air, Blows, Burns, Calamity, Danger, Death, Disgrace, Drowning, Earthquakes, Epidemics, Events, Falls, Famine, Fire, Flood, Grief, Heat, Highwaymen, Honour, Hurt, Injury, Misfortune, Murdered, Perils, Pestilence, Pirates, Public, Reputation, Reverses, Robbers, Ruin, Scandal, Shipwreck, Sickness, Sorrow, Storms, Thieves, Travel, Trouble, Vehicles, Violence, Weather, Wind, Wounds, etc. Also look in the alphabetical arrangement for the subject you have in mind).

MISERABLE — Misery — Miseries — Full of Afflictions — All manner of afflictions, and miseries, are ruled by the 12th H., and with ♄ or ♂ afflicted in this house; lord of the 12th in the 1st H., much misery, or illness from folly; the ☽ or ♃ Sig. □ or ☍ ♄. (See Affliction, Folly, Indiscretions, Misfortune, Sorrow, Suffering, Trouble, Twelfth House).

Dies a Miserable Death — (See Beheaded; "Miserable" under Death; Execution, Hanging, Murdered, Painful, Poison Death (see Poison); Tragical).

Has Many Miseries—(See "Many Afflictions" under Affliction).

Much Misery Everywhere—Much Misery Generally—♄ in ♍ at a Solar Ingress, or an Eclipse, in ☐ to ♂ in ♊, and the ☽ in ♐ in aspect with both ♄ and ♂, much misery, destruction of Kingdoms, and Revolutions, and espec. if the New ☽ immediately preceding or following these aspects should happen to be an eclipse, and the Countries affected most will be those ruled by the signs containing the malefics and the darkened Luminary. In cases of a Solar Eclipse, the miseries will be especially felt in places over which the central line of the eclipse passes. Saturn in ♎, ℞, and in ☍ the ☉, and the ☉ at the same time in evil configuration with ♂ ℞ at a Solar Ingress or Eclipse, there will be misery upon misery. (See Accidents, Affliction, Calamity, Casualties, Cholera, Comets, Crime, Dangers, Drought, Earthquakes, Eclipses, Epidemics, Events, Evils, Famine, Floods, Grief, Heat (Excessive); Humanity, Lightning, Lynching, Mankind, Mischief, Misfortune, Mobs, Mortality Great, Murders, Pestilence, Plague, Prevalent, Prisons, Public, Railroads, Riots, Robberies, Sadness, Seas, Ships, Shipwrecks, Sorrow, Storms, Suffering, Travel, Trouble, Twelfth House, Vernal Equinox, Violence, Volcanoes, Voyages, War, Water, Weather, Wind, etc.).

MISERLY—Avaricious—Covetous—Niggardly—Rapacious—Envious—Sordid—Selfish, etc.—A ♄ characteristic, and caused by ♄ afflictions; ♄ ruler of the Asc., or the horoscope, at B., and afflicted; ♄ Sig. in ♑; ♄ in ♉ or ♍, avaricious; ♄ in ♑, covetous; ♄ or ☋ in the Asc. or 10th H.; in Hor'y Q. ♄ as Sig. of the person; the ☉ Sig. ☐ or ☍ ♄; the ☽ Sig. ☌ ♄, extremely covetous; the ☽ Sig. in ♍; ♃ Sig. in ♍, ♏, or ♑; ☿ Sig. ☌ ♄; many influences in fixed signs at B.; ♒ and ♄ combinations in the 2nd H. (See Misanthropic, Penurious, Recluse, Secretive, Selfishness, Solitude).

MISFORTUNE—Adversity—Ill-Fortune—Calamity, etc.—The 12th H. is the house of sorrow, disgrace, and misfortune. The quality and time of the misfortune are usually denoted by the Map of Birth, and by the afflictions to that map by transits, directions, and progressions.

Causes His Own Misfortunes—Causes His Own Illnesses—(See "Brings Disease Upon Himself" under Disease; Disgrace; "His Own Worst Enemy" under Enemies; "Ruined by Women" under Love Affairs; Ruin, Self-Undoing).

Child of Misfortune—The Complete Child of Misfortune—♄ on the Meridian at B., or coming to it, and ill-aspected and ill-dignified; ♄ on or near the Nadir, the cusp of the 4th H., is almost as unfortunate.

Children—Misfortune To—(See "Accidents", and the various paragraphs under Childhood, Children, Infancy. Also for Misfortunes and Afflictions to members of the family, see the various paragraphs under Aunts, Brother, Daughter, Family, Father, Females, Friends, Grandparents, Husband, Males, Men, Mother, Relatives, Sister, Son, Uncles, Wife, Women).

Common People—Misfortune To—(See Public).

Face—Misfortune To—(See Cuts, Hurts, and the various paragraphs under Face. Also for misfortune and affliction to the various parts of the body, look in the alphabetical arrangement for the part you have in mind, such as Arms, Eyes, Feet, Hands, Head, Hips, Legs, Shoulders, etc.).

Liable to Misfortune—Subject To—Danger of—The ☉ rising at B., and afflicted by the ☌, ☐, or ☍ ♄; the ☉ Sig. ☐ or ☍ ♄; the ☽ to the ☌, ☐, or ☍ ♄ or ♂ by dir.; the ☽ to Deneb, misfortune by water or vehicles; the ☽ to the ☌ or P. Dec. South Scale; the ☽ decr. in light, sepr. from ♃ and apply. to ♄; the ☽ sepr. from ♂ and apply. to the ☉; ♄ rising or setting at B.; ♄ near the Meridian, or coming to, or on or near the Nadir; ♄ in the 10th H. in detriment or fall, sudden disgrace and irretrievable ruin; ♄ in the 10th H. in a Solar Rev., and elevated above the Lights; ♄ to his own bad aspects by dir.; ♃ and ♀ cadent and under the Earth; ♂ in detriment and ☍ the Asc.; malefics in the 10th H., and afflicted; malefics elevated above the Lights, and afflicted (see Elevated); malefics rising and in angles, and the benefics setting and ill-dignified; lord of the 12th H. in the 8th, and usually ends in a miserable death; the M.C. to the ☌ or P. Dec. the ☉ if the ☉ is afflicted at B. by malefics, or is in ☌ violent fixed stars. In Hor'y Q. the lord of the 12th H. also being lord of the Asc. Almost every subject in this book has to do with some affliction, or misfortune to the native. See the following subjects, and also look in the alphabetical arrangement for other subjects along this line you may have in mind. (See Accidents, Affliction, Air, Assassinated, Bathings, Blows, Burns, Calamity, Cuts, Destiny, Detriment, Directions, Disease, Disgrace, Drowning, Earth, Events, Evils, Execution, Exile, Falls, Fate, Fire, Folly, Fortune (see "Evil", "Ill-Fortune", "Malice of Fortune", under Fortune); Grief, Highwaymen, Honour (Loss of); Ill-Fortune (see Fortune); Ill-Health, Imprisonment (see Prison); Indiscretions, Injury, Malice of Fortune (see Fortune); Mischief, Miseries, Murdered, Pirates, Poverty, Recklessness, Reputation (Loss of); Reverses, Robbers, Ruin, Scandal, Sea, Ships, Sickness, Sorrow, Stabs, Thieves, Trouble, Tragical, Twelfth House, Unfortunate, Untimely, Vehicles, Violence, Water, Weather, Wind, Wounds, etc., and various other subjects too numerous to list here).

Malice of Fortune—(See "Malice" under Fortune).

Mankind—Misfortune To—(See "Much Misery Everywhere" under Miseries).

Much Misfortune Generally—(See Calamity, Drought, Eclipses, Epidemics, Famine, Grief, Humanity, Mankind, Mischief, Miseries, Panics, Pestilence, Plague, Prevalent, Public, Sorrow, Suffering, Trouble; "Liable to Misfortune" in this section).

Public Misfortune — (See Calamity, Drought, Earthquakes, Epidemics, Famine, Floods; "Much Misery Everywhere" under Misery; Pestilence, Plague, Public, Storms, etc.).

Remarkable Misfortunes — ♅ ascending at B., or with the chief Significator. (See Extraordinary, Mysterious, Peculiar, Strange, Sudden, Tragical, Uncommon, Untimely, etc.).

Some Misfortune Near — Mischief At Hand — (See "Threatened" under Calamity; "Near Some Danger" under Danger; Imminent; "Mischief At Hand" under Mischief; Perils, Public; "Near Relatives" under Relatives; Sudden, Tragedy, etc.).

Time of Misfortune—(See "Time" under Accidents; Directions, Disease, Events, Time; "Some Misfortune Near" in this section).

Vehicles—Misfortune By—(See Journeys, Railroads, Ships, Travel, Vehicles, Voyages).

Water — Misfortune By — (See Bathings, Drowning, Floods; "Hot Liquids" under Heat; Moisture, Rain, Scalds, Sea, Water, etc.).

Women — Much Misfortune, Sickness, Sorrow, and Trouble to Women — The ☽ incr. at B., and apply. to ♄; the ☽ to the ill-asps. the ☉, ♄, or ♀ by dir.; ♂ in ♉ at the Vernal Equi., occi., and Lord of the Year; ♄ in ♍ at the Vernal, ori., and Lord of the Year; ♎ ascending at a Vernal Equi., and ♀ afflicted, tends to much suffering, ill-health and trouble for women during the following Quarter. (See the various paragraphs under Females, Women).

Wounds — Hurts — Injuries — Misfortune By — (See Accidents, Ambushes, Assaults, Bloodshed, Blows, Burns, Cuts, Crushed, Duels, Enemies, Gunshot, Hurts, Injury, Instruments, Iron, Mobs, Operations, Plots, Poison, Robbers, Stabs, Stones (see "Flying Stones" under Stones); Sword, Trampled, Treachery, Weapons, Wounds, etc.).

MISHAPS—(See Accidents, Injury, Mischances, Misfortune, Wounds, etc.).

MISSHAPED — Misshaped Body — (See Contortions, Crooked, Deformities, Distortions; "Ill-Formed" under Ill; Malformations, Missing, Monsters, Twins, Ugly, etc.).

Misshaped Bones — (See "Misshaped" under Bones).

Misshaped Legs—(See Bad, Bent, Bow Legs, Crooked, Ill-Formed, Knock-Knees, One Leg Shorter, Strikes Legs Together, and the various paragraphs under Legs).

Organs Misshaped — Or Undersized — (See Diminished, Enlargements; "Misshaped" under Organs; Undersized, Undeveloped).

MISSING—Missing Members, or Parts Thereof — (See "Missing" under Arms, Feet, Forearm, Hands, Legs, Toes). The case of the famous Frog Child, with both forearms missing from birth, and both legs missing below the knees, is given under Forearm. There are cases of record born with both arms and both legs completely missing. I saw such a case, a lady, with a Circus, but failed to get her birth data. These cases are caused by Prenatal afflictions. (See Prenatal Epoch). The case of the Frog Child is illustrated and written up in the book, "The Prenatal Epoch", by Mr. Bailey, Editor of the British Journal of Astrology.

MISTRUSTFUL—Mistrustful of Others —Misanthropic—Suspicious—Cautious —The ☉ Sig. ☌ ♄; the ☉ ☌, □, ☍, or P. ♄; the ☽ Sig. ☌ ♄, much suspicious caution; ♄ to the ill-asps. his own place by dir. or tr.; ♄ Sig. ⚹ or △ the ☽; ♄ Sig. in ♓; the evil directions of ♄ to the ☉, ☽, ☿, the Asc. or M.C.; ♃ afflicted in ♍; ♀ ill-dig. at B.; ♂ or ☿ Sig. ⚹ or △ ♄. (See Jealousy, Misanthropic, Selfishness, Suspicious).

MISUNDERSTOOD—Misjudged—Misunderstandings—Not Easy to Understand —Eccentric—The ☉ ☌ ♅ at B.; the ☽ applying to the ☌ or any asp. of ♆ or ♅, difficult to understand; ♆ or ♅ in the Asc. or M.C.; ♂ afflicting the ☉ or ☽, apt to have many disputes and misunderstandings; afflictions between ☿ and ♃; the bicorporeal sign influence strong at B., on angles, and containing many planets; born when there are many □ aspects to a planet, and espec. to ♀ or ☿, or planets ascending at B. (See Eccentric, Fancies, Ideals, Ideas, Independent, Notions, Occult, Metaphysics, Mystical, Peculiar, Persecution, Quarrels, Reformers, Religion).

MITRAL DISORDERS — (See "Mitral" under Heart).

MIXED—Blends—Combinations—

Mixed Colors—Spotted Colors—(See "Clothing", "Mixed", under Colors).

Mixed Diseases—(See "Complications" under Disease).

Mixed Fevers — (See "Mixed" under Fever).

Mixed Fracture—Fracture with Laceration — (See "Compound" under Fracture).

Mixed Ideas — Mixed and Confused Ideas—(See Chaotic, Confused, Ideas).

MOBILITY—(See Action, Gait, Locomotion, Motion, Movement, Walk).

MOBS—Death or Injury By—Death by Mob Violence—Violent Death By—The ☉ □ or ☍ ♂ by dir. in a map where violent death is indicated; the □ and ☍ aspects of the ☽ to the Significators, death or injury by the Common People in Mobs or Riots; ♅ in the 8th H. and afflicting the hyleg by dir., and other testimonies concurring for a violent death; ♄ in a fixed sign, □ or ☍ the ☉, and contrary in condition, or with ♄ occi., and the ☽ be succedent to him. (See "Burned At Stake" under Burns; Common People (see Common); Crushed, Hanging, Impalement, Lynched, Riots; "Assaults" under Stone; Trampled).

MOCKERY — Shams — A False Show — Derisive—Delusive—♂ ruler at B., and afflicted. (See Deceitful, Dual-Minded, Hypocritical, Liars, Pretender, Sardonic, Scornful).

MODERATE — Moderate In Size — Moderate and Temperate In Habits, etc.—

Drink — Moderate Drinker — (See "Moderate" under Drink).

Eating—(See "Moderate" under Eating).

Habits—Moderate In—(See "Habits" under Temperance).

Hair—Moderate Growth of Hair—Moderate Curling—(See "Moderate" under Hair).

Immoderate—(See "Eating", "Habits", under Immoderate).

Stature—Moderate Stature—The ☉ in ♋, or ♋ on the Asc.; ♂ occi. at B.; ♄ in ♌ partile asp. the Asc.; ♈, ♉, ♎, or ♏ on the Asc., moderate in stature but rather long; ♈ on the Asc., a spare, dry, moderate-sized, strong body; ♑, ♒, or ♓ on the Asc., or the ☉ or ☽ in these signs. (See "Mean Stature" under Mean; "Medium Stature" under Medium; Middle; "Stature" under Moderately).

Vitality—Moderate Vitality—(See "Medium" under Vitality).

MODERATELY—Fairly Good—Medium—

Complexion—Moderately Good Complexion—Moderately Fair—(See Fair, Middling, Moderately, Tolerably, under Complexion).

Fortunate—(See "Moderately Fortunate" under Fortune).

Fruitful—(See "Moderately" under Fruitful).

Good Health—Moderately Good—(See "Tolerably Healthy" under Health).

Moderately Large Body—♄ in ♌ in partile asp. the Asc. (See "Middle Stature" under Middle; "Stature" under Moderate).

Proportioned—Moderately Proportioned Stature—♍, ♎, ♓, and the first parts of ♒ give a moderately proportioned body when on the Asc., but the latter part of ♒ on the Asc., a spare and thin body. (See Well-Proportioned).

Signs—Moderately Strong Signs of the Zodiac—(See "Moderately Strong" under Signs).

Stature—Moderately Large Body—(See "Moderately Large" in this section).

Temperate—Moderately Temperate—(See Temperate).

MODERATION—Amelioration—Under Better Control—Abatement—

Habits and Affairs—Exercises Moderation In—(See "Moderate" under Drink, Eating, Habits; Temperance).

Moderation of Disease—Abatement or Amelioration of—The ☉ or ☽ angular, ori., and elevated above the malefics, and also the benefics in a strong position and well-aspected; a Solar Eclipse falling on the place of the radical ♃; the ☽ coming to the ⚹ or △ the lords of the Asc., 9th, 10th, or 11th H. brings an interval of ease and amendment; the Prog. ☽ ☌, ⚹, or △ ♃ or ♀ in the radical map; ♃ or ♀ ori., and elevated above the malefics; a good aspect of ♃ or ♀ to the ☉, ☽, Asc., or hyleg at the same time there are evil aspects from the malefics, tends to moderate the disease. Also ☿ configurated with ♃ gives the addition of skillful Healers, or the proper remedies and treatment. When a malefic applying to the ☽ at decumbiture passes the ☽, the patient gets better. Any disease will tend to be mitigated, ameliorated, or curable if the benefics be elevated above the malefics which produce it, and the more angular, ori., and elevated above the malefics the benefics may be, the more they assist in the cure and amelioration of the disease. When a train of evil directions and aspects indicate ill-health or death, the course of disease is modified and ameliorated when the good asps. of ♃ or ♀ to the hyleg intervene. A strong map of birth tends to modify disease and give greater powers of resistance, no matter how evil the directions. If an afflicted planet causing the disease is well-aspected by the benefics, as by ☌ or P. asp., then the evil will be mitigated. The afflicting planet turning ℞ tends to modify the disease. Planets passing from cardinal to common signs tend to a falling off in the power and degree of morbid action in disease, and to moderation and improvement. (See Amelioration, Antipathy, Continuity, Course, Crises, Curable; "Better" under Disease; Duration, Ease; "Disease" under Force; "Improved" under Health; Minimizing, Modification, Opposites, Prognosis, Recovery, Recuperation, Remission, Resistance, Retrograde; "Illnesses" under Short; Termination, Treatment; "Good" under Vitality; Worse, etc.).

MODESTY—♃ is the author of; ♀ Sig. ⚹ or △ ♄, modest, shy, and retiring. (See Backwardness, Bashfulness, Blushing; "Chaste" under Females; Gentle, Immodest, Manners, Meek, Prudery, Quiet, Reserved, Retiring, Shy, etc.).

MODIFICATION OF DISEASE—The horoscope as a whole should be studied in judging of the force or outcome of a disease, and not any one aspect, as the good aspects from the benefics, the ☉ or ☽, will tend to modify the disease in a fortunate map. If the radical map is generally weak, the disease would tend to be more severe. Each planet imparts a special type of disease to an organ, but the disease may become disguised, modified, or changed by cross aspects from other planets, by the afflicting planet passing from one sign or house to another, or turning ℞. Also at the crisis time in a disease, if it is acute, it will either resolve itself, or go into a chronic form, and especially if the disease has progressed for about 28 days, one revolution of the ☽ from the time it began. (See the references under Moderation. Also see "Crises" under Acute; "Long Chronic Distempers" under Chronic; Complications, Diagnosis; "Complications" under Disease; Fatal; "Disease" under Force, Judgment, Nature, Quality, Severity; Polarity, Worse, etc.).

MOISTURE—Moist—Dampness—Vapors—Humidity—Wet—Water, etc.—Moisture is a feminine quality and passive, and is a benefic influence given by the ☽, and the benefics ♃ and ♀, and also by the watery signs ♋, ♏, and ♓. The airy signs ♊, ♎, and ♒, are next in degree of moisture. Dryness and moisture are passive qualities, and heat and cold are active qualities. The ☽ is moist in quality, and generates moisture, dampness, and vapors. The ☽ rules largely over the radical moisture of the body, and its distribution, and contributes moisture of temperament to the body. The ☽ makes the constitution moist from the New ☽ to the 1st Quarter. Jupiter is warm and moist, being temperate in nature, and produces moisture when occidental. Venus gives off much moisture, gathers the moist vapors from the Earth, and causes moisture when occidental. Venus denotes death by epidemics, rottenness, and putrefactions which proceed from too much moisture. White, the color ruled by the ☽, is passive, and is the sign of radical moisture. The colors of ♃ and ♀ combined are signs of heat and moisture combined, as blue and yellow. Mercury produces moisture when femininely constituted, and dryness when masculine. Moisture is prolific and nutritive. Heat and Moisture combined are positive and tend to fermentation. (See Zymosis). The feminine signs of the Zodiac, the even signs, predominate in moisture. The elementary qualities of moist and dry alternate in the signs of the Zodiac, one being moist, and the next one dry, etc., on around thru the 12 Signs. The ☽ and ♀ Groups of Herbs and Plants have a cold and moist action, but some Authors say that the Herbs of ♆ have a moist and warm influence. Moisture largely predominates in the female sex, and is a female and passive quality. Moisture is more feeble in the left side of the body, as the left side is ruled by Cold. Damp vapors are caused by the nearness of the ☽ to the Earth, thus tending to cause putrefaction and relaxation of animal bodies. Humidity is ruled by the ☽. The following subjects have to do with Moisture, its influences and action, the diseases caused by, and its general effects upon Humanity.

Abundance of Moist Humours — And Suffering From—Over-Moist Air—Excess of Rain and Floods—The ♒ sign ascending at a Vernal Equi., and espec. in places ruled by this sign. (See Floods, Rain; "Moist" in this section).

Air—Over-Moist Air and Suffering From — (See "Abundance" in this section).

Bodily Temperament — Moist Bodily Temperament — The ☉, ☽, and many planets in watery signs, and abounds especially in ♏; a watery sign on the Asc.; ♃ or the ☽ occi.; those born in cold climates and the Arctics. (See "Body" under Cold).

Body — Moist Body — Moist and Cold Body—Hot and Moist Body—(See Bodily Temperament, Cold and Moist Body, Hot and Moist Body, in this section).

Brain—Moisture of—The ☽ coming to the ☌ ☉, and ruled by ♄, or the ☽ at her Full being ruled by ♂, and espec. when it may happen in ♎, ♐, or ♓. Under these conditions if the malefics be in Eastern Parts and in angles, and the benefics in the West, tend to demoniacal affections, and ♄ and the ☽ cooperating in the scheme contribute to moisture of the brain; the ☽ and ☿ unconnected with each other or the Asc., ♄ and ♂ angular and ori., and with ♃ and ♀ setting and occidental. (See "Wild" under Delirium; Demoniac; "Outrageous" under Insanity).

Clothing—Damp Clothing and Linen, Illness and Colds From—(See "Colds" in this section; "Linen" under Wet).

Clouds — Excessive Rain From, and Suffering to Humanity — (See Clouds, Floods, Rain).

Cold and Moist Body—Cold and Moist Bodily Temperament—The Phlegmatic, or Lymphatic Temperament — The watery signs ♋, ♏, or ♓ predominant at B., or upon the Asc.; ♄ produces, and espec. when ori.; given by the Quadrant from the Winter Tropic to the Vernal Equi.; characteristic of those born in cold climates and in the Arctics. The ☽ and ♀ groups of plants and herbs are cold and moist. (See "Body" under Cold; "Temperament" under Lymphatic, Phlegmatic).

Cold and Moist Diseases—Distempers, or Humours — (See "Cold and Moist" under Humours).

Cold and Moisture — Dampness and Cold, and Diseases or Fevers Arising From—Caused by ♄ or ♅; ♄ diseases. (See "Cold and Dampness" under Exposure; "Humours" under Watery).

Colds—Colds Taken from Wet Linen, Wet Feet, or from Living In Cold and Damp Places—Afflictions in ♓, and are ♓ diseases. (See Exposure; "Cold Taken" under Feet; Pneumonia; "Linen" under Wet).

Constitution—A Moist Body and Constitution—(See "Bodily Temperament" in this section).

Corruption of Moisture—Diseases Arising From—Caused by ♀. (See Corruption; "Superabundance" in this section).

Damp and Cold Places—Diseases from Living In — (See "Colds" in this section).

Damp Vapors—Caused by the ☽, and tend to Putrefaction and Relaxation of Animal Bodies. (See Putrefaction, Relaxation, in this section).

Dampness and Cold—Diseases Arising From—(See "Cold and Moisture" in this section).

Death — From Diseases Arising from Moisture — ♀ denotes death by Epidemics, Rottenness, and Putrefaction which proceed from too much moisture. (See "Superabundance" in this section).

Diseases — Diseases Proceeding from Moisture—Water signs on the Asc. or 6th H. at B., or at decumb., or the Sig. of the disease in a watery sign at the beginning of an illness. (See "Cold and Moist" under Humours; "Superabundance" in this section).

Distempers—(a) Cold and Moist Distempers — ♓ diseases. (See "Cold and Moist" under Humours). (b) Hot, Moist, and Putrid Distempers — (See "Hot and Moist Diseases" under Heat).

Epidemics—From Too Much Moisture —Caused by ♀. (See Epidemics; "Death" in this section).

Exposure to Dampness — Diseases Arising From—(See "Cold and Dampness" under Exposure; "Colds" in this section).

Eyelids—Excessive Moisture of—(See "Watery Eyes" under Tears).

Feet—Moist Humours In—(See "Humours" under Feet).

Fermentation — (See Fermentation; "Hot and Moist Body" in this section).

Fevers—Arising from Dampness and Cold—(See "Cold and Moisture" in this section).

Fluids of the Body—Disorders of—(See Fluids).

Head—Moist and Watery Humours In—(See "Moist Humours" under Head).

Hips—Moist Humours In—(See "Cold and Moist" under Hips).

Hot and Moist Body—Hot and Moist Bodily Temperament — The Sanguine Temperament—This is a positive temperament, and tends to produce fermentation. Is given by the Quadrant from the Asc. to the Nadir, the Summer Tropic, or during the passage of the ☉ thru the ♈, ♉, and ♊ Signs. Also the Airy Signs are hot and moist, and with the ☉ and many planets in these signs, or with an airy sign upon the Asc., and especially the ♒ sign. The New ☽ is hot and moist. Also ♃ when ori. tends to produce this temperament. (See "Hot and Moist Diseases" under Heat, and in this section; "Sanguine Temperament" under Sanguine).

Hot and Moist Diseases—Hot, Moist, and Putrid Diseases—Distempers—(See "Hot and Moist" under Heat). The body abounds in heat and moisture with ♈, ♉, or ♊ on the Asc., or with the ☉ or ☽ in these signs; ♃ ruler of the Asc., a hot and moist constitution. (See Humidity).

Humidity — Much Affected By — (See Humidity).

Humours — Abundance of Moist Humours — Moist Diseases and Humours — (See Abundance, Diseases, Distempers, Moist Diseases, Superabundance, in this section; "Moist Humours" under Head, Humours).

Journeys—Danger from Dampness On —(See "Travel" under Exposure, Health; "Wet" under Journeys; "Dampness" under Voyages).

Lack of Moisture — Diseases Arising From — (See Drought; "Superabundance" under Dryness; "Heat" under Epidemics; Famine, Fountains; "Extreme Heat" under Heat; Pestilence, Scarcity).

Left Side of Body—Suffers from Lack of Moisture—Cold and Moist Humours In — (See "Cold and Moist Humours" under Humours; "Feeble" under Left).

Linen — Colds and Disease from Wet Linen—(See "Colds" in this section).

Liquids—(See Liquids).

Living In Damp Places — Colds and Diseases From — (See "Colds" in this section).

Moist Body — (See "Bodily Temperament" in this section).

Moist and Cold Body—(See "Cold and Moist Body" in this section).

Moist and Cold Diseases—Distempers — Humours — (See "Cold and Moist" under Humours).

Moist Constitution — (See "Bodily Temperament" in this section).

Moist Diseases and Humours — Moist Distempers—The Body Over-Charged with Moist Humours — The ☽ afflicted in ♓; the ☽ to the ☌, P., ☐ or ☍ ♄, cold and moist humours; ♓ diseases; watery signs on the Asc. at B., moist humours; many planets in watery signs. (See "Moist Humours" under Feet, Head; "Cold and Moist" under Humours; "Abundance", "Diseases", "Distempers", in this section).

Moist and Hot Body — (See "Hot and Moist Body" in this section).

Moist and Hot Diseases — (See "Hot and Moist" in this section).

Moist Humours—(See "Moist Diseases" in this section).

Moist Signs—(See "Signs" in this section).

Moist Warmth—Moist and Warm Diseases—The physiological action of the ☽, and in Nature tending to rottenness and putrefaction. In the human body afflictions to the ☽, or by the ☽, and especially when the ☽ is ☌ ♂, tend to warm and moist, or hot and moist diseases. Also warm and moist diseases are diseases of ♆, ♃, and ♀. (See "Hot and Moist Diseases" in this section; "Moist and Warm" under Heat).

Moisture — Diseases Which Proceed From—(See "Diseases" and the various paragraphs in this section).

Moisture of the Brain—(See "Brain" in this section).

Odors — Foul Odors or Vapors — (See Foul, Odors; "Foul" under Vapors).

Over-Moist Air—(See "Abundance" in this section).

Places — Locations — Diseases Arising from Living In Damp Places — (See "Colds" in this section).

Planets—The Moist Planets—♃, ♀, ☽, and also ☿ when femininely constituted. Also ♆ is classed as moist, as ♓ is the strong sign of ♆, and ♆ rules the Sea. These planets, along with ♆, tend to cause moist diseases, or moist and warm diseases.

Putrefaction—Putrid Diseases—Death By — (See "Hot and Moist Diseases" under Heat; the various paragraphs under Putrid; "Relaxation" in this section).

Rain—Excess of, and Suffering From —(See Rain).

Relaxation and Moisture—Relaxation of Animal Bodies—Damp vapors caused by the nearness of the ☽ to the Earth, tend to cause putrefaction and relaxation of animal bodies. Also ♆ and ♀ tend to relaxation of the body and tissues, and to bring on moist diseases. (See Decay; "Moist and Warm" under Heat; Putrefaction, Relaxation).

Residence—Colds and Disorders from Living In Damp Places—(See "Colds" in this section).

Rivers—Rivers Fail—Corruption of—(See Rivers).

Rottenness—♀ denotes death by rottenness which proceeds from too much moisture. (See Rottenness).

Sanguine Temperament — A Moist Temperament. (See "Temperament" under Sanguine).

Sea—(See the various paragraphs under Ocean, Sea, Ships, Voyages).

Signs—The Moist Signs of the Zodiac —The watery signs ♋, ♏, ♓. The airy signs ♊, ♎, and ♒ are next in degree of moisture. Libra and ♒ are warm and moist signs.

Sudden Exposure—To Dampness, and Diseases Arising From — (See "Exposure" in this section).

Superabundance—Of Moisture — Suffering and Disease From—♀ influence tends to when the dominion of death is vested in her. (See Abundance, Air, Colds, Death, Diseases, Epidemics, Fevers, Moist Diseases, in this section; Floods, Rain, Storms, Water).

Temperament—(See Bodily Temperament, Cold and Moist Body, Hot and Moist Body, Sanguine, in this section).

Thighs and Hips—Cold and Moist Humours In—(See "Cold and Moist" under Hips).

Too Much Moisture—Diseases Arising From—(See Colds, Death, Superabundance, in this section).

Vapors — Damp Vapors — (See Damp Vapors, Relaxation, in this section; Vapors).

Voyages—Danger from Dampness On —(See "Dampness" under Voyages).

Warm and Moist Diseases—(See Hot and Moist Diseases, Moist Warmth, Relaxation, in this section).

Warmth—(See Moist Warmth, Relaxation, Warm and Moist, in this section).

Water—(See Water).

Watery Signs — (See "Signs" in this section).

White Color—Ruled by the ☽, and is the sign of radical moisture. (See White).

MOLECULAR NUTRITION—Under the rule of ♃. (See Nutrition).

MOLES — A Small, Brown, Cutaneous Spot — Marks tend to be Moles when the part is not afflicted by ♂. The ☉ alone in a sign, away from ♂, tends to a Mole rather than a Scar or Wound. (See Blemishes, Defects, Freckles, Marks, Scars). For the influences which cause Moles on the various parts of the body, see "Moles" under the part you have in mind. See "Moles" under such parts as Arms, Back, Breast, Face, Feet, Front, Knees, Left Side (see Left); Legs, Neck, Right Side (see Right); Shoulders, Thighs, Throat, etc. Many of the rules as to the location of Moles are given in the Articles on Marks and Scars, and also in this section in what follows.

Location of Moles — Examples of —

(1) A masculine sign on the Asc., and a masculine planet in the Asc., as ♎ on the Asc., and ♃ in the Asc., tends to a mole on the right side of the face. (See "Left Side", "Marks", under Face).

(2) The latter degrees of ♎ on the Asc. would indicate a mole on the lower part of the Reins near the Haunches.

(3) The first part of ♈ on the 6th H., a mole on the head near the hair, or on scalp. The middle part of ♈ on the cusp of the 1st or 6th, a mole near the middle of the right side of the face.

(4) ♂ lord of the 6th, in ♐, near the middle of the sign, and under the earth, shows a mole on the back part of the right thigh, near the middle of the thigh, and not as noticeable. If ♂ had been prominent and above the earth, the mole would be on the front of the thigh and more prominent.

(5) The ☽ in a female sign, and under the earth, indicates a mole on the left foot, under and near the extremity of the foot.

(6) ♓, a feminine sign, on the Asc. would denote a mole on the left cheek, as the Asc. rules the head and face. Also as ♓ rules the feet there would be a mole on the left foot.

(7) ♌, a masculine sign, on the 10th denotes a mole, scar, or mark on the right side, below the breast, as ♌ rules the Sides. Other examples might be mentioned. Learn the rules and you can apply them to any case. (See "Moles" under Left; "Organs" under Lower, Middle; Naevus; "Lower Part" under Organs; Right; "Organs" under Upper).

MOMENT—The Time of Events—

Moment of Action — Hesitates In — (See Chaotic, Confused, Dreamy; "Doubts" under Fears; Inconstant, Mutable, Negative, Restless, Vacillating, etc.).

Moment of Birth—The time when the child takes in its first breath, and makes the first cry, for it is at this time that the magnetic forces and vibrations of the Planets, Aspects, and Universe, etc., are stamped upon the native, and not when the cord is cut. The cord may be cut some minutes after the first cry and intake of breath. However, some Authorities take either time as the Moment of Birth, as Wilson does in his Dictionary of Astrology under the subject of "Nativity". The Moment of Birth, and the actual Map of Birth intended for the native, are usually a fixed time, and predetermined, and interferences with normal birth may change the map, and thus considerably interfere with, or change and modify the destiny of the individual. (See "Planetary Baptism" under Baptism; "Causes of Birth", "Moment of Birth", under Birth; Calamity; "Born" under Children; "Map of Birth" under Map; Nativity).

Moment of Conception—(See "Moment" under Conception; Prenatal Epoch). See Events, Time.

MONARCHS—(See Kings, President, Queens, Rulers).

MONDAY—Ruled by the ☽. (See Week).

MONEY—Reckless and Extravagant In the Use of — Disease and Suffering From, etc. — (See Appetites, Conduct, Debauched, Dissipated, Dress, Drink, Eating, Excesses, Expense, Extravagant, Feasting, Food, Fortune, Gambling, Generous, Gluttony, Habits,

Harlots, Love Affairs, Luxuries, Men (see "Health Injured" under Men); Passion, Pleasures, Poverty, Prodigal, Property, Prosperity, Recklessness, Resources, Reverses, Riches, Ruin, Social Life, Sports, Travel, Wealth, Women, etc.).

MONOMANIA—(See this subject under Mania).

MONSTERS—Monstrosities—Monstrous Births — Teratism — An Anomaly of Conformation, and Usually Congenital —Too Many Parts or a Deficiency of—Abnormalities — Unnatural Conformations — Freaks of Nature—Congenital Conformations, etc.—Teratology is the Science, or Study of Monsters. The subject of Monsters, and especially of Congenital Monsters, is one largely for Prenatal study, and the conditions which existed at Conception and during Gestation, the aspects, position, and condition of the ☽ at her monthly return to the central line of impulse during pregnancy. The Map of Birth also may show conditions which indicate Monstrosity, if not at birth, that which may be acquired, and develop at some time later in life when certain directions and influences culminate. The Map of Birth is also apt to contain influences, aspects, and indications which supplement prenatal conditions. The Occult side of Monstrosities, and their relation to the Laws of Cause and Effect, and the Law of Karma, etc., are discussed in the book, "Cosmo-Conception", by Max Heindel.

Animal Forms — Resembles Animals or Fowls—The Luminaries in Bestial or Quadrupedal Signs at B., and the malefics in the Asc. or M.C. at the New or Full ☽ previous to birth, the birth will not be fully human. If the Lights in such case are supported by no benefic, but greatly afflicted by malefics, the person so born will be of a wild, savage, or indocile nature. In features such births often resemble the animals in appearance, as cats or dogs. Aspects from ☿ at the same time tend to bird features, or those of cattle or swine. Mercury in the foregoing configurations tends to a disposition agreeable to nature, but with an unnatural body, and not conforming altogether to human form. The Luminaries disconnected with the Asc. at a New or Full ☽ just previous to birth, and being in bestial signs, with no support from benefics, and afflicted by ♄ and ♂ at the same time, the offspring will then be like dogs, cats, or other creatures held in religious veneration, and used in worship. (See "Beastly Form", "Beastly Signs", under Beasts; "Dogs" under Children; Inhuman).

General Causes — General Considerations — Map of Birth and Prenatal Considerations—Monsters are often caused by an over-production of the secretion of the Pineal Gland under an afflicting influence of ♅, which planet rules this Gland. If at conception the Lights are in the 6th or 12th H., and the malefics angular, or if the place of the last Full ☽, or its lord, and the disposer of the Luminaries have no aspect to the Asc., monsters are gen-erated. Also may occur when the ruler of the last New or Full ☽ before birth, and the rulers of the ☉ and ☽ are un-connected with the preceding New or Full ☽. The Luminaries at the time of a New or Full ☽, or just previous to birth, are usually unconnected with the Asc. by aspect. In these cases the Luminaries at B. have been found cadent from the Asc., and forming no aspect to the Asc., and also with the malefics in angles, and espec. in the Asc. or M.C. Also the malefics in angles, and the ☉ and ☽ in ☍ in the 6th and 12th H., which would indicate great limitations. Are also said to be produced by the common sign influence predominant at conception, and at birth, the common signs on the angles, or the common signs much afflicted during gestation. Other influences along this line are given in the other paragraphs of this Article.

Monstrous In Quality — But with Proper Conformation of Body—The ☉ and ☽ in ♊, ♍, ♐, or ♒; the ruling planets discordant; the Luminaries in signs of human shape, and the other circumstances in the scheme of the nativity existing as before described, the body will be human, partake of human nature, but be defective in some peculiar quality. In order to ascertain the nature of the defect the shape and form of the signs containing the ☉ and ☽, and those on the angles occupied by malefics, should be considered. (See "Void Of" under Reason). For further and collateral study along this line see Abnormalities, Acquired, Armless Wonder (see Arms); Birth, Body, Born Blind (see Blindness); Congenital, Contortions, Cyclops, Deaf and Dumb (see Hearing, Mutes); Deaf, Dumb and Blind (see Deafness); Defects, Deficient, Deformities, Demoniac, Diminished, Distortions, Dwarfed, Enlarged, Eunuchs, Eyes Fused (Cyclops); Foetus, Freaks, Frog Child (see Forearm); Gestation, Giants, Growth, Heredity, Hermaphrodites, Idiots, Imbecile, Incomplete, Insanity, Irrational, Legs Missing Below Knees (see Forearm); Malformations, Mind (Weak Mind); Mutes, Organic, Perversions, Pineal Gland, Pregnancy, Prenatal Epoch, Reason, Savage, Structural, Twins (see United Twins); Undersized, Undeveloped, Unnatural, Virile, Void Of, Wild, etc.

MOODS — Moody—Moodiness—Melancholic Moods are given by ♄.

Subject to Moods—The ☉, ☽, or ☿ in ♑; the ☉ or ☽ to the ☌, P., □, or ☍ ♄ by dir.; the ☉, ☽, or ☿ afflicted by ♄ at B.; ♎ or ♑ on the Asc. The influences of the watery signs tend to moodiness, and espec. the ♓ sign, and also attended by a lack of cardinal influences strong at B., and the mutable signs predominant. The fiery signs strong at B. tend to emotional instability, but with greater power to throw off moods. (See Anxiety, Brooding, Dejected, Depressed, Despair, Despondent, Emotions, Fears, Gloom, Hope, Hypochondria, Introspection, Melancholy, Morbid, Morose, Obsessions, Regretful, Repining, Sadness, Serious, Sorrowful, Taciturn, Worry).

MOON—Lunar—The ☽ is one of the principle influences to be considered in Astrology, as her aspects, positions, influences, and progressed positions, tend to bring into action the vibrations of the ☉ and planets for good or ill over human life, as well as over the animal and vegetable kingdoms. The ☽ is the collector of the Solar forces, and reflects the heat and light of the ☉, and by her rapid course around thru the 12 Signs each month she is the distributor and conveyer of the forces of the ☉, and other planets she passes and aspects. The ☽ was thrown off from the Earth because it became a hard crystal and was holding back the evolution of the Earth. The bones in man's body were soft and cartilaginous before the ☽ was thrown off. The distant action of the ☽ now is to harden and crystallize, and after the ☽ was thrown off in the Hyperborean Epoch the bones of man began to harden, and a stronger skeleton was formed. The action of the ☽ today is to harden and crystallize man's body, and to bring on death. If man were to live on the ☽ his body would turn into stone and he would soon die. There is no plant, vegetable or animal life on the ☽. The ☽ is a corpse and gives off corpse-like emanations which makes her influence obnoxious. (See Decay, Moonlight). See the book, "Cosmo-Conception" by Max Heindel, for a full discussion of the origin of the ☽, and her present influences and destiny. The ☽ is feminine in quality, and along with ♀, a feminine planet, and is the general Significator of health in a female nativity, and also rules the female functions. The ☽ is the planet of Fecundation, the planet of fertilization and impregnation, and the ☽ stands at the head of the functional group, and is the chief index of functional activity. The ☽ rules the night, and the ☉ the day time. The ☽ has special affinity with the eyes, and when afflicted at B., and by dir., tends to eye disorders and blindness. The period of Gestation in man and beast is measured by the ☽. The ☽ is magnetic, and also an indicator of disease. She generates moisture, and causes putrefaction, rottenness, and relaxation of animal bodies by generating damp vapors. The ☽ has the greatest effect in infancy, and affects both mind and body. The ☽ weak and afflicted at B. rarely brings good health, and especially in females. In quality the ☽ is negative, feminine, magnetic, cold, moist, fruitful, changeful, lymphatic, plastic, romantic, and wandering. Her influence tends to change, and also to act as an expulsive, cleansing, and alterative agency. She is a receiver, and the preparer, and has strong influence over the breasts, stomach, and womb, and is of powerful import in a female nativity. A ☽ person is ever inconstant, restless, changeable, variable, and a rover. As the ☉ is typical of Spirit, so the ☽ represents Matter, organic decay, and transitory experience. (See Matter). What she represents is of an illusive nature, and has to do with present existence on the Earth Plane. The ☽ influence im-plies fate, thraldom of the flesh, and bondage to Matter. The ♋ sign is the home and only sign of the ☽. She has her exaltation in ♉, her fall in ♏, and her detriment in ♑. The ♋ and ♓ signs are the two best signs for the ☽, and the airy signs. The fire signs are not favorable for the ☽, and also ♏ and ♑ are considered bad signs for the ☽, as she has her fall and detriment in these signs. In order to get the ☽ influences in shape for more ready reference, this Article has been arranged into three Sections. Section One—Influences of the Moon, and General Considerations. Section Two—The Moon Rules. Section Three—Diseases and Afflictions of the Moon.

— SECTION ONE —

INFLUENCES OF THE MOON—

Above the Earth—The ☽ to be powerful should be above the Earth in a night nativity, and below the Earth in a day geniture. When the ☽ is above the Earth in a night map, the functional activities of the body are more normal and regular. The influence and power of the ☽ are weakened when above the earth by day, or below the horizon by night. (See "Below the Earth" in this section).

Absorbent Vessels—The ☽ rules the Absorbent Vessels, and when in the watery signs ♋ and ♓ is most at home and gives efficient and strong functions, and the action of the absorbent vessels and lymphatic system are regular and normal. (See Absorption; "Strong" under Functions; Lymph).

Action of the Moon—The Moon's action is reflective, and she has no basic nature of her own, but focuses the planetary influences upon the mind and body. The action of the ☽ by her different positions and aspects becomes chemically convertive, metamorphic, assimilating, integrative, and secreting. The Moon's action is periodic, mutational, changing, fluidic, and of the ebb and flow order, and traceable for the most part among the fluids. The action of the ☽ also is to harden and crystallize the body with age. (See the Introduction, "Qualities", and the various paragraphs in this Article).

Acts as a Medium—The ☽ acts as a medium of relationship between the ☉, planets, and human, animal and vegetable life and mundane affairs. She rapidly takes up the magnetic force from the other planets and distributes it, and quickly lets go, thus producing change and a great variety of conditions over mind and body.

Afflictions of the Moon—The ☽ afflicts by her □ and ☍ aspects, and by her progressed evil aspects to the radical ☉, planets, Asc., M.C., or hyleg. (See "Aspects" in this section).

Air Signs—Next to the watery signs, the airy signs are rather congenial to the ☽. (See "Air Signs" under Air).

Anareta—The ☽ as Anareta—(See Anareta).

Angel Of—Gabriel.

Appearance—The ☽, her sign and house position, have considerable influence over the personal appearance, and the positions of her nodes are also said to partly determine the height of the body. (See Appearance, Decanates, Height).

Aspects—Aspects and Position of the ☽—These tend to bring events to pass, as she is the time marker in human affairs and World conditions, the minute hand on the clock of destiny, and the ☉ is the hour hand. (See Events). The aspects and position of the ☽ affect and react on the general health, and also the aspects of the other planets to the ☽ have much to do with the general health. The ☽ is fortunate or evil in her influences according to the planets with which configurated, and in many respects is the most powerful of all the planets in health and other matters, the ☉ not even excepted. She afflicts by her □ and ☌ aspects, and tends to benefit the mind and body by her favorable aspects to the ☉, planets, Asc., M.C., and hyleg. (See Afflictions Of, Evil Aspects, in this section).

Below the Earth—The ☽ rules by night, and the ☉ by day, and the ☽ to be more powerful should be above the Earth in a night nativity, and below the earth in a day geniture. The influence and power of the ☽ are weakened when above the earth by day, or below the earth by night. Also when the ☽ is below the earth by day or night the functional activities are not as strong and regular as when the ☽ is above the earth, rising, elevated, dignified, and in a watery sign, as in ♋ or ♓. This is the rule with all the planets that they are more powerful when rising and elevated, and weaker when setting, or below the earth, or horizon at B. (See "Above the Earth" in this section).

Benefic—The action of the ☽ is more benefic in influence when increasing in light, and to some extent malefic and weaker in her action on the functions when in her decrease.

Best Signs—For the ☽—The watery signs ♋ and ♓.

Bodily Forces Weakest—At the New ☽. (See "New Moon" in this section).

Changeable and Variable—In the 12 Signs the influence of the ☽ is variable and changeable, and does not follow the same arrangement as the ☉ and Asc. The ☽ and ☿ are considered variable planets and take on much of the nature and attributes of the planets with which configurated. Thus the ☽ with ♄ gives a very serious, grave and despondent nature and personality, and also retarded and suppressed functions. The ☽ with ♃ gives a more fortunate and buoyant nature, and aids the functions, etc. (See Variable).

Changes of the Moon—The ☽ at her changes, as the New and Full ☽, has a very strong influence over Epileptics, Lunatics, Hysterical and Nervous people, and such people are very sensitive to these changes, and at the Full ☽ especially are very restless, and should never sleep in the open moonlight. (See "Full Moon", "New Moon", in this section).

Character and the Moon—The sign position of the ☽ at B. represents the personal character, the personality, the personal habits, and the functional activities, and to react on the general health according to the nature of the sign, house position, and aspects to the ☽.

Chemical Action Of—Is more deleterious at night by blending with the carbonic acid exhalations of the vegetable kingdom. (See Moonlight, Night, in this section).

Chief Index Of—The ☽ is the chief index of functional activity. (See Functions).

Children—The ☽ is the Sig. of children in Hor'y Q. The ☽ is classed as fruitful, and a giver of children. Females born at the time of an eclipse of the ☽, at a New ☽, are apt to die at birth, or soon after. (See "Death At Birth" under Birth; Eclipses, Fruitfulness).

Classification Of—The ☉ and ☽ are both reckoned as planets in Astrology. The ☽ is classified as a feminine, negative, passive, nocturnal, cold, moist, magnetic, fruitful, phlegmatic body. (See "Qualities" in this section).

Colors—The ☽ rules Green in the Solar Spectrum. Also rules white, or white spotted, or a light mixed color, silver, violet, spotted and mixed colors. The color of the ☽ has a passive power, and white is the sign of radical moisture. (See Colors).

Conduct and the Moon—The ☽ has much to do with the conduct and habits of life, the growth, the functional activities, and the general health.

Constitution—The Constitution Strengthened—(See "Strengthened" under Constitution).

Contracts Disease Easily—(See Contracts).

Crises In Disease—Ruled by the ☽. (See Crises).

Critical Days—Of the ☽ Influence—(See "Crises" under Acute; Amelioration; Crises, Critical, Decrease; "Disease" under Increase, Severe; Moderation; Full Moon, New Moon, Quarters, in this section).

Cycle of the Moon—(See "Metonic" in this section).

Damp Vapors—(See "Damp Vapors" under Moisture).

Dark of the Moon—(See "Decrease" in this section).

Day—The ☽ Above the Earth by Day —(See Above, Below, Night, in this section).

Death and the Moon—(See the Introduction, "Death" in Sec. 3 of this Article).

Decrease of the Moon—The vitality is usually less during the decr. of the ☽, and the body often loses two pounds in weight, and then regains it again during the light, or increase of the ☽. Sickness begun in the decr. of the ☽ is more apt to be depressing and weakening until after the New ☽. During the decr. of the ☽ the fluids of the body are at low ebb, and rise again, and fill the vessels of the body to a greater fullness during the incr. of the ☽. Goiter and Tumors decrease in size during the decr. of the ☽. The ☽ is more malefic during her decr. (See Benefic, Fluids, Last Quarter, in this section).

Diastole and Systole—Of the ☽—(See Full Moon, New Moon, in this section).

Diathesis—(See "Fifth Thoracic" under Ganglion).

Directions Of—The evil directions of the ☽ are especially dangerous during the Lunar Period of life in infancy, and from the 1st to 4th years especially. The directions of the ☽ along thru life bring to a climax other directions culminating and operating, and which are released by the ☽ entering into the configurations. Thus the time of crises in disease, and the critical times, months, and periods of life, can largely be predetermined by the movements of the ☽, and her aspects to the planets in the radical map. (See "Directions" under Children; Crises, Critical, Directions, Periods, Prognosis, Secondary).

Diseases Of—(See Section 3 of this Article).

Domain—Of the ☽—Is over Fluids. (See Fluids).

Dragon's Head—And Tail—The Nodes of the ☽. (See Dragon's Head).

Drugs Of—(See Herbs, Metal, Typical Drugs, in this section).

Earthy Signs—And the ☽—The ☽ is more fortunate in ♉, which is the sign of her exaltation, and tends to good health, regular functions, fixed and methodical habits. In ♍ the ☽ is not as fortunate, and tends to irregular bowel action, irregular functions, and digestive disorders. In ♑ the ☽ has her detriment, and is tinged with ♄ influence. (See "Earthy Signs" under Earth).

Eclipses Of—(See Eclipses, Lunations; "Full Moon", "New Moon", in this section).

Elementary Qualities—At the New ☽ the ☽ is hot and moist; at the 1st Quarter is hot and dry; at her Full is cold and dry, and the 3rd Quarter, cold and moist. (See First Quarter, Full, Last Quarter, New Moon, in this section).

Epoch—The sign the ☽ is in at the Epoch, or time of conception, or the opposite sign, is the Asc. at birth, as a rule. (See Prenatal Epoch).

Equivalent To—The ☽ is equivalent to a ℞ planet when slow in motion, and moving less than 13° 11′ in 24 hours. (See Retrograde).

Events and the Moon—(See Events; Aspects, Directions, in this section).

Evil Aspects Of—The ☽ Fortunate or Evil In Her Influences—(See Afflictions Of, Aspects, in this section). The evil aspects of the ☽ indicate the ailments which arise after birth, and to the detriment and injury of the native's health. (See Asquired).

Exaltation Of—The ☽ has her exaltation in ♉. (See "Earthy Signs" in this section).

Eyes—The ☽ has special affinity with the Eyes. (See Blindness, Eyes, Nebulous, Sight).

Fall—The ☽ has her fall in the ♏ sign. (See Scorpio).

Fecundation—Is the most salient characteristic of the ☽. (See Fecundation).

Females and the Moon—The ☽ is the principal ruler over the health of females, and the female functions, and is usually taken as the hyleg in female nativities when strong and well-aspected at B. Also ♀ is a ruler over females. (See Females, Functions, Menses, Women).

Fevers—The motion of the ☽ regulates fevers, and hot and dry diseases. (See Better, Crises, Fevers, Moderation, Recovery, Resolution, Worse).

Fire Signs and the Moon—The ☽ is not congenial in fiery signs and tends to disturbed functions and many disorders when in such signs, and also to give a hasty and excitable nature. (See "Fire Signs" under Fire).

First Quarter—Exerts a hot and dry influence, and acts especially on the Bile. The 1st Quarter of the ☽ is also concerned with the revitalization of the fluids and functions of the body, and with organic development.

Fluids—The ☽ rules the white fluids of the body, or the body oil; the lymph, chyle, synovial fluid, etc. (See Fluids).

Foetus—The ☽ Influence Over the Foetus—(See Foetus).

Fortunate or Evil—(See "Aspects" in this section).

Friendly To—The ☽ is friendly to all our planets except ♄ and ♂. (See Antipathy, Opposites, Sympathy).

Fruitfulness—The ☽ is fruitful and a giver of children. (See Fruitful).

Full Moon—The Full ☽ is of a cold and dry nature, and affects the Innervation. The Full ☽ corresponds to the Lunar Diastole, and is the Lunar expiration, while the New ☽ typifies the Lunar inspiration, preparation for a new cycle, and is the Lunar Systole. The Full ☽ is typical of maturity, or maturation, of the fullness or plenitude of fluids, the high tide, high tension, fruition, etc. Discharges are more profuse at the Full ☽. The Brain is largest at the Full ☽ and smallest at the New. Fits of nervousness are worse at the New and Full ☽, and also Lunatics are more affected, agitated or raving at these times, and the Insane, Hysterical, Nervous, and Epileptic patients are worse at the Full ☽, and should not sleep exposed to the Moonlight. At the New or Full ☽ the ☽ influence is not so manifest except with Lunatics, whose fluids are more violently disturbed at these times. A child born at the instant of the Full ☽, and especially females, usually dies at the next New ☽, and a child born at the New or Full ☽ rarely lives unless ♃ give a favorable aspect. The exact time of the Full ☽ is very dangerous for a surgical operation. White is the symbol of the Full ☽, which is the symbol of Initiation. (See Changes, First Quarter, Last Quarter, New Moon, in this section; Brain; "Death At Birth" under Children; Discharges;

Dropsy, Eclipses, Emissions, Entozoons, Evacuations; "Nervous Affections" under Fits; Fluids, Fluxes, Haemoptysis; "Profuse" under Hemorrhage; "Discharges" under Hemorrhoids; Insanity, Itching, Scabs, etc.).

Functions—The ☽ has rule over the Functions and the natural powers of the body, and especially over the female functions, childbirth, the menses, etc. (See Functions).

General Health—The ☽ has rule over the general health and habits. (See Habits; "General Health" under Health).

Generates—The ☽ generates moisture and damp vapors. (See "Damp Vapors", and the various paragraphs under Moisture).

Gestation — The period of Gestation for Man and Beast is measured by the ☽. (See Gestation).

Gives Life—The ☽ reflects the Solar Forces which helps to give life.

Growth—The ☽ has much to do with the growth and development of the body. (See Growth).

Habits of Life—The ☽ has an important influence over the personal habits. (See Habits).

Health—The ☽ weak at B., and afflicted tends to ill-health, and espec. in females. The ☽ strong at B., hyleg, and well-aspected, tends to good health in females, good vitality, and prospect of long life. (See Females, Health, Women).

Height of the Body—The Nodes of the ☽ have influence over. (See Height).

Herbs of the Moon — (See "Moon Group' under Herbs).

Home—The ☽ is at home in the watery signs ♋ and ♓, and also in her exalted sign ♉.

Horas—Lunar Horas—(See Horas).

Hour—☽ Hour—(See "Hours" under Planets).

House Position Of—The ☽ tends to disturb the functions more severly when in the 6th H., or ruler of the 6th, and afflicted by lords of the 1st, 6th, or 8th H.

Hyleg—The ☽ is hyleg in female nativities when she is strong, and can be taken for such. (See Hyleg).

Identified With—The ☽ is identified with the negative, passive, magnetic, and feminine forces in Nature.

Implies—The ☽ influence implies fate, thraldom of the flesh, and bondage to matter.

Increase Of—(See Benefic, Decrease, First Quarter, New Moon, in this section).

Indicator Of — The ☽ is an indicator of events, and of disease or health, and espec. in females.

Infancy — The ☽ has greatest effects over Infants, as Infancy is the Lunar Period of life. (See Infancy; "Directions" in this section).

Influence and Power Of—(See "Above the Earth", and the various paragraphs in this section).

Last Quarter — Third Quarter of the ☽—Is cold and moist, and acts especially on the Lymph. This Quarter is typical of the reaping period, the reaping of the harvest, and the application of power already generated. Sleep is more quiet during the last Quarter. (See "Quarters" in this section).

Life — (See "Gives Life" in this section).

Light of the Moon—Increase of—(See Benefic, Gives Life, Increase, Moonlight, in this section).

Lunar — Lunar Horas — Solar Lunar Forces — (See Horas; "Solar-Lunar" under Solar).

Lunations—(See Lunations).

Lymphatic System — Ruled by the ☽. (See Lymphatic).

Magnetic—The ☽ is a magnetic and negative body. (See Magnetic, Negative).

Mars and the Moon—The ☽ ☌ ♂ tends to cause the same diseases as does ♂ in the Asc. at B.

Malefic—When the ☽ is more Malefic—(See Benefic, Decrease, in this section).

Matter — The ☽ is typical of Matter. (See Matter; "Implies" in this section).

Mental Qualities — Given by the ☽ — The ☽ tends to make one timid and imaginative. (See Imagination, Timidity).

Metals—Ruled by the ☽—Aluminum, Silver. (See Therapeutics).

Metonic Cycle—Cycle of the ☽—The Nodes of the ☽ complete one revolution in about 1000 weeks, or 19 years, and the ☽ forms her ☌ with the ☉ on the same day every 19 years. The Eclipse at this time is very powerful for good or ill in health matters, according to her sign, aspects, etc., as related to the map of birth, and for People and Countries falling under the shadow of such an Eclipse. (See Eclipse).

Minerals Of—Emerald, Marcassite, Moonstone, Selenite. (See Minerals).

Moisture — The ☽ generates moisture and damp vapors. (See "Damp Vapors" under Moisture).

Moon People—A Moon person is ever inconstant, restless, changeable, variable, and a rover. Moon people, and with the ☽ afflicted at B., tend to contract disease easily, and usually have less vitality. The ☽ sign ♋ on the Asc. at B. tends to give a weak constitution. (See Cancer Sign; "Contracts Disease Easily" under Contracts; Restless; "Weak" under Vitality).

Moonlight — The night air and moonlight are noxious and tend to produce miasmic ailments, malaria, etc. (See "Full Moon", "Sleep", in this section; Malaria, Miasma, Noxious).

Moonstone—A Mineral ruled by the ☽.

Motion of the Moon—(See Equivalent, Fevers, in this section; "Planets" under Motion; "Motion" under Planets).

Mutation of Fluids—(See "Mutation" under Fluids).

Natural Powers—(See "Functions" in this section; "Natural Forces" under Natural).

Nebulous Spots — And the ☽ — The ☽ with at B. tends to Eye Trouble and Blindness. (See Blindness, Eyes, Nebulous).

Negative — The ☽ is a negative and magnetic body. (See Negative; "Classification" in this section).

New Moon—The New ☽ is the systole, or the low ebb of her influence, and implies death, disintegration, and the preparation for a new Cycle. The New ☽ is hot and moist in influence. The functional activities are lower at this time, and the bodily forces are weakest. A male child born at the time of the New ☽, which may also be a total eclipse of the ☉, may not survive. Much infant mortality is referable to the New ☽, which is a critical time with infants, and tends not only to weaken the constitution, but to make any contemporaneous malefic aspects and influences more powerful in their action upon the body. (See "New Moon" under Children). At the New and Full ☽ the ☽ influence is not so manifest except with Lunatics, whose fluids are more violently disturbed at these times. The New ☽ just previous to an event, an accident, or the beginning of a disease, has much to do with precipitating the event, and even before it would otherwise occur, and the aspects of a New ☽, or a Progressed ☽, tend to focus the hidden forces. Thus a New ☽ may hasten an event if it occurs previous to the natural time of a possible event, or tend to retard an event when it occurs soon after, or immediately after the time of the culmination of an event, accident, or the beginning of a disease. In a train of evil directions the focus of their action is often guided by a New ☽ at or near the time of their culmination. The influence of a New ☽ just previous to birth often tends to congenital malformations and monstrosities. (See Changes, Full Moon, in this section; Directions, Eclipses, Events; "Nervous" under Fits; Irritable; "Low Spirits" under Low; Lunations, Misery, Monsters, Prenatal Epoch).

Night Action Of — The ☽ by Night — The ☽ being magnetic helps to keep up the morbid action of germs at night, and make disease worse. The action of the ☉ being electric tends to destroy and overcome the morbid action of germs during the day, and to equalize the deteriorating action of the ☽ at night, and thus save life. (See Above the Earth, Chemical, Moonlight, in this section; Day, Electric, Germs, Magnetic, Night, Noxious).

Nodes — Of the ☽ — (See "Height" in this section; Dragon's Head).

Noxious — (See Chemical, Damp Vapors, Moonlight, Night Action, in this section).

Operations — Surgical Operations and the ☽—(See Operations).

Organic Development — The position, aspects, and influence of the ☽ at B. show the quality of the organic development. (See "First Quarter" in this section; Organic).

Origin of the Moon — (See the Introduction to this Article).

Pathological Action—Of the ☽—Tends to Atonicity, Critical Epochs, Dropsy, Disease Contracted Easily, Fluidic Secretions, Transudation; is also Sedative and Soporific.

Perigee Of — The ☽ in perigee tends to cause pains in various parts of the body. Also nightmares and dreams usually occur about 48 hours before the Moon's perigee, and when the ☽ is about an hour high. (See Perigee).

Personal Appearance—(See "Appearance" in this section).

Personality—(See "Represents" in this section).

Physiological Action—Of the ☽—Influences the Tears and Mutation of Fluids; influences the stomach; makes the womb receptive to the seminal fluid; rules and influences impregnation, inspiration, the animal instincts, and tends to inertia and sedentary habits. Movement in the body is a physiological action of the ☽. Moisture is a physiological action of the ☽, and tending to rottenness and putrefaction. The ☽ is classed as a physiological planet, and not pathological. The physiological action of the ☽ Group of Herbs has a cold and moist action, and tends to Mycrozymasis, Zymotic Periodicity, and to affect the Sympathetic Nervous System. (See "Moon Group" under Herbs; Microzymasis, Zymotic).

Plants Of—The general action of the ☽ plants tends to periodicity, and to be intermittent and zymotic. (See "Physiological Action" in this section).

Position Of—(See Above, Aspects, Below, House, Sign, in this section).

Power Of — (See Above, Below, Increase, and the various paragraphs in this section).

Principle of the Moon—Change, Harmony, Receptivity.

Quadratures—The 1st and 3rd Quarters of the ☽, and are very important in health matters. (See First Quarter, Last Quarter, in this section).

Quality Of—In quality the ☽ is moist, secreting, receptive, generating, mutational, relaxing, and pacific. (See "Qualities" in this section).

Qualities Of—The following Qualities are attributed to the ☽ — Alterative, Apathetic, Assimilative, Atonic, Attenuant, Binding, Changeful, Cleansing, Cold, Cold and Dry at the Full ☽; Cold and Moist at the 3rd Quarter; Collective, Convertive, Crystallizing, Decaying, Decomposing, Diluting, Dissipating, Dissolving, Distributing, Dreamy, Dry and Hot at the 1st Quarter; Dry and Cold at the Full ☽; Emetic, Emotional, Expulsive, Fecundating, Feminine, Fermenting, Fertilizing, Flaccid, Fluidic Fructifying, Fruitful, Functional, Generating, Hardening, Harmonious, Hot and Moist at the New ☽; Hot and Dry at the 1st Quarter; Illusory, Imaginative, Impregnating, Impressionable, Inconstant, Inertia, Instinctive, Integrative, Intermittent, Lethargic, Lymphatic, Magnetic, Materialistic, Metamorphic, Moist, Mutational, Negative, Neurasthenic, Nocturnal, Nutritive, Pacific,

Passive, Periodic, Phlegmatic, Plastic, Putrefying, Receptive, Reflective, Relaxing, Remittent, Restless, Rhythmic, Roaming, Romantic, Roving, Scattering, Secreting, Sedative, Sedentary, Self-Indulgent, Sensitiveness, Sequential, Sleep-Producing, Soporific, Timorous, Tumorous, Vacillating, Variable, Visionary, Wandering, Watery, Worrisome, Zymotic, etc. (See Classification, Elementary, in this section).

Quarters of the Moon — At the 1st Quarter, the Full ☽, and 3rd Quarter of the ☽ the Solar-Lunar forces are disturbed, and the functions and the constitution tend to be disordered. (See Decrease, First Quarter, Full Moon, Increase, Last Quarter, New Moon, Solar-Lunar, in this section).

Reflects—The ☽ reflects and collects the Solar Forces and the influences of the other planets as she passes around thru the 12 Signs. (See Action of the Moon, Acts As a Medium, Aspects, in this section).

Regulates—The ☽ regulates the period of gestation and time of; the female functions and menses, and also the course of disease, crises in disease, etc., and also the time of events. (See "Indicator" in this section).

Represents—The ☽ represents matter, organic decay, and transitory experiences. What she represents is of an illusory nature, and has to do with the present existence on the Earth Plane. The ☽ sign in the map of birth represents the Personality, the Lower Mind, the mind which denotes the contacts with the outer world, environment, externals, disease, pain, suffering, worry, social relations, etc. (See Personality).

Retrograde—(See "Equivalent" in this section).

Salient Characteristic— (See "Fecundation" in this section).

Scorpio Sign—Sign of the fall of the ☽, and in this sign at B. tends to disturbed functions, ill-health, sex disorders, etc. (See Scorpio).

Secretions — The ☽ and Secretions — The secretions are more normal and regular with the ☽ in ♋ or ♓ at B. In an airy sign also the secretions are more regular and normal, but with the ☽ in a fiery sign the functions and secretions are greatly disturbed. Of the earthy signs the ☽ in ♉ has the most favorable influence over the secretions. (See Secretions).

Shows the Quality Of—(See "Organic" in this section).

Sign Position—The ☽ is strong in ♉, ♋, and ♓; has her fall in ♏, and detriment in ♑. Is rather strong in the airy signs, but incongenital in fiery signs.

Significator Of—The ☽ is the general Sig. of the health in female nativities.

Sixth House — And the ☽ — (See "House" in this section; Sixth House).

Sleep—The ☽ is Sleep-producing. Hysterical and Nervous people should not sleep exposed to the Moonlight. (See Full Moon, Moonlight, in this section; "Sleep-Inducing" under Sleep).

Slow In Motion—(See "Equivalent" in this section).

Solar Forces — The ☽ reflects them. (See "Reflects" in this section).

Solar-Lunar Influences — (See "Solar-Lunar" under Solar).

Source Of—The ☽ is the source of the Natural Forces in the body. (See "Natural" in this section).

Strengthens Constitution—(See "Strengthened" under Constitution).

Strongest—The ☽ is strongest in the watery signs ♋ and ♓. Is weakest in ♏ and ♑. (See "Signs" under Water).

Systole Of—(See "Full Moon" in this section).

Temperament—(See Lymphatic).

Therapeutic Affinities — Ipecac has a strong affinity with the ☽, and is used as an emetic in stomach troubles. (See Emetics, Ipecac).

Therapeutic Qualities—Alterative, Attenuant, Emetic. (See these subjects).

Third Quarter — (See "Last Quarter" in this section).

Tides—The ☽ rules the Tides, and the ebb and flow. The Full ☽ is the high tide of fluids, and the New ☽ the low ebb. (See Full, New, in this section).

Time — The ☽ a Time Marker — (See "Aspects" in this section).

Typical Drugs Of—Agaricus, Argentum, Colocynth, Pellitory.

Typical Plants — (See "Moon Group" under Herbs).

Vapors—The ☽ generates moisture and damp vapors. (See "Damp Vapors" under Moisture).

Variable — (See Acts As a Medium, Changeable, in this section).

Vital Center — The ☽ is one of the three Vital Centers of the Map of Birth, along with the ☉ and Asc. The ☽ is usually hyleg in a female nativity. (See "Centers" under Vital).

Vitality — (See "Vitality" under Females).

Water Signs — The ☽ is strongest in the watery signs ♋ and ♓, and when in these signs at B. tends to more regular functions, and to good health. (See "Signs" under Water).

Weakened — Weaker — The Power of the ☽ Weakened — (See Below the Earth, Decrease, Fire Signs, in this section).

Weakest — The Bodily Forces are weakest at the time of the New ☽, and also when the ☽ is afflicted in ♏ or ♑ with females. (See "New Moon" in this section).

Weather and the Moon—(See Floods, Rain, Weather).

White Fluids—The ☽ rules the white fluids of the body. (See "Fluids" in this section; "Fluids" under White).

Women and the Moon — (See "Females" in this section).

— SECTION TWO —

THE MOON RULES—See the following subjects in the alphabetical arrangement — Abdomen and Abdominal Cavity; Absorbent Vessels; Acquired Diseases; Acute Diseases; Air, and the

Tidal Air in the Lungs; Alimentary Canal; Aluminum; Animal Lusts and Passions; Animal Propensities; Apathy; Atonicity; Automatic Action; Belly; Birth Place; Bladder; Blood—Flow of, or Rush of Blood to the Head; Body Oil; Bondage to Matter; Bowels; Brain Functions and Substance; Breasts; Canal (Intestinal); Cancer Sign; Cavities of Body; Cellular Tissue Building; Cerebellum; Changes in Life; Childbirth; Children — Period of Infancy; Chyle and Chylification; Cleansing of the Body; Colorless Lymph in the Body; Colors (see "Colors" in Sec. 1 of this Article); Common People; Constitutional Functions; Constructive Functions; Corpulency; Crises in Disease; Critical Days, Epochs and Years (see Critical); Crystallization; Day of the Week — Monday; Death; Decay (Organic; Decomposition; Deglutition; Deluges; Digestive Activity and Juices; Dilution; Disintegration; Dissolution; Dissolving Processes in the Body; Dropsical Swellings; Drugs of the ☽ (see "Drugs" in Sec. 1 of this Article); Ebb and Flow (see "Tides" in Sec. 1 of this Article); Emerald; Emissions; Emotions; Epileptics; Epochs; Etheric Double of Man (see Astral); Experiences (Transitory — See "Represents" in Sec. 1 of this Article); Expulsory Forces in the Body; Eyes—Left Eye in a Male and Right Eye in the Female; Faculties (the Sentient Faculties); Fate; Fecundation; Feelings; Female Functions; Female Relatives (see Relatives); Female—Right Eye in; Female Signs of Zodiac—The ☽ rules the first half of Female Signs, and the second half of Masculine Signs (see "Signs" under Female); Fermentation; Fertilization; First Seven Years of Life (Infancy Period); First Half of Life in General, and the ☉ Rules the 2nd Half of Life; Fleshiness (see Fleshy); Fluids of the Body and the White Fluids; Forces (Expulsory Forces); Fruitfulness; Functions—Brain Functions — Constitutional and Constructive Functions—Female Functions — Organic Functions and Development — Secreting Functions (see Functions); Gall Bladder as a Receptacle; Gastric Juices in General; General Health and General Habits of Life; Gestation; Glands of the Body and the Glandular Processes; Green Color; Habits of Life — Due to Automatic Action—Sedentary Habits (see Habits); Hardening; Health—The General Health, and especially among Females; Heart—Functions of; Herbs of the Moon (see "Moon Group" under Herbs); Home (the Home); Humidity; Humours; Humus; Impregnation; Inertia; Infancy (Period of); Inspiration (see Breath); Instincts; Intercellular Fluids (see Cells); Intermittent Action on the Body; Intermittent Fevers; Intestinal Canal; Irrational Faculties; Journeys by Water (see Voyages); Juices in the Body; Lachrymal Apparatus; Lacteals; Lassitude; Left Eye in a Male; Left Side of the Body (see Left); Lethargy; Life (Period of Infancy, from 1 to 7 Years); Light Mixed Colors; Liquids of the Body in General; Lower Mind (see "Represents" in Sec. 1 of this Article); Lunations;

Lungs—Tidal Air in Lungs; Lusts and Animal Passions; Lymph — Lymphatic System—Lymphatic Temperament; Mammae (see Breasts); Marcassite; Marriage Affairs; Masculine Signs — 2nd Half of (see "Masculine" under Signs); Maternity; Matter in General on the Earth Plane; Menopause; Menses; Metal (Silver); Metamorphosis; Miasma; Microzymasis; Midwives; Milk; Mind—The Instinctive Mind; Mixed Light Colors; Moisture — Moist Warmth; Monday; Moonlight; Moonstone; Mother (during Pregnancy); Motion; Movement; Mucous Surfaces; Mutation of Fluids; Native Place (Birthplace); Natural Functions in the Female — Natural Faculties — Natural Forces in the Body (see Natural); Nerves — Nerve Sheaths — Nervous People — Nerves in a General Way — Sympathetic Nervous System (see Nerves); Night (see Miasma, Moonlight, Night, Noxious); Obstetricians; Ocean; Oesophagus; Oils — Body Oils and White Fluids — Oozings; Organic Functions — Organic Decay; Osmosis; Ovaries; Palate; Parturition; Passions (the Animal Passions and Lusts); Pericardium; Periodic Action — Periodic Disease; Peristalsis; Personality; Perspiration; Physique; Plants (see "Moon Group" under Herbs); Powers (the Natural Powers of the Body); Pregnancy; Processes—The Dissolving Processes in the Body — The Glandular Processes; Putrefaction; Receptacles of the Body (see Cavities, Receptacles); Reception of Semen (see Semen); Relatives (Female Relatives); Remittent Action; Residence (Place of); Respiratory System (Absorbent and Lymphatic Vessels of); Restlessness; Returning Diseases; Rhythm; Right Eye in the Female; Right Side of the Body (see Right); Rivers; Saliva; Secretions; Sedatives; Sedentary Habits; Seeds; Selenite; Semen (Reception of); Sensation; Sensitive Faculties; Sensitives; Sensuous Faculties; Sentient Faculties; Serous Surfaces; Sheaths (Nerve Sheaths); Shot Violet Color; Signs of Zodiac — Rules the ♋ sign; Silver Cord and Silver Metal; Sleep-Inducing Drugs, Herbs and Habits (see Narcotics; "Drugs" under Sleep); Soft Tissues; Stamina; Stomach (Functions and Glands of); Surfaces (Mucous and Serous); Swallow (see Deglutition); Swamps; Sweat; Swellings (Dropsical); Sympathetic Nervous System; Synovial Fluid; Tears; Temperament (the Lymphatic); Testicle (the Left); Thoracic Cavity; Thraldom of the Flesh (see "Implies" in Sec. 1 of this Article); Throat; Thyroid Gland; Tidal Air in Lungs; Tides—Ebb and Flow of — Dropsical and Fluidic Tides in the Body, Swellings, etc.; Tissue—Tissue Building—Cellular—Soft Tissues; Tonsils; Transitory Diseases and Experiences (see "Represents" in Sec. 1 of this Article); Transudation of Fluids; Travel; Urine (as a Liquid); Uterus; Uvula; Vessels in General, and as Receptacles; Violet Color — Shot Violet Color; Vitality (Low, Lowered); Voyages; Water; Watery Tides in the Body; Weather; White — White Fluids of the Body — White Spotted Colors; Womb; Worldly

Conditions (see Acts As a Medium, Implies, Represents, in Sec. 1 of this Article); Zymotic Action.

— SECTION THREE —

DISEASES OF THE MOON—Diseases and Afflictions Ruled by the Moon — The ☽, by reflecting the aspects and influences of the ☉ and planets, tends to produce and regulate disease, and eventually to bring death. Her Quarters from the time of the beginning of a disease are the crises times. (See Crises). The ☽ rules and causes all Acute and Acquired Diseases. The ☽ joined with ♂ at B. causes the same diseases as ♂ does when in the Asc. The ☽ rules such diseases as return after a time, as Periodic Diseases. The ☽ rules the Functions and Health matters in females, and an afflicted and ill-dignified ☽ at B. tends to disturbed and irregular female functions. The ☽ is the Significator of Health in a female horoscope. Moon people contract disease easily. Over the body the ☽ normally represents a cleansing, alterative, and expulsive influence, and also with age to harden and crystallize the body, and the ☽ being a cold, ashy and cinder-like body, the body of man would quickly turn into stone if he lived upon the Moon, and death quickly result, as vegetable and animal life cannot exist on the ☽. See the following subjects in the alphabetical arrangement when not more fully considered here—

Abdomen — Gaseous Distention of — (See Abdomen, Flatulence, Tympanites).

Abscesses; Accommodation — Disorders of Vision — (See Accommodation).

Aches; Acute Diseases; Adaptation—Defective Powers of In the Eyes—(See Accommodation, Sight).

Alimentary Canal—Diseases of—(See Alimentary).

Anaemia; Aneurysm; Anxiety;

Apathy; Apoplexy; Arms—Gout In—Weakness In—(See Arms).

Arterial Blood—Defects In—(See Arteries).

Asthma; Astigmatism; Atonicity;

Back—Weakness In—(See Back).

Belly—Bellyache—Fluxes of the Belly —(See Belly, Fluxes).

Birth—Premature—(See Premature).

Bladder—Disorders of—(See Bladder).

Blemishes; Blindness; Blood—Cold Blood—Thin Blood—Defective Red Blood—(See Blood).

Boils; Bowels—Disorders of—Distempers In — Fluxes In — Disturbed Functions—Obstructions In—Pains In —(See Bowels).

Brain — Disorders of the Brain Substance—Inflammation of—(See Brain).

Breasts—Disorders of—See Breasts).

Bronchial Disorders—Bronchial Catarrh and Oedema—(See Bronchial).

Calculi—(See Stone).

Cancer Disease—(See Carcinoma).

Carcinoma; Carditis—(See Heart).

Catarrhs; Cellular Zymosis—(See Cells, Zymosis).

Children—Disorders of—Worms In— —(See Childhood, Children, Infancy).

Chlorosis; Cholic; Cold — Cold Diseases — Cold Blood — Cold and Moist Diseases—Cold, Phlegmatic Diseases— Taking Cold—Indigestion from Taking Cold—Cold Taken In the Feet—Cold, Rheumatic Diseases—Cold Stomach— Cold and Raw Humours In the Stomach—(See Cold).

Colds; Colic; Colliquative Sweats — (See Colliquative, Sweat).

Conjunctivitis—(See Conjunctiva).

Consumptions; Convulsions; Coughs —Rotten Coughs—(See Cough).

Crises In Disease—(See Crises).

Critical Days — In Disease — (See Crises, Critical).

Crystallization; Cysts; Death—The ☽ causes Death by Cold and Moist Diseases; Crystallization; Hardening; Drowning; Cold, Phlegmatic Diseases. (See these subjects).

Debauchery; Decay; Decomposition; Defluxions; Delirium Tremens — (See Delirium).

Diarrhoea; Digestive Disorders—(See Digestion, Indigestion).

Dilutions; Discharges — Menstrual, Mucous, Serous—(See Discharges).

Dissipation; Dissolution;

Distempers—In Bowels — Genitals— Reins—Secret Parts—Sex Organs— (See Distempers).

Distension—Of the Abdomen—(See Abdomen, Distentions).

Dizziness; Drink; Dropsies;

Drowning; Drowsiness—(See Sleep).

Drunkenness; Dry Bellyache — (See Belly).

Duration of Disease—(See Duration).

Dyspepsia; Effusions; Epilepsy; Eruptions—(See Eruptions, Face).

Excess—Of Mucous and Phlegm—(See Mucous, Phlegm).

Eyes—Disorders of—(See Accommodation, Blindness, Eyes, Nebulous, Sight).

Face—Eruptions On—(See Face).

Faintings—Falling Fits—(See Fainting).

Feet—Cold Taken In—Gout In— Lameness In—Pains In—Weakness In —(See Feet).

Female Complaints — (See Females, Women).

Fermentation; Fevers—The Motion of the ☽ Regulates Fevers—(See Fevers).

Fits—(See Fainting, Fits).

Flabbiness; Fluids—Of the Body— Disorders of—(See Fluids, Osmosis).

Fluor Albus—(See Leucorrhoea).

Fluxes; Functions—Disorders of— (See Females, Functions, Menses).

Gaseous Distentions—(See Abdomen, Distensions, Flatulence, Gas).

Generation—Diseases of Organs of— (See Generation).

Genitals—Diseases of—(See Genitals).

Genito-Urinary Disorders—(See Genito-Urinary).

Giddiness; Glands—Disorders of—(See Glands).

Gluttony; Goiter; Gout—In the Arms, Hands, Wrists, Legs, Joints, Feet, Knees—(See Gout).

Habits of Life—Diseases By—(See Habits).

Haemoglobin—Defects In—(See Haemoglobin; "Blood" under Red).

Hands—(See "Gout" under Hands).

Hardening; Head—(Defluxions of Rheum From).

Heart—(Inflammation of—Trembling of—Palpitation of).

High Strung—And Nervous—(See High, Nerves).

Hot and Dry Diseases—(See "Dry and Hot" under Heat; "Fevers" in this section).

Humours; Hurts to Eyes—(See Eyes).

Hydrocephalus; Hyperopia—(See Sight).

Hysteria; Imaginations; Indigestion; Infancy—(Disorders of).

Infiltrations; Inflammation—Of the Heart—(See Heart).

Injuries—To the Eyes—(See Blindness, Eyes).

Insanity; Intoxication;

Irregularities—Of the Bowels—Of the Female Functions—Of the Stomach—(See Bowels, Females, Fluids, Functions, Irregular, Menses, Stomach).

Joints—(Gout In).

Kidneys—Disorders of—Stone In—(See Kidneys).

King's Evil—(See Scrofula).

Knees—(See "Gout", "Pain", under Knees).

Lachrymal Apparatus—Disorders of—(See Tears).

Lacteals—Diseases of—(See Milk).

Lameness—(In Feet and Thighs).

Larynx—Disorders of—Laryngitis—(See Larynx).

Left Eye—Defects In—Hurts To—Blindness In—(See "Left" under Eyes; "Eyes" under Left).

Left Side of Body—Cold In—Disorders In—(See Left).

Legs—(Gout In—Pains In—Swellings In—Dropsy In).

Lethargy; Leucorrhoea; Limbs—(Obstructions In).

Liver—(Disorders of).

Lunacy; Lunar Diseases—Suffers from ☽ Diseases—The ☽ afflicted at B., and to the evil aspects the Asc. by dir.; the Asc. to the ☌, P., or ill-aspect the ☽ by dir. (See Lunar; also note the various paragraphs in this section).

Lungs—(Obstructions In).

Lymphatics—(Disorders of).

Mammae—Disorders of—(See Breasts).

Measles; Membranes—Diseases of the Mucous and Serous Membranes—(See Membranes, Mucous, Serous).

Menorrhagia—(See Menses).

Menses—Disorders of—(See Menses).

Mental Strain—(See "Strain" under Mental).

Miasma; Milk—(Disorders of).

Minor Ailments—(See Mild, Minor, Slight).

Miscarriage—(See Abortion, Miscarriage).

Moist and Cold Diseases—(See "Cold and Moist" under Humours; "Cold" in this section).

Moist Humours—Body Over-Charged With—(See Humours).

Morbid Action—Of Germs At Night—(See "Night Action Of" in Sec. 1 of this Article).

Mucous—Mucus—Mucous Discharges—Excess of Mucus and Phlegm—(See Discharges, Mucous, Phlegm).

Myopia—(See Sight).

Nausea; Near-Sighted—(See Sight).

Nervousness—(See "High Strung" under High; Hysterical; "Nervousness" under Nerves).

Neuralgia—In the Head—(See Head).

Night Diseases—(See Night).

Night Sweats—(See Phthisis).

Obstructions—(In Bowels, Limbs, Lungs).

Oedema—In Lungs—(See Lungs, Oedema).

Oesophagus—(Disorders of).

Oozings; Operations—Surgical—Influence of the ☽ Over—(See "Rules" under Operations).

Ophthalmia—(See Conjunctiva).

Osmosis; Pains—In Bowels—Feet—Knees—Legs—In Secret Parts—Painful Female Functions—(See "Pain" under these subjects; Menses, Pain).

Palsy; Periodic Irregularities—(See Irregularities, Periodic).

Periodical Diseases—(See Intermittent, Menses, Periodical, Returning).

Periods of Women—Disorders of—(See Menses).

Phlegmatic Diseases—Excess of Phlegm and Mucus—(See Mucous, Phlegm).

Phthisic; Phthisis—Night Sweats of—(See Phthisis).

Pimples; Pleurisy; Poison—Sickness From—(See Poison).

Premature Births—(See Premature).

Presbyopia—(See Sight).

Profluvial Effusions—(See Effusions).

Putrefaction; Quinsy; Raw Humours—(See Indigestion).

Red Blood—Defective—(See Haemoglobin; "Blood" under Red).

Reins—(Distempers In).

Relaxation—Of Animal Bodies—(See "Damp Vapors" under Moisture).

Renal Stone—(See "Kidneys" under Stone).

Respiratory Disorders—(See Breath, Bronchial, Lungs).

Restlessness; Returning Diseases—(See Periodical, Returning).

Rheum—(Defluxions of).

Rheumatism — (Cold, Rheumatic Diseases).

Right Eye—Of a Female—Hurts To, etc.—(See "Right" under Eyes; "Right Eye" under Females; "Eyes" under Right).

Ringworm; Salivation—(See Saliva).

Scrofula; Scurvy; Secret Parts—(Diseases In — Distempers In — Pains — Swellings).

Sedative Conditions — In the Body — (See Sedative).

Serous Membranes—Disorders of— (See Serous).

Severity of Disease — (See "Severe" under Disease; Duration, Severity).

Serum—(Disorders of—Infiltration of).

Sex Organs—Diseases of—Distempers In—(See Generation, Genitals, Genito-Urinary, Privates, Reproduction, Secret Parts, Sex, etc.).

Shingles—Herpes Zoster—(See Herpes).

Shoulders—(Weakness In).

Sight—Disorders of —(See Blindness, Eyes, Nebulous, Sight).

Signs—Diseases of the ☽ in the various Signs of the Zodiac — (See the Classified Lists in the various Textbooks and Dictionaries of Astrology).

Sixth House—The House of Health—Weakening Influence of the ☽ In— (See Sixth House; "House Position Of" in Sec. 1 of this Article).

Skin Diseases—Tendency To—(See Herpes, Pimples, Scrofula, Scurvy; "Tendency To" under Skin).

Sleep-Inducing—(See Lethargy, Sedative; "Drowsiness" under Sleep).

Smallpox; Soft Tissues—Disorders of —(See Tissues).

Somnambulism—(See Sleep).

Soporific — (See "Soporific" under Sleep).

Sore Throat—(See Throat).

Stomach — (Cold Stomach—Indigestion—Raw Humours In—Stomachache).

Stone—(In Kidneys).

Stoppage—In Throat—(See Throat).

Suffocation—(Death By—Drowning).

Surfaces — Disorders of the Mucous and Serous Surfaces — (See Mucous, Serous).

Surfeits; Sweats—Night Sweats—(See Phthisis, Sweat).

Swellings—(In Throat—Legs—Secret Parts—Dropsical).

Swoonings—(See Fainting).

Sympathetic Nervous System—Disorders of—(See Sympathetic).

Synovial Fluid—And Membranes—Disorders of—(See Synovial).

Tears—(Disorders of).

Tetters; Thighs — (Lameness In — Weakness In).

Thin Blood—(See Blood).

Throat—(Sore Throat—Stoppage In—Swellings In).

Transudations; Tumors — (Oedematous).

Tympanites; Ulcers—(In Arms—Legs —Throat).

Uterus—Disorders of—(See Womb).

Uvulitis; Varicose Veins — (See Varicose).

Vertigo; Vesicles—(Disorders of).

Vision—Disorders of—Errors of—Defects of—(See Blindness, Eyes, Sight).

Vitality—(Lowered).

Vomiting; Weakness—Weak—Weakness and General Debility—Weakness In the Arms, Back, Eyes, Feet, Shoulders and Thighs — Weak Sight — (See "Weakness" under Arms, Back, etc.; "General Debility" under Debility; "Ill-Health All Thru Life" under Ill-Health; "Weak" under Sight; "Low" under Vitality).

Whites In Women — (See Leucorrhoea).

Wind — In Bowels or Stomach — (See Wind).

Women—Diseases of—Liver Trouble In—Functional Disorders—Periodic Illnesses—Whites In—(See Females, Functions, Leucorrhoea, Liver, Menses, Women).

Worms—In Children—(See Worms).

Worry; Wrists—(Gout In).

Zymosis—(See Fermentation, Zymosis).

MOPING—Listless—Spiritless—♄ ruler at B., and characteristic of a ♄ person. (See Despondent, Dull, Listless; "Low Spirits" under Low; Melancholy, etc.).

MORALS—The Moral Faculties—The Moral Conduct—The Map of Birth may indicate a tendency to moral delinquency, or moral turpitude, but the native does not have to yield to them. It depends upon the age of the Soul as to how the influences of a map manifest, or do not manifest themselves. To get certain important influences in the birth map, many very Advanced Souls have an evil map in many ways, but the real and inner character of Advanced Souls cannot be told by the birth map. Only those who are drifting, or who may be young Souls, follow their maps, and especially where the evils are indicated. The following subjects have to do with the moral life, the principles, the motives, and conduct of the native. See these subjects in the alphabetical arrangement when not more fully considered here—

Abandoned—An Abandoned Person— (See Depraved, Profligate).

Adulterous — (See "Adultery" under Love Affairs).

Bad Company — Bad Courses — (See "Conduct" under Bad; Conduct, Courses, Evil, Harlots, Low; "Loose Morals" in this section).

Balance—Lack of Moral Balance—The lower influences and vibrations of ♅ tend to; ♅ in the ♀ signs ♉ or ♎, and afflicted by ♄, ♂, or ♀; ♅ ☌, □, or ☍ ♀. (See Balance; the various paragraphs in this section).

Chaotic Acts—Unnatural Acts—(See Chaotic, Perversions, Unnatural).

Character; Chastity — (See "Chaste", "Virgin", under Females).

Cheating; Conduct; Cravings — (See Cravings, Drink, Narcotics, Thirst).

Criminal; Debased; Debauched;

Deceitful; Depraved; Desires;

Deviations; Disgraceful—(See Disgrace, Lewd, Shameless).

Dishonest; Dissipated; Dissolute;

Drunken; Endurance — Moral Endurance — The fixed signs, and especially ♏, and also the planet ♄, tend to give moral endurance when well-aspected. The ♉ sign also gives endurance when strongly placed, occupied, and aspected. Venus when ill-aspected by malefics tends to give very little moral stamina or endurance. Uranus, ♂, and the masculine signs signify only sudden, temporary, or spasmodic efforts at moral endurance. The feminine signs give greater perseverance and patience in moral efforts. (See Endurance; "Moral Stamina" in this section).

Evil-Minded — Wicked — (See Evil, Lewd, Licentious, Obscene, Perversions, Shameless, etc.).

Excesses — Indulges In — (See Excesses).

Filthy Morals — (See "Loose" in this section; Filthy, Lewd, Obscene, Shameless, Wanton).

Flirting — (See "Unwomanly" in this section).

Folly — Moral Folly — (See "Free-Living" under Free; Folly; "High Living" under High; "Clandestine" under Sex; "Loose Morals" in this section).

Fornicators — (See "Clandestine" under Sex).

Free Love—(See Free).

Freedom—Unwomanly Freedom—(See "Unwomanly" in this section).

Gamblers; Good Morals—♄ Sig. ☌ ♃, extremely moral and grave; in Hor'y Q. ♃ Sig. of the person; ♀ ⚹ or △ ♄. (See "Chaste" under Females; Honest, Honorable, Sincere, etc.).

Habits—Loose Habits—(See Habits; "Habits" under Loose).

Harlots; Homosexuality; Honest;

Honour—(Loss of).

Husband—The Morals of—(See Husband).

Hypocritical; Imbecility—Moral Imbecile — (See Debauched, Depraved, Lascivious, Lewd, Obscene; "Loose Morals", and the various paragraphs in this section).

Immodest; Immoral—(See Conduct, Evil, Habits, Indecent, Lewd, Love Affairs, Lust, Passion, Perversions, Sex, Shameless, Vices; "Loose", and the various paragraphs in this section).

Imprisonment—(See Prison).

Improper; Impure Conduct — (See Lewd, Loose; "Amours", "Liaisons", under Love Affairs; Lust; "Impure" under Sex; Shameless; "Loose" in this section).

Incestuous—(See "Incest" under Perversions).

Indecent; Indiscretions; Indulgent;

Infamous; Inimical to Himself—(See Inimical).

Inhuman; Inordinate; Intemperate;

Intercourse—(Criminal In).

Intoxication; Introversion—(Moral).

Irresponsible; Judicial Condemnation —(See Judges).

Knavish; Lapsing—(Moral).

Lascivious; Law—Disregards Moral Laws—(See "Moral Laws" under Love Affairs).

Laxity—Lax Morals—(See Laxity; "Loose Morals" in this section).

Lewd; Liaisons—(See Love Affairs).

Liars; Libelers; Libidinous;

Licentious; Light-Fingered — (See Kleptomaniac).

Liquors—Indiscriminate Use of—(See Liquors).

Living — (See "Free Living" under Free).

Look—(Debauched, Dissipated, Wanton Look).

Loose Morals—Loose Living—Immorality—The ☉ ☌ ♀ in ♏, and afflicted; the ☉ to the bad aspects ♀ or the ☽ by dir.; ♆ affl. in the 5th or 7th H.; a ♆ disease and affliction; ♆ ☌, □, or ☍ ☽; ♆ by tr. in ☌ the radical ☽ or ☿ if ♆ is afflicted at B., tends to an unclean and polluted mind; the bad aspects of ♆ to the Sigs. tend to moral introversion, as the perverted influence of this planet is seductive; ♆ afflicted in ♏; the violent oppositions of ♆ and ♅ from the ♉ and ♏ signs, and affecting the 5th or 7th H.; ♅ by tr. ☌ ♀; the influence of ♅ by his afflictions and lower vibrations is to pervert the moral nature, lead to free love, unconventionalities, sex freedom, and clandestine love affairs; ♅ in the 5th or 7th H., and afflicting ♀; ♄ Sig. □ or ☍ ♀; ♄ in ♓, □ ♃ in ♐; ♃ □ ♄; ♂ ruler of the horoscope, and afflicted; ♂ ☌ or ill-asp. ♀ or the ☽; ♂ to the ill aspects ♀ by dir.; no direction of ♂ to ♀ is good for the morals; ♂ affl. in ♏, or afflicting ♀ from this sign, tends to sex diseases from sex abuses and sex immoralities; ♀ in ♏ and afflicted by ♆, ♅, ♄, ♂, or the ☽; ♀ afflicted at B., and to the ☌ or ill-asps. the Asc. by dir.; ♀ progressed, ☌, P., □ or ☍ ♅ or ♆ in the radical map, or vice versa; ♀ to the ☌ ♂ by dir.; ♀ or the ☽ to the ☌ or ill-asp. ♆, ♅, or ♂ by dir., and espec. if the ☽ or ♀ are afflicted by malefics at B., tends to loose morals, especially in women; ☿ progressed in □ or ☍ the radical ♅, a wayward state of mind; ☿ prog. to the □ or ☍ the radical ♆, if such is shown in the radix; the 3rd face of ♓ on the Asc. (See "Free Living" under Free; Infamous, Intercourse; "Loose Habits" under Loose; Love Affairs, Lust, Passion, Perverse, Perversions, Sex; the various subjects in this section).

Love Affairs—(See the various paragraphs under Love Affairs).

Low—(Low and Base—Low Character—Low Women).

Lower Nature — (See "Nature" under Lower).

Lustful; Luxuries—Fond of—(See Expense, Extravagance, Luxuries).

Malevolent; Malicious;

Manly and Sober—(See Manners).

Manners — (See the various paragraphs under Manners).

Marriage—Marriage Partner—(See the various paragraphs under these subjects).

Men—(See "Addicted to Women", and the various paragraphs under Men).

Methods — (See the subjects under Methods).

Mockery; Modest; Money — (Prodigal In the Use of).

Moral Folly—(See "Folly" in this section).

Moral Insensibiity—(See Debased, Debauched, Depraved, Infamous, Loose, Low, Obscene, Perversions, Shameless, Virtue, Wanton; the various paragraphs in this section).

Moral Lapses—(See Lapsing).

Moral Laws—Little Respect For—(See "Moral Laws" under Love Affairs).

Moral Nature Suffers—The moral nature tends to suffer under the evil aspects of ♆, as this planet is seductive. (See "Loose Morals" in this section).

Moral Perversions — ♆ diseases; ♀ ruler of the horoscope and afflicted by malefics. (See Deviations, Perversions, Shameless, Unnatural).

Moral Stamina Weakened—The ☉ afflicted by ♄; ♄ ☌ ♀; ♀ ☌ or ill-asp. ♂; ♆ ☌ ♀; ♅ ☐ or ☍ ♀. (See Endurance, Loose, and the various paragraphs in this section).

Morally Ruined — (See Debased, Depraved, Dishonest, Infamous, Love Affairs, Murderers, Passion, Profligate, Shameless, Thieves, Wanton, Wench, Wicked; "Loose" in this section).

Morbid Desires—Morbid Deviations—(See Desires, Deviations, Morbid, Nymphomania, Passion, Sex, etc.).

Motives; Murderers; No Moral Sense—Case—See "Mentally Defective", No. 408 in 1001 N.N. Also see Cases under Nymphomania.

Nymphomania; Obscene; Passion — (See the various paragraphs under Passion).

Perverse; Perversions—Moral and Sex Perverts—(See Passion, Perversions, Sex; "Moral Perversions" in this section).

Pious; Poisoners—(See Poison, Treachery).

Polluted; Principles; Prodigal;

Profligate; Promiscuity—(See "Clandestine" under Sex).

Rape; Respect — Little Respect for Moral Laws — (See "Moral Laws" under Love Affairs).

Riotous; Robbers; Ruined — By the Opposite Sex—(See Disgrace, Excesses; "Ruined" under Love Affairs, Women; "Injured" under Men; "Health Suffers" under Opposite Sex; "Poison Death" under Poison; Scandal, Tragical, Treachery).

Salacious—(See Effeminate, Lust).

Saloons — Frequenter of — (See Drink, Drunkenness, Harlots, Taverns).

Scandal; Scruples — (See Anarchists, Cheating, Conduct, Criminal, Deceitful, Dishonest, Hypocritical, Ideals, Ideas, Liars, Libelers, Motives, Principles, Thieves, etc., and also note the various paragraphs in this Article).

Seduction—(Liable To).

Sensuous—(See Amorous; Lascivious, Lewd, Licentious, Obscene; "Passional Excesses" under Passion; Perversions, Sensuality, Sex, etc.).

Sex Life — Given To — Excesses In — Sex-Perverts—(See Amorous, Excesses, Intercourse; "Amours" under Love Affairs; Passion; "Clandestine" under Sex, etc.).

Shameless; Sober and Manly — (See "Manly" under Manners).

Social Relations — (See Companions, Environment, External, Harlots; "Low Company" under Low; Social, Women).

Sodomists; Sordid; Stamina — (See "Moral Stamina" in this section).

Temptations—(See Influenced, Negative Nature, Temptation).

Thieves; Treacherous; Turpitude;

Unbridled Passion—(See Passion).

Unchaste—(See Immodest, Shameless; "Without Virtue" under Virtue).

Unclean; Unconventional—(See Love Affairs).

Unfaithful—(See Love Affairs).

Unnatural Practices—(See Depraved, Perversions, Unnatural).

Unrestrained—(See Inordinate).

Unwomanly Freedom — Flirtatious — The ☽ afflicted by ♄, and ♂ at the same time above the ☽ or ♀; ♂ ☌ or bad aspect the ☽; ♂ in any aspect to ♀ disposes to flirtation, intense affections, and without stability in love affairs with either sex. (See "Free Love" under Free; "Fickle" under Love Affairs; Nymphomania).

Upright—(See Honest; "Good Morals" in this section).

Vagabond; Venery; Vices; Virtue;

Wanton; Wayward—(See "Wayward" under Mind).

Weak Morals—(See "Loose", and the various paragraphs in this section).

Wench; Whoremongers — (See Harlots).

Wicked; Wife—The Morals of—(See Wife).

Women—Loose Morals In—(See Loose Morals, Unwomanly Freedom, in this section; Harlots, Imprudent, Nymphomania; "Unchaste" under Women).

Worldliness; Wrong — Has Many Temptations to Do Wrong—(See Evil, Habits, Love Affairs, Men, Passion, Sex, Temptations, Women). For other subjects along the line of Morals you may think of, and which are not listed here, look for the subject in the alphabetical arrangement.

MORBID — Pertaining to Disease — An Abnormal State—Saturn is responsible for morbid conditions generally, both of mind and body. (See Saturn).

Action — Morbid Action — The power and degree of morbid action shows a falling off as the planets pass from the cardinal to common signs. (See "Better" under Disease).

Anxiety — Morbid Anxiety About the Health—(See Hypochondria).

Blood—Morbid Blood Conditions— Morbid Changes In the Blood — (See "Morbid" under Blood).

Chronic Diseases—Those caused, and under the rule of ♄ are morbid. (See Chronic).

Compulsions—Morbid Compulsions— Morbid and Uncontrolled States of Mind Which May Lead to Crime, Death, Hallucinations, Insanity, Mania, Murder, Suicide, Violence, etc.—(See these subjects. Also see Fears; "Fixed Ideas" under Ideas; Jealousy; "Morbid" under Mind; Obsessions, Revenge, Spirit Controls, Treachery, etc.).

Deaths—Morbid Deaths—The Anareta In—(See Anareta).

Debility — Morbid Debility is caused by ♄. (See Debility).

Depression—Morbid Depression and Anxiety — (See Anxiety, Depressed, Hypochondria).

Desires — Morbid Sex Desires — (See Amorous; "Morbid", "Sensuous", under Imagination; "Erotic" under Mania; "Morbid" under Passion; Unsavory).

Deviations — Morbid Deviations—(See Deviations, Perversions, Unnatural, Unsavory).

Discharges—Morbid—(See "Offensive" under Discharges).

Diseases — Morbid Diseases and Distempers—Caused by ♄. Due to inhibited functions in the different organs governed by the sign ♄ is in at B., or the sign he occupies temporarily by tr. or dir., as ♄ action tends to a lack of vital activity, or circulation of the vital force in such parts of the body. Chronic diseases also tend to become morbid under ♄ action. (See Chronic).

Distempers—Morbid—(See "Diseases" in this section).

Enlargements — (See "Morbid" under Enlarged).

Evacuations—Morbidly Frequent— (See Diarrhoea, Dysentery, Evacuations).

Exudations — Morbid Exudations of Mucous Membranes—(See Exudations).

Face—(See "Morbid Red" under Face).

Fears—(See "Morbid" under Fears).

Fixed Ideas — Tending to Morbid States of Mind — (See "Morbid" under Fears; "Fixed" under Ideas; Obsessions).

Fluids—Morbid Oozing of—(See Exudations, Osmosis).

Germs—(See "Morbid" under Germs).

Growths — (See "Morbid" under Growths; "Vegetable Growths" under Vegetable).

Health—Morbid Anxiety Concerning— (See Hyponchondria).

Heart — (See "Morbid Action" under Heart).

Humours — Morbid — (See "Offensive" under Humours).

Hyponchondria — Morbid Anxiety About the Health—(See Hypochondria).

Imaginations — (See "Morbid" under Imagination).

Impulses — (See "Morbid" under Impulses).

Manifestations — Morbid manifestations are caused by ♄ and the ♄ sign ♑. (See Capricorn; "Peripheral Nerves" under Peripheral; Saturn).

Mind — (See Idiopathy; "Morbid" under Mind).

Mortification — (See Death, Decay, Gangrene, Mortification).

Obscure —Obscure Morbid Manifestations—(See "Morbid" under Obscure).

Particles—Collections of Morbid Particles In the Body—(See Deposits).

Product — Virus a Morbid Product — (See "Virus" under Pestilence; Virus).

Red Face—(See "Morbid Red" under Face).

Sadness—Morbid Sadness—(See Despair, Gloom, Hope, Hypochondria; "Low Spirits" under Low; Melancholy, Worry, etc.).

Secretions—Morbid Secretions—(See Discharges, Secretions).

Sensations—(See Paraesthesia).

Sex Desires—Morbid—(See "Desires" in this section).

Softening—Morbid Softening of Tissues—(See Malacia).

Stealing—A Morbid Desire to Steal— (See Kleptomania).

Throat—Morbid Exudations In—(See Diphtheria; "Exanthematous" under Throat; "Quinsy", "Tonsilitis", under Tonsils).

Tremors—Morbid Tremors and Twitchings — A ♅ disease. (See Subsultus; "Morbid" under Tremors).

Twitchings—Morbid—(See "Tremors" in this section).

Unclassified—Unclassified Morbid Conditions—The diseases caused by ♆ and ♅. (See Extraordinary, Mysterious, Obscure, Peculiar).

Unsavory Subjects—The Mind Morbid Upon—(See "Morbid" under Mind; Unsavory; "Desires" in this section).

Virus — A Morbid Product — (See "Virus" under Pestilence; Virus).

Vitality—(See "Morbid" under Vitality). For other conditions which may not be listed here, and which involve morbid conditions, look for the subject in the alphabetical arrangement.

MORGUES—A Place Where Corpses Are Kept—Are ruled by the 12th H. (See Corpse, Twelfth House).

MOROSE — Moroseness — Sullen and Austere—Fretful—Surly Temper—Bitter—Particular—The ☉ conciliated with the ruler of the mind, and being cadent and occidentally posited; the ☽ applying to ♄: ♄ ☌ ☿, a heavy mind, dejected, morose and dull; ♄ ruler of the Asc. at B., and afflicted; the 30° ♎ on the Asc. (See Austere, Dejected, Dull, Fears, Fretful; "Mind" under Heavy; Melancholy, Reserved, Rouse, Suicide, Taciturn, etc.).

MORPHINE HABIT—(See Narcotics).

Apomorphine—(See Emetics).

MORTAL ILLNESS — (See "Arguments for Death", "Sure Death", under Death; Fatal).

MORTALITY—The Death Rate—

Aged People—Much Mortality Among —(See "Mortality" under Old Age).

Children — Much Mortality Among — (See "Mortality" under Children).

Common People—Many Deaths Among —(See "Public Mortality Great" under Public).

Death Rate Augmented—The months of April and November tend to an increased death rate, as the action of the ☉ upon our planet is weaker during those months. In the intervals between these months the death rate is diminished.

Death Rate Diminished—(See "Death Rate Augmented" in this section; "Public Health Good" under Public).

Death Rate High — ♂ gives a high death rate when supreme at the Equinoxes or Solstices. (See "Public Mortality Great" under Public).

Depopulation—Great Mortality—Much Mortality, Slaughter and Bloodshed—♄ ☌ ♂ in the first three degrees of the ♋ sign. (See "Shedding of Blood" under Blood; Epidemics, Famine, Pestilence, War).

Eastern Parts—Much Mortality In—♂ in ♑ and Lord of the Year at the Vernal Equi. Comets appearing in ♈ or ♌ tend to much bloodshed in Eastern Parts. (See "Aries Rules" under Nations).

Great — Much Mortality Among The Great—(See "The Great" under Great).

Great Mortality — (See "Death Rate High" in this section).

Grievous Mortalities — Grievous and Petulant—An Eclipse of the ☉ in the 2nd Decan. of ♋. (See Grievous).

Infants — Much Mortality Among — (See "Mortality Great" under Children).

Just Men — Much Mortality Among— The ☉, ☽, and ♃ conjoined in ♎.

Many Deaths Generally — (See Death Rate Augmented, Death Rate High, in this section).

Men — Death of Many Men — (See "Death of Men" under Men).

Persons About to Die—(See Dying).

Petulant Mortalities—(See "Grievous" in this section).

Public Health Bad — Many Deaths Generally—(See "Death Rate High" in this section; Cholera, Drought, Epidemics, Famine, Pestilence, Plague; "Public Health Bad", "Public Mortality Great", under Public).

Public Mortality Great—(See "Death Rate High" in this section).

Summer — A Sickly Summer — (See "Excessive Heat" under Heat; Summer).

Women — Much Mortality Among — (See "Mortality" under Women).

Young Men — Much Mortality Among —(See "Young Men" under Young).

MORTICIANS—(See Undertakers).

MORTIFICATION—♂ causes death by. (See "Death" under Mars).

Foetus—Mortification of—(See Foetus).

Granulations — When Attended by Mortification—(See Granulations).

Soft Tissues—Mortification of—(See Gangrene, Tissues).

MOSSES—Ruled by ♆. (See Neptune).

MOTHER—The Mother—Motherhood—The ☽, ♀, and the 10th H. are allotted to the Mother. In Hindu Astrology the 4th H., the house of the ☽, always rules the mother. Also in European Astrology there is a finer ruling which says that the 4th H. rules the mother in a male nativity, and the 10th H. the mother in a female nativity, and this rule seems to work out in its practical application. The 10th H. is said to rule the affairs of the mother in a general way, and the 4th H., the affairs of the father. By day the ☉ and ♀ are the chief representatives of the parents, and the ☽ and ♄ by night. In Hor'y Q. the ☽ and ♀ are Significators of the mother. (See Father). The following influences are to be noted in the map of the child, and especially in the map of the first-born, if living. However, the influences may exist in the maps of any of the children. Also the map of the mother should be studied in regard to some of the paragraphs, which give influences which especially apply to her map, and show her indications. For the various conditions which affect the mother see the following paragraphs herein, and in the alphabetical arrangement—

Abortions—Miscarriage—Mother May Die By—(See Abortion).

Accidents To — Hurts, Injuries, or Wounds To—Death By—Danger of—The ☽ to the ☌ or ill-asp. ♂ by dir.; the ☽ in the 4th or 7th H., and afflicted by ♂; ♄ □ or ☍ ☽; ♄ or the ☽ cadent, and in □ or ☍ aspect each other; ♄ or the ☽ void of course, and espec. if ♄ is ℞; ♄ cadent, ℞, slow of motion, and afflicting the ☽; ♂ □ or ☍ the ☽ or ♀; ♂ and the ☽ angular, swift in motion, and ♂ □ or ☍ the ☽ and the ☽ ori.; ♂ succedent to the ☽ or ♀, and in □ or ☍ to them, the ☽ void of course, and both ♂ and ♀ ℞; ♂ in evil asp. to the ☽ or ♀, and in angular or succedent houses, and ♄ cadent, ℞ and slow of motion, and afflicting the ☽. An eclipse falling on the ☽ in a child's map. (See Eclipses).

Afflicted—The Mother Afflicted—The ☽ and ♀ in occi. angles or succedent houses denote her afflictions. The ☽ and ♀ in occi. angles and in □ or ☍ ♂; the ☽ ruler of the 4th or 10th H., and afflicted by ♄ or ♂, or malefics; ♄ and the ☽ in angles, swift in motion, and in □ or ☍ each other; ♂ succedent to the ☽ or ♀, or in □ or ☍ to them, and both swift in motion and in angles. (See "Short Life", and the various paragraphs in this section).

Ague — The Mother Afflicted With — (See "Mother" under Ague).

Breasts—Disorders of—(See Breasts, Milk).

Burns—The Mother Dies by Burns—The ☽ in the 4th or 7th H., and afflicted by ♂.

Caesarian Operation—(See "Excision" under Foetus).

Childbed Fever—(See Puerperal).

Childbirth — Danger In — Death In — Accidents In—(See Parturition, Puerperal).

Children—Sex of Her Children—(See "First-Born Child" under Children; "Birth of a Female" under Females; "Births" under Male; Predetermination; "Birth of a Son" under Son).

Cold—Diseases or Death By—♄ ori., and in □ or ☍ ☽. (See Cold).

Confinement — Bad Time During, and After—Danger In—(See Parturition).

Consumption — Afflicted With—Death By—The ☽ occi., and in □ or ☍ ♄; the ☽ in the 1st or 10th H., and affl. by ♄. (See Consumption).

Danger To—The ☽ eclipsed near the time of a Solar Rev., and afflicted by ♅, ♄, or ♂, and espec. if the place of the malefic at B. ascends at the Solar Rev.; the ☽ to the ☌ or P. Dec. Regulus if the ☽ be hyleg; ♄ in the 10th H. in a female nativity, or in the 4th H. in a male geniture, and afflicted by the ⊙ or ☽; the M.C. to the ill-asps. the ☽; the M.C. to the ☌ or P. Dec. the ⊙ if the ⊙ be afflicted at B., or in ☌ violent stars; an eclipse falling on the place of the radical ☽ in the child's horoscope. (See "Disease", and the various paragraphs in this section; "Danger" under Parturition).

Death Of—Indications of Death—Possible Time of Death of the Mother—Manner of Death of—The ⊙ in the 10th or 4th H. at B., (according to the sex of the nativity) or ruler of these houses, and to the ☌ or ill-asp. ♅; the ⊙ ruler of the 5th H. at B., and afflicted, and to the ☌ or P. Dec. the M.C. by dir.; the ☽ to the ill-asps. ♄ by dir., death from Colds or Cold Diseases; the ☽ in the 10th H., □ or ☍ ♄ from an angle; the ☽ weak and affl. at B., and to the ☌ the Asc. M.C., ♄ or ♂ by dir.; afflictions to the ☽ or ♀ in the map of the child; the ☽ afflicted at B., and to the ☌ or P. asp. the Asc. by dir.; the ☽ to the place of Rigel or Cor Scorpio; ♄ in the 10th H., □ or ☍ ☽; ♄ by dir. □ or ☍ the degree on the M.C. at B. The day of death may also occur when ☽ is in □ or ☍ the M.C. at B. by transit; ♄ passing over the place of the ☽ or ♀ at B. by tr., or at a Solar Rev.; ♄ in the 4th H. in a male nativity, or in the 10th H. in a female, and afflicted by the ⊙ or ☽; the M.C. to the ☌ or P. Dec. the ⊙ by dir. when the ⊙ rules the 5th H. at B. (See "Death" under Sister, Wife). For death by Abortion, Accidents, Burns, Childbirth, Cold, Consumption, Early Death, Fevers, Miscarriage, Sudden Death, see these paragraphs in this section.

Detriment To—(See the various paragraphs in this section).

Disease — Diseases Will Attend the Mother — The Mother Diseased — The Mother Subject to Many Diseases—The Mother May Suffer, etc.—In considering the question of the sickness of the mother, the nature of her diseases, the property of the signs in which the afflicting planets are posited should be noted. The ⊙ and ♀ by day should be observed, and ♄ and ☽ by night. There is a close bond of sympathy in these matters between the horoscope of the child and that of the mother, and by making a study of the child's map, the principle concerns of the parents may be ascertained. Evil directions in the child's map may not injure the child, but will tend to affect the parents or guardian. In such study the map of the first-born is preferable, then the map of the second child, etc. Along this line, the following influences are to be noted in the map of the child as to the causes of disease in the mother —The ☽ ori., and afflicted by ♄; the ☽ to the ☌ or ill-asp. ♄ or ♂ by dir.; the ☽ in the 1st or 10th H., and afflicted by ♄, the mother is diseased; the ☽ in the 10th H., □ or ☍ ♄ from an angle; the ☽ at a Solar Rev. passing the place of ♄ at B.; the ☽ to the □ or ☍ the ⊙ or ♀ by dir.; the ☽ to the ☌ or P. Dec. Regulus if the ☽ be hyleg; an eclipse falling on the radical ☽ in a child's map; ♄ passing over the place of the ☽ or ♀ at B. by tr., or at a Solar Rev.; ♄ affl. in the 10th H. at B.; ♄ in the 10th H., □ or ☍ ☽; ♄ or ♂ ☌ or evil asp. the ☽ in the 4th, 5th, 7th, or 8th H., the mother is subject to many diseases; ♄ in the 4th H. in a male nativity, or in the 10th H. in a female, and afflicted by the ⊙ or ☽; ♄ cadent, slow in motion, ℞, and afflicting the ☽; ♂ in evil asp. the ☽ or ♀, and in angular or succedent houses; ♂ succedent to the ☽ or ♀, and in □ or ☍ to them, and with ♂ and ♀ ℞; the Asc. to the □ or ☍ the ☽ or ♀ by dir.; the M.C. to the ☌, P., or evil asp. the ☽ or ♀ if either be weak or afflicted at B.; lord of the 6th in the 4th or 10th H., the mother is afflicted or sickly. (See Afflicted, Early Death, Fevers, Short Life, Sudden Sickness, and the various paragraphs in this section).

Early Death Of—♆, ♅, or ♄ in the 10th H., and afflicted by the □ or ☍ of planets; lord of the 10th a malefic in the 8th, and afflicted. These influences may also apply to the 4th H., according to the sex of the child, as the 4th H. rules the mother in a male nativity, and the 10th H. the mother in a female horoscope. (See Short Life, Sudden Death, in this section).

Eyes—Or Face—Hurts To—The ☽ in the 1st or 10th H., and afflicted by ♂; the ☽ to the ☌ or ill-asp. ♅ or ♂ by dir.; the ☽ ori. and angular, and □ or ☍ ♅ or ♂; ♅ or ♂ angular, □ or ☍ ☽. (See "Eyes" under Father).

Face—Injury To—(See "Eyes" in this section).

Fevers—Liable To—Death by Fevers —The ☽ or ♀ to the ☌ or ill-asp. ♂ by dir.; the ☽ ori., □ or ☍ ♄, tends to death from slow fevers; the ☽ in the 1st or 10th H., and afflicted by ♄ or ♂; ♂ □ or ☍ ♀, with ♂ angular and ♀ occidental. (See "Fevers" under Father).

Foetus — Caesarian Operation — (See "Excision" under Foetus).

Gestation—(See the various paragraphs under Conception, Gestation, Pregnancy, Prenatal Epoch).

Good Health For—Happiness For the Mother—♃ ☌, ✶, or △ the ☽ or ♀; ♀ ☌, ✶, or △ the ☽; the M.C. to the ☌, P., ✶, or △ ♀; the M.C. to the ☌ or P. the ☉ except when the ☉ is ruler of the 5th H. at B., which may cause her death. (See "Long Life" in this section).

Grandmother—Death of—(See Grandparents).

Grievously Afflicted—(See "Afflicted" in this section).

Happiness To—(See "Good Health" in this section).

Health Of—(See Afflicted, Good Health, and the various paragraphs in this section).

Hemorrhages—Floodings—(See Menses).

Hurts To—(See Accidents, Eyes, in this section).

Hysteria—(See "Mother" under Hysteria).

Ill-Fortune To—The ☽ to the place of Hydra's Heart. (See "Ill-Fortune" under Wife).

Ill-Health Of—Illness To—(See Afflicted, Disease, and the various paragraphs in this section; "Ill-Health" under Wife).

Inflammations To—The Possible Death of the Mother by Inflammations or Wounds—The ☽ to the ☌ or ill-asps. ♂ by dir.; the ☽ occi., and angular, and in □ or ☍ ♂. (See Accidents, Fevers, in this section).

Injuries To—(See Accidents, Eyes, Inflammations, in this section).

Kindred—On the Mother's Side—(See "Relatives" in this section).

Latent Disease—Illness or Death of the Mother From—♂ □ or ☍ the ☽ and ♀, with ♂ angular, and with the ☽ and ♀ occi. in the map of the child. (See Latent, Organic).

Leucorrhoea; Life Shortened—For the Mother—The ☽ Sig. □ or ☍ ♄, and caused at times by the evil ways of children. (See "Worries Thru Children" under Children; "Death of a Parent" under Parents; Early Death, Short Life, in this section).

Long Life For—The ☉ configurated with the ☽ or ♀, or ♀ in good asp. to the ☽; ♃ favorably configurated with the ☽ or ♀; ♀ ☌, ✶, or △ the ☽. (See "Good Health" in this section; "Long Life" under Females).

Mad Mother—The Mother a Lunatic—(See "Cases of Madness" under Madness).

Mammae—Disorders of—(See Breasts, Milk).

Mania—Puerperal Mania—(See Puerperal).

Many Diseases—Subject To—(See "Disease" in this section).

Maternal Instincts—(See Maternity).

Matricide—(See "Patricide" under Father).

Menses—Disorders of—(See Menses).

Milk—Disorders of—(See Breasts, Milk).

Miscarriage—Danger of Death By—(See Abortion, Miscarriage).

Misfortune To—(See Accidents, Affliction, Eyes, and the various paragraphs in this section; "Women" under Misfortune).

Mother Fixation—(See this subject under Marriage).

Mother-In-Law—Governed by the 4th H. in a male nativity, and by the 10th H. in a female. (See "Father-In-Law" under Father).

Mother May Suffer—(See Affliction, Disease, and the various paragraphs in this section).

Nervous Complaints—The ☽ in the 4th or 7th H., and afflicted by ♄. (See "Mother" under Hysteria; Neurasthenia, Nervousness, under Nerves).

Organic Trouble—(See "Latent" in this section).

Parents—(See the various paragraphs under Parents).

Parturition—Childbirth—Danger or Death In—(See Parturition, Puerperal).

Pregnancy—(See the paragraphs under Conception, Gestation, Pregnancy).

Puerperal Fever—Puerperal Mania—(See Puerperal).

Relatives—Of the Mother—(See "Aunts and Uncles" under Maternal).

Sex of Her Children—(See "Children" in this section).

Short Life For—The ☽ and ♀ in oriental angles or succedent houses, and in □ or ☍ ♂; ♄ and the ☽ in angles, swift in motion, and in □ or ☍ each other; ♄ and ♂ both afflicting the ☽; ♂ □ or ☍ the ☽ or ♀; ♂ succedent to the ☽ and ♀, or in □ or ☍ to them, and both swift in motion and in angles; lord of the 6th H. in the 8th, and afflicted, and espec. if the lord of the Asc. apply to the □ or ☍ the lord of the 6th. (See "Short Life" under Females).

Shortened—(See "Life Shortened" in this section).

Sickly—The Mother Sickly—(See Affliction, Disease, and the various paragraphs in this section).

Sickness Of—The Mother Suffers—Is Diseased—Sudden Sickness of—(See Afflicted, Disease, Sudden, and the various paragraphs in this section).

Significator Of—A planet in the 10th or 4th H., according to the sex of the child, is the Sig. of the mother if the ☉ or ☽ be not in these houses at B. (See the Introduction to this Article).

Slow Fevers—Death By—(See "Fevers" in this section; "Slow Fevers" under Fever).

Strangles Her Baby—Case—(See "Strangled", No. 922, in 1001 N.N.

Sudden Death Of—The ☽ in the 1st or 10th H., and afflicted by ♂; the ☽ or ♀ to the ☌ or ill-asp. ♅ or ♂ by dir.; the ☽ ori., and angular, and □ or ☍ ♅ or ♂; ♅ or ♂ angular, □ or ☍ the ☽, or to ♀ occidental. (See "Death" under Sudden).

Sudden Sickness Of—♂ in □ or ☍ the ☽ or ♀, with ♂ angular, and the ☽ and ♀ occidental.

Suffers—The Mother Suffers—(See Afflicted, Disease, and the various paragraphs in this section).

Swoonings—(See Fainting).

Time of Death—(See "Death" in this section).

Widows; Wife—(See the various paragraphs under Wife).

Womb Trouble—Possible Death From —The ☽ occi., in □ or ☍ ♄ in map of child. (See Womb).

Women—(See the various paragraphs under Women). Also see such subjects as Family, Fifth House, Fourth House, Fruitful, Home, Husband, Love Affairs, Marriage, Marriage Partner; "Influence Of" under Moon, Venus; Ovaries, Prenatal Epoch, Sister, Tenth House).

Wounds To—(See "Injuries" in this section).

MOTION — Mobility — Motility— Movement—Moving—Action—Kinetic Force, etc.—Mercury rules motion, as the influence of ☿ is excitable, quivering, and tends to ceaseless motion in mind and body. Life manifests as motion and vibration. Motion corresponds to the Mutable Signs, to the Legs, and to the Motive Temperament.

Accelerated Motion—Augmented Mobility—♂ influence. Mars when afflicted tends to tear the body apart and rupture organs and vessels. Augmented mobility is a plus condition, or tonic action of the ♂ influence. (See Action, Augmented, Exaggerated, Hernia; "Tonic" under Mars; Quick, Rapid, Rupture, Tonic, etc.).

Action—(See the various paragraphs under Action).

Amoeboid Action—(See "Amoeboid" under Cells).

Augmented Motion—(See Augmented).

Body—Motion In the Body—(See Action, Gait, Locomotion, Movement, Quick, Slow, Walk; the various paragraphs in this section).

Ceaseless Motion—In Mind and Body —(See the Introduction to this Article).

Energy—(See the subjects under Energy).

Exaggerated Motion—(See Exaggerated).

Excitability—(See Excitable).

Force—(See the paragraphs under Force).

Gait—(See Gait, Walk).

Increased Motion—(See Augmented, Exaggerated, Excitable, Increased, Motion, Movement, Tonic, etc.).

Kinetic Motion—(See Kinetic).

Locomotion; Mind—Motion In—(See Introduction to this Article).

Moon—Motion of—The motion of the ☽ has to be considered in cases of sickness, as the duration and severity of disease, and the crises and critical days, especially in fevers and acute diseases, depend upon her motion. (See Acute, Crises, Critical, Duration; "Motion Of" under Moon; Severity; "Planets" in this section).

Motor—Motor Nerves—Motor Disturbances—(See Motor).

Movement—(See the paragraphs under Motion, Movement).

Muscles—Action and Movement of— (See Locomotion, Muscles).

Nebuloid Motion—(See "Amoeboid" under Cells).

Planets—Motion of—(See "Motion Of" under Planets; "Moon" in this section).

Quick In Motion — Rapid — Active — Quick In Action—Nimble—Quick Walk, etc.—In Hor'y Q. when the Significator is in S. Lat., a quick and nimble person is indicated, and when the Sig. is in N. Lat., a person slow in motion and movement. (See Action, Active, Energy, Gait, Locomotion, Movement, Quick, Rapid, Walk; "Slow" in this section).

Rapid Motion—(See Rapid; "Quick" in this section).

Retarded Motion—(See Lameness, Legs, Paralysis, Retarded, Slow, Suppressed).

Rotational Motion—Rotary—Vortex Motion—♀ influence.

Slow Motion—Retarded Motion—♄ tends to slow motion of body, and to hinder and retard action and movement. (See Accelerated, Quick, in this section; Clumsiness, Dull, Idle, Impeded, Retarded, Slow).

Spasmodic Motion—(See Irregular, Jerky, Spasmodic).

Vibration; Vortex Motion—(See "Rotary" in this section).

Walk—(See the paragraphs under Gait, Locomotion, Walk).

Weak—Weak Motion and Action In the Body—Feeble Action—(See Debility, Feeble, Infirm, Lassitude, Lethargy, Malaise; "Weak Body" under Weak). There are many subjects which have to do with Motion, as related to the body, and to change the motion, as by disease, deformities, defects, habits, acquired tendencies, etc., and also which may be natural. See such subjects as Automatic, Brisk, Contortions, Coordination, Crippled, Defects, Deformities, Dexterity, Disturbed, Dynamic, Erratic, Feet, Graceful, Harmony, Incoordination, Inharmony, Knees, Lameness, Legs, Muscles, Paralysis, Tremblings, etc. For other subjects which you may have in mind look in the alphabetical arrangement. Especially see the subjects of Action, Gait, Locomotion, Motor, Movement, Muscles, Spasmodic, Walk, etc.

MOTIVE—

Motive Signs—♊, ♐, ♓. The ♐ sign especially gives motive force.

Motive Temperament—Motion corresponds to the Motive Temperament. The Common Signs are motive in temperament. Also indicated by ♄, and the 2nd face of the ♄ sign ♑ rising on the Asc. at B. The head in the motive temperament is flatter at the sides and square shaped. (See Decanates, Motion; "Mutable Signs" under Mutable).

MOTIVES—Purposes—Intentions—

Evil Motives — (See Cheating, Conduct, Criminal, Deceitful, Dishonest, Enemies, Evil, Forgers, Hatred, Liars, Libelers, Plots, Poison, Revenge, Thieves, Treachery, Wicked, etc.).

Good Motives—(See Character, Good, Honest, Humane, Kind; "Good Morals" under Morals; Noble, Pious, Purposes, Sincere, etc.).

Misunderstood—Motives Misunderstood—(See Misunderstood).

MOTOR—Motory—Motor Nerves—Motor Functions—Pertaining to Motion —Kinetic Force, etc.—The Motor Nerves are ruled by ♂, and also influenced strongly by ♅.

Arms—♅ in signs which rule the Arms, Hands, Legs, and Feet tends to affect the motor nerves of these parts, causing cramp, spasm, and paralysis.

Brain—Diseases of the Brain Affecting the Motor Functions—♅ afflicted in ♈ or ♉; Subs at AT. (See Brain).

Disturbances—Motor Disturbances—(See Coordination; "Movements" under Erratic; Incoordination).

Erratic Movements—(See Erratic).

Eyes—Oculo Motor Paralysis — (See "Motor" under Eyes).

Functions — Exalted Excito-Motory Functions — (See "Functions" under Exaltation).

Motor Nerves—Disorders of—♅ diseases and afflictions; ♅ afflicted in the 6th H.; ♅ ☌ ♂ in the 6th H.; ♅ afflicted by ♂. Uranus in any sign tends to disturbances of the motor nerves of the part, or parts, ruled by such sign. (See "Arms" in this section; "Motor Nerves" under Arms, Feet, Hands, Legs, Speech, Throat; "Disorders Of" under Coordination; "Nerve Action" under Incoordination).

Motor Vehicles — Death, Accident, or Injury By—Caused by the afflictions of ♅. (See Vehicles).

Neuroses — Motor Neuroses — (See "Movements" under Erratic).

Spinal Cord—Lesions of the Motory Columns Within the Spine—(See "Cord", "Lesions", under Spine).

Vaso-Motor System—(See Vaso). For disorders and diseases which are attended by disturbances of the motor nerves and functions see such subjects as Antiperistalsis, Ataxia, Colic, Contortions, Contractions, Coordination, Cramps, Deformities, Distortions, Energy, Epilepsy, Fits, Gait, Hiccough, Hysteria, Involuntary, Irregular, Jerkings, Kinetic, Locomotion, Motion, Movement, Muscles, Nausea, Nodding (see Head); Nystagmus (see Eyeballs); Paralysis, Saint Vitus Dance, Spasmodic Diseases, Speech (Impediments In); Tetanus, Tics, Tremors, Twistings, Twitching, Vomiting, Walk, Winking (see Eyelids); Wry Neck (see Neck).

MOUNTAIN FEVER—Rocky Mountain Fever—A ♌ disorder, and afflictions in ♌; ♂ afflicted in ♌; Subs at CP and KP. (See Fevers).

MOURNFUL—(See Bereavement, Complaining, Rejected, Depressed, Despond-

ent, Gloom, Grief, Lamenting, Low Spirits (see Low); Melancholic, Murmuring, Regretful, Repining, Sad, Sorrowful, Worry, etc.).

MOUTH—The Mouth—The Cavity At the Entrance to the Alimentary Canal —The Mouth is under the external rulership of the ♈ sign. Also ruled by ☿ and the ♎ sign. Mercury in ♈ has special rule and influence over the mouth, and its diseases when afflicted.

Affections—Of the Mouth—All Diseases of the Mouth—☉ diseases; the ☉ afflicted in ♈; the ☉ tends to cause all diseases of the mouth; ☿ afflicted in ♈; afflictions in ♈ or ♉, as ♉ rules the lower teeth and gums; afflictions in ♎ by reflex action; afflictions in the 1st House; Subs at MCP, LCP, CP, SP(7D), and KP (11D). (See the various paragraphs in this section).

All Diseases In—Signified by the 1st House. (See "Affections" in this section).

Aphthous Ulcers—Canker — Gangrenous Sores—Stomatitis—Thrush—Sore Mouth—(See "Mouth" under Aphthae, Gangrene).

Breathing—Mouth Breathing—(See "Mouth" under Breathing).

Broad Mouth—A Great Mouth—Large Mouth—Wide Mouth—The ☉ Sig. in ♉; the ☉ or ♂ in ♉ in partile asp. the Asc.; the ☉ in ♏; ♂ Sig. in ♉; ♉ gives, and with ♉ on the Asc.

Cankers—Aphthae—Mouth Sores—Cancrum Oris, etc.—(See "Mouth" under Aphthae, Gangrene).

Cleft Palate—Case—(See Palate).

Cystic Tumor—Under the Tongue—♀ afflicted in ♉. (See Ranula, Tongue).

Dentition—(See Teeth).

Dry Mouth—(See Fauces).

Foot and Mouth Diseases—(See "Foot and Mouth" under Feet).

Frothing At Mouth — (See Epilepsy, Fits, Hydrophobia, Saliva).

Gangrenous Sores — Cancrum Oris — (See Aphthae, Gangrene).

Glands — Glands of the Mouth Disordered—The ☽, ♆, or ☿ afflicted in ♈ or ♉; Subs at SP (7D). (See Glands, Saliva).

Great Mouth — (See "Broad" in this section).

Heat — Extreme Heat In the Mouth and Throat—(See "Heat" under Throat).

Infants — Sore Mouth In — Thrush — (See Aphthae).

Inflamed Mouth — Stomatitis — Aphthous Stomatitis—(See Aphthae).

Large Mouth — (See "Broad" in this section).

Lips — (See the paragraphs under Lips).

Lovely Mouth — ♀ in the Asc., and well dignified at B. (See "Lovely" under Face).

Mucous Membranes—Of the Mouth— Disorders of — Dryness of — ♄ afflicted in ♈ or ♉; ♂ afflicted in ♉; Subs at LCP and SP. (See Fauces; "Heat" under Throat).

Muscles — Nervous Catching of the Muscles of the Mouth — ♄ afflicted in the Asc. at B.

Nervous Disorders—Of the Muscles of the Mouth—(See "Muscles" in this section).

Palate — Roof of the Mouth — (See Palate).

Posterior Part — Of the Mouth — Disorders In—Dry Conditions In—Sore In, etc.—Caused by afflictions in the latter degrees of ♈, and in ♉; Subs at LCP (6,7C). (See Diphtheria, Fauces; "Heat" under Throat; Tonsils).

Pyorrhoea—(See Gums, Pyorrhoea).

Ranula—(See "Cystic Tumor" in this section).

Roof of Mouth—Palate—Cleft Palate —(See Palate).

Salivation—(See Saliva).

Sordes — Fetid Accumulations About the Teeth—(See "Sordes" under Teeth).

Sore Mouth — Sores In — Inflamed Mouth — Aphthous Stomatitis — (See Aphthae, Gangrene).

Stomatitis — Aphthous Stomatitis— (See "Mouth" under Aphthae).

Teeth — (See the paragraphs under Teeth).

Throat — (See the paragraphs under Fauces, Pharynx, Throat, Tonsils).

Thrush — Cankerous Sores In Mouth of Infants—Aphthous Stomatitis—(See Aphthae, Thrush).

Tongue — (See the subjects under Tongue).

Tumor—Under the Tongue—Epulis— (See "Cystic" in this section; Ranula).

Ulcers — Small, White Ulcerous Patches—Cankerous Sores—Aphthae— (See Aphthae, Gangrene, Thrush).

Uvula—Disorders of—(See Uvula).

Wide Mouth — (See "Broad" in this section).

MOVEABLE SIGNS—(See Cardinal).

MOVEMENT — Movements— Mobility — Motion—

Accelerated — (See "Accelerated" under Motion).

Arms—Inability to Move Arms—(See "Movement" under Arms).

Balance of Movement—In the Body— (See Balance, Coordination, Dexterity, Harmony).

Body—Movement In the Body—The Physiological Action of the ☽. Also caused by ♂. (See Action, Energy, Gait, Locomotion, Motion, Muscles).

Brisk Movements—(See Brisk).

Crippled—The Movements Crippled— (See Crippled, Deformities, Paralysis).

Erratic Movements—(See Erratic).

Gait — (See the paragraphs under Gait, Locomotion, Walk).

Jerky Movements—(See Jerkings).

Muscular Movements — Ruled by ♂. (See Muscles).

Quick In Movement — (See "Full of Action" under Action; "Active Body" under Active; "Choleric Temperament" under Choleric; "Abundance" under

Energy; "Energetic" under Gait; "Accelerated" under Motion; Quick, Rapid).

Retarded Movements—(See Retarded, Slow, under Motion; Retarded, Slow, Suppressed).

Slow Movements—(See "Retarded" in this section; "Slow Gait" under Gait; Slow).

Spasmodic Movements — (See Spasmodic).

MOVING PARTS — Of the Body — Such as the Arms, Extremities, Feet, Hands, Legs, Limbs, etc., are, as such, ruled by ☿ in a general way. (See these subjects).

MUCH — Abundant— Excessive — Along this line see such subjects as Abundance, Accelerated, Augmented; "Much" under Beard; "Too Much" under Blood; "Much Sickness" under Cattle; "Suffers Much" under Disease; "Great" under Energy; Enlargements; "Much Evil" under Evil; Excessive, Great; "Abundance" under Hair; Hyperacidity, Hyperactivity, Increased, Large, Many; "Too Much" under Moisture; "Great Mortality" under Mortality; Over (see the various subjects under Over); Plethora; "Much Rheum" under Rheum; "Much Sickness" under Sickness; "Much Suffering" under Suffering; Superabundance, Swellings; "Much Vitality" under Vitality, etc.).

MUCILAGINOUS—(See Demulcent).

MUCIPAROUS GLANDS — Producing Mucus—(See "Glands" under Mucus).

MUCOUS — Mucus — Muciparous — Mucous Surfaces — Mucous Membranes — Mucous Discharges and Exudations— The Mucous System—Phlegm—Sputum, etc.—Mucous Discharges are ruled in general, and as a fluid, by the ☽. The ♓ sign, and the watery signs in general, also rule over, and greatly influence the secretion, flow, and production of, and especially in pathological and disease conditions. Mucus is also strongly influenced and acted upon by the ♑ sign, which sign rules the Skin and Surfaces, and the ☉ and ☽ acting thru this sign tend to greatly influence mucous secretions, and especially those associated with skin disorders. (See what is said about the Mucous System, the ♑ sign, and the Splenic Diathesis, in the Introduction under Knees). The Saturn Group of Metals tends to have a pathological action on the Mucus, Cutaneous, and Osseous Systems, and especially the metal Lead, which is a ♄ metal. Sulphur, a strong ♄ remedy, also tends to greatly influence the mucous membranes and secretions, and to modify their action and functions. Arsenic, a ♂ remedy, when given in large doses, acts as a powerful irritant to the mucous membranes, and especially the bronchial membranes. Phlegm is mucus from the Bronchial Tubes, and a number of paragraphs concerning Mucus are considered in the Article on Phlegm.

Bowels—Mucus In the Bowels—(See "Mucus" under Bowels).

Catarrh — And with Mucous Discharges—(See Catarrh).

Colds — (See the paragraphs under Colds).

Colic—Mucous Colic—(See "Colic" under Bowels).

Conjunctiva — Mucous Membrane of the Eye—Inflammation of—(See Conjunctiva).

Cough — (See Cough, Expectoration, Spitting).

Discharges — Mucous Discharges — A ♓ disease, and afflictions in ♓. (See "Catarrhal" under Discharges).

Diseases—Mucous Diseases—Diseases of the Mucous Membranes — Largely under the rule of ♄ and ♑, and of which Eczema is typical. (See Eczema; the various paragraphs in this section).

Dropsy — (See "Mucus-Like Dropsy" under Dropsy).

Excessive Secretion Of—(See Catarrh; "Excessive", "Great Expectoration", under Phlegm).

Expectoration—(See "Great Expectoration" under Phlegm).

Exudations — Morbid Discharges On Mucous Membranes—(See Exudations).

Fluids—Mucous Fluids—(See "Mucous Membranes" in this section).

Glands—The Muciparous Glands—Those of the Generative Organs are ruled by the ♏ sign. Also the Muciparous Glands, the Mucus-Producing Glands of any part or organ, are ruled by the sign which rules the part. (See Glands).

Head—Mucous Discharges From—(See Catarrh; "Mucus" under Head; Nose).

Inflammation — Of the Mucous Membranes — Catarrhal Disorders are Inflammations of the Mucous Membrane of the part involved. Acute Inflammations of Mucous Membranes may be caused by ♂ in the sign ruling the part, as ♂ in ♊ tends to colds on the lungs. Saturn in signs tends to a chronic form of irritation and inflammation, as ♄ in ♊ to consumption, continued and morbid expectoration, etc. (See such subjects as Bronchitis, Catarrh, Conjunctivitis, Colds, Consumption, Defluxions, Diphtheria, Discharges; "Catarrh" under Nose; Pneumonia; "Inflammation", "Sore Throat", under Throat, etc.).

Larynx—Phlegm Collections In—(See "Phlegm" under Larynx).

Lungs — (See Catarrh, Consumption, Mucus, Obstructions, under Lungs).

Morbid Exudations—On Mucous Surfaces — (See Diphtheria, Exudations, Throat, Tonsils).

Mouth—(See Aphthous, Mucous Membranes, under Mouth).

Mucous Membranes—Mucous Surfaces and Fluids—Diseases of—The ☽ rules the internal mucous surfaces in a general way, and the ♑ sign rules the outer mucous surfaces, and the comparatively dry Epidermis. Arsenic, a ♂ drug, is an irritant to mucous membranes. The mucous membranes and vascular tissues are influenced by ♀ in such diseases as result from Impure Blood, Poisoning of the System, and Sloughing Sores resulting from Pustular Diseases. Afflictions to the ☽, and the ☽ ☌ or ill-asp. ♄, and af-

flictions in ♑, tend to disorders of the mucous membranes, surfaces, and the normal secretion of mucus. (See "Exudations", and the various paragraphs in this section).

Nose—Nasal Discharges of Mucus—(See Catarrh, Discharges; the various paragraphs under Nose).

Phlegm—Phlegmatic Diseases—Phlegmatic Temperament — (See Phlegm).

Respiratory Membranes—Deficient Secretion of Mucus On the Respiratory Membranes — ♄ ☌ or ill-asp. ☿. (See "Dry Cough" under Cough).

Rheum—(See Rheum).

Stomach — (See Irritations, Mucous Membrane, Obstruction, under Stomach).

Surfaces—The Mucous Surfaces—(See Exudations, Mucous Membranes, in this section).

Throat—Mucus Falling Into—(See "Mucous" under Throat).

Urine—Mucus In—(See "Mucus" under Urine).

Watery Humours — (See Defluxions, Fluxes, Rheum; "Humours" under Watery).

MUDDLING CREATURE — (See "Ill-Formed" under Ill).

MUDDY COMPLEXION — (See "Dull" under Complexion).

MULES—Hybrids—(See the Introduction under Barren; Horses, Hybrids).

MULATTO COMPLEXION—(See "Complexion" under Yellow).

MULLEIN—A Typical Drug of ♄. (See "Saturn Group" under Herbs; "Drugs" under Saturn).

MULTIPLE BIRTHS — (See Double-Bodied Signs, Fruitful, Quadruplets, Triplets, Twins).

MULTITUDE — The Multitude — (See "Common People" under Common; Humanity, Lynching, Mankind, Mobs, Public, Riots, Trampled, Tumults).

MUMPS — Parotiditis — (See "Mumps" under Parotid).

MUNDANE ASTROLOGY — This has to do with Events in the World At Large, and treats of the influence of the Planets, their Aspects, Conjunctions, Sign and House positions, as they affect different Countries, Nations, Cities, and Divisions of the World. This subject has much to do with the study of Calamities, Catastrophies, Cholera, Disasters, Drought, Earthquakes, Epidemics, Famine, Floods, Excessive Cold or Heat, Pestilence, The Plague, Wars, their causes and predetermination, etc. (See these subjects). Every student should make a study of Mundane Astrology, and a convenient Textbook is "Raphael's Mundane Astrology." Also see Pearce's Textbook of Astrology. (See "Planetary Aspects" under Aspects; Humanity, Mankind, Nations, Parallel, Perigee, Perihelion, Planets, Prevalent, Public).

Mundane Parallel Aspect — (See Parallel).

MURDER—Murders—Murderers—Murdered—Murderous—Mars and his afflicting aspects are the principal causes of murder, and of causing people to do things under sudden, exciting, and rash impulses. The afflictions of ♄ over the mind tend to premeditated murder, as resulting from malice, hatred, revenge, plots, jealousy, suspicion, treachery, etc., and especially when ♄ is conjoined with Mars. Murders which are committed under very sudden impulses are usually caused by ♅, and are of the unexpected and unpremeditated class, extraordinary, and unusual, tragical, etc.

A Murderer—Murderous Tendencies—An Assassin—A Potential Murderer—Has the Murder Complex—Not Averse to Shedding Blood—Homicidal—Ready to Rush Into Bloodshed—Criminally Inclined—Bloodthirsty—Violent Tendencies, etc.—The ☉ Sig. □ or ☍ ♂; the ☉ Sig. to the ☌ or ill-asp. ♂ by dir., if the map shows a tendency to violence, and ♂ be much afflicted and ill-dignified at B.; the ☉ joined to Hyades, Castor, Pollux, Pleiades, Ascelli, or Praesepe, danger of being a murderer, or being murdered, and espec. when the ☉ is with Praesepe; the ☉ conjoined with Caput Algol in an angle, and to come to an untimely end; the ☉ with Caput Algol in an angle, or with the hyleg, or if ♂ be there elevated above the Lights when Caput Algol is angular, denotes a murderer and an untimely end; the ☉ directed to all Nebulous Stars, and to Castor and Pollux; the ☉ or ☽ Sig. ☌ ♂, and ♂ ill-dignified; the ☽ in ♏ and afflicted by ♄ or ♂; the ☽ Sig. □ or ☍ ♂; the ☽ to the place of Caput Algol; ♆ afflicted in ♈; ♅ ☌ or ill-asp. ♂; ♅ afflicted in the 9th H.; ♅ ☌ ♂ in ♈; ♅ influence often provides the impulse to do wrong, and commit murder, or have moral lapses; ♅ ☌ or ill-asp. ♄; ♄ Sig. □ or ☍ ♂; ♄ Sig. to the ☌ or ill-asp. ♂ by dir., and especially if ♄ or ♂ were in the 1st, 3rd, 9th, or 10th H. at B.; ♂ Sig. ☌ ♄, and ♂ ill-dignified; the □ and ☍ aspects of ♂ are the aspects of cruelty and murder; ♀ Sig. □ or ☍ ♃, often a secret murderer or thief; ☿ ill-posited and □ or ☍ ♄ or ♂; ☿ Sig. ☌ or ill-asp. ♂, and espec. when in evil asp. to ♄ also; the M.C. to Algol or Hydra's Heart; the 3rd decan. ♌, or 1st dec. ♏ on the Asc. (See Anarchists, Assassins, Criminal, Cruel, Dangerous, Destructiveness, Execution; "Patricide" under Father; Homicidal, Malicious, Manslaughter, Poisoner; "Imprisonment" under Prison; Revengeful, Riotous, Robbers, Thieves, Treachery; "Tendency To" under Violence). Cases and Birth Data of Murderers—All taken from 1001 N.N. See "Wife Murderer", No. 189; "Holloway", No. 189; "Beach Murder", No. 134; "Schauman", A Political Murderer, No. 209; "H. G. R.", Shot and Killed a Man, No. 337; "Thaw Case", Murder of Stanford White, No. 340; "Who Was This?", Homicide, No. 560; "Pressed to Death", No. 626; "Murderer", No. 636; "Boy Murderers", No. 079.

Death by Murder—Murdered to Death—Danger of Being Murdered—Threatened with Murder—Meets with an Untimely End by Violence—The ☉ hyleg, and to the □ or ☍ ♂ by dir.; the ☉ to the place of Praesepe; the ☽ to the ☌ ♂ by dir., and especially if ♂ be Anareta; the ☽ to the place of Caput Algol or the Pleiades; the ☽ hyleg, and to the ☌, P., □ or ☍ ♂ by dir.; ♅ ☌ ♂ in the 7th H.; ♂ is Significator of; ♂ afflicted in fiery signs, and ☌, P., □ or ☍ the Asc. by dir.; ♂ in a human sign and afflicted by other malefics; ♂ ☌ the Asc. by dir.; ♂ ori., □ or ☍ ☉ from fixed signs, or ♂ occi., □ or ☍ ☽ from fixed signs, or death by Suicide, and caused by women if ♀ be with ♂; the Asc. □ or ☍ ♂ by dir., if in an earthy sign; cardinal signs show when strong at B., and containing several malefics, and the hyleg badly afflicted; the 26° ♊ on the Asc. Cases of Death by Murder—In 1001 N.N. See "Peasenhall", No. 170; "Whiteley", No. 336; "Prince", No. 744; "Russia", No. 763. (For further study along this line see Ambushes, Assassinated, Assaults, Attacks, Blows, Burning, Cuts, Duels; "Murdered" under Enemy; Executed, Feuds, Guillotine, Guns, Hanging, Highwaymen, Lynching; "Hand of Man" under Man; Mobs, Mutilation, Pirates, Plots, Poisoning, Public Death, Quarrelsome, Robbers, Ruffians, Stabs; "Flying Stones" under Stones; Suicide, Sword, Thieves, Tragical; "Treachery" under Women; "Untimely End" under Untimely; "Death" under Violence).

Great Men—Murder of—(See "Assassination" under Kings).

Journey—Murdered While On a Journey—Murdered During Travel—Lord of the 8th in the 3rd or 9th H., and afflicted; lord of the 3rd or 9th in evil asp. the ☽, or in the 7th or 8th H. (See Abroad, Assassination, Highwaymen, Journeys, Pirates; "Murder" under Ships; Travel, Voyages).

Many Murders Prevalent—Murderous Pandemics—The ☉ directed to all Nebulous Clusters, and to Castor and Pallux, threatens Murders, Rapes, and Quarrels, both committed upon, and by the native; an eclipse of the ☉ or ☽ in a fiery sign; an eclipse of the ☉ in ♏; the ☽ in the 8th H. at the Vernal Equinox, and Lady of the Year, and especially if in ♈, ♏, or ♑, and afflicted; ♂ sole ruler of an eclipse of the ☉; ♂ in ♏ at the Vernal, and Lord of the Year; ♂ ☌ the ☉ tends to many murders; ♂ elevated above and configurated with ☿ at a Solar Ingress or Eclipse; ♂ ☌ or P. ☿ near the Equator or Tropics; caused by fixed stars of the nature of ♂; caused by ♂ when he is in Perigee, nearest the Earth; ☿ in ♊ ☌ ♂ at the Vernal, and Lord of the Year; a maximum of planetary influences, as the ☌ of three or four of the superior planets in the signs of ♂, as in ♈ or ♏, tend to murderous pandemics. (See "Much Crime Prevalent" under Crime; Mobs; "Murderous Outrages" under Outrages; Robberies; "Much Slaughter Everywhere" under Slaughter; "Outbreaks of Violence" under Violence).

Murdered to Death—(See "Death" in this section).

Murderous Outrages—♂ in 8th H. at a Solar Ingress of ☉ into ♈, and afflicting the ☽ or planet ascending; ♂

in 7th H. at a Solstice, many murders, and criminals very active for the ensuing Quarter.

Noblemen—Murders of—(See Nobles).

Slaughter — Much Slaughter Everywhere—(See "Shedding of Blood" under Blood; Slaughter, War).

Travel — Murdered During — (See "Journey" in this section).

Women— Many Murders of Women— ☿ in ♋ at the Vernal Equi., Lord of the Year, and ☌ ♂ or ♀. (See Cases of Wife Murder under Wife. Also for cases of Men murdered by Women, see "Poison Death" under Poison; Tragical;"Female Treachery" under Treachery).

MURMURING — Regretful — Complaining—Lamentations—The ☽ Sig. □ or ☍ ♄; ♄ Sig. □ or ☍ ☽; many planets in double-bodied signs. (See Anguish, Complaining, Dejected, Discontentment, Exhibitionism, Grief, Lamentations, Misery, Peevish, Regretful, Repining, Sadness, Sorrowful, etc.).

Endures Disease Without Murmuring —Lord of the 5th in the 6th H. (See Complaining).

MUSCAE VOLITANTES — Floating Specks Before the Eyes—(See "Muscae" under Eyes).

MUSCLES — The Muscular System — Muscular — The Muscles, Tendons and Sinews are ruled principally by ♂. Also ruled by the ☽. Certain Groups of Muscles are ruled by other planets. Mars in any sign rules the muscles of the part, or organ, ruled by such sign. Thus, ♂ in ♈ rules the muscles of the head; ♂ in ♉, ♊, ♋, the Intercostal muscles; ♂ in ♋, the muscles of the stomach; ♂ in ♌, the muscles of the heart; in ♍, the abdominal muscles; in ♐, the thighs. Also ♐ rules the locomotor muscles of the hips and thighs. Mars in ♑, ♒, and ♓, the muscles of the knees, calves, feet, etc., and ♂ afflicted in any of these signs tends to affect and disturb the muscular action in the part. The Motor Nerves, which supply the muscles, are also ruled by ♂, and influenced by ♅, and afflictions to ♂ and ♅, or by them, tend to disturbed muscular action, cramps, spasms, paralysis, etc. The muscles of the Genito-Urinary Organs and System, as a whole, are ruled by ♂, as ♂ rules the external Genital Organs.

GENERAL CONSIDERATIONS—

Activity — Muscular Activity — Mars draws upon the Glycogen in the liver for fuel for the muscles during muscular activity. Also during muscular activity, ♄ deposits Uric Acid over the body, causing Gout and Rheumatism. (See Deposits, Glycogen, Gout, Rheumatism, Urea, Uric, Wastes).

Body—A Muscular Body—Athletic— The ☉ Sig. in ♉, proud of his physical strength; the ☽ in ♏; ♂ rising at B., more muscular than corpulent; ♂ in ♌ or ♏; given by ♂; ♄ in ♏. (See Athletics, Exercise, Sports; "Body" under Strong; "Strength" in this section).

Bony and Muscular — (See "Bony, Lean and Muscular", "Bony and Muscular", under Bones).

Cardiac Muscle—(See "Jupiter Group" in this section).

Coordination — Coordinated Muscular Action — (See Coordination, Dexterity, Harmony, Incoordination).

Dexterity—Harmonious Muscular Action—(See Coordination, Dexterity, Harmony).

Fibers and Filaments—Of the Muscles —Ruled by ♂. (See Fibers, Filaments, Ligaments).

Fuel for Muscles—(See "Activity" in this section).

Glycogen — The Fuel for Muscles — (See "Activity" in this section).

Harmony—Harmonious Muscular Action—(See "Coordination" in this section).

Jupiter Group—Of Herbs—This Group of Herbs tends to have a pathological action on the cardiac muscle, and also the Muscular, and Fibro-Ligamentous Systems, the Gastro-Intestinal Tunics, the Vesical Muscle (Bladder), and the Pulmonary Parenchyma. (See "Impar" under Ganglion; "Jupiter Group" under Herbs; "Pathological Action" under Jupiter).

Large Muscles — ♄ in ♌, partile asp. the Asc.

Lean, Bony, and Muscular — (See "Bony" in this section).

Ligaments—(See Ligaments).

Locomotor Muscles — Of the Hips — Ruled by ♐. (See Locomotion).

Motion In—(See Gait, Motion, Movement, Walk).

Motor Nerves — Which Supply the Muscles—(See Motor).

Movements — Muscular Movements— Are ruled by ♂. (See Action, Motion, Motor, Movement).

Muscular Activity—(See "Activity" in this section).

Muscular Body—(See "Body" in this section).

Muscular and Bony — (See "Raw-Boned" under Bones; "Bony" in this section).

Muscular Energy—Muscular Power— Ruled by ♂. (See Energy, Physical, Power, Strength, Strong; "Weak Body" under Weak; "Strength" in this section).

Muscular Movements — (See "Movements" in this section).

Muscular System—Ruled by ♂. (See Mars).

Nerve Supply—To the Muscles—(See "Motor Nerves" under Motor).

Power — Muscular Power — (See Activity, Energy, Muscular, Strength, in this section).

Sinews—(See Sinews).

Strength — Muscular Strength and Power — Strong Muscles — Given by ♂ and the ♂ signs ♈ and ♏. Also assisted by the good aspects of ♅ to ♂, and with the ☉ and ☽ in favorable asp. to ♂ also. The bad aspects of ♅, the ☉ or ☽ to ♂ tend to give strength, but with more danger of disease, strain, or accident. Neptune, ♄, ♀, and the ☽ tend to less muscular strength and power.

The ♉ and ♒ sign people often have strong and muscular bodies, and also ♍ develops muscular strength by exercises and physical culture. The ☉ Sig. in ♉, proud of his physical strength. The mutable signs do not tend to give much muscular strength, and especially ♓, which is weak, and tends to corpulency. The mutable signs tend to give agility rather than muscular strength, except ♓, which is a rather weak sign physically, and tends to dissipation, drink, lethargy, slovenliness, lassitude, etc. Some general aspects which give muscular strength are—♂ in the 6th H. in ♍, and well-aspected by the ☉ and ☽; ♂ rising at B. in ♈ or ♏, and well-aspected by the ☉, ☽, and ♅; ♂ ☌ ♅ in ♏ in the 6th H.; ♂ ✳ or △ the Asc., great muscular strength; the ☽ ☌ ♅ in ♊, and well-aspected by the ☉ and ♂. (See "Body" in this section).

Strong Muscles — (See "Strength" in this section; "Body" under Strong).

Tendons—(See Tendons).

Tensity—The muscles are rendered tense and trembling by ♂. (See Contractions, Spasmodic).

DISEASES OF THE MUSCLES—

Abdominal Muscles—Disorders of— Afflictions in ♍; ♂ in ♍, inflammation of; ♅ in ♍, cramps of; ♄ affl. in ♍, spasm of; Subs at PP (3L). (See Abdomen; "Ileac Passion" under Ileac).

Action — Incoordinated Muscular Action — Ataxia — ♅ influence and afflictions; ♅ afflicted in ♉, the organ of coordination. (See Action, Ataxia, Catalepsy, Contractions, Coordination, Erratic, Gait, Incoordination, Jerky, Lameness, Locomotion, Locomotor Ataxia, Motion, Motor, Movement, Spasmodic, Tics, Twitchings, Walk).

Arms—Muscular Rheumatism In— (See Muscles, Rheumatism, under Arms).

Arthritic Muscular Atrophy — (See "Arthritis" under Legs).

Ataxia—Incoordination—(See Ataxia; "Action" in this section).

Atrophy — (See Atrophy; "Arthritis" under Legs; "Progressive" in this section).

Catalepsy — With Loss of Muscular Activity—(See Catalepsy).

Back—Muscular Rheumatism In— (See Back).

Clonic Spasm—Of Muscles—(See Alternating, Involuntary, Myoclonia, Paramyoclonus; "Clonic" under Spasmodic).

Collapse—Muscular Collapse—Case— (See "Muscular" under Collapse; Flabby, Laxity, Relaxation, in this section).

Contortions—(See Contortions).

Contractions — Of the Muscles — ♅ in any sign, and afflicted, tends to erratic and spasmodic contractions in the part ruled by the sign. Also ♄ tends to contractions due to cold, deposits, impeded functions, as his influence is to hinder, suppress, and interfere with the nerve supply to a part, and as indicated by the sign he is in at B.

An alternating contraction is called a clonic spasm of the muscle. A continued rigid contraction is known as a tonic spasm. There are various movements in the muscles, due to contractions, such as jerkings, tremors, tremblings, irregularities, etc., due to the nature and aspects of the afflicting planet or planets. An exaggerated muscular contraction is often caused by a ☌ of ♂ with ♅, known as Hyperkinesia. Irregular, Alternate, and Spasmodic Contractions are the work of ♅, while a continued contraction is more apt to be caused by ♄, and to become chronic, which may result in a deformity. In intensified muscular contractions ♂ combines his influence in the configuration. (For Contractions in the various parts of the body see Contractions; "Contractions" under Anus, Arms, Face, Feet, Limbs, Neck; "Muscles and Limbs" under Father. Also see Action, Clonic, Cramps, Hyperkinesia, Involuntary, Myoclonic, Opisthotonos, Paramyoclonus, Spasmodic, Tetanus, and the various paragraphs in this section).

Control — Lack of Control Over the Muscles—A weak ♂ at B. (See "Muscles" under Control; "Involuntary" in this section).

Cramps—(See Cramps).

Crystallization — Of the Eye Muscles —(See "Crystallization" under Eyes).

Degeneration—Fatty Degeneration of the Muscles — Caused by ♃. (See Degeneration; "Fatty Degeneration" under Fat).

Diaphragm—Erratic Action of—(See Diaphragm).

Erratic Action — (See "Movements" under Erratic).

Exaggerated Contractions—(See Contractions, Exaggerated; "Hyperkinesia" in this section)..

Excitement—Involuntary Muscular Excitement — (See Contractions, Control, Involuntary, in this section).

Exercise — Inordinate Exercise — (See Exercise, Sports).

Extremities—Disorders of Muscles of —(See "Muscles" under Arms, Extremities, Feet, Hands, Legs; Atrophy, Progressive, and the various paragraphs in this section).

Eyes—Congestion and Crystallization of the Muscles of — (See "Crystallization" under Eyes).

Father — (See "Muscles and Limbs" under Father).

Fatty Degeneration—(See "Degeneration" in this section).

Flabby Muscles—(See "Muscular" under Collapse; Flabby).

Gout — In the Muscles — (See Gout, Rheumatism).

Hands—(See "Muscles" under Hands).

Head—(See "Muscles" under Head).

Heart Muscle—Inefficiency of—(See "Inefficiency" under Heart).

Hurts — To the Muscles — (See the various paragraphs under Blows, Bruises, Cuts, Hurts, Injuries, Stabs, Wounds, etc.).

Hyperkinesia—Exaggerated Muscular Contraction — ♂ ☌ or ill-asp. ♅. (See "Contractions" in this section).

Incoordination — Of Muscular Action —(See "Action" in this section).

Inefficiency—(See "Heart Muscle" in this section).

Inflammation—Of Muscles—Myostitis —May be caused by ♄, by excess deposits of acid wastes, as in Gout, Rheumatism, etc. Also caused by ♂, by excess heat in a muscle, or from hurts, etc. (See Gout, Inflammation, Rheumatism).

Intensified—Muscular Contractions Intensified—(See Contractions, Hyperkinesia, in this section).

Intercostal Muscles—(See Intercostal).

Involuntary Contractions — Involuntary Action of Muscles — Involuntary Muscular Excitement — ♅ or ♂ afflictions; ♂ ☌ ♅. (See Action, Clonic, Contractions, Control, Spasm, Tetanus, and the various paragraphs in this section; Involuntary, Nausea, Vomiting).

Jerkings; Laxity—Of Muscular Tissue —Caused by a weak ♂ at B. Also caused by ♀, and is classed as a ♀ disease. (See Flabby, Laxity, Relaxation).

Legs—(See "Muscles" under Legs).

Ligaments—(See Ligaments).

Limbs — Muscles of — (See Atrophy, Muscles, under Limbs).

Lock-Jaw—Spasm of the Muscles of Jaw—(See Lock-Jaw).

Locomotion—Disorders of Muscles of —(See "Muscular Spasm" under Feet; Gait, Locomotion; "Muscles" under Hips, Legs, Thighs; Walk).

Locomotor Ataxia—(See Ataxia, Locomotor Ataxia; "Action" in this section).

Mastication — Spasm of Muscles of — (See Lock-Jaw).

Mineral Salts — Deficiency of In the Muscles — (See "Blood" under Minerals).

Mouth—(See "Muscles" under Mouth).

Movements — Incoordinated Muscular Movements — ♅ influence. (See Gait, Incoordination, Locomotion, Motion, Motor, Movements, Walk; "Action" in this section).

Myoclonus—(See "Paramyoclonus" in this section).

Myostitis — (See "Inflammation" in this section).

Neck—Contractions and Cramps In— (See Neck).

Opisthotonos— (See Opisthotonos, Trunk).

Pain—In the Muscles—(See Inflammation, Rheumatism, in this section).

Paramyoclonus Multiplex—Myoclonus —A Nervous Disease with Clonic Spasms of the Voluntary Muscles—A ♅ disease and affliction; Subs at AT and AX. (See "Clonic" under Spasmodic).

Power—Lack of Muscular Power—A weak ♂ at B. (See Collapse, Control, Flabby, in this section; "Strength" in the first Division of this Article; "Weak Body" under Weak).

Progressive Muscular Atrophy— Tabes—A ♄ disease and affliction. (See Atrophy, Emaciation, Tabes, Thin, Wasting). Case Of—See "Living Skeleton", No. 053, in 1001 N.N.

Quiverings; Relaxation—Of Muscles —(See Collapse, Flabby, Laxity, Relaxation).

Rheumatism — Muscular Rheumatism —Pain In the Muscles—Caused by the afflictions of ♄, and the retention of wastes and Uric Acid in the tissues. Also caused by ♂ afflictions. (See "Muscular Rheumatism" under Back, Neck; "Rheumatism" under Arms, Feet, Hands, Legs, Limbs, Shoulders; Gout, Rheumatism).

Rigidity—Stiffness—(See Rigidity).

Saint Vitus Dance—(See Saint).

Shoulders — (See "Muscles" under Shoulders).

Sinews—(See Sinews).

Spasm of Muscles—Caused by ♅. (See Abdominal, Clonic, Contractions, Lock-Jaw, Saint Vitus, Tonic, and the various paragraphs in this section; Spasmodic).

Sphincter Ani Muscle—Contraction of —(See Anus).

Stabs—Muscles Wounded By—(See Stabs).

Sterno-Mastoid Muscle—Disorders of —(See Mastoid).

Stiffness—(See Rigidity).

Strain—(See "Muscular Strain" under Strain).

Strength—(See "Strength" in the first Division of this Article; Flabby, Power, Weak, in this section).

Tabes—(See "Progressive" in this section).

Tendons—(See Tendons).

Tetanus — Spasmodic and Continued Contraction of the Muscles — (See "Blood" under Minerals; Spasmodic, Tetanus; "Tonic Spasm" under Tonic).

Tissues — Muscular Tissues — Inflammation of—Laxity of—(See Collapse, Flabby, Inflammation, Laxity, Rheumatism, in this section; Tissues).

Tonic Spasm of Muscles—(See "Tonic" under Spasmodic; Tetanus, Tonic).

Tremors; Trismus—(See Lock-Jaw).

Twistings—(See Twistings).

Twitchings—(See Saint Vitus, Spasmodic, Tics, Twitching; "Involuntary" in this section).

Voluntary Muscles—Clonic Spasm of —Myoclonus — (See Clonic, Paramyoclonus, Spasm, in this section).

Wasting of Muscles—(See Consumptions, Emaciation, Tabes, Wasting; "Progressive" in this section).

Weak Muscular Action—♂ weak at B. (See Collapse, Flabby, Laxity, Power, Relaxation, in this section).

Wounds To—(See "Hurts" in this section). For other subjects along this line which may have been overlooked, and not listed here, look in the alphabetical arrangement for what you have in mind.

MUSHROOMS—Ruled by ♆.

MUSIC—Musicians—

Fond of Music—Has Musical Ability —Denoted by ♀ and ♆ strong at B. Venus especially rules music, and when well-aspected with ♆ gives the higher and inspirational musical genius. The ♊ sign favorably placed and occupied gives manual dexterity, and a good touch in musical work and piano playing. The fire and water elements are also strong in the map, as they rule strongly over the emotions. Taurus and ♎, the signs of ♀, are musical signs, but ♉ gives better executive ability than ♎. The ♋ and ♒ signs also give musical ability. The special areas of the signs which give musical ability and genius are the 16° ♉ and ♏; the 15° of the cardinal signs, and espec. of ♈ and ♋, and also the 24° of cardinal signs; the latter degrees of ♌ and ♒, and the first few degrees of ♍ and ♓. As ♄ rules the hearing, this planet when well configurated with ♀ and ♆, and otherwise favorably placed, tends to give a good ear for music, and to detect all inharmony. Other general influences found in the maps of musical people are the ☉, ☽, or ☿ in ♉ or ♎; ♃ and ♀ configurated with ☿; ♀ in ♉ or ♎; ♀ in the Asc. near the horizon, or ♀ in ♑ gives a musical voice; ☿ Sig. ☌, ⚹, or △ ♀; ♉ or ♎ on the Asc. or M.C.; many planets in bicorporeal signs. (See Geniuses, Prodigies; "Influence Of" under Libra, Taurus, Venus).

Music Halls—Case—Killed In a Fire In a Music Hall—See "Lafayette", No. 812, in 1001 N.N. (See Amusements, Theatres).

Singers—♀ ruler at B., rising in the Asc., and well-aspected, tends to make good singers, and espec. with ♀ rising in ♉. Also, ♉ or ♎ on the Asc., the signs of ♀. Loud singing and straining of the voice should be avoided when ☿ is afflicted in ♉ at B., as ☿ here often tends to nerve disorders of the larynx and vocal cords. (See "Hoarseness" under Larynx; "Musical Voice" under Voice).

MUSTARD—Sinapis—(See Rubefacient, Sinapis, Vesicant).

MUTABLE—Changeable—The Mutable Signs, etc.—

Diseases of the Mutable Signs—Diseases Ruled By—The Common Signs show Asthma, Blood (Poor Blood, Spitting of Blood); Bowel Disorders, Bronchial Disorders, Consumption, Cough, Dejection (Mental); Depression (Mental); Diabetes, Dropsy, Extremities (Diseases In); Kidney Disorders, Lung Diseases, Melancholy, Negative States of Mind, Nervous Diseases, Neurasthenia, Respiratory Disorders, Sciatica, Scurvy, Spasms, Tuberculosis, Worry, etc. (See these subjects).

Mutable Disposition—A Changeable, Vacillating, Restless, and Negative Nature—Given by the mutable signs, such signs on the angles at B., or many planets in them; the 3rd Decan. of ♓ on the Asc. (See "Lack Of" under Concentration; "Mind" under Instability; "Negative Nature" under Negative; Plastic, Restless, Vacillating, etc.).

Mutable Signs of Zodiac—Also called Common Signs, Flexed Signs, and Acute Signs. These signs are ♊, ♍, ♐, and ♓, and are closely allied with the cadent houses, the 3rd, 6th, 9th, and 12th Houses. (See Cadent). These signs relate to Thought. Flexibility is the main characteristic of the mutable signs, and people born with many planets in them are more amenable to suggestion and treatment. These signs form the Mutable Cross, and are all in □ or ☍ aspect to each other, and planets and afflictions in any of them tend to affect or afflict parts or organs ruled by all the common signs. (See "Disease" under Nature). These signs are ruled by ♃ and ☿. Resistance to disease is low with many planets in common signs at B., and especially if the planets are out of dignity, setting, ℞, below the horizon, and badly afflicted, and the mutable signs are more identified with disease than the cardinal and fixed signs. The ♍ people especially court disease, and think and brood much about their health conditions. (See Virgo). The ♍ and ♓ signs, and the 6th and 12th Houses, both have to do with matters of health and sickness, hospitals, asylums, etc. (See Asylums, Hospitals, Pisces, Sixth House, Twelfth House). People born under these signs are more passive, amenable to suggestion, and are subject to many diseases, but easily cured if under the right treatment, but disease may also be greatly prolonged with them, and become chronic, if under evil influences, and bad suggestions as to their condition and cure. People born with all four of the common signs on angles are more vacillating, changeable, and difficult to cure, as they are apt to change Healers frequently, go from one Healer, or System of Healing, to another, and for this reason they often become chronic invalids, and die an early death. Common signs on the angles also increase the chances of Insanity unless the mind is well controlled, and especially if the ☽, ☿, and the Asc. are badly afflicted at B. Pisces is considered the weakest of the common signs, and this sign on the Asc. at B. tends to give a very weak constitution, and also to corpulency, flabbiness of muscle and tissue, a watery constitution, and less vitality. Afflictions in ♓ tend to affect the lungs, bowels, thighs, and feet. (See Pisces). Gemini is the strongest of the common signs, is a positive and highly intellectual sign, and gives more power to resist and fight off disease. (See Gemini). Also, ♐ is a strong, fiery, masculine, and vital sign, and when on the Asc. at B. gives good vitality. (See Sagittarius). The mutable signs are Motive in Temperament, and correspond to the legs, and motion. Gemini, ♐, and ♓, are also called double-bodied signs, and tend to produce Twins, Monsters, and Hermaphrodites. (See Double-Bodied).

Rulership of the Common Signs—The Common, or Mutable signs, bear rule especially over the Arms, Bowels, Digestion, Extremities, Feet, Glandular System, Hands, Legs, Limbs, Lungs, Nervous System, Thighs. (See these subjects). For further study see Angles, Cardinal, Curable, Fixed Signs, Incurable, Mutation, Ninth House, Residence, Sixth House, Suicide, Third House, Twelfth House.

MUTATION — Mutations—Changes— Mutability—Mutations and changes are especially under the rule of the ☽.

Body—Mutations In—(See "Body" under Change).

Fluids — (See "Mutation" under Fluids).

Mind—The Mutability of the Mind Increased—(See "Instability" under Mind; "Mutable Disposition" under Mutable).

MUTE — Mutes — Dumb — Without the Power of Speech—Mute Signs, etc.—

Deaf and Dumb — Deaf Mute — (See "Deaf and Dumb" under Hearing).

Deaf, Dumb and Blind—(See this subject under Hearing).

Deaf, Dumb and Idiot—(See this subject under Hearing).

Mute or Dumb Signs — ♋, ♏, and ♓. Also known as the Reptilian Signs. Called Dumb, or Mute, because the creatures ruled over by these signs make no audible sound. (See Dumb).

Mutes — Dumbness — Deprived of Speech—(See Dumb).

MUTILATED — Mutilations — ♂ is Significator of Mutilations.

Death by Mutilation—♂ in the 7th H., and afflicted at a Solstice, as the ☉ is coming into ♋, or at a Solar Ingress. (See Beheaded; "Burned At Stake" under Burns; "Death By" under Cuts; Hanging, Lynching, Maimed, Mangled, Mobs; "Murdered" under Murder, Stabs; Tortured, etc.).

Degrees — The Mutilated Degrees of the Zodiac—♉ 6th to 10th degrees; ♋ 9th to 15th degrees; ♌ 18, 27, 28; ♏ 18, 19; ♐ 1, 7, 8, 18, 19; ♑ 26 to 29; ♒ 18, 19. These degrees on the Asc. at B., or when such degrees contain malefics, are supposed to cause Deformities, Distortions, Lameness, Mutilations, and especially Lameness. (See "Signs" in this section; "Azimene Degrees" under Azimene; Deformities; "Zodiac" under Degrees; Distortions, Lameness, etc.).

Foetus—Mutilation of At Birth—(See Foetus).

Limb—Mutilation of—(See Beheaded).

Mutilated Beyond Recognition—Case —Fell Under a Train—(See "Strafford", No. 814, in 1001 N.N.

Mutilated Degrees—(See "Degrees" in this section).

Mutilated Signs—(See "Signs" in this section).

Signs — The Mutilated Signs of the Zodiac—The Broken Signs—Imperfect Signs—These signs are ♌, ♏, and ♓. (See "Broken Signs" under Broken; "Causes Of" under Distortions; Imperfect).

MUTINY — Death In Abroad — (See "Battle" under Abroad; "Officer Killed" under Military).

MYDRIASIS—Abnormal Dilation of the Pupils—(See "Mydriasis" under Iris).

MYELITIS—Inflammation of the Spinal Cord—(See "Inflammation" under Spine).

MYOCARDITIS — Inflammation of the Heart—(See Heart).

MYOCLONUS — Myoclonia— (See "Myoclonia" under Arms; "Paramyoclonus" under Muscles; "Clonic", "Myoclonia", under Spasmodic).

MYOPIA — Nearsightedness — (See Accommodation; "Myopia" under Sight).

MYOSTITIS — (See "Inflammation" under Muscles).

MYSTERIOUS   Strange— Extraordinary—Peculiar—Vague—Obscure, etc.

Mysterious Death—Mysterious and Sudden Death—Caused by ♆ or ♅; ♆ the afflicting planet; ♆ afflicted in the 8th H.; ♅ afflicted in the 8th H., or afflicting the hyleg, tends to a strange and mysterious death, and in an uncommon, sudden, and extraordinary manner; the evil aspects of ♆ or ♅ to the hyleg at B., and by dir. (See "Mysterious Death" under Children; Curious, Extraordinary, Remarkable; "Death" under Strange, Sudden; Trance, Untimely, etc.). Case of Mysterious Death—See "Mysterious Death", No. 362, in 1001 N.N.

Mysterious Diseases—Obscure Diseases — Vague — Having a Psychic Rather Than a Physical Origin—♆ diseases. (See Extraordinary; "Imaginary Diseases" under Imagination; Obscure; "Diseases" under Peculiar; Praecipients, Pseudo, Psychic).

Mysterious Sayings—(See Demoniac).

Mystery—Fond of Mystery, Mysterious Doctrines and Studies, and of The Mysteries—(See Metaphysics, Mystical, Neptune, Occult, Philosophy, Perception, Psychic, Science, Truth; "Influence Of" under Uranus).

MYSTICAL — Inclined to Mystical Studies and Practices — Having the Power of Spiritual Sight and Illumination—Intuitive—People who are mystical usually have the Pineal Gland more fully developed than the ordinary person. This Gland is ruled by ♆, the planet of Spiritual Sight, and mystical people are born under the strong influence of ♆, and have ♆ in ♓, the Asc., M.C., 9th H., or ♆ ☌ ☿. Mystical people are in greater danger of obsessions by evil spirits, and Spirit Controls. Uranus is the planet of Occultism, rather than Mysticism, but ♅ conjoined with ♆ aids in giving mystical power, and a desire for Illumination and greater spiritual power and sight. Also ♄, when powerful in the nativity, or conjoined with ☿, renders one mystical, and a confederate in secrecy. (See Hypnotism, Magic, Metaphysics, Neptune, Ninth House, Occult, Philosophy, Psychic, Religion, Science, Spiritual, Truth, etc.).

MYXOEDEMA — Cretinism—Caused by afflictions to ☿, the ruler of the Thyroid Gland; Subs at AT, AX, LCP, SP. This is a disease with mucus-like dropsy, and also is often accompanied by spade-like hands, and with Idiocy, Goiter, and an undeveloped body. (See Cretinism, Dwarf, Goiter, Idiocy, Undeveloped).

N

NADIR — This is the point below the Earth, directly opposite to the Midheaven, or Zenith, and is the beginning of the cusp of the 4th H., and planets occupying the Nadir at B. are considered very strong in their influences to cause disease, and especially when malefics are so situated. The Nadir in a map of the Northern Hemisphere becomes the Midheaven if the native removes to the Southern Hemisphere. Therefore, if a group of malefic planets occupy the Nadir and the 4th H. at B., the native should remain in the Northern Hemisphere where they have less power to cause disease or misfortune, for if he removes to the Southern Hemisphere, he brings these planets to the Midheaven, and makes them powerful for disease, misfortune, or loss of vitality, according to their nature and aspects at B., etc. For this reason, people crossing the Equator, changing Hemispheres, tend to greatly change their fate in life, have misfortune, illness, early death, or good fortune, according to the conditions of their natal map. People born with ♃ ☌ ♀ on the Nadir would thus tend to have better fortune by crossing the Equator, and living in the Southern Hemisphere. If the malefics were all elevated at B., and near the Midheaven, they also would tend to benefit in health if they removed to the Southern Hemisphere, for they would then be on the Nadir of their map, and the polarity changed. Thus, in disease, and the cure of disease, and to change one's fate in life, the map of birth should be carefully studied along this line, and a proper location chosen according to the rules for location and residence. (See Abroad, Foreign Lands, Fourth House, Location, Misfortune, Nations, Native Land; "Place of Birth" under Place; Polarity, Residence, Travel, etc.).

NAEVUS—Nevus—Birthmarks—A Congenital Cutaneous Blemish—Birthmarks are supposed to correspond with the planetary positions at the time of birth.

Face—Naevus On—(See "Naevus" under Face. For further influences along this line see Blemishes, Congenital, Defects, Disfigurements, Freckles, Imperfections, Marks, Moles, Prenatal Epoch, Scars, etc.

NAILS—Nails of the Fingers and Toes —The Nails are connected with the ♍ sign, and are supplied by the Virgo Salt, Potassium Sulphate. Different kinds and shapes of Nails are given by the various Temperaments. In diagnosis, and as an index of disease, health, and the state of the constitution, the Nails make an interesting study. Thus pink nails indicate a good circulation, and a white background under the nails, an anaemic state, low vitality, etc. When there are many planets in one sign at B. the nails change shape as the native gets older. People born under ♀ tend to have

beautiful nails, to harmonize with the comeliness, grace and shapeliness of the rest of the body. Born under ♂ tends to make the nails strong, durable, and with resisting and fighting power when they are used in self-defense. When born under ♄, the nails are dryer, more brittle, lacking in vitality, circulation, etc., and break more easily, and are also more ugly and ill-shaped, and partake of the qualities of ♄. The nails of a ☿ person are usually thin, long, may have ridges and crack easily, and such characteristics are a strong sign of intellectuality, and of a studious and philosophical temperament. And so on with each of the planets. Judge the nature of the nails according to the characteristics of the ruling planet, and the predominating signs and planets at B. Note the following paragraphs about the Nails—

Blue Discolorations—The Half-Moons Dark—The sign of heart trouble, bad circulation, and caused by afflictions in the heart sign ♌, and especially ♄ in ♌. Also caused by ♌ on the Asc., and afflicted. (See Cyanosis; "Nails" under Heart).

Brittle Nails—Dry Nails—Caused by ♄, and also by ☿ when he partakes of the nature of ♄.

Broad Nails—Given by ♌, and ♌ on the Asc.; many planets in fixed signs, and fixed signs on the Asc. and angles. Also, ♌ on the Asc. gives large, broad nails.

Dark Discolorations — (See "Blue" in this section).

Discolorations — (See "Blue" in this section).

Distorted Fingers and Nails — (See "Distorted" under Fingers).

Eats Nails — Eats Glass, Nails, Iron, etc.—(See "Human Ostrich", No. 986, in 1001 N.N.).

Falling Out—Of the Nails—Whitlows —(See "Nails" under Toes).

Felon—Inflammation About the Nails —(See "Felon" under Fingers).

Fingers—(See the various paragraphs under Fingers). The description of the fingers, as clubbed, long, short, slender, etc., will also apply to the Nails.

Half Moons—Discolored—(See "Blue" in this section).

Horny Growths — Instead of Nails — (See "Horny" under Fingers).

Inflammation—About the Nails—(See "Felon" in this section).

Ingrowing Nails — Turned Down On the Sides—♌ influence, and afflictions in ♌.

Large and Long—Large and Broad— ♌ influence. Such nails usually indicate afflictions in ♌ or the 5th H., and heart trouble.

Long Nails—Long, Slender and Well-Shaped—The Psychic Type of Nails—

Many planets in the common and watery signs at B.; ♊ on the Asc. (See "Long" under Hands; Psychic).

Neck Of—Slender—♊ on the Asc.

Pallor Of—Pale or White Background —Lack of Circulation In—♄ influence; ♄ affl. in signs which rule the fingers and toes. (See Emaciation, Invalids, Pale, Sickly; "Weak Body" under Weak).

Phlegmonous Suppuration—Whitlows —(See "Nails" under Toes).

Psychic Type Nails—(See "Long" in this section).

Ridged Lengthwise—☿ influence; born under ☿; ♊ or ♌ on the Asc., and often indicates weak lungs or heart trouble.

Rounded Nails—Well-Shaped—Beautiful—♀ influence, and born under ♀; the ♀ signs ♉ or ♎ on the Asc.

Shape—The nails change shape with age when there are many planets in one sign at B.

Sides Turned Up—Or Down—♌ influence, and is indicative of heart trouble; afflictions in ♌, or ♌ on Asc.

Slender—(See "Long", "Neck", in this section).

Small Nails—With Slender Neck—♊ on the Asc.

Suppuration—About the Nails—Whitlows—(See "Felons" under Fingers; "Nails" under Toes).

Toes—(See "Nails" under Toes).

Turned Up or Down On Sides—♌ influence. (See Ingrowing, Sides Turned Up, in this section).

Well-Shaped—(See "Rounded" in this section).

White—Pallor of—(See "Pallor" in this section).

Whitlows—(See "Suppuration" in this section).

Yellowish—Indicative of Jaundice—♌ influence; ♌ on the Asc.; ♃ influence; ♃ afflicted at B., and especially by ♂. (See Jaundice).

NAKEDNESS—Wandering In Nakedness—(See "Outrageous" under Insanity).

NARCOTICS—Narcotic Drugs—Hypnotic Drugs—The Drug Habit—Drug Taking—Desire for Drugs and Opiates —Drug Addicts—The Cocaine, Heroin, Morphine and Opium Habits—Sleep-Producing Drugs—Soporifics—Stimulant Drugs, etc.—Neptune in general rules Narcotics, Opium, Soporifics, Sleep-Producing, Hypnotic, and Stimulant Drugs of this class. Narcotics are also partly ruled by ♄. (See Xanthalin). These drugs affect the Pineal Gland, which Gland is ruled by ♆, and the use of such drugs as Morphine, Cocaine, Heroin, Opiates, Alcohol, and other Narcotics, cause a supernormal rate of vibration of the Pineal Gland, causing, in many cases, Delirium Tremens and Demoniacal affections. (See "Delirium Tremens" under Delirium; Demoniac, Pineal).

Addicted to Narcotics—Has the Drug Habit—Addicted to the Use of Cocaine, Morphine, Heroin, or An Opiate In Some Form—The Inordinate Use of Drugs and Opiates—♆ influence, and ♆ weak and afflicted at B.; people born under the strong influence of ♆ are predisposed to; ♆ afflicted in ♈, brain disorders from the inordinate use of narcotics; ♆ afflicted in ♌, suspension of the heart action thru drugs, opiates, and narcotics; ♆ affl. in ♍, bowel disorders due to drugs and opiates; ♆ to the ☌, ⚹, or △ ♅ arouses the Pineal Gland, and to cause cravings and soul hunger which is often satisfied by narcotics with the weaker souls; ♆ ☌, P., □, or ☍ the ☉ or Asc., all ailments arising from injudicious use of drugs and narcotics; ♆ ☌, □, or ☍ ☽; ♆ in a weak sign at B., and especially in ♍ and afflicted; ♆ □ or ☍ ♄, ill-health by use of narcotics; ♆ afflicted in ♋, ♏, or ♓; ♆ afflicted in the 6th H., and espec. when in ♍ in this house; ♆ affl. in the 8th H.; progressed planets in ☌ ♆ tend to form the habit; ♆ in ♓ in the 12th H., and afflicted; ♆ afflicting the hyleg; the ☽ afflicted in ♓, the sign of ♆; the ☽ or ☿ afflicted by ♆; the Prog. ☽ to the ☌, P., □, or ☍ ♆, and espec. if ♆ is weak and afflicted at B., and in a watery sign; ♓ on the Asc. at B.; lord of the 6th or 12th H. in ♓; Subs at AT, AX, SP, KP. Cases of Narcotic Addiction—See "Marriage", No. 256; "Spendthrift", No. 262; "Opium Eater", No. 286; "Opium", No. 288, in 1001 N.N. Also in the book, "Astro-Diagnosis", by the Heindels, see Figures 18H, and 20B. (See the various paragraphs in this section).

Alcohol and Opium Habit—♆ in a watery sign, and especially in ♓ in the 6th or 12th H., and afflicted, tends to both inclination for Drink and Narcotics; ♓ on the Asc. Cases—See Nos. 262 and 288 in 1001 N.N. (See Neptune, Pisces).

Bowels Affected By—♆ affl. in ♍, and espec. in 6th H. (See "Opiates" under Bowels).

Brain Affected—By Alcohol or Opiates —(See "Drugs", "Softening', under Brain; "Delirium Tremens" under Delirium).

Cigarettes—And Narcotics—Given to Use of—Case—See Fig. 18H in "Astro-Diagnosis." Also see Case, "Self-Indulgence", No. 229, in 1001 N.N. (See Tobacco).

Cocainism—(See "Addicted To" in this section).

Craving for Narcotics—(See "Addicted To" in this section).

Death from Drug Habit—♆ setting in ☍ to the Luminaries indicates danger of death by taking Drugs, Opiates, Poisons; ♆ afflicted in the 8th H. (See "Death by Poison" under Poison).

Delirium Tremens—From Alcoholism and Narcotics—(See Delirium; Introduction to this Article).

Demoniacal Affections—From Use of Narcotics—(See Demoniac; Introduction to this Article).

Diseases from Drug Taking—♆ afflicted in ♍ or ♎; ♆ affl. in the 6th H. (See Addicted, Bowels, Brain, Heart, in this section).

Drink — (See the various paragraphs under Drink, Drunkenness, Intoxication).

Drug Habit—Drug Taking—Influences Causing — Toxic Psychoses — Principally ♆ influence and affliction; ♆ afflicting the hyleg. Also caused by ♓, the sign of ♆. (See "Addicted To" in this section).

Heart—Drug Heart—♆ affl. in ♌. (See "Drug Heart" under Heart; Tobacco).

Heroin—Use of—(See "Addicted To" in this section).

Hypnotic Drugs — (See "Hypnotic Drugs" under Hypnotic; "Soporifics", and the various paragraphs in this section).

Ill Habits of Body—Thru the Use of Narcotics—♆ diseases.

Injudicious Use Of — All Ailments Arising From—♆ ☌, □, ☍, or P. the ☉. (See "Addicted To" in this section).

Inordinate Use of Opiates—(See "Addicted To" in this section).

Morphine Habit—Morphomania—A ♆ disease and affliction; ♃ in ♊, □, or ☍ ☉, and especially if given first to alleviate pain and suffering; Subs at AT, AX. Cases—Death from An Overdose of Morphine—See "Marriage", No. 256, in 1001 N.N. Also see Fig. 20B in "Astro-Diagnosis". (See "Addicted To" in this section).

Narcotic Drugs — Ruled by ♆ and ♄, and ♄ configurated with ♆ tends to make their daily use more deadly, debilitating, and with greater danger of death.

Narcotic Troubles — And Diseases Arising from Their Inordinate Use—♆ diseases; ♆ afflicted by ♄ at B., and by dir. (See "Addicted To", and the various paragraphs in this section).

Obsessions from Narcotics—♆ □ or ☍ ♄ at B., bad for the health thru obsessions, and by taking narcotic drugs, medicines, and poisons. (See Medicines, Obsessions, Poisons).

Opium Habit—Addicted to Opiates— ♆ diseases; ♆ in ♌ tends to heart trouble from taking opiates; ♆ setting, and in ☍ the ☉ and ☽, tends to death by opiates; ♆ afflicted in ♎ tends to diseases arising from taking opiates, diseases such as weaken, debilitate, and emaciate the constitution, and which usually end in death unless the opiate is discontinued. Cases — See "Opium Eater", No. 286; "Spendthrift", No. 288, in 1001 N.N. (See "Addicted To" in this section; Opium).

Pain and Suffering — Morphine and Opiates should not be used to relieve pain and suffering when ♃ is in ♊, □ or ☍ ☉, and especially if also afflicted by ♆, as such subjects tend to become addicts to morphine, or some form of opiate. (See "Morphine Habit" in this section).

Pineal Gland — Stimulated by Narcotics—(See Pineal; the Introduction to this Article).

Poisoning by Drugs—And Narcotics— ♆, when afflicting, induces to the habit of taking drugs, opiates, hypnotic drugs, narcotics, and is also symptomatic of poisoning by drugs. (See Medicines, Poisons; "Obsessions" in this section).

Predisposed to Use Of—♆ afflicted at B.; ♆ afflicted in the 6th H. (See "Addicted To" in this section).

Sedatives—Given to Opium Sedatives and Sleep-Producing Drugs — ♆ afflicted at B.; ♆ □ or ☍ ♅; ♆ ☌ or ill-asp. ☿. (See "Addicted To" in this section; Drugs, Soporifics, under Sleep).

Sleeping Potions — Suffers Injury By —(See "Drug Heart" under Heart; Drugs, Sleeping Potions, Soporifics, under Sleep).

Smoking Habit — (See "Tobacco" in this section; "Drug Heart" under Heart).

Snuff — Pulverized Tobacco Snuffed Into the Nose—A habit fostered by ♆ influence. (See "Tobacco" in this section).

Soporifics—Narcotics—Sleep-Producing Drugs—Anaesthetics—Ruled by ♆, and ♆ influence and afflictions tend to their use. (See Anaesthetics, Sedatives, Soothing; "Soporifics" in this section and under Sleep).

Stimulants — All narcotic stimulants are under the rule of ♆. Cocaine, Morphine, Heroin, etc., have a stimulating and exhilarating effect for a time, then depression sets in, and weakness, calling for more. (See "Addicted To" in this section).

Suffering and Pain—Alleviation of by Narcotics—(See "Pain" in this section).

Therapeutics—Narcotics, Soporifics, Habit-Producing Drugs, Opiates, etc., are a Therapeutic Property of ♆. (See "Therapeutic" under Neptune).

Tobacco Habit—Snuff Habit—Under the rule of ♆, and ♆ influence and afflictions tend to make great smokers, and especially when ♆ is in the 6th H. (See "Cigarettes" in this section; Tobacco). See Debauched, Dissipated; "His Own Worst Enemy" under Enemies; Indulgent, Prodigal, Sensuous, Self-Indulgent).

NARES—The Nostrils—(See Nose).

NARROW—Narrowing—

Narrow Breast—(See "Narrow" under Chest).

Narrow Chest—Hollow Chest — (See "Narrow" under Chest).

Narrow Chin—(See "Narrow" under Chin).

Narrow Escapes — From Injury or Death—(See "Death" under Escapes).

Narrow Face—(See Decanates; "Narrow" under Face).

Narrow-Minded — Shallow Mind — Little Depth of Mind—(See "Shallow" under Mental).

Narrow Sides—(See Sides).

Narrow Sympathies — Not Humane — The Mind Narrow In Its Sympathies— ♄ influence in general. Also caused by the afflictions of ♂. (See Apathy, Cruel, Indifferent; "Shows No Pity" under Pity; Selfish, Treacherous, Vicious, Violent, etc.).

Narrowing of Parts—(See Constrictions, Contractions, Stenosis, Strictures).

NASAL — Nasal Bones — Nasal Duct — Nasal Fossae—Nares—Nostrils—Naso-Pharynx—Nasal Catarrh—Nasal Disorders, etc.—(See Nose).

NASTY—Foul—Disagreeable, etc.—(See Conduct, Corrupt, Dirty, Disagreeable, Discharges, Filthy, Foul, Habits, Immoral (see Morals); Indecent, Knavish, Lewd, Obscene, Odors, Offensive, Rotten, Temper, Unclean, etc.).

NATAL—Natal Place—The Birth Place — Native Land — (See "Moment of Birth" under Birth; Location, Native, Nativity; "Place of Birth" under Place; Residence, etc.).

NATES—(See Buttocks).

NATIONS—Countries—Peoples—Races —Rulership of the Various Nations— A list of the Rulership of Countries and Nations can be found in Lilly's Grammar of Astrology. A list will also be given here, as far as I have been able to gather up to this time. The ♐ sign is said to rule North America, and the benefic planets in ♐ at B. would make America more fortunate for residence. If a person born in England, ruled by ♈, should have ♃ and ♀ in ♐ at B., he would be apt to have more good fortune in North America than in England, and especially if he had malefics in ♈ at B. However, before removing from one's Native Land, the conditions over the 4th and 9th Houses should be noted, and to know whether the map is fortunate, or unfortunate, for Foreign Residence or Travel. For these rules see Fourth House, Location, Native Land, Ninth House; "Place of Birth" under Place; Residence, Removals, Travel, etc. The following paragraphs give the rulership of the Signs of the Zodiac over the various Nations, and in choosing residence Abroad, see what signs you have ♃ and ♀ in at B., and choose a Country ruled by such signs, if you leave your Native Land. Also it is well to travel and locate in the direction of the benefic planets in your map, provided there are no malefics with them at B., and in the same direction.

ARIES RULES—Great Britain, England, Wales, Germany, Denmark, Galatia, Lithuania, Spain, Portugal; Part of France; Lesser and Lower Poland; Morocco, Eastern Parts; Syria and Judea, and especially Lebanan and Damascus; Palestine, Iceland and adjoining Islands; Northern Soudan, New Zealand; a Small Part of Australia; Part of the Australasian Archipelago; Peru. The Cities and Towns of Lebanon, Damascus, Brunswick, Capua, Cracow, Florence, Leicester, Marseilles, Naples, Padua, Saragossa, Utrecht.

TAURUS RULES — Ireland, Persia, Italy, Great Poland, Asia Minor, The Archipelago, South Russia, Holland, Cypress, Samos, Greenland, Labrador, Newfoundland, Tasmania, New Guinea; the Main Body of Australia; the Atlantic Ocean Basin—the Site of the Ancient Atlantis, and a number of small Islands, and a corner of South America; Aderbijan, Caucasus, Georgia, Media, Mozendaran, White Russia. The Cities and Towns of Dublin, Leipsic, St. Louis, Franconia, Mantua, Palermo, Parma.

GEMINI RULES—North America as a whole; Eastern Canada; the United States east of the Mississippi River in particular; Belgium; West of England, Lower Egypt, Lombardy, Sardinia, West Indies, Colombia, Venezuela; Central America north to the Peninsula of Yucatan; the Southern Half of the Dutch West Indies; a Small Portion of Australia; Northern Ecuador and Islands Adjacent; Indian Ocean. The Cities and Towns of London, Versailles, Louvaine, Melbourne, New York City, San Francisco, Mentz, Nuremburg.

CANCER RULES—Holland, Scotland, Zealand, China, Africa, Armenia, Central Canada; the United States west of the Mississippi River and to the Eastern Part of California; Southern California, Lower California, the Greater Part of Mexico; Indian Ocean and Small Islands; Africa (North and West); Anatolia (near Constantinople); some Writers say Germany. The Cities and Towns of Constantinople, Algiers, Amsterdam, Venice, Genoa, Milan, Bern, Cadiz, Lubeck, Manchester (29th and 30th degrees); St. Andrews, Tunis, York. Some say New York City.

LEO RULES—France, Italy, Bohemia; Northern Part of Roumania; Sicily, Chaldea, Australia, the Alps, Madagascar, Zanzibar, East Africa; Part of Rhodesia; Western Canada; Washington and Oregon States; the Extreme Western Part of the United States; the Northern Half of California; Eastern and Central Alaska; a Large Area of the Pacific Ocean and Numerous Islands; Coast of Tyre and Sidon; Puglia, Cappadocia. Cities and Towns of Prague, Bath, Damascus, Bristol, Philadelphia, Rome, Taunton, Bolton-le-Moors; Ravenna, Chicago.

VIRGO RULES—Turkey in Europe and Asia; Switzerland, Mesopotamia, West Indies, Babylonia; Extreme Southern Siberia; Greece, Assyria, Thessaly, Uraguay, Western Alaska, Hawaiian Islands, Aleutian Islands, Pacific Ocean Basin, Rhodesia, The Congo, Babylon, Candia, Corinth, Croatia; the Country Between the Euphrates and Tiber; Lavadia, Morea, Lower Silesia, Brazil, Crete, New England States, State of Virginia. Cities and Towns of Jerusalem, Paris, Basil, Bagdad, Heidelberg, Cheltenham, Lyons, Navarre, Padua, Reading, Boston, East Side of Los Angeles; Corinth, Norwich, Strasburg, Brindisi.

LIBRA RULES — China, Japan, and Parts of India near them; Austria, Upper Egypt, Livonia, Tibet, Argentine, Siberia, South Pacific Islands, Savoy, Pacific Ocean (the South Pacific); Islands of the South Pacific. Cities and Towns of Lisbon, Vienna, Antwerp, Frankfort On Main; Charlestown, Fribourg, Speyer, Plasencia.

SCORPIO RULES—Barbary, Morocco, Norway, Bavaria, Transvaal, Brazil; Part of East Indies; Siberia, Korea, Manchuria, Philippines, Japan, China, Halifax, Algeria, Catalona, Judea, Uruguay, Paraguay, Eastern Bolivia, Eastern Argentine and Small Islands. Cities and Towns of Frankfort On Oder; Ghent, Algiers, Fez, Liverpool, Messina; Washington, D.C.; Baltimore, Cincinnati, New Orleans.

SAGITTARIUS RULES—Arabia, Spain, Hungary, Tuscany, Dalmatia, Moravia, Siberia, Mongolia, Siam, Burma, Tibet, Borneo, Northern Sumatra; China, Indo-China, Bolivia, Argentine, Chile, South Eastern Peru, Eastern Ecuador, Western Brazil, Southern Colombia, Cape Finisterre; France between Masien and La Garon; Italy (especially Tarante); Provence, Slavonia. Cities and Towns of Singapore, Cologne, Avignon, Toronto, Toledo. Buda, Narbonne, Naples, Sheffield (in Toledo).

CAPRICORN RULES—India, Thrace, West Saxony; Siberia, China, Tibet, Persia, Bulgaria, Afghanistan, Mexico, Orkney Islands, New Zealand; Small Islands in the Antarctic Region; the South Pacific Ocean Region; Bosnia, Circars, Hesse, Illyria, Morea, Khorassan, Lithuania, Macedonia, Mecklenburg, Punjab, Thrace, Styria, Saxony. Cities—Brandenburg, Brussels.

AQUARIUS RULES—Arabia, Russia, Prussia, Tartary, Poland, Siberia, Asiatic Turkey; Sweden, Lithuania, Muscovy, Abyssinia, the Holy Land, Syria, Persia, Cyprus, the Red Sea, the Black and Caspian Seas, Westphalia; Part of the Polynesian Islands; the South Pacific Ocean; Circassia; Lower Sweden, Piedmont. Cities and Towns of Hamburg, Bremen, Trent, Salsburg, Ingoldstadt.

PISCES RULES—Russia, Portugal, Galicia In Spain, Calabria, Scandinavia; Europe as a Whole; Algeria; a Small Part of England; Tripoli, Normandy, Cilicia, Egypt, Nubia, Tunis, the Mediterranean Basin, Polynesia, Samoa, Islands of the Antarctic Ocean, Southern Asia, North Africa, Desert of Sahara; Small Islands of the Mediterranean; Judea. Cities and Towns — Alexandria, Ratisbon, Seville, Worms, Tiverton, Cilicia, Compostella.

NATIVE—Natal—Native Country—Native Land, etc.—

Native Country—The Native Land— The Country of Birth—Hereditary tendencies, and also the nature of the individual environment, are indicated by the sign which rules the Country of Birth. If it is a positive sign, an electro-positive environment is indicated. If a negative sign, an electro-negative environment, etc. In long and chronic diseases the Native Land is often a curative agency in disease if the environment is suited to the constitution. The male is positive by nature, and the female negative. A male, or positive person, being born with the ☉ in ♓, a negative ♃ sign having a potentiality contrary to his own, would be out of place in a Country ruled by the ♓ sign, but such conditions would benefit a female. Thus ♃, ruler of ♓, may thus be evil for a male, but good for a female. Health conditions will tend to be better when a male having the ☉ in a positive sign at B. lives and locates in a Country

ruled by a positive sign, as ♈, ♊, ♌, etc., which location gives a potentiality similar to his own, etc. A female with the ☉ in a negative sign at B. would tend to thrive better in a Country ruled by a negative sign, as one ruled by ♉, ♋, ♍, etc. By following these illustrations up, and applying them to all the Signs, and choosing a Country for residence accordingly, the magnetic conditions over each individual may be better balanced. (See Location, Nations, Polarity, Residence; "Native Land" in this section).

Dangers and Perils—Many Dangers and Perils to the Native—(See "Many Dangers" under Danger; "Narrow" under Escapes; Perils).

Native Land—Should Remain In— Should Not Remain In—

(a) Should Remain In—The ☉, ☽, ♃, or ♀ well-aspected in the 3rd or 4th H.; Planets well-aspected in the 4th H., or Benefics in the 4th in good aspect to the ☉ or ☽; the ☉, ☽, ♃, or ♀ in the Asc., and well-aspected, will tend to give the native success and good health either at Home or Abroad.

(b) Should Remove from Native Land —Malefics in the sign ruling his Native Land; ♃ or ♀ in the 9th H., or rulers of the 9th, and with no malefics in the 9th, and also with the 4th H. badly afflicted by malefics. (See Abroad, Foreign Lands, Location, Nadir; "Place of Birth" under Place; Residence; "Fortunate In Travel", and the various paragraphs under Travel).

Native Place—(See "Place of Birth" under Place).

NATIVITY—Chart of Birth—Figure of the Heavens for the Moment of Birth —The Horoscope of Birth—The Time When the Child Draws the First Breath—The Nativity, or Horoscope of Birth, shows the tendencies and temperament of the native, the environment and external conditions he will encounter, and how he will manifest during the present Incarnation if he drifts with the influences shown. In every nativity there are the good and evil influences. The good should be allowed to manifest, and the evils overcome and transmuted. In every map of birth lies the secret of God's Will over the native, his place and work in life, the niche he is to fill if he finds out what it is. The Nativity shows what line of work to follow for success, advancement, and usefulness; shows the possible health conditions, the parts of the body weakest, most sensitive and ill-fated, and the prospects along health lines; the map shows the financial indications, the relation of the native to neighbors, relatives, children, friends, the Public, etc., for good or ill; shows the marriage conditions, the sign and birthday of the type of person to marry; the prospects of a happy or unhappy marriage; shows who will be the friends, and his possible enemies, and the signs they are born under. In fact, the Nativity deals with every possible condition that will be apt to confront the native, and the nature of the Personality, and the Lower Mind, and what he will have to contend with along moral lines. Man is born with Free Will to use this map as he will, and as he sows, so will he reap. Libraries have been written along this line, and the nature of the Chart of Birth, what it shows and indicates, and every student will have to make a deep and thorough study of the Elements of Astrology in order to understand life, himself, and destiny, and to obey the Axiom, "Man Know Thyself." More is said along this line under the following subjects. (See "Planetary Baptism" under Baptism; "Moment of Birth" under Birth; Character, Destiny, Environment, External, Fate, Heredity, Horoscope; "Map of Birth" under Map, Radix, etc.). Almost every subject in this book has to do with the Map of Birth, the Nativity, and your relation to it Mentally, Physically, and Spiritually. Look in the alphabetical arrangement for the subject you have in mind.

NATURAL—The ☽ rules the Natural and Expulsive Energies over the body, and also the Natural Functions, and especially the natural functions in the female. The ☽ is the source of the natural powers of the body, as the natural powers of each organ, or part, are maintained by the regular and proper functions of such part. (See Energy, Expulsion, Females, Functions; "Influence of the Moon" under Moon).

Natural Abilities—Innate—Inborn—Hereditary, etc.—

(a) Great Natural Abilities—(See the various paragraphs under Ability, Active, Ambition, Energetic, Excellent, Genius, Gifted, Good, Great, Inventive, Learning, Mathematical, Mechanical, Metaphysics; "Good" under Mind; Music, Orator, Philosophy, Prodigies, Qualities, Reading, Scholar, Speech, Study, Talents, Vocation, etc.).

(b) Poor Natural Abilities — Not Highly Gifted—(See Ambition, Chaotic, Concentration, Defects, Dreamy, Dull, Examinations, Idle, Imbecile, Impairments, Inability, Inactive, Incapable, Indifferent, Lack Of, Lazy, Learning, Limitations; "Shallow" under Mentality; "Light In Mind", "Quality", under Mind; Vacillating, Vagabond, Void Of, Wanderer, etc.).

Natural Death—Ordinary Death—Death from Natural Causes—Death In the Ordinary Course of Nature, and Not by Accident, Violence, or by Extraordinary Means—When a natural death is judged to ensue, the 6th and 8th H. are taken into consideration, and the signs in which the malefics are placed. Note the hyleg, the 8th H., and the nature of any planets in the 8th, and also the ruler of the 8th. A benefic planet well-aspected in the 8th H., as ♃ or ♀ in the 8th, or ruler of the 8th, and with no malefic influences in the 8th H., indicate a natural and easy death, and to die in comfort, and in order, and usually at home; ♃ or ♀ in the 8th H., and not afflicted by malefics; ♃ or ♀ in the 4th H., and not afflicted, and with no malefics in the 8th; ♃, ♀, ☿, or the ☽, in the 8th H., well-aspected, and the Asc. hyleg also

favorably aspected; ♄ in the 8th H., well-aspected, or in ♑ or ♎ in the 8th; in Hor'y Q. a natural death is indicated when ♃ or ♀ are lords of the 8th, or in the 8th, or aspecting the cusp of the 8th H. by a ✶ or △, and the death will be by such diseases as shown by the sign they are in, and the part of the body they govern; the lords of death possessing their own natural and peculiar properties, and the malefics ♅, ♄, or ♂ elevated above them, tend to death in the ordinary course of Nature; lord of the 8th in the 8th; lord of the 1st in good aspect to, or stronger than lord of the 8th, or planets in the 8th, or if the benefics be lord of the 8th, or in the 8th, or if there be translation by good aspect. (See "Easy Death" under Death; "Death" under Home).

Natural Defects—In Body or Mind—(See the various references and subjects under Blemishes, Body, Congenital, Defects, Mind).

Natural Faculties—Are ruled by the ☽. (See Faculties).

Natural Forces—In the Body—The Natural Powers—The ☽ is the source of the Natural Forces and Powers of the body. The ☉ and ♂ also tend to endow the bodily forces with life and greater activity. The ☽ afflicted in ♏ tends to lower the natural powers of the body, the vitality and tone, and especially the functions in females. Saturn tends to weaken, subdue, destroy, and to cause death and decay of the natural forces by his afflictions. (See Active, Diminished, Energies, Forces, Functions, Hindrances, Increased, Powers, Retarding, Suppressions, etc.).

Natural Functions—In the Female—Under the rule of the ☽. (See "Functions" under Females; Functions, Menses).

Natural Habits—(See "Natural" under Habits).

Natural Powers — (See "Natural Forces" in this section).

Natural Temperament — The Bodily Temperament—The Physical Temperament—This Temperament is ruled by the Asc., the sign rising, and especially by the Decanate of the rising sign. (Note the various paragraphs under Temperament which refer to the body, such as Cold, Cold and Moist, Hot, Hot and Dry, etc. Also see Decanates).

Unnatural—Contrary to Nature—(See Abnormal, Unnatural).

NATURE—

Active Nature — (See Active, Ambition, Angles, Brisk, Cardinal, Energy, Force, Movement, Motion, Positive, Powers, Quick, Rapid, Walk, etc.).

Curing—Nature-Curing—Nature Cure —♓ is the sign of, and this sign strong at B., and well-occupied, tends to give the magnetic forces which enable one to effect cures along Natural lines. Uranus strong at B. also tends to make Natural Healers, Magnetic Healers, Chiropractors, Naturopaths, Masseurs, Drugless Healers, Faith Healers, Spiritual Healers, Christian Science

Healers, etc. (See "Nature Cure", and the various paragraphs under Healers).

Death—Nature, Kind and Quality of the Death—The Terminus Vitae—Species of the Death—The nature and quality of the death are ruled over by the 8th H., the house of death, and indicated by the 8th H. and the nature of the planets in this house, or ruler of the 8th. The kind of death depends chiefly upon the nature of the planets which by direction tend to cause death, and also to forecast the nature of the final illness, the signs in which such planets were located at B. must be considered, and to know the part of the body liable to be attacked. The nature of the death is to be judged principally by the Directions in operation at the time. If ♄ is the afflictor, death will most likely be from some ♄ disease, as from Cold, Cough, Consumption, Rheumatism, etc., or by a blow or fall if violence is indicated. Saturn when afflicting the hyleg at B., or by dir., or holding the dominion of death, causes death by ♄ diseases, and so with each of the planets when they hold the dominion of death in the natal map, and afflict the hyleg at B., and by dir. Even the Benefics cause death when so situated. When the planet is known which afflicts the hyleg, see the diseases ruled by that planet for the one which may cause death, and the disease under that planet most likely indicated by the map of birth. The nature and kind of the death is also chiefly denoted by the planet which most afflicts the ☉ or ☽, and the sign and house in which placed, and also by the 6th H. conditions. (See "Death" in the Disease Section under each of the planets, where the kind and nature of death are noted under each planet. Also see Anareta; "Quality" under Death; "Death" under Kind, Quality, Species; "Kind of Death" under Old Age).

Disease—Nature of the Disease—Quality and Type of the Disease—The nature and state of the planet from which the ☽ is separating at decumb. shows the cause and nature of the disease, and the state of the sick. (See Sick). The nature and cause of the disease, or sickness, illness, fever, etc., are shown and indicated by the signs on the 6th H. and the Asc., and also by the position of the Significators. Also note the sign in which the majority of the planets are posited at B., and especially the signs which contain the malefics. Shown by the planets which afflict the ☉, ☽, or Asc. The nature of the disease is said to be known from the signs containing the lords of the 1st and 6th H., and the ☽, and whether they are fiery, airy, earthy, or watery signs, as each of these classes produce diseases of a different nature. (See "Signs" under Air, Earth, Fire, Water). In Hor'y Q., to judge of the nature of the disease, take the sign containing the ☽ for the nature and place of the disease. If not the ☽ take the sign on the cusp of the 6th H., and next to it the signs containing the Dispositors of the ☉ and ☽, and there can be little doubt

of the nature of the disease if all, or nearly all, of these agree. If they disagree it is an indication that the Querent has no particular anxiety in the matter. Cardinal Signs show Mental Derangement, Weak Stomach, Kidney and Liver Complaints, Fevers, Indigestion, Vertigo. The Fixed Signs indicate Heart Trouble, Diseases of Throat, of the Urinary Organs, Bronchitis, Stone, Gravel. The Common Signs show Poor Blood, Dropsy, Spitting of Blood, Consumption, Sciatica, Bowel Disorders. (See Ascendant, Cardinal; "Fixed Signs" under Fixed; "Mutable Signs" under Mutable; Parts, Rising Sign; "Quality" under Sickness; Sixth House, Species, Type).

Disposition—Mind—Temperament—Nature of—(See Conduct, Disposition, Evil, Good, Habits, Manners, Mentality; "Quality of the Mind" under Mind; Personality, Temper, Temperament).

Events—Nature of—(See Directions, Events).

Freaks of Nature—(See Freaks).

Healing Powers of Nature—(See Vis Conservatrix).

Magnetic Nature—(See Magnetism).

Nature Cure—(See "Curing" in this section).

Nature's Laws—(See Laws).

Naturopathy—(See this subject under Healers).

Operations—The Four Operations of Nature—These are based upon the four great Elements, Water, Air, Fire, and Earth, and are known respectively as Congelation, Volatilization, Combustion, and Condensation. These four fundamental and essential operations of Nature are synthetized by Hydrogen, Nitrogen, Oxygen, and Carbon. Hydrogen and Congelation are related to the Watery Signs of the Zodiac, ♋, ♏, ♓. Volatilization and Nitrogen are related to the Airy Signs, ♊, ♎, ♒. Oxygen and Combustion are related to the Fiery Signs ♈, ♌, ♐. Condensation and Carbon are related to the Earthy Signs ♉, ♍, ♑, and the fundamental operations in Nature result from the combinations of the elements in various degrees. Heat, Light, Electricity, and Magnetism are the forces which animate the elements of Water, Air, Fire, and Earth, and bring them into correlation with the Universe. (See Air, Earth, Fire, Water, and "Signs" under these subjects; also see Carbon, Combustion, Condensation, Congelation, Electricity, Ether, Heat, Hydrogen, Light, Magnetism, Nitrogen, Oxygen, Rhythm, Volatilization, etc.).

Planets—Nature of—(See each of the planets in the alphabetical arrangement, as Mars, Mercury, Moon, Saturn, etc. Also see Benefics, Malefics, Planets).

Requirements—Nature's Requirements, such as the Care of the Mind, Body, Health, etc.—♄ in ♏ tends to a laxness in attending to Nature's wants, and also ☿ afflicted in ♏, and forgetfulness and carelessness of Nature's requirements should be guarded against when these influences are in the star map of birth. (See Carelessness).

Weak Nature—The 6th Face of ♑ on the Asc. (See Apathy, Environment, External, Indifferent, Lassitude; "Shallow" under Mentality; "Weak Mind" under Mind; Mutable, Negative, Receptive, Suggestion, Susceptibility; "Weak" under Will, etc.).

NATUROPATHY—(See this subject under Healers; Medical Astrology; "Nature Cure" under Nature).

NAUSEA—Sickness At the Stomach—A Desire to Vomit—Caused by ♄ and the ♑ influences, rulers of the peripheral nerves, and tending to morbid manifestations; a ♋ and ♑ disease; the ☽ afflicted in ♋ or ♑; the ☽ in ♋ or ♑ and afflicted by ♂; the ☽ in ♑, and afflicted by the ☉ or ♂ when taken ill, nausea abounds; ♅, ♄, ♂, or ♀ afflicted in ♋ or ♑; ♀ afflicted in ♋ in the 6th H. Physic tends to nauseate if given when the ☽ is in ♈, ♉, or ♑, the Ruminant Signs. (See Antiperistalsis, Emetics, Incoordination, Peripheral, Physic, Ruminant; "Irritations" under Stomach; Vomiting, etc.).

Bilious Nausea—♂ in ♋, or in ☌ or ill-asp. the ☽. (See "Biliousness" under Bile).

NAVAMSA — This is a term used in Hindu Astrology, and is much discussed and mentioned in the British Journal of Astrology, and some mention of it will be given here. (See Hindu). The Navamsa is a division of each Sign of the Zodiac into nine parts of 3.20° each, and each part having a sub-influence of the 12 Signs in strict rotation. Thus ♈ from 0° to 3.20° is the ♈ Navamsa; from 3.20° to 6.40° is the ♉ Navamsa, etc., and so on around thru the Signs. By following this out you can erect and complete your own Table of Navamsas. Navamsa is a Sanscrit term, and means nine-fold division. This is a Hindu division of the Signs, and is not spoken of in European Astrology, but should be studied by Western students, as these sub-influences have been able to account for many diseases and conditions not found or explained in our Western Textbooks. The parts of an organ afflicted are shown by the Navamsa. Thus ♈ rules the head as a whole, but the subdivisions, as Eyes, Nose, Lips, Forehead, etc., would be indicated by the Navamsa. In the heart, the valves, pericardium, endocardium, auricles and ventricles, etc., would be shown by the Navamsa subdivisions of the ♌ sign, to show the rulership of the various parts. Consumption is an affliction of the common signs, and the common sign subdivisions of such signs. Thus the 28° of ♊ and ♐ govern Consumption, as they are in the ♊ and ♐ Navamsa of these signs. (See Consumption, Convulsions, Decanates).

NAVEL—Umbilicus—Under the external rulership of the ♍ sign. Also ruled by ♀ and the 7th H.

Diseases—Of the Umbilicus—♀ diseases, and caused by afflictions to ♀.

Umbilical Hernia—♄ or ♂ afflicted in ♍, and especially in the 6th H.; Subs at Spl.P.

NAVIGATION—Dangers In—Injury or Death In—Sickness In—

Dangers In—Danger In Travel by Water—Troubles by Sea—An eclipse of the ☉ or ☽ in ♓; malefics in the 9th H. in weak signs and afflicted; Comets appearing in ♓. (See "Dangers" under Seas, Ships, Voyages).

Much Loss of Life—Among Seamen and Maritime People—(See Maritime).

NEAR—Nearly—

Near Relatives—(See "Near" under Relations).

Near-Sighted—(See "Myopia" under Sight).

Near Some Danger—Near Some Misfortune—(See "Near Some Danger" under Danger).

Nearly Blind—(See this subject under Blindness).

NEAT—Orderly—Cleanly—Tidy—

Neat Appearance—Neat In Dress—Tidy—Fond of Dress—♂ Sig. in ♌ or ♎; ♀ in the Asc., and dignified at B.; ☿ ⚹ or △ ♀; ☿ Sig. in ♓ tends to make the native a Dandy, foppish, and fond of frivolous ornaments. (See Cleanliness, Dress, Extravagance, Luxuries).

Neat Body—♍ gives a neat and well-formed body; ♍ on the Asc., neat, compact, and well-formed; the ☽ in ♍; ♀ in the Asc. and dignified; ♀ ori., neatly composed, and not too tall or corpulent; ♂ Sig. in ♎. (See Beautiful, Compact, Handsome, Well-Formed, Well-Proportioned).

Neat and Cleanly—(See Cleanliness, Dress).

NEBULOID MOTION—Under the rule of ♆. (See "Amoeboid" under Cells).

NEBULOUS STARS—Nebulae—Nebulous Clusters—Nebular Areas—Nebular Spots—The principal Nebulous Stars mentioned in the Textbooks of Astrology are the Pleiades, Antares, the Ascelli, Hyades, Castor, Pollux, Praesepe, Cloudy Spot of Cancer, Mane of Leo, Sting of Scorpio, Arrow Head of Sagittarius. These Nebulous influences, and their places and degrees, signs, etc., as they appear thru the Zodiac, are given in the front Glossary of Simmonite's Arcana of Astral Philosophy, and also you can find them listed in the various Textbooks and Dictionaries of Astrology. They are listed in this book. Look for them in the alphabetical arrangement. The Nebulous Stars, when directed to the ☉, ☽, or Asc., or rising with the ☉ or ☽ in the Asc. or 10th H., tend to Banishment, Blindness, Cataracts, Decapitation, Disgrace, Dreadful Diseases; Bad Eyes, and Hurts to Eyes; Evils, and every Evil that can befall Humanity; Hurts to Face, Violent Fevers (see Fever); Glaucoma, Imprisonment (see Prison); Miseries, Murders, Quarrels, Rape, Ruin, Sickness, Stabs, Violent Death (see Violent); Wounds, Wretchedness, etc. (See these subjects). These Clusters impair the physical sight by interfering with the etheric vibrations sensed by the retina of the eye, and greatly afflict the sight, and especially when these Nebulous Areas are in ☌ or bad aspect the

☉ or ☽ at B., or in angles with the Luminaries. The ☽ in an angle, afflicted, and with Nebulous Stars, tends to a defect in the Sight. The ☉ or ☽ in a Nebulous place at B., and afflicted by a malefic, tend to eye trouble. Also if the malefic be in one of these places, and afflict the ☉ or ☽, there is danger to the eyes. The influence of ♆ is said to be with these Areas. The Nebulous Areas are mostly of the nature of ♂ and the ☽ combined. (See Blindness, Eyes, Optic, Retina, Sight; "Fixed Stars" under Stars).

NECK—The Part of the Body Between the Head and Trunk—The Cervical Region—The Neck is under the external rulership of the ♉ sign. Is also ruled by ♀. The Bones of the Neck are under the structural rulership of ♉. Also the Neck, and the hinder part towards the shoulders, are represented by the 2nd H. The Nerves and Blood Vessels of the Neck are under the internal rulership of ♉.

DESCRIPTIONS OF THE NECK—

Adam's Apple—(See "Long" in this section).

Bull Neck—Short and Thick—♉ on the Asc.

Fat Neck—Fat and Thick—(See "Thick", and the various paragraphs in this section).

Fleshy Neck—Fleshy and Full About the Neck—Thick Neck—The ☉ in ♉; ♉ or ♏ on the Asc. (See "Thick" in this section).

Full Neck—♉ on the Asc.

Hollow Neck—(See "Long and Thin" in this section).

Long Neck—Long and Thin—Long and Scraggy—Hollow—Long and Small—♈ gives a long, scraggy neck, and with ♈ on the Asc.; ♑ gives a long and small neck, a hollow, ill-shaped, ungainly, or disfigured neck, and especially with ♑ on the Asc. at B. Also ♈ or ♑ on the Asc. at B. usually give a prominent Adam's Apple.

Marks or Moles On—Scars On—Malefics in ♉ or the 2nd H., or very low in the Asc. at B.; ♂ affl. in ♉ in the Asc. tends to hurts, and a scar on the neck from a wound. (See Marks, Moles, Scars).

Moles—(See "Marks" in this section).

Scars On—(See "Accidents To", "Marks", in this Article).

Scraggy and Long—(See "Long" in this section).

Short Neck—♃ in the Asc.; ♉ or ♏ on the Asc.; ♉ on the Asc., short and thick. (See "Thick" in this section).

Small and Long—Scraggy—(See "Long" in this section).

Thick Neck—Fat Neck—Muscular Neck—Strong Neck—Full Neck—♉ or ♏ give, and espec. when on the Asc. at B.; ♂ well-aspected in ♉, and with this sign on the Asc., tends to a strong and muscular neck; ♃ affl. in ♉ may cause more fat than real muscular strength unless ♂ enters favorably into the configuration.

Thin Neck—Long and Scraggy—(See "Long" in this section).

DISORDERS OF THE NECK—Afflictions to the Neck—See the following subjects in the alphabetical arrangement when not more fully considered here—

Abscess Of—A ♉ disease, and afflictions in ♉; afflictions in or about the 16° ♉ or ♏; ♀ in ♉ in the 6th H., afflicted, or afflicting the ☽ or Asc.; ♃ afflicted in ♉. These same influences also tend to abscesses of the throat. Case of Abscess—See "Imperfectly Formed", No. 303, in 1001 N.N. (See Abscesses; "Abscesses" under Throat).

Accidents To—Hurts, Injuries, or Wounds To—♄ or ♂ affl. in ♉ at B.; the ♄ influence tends to blows, bruises, broken neck, etc., while the ♂ influence tends to cuts, stabs, incised wounds, flow of blood, or suicide by razor cuts to the throat.

Affected—The Neck tends to be affected when the ☉ is in ♍; ♄ in ♒ or ♓; ♃ in ♉ or ♑. (See Table 196 in Simmonite's Arcana. Also see "Affected" under Head).

Back Part of Neck—Lower Back Part—Disorders In—Afflictions and malefics in the 2nd H. at B., and especially when in ♉ in this house; afflictions in the latter degrees of ♉; Subs at AX.

Barber's Itch—Of the Face and Neck—(See Barbers).

Boils—Carbuncles On—(See "Neck" under Boils).

Bronchocele—(See Goiter).

Burns—To Face and Neck—(See "Face" under Burns).

Carbuncles—(See Carbuncles; "Neck" under Boils).

Cervical Region—Disorders of—(See Cervical).

Chronic Distempers—About the Neck—♄ in ♉ when he is the afflictor in the disease.

Contractions In—Muscles of Contracted—Spasmodic Contractions—♅ afflicted in ♉. (See "Wry Neck" in this section; Contortions, Contractions, Coordination, Incoordination; "Contractions" under Throat).

Cramps In—♅ affl. in ♉; Subs at MCP (3C). (See "Contractions" in this section; Cramps).

Diseases of the Neck—The Neck Disordered—Neck Complaints—The ☉ and ☽ acting thru the Paryngeal Plexus, and the Superior Cervical Ganglion, tend to affect the neck, Eustachian Tubes, the Throat and their dependencies, and give way to the Renal Diathesis (see "Cervical Ganglion" under Ganglion); caused by afflictions in ♉ or ♏; the ☉ in ♍—♄ in ♒ or ♓—♃ in ♈, ♉, or ♑, and ♀ in ♓, indicate and signify troubles about the neck when these planets are taken as Significators in Hor'y Questions (see Table "A" in Lilly's Astrology); ♃ affl. in ♐; a ♀ disease. (See the various paragraphs in this section).

Dislocations—Caused by ♄ afflicted in ♉, and death by hanging, and especially when the nativity shows violence, or a violent death. (See Dislocations, Hanging).

Distempers—(See "Chronic" in this section).

Enlarged Veins—(See "Veins" in this section).

Fever In—(See Glands, Inflammation, in this section).

Glands—Glandular Swellings—Glandular Fever—(See Goiter; "Mumps" under Parotid; "Glandular Swellings" under Throat; "Swellings" in this section).

Goiter—(See Goiter).

Guillotined; Hanging; Hurts To—(See "Accidents" in this section).

Inflammation In—♂ afflicted in ♉, and also to feverish conditions in neck; the ☽ in ♉ and afflicted by the ☉ or ♂ when taken ill, tends to inflammation in the neck, or hinder part thereof (Hor'y); ♂ affl. in ♉. (See "Swellings" in this section).

Injuries To—(See "Accidents" in this section).

Larynx—Disorders of—(See Larynx).

Left Side of Neck—Burns To—Case—(See "Face" under Burns).

Marks, Moles Scars—(See "Marks" in the first Division of this Article).

Men Suffer with Neck—♂ in ♐ and ℞ at the Vernal Equinox, and lord of the year.

Moles—(See "Marks" in the first part of this Article).

Muscles Of—Cramps and Contractions In—Stiffness of—Pains In—(See Contractions, Cramps, Inflammation, Pains, Rheumatism, Stiff, in this section).

Nervous Disorders Of—♅ or ☿ afflicted in ♉; ♅ ☌ ☿ in ♉, and afflicted by the □ and ☍ aspects of other planets.

Obscure Diseases In—♆ affl. in ♉. (See Obscure).

Obstructions In—♄ affl. in ♉. (See "Obstructions" under Throat).

Pains In—Pains In Neck and Throat—♂ affl. in ♉, extreme pain in the neck when taken ill, and ♂ the afflictor in the disease. (See Inflammation, Rheumatism, Stiff, in this section).

Parotid Gland—Inflammation of—Mumps—(See "Mumps" under Parotid).

Rheumatism—Muscular Rheumatism In—♂ affl. in ♉.

Scars On—(See "Marks" in the first part of this Article).

Scrofula—King's Evil—♉ denotes, and afflictions in ♉; a ♉ disease when in the neck. (See Scrofula).

Stiff Neck—Rigidity—♄ causes stiff neck from cold, and from the deposit of minerals and wastes in the muscles of the neck, and espec. when ♄ is afflicted in ♉ or ♏. Mars causes stiff neck from inflammation of the tissues, or by Mumps, and espec. when afflicted in ♉. (See Inflammation, Parotid, Rheumatism, in this section).

Subluxations—Of the Cervical Vertebrae—(See Subluxations; "Cervical Vertebrae" under Vertebrae).

Swellings In—The ☉ or ♂ affl. in ♉; the ☉ or ☽ in ♉, and afflicted by ♄ or ♂; the ☉ afflicted in ♍ when the ☉ is the afflictor in the disease; ♄ affl. in ♉, from deposits, wastes, or subdued functions; ♂ affl. in ♉, from inflammations of an acute nature; ♀ affl. in ♉, and generally from moist humours in the head when ♀ is the afflictor in the disease (see "Moist Humours" under Head); ☿ affl. in ♉; a ♉ disease and with ♉ on the Asc. Glandular swellings in the neck are signified by the 2nd H., and by afflictions in ♉. (See Glands; "Swellings" under Throat).

Throat—(See the various paragraphs under Throat).

Thyroid Gland—Disorders of—(See Thyroid).

Torticollis—(See "Wry Neck" in this section).

Tumors In—In Neck or Throat—The ☽ affl. in ♉, or afflicting the hyleg therefrom; ♄ affl. in ♉, from deposits of minerals and wastes of the body; ♃ or ♀ afflicted in ♉; ♂ ☌ ♃ in ♉. (See Tumors).

Various Disorders—Of the Neck—The ☽ hyleg in ♉, and afflicted, in a female nativity; the ☉, ☽, and malefics afflicted in ♉ or ♏.

Veins—Veins, Arteries, and Blood Vessels of the Neck Affected—Enlarged Veins—♃ or ♀ afflicted in ♉, or ☌ ♄ or ♂ in ♉. (See Arteries, Veins).

Voice—Vocal Organs—Disorders of—(See Larynx, Voice).

Wens—In the Neck—(See Wens).

Wounds To—(See "Accidents" in this section).

Wry Neck—Torticollis—Contraction of Muscles of the Neck—♅ affl. in ♉; ♄ ☌ ♅ in ♉. (See Contortions, Contractions, Spasmodic).

For disturbances of the Neck of the Bladder and Womb see "Neck" under Bladder, Womb.

NECROMANCY—Given To—☿ ill-dignified and afflicted at B. (See Magic).

NECROPHILISM—Necrophilia—The Desire To Have Sexual Congress with a Dead Body—♄ afflicted in ♏; ♄ ☌ ♆ in ♏; ♄ affl. in ♏ in the 8th H., the house of death. (See "Sex Perversions" under Perversions).

NECROSIS—The Death of a Circumscribed Piece of Tissue—♄ influence; ♄ in ♈ or ♉ tends to Necrosis of the bony sockets of the teeth; ♄ in any sign tends to necrosis, death, decay, or gangrene of the part. (See Decay, Gangrene, Pyorrhoea).

NEGATIVE—Negative Nature—Negative Signs—Negative Planets—

Negative Horas—(See Horas).

Negative Houses—The 2nd, 4th, 6th, 8th, 10th and 12th H. (See "Negative Houses" under Houses. Also see each of these Houses in the alphabetical arrangement, as Second House, Fourth House, Sixth House, etc.).

Negative Nature—The □ and ☍ aspects to the ☽ tend to make one negative and indifferent; the ☽ □ or ☍ ♆; the Prog. ☽ to the ☌, P., or ill-asp. ♆ if ♆ is afflicted at B., tends to negativeness and lassitude; the ☽ or ♀ strong and predominant at B., the native tends to be negative, more easily influenced, and more susceptible to disease, have less will power, live more in the feelings and emotions; give up more easily in the face of obstacles, disease and difficulties, and also be more easily hypnotized; ♆ and ♄, negative planets, tend to negative states of mind thru Psychic and Spiritual causes, Melancholy, Depression, Dejection, etc.; the majority of planets at B. in earthy and watery signs, the negative signs. (See Apathy; "Gives Up Easily" under Disease; Dull; "Fond Of" under Ease; Environment, External; "Hypnotic Subject" under Hypnotism; Improvident, Inactive, Indifferent, Influenced, Instability, Lassitude, Lethargy, Listless; "Low Spirits" under Low; Melancholy; "Shallow" under Mentality; "Light" under Mind; "Mutable Nature" under Mutable; Obsessions, Plastic, Psychic, Receptive; "Low" under Resistance; Spirit Controls, Susceptible, Vacillating; "Weak" under Will, etc.).

Negative Planets—The Magnetic Planets—♆, ♄, ♀, and the ☽, and they render the mind more negative, timid, receptive, susceptible to environment and outside influence, and the mind and body liable to a variety of diseases. They also tend to acidity in the body. (See Acid, Environment, External, Hyperacidity, Magnetic, Receptive. See these planets in the alphabetical arrangement, and note their special influences, and the diseases they foster. See the paragraphs in this Article).

Negative Psychism—(See Psychic).

Negative Signs—Of the Zodiac—Nocturnal Signs—Unfortunate Signs—Receptive Signs—Feminine Signs—♉, ♋, ♍, ♏, ♑, ♓, the earthy and watery signs. The fiery and airy signs are positive. The negative signs predominant at B., and well-occupied by planets, tend to make the native negative, weaker-willed, timid, receptive, somewhat lacking in daring, courage and individuality, and to be more easily influenced and persuaded, or dominated by others; to worry and brood over the troubles of life; to be more anxious and morbid along health lines, and to give up more easily to obstacles and difficulties. These signs on the Asc. at B. tend to give a weaker constitution and less vitality, except ♏, and the ♋ and ♓ signs on the Asc. at B. are considered the weakest of all the Signs when on the Asc., and to give low vitality and resistance, unless counteracted by many other favorable and powerful influences in the radix. Scorpio on the Asc. is considered the best of the negative signs for greater vitality and stamina. Taurus is next to ♏ in giving strength when on the Asc. at B. The negative signs are acid, and the positive signs alkaline. (See Acid, Alkaline, Deceitful, Dishonest; "Signs" under Feminine; Horas, Introspection; "Negative" under Magnetic; "Negative Nature" in this section. Also see each of the Negative Signs in the alphabetical arrangement, and note their influences, characteristics, diseases, qualities, and what they rule).

Polarity—Negative Polarity—(See Polarity).

NEGLECT—Neglectful—Privation—

Native is Neglectful—Is Negligent—Indifferent to Duty—Given to Laxity—Nothing Careful of the Things of This Life—(See Carelessness, Conduct, Debauched, Disgrace, Dissipated, Drink, Drunkenness; "Free Living" under Free; Habits, Idle, Imprisonment (see Prison); Improvident, Inactive; Indifferent; "Fear of Work" under Labor; Lassitude, Laxity, Lazy, Poverty, Procrastination; "Hard to Arouse" under Rouse; Vagabond, etc.).

Privation and Neglect—Diseases Arising From—♄ diseases; the ☉ or ☽ afflicted by ♄. (See "Internal Diseases" under Chill; Famine, Poverty, Privation, Starvation).

NEGRO—

Negro Lips—(See "Thick Lips" under Lips).

Negro Race—(See "Black Skin" under Black; Dark, Races).

NEIGHBORS—Are ruled by the 3rd H. Malefics in this house at B. tend to bad relations with, and possibly injury or hurt by neighbors. Benefics in this house, well-aspected, and with no malefic influence over the 3rd H., tend to benefits by neighbors. (See Brothers, Journeys, Sisters, Third House).

NEOPLASM—A New Growth or Tumor—(See "New Growths" under Growths; Tumors, Warts, Wens, Xanthoma).

NEPHEWS—(See Nieces).

NEPHRITIS—Inflammation of the Kidney—(See Kidneys).

NEPHROLITHIASIS — (See "Kidneys" under Stone).

NEPHROPTOSIS—Prolapse of the Kidney—(See Kidneys).

NEPTUNE—This planet was discovered in 1846. Some Writers say this planet does not belong to our Solar System, but is an outside planet exerting more of a psychic and spiritual influence over Humanity, and tending to Involuntary Clairvoyance, Mediumship, Psychic Diseases, Weird States of Mind, etc. The older Textbooks of Astrology, as Lilly's Astrology, do not mention this planet. Some Writers say that ♆ is the higher octave of ♀. Max Heindel says it is the higher octave of ☿, and exerts an inspirational influence over the mind, and corresponds to the higher vibrations of ☿ rather than those of ♀. Also ♆ is considered the higher octave of ☿ because he acts so strongly upon the Nervous System. (See the book, "Cosmo-Conception", by Max Heindel). At this writing not much is found about this planet in the Textbooks of Astrology, but the Magazines are well-filled with Articles on his nature and influence. Max Heindel, in his book, "The Message of the Stars", has given considerable information about ♆, and information given by the Rosicrucians, and The Elder Brothers of Humanity. In this Article, the information and influences of ♆ have been collected and arranged, both from Books and Magazine Articles. Neptune is especially affiliated with the 12th sign ♓, the sign which rules the Ocean, and the Seas, and also with the 12th House. Neptune is considered strongest in his influence when in ♓. He is said to have his exaltation in the ♋ sign. From observation the influence of ♆ is said to be similar to that of ♄, and is Astringent and Contracting. (See Astringent, Contractions, Ocean, Pisces, Sea, Twelfth House, Waters). This Article has been arranged into three Sections as follows: Section One—General Considerations. Section Two—Neptune Rules. Section Three—Diseases and Afflictions of Neptune. See the following subjects in the alphabetical arrangement when they are merely listed in any of the three divisions of this Article—

— SECTION ONE —

GENERAL CONSIDERATIONS—Also see the Considerations in the Introduction to this Article.

Abstract—♆ in the abstract is semi-spiritual, occult, supra-material, ensnaring, and illaqueative.

Action Of—The action of ♆ is aesthetic, magnetic, negative, moist, warm, fruitful, mysterious, inconstant, seductive, ensnaring, treacherous, etc. (See the various paragraphs in this Article).

Acts Upon—Acts upon the Nervous System, and also upon the Moral and Spiritual Nature, and the Psychic Powers. Acts strongly upon the Pineal Gland, which Gland it rules, which is the Spiritual and Intuitive center in the brain, and also greatly influences the Emotions, and especially in Religious matters. See Emotions, Intuition, Morals, Nerves, Pineal, Psychic, Religion, Spiritual).

Afflictions Of—Evil Aspects of—♆ afflicts by his ☌, P., □ and ☍ aspects. This planet is seductive by his evil aspects, and tends to greatly deprave the moral nature, and also lead to the Drug and Narcotic Habit. His afflictions tend to a chaotic mind, false fears, weird states of mind, obsessions, spirit controls, and Astral disturbances, etc. For the influence of his good aspects see "Aspects" in this section. (See the Diseases of ♆ in Sec. 3 of this Article).

Anareta—♆ may become the Anareta when powerful at B., and afflicting the hyleg, and he usually disposes to death in a riotous manner, by assassination, violence, etc., when Anareta. (See Anareta).

Aspects Of—Good Aspects of—The good aspects of ♆, his ✳, △, etc., to the ☉, ☽, and ☿ tend to greatly enhance the psychic, spiritual and intuitive powers, and to give true and genuine clairvoyance, spiritual sight and foresight, and power to discern Truth. For his Evil Aspects see "Afflictions" in this section).

Chaos—The Planet of Chaos, Doubt and Fear—♆ is the planet of Fear, and Chaos, and Doubt, to ordinary Humanity, as, it is said, the Human Race is not yet very responsive to the higher and better influences of this planet. (See Chaos, Doubt, Fear).

Colors—Lavender. (See Colors).

Discovered—In 1846. See the Article on Neptune, Chap. XVIII, in Pearce's Textbook of Astrology.

Doubt—The Planet of—(See Doubts, Fears).

Drugs—♆ has association with drugs and narcotics, such as Cocaine, Morphine, Heroin, Opiates, and other soporifics and stimulants. (See Narcotics).

Emotions—Influence of ♆ Over—(See Emotions).

Environment—The lower vibrations of ♆ are ensnaring, enticing, and often lead to passional excesses, and an immoral environment. (See Environment, External; "Morbid" under Imagination).

Evil Aspects Of—(See "Afflictions" in this section).

External Influences—The negative and afflicting influences of ♆ tend to unwise entanglements, sex excesses, and to lead the native astray, and into low and bad company. (See Companions, Environment, External, Licentiousness, Morbid, Nymphomania, Sensuality, etc.).

Eyesight and Neptune—(See "Nebulous" in this section).

Fear—♆, the planet of Chaos, Doubt, Fear, Timidity, etc.—(See these subjects).

Herbs Of—(See Herbs).

Hyleg and Neptune—♆ in evil asp. to the hyleg at B., and by dir., helps to destroy life, and to act as Anareta. (See Anareta, Hyleg).

Inclines To—♆ inclines to secrecy and hidden methods of work, deceit, treachery, etc., when afflicted at B., and by dir. (See Deceitful; "Secretive" under Secret; Treachery; "Tends To" in this section).

Indicates—♆ indicates Anaemia, Necrosis, Depletion, and Catalysis. (See Diseases in Sec. 3 of this Article).

Influence Of—The influences of ♆ by his afflictions are not always physical, but tend to be psychic, and to act upon the mind. The good aspects of ♆ to the ☉ tend to benefit the constitution psychically rather than in a physical way. Example of the Influence of ♆. Case—See "Neptune", No. 283 in 1001 N.N. (See the various paragraphs in this Article).

Inimical—The influence of ♆ is said to be inimical to the great majority of the Earth's inhabitants at this time, due to their materialistic tendencies, and lack of spiritual development. Neptune is attributed as the planet which will rule strongly over the new Sixth Sub-Race, and the Sixth Race, the foundations of which Races are now being formed. At this Stage and Era of the Evolution of the Earth, and of Humanity, people tend to respond more to the lower, or evil vibrations of ♆ than to his higher and spiritual ones, and to be greatly disturbed thereby, and especially along moral and sex lines, and to have chaotic, morbid, weird and sensuous states of mind. (See Chaos, Sixth Sub-Race, in this section).

Magnetic—♆ is a magnetic and negative planet, and tends to render the mind and body negative, timid, and subject to a variety of affections, and susceptible to external influences and environment. In this regard ♆ has an influence similar to ♄. (See Magnetic, Negative, Receptive, Susceptibility).

Mars and Neptune—These planets when in ☌ tend to make one lawless, unrestrained, self-indulgent, and to possibly become an Atheist or Anarchist, and go to extremes in whatever they do, and also to be more subject to obsessions, and the influences of discarnate spirits, and the influences on the Astral Planes. (See Anarchists, Astral; "Atheistical" under Religion; Self-Indulgent, Unrestrained, etc.).

Mental Qualities—♆ tends to make the native psychic, romantic, intuitive, spiritual, imaginative, and inspirational, according to his aspects. (See Aspects, Qualities, and the various paragraphs in this section).

Metals and Minerals—♆ is said to rule Potassium, and such substances as Ambergris and Meerschaum.

Morals and Neptune—His afflictions and lower vibrations tend to loose morals, and morbid sex desires, and especially when afflicting the ☉, ☽, or ♀ at B. (See Aspects, Inimical, Tends To, and the various paragraphs in this section; "Loose Morals" under Morals).

Most Evil In—♆ is most evil in his afflictions when in the 6th or 12th H. at B., or afflicted in ♍ or ♓. The 6th H. and ♍ are indicators of disease, while the 12th H. and ♓ tend to bring sorrow, self-undoing and trouble. (See Sixth House, Twelfth House).

Nebulous Areas—And ♆—The influence of ♆ is largely with the Nebulous Areas, which afflict the Eyes and the Eyesight. (See Blindness, Eyes, Nebulous, Sight).

Negative Planet—(See "Magnetic" in this section).

Neptune Persons—The ♆ person is often unconsciously deceptive, and without malice or predetermination. (See Inclines To, Tends To, and the various paragraphs in this section).

Nervous System—♆ acts strongly upon the Nervous System, and for this reason is considered the higher octave of ☿. (See Nerves).

Occult Influence Of—♆ is a Mystical Planet fundamentally, but Occult in the abstract. (See "Abstract" in this section).

Octave Of—(See the Introduction to this Article).

Orbit Of—It takes ♆ approximately 164½ years to make one revolution in his orbit, and he is about 14 years passing thru one Sign of the Zodiac, which tends to prolong his afflictions over the various Signs and Classes of people, as ♆ in any sign tends, more or less, to afflict the people born under that sign unless they are Advanced and highly spiritualized. (See the Diseases in Sec. 3 of this Article).

Pathological Action Of—(See the opening statements in Sec. 3 of this Article).

Period Of—(See "Orbit" in this section).

Persons—(See "Neptune Persons" in this section).

Physical Effects Of—(See "Influence Of" in this section).

Principle Of—Involution.

Qualities Of—As given by the Higher or Lower vibrations and influences of this planet—Abstract, Aesthetic, Analgesic, Astringent, Cataleptic, Changeable, Chaotic, Clairvoyant, Comatic, Confusing, Conserving, Constrictive, Contracting, Debilitating, Deceitful, Defensive, Delusive, Depraving, Destroying, Dissipating, Doubtful, Ecstatic, Effeminate, Elusive, Emotional, Ensnaring, Entrancing, Estranging, Exciting, Fearful, Fomenting, Frenzical, Fruitful, Generative, Habit-Forming, Hallucinating, Hidden, Hyperactive, Hypnotic, Illaqueative, Illusive, Imaginative, Immoral, Inconstant, Indulgent, Inimical, Inspirational, Intuitive, Lapsing, Lascivious, Lawless, Lethargic, Lewd, Licentious, Lustful, Lymphatic, Magnetic, Maniacal, Mediumistic, Misleading, Moist, Morbid, Mysterious, Mystical, Narcotic, Negative, Nervous, Neurotic, Obscuring, Obsessional, Occult (in the Abstract); Passional, Perverting, Poisonous, Producing, Protean, Psychic, Receptive, Relaxing, Religious, Romantic, Sardonic, Seclusive, Secretive, Sedative, Seductive, Self-Indulgent, Semi-Spiritual, Sensuous, Solitary, Somnambulistic, Soothing, Soporific, Speculative, Spiritual, Stimulant, Storing, Strange, Stupefying, Suffocating, Suggestive, Supra-Material, Susceptible, Timorous, Trance-Producing, Transforming, Treacherous, Unrestrained, Warm, Wasting, Weird, etc.

Revolution Of—(See "Orbit" in this section).

Sensitives—♆ has the most effect on Sensitives. (See "Sensitives" under Sensitive).

Shows—♆ shows distinct Nebuloid and Amoeboid motion, and is more relaxed, changeable, protean, and elusive than ♀, which planet is said by some Authors to be the lower octave of ♆. Also ♆ shows Depletion and Wasting diseases. (See "Amoeboid" under Cells; Depletion, Nebuloid, Wasting).

Sicknesses Caused By—(See the Diseases in Sec. 3 of this Article).

Sign Of—♓ is the strong and home sign of ♆. (See Pisces).

Signifies—(See the various paragraphs in this section).

Sixth Sub-Race—Sixth Race—♆ will be the strong ruler over them. The Pineal Gland, the center of ♆ in the brain, will be more highly developed in the future Ages to come, and people will have more Spiritual Sight, Intuition, Voluntary Clairvoyance, and the power to see and recognize Truth, Doctrine, and things as they are, and not as they seem to be, and when illusion, superstition, and fear will be done away with. (See "Inimical" in this section; Pineal, Pituitary).

Spiritual Influence Of—Is very great in his higher vibrations, and with those who are sufficiently advanced and developed spiritually to respond to his better influences. (See Inimical, Sixth Sub-Race, in this section; Retina).

Strong—♆ is strong in ♓, and also in the 12th H.

Temperament — (See "Temperament" under Lymphatic).

Tends To—Inclines To—Predisposes To—The lower vibrations of ♆ tend to moral lapses, perverted and loose sex morals, depravity, and to chaotic and morbid states of mind, obsessions, hallucinations, delusions, psychic diseases and disturbances, religious excitement and extremes, disturbances from the Astral Planes, Spirit Controls; peculiar, Mysterious and unusual diseases, weird and uncanny feelings, secrecy and hidden methods of work, etc. (See "Inclines To", and the various paragraphs in this section and Article).

Therapeutic Properties—Analgesic, Anodyne, Hypnotic, Soporific, Suggestive. (See these subjects).

Typical Drugs Of—Chloroform, Ether, Iodine, Narcotics, Opiates, Poppy. (See Anaesthetics, Narcotics).

Vitality Benefitted By—♆ ✳ or △ the ☉, in a psychic way rather than physical. (See "Influence Of" in this section).

— SECTION TWO —

NEPTUNE RULES—See the following subjects in the alphabetical arrangement—Ambushes; Amoeboid Motion (see "Amoeboid" under Cells); Anodynes; Appendix Vermiformis (see Appendix); Arms (Glands of when ♆ is in signs which rule the Arms); Assassinations; Astral Influences (see Astral, Spirit Controls); Asylums (see Insanity); Azoth; Blue Color; Brain (the Cerebral Ventricles and Pineal Gland); Canal (Spinal); Cells (Cell Development—Cell Reproduction—Cellular Tissue Building); Cerebral Ventricles; Clairaudience; Clairvoyance; Colors (Indigo and Blue); Conjunctiva; Conservation of the Functions (see Conservation); Cytoplastema; Death (see "Death" in Sec. 3 of this Article); Deceptions; Depressor Nerve (of the Heart); Disguises (see Deceptions) Dishonesty, Enemies, Plots, Treachery); Drowning; Ecstasy (Religious); Exiles; Eyes (The Eyesight—See Nebulous, Sight); Feet (Glands of); Fibers (Nerve Fibers); Fluidic System (Fluids —Spinal Fluids); Frauds (In Business —Deceptions—Defalcations—Thefts— See Dishonesty, Liars, Plots, Thieves, Treachery); Functions (The Conserving, Storing and Transforming Functions—The Telepathic Functions); Fungus Growths (Vegetable); Genito-Urinary System and Organs (Glands of); Glands (Glands of Arms, Hands, Feet—Glands of Genito-Urinary System—Pineal Gland); Growths (Fungus Growths—Vegetable Growths); Hands (Glands of); Heart (Depressor Nerve of); Higher Religious Experiences (see Religion); Hospitals; Humming; Hypnotic Powers; Ideals (Impractical Ideals); Impositions (see "Disguises" in this section); Indigo Color; Insane Asylums; Intuition (the Higher Intuitions); Kidnappings; Laughter; Lavender Color; Legs (Glands of); Life (the Period from 84 to 99 Years—See Periods); Lymphatic Temperament; Mediumship; Meerschaum; Metals and Minerals (see "Metals" in Sec. 1 of this Article); Methods Given By (see "Inclines To" in Sec. 1 of this Article); Minerals (see "Metals" in Sec. 1 of this Article); Mosses (Fungus Growths); Mushrooms; Mysterious Happenings (see Mysterious); Narcotics; Nebuloid Motion; Nerves (Nervous System—Depressor Nerves of Heart—Nerve Fibers —Optic Nerve—See "Nervous System" in Sec. 1 of this Article); Nutrition; Ocean; Odic Force (see Hypnotism); Odors from Man, Animals and Plants (see Odors); Optic Nerve; Period of Life from 84 to 99 Years; Pineal Gland; Pisces Sign; Plastic Fluid (see Cytoplastema); Poisons; Potassium; Prisons; Psychic States (see Psychic); Radium; Religious Experiences (see Ecstasy, Religion); Reproduction of Cells (see Cells); Respiratory System (Tissues of); Seas; Secret Societies; Secretions of Stomach (see "Secretions" under Stomach); Secrets of Life (see "Secrets" under Secret); Seduction; Soporifics; Spine (Spinal Canal and Azoth In—Spinal Cord—Spinal Fluids—Spinal Gas—Spinal Spirit Fire); Spirit Controls; Spiritual Nature and Spiritual Sight; Sponges; Stomach (Glands and Secretions of); Strange Conditions (see Mysterious, Strange); Sudden, Mysterious, Quick, and Unexpected Deaths; Talking to Oneself (see Speech, Talk); Tears; Telepathic Functions (see Telepathy); Throat (Tissues of); Tissues of the Throat and Respiratory System; Trance; Treachery; Twelfth House; Unusual Conditions in Mind and Body (see Extraordinary, Mysterious, Peculiar, Strange, Unusual); Vegetable and Fungus Growths; Ventricles (Cerebral); Vermiform Appendix (see Appendix); Wanderings (see Roving; "Given To" under Travel; Wandering); Waters (see Ocean, Sea, Water); Whistling.

— SECTION THREE —

DISEASES OF NEPTUNE—The Afflictions of Neptune—Neptune acts principally upon the Mind and Nervous System, the Emotions, the Psychic Powers, the Passions by his lower vibrations, and tends to chaotic and morbid conditions. The strong pathological action of ♆ over the Nervous System is considered a strong argument in favor of ♆ being the higher octave of ☿, as ☿ is the ruler of the Nervous System in general. Neptune has more of a Psychic and Mental effect than physical in causing disease. Also the vitality of the physical body is increased by the good aspects of ♆ thru psychic and mental effects, and by creating greater poise, and intensifying the Spiritual Powers, the Higher Intuitions, and Spiritual Sight. Neptune is closely related to the Nebulous Areas, and tends to affect the Eyes and Eyesight of Man. Neptune tends to strange and mysterious diseases and afflictions, hard to explain without a knowledge of the Occult and Mystical Sciences. Neptune has the most effect in a pathological way upon Sensitives, those very susceptible to Astral influences, and people who are nervous and high strung. The sicknesses caused by ♆ are chiefly of a depressive nature, and of a nervous tendency. The pathogenic and disease-producing influences of this planet are stronger when he is in the 6th or 12th H., or afflicted in the ♍ or ♓ signs, the signs affiliated with these two houses. (See "Most Evil In" in Sec. 1 of this Article). In a general way the pathological action of ♆ tends to Analgesia, Involuntary Clairvoyance and Mediumship, Obsessions, Spirit Controls, Psychic Disturbances; Dissipation of Functional Energy, and Atrophy of Process thru the cessation of functions; also causes laxity, relaxation, and lack of cohesion of parts. His pathological action is suggestive, delusive, ensnaring, hypnotic, analgesic, soporific, sleep-producing, anodyne, and with a feeling of torpor, lassitude, and a dreamy, chaotic, and weird state of mind, and even to demoniacal demonstrations, as in Obsessions and Spirit Controls. The following is a list of the Diseases and Afflictions of ♆, as far as I have been able to gather from my reading, study, observation, and the careful examination of nearly 10,-000 Maps of Birth of people, and their letters setting forth their diseases and complaints, during my career as a Physician Astrologer. See the following subjects in the alphabetical arrangement—

Absent-Minded—(See Chaotic, Dreamy; "Absent-Minded" under Mind; Visionary).

Accidents—♆ produces accidents, such as by Drowning, Water, Suffocation, in Sleep-Walking, and those of a Mysterious, Strange and Unusual Nature. (See these subjects, and also note the various paragraphs in this section).

Ambushes—Attacks By—Death or Injury In—(See Ambushes).

Anaemia; Analgesia; Appendicitis—(See Appendix).

Arms—Wasting of the Tissues of—(See "Arms" under Wasting).

Assassination; Astral Influences—Disorders, Obsessions, or Death From—(See Astral, Obsessions, Spirit Controls).

Asylums—Insanity and Confinement In An Asylum—(See "Asylums" under Insanity).

Atrophy—Of Function—(See "Atrophy" under Functions).

Beside Oneself—(See Excitable, Frenzy, Fury).

Blindness—(See Causes, Day Blindness, under Blindness).

Brain—Disorders of—(See Brain, Cerebral, Pineal).

Brooding; Cancer—(See Carcinoma).

Carcinoma; Carus—(See Carus, Coma).

Catalepsy; Catalysis; Cataphora;

Chaotic Mind—(See Chaotic).

Clairaudience; Clairvoyance;

Claustrophobia; Cocainism—(See Narcotics).

Cohesion—Lack of Cohesion of Parts —(See Cohesion).

Coma; Confusion of Mind—(See "Mental Chaos" under Chaotic).

Conjunctivitis—(See Conjunctiva).

Consumption — (See "Consumptive" under Consumption).

Crying Spells—(See Emotions).

Dark—Fear of—(See Claustrophobia).

Day Blindness—(See Blindness).

Day Dreaming—(See "Dreamy" under Dreams).

Death—♆ causes death by Ambushes, Assassination, Drowning, the Drug and Narcotic Habit, Obsessions, Poison, Riots, Spirit Controls, Trance, Treachery, and by Mysterious, Strange, Sudden, Unexpected, and Unusual Causes and Events. (See these subjects).

Debility—As General Debility, Depletion of the Vital Fluids, Fears, Nervous Complaints, etc. (See these subjects, and also note the various paragraphs in this section).

Deformities; Delirium —Delirium Tremens — The Delirium of Typhus Fever—(See Delirium, Typhus).

Demoniacal Affections — (See Demoniac).

Depletion — Of the Tissues and Vital Forces—(See Depletion).

Depravity; Depression—Mental—(See Depressed).

Destroys Life—By afflicting the hyleg at B., and by dir. (See Anareta).

Dispersions; Dissipation — Of Functional Energy—(See Dispersions).

Dreams—Dreamy—(See Dreams).

Drink Habit — (See Drink, Drunkenness).

Dropsy—(See "Dropsy" under Bowels; "Abdomen" under Dropsy).

Drowning; Drowsiness —Sleepiness—Stupor—(See Sleep).

Drug Habit—Drug Taking—(See Narcotics).

Ecstasy; Emissions—(See Semen).

Emotions—Disturbances of —(See Emotions).

Energy—Dissipation of Functional Energy — (See Dispersions; "Dissipation" under Functions).

Excesses—(See "Passional Excesses" under Passion).

Excitement — Religious— (See "Religious" under Excitement).

Extraordinary Diseases—Or Death—(See Extraordinary, Mysterious, Peculiar, Strange).

Eye Troubles—(See Blindness, Eyes, Nebulous, Sight).

Faculties—Disorders of the Spiritual Faculties — (See Ecstasy; "Religious" under Excitable; Pineal, Religion, Spiritual).

Faintings; Fears—False and Morbid Fears—(See Fears, Obsessions, Spirit Controls).

Feet — Wasting of the Tissues of — (See "Tissues" under Feet).

Fingers—Horny Nails On—(See Fingers).

Fluids—Disorders of—(See Fluids).

Forgetfulness—(See Memory).

Frenzy; Functional Energy—Dissipation of—(See Atrophy, Energy, in this section).

Fungus Growths—In the Body—(See Fungus).

Glands—(See Swelling, Wasting, under Glands).

Growths — (See Carcinoma, Fungus, Tumors).

Habits — (See Drink, Narcotics, Tobacco).

Hallucinations; Hands — (See "Wasting" under Hands).

Heart — (See Depressor, Drug Heart, Sleeping Potions, Stoppage, under Heart).

Hypnotic Disturbances — (See Hypnotism).

Hypochondria; Hysteria;

Infantile Paralysis—(See "Infantile" under Paralysis).

Influenza; Insanity; Insensibility—(See Analgesia, Carus, Coma, Insensibility).

Intemperance; Intoxication;

Intuitions Impaired—(See Intuition).

Involuntary—(See "Involuntary" under Clairvoyance, Mediumship).

Lapsing of Morals—(See Lapsing).

Legs—(See "Legs" under Wasting).

Lethargy; Limbs — Shrinking, Wasting and Withering of — (See "Arms" under Limbs).

Loose Morals—(See Morals).

Mania—(See All Forms Of, Neurotic, Religious, under Mania).

Mediumship; Mind — Diseases Originating In the Mind—(See Fears, Hallucinations, Imaginations, Insanity, Obsessions; "Diseases" under Psychic; Spirit Controls, etc.).

Moisture — (See "Moist and Warm" under Heat; "Relaxation and Moisture" under Moisture).

Morals—Moral Lapsing—Loose Morals — Moral Perversions — (See Lapsing; "Loose" under Morals; Perversions).

Morbid Manifestations—Of the More Obscure Types — (See "Morbid" under Mind, Obscure; "Unclassified" under Morbid).

Morphine Habit—(See Narcotics).

Myopia—(See Sight).

Mysterious Death — And Diseases — (See Mysterious, Peculiar, Strange).

Nails — Horny Nails — (See "Horny" under Fingers).

Narcotics—Use of—(See Narcotics).

Necrosis; Nervous Diseases—Nervous Depletion—Neuroses—Neurotic Affections—(See Depletion, Nerves).

Nightmare — (See Dreams; "Nightmare" under Sleep).

Noisome Diseases—(See Noisome).

Nyctalopia—(See "Day Blindness" under Blindness).

Obscure Diseases—(See Obscure).

Obsessions; Opium Habit—(See Narcotics).

Pain — Insensibility To — (See Analgesia, Insensibility).

Paralysis—(See "Infantile" under Paralysis).

Passional Desires—Excesses—Perversions — (See "Passional Excesses" under Passion; Perversions).

Peculiar Diseases — Or Death — (See Extraordinary, Mysterious, Obscure, Peculiar, Strange, Unusual).

Phenomena — Referable to Psychic Causes — (See Hallucinations, Obsessions, Psychic, Spirit Controls).

Pockmarks—(See Smallpox).

Poisoning — By Drugs and Opiates — (See Narcotics; "Death" under Poison; "Septic" in this section).

Psychic Powers — Disorders of — Hyperactivity of—(See Psychic).

Pus Diseases—(See Pus, Pyorrhoea).

Puzzling Diseases — (See Mysterious, Obscure, Peculiar, Strange).

Pyorrhoea; Relaxation of Tissues — (See Relaxation).

Religion—Religious Mania—Religious Ecstasy—Religious Excitement—(See Ecstasy, Excitable; "Religious" under Mania; Religion).

Saint Vitus Dance—(See Saint).

Self-Abuse—Solitary Vice—(See "Solitary" under Vice).

Self-Undoing — (See Self-Undoing, Twelfth House; "Most Evil In" in Sec. 1 of this Article).

Seminal Losses—(See Semen).

Sensitiveness—Hypersensitive — Sensitives—(See Sensitive).

Septic Poisonings—(See Septic; "Septic" under Throat).

Sex Abuses — Sex Perversions — Sex Excesses — (See "Loose Morals" under Morals; "Passional Excesses" under Passion; Perversions, Sex).

Shrinking Limbs—(See Shrinking).

Sleep — Disorders of — Drowsiness — Sleepiness — Soporifics — Nightmare — (See Dreams, Narcotics, Sleep).

Sleeping Sickness—(See Sleep).

Smoking — Disorders From — (See "Drug Heart" under Heart; Narcotics, Tobacco).

Snuff Habit—(See Narcotics).

Solitary Vice — (See "Solitary Vice" under Vice).

Somnambulism—(See Sleep).

Soothing Drugs — Use of — (See Narcotics, Sedatives; "Sleeping Potions" under Sleep; Soothing).

Soporific Drugs — Use of — (See Anodynes, Narcotics; "Soporifics" under Sleep).

Spirit Controls—Obsessions and Death By—(See Obsessions, Spirit Controls).

Spiritual Causes — Disease or Death By — (See Astral; "Religious" under Mania; Obsessions, Psychic, Spirit Controls, Spiritual).

Spiritual Faculties—Disorders of—(See "Faculties" in this section).

Strange Affections—Strange Death—(See Mysterious, Peculiar, Strange, Unusual).

Stupor—(See Sleep).

Suffocation — (See Drowning, Gases, Suffocation).

Suspended Heart Action—(See Heart).

Swellings—Glandular—(See Glands).

Talking to Oneself — (See Speech, Talk).

Therapeutic Properties — (See "Therapeutic" in Sec. 1 of this Article).

Throat — Septic Poisonings In — (See "Septic" under Throat).

Tissues—Wasting of—(See "Tissues" under Wasting).

Tobacco Habit — (See "Drug Heart" under Heart; Narcotics, Tobacco).

Trance—And Death By—(See Trance).

Treachery—Death or Injury By—(See "Death" under Poison; Treachery).

Treatment — The treatment of ♆ diseases should be mostly Psychic and Spiritual, and thru the Will Power, and also by proper knowledge of Astral Influences, the Astral Planes, and the Entities thereon; a knowledge of Spirits, Elementals, etc., and how to deal with them, drive out evil Spirits, and to bring relief to those who are under Obsessions and Spirit Controls. The use of Suggestion to patients in the Hypnotic State has proven very valuable in these cases to effect cures, but the Operator must know the nature of the Forces he is dealing with, and how to rid the patient of them. Evil Spirits do not linger long in the presence of a Master who knows and recognizes them, and gives them their orders. (See "Psychic Healers", "Spiritual Healers", under Healers; "Treatment" under Hypnotism).

Tumors; Typhomania — The Delirium of Typhus Fever—(See Typhus).

Unclassified Diseases — (See Extraordinary, Mysterious, Obscure, Peculiar, Strange, Uncommon, Unusual, etc.).

Unexplainable Diseases — (See Mysterious, Obscure, Strange, etc.).

Venereal Diseases—(See Venereal).

Vision—Eyesight—Disorders of—(See Blindness, Nebulous, Sight).

Warm and Moist Diseases — (See "Moist and Warm" under Heat; "Relaxation" under Moisture).

Wasting Diseases—(See Wasting).

Withering of Limbs—(See "Arms" under Limbs).

NERVES—Nervous System—Mercury is said to rule the Nerves in general, as ☿ rules the right Cerebral Hemisphere and the Motor Segment of the Spinal Cord. Neptune, as the higher octave of ☿, also rules over, and strongly influences the Nerves, and acts upon the Nerves thru the Brain Centers, the Mind, the Psychic and Spiritual Powers, the Emotions, and acts especially upon the Pineal Gland, which Gland is ruled by ♆. Uranus also has a very remarkable influence over the Nervous System, and especially upon the Motor Nerves, disturbing their action, and tending to Erratic, Spasmodic, and Jerky Movements over the body. The Motor Nerves are ruled by ♅ and ♂. Mercury exerts a nervous influence, and is usually badly afflicted in nervous and mental disorders. The Airy Signs are Nervous Signs, and on the Asc. at B. tend to nervousness. The ☉ is also said to rule strongly over the Nerves and the Brain. The Nerves, acting as sinews, or wires of transmission for nerve force and nerve impulses and messages from the Brain and other centers, are ruled by the ☉. The nerves of the brain are fed by the rays of the ☉. The Common, or Mutable Signs, also strongly influence the Nervous System, and especially ♊ and ♐. The Nerve Sheaths are connected with the ♌ sign, and are also under the rule of the ☽. The Third House also rules and influences the Nerves, and the conditions of the 3rd House, the house of ☿, should be studied in connection with Nervous Complaints. The Nerve Fibers are said to be under the internal rulership of the ♊ sign, the 3rd H. sign. The ♒ sign, the strong sign of ♅, also is a strong ruler over the Nervous System. For convenience of reference this Article is divided into two Sections. Section One — General Considerations. Section Two—Diseases of the Nervous System. See these subjects in the alphabetical arrangement when they are not more fully considered in this Article.

— SECTION ONE —

GENERAL CONSIDERATIONS—

Airy Signs — Are classed as Nervous Signs. (See "Air Signs" under Air).

Augmented — The Nerve and Vital Forces Augmented — H ✱ or △ the ☉ (See "Augmented" under Vital).

Blue Color — Blue Color is a nerve Palliative, and nervous patients benefit in a Blue Room. (See Blue).

Brain — Disorders of — (See "Nervous Disorders", and the various paragraphs under Brain; Cerebellum, Cerebral, Cerebrum).

Capillary — The Cutaneous Capillary Vaso-Constrictor Nerves — (See "Vaso-Constrictor" under Vaso).

Cells—Nerve Cells—(See Cells).

Centers—Nerve Centers—Are said to be under the internal rulership of the ♈ Sign. (See "Centers" in Sec. 2 of this Article).

Cerebellum; Cerebral Nerves — (See Cerebral).

Cerebro-Spinal Nerves—(See Cerebro-Spinal).

Cerebrum; Cervical Nerves — Cervical Ganglion—(See Cervical, Ganglion).

Color—(See "Blue Color" in this section).

Constrictor Nerves — (See Constrictions; "Vaso-Constrictor" under Vaso).

Control — The Nerves, Nervous System, and the Mind, should be kept under good control when ♅ is in ♒ at B., and afflicted.

Cranial Nerves—(See Cranial).

Depressor Nerves—(See Depressor).

Dilator Action — (See "Vaso-Dilator" under Vaso).

Discharge of Nerve Force — (See Innervation).

Disposition—The Nervous Disposition —(See "Temperament" in this section).

Dorsal Nerves—(See Dorsal).

Energy — Nervous Energy — (See "Nervous" under Energy).

Fibers — The Nerve Fibers are under the internal rulership of the ♊ sign. Also ruled by ♆ and ♅, and by the Anterior Lobe of the Pituitary Body, which Body is ruled by ♅. (See "Nerve Fibers" under Organs).

Filaments — The Nerve Filaments — (See Filaments).

Fluids — The Nerve Fluids are ruled by ♅. (See "Nerve Fluids" under Depletion; "Fluids" under Vital; "Depletion" in Sec. 2 of this Article).

Force — Nerve Force — (See "Nerve Force" under Force; "Fluid", "Force", under Vital).

Function — Of the Nerves — (See Innervation).

Ganglion—Nerve Centers—(See Centers, Ganglion).

Genito-Urinary System—Nerves of—(See Genito-Urinary).

Heart—Nerves of—(See Heart).

Impulses—The Nerve Impulses—(See Innervation; the Introduction to this Article).

Influx—The Nervous Influx—☿ adds to or subtracts from. (See Innervation).

Innervation—The Discharge of Nerve Force—(See Innervation).

Kinetic Force—(See Energy, Kinetic, Motion, Motor).

Lumbar Nerves—(See Lumbar).

Medulla Oblongata—(See Medulla).

Motor Nerves—(See Motor).

Nerve Centers—(See "Centers" in this section).

Nerve Fibers—(See Fiber; "Fibers" in this section).

Nerve Filaments—(See Filaments).

Nerve Fluids — (See "Fluids" in this section).

Nerve Force—(See "Life Force" under Force; "Force" in this section).

Nerve Sheaths—(See "Sheaths" in this section).

Nerve Tissue Building—(See "Tissue" in this section).

Nervine—An Agent Calming Nervous Excitement. A Therapeutic Property of ☿. Also the Blue Color is a Nervine, and soothing to nervous patients.

Optic Nerve—(See Optic).

Palliative — Nerve Palliative — Blue Color. (See Blue, Nervine, in this section).

Peripheral Nerves—(See Peripheral).

Plantar Nerves — (See Ligaments, Plantar).

Plexuses—(See Ganglion, Plexuses).

Pneumogastric Nerve — Vagus Nerve —(See Pneumogastric).

Pudic Nerves—(See Genitals, Pudic).

Renal Nerves—(See Kidneys).

Respiratory System—Nerves of—(See the Introduction under Breathing; "Nerves" under Lungs).

Sacral Nerves—(See Sacral).

Salt—The Nerve-Building Salt—Magnesium Phosphate, the Salt ruled by the ♌ sign. (See "Salts" under Zodiac).

Sciatic Nerves—(See Sciatic).

Secretory Nerves—(See Secretions).

Sensory Nerves — (See "Sensory Nerves" under Sensation).

Sheaths—The Nerve Sheaths—Ruled by the ☽. They are also connected with the ♌ sign, and the ♌ Salt, Magnesium Phosphate. Mercury rules the invisible rose-colored vital fluid which flows in the visible nerve sheath. (See "Fluid" under Vital).

Signs — The Nervous Signs of the Zodiac—The Airy Signs. Also ♉, ♍, ♎, ♏, ♑, are generally listed as the Nervous Signs, those which contribute to Nervousness.

Sinews—Nerve Sinews—Ruled by the ☉. (See the Introduction to this Article).

Solar Plexus — (See "Solar" under Plexus).

Speech—Nerves of—(See Speech).

Spinal Nerves—(See Spine).

Sympathetic Nervous System — (See Peripheral, Sympathetic).

Temperament — The Nervous Temperament — Melancholic Temperament —Cold and Dry Bodily Temperament—Ruled by ♅, ♄, ☿, and the Earthy Signs. Also influenced by the Airy Signs, as ♄ rules strongly over ♎ and ♒. This temperament is also said to be an exaggeration of the Bilious Temperament. The Nervous Temperament is one of thinking and feeling, and tends to Neurasthenia, restlessness, and a hurried, alert, and agitated manner. (See "Cold and Dry Body" under Dry; "Disposition" under Melancholy; Restlessness; "Temperament" under Saturn; "Neurasthenia" in Sec. 2 of this Article).

Tissue — Nerve Tissue-Building — The work of ♅ and ☿. (See Tissues).

Treatment — Of Nervous Disorders — Onions are nerve builders. The Blue Color is soothing to nervous and excitable patients. The Herbs of ☿ are Nervine. (See Blue, Nervine, Palliative, in this section; "Mercury Group" under Herbs; Onions).

Upper Dorsal Nerves—(See Dorsal).

Vagus Nerve—(See Pneumogastric).

Vaso-Constrictor Nerves — Vaso-Dilator—Vaso-Motor—(See Vaso).

Vital Fluid — In the Nerves — Vital Force—(See Augmented, Fluids, Force, in this section).

Voluntary Nervous System — (See Voluntary).

Weakest Part — The Nervous System the Weakest Part—The ☉ affl. in ♐.

— SECTION TWO —

DISEASES OF NERVOUS SYSTEM—See the following subjects in the alphabetical arrangement when not considered here—

Absorption Of—(See Resolution).

Acute Nervous Diseases—♄ diseases. (See the Introduction under Acute).

Affections—Nervous Affections—(See "Disordered", and the various paragraphs in this section).

Ailments—Arising from Nervous Conditions—The ☽ hyleg in ♈, and afflicted, and especially with females. (See "Disordered" in this section).

All Nervous Disorders—Diseases of ♄ and ☿; caused by the afflictions of ♄.

Anaemia; Analgesia; Apprehensive—Nervously Apprehensive—Afflictions to ☿; ☿ afflicted by ♄. (See Suspicious, Worry).

Arms—Nerves of Afflicted—(See "Motor Nerves" under Arms).

Ataxia; Attacked—The Nervous System Chiefly Attacked—The ☽ hyleg in ♐, and afflicted, in females.

Auditory Nerve—Clogging of—(See "Auditory" under Hearing).

Blue Color—A Nerve Palliative—(See "Blue" in Sec. 1 of this Article).

Bowels—(See "Nerves Of" under Bowels).

Brain—Disorders of—(See Brain Fag, Brain Storms, Nervous Disorders, and the various paragraphs under Brain).

Breakdown—Nervous Breakdown—(See "Prostration" in this section).

Burning Sensations—(See "Sensations" under Burning).

Centers—The Nerve Centers—Excitement and Irritation of—(See Erethism, Neuritis, in this section).

Chills—Nervous Chills—Caused by the strong afflictions of ♄ to the hyleg, and accompany Nervous Debility, Neurasthenia, etc. (See Debility, Neurasthenia, in this section).

Collapse—Complete Nervous Collapse—(See Collapse; "Prostration" in this section).

Color—In the Treatment of Nervous Disorders—(See "Blue" in Sec. 1 of this Article).

Complaints—(See "Disordered", and the various paragraphs in this section).

Constipation—(See "Nervous" under Constipation).

Contortions; Control—(See "Control" in Sec. 1 of this Article).

Convulsions—Convulsive Movements—(See Convulsions, Fits, Spasmodic).

Corrosions—Of the Nerves—(See Corrosion, Lesions, Paralysis).

Cramps; Crystallization—Of the Nerves and Muscles of the Eyes—(See "Crystallization" under Eyes).

Death—From Nervous Disorders—♅ afflicted in the 8th H., and afflicting the hyleg by dir.; ☿ denotes; ☿ afflicted at B., and especially by malefics, and ☿ afflicting the hyleg by dir., or taking part in a train of fatal directions. (See Case of Death under "Strain" in this section).

Debility—Nervous Debility—The ☽ hyleg, and to the ☌, P., □ or ☍ ♆ or ♅ by dir.; the ☽ in ♍ or ♒, and to the ☌ or ill-asp. any of the malefics as Promittors; the ☽ in fire signs, from haste and excitement, and espec. when afflicted in ♐; ♆, ♅, or ♄ in ♉ or ♏, and affl. the ☉ or ☽; ♄ diseases; ♄ affl. in ♐; a ☿ disease; ☿ affl. in ♍; ☿ affl. in the 6th H., from worry, overwork, or overstudy; ☿ afflicted in ♒, general debility of the Nervous System. Debility arising from nervous diseases is denoted by ☿. (See Depletion, Depression, Disordered, Neurasthenia, and the various paragraphs in this section).

Defects—In the Nervous System—Denoted by ☿, and with ☿ afflicted at B.

Depletion—Nervous Depletion—☿ afflicted by ♆; ♅ □ or ☍ the Asc. or ☿, depletion of the nerve and vital fluids. (See Depletion; "Depletion" under Vital; Debility, Depression, Disordered, Fluids, Neurasthenia, in this section).

Depression—Nervous Depression—♅, ♆, or ♄ in ♉ or ♏, and afflicting the ☉ or ☽; ☿ affl. by ♄, depression and brain fag. (See "Brain Fag" under Brain; "Mental" under Depressed; "Debility" in this section).

Derangement—Of the Nervous System—☿ diseases; ☿ ☌ ♂, and in □ or ☍ the ☽ or ♄. (See Debility, Disordered, Neurasthenia, and the various paragraphs in this section).

Diplegia—(See Paralysis).

Discharge—Excessive Discharge of Nerve Force—(See "Excessive" in this section).

Diseased Nervous System—(See "Disordered", and the various paragraphs in this section).

Disordered Nervous System—Deranged Nervous System—Predisposition to Nervous Complaints and Disorders—Liable To—Nervous Susceptibility, etc.—The ☉ affl. in ♊, ♐, or ♒; the ☉ in ♊ or ♐, and to the ☌ or ill-asp. ♄ or ♂ by dir.; the ☉ ☌ or ill-asp. ♅; a ☉ disease; the ☉ in any aspect to ♅, or vice versa; the ☉ or ☽ in the 6th H. in cardinal signs, and afflicted; the ☉ and ☿ affl. in ♓; the ☽ in ♒, ☌ or ill-asp. any of the malefics as Promittors; the ☽ to the ☌ or ill-asp. ♄ by dir.; the ☽ hyleg in ♊ or ♐ in female nativities, and afflicted; the ☽ to the ☌ or ill-asp. ☿ by dir., and ☿ afflicted at B.; the ☽ in ♐ in ☍ ♃ in ♊; the ☽ hyleg in ♈, and afflicted; ♆ ruler of the horoscope, and afflicted; ♆, ♅, ☿, and the ☽ when afflicted tend to make one nervous and high strung; ♆ afflicting ☿; ♆ in ♒ and afflicted; ♆ in ♒ and afflicting the Asc. or hyleg; ♆ afflicted in ♒ in the 6th H.; ♆ in the 3rd or 9th H., and afflicting the ☽ or ☿; ♆ in a prominent position at B., and afflicted; ♆ afflicting the Asc. at B., and by dir.; ♆ afflicted in ♐; ♅ in any asp. to the ☉ at B., and by dir.; ♅ afflicted in the 6th H.; ♅ afflicting the Asc. at B., and by dir.; ♅, ♄, or ♆ in ♏, and afflicting the ☉ or ☽; ♄ in ♌, ♍, ♎, or ♏, and afflicted; ♄ and ♂ in ♊; ♄ afflicted in a ☿ sign; born under strong ♄ influence; ♄ ruler of the horoscope, and afflicted; ♄ is one of the rulers of the Nervous Temperament, along with ♅, ♀, and the earthy signs; ♄ and ☿ combined in their influences, and afflicting the hyleg; ♃ afflicted in ♒; ♃ in perihelion when there is a Sun Spot tends to greatly aggravate the nerves of people generally; ♂ ☌, □, or ☍ the ☽ or ☿; ♂ Progressed, ☌ or ill-asp. ♆, or vice versa; ♂ afflicted in ♍; denoted by ☿, and is a ☿ disease; afflictions to ☿ or the ☽ by planets, as ☿ rules the sensory nerves; ☿ in a weak sign at B., and afflicted; ☿ afflicted in the 6th H., and usually from overwork or overstudy; ☿ affl. in ♓; ☿ afflicted by ♅; ☿ in ♐, ☌, or ill-asp. any of the malefics as promittors; ☿ afflicted by ♆; ☿ prog., ☌ or ill-asp. ♅, and vice versa; ☿ ruler of the horoscope, and afflicted by malefics; ☿ ill-dignified at B., and afflicted; ☿ ☌ or ill-asp. ♂; ☿ in the 1st H., and afflicted by ♄; ♊, ♐, ♑, or ♒ on the Asc. at B.; common signs show, and especially afflictions in ♊, ♐, or ♓; the malefics, or afflicting planets, in the flexed, or common signs; many planets, a Stellium, in the 3rd H. at B.; many planets in earthy signs; airy signs tend to worry and nervous disorders; the combined influence of two planets whose nature is cold and dry tends to nervousness, as that of ♄ and ☿; common signs on the cusp the 6th H. (For other influences along this line see the various paragraphs in this section. Also see "Mutable Signs" under Mutable; Perihelion; "Sun Spots" under Spots; Stellium). Cases of Disordered Nervous System, Maps, etc.—See Figures 1A, 14A, B, C, D, E, F, in the book, "Astro-Diagnosis" by the Heindels.

Dissolving Of—(See Resolution).

Disturbances — Of the Nervous System — Caused especially by afflictions in ♒, as this sign rules the nervous system. (See "Disordered", and the various paragraphs in this section).

Dreads and Fears — Nervous and Anxious Fears—(See Fears).

Drowsiness—Stupor—Sleepiness—(See Sleep).

Dyspepsia — (See "Nervous" under Dyspepsia).

Ears — Lack of Nerve Force to the Ears—(See Deafness).

Energy — Nervous Energy is upheld by ☿, and suppressed by ♄. (See "Suppression" in this section).

Enervation—A Weakening—(See Enervation; "Depletion" in this section).

Epilepsy; Erethism — Of the Nerve Centers—Abnormal Increase of Nervous Irritability—(See Erethism).

Erratic Movements—(See Erratic).

Excessive Nervous Power — Over-Activity of the Nervous System—Neurosthenia—The ☽ in ♐ and coming to the ☍ of ♃ at B. (See Highly Neurotic, Over-Activity, in this section).

Excitability— Nervous Excitability—(See "Nerves" under Excitable; "High Strung" under High; "Highly Neurotic" in this section).

Excitement—Nervous Diseases Arising from Excitement — Denoted by ☿; ♀ afflicted by ♅ or ♂. (See Excitable; Debility, Neurasthenia, Prostration, in this section).

Exhaustion — Of the Nerve Force — (See "Neurasthenia" in this section).

Eyes — (See "Crystallization" in this section).

Facial Nerve — Disorders of — (See "Nerves" under Face).

Fear — (See "Nervous Fears" under Fear).

Feet—(See "Feet" under Cramps; "Motor Nerves" under Feet).

Fibers — (See "Nerve Fibers" under Organs).

Fibroma — A Fibroma On a Nerve — Neuroma—Nerve Tumor—(See "Neuroma" in this section).

Fits — (See "Nervous Affections" under Fits).

Fluids—Depletion of Nerve Fluids—(See "Depletion" in this section).

Force — Lack of Nerve Force — (See "Force" under Vital; Collapse, Depletion, Loss Of, Nerve Force, Neurasthenia, Prostration, in this section).

Functional Disorders—Of the Nerves —(See Enervation; "Nerves" under Excitable; Hindered, Impeded, under Functions).

Gastric Neuroses — (See "Neuroses" under Stomach).

Genitals — Genito - Urinary System — Nervous Disorders of — (See "Nervous Affections" under Genitals, Genito-Urinary).

Gripings; Hands — Nerve Pains In — (See "Nerves" under Hands).

Hardening — Of Nerves — (See Corrosions, Crystallization, Lesions, Paralysis, in this section; "Nerves" under Hardening; Sclerosis).

Haste and Excitement — Nervous Debility From — (See Debility, Excitement, in this section).

Head — Nervous Disorders of — (See "Nervous Affections" under Head; Headaches).

Headaches — Nervous Headaches — (See Headaches).

Heart — Nervous Affections of — (See Cardialgia, Depressor, Nervous Affections, Neuralgia, under Heart).

Hemiplegia; Hiccough; High Strung —(See "Strung" under High).

High Tension—High Nervous Tension —(See "Nerves" under Excitable; "High Strung" under High; "High Nervous Tension" under Tension; "Highly Neurotic" in this section).

Highly Neurotic — Excessively Neurotic — Extremely Nervous — ♆ in a prominent position at B., and afflicting the ☽ or ☿; ♆ in the 3rd or 9th H. at B., and in adverse asp. to the ☽ or ☿; ♂ afflicting ♆ at B., and by dir.; ☿ afflicted in the 6th H. (See "Brain Storms" under Brain; Erethism; "Nerves" under Excitable; Frenzy, Fury; "High Strung" under High; Hyperaesthesia, Mania; Nervousness, Neurasthenia, Neurotic, in this section).

Hips—Nervous Pains In—(See Hips).

Horrors — Nervous Horrors — (See Horrors).

Hot Flashes — (See "Sensations" under Burning; Paraesthesia).

Hyperaesthesia; Hysteria;

Incoordination; Increase—Of Nervous Irritability — (See Erethism; "Nerves" under Excitable).

Indigestion—Nervous Indigestion—(See Indigestion).

Inflammation — Of a Nerve — (See "Neuritis" in this section).

Influx—The Nervous Influx—Mercury adds to or subtracts from. The ☿ Group of Herbs by their physiological action tend to modify the nervous influx and periodicity. (See "Alterations" under Cells).

Inhibition — ♄ has an inhibitory action over the Nervous System by his afflictions. (See Inhibitions, Retarded, Suppressions).

Insensibility—To Pain—(See Anaesthetics, Analgesia, Insensibility).

Irritability — Abnormal Increase of Nervous Irritability—The ☽ in P. asp. to ♄ in the Zodiac. (See Erethism, Irritability; Highly Neurotic, Neurasthenia, in this section).

Jerky Movements—(See Jerky).

Kidneys—Nervous Disorders of—(See Kidneys).

Lack of Nerve Force — (See Depletion, Neurasthenia, in this section; "Force" under Vital).

Leakage—Nervous Leakage—♆ strong at B., and holding a dominant position, or afflicting ☿ or the ☽. (See Depletion, Loss Of, Neurasthenia, in this section).

Legs—(See Motor Nerves, Nerves, under Legs).

Lesions—Of the Nerves—Denoted by ♅; ☿ afflicted by ♅. (See Corrosions, Lesions, Paralysis).

Locomotion—Nervous Disorders of—(See "Stoppage" under Gait; "Paralysis" under Legs; Locomotor Ataxia; "Incoordinated" under Walk).

Locomotor Ataxia—(See Locomotor).

Loss of Nerve Power—Denoted by ♐, and afflictions in this sign. (See Collapse, Depletion, Lack Of, Neurasthenia, Prostration, in this section).

Lumbar Nerves — Obstructions In — (See "Fifth Lumbar" under Lumbar).

Mania—Neurotic Mania—(See Mania).

Manners—(See "Nervous" under Manners).

Marriage Partner — (See "Neurotic" under Marriage Partner).

Medullary Substance — Inflammation of—Neuromyelitis—(See Medulla).

Mental Over-Strain — Nervous Diseases Arising from—☿ afflicted in the 6th H.; ☿ or ♅ afflicted in ♈; ♅ in ♊. (See "Exertion" under Mental; "Nerves" under Mind; Reading, Study).

Mother—(See "Nervous Complaints" under Mother).

Motion—Nervous Disorders of—(See "Spasmodic" under Motion).

Motor Nerves—Disturbances of—(See "Motor Nerves" under Motor).

Movements—Nervous Disorders of—(See Ataxia, Erratic, Incoordination, Jerky, Movement, Paralysis, Spasmodic; "Equilibrium" under Walk).

Neck and Throat—(See "Nervous Disorders" under Neck, Throat).

Nerve Force — Disturbances of the Circulation of the Nerve Force—♃ or ♀ □ or ☍ ☉. (See Fluids, Force, in this section; Fluid, Force, under Vital).

Nerve Power—Loss of—(See "Loss Of" in this section).

Nerveless—Lacking In Courage—♃ afflicted in ♓; ♂ weak and afflicted at B. (See Dejection, Depression; "Low Spirits" under Low; Timidity).

Nervine—(See "Nervine" in Sec. 1 of this Article).

Nervously Apprehensive — (See "Apprehensive" in this section).

Nervousness — Nervous — Neurotic — Unsettled Condition of the Nerves—Nervous Susceptibility—The Prog. ☉ or ☽ ☌, □, or ☍ ♅; the ☽ in P. asp. to ♄; nervous patients tend to be worse at the Full ☽, and more restless; ♆ and ♅ afflicted; ♆ □ or ☍ ♅; ♅ or ♂ afflicted in ♒ in the 6th H.; ♅ ☌ ♂; ♅ afflicted in ♊; ♅ in ♊ in □ or ☍ ♃ in ♍; denoted by an afflicted ☿; ☿ badly afflicted in ♈; a ♊ and ♒ disorder, and afflictions in these signs. (See Disordered, Excitability, Highly Neurotic, Neurasthenia, in this section).

Neuralgia—(See "Pain" in this section).

Neurasthenia — Exhaustion of Nerve Force—Nervous Depletion—Enervation—Nervous Debility—The Vital Fluid and Vital Forces Lowered, etc.—The ☉ to the ☌ or ill-asps. ♅ by dir., and with the ☉ affl. by ♅ at B.; ♆ afflicting ☿ predisposes to, and to nervous depletion; ♆ in a prominent position at B., and afflicting the ☽ or ☿, tends to depletion of the nervous energy and complete nervous collapse; ♅ ☌, □, or ☍ the Asc. at B., and by dir., nervous exhaustion from excessive excitement; a ☿ disease, and with ☿ afflicted by malefics at B., and by dir.; ☿ in a ♄ sign and afflicted; the Asc. to the ☌ or ill-asp. ♅ by dir.; a disease of the Nervous Temperament, ruled by ♅, ♄, ☿, and the earthy signs. The degrees usually involved are 10° ♉, the 25° ♊ and ♐, and the 26° ♒, and the ☉, ☽, or planets in these degrees at B. tend to greatly deplete the nervous system under evil directions; Subs at AT and PP. (See Collapse, Debility, Depletion, Enervation, Excitability, Highly Neurotic, Nervousness, Prostration, in this section).

Neuritis—Inflammation of a Nerve—Neuromyelitis—The bad aspects of ♆ to ☿, or to the Significators, the ☉, ☽, Asc., or M.C.; ♂ afflicted in ♊; ♂ afflicting ☿; ♂ in a ☿ sign, and afflicting ☿; ☿ afflicted by malefics, and especially by ♅ or ♂; those having the 29° ♌ or ♒ involved at B. are liable to this disease. Neuritis in the lower extremities is caused by ♆ in ♓ and afflicting the ☉ or ☽; ♂ in ♑, ♒, or ♓, ☌, or ill-asp.

☿, or with malefics afflicted in these lower signs at B., and by dir. Neuritis may occur in the nerves of any part of the body, according to the sign positions of the malefics and ☿ at B. (See Erethism, Medullary Substance, in this section; "Nerves" under Excitable).

Neuroma—A Nerve Tumor—Fibroma On a Nerve—♂ ☌ or ill-asp. ☿. (See "Fibroma" under Fiber).

Neuromalacia—Softening of Nerve Tissue—A ♀ and ♓ disease; ♀ afflicted in ♓. (See "Softening" under Brain; Malacia, Softening).

Neuromyelitis—(See Inflammation, Medullary, in this section).

Neurosis—Neuroses—Neurotic—Nervous Affection Without Lesion—A ♆ disease. (See "Anxiety Neuroses" under Anxiety; Catalepsy; "Movements" under Erratic; "Neuroses" under Motor, Stomach).

Neurosthenia—(See "Excessive" in this section).

Neurotic—Nervous—Pertaining to Neuroses—A ♆ disease and affliction. (See Erethism, Highly Neurotic, Mania, Marriage Partner, Nervousness, Neurasthenia, Neurosis, Sexual, Wasting, in this section).

Nodding Spasm—(See "Nodding" under Head).

Numbness of Nerves—Tingling of Nerves—(See Numbness, Paraesthesia, Tingling).

Nystagmus—Oscillating Eyeballs—Quivering of—(See Eyeballs).

Obstructed—The Nerves Obstructed—Vital Force Obstructed—The ☉ ☌ ♄ at B., and by dir.; ☉ ☌ ♄ in 6th H.; ♆ in the Asc., or in □ or ☍ to the Asc.; ♆ in ♊ in the Asc. or M.C., and afflicted by ♄; the Prog. ☽ ☌, P., □, or ☍ ♂ and ☿, planets which rule the motor and sensory nerves, tends to obstruct the vital flow along the nerves, and often results in paralysis; ♄ in ♊ ☌ ♆, ♅, or ☿. (See Fluid, Force, Nerves, under Vital; Lumbar, Pneumogastric, Sacral, in this section).

Operations—When Not to Sever a Nerve—Do not cut a nerve when the ☽ is passing thru the sign which rules the part. (See "Rules" under Operations).

Optic Nerve—Disorders of—(See Optic).

Over-Activity—Of the Nerves—Neurosthenia—(See Erethism, Excessive, Excitable, Highly Neurotic, in this section; "Over-Active" under Active; "Over-Activity" under Brain, Lungs, Stomach).

Over-Strain—Mental and Nervous Diseases Arising From—♅ or ♂ ☌ or bad asp. ☿; ♅ in ♊ at B. warns against over-strain of the mind and nervous system; the ☽ afflicted by ♅. (See "Brain Fag" under Brain; Fatigue; "Strain" in this section).

Over-Study—Nervous Diseases Arising From—♅ afflicted in ♊. (See Reading, Study).

Over-Work—Nervous Diseases Arising From—(See "Over-Worked" under Brain; "Inordinate", "Mind", under Exercise; Reading, Study; Over-Strain, Over-Study, Strain, in this section).

Pain In Nerve—Neuralgia—Caused by an afflicted ☿, and usually in the part ruled by the sign ☿ is in at B. Also caused by the afflictions of ♅ to ☿. (See Headaches, Neuralgia, Pain; Hands, Hips, Insensibility, Neuritis, Numbness, in this section).

Palliative—A Nerve Palliative—(See "Blue Color" in Sec. 1 of this Article; Anaesthetics, Anodyne, Sedatives).

Palsy; Paraesthesia; Paralysis—(See Paralysis; "Lesions" in this section).

Paramyoclonus—(See Muscles).

Paroxysms—Of Nervous Excitation—(See Collapse, Excitable, Prostration, in this section).

Peculiar Nervousness—Peculiar Nervous Diseases—Caused by ♅; ☿ in evil asp. to ♅. (See Peculiar).

Periodicity—Nervous Periodicity—(See Innervation; "Influx" in this section).

Pneumogastric Nerve—Obstruction of—(See Pneumogastric).

Power—Loss of Nerve Power—(See Depletion, Loss Of, in this section).

Pressure—Upon the Nerves—(See Pressure, Spine, Subluxations, Vertebrae).

Prickling Sensations—(See Burning, Numbness, Tingling, in this section).

Privy Parts—Disorders of Nerves of—(See "Genitals" in this section).

Prostration—Nervous Prostration—Nervous Breakdown—Complete Nervous Collapse—A ☉ disease; afflictions to the ☉ by ♅, ♆, or ♄; ♅ afflicting ☿ or the hyleg at B., and by dir.; ♄ ☌ the ☉ in ♊ or ♒; ♂ or ☿ in the 6th or 12th H., and in ☍ each other; ☿ weak and ill-dig. at B., and afflicted by malefics. The Mercurial man tends to exhaust his nervous energies due to the restless activity of Modern Life. Cases—See Fig. 14A and 14B in "Astro-Diagnosis". (See Collapse; "Nerves" under Excitable; Depletion, Neurasthenia, in this section).

Puffing—Puffing Up of the Sinews of the Nerves—The ☽ in ♑ and afflicted by the ☉ or ♂ when taken ill (Hor'y).

Quick and Nervous—(See "Quick and Nervous" under Speech, Walk).

Quiverings; Resolution—Of the Nerves—A ♄ disease. (See "Nerves" under Resolution).

Respiratory System—Nervous Disorders of—(See "Nerves" under Lungs).

Restlessness—Nervous Diseases Arising From—♊ on the Asc. (See Restlessness).

Sacral Nerves—Obstructed—(See Sacrum).

Saint Vitus Dance—(See Saint).

Sensations; Sensibility—Excessive Sensibility or Sensitiveness—Sensitive Nerves—♅ ☌ ☿. (See Hyperaesthesia, Sensibility, Sensitive; Excessive, Excitable, Highly Neurotic, Neurasthenia, in this section).

Sexual Neurotic—(See "Neurotic" under Sex).

Shock and Strain—(See Shock; "Strain" in this section).

Sinews—Puffing Up of Nerve Sinews —(See "Puffing" in this section).

Sleep — Nervous Disorders of — (See "Insomnia", and the various paragraphs under Sleep).

Softening—Of the Nerve Tissue—(See "Neuromalacia" in this section).

Somnolence — (See "Drowsiness" under Sleep).

Spasmodic Diseases—Spasmodic Movements—Spasms—(See Convulsions; "Movements" under Erratic; Fits, Jerky, Spasmodic, Tics, Twitchings).

Speech — (See "Quick and Nervous" under Speech).

Spinal Cord — Disorders of — (See "Cord" under Spine).

Stomach—Nervous Disorders of—(See Nerve Pains, Nerve Terminations, Nervous Indigestion, Neuralgia, Neuroses, under Stomach).

Storms — Psychic Storms—Violent Brain Storms — (See "Brain Storms" under Brain; Frenzy, Madness, Mania; "Psychic Storms" under Psychic).

Strain—High Nervous Strain and Tension, and Diseases Arising From—The ☽ afflicted by ♅; caused by afflictions to ☿; ♅ afflicted in ♈; airy signs on the Asc.; Aldebaran or Antares directed to the angles of the horoscope, the Asc., or M.C., tend to terrible periods of stress and nervous strain, the worst which may occur in a lifetime. (See Aldebaran, Antares; "Nerves" under Excitable; "Nervous Strain" under Headaches; "High Strung" under High; Strain, Stress; Highly Neurotic, Nervousness, Neurasthenia, Over-Strain, Stress, in this section). Case of Death from Nervous Strain and Shock—See "Leland", No. 813 in 1001 N.N.

Stress and Strain—Nervous Diseases Arising From, and from Over-Work and Worry—Denoted by ☿, and this planet afflicted by malefics at B., and by dir. (See Over-Strain, Over-Study, Over-Work, Strain, Worry, in this section).

Stupor—(See "Stupor" under Sleep).

Suppression — Of Nervous Energy — Caused by ♄ afflictions to ☿. (See Energy, Inhibition, in this section).

Susceptibility—Nervous Susceptibility —♄ afflicted in ♎. (See Disordered, Nervousness, Neurasthenia, in this section).

Swallowing — Deglutition Difficult — Dysphasia—(See Deglutition).

Sympathetic Nervous System—Disorders of—(See Peripheral, Sympathetic).

Tension—High Nervous Tension— (See "Nerves" under Excitable; "High Strung" under High; Tension; High Tension, Highly Neurotic, Strain, in this section).

Throat and Neck—(See "Neck" in this section).

Tics—Spasmodic Twitching—(See Spasmodic, Tics, Twitching).

Tingling — (See "Numbness" in this section).

Tissues—Wasting of Nerve Tissues— ♆ disease and affliction. (See Wasting).

Treatment—Of Nervous Disorders— (See "Treatment" in Sec. 1 of this Article).

Tremors — Tremblings—(See Tremors).

Tumor — Of the Nerve — (See "Neuroma" in this section).

Twitchings—(See Tics, Twitching).

Unsettled—The Nerves Unsettled— (See "Nervousness" in this section).

Urinary System — Nervous Disorders of—(See "Nervous Affections" under Urine).

Vascular Excitement—Of the Nerve Centers—(See Erethism).

Violent Brain Storms — (See "Brain Storms" under Brain).

Vital Flow — Obstructed — (See "Obstructed" in this section).

Vital Fluid — Vital Force—Exhaustion of—Lack of—(See Depletion, Exhaustion, Fluids, Force, Neurasthenia, Prostration, in this section).

Walk—(See "Quick and Nervous" under Walk).

Wasting—Neurotic Wasting—(See "Neurotic" under Marriage Partner; Wasting; "Neurotic" in this section).

Weakest Part—The Nervous System the Weakest Part—The ☉ afflicted in ♐.

Weakness—Nerve Weakness—♅ ☌, P., □, or ☍ the Asc., nerve weakness and depletion of nerve fluids; ☿ □ or ☍ Asc. (See Collapse, Enervation; Depletion, Exhaustion, Neurasthenia, Prostration, in this section).

Women—Nervous Disorders of—Afflictions to the ☽ and ☿; the ☽ ☌, □, or ☍ ♅. (See Emotions; "Women" under Headaches; Hysteria; "Disordered" in this section).

Worry — Nervous Disorders From — Afflictions to ☿, and especially ☿ afflicted by ♄; ☿ affl. in 6th H. (See Apprehensive, Depletion, Enervation, Fears, Strain, Stress, in this section; Dejection, Depressed; "Low Spirits" under Low; Melancholy; "Morbid" under Mind; Worry, etc.).

NERVINE—A Therapeutic Property of ☿. (See "Nervine" under Nerves).

NETTLE RASH—Urticaria—(See Hives, Itch, Urticaria).

NEURALGIA—Pain In a Nerve—Neuralgia may occur in any part, or organ of the body, and is caused principally by ☿ afflicted in the sign which rules the part or organ. Also ♄ causes Neuralgia, and lingering pains in a part due to the deposit of wastes and minerals in the part, and interfering with function, elimination, secretion, excretion, etc. Uranus also contributes to Neuralgia when configurated with Mercury. Mars causes acute neuralgic pains in a part; darting, sharp, shooting, or violent pains and Neuralgia in those parts ruled by the sign he may be in at B., as ♂ in any sign tends to draw heat to the part ruled by the sign, and to cause disturbances at times, pains, and an acute form of Neuralgia. The Neuralgia of ♄ is more chronic, dull, lingering, throbbing, more like an ache, but very severe and painful at times. Mercury afflicted in ♈ tends to Neuralgia and pains in the head, and headaches; ☿ in ♉, Neuralgia of the neck and throat; ☿ in ♊, of the chest and lungs; ☿ in ♋, of the stomach; ☿ in ♍, Neuralgia in the bowels and abdomen; ☿ in ♎, of the kidneys; ☿ in ♏, of the generative organs, womb, bladder, etc.; ☿ in ♐, in the hips and thighs; ☿ in ♑, in the knees and legs; ☿ in ♒, in the calves, ankles, and lower legs; ☿ in ♓, Neuralgia and pains in the feet, etc. For additional influences which may cause Neuralgia in the different parts and organs, see "Nerves", "Neuralgia", "Pains", under Arms, Bladder, Bowels, Face, Feet, Hands, Head, Heart, Intercostal, Kidneys, Legs, Stomach, Teeth, Womb, etc., and in other parts or organs which may not be mentioned here. Also note the various paragraphs in the Article on Pain, as the parts afflicted by Pains and Neuralgia are listed there, and also the various kinds of Neuralgic Pains, such as Darting, Sharp, Shooting, Violent, etc. In the treatment of Neuralgia the tonic remedies of ♂ will often relieve the Neuralgia caused by ♄, and where ♄ has caused a weak circulation, as ♂ opposes ♄, on the theory of opposites. (See Antipathy, Opposites; "Medicines" under Tonic).

NEURASTHENIA—(See Nerves).

NEURITIS—Inflammation of a Nerve—(See "Neuritis" under Nerves).

NEUROMA—Nerve Tumor—(See "Neuroma" under Nerves).

NEUROMALACIA—Softening of Nerve Tissue—(See this subject under Nerves).

NEUROMYELITIS—Inflammation of Nerve Tissue, or of the Medullary Substance—(See Medulla; "Inflammation" under Nerves).

NEUROSIS—Nervous Affection without Lesion—(See "Neurosis" under Nerves).

NEUROSTHENIA—Over-Activity of the Nervous System—(See this subject under Nerves).

NEUROTIC—Nervous—Pertaining to Neuroses—(See "Neurotic" under Nerves).

NEUTRAL—Neutral Planets—☿ is a neutral, or variable planet, and partakes of the nature of the planet with which configurated. This is important to note in making a study of the map of birth along health lines. Mercury with ♄ becomes like ♄, and causes the same diseases as ♄. Mercury with ♀ adds to the power of ♀ in musical and artistic matters. Mercury with ♂ adds to the hasty and impulsive tendencies of the mind, and to excitability of the nerve centers, etc. The ☽ is also variable, and takes on the nature of other planets when configurated with them, the same as does ☿. The ☽ ☌ ♄ gives a very depressed and despondent nature, or personality, and often leads to an increase of ♄ diseases, and to add to their power. (See Variable. Also study the Articles on the Moon and Mercury, and note their neutral, and variable influences).

NEW BORN—(See Birth, Children, Infancy, Parturition, Puerperal).

NEW GROWTHS—Neoplasm—Tumors—(See "New Growths" under Growths"; Tumors).

NEW MOON—(See "New Moon" under Moon).

NEWSMONGER—A Gossip—Busy-Body—Prattler—Meddler—Tale-Bearer—♃ afll. in ♎.

NEWTON—Sir Isaac Newton—Born Dec. 25, 1642. Died March 20, 1727. He came to be a great believer in Astrology. On one occasion, when upbraided by Mr. Halley, the discoverer of Halley's Comet, for his belief in Astrology, answered, "I have studied the subject, Mr. Halley, you have not". The only way to understand Astrology is to study it, observe the effects of the planetary influences over individuals, and not persecute what God has ordained as fixed Laws over His Universe. (See Kepler, Map, Medical Astrology, Nativity, Paracelsus, Star Map).

NICOTINE—(See Tobacco).

NIECES—Nephews—Ruled by the 3rd H., and come under the same rules as for the brothers and sisters of the native. (See "Case" under Aunt; Brothers, Sisters).

NIGHT—Nocturnal—The Night is ruled by the ☽, and the ☉ rules the Day. The night is magnetic, while the day is electric. At night the ☽ tends to keep up the action of morbid germs, while the electric action of the ☉ by day tends to destroy them. The night is less vitalizing than the day. Saturn is more malignant at night as the moisture of the night adds to his cold. Mars is less malignant by night as the moisture of the night moderates his heat and dryness. Thus ♄ is more malignant in night nativities, and ♂ less so. However, as Anareta, ♄ and ♂ are equally destructive to life whether they be diurnal or nocturnal. In a night nativity the ☽ is more powerful when elevated above the Earth, and tends to better functions. (See Day, Elevated). The planetary causes of disease, and even in the same disease, as in Insanity, tend to differ in a day and night nativity, due to the degree of malignancy of the afflicting planet. Thus in Insanity ♄ may cause and rule the scheme in a day nativity, and ♂ in a night nativity. (See Insanity). Moonlight and night air are noxious, and tend to Miasmic diseases. The exhalations of the vegetables at night, the prevalence of carbonic acid, and the chemical action of the Moon's rays, become very deleterious at night. People should not sleep with the Moonlight directly upon them. The Insane, Epileptics, the Hysterical and Nervous, are more affected by Moonlight, and at the Full Moon, and should not be allowed to sleep under the Moon's rays. (See Electric, Magnetic, Malignant, Miasma; "Full Moon", "Moonlight", "Night Action of the Moon", under Moon; Noxious). The following subjects have to do with the Night, and the Planetary Influences over Disease at Night.

Air—The Night Air Noxious, and Causing Miasma, etc.—(See Miasma, Noxious).

Danger to Life—In a Night Nativity —Influences Tending To—(See "Danger to Life" under Danger).

Diseases by Night—(a) Disease More Prevalent At Night—The ☽ in ♓, and afflicted by the ☉ or ♂ when taken ill (Hor'y). (b) The Disease Worse by Night—The Disease is worse at night if the ☽ was badly afflicted at B., as the ☽ rules the night, and also the ☽ be afflicted by direction at the time. The ☉ being more afflicted than the ☽ at B. tends to make the disease worse by day, as the ☉ rules the day. Females tend to suffer more at night in disease, as the ☽ rules strongly over female disorders, and the ☽ rules the night. Fevers and diseases which are strongly influenced by Miasmic conditions are usually worse at night. Also Chronic and Low Fevers usually get worse towards Sunset, and at night. (See "Chronic" under Fever; Miasma; "Night Action" under Moon).

Epilepsy—♂ ruling the scheme by day and ♄ by night. (See Epilepsy, Insanity).

Father—(See "Mother" in this section).

Fits—♄ by Day, and ♂ by Night, and Their Influences In Tending to Cause Fits—(See "Causes" under Fits).

Insanity—♄ Ruling the Scheme by Day and ♂ by Night. (See Insanity).

Insomnia—Loss of Sleep by Night— (See "Insomnia" under Sleep).

Losses—Night Losses—Wet Dreams— (See "Emissions" under Semen).

Malignant—♄ More Malignant In a Night Nativity—(See "Malignant"; the Introduction to this Article).

Mars—(See Day, Night, under Mars).

Miasma—Noxious Night Air—(See Miasma).

Moonlight—Influence of—(See "Full Moon", "Moonlight", "Night Action", under Moon; the Introduction to this Article).

Mother—Disease In—In studying the diseases of the mother note the positions and aspects of Venus in a day nativity, and the ☽ in a night nativity. (See "Disease" under Mother). With the father the ☉ is to be noted in a day nativity, and ♄ by night. Thus the ☉ and ♀ represent the parents in a day geniture, and the ☽ and ♄ by night.

Nativity—Night Nativity—(See the Introduction, and the various paragraphs in this Article).

Nightmare — Horrible Dreams — (See Dreams; "Nightmare" under Sleep).

Night Study—(See "Night Study" under Study).

Night Sweats—Of Phthisis—(See Phthisis).

Night Vision—Vision Best At Night— (See "Night Vision" under Sight).

Nocturnal Life—Night Life—Disposed To—The 3rd Decan. of ♒ on the Asc. at B. More common among people born between Sunset and Midnight, and with the ☽ in this Quarter and afflicted by malefics, and also with the ☽ and many planets in watery signs in this Quarter, which influences may lead to dissipations of various kinds. Also people born between Noon and Midnight may be inclined to a night life. People born between Midnight and Noon, and with the ☉ and many planets rising in the East, are more active during the day, and inclined to rest and relax at night.

Nocturnal Signs—The Feminine Signs —♉, ♋, ♍, ♏, ♑, ♓, and called nocturnal because they excel in dryness or moisture. These are also the night signs, or night houses, of the planets, except ♋, which is the only sign of the ☽, and serves as the home and strong sign by day or night. The diurnal signs are ♈, ♊, ♌, ♎, ♐, ♒, as their rulers are stronger in them by day than at night. The ☉ has only one sign, that of ♌, and the ☉ is equally strong in this sign, day or night.

Noxious Air At Night—(See Miasma).

Pain Greater At Night—The ☽ ☌ or ill-asp. ♄ (or ☿ if he be of the nature of ♄) at the beginning of an illness, or at decumbiture (Hor'y). (See "Diseases by Night" in this section).

Parents—Significators of the Parents In a Night Nativity—(See "Mother" in this section).

Patient Worse At Night — (See "Disease" in this section).

Saturn by Night — ♄ is more malignant when afflicting in a night nativity. (See Introduction to this section).

Study At Night—(See "Night Study" under Study).

Vision At Night — Better At Night Than In Day—(See "Night Vision" under Sight).

Worse — Disease Worse At Night — (See "Diseases by Night" in this section).

NIMBLE BODY — Nimble Step — (See "Energetic" under Gait; "Quick" under Motion).

NINTH HOUSE—The house of ♃ and ♐, and a masculine house. Denotes the Fundament, the Hips, Thighs, Hams. This is the House of Religion, Philosophy, the Higher Mind, Dreams, Dream Consciousness, Visions, Kindred of the Marriage Partner, Long Journeys, Foreign Travel, Voyages, Residence Abroad. In the body this House rules the Hips, Thighs, and Fundament, and signifies all diseases in these parts. Malefics in the 9th H. at B. tend to disturb and unbalance the mind, or cause Religious Excitement, Religious Fanaticism, Distorted Religious Views, Religious Mania, Unorthodox Views, and trouble with Religious Authorities. Malefics in the 9th H. also tend to dangers in Foreign Travel, Injury, loss or death at Sea, and ill-health, dangers, or death Abroad. Mars afflicted in this House at B. tends to dangers at Sea by Lightning, Fire, or Shipwreck, and also to cause many conflicts with the Clergy and Orthodox Leaders. Neptune or H well-aspected in this house at B. tend to give an Occult and Mystical mind, Advanced Views, and with good powers to comprehend and appreciate Truth wherever found. People having malefics in this house at B., and afflicted, and with no benefics in the house, or favorably influencing the house, should remain in their Native Land, and not take voyages, or go Abroad, as such might bring them disease, ill-health, accident, injury, capture, death, failure, or disaster. The benefics ♃ and ♀ in this house, and with no malefic in, or ruling, the house, tend to give a religious and devotional mind, and with greater success along Orthodox lines and the Ministry, and to have more success in ordinary Church work. Uranus here tends to make the native soon rebel against the Orthodox interpretations of the Bible, and to study into the Mysteries, and the Esoteric explanations of Christianity, and of all Religions, and to delve into the Secret Doctrines of the Ages. These tendencies for Esoteric study are also given by the ☉ or ☿ ☌ ♅ at B., or with ♅ rising in the Asc. or M.C. Neptune well-aspected in the 9th H. gives strong Psychic, Clairvoyant, Mediumistic, and Spiritual Powers. The Colors ruled by this house are Green and White. (See Abroad, Foreign Lands, Jupiter, Religion, Sagittarius, Third House, Voyages, etc.).

NIPPLES—Paps—Ruled by the ♋ sign. Afflictions in ♋, and Subs at Lu.P. (3D), tend to Imperfections in, Disorders of, and Injuries to, etc.

Pain Under Nipples—♅ or the ☽ in ♋, ☌, or ill-asp. ♄ (or ☿ if he be of the nature of ♄) at the beginning of an illness or at decumbiture; the ☽ ☌ ♄ in ♓ (or ☌ ☿ in ♓ if he is of the nature of ♄) at the beginning of an illness, or at decumb., tends to pain under the Nipples, and in the chest, and caused by wet feet or damp linen; ♂ affl. in ♋, or in ♋ in the Asc. (See "Pain" under Breast, Chest).

Sore Nipples—♄ or ♂ afflicted in ♋.

Suppurative Inflammation — Of the Areola About the Nipple—Phlegmon—♄ affl. in ♋. (See "Phlegmon" under Pus). See Milk, Nursing.

NITROGEN—Ozote—A Gaseous Element and Constituent of the Air—Is the base of a number of compounds ruled by ♅. Nitrogen is ruled by ♅ and the Airy Signs, and is a dominant element of the Airy Signs. Nitrogen is unstable, highly explosive, and tends to explosions and accidents, and death by explosions when ♅ is afflicted in the 8th H. at B., and by dir. Hydrogen, Nitrogen, Oxygen and Carbon correspond to the four elements of Nature, as Water, Air, Fire, and Earth respectively, and the four fundamental and essential Operations of Nature are synthetized by their qualities, namely—Congelation, Volatilization, Combustion, and Condensation. (See these subjects. Also see Air, Carbon, Explosions, Gases, Hydrogen; "Operations" under Nature; Oxygen, Uranus, Urea).

NOBLE—Noble-Minded—A Just Mind and Disposition—The ☉ Sig. in ♈, ♌, ♎, or ♑; the ☽ Sig. in ♉; the ☽ Sig. ⚹ or △ ♃; ♄ Sig. ⚹ or △ the ☉; ♃ Sig. in ♈, ♌, ♎, ♐, or ♒; a ♃ trait; ♃ well-aspected in the Asc.; ♃ ⚹ or △ the ☉; ♂ Sig. ☌ ♃; ♀ Sig. in ♊ or ♓; ☿ Sig. in ♎; ♎ on the Asc.; many influences in fixed signs. (See Honest, Humane, Kind, Philanthropic, Royal, Sincere, Sympathetic, etc.).

NOBLES—Noblemen—Grandees—The ☉ rules Nobles and Noblemen.

Death Of—Suffering or Evils To—♃ or ♂ conjoined in ♓; Comets appearing in ♌; Comets appearing in ♈, detriment and evils to Grandees and Nobles in Eastern Parts. (See Famous; "Great Men" under Great; Kings, Rulers).

Injury To—♃, ♂, ♀, and the ☽ conjoined in ♉.

Murders Of—☿ in ♋ at the Vernal Equi., Lord of the Year, and ☌ ♂ or ♀. (See Assassination).

Sickness and Infirmities—♄ Lord of the Year at the Vernal, in ♊, and ori., tends to much sickness to Nobles or Grandees.

Suffer—Nobles, Grandees, and the Associates Suffer—♄, ♃, and ♂ conjoined in ♓; ♃ and ♂ conjoined in ♎; Comets appearing in ♌.

NOCTURNAL—(See Night).

Nocturnal Signs—(See "Signs" under Night).

NODDING SPASM—Of the Head—(See "Nodding" under Head).

Nods Head to One Side—When Speaking—(See Skippish).

Nodding of the Eyeballs—Rolling of—(See "Nystagmus" under Eyeballs).

NODES—The points where planets cross the Ecliptic from South Latitude into North Latitude, and also where they cross again from N. Lat. to S. Lat. The Nodes of the ☽ are the ones mostly used and studied. The North Node of the ☽, when she crosses the Ecliptic going North, is called Caput Draconis, or the Dragon's Head, and is considered a fortunate influence in health, and other matters, when falling on the place of the Asc., or M.C. in a nativity. (See Dragon's Head). The South Node of the ☽, where she crosses the Ecliptic going South, is called the Dragon's Tail, and is considered unfortunate, and to have an influence similar to ♄ in health matters when it falls in the Asc., M.C., and other vital centers of the map of birth. (See "Nodes" under Moon). However, in the consideration of the power and force of the planets in disease, the Nodes of all the planets should be considered, and their Latitudes. A planet is stronger in its influence when near its node, and on or near the Ecliptic, and the further from the Ecliptic the afflicting planet may be, the less is its power to cause affliction and disease. Also the aspects between planets which have a wide difference in Latitude are not as important to consider as those which are in aspect in and near the same degree of Latitude, either North, or South. If several planets are on the Ecliptic at B., near their Nodes, and afflicting the hyleg, their power is greater to cause disease, or great suffering and affliction. It is very important, therefore, for every student and Diagnostician in Astrology to have an Ephemeris which gives the Latitudes of the planets, and to study their positions as to Latitude and Declination, as well as Longitude. (See Latitude). Declination is the distance of a planet North or South of the Equator, and planets with the same Declination, or within 1° of the same, are said to be in Parallel Aspect, which is a very strong aspect for good or evil in health matters, according to the nature of the planets so aspected. (See Parallel).

Nodules — Tubercles — Tophus — A ♄ disease. (See "Nodes" under Ears; "Adiposa Dolorosa" under Fat; Tubercles).

NOISE—Noisy—Noisome—

Noise In the Head — Rumbling or Ringing Noises In the Head — (See "Noises" under Head).

Noisome Diseases — ♆ afflicted in the 12th H., and bordering on Fury or Insanity. (See Fury, Insanity, Madness, Mania).

Noisy Breathing—(See "Noisy" under Breathing).

Noisy and Contentious—A Brawler—A Scold—A ♄ characteristic. (See Harlots, Riotous, Scolding).

NON—The Latin word for "Not".

Non-Malignant Growths—(See "Non-Malignant" under Growths).

Non-Oxygenation—Of the Blood—(See Oxygen).

Non-Sensitives — (See Dull, Indifferent, Inertia, Lethargy, Mild; "Dulling of the Senses" under Senses).

NORMAL—According to Rule or Type—

Normal Births—(See "Normal Birth" under Parturition).

Normal Constitution — (See Good, Sound, Strong, under Constitution).

Normal Functions — (See "Normal" under Functions).

Normal Growth — Of the Body — (See "Normal" under Growth).

Normal Health — (See "Abundance", "Good Health", under Health; Immunity; "Good" under Vitality).

Normal Mind — ☿ strong, dignified, and well-aspected at B., and free from the affliction of malefics; ☿ in good aspect to the ☽ and Asc., and otherwise free from the afflictions which tend to an unbalanced mind. (See "Quickened" under Mentality; "Good Mind" under Mind).

Planets — Normal Action of — (See "Perverted" under Planets).

NORTH—Northern—

North Scale — A Star of the second magnitude, of the nature of ♃ and ♂, in the 17° ♏. The Asc. ☌ this star at B. tends to unusual melancholy. (See "Tendency To" under Melancholy).

North-Western Parts — War and Bloodshed In—☿ in ♋ and afflicted by ♂ at the Vernal Equi., and Lord of the Year.

Northern Parts — Effusion of Blood Prevalent In Northern Parts — (See Effusions).

Northern Signs — Of the Zodiac — Called Commanding Signs—♈, ♉, ♊, ♋, ♌, ♍. Planets in these signs are said to command, and those in opposite signs to obey. The Southern Signs are ♎, ♏, ♐, ♑, ♒, ♓, and a planet in these signs, in direct ☍ to a planet in a Northern sign, and with the same Declination, is weaker, and is said to obey the northern planet, and the Southern Signs are called Obeying Signs.

NOSE — Nostrils — Nares—Nasal Fossae —Nasal Bones — Nasal Septum — Turbinated Bones—The Nose, taken as a whole, is ruled by the ♏ Sign. It is also said to be under the external rulership of the ♈ sign, and influenced by ♈, and planets in this sign, and especially by ♂ in ♈, as ♂ rules both the ♈ and ♏ signs. The Nose has special affinity with the ♏ sign, and is one of the organs of Excretion. The nasal bones, and the nasal orifice, are ruled by ♏. Ptolemy says the Nostrils are ruled by ♀. Wilson, in his Dictionary, says the Olfactory Nerves are ruled by ♀. The Nerves to the Nose pass thru the 3rd, 4th and 5th Cervical Vertebrae, known as MCP, Middle Cervical Place, and these nerves when impinged tend to nasal disorders. The Naso-Pharynx is especially affected when planets are in both the ♈ and ♉ signs, or with ♂ in ♉. The Nasal Duct is the Tear Duct, or Lachrymal Duct. (See Aries, Excretion, Scorpio, Tears).

DESCRIPTIONS OF THE NOSE—

Broad Nose—☿ Sig. in ♌, broad and high. (See Thick, Wide, in this section).

Conspicuous — And High — ♊ on the Asc.

Great Nose—(See "Large" in this section).

Grecian Nose — ☿ in ♐, or ♐ on the Asc.

High Nose—♃ Sig. in ♈; ☿ Sig. in ♌, high and broad; ♊ on the Asc., high and conspicuous.

Large Nose—The ☉ Sig. in ♉, or in ♉ in partile asp. the Asc.; ♄ Sig. in ♎, or in ♎ in partile asp. the Asc.; ☿ Sig. in ♐ or ♑; ☿ in ♐ partile asp. the Asc.; ♉ on the Asc., large or wide.

Long Nose — Long and Straight — ☿ gives when strong at B., or the ruler.

Pointed Nose — (See "Sharp" in this section).

Prominent Nose—♄ in ♎, ♏, or ♐; ☿ in ♊ or ♌; ☿ in ♐, a prominent Grecian Nose; ♈ on the Asc., a prominent Roman Nose. (See "Large" in this section).

Roman Nose—♈ on the Asc., prominent Roman Nose.

Rounded and Short—♋ on the Asc.

Sharp Nose—Pointed—A ☿ person has a long, thin, and sharp nose; ☿ Sig. in ♈, or in this sign in partile asp. the Asc.

Short Nose — Short and Rounded — ♋ on the Asc.

Smell—Sense of—(See Smell).

Straight Nose — Straight and Long — ☿ gives; ☿ ascending at B., and free from the rays of other planets; ♐ gives a straight, Grecian nose.

Thick Nose — Thick Nostrils — Given by ♄ when he forms the body; ♄ ascending at B.

Thin Nose—☿ gives a long, straight, thin, and sharp nose; ☿ ascending at B., and free from the rays of other planets.

Wide Nose — ♉ gives, and with this sign on the Asc. (See "Broad" in this section).

DISEASES OF THE NOSE—Afflictions to the Nose — See the following subjects in the alphabetical arrangement when not more fully considered here—

Abscess — Frontal — (See "Frontal" under Abscesses).

Accidents To — Hurts — Wounds To — Injuries To—♄ or ♂ afflicted in ♏, and especially when in the 1st H. at B.; ♂ afflicted in ♈ tends to accidents to the head, which may involve the nose. (See "Accidents" under Face, Head).

Adenoids; All Diseases—In the Nose—Signified by planets in the 1st H., or by afflictions in ♈, ♉, or ♏.

Asthma—Hay Asthma—(See Asthma; "Hay Fever" in this section).

Bleeding — At the Nose — (See Epistaxis, Vicarious, in this section).

Capillaries — Of the Nose — Red and Swollen—Obstructed—Red Nose—Usually caused by ♄ influence, and ♄ afflicted in ♈ or ♏, due to deposits, or afflictions to ♃ or ♀ if these planets also are in ♈ or ♏; ♃ in ♈, ☌, or ill-asp. ♄; ♂ afflicted in ♈ tends to a general redness of the face. Is also caused by Alcoholism, and gives the Toper's Nose when there are many planets in watery signs at B., and especially in ♏ or ♓. (See Capillaries, Drink, Drunkenness; "Red Face" under Face).

Caries—Of the Cartilage of the Nose —♄ afflicted in ♏. (See Caries).

Cartilage — Caries of — (See "Caries" in this section).

Catarrh—Nasal Catarrh—Foul Odors of—Catarrhal Headaches—A ♏ disease, and afflictions in ♏; the ☉ afflicted in ♈ or ♉; ♄ afflicted in ♈, ♉, ♎, or ♏; ♃ afflicted in ♉; Subs at MCP. (See Catarrh, Colds, Defluxions, Discharges; "Noises In" under Head; "Catarrhal" under Headaches; "Coryza" in this section).

Cold Nose — Coldness and Whiteness of—A ♄ disease. (See "Raynaud's Disease" under Fingers).

Colds — (See Colds; Coryza, Rhinitis, in this section).

Constrictions In — Stenosis of—Stricture of the Nasal Passage—♄ afflicted in ♏; Subs at MCP (3, 4C).

Coryza—Catarrhal Inflammation of the Nose—♄, ♃, or ♂ afflicted in ♉; a ☿ disease. Subs at MCP (4C), and KP. (See Colds; "Colds" under Head; Hay Fever, Rhinitis, in this section).

Cut Off — The Nose Nearly Cut Off — Case—See Chap. XIII in Daath's Medical Astrology).

Destroyed — The Nose Partially Destroyed by Lupus—Case—See "Lupus", No. 363, in 1001 N.N. (See Lupus).

Discharges — Much Discharge At the Nostrils—The ☽ in ♈, □ or ☍ ♄ (or ☿ if he be of the nature of ♄) at the beginning of an illness, or at decumb. (Hor'y). (See Catarrh, Colds, Discharges, Rheum; "Coryza" in this section).

Diseased Nose—The ☉ afflicted in ♏; ♂ diseases; ♂ affl. in ♏; afflictions in ♏. (See the various paragraphs in this section).

Disorders—Nasal Disorders—♂ afflicted in ♈; Subs at MCP (4C). (See the various paragraphs in this section).

Ducts — Nasal Ducts — (See "Ducts" under Tears).

Epistaxis — Nose Bleed — Hemorrhage from the Nose—A ♃ disease, due to fullness and plethora of blood vessels; ♃ afflicted in ♈, ♉, or ♏; ♂ affl. in ♉ or ♏; ♂ afflicted in ♏ in the Asc. or 6th H.; ♏ on the cusp the 6th H.; Subs at MCP (4C). (See Hemorrhage, Plethora; "Vicarious" in this section).

Epithelioma — Of the Nose — ♂ afflicted in ♏; ♂ in ♏ and afflicting the Asc.; ♂ in ♏ in the 7th H., angular, and in ☍ the Asc.; the ☽ in ♑, afflicted by malefics, and conjoined with afflictions in ♏, and especially ♂ afflicted in ♏ at the same time, and with ♂ in the Western angle. Case — See "Epithelioma", in Chap. XIII, in Daath's Medical Astrology. (See Epithelioma).

Eustachian Tubes—Disorders of—(See Eustachian).

Fluids—Regurgitation of Fluids Thru the Nose — ♄ influence; ♄ afflicted in ♈, ♉, or ♏; Subs at MCP (4C). (See "Obstruction" in this section).

Floor of Nose—(See Palate).

Fossae Diseased—Disorders of the Nasal Fossae — ♏ diseases, and afflictions in ♏; malefics in ♏.

Foul Odors From — ♄ afflicted in ♈, ♉, ♎, or ♏. (See "Catarrh" in this section; "Foul Breath" under Breath; Foul).

Frontal Bones—Frontal Sinuses—Abscess In—(See "Frontal" under Abscesses).

Growths In — (See "Polypus" in this section).

Hay Fever—Hay Asthma—Rose Cold —A Microbic Disease of the Nasal Mucous Membrane, and accompanied by Inflammation, Coryza, and Lacrimation—Caused by afflictions in ♉, ♊, or ♏; the ☽ afflicted in ♉ or ♏; ♆ afflicted in ♊, due to disturbances of the bronchioles from breathing Pollen in the Summer time; ♄ or ♂ ☌ ♃ or ♀ in ♏; ♅ afflicted in ♏; ♂ afflicted in ♉ or ♏; ♀ in ♉, ☌, □, or ☍ ♂; Subs at MCP (4C), LCP (6C), and AP (1D). (See Asthma, Hay Fever; "Sneezing" in this section).

Hemorrhage Of—(See Epistaxis, Vicarious, in this section).

Humours In—A ☿ disease; ☿ afflicted in ♈, ♉, or ♏. (See "Humours" under Head).

Hurts To — (See "Accidents" in this section).

Hypertrophy — Of the Nasal Membranes—♃ or ♂ afflicted in ♈, ♉, or ♏. (See Hypertrophy).

Inflammatory Action—In the Nose—♂ afflicted in ♈, ♉, or ♏; ♀ in ♉, ☌, □, or ☍ ♂. (See Coryza, Hypertrophy, Polypus, Rhinitis, in this section).

Influenza—The Nose Affected By—Afflictions in ♉ or ♏ prevailing at the time; ♃ in ♉ or ♏ in ☌ or ill-asp. ♄; Subs at MCP (4C), CP, and KP. (See Influenza, La Grippe).

Injuries To—(See "Accidents" in this section).

Lachrymal Disorders — And of the Nasal Duct—(See Tears).

Lupus—(See "Destroyed" in this section).

Menses—Menstruation Thru the Nose—(See "Vicarious" under Menses).

Mucous Membranes—Of the Nose—Inflammation of—(See "Inflammation" in this section).

Mucus—In the Nose and Head—The ☽ or ♀ afflicted in ♈. (See Catarrh, Discharges, in this section; "Mucus" under Head; "Humours" under Throat).

Nares — (See "Nostrils" in this section).

Nasal Catarrh—Nasal Disorders—(See "Catarrh", and the various paragraphs in this section).

Naso-Pharynx—Disorders In—♂ afflicted in ♉. (See Pharynx).

Noises In Head—(See "Noises" under Head).

Nose Bleed—(See "Epistaxis" in this section).

Nostrils — Nares — Much Discharge From—Stenosis of—Stricture of—(See Constriction, Discharges, Obstruction, in this section).

Obstruction—In the Nasal Passages—An afflicted ♄ in ♏ tends to, and to growths, such as Adenoids and Polypus, and especially when the mutable signs are also prominent. Throat troubles usually result, and enlarged Tonsils. (See Adenoids; "Obstructions" under Head; Tonsils; Constrictions, Fluids, Hypertrophy, Polypus, Spurs, in this section).

Odors—(See "Foul" in this section).

Olfactory Nerve—Disorders of—Loss of Smell—Anosmia—(See Smell).

Palate—(See Palate).

Passages—Nasal Passages—Disorders In—(See Catarrh, Colds, Constriction, Discharges, Inflammation, Nostrils, and the various paragraphs in this section).

Pharynx—The Naso-Pharynx—Disorders of—(See "Naso-Pharynx" in this section).

Polypus—Nasal Polypus—The ☉ afflicted in ♉; ♄ afflicted in ♉ or ♏, obstructions and growths; ♂ afflicted in ♉; an ♈ and ♉ disease, and afflictions in these signs; ♀ in ♉, ☌, □, or ☍ ♂; Subs at MCP (4C). Case—See Fig. 18B in "Astro-Diagnosis" by the Heindels. (See Hypertrophy, Inflammatory, Obstruction, Turbinated Bones, in this section; Adenoids, Polypus).

Posterior Nares—Disorders In—♄ or ♂ afflicted in ♉; afflictions in ♉; Subs at MCP (4C). (See Adenoids, Pharynx; "Naso-Pharynx" in this section).

Raynaud's Disease — Coldness and Whiteness of the Nose and Fingers—(See "Raynaud" under Fingers).

Red Nose—(See "Capillaries" in this section).

Regurgitation—Of Fluids—(See "Fluids" in this section).

Rheum In—(See Rheum).

Rhinitis—Inflammation of the Nasal Mucous Membrane—Acute Rhinitis—Coryza—Cold In the Head—♂ afflicted in ♉. (See Colds, Coryza, Inflammation, in this section; "Colds" under Head).

Rose Cold—(See "Hay Fever" in this section).

Sneezing—♅ or ☿ afflicted in ♈ or ♉, from nerve irritations and excitement; ♄ in ♈, ♉, ♎, or ♑, from chill and cold; ♄ rising at B., in evil asp. the hyleg, and also with many planets in the earthy or watery signs, are subject to a cold body, chill, to take cold easily, and to sneezing spells, and should dress warmly, and wear wool next to the skin. (See Chill; "Body" under Cold; "Causes of Colds" under Colds; "Hay Fever" in this section).

Snuffling — Snaffling — Snuffles — A ☿ disease, and with ☿ badly afflicted at B. Usually exaggerated in Infancy and Childhood.

Spurs — Elongated Projections from the Septum—Projected Turbinated Bone—♄ afflicted in ♉ or ♏, tending to obstruction of the passage; many afflictions in fixed signs, fixed signs on the angles, and many afflictions in or to ♏ especially. (See Hypertrophy, Obstruction, Polypus, in this section).

Stenosis — Of the Nares — (See Constrictions, Obstruction, in this section).

Stoppage—Caused principally by the ♄ influence, and ♄ afflicted in ♈, ♉, or ♏. (See Catarrh, Colds, Constrictions, Polypus, Rhinitis, Spurs, in this section; Stenosis, Strictures, Stoppages).

Stricture—Of the Nares, and Nasal Passage—(See Constrictions, Stoppage, in this section).

Throat—All Inflammations In the Throat and Naso-Pharynx—♂ afflicted in ♉. (See Throat, Tonsils).

Turbinated Bones—Swelling and Inflammation of — Projection of — (See "Spurs" in this section).

Ulcers—Venereal Ulcers In the Nose—♂ afflicted in ♏. (See Ulcers, Venereal).

Venereal Ulcers—In the Nose—(See "Ulcers" in this section).

Vicarious Menstruation — Thru the Nose—(See "Vicarious" under Menses).

Whiteness and Coldness—Of the Nose—(See "Raynaud" in this section).

Wounds To—(See "Accidents' in this section).

NOTABLE PEOPLE—Death of—(See "Great Men", "The Great", under Great; "Death" under Famous, Kings, Nobles, Princes, Rulers, etc.).

NOTIONS—Conceptions—Ideas—Intentions—Opinions, etc.—

Chaotic Notions—Chaotic and Fanciful—♆ afflicted in ♊; ☿ affl. in ♒, fanciful notions should be guarded against. (See Chaotic, Dress, Fancies, Food, Ideas).

Impractical Notions—Notions Which Outrage Common Sense—♆ afflicted in ♈. (See Confusion, Erratic, Ideals, Ideas, Impractical; "Bad" under Judgment).

Wrong Notions — In General — ☿ afflicted by the ☽ or ♃ at B., and by dir. (See Delusions, Expense, Imaginations, Improvident, Impulses, Opinions, Purposes, Recklessness, etc.).

NOTORIETY—Of the Passions—Exposure of the Passions—Exhibitionism—(See "Sex Organs" under Exhibition; "Notoriety" under Passion).

NOTORIOUS DEATH—(See "Notorious" under Death).

NOURISHMENT—(See Absorption, Assimilation, Digestion, Nutrition).

NOVELTIES—Novelty—

Fond of Novelties—The ☽ ascending at B., fond of novelties, and roaming about.

Many Novelties — Strikes Out Many Novelties—♅ strong at B., ascending, and well-dignified. (See Eccentric, Genius; "Inventive" under Learning; "Influence Of" under Uranus).

NOXIOUS — Poisonous — Harmful — Destructive — Obnoxious — Mephitic — Moonlight and Night Air are noxious. Also cold and dryness are noxious and destructive. (See "Obnoxious" under Air; Cold, Dryness, Epidemics, Foul, Gases, Malaria, Miasma; "Moonlight" under Moon; Obnoxious, Pestilence, Poisonous, Putrefaction, Stagnant, Venomous, Vermin, etc.).

Noxious Growths—(See Growths).

NUCLEUS — Nucleolations — Nuclei — Neucleolus — The Nucleus of Cells is ruled and supported by the ☉ influence. Neucleolations are the work of ♄ and the ♑ sign. (See "Nucleus" under Cells; Protoplasm).

NUMBNESS — Tingling of a Nerve — Lack of Feeling In a Part—Caused by an afflicted ♄ in the sign ruling the part, or in a sign in □ or ☍; ♄ ☌ or ill-asp. ☿; also caused sometimes by ♅, and ♅ ☌ ☿ in the sign ruling the part. This is generally due to pressure upon a nerve, and the spine and vertebrae should be relieved of subluxations. Also caused by poor circulation, due to the cold, restraining and suppressing influence of ♄, and ♄ ☌ ☿, ♃, or ♀ tends to considerable numbness, and disturbance in the part ruled by the sign so occupied. (See Analgesia; "Poor Circulation" under Circulation; "Raynaud's Disease" under Fingers; Paraesthesia, Tingling).

Arms—Numbness In—♄ in ♊, ☌ ♃ or ♀; ♄ afflicted in common signs; ♃ in ♊ ☍ ♄; ♅ afflicted in ♊, as ♅ in any sign, if afflicted, tends to a numbness and peculiar prickling sensation in the part ruled by the sign.

Legs—Numbness In—(See "Cold and Numb", "Numbness", under Legs). Saturn in the signs which rule the Legs, as in ♐, ♑, ♒, or ♓, tends to a coldness of the legs, which often is accompanied by numbness, slow and disturbed circulation, lack of sensation in the lower limbs, etc. (See "Body", "Temperament", under Cold).

NURSES — Trained Nurses — Practical Nurses—The ☉ in ♍, or ♍ on the Asc., is not as favorable for a Nurse, as ♍ is too negative, susceptible, and takes on the diseases of others. (See Virgo).

Successful As a Nurse—Fortunate In the Care of the Sick—The ☉ well-aspected in ♏; the ☽ ruler of the horoscope, or ☽ well-aspected in the 10th H.; influences in ♍, the sign of health, or in the 6th H., the house of health, or in the 12th H., the house of Confinement, Asylums, Hospitals, Prisons, etc.; the 6th H. well-aspected at B.; ♃ or ♀ well-aspected in the 6th or 12th H., and especially when in ♓, the home sign of ♃, and the exalted sign of ♀; ♃ well-aspected in ♓ in the 10th H.; ♂ well-aspected in ♍; common signs on angles. For a Nurse to be compatible with the patient, the places of the malefics in her nativity should not fall in the 6th H. of the patient, or her vibrations and magnetism would tend to injure, worry, and weaken the patient. This is also true of the Healer and patient. The same influences which are good for the work of a Healer, Physician, Midwife, etc., may also be good for Nursing and the care of the sick. (See "Compatibility", and the various paragraphs under Healers; Hospitals, Midwives, Obstetricians).

NURSING — The Nursing of Infants — (See Breasts; "Nursing" under Children; Milk, Nipples, Weaning).

NUTRITION — Nutriment — Nurture — Nourishment—Sustenance—Nutritive—Nurturing—Alimentation, etc.—The ☽ is nurturing, and nourishment and alimentation are ruled largely by the ☽ and the ♋ sign. The influences of ♆, ♃, and ♀ are also nutritive, and are concerned with the nourishment, sustenance, conservation, preservation, and the aphetic processes in the body. The functions of growth and nutrition are ruled by ♀ and ♅. Venus rules growth and nutrition until puberty and adolescence, and then the ♅ influence takes charge of growth and assimilation. The Kidneys, being under the rule of ♀, tend to play an important part in the nutrition of the body, as well as to eliminate wastes and poisons. Physiologically ♂ acts thru the demands of sustenance and evolution. Heat and moisture are nutritive. The Venus Group of Planets are nutritive. Fermentation, which is produced by heat and moisture, plays and important part in nutrition and alimentation. Venus rules the fermentative, or nutritive process, and also the distillatory processes in the body. Molecular Nutrition is under the special rule of ♃. (See Alimentary, Assimilation, Conservation, Diet, Digestion, Distillation, Eating, Fermentation, Food, Growth, Heat, Jupiter, Moisture, Neptune, Pituitary, Preservation, Processes, Venus, Zymosis, etc.). The following are Diseases and Disorders of Nutrition, and conditions which tend to disturb Nutrition. See these subjects in the alphabetical arrangement when not considered here—

Absorption — Disorders of — (See Absorption).

Alimentary Tract—Alimentation—Disorders of—(See Alimentary).

Alteratives—Drugs which change the Process of Nutrition—(See Alterative).

Assimilation—Disorders of—(See Assimilation; "Malnutrition" in this section).

Atrophy; Blood Disorders—From Improper or Excessive Nutrition—(See "Poor", "Thin", under Blood; "Impure Blood" under Impure).

Cachexia—A Depraved Condition of Nutrition—(See Cachexia; "Malnutrition" in this section).

Defective Nutrition—Dystrophia—Faulty—Imperfect—(See "Imperfect" under Assimilation; "Malnutrition", and the various paragraphs in this section).

Diet—Ailments from Improper Diet—(See Diet).

Digestion—Disorders of—(See Digestion, Indigestion).

Eating—Excesses In—Fast Eating—(See Eating).

Emaciation; Embryo Not Nourished—(See "Nourishment" under Foetus).

Faulty Nourishment—(See "Defective" in this section).

Food—(See "Indigestible Food" and the various paragraphs under Food).

Growth and Nutrition—(See Abnormal, Arrested, Increase, and the various paragraphs under Growth).

Illness—From Want of Proper Nutrition—The ☉ afflicted in ♑; ♄ afflicted in the 6th H. (See Ailments, Evil Diet, under Diet; Meat, Starches, Sugar, Sweets, Unnatural, Wrong, under Food).

Imperfect Nutrition—(See Defective, Illness, in this section).

Incapable of Nurture—Dies Immediately After Birth—Either the ☉ or ☽ in an angle in ☌ a malefic, and a malefic equally distant from the ☉ or ☽, and no benefic configurated with the ☉ or ☽, and the rulers posited in a place ruled by the malefics, the child then born will not be susceptible to nurture, and will immediately die. The ☉ or ☽ in an angle, and the malefics be succedent to the Lights, or in ☍, or with one malefic succedent, and the other in ☍ to the ☉ or ☽, and with no good aspects from ♃ or ♀, then no duration of life is allotted. All the Significators of life afflicted, as the ☉, ☽, Asc., and lord of the Asc., and with no assistance from benefics. The ☽ besieged between ♄ and ♂, or between ♅ and ♂, and the hyleg severely afflicted by malefics. Uranus, ♄, or ♂ ☌ ☋ in the 4th H., and the hyleg afflicted also by malefics. (See "Imperfect" under Assimilation; Emaciation; "Death Soon After Birth" under Infancy; "Malnutrition" in this section).

Indigestion; Infants—Not Capable of Nurture—(See "Incapable" in this section).

Lack of Nutrition—Illness from Lack of Proper Nourishment and Assimilation—(See "Imperfect" under Assimilation; Atrophy, Famine, Neglect, Poverty, Starvation; "Illness" in this section).

Malnutrition—Mal-Assimilation—Starved Condition of the Body—Imperfect Assimilation—Afflictions in ♋, ♍, or ♎; the ☉ afflicted in ♍; the ☽ in ♋ or ♍ in the 6th H., and afflicted; ♆ afflicted in ♋ or ♍; ♆ in ♋, □, or ☍ the ☉ or ☿; ♆ afflicted in the 6th H.; ♆ in ♍ and afflicting the ☉, ☽, Asc., or hyleg; ♄ or ♃ afflicted in ♍, due to over-eating, and great energy required to eliminate wastes; ♄ afflicted in ♋ or ♎; caused by ♄ through decay of the teeth; ♄ ☌ ♃ or ♀, by impeding the circulation, retention of carbonic acid, and insufficient oxygenation; ♂ in ♋, □, or ☍ ♃ or ♀, which latter governs the circulation; a ♍ disease. (See "Imperfect" under Assimilation; Atrophy, Emaciation, Tabes, Wasting; "Incapable" in this section).

Mastication—Does Not Masticate Food Sufficiently—(See "Fast Eater" under Eating).

Molecular Nutrition—Under the rule of ♃. Interferences with this function may occur when ♃ is weak and afflicted at B.

Not Susceptible To Nurture—(See "Incapable" in this section).

Nurture—Infants Incapable of—(See "Incapable" in this section).

Nutritive Process—Ruled by ♀, and ♀ weak and afflicted at B., and by dir., tends to disorders of, and especially when ♄ afflicts ♀.

Obesity; Perverted Nutrition—♅ diseases, and this planet afflicting the hyleg.

Plants—The ♀ Group of Plants are nutritive. (See "Venus Group" under Herbs).

Process—(See "Nutritive Process" in this section).

Stomach Disorders—From Improper Nutrition—(See Indigestion, Stomach).

Superfluous Nutriment—A ☉ and ♃ affliction. (See "Abnormal" under Appetite; Epicureans, Fat, Feasting; "Rich Food" under Food; Gluttony, Plethora).

Textural Nutrition—Changes In the Process of Textural Nutrition—♀ diseases.

Tissues—Nutrition of the Tissues Affected—The ☉ and ☽ acting thru the ♒ sign. (See the Introduction under Lymph).

Venus Group of Herbs—And Plants—Are nutritive. (See "Plants" in this section).

Wasting Diseases—From Imperfect Assimilation, or Disorders of Nutrition—(See Anaemia, Cachexia, Emaciation, Tabes, Wasting; "Malnutrition" in this section). For other subjects along this line, and which may have to do with Nutrition, look in the alphabetical arrangement for the subject you have in mind.

NUTS—For the various rulership of Nuts, Seeds, Plants, etc., and the Planetary influences over them, see Fruit, Herbs, Seeds, etc.

Nut Butters—Successful Makers of As a Specialty—(See "Specialties" under Healers).

NUX VOMICA — Is one of the typical Polycrest Remedies, corresponding to the ♍ sign, the sign ruled by ☿. Some Writers, therefore, class it is an Herb of ☿. The Herbs of ☿ are Nervine, and tend to calm nervous excitement. Nux Vomica, and its alkaloid, Strychnine, are, on the other hand, stimulant, supporting, tonic, and exciting, and have the action of ♂. This Writer has, therefore, taken the liberty of classing Nux Vomica as a ♂ Drug, even though it is assigned to the ♍ sign in the Polycrest classification. However, ☿ may also have some rule over Nux Vomica, as excitability and irritation are ☿ qualities, and a few drops of the Tincture of Nux Vomica given before meals excite the nerves of the stomach, increase the appetite, and aid digestion. Mercury is a variable planet, and partakes much of the nature of ♂ at times, and ☿ and ♂ can both have rulership over Nux Vomica. (See "Polycrest" under Zodiac).

NYCTALOPIA — (See "Day Blindness" under Blindness).

NYMPHOMANIA—Unbridled Passion In Women—Sexual Obsession In Women—Excessive Sexual Desire—The ☽ to the ill-asps. ♀ by dir., and the ☽ or ♀ afflicted by ♂ or ♆ at B.; ♂ Sig. ☌ or ill-asp. ♀, and especially with ♀ in ♏ and also afflicted by ♄; ♀ Sig. ☌ or ill-asp. ♂; ♀ ruler of the horoscope and afflicted by malefics. Cases—See "Nymphomania", Nos. 289 and 306, in 1001 N.N. (See Amorous, Erotic; "Morbid" under Imagination; Lascivious, Licentious, Lust; "Abnormal" under Passion; "Solitary" under Vice, etc.).

NYSTAGMUS—(See Eyeballs).

O

OBESITY—Fatness—Corpulence—Excess of Corpulence—The ☉ or ☽ in the ♋ sign tends to direct the mind to the stomach, causing over-eating or gluttony, and resulting in Obesity; the ☽ afflicted in ♋; the ☽ afflicted in ♏, an impure kind of obesity in females; the ☉ or ☽ afflicted in the first few degrees of ♒; ♃ conduces to blood changes and accumulation of fluid, either in the form of obesity or tumors; ♃ afflicted in the 6th H., from over-eating; ♃ is usually found in ♍, and afflicted by ♅ or ♄; ♃ ☌ ♅ or ♄; ♃ badly aspected by the ☉, ☽, or any of the planets except ♂; ♀ influences and an afflicted ♀ tends to, and especially brought on by bad habits, lack of exercise, sedentary habits, and gastonomical indiscretions; the fixed signs are usually prominent, except ♏; ♉ influence tends to, and with ♉ on the Asc., and ♀ as ruler, and afflicted; ♋ on the Asc., and the ☽ □ or ☍ the Asc., tends to bad results from over-eating; Subs at AT, CP, and KP (11D). (See "Abnormal" under Appetite; "Accumulation" under Blood; Corpulent; "Excesses" under Diet, Eating, Food; "Lack Of" under Exercise; Fat, Feasting, Fleshy; "Large Quantities" under Food; Gluttony, Plethora, Puffing, Sedentary, Stout, Surfeits, Tumors, etc.).

OBEYING SIGNS—Southern Signs—(See "Northern Signs" under North).

OBNOXIOUS—Offensive—Odious—Poisonous—Noxious—

Obnoxious Air—(See "Obnoxious" under Air; Noxious).

Obnoxious Creatures — Bites, Stings, Injury, or Death By—(See Adder, Bites, Reptiles, Serpents, Stings, Venomous).

Obnoxious Signs—Of the Zodiac—(See "Hurtful Signs" under Hurtful).

OBSCENE—Obscenity—Foul Mind—A Filthy Mind—Infamous—Immoral—Shameless—Lewd—♄ ill-dignified at B. tends to a foul mind; ♄ afflicted in ♋ or ♓; ♆ and ♂ afflictions involving the 5th H.; ♂ ill-dig. at B., and afflicted; ♀ Sig. □ or ☍ ♂, if a female, and often becomes a harlot; in male nativities affliction of malefics to the ☽, and tend to coarsen the nature; afflictions in the 5th H., and in the earthy and watery signs. (See Depraved; "Sex Organs" under Exhibition; "Habits" under Filthy; Harlots, Immodest, Infamous, Knavish, Lewd, Lust; "Loose Morals" under Morals; "Notoriety Of" under Passion; Perversions; "Women" under Scandalous; Shameless, Vices, etc.).

Obscene In Speech — (See "Obscene" under Speech).

OBSCURE—Obscuration—Obscurity—

Air—(See "Obscuration" under Air).

Complexion — (See "Obscure" under Complexion).

Diseases—Obscure Diseases—Vague—Puzzling—Unclassified—Having a Psychic Rather Than a Physical Origin—♆ diseases; ♆ afflicted in ♉, obscure diseases of the neck or throat; ♆ in any sign tends to obscure diseases in the part, parts, or organs ruled by such sign; ♆ afflicted in the 6th H.; ♆ has dominion over certain vague and obscure diseases of Psychic origin; ♄ ☌ or ill-asp. ♆ tends to obscure ailments, puzzling, and difficult to explain. (See Extraordinary, Mysterious, Peculiar, Praeincipients, Pseudo, Psychic, Strange, Vague, etc.).

Marks—Moles—(See "Obscure" under Marks).

Mind — Obscure Mind — (See Chaotic, Confusion, Delusions; "Dreamy" under Dreams; Dull, Fears, Hallucinations, Ideas, Imaginations, Obsessions, Psychic, Vague, Weird, Worry, etc.).

Morbid Manifestations—Obscure Morbid Manifestations are due to the influences of ♆ and ♅, and afflictions to the ☉, ☽, ☿, Asc., M.C., and Significators by these planets; caused by ♄ and the ♑ sign influences; ♄ afflicting the ☉, ☽, Asc., M.C., or hyleg. Morbid Mental Manifestations are caused, and complicated, and made more mysterious, extraordinary, obscure and peculiar by the afflictions of ♆ and ♅, in addition to the ♄ configurations, and especially when afflicting ☿, the mental ruler. (See Dejected, Depression, Despondency, Gloom, Hope, Hypochondria; "Low Spirits" under Low; Melancholy, Morbid, Obsessions, Spirit Controls, Worry, etc.).

Obscure In Life—Dies In Obscurity—The ☽ separating from ♄ and applying to ☿, and the ☽ increasing in light; the ☉ or ☽ far below the horizon, afflicted by malefics, and no benefics angular; ♃ Sig. ☌ ♄, dies in obscurity.

OBSESSIONS—Possessed by a Demon, or An Evil Spirit—Obsessed with Fears, Hallucinations, Wrong Ideas—

Cases of Obsession—See "Obsession", No. 130 in 1001 N.N. See Fig. 16B and 10C in "Astro-Diagnosis" by the Heindels.

Demoniacal Obsession—Principally caused by ♆ and his afflictions. The ♅ afflictions also tend to, and especially when configurated with ♆, ♄, or ☿; ♆ afflicted in ♓; ♆ in ♓ in the 6th H., and afflicted; ♆ in the 6th H., afflicting the Asc. or hyleg, liable to death from obsessions; ♆ afflicted in the 1st, 3rd, 6th, 8th, 9th, 10th, or 12th H.; ♆ □ or ☍ ♅ or ♄, and ill-health by obsession; ♆ afflicted in ♈ in the 12th H.; ♆ ☌ ☽ in the 12th H.; ♆ ☌ ♄ in the 8th H., and in □ asp. to ☿; ♆ afflicted in ♍ or the opposite sign ♓; ♆ afflicted in the 1st H., tends to spirit obsession; ♆ afflicted in a water sign; ♆ ruler of the horoscope and afflicted; ♆ in ♒ in the 6th H., and afflicting the Asc. or hyleg; ♆ afflicting the hyleg, and adding his influence to that of ♄ or ♂; ♅ afflicted in the 6th H.; the ☽ or ☿ afflicted by ♆; ♓ on the Asc., and especially the 27° ♓; the Prog. ☉ to the ☌, P., □ or ☍ ♆; Subs at AT or AX. (See Darkness; "Wild" under Delirium; Dementia, Demoniac, Fears, Forebodings, Hallucinations, Horrors, Madness, Mania, Mediumship, Premonitions, Psychic, Spirit Controls, Terrors, Visions, Weird, etc.).

Fears—Obsessed With—(See "Obsessions" under Fears).

Fits of Obsession—The ☽ ☌, □, or ☍ ♄ at B., and by dir. (See Depressed, Despondent; "Low Spirits" under Low; Melancholy, Prophetic, Worry, etc.).

Medicines and Obsessions—♆ □ or ☍ ♄ at B., bad for the health through obsessions by taking medicines.

Narcotics and Obsessions—(See "Obsessions" under Narcotics).

Sexual Obsession In Women—(See Lewd, Nymphomania, Shameless).

OBSTETRICIANS—The ☽ as ruler of the horoscope tends to make good Obstetricians. (See Healers, Midwives, Nurses).

OBSTINATE—Stubborn—Resisting—

Obstinate Diseases—Stubborn Diseases—Tedious—Prolonged—(See Chronic, Consumptions, Lingering; "Diseases" under Long; Prolonged, Tedious, Wasting, etc.).

Obstinate Nature—Headstrong—Stubborn—Tenacious—Resisting—The ☉ Sig. ☌ ♂; the ☉ in the Asc. □ ♂ in the 10th; the ☉ or ☽ afflicted in ♉; ♂ afflicted in the 1st H.; ♂ affl. in ♉, ♏, ♑, or ♒; many planets in fixed signs at B., and with fixed signs on the angles; ♉ on the Asc., the sign of "The Bull", especially obstinate in nature. (See "Fixed Signs" under Fixed; Inflexible, Rebellious).

OBSTRUCTIONS—Stoppages—Hindrances—Occlusions—Obstruction is the keynote, and the most salient characteristic of ♄. Also Cauda (☋) is of the nature of ♄, and tends to obstructions when in ☌ the ☉, ☽, Asc., M.C., or hyleg at B., and to especially obstruct and afflict the part of the body, or matters ruled by the sign ☋ is in at B. (See "Dragon's Tail" under Dragon; "Influence Of" under Saturn). Saturn tends to obstructions in the body, in the tissues, blood vessels and organs, by retaining the wastes and poisons of the system, hindering and suppressing elimination, functional activity, secretion, and by causing hardening of the tissues, crystallization, retardation, deposit of mineral wastes, and the deposit of too much Urea over the body. The good aspects of ♄ tend to obstruct when coming to the other planets. Saturn in an angle, occi. of the ☉, and ori. of the ☽, tends to obstruct. Caused by ♄ or ☿ when the dominion of death is vested in them. Signified by ♄ in ♈ when ♄ is the afflictor in the disease. Saturn in any sign tends to obstructions in the part, parts, or organs ruled by the sign so occupied, and even ♄ in his own signs ♑ and ♒ tends to afflict the knees and lower legs, and make them subject to cold, obstructions, etc. Saturn causes all diseases proceeding from obstructions in any part of the body. In this regard the influence of ♄ is normal, as it is necessary for the planetary influences to be balanced, otherwise the influence of any one planet in excess, as that of ♂, would tend to tear people apart, or bring instant death, if not opposed and balanced by ♄, ♃, and ♀. To grow old in the body here is normal, natural, and the only way to progress, as continued life in the body on Earth would be a hindrance to the evolution and progress of the Soul. Also the ☉ in the 6th H. has an obstructing influence in health matters, and invites disease; the ☉ or ☽ afflicted by ♄; the ☽ afflicted in ♊, or afflicting the hyleg therefrom. The ☽ afflicted in ♊ tends to great obstructions; the ☽ or ☿ afflicted in ♍ or ♎. Obstructions may take place in any part of the body, and go under the names of various diseases. A few of these conditions are listed as follows. See these subjects in the alphabetical arrangewhen not commented upon here, as they are all caused by the obstructing work of ♄, and by his deposits, or work of suppression, retardation of function, etc.

Arms—Circulation In Obstructed—(See "Circulation" under Arms).

Arterial Circulation—Obstruction of—(See "Arterial" under Circulation).

Bile Passages—Obstruction of—(See Bile).

Bladder—Obstructions In—(See Gravel, Stone, Stricture, under Bladder).

Blindness—(See Blindness, Cataracts; "Growths" under Eyes).

Blood—Circulation of Obstructed — Oxygenation Obstructed — (See "Obstructions" under Circulation; "Non-Oxygenation" under Oxygen).

Blood Vessels Obstructed—(See Clots).

Body—Obstructions Over the Body— The ☽ in ⊓ and afflicted by the ☉ or ♂ when taken ill (Hor'y).

Bowels Obstructed — (See "Obstructions" under Bowels).

Brain—(See "Obstructions" under Brain).

Breasts — (See Adenoma; "Obstructions" under Breasts).

Breathing—(See "Obstructions" under Breathing).

Bronchial Tubes—(See "Obstructions" under Bronchial, Lungs).

Calculus—Obstruction By—(See Calculus).

Capillaries Obstructed — (See Capillaries; "Capillaries" under Lungs).

Cataracts; Circulation—(See Blood, Fluids, in this section).

Clots; Cold—The Body Obstructed By —(See the various paragraphs under Cold, Colds).

Colon — (See "Obstructions" under Colon).

Congestions—Obstructions By—(See Congestion).

Constrictions; Contractions;

Crystallization— (See Crystallization, Hardening, Petrifaction, Stone).

Death from Obstructions—♄ (or ☿ if he be of the nature of ♄) afflicting the hyleg at B., and by dir., if either hold the dominion of death; ♄ Anareta, and to the ♂ or ill-asp. his own place by dir., and especially if the direction fall in the 8th H.

Deformities; Digestion Obstructed — (See "Hindered" under Digestion).

Diseases—Arising from Obstructions —♄ diseases; ♄ in the 6th H., or afflicting the hyleg or the Asc.

Dropsy; Ducts—Obstruction of—(See the subjects under Ducts).

Ears—Obstructions In—(See "Circulation" under Ears; "Auditory", "Deafness", under Hearing).

Elimination—(See "Hindered" under Elimination).

Embolism; Excretion—(See "Obstructions" under Excretion).

Eyes Obstructed — (See Blindness, Cataracts; "Growths" under Eyes; Optic; Sight).

Fevers—Obstructions From—(See "Fever" under Heart, Liver).

Fluids Obstructed — (See "Obstructions" under Fluids, Gastric, Juices, Secretions, Spine; "Fluids" under White).

Functions — (See Hindered, Impaired, Impeded, Inhibited, Obstructed, Retarded, Slow, Stagnation, Suppressed, under Functions).

Gall Ducts Obstructed—(See Bile).

Gas — Spinal Gas Obstructed — (See Gas, Obstructed, under Spine).

Gastric Juices Obstructed — (See Digestion, Gastric, Indigestion, Juices; "Obstructions", "Stopped", under Stomach).

Generative Organs — (See "Obstructions" under Generative).

Goiter; Gout; Great Obstructions — The ☽ afflicted in ⊓. (See "Body" in this section).

Growths; Hardening; Head — (See "Obstructions" under Head).

Hearing Obstructed — (See "Ears" in this section).

Heart Obstructed—(See Blood, Fever, Obstructions, Valves, under Heart).

Hindrances; Hydronephrosis—(See "Dropsy" under Kidneys).

Ileum — (See "Obstructions" under Ileum).

Impairments; Impediments; Infarcts —(See Clots, Embolus, Infarcts, Thrombus).

Inhibitions; Interferences; Intestines —(See "Bowels" in this section).

Intussusception—(See Bowels).

Jaundice — (See "Obstructive" under Jaundice).

Judgment—The Judgment Obstructed —(See "Bad" under Judgment).

Juices Obstructed — (See "Fluids" in this section).

Kidneys Obstructed — (See "Obstructions" under Kidneys).

Legs — (See "Obstruction" under Legs).

Life Forces Obstructed — (See "Obstructed Life Forces" under Life; "Obstructed" under Nerves, Vital).

Limbs — (See "Obstructions" under Limbs).

Limitations; Liver — (See Deranged, Fever, Infirmities, Obstructions, under Liver).

Lower Limbs—Obstructions In—Circulation Obstructed — (See Blood, Obstruction In, under Legs).

Lungs — (See "Obstructions" under Breathing, Lungs; Bronchial, Consumption, Oxygen, Phthisis, Tuberculosis).

Lymph Obstructed—(See Lymph).

Menses Obstructed — (See "Obstruction" under Menses, Womb)

Mind Obstructed—(See Fears, Idiocy, Imbecile, Insanity, Obsessions; "Obstructed" under Mind; Spirit Controls, Worry, etc.).

Mucus — Obstructions By — (See Mucus; "Mucus" under Bowels, Head, Nose, Stomach, Throat).

Neck and Throat Obstructed — (See Goiter; "Obstructions" under Neck, Throat).

Nerves Obstructed—Nerve Force Obstructed—(See "Obstructed" under Nerves; "Nerves" under Pressure; "Life Forces" in this section).

Nose Obstructed—(See "Obstruction" under Nose).

Oesophagus Obstructed—(See "Stricture" under Oesophagus).

Oxygenation—Of the Blood Obstructed —(See "Non-Oxygenation" under Oxygen).

Phlegm—Obstructions By—(See the various paragraphs under Humours, Mucus, Phlegm).

Plugs; Pneumogastric Nerve—Restricted Action of — (See Pneumogastric).

Poisons and Wastes — In the Body — Obstructions Caused By—(See Deposits, Elimination, Excretion, Fevers, Filth, Gout, Hyperacidity, Impure, Inflammation, Inhibition, Minerals, Poisons, Retention, Rheumatism, Stoppages, Suppressions, Urea, Uric Acid, Wastes).

Pressure; Private Parts — (See "Obstructions" under Generative; "Diseases" under Private).

Prohibitions; Prolapse; Reason—(See "Impaired" under Reason).

Recovery Obstructed—(See Incurable; "Slow" under Recovery).

Rectum — (See "Obstructions" under Rectum).

Reins—(See "Obstructions" under Reins).

Renal Obstructions—(See Circulation, Dropsy, under Kidneys).

Respiration Obstructed — (See Interrupted, Labored, Obstructions, under Breath).

Restraints; Restrictions; Retarded; Retentions; Rheum—Obstructions By —(See Rheum).

Rheumatic Obstructions—(See Rheumatism).

Rigidity—Stiffness—(See Rigid).

Secretions Obstructed — (See Secretions).

Senses Obstructed — And Inhibited — (See Senses).

Sex Organs—(See "Obstructions" under Generative).

Slow — (See "Slow" under Motion, Speech; Slow).

Sluggish Conditions—(See Sluggish).

Smell Obstructed—(See "Loss Of" under Smell).

Speech—(See Halting, Impediment, under Speech).

Spine—(See "Obstructions" under Spine).

Stagnation; Stamina Obstructed—(See "Void Of" under Stamina).

Stammering—(See Speech).

Stiffness; Stomach—Obstructions In—(See "Inability" under Digestion; Indigestion; "Obstructions" under Stomach).

Stones — Calculi — (See Gravel, Sand, Stone).

Stoppages; Strictures; Suppressions;

Throat Obstructed — (See "Neck" in this section).

Thrombus; Too Much Blood—Obstructions From—(See "Too Much" under Blood).

Trachea Obstructed—(See Trachea).

Transverse Colon—Obstructions In—(See Colon).

Tumors—Causing Obstructions—(See Abscesses, Boils, Carbuncles, Carcinoma, Growths, Swellings, Tumors).

Urea—Urates—Uric Acid—Deposit of, and Causing Obstruction — (See Deposits, Gout, Hyperacidity, Minerals, Poisons, Rheumatism; "Influence Of" under Saturn; Urates; Urea, Uric Acid, Wastes).

Ureters Obstructed—(See Ureters).

Urethra Obstructed—(See Urethra).

Urine Obstructed — (See "Obstructions" under Urine).

Venous Circulation—Obstruction of—(See "Obstruction" under Veins).

Viscera Obstructed—(See Viscera).

Vision Obstructed — (See Blindness, Cataract; "Growths", "Obstructions", under Eyes; Sight).

Walk — Obstructions To — (See Crippled, Deformities, Feet, Gait, Lameness, Legs, Locomotion, Locomotor Ataxia, Paralysis, Walk).

Wastes of System — Obstructions Caused by Deposit and Retention of—(See Deposits, Gout, Minerals, Wastes).

White Fluids Obstructed — (See "Fluids" under White).

Womb Obstructed — (See "Obstructions" under Womb). The subject of Obstructions in the Mind and Body is a large one, and the conditions too numerous to list here. Nearly all disease is caused by some obstruction, limitation, hindrance, suppression, excess, etc. For subjects along this line which may not be listed here, look in the alphabetical arrangement for the subject you have in mind.

OCCASIONAL INDISPOSITION—(See Indisposition).

OCCIDENTAL—Planets Occidental— The ☉, ☽, and planets in the Occidental Quarters of the Heavens at birth show disease, and in the Oriental Quarters indicate Acute Pains and Accidents. Malefics occi., and afflicting the ☉ or ☽, tend to cause disease. Planets are considered Occidental, in a general way, when setting in the West between the M.C. and Nadir, and Oriental when rising between the Nadir and Midheaven. The Occidental Quarters of the Heavens are those from the Nadir to the Asc., and from the M.C. to the Descendant, and the ☉ or ☽ found in these Quarters at B. are said to be Occidental. Also planets are said to be occidental when rising and setting after the ☉, and oriental when rising and setting before him. (See the lengthy Article on "Oriental" in Wilson's Dictionary of Astrology, which also deals with Occidental conditions). In Health matters, and in judging of the effects of disease, or the liability to the predisposition to disease or accidents, it is necessary for the student to understand these differences between Oriental and Occidental in order to be able to more accurately diagnose ailments, and to know the severity or mildness of the complaint, its nature, prospects, and possible outcome. Mercury rising before the ☉ tends to give a keener and better mind, but rising after the ☉, to dull the mentality. The ☽ in an Oriental Quarter at B., indicates an early marriage, and a late marriage when in an Occidental Quarter, etc. Jupiter oriental, and rising before the

⊙, or elevated above the ⊙, is more powerful in health matters than when he is occidental, or rising after the ⊙. In this book, many references are made to oriental and occidental, and such influences listed under the various diseases, and it is very important to note these causes in making a planetary study of disease, accidents, affliction, etc., as well as in matters of joy, happiness, abundance, good health, success, long life, etc. (See Elevated, Majority, Oriental, Quadrants, Quarters, Rising, Rouse, Setting).

OCCIPITAL REGION—Occiput—Ruled by the ♉ Sign.

Occipital Headache—(See Headache). See Brain, Head, Medulla, Skull.

OCCLUSION—Stopping Up of An Opening In the Body—Generally caused by ♄ influence. (See Anus, Canals, Clots, Constrictions, Contractions, Ducts, Growths, Hernia, Nipples, Nose, Obstructions, Orifices, Polypus, Stenosis; "Pylorus" under Stomach; Stricture, Tubes, Urethra, Valves, etc.).

OCCULT STUDY—Fond of—Given To— Occult Powers — ♅ strong, dignified and well-aspected at B.; ♅ in the 1st, 9th, or 10th H. at B.; ♅ ☌ the ⊙ or ☿ at B. Also ♆ prominent, rising, elevated, and well-aspected, tends to give Occult, Mystical, and Spiritual Sight of a high order. (See Eccentric, Ideals, Independent, Magic, Metaphysics, Misunderstood; "Mystery" under Mysterious; Mystical, Ninth House, Reformers; "Occult Science" under Science).

OCCUPATION—The Employment or Vocation—

Accidents In — Death or Injury In — (See Employment).

Strange Occupational Diseases—♅ afflicted in the 6th H. (See Strange).

OCEAN—The Sea—Ocean Travel—The Salt Water—The ☽, ♆, and the ♓ Sign rule the Ocean and the Seas.

Danger On—(See Maritime; "Danger" under Voyages).

Fire On Ships At Sea — (See "Ships" under Fire).

Fish — Death of In the Seas — (See Fish).

Fortunate Upon the Ocean — (See Maritime; "Fortunate" under Seas).

Good Time For Voyages — Bad Time For—(See Bad Time, Good Time, Long Journeys, under Journeys, Voyages).

Misfortunes At Sea—(See Sea, Ships, Shipwreck).

Unfortunate On the Sea — (See Sea). See Abroad, Bathings, Drowning, Events, Foreign Lands, Navigation, Sailors, Travel; "Perils by Water" under Water.

OCULAR—Pertaining to the Eyes—(See Accommodation, Blindness, Cataracts, Eyes, Nebulous, Sight).

Ocular Defects—(See "Defects" under Eyes).

OCULUS TAURUS—Bull's South Eye—der Headaches).

Ocular Headaches—(See "Ocular" under Headaches).

A Star in 6° 13′ ♊, and of the nature of ♀. Men born with ♃ in ♊ near Oculus Taurus tend to be addicted to women. This star is mentioned only a few times in Astrological books, but is listed in the Tables of Stars in the various Textbooks of Astrology. Aldebaran is the North Eye of the Bull, and of the nature of ♂. (See Aldebaran, Bulls, Chances; "Addicted to Women" under Men; Stars).

ODD—Peculiar—Singular—Queer—Unusual, etc.—

Odd Diseases — (See Extraordinary, Mysterious, Obscure, Peculiar, Psychic, Strange, Unusual).

Odd Disposition—(See Eccentric, Fanatical, Fancies, Independent, Misunderstood, Occult, Peculiar, Recluse).

Odd Signs—Of the Zodiac—The positive and masculine signs, as ♈, ♊, ♌, ♎, ♐, ♒. The Odd Houses also correspond to these signs, as the 1st, 3rd, 5th, 7th, 9th, and 11th H. Many planets in the Odd Signs at B. tend to give a strong will, determination, greater vitality, as a rule, and with greater power to resist and overcome disease. (See "Positive Signs" under Positive; "Masculine Signs" under Signs).

ODIC FORCE — (See Hypnotism, Magnetism; "Powers" under Psychic).

ODORS—A Scent or Smell—

Foul Odors — (See "Sweating" under Axillae; "Foul" under Breath; Carcinoma, Corpse, Corruption, Dead, Decay, Discharges, Disintegration, Excrement, Faeces; "Fetid" under Feet, Sweat; Fetid, Foul, Gangrene, Gases, Leprosy, Noxious, Obnoxious, Offensive; "Stagnant" under Pools; Pungent, Pus, Putrid, Rottenness, Sores, Ulcers).

Foul Vapors—(See Vapors).

Man, Animals and Plants — Odors From—Ruled by ♆.

Pungent Odors — Ruled by ♂. (See "Hot Acids" under Acids; Perfumes, Pungent).

OEDEMA — Edema — Oedematous Tumors — Accumulation of Serum In the Cellular Tissue—A ☽ disease, and the ☽ afflicted in watery signs. (See Accumulative; "Fluids" under Cells; Dropsy, Elephantiasis, Enlargements, Hypertrophy; "Oedema" under Lungs; Osmosis, Puffing, Resolvent, Serum, Swellings, Tissues, etc.).

OESOPHAGUS — Esophagus — Gullet— The Canal from the Pharynx to the Stomach — Ruled by the ☽ and the ♋ sign. Also under the internal rulership of ♉, and is greatly influenced and affected when the ☽ is in ♉. The upper part of the Oesophagus is more under the rule of ♉.

Disorders Of — ♄ afflicted in ♉; Subs at SP (7D), and KP.

Obstruction Of — Stricture of—Sluggish Action of—♄ afflicted in ♋; the ☽ in ♋, □, or ☍ ♄; Subs at SP.

Stricture Of — (See "Obstruction" in this section).

OFFENDED—Offending—

Easily Offended—♂ afflicting ☿. (See "High Strung" under High; Hyperaesthesia; "Sensitiveness" under Sensitive; "High Temper" under Temper).

Offending Humours — (See "Offending" under Humours).

Stomach Offended — (See "Raw Humours" under Indigestion).

OFFENSIVE—Peccant—Corrupt—Putrid—

Offensive Breath—(See "Foul" under Breath).

Offensive Discharges — (See "Offensive" under Discharges).

Offensive Manners — (See Disagreeable, Rough, Unpleasant, under Manners).

Offensive Odors — (See Decay, Odors, Pus, Putrid).

OFFICERS OF THE LAW — Killed by Police Officers—♂ Sig. □ or ☍ the ☉, and also ☿ □ ♂ concurring. (See Judge, Law).

Officer Killed—(See Military).

OFFSPRING—Issue—(See Children).

OFTEN AILING—(See "Many Diseases" under Disease; "Ill-Health All Thru Life" under Ill-Health; "Much Infirmity" under Infirmity; "Much Sickness" under Sickness).

OIL—Oils—Oils of the Body—The Body Oil—Ruled largely by the ☽, ♃, and ♀. The White Fluids, or the Body Oil, are ruled by the ☽. The Oils of the body are connected with the ♍ sign, and Potassium Sulphate, the Virgo Salt. (See Fat; "Fluids" under White).

Emollients — Oils As An Emollient — (See Emollient).

Oily Face—Oily and Shining Skin—♃ gives. (See "Oily" under Face).

Oily Hair — Glossy and Shiny — (See "Glossy" under Hair).

OINTMENTS—Unguents—Ointments are principally ♄ remedies, and applied to combat the evil effects of Bruises, Injuries, Eruptions, Excoriations, Ulcers, Sores, Inflammations, Skin Diseases, etc. Treating on the basis of Antipathy, ♄ remedies are used in Ointments to combat the diseases, hurts, eruptions, and afflictions of ♂, and the remedies of ♂ in ointments to combat ♄ diseases. On the basis of Sympathy, the ♄ remedies in ointments are used to combat ♄ diseases, and ♂ remedies to combat ♂ diseases. The Oxide of Lead, a ♄ remedy, mixed with Olive Oil, is a common Lead Plaster. Also Zinc, ruled by ♅, is much used in Ointments where a mild astringent action is desired. (See Antipathy, Lead, Opposites, Sympathy, Zinc).

OLD—Mature—Old Maladies—

Old Aches—In Hips and Thighs—(See "Aches" under Hips).

Old Age—(See Old Age, the Article following this one).

Old Maladies Return—(See Return).

OLD AGE—Old People—Elderly People—Conditions Affecting the Aged—The Latter Part of Life—The conditions at the close of life, and in Old Age, are denoted by the 4th H. and its influences in the map of birth. The 4th H. is one of the Terminal Houses, along with the 8th and 12th H. (See Fourth House, Terminal). Saturn also rules Old Age, and is the Star of Old Age, and the planet which rules hoary hairs. In the Kabala, Old Age was dedicated to ♄. The 3rd Decan. of ♍ denotes Old Age, Weakness, Infirmity, Decay, and Dissolution. The ruling places situated in the West at a Solar Eclipse tend to affect the Aged, and persons about to die, for good or ill, according to the aspects and influences at B., and by Direction, Transit, or Progression. The following paragraphs give the planetary influences which affect Old Age, making it fortunate or unfortunate, and the conditions which the native is apt to meet with at the close of life.

Adult Life—(See Adults).

Aged Female Relative — Death of — (See "Female" in this section).

Aged People—Those of Frail Constitution—Death of—Caused by the ill-aspects of malefics to the ☉, ☽, Asc., M.C., or Hyleg, by dir.; the ☉ to the bad aspects ♆, ♅, ♄, or ♂ by dir. with males, or the ☽ to these bad aspects in females.

Aged Person In the Family—Death of —(See Grandparents).

Asylum—Ends Life In An Asylum or Institution — ♆ afflicted in the 4th or 12th H. (See Confinement; "Asylums" under Insanity; Prison, Twelfth House).

Aunt—Death of An Aged Aunt—(See Aunts).

Bad End — Frequently Meets with a Bad End—The ☉ Sig. □ or ☍ ♄; ♄ or ♂ afflicted in the 4th H. (See "Bad End" under End; "Sad" in this section).

Childish—In Old Age—☿ afflicted at B., in a weak sign, and afflicted by dir., and especially by ♄ and the ☽. (See "Weak Mentality" under Mental; "Weak Mind" under Mind).

Chronic Ill-Health — In Old Age — ♄ rising at B. tends to chronic ill-health in the latter part of life; ♄ afflicting the ☉, ☽, Asc., or Hyleg at B., and by direction in old age; the ill-asps. of the ☉ or ☽ to ♄ by dir. (See "Ill-Health" in this section).

Close of Life — (See "Close of Life" under Close; Death, End, Terminal; the paragraphs in this section).

Complexion — In Old Age — (See Pimples, Ruddy, in this section).

Dangerous Illness—In Old Age—Malefics in the 4th H., and afflicted at B., and by dir.; ♅ afflicted in the 4th H.; the hyleg afflicted by malefics by dir., and with little or no help from benefics; the ☽ in ♊, □, or ☍ ♄ (or ☿ if he be of the nature of ♄) at the beginning of an illness, or at decumbiture, if at decumb. the ☽ shall be under the beams of the ☉, or with ♄ or ♂, there is great peril even tho the ☽ be in ☌ a benefic.

Death of Aged People — (See "Aged People" in this section).

Decrepit Old Men—(See "Men" in this section).

Dies In Old Age — (See "Long Life" under Life).

Easy Death—Natural and Peaceful Death In Old Age—Benefics in the 4th or 8th H., and no malefic influences over these houses. (See "Easy Death" under Death).

Elderly People—Ill-Health of—(See "Ill-Health" in this section; Grandparents).

Father—The Father Lives to Old Age —(See "Long Life" under Father).

Feebleness—Decrepitude—(See Men, Senility, in this section).

Female—Death of An Aged Female— (See Aunts, Grandparents).

Fortunate Old Age—The ☉ in the 4th H., and well aspected; ♄ in ♎ or ♑, and not afflicted; ♃ or ♀ in the 4th H., and well-aspected.

Good Health—In Old Age—The ☉, ♃, ♂, or ♀ in the 4th H., and well-aspected; the 19° ♓ on the Asc. at B., but sickly in youth.

Grandparents—Sickness and Death of —(See Grandparents).

Gray Hair—(See "Gray" under Hair).

Great Age—Will Live To—Will Not Live To — (See "Long Life", "Seldom of Long Life", "Short Life" under Life).

Health—The Health Good In Old Age — Health Bad — (See "Good", "Ill-Health", in this section).

Ill-Health—Of the Aged and Elderly People—The ill-asps. of the ☉ to malefics by dir., and the ☉ hyleg, even tho they did not aspect the ☉ at B., and especially among the Aged and Feeble, or others of frail constitution; the ill-asps. of malefics to the ☉ by dir.; ♄ rising at B., ill-health or chronic troubles in old age. (See Chronic, Dangerous Illness, Incurable, Senility, in this section).

Illness—(See "Dangerous Illness" in this section).

Incurable Infirmity—♅ afflicted in the 4th H. (See Incurable).

Infirmity—Incurable Infirmity In Old Age—(See "Incurable" in this section).

Kind of Death—The nature and kind of death in old age are largely determined, and modified, by the conditions over the 4th and 8th H. at B., the lord or ruler, of these houses, and their aspects towards the end of life, and also the nature of the directions, transits, or progressions which may be affecting the hyleg. (See "Quality Of" under Death; "Death" under Kind, Nature, Quality, Species).

Many Deaths — Of the Aged — (See "Mortality" in this section).

Meets With a Bad End — (See "Bad End" in this section).

Men—Decrepit Old Men—Ruled by ♄; ♄ in the 4th H. at B., and afflicting the ☉, and also ♄ afflicting the ☉ or hyleg by dir., tend to make old men more decrepit and feeble, or to suffer with a chronic ailment, lameness, gout, rheumatism, or paralysis. (See "Chronic", "Senility", in this section).

Mind—An Uneasy Mind In Old Age— ♆ afflicted in the 4th H.

Mortality—Much Mortality Among the Aged—The evil aspects of the ☉ to the malefics ♆, ♅, ♄, or ♂ by dir., many deaths of those who are under such

aspects, and especially among those of frail constitution; ♄ Lord of the Year at the Vernal Equi., and espec. in places ruled by ♄, as those ruled by ♑ and ♒, or in places ruled by the sign in which ♄ is located; ♄ sole ruler at an eclipse of the ☉; ♂ in ♍, and ori. at the Vernal, and Lord of the Year; the ruling places situated in the West at a Solar Eclipse. (See Mortality).

Mother — (See "Long Life" under Mother).

Natural Death—(See "Easy Death" in this section).

Paralysis—In Old Age—Danger of— ♅ afflicted in the 4th H. at B. (See Paralysis).

Peaceful End to Life—Benefics well-aspected in the 4th H. at B. (See "Easy Death" in this section).

Pimples—Usually Afflicted with Pimples At Middle Life and In Old Age — A Highly Colored Complexion and Pimples—Given by ♎; ♎ on the Asc. at B., and many planets in ♎, and giving a deep red color, with pimples, but the complexion is usually clear and fair in youth. (See "Ruddy" in this section; Pimples, Ruddy).

Premature Old Age—(See Juvenility; "Senility" in this section).

Recluse—In Old Age—♆ or ♄ in the 4th H. at B., and prefers to end life in seclusion. (See Recluse).

Relative—Death of An Aged Relative —(See Aunts, Grandparents). For influences indicating that Brethren do not live to Old Age, see "Old Age" under Relatives).

Ruddy Complexion — In Old Age — ♎ gives, and ♎ on the Asc. at B., and with pimples. (See "Pimples" in this section).

Sad Old Age—Sad and Unfortunate— ♆, ♅, ♄, or ♂ in the 4th H. at B., near the lower Meridian, and afflicted; adverse afflictions of the malefics falling in the 4th H. in old age, and especially of ♄. (See Sadness).

Seclusion — Ends Life In Seclusion — (See Asylum, Recluse, in this section).

Senility — The Weakness of Old Age, or Imbecility — Senile Feebleness — Tendencies in the body to dryness, contraction, decrepitude, and immobility, are the work of ♄. Also, ♄ tends to harden the tissues and blood vessels with age, and to increase the mineral deposits over the body, and with the powers of elimination weakened. (See Feeble, Imbecility, Infirm).

Shrinkage—Of the Limbs In Old Age — Withering of — ♆ or ♄ afflicted in signs which rule the Arms or Legs. (See Shrinking, Withering).

Stout In Later Years—♃ in the 1st H., and well-aspected; ♃ in ♋ on the Asc., and afflicted. (See "Corpulent" under Middle Life; Stoutness).

Uneasy Mind — In Old Age — (See "Mind" in this section).

Unfortunate—In Old Age—(See Bad End, Sad, and the various paragraphs in this section).

Vision—Old Age Vision—(See "Presbyopia" under Sight).

Vitality Good — In Old Age — (See "Good Health" in this section; "Long Life" under Life; "Good" under Vitality).

Weakness — In Old Age — (See Ill-Health, Senility, in this section).

Will Not Live to Old Age—(See "Seldom of Long Life" under Life).

Withering—(See "Shrinkage" in this section).

Wrinkles—(See Wrinkles).

OLFACTORY — Olfaction —Olfactory Nerves—(See Smell).

OLIVE—

Olive Complexion—Olive Brown Complexion — (See Olive, Sunburnt, under Complexion).

Olive Tree — Ruled by the ⊙. (See "Sun Group" under Herbs).

OMENS — Ominous— Forebodings — A Prophetic Sign—(See Forebodings).

Ominous Fevers — (See "Portentous" under Fever).

OMENTUM—A Fold of the Peritoneum —(See Peritoneum).

ONANISM — Self-Abuse —(See "Solitary Vice" under Vice).

ONE—Single—

One Child At a Birth — (See "Single Births" under Children).

One Ear — Deafness In — (See "One Ear" under Hearing).

One Eye—Loss of One Eye—(See "One Eye" under Blindness, Eyes).

One Passage — A Common Outlet to the Rectum and Bladder—(See Cloaca).

One Side of Body—Paralysis In—(See "Hemiplegia" under Infancy, Paralysis).

ONION—Allium Cepa—A Bulb of the Lily Family—The Onion is classed as an Herb of Mars in most books, due to its pungent taste and odor, stimulating and nerve-building qualities. Other Authors list it as ruled by ♄, due to the fact that it opposes the excitability of ♅ and ♂, and as a poultice is excellent to relieve the inflammation of bruises, contusions, etc. On the theory of Antipathy or Sympathy in treatment, the Onion could be ruled by either ♄ or ♂, or both, as it is both building and soothing. Saturn tends to suppress the nerves, and as a nerve builder, ♂ is the more suitable ruler of this vegetable. Onions are very stimulating, a ♂ characteristic, while ♄ depresses. An onion sandwich taken at bed time is said to purify the kidneys and liver, and to build up the nervous system. (See "Treatment" under Nerves).

OOZING — Of Fluids — Oozings — (See Dropsy, Exudations, Oedema, Osmosis, Transudations).

OPEN—

Open Countenance—(See "Open" under Face).

Resentment—Open In—(See Resentment).

Sex Organs—Open Display of—(See "Sex Organs" under Exhibition).

Sores—Open Sores—Ulcers—(See Sores, Ulcers).

OPENING—Opening Medicine—Yellow Color acts as an opening medicine, the color ruled by ☿ in the Solar Spectrum. (See Physic, Yellow).

OPENLY—Openly Scandalous—Infamous—(See Exhibitionism, Harlots, Infamous, Lewd; "Women" under Scandalous; Shameless).

OPERATIONS — Surgical Operations — Incisions—Surgical Incisions are ruled by ♂, and this planet causes Operations and Violence.

Abdominal Operations—Avoid when the ☽ is passing thru ♍, ♎, or ♏. Good times for are when the ☽ is passing thru ♐, ♑, or ♒, when the ☽ is passing down and below the vital signs. Operations for Appendicitis, or upon the Womb, or any abdominal location, when the ☽ is in ♍, ♎, or ♏, are apt to result in inflammation, infection, and often result in death. (See "Appendicitis" under Appendix; "Operations" under Womb).

Amputations—Danger From—Danger of Death By—♂ in ♉ or ♏ and afflicting the hyleg; ♂ in ♉ near Caput Algol, or in ♉ aspect in ♏, and at the same time in □ or 8 the ⊙ or ☽, a dangerous time to operate, and especially if the radical map also shows this position of ♂; the ☽ under the Sun's beams, and opposed by ♂, is considered a dangerous, or fatal time for amputations, and brings danger in the loss of a member at such a time. (See "Rules" in this section).

Death by Operations—Danger of—The ⊙ to the ☌ or ill-asp. ♂ by dir.; ♂ in ♉ or ♏ and afflicting the hyleg; ♂ ori. in ♉ or ♏, □ or 8 the ⊙ at B., or ♂ occi. in ♉ or ♏, □, or 8 the ☽ at B.; death may result if the ☽ is afflicted and passing thru the sign ruling the part to be operated upon, and also if the ☽ is in the same sign as at birth.

Eyes—Operations Upon—(See "Operations" under Eyes).

Hemorrhage—Greater Hemorrhage from An Operation—(See "Operations" under Hemorrhage).

Immediate Causes—For An Operation —♂ influence and affliction is usually the immediate cause for an operation, and resulting either from inflammation, infections, or an accident. Caused by the ⊙ or ♂, which are the positive, electric, and heat-producing planets; caused by the evil directions, transits, or progressed positions of ♂ to the ⊙ or ☽; the ⊙ to the ☌ or ill-asp. ♂ by dir.; ♂ □ or 8 the ⊙ or ☽ by dir. (See "Certain" under Disease).

Liable to Operations—♂ strong at B., as in the Asc. or M.C., and afflicting the ⊙ or ☽; ♂ afflicting the ⊙, ☽, Asc., or hyleg by dir. tends to precipitate conditions making an operation necessary, or more likely; ♂ afflicted in the 6th H.; the ☽ in the 6th H., ☌ or □ ♂. (See "Immediate Causes" in this section).

Loss of Blood—Undesirable Elemental Spirits often are present at Operations to absorb the life force from the blood of the patient, introduce Astral infections, and prevent recovery. Every operation should be preceded with prayer to prevent the presence of Elementals, and to place an Aura of Protection about the patient.

Major Operations—Time and Rule For—(See "Rules" in this section).

Nature—The Four Operations of Nature—(See "Operations" under Nature).

Operations Dangerous—Performed when the ☉ is in the 12th H., in ☌ ♄ or ☋, and ♂ afflicted in the 6th H. at the same time. (See Death, Rules, in this section).

Ovariotomy—Rules For—(See Ovaries).

Pelvic Operations—(See "Operations" under Hips; Pelvis).

Rhythmic Operations—In the Body—(See Rhythm).

Rules for Operations—Statistics show that operations are more successfully performed when the ☽ is increasing in light, between the New and Full ☽, and heal more quickly, and are less liable to complications than when the ☽ is past the full and decreasing. Note the following Rules—

(1) Operate in the increase of the ☽ if possible.

(2) Do not operate at the exact time of the Full ☽, as the fluids are running high at this time.

(3) Never operate when the ☽ is in the same sign as at birth.

(4) Never operate upon that part of the body ruled by the sign thru which the ☽ is passing at the time, but wait a day or two until the ☽ passes into the next sign below, and especially if the ☽ be in ☌, □, or ☍ ♆, ♅, ♄, or ♂ at the time. This rule should be especially followed in major operations. Ptolemy says, "Pierce not with iron that part of the body which may be governed by the sign actually occupied by the Moon".

(5) Do not operate when the ☽ is applying closely to the □ or ☍ the ☉, ♄, or ♂.

(6) Let the ☽ be increasing in light, and in ⚹ or △ ♃ or ♀, and not afflicted by ♂.

(7) Let the ☽ be in a fixed sign, but not in the sign ruling the part to be operated upon, and such sign of the ☽ also not on the Asc.

(8) Do not operate when the ☽ is applying to any aspect of ♂, as such tends to danger of inflammation and complications after the operation.

(9) Avoid operation when the ☉ is in the sign ruling the part upon which the operation is to be performed.

(10) Never operate when the ☽ is combust, or within 17° of the ☉, and with the ☽ ☍ ♂ at the same time.

(11) The ☽ should be free from all manner of impediment.

(12) ♃, ♀, and the ruler of the Asc. should be in the Asc. or in the M.C., if possible, and free from ♂ affliction.

(13) Fortify the Sign ruling the part of the body to be operated upon.

(14) A ♂ hour is evil for surgical operations.

(15) Do not cut a nerve when ☿ is afflicted. (See Amputations, Death, and the various paragraphs in this section).

Surgeons—(See Surgeons).

Successful Operations—(See "Rules" in this section).

Times for Operations—(See "Rules" in this section).

Undergoes An Operation—(See Immediate Causes, Liable To, in this section).

Womb Operations—(See "Abdominal" in this section).

OPHIUCUS—Stars in the last part of ♏ and the first half of ♐, of evil import, and threaten disease, disgrace, ruin, sickness, every evil, and debauchery when with the ☉ or ☽ at B., or when the Lights are directed to them. The Right Knee and Leg, and the Left Hand of Ophiucus, are mentioned. (See Debauchery; "Threatened" under Disease; Disgrace).

OPHTHALMIA—(See "Conjunctivitis" under Conjunctiva; Xeroma).

OPINIONS—Views—Notions—

Distorted Opinions—Wrong Notions In General—Wrong Opinions—(See Anarchists, Confused, Eccentric, Erratic, Fanatical, Ideals, Ideas; "Bad" under Judgment; Notions; "Atheistical", and the various paragraphs under Religion).

Fixed Opinions—(See "Obstinate" in this section).

Forms Bad Opinions—Of Every One—♄ Sig. □ or ☍ ☿. (See Mistrustful, Suspicious).

Inconstant In Opinions—Constant In No Opinion—☿ ill-dignified at B.; ☿ afflicted in ♓. (See Inconstant).

Independent Opinions—(See Independent).

Obstinate In Opinions—Fixed Notions and Opinions—Born under strong ♄ influence; many planets in fixed signs at B., or fixed signs on angles. (See "Fixed Signs" under Fixed; Inflexible, Misunderstood, Obstinate, Reformers, Riotous, etc.).

Opinionated of Himself—Egotistical—(See "Egotistical" under Ego).

OPISTHOTONOS—A Spasmodic Rigidity of the Body in which the Trunk is Thrown Backward and Arched Upward—A ♅ disease and affliction; ♅ afflicted in ♌; ♅ ☌ ♂ in ♌, or in fixed signs; ♆ ☌ ♄ in ♌. (See Contractions; "Movements" under Erratic; Incoordination; "Contraction" under Muscles; Rigidity, Spasmodic, Trunk).

OPIUM—Opiates—Poppy Plant—Papaver—Ruled by ♆. (See "Neptune Group" under Herbs; Narcotics).

OPPOSITE—Opposites—Opposition—

Aspect—The Opposition Aspect—The 180° aspect (☍)—In health, and other matters, this is a very evil aspect, and is of the same nature as the □ aspect, or 90° aspect, the ☍ being a double square. When the ☽ is in ☍ the ☉ at B., as at the exact time of Full ☽, the vitality tends to be weakened. Also malefics in ☍ the ☉, ☽, Asc., or hyleg, or in ☍ to each other, tend to weaken the nativity, invite more disease, affliction, and trouble. (See Aspects).

Fond of Opposition—The ☉ Sig. in ♉. (See Obstinate, Taurus).

Opposite Sex—(See the next Article after this one).

Opposite Signs—Of the Zodiac—The Opposite Signs, as ♈ and ♎, ♉ and ♏, etc., are complementary, or supplementary signs, and both rule and effect the same parts, or organs by their reflex action, and there is great sympathy between opposite signs, especially in health matters. Planets in ♏ not only affect the sex organs and nature, but also the throat, and vice versa. There is Polarity and affinity between opposite signs. These signs are 180° apart, and planets in them at B. are in ☍ aspect, if within orb of the aspect. Many planets in opposite signs at B., and in the signs which are in □ to each other, indicate weakened vitality, a more difficult fate, and many troubles and vicissitudes to be overcome. (See Kinetic; "Aspect", "Planetary Opposites", in this section).

Planetary Opposites—Planets ruling opposite signs oppose each other in their action. Mars, ruler of ♈, opposes ♀, the ruler of ♎. Saturn, ruler of ♒, opposes the ☉, the ruler of ♌. The remedies of the ☉ will cure the diseases caused by ♄, and on the theory of Antipathy. Jupiter, the ruler of ♐ and ♓, opposes ☿, the ruler of ♊ and ♍, the opposite signs, and ♃ remedies tend to offset and heal the diseases of ☿, etc. Mars is strong in ♈, and ♄ has his exaltation in ♎, the opposite sign, and also ♄ has his fall in ♈, and the remedies of ♂ tend to bring cure and relief to ♄ diseases, and the diseases and afflictions of ♂ are relieved by ♄ remedies. By observing this rule of Opposites, the student can soon quickly learn how to analyze and treat disease Astrologically and scientifically. In treating disease by sympathy, a ♄ remedy is used to relieve a ♄ disease, and a ♂ remedy to alleviate a ♂ disease, and this is the theory of Homeopathy. The Planetary Opposites are as follows—The ☉, ruler of ♌, opposes ♄, ruler of ♒. The ☽, ruler of ♋, opposes ♄, ruler of ♑. Mars, ruler of ♈ and ♏, opposes ♀, ruler of ♉ and ♎. Saturn, ruler of ♑ and ♒, opposes the ☉ and ☽, rulers of ♋ and ♌. Jupiter, ruler of ♐ and ♓, opposes ☿, ruler of ♊ and ♍. Venus, ruler of ♉ and ♎, opposes ♂, ruler of the opposite signs ♏ and ♈. Mercury, ruler of ♊ and ♍, opposes ♃, ruler of ♐ and ♓. (See Antipathy, Aspects, Chemical, Complications; "Allopathy" under Healers; Herbs, Homeopathy; "Disease" under Mild; Minimizing, Signature, Sympathy, Treatment).

OPPOSITE SEX—The Relations of the Opposite Sex and Their Dealings with Each Other—

Addicted to Women—(See Love Affairs, Marriage; "Addicted To", "Fascinating", under Men; Passion, Sex).

Aversions—To the Opposite Sex—Indifferent To—(See Apathy, Aversions, Bachelors, Celibacy, Deviations, Indifferent; "Aversion" under Marriage; "Free From" under Passion; Perversions).

Health Suffers—Through the Opposite Sex—Energies Wasted On the Opposite Sex—♂ diseases; ♂ ☌ or ill-asp. the ☽ or ♀; lord of the 6th in the 5th or 7th H. (See Amorous; "Energies Wasted" under Love Affairs; "Health Injured" under Lust, Men; "Passional Excesses" under Passion; Venereal).

OPPRESSED—Oppression—♄ influence, and ♄ in any sign tends to oppression, suppression, and affliction to the part ruled by the sign he is in at birth. (See Depressed; "Oppression" under Heart; "Oppressed" under Lungs; Saturn, Suppression).

OPTIC—Pertaining to Vision and Its Organs, the Eyes—

Decay of Optic Nerve—Atrophy of—Crystallization of—Hardening of—Inhibition of—Weakness of—Sight Destroyed or Dimmed By—The ☽ or Asc. in Nebulous Parts at B., and afflicted by ♄; the ☉ and ♆ in angles at B., and the ☉ afflicted by ♆, tends to weakness of the optic nerve; ♆ in the Asc. at B., near Nebulous Spots, and afflicted by the ☉, ☽, or ♃, tends to some affection of this nerve; Subs at MCP (3, 4C). (See Blindness; "Crystallization" under Eyes; Nebulous, Retina, Sight).

Optic Nerves—Ruled by ☿ and the ♈ sign. Also ruled and affected by ♆ when in ♈. Also strongly influenced by ♅.

OPTIMISM—Optimistic—Hopeful—Cheerfulness—People who are optimistic, cheerful, and hopeful, who have developed an inner vision of power, and who avoid worry, have better health, and avoid loss of nerve and vital force, while the pessimistic, negative, despondent, worrisome, melancholic Saturn person, full of fear, is apt to weaken, become a chronic sufferer, and die an earlier death. The following influences tend to Optimism and Good Health. The ☉ and ☽ well-aspected by ♃, and with ♃ in one of his own signs, and favorably aspected; the ☉ and ♂ strong and well-aspected at B., and especially when in ♈ or ♌; ♃ is considered the planet of optimism and hope, and this planet when in the Asc. or M.C. at B., and in favorable aspect to the ☉, ☽, ♀, or ☿, tends to optimism; ♀ alone does not tend to optimism as much as she does to resignation and contentment in life, when strong and well-aspected at B. However, ♀ in the 10th H. at B., and favorably aspected, tends to optimism, cheerfulness, and success in life, which favors better health. Mercury in the 3rd H., and well-aspected by the ☽, ♃, and ♀, tends to hopefulness, a cheerful and optimistic spirit; ☿ progressed, and to the ✶ or △ ♂, favors an optimistic and enthusiastic state of mind for the time. (See Cheerfulness, Contentment; "Resigned" under Fate; Happiness, Hope, Joy; "Peace of Mind" under Mind; "Sanguine Temperament" under Sanguine).

Optimism Destroyed—A Pessimistic State of Mind—Fears—Doubts—Gloomy State of Mind—Saturn strong at B., rising in the Asc. or M.C., and afflicting the ☉, ☽, ☿, Asc., or Hyleg, tends to destroy hopefulness and optimism, and to bring grief, sorrow, sadness, gravity, a less hopeful outlook upon life, and to invite mental depression, ill-health, chronic diseases, loss of nerve and vital force, and with more of a desire for seclusion, separateness, and to lead a solitary life. Also ♆ is called the planet of Doubt and Fear. (See Doubts, Gloom; "Hopes Cut Off" under Hope; "Low Spirits" under Low; Melancholy, Misanthropic, Miserable, Miserly, Pessimistic, Recluse, Secretive, Selfishness, Unhappy, Worry, Wretched, etc.).

ORANGE COLOR—Saffron—This Color in the Solar Spectrum is ruled by the ☉. Orange Color tends to sharpen the appetite, and rooms papered with Orange tend to increase the appetite, and stimulate the forces of the body to better action, as Orange color is pregnant with the vital Sun forces. Gold, the orange-colored metal, is also ruled by the ☉. (See "Planets and Color" under Colors; "Saffron" under Complexion; Gold, Saffron).

Orange Fruit—Citrus Aurantium—The Gold-Colored Fruit or Berry—Ruled by the ☉. The juice of the Sun-kissed Orange contains the vital forces of the ☉, and is health-restoring, nerve building, a purifier and eliminator of the poisons, wastes, and over-acidity of the body. (See "Sun Group" under Herbs).

ORATOR—Oratorical Ability—A Good Voice—No Stammer or Defect of Speech—(See Eloquent, Fluency, under Speech; "Gifted" under Voice).

ORBS OF PLANETS—The planets in forming aspects with each other are said to be within orb of the aspect, and to cause the aspect to act, if within a certain number of degrees of the exact aspect. The Orbs of the planets are as follows: The ☉—17°; ☽—12°, 30'; ♆—8°; ♅—8°; ♄—10°; ♃—12°; ♂—7° 30'; ♀—8°; ☿—7°. Example—The orb of the ☉ plus the orb of the ☽ are equal to 29° 30'. One-half of this is 14° 45', the distance on either side of the exact aspect. The ☉ and ☽ to be in △ aspect each other at B. must be within the orb of 14°. The ☉ in 4° ♌, and the ☽ in 18° ♐ would still be within the orb of the △ aspect, and fortunate for good health. The smaller orbs of the other planets make the range of the aspects smaller. The student should study carefully the subject of Orbs in the Textbooks and Dictionaries of Astrology, and how to calculate aspects. (See Aspects, Reaction).

ORDINARY—(See "Ordinary" under Complexion, Death).

ORGANIC—Pertaining To, Or Having Organs—The Physical Body—Structural—

Organic Constitution—The ☉ is the chief index of the Organic Constitution. Also the Asc. rules largely over, and determines the nature and quality of the physical constitution. (See Constitution, First House, Structural).

Organic Decay—(See Decay).

Organic Defects—Those inherent in the body, and congenital. Caused by the ☉ afflicted in signs, and also by prenatal conditions. The ☽ rules Ac-

quired Defects. (See Acquired, Congenital, Defects, Heredity, Structural).

Organic Development—The ☽ shows the quality of Organic Development. (See "First Quarter" under Moon).

Organic Diseases—Constitutional Diseases—Structural Diseases—Inherent—Hereditary—Innate—Organic diseases are due to afflictions to the Signs of the Zodiac, while Functional Disorders are caused by afflictions to the Planets. The ☉ is the chief index of the organic constitution, and to determine organic diseases, note the nature of planets afflicting the ☉, and the signs they occupy, and the sign and house the ☉ is in at B. Organic diseases are denoted by conditions in the radical map, and by the afflictions to the ☉. The organic elements of the body, and the organic resistance against disease, are largely ruled by the sign on the Asc. at birth. Organic diseases are those which take a deeper hold upon the constitution, and tend to be chronic, slow, tedious, or fatal. The nature of structural and functional disorders can be inferred from the combination of the sign, planet, house and aspects of the ☉, ☽, and other planets. The Organs of the body are ruled by the different Signs, and a planet, or planets, in each sign will definitely affect the organs, and part, ruled by such sign. Also the position of the ☉ in the houses plays some part in the development of an organic disease, and whether the ☉ is rising, elevated, above, or below the horizon at B., and according to the degree of the power of the ☉ in the map of birth. The ☉ below the horizon at B., between the middle of the 6th H., and the middle of the 1st H., tends to a weakening of the constitution and vital powers, and if much afflicted to bring the danger of serious constitutional and organic diseases. The ☉ □ or ☍ the Asc. tends to organic diseases. Organic diseases which tend to mental disorders are indicated by the ☽ and Asc. (See "Organic" under Mind). The following influences are some of the principle causes of organic diseases. The ☉ in each sign, from ♈ on around to ♓, tends to organic diseases, and structural defects in those parts which are under the special rule of the ☉. Thus the ☉ in ♈ would tend to affect the Brain and Eyes; the ☉ afflicted in ♉, organic defects of the throat and neck; the ☉ afflicted in ♊, organic defects and weakness of the lungs; the ☉ afflicted in ♌, organic weakness of the heart, etc., and on around thru the Signs. Afflictions in the Fixed Signs tend to organic diseases. (See "Fixed Signs" under Fixed). The evil aspects between the ☉ and ☽ tend to disturbances of the organic functions ruled by the ☽. (For a list of Constitutional and Organic Diseases see "Constitutional Diseases" under Constitution; Structural; "Diseases of the Sun" under Sun).

Organic Force—(See Force).

Organic Functions—(See "Organic under Functions).

Organic Headaches—(See Headaches).

Organic Power—Given by the fire signs on the Asc. at B. (See "Fire Signs" under Fire).

Organic Resistance—The ☉ or ♂ ✶ or △ the Asc. (See "Abundance of Health" under Health; Immunity, Resistance; "Body" under Strong; "Good" under Vitality).

Organic Weakness — Structural Defects—Afflictions to the ☉ at B., and usually in the part or organ ruled by the sign the ☉ is in; the ☉ or ☽ in the 6th H., and afflicted by malefics. (See Congenital, Heredity; "Ill-Health All Thru Life" under Ill-Health; Organs; "Low" under Vitality; "Weak Body" under Weak).

ORGANS — Organs of the Body — The Organism—Members of the Body—In a general way the ☉ rules the structural organization of the organs of the body, and the organic functions are ruled by the ☽. The ☉ in the different signs tends to organic and structural diseases of the part, or organs, ruled by the sign the ☉ is in at B. Also the Organs are ruled by the different Signs, and a planet, or planets, in each sign will definitely affect only certain parts of an Organ. Thus ♈ rules the head and face, and the ☉ in ♈ affects the Brain and Eyes, and tends to organic Brain trouble. The ☽ in ♈ affects the Glands and Eyes. Venus in ♈, the Skin and Complexion. Jupiter in ♈, the Arteries and Right Ear. Saturn in ♈, the Skull, Teeth, and Left Ear (some Authorities say the Right Ear). Uranus in ♈, the Membranes of the Brain and the Pituitary Body. Neptune in ♈, the Optic Nerve and the Pineal Gland, etc. The various Organs of the body, and the planetary influences relating to them, and the Diseases of Organs, are listed alphabetically in this book, and only the general conditions tending to affect the Organs will be listed in this Article. Also see the Articles on Body, Constitution; "Left Side" under Left; Lower, Members, Middle, Parts; "Right Side" under Right; Upper. Also there are subjects which may include and deal with Parts containing several Organs, such as Abdomen, Chest, Head, Thorax, Trunk, etc. The following subjects have to do with the Organs of the Body—

Ablation of Organs — (See Remote, Removal, Suppression; "Ablation" under Tonsils).

Affected—The Organs affected in disease are denoted by the Sign occupied by the afflicting planet. The House position of the afflicting planet shows which part of the organ is affected, and whether on the right or left side of the body, according to the sex of the native. (See "Left Side" under Left; "Disease" under Members; Navamsa; "Right Side" under Right).

Atrophy of Organs—(See Atrophy).

Birth—Organs Afflicted from Birth—(See Birth, Blindness, Congenital, Crippled, Cyclops, Deafness, Deformities, Distortions, Dumb, Forearm, Frog Child, Hearing, Hermaphrodites, Idiocy, Lameness, Limitations, Maimed, Missing, Monsters, Mutes, Prenatal

Epoch, Twelfth House; "United" under Twins; Virile, etc.).

Bulky Organs—(See "Organs" under Enlarged; "Over-Developed" in this section).

Chest—Organs of, and Afflictions To —(See the subjects under Chest).

Cold Organs—♄ rules Cold, and the Organ, or Organs, ruled by the sign in which ♄ is posited at B., tend to be cold, and more subject to disease, poor circulation in, etc., and especially if it is a weak sign for ♄, and ♄ is badly afflicted by the ☉, ☽, or malefics. (See Cold, Saturn).

Compression of Organs—(See Compressed).

Conformity of Members—(See Conformity, Harmony, Well-Proportioned).

Coordinated Action—Of Organs—(See Coordination, Incoordination).

Deficient Development—Of the Organism—(See Cretinism, Deficient, Development, Diminished, Undersized, Undeveloped).

Degeneration Of—(See Decay, Degeneration).

Development Of—(See Cretinism, Development, Diminished, Enlarged, Growth; "Organic Development" under Organic; Overgrowth, Undersized, Undeveloped).

Digestion—Organs of—(See "Organs" under Digestion).

Diminished—In Size—(See "Body" under Diminished; "Arrested" under Growth; Undersized, Undeveloped).

Displacement—Of Organs—(See "Organs" under Dislocations; Displacements).

Elimination—Organs of—(See Elimination).

Enlarged Organs—(See "Organs" under Enlarged; "Over-Developed" in this section).

Erratic Action—Of Organs—Caused by ♅. (See Erratic, Spasmodic).

Excretion—Organs of—(See Excretion).

External Organs—(See "External" under Genitals).

Functions—Of Organs—(See Functions).

Generative Organs—External and Internal—(See External, Internal, under Generative; "External" under Genitals; Ovaries, Reproductive, Sex, Womb).

Glandular Organs — (See Glands, Secretion).

Hardening Of — (See Crystallization, Hardening, Sclerosis).

Head—Organs of—(See "Organs" under Head).

Heart—The Heart On the Right Side —(See "Right Side" under Heart).

Ill-Placed Organs — (See "Displacement" in this section; "Right Side" under Heart; Floating, Prolapsed, under Kidneys; "Falling Of" under Womb).

Incomplete Organs — (See "Born Incomplete" under Incomplete).

Incoordination—Of Organs—(See Incoordination).

Inhibition—Of Organs—(See Inhibition, Suppression; "Ablation" in this section).

Intermittent Action—Of Organs—(See Erratic, Intermittent, Irregular, Jerky, Spasmodic).

Internal Organs—(See Internal).

Irregular Action — Of Organs — (See "Intermittent" in this section).

Kidneys — (See Floating, Prolapsed, under Kidneys).

Left Side — Of the Body — Organs of Affected—(See Left).

Lower Part of Organs—Is shown by the latter part of a Sign, or the 3rd Decanate. The upper and lower parts of an organ may be ruled by a different sign. The ♋ Sign rules the upper part of the Stomach, while ♍ rules the lower part. Gemini rules the upper lobes of the Lungs, while ♋ rules the lower lobes. The upper lobes of the Liver are ruled by ♋, while ♍ rules the lower lobes, etc. Thus, ♄ in ♊ would tend to affect the upper lobes of the Lungs, and ♄ in ♋, the lower lobes, etc. (See "Lobes" under Liver, Lungs). The upper part of an organ is shown and indicated by the early degrees of a Sign, or the first Decanate, and planets in this decan. tend to affect the upper part. The middle part of an organ is shown by the second decan., or from 10 to 20° of the sign. Thus, to judge which part of an organ is the more afflicted, or diseased by the action of a malefic, or afflicting planet, note the position of the planet in the sign. (See Decanates; "Organs" under Lower, Middle, Upper; Navamsa).

Middle Parts of Organs—(See "Lower" in this section; "Organs" under Middle).

Misshaped Organs—♆ influence; ♆ afflicted by ♄, and in the part ruled by the sign ♆ is in at B. (See Misshaped; "Development Of" in this section).

Nerve Fibres — Of Organs — ☿ rules Complaints which affect the nerve fibers of organs; also diseases of the ☿ sign ♊; caused by the afflictions of ♆ and ♅ to ☿. (See "Fibers" under Nerves).

Organic Diseases—(See Organic).

Over-Activity Of—(See Over-Active).

Over-Developed Organs— Enlarged— Bulky—♆ influence; ♆ ☌ ☉, ♂, or ♀ in airy signs; ♆ afflicted by ♄, and the organ afflicted is that ruled by the sign containing ♆; ♂ □ or ☍ the ☉ and ♀, abnormally enlarged organs according to the sign containing the ☉ and ♀. Also the overgrowth of connective tissue, or an organ, often result from ♄ affliction, and the mineral deposits of ♄. (See Development; "Organs" under Enlarged; "Abnormal" under Growth).

Over-Growth — Of Organs — (See "Over-Developed" in this section).

Parenchyma Of—(See Parenchyma).

Part of Organ Afflicted—(See Lower, Middle, Upper, in this section).

Perversion—Of the Natural Function of An Organ—(See "Perversion" under Functions; Perversions).

Polarity of Changed—(See Polarity).

Prolapsus of Organs—(See Prolapse; "Ill-Placed" in this section).

Right Side—Of the Body—Organs of Affected—(See Right).

Rulership of Organs — Each Sign of the Zodiac rules over a different Organ, or part of the body, and also each of the Planets rules one or more organs. A Sign of the Zodiac may rule an organ as a whole, yet the different parts of an organ may be ruled by different Signs, as explained in the paragraph on "Lower Part Of" in this Article. Also the Decanate and Navamsa divisions of a sign indicate what part of an organ may be afflicted. (See Decanates, Navamsa; also see "Lower Part" in this section). The Head, as a whole, is ruled by the ♈ Sign, but the Nose is ruled by ♏. The ☉ and ♌ rule the Heart, yet the various forms of disease which attack the heart may be caused by the afflictions of other planets when in ♌, and especially the malefics in ♌. The different parts of the heart, as the auricles, ventricles, endocardium, pericardium, etc., and how to know which part of the heart is afflicted, is explained in the Article on Navamsa. The ☉ and the ♌ Sign also rule the Spine, taken as a whole, but the Spinal Canal is ruled by ♆, and the rulerships of the different parts of the Spine need to be studied carefully to diagnose Spinal Disorders. (See Spine). For the rulerships of the various organs of the body, see the Articles on each of the Planets, as Sun, Moon, Neptune, etc. Also see each of the 12 Signs, as Aries, Taurus, Gemini, etc. Also look in the alphabetical arrangement for each of the Organs of the body, as Brain, Ears, Eyes, Heart, Larynx, Liver, Lungs, Nose, Spleen, etc. (See "External Rulership" under Signs; the Introduction to this Article).

Rupture of Organs — (See "Accelerated" under Motion; Rupture).

Secretory Organs — (See Glands, Secretions).

Sensitive Organs—(See "Organs" under Sensitive).

Shrinkage Of—(See Shrinkage).

Spasmodic Action—Of Organs—(See "Organs" under Spasmodic).

Suppression—Of Organs—(See "Ablation" in this section).

Undersized Organs— Undeveloped— (See Atrophy, Diminished, in this section).

Upper Parts of Organs—(See "Lower" in this section; "Organs" under Upper).

Vital Organs — The Internal Organs, such as Bowels, Brain, Heart, Liver, Lungs, Stomach, etc.—(See these subjects).

Weak Organs—Weakened—♄ in any sign tends to weaken, and make more liable to disease, the part ruled by the sign he is in at B., and the sign so occupied is usually considered the most vulnerable part of the organism, or to cause death eventually thru disease and breakdown of the organ, organs, or parts, ruled by such sign. Thus ♄ afflicted in ♌ usually brings death by heart trouble; ♄ afflicted in ♎, by kidney disorder, etc., and especially if ♄ holds the dominion of death, and otherwise afflicts the ☉, ☽, Asc., or Hyleg. (See Saturn Diseases and Afflictions under Saturn).

ORIENTAL — Planets Oriental — The more oriental and angular a planet is at B., whether benefic or malefic, the more powerful will be its effects for good or ill. The ☉ and ☽ are oriental from the 1st to 10th H., and from the 7th to 4th House, and when in these Quarters at B. tend to have different effects in health matters. Planets rising between midnight and noon are considered oriental, and occidental when setting between noon and midnight. Planets in the Oriental Quarters at B. indicate Acute Pains and Accidents, and when in the Occidental Quarters tend to Disease. Planets are also said to be oriental when rising and setting before the ☉. Malefics ori., and afflicting the ☉ or ☽, tend to cause Blemishes. (See Benefics, Blemishes; "Total Blindness" under Blindness; Fits, Lunacy, Malefics, Occidental). The oriental influences of the planets are listed and mentioned many times in this book, under the different diseases and condtions, and the student should make a careful study of this subject in the Textbooks of Astrology, and thoroughly know the Elements of Astrology before he can expect to make a good Diagnostician, or Medical Astrologer. (See Quadrants).

ORIENTATION—Ability to Know Correctly One's Position In a Given Environment—(See Balance; "Coordinated Action" under Coordination; "Sound Mind" under Mind).

Disorientation — Loss of Identity — (See Identity, Memory).

ORIFICES — Of the Body — A Mouth, Opening, or Entrance Into the Body from the Outside World. (See Ears, Eyes, Mouth, Navel, Nose, Rectum, Urethra, Vagina, etc). Also in Infancy the Fontanelle is an opening in the Skull, covered by a thin membrane. In Occult Literature considerable is said about the 12 openings into the human body, and their Mystical meaning. There are also many internal orifices in the body, as the Valves, the Pylorus, the Inguinal Canals, the Ducts, etc. The Orifices in the different parts of the body are under the rulership of the Signs ruling the part. In Ancient Times, it is said, there was a Third Eye in the human head, enabling one to see on all sides, and to avoid dangers when the Earth was in a more molten stage, but that opening has long since been closed. (See Pineal Gland).

ORION—Constellation of Orion—

Orion's Belt—Cingular Orionis—Three stars, from 21° to 24° ♊, of 2nd magnitude, of the nature of ♄ and ♃. These stars are mentioned in the following subjects — (See Assassination; "Causes" under Blindness; Drowning; "One Eye" under Eye, as causing loss of one eye). Other references to subjects and diseases are given under Bellatrix and Rigel.

Orion's Foot—(See Rigel).

Orion's Left Shoulder—(See Bellatrix).

Orion's Right Shoulder — Betelgeuse —A fixed star of the first magnitude in the last face of ♊, of the nature of ♂ and ☿. (See "Many Calamities" under Calamity; "Many Dangers" under Danger; Disgrace, Drowning; "Hot Diseases" under Heat; "Fevers" under Putrid; Ruin; "Danger Of" under Sickness; Trouble; "Death" under Violent).

ORNAMENTS— (See "Adornment" under Dress; Neat).

ORPHANS — (See Adoption; "Early Death", "Separated from Parents", under Parents).

ORTHOPEDIST—One who corrects Deformities—One with the Qualities of a Surgeon — ♂ strong at B., as in the Midheaven, makes good Orthopedists. (See Surgeons).

OS CALCIS—The Heel Bone—Ruled by ♓. (See Feet).

OS COCCYX — (See Coccyx, Sacrum, Spine).

OS SACRUM—(See Sacrum).

OSCILLATION—Of the Eyeballs—(See "Nystagmus" under Eyeballs).

OSMOSIS—The Transudation or Oozing of Fluids thru the Walls of Vessels, or thru Membranes — The Oozing of Fluids—Osmosis is a ☽ influence. Endosmosis is the transudation, or osmosis, of fluids inward, and is generally a ☽ influence. Exomis is the outward oozing, or transudation of fluids, and is under the rule of ♀, and in abnormal conditions is a ♀ disease. Osmosis may also be caused by ♄ affliction, due to stoppages, and with the ☽ afflicted by ♄, as in Dropsies. (See Dropsy, Effusions, Exudations, Fluids, Oedema, Serum, Transudations).

OSSEOUS—The Osseous System—Ossification—Resembling Bone—The Bones —Concretions, etc.—

Osseous Deposits — Mineral Deposits —(See Calculus, Concretions, Crystallization, Deposits, Gravel, Hardening; "Fontanelles" under Head; Mineral, Sand, Sclerosis, Stone; "Influence Of" under Saturn; Urea, Uric, Wastes, etc.).

Osseous System — The Bones — The Skeleton — Ruled generally by ♄ and the ♑ Sign. The Osseous System is especially affected with the ☉ and ☽ acting thru the ♑ sign. (See Bones; the Introduction under Knees; Minerals).

Ossification — Bone-Building — Ruled and denoted by ♄, and is a ♄ process. (See "Ossification" in Sec. 1 under Bones; "Morbid Ossification" in Sec. 2 under Bones).

OSSICLES — The Small Bones of the Ears—Ruled by ♉, and also influenced by ♈. (See "Bony Parts" under Ears).

OSTEITIS — Inflammation of a Bone — (See "Bones" under Arms; "Inflammation" under Bones).

OSTEOMYELITIS— (See "Osteomyelitis" under Bones; "Marrow" under Femur; "Inflammation" under Marrow).

OSTEOPATHY — Osteopathic Physician —Good Influences For—Successful As An Osteopath—(See "Osteopathy" under Healers).

OSTRICH—A Human Ostrich—Swallows Glass, etc.—(See "Human Ostrich" under Human).

OUT—Words beginning with "Out"—

Outbreaks of Violence—(See "Outbreaks" under Violence).

Outbursts of Passion—(See "Outbursts" under Passion).

Outbursts of Rage—(See Anger, Choleric, Rashness; "High Temper" under Temper; "Becomes Violent" under Violent).

Outcaste—A Social Outcaste—♂ afflicted in the 12th H. (See Social Relations).

Outcome of the Disease—(See "Outcome" under Disease).

Outdoor Sports—(See Exercise, Hunting, Sports).

Outlaw—(See Banishment, Exile).

Out-of-Sorts—(See Anguish, Anxiety, Irritable; "High Temper" under Temper; Worry, etc.).

Out-of-the-Way Places—Detention In—Detention In a Foreign Land—(See "Accidents" under Abroad; Banishment, Captivity, Exile).

Outgrowth—(See Exostosis).

Outrageous—The Patient Becomes Outrageous and Unmanageable—(See "Outrageous" under Insanity).

Outrageous Diseases—(See "Private Diseases" under Private; Scandalous, Venereal).

Outrages—(1) Murderous Outrages—(See "Murderous Outrages" under Murder). (2) Outrages Prevalent—Outrages Numerous—☿ in ♊, ☌ ♂ at the Vernal Equi., and Lord of the Year. (See "Much Crime" under Crime).

Outraging Nature's Laws—(See "Nature's Laws" under Laws).

Outside Influence Over Body—(See Contagions, Environment, External, Susceptibility).

Outward—The Blood and Fluids Drawn Outward to the Surface—(See Caustics, Centrifugal, Congestions, External, Irritations, Rubefacients, Surface).

OUTER PARTS—The Outer and Upper Part of the Kidney—(See Kidneys).

Outer Parts of the Body—(See External, Skin, Surface).

OVAL—Oval Face—(See "Oval" under Face).

OVARIES—Ova—Ruled by the ☽, ♀, ♎, and ♏. The ☉ rules the right ovary, and the ☽ the left. The Ovum is ruled by ♀. They are also affected by planets in the cardinal signs, as in ♈, ♋, ♎, or ♑.

Ablation Of—Suppression of the Ovaries—♄ afflicted in ♉, by reflex action to ♏, from the opposite sign; ♄ afflicted in ♏. (See Ablation, Remote, Removal, Suppressions).

Abscess Of—♂ afflicted in ♏. (See Abscess).

Afflicted Ovaries—Diseased Ovaries—The ☉ or ☽ afflicted in ♏; the ☽ afflicted, and especially when in ♉, ♏, and fixed signs; a ☽ disease; ♀ affl. in ♏; ♀ in ♏ and afflicting the ☽ or Asc.; ♀ afflicted in ♏ in the 6th H.; a ♏ disease, and afflictions in ♏; a ♉ disease by reflex action to ♏; Subs at PP.

Dropsy Of—The ☽ afflicted in ♏; ♄ ☌ ☽ in ♏; ♃ or ♀ ☌ ♄ in ♏; Subs at PP (2L). (See Dropsy).

Inflammation Of—Abscess of—Ovaritis—Ulceration of—♂ afflicted in ♏; Subs at PP (2, 3, 4L).

Ovariotomy—Surgical Removal of the Ovaries—Never operate upon the Ovaries or Womb when the ☽ is in ♍, ♎, or ♏, and especially applying to ♄ or ♂, or other malefics, as death or inflammation may result. (See "Rules" under Operations).

Ovaritis—(See "Inflammation" in this section).

Oviducts—Fallopian Tubes—Disorders of—(See Fallopian).

Suppression Of—(See "Ablation" in this section).

Ulceration Of—(See "Inflammation" in this section; Ulcers). See Barren, Conception, Fallopian, Fecundation, Fruitful, Menses, Pregnancy, Reproduction, Womb.

OVER—Words Beginning with "Over"—

Over-Abundance—(1) Over-Abundance of Animal Heat, and Disease From—(See "High Fever" under Fever; "Animal Heat" under Heat). (2) Over-Abundance of Life Force—(See "Excess Of" under Force; "Force" under Vital; Vitality).

Over-Activity—Over-Active—Many planets in one sign at birth, and especially the ☽ and ♂ in the same sign, tend to over-activity of the organ, or organs ruled by such sign. (1) Over-Active Brain—(See "Over-Active" under Brain; "Over-Active Mind" under Active). (2) Over-Active Body—(See "Body" under Hyperactivity). (3) Over-Activity of the Lungs, Stomach and Nerves—(See "Over-Activity" under Lungs).

Over-Ardent—(See "Ardent" under Love Affairs).

Over-Braced Tonic Fibers—(See "Tonic Fibers" under Fiber).

Over-Charged—The Body Over-Charged with Moist Humours—(See "Moist Diseases" and Humours" under Moisture).

Overcoming—(1) Power to Overcome Evil Directions—(See "Overcoming" under Directions). (2) Overcomes Disease—(See "Overcoming" under Disease; Immunity; "Strong Resistance" under Resistance; "Good" under Vitality).

Over-Eating—(See "Over-Eating" under Eating; Feasting; Gluttony; "Over-Indulgence" in this section).

Over-Emotional—(See Ecstasy; "Intensified" under Emotions; Hysteria).

Over-Excitement—(See Excitement).

Over-Exercise—Disease or Fatigue From—(See "Inordinate" under Exercise; Fatigue, Sports).

Over-Exertion—Illness From—(See Exertion).

Overflowing—♃ is overflowing in action. (See Excesses, Flooding, Flow, Jupiter, Redundant).

Over-Growth—(See "Thickening" under Cells; "Abnormal" under Growth; Hypertrophy; "Over-Growth" under Organs; Sclerosis).

Over-Heated — (See "Over-Heated" under Blood, Heat; "Sunstroke" under Sun).

Over-Indulgence — (1) Appetites — Over-Indulgence of the Appetites and Sickness From—♃ afflicted in ♉; ♃ in ♋ on the Asc., and afflicted; ♃ afflicted in the 6th H.; ♂ afflicted in ♍; ☿ Sig., and to the ☌ ♀, and ♀ ill-dignified at B.; ♉ influence; the 11° ♊ on the Asc. (See Amorous; "Over-Indulgence" under Appetites; Desires, Epicureans; "Excesses" under Diet, Drink, Eating, Food, Passion, Pleasure; Excesses; "Inordinate" under Exercise; Feasting, Gluttony; "High Living" under High; Indiscretions, Indulgences, Living; "Health Injured" under Men; Plethora; "Intemperate" under Sports; "Over-Indulgence" under Sugar; Surfeits).

(2) Of the Passions—(See Amorous; "Health Suffers" under Opposite Sex; "Passional Excesses" under Passion).

Over-Loaded Stomach — (See "Over-Loaded" under Stomach).

Over-Secretion — (See the various paragraphs under Excess, Fluids, Secretion; "Excess" under Urates, Urine).

Over-Strain—Of the Mind and Body, and Diseases Resulting From — (See "Over-Active Mind" under Active; "Inordinate", "Mind", under Exercise; "Over-Exertion" under Exertion; "Mind" under Fatigue; Hyperactivity; "Exertion". "Strain", under Mental; "Over-Strain", "Strain", under Nerves; Reading, Strain, Stress, Study, etc.).

Over-Study — Disorders From — (See "Reading and Study" under Blindness; "Brain Fag" under Brain; "Eyestrain" under Eyes; "Mind" under Fatigue; Reading, Study, etc.).

Over-Time Children — (See Prenatal Epoch).

Over-Work—(See Over-Activity, Over-Exercise, Over-Exertion, Over-Strain" in this section; "Over-Work" under Nerves).

OVUM—Ruled by ♀. (See Ovaries).

OWN—Relating to the Individual—
(1) Causes His Own Death — (See "Causes His Own Death" under Death).
(2) Fears His Own Death — (See "Death" under Fear).
(3) His Own Worst Enemy—(See this subject under Enemies).
(4) Causes His Own Illnesses—(See "Brings Disease Upon Himself" under Disease).
(5) Causes His Own Misfortunes — (See this subject under Misfortune).

OXEN—Large Cattle—Death of Many Great Cattle—Injury or Attacks By—(See "Death", "Hurts By", under Animals; "Great Beasts", "Hurts", under Beasts; "Death", "Destruction", "Diseases", "Great Cattle", under Cattle; "Cattle" under Detriment; "Great Beasts", "Great Cattle", under Great; "Cattle" under Large; "Epidemics" under Sheep).

OXYGEN—Oxygenation—Non-Oxygenation, etc.—Oxygen is one of the Gaseous Elements, and the Supporter of Life, and is an important element in Heat and Combustion. Oxygen is essential in the four Operations of Nature. (See Combustion; "Operations" under Nature). The ☉ rules Oxygen, and also the oxygen in the blood is supplied and ruled by the ☉. The oxygen of the ☉, and the iron of ♂, maintain the heat of the blood. (See Haematopoiesis). Also, oxygen is ruled largely by the Fiery Signs of the Zodiac. Oxygenation of the blood is ruled by, and is a function of the ♊ sign, the sign which rules the Lungs, and people born under Airy Signs require more oxygen, and should sleep in well-ventilated rooms. The atmosphere about us is made up of about 23 per-cent of oxygen by weight, and Nature gives this gas to us freely, if we will breathe it in, to replenish, purify, and revitalize the blood. People who have ♄ afflicted in ♊, the lung sign, tend to shallow breathing, and for lack of sufficient oxygen, tend to Anaemia, and also to be more liable to go into Consumption. Sunlight, Oxygen, and the most of the vital, and life-giving forces about us, both in drink, and our food, are ruled by the ☉, as the ☉ is the Giver of Life. The fruits and vegetables which are ruled by the ☉ are strong with oxygen.

Non-Oxygenation of the Blood — Insufficient Oxygenation — Oxygenation Interfered With—Obstructed—Poor, etc.—The ☉ in ♊ ☌ ♅; the ☉ in ♊, ☐ or ☍ ♂ at B.; ♆, ♅, ♄ in ♊, ☐ or ☍ ♃ or ♀; ♆ in ♊ in the 12th H., ☐ or ☍ ♅, the capillaries are incapable of taking in sufficient oxygen for the blood; ♅ ☌ ♂ in ♊, and in ☐ or ☍ the ☉ or ☽; ♅ in ♊ on the Asc., and in ☍ ♃, ♀, or the ☽, oxygenation is spasmodic, and the capillaries contracted; ♅ or malefics in ♊, and afflicting ♃ or ♀, rulers of the Arterial and Venous circulation; ♄ in ♊, ☍ the ☽, insufficient tidal air and oxygen to cleanse the blood of carbon dioxide; ♄ in ♊, ☌, ☐, or ☍ ♃ or ♀; ♄ in ♊, ☐ ♂, ♀, or ☿, expulsion of carbonic acid, and proper oxygenation of the blood prevented; ♄ ☌ ♃ in the 6th H.; ♄ ☌ ♃, and ☐ ♅; ♄ afflicted in ♌, due to a weak heart; ♂ afflicted in ♊, the oxygen in the lungs is burned up too fast; ☿ afflicted in ♊; malefics in ♊ in the 12th H.; many afflictions in ♊ or common signs; common signs on the angles. Aquarius causes incomplete oxygenation, morbid blood conditions, blood poisoning, etc. Case of Insufficient Oxygenation — See Fig. 24 in the book, "Message of the Stars", by the Heindels. (See Air, Carbon, Combustion, Gases, Hydrogen, Iron, Nitrogen).

Sickness from Non-Oxygenation — Disease and Illness From — Afflictions and Disturbances By — (See Anaemia, Asphyxiation; "Labored", "Obstructions", under Breathing; "Delayed Birth" under Children; "General Causes" under Cough; Cyanosis; "Impure Blood" under Impure; "Blood Poisoning" under Poison; Suffocation; "Tidal Air" under Tidal).

P

PAIN — Pains — Painful — Painless— Aches—Acute Suffering, etc.—The various parts of the body are more apt to suffer with pains at the time of the Moon's Perigee. Also Pains, Tumors, and Fluxions follow a Solar Periodicity. The afflictions of the malefic planets, and especially of ♄ and ♂, are the principal causes of pain and distress in suffering, and especially when they afflict the Asc., or are in the 6th H., or lords of this house. (See "Pain" under Jupiter, Mars, Mercury, Moon, Neptune, Saturn, Uranus, Venus). Every part of the body is subject to pain and disease at times, and each of the planets when afflicted tends to cause pain in the part, parts, or organ ruled by the sign in which posited. Mars tends to acute, sharp, darting pains. Saturn gives dull pains and aches. Uranus tends to spasmodic pains. For pain in the various parts and organs of the body see "Pain", or "Pains", under the subject you have in mind. In this Article a partial list of the organs and parts affected by pain are listed, and also general considerations and conditions concerning pain. For subjects not listed here, look in the alphabetical arrangement for what you have in mind.

Abdomen — Pain In — (See Abdomen, Appendicitis; "Pain" under Bowels; Colic, Flatulence, Ileac Passion, Tympanies; "Bowels" under Wind).

Abscesses—Painful Abscesses — (See Abscesses, Boils, Carbuncles).

Accidents—(See "Painful" under Accidents).

Aches—Heavy and Dull Pains—(See "Heavy" under Aches; "Dull Pains" under Head; Headaches, Neuralgia).

Acute Pains — Acute Nerve Pains — Acute Pains In the Body—Caused principally by the afflictions of ♂; the ☉ or ☽ afflicted in the Oriental Quarters of the map. (See "Suffering" under Acute; "Acute Diseases" under Head; Fierce, Sharp, Shooting, Violent, in this section)

All Over the Body — Pains Over the Whole Body—(See Whole).

Alleviated—The good aspects of the benefic planets ♃ and ♀ to the afflicting planets tend to alleviate pain and suffering. (See Amelioration, Moderation).

Analgesia — Insensibility to Pain — (See Analgesia, Insensibility).

Angina Pectoris — Pain About the Heart—(See Angina).

Anguish of Mind—(See Anguish).

Anodynes—A Drug Relieving Pain— (See Anodyne; "Pain and Suffering" under Narcotics).

Arms—Pains In—(See "Pains" under Arms, Hands, Shoulders).

Arthralgia—(See "Pain" under Joints).

Asthenopia — Painful Vision — (See Sight).

Back—(See "Pains" under Back).

Backbone —-Spine — Pains In — (See "Pain" under Spine).

Bladder—(See "Pains" under Bladder, Bile).

Boils; Bones — (See "Pain" under Bones).

Bowels — (See "Pain" under Bowels; Cholera, Colic, Dysentery, Enteralgia).

Breasts—(See "Pain" under Breast).

Burning Pains — Burning Sensations —Burning Pains In the Chest or Stomach—(See Belching; "Heartburn" under Heart).

Catamenia Painful — (See "Painful" under Menses).

Chest—(See "Pains" under Chest).

Children — (See "Pain" under Children).

Cholera Pains—(See Cholera).

Chordee—(See "Chordee" under Gonorrhoea).

Colic; Complaints—Painful Complaints —(See "Diseases" in this section).

Consumptive Pains—(See "Consumptive Pains" under Knees, Thighs).

Cramps; Darting Pains — (See "Darting Pains" under Head; "Sharp" in this section).

Day Time — Pains Less In the Day Time, and Greater At Night — (See "Pain" under Night).

Death—(1) Painful Death—♂ in the 8th H. at B., and afflicting the hyleg; ♂ lord of the 8th., or afflicting the lord of the 8th H., or afflicting the cusp of the 8th H. at B., or by dir.; ♂ having sole dominion at a Solar Eclipse, many painful deaths; a malefic planet in the 8th H., and when other testimonies do not show a violent death. (See "Death" under Accidents, Blows, Burns, Cuts, Duels, Hurts, Injuries, Iron, Stabs, Sword, Wounds; "Diseases" in this section). (2) Death Without Pain — (See Comforts; "Easy Death" under Death; "Natural Death" under Natural). (3) Death of Females from Pain and Long Illness—(See "Death" under Females).

Delivery Painful—Childbirth Difficult and Painful — (See "Painful" under Parturition).

Dengue — Pain In the Bones — (See Dengue).

Diseases — Painful Diseases—Suffers Much Pain In Sickness—Distressful— Poignant—Fierce—Sharp—Swift—Violent—Vehement, etc.—Caused by the ☉ and ♂, the positive, electric, and heat-producing planets; the afflicting planets, or malefics, in the Oriental Quarters tend to painful, short, and acute diseases; the ☽ afflicted by ♂ tends to painful complaints and irregularities due to rashness and want of forethought. At the time of a crisis in disease, if the ☽ is ☌, □, or ☍ a planet which afflicts the Asc., lord of the Asc., or if the ☽ is in evil aspect the lord

of the 6th H., the patient suffers much
pain and distress, the disease runs
high, and medicines do little good.
(See "Suffering" under Acute; "Gall
Stones" under Bile; Colic; "Worse"
under Crises; Distressful, Fierce,
Gnawing, Grievous; "High Fever" under High; "Mars Diseases" under Mars;
Poignant, Quick, Severe, Sharp, Shooting; "Suffering" under Sickness; Swift,
Terrible, Vehement, Violent, etc. Also
for the various painful diseases note
the paragraphs in this Article).

Distressful Maladies—(See "Diseases"
in this section; Distressful).

Dull Pains—Dull Aches—Given by ♄
and ☿. (See "Pains" under Dull).

Dyspnoea — Painful Dyspnoea — (See
Dyspnoea).

Ears—(See "Pain" under Ears).

Electric Pains — Caused by ♅. (See
Electric).

Enteralgia—(See "Pain" under Bowels;
Enteralgia).

Erections Painful — (See "Chordee"
under Gonorrhoea; "Priapism" under
Penis).

Extremities — (See "Pain" under Extremities).

Eyes—(See "Pain" under Eyes).

Father—(See "Pain" under Father).

Feet—(See "Pains" under Feet).

Females — Pains To — (See Accidents,
Death, Functions, Painful, under Females).

Fierce and Painful — (See "Fierce
Maladies" under Fierce).

Flying Pains—(See Flying).

Forethought—Pain and Disease from
Lack of—(See Forethought).

Functions — (See "Painful" under
Functions).

Gall Bladder—(See Cholic, Gall Stones,
under Bile).

Generative System—(See "Pains" under Generative).

Genitals—(See "Pain" under Genitals).

Gnawing Pains—(See Gnawing).

Gouty Pains — (See "Pains" under
Gout).

Groins—(See "Pain" under Groins).

Head—(See "Pains" under Head).

Headaches; Heart—(See "Pain" under
Heart).

Heartburn—(See Heart).

Heavy Pains—(See "Heavy" under
Aches).

Hips—(See "Pain" under Hips).

Hurts — Pains By — (See the paragraphs under Hurts).

Illness — Painful Illness and Death
From—♂ in the 8th H., lord of the 8th,
or afflicting the lord of the 8th, or
cusp of the 8th, indicates death from
a painful illness (Hor'y). (See Death,
Diseases, in this section).

Increased—Pain Increased At Night—
Pain and Suffering Increased — (See
"Worse" under Crises, Disease; "Pain"
under Night; "Suffering" under Sickness; "Diseases" in this section).

Inflammation—Painful Inflammations
—(See Inflammation).

Injuries—Painful Injuries—(See Injuries).

Insensibility to Pain—(See Analgesia,
Insensibility).

Irregularities—Painful Irregularities
Due to Lack of Forethought—(See
"Painful" under Forethought, Rash-
ness).

Joints—(See "Pain" under Joints).

Kidneys—(See "Pain" under Kidneys).

Knees—(See "Pains" under Knees).

Left Ear—Pains In—(See "Left Ear"
under Ears).

Legs—(See "Pain" under Legs).

Limbs—(See "Pain" under Limbs).

Lingering Pains—(See Aches; "Death"
under Females; Headaches, Lingering,
Neuralgia).

Liver—Pains In—(See Inflammation,
Pain, under Liver).

Loins—(See "Pain" under Back, Loins;
Lumbago).

Lumbago; Lumbar Region — Pain In
— (See "Pain" under Back, Lumbar;
Lumbago).

Mad with Pain — Almost Mad with
Pain — The ☽ in ♈ and afflicted by
the ☉ or ♂ when taken ill (Hor'y).
(See Darting, Fierce, Sharp, Shooting,
Violent, in this section).

Menses Painful — (See "Painful" under Menses).

Micturition Painful—(See "Strangury"
under Urine).

Motor Functions—Pains and Cramps
from Exalted Excito-Motory Function
—(See "Functions" under Exaltation).

Muscles — Pains In — (See "Pain" under Muscles).

Neck—(See "Pains" under Neck).

Nerve Pains — Nervous Pains — (See
"Pain In Nerve" under Nerves; "Acute"
in this section).

Neuralgic Pains—(See Neuralgia).

Night—Pain Greater At Night—(See
"Pain" under Night).

Nipples—(See "Pain" under Nipples).

Painful Diseases — (See "Diseases",
and the various paragraphs in this
section).

Painless—(See "Painless" under Functions).

Poignant and Painful—Severely Painful and Distressing—Keen—Cutting—
(See Acute, Diseases, Distressful,
Fierce, Severe, Sharp, Shooting, Violent, in this section; Poignant).

Priapism — Painful Erections — (See
"Erections" in this section).

Private Parts — (See "Pain" under
Generative, Genitals, Penis, Secrets).

Pyrosis—Burning Pains At the Stomach—(See Belching).

Rashness — Painful Diseases from
Rashness and Lack of Forethought—
(See Forethought, Rashness).

Reins—(See "Pain" under Reins).

Rheumatic Pains — (See "Pains", and
the various paragraphs under Rheumatism).

Ribs — (See "Shooting Pains" under
Ribs).

Running Pains — (See Flying, Running).

Secret Parts—(See "Private Parts" in this section).

Sharp Pains—(See Diseases, Poignant, in this section; "Pains" under Sharp).

Shooting Pains—(See Acute, Darting, Flying, Ribs, Running, in this section; Shooting).

Shoulders— (See "Pains" under Arms, Shoulders).

Sores—Painful Sores—(See Abscesses, Boils, Carbuncles, Pus, Sores, Ulcers).

Spasmodic Pains—(See Colic, Cramps, Gripings, Spasmodic).

Spine—(See "Pain" under Spine).

Stomach — (See "Pains" under Stomach).

Strangury—Painful Micturition—(See "Strangury" under Urine).

Suffers Much Pain—In Sickness—(See "Disease" in this section).

Swellings—Pain From—Painful Swellings — (See the paragraphs under Swellings).

Teeth — Pain In — (See "Toothache" under Teeth).

Thighs—(See "Pains" under Thighs).

Throat—(See "Pains" under Neck; the various paragraphs under Throat).

Urination Painful—(See "Strangury" under Urine).

Violent Pains — Caused by ♂. (See Fierce, Poignant, Sharp, Swift, Vehement, Violent).

Vision— Painful Vision —Asthenopia —(See "Painful" under Sight).

Whole Body—Pains Over the Whole Body—(See Gnawing, Shooting; "Pains" under Whole).

PAINTERS' COLIC—(See "Lead Colic" under Colic, Lead).

PALATE—The Roof of the Mouth and Floor of the Nose—Ruled by the ☽, ♀, and the ♉ sign, and the ☽ or ♀ afflicted in ♉ tend especially to affect the Palate. (See Mouth).

Cleft Palate—Case—Mouth a Series of Roofs, with none joining. Can return food out of nostrils. See "Cleft Palate", No. 679 in 1001 N.N.

PALE—Pallor—Pallid—Anaemic— Sickly-Looking — Ghastly-Looking — Wan Face—Pale Complexion—Pale Countenance—Unhealthy Countenance —White and Chalky Face—Cadaverous —Thin and Impoverished Blood, etc.— The ☽ and ♄ make the complexion paler and also darker; the ☉ Sig., and afflicted in ♋, ♑, or ♓, the weaker signs, and especially when these signs are upon the Asc. at B.; the ☉ in ♋ in partile aspect the Asc.; the ☉ in ♑, partile the Asc., pale and sickly; the ☽ and the ♋ sign tend to paleness; the ☽ gives a fair, pale countenance; the ☽, the planet ruling white, rising in the Asc., and afflicted, pale and white; the ☽ ascending at B.; the ☽ Sig. in ♋, ♑, or ♓; the ☽ in ♋, partile the Asc., pale, dusky complexion; the ☽ in ♓, partile the Asc., pale and sickly looking; the ☽ Sig. in ♓, a pale and bloated face; the ☽ Sig. ☐ or ☍ ♄; in Hor'y Q. the ☽

is Sig. of persons more white than red; the ☽ gives a whitely colored stature; the ☽ strong at B. gives a white and red mixed complexion, but tending to paleness; ♆ rising in the Asc. gives pallor; ♆ when setting at B. often gives a pallid complexion; ♅ afflicted in ♉, ♋, ♎, ♑, or ♓; ♄ influence tends to paleness, and especially when ♄ is in the Asc., or a ♄ sign on the Asc. at B.; in Hor'y Q. ♄ as Sig. indicates a pale and sickly-looking person; ♄ ascending at B.; ♄ Sig. in ♋ or ♓; ♄ in ♋, partile the Asc.; ♄ in ♓, partile the Asc., pale, but with dark hair; ♄ ☐ or ☍ the ☽; the two ♄ signs ♑ and ♒ tend to give a pale, tanned, and dusky complexion, even though the native is otherwise healthy; ♃ afflicted in ♋ or ♑; ♃ in ♋, partile the Asc., pale, sickly, and unwholesome countenance; ♃ in ♑, partile the Asc., a fragile appearance; ♃ afflicted in ♋ or ♑; ♂ in ♋ if afflicted by the ☉ and ☽; ♂ Sig. in ♋ or ♓; ♀ Sig. in ♋ or ♑; ♀ in power at B., pale and white, but with a dark hue; ♀ afflicted in ♋ or ♑; ♀ in ♋, partile the Asc., a sickly complexion; ♀ in ♑, partile the Asc., pale, thin, and sickly visage; ♀ Sig. ✶ or △ ♄, rather pale, but comely; ☿ Sig. in ♋; ☿ Sig. in ♓ when in the term of ♄; ☿ in ♓, partile the Asc., pale, sickly face; ♋ or ♓ on the Asc.; the ♋ sign gives a pale, sickly, and white complexion; ♓ gives a white, ghastly, chalky appearance, and a pale, large and bloated face; ♋ on the Asc., a round, pale, white face; ♓ on the Asc., pale, sickly, short, fleshy, crooked, and usually with stooping shoulders; ♑ or ♒, the signs of ♄, on the Asc.; ♒ on the Asc., rather pale complexion, delicate, but usually very beautiful, and with white hair early in life; a planet in the 1st H. which has the signification of white, as the ☽; given by the Lymphatic Temperament. People living in shaded and wooded places, or working in Mines, and who do not get the Sunshine, tend to paleness and anaemic conditions if such manner of living is continued over a long period of time. (See Anaemia; "Poor", "Thin", under Blood; "Bad", "Poor", "Sickly", under Complexion; "Weak Constitution" under Constitution; Delicate, Emaciation, Fading, Feeble; "Bad Health" under Health; Invalids, Sickly, Unhealthy; "Low" under Vitality; "Weak Body" under Weak; "Complexion" under White).

Fingers and Toes—The Fingers and Toes Pale, White, and Cold—(See "Raynaud's Disease" under Fingers).

Marks—Marks on the Body of a Pale, Lead Color— ☿ influence. (See Marks).

PALLIATIVES—Mitigating and Relieving Remedies—(See Amelioration, Anaesthetics, Anodynes, Antidotes, Antipathy, Blue Color, Cure, Drugs, Emollients, Healers, Medicines, Moderation, Modification, Opposites, Remedies, Sedatives, Soothing, Sympathy, Treatment, etc.).

PALMISTRY—The Birth Data of Cheiro. (See "Palmist", No. 083 in 1001 N.N. For planetary influences which incline to the study of Palmistry see "Occult Study" under Occult).

PALPITATION—Palpitations—The dynamic energy of ♂ causes palpitations. Also the influences of ♅ tend to tremblings, palpitations, spasmodic, and erratic movements, incoordination, etc. (See "Movements" under Erratic; Incoordination, Jerky, Spasmodic, Tremblings).

Heart—Palpitation of—(See "Palpitation" under Heart).

PALSY—Palsies—A ☽ disease; the ☽ afflicted at B., and by dir.; the ☽ hyleg, and to the ☌, P., □ or ☍ ♄ by dir.; a ♅ disease; a ♄ disease; ♄ in ♏, occi., and afflicting the ☉, ☽, or Asc.; denoted and caused by fixed stars of the nature of ♄; ♄ afflicted in the 6th H.; ♄ afflicting the hyleg or Asc.; an ♈ disease when malefics are in this sign. These influences may also cause death by Palsy. (See Paralysis).

Face—Palsy of—(See "Palsy" under Face).

Shaking Palsy—Paralysis Agitans—Trembling—Tremors—A ♅ and ♄ disease; ♅ afflicted in the sign ruling the part; ♅ or ♄ afflicted in ♓ tends to the peculiar walk in cases of Paralysis Agitans. (See Incoordination, Paralysis, Tremors; "Festination" under Walk). Subluxations in the Vertebrae, and pressure upon a Nerve, and improper distribution of nerve force, are often a contributing cause to these Shakings and Tremblings. (See Subluxations, Vertebrae).

PANARIS—(See "Whitlows" under Fingers, Toes).

PANCREAS—The Sweetbread—A Racemose Gland In the Abdomen—Ruled by the ♋ and ♍ Signs. The Pancreatic Diastase is ruled by ♋.

Cancer of Pancreas—Caused by the afflictions of ♃.

Cyst Of—♀ afflicted in ♋, and especially in the 6th H.; Subs at SP (8D).

Inflammation Of—♂ afflicted in ♋ or ♍ in the 6th H.; Subs at LSP (8D).

PANDEMICS—Widespread Epidemics—Due to the maximum of planetary influence, as the ☌ of several superior planets in the airy signs. (See Epidemics).

Pandemic of Murders — (See "Many Murders" under Murder).

PAPAVER—The Poppy Plant—Opium—Ruled by ♆. (See Narcotics).

PAPILLAE—The Renal, or Kidney Papillae are ruled by ♀. (See Kidneys). The Papillae of the Tongue are ruled by ☿ and the ♉ sign. Also influenced by ♂. (See Taste, Tongue).

Papilloma—Hypertrophied Papillae of the Skin—♀ affl. in □.

PAPULES—Small Elevations on the Skin—Caused by ♄ and ♄ deposits. (See "Condyloma" under Anus; "Pustules" under Ears; Warts).

PARACELSUS—A Great Physician and Astrologer. Born Dec. 17, 1493, near Zurich. Died Sept. 23, 1541, at Salzburg. He was the first Physisian to advocate giving Similars, and drugs to produce symptoms similar to those of the malady. Hahnemann afterwards demonstrated this principle in Homeopathy. (See Homeopathy, Sympathy). The ♈ and ♏ signs are called "The Poles of Paracelsus." Aries is the Cerebral Pole of Paracelsus, and Scorpio the Genital Pole. (See Aries, Cerebral, Genitals, Scorpio). Paracelsus said, "Man is related to the Stars by reason of his Sidereal Body." (See Astral, Sidereal).

PARAESTHESIA—A Morbid or Altered Sensation—May be caused by ♅, ♄, or ☿, and due to nerve irritations. (See "Sensations" under Burning; "Buzzing" under Ears; "Heartburn" under Heart; "Flushings" under Heat; Hyperaesthesia, Itch, Numbness, Sensations, Tingling).

PARALLEL ASPECT — The Mundane Parallel—In health matters this aspect is considered as evil as a ☌, □, or ☍, and should not be overlooked in calculating the influences of the star map of birth, and the aspects forming over it along thru life. Also all Progressed Parallels should be noted, as a Prog. P. aspect from a malefic to the ☉, ☽, Asc., or Hyleg, or Prog. P. aspects between two malefics, tend to cause great disturbances of the health or mind while such aspects last. The P. Aspects are strong factors in causing disease, as they are usually of long duration. Two planets are in P. aspect when they have the same Declination, North or South of the Equator, but of greater severity when both are North, or both South, and of the same Declination. P. Aspects between the malefics, or of the malefics to the ☉ or Hyleg, are very dangerous and annoying for the time, and may cause death, injury, or severe illness. P. Aspects between the Benefics, or of the Benefics to the ☉, ☽, Asc. or Hyleg, or very beneficial to the health and general prospects of the native. (See Aspects, Nodes).

PARALYSIS—Loss of Sensation or Voluntary Motion—Depressed Motility—Nerve Lesions—Corrosion and Hardening of the Nerves—Interference of the Nerve Force to a Part, or Parts of the Body, as by Vertebral Subluxations—

Agitans—Paralysis Agitans—(See "Shaking" under Palsy).

Arms—(See "Paralysis" under Arms).

Birth — Paralyzed from Birth — (See Distortions, Excrescences).

Blows—Paralysis From—(See Distortions).

Bulbar Paralysis—(See Medulla).

Cases of Paralysis—Birth Data, etc.—See "Tunnison", No. 113, and "Seventeen Years In Bed", No. 843, in 1001 N.N. See "Stone In Kidney", Case in Chap. XIII, Daath's Medical Astrology. See Figures 13A, 13B, 13C, 13D, 13F, 13G, 14A, in the book, "Astro-Diagnosis" by the Heindels.

Causes of Paralysis—The ☉ rising at B., and afflicted by ♄; the ☉ afflicted in ♐; the Prog. ☽ ☌, P., □, or ☍ ♂ and ☿; ♆ afflicting ☿ at B., and by dir.; ♅ and ☿ afflicted in signs which rule the part, or parts affected; ♅ brings danger of by corrosion of the nerves, and by nerve lesions; ♅ afflicting ☿; ♅ afflicting the Significators, as the ☉, ☽, Asc., or M.C.; ♄ afflicted in ♈; ♄ ☌ or ill-asp. the ☉; due to the atonic action of ♄; a ♄ disease; ♄ and ♃ combined afflictions to the Significators or the hyleg; ♄ affl. in the 6th H.; ♄ afflicting the hyleg or the Asc.; ☿ afflicted by ♆, ♅, or the ☽; ☿ affl. in ♐; many planets in ♉, ♋, ♏, or ♑; planets afflicted in and about the 8° ♋ or ♑; cardinal signs on the angles, more subject to paralysis. (See Corrosions, Distortions, Excrescences, Lesions; "Lesions" under Nerves; Spasmodic; the various paragraphs in this section).

Corrosion—Of the Nerves, and Resulting In Paralysis—(See Corrosion).

Cuts—Paralysis From—(See Distortions).

Death from Paralysis—The ☉ afflicted at B., and in □ or ☍ the ☽ or Asc., whichever may be hyleg, and the hyleg afflicted by a fatal train of directions; ♅ afflicted in the 8th H.; ♄ occi. at B., and afflicting the hyleg by dir.; ♄ in the 8th H. at a Solar Ingress into ♈, and afflicting the ☽ or planet ascending, tends to be very fatal according to the sign occupied by ♄; ♄ afflicting the hyleg by dir., and ♄ holding the dominion of death. (See Palsy).

Diaphragm — (See "Paralysis" under Diaphragm).

Diplegia—Double Symmetric Paralysis—Paralysis of both sides of the body may result in cases where both sides are afflicted by planets which cause paralysis, as ♄ in ♑, a feminine sign, and ♅ in ♐, a masculine sign, in cases with males. (See Left, Right). Also where the nerves which leave the Spine supply both sides, and are impinged in their exits thru the vertebrae, can cause a double Paralysis. Also Diplegia is caused by Subs at AT and AX, and by interferences with the Organ of Coordination situated in the ♉ sign. (See Coordination, Incoordination, Hemiplegia).

Distortions — Caused by Paralysis — (See Distortions).

Excrescences—Caused by Paralysis—(See Excrescences).

Eyes—(See "Paralysis" under Eyes).

Face—(See "Paralysis" under Face).

Falls—Paralysis From—(See Distortions, Excrescences).

Feet—(See "Paralysis" under Feet).

Hands — (See "Paralysis" under Hands).

Hemiplegia—Paralysis of One Side of the Body — The affliction of a single planet tends to this condition, or where the nerves leading out from the spine are only partially impinged. Caused by the afflictions of ♅ or ♄ to the ☉; ♄ in ♑, occi., and afflicting the ☉, ☽, or Asc.; Subs at AT, AX, or CP. (See "Hemiplegia" under Infancy).

High Places — Heights — Paralysis from Falls From — (See Distortions, Excrescences).

Infantile Paralysis—Poliomyelitis—♆ is the chief afflictor; ♆ in ♋ and afflicted by ♅ and ♄; ♅ in ♑ and afflicted by ♆ and ♄; ♅ afflicted in ♌ or ♒. (See "Paralysis" under Infancy; "Poliomyelitis" under Spine).

Injuries—Paralysis From—(See Distortions, Excrescences).

Lameness — From Paralysis — (See "Paralysis" under Feet, Legs, Limbs).

Legs—(See Locomotor Ataxia, Paralysis, under Legs).

Lesions—Paralysis from Nerve Lesions—(See Corrosions, Lesions; "Lesions" under Nerves).

Limbs — (See "Paralysis" under Limbs).

Locomotor Ataxia—(See Ataxia; "Argyll-Robertson Pupil" under Iris; "Knee Jerk" under Knees; Locomotion, Locomotor Ataxia).

Medulla—(See "Bulbar Paralysis" under Medulla).

Mobility Decreased—(See "Paralysis" under Feet, Legs; Gait, Locomotion, Locomotor Ataxia, Motion, Movement, Walk).

Moment of Birth—Paralysis from the Time of — (See Distortions, Excrescences, Prenatal Epoch).

Motor Nerves—Paralysis of—(See "Arms", and the paragraphs under Motor).

Nerve Lesions — (See Corrosions, Lesions; "Lesions" under Nerves).

Neuroses — (See "Neurosis" under Nerves).

Old Age—(See "Paralysis" under Old Age).

One Side of Body—Paralysis In—(See "Hemiplegia" in this section).

Ophthalmoplegia — (See "Paralysis" under Eyes).

Palsy—Shaking Palsy—(See Palsy).

Paraplegia—(See Legs).

Paresis—Slight Paralysis—Caused by the milder afflictions of ♅, and where the benefics give a favorable and saving aspect in the configuration. Also the subluxations are or a minor order, and not major, and the "Stroke" may be only temporary.

Partial Paralysis — Limited to One Organ or Part of the Body — Usually due to the affliction of one planet in a sign, and in the part, or organ, ruled by the sign, as ♅ afflicted in ♈ causes paralysis of an eye muscle. Also indicated in cases of Paralysis in the Arms, Hands, Feet, etc. Case—See No. 843 under "Cases" in this section.

Poliomyelitis — (See "Infantile" in this section).

Quadrupeds—Paralysis Due to Injury By—(See Distortions, Excrescences).

Robbers — Paralysis Resulting from Injuries By—(See Distortions, Excrescences).

Shaking Palsy — Paralysis Agitans — (See Palsy).

Shipwreck—Paralysis from Injury In —(See Distortions).

Slight Paralysis — (See "Paresis" in this section).

Speech — Paralysis of — Paralysis of Tongue — Loss of Power of Speech —(See "Deaf and Dumb" under Hearing; Mutes; "Aphasia" under Speech; "Paralysis" under Tongue).

Stabs—Paralysis From—(See Distortions).

Thought—Paralysis of—(See Chaotic, Confused, Delusions; "Dreamy" under Dreams; Hallucinations, Idiocy, Imbecility, Insanity; "Weak Mind" under Mind; Vague, etc.).

Walk—Interferred with by Paralysis —(See "Paralysis" under Feet, Legs; "Festination" under Walk).

PARAMYOCLONUS MULTIPLEX—(See Muscles).

PARANOIA—A Chronic Form of Insanity with Delusions—A Toxic Psychosis —Delusions of Persecution—Principally a ♆ disease and affliction; ♆ afflicted in ♈; ♆ in the 6th H. in ♈, and afflicted; ♆ in ♈, and afflicting the ☉, ☽, Asc., or Hyleg. (See Delusions, Hallucinations, Illusions, Insanity).

PARAPLEGIA — (See "Beriberi" under Dropsy; "Paraplegia" under Legs).

PARASITES—An Organism That Inhabits Another Organism, and Feeds Upon It.

Contagious Parasitic Disease—Of the Skin—(See Favus).

Intestinal Parasites—Caused by afflictions in ♍; ☿ or ♀ afflicted in ♍. (See Cestode, Entozoons, Taenia, Tapeworm, Worms).

Parasitic Diseases—Caused by afflictions in ♑, and tend to the external form; afflictions in ♋ or ♍ tend to internal parasitic disorders, as in the stomach or bowels, such as worms. (See "Pruritis" under Itch; Scabies; "Worms" under Stomach; Worms).

Worm Remedy—(See Anthelmintic).

PARCHED — Parched Body — The ☽ in ♌ and afflicted by the ☉ or ♂ when taken ill (Hor'y). (See "Hot and Dry Body" under Dry; "Liable to Fever" under Fever; "Animal Heat", "Excessive Bodily Heat", under Heat).

Parching Diseases — (See "High Fever", "Parched", under Fever; "Dry and Hot Diseases" under Heat).

PARENCHYMA — Connective Tissue — Soft, Cellular Tissue — The Functioning or Secreting Structure of an Organ — The Pathological Action of the ♃ Group of Herbs tends to especially affect the Pulmonary Parenchyma. (See Cells, Glands, Secretions, Tissues).

PARENTS — The 10th and 4th Houses, and the planets in them, and their rulers, show the parents and the conditions affecting them. The ☉ and ♄ are allotted to the person of the father, and the ☽ and ♀ to the mother. The 10th H. rules the father in a male nativity, and the mother in a female horoscope. The 4th H. rules the father in a female nativity, and the mother in a male nativity. Guardians and Godfathers come under the rule of ♃. In diseases and afflictions to the parents the ☉ and ♀ should be principally observed by day, and the ☽ and ♄ by night. Many subjects in this book which have to do with parents are given in the Articles on Children, Family, Father, Husband, Mother, Wife. (See these subjects). The following planetary influences are to be considered in the map of the child, as the radical map and directions of the child show many of the conditions which will affect the parents, and show the nature of the possible events in the life of a parent, the diseases, afflictions, possible length of life, etc.

Accident to a Parent — Danger to a Parent—Danger of Accidents, Hurts, Injuries, Wounds, etc.—♆ in the 10th H., and possibly by water, and during early youth or childhood; ♂ to the ☌, P., □ or ☍ the ☉, ♄, ☽, or ♀ by dir.; the Asc. to the ☌, P., □ or ☍ ♂ by dir.; malefics afflicted in the 4th or 10th H. at B., and by dir.; malefics in the 4th or 10th H. at a Solar Rev. (See "Accidents To" under Father, Mother).

Adoption of Children—(See Adoption; "Death", "Separation", in this section).

Affection—The Love and Affection of Parents for Children—(See "Love" in this section).

Afflicted—Affliction to the Parents—Sickness—Illness—Indisposition—The Parents Suffer—The ☉ directed to Cor Leo; the ☉ afflicted in the 12th H.; the M.C. or Nadir to the ☌, P., □ or ☍ ♄ or ♂ by dir.; malefics in the 4th or 10th H. at a Solar Rev.; the 1st Decan. of ♓ on the Asc., affliction of a parent, or the early death of one. (See the various paragraphs in this section).

Bad Children — Worries and Sorrows to Parents Thru Bad and Unfortunate Children—(See "Parents" under Children; "Injured" in this section).

Benefits — To Parents — (See "Good Health" in this section).

Creative Powers Of — (See Barren, Fruitful, which influences are in the map of the parent).

Danger To—(See "Accidents" in this section).

Day and Night Nativities — Diseases of the Parents In—(See "Mother" under Night).

Death of Parents—Or a Parent—

(1) Death of Parents—The ☉ or ☽ to the ☌ or ill-asp. ♄ by dir., and especially with women; ♄ or ♂ afflicting the ☉, ☽, Asc., M.C., or Nadir by dir., often kills or afflicts a parent; ♄ in the 4th or 10th H., and afflicted by the ☉ or ☽; the Asc. or M.C. afflicted by the malefics ♄ or ♂; the Asc. ☌ ♆, ♄, or ♂ by dir., often corresponds to the time of death of a parent; the M.C. to the ☌, P., □ or ☍ ♄, and espec. if the ☉ be elevated above the Earth, and ♄ be ori. of the ☉; the M.C. to the ☌ or ill-asp. ♂ by dir.; lord of the 8th H. in the 5th H., and caused by worries thru bad children; transits of malefics thru the 4th or 10th H. if they afflict these houses at B.; malefics in the 4th or 10th H. at a Solar Rev.; the Nadir afflicted by the ☌ or ill-asps. of ♄ or ♂ by dir.; ♀ by dir. afflicting the M.C. or Nadir, as by the □ aspect. (See "Early Death", and the various paragraphs in this section: "Directions", "Worries", under Children; "Early Death" under Early; "Death' under Father, Mother; "Short Life" under Life).

(2) Death of Parents Before the Native—♄ afflicted in the 10th or 4th H., by disease; ♂ afflicted in the 10th or 4th, danger of, by an accident or swift fever. (See (1) in this paragraph).

(3) Death of Parents, or a Parent, Thru Bad Children—(See (1) in this paragraph).

(4) Death of Parents In the Youth of the Native—Case—See "Saturn in the Tenth", No. 831, in 1001 N.N. (See (1) in this paragraph).

Directions — Parents Affected by the Directions of Children — With young children, the directions of the M.C., the Nadir, and the ☉ and ☽ to the malefics, tend to affect the parents, and often cause their sickness, and in some cases their death, or the death of one parent, according to the rules of a male, or female nativity. (See "Directions" under Children).

Drink — Drunkenness — Parents, or a Parent, Liable to Drunkenness and Neglect of Children — The ☽ in ♓ in the 12th H., and afflicted. (See "Lewdness" in this section; "Father" under Drunkenness; "Drink" under Husband, Wife).

Early Death of Parents—Or of a Parent—Short Life For — Parents Do Not Live to be Old—Malefics in the 4th or 10th H. at B., and by dir., or at a Solar Rev., or by transit; the death of one parent is indicated by an affliction to the 4th or 10th H., and may be the father or mother, according to the sex of native; the death of both parents may take place at nearly the same time, or soon apart, if both the 4th and 10th H. are afflicted by malefics at B., and by dir., or at a Solar Rev.; the ☉, ☽, ♄, or ♀ severely afflicted at B. in map of child; the ☽ increasing, or at Full, sepr. from ♃ and applying to ♄; ♅ in the 10th H., and near the Meridian, early loss of one; ♄ in the 10th or 4th H., and afflicted; the Asc. or M.C. afflicted by ♄ or ♂; lord of the 8th or 11th H. a malefic, and in the 4th H., and afflicted; the 8° ♎ on the Asc; the 11° ♎ on the Asc., early death of the father, or the father unknown to him; the 1st Decan. of ♓ on the Asc., ruled by ♄. (See "Early Death" under Father, Mother; "Separation" in this section).

Family—(See the various paragraphs under Family).

Father—Illness of—Death of—Length of Life—(See the paragraphs under Father).

Females — (See "Parents" under Females).

Fever—Parents Suffer from Fevers—(See "Fevers" under Father, Mother).

Good Health—Benefits to the Parents—The ☉ and ☽ well-aspected at B., and free from serious afflictions; the progression of the benefics into the 4th and 5th H. of the child indicate a period of good health and good fortune for the parents if these houses are also free from the affliction of malefics, and the map of the child otherwise shows good health and long life for the parents; the M.C. to the ☌ or P. asp. the ☉ except when the ☉ is ruler of the 5th H. (See "Long Life" under Father, Mother).

Godfather—Godmother—(See Guardians).

Grandparents—(See Grandparents).

Guardians—Godfather—Godmother—(See Guardians).

Health Good—Health Bad—(See Afflicted, Early Death, Fever, Good Health, Long Life, Short Life, and the various paragraphs in this section).

Heredity—(See the various paragraphs and references under Heredity).

Hurts To—(See "Accident To" in this section; the various paragraphs under Father, Mother).

Husband—(See the various paragraphs under Husband).

Illness To—(See Afflicted, Fever, and the various paragraphs in this section).

Indisposition—(See "Afflicted" in this section).

Inflammatory Attacks — Fevers and Inflammations—(See "Infirmities" under Father; Fevers, Inflammations, under Mother).

Injured by Children—Lord of the 7th H. in the 5th, or lord of the 7th a malefic. (See Bad Children, Love, in this section).

Injured by Parents—Children Suffer Injury Thru Parents—Malefics in the 4th or 10th H., or lords of the 4th or 10th a malefic in map of child; lords of the 4th and 10th H. in □ or ☍ asp. each other. (See Drink, Love, Separation, in this section).

Injuries To—(See "Accident To" in this section).

Killing of a Parent—(See "Patricide" under Father).

Lewdness—Of Both Parents—♆ in the 10th H., ☍ ♄, ♀, and ☿ in the 4th; ♆ ☌ ☽ in the 10th H., and ♄ or ♂ ☌ ♀ in the 4th H. (See Lewd).

Life Endangered—♆ in the 10th H., according to the sex of the nativity, the father in a male horoscope, and the mother in a female nativity. (See "Accident To" in this section; "Danger To" under Father, Mother).

Long Life—(See "Long Life" under Father, Life, Mother).

Love and Affection — The Love and Affection of Parents for their Children is ruled and denoted by the 7th H. and its conditions. Benefics in this house tend to a greater love and affection, which is also strengthened by a benefic in the 5th H. of a parent, or a benefic ruling the 5th and 7th. Malefics in the 7th H. may make the parents cold and ill-disposed towards their children, which may be added to by the influence of malefics in the 5th or 11th H., causing the children to bring sorrow and misfortune upon the parents. Saturn weak and afflicted in the 7th H. of the child denotes antipathy from the father, and the ☽ so situated, antagonism from the mother. Also the conditions of the 10th and 4th H. should be noted, and judgment formed according to the sex of the native. (See Injured by Children, Injured by Parents, Separation, in this section; "Worries" under Children).

Matricide — (See "Patricide" under Father).

Mother—(See the various paragraphs under Mother).

Night Nativities—When the Parents are Afflicted In—(See "Mother" under Night).

Old Age—Parents Live To—Do Not Live To—(See Death, Early Death, Long Life, Short Life, in this section; "Death At Middle Life" under Middle Life).

Parents Die Before Native — (See Death, Early Death, in this section).

Patricide — (See "Patricide" under Father).

Relation of Children to Parents — Children a Blessing or Misfortune— (See Blessing, Parents, Worries, under Children; Eleventh House; "Drink", "Love and Affection", in this section).

Separation from Parents—The ☽ sepr. from ♃ and applying to the ☉, and especially if the ☽ be in ♈, ♏, ♑, or ♒; the ☽ sepr. from the ☉ and apply. to ♄ in a day geniture; the ☽ sepr. from ♀ and apply. to the ☉, separation from parents thru a bitter dispute; the ☽ increasing, or at Full, sepr. from ♃ and applying to ♄, separated and adopted by a stranger. (See Adoption; Death, Drink, Love and Affection, in this section).

Separation of Parents—A Separation In the Family—♅ afflictions and influences cause separations of all kinds; ♅ afflicted at B., and by dir., or ♅ afflicting the Midheaven, cusp of the 4th H., the Asc., ☉, ☽, or hyleg. (See "Death In the Family" under Family; "Unhappy Marriage" under Marriage; Death, Early Death, in this section).

Short Life—(See Death, Early Death, in this section).

Sickness of Parents — (See "Directions" under Children; Afflicted, Fever, and the various paragraphs in this section).

Significators of Parents—The ☉ and ♀ are Significators of the parents in a day nativity, and the ☽ and ♄ by night. The ☉ by day represents the father, and ♄ by night; ♀ by day, the mother, and the ☽ by night. In making a study of the diseases and afflictions to a parent, the severity, prognosis, nature of the disorder, etc., these distinctions should be noted.

Sorrow Thru Children—(See "Injured by Children" in this section).

Suffer—The Parents Suffer—(See Afflicted, Directions, Fever, Injured, and the various paragraphs in this section).

Violent Death — Danger of — The ☽ sepr. from the ☉ and applying to ♂ in a day geniture. (See "Patricide" under Father; "Death" under Violent).

Wicked Children — (See Eleventh House).

Wife—(See the various paragraphs under Wife).

Worries Thru Children — (See "Injured" in this section; Parents, Worries, under Children).

Wounds To—(See "Accidents" in this section).

PARESIS—Slight Paralysis—(See "Paresis" under Paralysis).

PAROSMIA — (See this subject under Smell).

PAROTID GLAND—The Parotids—A large Salivary Gland in front of the Ear—Ruled by the ♉ Sign.

Diseases Of—Afflictions in ♉ or ♏. (See Bubo).

Mumps—Inflammation of—Parotiditis —Glandular Fever In the Neck—An Acute Infectious Disease Attended with Swelling of the Parotid Gland, and also Swollen Testes in some Cases —A ♉ disease, and afflictions in ♉; ♄, ♂, or ♀ afflicted in ♉; ♀ in ♉ in the 6th H., afflicted, or afflicting the ☽ or Asc.; Subs at LCP, SP (7D), and KP. (See Saliva).

PAROXYSMS—A Period of Increase, or Crisis of a Disease—A Spasm or Fit—

Asthma—Paroxysmal Dyspnoea—(See Asthma).

Coughing—Paroxysms of—(See "Convulsive" under Cough).

Crises In Disease—(See Crises).

Dyspnoea — Paroxysms In Breathing — (See "Labored" under Breathing; Dyspnoea).

Facial Paroxysms—(See "Paroxysms" under Face).

Headaches—Paroxysmal Headaches— (See Migraine).

Nervous Excitation—Paroxysms of— (See "Excitable" under Excitement).

Renal Paroxysms—(See "Paroxysms" under Kidneys).

Spasm or Fit—A ♅ disease, and caused by ♅ afflictions. (See Fits, Spasmodic).

Tachycardia — Heart Paroxysm—(See "Spasm" under Heart).

PARRICIDE — (See "Patricide" under Father).

PARROT FEVER—(See Psittacosis).

PARTIAL—

Partial Blindness — (See Gutta Serena).

Partial Deafness—(See "Partial" under Hearing).

Partial Paralysis—(See Paresis, Partial, under Paralysis).

PARTICULAR DISEASE—To Determine the Course Any Particular Disease May Follow—(See Amelioration, Continuity, Course, Crises, Decumbiture; "Better" under Disease; Duration, End, Fatal; "Course" under Irregular; Moderation, Prognosis, Termination, Worse).

PART OF FORTUNE—(⊕)—A point in the Horoscope where the rays of the ☉ and ☽ converge, and where the ☽ would be if the ☉ were exactly rising. Many Authors refer to the Part of Fortune as a benefic influence, and to indicate good fortune, good health, etc., when in favorable aspect to the Significators in the map. Wilson in his Dictionary says that the Part of Fortune is but a "Phantom hatched in the brain of Ptolemy", and has no influence whatever. Some Writers say the Part of Fortune may become Hyleg in a Nocturnal Horoscope if the ☽ be decreasing in light, and both the ☉ and ☽ are below the horizon, and not in a hylegiacal place. They also say the Part of Fortune may become Anareta when the ☉, ☽, or Asc. are hyleg.

The student should learn how to compute the place of the Part of Fortune, both in the Zodiac, and Mundane, and there are good Chapters and Articles on the subject in the various Textbooks and Dictionaries of Astrology. (See Anareta, Hyleg).

PARTNER—Companion—Associate—

Business Partner—Illness or Death of —♄ afflicted in the 12th H., from some lingering and chronic disease; ♂ afflicted in the 12th H., from some fever or inflammatory disease. Also malefics afflicted in the 7th H. tend to afflictions to, death of, or unfortunate relations with a business partner. (See "Lawsuits" under Public).

Marriage Partner—Illness or Death of—(See Husband; "Death", "Sickly", under Marriage Partner; Wife).

PARTS OF THE BODY—Members—Organs—

Absence of a Part—(See Missing).

Afflicted Parts—The Parts, Organs, or Members of the body usually afflicted are those ruled by the signs containing the malefics, or a badly afflicted ☉ or ☽. The Asc. denotes the part of the body liable to affliction from external causes. (See External). The Sign in which the Significator of disease is found indicates the Part, or Organs, principally affected. The Parts afflicted are also those containing the ☉ or ☽ if the Lights are in ♂ or ill-asp. with malefics. The places occupied by the malefics at B. are always considered places of affliction. (See Malefics). The Part of the Body afflicted is also shown by that part of the Sign, Face or Decanate of the Sign, which is rising upon the Eastern horizon at B., and especially if afflicted, or containing a malefic. (See "Locating the Disease" under Diagnosis). The Part of an Organ afflicted is denoted by the Face, Decanate, or Division of the Sign containing the afflicting planet, and which indicates whether the upper, middle, or lower part of the organ is afflicted. (See Decanates; "Organs" under Middle; Navamsa; "Lower Part" under Organs; "Organs" under Upper). The Asc. afflicted by a malefic tends to trouble in the head. (See "Disorders Of" under Head). For the influences causing diseases, infirmities, and afflictions to the various parts and organs of the body, see the Part, Organ, or Member in the alphabetical arrangement. The Sixth House should be noted, as this is the House of Health, and the Sign, Signs, and Planets ruling this house at B., and the parts of the body coming under these influences, are very subject to disease and weakness when the vitality becomes lowered for any reason, or thru worry and anxiety, bad thinking, and adverse planetary influences by Direction, Transit, or Progression, etc. Also observe the Sign and House containing the ☽, and especially with females, and the planets to which the ☽ may be applying, or from which she is separating, as such influence of the ☽ helps to form a judgment as to the part of the body afflicted, and also the nature of the disease. (See "Disease"

under Nature; Quality, Sixth House, Type, Vulnerable).

Blemishes — (See Blemishes, Defects, Deformities, Imperfections, Marks, Moles, Scars, etc.).

Conformity Between the Parts—Conformity in the Members—(See "Conformity" under Members).

Defects—(See "Blemishes" in this section).

Disease—Members or Parts Afflicted by Disease—(See "Afflicted Parts" in this section; Disease, Members, Organs).

Enlargement of Parts—(See Enlarged; "Abnormal Growth" under Growth; "Over-Developed" under Organs).

External Causes—Parts Afflicted By —Are denoted by the Asc., and the part, or parts, ruled by the Asc. at B. (See Ascendant, External).

Fever In a Part—Or Organ—(See the paragraphs under Fever).

Induration of a Part—(See Hardening, Hypertrophy, Sclerosis, Thickening).

Inflammation In a Part — (See the paragraphs under Inflammation).

Injury to a Part—(See Injuries).

Intellectual Parts—All Imperfections In—All Evils In—(See Intellect, Mental, Mind).

Internal Parts — Disorders In — (See Internal).

Irregular Action Of—(See Erratic, Irregular, Spasmodic).

Left Side Suffers—(See Left).

Lower Parts — (See Lower; "Lower Part" under Organs).

Marks, Moles, Scars—(See these subjects).

Members—(See the paragraphs and references under Members).

Middle Parts—(See "Organs" under Middle).

Missing Parts—(See Limbs, Missing).

Moving Parts—(See Moving).

Organs—(See the subjects under Organs).

Parts Liable to Suffer—(See Afflicted Parts, Disease, in this section; Ascendant, Malefics, Sixth House).

Right Side Suffers—(See Right).

Rush of Blood — To a Part — (See Rush).

Sensitive Parts—(See "Organs" under Sensitive).

Spasmodic Action of Parts—(See Erratic, Jerky, Spasmodic, Tics, Tremors, Twitchings).

Upper Parts—(See "Lower Part" under Organs; Upper).

Vulnerable Parts—(See Vulnerable).

Weak Parts — Those ruled by the Signs and Houses containing the malefics, and especially ♄, if afflicted. (See "Weak Spots" under Weak).

Weakest Part—The part ruled by the sign containing ♄, or several malefics. (See Vulnerable; "Weakest" under Weak).

PARTURITION — Childbirth — Delivery —Confinement — Accouchment—Puerpera—Puerperal—Pertaining to Child-Bearing, etc.—Ruled by the ☽ and the 5th H. conditions. The time of birth of a child is ruled by the movement of the ☽, but it is the influence of ♂ which ushers the child into the world. The rules of the Prenatal Epoch govern the time of the Accouchment. (See "Moment of Birth" under Moment; Prenatal Epoch). Normal births are ruled by ♃. Abnormal births, and dangerous and difficult parturition, are caused by the influences of the malefics at the time, or such influences in the 5th H. of the mother at B. The following subjects have to do with Parturition, Childbirth, and the normal, abnormal, dangerous, difficult, premature, or delayed entrance of the child into the world. See these subjects in the alphabetical arrangement when not more fully considered here—

Abortion; Accident At Birth—Extreme Danger In—Danger to the Mother and Child—The ☉ or ☽ to the ☌ or ill-asp. ♂ by dir. at the time; ♅ afflicted in the 5th H. at B., and afflicting the 5th H., or ruler of the 5th by dir.; ♅ afflicted in ♌ at B.; ♂ afflicted in the 5th or 11th H.; ♂ afflicted in ♌, the sign affiliated with the 5th H.; the afflictions of ♂ are very dangerous in cases of childbirth, and especially if ♂ is in the sex sign ♏ at B., or in ♏ by transit or direction at time of the Accouchment. These influences also often make it necessary for an instrumental delivery (and especially if ♄ is involved in the configuration causing delay), excision of the foetus (Caesarian Operation), or extraction of the foetus in mutilated parts. The ☽ or ♀ badly afflicted by ♄ or ♂ during pregnancy at the times corresponding to the monthly periods, bring danger of an accident, or dangerous trouble to the mother during parturition. (See "Death At Birth" under Children; "Excision", "Mutilation", under Foetus; "Accidents At Birth" under Infancy; "Injured" in this section).

Almost Died In Confinement—Case—See "Four", No. 954 in 1001 N.N.

Asphyxiation—At Birth—(See "Birth" under Asphyxia; "Delayed Births" under Children).

Bad Time For Confinement—Bad Time for the Mother After Confinement — The ☽ afflicted at the time of birth of the child may cause death of the mother, puerperal fever, and dangerous complications. (See Accident, Death, Difficult, Excision, Fever, in this section).

Birth—(See the various paragraphs under Birth).

Born Before Time—Cases and Influences—(See Abortion; "Eight Months Children" under Children; Miscarriage, Premature).

Born Dead—(See Stillborn).

Breathing—Child Does Not Breathe Until Two Hours After Birth—Case—See "Foot", No. 106 in 1001 N.N.

Breech Presentation—Usually caused by ♄ in ♏ in the map of the mother.

Case—See "Breech Presentation", No. 075 in 1001 N.N.

Caesarian Operation—(See "Excision" under Foetus).

Caul—Child Born with Caul Over Face —(See "Caul" under Face).

Child—For the various conditions affecting the Child at birth, see the paragraphs under Birth, Children, Foetus, and in this Article.

Childbed Fever—(See "Puerperal Fever" under Puerperal).

Conception—(See the paragraphs under Conception).

Convulsions—(See "Convulsions" under Puerperal).

Danger In Childbirth—A Dangerous Event — (See Accident, Bad Time, Death, Difficult, Excision, Injury, and the various paragraphs in this section).

Dead—Child Born Dead — (See Stillborn).

Death—(1) Of Child—(See "Death of Children", Sec. 3, under Children). (2) Death of Mother In Childbirth—Danger of—The ☉ or ☽ to the ☌ or ill-asp. ♂ at time of delivery, and especially if ♂ afflict the ☉ at B., or occupy the 5th H.; the ☉ or ♂ in the 5th H. at B., and the ☉ to the ☌ or ill-asp. ♂ by dir. at delivery. Case—Death In Childbirth— See "Elizabeth", No. 562 in 1001 N.N. (See "Death by Miscarriage" under Abortion; "Death" under Hemorrhage, Mother; "Puerperal Fever" under Puerperal; Almost Died, Bad Time, Caesarian, Difficult, Hemorrhage, in this section).

Delayed Birth — (See "Birth" under Asphyxia; "Delayed Births" under Children; Prenatal Epoch; "Difficult" in this section).

Delivery—(See Danger, Delayed, Difficult, Excision, Premature, and the various paragraphs in this section).

Difficult Parturition—Birth Delayed— Extreme Danger In — A Dangerous Event—Painful and Difficult—The ☽ afflicted in ♏; the ☽ to the ☌ or ill-asp. ♂ by dir., and ♂ in the 5th H. at B., or afflicting the ☽; ♅ or ♂ afflicted in ♏; ♅ afflicted in ♌ or the 5th H.; ♂ afflicted in the 5th H.; ♀ in bad aspect to the ☽ at B., or at delivery. (See Delayed, Instrumental, Painful, and the various paragraphs in this section; "Danger To" under Wife).

Excision of Foetus—(See "Excision" under Foetus).

Feet First—Born Feet First—♄ afflicted in ♏ tends to malposition of the foetus, and to be born feet first, or breech. Case—See "Soraby", No. 089 in 1001 N.N.

Fever—Danger of Childbed Fever— (See "Puerperal Fever" under Puerperal).

Foetus—Excision of—(See Foetus).

Gestation — (See the various paragraphs under Gestation).

Hemorrhage—Flooding at Delivery— Great Loss of Blood—Danger of Death By—The ☉ or ☽ to the ☌ or ill-asp. ♂ by dir., and ♂ afflicting the ☉ or ☽ at

B., or in the 5th H.; the ☽ in the 8th H., and afflicted by ♂; ♂ afflicted in ♉ or ♏, and especially if in the 5th H. at B.; ♂ afflicted in the 8th H.; ♂ in the 8th H., and afflicting planets in the 5th H. Case—See Fig. 8-I, Chap. XIX, in the book, "Astro-Diagnosis", by the Heindels. (See "Death" under Hemorrhage; Miscarriage).

Incommodities—To Those Bearing Children—An Eclipse of the ☉ in the 2nd Decan. of ♉.

Infancy—(See the various paragraphs under Infancy).

Infant Dies At Birth—(See "Death At Birth" under Children, Infancy).

Infection At Birth—(See "Infections" under Infancy).

Injury At Birth—Instrumental Delivery—♅ afflicted in ♏ in map of the mother. (See Accident, Maimed, Mangled, in this section; "Death At Birth" under Children).

Instrumental Delivery—Necessity For —♅ afflicted in ♏; ♂ in the 8th H., and afflicting planets in the 5th H. Cases —See Fig. 8-I mentioned under "Hemorrhage" in this section. Also see "Four", Nos. 953 and 955, in 1001 N.N. (See Accidents, Injury, in this section; Prenatal Epoch).

Killed—Child Had to be Killed to Deliver—Case—See "Four", No. 952 in 1001 N.N. (See "Mangled" in this section).

Large At Birth—(See "Birth" under Large).

Lateral Position—Of Foetus—(See "Lateral" under Foetus).

Loss of Blood—In Childbirth—(See "Hemorrhage" in this section).

Maimed—Child Maimed At Birth, or Maimed from Birth—(See Accident, Injury, Instrumental, in this section; Maimed).

Mangled—Child Mangled or Mutilated At Birth—(See "Killed" in this section; "Mutilated" under Foetus).

Mania—Puerperal Mania—(See "Mania" under Puerperal).

Metritis—Inflammation of the Womb Complications—(See "Metritis" under Womb).

Midwives—(See Midwives, Nurses, Obstetricians).

Miscarriage—(See Abortion, Miscarriage).

Mother—For the various conditions affecting the mother in childbirth see the subjects in this Article. Also see the paragraphs under Birth, Children, Congenital, Foetus, Gestation, Maternity, Mother, Pregnancy, Prenatal Epoch, Wife).

Nervous Shock—In Childbirth—Case —See Case mentioned under "Hemorrhage" in this section.

Normal Births—Are ruled by ♃; ♃ in ♌ or ♏, or in the 5th H. at B., and well-aspected. (See "Astral Body" under Astral; "Cause of Birth" under Birth; "Birth Of" under Foetus).

Obstetricians—(See this subject).

Painful Parturition—Painful and Severe—♄ afflicted in ♉ or ♏; ♄ ☌ ♆ in ♉ or ♏; ♂ afflicted in ♏; afflictions in ♉ or ♏; Subs at PP. Case of Painful Delivery—See the Case under "Feet First" in this section. (See Difficult, Instrumental, in this section).

Pains—Suffers with After-Pains—♄ or ♂ afflicted in ♉ or ♏ at B.; Subs at PP.

Pregnancy—(See the various paragraphs under Conception, Gestation, Pregnancy, Prenatal Epoch).

Premature Birth—(See Abortion; "Eight Months Children" under Children; Miscarriage; "Premature Birth" under Premature).

Prevented—(See "Difficult" in this section; "Prevented" under Children; "Excision" under Foetus).

Puerperal Fever—Puerperal Convulsions — Puerperal Mania — (See Puerperal).

Quadruplets—(See Multiple).

Seven Months Children—(See "Seven Months Children" under Children. Also for Cases of, see Premature).

Severe and Painful—(See "Painful" in this section).

Shock—Suffers Great Nervous Shock In Childbirth—(See "Nervous Shock" in this section).

Single Births—(See "Single Births" under Children).

Stillborn—Cases—(See Stillborn).

Suffocation At Birth—(See "Asphyxiation" in this section).

Time of Delivery—To Know the Time Of—Time of Advent of a Child—When a pregnant person wishes to know the time of delivery, it is usual to direct the lord of the Asc., or the ☽, to the cusp of the 5th H. by oblique ascension, according to which of the two is nearer, and allow a day for every degree in the arc of direction. Or observe on what day ♃ or ♀ will transit the cusp of the 5th H., and look for the birth on that day. (Hor'y). (See "Cause of Birth", "Moment of Birth", under Birth; "Birth of a Child", "Born", under Children; "Moment of Conception" under Conception). The time of birth, or delivery, may be some days before, or after what would appear to be the normal time, according to the Order to which the case belongs in the Prenatal Epoch considerations. (See Prenatal Epoch; Delayed, Premature, in this section).

Triplets Born—(See Triplets, Twins).

Twins Born—(See Twins).

Two Weeks Premature—(See Case under Premature).

Unusual Diseases—At Childbirth—(See "Eyes", "Infections At Birth", under Infancy). For unusual complications to the mother see the various paragraphs in this section and under Puerperal.

When Will the Child Be Born?—(See Delayed, Premature, Time of Delivery, in this section).

Wife Benefits by Childbirth—♃ well-aspected in the 11th H. (See the various paragraphs under Wife).

PASSAGES—Channels—Canals—

Narrowing Of — Caused by ♅ or ♄. (See Constrictions, Stricture).

One Passage — A Common Outlet to the Rectum and Bladder—(See Cloaca).

Sex Channels — Lack of Proper Sex Channels—(See Canals; "Channels and Vents" under Genitals).

PASSION — Intense Emotion — Intense Sexual Desire—Erotic Disturbances— Abuses of the Passional Nature—Morbid Passions—Excess of Passion—Passionate Diseases and Disorders from Passional Excesses, etc.—The Passions are ruled principally by ♂ and the ♏ sign. Are also ruled by the ☽ and the Asc. Animal Lust and Passion are ruled by the ☽ and ♂. The Liver is the seat of the passional desires. (See "Desire Body" under Desire; the Introduction under Liver. Also see Reins). The afflictions of ♂ tend to increase of the passion. Mars rules passion in men, and ♀ in women. The good aspects of ♂ stimulate the sex feelings along lawful lines, but the bad aspects of ♂ tend to destroy it by over-stimulation and excesses. In good aspect, ♄ tends to control passion, but in evil aspect perverts, destroys, or suppresses it. The ☉ also tends to give passion. Mercury in ♏ tends to center the mind upon sex and to give morbid sex desires. Since the separation of the sexes in the Lemurian Age, it is said the greatest problem of Earth life is to learn to properly control and use the creative force, avoid its abuse, perversion, waste. The creative function is at present under the control of Man, and to use at his will for pleasure or propagation, whereas in the earlier Races this function was under the control of the Higher Powers, and propagation was limited to certain times of the year when the planetary influences were favorable for such. The abuse of sex, sex excesses, and misuse of the creative power, is said to be the cause of sickness, suffering, sorrow, and earlier death upon the Earth today. From the Occult standpoint the question of Sex, its proper use, and how to transmute it to its proper use, is elaborately considered in the book, "The Key of Destiny", and other books by Dr. Homer and Mrs. Curtiss, Founders of the Order of Christian Mystics, or "The Order of the Fifteen." Passion is legitimate when properly used, and should not be killed out, but controlled. Each of us has within us much of the animal, but the Higher Mind should rule, and the animal in us guided, directed and controlled. From the human, or lower mind side, much is given in the Textbooks of Astrology along the lines of passion, its abuse, excesses, deviations, perversions, etc., and the following paragraphs and subjects have to do with such matters, as gathered, tabulated, and arranged from my Library of books. See the following subjects in the alphabetical arrangement when not more fully considered here—

Abnormal Sex Desires—♂ ☌ or P. asp. the ☽; ♂ ☌ the ☽ or ♀ in ♏. (See

Amorous, Venery; "Passional Excesses", and the various paragraphs in this section).

Addict — A Sex-Addict — (See "Sex-Addict" under Marriage Partner; "Addict" under Sex).

Adulterous—(See "Adulterous" under Love Affairs).

Affection—Inordinate Affection—(See "Free Love" under Free; "Unlawful Affections" under Love Affairs).

All Sensuous Enjoyments — Given To —(See "Sensuous" under Sensuality).

Amativeness; Amorous; Amours — Illicit Amours—(See "Amours" under Love Affairs).

Anaphrodisiacs — Remedies which Lessen Passional Desire—(See Anaphrodisiacs).

Anger; Animal Propensities — (See "Animal Instincts" under Animal).

Apathy—Lack of Passion — (See Apathy; "Free from Passion" in this section).

Aphrodisiacs — Medicines Which Increase Passional Desire—(See Aphrodisiacs).

Appetites — Over-Indulgence of the Sex Appetites—(See Amorous; "Over-Indulgence" under Appetites; "Love Affairs", "Sex Excesses", under Excesses; "Passional Excesses" in this section).

Ardent Passion — Over-Ardent — (See "Ardent" under Love Affairs).

Attackers of Women—(See Rape).

Bohemian Pleasures — (See "Bohemian" under Pleasure).

Celibacy; Chaotic Acts — Chaotic and Unnatural Acts—(See Unnatural).

Chastity — (See "Chaste" under Females).

Childhood—Unusual Passion In At Puberty—(See Puberty; "Young People" in this section).

Choleric Passion—(See Choleric).

Clandestine Relations—(See "Clandestine" under Sex).

Command—Control—Has Great Command and Control Over the Passions— The ☉ exalted and dignified at B., and the ☽ well-aspected by ♃ and ♀. (See Apathy, Celibacy, Cohabitation, Self-Control; "Regulated" under Sex).

Debauchery; Deportment — (See the subjects and references under Conduct, Love Affairs, Morals, Sex, and also in this Article).

Depraved; Desires—(See the subjects under Desire).

Deviations; Diseases — Arising from Sex Excesses or Irregularities — (See Amorous; "Diseases" under Excesses; "Health Injured" under Men; "Diseases" under Sex; Venery; Passional Excesses, Too Much Passion, Wastes Energies, in this section).

Emotions—(See "Intensified" under Emotions).

Enjoyments — All Sensuous Enjoyments—(See "Sensuous" under Sensuality; the various paragraphs in this section).

Erotic Mania—Morbid Sex Desires— (See "Erotic" under Mania).

Exaggerated Sex Desires—(See Amorous, Lewd; "Erotic" under Mania; Nymphomania; Abnormal, Passional Excesses, Unbridled, Violence, and the various paragraphs in this section).

Excess of Amorous Indulgence—(See Amorous).

Excess of Passion—The ☉, ☽, ♂, and ♀ in ♌ in the 5th H.; ♂ Sig. ☐ or ☍ ♀; ♀ Sig. ☐ or ☍ ♂; ♌ on the cusp of the 5th H. (See Abnormal, Morbid, Passional Excesses, Strong Passions, and other paragraphs in this section).

Excesses—(See "Passional Excesses" in this section).

Exhibitionism—Public Exposure of the Sex Organs—(See Exhibition; Notoriety" in this section).

Eyes—The Eyes Full of Amorous Enticements—(See "Amorous" under Eyes).

Flower—Passion Flower—(See "Sun Group" under Herbs).

Fornicators—(See "Clandestine" under Sex).

Free from Passion—Apathy—Little or No Passion—The ☽ Sig. in ♋; the ☽ in partile the Asc.; the ☉, ☽, and ♀ free from the affliction of malefics at B.; ♄ afflicted in ♈ or ♌. (See Apathy, Aversions, Bachelors, Celibacy, Cohabitation, Deviations; "Anchorite" under Husband; Indifferent; "Aversion" under Marriage).

Free Love—(See "Free Love" under Free).

Genitals—Diseased from Passional Excesses and Irregularities—(See "Diseases" under Genitals).

Gratification—Of the Passions—Men Prone to Violence In—(See "Violence" in this section).

Great Command—Of the Passions—(See "Command" in this section).

Habits—(See Bad Habits, Diseases, Sex Habits, under Habits).

Harlots—Becomes One—Injured By—(See Harlots).

Heart—Passion or Trembling of—(See "Passion" under Heart).

Homosexuality; Ileac Passion—(See Ileac).

Illicit Amours—(See "Amours" under Love Affairs).

Immodest; Immorality—In Sex Matters—(See "Free Love" under Free; Homosexuality; "Adulterous" under Love Affairs; "Loose Morals" under Morals; Perversions; "Clandestine" under Sex; the various subjects in this Article).

Incest—(See "Incest" under Perversions).

Indulgence—Over-Indulgence of the Passions—Excesses In—(See Amorous, Lascivious, Lewd, Licentious, Lust, Venery; "Passional Excesses" in this section).

Infamous; Inflamed with Passion—(See Amorous; "Erotic" under Mania; Nymphomania; "Exaggerated" in this section).

Lack of Passion—(See "Free From" in this section).

Lascivious; Lewd; Liaisons—(See "Liaisons" under Love Affairs).

Libidinous; Licentiousness;

Love Affairs—(See the various paragraphs under Love Affairs).

Love Passion—(See "Love Passion" under Love Affairs).

Low and Base—(See Low).

Lower Passions—Carried Away By—(See Amorous, Lascivious, Licentiousness, Lust; "Low Pleasures" under Pleasures; "Excess of Passion" in this section).

Lust; Mania—Sex Mania—(See "Erotic" under Mania).

Marriage—(See the various paragraphs under Husband, Marriage, Marriage Partner, Wife).

Masturbation—Self-Abuse—(See "Solitary" under Vice).

Men—(See "Sex Gratification", and the various paragraphs under Men; "Violence" in this section).

Middle Life—Dies Before Middle Life from Sex Excesses—(See "Death Before Middle Life" under Middle Life).

Mind Absorbed with Passion—The ☉, ☽, ♀, ☿, and many planets in the sex sign ♏. (See Excess, Mania, Nymphomania, and the various paragraphs in this section).

Modesty; Morals—(See "Loose Morals", and the various paragraphs under Morals).

Morbid Passional Desires—Morbid Imaginations—(See "Morbid" under Imagination; "Erotic" under Mania; "Desires" under Morbid; Nymphomania, Perversions, Unsavory, Vice; the various paragraphs in this section).

Nakedness—Exposure of the Sex Organs—(See Exhibitionism, Notoriety, in this section; "Outrageous" under Insanity).

Notoriety of the Passions—Exposure of the Passions—Immodest—In male horoscopes, ♀ afflicted by ♄, ♂, and ☿, and ♀ be in the West at B., tends to make men wanton, licentious, and to display their passions publicly. In a female horoscope, the ☉, ☽, ♂, and ♀ in male signs, and ♀ sorely afflicted by ♄, ♂, and ☿, and with ♂ and ♀ oriental and diurnal, tend to notoriety of the passions, and to make women shameless. Saturn and ♀ in the Eastern Angles, in the Asc. or M.C., tend to a total exposure of the passions. (See Exhibitionism; "Outrageous" under Insanity; Perversions, Shameless).

Nymphomania—Unbridled Passion In Women—(See Nymphomania; "Unbridled" in this section).

Obscene; Obsessions—Sexual Obsessions In Women—(See Nymphomania; "Morbid" in this section).

Opposite Sex—Fond of—Addicted To—(See the paragraphs under Opposite Sex).

Outbursts of Passion—Should guard against when ♀ and ☿ are in ♌ at B.; ♂ ☌ ♀ in ♌ or ♏; the ☽ afflicted in ♏. (See Inflamed, Storms, in this section).

Outrages Nature's Laws — (See "Nature's Laws" under Nature; Perversions).

Over-Indulgence — Of the Sex Nature — (See "Passional Excesses" in this section).

Passional Excesses—Over-Indulgence of the Sex Nature—Excessive Venery —Excess of Amorous Indulgence—Caused principally by ♂, the ruler of the Genital Organs. Due also to ♆ and ♅ afflictions to ♀; the ☉ in a weak sign at B., and afflicted; the ☉ afflicted in ♐, the half man and half horse sign, and especially when other influences contribute to lowered moral standards; the ☉, ☽, ♂, or ♀ in ♌ in the 5th H.; the ☉ to the ill-asps. ♀ or the ☽ by dir.; the ☽ afflicted in ♏; the ☽ in ♏, □ or ☍ ♆; the Prog. ☽ to the ☌ or ill-asp. ♂; the ☽ to the ill-asps. ♀ by dir.; ♆ afflicted in ♏; ♆ ☌, □, or ☍ the ☽ or ♀ at B., and by dir.; ♅ afflicted in ♏; ♅ ☌, □, or ☍ ♀; ♄ Sig. □ or ☍ ♀; ♃ afflicted in ♉, ♎, or ♏; ♂ afflicted in ♏; ♂ in ♏ in the 12th H., and afflicted; ♂ or ☿ Sig. to the ☌ ♀ and ♀ ill-dignified at B.; ♂ afflicted in the 5th H.; ♂ Sig. ☌, □, or ☍ ♀; ♂ Prog. to the ☌, P., □ or ☍ ♀, or vice versa; ♀ affl. in ♌ or ♏; ♀ in ♏, ☌ the ☽ or ♂; ♀ affl. at B., and to the ☌, P., or evil asp. the Asc. by dir.; ♀ to the ☌ ♂ by dir.; ♀ in the Asc. or M.C., and afflicted, prone to venery; ♀ Sig. □ or ☍ ♂; the tonic action of ♀ tends to venereal excesses; ♌ on the cusp of 5th H.; the 17° ♏ on the Asc., apt to be carried away by the lower passions. Remember that these influences apply only to unregenerate people, and those who may be drifting with their stars instead of ruling them. (See Amorous, Depraved, Dissipated, Dissolute; "Free Living", "Free Love", under Free; "Loose Morals" under Morals; Venery; Abnormal, Exaggerated, Excess, Too Much Passion, Unbridled, and the various paragraphs in this section).

Passional Violence — (See "Violence" in this section; "Violent" under Men).

Perversions; Pleasures—Given to Sexual Pleasures—(See Amorous, Pleasure; "Sensuous" under Sensuality; "Passional Excesses", and the various paragraphs in this section).

Prodigal; Profligate; Promiscuity—(See "Clandestine" under Sex).

Rape; Restraint — Unnatural Sex Restraint — ♄ influence and affliction; ♄ afflicting the ☽ or ♀ at B., and by dir. (See Apathy, Aversions, Bachelors, Celibacy, Indifferent). For influences which tend to lack of Restraint over the sex nature see Excess, Passional Excesses, and the various paragraphs in this section.

Salacious—(See Effeminate, Lust).

Same Sex—Sex Perversions with the Same Sex—Sodomy — (See Homosexuality).

Scheming and Underhanded—Resorts to Such Measures to Gratify Passion—♀ ☌, □, or ☍ ♄.

Seduction; Self-Abuse — (See "Solitary" under Vice).

Sensuous Enjoyments—(See Amorous; "Sensuous" under Sensuality; the various paragraphs in this section).

Sex-Conscious—(See Amative).

Sex Desires — Variations of — (See Amorous, Apathy, Desire, Love Affairs, Men, Sex, Women; the various paragraphs in this section).

Sex Gratification—Various Manners of —(See Rape, Scheming, Violence, and the various paragraphs in this section; Perversions, Sex, Venery).

Sex Perversions—(See Perversions).

Sex Relations—(See Cohabitation, Intercourse, Love Affairs, Morals, Sex; the various paragraphs in this section).

Sexual Immorality—(See "Free Love" under Free; "Loose Morals" under Morals; Perversions; "Clandestine" under Sex; the various paragraphs in this section).

Sexual Obsessions—(See "Morbid" under Imaginations; "Erotic" under Mania; Nymphomania, Perversions; "Sensuous" under Sensuality).

Shameless Practices — (See Exhibitionism, Perversions, Rape, Shameless; Notoriety, Violence, in this section).

Social Relations—(See Harlots, Love Affairs; "Low Company" under Low; Men, Social, Women).

Sodomy — (See Homosexuality, Perversions).

Solitary Vice — (See "Solitary" under Vice).

Storms — Sudden Storms of Passion, and with Violence—♂ ☌ the ☽ or ♀ in ♏; ♂ ☌ ♀ in ♈; ♂ afflicting ♅ or ♄ by dir., or ♄ to the ill-asps. ♂ by dir., and where other influences indicate great passion or sex perversions. (See Mania, Outbursts, Violence, in this section; "High Temper" under Temper).

Strengthened — The Passional Nature Strengthened — (See "Strong Passions" in this section).

Strong Passions — The Passional Nature Strengthened—The ☽ ☌ ♂ and ♀ in ♏; ♆ afflicted in ♉ or ♏; ♄ Sig. in ♌ or ♏ in Hor'y Q.; ♂ ☌ ♀ in any part of the map, and espec. in ♏; ♂ Sig. □ or ☍ ♀; ♂ in the 10th H.; ♀ in ♏; ♀ Sig. □ or ☍ ♂; the 3rd Decan. of ♈ on the Asc., ruled by ♀; the 3° ♎ on the Asc.; the 25° ♌ on the Asc.; the 3rd Decan. of ♐ on the Asc., ruled by ♄; the 3rd Decan. of ♓ on the Asc., ruled by ♂; the 30° ♓ on the Asc. (See Excess of Passion, Passional Excesses, in this section).

Sudden Storms of Passion — (See "Storms" in this section).

Too Much Passion—Diseases Arising From—Caused by ♂; ♂ Sig. □ or ☍ ♀, and vice versa. (See Diseases, Passional Excesses, in this section; Venery).

Unbridled Passion — Lustful — Profligate—The ☽ to the ill-asps. ♀ by dir.; ♂ afflicted in ♉, profligate; ♂ Sig. □ or ☍ ♀; ♀ ill-dignified at B.; ♀ ruler of the horoscope and afflicted by malefics; ♀ on the Meridian at B., and ill-aspected by ♂, tends to be unchaste; ♀ Sig. □ or ☍ ♃, void of virtue and prudence; ♀ Sig. □ or ☍ ♂; the 11° ♌

on the Asc., loss of virtue. (See Imprudent, Indecent, Infamous, Lust. Nymphomania, Obscene, Profligate, Shameless, Unchaste, Virtue, Wanton; "Passional Excesses", and the various paragraphs in this section).

Unnatural Desires — (See Aversions, Celibacy, Deviations, Homosexuality, Indifferent, Perversions, Unnatural; "Restraint" in this section).

Unsavory Subjects — Given To — (See Unsavory).

Unwomanly Freedom—(See "Unwomanly" under Morals; "Unchaste" under Women).

Vehement Passions—(See Vehement).

Venery; Vices; Violence — Violence Attending Passion—Men Prone to Violence In Sex Gratification — Sudden Storms of Passion with Violence—The ☉ □ or ☍ ♂; ♀ afflicted by ♂. (See Cruel, Libidinous, Lust, Masochism, Perversions, Rape, Sadism; "Shameless Practices" under Shameless; Vehement, Virile; "Storms" in this section). The lord of the 8th H. in the 7th H. tends to death from violent outbursts of passion.

Virtuous—Is Virtuous—Is Not Virtuous — (See "Chaste" under Females; Immodest, Modesty, Shameless, Virtue; "Unchaste" under Women; "Unbridled Passion" in this section).

Vitality Depleted — From Sex Excesses—(See "Wasted" under Vitality).

Voluptuous; Wanton; Wench — (See Harlots).

Women—Fond of—Given to Company of Lewd Women—Passional Excesses In Women—(See Addicted To, Fascinating, Harlots, under Men; Nymphomania, Opposite Sex, Women; "Virtuous" in this section).

Young People—Passion Strong In At Adolescence — (See "Passional Excesses under Children; Puberty).

PASSIVE—Unresisting—Cold is a negative and passive quality, and predominates in the left side of the body. (See Cold). Dryness is passive and feminine when acting alone. (See Dry). Moisture is a feminine and passive quality. (See Moisture). The Earthy and Watery Signs of the Zodiac are feminine, and considered more passive and negative than the fiery and airy signs, which are masculine and positive.

Passive Disposition — (See Apathy, Dull, Inactive, Influenced, Mutable, Negative, Receptive, Rouse, Susceptible).

Passive Faculties — Deviation of the Passive or Sensitive Faculties—(See Deviations; "Passive Faculties" under Faculties).

Passive Planets—The ☉, ☽, and ☿ are considered passive planets, and passive subjects of the other planets according to the nature of the aspects and planets with which configurated. In the Zodiac, the M.C. and the Asc. are considered passive points, and very strong for good or evil according to the aspects formed with them at B., and by direction. (See Ascendant, Mercury, Midheaven, Moon, Sun, Variable).

PAST EVENTS—(See "Past Events" under Events).

PASTIMES — (See Amusements, Exercise, Hunting, Journeys, Love Affairs, Pleasures, Reading, Recreations, Sports, Study, Theatres, Travel, Voyages, etc.).

PASTRIES—Fond of—(See "Pastries" under Food).

PATELLA—Knee Cap—(See Knees).

PATERNAL—Pertaining to the Father —Paternal Aunts and Uncles — Relatives On Father's Side—(See "Paternal" under Aunts; "Relatives" under Father).

PATHOLOGICAL—Pathogenic—Causing Disease—♄, ♃ and ♂ are considered the Pathological Planets, and their afflictions tend to cause disease. (See "Pathological Action" under each of the Planets).

    Ganglion—Pathological Formation of —(See "Pathological" under Ganglion).

PATIENCE—Patient—This is a quality of ♄, and ♄ people are very patient in disease, suffering, and affliction, and have great power to wait tranquilly for events. The good aspects of ♄ to the ☉, ☽, and ☿ give patience, or any aspect of ♄ to ☿. Also given by many planets in the fixed signs at B. Uranus and ♂ more prominent at B. than ♄, or afflicting ♄, tend to give impatience. (See Contentment, Discontentment, Endurance, Fretful; "Peace of Mind" under Mind; Persevering, Resignation, Restless, Saturn).

PATIENT—The Patient—Condition of— —Conduct of—Prospects of—(See "Patient" under Disease).

PATRICIDE — (See this subject under Father).

PEACE—Peaceable—Peaceful—

    Death — A Peaceful Death—(See "Peaceful" under Death, Old Age).

    Lover of Peace—A Peaceful Disposition—(See Cheerfulness, Contentment, Gentle, Good, Harmless, Honest, Humane, Kind, Mild, ·Quiet, Sincere, etc.).

    No Peace of Mind—(See "No Peace" under Mind).

    Peace of Mind—(See "Peace of Mind" under Mind).

PECCANT HUMOURS—(See "Offensive" under Humours).

PECTORAL—Pectoral Affections—(See Breast, Chest, Lungs, Thorax).

PECTORIS—Angina Pectoris—(See Angina).

PECULIAR—Peculiarity—Peculiarities —Strange—Unusual, etc.—

    Accidents—Peculiar and Sudden Accidents — (See "Extraordinary" under Accidents).

    Appetites—Peculiar Appetites and Tastes—Capricious — Whimsical — Illusory—Fantastic—♆ in ♋ or the 6th H.; the ☽ in ♒, fantastic appetites. (See Appetites, Cravings, Diet, Eating, Fancies, Food, Ideals, Tastes, etc.).

    Brain Diseases—(See "Peculiar" under Brain).

    Clothing — Dress — Food—Peculiar Tastes In Food and Clothing — (See "Peculiar" under Dress, Food).

Course of Disease — Peculiar Course In Disease—Peculiar Symptoms— Caused principally by the afflictions of ♅ to the ☽ during the course of the disease. Also the afflictions of ☿ cause a various course in disease. (See Course, Erratic; "Disease" under Extraordinary; "Course of Disease" under Irregular; Mysterious, Strange, Symptoms, Unusual, Variable, etc.).

Death—Peculiar Death—(See "Death" under Extraordinary).

Diseases—Peculiar Diseases—Difficult to Understand—Ill-Health of a Peculiar Nature—The ☉ hyleg, and ♅ ☌ or P. the ☉ at a Solar Rev.; the ill-asps. of the ☽ by dir. to the hyleg; ♆ and ♅ diseases; ♆ or ♅ afflicted in the 6th H.; ♒ on the Asc. (See "Diseases" under Extraordinary; "Imaginary Diseases" under Imagination; Mysterious, Periodic, Praeincipients, Pseudo, Psychic, Strange, Uncommon).

Disposition—A Peculiar Disposition— (See Eccentric, Misunderstood).

Fears—Peculiar Fears—(See the various paragraphs under Fear).

Food and Clothing — (See Appetites, Clothing, in this section).

Forebodings—Peculiar Forebodings— (See Forebodings).

Head—(See "Peculiar Shaped" under Head).

Hurts—(See Extraordinary; "Strange" under Hurts).

Imaginations—(See "Peculiar" under Imagination).

Mind—A Peculiar Mind—(See Chaotic, Eccentric, Fancies, Ideals, Mentality, Mind, Misunderstood, Notions, Occult, Religion, Vagaries, Weird, etc.).

Nervous Diseases—A Peculiar Nervousness—(See "Peculiar" under Nerves).

Pleasures—Given to Peculiar Pleasures—(See "Peculiar" under Pleasure).

Symptoms — Peculiar Symptoms In Disease—(See "Peculiar" under Symptoms; "Course" in this section).

Tastes — Peculiar Tastes and Appetites—(See Appetites, Clothing, in this section).

Vagaries—(See "Peculiar" under Vagaries).

Vision—(See "Peculiarity of Vision" under Sight).

PEDESTRIANISM—A Fondness For Walking—A ♐ characteristic. Where ♄ is prominent, however, and afflicted, the Sagittarian may be averse to walking, exercise, out-door sports, or recreations. (See Exercise, Sports, Walk).

PEDUNCULATED TUMORS—(See "Polypus" under Nose; Polypus).

PEEVISH—Fretful—Irritable—Childish—Mostly a ♄ and ♑ influence; ♄ Sig. in ♋ or ♑; the ☽ ☌ or P. ♄ at B., and by dir., peevish and fearful; ♃ Sig. in ♑; ☿ Sig. in ♑ or ♓; ♏ upon the Asc. (See Dejected, Discontentment; "Brings Disease Upon Himself" under Disease; Fears, Fretful, Irritable; "Low Spirits" under Low; Murmuring, Patience, Regretful, Repining, Restlessness, Scolding, Worry, etc.).

PELLAGRA — An Endemic Erythematous Disease of Italy—Caused by the same general influences as given under Endemic and Erythema. (See Endemic, Erythema).

PELLITORY — Pyrethrum — A Typical Drug of the ☽. A Sialagog, increasing the flow of saliva. (See "Moon Group" under Herbs; Saliva).

PELVIS — Pelvic — The Bony Basin of the Trunk, formed by the Innominate Bones and the Sacrum—The Pelvis is ruled by the ♐ Sign. The Pelvic Bones are ruled by ♏. (See Hips, Innominate, Pubes, Sacrum).

Pelvic Operations—Are indicated by ♂ afflicted in ♐.

Pelvis of the Kidneys—Ruled by ♏. Stone is formed in the pelvis of the kidneys by the action of ♄. (See Kidneys).

PENETRATING— See "Penetrating" under Eyes, Mind; Pungent.

PENIS—Glans Penis—The Male External Sex Organ—The Organ of Copulation — Ruled by ♂. The Penis, the Urethra, and the Scrotum, are ruled by the ♏ Sign. The Muscles of Erection are ruled by ♏. The Uro-Genital Orifice is ruled by ♏.

Balanitis—Inflammation of the Glans Penis—♂ afflicted in ♏ or ♓.

Chancre — Hard Chancre — Accompanies Syphilis—(See Syphilis).

Chancroid—Soft Chancre—Accompanies Gonorrhoea—(See Gonorrhoea).

Channels and Vents—Lack of Proper Sex Channels—(See "Channels" under Genitals).

Chordee—Painful Down-Curved Erection—(See Gonorrhoea).

Circumcision Indicated—(See Circumcision).

Erections Painful — (See "Chordee" under Gonorrhoea; "Priapism" in this section).

Eunuchs — A Castrated Male — (See Eunuchs, Testes).

Genitals—Diseases of—(See Genitals).

Genito-Urinary Diseases—(See Genito-Urinary).

Glans Penis—Inflammation of—(See "Balanitis" in this section).

Gleet—(See "Chronic" under Gonorrhoea).

Gonorrhoea—(See Gonorrhoea).

Hermaphrodites—(See this subject).

Inflammation — (See "Balanitis" in this section).

Injuries To — (See "Mens' Genitals" under Genitals; Maimed).

Masturbation—(See "Solitary" under Vice).

Mens' Genitals—Diseases of—Injuries To—(See "Mens' Genitals" under Genitals; the various paragraphs in this section).

Natural Channels—(See "Channels" in this section).

Pain In—(See "Pain" under Genitals).

Painful Erections — (See "Priapism" in this section).

Prepuce—(See Circumcision).

Priapism—Painful Erection—A ♏ disease; a ♀ disease and caused by afflictions to ♀; ♂ influence at B. overlaid and intermixed with other planets, as ♄, ♅, and ♆; afflictions in ♏. (See "Chordee" under Gonorrhoea).

Scrotum — Complications Affecting — (See Scrotum, Semen, Testes).

Soft Chancre—(See Gonorrhoea).

Stricture of Urethra—(See Urethra).

Undeveloped — Sex Organs Undeveloped—(See Undeveloped).

Urethra—Disorders of—(See Urethra).

Venereal Diseases—(See Venereal).

PENSIVE—A Pensive or Sad Aspect—(See "Appearance" under Sadness).

PENURIOUS—Parsimonious—Sordid—Indigent—♄ ruler of the Asc. and the horoscope at B., and afflicted; ♄ in ♉, avaricious. (See Misanthropic, Miserly, Selfish).

PEOPLE — The People — The Public — Humanity—The Common People—Are ruled generally by the ☽. (See Common People, Humanity, Mankind, Mobs, Nations, Public).

Aged People—(See Grandparents, Old Age).

Middle-Aged People — (See Middle Life).

Young People—(See Children, Young, Youth).

PEPPER—Cayenne Pepper—Capsicum—Ruled by ♂. (See "Mars Group" under Herbs).

PEPPERMINT—Mentha—A Typical Drug of ♃. (See "Jupiter Group" under Herbs).

PEPSIN—Ruled by the ♋ Sign. (See "Fluids" under Digestion; "Juices" under Gastric; "Pepsin" under Stomach).

PERCEPTION — Perceptions — Perceptive Faculties—

Acute Perceptive Faculties — Saturn well-dignified at B., as in ♎, ♑, or ♒, and well-aspected by the ☽ and ☿; ♂ a strong ruler at B., well-aspected and dignified; ♂ Sig. in ♏, excelling in mystery. (See "Active Mind" under Active; Knowledge, Learning; "Quickened" under Mentality; "Good Mind" under Mind; Understanding, etc.).

Disorders of Perception—☿, the mental ruler, weak and afflicted at B.; ☿ in no aspect to the ☽ or Asc., and with ☿ otherwise weak and afflicted at B. (See Comprehension; "Mind" under Dull; Fears, Hallucinations, Illusions; "Mental" under Impaired; Inactive, Intuition; "Weak" under Intellect, Mentality, Mind, Senses, Smell, Understanding).

False Perceptions — (See Delusions, Hallucinations, Illusions).

Sense Perceptions—☿ rules all sense perceptions. (See Senses).

PEREGRINE—A Planet in a Sign having no essential dignity of any kind, and is reckoned a debility of five degrees. In Hor'y Q. a peregrine planet in an angle, or the 2nd H., is taken as the thief in matters of theft. (See Thieves). A benefic planet, when peregrine, also does not lend as much support in health matters, and a malefic planet, when so situated, and afflicted, is more mischievous in causing disease, affliction, suffering, misfortune, and trouble. (See Benefics, Malefics).

PERFECT—Perfection—Physical Harmony—Perfection of Mind and Body—A "Perfect" Physical Body—(See "Perfect" under Eyes, Functions; Harmony; "Perfection" under Mind; "Free Will" under Will).

PERFORATED—Perforated Ear Drum—(See "Discharges" under Ears).

PERFUMES—Ruled by ♀. (See "Vocation" under Color; "Dealing In Medicines" under Medicine; Odors).

PERICARDIUM—The Membranous Sac Around the Heart — Ruled by the ♌ sign, and especially affected by the ☽ in ♌. (See Carditis, Endocarditis, Pericarditis, under Heart).

PERIGEE—A Planet in its Orbit nearest the Earth. Planets in Perigee tend to be very strong in causing disturbances, diseases, distempers, epidemics, etc. (See Cholera, Epidemics, Malefics; "Perigee" under Moon; Perihelion).

PERIHELION—A Planet in its Orbit nearest the Sun. The Superior Planets when in Perihelion tend to cause epidemics, weather and atmospheric disturbances, and many troubles upon the Earth. (See "Corrupt Air" under Air; Cholera, Dreams, Epidemics; "Disordered" under Nerves; Perigee, Pestilence; "Sun Spots" under Spots; Typhus, Volcanoes).

PERIHEPATITIS— (See "Inflammation" under Liver).

PERIL—Perils—Dangers—(See the various paragraphs under Accidents, Dangers, Death, Hurts, Injuries, Travel, Wounds, etc. Also look in the alphabetical arrangement for the subject you have in mind).

Danger and Peril—To the Native—The ☽ Sig. □ or ☍ ♂, passes thru innumerable dangers; the ☽ incr. in light, sepr. from ♃ and applying to ♂ in a nocturnal nativity; the ☽ with Antares or Aldebaran in the Asc. or M.C.; ♃ ruler of the 1st H., and to the ill-asps. ♄ by dir.; ♂ ☌ ☋. (See "Many Dangers" under Danger).

Great Perils Generally—Comets appearing in ♏. (See Abroad, Calamity, Comets, Drowning, Falls, Heights, Highwaymen, Pirates, Quadrupeds, Robbers, Shipwreck, Travel, Voyages, War, etc.).

PERINEUM — The Space between the Thighs from the Anus to the Genitals—Ruled by ♏. (See Fundament).

PERIODIC — Periodical — Recurrent — Returning—Intermittent, etc.—

Periodic Diseases—Periodic Sickness and Illness—Periodic Irregularities—The ☽ rules diseases and afflictions which return after a time, such as Vertigo, Epilepsy, Faintings, Falling Fits, Falling Sickness, Periodic Illnesses in Females, Giddiness, Gout, Swimming in the Head, etc. (See these subjects). Those who have the ☉ critically afflicted at B. tend to have peculiar trouble and serious illness every tenth year of life. The hyleg afflicted by ♄ at B., or ♄ in the Asc. or

M.C., or afflicting the ☉, ☽, or Asc., tends to cause the return of some chronic ailment, or cause some chronic disease every seven years when ♄ passes the evil aspects of □, ☍, and ⚹ to his place at B., and also again when he reaches his place in the map of birth at from the 28th to 30th years of life, and also at about the 58th and 59th years of life, when ♄ finishes his second revolution in his orbit after birth. The ☽ in bad asp. to ♄ at B. tends to ill-health every seven years. The ☽ ruler of the 1st or 6th H. at B., and in bad asp. to ♀, tends to ill-health periodically, both by transit and the directions of ♀, when the ☽ is in bad asp. to ♀ at B.; the ☽ □ or ☍ Asc., periodic illness. (See Climacteric, Critical Years, Cycles; "Periods of Bad Health" under Health; Periods; "Returning Diseases" under Return).

Periodic Fevers — (See Ague, Intermittent, Malaria, Quartan, Quotidian, Remittent, Semi-Tertian, Tertian, etc.).

Periodic Headache — (See "Periodic" under Headaches).

Periodic Insanity—Returning At Intervals — (See "Periodic" under Insanity).

Periodic Irregularities—Ruled by the ☽. (See Irregularities).

Periodic Lunations—The time the ☽ returns to her place each month in the map of birth, a period of 27d. 7h. 44m. This is a sensitive place for the ☽ in health matters, and also a very dangerous time for an operation. It may also be a crisis time in a fever, if the ☽ was on her place when the fever began, and when an acute disease will either resolve itself or go into a chronic form of disease, being the 28th day of the disease. (See Crises, Lunations; "Rules" under Operations).

Periodic Remedies — The Moon and Mercury Groups of Herbs are periodic in their general action. (See Antiperiodic; "Mercury Group", "Moon Group", under Herbs; Innervation).

Periodic Revolution—Of a Planet—The return of a planet to its place in the radix after making a revolution in its orbit. A planet at such times exercises considerable influence in health matters for good or ill according to the nature and aspects of the planet at the time. (See the ☿ influences in the paragraph, "General Causes" under Epilepsy; "Solar Revolution" under Revolution; "Periodic Lunations" in this section).

Periodic Vomiting—(See Vomiting).

Women—Periodic Illness In—(See Menses).

PERIODICITY—Regularly Recurrent—

Cellular Periodicity — (See "Periodicity" under Cells).

Nervous Periodicity — Innervation — (See "Periodicity" under Nerves).

Solar Periodicity—(See "Periodicity" under Sun).

Zymotic Periodicity—(See Zymotic).

PERIODS—Periods of Life—Periods of Good or Bad Health—

Acute Diseases — (See "Periods Of" under Acute).

Childhood—Periods of—(See Childhood).

Gestation — Period of — (See Gestation).

Good Health—Periods of—(See "Periods of Good Health "under Health).

Ill-Health — (See "Periods of Bad Health" under Health).

Infancy—Period of—(See Childhood, Infancy).

Life—Periods of Life Ruled by the Planets—Authorities seem to differ on the Periods of Life, as ruled over by the different Planets. The first four years of life are ruled by the ☽, and also it is generally understood that the ☽ rules the first seven years of life. Mercury rules from the 4th to 10th years. From the 10th to 18th years, by ♀. From the 18th to 37th years by the ☉. From the 37th to 52nd years by ♂. From the 52nd to 64th years by ♃. After the 64th year, by ♄. Another division given by some Authors is as follows: The ☽ rules the first seven years of life; ☿ from 7 to 15; ♀ from the 15th to 24th years; the ☉ from the 24th to 34th years; ♂ from the 34th to 45th; ♃ from the 45th to 57th; ♄ from the 57th to 70th. If a person lives beyond 70, then ♅ rules from 70 to 84, and ♆ from 84 to 99. When the ruler of any of these periods is severely afflicted at B., it indicates that that part of the life ruled by such planet will tend to be especially unfortunate, and filled with trouble, trials, misfortune, or illnesses of the nature attributed to such planet. The ☽ badly afflicted at B. tends to more danger in infancy. In the Kabala, Infancy was dedicated to the ☉; childhood to the ☽; youth to ♂ and ♀; mature age to ♃, and old age to ♄. (See Climacteric; "Critical Periods" under Critical; Cycles).

Middle Life—Period of—(See Middle Life).

Old Age — Period of — (See Fourth House, Old Age, Terminal).

Planetary Periods — Periods of the Planets — The revolution of ♄ takes 29y. 167d. 4h.; of ♃, 11y. 314d. 20h.; of ♂, 1y. 321d. 22h.; of ♀, 224d. 7h.; of ☿, 87d. 23h.; of ♅, about 84 years, or 7 years in a Sign; of ♆, 165 years, or about 14 years in one Sign of the Zodiac; of the ☽, 27d. 7h. 43m., her periodical course, but the period between her actual conjunctions is 29d. 12h. 44m. The ☉, about 365 days to pass thru the 12 Signs, as seen from the Earth. (See "Direct Motion" under Direct; Retrograde).

Seven-Year Periods—Every 7th year of life is said to be a changing, and more critical year in life, which years correspond to the Quarters of the ☽. Life is divided into seven-year periods, as 7, 14, 21, 28, 35, 42, 49, 56, 63, 70, etc., which are considered crisis years in life, or more dangerous years. Also every 7th year from birth corresponds to the ∠, □, ☍, and ⚹ aspects of ♄ from his place in the radix, as his period is about 28 years, which makes every seventh year more critical for the health. The 49th and 63rd years of adult life are considerel dangerous years, being doubly climateric, and many deaths occur in such years of life. (See Aspects, Climacteric, Crises, Seven).

Youth—The Period of—(See Puberty, Young, Youth).

PERIOSTEITIS — Inflammation of the Periosteum—(See Bones).

PERIPHERAL — The Outer Boundary, Circumference, or Surface of the Body—

Peripheral Lesions — (See "Aphonia" under Voice).

Peripheral Nerves — Peripheral Sympathetic Nerves — Ruled by ♄ and ♑. Remedies used in the treatment of acute diseases begin their action at the peripheral nerves. These nerves also ruling the skin and mucous membranes, and also being ruled by ♄, tend to morbid diseases and manifestations. Cold, ruled by ♄, also affects these nerves, driving the blood inward, and causing internal congestions, and acute diseases start with disturbances in the peripheral nerves. (See Acute, Capillaries, Centripetal, Chilblain, Chill; "Blood' under Circulation; Cold, Colds, Congestion, Constrictions, Ganglion; "Congestion" under Internal; "Mydriasis" under Iris; the Introduction under Knees; Nausea, Saturn; "Arms" under Skin; "Sympathetic Nervous System" under Sympathetic).

PERISTALSIS—Peristaltic Action—The peristaltic action of the stomach is ruled by ♋, and of the bowels by ♍. Saturn when in these signs tends to impede this action. Antiperistaltic action is usually caused by the affliction of ♄ from an opposite sign, as from ♑ or ♓. (See Antiperistalsis; "Peristaltic Action" under Bowels, Stomach; Emetics, Expulsion, Nausea, Physic, Vomiting).

PERITONEUM — Mesentery — Omentum —Ruled by ♍ The Serum of the Peritoneum is connected with the ♓ sign. (See Mesentery, Omentum, Serous).

Diseases Of—Caused by afflictions in ♍.

Dropsy Of—Ascites—(See "Abdomen" under Dropsy).

Inflammation Of—Peritonitis—The ☉, ☽, or ♂ afflicted in ♍; ♂ afflicted in ♍ in the 6th H.; afflictions in ♍; Subs at PP. Cases—See Fig. 18E in "Astro-Diagnosis", by the Heindels. See "Marriage", No. 256, in 1001 N.N.

Rupture Of — ♂ afflicted in ♍. (See Rupture).

PERITYPHLITIS—Inflammation Around the Caecum—(See Caecum).

PERJURY—Perjured—Given to Perjury —♃ to the ill-asps. ☿ by dir.; ♂ ill-dignified at B., and afflicted; ☿ is the author of perjury; ☿ afflicted at B., and by dir. (See Deceitful, Dishonest, Liars; "Perjured" under Religion).

PERMANENT — Tending to Endure — More Lasting In Effects—Lingering—Chronic—

Permanent Diseases — These diseases proceed from ♄, and are generally regulated by the motion of the ☉. (See Chronic, Incurable, Lingering; "Diseases" under Long; "Incapable Of" under Remedy; Tedious, Wastings).

Permanent Habit In Disease—(See Diathesis, Hexis).

Permanent Habits—(See "Permanent" under Habits).

Permanent Hurts—Or Injuries—Those Tending to Cripple, Deform, Blemish, or Incapacitate—The ☉ in the 6th H., in cardinal signs, and afflicted by malefics. (See Blemishes, Crippled, Deformities; "Hurts" under Remedy).

PERNICIOUS — Fatal — Vehement — Highly Destructive—

Pernicious Anaemia—(See Anaemia).

Pernicious Diseases — Caused by ♂. (See Fierce, Quick, Sharp, Swift, Vehement, Violent).

Pernicious Fevers—(See "Destructive Processes" under Destructive; High, Violent, under Fever).

PERPLEXITIES — (See Affliction, Anguish, Anxiety, Cares, Disgrace, Gloom, Grief; "No Peace of Mind" under Mind; Miseries, Misfortune; "Loss Of" under Reputation; Reverses, Ruin, Sorrow, Trouble, Vexations, Worry, etc.).

PERSECUTION—Persecutions are ruled and denoted by the 12th H.

Delusions of Persecution — See Paranoia).

Religious Persecution — Persecuted Because of Religious Beliefs, or Advanced and Independent Views—☿ Sig. □ or ☍ ♃. (See Eccentric, Independent, Misunderstood, Occult, Opinions, Reformers, Religion, Revolutionary, etc.). Death from Religious Persecution may result when the lord of the 9th H. at B. is afflicted in the 8th H. (See "Injured" under Religion).

PERSEVERING — Perseverance — Persistent—Tenacious—Constant—Steady In Purpose — Unwavering — The ☉, ☽, and ☿ in fixed signs at B., and in angles; the ☉ influence strong at B.; ♄ strong at B.; ♃ to the ☌ and good asps. ♀, the mind is steady; many planets in fixed signs, or fixed signs on the angles. (See Constancy; "Fixed Habits", "Fixed Signs", under Fixed; Inflexible, Obstinate, Patience, Positive, Resolute, Self-Reliant, etc.).

PERSONAL—Pertaining to the Person—

Personal Appearance — (See Appearance, Beautiful, Body, Countenance, Crooked, Decanates, Deformities, Expression, Eyes, Face, Figure, Fleshy, Form, Hair, Height, Ill-Formed, Large, Look, Middle-Sized, Neat, Robust, Short, Sickly, Stature, Tall, Thin, Ugly, Weight, Well-Proportioned, etc.).

Personal Beauty — (See Beautiful, Comely, Complexion, Handsome, Harmony, Well-Proportioned, etc.).

Personal Cleanliness — (See Cleanly, Dress, Neat, etc.).

Personal Habits—The ☽ has an important influence over the personal habits, and represents the personal character. (See Character, Conduct, "Personal Habits" under Habits).

Personal Marks—(See Blemishes, Defects, Marks, Moles, Scars, etc.).

PERSONALITY—The Lower Mind—The Desires — The Animal Instincts — The Sense Mind—Denoted by the sign in which the ☽ is posited at B. The sign containing the ☉ indicates the Higher Mind, or the Individuality. (See Adrenals; "Animal Instincts" under Animal; Character, Desires, Habits, Individuality, Instincts; "Lower Mind" under Mind; Temperament).

Dual Personality—(See "Double-Bodied Signs" under Double-Bodied; "Dual-Minded" under Dual; Memory).

Erratic Personality—Caused by the □ and ☍ of ♅ to planets; ♅ □ or ☍ the ☉, ☽, ♃, ♂, ♀, or ☿; ♅ afflicted in ♊, ♍, ♐, ♑, ♒, or ♓; afflictions to the ☽; the ☽ □ or ☍ ☿ or ♅; ☿ ruler of the horoscope and afflicted by malefics. (See Conduct, Eccentric; "Mind" under Erratic).

Good Personality—(See Pleasant).

Triple Personality—Case—(See "Triple", No. 369, in 1001 N.N.

PERSPIRATION—Sweating—(See Axillae, Excretion; "Bromidrosis" under Feet; Fetid, Sweat).

PERTUSSIS—Whooping Cough—(See "Convulsive Coughing" under Cough; Whooping).

PERUVIAN BARK—Cinchona—Quinine—(See Cinchona).

PERVERSE—Perversity—Perverted—An afflicted ♅ tends to make one perverse, and to rebel against established customs, and often unreasonably so. The good aspects of ♃ to ♅ tend to modify this, but with no good aspect from ♃, and ♃ also sorely afflicted, the perversity tends to be uncontrolled. Aquarius and ♓ when afflicted tend to perversity, and to be unconventional. Aquarius afflicted tends to perversions in sex relations, and to immorality. Saturn Sig. in ♊ tends to perversity; ♂ afflicted in ♒, perversity, and to be unruly and controversial. Also caused by the ☽ applying to the evil aspects of ♂. (See Anarchists, Eccentric, Erratic, Erring, Independent, Irrational; "Bad Judgment" under Judgment; Misunderstood, Perversions; "Unreasonable" under Reason; Rebellious, Riotous, Uncontrolled).

PERVERSIONS—Abnormal—Abnormalities of the Sexual Instincts—Perverted Action—Are due to the tonic action of ♅; ♅ afflicting the ☉, ♆, or ☿, a perverting agency, and disruptive.

Activity—Perverted Activity—Caused by the afflictions of ♅ and ♆, and especially when afflicting the ☉, ☽, ♀, or ☿. (See Action, Activity).

Appetites—Perverted Appetites—♆ afflicted in ♎; ♆ afflicted in the 3rd or 12th H.; ♄ affl. in ♎. (See "Abnormal" under Appetites).

Contrary Manner—Men Seek Sex Connection In a Contrary Manner, but In Secret, and Not Openly—(See Homosexuality; "Licentious" under Men).

Desires—Perverted Desires—♆ afflicted in the 5th H., perverted and depraved desires; ♆ afflicted in the 1st H.; ♅ ruler of the horoscope, and afflicted; ♀ afflicted at B., tends to faulty desires, dissipation, and debauchery. (See Debauchery, Depraved, Desires, Dissipation; "Low and Base" under Low; "Loose Morals" under Morals; Perverse, Prodigal; the various paragraphs in this section).

Deviations—Deviations from the Usual Limits of Nature—(See Aversions, Deviations; "Nature's Laws" under Nature; Unnatural, Vices).

Easily Perverted—☿ ill-dignified at B. (See Influenced).

Effeminate—Men Effeminate and Women Masculine—(See Effeminate).

Emotional Perversion—(See "Desire Body" under Desire; Emotions).

Food—(See "Perverted Tastes" under Food).

Functions—(See "Perversion" under Functions).

Homosexuality—Sodomy—(See Homosexuality).

Imagination Perverted—(See "Perverted" under Imagination).

Incest—Sex Connection with a Near Relative—♂ and ♀ both in masculine signs, and ori., inclines to, and with danger of; ♀ ill-dignified at B.

Judgment Perverted—(See "Bad" under Judgment).

Masochism—Cruel Treatment In Sex Relations—(See Masochism).

Men—Sex Perversions In—(See "Contrary", and the various paragraphs in this section).

Moral Perversions—(See "Adulterous" under Love Affairs; Loose Morals, Moral Perversions, under Morals; "Clandestine" under Sex; the various paragraphs in this section).

Morbid Perversions—(See Compulsions, Unsavory, and the various paragraphs under Morbid).

Necrophilism—Sex Congress with a Dead Body—(See Necrophilism).

Nutrition Perverted—(See "Perverted" under Nutrition).

Planets—Perverted Action of—(See "Perverted Action" under Planets).

Practices—Perverted Practices—♆ afflicted in the 1st, 3rd, 5th, 6th, 7th, 9th, or 12th H.; ☿ ruler of the horoscope, and afflicted by malefics. (See Practices).

Sadism—Sex Gratification Attended by Violence—(See "Violence" under Men, Passion; Sadism).

Sex Perversions—Largely caused by the afflictions and lower vibrations of ♅, which tend to make the unawakened and unspiritualized native careless, unconventional, and to believe in free love, and to disregard the laws of Society; ♅ ☌ ☽ in ♏; ♅ afflicted in ♏; ♆ afflicted in the 1st, 3rd, or 12th H.; ♆ □ or ☍ ☽; ♄ ☌, P., □, or ☍ ♀, perverted sex desires, and usually directed against a younger person; ♀ in a female sign, and afflicted by ♂ in a male nativity, tends to make men wanton, and to seek connection contrary to nature, but privately, and not openly. If ♂ also be in a female sign, men will be shameless and public in their sex practices. The same conditions may exist in women if ♂, ♀, and the Lights are in masculine signs and sorely afflicted, and with ♄ also in evil configuration, tends to greater obscenity and impurity. (See Infamous, Lewd; "Low and Base" under Low; Obscene, Secret, Shameless, Unnatural; the various paragraphs in this section).

Shameless Practices—(See Shameless; "Sex Perversions" in this section).

Sodomy—Sex Connection by the Anus —(See Homosexuality).

Solar-Lunar Activity — Perversion of —(See "Solar-Lunar" under Solar).

Spiritual Perversions—(See Spiritual).

Talents — Perverted Talents — (See Talents).

Tastes — (See "Perverted" under Tastes).

Tonic Action—Perverted Tonic Action of Planets — (See "Perverted Action" under Planets; Tonic).

Violence—Men Given to Violence In Sex Gratification — (See Masochism; "Licentious" under Men; "Violence" under Passion; Sadism).

Vital Stimulus—Perversion of—(See "Stimulus" under Vital).

PESSIMISTIC—♄ strong at B., or born under ♄. (See Dejected, Despondent, Doubts, Fears, Gloom, Hope, Mistrustful; "Optimism Destroyed" under Optimism; Recluse, Reserved; "Secretive" under Secret; Suspicious, etc.).

PEST—

Black Pest—(See Pestilence, Plague).

Insect Pests — Vermin — (See Insects, Vermin).

Pest to Society — (See "Pest" under Society).

PESTILENCE — Pestilential—Deadly Epidemic Disease — Principally ♌, ♏, and ♐ diseases — and caused by afflictions in these signs. The Causes of Pestilence are discussed in the Article on Epidemics. (See "Causes" under Epidemics).

Air—Pestilential Air—(See "Corrupt Air" under Air; "Winds" in this section).

Danger by Pestilential Disease—The ☽ to the ☌ ♂ in ♌; the Asc. to the □ or ☍ ♂ by dir.; the ☽ directed to Antares or the Bull's Eye.

Death by Pestilence—Danger of—The ☉ directed to the Pleiades; ♂ ☌ the Asc. by dir. (See "Illness" in this section).

Eruptions — (See "Pestilential" under Eruptions).

Fevers — Pestilential Fevers — Pestilential Burning Fevers—The ☉ afflicted in □ when the ☉ is the afflictor in the disease; the ☽ in ♐ and afflicted by the ☉ or ♂ when taken ill; a ♂ disease and affliction; ♂ causes pestilential burning fevers; ♂ in the 6th H., or under the Sun's beams at a decumbiture, and if the ☉ or ♂, the planet signifying the disease, be in ♌ or ♏, the disease will be pestilential; ♂ in an earthy sign, and to the ill-asps. the Asc. by dir. (See "Epidemic Fevers" under Epidemics; "High" under Fever; "Illness" in this section).

Great Pestilence Signified—Pestilence Over the World—Pestilence Prevalent —A Solar Eclipse in the 2nd Decan. of

♍, and especially among People and Countries ruled by ♍. (See "Virgo" under Nations). An Eclipse of the ☉ or ☽ in airy signs, and especially in places ruled by the Signs in which it occurs; an eclipse of the ☉ in the 3rd Decan. ♎; an eclipse of the ☉ in ♎, and especially in the 1st Decan. of this sign, and due to corrupt air; an eclipse of the ☽ in the 2nd Decan. of ♈ or the 3rd Dec. of ♐; ♄ ☌ ♂ in the 6th or 8th H., in a human sign, and ♄ Lord of the Year at the Vernal Equinox (see "Human Signs" under Human); a malefic planet in power at a Summer Solstice, and afflicting the ☉ or ☽, or planets in the 6th H., and also a malefic in the 8th H.; caused by the ☌ of several superior planets in airy signs, and due to the maximum of planetary influence; coincident with the appearance of Comets; Comets appearing in ♋, ♑, or ♒. (See "Corrupt Air" under Air; Cholera, Comets, Drought; "Fountains" under Dry; Eclipses, Epidemics, Famine; "Extreme Heat" under Heat; Pandemics, Perihelion, Plague; Virus, Winds, in this section).

Illness by Pestilence—Pestilential Complaints — Danger of Death By — The ☉ afflicted in □; the ☉ directed to the Pleiades; the ☽ Sig. □ or ☍ ♂; the ☽ hyleg, and to the ☌ or ill-asp. ♂, and with ♂ in ♌ near the Ascelli, or if ♂ be near Cor Scorpio, there is danger of illness or death by pestilence, and especially if ♂ also be ill-aspected by the ☉ or ♄; ♄ ☌ ♂ in the 6th or 8th H., in a sign of human form, and ♄ Lord of the Year at the Vernal; ♂ afflicted in □ or ♍, and ☌, P., □ or ☍ the Asc. by dir.; ♂ ☌ the Asc. by dir.; ♂ afflicted in earthy signs, and ☌ or ill-asp. the Asc. by dir. The crisis in any pestilential illness or fever may be terminated from the 3rd to 8th day after the beginning. (See Death, Fevers, in this section).

Immunity to Pestilence—Passes Thru Unharmed—(See Immunity).

Virus — Pestilential Virus — Eclipses of the ☉ or ☽ in airy signs, or in ♍, tend to develop pestilential virus, and to cause great Pestilences, afflicting humanity, as well as horses, cattle, sheep, goats, dogs, cats, fish, fowl, and also vegetables and fruits. (See Virus).

Winds — Pestilential Winds — The ☉ and ☿ conjoined in fiery signs, heat and pestilential winds; ♂ ☌ ♃, and ♂ have more Northern Latitude; ♂ in power, and Lord at Equinoxes and Solstices, or Lord of the Year at the Vernal Equinox. (See "Corrupt Air" under Air; "Fountains Dry Up" under Dry; Epidemics, Equinoxes, Solstices, Vernal, Wind).

PETIT MAL—A Mild Form of Epilepsy —(See Epilepsy).

PETRIFACTION — Conversion Into a Stony Substance — (See Calculus, Gravel, Hardening, Sand, Stone).

PETS — Domestic Pets — Ruled by ♃. Also Small Animals are ruled by the 6th H. (See "Small Animals" under Animals; Cats, Dogs; "Virus" under Pestilence).

PETTIFOGGING—Tricky—An Inferior Lawyer—☿ afflicted in ♊; ☿ □ or ☍ ♄ indicates those who very seldom treat their clients honestly. (See Cheating, Deceitful, Dishonest, Liars, Libel, Mischief, Politics, Shrewdness, Thieves).

PETULANT—Fretful—Capricious—Captious—Fault-Finding—Vituperative—Hypercritical—The ☽ □ or ☍ ☿; a ♄ characteristic; ♄ afflicted in ♏; ♂ afflicted in the 10th H.; ♀ Sig. in ♌; ♍ on the Asc. (See Fretfulness, Prejudice, Scolding, Virgo).

Petulant Mortalities—(See "Petulant" under Mortality).

PHAGOCYTES—Vis Conservatrix—Cells Which Have the Property of Absorbing—Healing Forces In the Body—Defensive Forces—Ruled by the ☉, ♃, ♂, and ♀. The planetary influences showing strong vitality also favor the power of the Phagocytes. In cases of a weak body the workings and power of the Phagocytes are hindered. (See Absorption, Defensive, Immunity, Preservation, Recuperation, Resistance, Stamina, Tone; "Good", "Low", under Vitality; "Weak Body" under Weak).

PHALANGES—The Bones of the Fingers and Toes—(See Feet, Fingers, Hands, Toes).

PHANTASIES—Fantasies—

Mental Fantasies—(See "Dreamy Mind" under Dreams).

The Phantasies Prejudiced—(See "Prejudiced" under Fancies).

PHARMACY—The Influences Which Favor Pharmacists—(See Chemists).

PHARYNX—The Musculo-Membranous Sac Behind the Mouth—The Naso-Pharynx—Ruled by the ♉ sign.

Abscess—Retropharyngeal Abscess—Abscess Behind the Pharynx—♀ afflicted in ♉; Subs at LCP, SP, and KP.

Adenoids—(See Adenoids).

Diphtheria—Membranous Exudation On the Mucous Surface of the Pharynx—(See Diphtheria).

Diseases Of—Afflictions in ♉. (See Fauces, Neck, Throat).

Mucous Surface Of—Infectious Disease of, with Membranous Exudation—(See Diphtheria).

Naso-Pharynx—Inflammation of—♂ afflicted in ♉; Subs at MCP (4C). (See Nose).

Pharyngitis—Inflammation of—♂ afflicted in ♉.

Plexus—The Pharyngeal Plexus—(See "Diseases of the Neck" under Neck).

PHENOMENA—Phenomenon—A Symptom—Uncommon Occurrences—

Apparitions In the Air—Eclipses of the ☉ or ☽ in fiery signs, and especially in those places ruled by the Signs in which the Eclipse occurs. Also caused by Comets appearing in ♓. (See Air, Illusions).

Psychic Phenomena—Phenomena Referrable to Psychic Causes—(See Psychic). See Dreams, Extraordinary, Fears, Forebodings, Imagination, Mysterious, Obsessions, Obscure, Spirit Controls, Strange, Symptoms, Vagaries, Weird, etc.).

PHILANTHROPIC—Humane—A Lover of Mankind—The ☉ in ♒, or ♒ on the Asc. at B. (See Humane).

PHILOSOPHY—Philosophical—Philosophy and Religion are ruled by ♐ and the 9th H.

Philosophical—♃ in ♐ in the 9th H., and well-aspected. (See Metaphysical, Occult, Religion, Renunciation, Science, Study).

PHILTRES—Love Potions—Ruled by ♀. (See Aphrodisiacs).

PHLEBITIS—Inflammation of a Vein—(See Veins).

PHLEGM—Phlegmatic—Watery Humour—Mucus—Phlegmonous—Mucus from the Bronchi—The Phlegmatic Signs are ♋, ♏, and ♓, the watery signs. Phlegm is ruled by ♄, and also by ☿ when this planet partakes of the nature of ♄. The ♓ sign produces Phlegm. Also the ☽ in aspect to ♄ or ☋ tends to produce phlegm, and to cause its excessive discharge.

Body—Phlegmatic Body—The ☽ gives a smooth, corpulent and phlegmatic body. (See Corpulent, Fleshy).

Breast—Much Afflicted with Tough Phlegm and Slimy Matter In the Breast, Chest, and Lungs, and the Trachea Obstructed—The ☽ in ♋, ☌, P., □, or ☍ ♄ (or ☿ if he be of the nature of ♄) at decumbiture or the beginning of an illness. If the ☽ be decreasing, and near the body of ♄, the disease will continue a long time. (See Bronchial, Consumption, Cough, Lungs).

Catarrh—(See the various paragraphs under Catarrh).

Chest—Tough Phlegm In—(See "Breast" in this section).

Cold, Phlegmatic Diseases—And Death By—Caused by the ☽; the ☽ and many planets afflicted in watery signs, and with a water sign on the Asc. The ☽ assists in causing death by phlegmatic diseases, when the ☉ or Asc. are hyleg, by her evil directions to the hyleg when she holds the dominion of death. (See Cold).

Colds—(See the paragraphs under Colds).

Cough—(See "Rotten Coughs", and the various paragraphs under Cough).

Defluxions—(See this subject).

Discharges of Phlegm—A ♄, ☽, and ☿ disease. Also a ♉ disease. (See Discharges; "Discharges" under Mucous; Rheum).

Diseases—Phlegmatic Diseases—Caused by ♄, ☿, and the ☽, and by the ♉ and ♓ Signs; the ☽ to the ☌ ♄ or ☋ by dir.; the Asc. to the ill-asps. ♄. (See the various paragraphs in this section).

Enteritis—Catarrhal and Phlegmonous Enteritis In Bowels—(See "Enteritis" under Catarrh).

Excessive Phlegm—Excess of—♄ in an angle, occi. of the ☉, and ori. of the ☽. (See "Throat" in this section).

Great Expectoration—Of Phlegm—The ☽ in ♓, and afflicted by the ☉ or ♂ when taken ill, great expectoration, and almost suffocated with phlegm. (See Bronchial, Cough, Lungs; "Humours", "Rheum", under Throat).

Humours—(See "Flow of Humours", and the various paragraphs under Humours).

Larynx — Collections of Phlegm and Mucus In—(See "Phlegm" under Larynx).

Legs—(See "Phlegmasia Alba Dolens" under Legs).

Lungs — Phlegm In — (See Breast, Great Expectoration, in this section; "Bronchitis" under Bronchial; Consumption; "Phlegm" under Lungs; Phthisis, Tuberculosis).

Melancholic Disease—Proceeding from Phlegm—(See "Diseases" under Melancholy).

Obstructions by Phlegm—♄ diseases and affliction. (See Breast, Great Expectoration, Larynx, Lungs, in this section; "Obstructions" under Bronchial, Lungs, Stomach).

Phlegmatic Dolens—(See "Milk Leg" under Legs).

Phlegmon—Suppurative Inflammation —(See Phlegmon, Pus).

Rheum — (See the paragraphs under Rheum).

Salt Phlegm — A ♋ sign disease, and caused by afflictions in this sign. (See "Salt Rheum" under Eczema).

Stomach — Phlegm In the Stomach — ☿ afflicted in ♋. (See Catarrh, Phlegm, under Stomach).

Suffocated — Almost Suffocated with Phlegm — (See "Great Expectoration" in this section).

Temperament—Phlegmatic Temperament—The Phlegmatic Attitude—The Lymphatic Temperament — Given by the ☽; the ☽ in ♓; the ☽ ascending at B.; is also produced by ♄, and is a cold and moist bodily temperament. The Phlegmatic Attitude is especially caused by heavy ♄ afflictions at B., and by dir., and also by a preponderance of influences in the fixed signs. The ♉, ♋, and ♓ signs are phlegmatic. Given by ♓, and with ♓ on the Asc. (See "Dull Eyes" under Eyes; "Temperament" under Lymphatic; Pituitary).

Throat—Excess of Phlegm In — (See "Phlegm" under Throat).

Trachea—Windpipe Obstructed by Phlegm — (See "Breast" in this section).

Whitlows—Phlegmonous Inflammation About the Nails — (See "Nails" under Toes).

PHLEGMASIA ALBA DOLENS — (See "Milk Leg" under Legs).

PHLEGMON—Suppurative Inflammation of Areolar Tissue—(See Nipples; "Phlegmon" under Pus; Suppuration; "Whitlows" under Toes).

Phlegmonous Enteritis—(See "Inflammation" under Bowels).

Phlegmonous Ulcer—(See Ulcers).

PHOBIAS—Fears—Dreads—(See Fear).

PHONATION — The Emission of Vocal Sounds—(See Articulation, Dysphonia, Hoarseness, Larynx, Speech, Voice).

PHOSPHATE — Salts of Phosphoric Acid—

Phosphate of Iron—Ferrum Phosphate —Ruled by the ♓ Sign. (See "Iron Phosphate" under Iron).

Phosphate of Lime — Calcium Phosphate—Ruled by ♑. (See Lime).

Phosphate of Magnesia—Ruled by the ♌ sign. (See Magnesia).

Phosphate of Potassium—Ruled by ♈. (See Biochemistry, Potassium; "Salts" under Zodiac).

PHREN—Phrenic—(See Diaphragm).

Phrenasthenia—(See "Paralysis" under Diaphragm).

Phrenasthesia—(See Idiocy).

Phrenitic Man—(See "Wild Delirium" under Delirium).

Phrenitis—(See "Inflammation" under Brain).

Phrenologist — Case and Birth Data of a Phrenologist and Mesmerist—(See "Mesmerist" under Hypnotism; Mesmerism).

Phrenzy—(See Frenzy).

PHTHISIC — Consumptive — Asthma — (See Asthma, Consumption).

PHTHISIS—A Wasting or Consumption — Pulmonary Tuberculosis — Low and Hectic Fever—

Abdomen — Phthisis Abdominalis— Consumption of the Bowels—♆ in ♍ and afflicting the ☉, ☽, Asc., or Hyleg; ♆ afflicted in ♍ in the 6th H.; ♄ in ♍, occi., and afflicting the ☉, ☽, or Asc.; ♂ afflicted in ♍, inflammatory tubercular trouble in the bowels, and especially if ♂ is in a common sign division of ♍; many afflictions in common signs, and with these signs on the angles. (See "Inflammation" under Bowels; "Consumptive" under Consumption; Navamsa; "Acute" in this section).

Acute Phthisis—♂ in ♊ and afflicted by the ☉ in ♍, and by the ▢ aspect of ♄ or ♆; ♂ in ♊ at B., and afflicted by the ill-aspects of the ☉ by dir. Case— See Chap. XIII, page 90, in Daath's Medical Astrology.

Bowels—Phthisis In—Consumption of —(See "Abdomen" in this section).

Colliquative Sweats — Of Phthisis — (See "Night Sweats" in this section).

Death by Phthisis — Death by Consumption or Tuberculosis—The ☉ hyleg, and afflicted by ♄ from an angle; the afflictions of ♄ and ☿ to the hyleg denote death by Phthisis; ♄ afflicting the hyleg by dir., and holding the dominion of death; ♄ ☌ or evil asp. the Asc. by dir. when not the ruler of the Asc. at B.; ♄ in the 8th H. at B., and afflicting the hyleg; ♄ in the 8th H. at a Solar Ingress into ♈, and afflicting the ☽ or planet ascending, tends to be very fatal according to the sign occupied by ♄; ♅ ☌ ♄ in ♉ or ♊ in the 8th H. at B., and afflicting the ☉, ☽, Asc., or Hyleg; common signs show death by consumptions, and with many planets in these signs at B., with common signs on the angles, or a common sign on the cusp the 6th H., and especially with ♄ therein in the 6th H., and afflicting the hyleg. (See "Death By" under Consumption). For Cases of Death by Phthisis see the Cases at the end of the paragraph "Consumptive" under Consumption).

Fever—The Hectic Fever of Phthisis —(See "Hectic" under Fever).

Fibroid Phthisis — In Lungs — (See "Pulmonary" in this section).

Larynx—Phthisis of—(See "Consumption" under Larynx; "Tubercular" under Throat).

Night Sweats — Colliquative, Excessive, and Profuse Sweats of Phthisis— A ☽ and ♂ disease. A preparation of Lead (Tinct. Saturnina) is good for restraining the profuse sweats of hectic fevers, and in Phthisis. (See Lead, Sweat).

Pulmonary Phthisis—Pulmonary Consumption—Phthisis Pulmonalis—Consumption of the Lungs—Fibroid Phthisis — Pulmonary Tuberculosis — The ☉ ☌ ♄ in ♊ or ♐; the ☉ ☍ ♄ from ♊ or ♐; the ☉ ☌ or P. ♄ in ♊; the ☉ rising at B., and afflicted by ♄; the ☉ or ☽, or both, in common signs and in cadent houses, and especially in the 6th and 12th H., and afflicted by ♄ and ♂; the ☉ in ♒, ☌, P., or ill-asp. ♄, and espec. when ♄ is in the 12th H. and afflicting the ☽ in ♊ at the same time; the ☉ or ☽ in the 6th H., in common signs, and afflicted by ♄; the ☽ in ♊ or ♐, in a cadent house, and afflicted by ♄; ♄ in ♊ when ♄ is the afflictor in the disease; ♄ people become an easy prey to the germs of Phthisis from catching cold from drafts or wettings; a ♄ disease; ♄ afflicted in ♋ or ♓; ♄ in ♋, occi., and afflicting the ☉, ☽, Asc., or Hyleg; caused by ♀ when the dominion of death is vested in her; ☿ afflicted in ♓ or the 8th H.; ☋ in ♊; a ♉, ♊, ♋, and ♓ disease, and caused by afflictions in these signs; a ♉ disease, especially when there are malefics in this sign, and tend to bronchial consumption; planets in ♊, and afflicted by malefics in ♐; the Asc. ☌, P., □, or ☍ ♄ by dir., and ♄ occi. at B.; the 6th Face of ♒ on the Asc. if ♄ be there; the 6th Face of ♓ on the Asc.; Subs at Lu.P., CP, and KP. (See Consumption; "Diseased Lungs", "Pulmonary Affections", under Lungs; Pulmonary, Tuberculosis, Wastings). Case — See "Pulmonary Consumption", Chap. XIII, in Daath's Medical Astrology.

PHYSIC—A Purge—Cathartics—Laxatives—Medicine—An Opening Medicine —Yellow color acts as an opening medicine. Physic works less when the ☽ is in a fixed sign. Dr. Pearce, in his Textbook of Astrology, says, "Healthy Persons should never take Physic." In purging, the ☽ and lord of the Asc. should be descending and under the Earth. Do not give a physic when the ☽ is in a fixed sign, but give it when the ☽ is in a watery sign, as in ♋ or ♓, for the best and quickest results. A physic given when the ☽ is in ♈, ♉, or ♑, the Ruminant Signs, tends to nausea and vomiting. Avoid physic when the ☽ is in ♏, as this sign governs the Excretory System. (See Antiperistalsis; "Biliousness" under Bile; Constipation, Costiveness, Emetics, Enema, Faeces; "Organic" under Functions; "When to Give", "When Not to Give", under Medicine; Nausea, Peristalsis, Podophyllin, Vomiting, Xylostein; "Bowels" under Yellow).

PHYSICAL — Physique — Pertaining to the Physical Body—Physiological—The Physical Body is ruled largely by the sign on the Asc. at B., and the Asc. rules the physical strength, the body, and the organic force. Also as the Sign the ☽ is in at B. is either the Asc. or Descendant at Epoch, this sign should be considered in judging of the physique, as the ☽ is the Astral Mould upon which the body is built. When the ☽ is setting at B., or decr. in light, people come very much under the influence of the sign on the Descendant at B. (See Ascendant, Astral, Body, Descendant, First House; "Organic" under Force; Moon, Prenatal Epoch, Seventh House).

Activity — (1) The Physical Activity Increased — The cardinal signs and ♂ relate especially to physical activity. The ☉ and ☽ to the good aspects ♂ by dir., and ♂ in good asp. to the ☉ and ☽ at B. (See Action; "Active Body" under Active; "Body", "Strength", under Muscles; Strength, Strong). (2) Physical Activity Decreased — (See Apathy, Decrease, Diminished, Dull; "Bad Health" under Health; Inactive, Inertia, Sickly; "Low" under Vitality; "Weak Body" under Weak).

Ailments — (1) Many Physical Ailments—(See "Ill-Health All Thru Life" under Ill-Health; Sickly; "Much Sickness" under Sickness; "Weak Body" under Weak). (2) Physical Ailments Rare—(See "Abundance of Health" under Health; Immunity; "Good" under Vitality).

Appearance—Of the Physical Body— (See the paragraphs and subjects under Appearance, Body, Complexion, Countenance, Eyes, Face, Form, Hair, Height, Shape, Stature, Weight, etc.).

Aura—The Physical Aura—(See Aura).

Being — The Physical Being — The ☉ is the Soul of the Physical Being, and contains in itself every form of manifestation of Phenomena. (See Sun).

Body—The Physical Body—(See the subjects under Body; the various paragraphs in this section).

Comforts—Loss of Physical Comforts —(See Comforts).

Condition—The Physical Condition— Is denoted by the 1st H., and the Sign rising. (See Introduction to this Article; Body, Constitution; "Judging the Health" under Health).

Constitution—The Physical Constitution—(See Body, Constitution).

Debility—Physical Debility—(See Debility, Disease, Ill-Health, Sickly, Weak, etc.).

Defects—Physical Defects—(See Defects).

Degree of Physical Strength — (See Degree).

Derangements—(See Deranged).

Description Of — (See Description; "Appearance" in this section).

Development — Perfect Physical Development—(See Development).

Diseases Of—Disorders—(See the subjects under Disease).

Endurance—Physical Endurance—Strong or Weak, etc.—(See Endurance, Resistance, Stamina, Strength, Tone, Vitality, Weak).

Faculties—(See "Physical" under Faculties).

Feeble Physical Powers—(See Feeble).

Foetus—Physical Plasm of—(See Foetus).

Great Physical Powers—The ☉ in ♐, well-aspected by ♂; the ☉ ✱ or △ ♂; ♂ ✱ or △ ♅. (See Endurance; "Good Health" under Health; "Strength" under Muscles; "Increased" under Strength; "Body" under Strong; "Good" under Vitality, etc.).

Functions—(See the various paragraphs under Functions).

Harmony—Physical Harmony—(See Harmony).

Herbs—Physiological Action of—Therapeutic Action of—(See Herbs).

Judging the Physique—(See the Introduction, "Appearance", and the various paragraphs in this Article).

Limitations—Physical Limitations—(See Limitation).

Muscular Power—(See Muscles).

Planets—The Physiological Planets—(See "Physiological Planets" under Planets).

Resistance—The Physical Resistance Strong or Weak—The fiery signs give the greatest physical resistance and strength, while the watery signs are weakest when on the Asc. at B., and especially ♋ and ♓, and give little physical resistance. (See "Low", "Strong", under Resistance).

Restrictions—Physical Restrictions—(See Limitations).

Sensation; Senses—The Physical Senses—(See Senses).

Strain—Physical Strain—Over-Strain—(See "Body" under Strain).

Strength—The Physical Strength—Strong Body—Weak Body, etc.—(See Feeble; "Body", "Strength", under Muscles; Proud; "Body" under Strong; "Weak Body" under Weak).

Temperament—The Physical Temperament—(See "Natural Temperament" under Natural; the Bodily Temperaments under Temperament).

Vitality—The Physical Vitality—(See Vitality).

Weak—Weak Physical Constitution—(See "Weak" under Constitution; Debility, Feeble; "Low" under Vitality; "Weak Body" under Weak).

Wear and Tear—The Physical Body Able to Withstand Much Wear and Tear—(See Endurance, Immunity; "Strong" under Resistance; "Body" under Strong; "Good" under Vitality; Wear; "Resistance" in this section).

PHYSICIANS—Influences Which Make a Successful Physician—(See "Physicians" under Healers).

PIERCING—Darting—Penetrating—

Eyes—(See "Piercing" under Eyes).

Pains—(See Darting, Sharp, Shooting, under Pain).

PIETY—Pious—Much Given to Religion—(See "Pious" under Religion).

PIGMENT—Pigmentation—(See "Pigmentation" under Skin).

PILES—Hemorrhoids—(See Hemorrhoids).

PILFERING—(See Cheating, Dishonesty, Kleptomaniac, Thieves).

PIMPLES—Pimpled—A Small Pustule or Blotch—The ☉ in ♎, or ♎ on the Asc., tend to cause Pimples, and especially in Middle Life, and Old Age. Also caused by the ☽ in the Winter Tropic ♑ at B.; the ☽ afflicted in ♒ or ♓; ♃ afflicted in ♈, ♋, ♎, or ♑.

Face—Pimples On the Face—Rash On the Face—Face Eruptions—A disease of the ☉; the ☉ afflicted in ♈ or ♎; the ☉ in ♎ in partile asp. the Asc.; the ☽ afflicted in ♈, ♉, or ♊; the ☽ in the Winter Signs ♑, ♒, or ♓; ♃ Sig. in ♈ or ♎; ♃ in ♈ or ♎ in partile the Asc.; born under ♂, a breaking out on the face or skin; an ♈ and ♎ disease, and with these signs on the Asc.; ♎ on the Asc., inclined to pimples when old; the 6th face of ♈ on the Asc. at B.; the 4th face of ♉ on the Asc.; Subs at KP. (See Acne, Blemishes, Blotches; Eruptions; "Eruptions" under Face; Impetigo; "Pustules" under Pus; Skin).

Middle Life—Old Age—Pimples At Middle Life and In Old Age—The ☉ in ♎, or ♎ on the Asc.; many planets in ♎, but the complexion is usually clear and fair in youth. (See "Pimples" under Middle Life).

Red Face and Pimpled—♃ Sig. in ♈. (See "Red" under Face).

PINE—Pine Cone—Pineapple—Ruled by ♂. The Pineapple is a good digestive stimulant. (See "Mars Group" under Herbs).

PINEAL GLAND—The Hypophysis or Conarium—A Small, Reddish, Vascular Body In the Posterior Part of the Third Ventricle—The Third Eye—The Spiritual Center In the Body—The Organ of Spiritual Sight and Spirituality—The Seat of the Soul In the Body—The Organ of Thought Transference—This Gland, or Organ, is ruled by ♆, and ♆ in ♈ especially rules and affects this Gland. In the earliest Races of Humanity this organ is said to have been a Third Eye in the back of the head, so the people of that time, when the Earth was hot and full of dangers, could see in all directions at the same time for protection. In later Ages, when sight in so many directions became less necessary, this organ was withdrawn into the brain, and is now known as the Pineal Gland. (See Orifices.) This Gland in present Humanity is not very well developed, but is now becoming very well developed again in certain types of Humanity, and is especially connected with what is termed "The Sixth Sense". In the coming Sixth and Seventh Races, the Pineal Gland will be very highly developed, and be a powerful organ for high spiritual development and perception. The Pineal Gland is vibrated by the Ether, or Luminous Gas, in the Spinal Canal, and tends to produce Spiritual Sight and Religious Ecstasy.

A high rate of vibration of this gland tends especially to religious ecstasy. Drink, Drugs, and Narcotics produce a supernormal rate of vibration of the Pineal Gland, causing Delirium, and the seeing of Demoniacal Shapes, due to ♆ afflicted in the map of birth, and especially when ♆ is in the watery sign ♓, or in the 12th H. The Pineal Gland is stimulated and awakened also by the ⚹ and △ aspects between ♆ and ♅ at B. Also progressed planets, except ♄, in ☌, ⚹, or △ ♆ tend to awaken the Gland, and to cause unusual cravings and Soul hunger, and often to lead to the use of Narcotics. (See Delirium, Demoniac, Ductless Glands, Ecstasy, Monsters, Narcotics; "Sixth Sub-Race" under Neptune; Pituitary; "Canal" under Spine; Spiritual). See the Chapter on the Pineal Gland in the book, "The Message of the Stars", by Mr. and Mrs. Max Heindel, of the Rosicrucian Fellowship at Oceanside, California.

PIOUS—Reverent—Religious—Godly—(See "Pious" under Religion).

PIRATES—Piracy—

Danger from In Travel—The Significators of Travel in evil aspect to ☿; the afflictor to the Sig. of Travel in the 12th H., and in ♊ or ♍. (See "Danger" under Travel).

Death by Pirates—Danger of—The ☉ conjoined with Antares, Hercules, Hyades, Regulus, Aldebaran, or any eminent star of the nature of ♂ at B., brings this danger. (See "Battle" under Abroad).

Piracy Prevalent—An eclipse of the ☉ or ☽ in ♓; an eclipse of the ☽ in the 3rd Decan. of ♓.

PISCES—The 12th Sign of the Zodiac, and closely related to the 12th H. (See Twelfth House). Symbol of—The Two Fishes. This Sign is the night house of ♃, the exaltation of ♀, and the fall of ☿. The planet ♆ is also strong in this Sign, as ♓ and ♆ rule the Sea. (See Neptune). Pisces is a double-bodied sign, and the most fruitful of all the signs, and tends to a large family when strong at B., and to the production of Twins, Triplets, and multiple births. This Sign is connected with the Hebrew letter Qoph (K), and is also predominant in mirth. Pisces is a sign of restraint and confinement, as symbolized by the Fishes joined together, and a sign of self-undoing. It is called "The Sign of Sorrows", and people born with the ☉ and ♄ in this sign are subject to great sorrows, tribulations, secret enemies, plots, treachery, self-undoing, restraints, confinement, isolation, as well as to reserve, and more of secrecy and seclusion. Pisces is classified as a bicorporeal, broken, changeable, cold, cold and moist, cold-blooded, common, crooked, double-bodied, effeminate, feminine, fruitful, humid, hyemal, imperfect, lymphatic, moist, motive, mutable, mute, negative, nocturnal, obeying, phlegmatic, plastic, relaxing, sickly, southern, torpid, unfortunate, watery sign. Also other qualities assigned to ♓, and which often characterize the Pisces people are—Brooding, clairvoyant, compassionate, confining, consumptive, debauched, dissipated, erratic, fretful, generous, grievous, idle, indifferent, intoxicating, jovial, kind, loquacious, mediumistic, mirthful, obsessional, prodigal, psychic, receptive, reserved, restless, restraining, scattering, secretive, self-undoing, slothful, sorrowful, spiritual, stagnant, susceptible, sympathetic, treacherous, vacillating, weak and of low vitality, worrisome, etc. This sign, when on the Asc. at B., gives the least vitality of all the Signs. It tends to a softening and relaxing effect upon the tissues, and to produce phlegm and mucus. It has a torpid, lymphatic, plastic, and humid action, and leads to many ailments thru carelessness, forgetfulness, or dissipation. This sign, when afflicted at B., and containing the ☉ and malefics, tends to affect the lungs, and many Consumptives have the ☉ or ♄ in this sign, or ♓ upon the Asc. at B. Pisces is said by many Authors to be the most Spiritual Sign of the Zodiac in its higher vibrations, and being the last Sign of the Zodiac, denotes the end of material experiences, and the transition to a higher Spiritual State if the Soul is ready for it. However, with the unregenerate person, those who are drifting with Earth-life tendencies, and being dominated by Personality, it is considered a sign of Drink, Dissipation, Debauchery, and Self-Undong. Being a watery sign, it is restless, changeable, and vacillating, and tends to idleness, slothfulness, and indifference to life's duties in the unawakened person.

PISCES RULES—Externally, ♓ rules the feet and toes. Internally, rules the Glandular System, the Lymphatic System, the Synovial Fluids. Structurally, the Bones of the Feet, the Tarsus, Metatarsus, and Phalanges. Pisces rules the following matters, powers, subjects, habits, organs, functions, conditions, and parts of the body, which subjects see in the alphabetical arrangement—Abdomen and Abdominal Cavity, by reflex action in ♍; Asylums; Banishment; Blood (Fibrin of); Bones of Feet and Toes; Carelessness; Clairvoyance (Psychic and Mediumistic conditions); Cold; Cold and Moist Conditions; Color—Pure White or Glistening White; Confinement (Restraints and Limitations); Drink Habit (Alcoholic Liquors, Dissipation and Debauchery); Exiles; Feet—The Feet from the Ankles to the extremity of Toes; Ferrum Phosphate; Fibro-Ligamentous System and Fibrin of the Blood; Fluidic System; Forgetfulness; Gastro-Abdominal System, by reflex action in ♍; Glandular System; Hospitals; Idleness; Imprisonment; Indifference; Intestinal Mucus; Limitations, and especially those affecting the five Senses, thus restraining the expression of the Soul upon the Material Plane; Iron Phosphate Salt; Lost in out-of-the-way Places; Lymphatic System; Matrix and Secrets where Syphilitic contagion is involved; Mediumship; Misfortune; Moisture (Cold and Moist Conditions); Mucus (the Intestinal Mucus, and Mucus in the

Lungs); Nurses; Ocean; Peritoneal Serum; Phlegm; Pleural Serum; Prisons; Psychic and Spiritual Powers, which are normal, and strengthened by good influences in ♓, and perverted by afflictions in this sign); Relaxation of Tissues; Respiratory System; Restraints and Limitations of Life; Sea (The Seas); Secret Enemies; Secret Parts and the Matrix, and especially where Syphilitic Contagion is involved; Self-Undoing; Serum (the Pleural, Peritoneal, and Synovial); Slothfulness; Softening of Tissues; Sorrow; Spirituality (the Higher Spiritual Consciousness in Advanced and Highly Evolved Souls); Stagnant and Standing Pools of Water; Synovial Serum; Syphilitic Contagion; Tarsus Bones (the Tarsus, Metatarsus, and Phalanges of Feet); Toes; Torpidity; Trouble; Twelfth House; Veratrum Album (one of the 12 Polycrest Remedies); Water (the Ocean, Sea, and Standing and Stagnant Pools of Water); White, and Glistening White Color, etc.

PISCES DISEASES—The Morbid Action of Pisces — The Afflictions of Pisces—See the following subjects in the alphabetical arrangement when not more fully considered here—

Abdominal Diseases — (See the paragraphs under Abdomen, Bowels).

Alcoholism; Blood — Putrefaction In —(See "Putrefaction" under Blood).

Blotches; Boils; Bowel Disorders —- From Wet Feet, and Living In Damp and Cold Places—Colic—Mucus In the Bowels—(See Colic, Mucus, Wet Feet, and the various paragraphs under Bowels).

Breakings Out — (See Eruptions, Pimples, Skin).

Bunions; Carelessness — Ailments From—(See Carelessness).

Chilblains; Chronic Diseases—In the Lungs, such as Consumptions, Tuberculosis, etc.—(See Consumption, Lungs, Phthisis, Tuberculosis, Wastings, etc.).

Club Feet—(See Feet).

Cold and Moist Diseases—Cold, Phlegmatic Diseases—(See "Cold and Moist" under Humours; Phlegm).

Colds—Taken by Wet Feet, or Living In Cold and Damp Places—(See "Cold Taken" under Feet).

Consumptions; Contagious Diseases— Danger From — (See Contagions, Infections).

Corns; Corrupt Blood—(See "Impure Blood" under Impure).

Damp Feet — Colds By — (See "Cold Taken" under Feet).

Debauchery; Defluxions of Humours —(See "Flow Of" under Humours).

Deformities—Of the Feet and Toes— (See "Deformities" under Feet).

Delirium Tremens—(See Delirium).

Demoniacs; Dissipation; Drink Habit —(See Drink, Drunkenness).

Dropsy; Effeminate; Eruptions; Feet —All Diseases and Infirmities In—(See Feet).

Forgetfulness — Ailments Arising From — (See "Forgetfulness" under Memory).

Frenzy; Glandular Tissue—Softening of (See "Softening" under Glands).

Gonorrhoea; Gout; Habits—The Drink and Narcotic Habits — (See Drink, Drunkenness, Narcotics).

Hallucinations; Humours—Defluxion of—(See Defluxions; "Flow Of" under Humours).

Imprisonment—(See Prison).

Insanity; Intestinal Diseases — (See "Bowel Disorders" in this section).

Intoxication; Itch—(See Scabies).

Lameness — (See "Lameness" under Feet).

Lungs —Consumption of —Tuberculosis—(See Consumption; "Pulmonary Affections" under Lungs; Phthisis, Tuberculosis, Wastings).

Mania — Alcoholic Mania — (See "Delirium Tremens" under Delirium).

Matrix —-Womb — Syphilis of — (See "Syphilis" under Womb).

Moist and Cold Diseases—(See "Cold and Moist" in this section).

Mucus—Mucous Disturbances and Discharges—(See Mucous).

Narcotic Habit—(See Narcotics).

Obsessions; Pale and Sickly — (See Pale, Sickly; "Low" under Vitality; "Weak Body" under Weak).

Phlegmatic Diseases—(See Phlegm).

Phthisis; Putrid Blood—(See "Putrefaction" under Blood).

Relaxation of Tissue—(See "Tissues" under Relaxation; Softening).

Rheumatism; Scabies; Secrets — Private Parts — Diseases In — Contagions In—(See Gonorrhoea; "Distempers" under Secrets; "Syphilis" under Womb).

Self-Undoing; Sickly; Softening—Of the Glandular Tissues — (See "Softening" under Glands; "Tissues" under Relaxation; Softening).

Sores—Ulcerous Sores—(See Ulcers).

Spiritual Perversions — (See "Perversions" under Spiritual).

Swollen Feet—(See "Swelling" under Feet).

Syphilitic Contagion — (See Syphilis; "Syphilis" under Womb).

Tender Feet — (See "Tender" under Feet).

Toes —Diseases of—Deformities of— (See Toes).

Tuberculosis; Tumors; Ulcers;

Vitality Low—(See "Low" under Vitality; "Weak Body" under Weak).

Weak Body—(See "Weak Body" under Weak).

Weakness In the Feet—(See "Weakness" under Feet).

Wet Feet — Colds Taken By — (See "Cold Taken" under Feet).

PITCH-BLENDE — A Mineral ruled by H. It is a source of Uranium and Radium. (See Radium, Uranium; "Metals and Minerals" under Uranus).

PITTED DEGREES — Of the Zodiac — Pitted or Deep Degrees of the Zodiac —The Asc., or its lord, in any of these degrees makes the native subject to deep marks by scars or the pockmarks of smallpox. They also cause an impediment in the speech. These degrees are as follows—♈ 6, 11, 16, 23, 29; ♉ 5, 12, 24, 25; ♊ 2, 12, 17, 26, 30; ♋ 12, 17, 23, 26, 30; ♌ 6, 13, 15, 22, 23, 28; ♍ 8, 13, 16, 21, 22; ♎ 17, 20, 30; ♏ 9, 10, 22, 23, 27; ♐ 7, 12, 15, 24, 27, 30; ♑ 7, 17, 22, 24, 29; ♒ 1, 12, 17, 22, 24, 29; ♓ 4, 9, 24, 27, 28. (See "Face" under Smallpox).

PITUITARY BODY—Pituitary Gland—Hypophysis Cerebri—A Small Reddish Body in the Sella Turcica in the Pituitary Fossa of the Sphenoid Bone — Pertaining to Phlegm — The Pituitary Body is a Ductless Gland, and is ruled by ♅ and the ♏ Sign. Uranus in ♈ especially rules and affects this Gland. The Anterior Lobe of this Gland rules over the Creative, or Sex Force, and over the Nerve Fibers. (See "Fibers" under Nerves). The Posterior Lobe rules over the circulation of the Fluids of the body, and especially the circulation in the Kidneys. (See "Circulation" under Kidneys). The Pineal Gland, ruled by ♆, and the Pituitary Body, ruled by ♅, are closely related to the spiritual side of our natures. The Thyroid Gland acts as a connecting body between the Pineal and Pituitary Glands. The Pituitary Body, and also the Pineal Gland, are now more or less dormant and inactive in their workings in the majority of people, but are gradually becoming awakened in the more highly advanced and evolved Souls, and form the link between the Soul and the Spirit World about us. These Glands are gradually coming under the control of the Cerebro-Spinal Nervous System, which system rules the voluntary muscles. The Pineal and Pituitary Glands, acting as Spiritual Centers in our Being, rule over Voluntary and genuine Clairvoyance, Mediumship, Spiritual Sight, etc., and in a coming distant Age will be very highly developed, so that people can see and know what is going on in all parts of the Universe. These organs, or Glands, are not atrophied, as is usually thought by the Medical Profession, but are merely dormant, awaiting their future time and renewed development, and in the coming Sixth Race these Organs will be highly developed and very active. (See "Sixth Sub-Race" under Neptune). The Pituitary Body is awakened and stimulated by the ✶ and △ aspects of ♆ to ♅. Also progressed planets, except ♄, when in ☌, ✶, or △ ♅, tend to arouse and awaken the organ, and to cause unusual cravings and Soul hunger. Uranus acting too freely upon the Pituitary Body often causes too much Pituitary Secretion, and overgrowth of the body, Giants, and Freaks of Nature. (See Freaks, Giants; "Abnormal Growth" under Growth). Lethargy of the Pituitary Body is given by the Lymphatic Temperament. (See "Temperament" under Lymphatic). Uranus in ♉ also tends to diminish the Pituitary Secretion. The Pituitary Body supplies a secretion made up by the Uranus Alchemistry, which, by passing into the blood, aids the growth and nutrition of the body. The assimilation of food is also regulated by ♅ through the Pituitary Body. (See Assimilation, Cerebro-Spinal, Clairvoyance, Ductless Glands, Dwarfed; "Basal Ganglia" under Ganglion; Glands, Leprosy, Mediumship, Nutrition, Phlegm, Pineal; "Creative Force" under Sex; Sphenoid, Spiritual, Thyroid, Uranus). See the Chapter on the Pituitary Body in the book, "The Message of the Stars", by the Heindels.

PITY—Compassion—Mercy—Sympathy—

Has Pity for Others — The watery signs tend to be more emotional, and to soften the nature and create sympathy for others. Venus in ♓ is a strong symbol of sympathy, but if ♄ or ♂ afflict ♀ in this sign, the sympathies and pity may be unwisely or foolishly bestowed. (Pisces is a strong sympathetic sign, being the sign of ♃, the planet of benevolence, and also ♃ in his exalted sign ♋ tends to pity and a sympathetic nature. The Airy Signs ♎ and ♒, when well-aspected at B., and occupied by benefics, are considered very sympathetic signs, and to make the native kind and pitiful of those in sorrow, trouble, illness, or distress. Aquarius is the sign of "The Water Pourer", and people born with the ☉ in ♒, or ♒ on the Asc., tend to be humane and full of mercy for others, and Emancipators, as was Abraham Lincoln, who was an Aquarian. (See Aquarius, Humane, Kind, Merciful, Sympathetic, Well-Disposed).

Shows No Pity — Cruel — Rough — Without Compassion—Merciless—Cold-Blooded, etc. — Born under the strong influence of ♂, and ♂ afflicted and ill-dignified at B. The ♂ signs ♈ and ♏, when afflicted tend to make the nature harder and more severe and cruel, and especially under provocation. The malefics, ♄ and ♂, when rising and elevated at B., and afflicting the mental ruler, ☿, tend to make the nature harder, more cruel, unsympathetic, revengeful, fierce and savage. The ☿ signs tend to be hard and self-occupied, and especially if ♄ be in the Asc., or afflicting the Asc. (See Brutish, Cruel, Fierce, Inhuman; "Rough", "Violent", under Manners; Merciless, Raving, Rough, Savage, Vicious, Violent).

PLACE—Location—Residence, etc.—

Place of Birth—Is ruled by the 4th H. When ♃ is in this house at B., and well-aspected, and with no malefics in this house, the place of birth is the most fortunate location for the native. The native should remain at the place of birth when the 3rd and 9th Houses, the Houses of Home and Foreign Travel, are afflicted by malefics, or ruled by them, as danger, injury, accident, sickness, or death, would be indicated by travel, making the place of birth the safest and most fortunate location. Also if the ☉, ☽, ♃, and ♀ are all above the Earth at B., remain at the place of birth. However, the native should remove from the place of birth when ♃ is in the 4th H. at B., and afflicted by malefics, or when there are malefics in the 4th H., and no benefics there, or when a malefic rules the 4th H., and is evilly aspected. Uranus or ♂ in the 4th H. at B., and afflicted, tend especially to make the birthplace very unfortunate and full of trouble. Also ♄ afflicted in the 4th H. tends to bring many sorrows, delays, hindrances, and disappointments if the native continues to live at the birthplace. (See Abroad, Environment, External, Foreign Lands, Fourth House, Location, Nadir, Native Land, Removals, Residence, Travel, etc.).

Place of Death—The Killing Place In the Map of Birth — The Anareta — Is indicated by the foremost, or most malevolent direction, in a train of evil directions to the hyleg. (See Anareta). For the actual place of the death, and the conditions under which death is apt to occur, see such subjects as Abroad, Accident, Desert, Exile, Foreign Lands, Home, Native Land, Prison, Shipwreck, Travel, Voyages, etc.).

Place of Residence — (See the paragraphs under Residence. Also see Abroad, Location, Native Land, Removals; "Place of Birth" in this section).

PLACENTA—(See "Placenta" under Womb).

PLAGUE—A Contagious, Malignant, Epidemic Disease — Pest — Pestilence, etc. — Plagues are usually coincident with the appearance of Comets in the sign ruling the different Countries and Nations. The appearance of Halley's Comet is usually followed by a Plague, and especially in the Country ruled by the Sign of the Zodiac in which the Comet appears. Plagues are also caused by afflictions in ♌, and are a ♌ and ☉ disease. Also caused by the ☌ of two or more Superior Planets. (See Comets, Eclipses, Epidemics, Pandemics, Perihelion, Pestilence).

Black Death — An Epidemic Disease with dark blotches upon the skin, and caused by the ☌ of several superior planets, and especially in airy signs. In March, 1866, this disease broke out in Dublin, Ireland, at a time when ♂ was badly afflicted in ♒, the sign which rules the blood, and when ♄ was also afflicting Ireland. Also the Black Death occurred in England in the 14th Century.

Bubonic Plague—(See Bubo).

Madness Plague—(See Madness).

Plague Sores—A ♂ disease, and caused by ♂ afflictions. (See Sores).

Spotted Fever—(See Spotted).

PLANETS—Planetary—Dominion of the Planets — From Ancient Times seven Planets have been referred to in Sacred Writings as belonging to, and making up our Solar System. In the Christian Bible, in Rev. 1:4, it speaks of the Seven Churches in Asia, and the Seven Spirits which are before the Throne. In Rev. 1:20 it says, "The Seven Stars are the Angels of the Seven Churches". Occult Writers refer to these verses as meaning our Planets, and the Seven Great Planetary Angels, the Planetary Hierarchies, the Seven Archangels, and that each Planetary Angel is an Aspect of God, and doing the work the Higher Powers have ordained to be done in our Universe. No Planet is, therefore, evil, but may have its disciplinary action for the good of Humanity, and to help Souls on in their Evolution. For the names of the Planetary Angels see "Angel" under each of the Planets. The seven Planets which make up our System are the ☉, ☽, ♄, ♃, ♂, ♀, and ☿. Neptune and ♅ are not spoken of by early Writers, and many Writers say that these two Planets are outside of our Solar System, but have a certain spiritual influence over us, acting thru the Pineal Gland, and the Pituitary Body, which influence is to gradually awaken Humanity to Powers which will be needed, and brought into greater manifestation in the people of the coming Sixth Race. (See Pineal, Pituitary; "Sixth Sub-Race" under Neptune; Pluto; "Influence Of" under Uranus). Much has been written upon the Occult and Mystical side of planetary influence, and the student can find these Teachings in the various Occult and Mystical Societies, such as The Rosicrucians, The Theosophical Society, The Order of Christian Mystics, etc. For the action and influence of the Planets, and the nature of their good and bad aspects over Humanity, see each of the Planets in the alphabetical arrangement. The Masters, Adepts, Initiates, and very Advanced and highly evolved Souls, have conquered the Planetary and Zodiacal influences, and are no longer affected by them, but ordinary Humanity, those who are still drifting with their Stars, and who may be still living in their lower minds, and who also may be breaking the Laws of God and Nature, are considerably affected by the Planetary influences for ill at times, which influences are placed over us for testings, training, education, experience, etc., and all which in the end are for our good and advancement. (See Aspects, Character, Destiny, Fate, Map; "Free Will" under Will). The following paragraphs have to do with the Planets, their Action, Classification, Influence, etc., and along lines which are generally spoken of in the Textbooks of Astrology.

Accidents—And Planetary Influence— (See Accidents, Directions, Events).

Acid Action Of—(See Acids).

Action of the Planets—(See "Action", and the various paragraphs under each of the Planets. Also see Pathological, Perverted, Physiological, Polarity, Tonic, in this section).

Afflictions Of — The Planets may afflict by their evil aspects to the Significators in the Map of Birth, and benefit by their good aspects. The ☉, ♃, ♀, ☿, and the ☽ afflict only by their □ or ☍ aspects. The malefics afflict by their ☌, P., □, or ☍ aspects. However, any aspect of ♄ is considered an affliction in the life of the ordinary person, but his evil aspects are more inimical. Saturn in any part of the horoscope is considered an affliction to the Sign, House, and part of the body so ruled. Judgment cannot be based upon any one affliction, but the progressed planets, transits, directions, and the last New Moon, should be studied. (See Affliction, Aspects, Directions, Lunations).

Alkaline Action Of—(See Alkaline).

Angels—The Planetary Angels—These Angels have charge of the affairs, and various Departments in the rule of our Solar System. They are called "The Elohim" also in the Bible. They each manifest under a different Ray, or Color, and represent the seven principal Planetary Colors, or the seven Primary Colors of the Solar Spectrum. (See "Planets and Color" under Colors; "Angel" under each of the Planets).

Aspects Of—(See Aspects; Afflictions Of, Perverted Action, in this section).

Atonic Planets—(See Atonic).

Baptism — The Planetary Baptism — (See Baptism).

Barren Planets—(See Barren).

Benefic Planets—(See Benefics).

Chemical Action Of—(See Chemical).

Climacterical Years—Of the Planets—(See Climacteric, Cycles, Periods).

Clonic Action Of—(See Clonic).

Cold Planets—♄ is classed as the Cold Planet. The ☽ exerts a cold and moist influence. Mercury is cold when he partakes of the nature of ♄. (See Cold).

Colors and Planets — (See Colors; "Angels" in this section).

Conjunctions Of—(See Aspects; "Afflictions Of" in this section).

Cycles Of — (See Climacteric, Cycles, Periods, Years).

Daily Motion Of — This varies from time to time. A fast motion tends to make diseases more speedy and sharp, and to terminate more quickly. A slow, stationary, or ℞ motion, when such a planet is the afflictor in the disease, tends to make the ailment more protracted and difficult to cure, and especially until such planet assumes a direct, faster, and more normal motion, as seen from the Earth. A Table of the standard Daily Motions of the Planets can be found in the Textbooks of Astrology. Also see the Article on the Motional Strength of the Planets in Chap. XI, in Daath's Medical Astrology.

Debilities Of—Dignities of—Exaltation of—Fall of—Detriment of, etc.—These are mentioned in the Articles on each of the Planets in this book. Also see the Tables of Dignities of the Planets in the various Textbooks of Astrology.

Dignities Of—(See "Debilities" in this section).

Direct Motion — The forward motion of a Planet, as seen from the Earth. The influence of a planet is more fortunate when direct in motion, and also more prompt and swift in disease. (See Direct).

Directional Strength—(See Directions. Also see the Article on "Directional Strength" in Chap. XI, in Daath's Medical Astrology).

Disease — The Planets and Disease — (See Complications, Course, Disease, Ill-Health, Sickness).

Dryness — Planets Exercising a Dry Influence—(See Dryness, Heat).

Electric Planets—(See Electric).

Elevated Planets—(See Elevated).

Exaltation Of — (See "Debilities" in this section).

Fall of Planets — Planets have their fall in the sign in ☍ to the sign of their exaltation, and planets in their fall at B. tend to be more troublesome and evil in health, and other matters. (See "Debilities" in this section).

Feminine Planets—The ☽ and ♀.

Fiery Planets — The ☉ and ♂. (See "Fire Signs" under Fire).

Forms—Planetary Forms—(See Chap. III, on the Planets, in Sepharial's Manual of Astrology).

Fruitful Planets — The ☽, ♃, and ♀. (See Fruitful).

Functions Of—(See "Action", "Functions", and the various paragraphs under each of the Planets).

Geocentric System—Of the Planets—(See Geocentric).

Heliocentric System — Of the Planets —(See Heliocentric).

Herbs—Herbs Ruled by the Planets—(See Herbs).

Hot and Fiery Planets—The ☉ and ♂.

Hours—Planetary Hours—The Hours of the day are ruled by the Planets. There are 24 Planetary Hours in each day. The time from Sunrise to Sunset is divided by 12, which gives the time of the day-time planetary Hours. The Planetary Hours at night are from Sunset to Sunrise, and this time also divided by 12 gives the length of the night Planetary Hours. The Planets rule these hours, from sunrise to sunset, in the following order. On Sunday, the first hour after sunrise is ruled by the ☉; the 2nd planetary hour by ♀; the 3rd hour, by ☿; the 4th hour, by the ☽; the 5th hour by ♄; the 6th hour, by ♃; the 7th hour, by ♂, and the 8th hour by the ☉ again, etc., and in this order on thru the 24 hours. The first planetary hour of each day at sunrise is ruled by the planet which rules the day. Thus, Sunday, ruled by the ☉, the first hour at sunrise is ruled by the ☉. The ☽, ruling Monday, rules the first planetary hour after sunrise. Tuesday is ruled by ♂, and ♂ rules the first planetary hour after sunrise; ☿ the first hour after sunrise on Wednesday; ♃ the first hour after sunrise on Thursday; ♀ the first hour on Friday, and ♄ the first hour after sunrise on Saturday, etc. The planetary hours of each day of the week follow the same order of the planets as given for Sunday in this paragraph. The planetary hours are longer in the daytime in the Summer, as the days are longer, and shorter at night, with the shorter nights. In the Winter time, the night planetary hours are longer, due to the longer nights, and longer time between sunset and sunrise, and the daytime planetary hours shorter, etc. The happenings of each hour are said to be of the nature of the planet ruling the hour. Thus, the ♄ hour brings delays, trouble, hindrances, despondency, increased suffering, and is also known as the hour of death. To take sick in a ♄ hour tends to prolong the disease. (See Calm). The ♂ hour tends to accidents, injury, quarrels, etc., and so on with each of the planetary hours. The important planetary hours to be considered in connection with the health are the ♄ and ♂ hours, which are usually bad hours for the health, or for an operation. The ♃ and ♀ planetary hours also tend to bring alleviation and moderation in disease, and happier conditions. The student should make a study of Planetary Hours in the Textbooks of Astrology. In Dr. Broughton's book, "The Elements of Astrology", the subject is treated quite at length, and also a Perpetual Table of the Planetary Hours given for each of the 12 months of the year, and which can be used and adapted to any location. Also see the Articles on "Hours" in Wilson's Dictionary of Astrology, and in Alan Leo's Dictionary of Astrology. Also read the book, "The Silver Key", by Sepharial. (See "Order of the Planets" in this section; "Hour" under Saturn, Sun; "Days of the Week" under Week).

Houses — The House Position of the Planets—(See each of the 12 Houses, as First House, Second House, Third House, etc.).

Humid and Moist Planets — The ☽ especially rules Moisture. Also ♃ and ♀ give off moisture. (See Moisture).

Illnesses Caused By—(See the section on "Diseases" under each of the planets. Also see Disease, Ill-Health, Infirmities, Sickness).

Inferior Planets—♀, ☽, and ☿.

Influences Of — (See the section on "Influences" under each of the Planets).

Intrinsic Nature—Each planet has its own intrinsic and fundamental nature, rules over a certain Department of life and Human Affairs, and always acts in this manner unless modified by the aspects of other planets, and its sign or house position. Thus, ♄ is cold, contracting, suppressing, hindering, hardening, obstructing, etc. Mars is hot, fiery, hasty, combative, and tends to anger, fevers, inflammation, etc. The nature of the planets is given in the Articles on each of the Planets. Also good Articles on each of the Planets, and their nature, are given in the book, "The Message of the Stars", by the Heindels, and also in the Textbooks and Dictionaries of Astrology. Also see "Action", "Perverted", and the various paragraphs in this section).

Keywords—The Keywords, or the Intrinsic Principle of Each Planet—(See "Principle Of" under each of the Planets).

Kinetic Points — The Static and Kinetic Points for each planet are quite fully considered in Chap. XII, in Daath's Medical Astrology. These points have an effect upon the physical organism. The static point of a planet is its degree of Longitude in a Sign, while its kinetic points are those places in the map affected by its aspects. Thus ♄ in ♏ tends by his static

position to affect the sex nature and organs, and by his reflex aspect, or kinetic point in ♉, to greatly affect the throat and cause throat disorders. (See Ablation, Antipathy, Aspects, Opposites).

Life — The Period of Life Ruled by Each of the Planets—(See Periods).

Magnetic Planets—(See "Negative Planets" under Negative).

Major Planets—(See Major).

Majorities — Of the Planets — (See Majority).

Malefic Planets—(See Malefics).

Mars—(See Mars).

Masculine Planets — The ☉, ♅, ♄, ♃, and ♂ are classed as masculine planets. Also planets are classed as masculine when rising before the ☉ between the 1st and 10th Houses, or setting before the ☉ between the Descendant and Nadir. The ☽ and ♀ are classed as feminine. Mercury is variable according to the sex of the planet with which aspected and configurated.

Mental Planets—♅ and ☿.

Mercury—(See Mercury).

Metals—Metals Ruled by the Planets —(See Metals).

Mind and Planets — (See Intellect, Mental, Mind, Perception, Understanding, etc.).

Minerals — Minerals Ruled by the Planets—(See Metals, Minerals).

Minor Planets—Inferior—☽, ♀, ☿.

Moisture—Planets Exerting a Moist Influence—☽, ♃, ♀. (See Moisture).

Moon—(See Moon).

Motion of the Planets — The motion of the planets tends to modifications in health, disease, and states of the mind, and the planets have various effects in their vibrations over the mind and organism, according to their motion, whether slow, rapid, retrograde, or direct, and the aspects they form to each other, and their sign and house positions from time to time, by transit, direction, or progression. However, the motional strength of planets as related to disease is still considered an uncertain factor by some Authors. (See Daily Motion, Direct, Retrograde, Slow, Stationary, in this section; "Degree of Disturbance" under Disturbed).

Mystery Planet—(See Violet).

Nature Of — (See "Intrinsic" in this section).

Negative Planets—♆, ♄, ♀, and the ☽. (See "Negative Planets" under Negative).

Neptune—(See Neptune, Pineal).

Neutral Planets—(See Neutral).

Nutritive Planets—(See Nutrition).

Occidental—Planets Occidental—(See Occidental).

Orbs of the Planets—(See Orbs).

Order of the Planets—Esoteric Order of the Planets—The Planets considered in this order are as follows—☉, ♀, ☿, ☽, ♄, ♃, ♂. This is also the order of the Planetary Hours in their rotation. (See "Hours" in this section).

Oriental—Planets Oriental—(See Oriental).

Passive Planets—(See Passive).

Pathological Planets—(See Pathological).

Peregrine Planets—(See Peregrine).

Perigee — Planets In Perigee — (See Perigee).

Perihelion — Planets In — (See Perihelion).

Periods of Life—Ruled by the Planets —(See Periods).

Perverted Action Of—Each planet in its action is intrinsically normal, tonic, or above normal; atonic, or below normal; electric, or magnetic, positive or negative. A planet in its fundamental nature is always the same. The action of the planets is changed, perverted, and mutated by the constantly new-forming polarizations formed by aspects to other planets. Also in a nativity there may be too much of the action of a planet, or an insufficiency or permutation, which may lead to disease, mental disorders, etc. Thus, the action and reaction of the planets upon each other is what causes the many contingencies of life, such as sin, suffering, misfortune, disease and death by their evil aspects, and good health, good fortune, peace of mind, etc., by their more favorable aspects, progressions, and directions after birth. (See Aspects, Atonic, Polarity, Tonic; Afflictions Of, Intrinsic Nature, and the various paragraphs in this section).

Physiological Action Of—(See "Physiological Action" under each of the Planets).

Physiological Planets — The ☉, ☽, ♀, and ☿.

Pluto—(See Pluto).

Polarization Of—(See Aspects, Polarity; "Perverted Action" in this section).

Positive Planets—☉, ♅, ♃, ♂. (See Electric, Positive).

Principle Of—(See "Principle Of" under each of the Planets).

Progression Of — (See Directions, Events, Progression).

Prolific Planets — (See "Fruitful" in this section).

Retrograde Planets — (See Retrograde; "Motion" in this section).

Rising Planets—(See Rising).

Rules — What Each Planet Rules — (See the section on "Rules" under each of the Planets).

Setting Planets—(See Setting).

Signs Ruled By—☉ rules ♌; ☽ rules ♋; ♄ rules ♑ and ♒; ♃ rules ♐ and ♓; ♂ rules ♈ and ♏; ♀ rules ♉ and ♎; ☿ rules ♊ and ♍. (See each of the Signs and Planets in the alphabetical arrangement; "Debilities" in this section).

Slow Motion Of—The slow motion of a planet which is the afflictor in the disease tends to make the disease more tedious, lingering, and prolonged, until the planet changes to a direct, or faster motion. (See "Motion" in this section; Slow).

Static Points Of — (See "Kinetic" in this section).

Stationary Position—Of Planets—Denotes constancy and duration of effects when such a planet is the afflictor in the disease, or in matters which it may rule. (See Stationary; "Motion" in this section).

Sun—(See Sun).

Superior Planets—(See Major, Superior).

Tempo and Daily Motion—(See "Daily Motion" in this section).

Therapeutic Properties Of — (See "Therapeutics" under each of the Planets).

Tonic Planets—Tonic Action of—(See "Planets" under Tonic; "Perverted Action" in this section).

Transits of Planets—(See Transits).

Uranus—(See Uranus).

Variable Planets—(See Variable).

Venus—(See Venus).

Vibrations Of—(See Vibration).

Violent Planets — The Malefics — (See Malefics; "Planets" under Violent).

Years—Planetary Years, Periods, and Cycles — (See Climacteric, Cycles, Periods, Years).

PLANTAR—Plantar Nerves—Ruled by ♓. (See Feet).

PLANTS — (See Fruits, Herbs, Odors, Rottenness, Trees, Vegetation; "Plants" in the Articles on each of the Planets, as "Plants" under Mars, Moon, etc.).

PLASM—Plasma—The Fluid Part of the Blood and Lymph—The physical Plasm of the Foetus is formed by ♄. (See Foetus). For Disorders of the Plasm of the Blood and Lymph, see the various paragraphs under Blood, Lymph.

PLASTIC—Capable of Being Moulded— The ☽ is plastic. Also the ♋ and ♓ Signs are plastic, which signs are very agreeable to the ☽, being of a plastic and watery nature. Cell development in a plastic fluid is presided over by ♆. (See Cancer Sign; "Cytoplastema" under Cells; External; "Flexible Mind" under Flexible; Influenced, Moon, Mutable, Negative, Pisces Sign, Receptive, Susceptible; "Signs" under Water).

PLAY — Injuries, Accidents, or Death While At Play, or At Some Amusement, or In Sports—(See Amusements; "Causes" under Blindness; Exercise, Hunting, Sports).

PLEASANT—Pleasing—

Companion—A Pleasant Companion— ☿ ⚹ or △ the ☽, because of his extensive knowledge, and sometimes a pleasant companion. (See Antipathy, Companions, Friends, Sympathy).

Disposition — Pleasant Disposition — (See Cheerfulness, Gentle, Happy, Harmless, Humane, Joy, Kind; "Amiable" under Manners; Mild, Quiet; "Popular" under Reputation; "Sanguine Temperament" under Sanguine).

Expression—A Pleasing Expression— (See "Pleasant" under Face).

Face—A Pleasing Face—(See Beautiful; "Beautiful" under Eyes; Beautiful, Pleasant, Smiling, under Face; Handsome).

Personality — A Pleasing Personality —Good Disposition—Pleasing Manner —A Good Personality—The ☉ well-aspected in ♎; the ☉ Sig. ☌ ♀, a pleasing address; the ☽ Sig. in ♎; ♃ or ♀ well-aspected in ♎; ♀ well-aspected in the Asc.; ☿ Sig. in ♎; ☿ Sig. in ♏, not in any way pleasing or elegant in manner. (See "Disposition" in this section).

Pleasing Address — (See "Pleasing" under Speech).

PLEASURE— Pleasures—Delights—Enjoyments—Amusements — Recreations —Sports—Pleasures, and the nature of the pleasures, are ruled by ♀, the ♌ sign, and the 5th H. Also ♐ is a pleasure-loving sign. The Animal and Worldly Pleasures are ruled over largely by ♂ and ♀, and by afflictions to the planets. The Higher, or Spiritual Pleasures, usually come from the good aspects to the ☉, ♆, ♅, ☿, or to any of the planets in the map of a more Advanced, Awakened, and Spiritualized Soul. Pleasures may be of a high or low nature, and the following subjects have to do with Pleasure in its various forms, and its effects upon the Native. See these subjects in the alphabetical arrangement—

Abandoned Persons—(See Debauched, Depraved, Profligate).

Abnormally Fond of Pleasure—Much Given to Pleasure and Enjoyment, and Especially of a Worldly Nature—Addicted to Pleasure—The ☉ Sig. in ♋, ♎, or ♓; the ☽ in the 5th H. at B.; the ☽ to the ☌ ♀ by dir.; the ☽ to the place of Canis Majoris; the ☽ at full in a nocturnal geniture, sepr. from ☿ and applying to ♀; ♄ Sig. ☌ ♀; ♄ to the ☌ or good asps. ♀; ♃ Sig. in ♉, ♎, or ♐; ♃ in ♐, fond of outdoor pleasures; ♂ ☌ ♀, and especially in ♏, fond of sexual pleasures; ♀ ascending at B., strong inclination for pleasure; ♀ in ♓; ♀ in ♋, a pleasure-loving disposition; ♀ by Periodic Rev. to the ☌ the radical ☉; ♀ in the Asc. near the horizon; ♀ to the good asps. her own radical place by dir.; ♀ Sig. in ♑, fond of enjoyment; ☿ in ♐; ☿ at a Solar Rev. passing the place of the radical ♀; ☿ to the good asps. ♀ by dir.; the 2nd Decan. ♉ on the Asc., ruled by the ☽; the 1° or 6° ♍ on the Asc. at B.; the 6th face ♌ on the Asc. (See the various paragraphs in this section).

Accidents—While Seeking Pleasure— Accidents At Pleasure Parties—♂ in the 5th H., □ or ☍ the ☉ or ☽. (See Amusements, Exercise, Play, Sports).

Addicted to Pleasure — (See "Abnormal", and the various paragraphs in this section).

Amusements—Given To—(See Amusements).

Appetites—Seeks Pleasure Thru Gratification of—(See the paragraphs under Appetites).

Averse to Pleasure—Seeks Very Few Pleasures—♄ in ♌ or the 5th H. (See Apathy, Aversions, Celibacy, Deviations, Miserly; "Free from Passion" under Passion; Recluse, Secretive, Selfishness).

Bohemian Pleasures — Given To — ♅ strong at B.; ♅ by transit ☌ the radi-

cal ♀; ♆ afflicted in the 5th H.; ♀ to the ☌ or ill-asp. ♅ or ♂ by dir.; ♀ afflicted at B., and to the ☌, □, ☍, or P. the ☽, ♅, ♂, the Asc. or M.C. by dir.; ♀ by Periodic Rev. to the ill-asps. the radical ☉; ☿ strong at B. (See "Free Living", "Free Love", under Free; "Unconventional" under Love Affairs; "Loose Morals" under Morals; "Clandestine" under Sex).

Cruel Pleasures — (See Cruel, Masochism, Sadism; "Violence" under Passion).

Danger—In the Pursuit of Pleasure— ♅ afflicted in the 5th H. (See Accidents, Ill-Health, in this section).

Death—From Excess of Pleasures— Death In the Pursuit of Pleasure — (See "Causes His Own Death" under Death; "Death" under Bathings, Debauchery, Eating, Drink, Intoxication, Love Affairs, Sports, etc.).

Disease—From Excessive Pleasures— ♀ diseases; ♀ afflicted at B. by ♂, ♅, or ♆; ♀ or ♂ afflicted in the 5th or 6th H. (See Amorous; "Brings Disease Upon Himself" under Disease; Dissipation, Drink; "His Own Worst Enemy" under Enemies; Excesses, Gluttony, Intemperance, Lust; "Health Injured" under Men; Opposite Sex; "Diseases" under Passion, Sex; Venery).

Drink — Pleasure from Drink and Liquors—(See Drink).

Eating—The Pleasures of — (See Appetites, Cravings, Drink, Eating, Epicureans, Feasting, Food, Gluttony).

Energies Wasted—In Pleasure Seeking—♂ afflicted in the 5th H.; ♂ afflicting ♀. (See "Wasted" under Energies).

Enjoyment — Abnormally Fond of — (See "Abnormally" in this section).

Epicureans—Given to Pleasure, Luxury and Feasting—(See Epicureans).

Excessive Pleasures — Excesses In — The 6th face of ♋ on the Asc. (See "Diseases", and the various paragraphs in this section).

Extravagant Pleasures — (See Dress, Eating, Expense, Extravagance; "Rich Food" under Food; Habits, Luxuries, Prodigal).

Feasting—Given To—(See Epicureans, Feasting, Gluttony).

Fond of Pleasure—(See "Abnormally Fond Of", and the various paragraphs in this section).

Food — Extravagant In — (See "Extravagant" under Food).

Free Living—Free Love—(See Free).

Given to Pleasure — (See "Abnormally", and the various paragraphs in this section).

Gluttony — Gormandizing—(See Gluttony).

Gratification — Of the Animal Appetites — Excesses In—(See Appetites, Excesses, Gratification, Indulgences, Self-Indulgent).

Habits—(See the various paragraphs under Habits).

Health Injured—By Lustful and Inordinate Pleasures—(See Amorous; "Wasted" under Energies; Excesses, Inordinate, Lust; "Health Injured" under Men).

Hedonism—(See Self-Indulgent).

High Living—(See High).

Ill-Health—Thru Inordinate Pleasures—(See Diseases, Health Injured, and the various paragraphs in this section).

Inclined to Pleasure—(See "Fond Of" in this section).

Indulgent — (See Indulgent, Self-Indulgent).

Injudicious Pleasures—Diseases From—♀ diseases. (See Imprudent, Indiscretions, Injudicious).

Injuries Thru Pleasure—(See "Accidents" in this section).

Inordinate Pleasures—(See Excesses, Inordinate).

Jovial—Joyous—(See Joy).

Lascivious; Lewd; Libidinous — (See Lewd).

Licentiousness; Loose Pleasures—Immorality—(See "Loose Habits" under Loose; "Adulterous" under Love Affairs; "Loose Morals" under Morals; "Clandestine" under Sex).

Love Affairs—(See the various paragraphs under Love Affairs).

Low Pleasures — Given to Low and Sensuous Pleasures—♆ afflicted in the 5th H.; denoted by the 5th H.; ♂ □ or ☍ ♀; ♀ to the ☌ ♂ by dir.; ♀ afflicted at B., and to the ☌ or ill-asp. the Asc. by dir. (See Low Company, Low Public Houses, Low Women, under Low).

Lustful Pleasures — Given To — (See Amorous, Lust; "Passional Excesses" under Passion; "Sensuous" under Sensuality).

Luxuries; No Love of Pleasure—(See "Averse" in this section).

Opposite Sex—Seeks Pleasure With—(See Opposite Sex).

Outdoor Pleasures — Fond of — (See Exercise, Hunting, Sports).

Parties—Accidents At Pleasure Parties—(See "Accidents" in this section).

Passional Pleasures — (See Amorous, Love Affairs, Lust, Passion, Perversions, Sensuality, Sex).

Peculiar Pleasures—Given To—♅ in the 5th H. (See Peculiar).

Play — Accident or Death While At Play — (See Play; "Accidents" in this section).

Pleasure Parties—(See "Accidents" in this section).

Pleasure Seeking Generally — ♀ elevated above, and configurated with the ☽ at a Solar Ingress or Eclipse.

Plethora—From Excesses, Indulgences and Pleasure Seeking—(See Plethora, Surfeits).

Profligate—Profligate Love of Pleasure, and Sickness From—Lord of the 6th or 12th H. in the 5th H., and afflicted. (See Profligate).

Reckless—In the Pursuit of Pleasure—(See "Pleasure" under Recklessness).

Recreations; Religious Enjoyments—(See "Exaltation" under Emotions; "Devotion", "Ecstasy", and the various paragraphs under Religion).

Sensuous Pleasures—Sex Pleasures—(See Amorous, Love Affairs, Lust, Passion, Sensuality, Sex, etc.).

Sex Pleasures — (See Passional, Sensuous, in this section).

Sickness—From Pleasurable Excesses—(See Disease, Health Injured, in this section).

Social Pleasures — (See Companions, Friends, Love Affairs; "Popular" under Reputation; Social Relations).

Study—Pleasure and Enjoyment In—(See Learning, Reading, Study).

Surfeits — From Excesses In Eating, Drink, and Pleasures — (See Plethora, Surfeits).

Table—Given to the Pleasures of the Table, and to Feasting—(See Diet, Eating, Epicureans, Feasting, Gluttony).

Temperate—Should Be Temperate and Moderate In Pleasure, and Excesses Avoided—When the 6th face of ♉ is on the Asc. at B. (See Temperate).

Theatre—A Lover of—(See Theatres).

Too Much Pleasure — Inclined To — (See "Abnormally Fond Of" in this section).

Travel — Takes Pleasure In — (See Travel).

Unfortunate Pleasures — Health Undermined By—♆, ♅, or ♂ afflicted in the 5th H.; ♂ ☌ or ill-asp. ♀; ♀ in the 5th H., and afflicted by malefics; ♀ afflicted in the Asc. at B.; ♀ afflicted at B., and to the ☌ or ill-asps. the Asc. by dir.; ♀ ascending at B., and afflicted or ill-dignified; ♀ by Periodic Rev. to the ill-asps. the ☽, ♂, or M.C. (See Amorous, Drink, Excesses, Indiscretions, Inordinate, Lust; "Health Injured" under Men; Passion, Sex, Venery, etc.).

Unrestrained Pleasures — (See Depraved, Dissipated, Dissolute, Drink, Drunkenness, Lewd, Licentiousness, Lust, Passion, Profligate, Venery, Wanton, etc.).

Venery; Vices; Vicious Pleasures — Fond of—(See Vicious).

Violence — Resorts to Violence In Seeking Sex Pleasures — (See "Violence" under Passion).

Vitality Wasted — And Lowered by Excessive Pleasures and Wasted Energies—(See "Wasted" under Energies; Excesses, Inordinate, Lust; "Passional Excesses" under Passion; "Waste" under Vitality).

Wanton Pleasures — (See Lust, Passion, Wanton).

Waste of Energies—In Seeking Pleasure—(See Disease, Energies Wasted, Health Injured, Vitality Wasted, in this section).

Whoremongers — (See Harlots; "Low Company" in this section).

Women—Fond of—(See "Addicted to Women", "Women", under Men).

PLEIADES—Lucida Pleiadum—A Nebulous Group of seven Stars in the 27° ♉, in the Bull's Neck, stars of the 5th magnitude, except the middle star, which is of the third magnitude. Many of the evils which befall Humanity are connected with the influences of these stars when they rise with the Lights, or are directed to the Asc. The Pleiades are of the nature of the ☽ and ♂, and have special affinity with the Eyes. Blindness is one of the principal afflictions caused by the Pleiades, and resulting from Accidents, Measles, or Smallpox complications. The Pleiades tend to injuries to the eyes, bad eyes, hurts and injuries to the face; illness, sickness, disgrace, ruin, imprisonment, violent death, and every evil that can befall Humanity. (See Nebulous). The Pleiades are mentioned many times in the Textbooks of Astrology, in connection with the Eyes, Disease, Calamity, and the various afflictions which come to Humanity. These influences have been gathered up and listed in this book under the subjects where the Pleiades have a part. These subjects are as follows, which see in the alphabetical arrangement—

Accidents to Eyes—(See "Accidents" under Eyes).

Arms—(See "Wounds" under Arms).

Bad Eyes—(See "Bad" under Eyes).

Beheaded; Blindness—In One or Both Eyes—Partial Blindness— (See Blindness).

Blows—(See "Death By" under Blows).

Both Eyes—Blindness or Injury To—(See "Total Blindness" under Blindness; Accidents, Injury, under Eyes).

Calamity — (See "Many Calamities" under Calamity).

Conjunctivitis; Controversies — (See "Quarrelsome" under Quarrels).

Cuts; Death — Violent Death — (See "Death" under Violent).

Defects In Eyesight—(See Defective, Weak, under Sight).

Disgrace; Evil—Every Evil Upon Humanity — (See "Every Evil" under Evil).

Exile—(See Banishment).

Eyes—Blindness In—Hurts and Accidents To—Diseases of—Defects In—Weak Eyes — Bad Eyes, etc. — (See Blindness, Conjunctivitis, Eyes; "Eyes" under Left, Right; Retina, Sight).

Face—(See "Hurts" under Face).

Fever—(See Death from Fever, High Fever, Violent Fever, under Fever).

Goiter; Hurts—To Eyes and Face—(See "Hurts" under Eyes, Face).

Imprisonment—(See Prison).

Injuries — To Eyes and Face — (See "Eyes" under Exercise; Accidents, Hurts, Injuries, under Eyes, Face; Sword).

Lustful—(See Lust).

Measles—(See "Measles" under Blindness).

Murder—(See A Murderer, Death by Murder, Many Murders Prevalent, under Murder).

Nearly Blind — (See "Nearly Blind" under Blindness).

Nebulous Stars—(See Nebulous).

One Eye—Blind In One Eye—Loss of One Eye—(See "One Eye" under Blindness).

Ophthalmia—(See Conjunctivitis).

Pestilence—(See "Death" under Pestilence).

Quarrels—(See "Quarrelsome" under Quarrels).

Ruin; Sharp Instruments—Death By —(See Instruments).

Shipwreck; Sickness; Sight—Defects In—Blindness—(See Blindness, Sight).

Smallpox — (See "Smallpox" under Blindness; "Face" under Smallpox).

Stabs; Throat — (See "Cuts" under Throat).

Total Blindness—(See "Total" under Blindness).

Tragical Death—(See Tragical).

Trouble — (See "Causes" under Trouble).

Unfortunate; Untimely Death — (See Untimely).

Violent Death—Violent Fevers—(See "Violent" under Fever; "Death" under Violent).

Weak Eyes—(See "Weak Eyes" under Eyes).

Women—Tragical Death by Means of —(See Tragical; "Female Treachery" under Treachery).

Wounds — To Eyes and Face — (See "Injuries" in this section).

PLENTY—Plentiful—Plenitude—Abundance—Fullness—

Fluidic Plenitude—(See "Full Moon" under Moon).

Hair—(See "Abundance" under Hair).

Health — (See "Abundance" under Health).

Heat — (See Abundant, Excessive, Plenty, under Heat).

Vitality—(See Good, Superabundance, under Vitality). See the subjects and paragraphs under Abundance, Exaggerated, Excess, Excesses, Hyper, Increase, Much, Over, Super, Tonic, etc.

PLETHORA—Abnormal Fullness of the Blood Vessels—Too Much Blood—The Plethoric Habit—Hyperaemia—Localized Swellings — Plethoric conditions in the body tend to be at their worst at the time of the Full Moon, when the fluids of the body are at high tide. Plethora tends to High Blood Pressure, Hyperaemia, Localized Swellings; Fullness at the Stomach, and Gas in Stomach from Gormandizing; Apoplexy; Epistaxis (Nose Bleed); Excessive Menses. Jupiter rules all diseases that arise from a Plethoric Habit. Plethora is a condition caused by the ☉, ♃, or ♀, and by afflictions to these bodies. Is a ☉ disease, and especially caused by superfluous nourishment; the ☉ afflicted by ♃; the ☉ to the □ or ☍ ♃ by dir.; a ♃ disease, as ♃ is plethoric, and tends to surfeits, fullness, thick and impure blood, and especially caused by gormandizing and bad habits in eating, and by gluttony, etc.; ♃ afflicted in ♉, plethora from high living; ♃ □ or ☍ the ☽, plethora and malaise; ♃ □ or ☍ Asc.; ♃ ☌ or P. ♂; the ☽ □ or ☍ ♃, ♅, or ♀; ♀ afflicting the ☉, ☽, or ♃; ♀ afflicted in the 6th H.; the Asc. to the □ or ☍ ♃ by dir.; the ☉ □ or ☍ ♃.

Asthenic Plethora—A ♀ disease, and due to the atonic action of ♀. This is a more feeble form of plethora. (See Asthenia, Atonic).

Sthenic Plethora — Sthenic Distentions—A ♃ disease and affliction, and caused by the plus, or tonic action of ♃. Jupiter causes plethora from too full a habit, over-eating, too much blood, etc., and especially when afflicted, or afflicted in the 6th H. (See "Too Much Blood", "Pressure", under Blood; "Excesses" under Eating; "Full Habit" under Habits; "Impure Blood" under Impure; Sthenic, Tonic). Also, for further study along this line, see Apoplexy, Carbuncles, Decay; "Complications" under Disease; Distentions, Excess, Excesses, Flatulence, Fullness; "Stomach" under Gas; Gluttony; "High Living" under High; Hyperaemia, Malaise; "Profuse" under Menses; "Full Moon" under Moon; "Epistaxis" under Nose; "Superfluous" under Nutrition; Pressure, Surfeits, Swellings; "Rupture" under Vessels, etc.).

PLEURA — The Serous Membrane Enveloping the Lungs—The Pleural Cavity—Pleurisy—The Pleura is ruled by the ☽, ♃, and the ♋ sign. Cancer also rules the Pleural Cavity. The Pleural Serum is connected with the ♓ sign. (See Serum; "Fifth Thoracic" under Ganglion). The Serous Membranes, Surfaces, and Fluids are under the rule of the ☽ generally.

Crisis In Pleurisy — May be terminated from the 3rd to 8th day after the beginning.

Death by Pleurisy — Denoted by the ☉; the ☉ to the ill-asps. ♃ by dir.; the ☽ in ♎, ☌, or ill-asp. any of the malefics as promittors; ♃ much afflicted at B., and afflicting the hyleg by dir.

Emphysema—Pleural Emphysema—A ♊ disease, and afflictions in ♊; a ♅ disease; ♅ in ♊; Subs at Lu.P. (See "Emphysema" under Chest; Emphysema).

Inflammation of the Pleura—Pleurisy — Pleuritis — The ☉ hyleg, and to the □ or ☍ ♃ by dir.; the ☽ in ♐, ☍ ♃ in ♊; the ☽ hyleg, and to the □ or ☍ ♃, and ♃ afflicted at B.; the ☽ afflicted in ♎, and afflicting the hyleg therefrom; a ♃ disease; ♃ afflicted in ♉, ♊, or ♋ tends especially to affect the pleura; ♃ afflicted in ♌ or ♎; ♃ afflicting the ☉ by dir; ♂ in ♊ and ☌ the Asc. by dir.; ♂ in watery signs, and ☌, □, or ☍ the Asc. by dir.; a ♊ disease and afflictions in ♊; the Asc. to the □ or ☍ ♃ by dir., and ♃ afflicted by ♂; the Asc. to any aspect ♃ by dir., and ♃ afflicted at B., and especially if ♃ be in ♌ or ♒; the Asc. to the ☌ ♃ by dir., and ♃ afflicted at B.; caused by afflictions in ♉, ♊, ♋, ♌, ♎, or ♒; Subs at Lu.P. (See "Inflammation" under Lungs).

Pleurisies—The ☉ afflicted in ♊; the ☽ afflicted in ♎; ♄ afflicted in ♊; ♃ afflicted in ♊, ♌, ♎, or ♒; ♃ afflicting the ☉ by dir.; ♃ by direction in ♌ or ♒, and ☍ the Asc.; ♂ afflicted in ♊ or ♐; ♂ in ♌ in the 6th H.; ♂ affl. in ♋; ☿ afflicted in ♊ or ♐; caused by afflictions in ♊, ♋, ♌, ♎, and ♒; a ♊, ♋, and ♌ disease.

Pleurisy—(See "Inflammation" in this section).

Pleurodynia — Pain—(See "Pain" under Intercostal).

Pleuro-Pneumonia — ♂ afflicted in ♊ in the Asc. or 6th H.; Subs at Lu.P. and KP. (See Pneumonia).

PLEXUS — Plexuses — A Network of Nerves or Veins—The seven great and important Nerve Plexuses are the Cardiac, Cavernous, Pharyngeal, Laryngeal, Solar, Prostatic, and Sacral.

Aortic Plexus—(See Hypogastrium).

Brachial Plexus—The action of the ☿ Group of Herbs tends to pulmonary innervation thru the Brachial Plexus. The ☉, ☽, and other planets, acting thru the ♊ sign tend to affect this Plexus and the Respiratory System. (See Brachial; "Middle Cervical" under Ganglion).

Cardiac Plexus — The Deep Cardiac Plexus—(See "Middle Cervical" under Ganglion).

Carotid Plexus—(See Carotid; "Ribes" under Ganglion).

Cavernous Plexus—(See "Ribes" under Ganglion).

Coronary Plexus—The Right and Left Coronary Plexuses—(See "Middle Cervical", "Fifth Thoracic", under Ganglion).

Diaphragmatic Plexus — (See Diaphragm).

Ganglion — (See the various paragraphs under Ganglion).

Gastric Plexus — (See "Fifth Thoracic" under Ganglion).

Hemorrhoidal Plexus — (See Ductless Glands).

Hepatic Plexus—(See Hepatic).

Hypogastric Plexuses—(See "Impar", "Lumbar", under Ganglion; Hypogastrium).

Intestinal Plexuses — (See the Introduction under Bowels; "External Humours" under Humours).

Laryngeal Plexus—(See Larynx).

Mesenteric Plexus—(See "Splanchnic" under Ganglion; Mesentery).

Pharyngeal Plexus—(See Pharynx).

Post-Pulmonary Plexuses — (See "Middle Cervical" under Ganglion; Pulmonary).

Prostatic Plexus—(See Prostate).

Renal Plexuses—(See Ductless Glands; "Lumbar" under Ganglion; Kidneys).

Sacral Plexus—(See Sacrum)

Solar Plexus — Is under the internal rulership of ♍, and is the seat of the Life Force, or Prana, in the physical body. Good descriptions of the nature and functions of the Solar Plexus are given in the books, "The Key to the Universe", by Dr. and Mrs. Homer Curtiss. Also in the book, "Cosmo-Conception", by Max Heindel. (See Ductless Glands; "Splanchnic" under Ganglion; "Innervation" under Gastric; "Force" under Vital).

Spermatic Plexus — (See Ductless Glands).

Splenic Plexus—(See "Fifth Thoracic" under Ganglion; Spleen).

Supra-Renal Plexus — (See Ductless Glands).

PLIABLE—(See Bending, Flexible, Influenced; "Mutable Disposition" under Mutable; "Negative Nature" under Negative).

PLODDING—A Plodding and Laborious Nature — (See "Laborious" under Labor).

PLOTS—Conspiracies—Secret Enmities —Caused by ♆ and the 12th H. influences, and afflictions in the 12th H., and especially malefics in this House.

Active In Plots — Schemes and Intrigues—☿ afflicted in the 12th H.

Death by Plots—Injury by Plots—♄ and ♂ elevated above, and in evil aspect to the ruler of the horoscope, enemies conspire against the native. (See "Death" under Ambushes, Enemies, Enmity, Murder, Poison, Treachery, Violence).

Many Plots Generally—An eclipse of the ☉ in the 1st Decan. of ♏; an eclipse of the ☽ in ♑; Comets appearing in ♎.

Prison — Imprisoned Thru the Plots of Relatives or Children—(See "Plots" under Prison).

Society—A Plotter Against Society—Bomb Plotters—(See Anarchists). For other influences along this line, which may lead to plots and treachery, see Artifice, Contests, Criminal, Dangerous, Destructive, Duels; "Secret Enemies" under Enemies; Hatred, Kidnapped, Libel, Malevolent, Malice, Mischief; "A Murderer" under Murder; Neptune; "Death by Poison" under Poison; Revengeful, Shrewdness, Treachery, Twelfth House, Vicious, Violent, etc.

PLUGS — Clots—Obstructions—(See Clots, Embolism, Infarcts, Obstructions, Thrombus).

PLUMBAGO—(See Graphite, Lead).

PLUMBUM—(See Lead).

PLUMP—Plump Body—Somewhat Fat —Distended—Filled Out—

Plump Body—The ☉ Sig. in ♓, plump and fleshy; the ☽ Sig. in ♈, rather plump; the ☽ in ♈ in partile asp. the Asc.; the ☽ Sig. in ♓, plump or fat; the ☽ in ♓, partile the Asc., plump or fat, and with a mean, short stature; the ☽ increasing causes a fat, plump, full, and tall body; ♄ Sig. in ♒, corpulent and plump; ♃ Sig. in ♓, plump and fleshy; ♃ Sig. in ♉, ♊, ♋, ♒, or ♓; ♃ Sig. in ♋, rather plump, but disproportioned; in Hor'y Q., ♃ as Sig. denotes a fat and plump person; ♀ Sig. in ♉, plump but not gross; ♀ Sig. in ♓, plump and fleshy; ♀ in ♓, partile the Asc., plump, middle-sized, and rather fleshy; ♀ rising in the Asc.; ♒ on the Asc., plump, robust, strong, well-set, healthy make; ♓ on the Asc.; given by the Sanguine Disposition. (See Compact, Corpulent; "Plump" under Face, Hands, Lips; Fat, Fleshy, Full, Lumpish, Sanguine, Stout).

PLUTO—The Planet Pluto—This planet will not be considered in this Edition of this book, as very little is known of it, and at present is considered by many Authorities to be a hypothetical planet. It is also doubted by some Writers as being a part of our Solar system, and is said to be outside of the Earth's Zodiac in the greater part of its orbit. (See Planets). Mr. E. H. Bailey, Editor of the British Journal of Astrology, writes in the October, 1931 issue of his Journal, and says—"I have no belief whatever in the alleged influence of this planet. It is a very great question whether it is a member of our Solar System . . . and I would warn my readers not to accept anything at the present time. It is far too early to lay down definite information with regard to a body which may, or may not, have any astrological influence." Also in the November, 1932 issue of the British Journal, Mr. Bailey further says—

"Several correspondents have written me asking for my opinion respecting this planet, and whether I consider it has any real influence in Astrology, and if so, in what way its influence will be felt. Also what sign it rules. To be quite candid, I must confess that I have little or no belief in this planet, and from the evidence which I have obtained personally, and what has been sent to me by students, I see no reason whatever to include it when dealing with horoscopes. It is far too early in the day for students to lay down any definite information as to its influence, real or imaginary, yet one would think from published statements that certain students were fully aware of its action in horoscopes, and knew nearly all there was to be known about it. A number of horoscopes have been sent to me from readers, in which they allege that certain events have been shown by this planet, but in all the cases sent, I have been able to detect the real cause without incorporating Pluto, or any other hypothetical planet."

PNEUMOCONIOSIS — Lungs Diseased by Dust Inhalation—(See this subject under Lungs).

PNEUMOGASTRIC NERVE — Vagus Nerve—Ruled by ♄. Saturn badly afflicted at B. tends to restrict and obstruct the action of this nerve, and to cause indigestion, irregular heart action, lung disorders, suppression of the urine, stools (faeces), and also to cause worry and fears. Case of Obstruction of this Nerve—See Fig. 14F in the book, "Astro-Diagnosis" by the Heindels. (See "Suppression" under Faeces; "Pneumogastric" under Fears; "Impeded" under Heart; Indigestion; "Obstructions" under Lungs, Nerves; Retentions, Suppressions, Urine, Worry, etc.).

PNEUMONIA—Inflammation In the Lungs—Lung Fever—The ☉, ☽, or ♄ afflicted in ♓, from catching cold, wet feet, or living in a damp place, and especially when these planets are in ☌ malefics in the 12th H.; the ☉ in ♓, □ the ☽ in ♐; the ☽ ☌ ♆ in ♓ in the 12th H., from catching cold; the ☽ afflicted in ♊; ♅ afflicted in ♊; ♅ in ♊ in the Asc., and afflicted by ♃, ♀, and the ☽; a ♄ disease; ♄ afflicted in ♊, and tending to consolidation; ♄ afflicted in ♓, from catching cold thru the feet; ♄ afflicted in ♐; ♄ in a strong sign of the ☽, and the ☽ in a ♄ sign; a ♃ disease, and due to surfeits caused by ♃, congested blood vessels, corrupt and impure blood, the result of gluttony and gormandizing, and Pleurisies also result from the afflictions of ♃; ♂ afflicted in ♉, ♊, ♎, or ♐; ♂ afflicted in ♊ in the Asc. or 6th H.; a ♊ disease, and afflictions in ♊; malefics in ♊ and common signs; malefics in ♊, and afflicting ♃ and ♀, the rulers of the circulation, and interfering with oxygenation, tends to colds, coughs, and even running into double pneumonia; the 3rd H. and ☿ are often involved with the afflictions which cause this disease; Subs at Lu.P., CP, and KP. Case—See "Pneumonia", in Chap. XIII, in Daath's Medical Astrology. (See "Pulmonitis" under Lungs; the paragraphs in this section).

Broncho-Pneumonia — (See "Pneumonia" under Bronchial).

Catarrhal Pneumonia—The ☽ afflicted in ♊. (See Catarrh).

Catching Cold — Pneumonia From — The ☉, ☽, or ♄ afflicted in ♓, from wet feet, or living in damp places. (See "Cold Taken" under Feet).

Consolidation In—♄ afflicted in ♊. (See Consolidation).

Croupous Pneumonia—Lung Fever—Generally caused by the same influences which lead to Croup, such as afflictions in ♉, which may also be combined with afflictions in ♊. (See Croup; "Lung Fever" under Lungs).

Death from Pneumonia—♂ afflicted in ♊ at B., occi., and also afflicting the hyleg by dir. (See "Death" under Bronchial, Lungs).

Delayed Resolution—♄ in ♊ and afflicting the ☉, ☽, Asc., or hyleg.

Pleuro-Pneumonia—(See Pleura).

Typhoid Pneumonia — Pneumonia accompanied by Typhoid Symptoms — Afflictions in ♊ combined with afflictions in ♍, ♐, and common signs at the same time; the ☽ afflicted in ♍. (See Typhoid).

POCK-MARKED—(See "Pitted Degrees" under Pitted; "Face" under Smallpox).

PODAGRA — Gout In the Feet — (See "Feet" under Gout).

PODOPHYLLIN — Podophyllum — May Apple—A Typical Drug of ☿. A Cathartic. (See "Mercury Group" under Herbs; Physic).

POIGNANT—Sharp—Severe—Poignant action over the body is ♂ action.

Poignant Diseases — And Maladies — Caused by the ☉ and ♂, the positive, electric, and heat-producing planets. (See "Poignant" under Diseases, Pain).

POINTED—(See "Pointed" under Chin; "Narrow" under Face; "Sharp" under Nose).

POISE — Balance — Equilibrium — (See Adrenals, Calm, Equilibrium; "Disposition" under Excellent; Harmony; "Mild Disposition" under Mild; "Even Temper" under Temper).

POISON—Poisons—Poisoning—Poisonous—Poisonings—Toxins—Virulent—Malignant—Noxious, etc.—Mars governs poison drugs, as a rule. Neptune rules poisons, as Narcotics and Opiates. The poisonous wastes and deposits in the system are ruled by ♄, and also ♄ tends to prevent the elimination of poisons from the body. Dealers in poisonous drugs are ruled by ♀, as a class. The following subjects have to do with poison, the poisons in the body, and the various uses and practices with poison.

Acidity — Excessive Acidity In the Body—(See Acids, Deposits, Gout, Hyperacidity, Rheumatism, Uric, Wastes).

Air—(See "Corrupt" under Air).

Alexipharmics — (See Alexipharmic, Antidotes).

Antidotes to Poisons — (See Alexipharmic, Antidotes, Antipathy, Opposites).

Arms—Blood Poisoning In—The ☉, ♃, or ♀ afflicted in signs which rule the Arms, Hands, Legs, and Feet tend to blood poisoning and blood impurities in these parts. (See "Blood In Arms" under Arms; "Disordered Blood" under Blood; "Corrupt Blood" under Hands; "Arms" under Impure).

Bites—Poisonous Bites—(See Bites).

Blood Poisoning — Septicemia — Toxic Blood — Impure Blood—Caused principally by afflictions in ♒, as this sign rules strongly over the blood. Also caused by afflictions to ♃, which planet rules the arterial blood. An ♒ disease, and ♒ causes blood poisoning, morbid blood conditions, and incomplete oxygenation of the blood; ♃ or the ☽ afflicted in ♒; the ☽ to the ☌ or ill-asps. ♂ by dir., and ♂ afflicting the ☽ at B., tends to death by blood poisoning; ♂ afflicted in ♒; ♂ afflicted in ♒ in the 6th H.; ♂ in ♒, and afflicting the ☽ or Asc.; caused by ♀ when the dominion of death is vested in her. (See Autointoxication; "Blood" under Impure; Septic, Toxaemia, Uremia).

Body — Poisoning of the System — Saturn obstructions retain the wastes of the body, retard the functions, weaken elimination and excretion, which tends to poisoning of the system. This surplus of poison and waste is burned out by ♂, and, if necessary, by high fevers and inflammation. Also an afflicted ♃ or ♀ tend to diseases which arise from poisoning of the system, and which may result from bad habits, gluttony, and indiscretions. (See Plethora, Pressure, Surfeits).

Carbonic Acid—Poisoning of the System By—(See Carbon).

Danger from Poisons — (See Death, Life Endangered, and the various paragraphs in this section).

Dealers In Poisons—Ruled by ♀. (See Chemists).

Death by Poison — Poison Death — Poison Death by Treachery — The ☽ hyleg, and to the ☌ or ill-asp. ♂ by dir., and especially if ♀ gives an evil aspect in the configuration; the ☽ hyleg, afflicted, and to the ☌ ☋ by dir.; the ☽ with Cor Hydra, ☌, □, or ☍ ♄ or ♂, death by poison, and especially if ♂ be angular; ♆ afflicting the hyleg, and elevated above it, indicates death by poison, and especially by Narcotics; ♆ afflicted in the 8th H., or afflicting the hyleg therefrom; ♆ setting in ☍ to the ☉ or ☽; ♄ in the Asc. in ☍ the ☉ or ☽, and ♀ attached to ♄ and ☿ combined; ♄ in ♏, afflicting the hyleg, and conjoined with ♀ by aspect, death by treachery or poison; ♄ afflicted in the 12th H.; ♄ Sig. of death, and in □ to ♀ (Hor'y); ♄ in ♏ in the 8th H., and both afflicting the hyleg at B., and by dir.; caused by ♄ and ♀ influences when these planets are conjoined, and thru the treachery of ♄; ♂ Sig. □ or ☍ ♄, if either be in the Asc., or ♄ in the M.C.; ♂ ☌ ♄ in ♏ in the 8th H., and both afflicting the hyleg at B., and by dir.; ♀ denotes death by; ♀ much afflicted at B., and afflicting the hyleg by dir., and taking part in a fatal train of directions to the hyleg; ♀ afflicting the hyleg, or giver of life, by dir.; ♀ or ☿ conjoined with ♄ and ♄ afflicting the hyleg; in a train of evil directions indicating death, if ♀ also cast a □ or ☍ to the hyleg, and ♀ be afflicted by malefics at B., danger of a poison death; ♀ afflicted at B., and afflicting the hyleg by dir., and holding the dominion of death, and especially if ♀ be in the 8th H., or afflicting the cusp of the 8th at the same time, and if the radical map also shows death by violence; ruled by the 8th H., and malefics in the 8th, or afflicting the lord of the cusp of the 8th, and ♀ in □ aspect to the Significator at the same time, death by poison, or from fear of a poison death; lord of the Asc. in ♏ in the 7th or 8th H., and afflicted by ♀ and malefics; Cor Hydra joined to ♂, and in evil asp. the ☉ or ☽. (See Enemy, Husband, Kings, Treachery, Women, in this section). Cases of Death by Poison—All in 1001 N.N. See "Husband", No. 162; "Allenby", No. 298; "Ladislaus", No. 450; "Medici", No. 525; "Hickman", No. 774.

Deposits — The System Poisoned by Mineral Deposits—(See Deposits).

Diseases Arising From—Sickness and Diseases Arising from Poisons In the System—Denoted by ♄ afflictions, retaining the wastes and poisons of the body. Also denoted by ♀. (See "Blood Poisoning", and the various paragraphs in this section; "Vascular Tissues" under Vascular).

Drugs—Poison Drugs are ruled by ♂, ♀, and the 8th H., and also poison death from such drugs.

Elimination — Of Poisons from the System—The elimination of the poisons from the body is done by ♂ in a normal way, but when there is too much surplus of poison and waste products, ♂ burns them out by causing high fevers and inflammations. (See Elimination, Fever, Inflammation; "Body" in this section).

Enemy — Poisoned by An Enemy — Danger of Secret Poisoning—Poisoned by Plots or Treachery—♄ afflicted in the 12th H.; lord of the 7th H. a malefic, in the 12th H., and afflicted. (See Death by Poison, Secret, Treachery, Women, in this section; "Death by An Enemy" under Enemies).

Fear of Poison Death — (See "Death by Poison" in this section).

Feet — Blood Poisoning In — (See "Arms" in this section).

Females Poisoned by Treachery of —(See "Women" in this section).

Fevers—Purpose of to Burn up Poisons and Wastes—(See Body, Elimination, in this section).

Gases — Poison Gases — Death By — (See "Poisoning" under Gases).

Gastritis — The Toxic Form from Swallowing Poison — (See "Gastritis" under Gastric).

Gout — From Retention of Poisons — (See Gout).

Hands — Blood Poisoning In — (See "Arms" in this section).

Healer — Poisoned By — (See "Poisoned" under Healers).

Heart Afflicted by Poison—(See "Poison" under Heart).

Herbs—Poison Herbs—(See Herbs).

Husband—Commits Suicide by Poison — Case — (See "Poison" under Husband).

Illness from Poison—(See "Sickness" in this section).

Improper Medicines — Poisoned by Taking — (See "Improper Medicines" under Medicines).

Impure Blood — Poisoned By — (See "Blood Poisoning" in this section; "Blood" under Impure).

Inflammation—Poisons Eliminated By —(See Body, Elimination, in this section).

Ivy Poison—(See Ivy).

King—Death of a King by Poison—(See "Dethroned" under Kings).

Lead Poisoning—(See Lead).

Legs — Blood Poisoning In — (See "Arms" in this section).

Life Endangered—By Poison—The ☽ hyleg at B., afflicted, and to the ☌ ♄, ♂, or ☋ by dir., and especially if ♀ take part in the configuration; ♄ afflicted in ♌; ♄ afflicted in the 12th H. (See Death, Enemy, Treachery, in this section).

Malaise — From Poisons In the Body —(See Malaise).

Medicines — Poison Drugs and Medicines—(See Medicines, Remedies).

Metals—Poison Metals—(See Metals).

Minerals—Poison Minerals—(See Minerals).

Mineral Deposits — The System Poisoned and Injured By—(See Deposits, Gravel, Minerals, Sand, Stone, Wastes).

Mucous Membranes — Arsenic, a ♂ drug and poison, is a powerful irritant to the mucous membranes. (See Introduction under Mucous).

Narcotic Poisons—(See Narcotics).

Neutralization of Poisons—(See Alexipharmics, Antidotes, Antipathy, Opposites).

Noxious Poisons—(See Noxious).

Obstructions—From Poisons Retained In the Body—(See "Hindered" under Elimination; Obstructions, Retarded, Retentions, Suppressions).

Opiates — Poisoned By — (See Narcotics).

Oxygenation — The System Poisoned by Improper Oxygenation—(See Oxygen).

Physician—Healer—The Patient Poisoned By — (See "Poisoned" under Healers; "Improper Medicines" under Medicines).

Plots—Poisoned Thru Plots—(See Enemy, King, Women, in this section).

Poisoner—A Poisoner—The ♏ influence strong at B., and with afflictions in this sign; ♂ ill-dignified and afflicted at B., and adversely configurated with ♀; ♀ is usually badly afflicted at B., and in a weak sign, as in ♏, and also afflicted by ♄ and ♂, which leads to enmity, jealousy, hatred, revenge, etc. The same influences apply here as in the cases of murderers, but with ♀ strongly involved, if caused by some love affair, or where ♄, ♂, and ♀ are configurated in cases of business and financial grievances. (See "A Murderer" under Murder; "Tendency To" under Violence). Cases of a Poisoner—All in 1001 N.N. See "Poisoner", No. 271; "Horsford", No. 764; "Maybrick", No. 969.

Remedies — Poisons As Remedies — Poisons, such as Strychnine, when given in very small doses, act as a stimulant and tonic. Most drugs are poisonous if given in large doses. (See Cure, Drugs, Medicines, Remedies, Treatment; "Herbs", "Metals", "Minerals", "Therapeutic Properties", "Typical Drugs", under each of the Planets).

Retention of Poisons—In the System —(See Crystallization, Deposits, Hardening, Minerals, Retentions, Suppressions, Uric, Wastes; Blood Poisoning, Body, Elimination, in this section).

Rheumatism—From Retained Poisons and Wastes—(See Rheumatism, Uric).

Secret Poisoning — ♄ afflicted in the 12th H. (See Death by Poison, Enemy, King, Women, in this section).

Septic Poisoning — Septicemia — (See "Blood Poisoning" in this section; Putrefaction, Septic).

Sickness — From Poisoning — The ☽ afflicted in ♏; the ☽ to the ☌ or ill-asps. ♂ by dir.; ♆ setting in ☍ to the ☉ or ☽, sickness or death by; lord of the Asc. in ♏ in the 7th H., and afflicted by malefics. (See Death by Poison, Diseases Arising From, and the various paragraphs in this section).

Sloughings — Arising from Weakness and Poison—(See Sloughings).

Stings—Poisonous Stings—(See Bites, Stings, Venomous).

Suicide by Poison — ♆ in the 8th H., and afflicting the hyleg. (See "Poison" under Husband; Narcotics, Suicide).

Surplus Poisons — In the Body — Diseases or Death By—(See Blood Poisoning, Body, Death, Diseases, Elimination, Retention, Sickness, and the various paragraphs in this section).

Swallowing Poison — (See Gastritis, Suicide, in this section).

System—Diseases Arising from Poisons In the System — (See "Surplus" in this section).

Throat — Septic Poisoning In — (See "Septic" under Throat).

Toxaemia—Toxic Blood—(See "Blood Poisoning" in this section; Toxaemia).

Travel — Poisoned During Travel — ☿ in evil asp. to the Significators of Travel. (See Danger, Death, under Travel).

Treachery — Poison Death By — (See Death, Enemy, King, Women, in this section).

Uremia—Toxic Blood with Excess of Urea—(See Uremia).

Vegetable Poisons—(See Herbs, Vegetation).

Violent Death — By Poison — (See Death, Enemy, Women, in this section).

Virulent Poisons—(See Malignant, Noxious, Venomous).

Wastes and Poisons—In the Body—(See Body, Elimination, Retention, in this section).

Women — Poisoned Thru the Treachery of—The ☉ or ☽ afflicted in ♏, and ill-aspected by ♀; the ☽ hyleg, and to the ☌ or ill-asp. ♂ by dir., and ♀ throw in an aspect; ♄ in ♏, ☌, or evil asp. the Asc. by dir.; ♀ in ♏ and afflicting the ☉ or ☽; adverse ♀ influence at B. makes liable to, and afflictions in or from the ♏ sign. (See Death, Enemy, in this section; Enmity, Jealousy; "A Murderer" under Murder; Revengeful; "Female Treachery" under Treachery; Vicious; "Tendency To" under Violence).

Wrong Medicine—Poisoned By—(See "Improper Medicines" under Medicines).

POLARITY — Polarization — The fresh polarizations of the Planets cause their changing influences. Each planet has a certain and definite polarity in itself, and when unaspected will always act in a certain manner, and produce certain effects from the causes it generates. The aspects, and the changing and modified polarities of the planets, tend to produce the different diseases, different states of mind, and the afflictions and testings of life, according to the vibrations. Plants and Herbs gather the different properties given by the Planets, and individualize these properties, or vital forces, according to their form. The Plants contain particles of matter and colors corresponding to the seven planetary rays. The organs, tissues, and cells of the body also contain a polarity, and are ruled by planets, and when an herb is used as a remedy, by the law of antipathy or sympathy, such remedy can change the polarity of an organ or tissue, and thus modify, cure, or heal a disease, or make it worse, according to the reaction between the remedy and the organ. The location, or place of residence, also have a polarity which may, or may not agree with the native, and a change of residence in case of sickness often brings relief and a cure if the polarity of the new location is harmonious with the vibrations of the patient. Certain Adepts and Masters have the power to change their polarity, overcome the law of gravitation, cause their bodies to rise or float in the air in Levitation, and also to perform various unusual phenomenon. (See Antipathy,

Aspects; "Cure of Disease" under Cure; Location, Nadir; "Native Country" under Native; Negative, Opposites; "Action", "Polarity", under Planets; Positive, Residence, Sympathy; "Direction to Travel" under Travel, etc.).

POLES—The Cerebral and Genital Poles of Paracelsus—(See Paracelsus).

POLICE OFFICERS—Killed or Injured By—(See Officers).

POLIOCEPHALITIS—(See Brain).

POLIOMYELITIS—(See "Infantile" under Paralysis).

POLITE—Courteous—(See "Polite" under Manner).

POLITICS—Politician—Public Life—
  Fond of Political Life—Of Public Life—Born under the strong influence of the tropical signs ♋ and ♑.
  Political Murderer—Case—(See Murder).
  Political Strife—Much Public Discord—(See "Dissentions", and the various paragraphs under Public; "Discord" under Quarrels; Reformers, Religion, Revolutionary; "Civil War" under War).
  Public Life—Execrated by the Multitude In Public Life—(See Anarchists, Execrated).
  Subtle Politician — ☿ Sig. in ♊, and not afflicted. (See Pettifogging).

POLLUTION—Polluted—
  Polluted Blood — (See "Blood" under Impure).
  Polluted Mind — (See Amorous, Debased, Debauched, Degenerate, Depraved, Disgrace, Dissolute, Evil, Harlots, Infamous, Lascivious, Lewd, Licentious; "Loose Morals" under Loose; "Adulterous" under Love Affairs; "Low and Base" under Low; "Licentious" under Men; Obscene; "Pasional Excesses" under Passion; Perversions, Profligate; "Clandestine" under Sex; Shameless; "Solitary" under Vice; Vile, Wanton; "Dissolute Habits" under Women, etc.).

POLLUX—Hercules—Caput Hercules—One of the two stars known as "The Twins", Castor and Pollux. (See Castor). Pollux is a violent star of the 2nd magnitude, in the 4th face of ♋, and of the nature of ♂ and the ☽ combined, and denotes ruin, disgrace, death, and every calamity. The stars in the knees and feet of Castor and Pollux are equally injurious. The ☉ directed to the place of tends to cause blindness in one or both eyes, and if Praesepe be also with the ☉ and ☽ in an angle, or on the Asc., certain blindness is almost sure to result, or hurts to the face. The danger of a violent death is also denoted, and much evil to the native, if the ☉ is with Pollux at B. The ☽ to the place of Pollux often denotes blindness, or a great defect in the sight, and especially if the ☉ or ☽ at B. were with Nebulous Stars. The ☽ to the place of Pollux also tends to ill-health, danger of a violent death, or damage to the wife or daughter. Disgrace and ruin are also indicated if the ☉ or ☽ be with this star at B., or by dir. The ☽ directed to the Belly of the Twins, and the Knees of Castor and Pollux, tends

to danger by thieves. The star Pollux is mentioned many times in the Text-books of Astrology, and these influences have been gathered up for this book. Pollux is referred to under the following subjects as Pollux, Hercules, Caput Hercules, The Twins, or Violent Fixed Stars. See Assassination, Banishment, Beheaded, Blindness, Blows, Calamity, Daughter; "Tragical", "Violent", under Death; Disease, Disgrace, Dreadful, Drowning; "Every Evil" under Evil; "Bad Eyes", "Accidents To", under Eyes; "Hurts To" under Face; "Death By", "Violent", under Fever; Ill-Health (see "Much" under Sickness); "A Murderer", "Many Murders", under Murder; Pirates, Prison; "Quarrelsome" under Quarrels; Rape, Ruin, Shipwreck, Shot to Death (see Gunshot); "Extreme Sickness", "Much Sickness", under Sickness; Stabs, Suffocation; "Danger By" under Thieves; "Tragical Death" under Tragical; "Death" under Violent; "Danger To" under Wife; "Danger Of" under Wounds; Wretchedness.

POLONIUM — A Radioactive Substance ruled by ♅, and closely related to Radium. (See Radium).

POLYCREST REMEDIES—(See "Polycrest" under Zodiac).

POLYPUS—A Pedunculated Tumor, and generally located in the Nose, Throat, Ear, or Rectum.
  Ear or Throat—Polypus In—An ♈ or ♉ disease; the ☉ or ☽ afflicted in ♈ or ♉; ♄ or ♂ in ♈ or ♉; Subs at AT.
  Nasal Polypus—(See "Polypus" under Nose).
  Rectal Polypus — The ☉, ☽, ♄, or ♂ afflicted in ♏; ♏ on the Asc. at B. (See Rectum).

POLYURIA — Excessive Secretion of Urine—(See "Polyuria" under Urine).

POMPHOLYX — A Disease with Bullas of the Hands and Feet — (See Dysidrosis).

PONS VAROLII—Vital Knot, located at the base of the Brain. Ruled by the ☉ and ♉. (See Brain).

POOLS — Stagnant Pools — Ruled by ♓. Saturn sole ruler at an eclipse of the ☉ tends to diseases arising from stagnant pools. (See Foul, Odors).

POOR—Deficient—Lacking—Poorly—Indifferent—Not Up to Standard—Below Par—The Poor, etc.—
  Poor Abilities—Not Highly Gifted—(See "Fails In" under Examinations; Inability, Inactive; "Incapable", "Void Of", under Learning; "Shallow" under Mentality; "Light In Mind" under Mind; Talents, etc.).
  Poor Assimilation—(See Assimilation).
  Poor Blood — (See "Poor" under Blood).
  Poor Body—(See Crippled, Deformed; "Ill-Formed" under Ill; "Ill-Health All Thru Life" under Ill-Health; Invalid, Sickly; "Weak Body" under Weak).
  Poor Circulation—Of the Blood—(See "Poor" under Circulation).
  Poor Complexion—(See "Poor" under Complexion).

Poor Digestion — (See "Poor" under Digestion; Indigestion).

Poor Health — (See "Poor" under Health).

Poor Heart Action — (See "Poor Action" under Heart).

Poor Mentality—(See "Poor and Shallow" under Mental).

Poor Oxygenation — (See "Non-Oxygenation" under Oxygen).

Poor Vitality — (See "Low", "Weakened", under Vitality).

The Poor — The Poorer Classes, and the Common People are ruled by the ☽. Venus Sig. in ♋ at B. is in indication and influence in the map of a female that she may belong to the Poorer Classes. (See Common People, Humanity, Mankind, Poverty, Public).

POPPY PLANT—Opium—Ruled by Neptune. (See Narcotics, Opium).

POPULACE—The People—(See Common People, Humanity, Mankind, Public).

POPULAR—A Popular Person—Popularity — (See "Many Friends" under Friends; "Popular" under Reputation). For Unpopular, see "Many Adversaries" under Enemies; Execrated; "Hated by Others" under Hate; Recluse, Secretive).

POPULATION—The People—

Decreased — The Population Rapidly Decreased — (See "Death Rate High", "Depopulation", under Mortality).

Increased—The Birthrate Increased—(See "Birthrate" under Birth). See Common People, Mankind, Public.

PORES—(See "Pores" under Skin).

PORRIGO — Favus of the Scalp — (See Favus).

PORTAL BLOOD STREAM—The wastes of the Portal Blood Stream are converted into Glycogen in the Liver by ♃, to act as fuel for the body. (See Glycogen, Liver).

PORTENTOUS FEVERS—Dreadful—Ominous — (See "Portentous" under Fever).

PORTLY BODY—Full—Somewhat Stout—Commanding—♃ and ♀ make the body more portly and commanding. Also the ☉ Sig. in ♌, and especially with the ☉ in the Asc. in ♌, or elevated in the East in this sign; the ☉ ☌ ♃ and ♀ in ♌, and elevated in the East at B. (See Commanding, Corpulent; "Body" under Large; Stout, Tall).

POSITION IN LIFE—(See Low, Popular, Poverty, Reputation, Riches, Social, Vagabond, Wealth, etc.).

POSITIVE—

Positive Constitution—Positive Form—The ☉ in ♎, or ♎ on the Asc. at B. (See Constitution).

Positive Horas—(See Horas).

Positive Houses—(See "Positive" under Houses).

Positive Nature—Positive Disposition — A Firm, Ruling, and Commanding Nature—The ☉ rising and oriental at B. has a positive and electric influence upon the mind and body. A positive state of mind is given by the ☉, ♃, and ♂ when rising, elevated in the East, dignified, and well-placed at B.; ♂ well-aspected at B., and especially when rising and elevated; many planets in the masculine signs at B.; many planets elevated in the East at B., and more so if in masculine signs. (See Commanding, Electric; "Great Energy" under Energy; Environment; Independent, Majority, Resolute, Rule, Self-Assertive, Self-Confident, Self-Reliant; "Strong Will" under Will).

Positive Planets — Postive and Electric—(See Electric).

Positive Signs — Of the Zodiac — The masculine Signs, such as ♈, ♊, ♌, ♎, ♐, and ♒. The fiery signs ♈, ♌, and ♐ are extremely positive and fiery. The positive Signs are alkaline, and the negative, or female signs, are acid. (See Acid, Alkaline). Hot and Dry, and Hot and Moist combinations are positive. Hot and Dry are positive, and belong to the positive and fiery signs ♈, ♌, ♐. Also the Signs presiding over the right side of the body are positive, and especially in the female. (See Horas; "Hot and Dry", "Hot and Moist", under Heat; Left, Right; "Positive" under Signs).

POSTURE—Position—Attitude—

Awkward Posture — (See Awkwardness).

Body Bent Forward — Hooked Forward — Stooping — (See "Downward" under Look; Stooping).

Downward Look — (See "Downward" under Look; Stooping).

Erect Posture—(See Erect, Upright).

Stooping Head—(See Stooping).

Straight and Tall—(See Erect).

Walk—(See Gait, Walk). See Appearance, Body, Form, Shape, Stature.

POTASSIUM—Is ruled by ♆. Potassium Phosphate is ruled by the ♈ Sign, and supplies the Brain Tissues. Potassium Chloride is the Zodiac Salt, or Tissue Remedy, ruled by the ♊ sign, and is connected with the Animal Tissues. Potassium Sulphate is the Salt ruled by the ♍ sign. This Salt supplies the Hair, Nails, and Oils of the body. Injections of Potassium are said to cure Carcinoma, or Cancer. (See Carcinoma, Hair, Nails, Oils; "Salts" under Zodiac).

POTATO-LIKE CANCER — (See "Solanoid" under Carcinoma).

Potato Blight — Coincident with the appearance of Comets. (See Comets, Vegetation).

POTENTIALITY—Inherent Capacity—(See Heredity, Inherent, Innate; "Native Country" under Native; Polarity).

POTIONS—Love Potions—Philtres—Ruled by Venus. (See Philtres).

Sleeping Potions—Ruled by the ☽ and ♆. (See Narcotics; "Sleeping Potions" under Sleep).

POTT'S CURVATURE—Of the Spine—Pott's Disease — (See "Pott's" under Spine).

POUCH—A Pocket-Shaped Cavity—(See Cavities, Cysts, Sacs, Scrotum).

POULTICES — (See Emollient, Resolvent).

POVERTY—Neglect—Privation—Poor—Indigent—Poverty and Indigence are governed by ♄; ♄ in the 2nd H., and afflicting ♃; the ☉ and ☽ far below the horizon, with no benefic angular, and the Lights afflicted by malefics; the ☽ sepr. from the ☉, and applying to ♄, often in want and misery; the ☽ decr., sepr. from ♂ and applying to ♄; the ☽ sepr. from ♀ and applying to the ☉; the ☽ Sig. ☌ ♄, often poor and poverty stricken; the ☽ Sig. □ or ☍ ♀, tends to indigence and poverty; ♃ Sig. □ or ☍ ☿, becomes indigent thru lawsuits and losses; planets ℞ at B. are said to cause poverty and sickness, and especially ♄ and ♂ retrograde; the Ruler, or Significator, being in his own decanate or face signifies a person in want, and hardly able to support himself (Hor'y). (See Begging, Careless, Destiny, Dissolute, Dull, Failure, Famine, Fate, Fortune, Idle, Improvident, Indifferent, Indigent, Indolent; "Bad" under Judgment; Laborious, Lack Of, Lazy, Livelihood, Loss Of; "Shallow" under Mentality; Misery, Misfortune, Neglect, Poor, Privation, Property, "Many Changes" under Residence; Resources, Reverses, Riches, Ruin, Unfortunate, Vagabond, Void Of, Wretchedness, etc.).

Beggarly—Lives Beggarly and Carelessly—(See Begging).

Diseases—Diseases Arising from Neglect, Privation, and Poverty—♄ diseases; the ☉ and ☽ afflicted by ♄.

Fear of Poverty—♆ afflicted in the 2nd H. at B. (See Fear).

Indigent—(See Apathy, Careless, Dull; "Lack of Forethought" under Forethought; Idle, Indigent, Indifferent, Indolent, Lazy, Vagabond, etc.).

Journeys—Danger from Privations On Journeys or Voyages—(See "Privations" under Sea).

Property and Riches—Loss of—(See Expense, Money, Prodigal, Property, Reverses, Riches, Ruin, etc.).

Voyages—Privations On—(See Famine; "Privations" under Seas).

Want—Fear of Coming To—(See "Fear" in this section).

POWDER BURNS—(See Gunshot).

POWER—Powers—Powerful—Energy—Force—Strength, etc.—The ☉ and ♂ when strong at B., and supporting each other by aspect, tend to give the native more power, force, and energy on the physical plane, and in health matters, with increased vitality. The ☉ and ♂ weak and ill-dignified at B., and the ☉ not supported by ♂ by a good aspect, or no aspect, and at the same time with a weak sign rising in the Asc., tend to weaken the powers of the native, lower resistance to disease, etc. (See Mars, Sun).

Application of Power—(See "Last Quarter" under Moon).

Creative Powers—(See Creative).

Dynamic Power—♂ is the planet of. (See Dynamic, Mars).

Energy—(See the various paragraphs under Action, Energy, Force, Life, Motion, Movement, Muscles, Physical).

Men In Power—(See "Power" under Men).

Mental Powers—(See Intellect, Mental; "Active Mind" under Mind; Perception, Understanding, etc.).

Natural Powers—(See "Natural Forces" under Natural).

Organic Power—(See Organic).

Physical Powers—(See Body, Physical, Strength, Strong, Weak, etc.).

Psychic Powers—(See Psychic).

Sources of Power—All of the Planets endow certain powers, according to their nature, sign and house positions, aspects, etc. For the nature and quality of the powers given by the Planets, see each planet in the alphabetical arrangement, and especially note the sections on "Influences", and the Qualities endowed by each planet. Also note the various paragraphs in this section.

Spiritual Power—(See Pineal, Pituitary, Spiritual).

Strength—(See the various paragraphs under Strength, Strong).

Vital Powers—(See "Life Force" under Life; Vital, Vitality).

Weak—The Powers Weakened—(See Diminished, Feeble, Lack Of, Loss Of, Void Of; the various paragraphs under Weak).

Will Power—(See Will).

POX—Syphilis—A Contagious, Eruptive, Pustular Disease—(See Eruptions, Pustular, Syphilis).

PRACTICAL—Utilitarian—The Earthy Signs strong at B. tend to make one practical, as these signs have more to do with the material, or Earth Plane. The Fiery Signs are also usually practical, and the ☽ influence, and the ♋ sign. Also ♅ when well dignified at B. tends to practicability in the business affairs of life, but with some dangers of going to extremes and being eccentric, peculiar, and misunderstood when ill-dignified and ill-aspected at B.

Impractical—The ♎, ♒, and ♓ signs do not tend to be as practical, and are usually more impractical and dreamy. The ♆ afflictions at B. also tend to make one less practical, and to be more liable to obsessions, hallucinations, dreamy ideas and notions, and to resort to strange, weird, uncanny, or unusual methods in their procedures. (See Chaotic, Dreamy, Eccentric, Erratic, Fanatical, Fancies, Ideals, Imaginations; "Bad" under Judgment; Notions, etc.).

PRACTICE OF MEDICINE—And Healing—(See "Physicians" under Healers).

PRACTICES—(See Conduct, Evil, Excesses, Good, Habits, Ideals, Ideas, Manners, Morals, Notions, Perversions, Religion, Vices, Wicked, Unnatural).

PRAEINCIPIENTS—In Disease—Incipients—♅ and ♆, as related to disease, and as incipients and praeincipients in disease, are classed as planets which tend to obscure, extraordinary and mysterious causes in disease, and peculiar complications. Incipient diseases, those at their very beginnings, if taken when they first manifest themselves, as indicated by the diathesis and idiosyncrasies, habit in disease, etc., can usually be broken or neutralized by the proper remedy and treatment. Thus ♄ and ♂ in □ predispose to lung disorders, colds on the lungs, etc., and if this is known to the native who has such influences at B. he can safeguard these tendencies, remove the causes of nose, throat, and lung troubles in the body, and also have a remedy at hand always to quickly disseminate and break up the first symptoms of disease when they appear. Each person should make a study of his own case, know the tendencies of his body and mind, and then set out to control and rule conditions, and be Master of his Fate and Destiny, and thus avoid much unnecesary suffering, pain, sorrow, and tribulation. (See Antipathy; "Cure of Disease" under Cure; Diagnosis, Diathesis, Hexis, Opposites, Prevention, Prognosis, Remedies, Sympathy, Treatment, etc.).

PRAESEPE — The Cratch—The Crab's Claw—The Ascelli—A Nebulous Cluster in the first Decanate of ♌, of the nature of ♂ and the ☽, and said to cause blindness, or hurts to the face, when rising in ☌ the ☉ or ☽, and especially when in an angle. (See Ascelli). Also said to cause disgrace, diseases, and every calamity and evil upon humanity. The ☉ directed to Praesepe tends to blindness in one or both eyes, and if Praesepe be on the Asc., or with the ☉ or ☽ in an angle, certain blindness. The ☉ directed to the Cratch, in the 6° ♌, tends to danger to the head and eyes, injury by machinery, gunshot, falls, or bruises. The ☉ with Praesepe at B. also is indicative of evil, and the danger of a violent death. Also the ☉ and ☽ with Praesepe at B., and especially in an angle, tend to every kind of calamity upon the native, disgrace, and to cause diseases of various kinds. The ☽ to the place of tends to great defects in the sight, and often blindness, and especially if the Lights are with Nebulous stars at B. The ☽ with Praesepe, and espec. in an angle, tends to blindness, or injury to the eyes. The ☽ Sig. ☌ the ☉, and near Praesepe at B., the native is likely to be nearly blind. The Ascelli, Praesepe, and the Cratch, are all very close together in the first Decan. of the ♌ sign, and of the same nature, and make up a Nebulous Cluster, and in the Textbooks seem to be used interchangeably, and the influences given in the Article on The Ascelli in this book will also apply to those for Praespe, or Praesepe, as this word is spelled both ways in the books. Praesepe is mentioned many times in the Textbooks of Astrology. In this book Praesepe, the Cratch, or the Ascelli, are mentioned in the following subjects, and as taking a part in causing these diseases, afflictions, or injuries. See these subjects in the alphabetical arrangement — Arms (Wounds To); Banishment, Beheaded, Blindness, Bruises, Calamity, Conjunctivitis, Disgrace, Evil (Every Evil); Exercise (Death By); Eyes (Bad Eyes, Danger To); Face (Hurts To); Fevers (Violent); Fire (Death By); Gunshot (Danger, Death, or Wounds By); Head (Danger To); Imprisonment (see Prison); Iron (Death By); Machinery (Accidents By); Murder (Death By); Nebulous Stars (see the Article on Nebulous); Ruin, Shipwreck, Shot to Death (see Gunshot); Sight (see Blindness, Sight); Stabs, Stars, Trouble, Untimely Death (see Untimely); Violent Death (see "Death" under Violent); Wounds, etc.

PRANA — The Hindu name for Vital Force, Life Force, etc. Ruled by the ☉. (See "Life Force" under Force; "Force" under Vital). Prana is Life Force in the Air, in Food and Drinking Water, and gives force, energy, strength, and nourishment to the body. It is an etheric force, and separate from the actual ingredients in air, food or water, and it is said that we absorb more of this Prana when we are conscious of its presence, and hold the thought that we are taking in this Force when breathing or eating. Orange is the color of the Pranic life forces in the blood. Occult books on the Science of Breath, and Breathing, deal with this subject quite fully. Read the Chapter on "Prana Absorption" in the book, "Hatha Yoga", by Yogi Ramacharaka (William Walter Atkinson). Prana is also said to increase the Spiritual Powers when taken in consciously, and directed by the thoughts and prayers to such Centers. (See "Fire Signs" under Fire; "Solar Plexus" under Plexus).

PRECARIOUS — Perilous — Uncertain — Subject to Dangers—(See "Many Dangers" under Danger; Escapes; "Precarious Life" under Life; Perils).

PRECIPICES—High Places—Falls From — (See Heights; "Dangers" under Travel).

PRECIPITATE — Hasty — Hurried — Without Due Deliberation—

Precipitate Actions — Accidents from Precipitate and Impulsive Actions—♂ in the 1st H., □ or ☍ the ☉ or ☽ at B. (See Foolhardy; "Lack Of" under Forethought; Hasty, Impulsiveness, Rashness, Recklessness, etc.).

Precipitate Fancies — (See "Foolish" under Fancies).

PRECIPITATION— The Throwing Down of Solids from Liquids—In the human body this is usually the work of ♄, thus causing excessive mineral deposits in the tissues, and resulting in disease, such as Gout, Rheumatism, Uric Acid Poisoning, etc. (See Deposits, Gout, Minerals, Rheumatism, Uric, Wastes, etc.).

PRECOCIOUS—Premature Development — Precocious Mental Development — (See Backwardness, Genius, Mathematician, Premature, Prodigies).

PREDETERMINATION — Of Sex — To Foretell Whether Male or Female During Pregnancy—Judgment of the 5th H. of a parent indicates whether the first child will be male or female. Also the time of conception, if known, and the planets in the signs at that time, are to be considered, and the nature of the signs and planets. The ☉, ☽, and Asc. are principally to be observed, and the planets which have prerogative over them. If the ☉, ☽, and Asc. are femininely constituted, then judge a female child. The masculine planets are the ☉, ♅, ♄, ♅, and ♂, and the ☽ and ♀ are feminine. Mercury partakes of both genders, according to his location and aspects with the masculine and feminine planets. The odd signs, as ♈, ♊, ♌, etc., are considered masculine, and the even signs, as ♉, ♋, ♍, etc., are feminine. The watery signs are very fruitful, and also feminine. In judging of the sex keep the gender of the planets, signs, and the degrees of the signs in mind. A Table of the Masculine and Feminine Degrees of the Zodiac is given in the book, "The Prenatal Epoch" by Mr. E. H. Bailey. Also see "Degrees" under Feminine, Masculine. For further consideration of this subject see "Female Children", "First-Born Child", under Children; Conception; "Birth of a Female" under Female; "Births" under Male; Prenatal Epoch, Quadrants, Quickening, Triplets, Twins).

PREDICTIONS—Predicting—(See Character, Curable, Destiny, Diagnosis, Directions, Events, Fatal, Fate, Foretold, Incurable, Judgment, Predetermination, Prognosis, Progressions, Prophetic, Quality, Secondary Directions, Transits, Type, Will, etc.).

PREDISPOSED — Predisposition — Inherent— Innate — Hereditary—Tendencies— Idiosyncrasies — Diathesis, etc.— The Signs occupied by planets at B., the rising sign, the signs on the Midheaven, and the 6th H., especially indicate what parts of the body are more predisposed to disease, afflictions, accidents, etc., and especially the signs occupied by malefics. The degree on the Asc. at B. gives predisposition to certain diseases and afflictions, according to the sign rising. (See the book, "Degrees of the Zodiac Symbolized", by Charubel). The part ruled by the sign occupied by the ☉ denotes a sensitive part, or organ, and more liable to disease if the ☉ is badly afflicted at B. (See Congenital, Constitutional, Diathesis; "Strong" under Disease; Environment, External, Heredity, Hexis, Inherent, Innate, Organic, Praeincipients, Prenatal, Propensities, Structural, Susceptibility, Temperaments, Tendencies, etc.).

PREGNANCY — Impregnation — Pregnant — Gestation — Prenatal Period — Fertilization—Conception, etc.—The ☽ and the 5th H. rule pregnancy, and the ☽ is the planet of impregnation and fertilization. (See Fifth House, Moon). The conditions for fruitfulness must exist, and the ☽ and watery influences strong and prominent at B., before impregnation can take place. Barren conditions in the map prevent pregnancy. Note the following subjects—

Barrenness—Not Capable of Becoming Pregnant—(See Barren).

Conception — Conception Has Taken Place — (See the paragraphs under Conception).

Delivery — To Know Time of — (See "Time of Delivery" under Parturition).

Fancy—A Pregnant and Ingenious Fancy—(See "Pregnant Genius" under Genius).

Fecundation—(See this subject).

Female — Male or Female During Pregnancy—(See Predetermination).

Fertilization—(See Fecundation, Fertilization).

Foetus — (See the paragraphs under Foetus).

Fruitful — May Often Become Pregnant — (See "Many Children" under Children; Fruitful).

Genius — A Pregnant Genius — (See Genius).

Gestation — (See the paragraphs under Gestation).

How Long Pregnant?—Observe the ☽ and lords of the Asc. or 5th H., and find the nearest past aspect they make to any planet. If separating from a ☌ of a planet, it is the first month of pregnancy; if sepr. from the ⚹ aspect, judge she is in the 2nd or 6th month; from the □ aspect, in the 4th month; from the △ aspect, in the 3rd or 5th month; from an ☍ aspect, in the 7th month, etc. These are the rules for judging the matter in Hor'y Questions.

Male or Female — During Pregnancy —How to Judge the Matter—(See Predetermination).

Maternity — (See the paragraphs under Maternity, Mother).

Mother—Motherhood—(See Maternity, Mother).

Parturition — The Puerperal State — Childbirth—(See Parturition, Puerperal).

Party Has Just Conceived—(See this subject under Conception).

Period of Gestation—(See Gestation, Prenatal Epoch).

Prenatal Epoch—(See Prenatal).

Quickening—Of Foetus—(See Quickening).

Sign of Pregnancy—A Benefic in Cazimi. (See "Woman Is with Child" in this section).

State of a Woman With Child — This is judged by the 5th H. and its influences. Also the last application of the ☽, before she leaves the Sign she is in, denotes the state of the mother (Hor'y).

Uterus In Pregnant Women—Is especially affected and influenced by the ☉ and ☽ acting thru the ♎ sign.

Vexations During Pregnancy — Malefics in the 5th H. at B. and by dir.

When Will the Child Be Born?—(See "Born" in Sec. 1 of the Article on Children; "Time of Delivery" under Parturition).

Woman Is With Child—In Hor'y Q., the following influences indicate that she is with child—If the lord of the 5th H. behold a planet in an angle, and with reception; lords of the Asc., 5th, or 7th H., or the ☉, ☽, ♃, ♀, or ☿ be in the 5th H., and fortified, except when ☿ is in the 5th H. in aspect to a malefic, and with no aspect to a benefic, when ☿ cannot be relied upon; if translation of light has passed between the lords of the 1st and 5th, or if the ☽ be just separating from the latter in a fruitful sign, or in the 5th, 7th, or 11th H.; lords of the 1st and 5th, or the ☽, in reception to a planet angular; the ☽ and the lord of the triplicity she is in both be in fruitful signs, or if ♃ and ♀ be both angular and free from affliction, these are symbols of conception having taken place. If at the time any of these symptoms appear, ♃ be cadent, or afflicted, or ♄, ♂, or ☋ be present at the place of the aspect, or on the cusp the 5th H., there is either no conception, or there will be an abortion. It is the same if they afflict the ☽, ♀, or lord of the 1st or 5th H. (See "Signs of Children" under Children; Conception, Fruitfulness).

Woman Is Not With Child—Signs of No Conception In Hor'y Questions—Denoted when the ☽ is void of course; ♃ and ♀ afflicted; ♀ joined to ♄ or ♂, or to ♅ if he be afflicted, and these planets ℞, combust, or in ♌, ♍, or ♑; ♄ in the 11th H. frustrates hope; ♄ or ♂ in the 5th H., □ or ☍ the lord of the 5th; a barren sign on the Asc., or malefic planets there, or afflicting their lords or the ☽; a barren sign on cusp the 4th or 5th H.; lord of the Asc. joined to a ℞ planet, or to one in a cadent house, or received by a ℞ or combust planet, or if there be no translation of light or aspect between lords of the 1st or 5th, are all signs of no conception. (See Barren).

PREJUDICE—Prejudiced—

Fancies—Prejudiced Fancies—(See Fancies).

Heat or Fire—Prejudice By—(See "Danger" under Fire).

Mind—Prejudiced Mind—Narrow-Minded—A characteristic of the fixed signs, and with ☿ and many planets in these signs at B.; ☿ afflicted by ♄ tends to prejudices and narrowness of mind; the ♍ sign and its influences tend to prejudice of mind, and to make one more critical and fault-finding, and less tolerant of the views and opinions of others. The ♊ and ♐ signs are more liberal. (See Doubts, Fears; "Shallow" under Mentality; "Light In Mind" under Mind; Mistrustful, Reason, Scepticism, Suspicious; "Weak" under Understanding, etc.).

PREMATURE—Precocious—

Premature Baldness—(See "Early In Life" under Baldness).

Premature Birth—Premature births may be attributed in some cases to the mother, and her tendency to habitual abortion. (See Abortion). In other cases the afflictions to the ☽ during the gestation period, when the ☽ crosses, or does not cross the central line of impulse at the monthly periods during the prenatal period, may cause it. If several of the Moon's librations do not return to, and cross the central line of impulse during pregnancy, there tends to be a lack of equilibrium, and an unbalanced condition of the foetus, which may lead to its expulsion. (See Prenatal Epoch). Diseases of the Foetus are also a cause.

CASES OF PREMATURE BIRTH—

(1) Born Two Weeks Before Time—See "Weak Mind", No. 146, in 1001 N.N.

(2) Born Three Weeks Too Soon—See "Deaf and Dumb", No. 166, in 1001 N.N.

(3) Born At Eighth Month—(See "Eight Month's Children" under Children).

(4) Born Six Weeks Too Soon—(See Chap. XIV, in Daath's Medical Astrology).

(5) Born At the Seventh Month—See "Weak Mind", No. 145; "Twins", No. 681; "Sight Defective", No. 684, all in 1001 N.N. (See Abortion; "Eight Months Children" under Children; Miscarriage).

Premature Burial—Danger of Being Buried Alive—(See Burial).

Premature Death—(See "Death by Accident" under Accidents; Burial; "Death" under Childhood, Children, Early, Extraordinary, Hurts, Infancy, Injuries, Mysterious, Peculiar, Strange, Sudden, Untimely, Unusual, Violent, Wounds; "Short Life" under Life, etc. Also note the various paragraphs under Death).

Premature Decay—(See Decay; "Fluid" under Vital).

Premature Mental Development—Precocious—The favorable aspects of the ☉, ♅, ♂, or ☿ all tend to early mental development. (See "Active Mind" under Active; Backwardness, Genius; "Mind" under Growth; Mathematical; "Quickened" under Mentality; Precocious; Prodigies).

Premature Old Age—(See Juvenility; "Senility" under Old Age).

Premature Wrinkles—(See Wrinkles).

PREMONITIONS—Presentiments—Forebodings—(See "Impending" under Calamity; "Mental Chaos" under Chaotic; Dreams (Case of Strange Dreams and Premonitions); Fears, Forebodings; "Hallucinations, Hauntings, Imaginations, Obsessions, Spirit Controls, Terrors, Visions, Weird, etc.).

PRENATAL EPOCH—The Epoch—Conception—The time of conception is called The Epoch, and this time has a definite and fixed relation to the time and moment of birth, as these two points are connected by a fixed and determined arc, and when the time of birth is approximately known, the time of conception can be accurately determined by the proper astronomical calculations, and also when the time of conception is determined, the true time of birth can also be found, and the exact degree rising on the Asc. at the true moment of birth. Thus, by this method, the time of birth can be rectified, if such time is approximately known. Ptolemy, in his "Tetrabiblos", laid down many of the rules for the Epoch and its determination, which rules have been further worked out, amplified, and systematized by the Modern Astrologers Sepharial, and Mr. E. H. Bailey, Editor of the British Journal of Astrology. Read the books, "Sepharial's Manual of Astrology", and "The Prenatal Epoch", by Mr. E. H. Bailey. The fundamental rule of the Epoch is that the sign and degree of the ☽ at Epoch, or Conception, becomes the exact sign and degree on the Asc. or Descendant at the quickening, and at birth. (See Quickening). If at birth the ☽ is increasing and above the Earth, the place of the ☽ at conception becomes the Ascendant at B. If at birth the ☽ was below the Earth, and decreasing, the place of the ☽ at the Epoch becomes the Descendant at B. Thus, when the hour of birth is known approximately, the Prenatal Epoch calculations give us one of the best methods for rectifying the exact moment of birth, for when once the time of conception is determined, according to the Order, it is an easy matter to calculate the exact degree on the Ascendant or Descendant at the time of birth.

Orders of the Epoch—The Epoch may be regular or irregular, and the Epochs are classified into four Orders.

(1) The ☽ increasing and above the Earth at B., which gives a time of conception 273 days before birth, less the days for correction, which makes the period of gestation less than the ordinary time, or what we would call an "undertime" child.

(2) The ☽ above the Earth and decreasing, which makes the time of conception 273 days, plus the days for correction, and an "overtime" child. These two Orders of the Epoch have to do with the true Asc. at B., and the degree rising.

(3) The ☽ below the Earth and increasing at B., which gives a count back of 273 days, and plus the days for correction, and gives an "aparently overtime" child.

(4) The ☽ below the Earth and decreasing, which gives a pregnancy of 273 days, minus the days for correction, or an "undertime" child. In the book, "Prenatal Epoch", By Mr. Bailey, the Irregular Epochs are considered, and how they are calculated. The Index Date, or the ordinary day of conception, is found by counting back nine calendar months to the day and date when the ☽ is in the same sign and degree as at birth, or near the same degree. The distance in degrees of the ☽ from the Asc. in the first Order, and this distance divided by 13, gives the number of days for correction to the Index Date, to be subtracted, and the conception took place within 14 days following the Index Date. In the 2nd Order, the distance of the ☽ from the Asc. at B., divided by 13, gives the number of days to be added to the Index Date, and which may make the time of conception as much as 14 days before the Index Date, and an apparently overtime child. A knowledge of these Laws, and how to calculate the map for the time of conception, helps to clear away many of the mysteries of why children are not born on the exact times expected, some being born two weeks "ahead of time", and others two weeks late, etc. The time of birth is fixed by the arc of direction between conception and birth, and the child under normal conditions has to be born at the time fixed and set by Nature.

Therefore, birth should not be forced, or instruments used, if the mother seems to be in Labor too long, according to the Physician's views, or the opinions of the family. The child will be born when its time comes, if things are normal and allowed to have their way. This Article is not intended to be a full elaboration on the subject of the Pranatal Epoch, but only to give the student some ideas of the work, its importance, and then you must follow this up for yourself, and study the books mentioned. The Chart of Descent is a perpendicular line drawn from the place, sign and degree of the ☽ at Epoch to the degree of the Asc. at B. This line of descent is also known as "The Descent of the Monad." The date each month during Gestation when the ☽ is nearest to the ascending or descending degree at B. should be noted, and a line drawn on the Chart of Descent to this point. A Figure for a Chart of Descent is given on page 155 in Mr. Bailey's book. The ☽ at her return to this degree each month may come to the central line, fall short of it, or cross it. In a normal child, the ☽, at her return each month, should cross back and forth over the central line. If for several months the ☽ does not touch or cross this line at the time mentioned, it indicates an unbalanced condition of the child, lack of equilibrium, and when disease, malformation, idiocy, mental disorders, insanity, defects or even premature birth, abortion, or miscarriage may take place. Cases and illustrations of these unbalanced conditions are given in Mr. Bailey's book, such as The Frog Child, born minus a forearm and legs below the knees. Many weaknesses that exist in the child after birth, or at birth, such as deformity, malformation, tendency to certain diseases, etc., can be explained by the Prenatal Map, and by noting the descent of the ☽ thru gestation, and the relation of the ☽ to the line of central impulse, and also the aspects to the ☽ at these times. The Map of Birth is valuable to study in connection with the Epoch Map, and the maps for each month during the descent of the Monad. The map of the Epoch helps to explain many things. Infant Mortality is caused by afflictions to the ☽ at conception, or the Epoch. Procreation may be controlled, and even the sex of the child predetermined, if coitus and conception can take place at a time which will predetermine the Epoch map, which map is then reflected in the map of birth. Mr. Bailey deals with this subject, and many others, in his book, and it would take a whole volume to go into these matters here. The address of Mr. Bailey is 10 Red Lion Court, Fleet St., London, E. C. 4, England. The ☉, ☽, and Ascendant at birth are controlling factors in the calculation of a Prenatal Epoch Map. Also the gender of the degrees of the Zodiac have to be considered, and to ascertain the sex positions of the ☽ and Asc., and as given in the Table of Genders of Degrees, on page 40 of Mr. Bailey's book. The map for the time of conception also shows the nature of the incoming Ego, the innate character developed in previous Incarnations, the stage of the evolution of the native, etc., while the map of birth shows the environmental conditions, the contacts with the world which are laid out for the native in the present life; shows the Personality, tendencies of the mind and body, lessons and tests to be encountered, the diseases and afflictions apt to come to the native, and also his relation to Society, etc. In this Encyclopaedia, the Prenatal Epoch, its workings, and the conditions it causes in the body before birth, at birth, and after birth, are mentioned, or have to do with the following subjects, which see in the alphabetical arrangement, and the Epoch Map, and Chart of Descent, will help to explain the causes and presence of these diseases and conditions when such indications may be absent from the map of birth. Also the causes of many diseases, afflictions, defects, deformities, malformations, etc., are gone into quite fully in Mr. Bailey's book, and in Sepharial's Manual of Astrology. See Abortion; "Beastly Form" under Beasts; "Cause of Birth", "Moment of Birth", under Birth; "Born Blind" under Blindness; Character; "Born", "Delayed Births", "Eight Months Children", "Dogs", under Children; Conception, Congenital, Cyclops, Deafness, Deaf and Dumb; Defects, Deformities, Dumbness, Embryo, Fecundation, Fertilization, Foetus; "Foolish Mind" under Foolish; Forearm, Freaks, Gestation, Heredity, Idiocy; "Ill-Formed Body" under Ill; Imbecile, Imperfections, Incomplete; "Deformed from Birth", "Premature Birth", "Signs of Death", under Infancy; Inhuman, Insanity, Intellect; "Disease" under Judgment; Lameness; "No Limbs" under Limbs; Lunacy, Maimed, Miscarriage, Malformations; "Hereditary" under Mania; Map, Marks; "Mising Members" under Members; "Retarded" under Mental; "Weak Mind" under Mind; Missing; "Moment of Birth" under Moment; Monsters; "Epoch" under Moon; Mute, Naevus, Nativity; "Incapable Of" under Nutrition; Organic; "Birth" under Paralysis; Parturition, Personality, Perversions, Physical, Predetermination, Pregnancy, Premature, Ptolemy, Quadrants, Radix; "Void Of" under Reason; Rectification, Reproduction, Savage, Stillborn, Structural; "Birth" under Time; Triplets, Twins, etc.

PRESBYOPIA—(See Sight).

PRESENTIMENTS — (See Forebodings, Premonitions).

PRESERVATION—Preservatives—Preserved—Preservation is a Therapeutic Property of ♃, and this planet exerts a preservative and conserving influence over the body and tissues. The Sun Group of Herbs are preservative. In the physical world Sugar is a preservative, and is the result of ♃ action, and is ruled by ♃. (See "Substance" under Cells; Conservation, Defensive, Jupiter, Nutrition, Phagocytes, Prevention, etc.).

Life Preserved—(See Escapes; "Spared" under Life; "Disease Pre-

vented" under Prevented; "Patient Will Recover" under Recovery).

Preserves—Sweets—Sugars—Over-Indulgence In—♀ afflicted in ♎. (See Sugar).

Self-Preservation—(See this subject).

Well-Preserved—In Body—(See Juvenility).

PRESIDENT OF THE U. S. A.—Danger To — Danger of Assassination — Death or Injury To—These influences are the same as for Kings, Rulers, and Prominent People. (See Assassination, Famous; "Great Men" under Great; "Assassination" under Kings; Nobles, Princes, Queens, Rulers, etc.).

PRESSED TO DEATH—(See Crushed).

PRESSURE—Force—Weight—

Atmosphere—Excessive Atmospheric Pressure—Diseases Arising From—♀ diseases and influence. (See "Pressure" under Air, Gases; Caisson Disease, Compressed).

Blood Pressure—High or Low Blood Pressure — (See "Pressure" under Blood).

Nerves — Pressure Upon, and especially in the Spine, and as the Nerves make their exits thru the Vertebrae, as in Subluxations. (See Subluxations, Vertebrae). Undue, or abnormal pressures may be exerted upon any part, or organ of the body, due to diseased conditions, the deposit of minerals, poisons and wastes of the system by ♄ influence, as in Gout and Rheumatism. Pressure of the skull upon the brain by congenital defects, or by accidents to the head, is caused by ♂ in ♈ at B., or ♈ upon the Asc. There may be pressure upon the heart, due to stomach gases and indigestion, as caused by afflictions in ♋. Too much blood may cause undue pressure upon the blood vessels, resulting in rupture of the vessel, Apoplexy, Hemorrhage, Plethora, etc. Falls, caused by ♄, may result in too much pressure upon a part, causing a rupture of the tissues, as in Inguinal Hernia. (See these subjects).

PRETENDER—Pretenses—Pretended—Pretentions—

Pretended Ailments—♆ in evil asp. to ☿. (See Complaining, Delusions, Exhibition, Hysteria, Illusions, Imaginations, Lamentations, Mysterious, Neptune, Obscure, Obsessions, Peculiar, Spirit Controls, Strange, Weird, etc.).

Pretender—A Pretender to All Kinds of Knowledge—(See "Void Of" under Learning).

Pretenses — Outwardly of Great Decorum—♏ influence.

Pretensions — Pretentious — Ostentatious—

(1) Adornment — Fond of Personal Adornment, Fine Clothes, Jewelry, etc. —Governed by ♀; ♀ in the Asc., and dignified; ♂ Sig. in ♌ or ♎. (See Dress, Expense, Extravagance, Luxuries, Neat).

(2) Boastful—Bragging—Conceited—The ☉ ill-dignified at B., and afflicted; the ☉ Sig. ✶ or △ ♄; ♃ Sig. in ♍; ♂ Sig. in ♌ or ♎; in Hor'y Q. ♄ Sig. in ♈;

☿ ill-dignified at B.; ☿ Sig. in ♌, and apt to be full of idle words. (See "Exaggerated Ego" under Ego).

(3) Bombastic—Caused by the □ and ⚹ aspects to ♃.

(4) Ostentatious — The ☉ Sig. in ♒; the ☉ Sig. ✳ or △ ♄; the □ and ⚹ asps. to ♃; ♀ in the Descendant at B., and in a strong sign. (See Hypocritical, Proud, Religion).

PREVALENT — Prevailing Generally Among the People or Nations — The Mundane, or House positions of the Planets from day to day, rule over World Affairs, and tend to bring disease, epidemics, pestilence, famine, earthquakes, storms, calamity, catastrophy, public sorrow and distress, outrages, panics, etc., and the student should make a study of Mundane Astrology. Planetary influences at the Vernal Equinox, and at Solar Ingresses, tend to a general prevalence of World conditions, for good or ill. Comets, Eclipses, the conjunction of several Superior Planets, Planets in perihelion or perigee, etc., tend to unusual World conditions. (See Comets, Eclipses, Ingresses, Mundane, Perihelion, Vernal). Under the following subjects the planetary influences are given which tend to some of these prevailing conditions, and by which Mankind is afflicted in various ways. See these subjects in the alphabetical arrangement, and especially look for "Prevalent" in these Articles. See Abdominal Diseases; Aged — (Great Mortality Among— (see Old Age); Bereavement; Bloodshed (see Blood); Boils, Calamity, Carbuncles, Catastrophy, Chest Diseases, Cholera, Colds, Colic, Conjunctivitis, Consumptions, Contempt for Religion (see Religion); Crime; Dangers (see Great Perils Generally" under Danger); Death (Painful Deaths Prevalent — see "Death" under Pain); Diarrhoea, Dissipation, Dropsy, Earthquakes; Effusion of Blood (see Effusions); Enemies (see "Fear Of" under Enemies); Epidemics, Eye Diseases, Famine, Fevers, Fluxes, Grief, Hatred; Head Diseases (see "Disorders" under Head); Heat (see "Extreme Heat" under Heat); Highwaymen, Incendiarism, Influenza, La Grippe, Lung Diseases, Mania, Measles; Melancholy (see "Much" under Melancholy); Mischief (see "Every One" under Mischief); Misery, Misfortune, Mortality, Murders, Nervous Diseases; Night (Diseases by Night); Outrages; Painful Deaths (see "Death" under Pain); Pandemics, Perils, Pestilence, Piracy, Plague, Pleasure Seeking, Plots; Public (see the paragraphs under Public); Railroad Accidents, Rapine; Reproductive Organs (Diseases of Prevalent); Robberies; Sadness (Much Sadness Generally); Sex Diseases (see "Diseases" under Sex); Shipwrecks; Skin Diseases, Slaughter, Smallpox; Sorrow (see "Sorrow" under Public); Suffering; Terrible Diseases (see Terrible); Trouble, Urinary Diseases, Violence, War, etc.

PREVENTED — Prevention — Averted — Preventive—

Birth Prevented — (See Abortion; "Birth" under Asphyxia; Barrenness; "Delayed Births" under Children; "Excision" under Foetus; Miscarriages).

Death—Death In Sickness Averted— (See Averted).

Disease Prevented—Averted—"To be Forewarned is to be Forearmed", is an old saying. Much of the sickness, suffering, and sorrow in the world today could be prevented if people would live and think right. It is said the abuse of the sex nature is the cause of sickness, weakness, and premature death, and that by the proper use and conservation of the sex fluids and vital forces of the body, man would live to an extreme old age, as they did in Ancient Times. The greatest problem of Earth Life is to learn to control the creative force under the regime of the Separated Sexes, and to not abuse and misuse it for sensuous purposes. This question is discussed in the book, "The Voice of Isis" by Dr. and Mrs. Homer Curtiss. (See "Separation of the Sexes" under Sex). The more Advanced Souls are born with star maps which do not have the aspects which increase passion, and it is easier for such people to properly use their creative forces. People born with good and well-balanced maps, showing strong vitality and practical immunity to disease, have more power to prevent or throw off disease when it comes. (See Immunity; "Strong" under Resistance; "Body" under Strong; "Good" under Vitality). There are also Herbs, Remedies, and many Natural Methods, and the regulation of Diet, to combat and prevent disease. People who overeat, and clog the system, invite disease. Also worry, anxiety, fear, melancholy, despondency, depression, low spirits, etc., tend to bring on disease, and lower the vitality and powers of resistance. (See these subjects). The proper remedies, or treatment given at the beginning of a disease, can often scatter and prevent its progress, as remedies change the polarity of the disease. (See Polarity, Praecipients, Remedies, Treatment). Many diseases originate in the Mind, and may be imaginary, and the power of Suggestion is a strong factor in the prevention or elimination of disease, if rightly used by the Healer. (See "Disease" under Fear; Healers, Hypnotism, Imaginations, Psychic, Suggestion). The Occult Masters teach that perfect health is the right of every one, and when we learn to think in terms of perfect health, and not in terms of disease, we will have health, for "As a Man Thinketh in His Heart, so is He". Spiritual Attainment and Spiritual Sight, the New Birth, and the proper use of our Forces, are essential to good health and the prevention of disease. The Masters, Adepts, and Initiates among us today in physical bodies have the spiritual power to control their health conditions, keep their bodies young, vigorous and healthy, and to renew their youth, and it is said they can renew their physical bodies, and keep them as long as they wish, and throw off the body also at their pleasure. Also Hygiene, Sanitation, and Cleanliness, play a large part in health, and the prevention of disease. (See these subjects. Also see Antipathy; "Cure of Disease" under Cure; Diathesis, Opposites, Medicines, Prognosis, Subluxations, Sympathy).

Events—Prevention of—(See Events).

Functions Prevented—Impeded—(See "Impeded" under Functions).

Preventive Remedies — (See Cleanliness, Diet, Discernment, Drugs, Healers, Hygiene, Knowledge, Power, Praeincipients, Remedies, Sanitation, Spirituality, Treatment, Wisdom, etc.).

PREY—Birds of Prey—(See "Birds of the Air" under Air; "Body Devoured" under Burial; Fowls, Vultures).

PRIAPISM — Painful Erections — (See Erections).

PRICKLING SENSATIONS—♅ influence. (See "Sensations" under Burning; Numbness, Paraesthesia, Sensations, Tingling, etc.).

PRIDE—The ☉ in the Asc., or in aspect to the Asc.; the ☉ in ♒, tinctured with pride; the ☉ afflicted tends to; the ☉ ☌ or P. ☿; the Dispositors of the ☉ and ☽ weak and afflicted, and the ☽ □ the Asc.; ♃ in ♈, a becoming pride; ♀ in ♌, proper pride and dignity; ♂ Sig. □ or ☍ ♃. The Hebrew letter Ayin is connected with Pride and the ♑ sign. (See Ego, Pretender, Self-Esteem, Self-Laudation).

PRIESTS—The Clergy—Ministers—Churches—Sadness and Anxiety To—(See Clergyment).

PRIMARY DIRECTIONS — The Effects of — (See Directions). Rules for the working out of Primary Directions, and examples, etc., are given in Wilson's Dictionary of Astrology; Simmonite's Arcana of Astral Philosophy, and other standard Textbooks of Astrology. Simmonite's Arcana is considered the most complete work on the subject, as Tables, Formulae, various Examples and Helps are given in this book. Primary Directions are very powerful in their action, and especially when assisted by a Secondary Direction, a Revolution, or Transit. They are also enduring in their effects, slower to form, and slower to pass away, and the student of Diagnosis, Prognosis, and the Causes of Disease, should be well up in the Mathematics of Astronomy and Trigonometry to do this work when required. (See Progression; "Solar Revolution" under Revolution; Secondary, Transits).

PRINCES—Princes and Kings are signified by the 10th H., and also by the ♌ sign.

Death by Wrath Of — (See this subject under Kings).

Death of a Prince—An Eclipse of the ☉ in the 1st Decan. of ♌; Comets appearing in ♌, ♑, or ♒. (See "Death of a King" under Kings).

Has the Favor of Princes — Or the Favor of Kings and Rulers—♂ Sig. ☌ the ☉, and also it may be their frowns to the utter undoing of the native. (See Famous; "Great Men" under Great; Queens, Rulers).

PRINCIPLE—Principles—

Planets — Principle of the Planets — (See "Principle" under each of the Planets).

Principles—Scruples—There are many subjects listed in this book which have to do with the Mental Traits, Tendencies of Temperament, Scruples, Principles, Motives, Character, etc. Look in the alphabetical arrangement for the subject you have in mind. Many of these subjects and traits are listed in the Articles on Conduct, Habits, Love Affairs, Men, Mentality, Mind, Morals, Passion, Religion, Sex, Temperament, Women, etc.

PRISONS — Imprisonment — Places of Confinement and Retention — Detentions — Restraints, etc. — Prisons and places of Confinement are ruled by ♆ and the 12th H., which house rules confinement, limitations, restrictions, plots, treachery, misfortune, Institutions where people are confined, as Asylums, Sanitariums, Hospitals, Prisons, Exiles, Banishments, Seclusion, etc. If the influences at B. indicate the danger and liability of Imprisonment, the time of such confinement will be apt to come under the evil transits, directions, and afflictions to the 12th H. and its influences at B. The following subjects have to do with Prisons, Imprisonment, Loss of Liberty, Confinement, Restraints, Limitations, and Misfortunes which tend to imperil the life and liberty of the native. See these subjects in the alphabetical arrangement when they are not more fully considered here—

Abroad—Detention Abroad—(See "Detention" under Abroad; Captivity).

Absent Party In Prison—(See "Prison" under Absent Party).

Anarchists; Asylum — Confined In — (See "Asylum" under Insanity).

Banishment; Beaten In Prison — Put In Irons, Beaten, and Severely Punished—The ☽, or lord of the 1st H., in ♉ or ♌, and in ☍ ♄ or ♂; ♂ ascending, or ruler of the Asc., when put in prison (Hor'y). (See "Injured" in this section; Cruel).

Captivity; Confined In Prison — (See "Imprisonment" in this section).

Confinement; Crime — Imprisoned for Criminal Acts—(See Crime).

Danger of Imprisonment—Liable To — Subject To — The influences at B. will be given here, and the directions, progressed influences, etc., will indicate the time of, and the immediate danger of imprisonment, unless the character, life, conduct, and habits of the native are properly regulated. The SUN afflicted in the 12th H. at B., and to the ill-asps. the ☽ by dir.; the ☉ afflicted at B., and to the evil asp. the Asc. by dir.; the ☉ to the cusp the 10th H., and this house afflicted; the ☉ directed to the Ascelli, or to Caput Hercules; the ☉ progressed to the □ or ☍ the M.C.; the ☉ in the 12th H., and afflicted at the Vernal Equi., and lord of the year; the ☉ Sig. □ or ☍ ♂, falls a victim to the Law; the ☉ afflicted in the 12th H. at B.; the ☉ to the ill-asps. ♃ by dir.; the ☉ to the ☌ or ill-asp. ♅ by dir.; the MOON in the 12th H. at B., and to the ☌ or evil asp. ♅ by dir.; the ☽ to the ☌, □, or ☍ ♄ or ♂ by dir., and especially if the direction falls in the 8th or 12th H.; the ☽ at a Solar Rev. passing the place of the radical ♄; the ☽ to the ill-asps. ☿ if this planet be ruler of the 4th, 8th, or 12th H.; the ☽ at Full, or incr. in a day nativity, sepr. from ♀ and applying to ♂; the ☽ incr. in a night geniture, sepr. from ☿ and apply. to ♄, if malefic planets afflict them; the ☽ to the ill-asps. ☿ by dir., and ☿ afflicted at B.; the ☽ afflicted at B., and to the cusp the 12th H. by dir.; the ☽ or M.C. to the place of Algenib, thru Forgery and Writings; the ☽ to the place of the Pleiades or Praesepe; NEPTUNE or ♅ afflicted in the 12th H.; ♆ afflicted in ♈, and possibly to Anarchistic tendencies; ♆ afflicted in ♓; ♆ by transit ☌ the ☽ or ☿ in the radix, and thru crime if ♆ is afflicted at B.; URANUS afflicted in the 12th H.; ♅ ☌ ♂ in ♈, thru criminal acts; ♅ to the ☌ or ill-asp. ♄, for neglect of family; ♅ to the ☌ or ill-asp. ♂ by dir., and espec. if ♅ or ♂ were in the 12th H. at B.; ♅ ☌ ♄ in the 12th H.; ♅ in the 12th H., and afflicted by ♄; SATURN afflicted in the 10th or 12th H.; ♄ afflicted in ♓; ♄ ruler of the 12th H. at B., and afflicted, and ♄ ☌ or ill-asp. the Asc. by dir.; ♄ to the ☌ or ill-asp. ♂ by dir.; ♄ Sig. ☌ ♂, may end days in prison (Hor'y); ♄ Sig. ☌ the ☉, for contempt of the Law; ♄ in the 12th H., and affl. by ♅ or ♂; MARS to the ☌ or ill-asp. the ☉ by dir.; ♂ afflicted in ♓ or the 12th H.; ♂ in fiery signs, afflicted, and ☌ or evil asp. the Asc. by dir.; ♂ in the 12th H., and affl. by ♅ or ♄; ♂ ☌ the Asc. by dir.; ♂ afflicted at B., and to the ☌ the M.C.; ♂ lord of the 12th H. at B., and the M.C. to the ☌ or ill-asp. ♂ by dir.; ♂ prog. to the ☌, □, or ☍ the radical ♄, or vice versa, the result of crime or murder; ♂ in the 12th H., but well-aspected, may be imprisoned, but escapes; the ASCENDANT to the □ or ☍ the ☉ by dir.; the 1st face of ♎, or the 7° ♎ on the Asc.; lord of the Asc. afflicted by lord of the 12th H. from bad houses; lord of the 1st in the 12th H.; the MIDHEAVEN to the cusp the 12th H. by dir.; the M.C. to the place of Procyon, the Pleiades or Pollux; the M.C. directed to Algenib, imprisonment thru writings, signings, forgery, bonds, libel; lord of the 10th a malefic, and in the 12th H.; the M.C. to the □ or ☍ the ☉; lord of the 10th in the 12th; the M.C. to the □ or ☍ ♂ by dir.; lord of the 3rd or 9th in the 12th H., imprisoned on a journey; lord of the 6th H. in the 10th H., and afflicted; lord of the 6th a malefic, and in the 12th H., and afflicted; lord of the 6th by transit over the cusp the 12th H.; lord of the 6th in the 12th H., sickness from imprisonment; the ruler of the 7th H. at B. in the 12th H. at a Solar Rev.; lord of the 8th a malefic, and in the 12th H., and afflicted; LORD OF THE 12TH in the 3rd or 9th, and especially while engaged in travel; lord of the 12th a malefic, and in the 12th, and afflicted, and afflicting the lords of the 1st or 4th, apt to end days in prison; lord of the 12th a malefic, and in the 1st H., thru his enemies; lord of the 12th a malefic, and in the 2nd H., thru money matters; lord of the 12th a malefic, and in the 3rd H., thru relatives; lord of the 12th a malefic, and in the 5th H., thru the influence of his children; lord of the 12th a malefic, in the 7th H., thru the wife's influence; lord of the 12th a malefic, and in the 10th, thru corrupt Judges, or his enemies in business swearing falsely; lord of the 12th a malefic, and afflicted in the 12th; lord of the 12th afflicted in ♓ in the Asc. (Hor'y); malefics, or a planet in the 12th H. at B., and afflicting the ☽; Fixed Stars of the nature of ♂ and the ☽ culminating at B., such as the Pleiades and other Nebulous stars of this character; the Ascelli, Pleiades, Hyades, Castor, Pollux, Praesepe, or Antares, directed to the Asc. or Lights, disgrace, imprisonment, and every evil that can befall the native; the Pleiades rising, or with the ☉ or ☽, or directed to the Asc. Cases of Imprisonment — All in 1001 N.N. See "Krishnananda", No. 225; "Tilak", No. 228, and "Scandals", No. 653. (See "Fixed Stars" under Stars; Twelfth House).

Danger to Those In Prison — Injured by Convicts or Other Prisoners—(See "Injured" in this section).

Death In Prison—Ends His Days In Prison—The ☉ or ☽ setting at B., and in ☍ to ♄ in the Asc.; the ☉ or ☽ rising and ♄ in ☍ to either; the ☉ Sig. □ or ☍ ♄, sometimes dies in prison; ♄ Sig. ☌ ♂, often ends days in prison; ♃ Sig. ☌ ♄, and especially if ♂ afflict ♃ and ☿ at the same time; lord of the Asc. in the 12th, and afflicted; lord of the Asc. disposed of by a malefic in the 8th (Hor'y); lord of the Asc. in the 4th, and afflicted by lords of the 7th, 10th, 11th, or 12th; lords of the 1st and 12th applying to a ☌ each other, and lord of the 12th stronger, or a malefic, denotes a fatal imprisonment; lord of the 1st also lord of the 12th; lord of the 1st, or the ☽, applying to the evil asps. ♄ or ♂, and especially if the malefic be lord of the 8th, or going into combustion without any good aspect of a benefic, or if ♄ and ♂ be in ☍ the ☉ or ☽, or the ☽ or lord of the 1st be near any violent fixed stars, as Caput Algol, it denotes that the whole will end in a violent death, or he will die in prison (Hor'y); lord of the 6th in the 12th, and afflicting the lords of the 1st, 4th, or 8th; lord of the 8th in the 12th, and afflicting the lord of the Asc., and with no benefics in the 12th; lord of the 8th in the 12th, or lord of the 12th in the 8th H.; afflictions in the 12th H.; lord of the 12th a malefic, and in the 12th, and afflicting the lords of the 1st or 4th; common signs show, and several malefics in them, and upon the angles.

Employment In Prisons — Successful In Prison or Hospital Work — (See "Employment" under Hospitals).

Ends Days In Prison—(See "Death" in this section; "Low Business" under Low).

Enemies—Imprisoned Thru Influence of Enemies—Lord of the 12th a malefic, and in the 1st or 10th H., and usually over money and business matters. (See Danger Of, Plots, in this section).

Escapes from Prison—♂ in the 12th H., and well-aspected. (See Fugitive).

Exile; Fear of Imprisonment—The ☽ afflicted at B., and to the cusp the 12th H. by dir. (See Fears).

Forgery—Imprisoned For—(See Forgers; "Danger Of" in this section).

Fugitive — The Fugitive Is Dead — Escaped from Prison—(See Fugitive; "Escapes" in this section).

Hospitals; Ill-Treated In Prison—(See Beaten, Injured, in this section).

Imprisonment — (See "Danger of" in this section).

Injured In Prison—By Convicts and Other Prisoners—♂ afflicted in fiery signs at B., and to the ☌, □, or ☍ the Asc. by dir.; a malefic ruler of the 12th at B., and at a Solar Rev. (See "Beaten" in this section).

Insanity — Confined In An Asylum — (See "Asylums" under Insanity).

Invalids; Irons — Put In Irons In Prison—(See "Beaten" in this section).

Judges—Imprisoned by Sentence of—(See Judges, Law).

Kidnapped; Liable to Imprisonment—(See "Danger Of" in this section).

Libel—Imprisoned For—(See Libel).

Limitations—(See this subject).

Long Imprisonment—In Prison Most of His Life—The ☽ disposed of by a malefic or lord of the 12th H.; the ☽ disposed of by a planet in an angle, and especially in the 4th H., and the planet B; the ☽ or lord of the 1st in the 8th or 12th H.; the ☽ or lord of the Asc. combust; the ☽ or lord of the Asc. in a fixed sign, or in ♓ at the time of arrest, or a fixed sign upon the Asc.; the ☽ in ♒ and afflicted by malefics, or a malefic in ♒, and espec. if the 12th H. is concerned and afflicted at the same time; ♄ or ☿ ascending, or ruling the Asc. at the time when imprisoned; a malefic in the 12th, and in evil asp. to the lord of the 1st or 10th; a fixed sign on the 12th, or lord of the 12th angular and in a fixed sign; lord of the Asc. in detriment or fall; lord of the 12th a malefic, and in the 12th H. (See "Fixed Signs" under Fixed).

Many Taken Prisoners—Held In Captivity—(See Captivity).

Murder — Imprisoned For — (See "A Murderer" under Murder).

Plots — Imprisoned Thru Plots and Treachery, as by Enemies, Children, Relatives, Competitors, etc.—The lord of the 12th H., and his position in the houses, and his afflictions, are the principal factors to be considered. (See the 12th H. influences in the paragraph "Danger Of", and also "Enemies" in this section; also see "Imprisonment" under Children; "Secret Enemies" under Enemies; "Asylums" under Insanity; Kidnapped, Plots, Revenge, Treachery).

Punishment—(See this subject).

Relatives — Imprisoned Thru Treachery of—(See Danger Of, Plots, in this section).

Restraints — Restrictions — (See Restraints).

Stealing—Imprisoned For—(See Kleptomaniac, Robbers, Thieves).

Surgeons In Prisons—Good Influences For—(See "Employment" under Hospitals).

Thieves — Imprisoned for Stealing — (See "Stealing" in this section).

Time of Imprisonment—Indicated by the directions, progressions, and transits to the 12th H., its lord, or to planets in the 12th at B.; also denoted by the ☌ or ill-asps. of lord of the 12th with malefics by dir. (See Directions, Events; the Introduction to this Article).

Travel—Danger of Being Held Captive, or Imprisoned During Travel—☽ in evil asp. to the Significator of Travel; the planets afflicting the Sigs. of Travel being in the 12th H. at the time; lord of the 12th a malefic, and afflicted in the 3rd or 9th H.; lord of the 3rd or 9th in the 12th, and afflicted. (See Captivity, Highwaymen, Pirates, Robbers, Travel; "Danger Of" in this section).

Treachery — Imprisoned By — (See Danger Of, Enemies, Plots, in this section).

Wife—Imprisoned by Influence of—Lord of the 12th a malefic in the 7th H. (See Marriage, Wife).

PRIVATE—Privacy—Secret—

Blindness by Private Injury — (See "Artifice", "Private Injury", "Treachery", under Blindness).

Loves Privacy and Seclusion — (See Grave; "Coldness" under Manner; Miserly; "Recluse" under Old Age; Recluse, Reserved, Retiring, Saturn, Seclusion; "Secretive" under Secret; Solitary, Suspicious).

Private Diseases—Diseases Connected with the Genitals and Organs of Sex and Reproduction—(See the subjects under Generative System; Genitals, Genito-Urinary, Penis, Reproduction, Secret Parts, Sex Organs, Venereal, Womb, etc.).

Private Enemies — (See "Secret Enemies" under Enemies; Enmity, Feuds, Hatred, Plots; "Death by Poison" under Poison; Revenge, Treachery, etc.).

Private Injury—Blindness By—Suffering By—(See Blindness, Private Enemies, in this section).

Private Parts — (See Genitals, Privates, Secrets, Sex Organs, etc.).

Private Sex Practices—(See "Liaisons" under Love Affairs; Perversions; "Clandestine" under Sex; "Solitary" under Vice).

PRIVATES — Secrets — Secret Parts — Private Parts—

Diseases In—(See "Private Diseases" under Private).

Injury To—The Asc. to the □ or ☍ ♄ by dir.; ♂ in ♏. (See "Mens' Genitals" under Genitals; Maimed, Testes; "Injuries To" under Womb).

Obstructions In—(See "Obstructions" under Generative). See the paragraphs under Generative, Genitals, Genito-Urinary, Penis, Ovaries, Reproduction, Secret Parts, Sex Organs, Vagina, Womb, etc.

PRIVATION—Privations—Poverty—Neglect—The strong afflictions of ♄ at B., and by dir., tend to privations, neglect, poverty, losses, or ruin, and especially when ♄ is afflicted in the 2nd H. (See Begging, Famine, Indifferent, Neglect; "Privation" under Seas; Starvation).

Functions Disordered—Thru Privation and Neglect—The ☽ afflicted by ♄. (See "Privation" under Functions).

Internal Disorders—Arising from Privation, Chill, Cold, and Neglect—(See "Internal Diseases" under Chill).

PROBABILITY—Probable—

Children—Probability of—(See "Promise of a Child" under Children; Fruitful).

Consumption—Probability of—(See "Consumptive" under Consumption).

Fainting—Probability of—(See Causes, Sudden, under Fainting).

Health—Probability of Good or Bad Health—(See Health, Stamina, Strength, Tone, Vitality, Weak, etc.).

Life—Probable Length of Life—(See "Probable Length" under Life).

Mental Disorders—Probability of—(See the paragraphs under Intellect, Judgment, Mental, Mind, Perception, Reason, Understanding).

Pleurisy—Probability of—(See Pleura). See the paragraphs under Danger, Diathesis, Disease, Health, Heredity, Idiosyncrasies, Ill-Health, Inherent, Liable, Receptivity, Susceptibility, Temperament, Tendencies, etc.

PROCEDURE—(See Action, Character, Conduct, Ideals, Ideas, Manners, Methods, Motives, Purposes, etc.).

PROCESS—Processes—

Alimentation—The Process of Nourishment—(See Alimentation, Nutrition).

Aphetic Process—(See Nutrition).

Asthenic Process—(See Asthenia).

Atrophy of Process—(See "Atrophy" under Functions).

Cell Processes—(See "Alteration" under Cells; Metabolism).

Coction Process—(See Combustion, Digestion).

Conservation Processes—(See Conservation).

Constructive Processes—In the Body—(See "Building the Body" under Build; Constructive).

Destructive Processes—(See Destructive).

Digestion—Process of—(See Alimentation, Assimilation, Diet, Digestion, Food, Nutrition).

Distillatory Process—(See Distillation).

Fermentation—(See Fermentation, Zymosis).

Gustatory Process—(See Gustativeness).

Hepatic Process—(See Hepatic).

Hypertrophic Process—(See Hypertrophy).

Inflammatory Process—(See Inflammation).

Metabolism; Metamorphosis;

Nerve Process—(See "Influx" under Nerves).

Preservative Processes—(See Preservation).

Renal Process—(See Kidneys, Renal).

Reproductive Processes—(See Conception, Fecundation, Fertilization, Foetus, Generative, Gestation, Parturition, Pregnancy, Prenatal Epoch; "Processes" under Reproduction).

Splenic Process—(See Spleen).

Sthenic Process—(See Mars, Sthenic).

Thoracic Process—(See Thorax).

PROCRASTINATION—Caused by the □ and ☍ aspects to ♃; ♃ □ or ☍ ☿. (See Dull, Idle, Inactive, Indifferent, Lassitude, Lazy, Lethargy, Negative, etc.).

PROCREATION—Ruled by the ☽ and ♀. (See Amativeness, Childhood, Conception; "Desire Body" under Desire; Fecundation, Fertilization, Fruitful, Gemmation, Puberty, Reproduction).

PROCYON—A violent star of the 1st magnitude in the 5th face of ♋, and of the nature of ♂ and ☿ combined. Tends to cause much evil in the life of the native, and dissipation. The ☽ to the ☌ Procyon tends to dissipation. The M.C. directed to brings danger of imprisonment, and many calamities. (See "Fixed Stars" under Stars).

PRODIGAL—Prodigality—Wasteful—Extravagant—Debauched—Dissipated—Prodigal of Expense—Fond of Luxuries—Diseases and Afflictions Arising from Prodigality, etc.—The ☉ to the ☌ ☽ by dir., and the ☽ badly afflicted at B.; the ☉ to the P. aspect the ☽; the ☉ or ☽ in a watery sign and afflicted; the ☉ Sig. □ or ☍ ♃; the ☉ and ♂ in the 1st H. in a fiery or airy sign; the ☽ strong at B. in the Asc., M.C., or ruler; the ☽ Sig. □ or ☍ ☉, ambitious but prodigal; ♄ or ♃ as Significators □ or ☍ ☉; ♄ Sig. ⚹ or △ ♀; ♃ ☌ or ill-asp. ♂; ♃ afflicting the ☉ or ☽; ♂ diseases and affliction; ♂ in bad asp. to ♃; ♂ Sig. □ or ☍ ♀, or vice versa; ♀ afflicted at B.; water signs on the Asc. at B.; the 6th face of ♒ on the Asc., and ♀ therein; the 3rd face, or 3° ♓ on the Asc.; the cusp of the 2nd H., or its ruler, to the ill-asps. the ☉. (See Conduct, Debauched, Dissipated, Dissolute, Drink, Drunkenness, Eating, Excesses, Expense, Extravagance, Feasting, Food, Free Living, Gluttony, Habits, High Living, Imprudent, Indiscretions, Indulgent, Low Company, Luxuries, Morals, Profligate, Reckless, Riotous, Self-Indulgent, Wanton, etc.).

PRODIGIES—Genius—Evolved Types—Precocious Mental or Spiritual Development—Mental or Physical Prodigies—♆ and ♅ strong at B., and in good asp. to ☿, tend to Geniuses and youthful Prodigies. This subject is further explained in the Articles on Genius, and Mathematical.

Chess Players—In the case of Chess Players, Lightning Calculators, Inventors, Mechanical Geniuses, Cranks, etc., the fundamental responsibility depends upon the association of ♂ and ☿, and especially by the ☌ and ☍, and with these planets in angles or the 3rd or 9th H. Case—See Chap. XIII in Daath's Medical Astrology. (See Genius, Mathematical).

Child Prodigy—Case—Began to Read at three years of age, and read Darwin and Huxley at eight years of age—See "Wiener", No. 353, in 1001 N.N.

Does Two Things At Once—Writes a Letter and Solves a Problem at same time—Case—See "Neptune", No. 352 in 1001 N.N.

Genius — (See the subjects under Genius).

Inventive—(See Genius).

Lightning Calculator — (See "Chess Players" in this section; Genius, Mathematical). Cases — See Daath, Chap. XIII. Also see "Bidder", No. 787 in 1001 N.N.

Mathematical Mind — ☿ is especially associated with mathematical ability. Also ☿ aspected by ♂. (See Genius, Mathematical. See Cases under "Lightning Calculator" in this section).

Mechanical Genius—(See Mechanical). Case—See Daath, Chap. XIII.

Musical Genius—(See Music).

Performing Pig—Case—(See Hogs).

Physical Prodigies—The 26° ♐ on the Asc. tends to make physical or mental prodigies. (See Freaks, Giants; "Premature Mental Development" under Premature).

PROFANE — Given to Profanity — In coarse maps profanity is caused by severe ♂ affliction; ♂ afflicting ♃ or ☿; ♂ afflicted in the 9th H., the house of religion. (See Anger, Evil, Excitable, Filthy, Irritable, Quarrelsome, Rough; "High Temper" under Temper; Vicious, Violent, etc.).

PROFESSION—The Profession—The Employment or Vocation — Ruled by the 10th H. (See Business, Employment, Vocation).

PROFESSIONS—Declarations—Avowals—Claims—Pretenses, etc.—The Principles, Character, Temperament and Tendencies, etc.—There are many subjects in this book listed along this line. Look in the alphabetical arrangement for the subject you have in mind. See such subjects as Anarchists, Bad, Character, Conduct, Deceitful, Disgrace, Dishonest, Dual, Enemies, Evil, Fanatical, Fancies, Friends, Habits, Honest, Honor, Hypocritical, Ideals, Ideas, Liars, Libelers, Love Affairs, Low, Metaphysics, Mind, Morals, Motives, Occult, Pretender, Principles, Purposes, Reformers, Religion, Reputation, Revolutionary, Riotous, Science, Temperament, Visionary, etc.

PROFICIENT — Proficient In Learning and In the Arts and Sciences — (See Learning).

PROFILE—(See "Profile" under Face).

PROFIT — Profit and Support from the Exhibition of Maladies — (See Exhibitionism).

PROFLIGATE — An Abandoned Person—Debased — Debauched — Depraved — Dissolute — Drunken — Indecent — Immoral — Corrupt — Low — Prodigal — Vicious—Of Little or No Virtue, etc.— (See these subjects. Also see Conduct, Habits, Morals, Passion, Pleasures, Self-Indulgent, Wanton, etc.).

Husband a Profligate — (See "Profligate" under Husband).

Pleasure — Profligate Love of — (See "Profligate" under Pleasure).

Wife Profligate—Dissolute—(See Dissolute, Drink, under Wife).

PROFLUVIAL EFFUSIONS—(See Effusions).

PROFOUND—

Profound Mental Incapacity — (See "Incapacity" under Mental).

Profound and Deep Mind—(See "Deep and Profound" under Mind).

PROFUSE—Excessive—Colliquative—

Profuse Diarrhoea — (See Cholera, Diarrhoea, Discharges, Dysentery, Evacuations, Faeces, Fluxes, Watery).

Profuse Expectoration — (See Expectoration).

Profuse Functions — (See "Irregular" under Functions).

Profuse Hemorrhage—(See Effusions, Hemorrhage; "Flooding" under Menses; "Epistaxis" under Nose).

Profuse Living—(See Living).

Profuse Menses—(See Menses).

Profuse Sweats—(See "Night Sweats" under Phthisis; "Excessive" under Sweat). See Abundance, Defluxions, Excess, Excesses, Humours, Hyperidrosis, Increased, Much, Over-Abundance, Plenty, Superabundance, Too Much, etc.).

PROGENY—(See Children).

PROGNOSIS — Prognostication — Prediction of the Course and End of a Disease—Possible Outcome of the Disease—The Planetary influences operating over the lives of people at B., and by transit, progression, or direction, give a very important clue to the possible beginnings of disease, of affliction, misfortune, and the time, nature and outcome of events, and especially with people who are drifting with their stars, following their tendencies, and who are dominated by their lower minds and the personality. By self-control, will-power, knowledge, wisdom, discretion, discrimination, spiritual sight, etc., it is usually possible to change the nature of events, or forestall them altogether, except in the case of ripe fate. (See Events, Fate; "Free Will" under Will). It is very difficult to give a correct prognosis as to the outcome of disease, suffering, or temporary affliction, in the case of Advanced Souls, Adepts, Initiates, etc., as the planetary influences have less power over them, and they have learned how to live more in harmony with Law, rather than to go against, and break them. (See "Disease Prevented" under Prevented). Predictions, therefore, and prognostications, may fail in proportion to your degree of spiritual attainment and development. The Art of Prediction has its foundations in Nature, and the movements of the Planetary Bodies. Events on the Earth Plane are but repetitions of similar occurrences, diseases, accidents, afflictions, trials, or sorrows of the Past, and which were produced by similar planetary aspects and influences in some remote Age of the World. Observations of these influences for thousands of years have enabled Astrologers to recognize, discover, and tabulate into a Science the Laws of Nature as they affect the destiny of the Individual, of Races, and Nations. Any possible event in a human life, from the cradle to the grave, can be reasonably foretold by the study of the coming aspects, conjunctions, and influences which will be culminating over the native and his map of birth, and even the time of death can ordinarily be predicted if the native drifts along, and follows the leadings of his planets, gives way to his weaknesses and tendencies, instead of controlling himself, and listening to the voice of Intuition and his Higher Mind. (See "Future Events" under Future).

Rules for Prognostication—
(1) Never predict the possible time of death.
(2) Never predict the actual future, or say what disease will actually come.
(3) Never predict that sickness, accident, or misfortune will actually come at a certain time.
(4) Do not say discouraging things to a patient.
(5) Do not tell the patient when crises are due.
(6) Never suggest sickness to a well person, or tell them they look pale and sickly, and especially to a Virgo person. (See "Time Of" under Accidents, Disease, Death; Calamity, Character, Danger, Diagnosis, Directions, Events, External, Fate, Future, Healers; "Good Health", "Periods of Bad Health", under Health; Individuality, Influenced, Map, Misfortune, Mutable Disposition, Nativity; "Death", "Disease", under Nature; Negative Disposition, Personality, Planets, Positive Nature, Predictions, Progressions, Prophetic, Receptive, Secondary, Spiritual, Susceptibility, Time, Transits, etc.). The following are a few subjects which have to do with Prognosis in Disease, either directly or indirectly.

Acute Diseases — Crises In — (See "Acute Diseases" under Crises).

Better — The Disease Will Turn for the Better — (See "Better" under Disease).

Course of the Disease—(See Course).

Crises In Disease—Favorable or Unfavorable—(See Crises).

Curable Diseases—(See Curable).

Death Almost Certain—(See "Certain Death" under Death; Fatal, Incurable).

Debility — Greater Debility and Continued Weakness In Disease—(See Debility, Duration, Lingering, Long Diseases, Prolonged, Protracted, Slow, Tedious).

Diagnosis — (See the paragraphs under Diagnosis).

Duration of the Disease—(See Duration, Long, Short, etc.).

End of the Disease—(See "End" under Disease).

Erratic Course — In Disease — (See "Course" under Erratic).

Favorable Prognosis — In Disease — (See "Disease" under Improved).

Fevers — Prognosis In — Fever Will Run High — The Fever Will Abate — (See "Curtailed", "High", under Fever).

Good — The Prognosis In Disease Is Good—(See "Disease" under Improved).

Incurable — The Disease Is Incurable — (See "Certain Death" under Death; Fatal, Incurable, Invalids, Wasting).

Judgment of the Disease—(See "Disease" under Judgment).

Long Diseases — (See "Diseases" under Long).

Moderation — Of the Disease — (See Moderation).

Modification — Of the Disease — (See "Better", "Complications", "Worse", under Disease; Modification).

Old Age — Prognosis of Disease In — (See "Health" under Old Age).

Peculiar Symptoms—In Disease—(See "Symptoms" under Peculiar).

Peril — Danger — The Disease Is Attended with Great Peril — (See "The Sick Will Hardly Escape" under Escape).

Prevention of Disease—(See Prevention).

Recovery In Disease—Will Recover—Will Not Recover—Recovery Doubtful —(See Curable, Fatal, Incurable, Recovery).

Resolution of Disease — (See Amelioration, Crises; "Better" under Disease; Moderation, Resolution, Termination).

Short Diseases — (See Acute; "Short" under Disease).

Suffering — Serious Suffering In Disease Forecasted—(See Grievous; "Diseases" under Pain).

Symptoms In Disease—(See Continuity, Course, Crises, Decumbiture, Diagnosis, Duration, Symptoms, etc.).

Tedious Diseases—(See Chronic, Consumption, Lingering, Long, Slow, Tedious, etc.).

Unfavorable Prognosis—(See "Worse" under Crises, Disease; "Illness" under Dangerous; "Certain Death" under Death; Fatal, Incurable, Majority, Malignant, Relapses).

Worse—The Disease Becomes Worse —(See "Worse" under Crises, Disease; Relapses).

PROGRESSION—Progressed—Progress — The Progressed Horoscope — Directions, etc.—According to the System of Primary Directions, the movements of the planets for each day after birth correspond to a year of life, or very close to a year. Thus, if ♂ be in the 1st degree of ♈ at B., and the Asc. in 6° ♈, we know that at about the 5th year of life ♂ will have progressed to the ☌ the Asc., and with the danger of an accident, injury, smallpox, hurts to the head or face, or a serious quarrel, etc. (See Primary). Secondary Directions, or Progressions, are based upon the movements of the ☽ on the days immediately after birth, and are calculated at the rate of two hours for every month, and the aspects thus formed by the ☽ to the positions of the radical planets are important to note, and tend to bring events, diseases, and efflictions, according to the nature of the planets, or planets aspected at such times. (See Secondary). The movements of the planets after birth are known as Progressions, Directions, Transits, etc., and the aspects, conjunctions, parallels, etc., formed to the radical planets by these progressions and movements of the planets after birth, indicate the possible time of events, disease, trouble, sorrow, misfortune, gloom, joy, happiness, good or bad health, prosperity, reverses, and possible death, etc., according to the nature of the planets aspected, and also the directions and transits which may be operating at the time. (See Aspects, Directions, Disturbances, Events, Fate; "Directions Of" under Moon; "Moon" under Motion; "Motion Of" under Planets; Prognosis, Progressive, Transits, etc.).

Disease—Progression In Disease—(See Chronic, Constancy, Continuity, Course, Crises, Duration, Progressive, Sequence, Slow, Tedious, Termination).

PROGRESSIVE—Gradually Extending—

Progressive Emaciation — (See Consumptions, Decay, Degeneration, Emaciation, Tabes, Wasting).

Progressive Muscular Atrophy — (See "Progressive" under Muscles).

Progressive Wasting — (See Emaciation, Tabes, Wasting, etc.).

PROHIBITION—Prohibitions—Prohibiting—In the human body, ♄ by his evil aspects and influences, tends to prohibit, retard and suppress function, secretion, elimination, excretion, etc., and to cause excess deposit of the poisons and wastes of the body, tending to hardening of the tissues, crystallization, thickening, stiffness, etc. In human affairs ♄ tends to bring limitations, confinement, sadness, sorrows, prohibitions, chastenings, testings, restraints, etc. (See Hardening, Limitations, Retentions, Suppressions).

Prohibition — The Prohibition of Intoxicating Liquors—Ruled over by ♃, and his good influences and aspects in Mundane Affairs. Also people born under the strong influence of ♃ tend to be sober and upright, religious, and not given to strong beverages. (See Temperance).

PROJECTING — Protruding — (See Protruding).

PROJECTS — Confusion of — Confusion of Mind — ♆ diseases and afflictions; the afflictions of ♆ to ☿, or to the Significators, the ☉, ☽, or Asc. at B., and by dir.; ♆ afflicted in ♒. (See Chaotic, Confusion; "Dreamy Mind" under Dreams; Ideas, Visionary, etc.).

PROLAPSE — Prolapsus — Prolapsed — Ptosis—A Falling Down of a Part—♅ and ♄ influence.

Abdominal Prolapsus — ♄ afflicted in ♍; Subs at PP (2L).

Bowels — (See "Prolapse" under Bowels).

Eyelid—(See "Ptosis" under Eyelids).

Hernia—The Prolapse and Protrusion of a Viscus—(See Hernia).

Kidneys—(See "Prolapsed" under Kidneys).

Spleen—(See "Prolapse" under Spleen).

Viscera — (See "Prolapse" under Viscera).

Womb — (See "Falling Of" under Womb).

PROLIFERATION — Cell Genesis — Reproduction — The general action of ♀ and her signs ♉ and ♎, and also of the ♀ Group of Herbs. (See "Gemmation" under Cells).

PROLIFIC—Fertile—Fruitful—♋ influence, and ♋ on the Asc., females are very prolific. (See "Many Children" under Children; Fertile, Fruitful).

Prolific Planets—(See "Fruitful" under Planets).

Unprolific—(See Barren).

PROLONGED — Prolongation — Protracted—Lengthened—

Disease Prolonged—The Disease Protracted—The Disease Will Continue—The ☉ or ☽ ill-aspected at B., or by dir., long and serious sicknesses; the ☉ or ♄ in the 6th H. in ☌, □, or ☍ denotes heavy affliction; the ☽ slow of motion, and in any asp. to the lord of the Asc., but with hope of a cure; the ☽ decr. in light, and near the body of ♄, the disease will continue a long time; ♅ ☌ ♄ in the 6th H., heavy and prolonged sickness; ♄ lord of the 6th H., in a fixed sign, ℞, and slow of motion; ♄ in the 6th H. and afflicted, or afflicting the hyleg, sad and heavy sickness; ♄ or ♂ occi. at B., between the 10th and 7th H., or in the 7th; to be taken sick in a ♄ hour tends to prolong the disease; lord of the 6th in the Asc., and lord of the Asc. in the 6th, the disease will continue until one of the Significators changes signs; lord of the 6th in the Asc., but the pain small at times; malefics in the occidental Quarters, the disease will be prolonged and tedious; signs of long ascension ascending. (See Chronic, Constancy, Continuity, Consumptions, Crises, Emaciation; "Hectic", "Low", under Fever; Grievous, Heavy; "Long Siege" under Ill-Health; Incurable, Invalids, Lingering; "Diseases" under Long; Serious Diseases, Severe, Slow Diseases, Tedious, Wastings, etc.).

Life Prolonged — The Life May Be Prolonged—The lord of the Asc. well-placed and free from affliction; ♃ or ♀ in the Asc. at B., and free from affliction; the hyleg well-aspected and free from the affliction of malefics. (See "Long-Lived", "Life Prolonged", under Children; Endurance; "Good Health" under Health; Immunity; "Long Life" under Life; Recuperation, Recovery, Resistance, Strength, Strong; "Good" under Vitality).

PROMINENT — Protruding — Conspicuous Parts of the Body—

Prominent Abdomen — (See "Prominent" under Abdomen).

Prominent Eyes — (See "Goggle" under Eyeballs; "Large", "Prominent", under Eyes; "Exophthalmic" under Goiter).

Prominent Forehead—(See Forehead).

Prominent Marks—Moles, or Scars—(See Marks, Moles, Scars).

Prominent Nose—(See Nose).

Prominent People — Death of — (See Famous; "Great Men", "The Great", under Great; Kings, Nobles, President, Rulers). See the subjects under Protruding.

PROMISCUITY — (See "Free Love" under Free; "Adulterous", "Liaisons", under Love Affairs; "Clandestine" under Sex; Shameless, Venery).

PROMISE—

Children—Promise of—(See "Promise of a Child" under Children; Fruitful).

Good Health—Promise of—(See "Good Health" under Health).

Long Life—Promise of—(See "Long" under Life).

Riches—Promise of — (See "Accumulates", "Confers", under Riches).

PROMISES—Profuse In Promises Thru Excess of Good Nature — ♄ well-aspected in ♐ at B.; ♃ influence; ♃ ruler, strong by sign, and well-aspected at B. (See Humane, Kind; "Obliging" under Manner).

Insincere Promises — (See Deceitful, Dual, Hypocritical).

PROMISSOR — Promittor — The Planet which promises, or indicates the kind or nature of the disease, affliction, or benefit, and to fulfill some event. The malefics, ♄ and ♂, tend to be evil Promittors, or the Anareta, when the hyleg is directed to them. The benefics, ♃ and ♀, promise good fortune, and are promittors of good when favorable directions to them are fulfilled. The planet signifying the event is the Promittor in Hor'y Questions. If the question is concerning health, take the lord of the 6th H. as the Promittor. If concerning marriage, the lord of the 7th, and its aspects, dignities, weaknesses, etc. If concerning money, the lord of the 2nd H. becomes the Promittor, etc. See the Articles on Promittor in Wilson's Dictionary of Astrology, and in Sepharial's New Dictionary of Astrology.

PROMOTED—

Health Promoted — (See "Improved" under Health).

Rheumatism Promoted — (See "Continued and Promoted" under Rheumatism). See Continuity, Crises; "Worse" under Disease; "Disease" under Increase).

PROMOTER — A Great Promoter — A Speculative Mind—(See Speculative).

PRONOUNCED — The Disease Is More Pronounced—(See Diathesis; "Certain" under Disease; "Disease" under Severity).

PROOF—Proof Against Attacks of Disease—(See "Good Health" under Health; Immunity; "Good" under Resistance; Robust; "Body" under Strong; "Good" under Vitality).

PROPAGATION — A Strong Desire to Propagate—(See Amativeness).

PROPENSITIES—Tendencies—

Animal Propensities — (See "Animal Instincts" under Animal).

Evil Propensities — (See Cheating, Conduct, Crime, Evil, Forgers, Gamblers, Liars, Murderous, Prodigal, Thieves, Wicked, Wanton, etc.).

Good Propensities — (See Good, Honest, Humane, Kind; "Good Morals" under Morals; Noble, Sincere, etc.).

Mental Propensities — (See the paragraphs and subjects under Mental, Mind).

Sensual Propensities— (See Amorous, Lascivious, Lewd, Licentious, Passion, Perversions, Sex, Vices, Wanton, etc.).

Tendencies—Of Mind and Body—(See Acquired, Character, Congenital, Constitution, Diathesis, Heredity, Intellect, Mind, Organic, Structural, Temperament, Tendencies, etc.).

PROPER STATURE — (See Beautiful, Comely, Handsome, Harmony, Well-Proportioned, etc.).

PROPERTY—Possessions—Riches—

Acquires Property—(1) By Honorable Means—(See Honest; "Confers" under Riches). (2) By Dishonest, Unfair, and Selfish Means—♃ Sig. ☌ ♄, and seldom enjoys it like other persons. (See Cheating, Deceitful, Dishonest, Forgers, Gambling, Thieves, etc.).

Duped of His Property — And Dies a Miserable Death—♃ Sig. ☌ ♄. (See Inheritance).

Loss of Property — Death from the Vexation of — Lord of the 8th in the 4th H. (See Misfortune, Resources, Reverses; "Losses" under Riches; Ruin, Wealth).

Property of Others—No Respect For —(See Respect).

Sickness—From Waste of Property—Lord of the 6th in the 2nd H. (See "Undermined" under Health; "Health Injured" under Men).

Wastes Property—By Riotous Living — (See Debauchery, Dissipation, Excesses; "Free Living" under Free; "High Living" under High; Indiscretions, Indulgences, Intemperance, Prodigal; "Property" under Religion; Riotous, Speculation).

PROPHETIC — Foretelling the Future — Seers — ♆ strong and well-aspected at B.; ♆ in the Asc. or M.C.; 4th face of ♍ on the Asc. (See Clairaudience, Clairvoyance, Dreams, Fears, Forebodings, Hypnotism, Intuition, Mediumship, Obsessions, Psychic, Religion, Seers, Spirit Controls, Visions, etc.).

PROPITIATIONS — (See the Introduction under Events).

PROPORTIONATE — (See Beautiful, Comely; "Fair Proportions" under Fair; Handsome, Harmonious; "Proportioned" under Moderately; Stature, Well-Proportioned).

PROPUS—Left Foot of Castor—In 29° ♊, of the nature of ♂. (See Castor).

PROROGATOR—Apheta—Hyleg—The Giver of Life—(See Hyleg).

PROSPECTS—

Good Fortune — Prospects of — (See Fortunate).

Good Health — Prospects of — (See "Good Health", "Prospects", under Health).

Ill-Fortune—Prospect of—(See "Ill-Fortune", "Malice of Fortune", under Fortune).

Ill-Health—Prospects of—(See "Bad Health", "Periods of Bad Health", under Health; "Ill-Health All Thru Life" under Ill-Health; "Much Sickness" under Sickness; "Low" under Vitality).

Long Life—Prospects of—(See "Long Life" under Life).

Short Life—Prospect of—(See "Death" under Childhood; "Early Death" under Early; "Death In Infancy" under Infancy; "Short Life" under Life).

Wealth—Prospect of—(See "Accumulates", "Confers", under Riches).

PROSPERITY—Success—The ☉, ☽, ♃, and ♀ rising and above the Earth, and especially when well-aspected in the 10th H.; ♃ ☌ ♀ in the 2nd H., well-aspected, and no malefics in this house. (See Contentment, Fortunate, Happiness; "Peace of Mind" under Mind; Property; "Prospers Anywhere" under Residence; Riches, Wealth, etc.).

PROSTATE GLAND—Ruled by the ♏ Sign.

Diseases Of—The ☉ afflicted in ♏; afflictions in ♏; Subs at LPP (4L).

Enlargement Of—Hypertrophy of—The ☉ ☌ ♄ or ♂ in ♎ or ♏, and affl. also by the □ or ☍ ♆; ♆ in ♏, ☌, □, or ☍ ♄; ♂ affl. in ♏. (See Enlarged, Hypertrophy).

Inflammation Of—Prostatitis—♂ afflicted in ♏.

Prostatic Plexus—Ruled by ♏.

Prostatic Stricture—A ♏ disease; ♅ or ♄ afflicted in ♏; ♄ ☌ ♅ in ♏. (See Stricture).

PROSTITUTES—(See Harlots).

PROSTRATION—Collapse—Fainting—Feeble—Weak—(See Collapse, Debility, Fainting, Feeble, Infirm, Languishing; "Low" under Resistance, Vitality; "Weakened" under Strength; "Weak Body" under Weak).

Heat Prostration—(See "Excessive Heat" under Heat; "Sunstroke" under Sun).

Nervous Prostration—(See Collapse; "Nerves" under Excitable; "Prostration" under Nerves).

PROTECTION—Protects—Protective Influence—The Benefics, ♃ and ♀, exert a protecting, saving and beneficial influence over the body and mind. Also the ☉ dignified, well-placed, and well-aspected at B. (See Benefics).

Protects the Health—The ☉ ☌ or P. ♃ or ♀ acts as a protective influence against the evil aspects of the other planets; the ☉ ☌, P., ✶ or △ ♃ is a protective influence, increases the vitality, strengthens the constitution, and helps to overcome disease; the benefics well-aspected in the 6th H., and with no malefics in the 6th, or ruling the 6th. (See Endurance; "Good Health" under Health; Immunity; "Good" under Recuperation, Resistance, Vitality).

PROTEIDS—An Albuminoid Constituent of An Organism—Ruled by the ☉. Also strongly influenced by the ♒ sign. The clotted Proteids of Milk are ruled by the ☉. (See Albumen, Casein; "Proteids" under Food).

Eats Excess Of—And of Starches and Sugars—(See "Proteids", "Sweets", under Food).

PROTOPLASM—Protoplasma—Germinal Matter—Primitive Organic Cell Matter—Ruled by the ☉, as the ☉ is the center of our Solar System, ruler of the Nucleus, or Germinal Center of Organisms. The irritation and activity of the Protoplasma are furnished by ☿, as ☿ is near the ☉, and less than 30° from the ☉ at all times. (See Cells, Nucleus).

PROTRACTED—Prolonged—Extended—Long Drawn Out—

Protracted Fevers—(See "Chronic", "Hectic", "Low", under Fever).

Protracted Illness—(See Chronic, Consumptions, Invalids, Lingering, Long Diseases, Phthisis, Prolonged, Slow Diseases, Tabes, Tedious, Tuberculosis, Wastings, etc.).

PROTRUDING—Protrusions—Projecting—Prominent—

Abdomen—A Protruding Abdomen—(See "Prominent" under Abdomen).

Breastbone—Protrusion of—(See "Breastbone" under Breast).

Chin—Protruding Chin—(See "Long" under Chin).

Ears—Protruding and Large Ears—(See the Introduction under Ears).

Eyeballs—Protruding—(See "Goggle Eyes" under Eyeballs).

Eyebrows—Bushy and Overhanging—(See "Beetle Brows", "Bushy", under Eyebrows).

Hernia—Hernia Protruding Thru the Abdominal Ring—(See "Inguinal" under Hernia).

Nose—Protruding Nose—(See "Long", "Prominent", under Nose).

Piles—Protruding Piles—(See "Blind Piles" under Hemorrhoids). See the subjects under Prominent.

PROUD—Haughty—Lofty-Minded—Disdainful—Lordly—Conceited—The ☉ rising in ♌; ♌ gives a haughty air, carriage and walk, and especially when the ☉ is rising in ♌; the ☉ Sig. in ♉, proud of his physical strength; the ☉ Sig. in ♐, lofty and proud-spirited; the ☉ Sig. in ♒; the ☉ ill-dignified at B., and afflicted; planets in ♌; the ☽ Sig. in ♌, lofty and proud; the ☽ Sig. ✶ or △ the ☉, proud and aspiring; ♄ Sig. in ♎; ♃ Sig. ☌ ♂; ♃ Sig. in ♌; ♃ Sig. □ or ☍ the ☉; ♂ in ♌; ♂ Sig. in ♈, ♌, ♍, or ♐; ♂ a strong ruler at B.; ♂ strong at B., and in the sign or house of the ☉; in Hor'y Q. ♂ Sig. of the person or querent; ♀ Sig. ☌ the ☉; ♀ Sig. in ♌ or ♐; ♀ Sig. ✶ or △ ♂; ☿ Sig. in ♌; the Ruler or Significator in its exalted sign, angular, and in no way impedited, the native is arrogant, haughty, and assuming to himself more than his due. (See Commanding; "Proud" under Gait; Pretender).

PROVISIONS—Scarcity of—(See Crops, Drought, Famine, Fountains, Privation, Scarcity).

PROWESS—Fearlessness—Daring In Battle—(See Bold; "Fearless" under Fear).

PRUDENT—Prudence—Cautious—Sagacious — Circumspect — Discreet — Good Judgment — Thoughtful — Thrifty, etc. —The good aspects of ♄ to the ☉, ☽, and ☿; the ☽ applying to the good asps. ♀ or ☿; ♃ in the Asc.; ♂ Sig. ⚹ or △ ♄; ☿ Sig. in ♎; ☿ Sig. ⚹ or △ ♄. (See "Good" under Judgment).

Excess of Prudence—The ☽ Sig. ☌ ♄, and doubts and deliberates too much in the moment of action. (See Doubts, Fears, Mistrustful, Suspicious).

Imprudent—Void of Prudence—(See Imprudent, Indiscretions, Foolhardy; "Bad" under Judgment; Recklessness).

PRUDERY—Excessive Modesty—Coyness—Most common with people born with the ☉ in ♋, ♍, ♎, and ♏, and especially with females. The fiery signs, and also ♉, ♑, and ♒, are devoid of exaggerated, or false modesty. The ♍ people especially have more sex modesty, this being the sign of the Virgin. (See Bashfulness; "Chaste" under Females; Modesty, Shy).

PRURITUS—Intense Itching—(See Itch).

PSEUDO—False—There are a number of conditions, or manifestations in mind and body, which may resemble a disease, and have its symptoms, but which may be false, unreal, and imaginary. The planets ♆ and ♅ are largely responsible for such conditions. Also the malefics in the Signs of the Zodiac which rule, or cause a disease, may for a time lead to false, or exaggerated conditions, and mental impressions. (See Curious, Extraordinary, False, Illusions; "Imaginary Diseases" under Imagination; Mysterious Diseases; "Diseases" under Obscure, Peculiar, Psychic, Strange, Uncommon; "Pretended Ailments" under Pretended; Vague, Weird, etc.).

Pseudo Angina—False Angina—(See "False Angina" under Angina).

Pseudo Ischuria—Spurious Ischuria —(See "False Ischuria" under Urine).

PSITTACOSIS—A Disease of Birds Communicable to Man, marked by High Fever and Pulmonary Disorders—Parrot Fever—A ♊ disease, and afflictions in ♊; the ☉, ☽, or ♄ afflicted in ♊, susceptible to if exposed to birds with the disease, as Parrots; ♊ on the Asc. at B.; Subs at Lu.P. (See Fowls).

PSORIASIS—A Chronic Inflammatory Skin Disease with Scale Formation—♂ or ☿ afflicted in ♑. (See Scales, Skin Diseases).

Face—Psoriasis of—♄ or ♂ afflicted in ♈; Subs at MCP (4C), and KP. (See "Tetter" under Face).

PSYCHIC—Pertaining to the Mind—Psychic Powers—Psychic Conditions—Psychopathic—Psychosis—Psychoses—Psychism, etc.—The Psychic Powers and Psychic Mental Traits are largely ruled over by ♆, and this planet in his strong sign ♓ tends to enhance these powers, to make the native very psychic, clairvoyant and mediumistic, and to good advantage when ♆ is not sorely afflicted by malefics. The ♋ sign is a very Psychic Sign. The following subjects have to do, more or less, with the Psychic Powers and the Mind. The Psychic Powers are also dealt with in this book in the Articles on the Intellect, Intuition, Mentality, Mind, Perception, Reason, Understanding, etc. See these subjects, and also see the following subjects in the alphabetical arrangement when only listed here—

Abeyance—Of the Psychic Powers—(See Coma, Consciousness, Delirium, Insensibility, Unconsciousness).

Apparitions—(See Phenomena).

Auto-Toxic Psychoses—(See "Psychoses" in this section).

Catalepsy; Chaotic Mind—(See Chaotic, Confusion).

Clairaudience; Clairvoyance; Coma;

Confusion; Consciousness;

Constitution—The Constitution and Vitality Benefitted Psychically—♆ ⚹ or △ the ☉ at B.

Curious Diseases—(See Curious, Extraordinary, Pseudo, Strange, etc.).

Death—Of the Psychic Nature—Shown by the 12th H. and ♓ sign, as this is the last, or end of the signs and houses, when life on earth is finished, and the Soul is ready to pass out of the influence of the physical body. (See Terminal, Twelfth House).

Delirium; Delusions; Demoniac;

Diseases—Disorders—Psychic Diseases and Disturbances—Psychic Distempers—Psychic Origin of Disease—The Disease Originates In the Mind Rather Than In the Body—Caused principally by ♆; ♆ afflicted in the brain sign ♈; ♆ ☌, □, or ☍ the Asc.; the ☽ afflicted by ♆; the ☽ □ or ☍ lord of the 1st H.; ♄ ☌ or ill-asp. ♆; if ♄ afflict the Asc., the ☽, and dispositors of the ☉ and ☽ (as the 1st H. and the dispositors of the ☉ and ☽ signify the mind), and the trouble may be over some business loss; ☿ ☌ ♆; the Asc. afflicted by ♆ or ♅. (See "Centered on Disease", "Disease", "Diseased Mind", "Mind and Body", under Disease; "Imaginary Diseases" under Imagination; Mysterious Diseases, Obscure Diseases, Peculiar Diseases, Strange, Vague).

Dreams; Ecstasy; Emotions;

Experiences—Psychic Experiences—Predisposition To—♆ or ♅ in the 6th or 8th H. at B.; ♆ progressed, afflicting the ☉, ☽, ♀, ☿, or the Asc., and tends to undesirable phases of. (See "Involuntary" under Clairvoyance, Mediumship; Imaginations, Obsessions, Spirit Controls, Uncanny, Weird, etc.).

Fainting; Fears; Feelings; Functions —The Psychic Functions Strengthened —♆ ⚹ or △ the Asc.

Hallucinations; Healing—Psychic Healing—(See "Psychic" under Healers).

Hyperactivity—Of the Psychic Powers —Over-Activity of—Caused by the afflictions of ♆ or ♅ at B.; these planets in the 8th H. at B., and afflicting the hyleg, the ☉, ☽, or Asc.; ♆ afflicting ☿, the mental ruler; ♆ in the Asc. or M.C., and afflicted by the ☉, ☽, ☿, or malefics. (See "Over-Active Mind" under Active; Coma, Effervescent, Excitable; "Mind" under Hyperactivity; Lethargy).

Hypnotism; Illusions; Imaginations; Insanity; Intellect; Introspection;

Intuition; Low Grade — The Psychic Powers of a Low Grade—♆ ruler of the horoscope and afflicted. Involuntary Clairvoyance, Undesirable Mediumship, Crystal Gazing, etc., are usually practiced by people with a low grade of Psychic Power, or who resort to Black Magic for commercial purposes. Neptune strong, dignified, and well-aspected at B. tends to give Psychic Powers of a very high grade, Spiritual Sight, and to use such powers only for the benefit of Humanity, and rarely for financial gain. (See Clairvoyance; "Practices Hypnotism" under Hypnotism; Magic, Mediumship).

Magic; Magnetic—(See "Healers" under Magnetism).

Mania—(See Madness, Mania, Fury).

Mediumship; Mental — (See the subjects under Mental, Mind).

Metempsychosis—(See Reincarnation).

Mind—The Disease Originates In the Mind—Of Psychic Origin— (See "Diseases" in this section).

Mysterious Diseases — (See Curious, Extraordinary, Mysterious, Obscure, Peculiar, Strange, Uncommon, etc.).

Nails—Psychic Type of—(See "Long" under Nails).

Negative Psychism—♆ □ or ☍ ♃ tends to. (See Negative).

Obscure — Obscure and Psychic Diseases—(See "Diseases" under Obscure).

Obsessions; Over-Activity — Of the Psychic Powers—(See "Hyperactivity" in this section).

Passive — (See Influenced, Negative, Passive, Receptive, Susceptibility).

Perception; Phenomena — Psychic Phenomena—Phenomena Referable to Psychic Causes — ♂ ☌ or ill-asp. ♆. (See Catalepsy, Clairvoyance, Consciousness, Delirium, Delusions, Hallucinations, Hypnotism, Illusions, Magic, Mediumship, Obsessions, Spirit Controls, Trance).

Photographer—Psychic Photographer —Case—See "Psychic Photographer", No. 935, in 1001 N.N.

Pineal Gland — This Gland is closely related to the higher Psychic and Spiritual Powers, and is ruled by ♆. (See Pineal, Pituitary).

Powers — Strong Psychic Powers — Odic Force—♆ ☌ or P. the ☽, and especially in ♋ or ♓; ♆ ⚹ or △ the Asc., the psychic functions strengthened; the 10° ♓ on the Asc. at B., tends to give much psychic power. (See "Active Mind" under Active; "Psychic" under Healers; Hypnotism, Intuition; "Quickened" under Mentality; Pineal, Spiritual; "Hyperactivity", "Low Grade", in this section).

Predisposition — To Psychic Experiences—(See "Experiences" in this section).

Predominance—Of the Psychic Powers Over the Physical—♆ rising in the Asc. or M.C., and with the ☉, ☽, and many planets setting in the West; ♆ rising in ♋ or ♓. Also caused by the afflic-

tions of ♆ and ♅, and especially of the lower grade of psychic powers, and involuntary conditions. (See Experiences, Hyperactivity, Low Grade, Phenomena, Powers, Sensitive, in this section).

Premonitions; Pretended Ailments — (See Pretended).

Prophetic; Psychic Experiences—(See "Experiences", and the various paragraphs in this section).

Psychic Nature — Psychic Tendencies —♆ and ♅ strong at B.; the 4th face of ♉ on the Asc., soft and negative; the 5th face of ♋, the 6th face of ♍, or the 5th face of ♓ on the Asc. (See Experiences, Powers, Predominance, and the various paragraphs in this section).

Psychic Storms—Afflictions to ♆ at B.; ☽ □ or ☍ ☿.. (See "Brain Storms" under Brain; Emotions, Excitable, Hysteria).

Psychic Tendencies — (See Predominance, Psychic Nature, and the various paragraphs in this section).

Psychic World—Experimenting In, or Tampering with the Psychic Powers— (See "Tampering" in this section).

Psychism—Favorable To—Tendencies To—♅ in △ aspect to ♆. Negative Psychism is caused by the □ or ☍ asp. of ♆ to ♃. Adverse Psychism and Obsessions are caused by ♆ □ ♄ in the 8th H., and in □ asp. to ☿ at the same time.

Psychoses—(1) Auto-Toxic Psychoses —(See Diabetes, Uremia). (2) Toxic Psychoses — Occurs in such disorders as Alcoholism, Dementia, Delirium Tremens, Mania, Narcotic Habit, Paranoia, etc. (See these subjects).

Reason—(See the paragraphs under Reason).

Religion—Ecstatic and Psychic Experiences In—(See "Religious Excitement" under Excitable; "Ecstasy" under Religion).

Seances—(See Spiritualism).

Sensitive — To Psychic and Spiritual Conditions—♆ strong at B.; ♆ or ♅ in the 3rd, 6th, or 9th H. at B., and if these planets are afflicted in these houses, in an adverse manner, or to cause hyperactivity of the psychic powers, or involuntary conditions; the ☽ in ♋, and especially when aspected by ♆ or ♅, and for good or evil according to the aspect. (See Diseases, Experiences, Hyperactivity, Low Grade, Predominance, Psychic Nature, in this section).

Sensitives — The aspects and influences of ♆ along Psychic or Spiritual lines have the most effect upon Sensitives for good or ill. (See "Sensitives" under Sensitive).

Spirit Controls; Spiritualism — Is strongly ruled by ♆. (See Spiritualism).

Spirituality — Spiritual Sight — (See Spiritual).

Storms—(See "Psychic Storms" in this section).

Strange Diseases—Of a Psychic Origin—♆ and ♅ diseases. (See Strange).

Strengthened — The Psychic Powers Strengthened—(See Functions, Powers, in this section).

Strong Psychic Powers — (See Functions, Powers, in this section).

Subconscious Mind — (See "Subconscious" under Mind; Subconscious).

Tampering—With the Psychic Powers — Experimenting with the Psychic World—Born with ♆ in ♓, the Asc., 12th H., or in the 10th H.; ♆ ☌ ☿ or the ☽. The Psychic Powers should not be forced, or prematurely developed, but be allowed to unfold naturally, otherwise they bring great dangers to the native, danger of Obsessions, involuntary Clairvoyance or Mediumship, Spirit Controls, etc.

Telepathy; Tendencies—Psychic Tendencies—(See Experiences, Psychic Nature, and the various paragraphs in this section).

Undesirable Experiences—In Psychism—♆ afflicted by ♅ or the ☽. (See "Involuntary" under Clairvoyance, Mediumship; Spirit Controls; Experiences, Hyperactivity, Low Grade, Predominance, Tampering, in this section).

Vitality—The Vitality Benefitted Psychically—(See "Constitution" in this section).

PTOLEMY—Claudius Ptolemy was the Author of the great Textbook on Astrology, known as "The Tetrabiblos". This book is still considered the basis of our Modern Teachings on Astrology, and is quoted very much. Ptolemy was born 132 A.D., and passed out in A.D. 160. Ptolemy gave us the fundamental teachings and theories about the Prenatal Epoch, and its various Orders and Modifications, and of the close relationship between the time of conception, and the time of birth. His book is quite a valuable Treatise on Medical Astrology, and should be in the hands of every student of Astral Philosophy. Ptolemy's book has been translated by Mr. J. M. Ashmand in recent years, and is now available in the Occult and Metaphysical Book Stores. (See Prenatal Epoch).

PTOMAINES—A Putrefactive Alkaloid — (See "Offensive Humours" under Humours).

PTOSIS—A Falling—Drooping—Prolapsus—(See Prolapse).

PTYALISM—An Excess of Saliva—Salivation—(See Saliva).

PUBERTY — Adolescence — The Age of Capability of Reproduction — Adolescence is the age between Puberty and Maturity. In the Kabala, Puberty was dedicated to Mercury.

Delayed Puberty — ♄ afflicted in ♏; Subs at PP (2, 3, 4L). (See the Introduction under Menses; "Early", "Time Of", in this section).

Dementia Praecox—At Puberty—(See "Trouble" in this section).

Disturbed—The removal of the Tonsils in childhood (the Tonsils are ruled by ♉, the opposite and complementary sign to ♏, the sign which rules the sex organs) tends to make the puberty period more disturbed, and also to later make childbirth more difficult and painful. Afflictions in ♏ also tend to disturb the puberty period, as ♄ or ♂ afflicted in ♏. Also caused by afflictions in ♉ at B. (See "Puberty Weakened" under Menses; "Operations" under Tonsils; "Females", "Trouble", in this section.

Early Puberty — The ☽ progressing thru signs of short ascension after birth, and at a later age when passing thru signs of long ascension. (See the Introduction under Menses; "Time Of" in this section).

Females — Ill-Health In Females At Puberty—Weakness In Females At Time of—The ☽ ☌ ♄ in ♍, ♎, or ♏; the Asc. to the □ or ☍ the ☽ or ♀ when occurring near the age of adolescence. The regularity of the female system, and the health after puberty, will depend largely upon the conditions, positions, and affections of the ☽ and ♀. (See "Painful", "Profuse", under Menses).

Imaginations — Morbid and Sensuous Imaginations Upon Passion and Sex Life At Time of Adolescence—♆ in the 6th or 12th H., and especially if in ☍ to ♅, or if ♆ is ☍ ♅ from an angle. (See "Morbid" under Imagination; "Sensuous" under Sensuality).

Insanity—At Puberty—(See "Puberty" under Insanity).

Menses—The Menses Begin—(See Menses; Delayed, Early, Time Of, in this section).

Mental State—And Puberty—See Fig. 13 in "Message of the Stars" by the Heindels, page 630, and the comments on page 610 of the same book. Puberty usually occurs at about the 14th year of life, and at the beginning of the third seven-year cycle, and when the Mind begins to take a deeper hold upon the life. The voice in males also changes to a deeper tone at this time, due to the reflex action upon the Larynx (♉) from the ♏ sign, the sex sign. (See Larynx).

Morbid Brooding — On Sex Life At Time of Adolescence—(See "Imaginations" in this section).

Passion — The Passion Increased At Puberty, and Brooding Upon — (See "Imaginations" in this section).

Procreation — Strong Desire For At Puberty—(See Amativeness).

Sensuous Imaginations — At Puberty —(See "Imaginations" in this section).

Sex Activity—Great Sex Activity At Adolescence—Children who have ♆ in the 6th or 12th H. at B. tend to greater sex activity at adolescence and during puberty, and to have morbid sex desires, and should be carefully trained, advised, and watched at this time. (See "Imaginations" in this section).

Time of Puberty—The Menses Begin —The Voice Changes In Males—The ☽ by progression in ☍ to her place at B. tends to precipitate the adolescent period, and the menses begin in females, the voice changes in males. (See Childhood, Larynx; the Introduction under Menses; Delayed, Early, Mental State, in this section).

Trouble At Puberty—Danger of Dementia Praecox At Puberty—Afflictions in ♉ or ♏, or in both signs; ♄ ☌ ♆ in ♉ or ♏; ♄ afflicted in ♉ or ♏; ♃ ☌ ♆ or ♂ in ♉ or ♏; Subs at PP. (See Disturbed, Females, Insanity, and the various paragraphs in this section).

Voice Changes—In Males At Time of—(See Larynx; Mental State, Time Of, in this section).

Weakened—(See "Puberty Weakened" under Menses; Disturbed, Females, in this section).

Weakness Incident To — (See "Females" in this section).

Young Females — Weakness and Ill-Health In At Adolescence—(See "Females" in this section).

PUBES — The Anterior Portion of the Innominate Bone—Ruled by ♑. The Hair of the Pubic Region is also ruled by ♑. Some Writers also say that the ♏ sign rules the Pubic Bone. (See Innominate, Pelvis).

PUBLIC—The Public—The People—The Common People — The Community — The Multitude—Humanity—Mankind—The Public Welfare—Public Benefits or Evils—Public Joys or Sorrows—Prevalent Conditions, etc.—The ☽ rules the Public, and especially the Common People. Also the Common People and Laboring Classes are ruled by the 6th H. (See Common People, Humanity, Mankind). The ☽, (unless ♒ be on the Meridian) and the planet ascending, or ruling the Asc., are the Significators of the People at a Vernal Ingress. The following subjects have to do with the Public, the State and Condition of the Public, as Accidents, Anxieties, Benefits, Births, Calamities, Crime, Dangers, Deaths, Discords, Diseases, Epidemics, Evils, Health, Pestilence, Pleasures, Punishments, Sufferings, etc. See these subjects in the alphabetical arrangement when not more fully considered here—

Abdominal Diseases—Prevalence of—(See "Diseases" under Abdomen).

Accidents Prevalent—♂ rising in the Asc. at the Vernal Equinox; ♂ ☌ the ☉ at an eclipse of the ☉. (See the paragraphs under Accidents; "Accidents" under Journeys, Railroads, Travel, Vehicles, Voyages, etc.).

Acute Fevers Prevalent—(See "Prevalent" under Acute, Fever; "High Fever" under Fever).

Aged — Much Mortality Among the Aged — (See "Mortality" under Old Age).

Air—Unhealthy Air Affects the Public—(See "Corrupt Air" under Air).

Assassinations;

Assaults and Batteries — (See Assaults).

Birth Rate—Increase of—Decrease of—(See "Birth Rate" under Birth).

Blood—Effusion of Blood Prevalent—Expectoration of Blood Prevalent—(See Effusions; "Expectoration" in this section).

Bloodshed Prevalent — (See "Bloodshed" under Blood; Shedding, Slaughter, War).

Boils Prevalent—(See Carbuncles).

Captivity—Many Taken Into Captivity—(See Captive).

Carbuncles Prevalent — (See Carbuncles).

Cattle—Loss of—(See Cattle, Goats, Sheep).

Cheating—Prevalence of—(See Cheating).

Chest Affections—Prevalence of—(See "Prevalent" under Chest).

Children — Much Mortality Among — (See "Mortality" under Children).

Cholera Prevalent—(See Cholera).

Civil War—Civil Revolution—Danger of—(See "Civil" under War).

Comets—Influence of on Humanity—(See Comets).

Common People — Mischief and Misfortune To—♃ ☌ ♂ in the Asc. at the Vernal E. (See Common, Mischief, Misfortune).

Conspiracies—Plots—(See Plots).

Controversies — Much Public Discord—(See "Discord" under Quarrels).

Countries — Nations — Rulerships of, and Conditions Over—(See Countries, Eastern Parts, Nations, Northern). Afflictions in the Signs which rule the different Nations, Comets appearing in such signs, or Eclipses, tend to bring afflictions upon such Countries. (See Comets, Eclipses).

Crime Prevalent—(See Crime).

Crushed — By Avalanches, Fall of Buildings, Mobs, etc. — (See Crushed, Trampled).

Cursed by the Multitude—(See Execrated).

Death—(See "Public Death" in this section).

Diarrhoea Prevalent—(See Diarrhoea).

Discord—Much Public Discord—(See "Discord" under Quarrels).

Disgrace—Public Disgrace—(See Disgrace).

Dissensions — Many Dissensions Generally—(See "Discord" under Quarrels).

Drought—Much Suffering From—(See Drought).

Earthquakes; Eclipses—Effects of—(See Eclipses).

Effusion of Blood — Prevalence of — (See Blood, Bloodshed, in this section).

Enemies—Much Fear of Generally—(See "Fear Of" under Enemies).

Epidemics; Events; Evil—Every Evil Upon Humanity — (See "Every Evil" under Evil).

Execrated — By the Multitude — (See Execrated).

Execution — Public Execution — (See Execution).

Exhibition—Public Exhibition of Maladies—(See Exhibition).

Expectoration of Blood — Prevalence of—☿ in ♒ at the Vernal E., lord of the year, and afflicted by ♂. (See Expectoration, Haemoptysis).

Eye Diseases — Prevalence of — (See "Males", "Prevalent", under Eyes).

Famine; Feuds; Fevers—(See High, Low, Prevalent, under Fever).

Fires—Great Fires—(See "Great Fires" under Fire; Incendiarism).

Floods; Fluxes—(See "Prevalent" under Fluxes).

Foes—(See "Enemies" in this section).

Great—Death to The Great—Much Mortality Among—(See Assassinations, Famous; "Great Men", "The Great", under Great; Nobles).

Grief—(See "Public" under Grief).

Grievous Infirmities—Among the People—(See "Public Health Bad" in this section).

Grievous State of the People—♄ ruler of the year at the Vernal Ingress, and ♄ ℞ in an angle.

Hatred Prevalent—(See Hatred).

Health—The Public Health—(See Public Health Bad, Public Health Good, and the various paragraphs in this section).

Health of the Nations—(See Countries, Public Health, in this section).

Heat—Much Suffering, and Many Deaths from Extreme Heat—(See Drought, Famine; "Extreme Heat" under Heat; Summer; "Hot Winds" under Wind).

Humanity—Suffering To—(See Humanity, Mankind; the various paragraphs in this section).

Incendiary Fires—(See Incendiarism).

Internal Revolutions—Civil War—Danger of—(See "Civil" under War).

Judges—Sentences By—(See Judges).

Kingdoms—Danger of Destruction of—(See Kingdoms).

Kings—Danger To—Death of—(See Kings).

Lamentations—♃ in aspect with, and elevated above ♄ at a Solar Ingress or Eclipse. (See Lamentations).

Lawsuits—Many Lawsuits Generally—Lawsuits are ruled by the 7th H. Malefic planets in this house at the time of the Vernal or Autumnal Equinox; an Eclipse of the ☉ falling in the 7th H. Also tends to much trouble between Partners in Business, and in the Marriage relation, causing separations and divorces. (See Quarrelsome).

Lightning—Many Deaths From—(See Lightning).

Low Fevers Prevalent—(See "Low Fevers" under Fevers).

Low Public Houses—Frequenters of—(See Harlots, Taverns).

Lynchings; Maladies—Public Exhibition of—(See Exhibition).

Mankind—Many Evils Upon—(See "Every Evil" under Evil; Mankind, Misery, Misfortune, Trouble).

Measles Prevalent—(See Measles).

Men—Diseases Among—Many Deaths Among—Men In Power—Men Suffer with Their Eyes—Young Men Suffer—(See "Males" under Eyes; the various paragraphs under Men; "Young Men" under Young).

Mischief and Misfortune—To the Common People—(See "Common People" in this section; Mischief; Misery, Misfortune, Poverty, Reverses, Ruin).

Misery—Much Misery Everywhere—(See Misery).

Misfortune—Public Misfortune—(See "Common People" in this section; "Much", "Public", under Misfortune).

Mobs—Mob Violence—(See Mobs).

Monarchs—Danger To—Death of—(See Kings, Monarchs, Princes, Rulers).

Mortality Great—(See Mortality).

Murders Numerous—(See "Many Murders" under Murder).

Nations—The Health of—(See "Countries" in this section).

Nobles—Noblemen—Death of—Murder of—(See Nobles).

Outrages Numerous—(See Outrages).

Pandemics; Pestilence; Piracy;

Plague; Pleasure Seeking Generally—(See Pleasure).

Plots; Politics—Political Strife—(See Politics).

Poor—The Poor—(See Poor).

Population—Increased—Decreased—(See Population).

Poverty; Power—Men In Power—(See "Power" under Men).

Prevalent—(See the subjects under Prevalent).

Priests—Clergymen—Churches—Anxieties To—(See Clergymen).

Princes—Death of—(See Princes).

Prisons; Privations; Prohibition;

Public Death—Death In the Streets—Death by Day—Death in a Public Resort—Death by Public Execution—The ☽ afflicted in the 8th H. at B., and by dir., death in the streets, in a public hospital, in the presence of strangers, and in a public place; ♅ afflicted in the 8th H., and afflicting the hyleg, denotes an extraordinary and unusual death, and one that may create much public interest and concern; ♄ or ♂ in the angles at B., or any malefic in an angle and afflicting the hyleg. (See "Notorious Death" under Death; Extraordinary, Hanging, Judges; "Death" under Journeys, Mobs, Railroads, Sea, Ships, Strangers, Tragical, Travel, Vehicles, Voyages; "Wild Beasts" under Wild).

Public Discord—(See "Discord" under Quarrels).

Public Disgrace—(See Disgrace; "Loss Of" under Honor; "Imprisonment" under Prison; Reputation, Ruin, Scandal, etc.).

Public Dissentions—(See "Discord" under Quarrels).

Public Execution—(See Execution; "Public Death" in this section).

Public Exhibition—Of Maladies—(See Exhibition).

Public Grief—(See Grief; "Much Sadness" under Sadness).

Public Health Bad—A Bad Year for the Health of the People Generally—An Unhealthy Season—Much Sickness Generally—The ☉ lord of the year at the Vernal, and afflicted; the ☽ lady of the year, and badly afflicted; the ☽ in the 6th H. at the Vernal E., or at a

Solstice, and afflicted by malefics; ♄ lord of the year and afflicted at the Vernal Ingress; ♄ near the cusp of the 4th H. at the Vernal; ♄ in ♊, direct in motion and angular at the Vernal, and tends to much lung trouble; ♄ in ♌, ori., and ruler of the year at the Vernal; ♄ in ♎, ℞, and ruler of the year at the Vernal; ♄ ☌ ♂ in a human sign at the Vernal, and especially if in the Asc., tends to many infirmities among men for the time; ♂ lord of the year at the Vernal, in ♈, and afflicted by ♄; ♂ lord of the year in ♉, and occidental; ♂ in ♍ in N. Lat., and lord of the year at the Vernal; ♂ in ♎ in S. Lat., or ℞, at the Vernal, and lord of the year; ♂ in ♏ at the Vernal, ori., and lord of the year, much sickness generally and ♏ diseases; ♂ in ♐ at the Vernal, lord of the year, and especially in places under the rule of ♐; ♀ in ♌ at the Vernal, afflicted, and lady of the year; ☿ in ♊, ☌ ♂ at the Vernal, and ☿ lord of the year; ☿ in ♎ at the Vernal, afflicted, and lord of the year; ☿ in ♐, ☌ ♄ at the Vernal, lord of the year, and otherwise afflicted; ☿ in ♓ at the Vernal, and afflicted; if the ☽ or the planet ascending at a Solar Ingress into ♈ be under the beams of the ☉, combust, and afflicted by one or more of the malefics; a malefic in the Asc. at the Vernal, and afflicting the lord of the year; lord of the year afflicted, and in evil asp. to the ruler of the sign in which located; lord of the year afflicted, unfortunate, and impedited at the Vernal; the ☌ of malefic planets in fiery signs at the Vernal or a Solar Ingress, and due to corruption of the air and the fruits of the Earth. (See "Corrupt Air" under Air; Famine; "Drying Up Of" under Fountains; "Corruption Of" under Fruit; "Bad Health", "Periods of Bad Health", under Health; "Extreme Heat" under Heat; "Sickly Summer" under Summer; "Public Mortality Great" in this section).

Public Health Good—A Healthy Year for the People—Death Rate Diminished—The 1st H., or the Asc., rules the Public Health generally. If the planet ascending be swift in motion, and more than 17° from the ☉, and well-aspected by ♃ or ♀, or both, or the ☽ so placed at a Solar Ingress into ♈, the Public Health tends to be good; the ☽ lady of the year and free from affliction; ♃ lord of the year at the Vernal, and well-aspected; ♃ in the Asc. at the Vernal, and well-aspected; the ☉ lord of the year at the Vernal, and free from affliction; ♂ in ♓, direct in motion at the Vernal, and lord of the year; ♀ lady of the year at the Vernal, in the Asc., and free from affliction; ♀ in ♉ or ♎ at the Vernal, lady of the year, and well-aspected; ☿ in ♒ at the Vernal, lord of the year, and in ⚹ or △ ♃; ☿ in ♐, ☌ ♃ at the Vernal, lord of the year, and well-aspected; a benefic in the Asc., not afflicted by a malefic, and the ☽ applying to it by ☌, ⚹, or △ aspect; lord of the year free from affliction, well-aspected and dignified at the Solar Ingress into ♈; lord of the year in good aspect to the planet ruling the sign in which it is located, and free from the affliction of malefics. (See "Good Health" under Health; "Death Rate Diminished" under Mortality).

Public Life—Politics—Engaged In—(See Politics).

Public Mortality Great—Many Deaths Among the People—A Sickly Time—An eclipse of the ☉ or ☽ in watery signs; the ☽, or the planet ascending, afflicted by a malefic planet in the 8th H. at the Vernal; the ☽ in the 8th H. at the Vernal, afflicted, lady of the year, and espec. if the ☽ be afflicted in ♈, ♏, or ♑; an eclipse of the ☽ in the 3rd Decan. of ♏; ♄ in ♉ at the Vernal, afflicted by ♂ and the ☽, direct in motion, and in an angle; ♄ near the cusp the 4th H. in S. Lat. at the Vernal; ♄ ℞ in ♌, and ruler of the year at the Vernal; ♄ or ♂ supreme at the Vernal or Solar Ingresses; ♄ ☌ ♂ at the Vernal, or a Solar Ingress, afflicting the lord of the year, and espec. when in the first three degrees of ♒; ♄ in a fixed sign at the Vernal, or a Solar Ingress, and afflicting the lord of the year, and tends especially to the death of many men; ♂ ☌, □, or ☍ the lord of the year at the Vernal, and especially from angles, and being in a sign of human form; ♂ in ♉ at the Vernal, lord of the year, and occidental; ♀ in ♓ at the Vernal, lady of the year, and afflicted. (See the paragraphs under Mortality; "Public Health Bad" in this section).

Public Quarrels—(See "Discord" under Quarrels).

Public Sadness—(See "Public Grief" under Grief; "Much Sadness Generally" under Sadness).

Public Streets—Death In—(See "Public Death" in this section).

Quarrels Prevalent—(See "Discord" under Quarrels).

Railroad Accidents—(See Railroads).

Rapine Prevalent—(See Rapine).

Religion—Much Religious Intolerance—♄ lord of the year at the Vernal, and ♄ afflicted in the 9th H. Also ♅ falling in the 9th H. at the Vernal, or a Solar Ingress, rebellious against established Orthodoxy. (See "Intolerance" under Religion).

Revolution—Civil and Political—(See Politics; "Civil" under War).

Riots—Danger of—(See Riots).

Robberies Prevalent—(See Robberies).

Rulers—Danger To—Death of—(See Assassinations, Kings, Monarchs, Rulers).

Sadness—Public Sadness and Sorrow—(See "Public Sadness" in this section).

Scarlatina Prevalent—(See Scarlet).

Scorpio Diseases Prevalent—(See "Public Health Bad" in this section; "Prevalent" under Scorpio).

Secret Foes—Much Damage From Generally—(See "Fear Of" under Enemies; Plots, Poisonings, Treachery).

Sedition—Deadly Seditions—(See Sedition).

Sheep—Many Deaths Among—(See Sheep).

Shipwrecks; Sickness—Much Sickness Generally—(See "Public Health Bad", "Public Mortality", in this section).

Skin Diseases Prevalent—(See "Prevalent" under Skin).

Slaughter Everywhere—(See Slaughter. Also see "Bloodshed" in this section).

Smallpox Prevalent—(See Smallpox).

Society — Much Discord Between the Different Classes of Society—(See "Discord" under Quarrels; Revolutions, Riots; "Civil War" under War).

Sorrow — Public Sorrow and Grief — (See "Public" under Grief, Sorrow).

Stones — Many Injured by Flying Stones and Mob Violence — (See Assaults, Mobs; "Flying Stones" under Stones).

Storms—Much Suffering and Distress By — (See Floods, Lightning, Rain, Storms, Tornadoes, Wind).

Streets—Public Death In the Streets —(See "Public Death" in this section).

Thefts Prevalent — Thieves Active — (See Highwaymen, Piracy, Rapine, Robbers, Thefts, Thieves).

Throat Diseases Prevalent — (See "Prevalent" under Throat).

Tornadoes—Hurricanes—(See "Tornadoes" under Wind).

Trampled by Mob—(See Trampled).

Travel—Many Accidents In—Dangerous to Travel — (See Journeys, Railroads, Travel, Voyages).

Treachery Everywhere—(See Treachery).

Trouble Generally—(See Trouble).

Tumults; Unhealthy Year—Unhealthy Time—Unhealthy Air—(See "Corrupt", "Obnoxious", under Air; "Public Health Bad" in this section).

Untimely Deaths—(See Untimely).

Violence Everywhere—(See Highwaymen, Murders, Pirates, Robbers, Slaughter; "Mob Violence", "Outbreaks", under Violence; War).

Volcanoes Active—(See Volcanoes).

War; Weather—Much Suffering from Extremes of Heat or Cold—(See Blizzards, Cold; "Extreme Heat" under Heat; Lightning, Snow, Storms, Weather, Wind, etc.).

Welfare—The Public Welfare—(See the various paragraphs in this section).

Wind — High Winds — Hot, Blasting Winds — Much Suffering From — (See the paragraphs under Wind).

Women—Many Deaths Among—Much Suffering Among — Murders of Many Women—(See Females; "Women" under Misfortune; Murder; "Mortality", and the various paragraphs under Women).

Young Men—Great Mortality Among —(See Young, Youth).

PUDIC—Pertaining to the Genitals—

Pudic Nerves—Ruled by ♏. Disorders of these nerves are caused by ☿ afflicted in ♏. (See "Nervous Affections" under Genitals).

PUERPERAL — Pertaining to Child-Bearing—Puerpera—A Female In Labor—Parturition—The Puerperal State —This subject is considered in the Article on Parturition.

Puerperal Fever—Child-Bed Fever—Eclampsia — Danger of Death By—Puerperal Convulsions—♂ afflicted in the 5th H. of the mother; ♂ afflicted in ♋ in the 6th H.; Subs at AT, AX, and PP. (See "Death of Mother" under Parturition).

Puerperal Mania — The ☽ afflicted by ♄ and ♂ at childbirth; ♂ afflicted in the 5th H. of the mother. (See Foetus, Gestation, Maternity, Mother, Parturition, Pregnancy, Prenatal Epoch).

PUFFING—Puffy—Soft—

Puffing of the Body—Soft Body—The watery signs prominent at B.; a water sign on the Asc.; the ☉ and ☽ in water signs, due to excess of fluids in the body. (See Bloating; "Puffy" under Cheeks; Corpulent, Dropsy, Fat, Flabby, Flatulence, Fleshy, Fluids, Gases, Gluttony, Obesity, Oedema, Plethora, Surfeits; "Puffy" under Swellings; Water Signs, etc.).

Sinews—Puffing Up of—(See "Puffing" under Nerves).

PUGILIST — A Pugilist—Case—(See "Pugilist" under Athletics).

PULMONARY—Affecting the Lungs—

Pulmonary Affections—(See "Pulmonary Affections" under Lungs).

Pulmonary Apoplexy — (See "Pulmonary" under Apoplexy).

Pulmonary Circulation—Ruled by ☿. (See "Pulmonary" under Circulation; "Blood" under Lungs).

Pulmonary Congestion — (See "Congestion" under Lungs).

Pulmonary Consumption — (See Consumption; "Pulmonary" under Phthisis; Tuberculosis, Wasting).

Pulmonary Diseases—(See Bronchial, Consumption; "Pulmonary" under Lungs; Phthisis, Pleura, Tuberculosis; the various paragraphs in this section)

Pulmonary Haematosis — (See Haematopoiesis).

Pulmonary Hemorrhage—(See "Hemorrhage" under Bronchial, Lungs).

Pulmonary Inefficiency—(See "Lungs" under Inefficiency).

Pulmonary Innervation — (See Innervation).

Pulmonary Parenchyma—(See Parenchyma).

Pulmonary Phthisis—(See Phthisis).

Pulmonary Plexus — Post-Pulmonary Plexuses—(See "Middle Cervical" under Ganglion).

Pulmonary Stenosis—(See "Stenosis" under Lungs).

Pulmonary Tuberculosis — (See Consumption, Phthisis, Tuberculosis, Wastings).

Pulmonitis—Inflammation of the Lungs — (See "Pulmonitis" under Lungs).

PULSATILLA — An Alterative and Depressant Herb. A Typical Drug of ♀. Is also a Polycrest Remedy corresponding to the ♏ Sign. (See "Typical Drugs" under Venus; "Polycrest" under Zodiac).

PULSE—The Expansile Impulse of the Arteries—

Accelerated Pulse — (See "High" in this section).

Bradycardia—(See "Slow" in this section).

Failing, Weak Pulse — The ☽ ☌ ♂ in the Asc., and ♄ ruler of the 6th H. when taken ill (Hor'y). (See Faint, Rare and Weak, Slow, in this section).

Faint—Faint Pulse—Often Faint and Beats Slowly and Feebly—The ☽ in ♐, and afflicted by the ☉ or ♂ when taken ill (Hor'y). (See Faintings, Feeble, Weak, under Heart).

Feeble Pulse — (See Failing, Faint, Rare and Weak, Slow, in this section; "Weak Heart" under Heart).

High Pulse—High and Immoderate—Rapid—Accelerated Heart Action—The ☉ ☌ or ill-asp. ♂ when taken ill; the ☽ in ♈ or ♉, and afflicted by the ☉ or ♂ when taken ill (Hor'y); the ☽ in ♉, ☌, □, or ☍ ♄ (or ☿ if he be of the nature of ♄) when one is taken ill, or takes to his bed, which is generally due to high living, surfeits, etc., and is attended with high fever (Hor'y); the ☽ in ♎, afflicted by the ☉ or ♂ when taken ill, and due to too much blood (Hor'y); the ☽ in ♒, afflicted by the ☉ or ♂ when taken ill, and due to too much blood (Hor'y); the ☽ in ♒, afflicted by the ☉ or ♂ when taken ill, and the ☽ slow in motion and decreasing, and is usually attended with a hot and violent fever. (See High Pressure, Too Much Blood, under Blood; Accelerated, Palpitation, Pulse, Rapid, Spasm, under Heart).

Immoderate Pulse — (See "High" in this section).

Impeded Pulse—(See "Impeded" under Heart; "Slow" in this section).

Irregular Pulse — (See Interrupted, Irregular, Palpitation, Rhythm, Uncertain, under Heart).

Rapid Pulse—(See "High" in this section).

Rare and Weak—Weak Pulse—Afflictions in ♌ or ♒; the ☽ in ♌ ☌ ♄ at the beginning of an illness; ♄ afflicted in ♌. (See "Weak Heart" under Heart; Failing, Faint, Feeble, in this section).

Remits—(See "Remits" under Heart; "Slow" in this section).

Rhythm—Interrupted Rhythm—(See "Rhythm" under Heart).

Slow Pulse—The Pulse Remits and Is Slow—Bradycardia—The ☽ in ♑, and afflicted by the ☉, ♄, or ♂ when taken ill (Hor'y); ♄ afflicted in ♌; Subs at HP. (See "Slow" under Heart; Failing, Faint, in this section).

Suspended Pulse — (See "Suspended" under Heart).

Troubled Pulse—The ☽ in ♌, ☌, or ill-asp. ♄ (or ☿ if he be of the nature of ♄) at the beginning of an illness, or at decumbiture, and death may result if the ☽ comes to the ☍ ♄ during the sickness (Hor'y). (See "Troubled" under Heart; the various paragraphs in this section).

Uncertain — (See "Uncertain" under Heart).

Weak Pulse — (See Failing, Faint, Feeble, Rare and Weak, in this section).

PUNGENT—Acrid—Bitter—Penetrating—The Acrid, Bitter, and Pungent Drugs and Odors are ruled by ♂. (See "Hot Acids" under Acids; Astringent, Bitter, Odors).

PUNISHMENT — Penalties — Operation of the Law of Cause and Effect—Sowing and Reaping—Punishments, Chastenings, Afflictions, Suffering, Troubles, and Sorrows are usually brought upon us because we have broken some Law, and are not living right, or in harmony with the Laws of God, Man, or Nature. The Human Race is punished in thousands of ways, to adjust and restore the balance of harmony. Ill-Health is a punishment, and we usually bring sickness upon ourselves by our manner of living and thinking, and by engaging in excesses and indiscretions in some way. It is said that "Character is Destiny", and our fate in life is much as we make it by our character, innate and acquired tendencies, conduct, habits, etc. (See Character, Fate). Saturn is said to be "The Chastener", and it is principally into the hands of the Angel of Saturn that the chastenings, testings, and disciplinary measures have been given by the Higher Powers. (See Saturn). The Twelfth House also denotes sorrows, punishments, limitations, confinements, self-undoing, restraints, and if this house is badly afflicted at B., or had a malefic as its ruler, the native is apt to have his trials and afflictions considerably increased until he gets the New Birth, and learns how to live in harmony with the Law. (See Twelfth House). Our God is not an "Angry God", as is taught by some Creeds, nor does He seek revenge upon His Children, and, in the spiritual sense, there are no punishments inflicted upon us, but what we call punishments are merely trials, chastenings, suffering, and afflictions brought upon us to teach us lessons, increase our wisdom and understanding of life and destiny, and to show us the folly of sin, debauchery, wickedness, and an evil life. Good living always has its rewards and blessings, and the person who is living right, and in harmony with Law, and who has made conscious contact with his Higher Mind, and the Divine Within Himself, and who has learned to rule the animals within himself, and to not be dominated by personality and the lower mind — to such there are no "Punishments", but constant progress and attainment. Most every subject in this book deals in some way with the "Punishments" of life. Look in the alphabetical arrangement for the subject you have in mind. The following are a few of the important subjects along this line. See these subjects — Accidents, Affliction, Anguish, Anxiety, Assassination, Banishment, Beheaded, Bloodshed, Calamity, Casualties, Catastrophies, Confinements, Disaster, Discomforts, Discord, Disease, Disgrace, Dishonour, Distress, Early Death, Enemies, Events, Evils, Execrated, Executed, Exile, Failure, Fate, Fears, Fortune, Gloom, Grief, Grievous, Hanging, Horrors, Hurts, Ill-Fortune, Ill-Health, Imprisonment, Inharmony, Injuries, Insanity, Judges (Sentenced By); Lamentations, Limitations, Lingering Diseases, Madness, Mania, Mental Disorders, Mischief, Misery, Misfortune, Murdered, Murmurings; "No Peace of Mind" under Mind; Pain, Plots (Victim of)); Poverty, Prison, Privations, Reputation (Loss of); Restraints, Reverses, Ruin, Sadness, Scandal, Self-Undoing, Sickness, Sorrow, Starvation, Suffering, Suicide, Tragedy, Treachery, Trials, Tribulations, Trouble, Unfortunate, Untimely End, Vexations, Violent Death, War, Worry, Wounds, etc., and many other subjects throughout this Encyclopaedia.

PUPILS—Pupils of the Eyes—The Aperture In the Iris of the Eye—For Disorders of the Pupils, see the various paragraphs in the Article on Iris.

PURE—Purity—Unalloyed—Unstained— **Air** — Pure Air — (See "Pure" under Air).

Blood — The Blood Should Be Kept Pure—(See "Pure" under Blood).

Morals — Pure Morals — Has Good Morals — (See "Good Morals" under Morals).

Skin—A Pure Skin—(See "Pure" under Skin).

PURGATION—Purging—(See Cleansing, Enema; "Organic" under Functions; Physic).

PURPLE—The Color of the ☉ is Yellow, or inclined to Purple. The Colors of ♀ are white and purple. Some Authors say ♃ rules Purple (or Violet) in the Solar Spectrum. (See Colors, Indigo, Violet). The Purple rays and color are valuable in the treatment of Blood and Liver Disorders. (See "Remedies" under Blood; "Treatment" under Liver).

Marks — Purple Marks on the body are given by ♃. (See Marks).

PURPOSES—Aims—Intentions—Motives, etc.—

Aims—Aiming At Great Things—The ☉, ☽, or ♀ Sig. in ♐. (See Ambition; "Elevated Planets" under Elevated; "Majorities of the Planets" under Majority; Positive Nature, Resolute; "Rising Planets" under Rising).

Constant In Nothing — (See Changes, Concentration, Discontentment, Idle, Improvident, Indifferent, Instability, Location, Mutable Nature, Residence, Restlessness, Roamer, Vacillating, Vagabond, Wanderer, etc.).

Dishonest Purposes — (See Cheating, Criminal, Deceitful, Dishonest, Evil, Forgers, Hypocritical, Liars, Libelers, Plots, Thieves, Treachery, etc.).

Honest Purposes — (See Honest, Humane, Kind, Noble, Sincere, etc.).

Motives—Good—Evil—(See Motives).

Persevering — Steady In Purposes — (See "Good Powers Of" under Concentration; "Fixed Signs" under Fixed; Persevering, Positive Nature, etc.).

PURPURA—Hemorrhage Into the Cutis of the Skin—♄ afflicted in ♋. Scurvy is a form of Purpura, and due to improper diet. (See Derma, Scurvy).

PURSUITS — Trades — Callings — Professions — Success In — Dangers In — (See Business, Chemists, Employment, Healers, Nurses, Occupation, Surgeons, Vocation, etc.).

PURULENT—Having the Character of Pus—(See Pus).

PUS—Purulent—Pus-Forming Diseases —Pustular—Pustules — Festering Diseases—Suppurations—Phlegmon—Phlegmonous—Putrid—Putrefaction—Septic—Toxic—Contagions—Infections, etc.—Pus diseases are said to be caused especially by ♆. Also caused by afflictions to, or by the ☉, ☽, ♄, ♃, ♂, and ♀, depending upon the part, or parts of the body afflicted, and the parts ruled by the planet. The following diseases and conditions have to do with Pus, and where Pus is present in smaller or larger quantities. See these subjects in the alphabetical arrangement when only listed here—

Abscesses; Areolar Tissue—(See "Suppurative Inflammation" under Nipples).

Blood — (See "Putrefaction" under Blood).

Blotches; Bones — (See "Pus" under Bones).

Breast—(See "Abscess" under Breast).

Carbuncles; Carcinoma; Cavities—Pus Cavities—(See Cavities, Cloaca).

Chickenpox; Cloaca; Contagions;

Corruption; Decay; Decomposition;

Discharges — (See "Offensive" under Discharges; Fetid, Foul).

Ears—(See Abscesses, Discharges, Pustules, under Ears).

Eruptions; Festering; Fevers — (See "Fevers" under Putrid).

Finger Nails—Toe Nails—Pus Formations Around—(See "Whitlows" under Toes).

Free Surfaces—Suppuration of—Open Sores—(See Sores, Ulcers).

Gangrene—Malignant Gangrene with Pus—A ♄ disease; Subs at CP and KP. (See Gangrene, Malignant).

Granulations; Gums—Putrid Gums — (See Gums, Pyorrhoea).

Impetigo—Acute Pustular Inflammation of the Skin—(See Impetigo).

Kidneys—Pus In—(See "Pyonephrosis" under Kidneys).

Malignant — (See "Gangrene" in this section).

Measles; Morbid Discharges — (See "Offensive" under Discharges; Morbid).

Nails—Suppuration of—(See "Finger Nails" in this section).

Nipples — (See "Suppurative" under Nipples).

Offensive Discharges — (See Discharges, Odors, Offensive).

Osteomyelitis — (See "Pus" under Bones).

Papules; Phlegmon—Suppurative Inflammation of Areola Tissue, such as in the colored ring about the Nipple—Phlegmonous Suppuration About the

Nails—Phlegmonous Ulcers—(See Nipples; "Whitlows" under Toes; Ulcers).

Pimples; Pustular Diseases—Pustules—Pustular diseases arising from blood impurities and poisoning of the system are denoted by ♀. Acute pustular inflammation of the skin occurs in Impetigo, a ♑ disease. Mars is active in causing the pustules in eruptive diseases, as in Chickenpox, Smallpox, etc. Also ♄ causes Festerings. (See the various paragraphs in this section; Blotches, Chickenpox; "Pustules" under Ears; Impetigo, Measles, Pimples, Pox, Sloughing, Smallpox; "Vascular Tissues" under Vascular).

Pustules—A Small Purulent Papule—(See "Pustular Diseases" in this section; "Pustules" under Ears; Pimples).

Putrid Diseases—(See Putrid).

Pyemia; Pyorrhoea; Quinsy — (See Tonsils).

Septic Diseases—(See Putrid, Septic).

Skin — Pustular Inflammation of — (See Impetigo).

Sloughings; Smallpox; Sores;

Syphilis; Teeth—Suppuration Around—(See Gums, Pyorrhoea, Teeth).

Throat — Pus Sores In — Putrid Sore Throat — (See Diphtheria; Putrid, Ulcerated, under Throat; Tonsils).

Toe Nails—Suppuration About—(See "Whitlows" under Toes).

Tonsils — (See Quinsy, Suppuration, under Tonsils).

Ulcers; Urine — (See "Pus" under Urine).

Vascular Tissue — Suppuration of — (See Vascular).

Whitlows—(See Toes).

Xanthopsydracia — A Skin Disease with Yellow Pustules—(See this subject).

PUTRID—Putrefaction—Rottenness—Decay—Decomposition—Fetid—Offensive—Septic, etc.—The following subjects have to do with Putrefaction, Rottenness, Foul, Fetid, Offensive and Septic Conditions, which subjects see in the alphabetical arrangement when only listed here—

Abscesses; Animal Bodies—The putrefaction of animal bodies is caused by the damp vapors generated by the ☽, and caused by the nearness of the ☽ to the Earth. Putrefaction is also caused by ♄ or ♂ in the 1st or 7th H. in ♋, ♑, or ♓, and all signs ascribed to terrestrial animals or fishes. (See "Animal Signs" under Animal; Decay, Fish; "Damp Vapors", "Relaxation", under Moisture).

Blood—Putrefaction In—(See "Putrefaction" under Blood).

Bowels — Bowels Filled with Putrid Matter—(See "Putrid" under Bowels).

Breath—Putrid Breath—(See "Foul" under Breath).

Catarrh—Putrid Catarrh—Foul Odors of—(See "Catarrh" under Nose).

Cough—Rotten Cough—(See "Rotten" under Cough).

Death—Death from Putrid Diseases—♀ denotes death by, and by putrid sore throat, and from diseases arising from putrefaction and rottenness; ♀ afflictions at B., or afflicting the hyleg, and holding the dominion of death. (See "Death" under Moisture).

Decay; Decomposition; Dissolution;

Distempers — Putrid, Hot, and Moist Distempers—The ☉ or ☽ Sig. ☌ ♂. (See "Hot and Moist Diseases" under Heat).

Excretions; Faeces; Fermentation;

Fetid; Fevers—Putrid Fevers—The ☉ directed to Aldebaran, Deneb, Regulus, Antares, Bellatrix, or Frons Scorpio. The ☉ gives putrid fevers, and also ♃ and ♂; ♃ in fiery signs at a decumbiture, and ♂ behold him, and with the ☉ weak and afflicted; watery signs threaten putrid fevers if ♂ be in one of them at a decumbiture. (See "Eruptive Fevers", "Septic", under Fever; Septic).

Gums—(See "Putrid" under Gums).

Herbs—Rotten Herbs—Rottenness of Seeds—Putrid Condition of—(See "Seeds and Herbs" under Rotten).

Hot and Moist—Hot, Moist, and Putrid Distempers—(See "Distempers" in this section).

Moisture — Putrid Diseases From — (See Decay; "Hot and Moist Diseases" under Heat; "Damp Vapors", "Putrefaction", under Moisture; "Physiological Action" under Moon; Rottenness).

Odors—Offensive Odors—(See Odors).

Ptomaines; Pus Diseases—(See Pus).

Rottenness—(See Decay, Decomposition, Fermentation, Rotten, Zymosis).

Scrofula — When Attended with Putridity—(See Scrofula).

Septic Poison — Septic Fever — (See Septic).

Sores — Open Sores — (See Sores, Ulcers).

Sweat—Putrid and Fetid Sweat—(See "Fetid" under Sweat).

Throat — Putrid Sore Throat — (See "Putrid" under Throat).

Ulcers; Vegetation — Putrefaction of —(See Corruption, Fruit, Rotten, Vegetation).

Zymosis — Fermentation — (See Zymosis).

PUZZLING DISEASES—Obscure Diseases—Mysterious—(See Extraordinary, Mysterious, Obscure, Peculiar, Strange, Uncommon, etc.).

PYELITIS—Inflammation of the Pelvis of the Kidney—(See "Pyelitis" under Kidneys).

PYELONEPHRITIS—(See "Pyelitis" under Kidneys).

PYEMIA — Pyaemia — Septicemia with Abscess Formations—This condition is usually caused by afflictions to ♃ or ♀, and by acting upon the blood, causing impure blood, and blood poisoning. (See Abscesses; "Impure Blood" under Impure; "Blood Poisoning" under Poison; "Pustular Diseases" under Pus; Septic).

PYLORUS — The Opening of the Stomach Into the Duodenum—Constriction of—(See "Pylorus" under Stomach).

PYONEPHROSIS—Pus In the Kidney—(See this subject under Kidneys).

PYORRHOEA—A Discharge of Pus—

Alveolar Pyorrhoea — (See Necrosis; "Alveolar" under Teeth).

Pyorrhoea — Pus Around the Gums — A ♅ disease; ♄ afflicted in ♋ or ♑, and due to eating an excess of sugar and sweets. (See Gums).

PYRETHRUM—(See Pellitory).

PYREXIA—An Elevation of Temperature—(See Fever).

PYROMANIA—(See Incendiarism).

PYROSIS — A Gastric Burning Pain, with Eructations—(See Belching).

PYURIA—Pus In the Urine—(See "Pus" under Urine).

Q

QUADRANTS—Quarters of the Heavens —The three Houses, or the Quadrant from the Asc. to the Midheaven, and the three opposite Houses from the Descendant to the Nadir, are called the Male Quadrants, and are positive, and many planets in these Quadrants at B., and especially in the houses between the 1st and 10th H., tend to make the native very positive, forceful, energetic, and also to have more vitality, and greater resistance to disease. (See Quadratures, Quarters). The other Quadrants are the negative or feminine ones, those from the Nadir to the cusp of the 1st H., and from the Midheaven to the cusp of the 7th H., or Descendant. The Male Quadrants, and with the ☽ in such at conception, tend to produce male children, and with the ☽ in a female Quadrant at conception, the child conceived will usually be a female. These distinctions are important to note in connection with the study of the Prenatal Epoch, and the determination of sex. (See Predetermination, Prenatal Epoch). The Male Quadrants are also classed as Oriental as regards the position of the ☉ and ☽ at B., and the Female Quarters are Occidental, and the ☉ or ☽ in these Quarters at B., are oriental or occidental. With the other planets they are called oriental when in the Eastern Quadrants, occidental when in the Western half of the map. Planets are also called oriental when rising before the ☉. (See Occidental, Oriental). A planet rising before the ☉ is much more powerful over the mind and body, for good or ill, according to the nature of the planet, and its aspects, etc. (See Elevated, Majority, Rising, Setting). The ☽ in an oriental Quarter at B. indicates an early marriage, and a late marriage when in an occidental Quarter. (See "Early Marriage" under Marriage).

QUADRATURES — Quarters — This refers principally to the Quarters of the ☽, and to the position of planets in their orbits when the □, ☍, and ☌ aspects to their place in the map at B., and these aspects, or Quarters, are very important to note in health matters, as they usually precipitate some crisis in the life of the native. (See Crises; Decrease, First Quarter, Full Moon, Increase, New Moon, Quarters, Third Quarter, under Moon; "Planetary Periods" under Periods; Quadrants, Quarters).

QUADRUPEDS — Quadrupedal — Four-Footed — Four-Footed Beasts — The Four-Footed, Terrestrial, or Animal Signs of the Zodiac, are ♈, ♉, ♌, ♐, and ♑, all typical of the four-footed beasts which are symbolds of these signs. People born with malefics in these signs, and especially when they are on, or in the Asc., are more liable to attacks and injuries by Quadrupeds when under evil directions or transits. They also tend to have more of the animal nature in them, and to partake somewhat of the form, shape, and characteristics denoted by the animal symbol of the sign. (See "Animal Signs" under Animal; Beasts, Brutish, Four-Footed; "Human Signs" under Human; Hurtful, Ruminant. Also see each of these Signs in the alphabetical arrangement).

Animals — Injuries By — (See "Hurts By" under Animals, Beasts).

Attacks By—Malefics in the M.C., elevated above the Lights, or in ☍ to each other; ♄ in ♉, ♂, □, or ☍ the Asc. by dir., and probably an attack by a bull; ♂ in the 12th H., and afflicted by ♅ or ♄. (See Bites, Ferocious, Hurts, Kicks, Wild Animals, under Animals; "Attacks By", "Injury By", under Beasts; "Animals" under Bites; Cattle, Distortions, Elephants; "Great Beasts" under Great; Kicks; "Cattle" under Large).

Beasts—Attacks or Injury By—Death By—(See the various paragraphs under Animals, Beasts, Cattle; the paragraphs in this section).

Bull—Attack By—Malefics in the ♉ sign, and afflicted. (See "Attacks By" under Cattle, and also in this section).

Cattle—Attacks By—Danger or Death By—(See "Attacks By" under Cattle; "Great Beasts", "Great Cattle", under Great).

Death By — (See "Hurts By" under Animals; "Death By" under Beasts).

Distortions—Due to Injury by Quadrupeds—(See Distortions, Excrescences).

Elephants—Injuries, Hurts, or Death By—(See Elephants).

Excrescences — Due to Attacks of Quadrupeds—(See Excrescences).

Great Beasts — Great Cattle — Hurts, Injury, or Death By — (See Beasts, Cattle, Elephants; "Great Beasts", "Great Cattle", under Great; Horses; "Cattle" under Large).

Horses — Injury By — (See Horses, Kicks).

Injury By—Hurts By—(See "Attacks By", and the various paragraphs in this section).

Kicks—(See Horses, Kicks).

Lameness—Due to Injury By—(See Distortions, Excrescences).

Large Quadrupeds—Hurts By—(See "Great Beasts" in this section).

Paralysis—Due to Injury By—(See Distortions, Excrescences).

Signs—Quadrupedal Signs—(See the Introduction to this Article).

Thrusts—(See Kicks).

Wild Beasts—Attacks or Injury By—(See "Wild Animals" under Animals; "Wild Beasts" under Beasts; Wild).

QUADRUPLETS—Case—The four Doyle sisters, of Hollywood, Calif. Born August 10th, 1912. They are all living, and their picture appeared together in a Los Angeles paper in June, 1931. Hour and place of birth not known to me. (See Multiple, Triplets, Twins).

QUALITY—Qualities—Nature of—Type of—Attributes—Traits—Characteristics—

Body—Qualities of the Body—(See Body; "Body" under Cold; "Body", "Cold and Dry Body", under Dry; Elemental, Form, Good, Health; "Animal Heat", "Hot Bodily Temperament", "Hot and Dry Body", "Moist and Warm", under Heat; Height; "Cold and Moist", "Hot and Moist", under Moisture; Physical, Shape, Size, Stature, Strength, Strong; "Bodily Temperaments" under Temperament; "Weak Body" under Weak; Weight, etc. Also look in the alphabetical arrangement for the subject you have in mind).

Death—Quality of—(See Anareta; "Kind of Death", "Quality of the Death", under Death; Directions, Dominion, Events; "Death" under Nature, Species).

Disease—Quality of the Disease—(See "Causes", "Quality", under Disease; "Disease" under Nature, Species, Type; "Quality" under Sickness).

Disposition—Qualities of—Many of these Qualities are given and listed alphabetically throughout this book. Look for the subject you have in mind. A special list of the traits of Mind and Disposition are given in the Article on Mind. (See Conduct, Fancies, Habits, Ideals, Ideas, Mentality; "Desirable", "Undesirable", under Mind; Morals, Motives, Principles, Propensities, Purposes, Temperament, Tendencies, etc.

Eyes—(See "Quality Of" under Eyes).

Fever—(See "Quality Of" under Fever).

Intellect—Mind—Qualities of—(See Intellect, Mentality, Mind, Perception, Reason, Understanding; "Disposition" in this section).

Mind—Qualities of—(See Disposition, Intellect, in this section).

Passive Qualities—(See "Qualities" under Active; Negative, Passive).

Positive Qualities—(See Positive).

QUARRELS—Quarrelsome—Contentious—Discord—Disagreeable—Turbulent—Dissensions—Fights—Violent Outbreaks—Frays—Strife—Anger—Commotions—Dissimulations—Disputes—Misunderstandings, etc.—The planet ♂ is the principal author of quarrels and disputes, bloodshed, etc., and where violence may attend. For the general influences which tend to give a quarrelsome nature see "Quarrelsome" in this section. The following subjects have to do with Quarrels, the Causes leading to Quarrels, Attending Circumstances, States of Mind, and the Results of Quarrels. See these subjects in the alphabetical arrangement when merely listed here—

Ambushes; Anarchists; Anger;

Antipathy; Argumentative—(See Argumentative, Independent, Obstinate).

Assassinations; Assaults;

Banishment; Battle—(See Battle, Contests, Duels, Feuds, War).

Beside Oneself—(See Excitable).

Blackmailers—(See Libel).

Blasphemers—(See "Blasphemy" under Religion).

Bloodshed—(See "Bloodshed" under Blood; Murder, Shedding, Slaughter, War).

Bloodthirsty—(See Cruel; "A Murderer" under Murder; Vicious; "Tendency To" under Violence).

Bold; Causes of Quarrels—(See "Quarrelsome", and the various paragraphs in this section).

Chartering; Choleric; Contests;

Crime; Cruel; Cuts; Dangerous—To Society and the Community—(See Anarchists, Dangerous).

Death In Quarrels—Danger of—♂ holding dominion at B., and elevated above the Lights, and afflicting the hyleg; the ☉ Sig. ☌ ♂, death, or terribly wounded; ♃ Sig. ☌ ♂, sometimes wounded in a quarrel; ♀ Sig. ☌ ♂, and usually in a quarrel with a woman; the Asc. to the ☌, P., □, or ☍ ♂ by dir., and ♂ in a sign of human form at B.; lord of the 8th in the 7th H.; 26° ♊, or the 9° ♎ on the Asc. (See "Death" under Contests, Duels, Fighting, and under the various subjects mentioned in this Article).

Destructiveness; Disagreeable;

Discord—Much Public Discord Prevalent—Political Strife—Many Quarrels Prevail—Discord Between the Various Classes of Society—The ☽ elevated above, and configurated with ♄ at a Solar Ingress or Eclipse; an eclipse of the ☉ or ☽ in a fiery sign; an eclipse of the ☽ in ♍, or the 3rd Decan. of ♏; ♄ Lord of the Year at the Vernal Equi., direct in motion, and in an angle; ♄ ℞ in ♊, and angular at the Vernal; ♂ elevated above, and configurated with ☿ at a Solar Ingress or Eclipse, much discord everywhere. (See Anarchists, Politics, Prevalent, Public, Reformers, Revolutions, Sun Spots (see Spots); "Civil War" under War).

Disputes—Fond of War and Disputes—♂ strong at B.; ♂ Sig. in ♈ or ♏, and often gains by them; ♂ Sig. in ♌, ready for warlike occupations at any time; ♂ in the Asc. or 10th H. at B.; many cross aspects at B. to a planet, or planets ascending, and often not of their own seeking. (See "Quarrelsome", and the various paragraphs in this section).

Dissentions — Many Dissentions Generally—(See "Discord" in this section).

Dissimulation — (See "Quarrelsome" in this section).

Duels; Emotions—Disorders of—(See Anger, Emotions, Excitable, Feelings, Hatred, Jealousy, etc.).

Enemies—Quarrels With—Injury By—His Own Worst Enemy—Secret Enemies Active—(See Enemies).

Enmity; Excitable; Executed;

Exile; Family Quarrels—(See "Relatives" in this section).

Females—Quarrels With—(See Quarrels, Treachery, Vexations, under Females; "Injured Thru Women" under Men; "Death by Women" under Women).

Feuds; Fierce; Fiery; Fighting;

Fratricide; Gross—(See "Gross Manners" under Gross).

Gunshot Wounds — (See Gunshot; "Murdered" under Murder).

Hanging; Hasty; Hatred;

High Temper — (See "High" under Temper).

Highwaymen; His Own Death — (See "Causes His Own Death" under Death).

Homicide; Hot-Headedness — (See Anger, Choleric, Hasty, Irascible, Obstinate; "High Temper" under Temper; Vicious, Violent).

Hurts—(See "Quarrels" under Hurts).

Imprisonment—(See Prison).

Incised Wounds--(See Incised).

Incompatibility; Inhuman — (See "Inhuman Disposition" under Inhuman).

Injuries During Quarrels — (See Blows, Cuts, Duels, Gunshot, Stabs; the various paragraphs in this section).

Insanity — (See Dangerous, Outrageous, under Insanity).

Instruments—Injury By—(See Instruments).

Irascible; Irrational; Irresponsible;

Irritable; Jealousy; Judges—Sentenced By—(See Judges).

Kings—(See "Death By" under Kings).

Law—Killed by Officers of the Law—Sentenced by Law—(See Judges, Law, Officers).

Lawsuits—(See Law; "Lawsuits" under Public).

Libel; Love Affairs — Quarrels In — (See the paragraphs under Husband, Love Affairs, Marriage, Marriage Partner, Wife).

Lynchings; Madness — (See "Brain Storms" under Brain; "Beside Oneself" under Excitable; Frenzy, Fury, Madness; "Psychic Storms" under Psychic).

Maimed; Malicious—(See Malice).

Manners — (See "Rough" under Manners).

Manslaughter; Marriage—(See "Quarrels" under Marriage).

Mars — (See "Author of Strife", and the various influences under Mars).

Mean — (See "Mean-Spirited" under Mean).

Men — (See "Injured Thru Women" under Men).

Merciless; Military Life — Killed or Murdered In—(See Military).

Misanthropic; Mischief—(See "Active to Do Mischief" under Mischief).

Misunderstandings; Mob Violence — (See Mobs).

Monarchs—Death by Wrath of—(See ("Death by Wrath Of" under Kings).

Moods; Motives; Murder; Mutilations;

Neighbors; Obstinate; Offended—(See "Easily Offended" under Offended).

Officers—Killed by Officers of the Law —(See Officers).

Opinions; Opposite Sex—(See "Aversions" under Opposite Sex).

Outrages; Parents—(See "Injured by Children", "Killing of a Parent", under Parents).

Passion—(See "Violence" under Passion).

Patricide — (See this subject under Father).

Perils; Perplexities; Perverse;

Petulant; Pirates; Pity—(See "Shows No Pity" under Pity).

Plots; Poison Death — (See "Death" under Poison).

Politics—Much Strife In—(See "Discord" in this section; Politics).

Power — Ruined by Men In Power — (See "Power" under Men).

Prejudice—(See "Mind" under Prejudice).

Prevalent — (See the subjects under Prevalent).

Prison—(See "Beaten In Prison", "Injured", under Prison).

Profane; Propensities; Property—Disputes Over—(See "Duped of His Property" under Property).

Prowess — Daring In Battle — (See Bold, Prowess).

Public Discord — (See "Discord" in this section; the various paragraphs under Public).

Punishment; Purposes — (See Character, Motives, Principles, Purposes).

Quarrelsome—A Quarrelsome Nature —Warlike—Combative — Mars is the planet of War, and the ♂ influence must be strong at B., and the Significators afflicted by ♂, to give a warlike nature; ♂ ruler at B. and afflicted; ♂ afflicted in the 1st H. and near the cusp; ♂ afflicted and ill-dignified at B., and in his own signs or houses; people born under ♂, and with ♂ afflicted and ill-dignified at B., are always ready to rush into quarrels, disputes, war, and bloodshed; ♂ is the principal Sig. of strifes and contentions by his evil aspects and directions to the Significators, the ☉, ☽, Asc., or M.C.; ♂ Sig. in ♈, ♌, or ♏; ♂ afflicted in the Asc. or 10th H. at B.; ♂ to the ill-asps. ☿ by dir.; ♂ Sig. □ or ☍ the ☉; ♂ afflictions to the ☉, ☽, ♄, or ☿ at B.; ♂ afflicted in the 3rd H.; ♂ Sig., and afflicted in ♈, ♉, ♊, ♍, ♏, ♐, ♒, or ♓; ♂ ☌ the ☉ at a Solar Rev.; ♂ passing over the place of the ☽, ♃, or ☿ at a Solar Rev.; ♂ afflicted in ♊ or ♍, and

☌ or ill-asp. the Asc. by dir.; ♂ to the ☌ the North Node of the ☽ (☊); ♂ by Periodic Rev. to the ill-asps. the ☉; ♂ holding dominion at B., and elevated above the Lights; the ☉ afflicted at B., and the ☉ to the bad asps. the Asc. by dir.; the ☉, ☽, or ☿ to the ☌, P., □ or ☍ ♂; the ☉ to the □ or ☍ the ☽ by dir., or vice versa; the progressed ☉ or ☽ to the ☌ or ill-asps. ♅ or ♂; the ☉ Sig. □ or ☍ ♂; the ☉ afflicted at B. by malefics, or ☌ violent fixed stars; the ☉ ☌ ♂ at a Solar Rev.; the ☉ directed to all nebulous clusters, and to Castor and Pollux, threatens quarrels; the ☽ □ ♂; the ☽ afflicted in ♏; the ☽ to the ☌ or ill-asp. ♂ by dir.; the ☽ to the ☌ ♂ by transit, or passing the place of the radical ♂ by tr., progression or dir.; the ☽ Sig. ☌ ♂; the ☽ Sig. □ or ☍ the ☉; the ☽ to the □ or ☍ ☿ by dir., and the ☽ hyleg, and ☿ afflicted at B.; the ☽ to the □ or ☍ ♃ by dir.; the ☽ Sig. in ♈ or ♏; the ☽ ☌ ♂ in the Asc. or 10th H.; the ☽ to the ☌ the Pleiades, Ascelli, or Praesepe; ♄ to the ill-asps. ♂ by dir.; ♄ ☌ or ill-asp. ♂ at B.; ♄ ☍ ♂ at B. in angles; ♄ Sig. in ♈, ♎, ♏, or ♓; ♃ Sig. □ or ☍ ☿, involved in strife, contention, and lawsuits; ♃ Sig. ☌ ♂, loses much by strife and contention; ♀ afflicted in ♏, contentious and jealous; ☿ afflicted at B., and ☿ to the evil asps. the Asc. by dir.; ☿ Sig. □ or ☍ ♄, ♃, or ♂; ☿ Sig. ☌, P., □, or ☍ ♂; ☿ Sig. in ♈ or ♌; the Asc. to the ☌ ♂ by dir.; the M.C. to the place the Pleiades or Pollux; the M.C. to the ☌ or P. asp. the ☉ if the ☉ is afflicted at B. by malefics, or ☌ violent fixed stars; the M.C. to the □ or ☍ the ☽; the M.C. to the ☌, P., □, or ☍ ♂ by dir.; lord of the 6th in the 7th, sickness caused by quarrels and fighting; many influences in fixed signs at B.; the 16° ♓ on the Asc. at B.; the 7th H., and its influences rule and concern quarrels; malefics afflicted in the 7th H. (See "Disputes", and the various paragraphs in this section).

Quarrelsome Persons — Danger From —♂ badly afflicted at B., and ♄ passing over the place of the radical ♂ by transit, or at a Solar Rev. (See Cuts, Death, Injury, Maimed, Mutilated, Stabs; "Quarrelsome", and the various paragraphs in this section).

Rape; Rash Disposition — (See Rashness).

Ravings; Reactionary; Reason—(See "Void Of" under Reason).

Rebellious; Recklessness; Reformers;

Refractory; Relatives—Quarrels With —Indicated by malefics in, or ruling the 3rd, 6th, 7th, 9th, or 12th Houses, according to which class of relatives. (See Brethren, Brothers, Family, Husband, Relatives, Sisters, Third House, Wife, etc.).

Religious Quarrels—(See Clergymen; Fanatical, Intolerance, under Religion).

Resentful; Resisting—(See Obstinate, Rebellious).

Restraint—(See "Lack Of" under Restraint).

Retains Anger—(See Anger).

Revengeful; Revolutionary; Riotous; Robbers; Rough; Ruffians;

Ruling Nature — (See Commanding; "Positive Nature" under Positive; Rule).

Sanguinary; Sarcastic; Saucy;

Savage; Scolding; Scornful;

Secret Enemies—Injury or Death By —(See "Secret Enemies" under Enemies).

Seditions; Self-Control—Lack of—(See Self-Control).

Self-Undoing; Servants—Hurts By—(See Servants).

Seventh House — Rules Quarrels, etc. (See "Rules" under Seventh House).

Severe Disposition—(See Severe).

Sharp Instruments—Hurts By—(See Instruments).

Shedding of Blood—(See "Bloodshed" in this section).

Sickness from Quarrels—Lord of the 6th in the 7th H.

Slaughter; Social Relations — Much Trouble In—(See Execreted, Love Affairs, Marriage, Neighbors, Relatives, Social, Society, etc.).

Socialism; Society—Much Discord In —(See "Discord" in this section).

Stabs; Stones — Injured by Flying Stones—(See "Assaults" under Stones).

Strangulation; Strife—Fond of—(See "Quarrelsome" in this section).

Stubborn—(See Obstinate, Rebellious).

Suicide; Suspicious — (See Jealousy, Mistrustful, Suspicious).

Sword—Injury by During Quarrels—(See Duels, Stabs, Sword).

Temper—(See Choleric, Fierce, Fury; "High Temper" under Temper; Vicious, Violent).

Thieves; Tragical Death—(See Tragical).

Treachery; Trouble-Maker — (See "Quarrelsome", and the various paragraphs in this section).

Tumults; Turbulent; Unbalanced;

Uncompromising — (See Independent, Obstinate, Positive, Stubborn).

Uncontrolled; Ungovernable;

Unreasonable; Unreliable; Vicious;

Violent; War; Weapons; Wicked;

Wife—(See "Troublesome" under Wife).

Women — (See "Quarrels" under Women).

Wounds — Received During Quarrels —(See Death, Hurts, Injuries, and the various paragraphs in this section. Also see the paragraphs under Wounds).

Wrath—(See Anger, Wrath).

QUARTAN AGUE — Quartan Fever — Quarternaries—An Intermittent Fever with a Paroxysm Every Fourth Day—(See "Quartan Ague" under Ague; Intermittent, Malaria, Remittent, Semi-Tertian).

QUARTERS — Quadrants — Quadratures —Quarters of the Heavens—Quarters of the Year—Quarters of the Moon—(See "Fullness of Fluids" under Fluids; "Women" under Misfortune; "Quarters" under Moon; Occidental, Oriental, Quadrants, Quadratures; "Quarters of the Year" under Year).

QUARTZ—(See Silica).

QUEENS — Danger of Death of — The appearance of a Comet in ♒. An Eclipse of the ☽ in the 2nd Decan. of ♉, death of a Queen in a Country ruled by ♉. Comets, or an eclipse of the ☽, in the ruling sign of any Country tend to the death of a Queen over such a Country, while an eclipse of the ☉ in such a sign tends to the death, murder, or assassination of a male Ruler. (See Famous; "The Great" under Great; "Death" under Kings; Lady).

QUEER—Queer Ideas, Actions, and Disposition—(See Eccentric, Fanatical, Fancies, Ideals, Ideas, Independent, Misunderstood, Notions, Opinions, Peculiar, Persecution, Reformers; "Ranters" under Religion, etc.).

QUERENT—Quesited—In Hor'y Questions, the Querent is the person who asks the question. The Significator of the Querent is the Asc., lord of the Asc., or a planet in the Asc. The Quesited is the person or thing asked about by the Querent. The Significator of the Quesited varies, and is usually the planet, house, or lord of a house, which rules the matter about which the Querent asks. (See Horary).

QUICK — Quickness—Quickened—Quickening—Quickened Action—

Action — Quick In Action — ♂ people are usually quick and active, and move about freely; ☿ ✶ or △ the Asc., quick, and with an active body; ☿ Sig. in Hor'y Q. denotes a quick walk. (See Acceleration, Action, Active, Energy, Motion, Movement; the various paragraphs in this section).

Death—A Quick Death—♂ afflicted in the 8th H., or afflicting the hyleg from this house; ♅ afflicted in the 8th H. tends to a quick death, as by explosion, accident, electricity, machinery, or on a Railroad, etc. (See "Death by Accidents" under Accidents; Assassination, Extraordinary, Gunshot, Heights (Falls From); Murdered; "Death" under Sudden, Tragical, Untimely, etc.).

Dexterity — Quickness of Mind and Body—(See Dexterity).

Diseases — Quick Diseases—The Disease Terminates Quickly — A Rapid Disease—♂ rules quick and rapid diseases. The afflictor, or afflictors, in cardinal signs tend to a quick disease, severe, and soon over. The ☽, or cusp of the 6th H. in a cardinal, or movable sign, the disease terminates quickly, either in death or recovery. (See Acute, Course, Curtailed; "Illness" under Dangerous; "End of the Disease" under End; Ephemeral; "High Fever" under Fever; Fierce, Fulminating; "Diseases" under Painful; Pernicious, Poignant, Rapid; "Rapid" under Recuperation; Severe, Sharp; "Illnesses" under Short; Slight, Swift, Termination, Vehement; "Diseases" under Violent, etc.).

Disposition — A Quick Disposition — (See Anger, Choleric, Excitable, Hasty, Impulsive, Irascible, Irritable, Rashness; "High Temper" under Temper; "Tendency To" under Violence, etc.).

Energy—(See "Abundance of Energy" under Energy).

Eyes — A Quick Eye — (See "Quick Eye" under Eyes).

Fevers—Quick Fevers—Fierce Fevers—Sharp—(See "High Fevers", "Pernicious", "Violent", under Fevers).

Foetus Quickened—(See "Quickening" in this section).

Light and Quick — In Action — (See "Action" under Light).

Mentality — (See "Quickened" under Mentality, Mind).

Mind—A Quick Mind—Quick-Witted—Clever—(See "Active Mind" under Active; "Quickened" under Mentality).

Motion—Movement—Quick In—(See "Quick" under Motion, Movement).

Muscular Action—Quick Action—(See "Action" under Light; "Quick" under Motion, Movement; "Movements" under Muscles).

Nervous and Quick—(See Excitable; "Energetic" under Gait; Hasty; "High Strung" under High; "Quick and Nervous" under Speech).

Quickening — Of the Foetus — The ☉ produces the Quickening of the foetus. The quickening occurs, as a rule, at about the end of the fourth month of pregnancy, and when the ☽ is passing the same sign and degree she will be found in at birth. The position of the ☽ at the quickening, and at birth, is also said to be the Ascendant at conception, and the position of the ☽ at conception becomes the ascendant or descendant at birth. Also the Ascendant at the time of the quickening is said to be the sign and degree position of the ☽ at conception, or very near it. By a study of the Prenatal Epoch, and the Chart of Descent, it is an easy matter for the student to determine beforehand the exact time of the quickening, as it is so closely related to the ☽ and Asc. at conception, and the positions of the ☽ and Asc. at birth. This matter is quite thoroughly discussed, and with illustrated Charts, in Chap. XXVIII, in the book, "The Prenatal Epoch" by Mr. E. H. Bailey. The quickening occurs approximately at the half-way point between conception and birth, and at the time of the fifth libration of the ☽, as shown in the Chart of Descent. In a Horary Map the Quickening has taken place if the Dispositor of the ☽, and the lord of the hour be angular, or ♄ in the 7th H. If ♃ be in the 7th H. a male is indicated. (See Conception, Foetus, Gestation, Pregnancy, Prenatal Epoch).

Quicksilver—(See "Metal" under Mercury; Therapeutics).

Rapid — (See the paragraphs under Rapid).

Recovery—Recuperation—Quick Recovery from Disease — (See "Throws Off Disease Quickly" under Disease; Recovery, Recuperation; "Strong Resistance" under Resistance).

Sight—Quick Sight—(See Keen, Penetrating, Quick, under Eyes).

Speech — (See "Quick and Nervous" under Speech).

Temper—Quick Temper—(See Anger, Choleric, Excitable, Hasty, Irascible; "High Temper" under Temper).

Walk — A Quick Walk — (See "Energetic" under Gait; "Quick" under Walk).

QUICKENING — Of the Foetus — (See "Quickening" under Quick).

QUICKSILVER—The Metal ruled by ☿. (See "Metal" under Mercury; Therapeutics).

QUIET—Calm—Peaceful—Without Excitement—Tranquil—

Quiet Body—Quieting Influences Over the Mind and Body—(See Anaesthetics, Anaphrodisiacs, Anodyne, Calm, Contentment, Emollient, Happiness, Insensibility, Narcotics; "Peace of Mind" under Mind; Palliatives, Poise; "Illumination" under Religion; Sedatives, Sleep, Soothing, etc.).

Quiet Death—(See "Quiet Death" under Death).

Quiet Disposition — Harmless — Inoffensive—(See Calm, Cheerfulness, Contentment, Easy-Going, Gentle, Grave, Harmless, Humane, Indifferent, Inoffensive, Kind; "Amiable" under Manners; "Mild Disposition" under Mild; Modesty, Patient, Peaceful, Pleasant, Poise, Recluse, Reserved, Retiring, Shy, Spiritual, Taciturn; "Even Temper" under Temper, etc.).

Quieting Remedies—(See Anaesthetics, Anaphrodisiacs, Anodynes, Narcotics, Palliatives, Sedatives, Soothing, Soporific, etc.).

Sleep More Quiet — (See "Quiet" under Sleep).

QUININE — (See Cinchona; "Typical Drugs" under Mars).

QUINSY—(See "Quinsy" under Tonsils).

QUIVERING — Tremor—Trembling — Jerkings—Thrills—Spasmodic—

Eyeballs—Quivering of—(See "Quivering" under Eyeballs).

Muscles — Quiverings of — Spasmodic Action of — (See Contractions, Coordination, Cramps; "Movements" under Erratic; Incoordination, Intermittent, Involuntary, Irregular, Jerkings; "Motor Nerves" under Motor; Muscles (see the paragraphs under Muscles); Palpitation, Palsy, Paralysis, Paroxysms, Saint Vitus Dance, Spasmodic, Tics, Tremors, Twitchings, etc.).

QUOTIDIAN FEVER—Intermittent, and with a Daily Paroxysm—☿ influence; ☿ afflicted by ♂; ☿ sole ruler at an eclipse of the ☉ tends to a greater prevalence of daily fevers. (See Ague; "Fever" under Intermittent; Malaria, Remittent, etc.).

R

RABIES—Rabid—(See Hydrophobia).

RACEMOSE GLAND — A Gland Resembling a bunch of Grapes. The Pancreas is such a Gland. Also the Meibomian Glands of the Eyelids. These Glands are also called Aggregate Glands, as they are composed of a number of vesicles arranged in groups, or globules, and their arrangement gives the largest amount of secreting surface in the smallest space. These Glands come under the rule of the Sign ruling the part in which located. The Racemose Glands of the Eyelids are ruled by the ♈ sign. The Pancreas by the ♋ and ♍ signs. (See Glands, Pancreas).

RACES—The different Races and Nations of the Earth come under the rulership of the various Signs of the Zodiac. These rulerships are given in the Article on Nations. Races, their color of skin, and their special characteristics, have been established in the various parts of the Earth, and adapted to their location, and to play their part in the Grand Plan of Humanity. There are Sixteen Races in all in the scheme of the Evolution of our Planet. For a good discussion of the Origin of Races, their time and endurance, destiny, etc., see the book, "Cosmo-Conception" by Max Heindel. (See Barrenness; "Black Skin" under Black; Complexion, Hair, Nations, Negro; "Sixth Sub-Race" under Neptune; Pigment, White; "Complexion" under Yellow).

RACHITIS—Rachitic—(See Rickets).

RADICAL MAP—(See Horoscope, Map, Nativity, Radix, Star Map).

RADICALISM—(See "Impractical Ideals" under Ideals; Reactionary, Religion).

RADIUM—Ruled by ♅. This planet has a radio-active influence. Pitch-Blende and Polonium, radio-active substances, and closely related to Radium, are also ruled by ♅. Some Writers also say Radium is ruled by ♆. (See Neptune, Pitch-Blende, Polonium, Uranus).

RADIUS—The Small Bone of the Forearm—The Radius is under the structural rulership of the ♌ sign, and also influenced by ♊, and disorders, or fractures to the bones of the forearm, as the Radius and Ulna, and also the Wrists, are caused by afflictions in ♌, and especially ♄ or ♂ afflicted in this sign, or in ♊. (See "Accidents", "Broken Arms", under Arms; Forearm). Case—Radius of Left Arm Fractured—See "Saturn in the Tenth", No. 831 in 1001 N.N.

Radius Missing — (See "Missing" under Forearm).

RADIX—The Radical Map—The Chart of Birth—The Nativity—Radix means "Root", and the Map of Birth is the Root Map, a foundation map upon which you are to build. The Radix Map shows the Permanent Habit, or Hexis, of the diseases to which you will be subject, your fundamental tendencies, and your relationship to external conditions, environment, etc. The Directions and Progressions of the planets over this map show the Diathesis, or Transient Disposition of the disease. Diseases indicated by the radical map tend to be constitutional, organic, structural, deep-seated, and if neglected and allowed to progress, to become chronic, morbid, malignant, and fatal. The Prenatal Epoch Map also shows fundamental conditions and tendencies, and should be studied in connection with the radical, or map of birth. (See Acquired, Character, Chronic, Diathesis, Directions, Fate, Fortune, Heredity, Hexis, Map, Nativity, Organic, Prenatal Epoch, Progressions, Star Map, Structural, etc.).

RAGE—Anger—Fury—Fierce—Raging—Raging Fevers, etc.—(See Anger; "Brain Storms" under Brain; "Beside Oneself" under Excitable; "High Fevers" under Fever; Fierce, Frenzy, Fury, Madness, Quarrels, Ravings, Riotous; "High Temper" under Temper; Violent, Wrath, etc.).

RAILROADS—Public Conveyances—Vehicles—Street Railways, etc.—The Third House is the house of Short Journeys, Inland Journeys, as by Rail, or any class of Vehicle. Also ☿, the ruler of the 3rd H. influences fundamentally, and the ♊ sign, which sign is affiliated with the 3rd H., have strong rule over short journeys and travel by land. Uranus is said to especially rule Railroads. Benefics in the 3rd H. at B., and with no malefics afflicting this house, make short journeys fortunate, and with less liability of accidents, injury, or death during inland travel. Malefics in, or ruling this house, make travel and short journeys, railroad, bus, automobile, or aeroplane travel very dangerous, and especially when the directions to the 3rd H., planets in this house at B., or to the ruler of the 3rd H., are bad. Before going on a journey by train, or other vehicle, every person should study the planetary conditions over them at the time, and be warned of impending dangers, or benefits, and by so doing travel could be reduced to a scientific basis, and many deaths and serious injuries avoided. In a serious railroad accident, those who are under bad directions are the ones who usually suffer, while the more fortunate escape. The opposite house, the 9th H., rules voyages, long journeys, and Foreign Travel. (See Journeys, Third House, Travel, Vehicles).

Accidents—Danger of Accidents, Injury, Misfortune, Delays, etc., on Short Journeys, Railroads, Vehicles, and Inland Travel—The ☽ in the 3rd H. at B., ☌, or evil asp. any of the malefic planets, and especially ♅; the ☽ in the 3rd H. at B., and to the ☌ or ill-asp. ♅ by dir.; the ☽ in the 3rd H. at the Vernal Equinox, and afflicted, greater danger in travel, and a prevalence of railroad accidents; ♅ afflicted in ♊ or the 3rd H. at B.; ♃ afflicted in the 3rd H., but escapes injury, or serious hurt; ♄ ℞ by transit, and in ☌, □, or ☍ ☿ ℞; ♂ afflicted in ♊ or the 3rd H. at B., and also ♂ afflicted by dir.; ♂ in the 1st H., and afflicted by ♃; ♂ to the cusp the 3rd H. by dir.; ♂ progressed to the ☌, P, □, or ☍ ☿, or vice versa; ♂ by Periodic Rev. to the ☌, □, or ☍ ♅, or to the ill-asps. the ☽, and especially if ♂ is in the 3rd H. at B.; ♂ in the 3rd H., in □ or ☍ the ☉ or ☽; ☿ afflicted in the 8th H.; malefics afflicted in the 3rd H.; lord of the 8th a malefic, in the 3rd H., and afflicted; lord of the 11th a malefic, and afflicted in the 3rd H. at B.; the 2nd Decan. of ♊ on the Asc., which decan. is ruled by ♂. (See "Short Journeys" under Journeys; "Accidents" under Travel; Vehicles; the various paragraphs in this section). Case—Injured In a Railroad Accident—See Fig. 21 in "Message of the Stars" by the Heindels. See "Strange Case, No. 405 in 1001 N.N. Also see Cases under Vehicles.

Death On Railways—Death On a Short Journey—Principally caused by the afflictions of ♅ to the hyleg if ♅ afflict the 3rd H. at B., and especially if this planet holds the dominion of death, and the radical map denotes a violent death; ♅ afflicting the hyleg by dir.; ♅ afflicted at B., and to the ☌, P, □ or ☍ the Asc. by dir., and especially if the Asc. be hyleg; the ☽ in the 3rd H. at B., and to the ☌ or P. asp. ♅ by dir.; the ☽ in the 3rd H. at the Vernal, lady of the year, and afflicted, many deaths on railroads; lord of the 8th H. a malefic, and afflicted in the 3rd H.; many afflictions in cardinal signs show. (See Avalanches; "Notorious Death" under Death; "Death" under Journeys, Travel, Vehicles). Cases of Death in Railroad Accidents—See "Luckless Youth", No. 390; "Run Over", No. 853; "Dey", No. 803; "Strafford", No. 814, all in 1001 N.N. Also see the Cases of Death under Vehicles.

RAIN—Moisture—Rain Storms—

Too Much Rain—Violent Rains—Floods—Excess of Rain, and Much Damage, Suffering, and Loss of Life by Rain, Storms, Water, etc.—An eclipse of the ☉ or ☽ in watery signs, and especially in places ruled by them; the ☽ applying to ♄; there tends to be more rain during the increase of the ☽; ♄ lord of the year at the Vernal, and with ♄ in an angle and direct in motion; ♄ in ♊ at the Vernal, angular, and direct in motion; ♄ ☌ ♃ in a water sign; ♃ ☌ ♂, mischief by rains; malefics in the 3rd or 9th H., in watery signs, and afflicting the ☉ or ☽, the native is more apt to encounter floods and severe storms on journeys or voyages; coincident with the appearance of Comets, and especially Halley's Comet; Comets appearing in Western Quarters of the heavens tend to cause aqueous vapors; the ♒ sign ascending at the Vernal tends to over-moist air, excess of rain, and much damage and suffering, and espec. in places ruled by this sign; ♋ or ♏ ascending at the Vernal, and the ☽ weak and afflicted, Countries under these signs suffer much damage and sickness from excessive rains and floods. (See Clouds, Comets, Floods; "Wet Journeys" under Journeys; Lightning; "Abundance", "Superabundance", under Moisture; Storms, Thunder, Waters, Weather).

Not Enough Rain—(See Drought, Famine, Fountains).

RAKISHNESS—(See Debauched, Dissolute, Lewd, Prodigal, Profligate, etc.).

RAMBLING—

Rambling Nature—(See "Many Changes" under Residence; Vagabond, Wanderer).

Rambling Speech—(See "Mental Chaos" under Chaotic; "Mind" under Confusion; "Rambling" under Speech).

RANSOM—Held for Ransom—(See Captive).

RANULA — A Cystic Tumor Under the Tongue — (See "Cystic Tumor" under Tongue).

RAPACIOUS — Extortionate — Plundering—Grasping—Caused principally by a weak, afflicted, and ill-dignified ♄ at B., and when ♂ adds his adverse influences, violence in attaining ends may be added. (See Assassins; "Evilly Disposed" under Evil; Highwaymen, Miserly, Pirates, Rapine, Ravenous, Selfishness, Thieves, Violent, etc.).

RAPE — Attackers of Women — The ☉ directed to all Nebulous Clusters, and to Castor and Pollux, threatens the native with Rape, or to commit such; ♅, ♄, or ♂ in ♏; ♂ ☌ ♀ in ♏. (See Cruel, Degenerate, Depraved, Lewd; "Low and Base" under Low; "Violence" under Passion; Perversions, Seduction, Shameless).

RAPID—Accelerated—

Rapid Action—(See Acceleration, Action, Active, Exaggerated, Quick).

Rapid Breathing—(See "Rapid" under Breathing).

Rapid Dyspnoea—(See Dyspnoea).

Rapid Fevers — (See "High Fevers" under Fever).

Rapid Heart Action — (See "Rapid" under Heart, Pulse).

Rapid Motion — (See Motion, Movement, Quick).

Rapid Physical Growth—(See Giants; "Abnormal Growth" under Growth).

Rapid Planets — The Effect of the Planets When More Rapid, or Direct In Motion — (See Direct; "Degree of Disturbance" under Disturbance).

Rapid Pulse — (See "Rapid" under Pulse).

Rapid Recovery—From Disease—(See Recovery; "Rapid" under Recuperation; "Good" under Resistance).

Rapid Respiration—(See "Rapid" under Breathing).

Rapid Speech — (See "Rapid" under Speech).

Rapid Walk—(See "Energetic" under Gait).

RAPINE—Thefts—Spoliation—Pillaging—Plundering—Rapacious, etc.—Prevalence of—An eclipse of the ☉ in the 3rd Decan. of ♌, or the 2nd Decan. of ♒; an eclipse of the ☽ in the 1st Decan. of ♊, the 1st Decan. of ♐, or the 3rd Decan. of ♓. (See Bandits, Highwaymen, Piracy, Rapacious, Robberies, Thefts, Thieves).

RARELY ILL — (See "Abundance of Health" under Health; Immunity; "Good" under Vitality).

RASHES—Eruptions—An Exanthematous Eruption on the Skin—Rashes are diseases of ♂, and also strongly ruled by the ♑ sign, and afflictions in ♑. (See Efflorescence; "Hot Eruptions" under Eruptions; Itch, Measles, Nettle Rash (see Hives, Urticaria); Pimples, Pruritis, Roseola, Rubefacient, Scarlatina, Skin Diseases).

RASHNESS—Rash Acts—Hasty—Rash Disposition—Self-Motived Acts—Precipitate—Turbulent—Inconsiderate—Foolhardy—Recklessness—Choleric—Lack of Forethought—Indiscreet—Lack of Judgment and Discrimination, etc.—Rashness is principally a ♂ influence, and with ♂ strong at B., in the Asc. or M.C., or afflicting the ☉, ☽, or Asc.; ♂ in an angle, and afflicted by the ☉, ☽, or other planets, by the □ or ☍ aspects from angles; the ♂ signs ♈ and ♏ when strong, and especially with ♂ therein, tend to rashness; ♂ afflicted in the 1st H.; ♂ to the cusp of the 1st H. by dir.; ♂ ill-dignified at B., and afflicted; ♂ configurated with ☿; ♂ elevated above, and in evil asp. to the ruling planet; ♂ ☌ ☿ at B.; ♂ to the place of ☋ by dir.; ♂ afflicted in ♈, ♉, ♏, ♐, ♑, or ♒; ♂ progressed to the ☌, □, or ☍ ☿; fixed stars of the nature of ♂ and ☿ ascending at B.; the ☉ ☌, □, or ☍ ♂ at B.; the ☉ to the ☌ or ill-asp. ♂ by dir. or progression; the ☉ rising at B., and afflicted by ♂; the ☉ in the Asc., and in □ to ♂ in the 10th; the ☉ □ or ☍ ☽, and especially when the Lights are also afflicted by ♂ or ♅; the ☽ ☌ or ill-asp. ♂ at B. and by dir.; the ☽ Sig. ☌ the ☉ or ♂; the ☽ Sig. in ♈ or ♏; ♅ ☌, P, □ or ☍ the ☽, ♂, or ☿ at B., and by dir.; ♃ afflicted in ♈; ♃ to the ☌ or ill-asp. ♂ by dir.; ♃ in ♊ near violent fixed stars; ♃ Sig. in ♍, rashness, and often resulting in serious losses; ♃ Sig. in ♊ near Aldebaran or the Bull's North Horn; ♄ Sig. ☌ ♂, or vice versa; ♀ Sig. ✱ or △ ♂, rash and inconsiderate; ☿ Sig. ☌, P, □, or ☍ ♂; ☿ Sig. in ♐, rash to his own injury; the 16° ♌ on the Asc. Rashness is a characteristic of the Choleric, or Bilious Temperament, ruled by the ☉, ♂, and the Fiery Signs. (See Anarchists, Anger; "Animal Instincts" under Animal; Bold, Choleric, Cruel, Dangerous; "Causes His Own Death" under Death; Destructiveness, Duels; "His Own Worst Enemy" under Enemies; Emotions, Erratic, Excitable; "Mental Extremes" under Extremes; Feelings, Fierce, Fiery, Fighting, Folly, Foolhardy; "Lack Of" under Forethought; Frenzy, Fury, Hasty, Imprudent, Impulses, Indiscreet, Inordinate; "Bad" under Judgment; Madness, Malicious; "Unbalanced" under Mentality; Murderous, Obstinate, Perverse, Precipitate, Quarrelsome, Recklessness, Revengeful, Riotous, Savage, Self-Control, Self-Undoing, Severe Disposition; "High Temper" under Temper; Temperaments, Treachery, Turbulent, Unbridled, Uncontrolled, Ungovernable, Vicious, Violent, etc.).

Death — From Rash Actions — (See "Causes His Own Death" under Death; Folly; "Death" under Imprudence).

Disease or Injury — The Result of Rash Acts and Irregularities—Caused by the ☉ and ♂, the positive, electric, and heat-producing planets, and by afflictions to these bodies. (See "Brings Disease Upon Himself" under Disease; Folly; "Lack Of" under Forethought; Imprudent, Indiscretions, Intemperance; "Disease" under Irregularities; "Health Injured", "Injured Thru Women", under Men; Recklessness).

Free from Rash Actions—The ☽ Sig. in ♋, and well-aspected. (See Gentle, Harmless, Humane, Kind, Mild; "Even Temper" under Temper).

Painful Complaints—Due to Rashness—The Result of Self-Motivated Acts—Caused by the afflictions of the ☉ and ♂. (See "Painful Complaints" under Forethought; "Disease or Injury" in this section).

RATIONAL FACULTIES—The Reasoning Faculties—Ruled by ☿. (See Comprehension, Coordination, Faculties, Fears, Insanity, Intellect, Intuition, Irrational, Judgment, Mentality, Mind, Perception, Reason, Thinking, Understanding). Aquarius is classed as a Rational Sign of the Zodiac.

RATIONALISM—The Formation of Opinions from Reason Alone—Not Drawing Upon the Intuitive or Spiritual Powers to Reach Conclusions—The Earthy Signs strong, predominant, and well-filled with planets at B., and holding the Asc., angles, etc. Also ♄ strong and predominant at B., and in an earthy sign, tends to Rationalism. Also caused by ☿ when this planet partakes of the nature of ♄, and is in an earthy sign. The watery signs, when prominent and well-occupied at B., are quite free from Rationalism and Materialism. (See Materialism, Radicalism, Reactionary, Revolutionary).

RATTLE-BRAINED—Rapid and Noisy Talk—Talking Rapidly, Foolishly, and with Little Depth of Thought—(See "Shallow" under Mentality; "Light in Mind" under Mind; "Rapid" under Speech).

RAVENOUS—Furiously Rapacious or Hungry—Rapacious—Violent—♂ ill-dignified at B., and afflicted. (See Rapacious, Rapine; "Tendency To" under Violence).

Ravenous Appetite—(See "Abnormal" under Appetite; Cravings, Gluttony, Hunger).

RAVING—Ravings—The ☽ in ♌ and afflicted by the ☉ or ♂ when taken ill (Hor'y). (See Cruel, Delirium, Demoniac, Drink, Fanatical, Frenzy, Fury; "Outrageous" under Insanity; Madness, Mania, Vicious, Violent, etc.).

RAW—Crude—Unrefined—Bleak—Chilling—Coarse—Caused by the ♄ and ♑ influences; ♄ rising in the Asc.; ♑ on the Asc.

Raw-Boned Body—(See "Raw-Boned" under Bones; Spare, Thin, Ugly, Ungainly).

Raw Food—(See "Cooked Foods" under Food; "Vegetarians" under Vegetables).

Raw Humours—In the Stomach—(See "Raw Humours" under Indigestion).

Raw, Tanned Appearance—Raw, Tanned, Leathery Appearance—(See "Tan" under Complexion).

RAYNAUD'S DISEASE—(See Fingers).

REACTION—Opposite Signs of the Zodiac, as ♉ and ♏, affect each other by reaction. Also signs in □ aspect to each other tend to have an unfavorable reactionaly influence upon each other, as ♈, ♋, ♎, and ♑. There is also the reaction of the Planets upon each other by their ☌, □, ☍, and other aspects, when within orb of aspect. The unfavorable reactions of Signs and Planets upon each other tend to produce affliction, discord, disease, and inharmony, except as they are ruled and transmuted. Planets in any of the fixed signs tend to react upon all of the fixed signs, and also with the cardinal and mutable signs. The stomach, ruled by the ♋ sign, is afflicted by planets in all the cardinal signs, or when these signs are on the Asc. Planets in ♏, the sex sign, also afflict the throat, ruled by the ♉ sign, etc. (See Action, Antipathy, Aspects, Opposites, Orbs, Removal, Sympathy).

REACTIONARY TENDENCY—Violent or Sweeping Methods of Procedure—The Fixed Sign influences, combined with a very strong ♄ influence at B., and with the cardinal and mutable signs in weaker positions; ♅ strong and prominent at B., as in the Asc. or M.C., and ☌ the ☉, ☽, or ☿, often tends to very radical characteristics, and a desire to bring about great Reforms, even tho resorting to violence. (See Anarchists, Fanatical, Radicalism, Rationalism, Reformers, Religion, Revolutionary, Sedition, Violence, etc.).

READAPTATION—In the System—♏ influence. (See Recovery, Restoration, Scorpio).

READING—Study—

Blindness—Blindness from Over-Study and Too Much Reading—(See "Reading and Study" under Blindness).

Brain Fag—From Too Much Reading and Study—(See "Brain Fag" under Brain; "Mind" under Fatigue; "Ocular Headaches" under Headaches; "Over-Study" under Study).

Disease—And Ill-Health from Too Much Reading and Study—☿ afflicting the Asc., the ☽, and the Dispositors of the ☉ and ☽, causes disease from too intense application. (See "Over-Exertion" under Exertion).

Fond of Reading—(See Learning, Scholar, Study).

Myopia—From Too Much Reading—The ☽ Sig. ☌ the ☉, danger of. (See "Myopia" under Sight).

Reading Prodigy—Child Reads at Three Years of Age—Reads Darwin and Huxley at Eight Years of Age—(See "Child Prodigy" under Prodigies).

REAR PARTS—Of the Body—Hinder Parts—(See Back, Buttocks, Dorsal, Front, Loins; "Back Part" under Marks; Shoulders, Spine, Vertebrae, etc.).

REARED WITH DIFFICULTY—(See "Reared" under Children).

REASON—The Reasoning Faculties—The Rational Faculties—The Rational Mind—Ruled by ☿, and the Principle of ☿ is Reason. Uranus and ☿ are termed the Mental Planets, and greatly influence the Mind. Reason finds expression thru the planet ☿, and the good aspects to ☿ tend to a good mind, and to act as a check upon the lower nature. By many Authors ♅ is considered the higher octave of ☿. The Rational Mind corresponds to the Stars;

the Subconscious Mind to the ☽, and the Superconscious Mind to the ☉. (See "Influence Of" under Mercury, Uranus. Also see the paragraphs under Intellect, Mental, Mind, Perception, Rational, Thinking, Understanding). The following subjects and paragraphs have to do with the Reasoning Faculties, which see in the alphabetical arrangement when only listed here—

Detriments—To the Reasoning Faculties—(See "Mental Chaos" under Chaotic; Confusion, Idiocy, Insanity; "Bad" under Judgment; "Weak Mind" under Mind; "Weak" in this section).

Emotions—(See "Arrested Emotions" under Emotions).

Erratic Mind—(See "Mind" under Erratic).

Erring; Fears; Feelings — Predominance of Feeling Over Intellect—(See Feelings).

Forethought — Lack of — (See Forethought).

Ideals; Ideas; Idiocy; Imbecility;

Impaired — The Reasoning Faculties Impaired—The ☽ □ or ☍ ☿, and neither in any way connected with the Asc.; ♃ □ or ☍ the ☽. (See Idiocy, Insanity; "Bad" under Judgment; "Weak Mind" under Mind).

Impulses — (See "Blind" under Impulses).

Insanity; Intellect — (See the paragraphs under Intellect).

Irrational; Irresponsible; Judgment—(See "Bad" under Judgment).

Loss of Reason—(See Foolish, Idiocy, Imbecile, Insanity, Irrational; "Void Of" in this section).

Mental—Mind—(See the subjects under Mentality, Mind).

Monsters; Not Governed by Reason—(See Feelings, Foolhardy; "Impractical" under Ideals; Impulses, Irrational, Rashness, Recklessness, etc.).

Perception; Prejudiced;

Reasonableness—An Open Mind—The Airy Signs prominent at B., and ☿ strong and well-aspected, tend to give a reasonable mind, open to conviction, the study of Truth, and to gain new viewpoints. The ♊, ♍, ♎, and ♒ people are especially open to discussion and new points of view, while the watery signs strong at B. tend to prejudice, aversion to new ideas which disturb their fixed beliefs, while the earthy signs tend to give narrow and materialistic views and opinions. The planet ♅ strong at B. tends to give a wide mental outlook, and the ☉ influence the widest range for the emotions. (See Ideals, Ideas, Judgment, Materialism, Metaphysics, Occult, Opinions, Prejudiced, Rationalism, Reactionary).

Strengthened—The Reasoning Faculties Strengthened—♃ in good asp. to the ☽ and ☿; ☿ well-aspected by the ☽, and with ☿ in good aspect to the Asc.; ☿ free from the affliction of malefics. (See "Good" under Judgment; "Quickened" under Mental; "Strong Mind" under Mind).

Thought—Little Depth of Thought or Mature Reasoning — ☿ afflicted in ♒. (See "Void Of" under Learning; "Shallow" under Mentality; "Light In Mind" under Mind; Pretender).

Unbalanced Mind—(See Balanced, Incoordination, Insanity, Irrational, Madness, Mania; "Unbalanced" under Mentality; "Void Of" in this section).

Understanding — (See "Weak" under Understanding).

Unreasonable—Not According to Reason — Irrational — (See Anarchists; "Mind" under Erratic; Erring; "Mental Extremes" under Extremes; Fanatical; "Fixed Signs" under Fixed; "Impractical" under Ideals; Ideas, Intractable, Irrational, Obstinate, Perverse, Radicalism, Rashness, Reactionary, Rebellious, Recklessness, Revolutionary, Ungovernable, Unruly).

Unsound Mind — (See "Unsound" under Mind).

Void of Reason — This condition is usually caused by prenatal conditions, and the afflictions during gestation, as in cases of Idiots, Imbeciles, Monsters, etc. Some important Prenatal causes are—The ☉ and ☽ at the time of the New or Full ☽ previous to birth forming no aspect to the Asc., and having no help from the Benefics ♃ and ♀, and also the angles, as the 1st and 10th H., occupied by malefics. Evil aspects to ☿ at the same time tend to unbalance the mentality, make void of reason, and the mind undefinable. If ♅, ♄, or ♂ give testimony in any of the foregoing positions, what is then generated will have ungovernable and irrational qualities. (See Foolish, Idiocy, Imbecile, Inhuman, Insanity, Monsters, Prenatal Epoch).

Weak Reasoning Faculties — (See "Mental Chaos" under Chaotic; Confusion; "Mind" under Erratic; Erring, Foolish; "Lack Of" under Forethought; Idiocy, Imbecile; "Mental" under Incompetency; Irrational; "Bad" under Judgment; "Weak Mind" under Mind; Precipitate; "Impaired", and the various paragraphs in this section).

Well-Balanced Mind—(See "Strengthened" in this section; "Good" under Judgment, Intellect, Understanding; "Quickened" under Mentality; "Good", "Strong", "Sound", "Talented", under Mind; "Acute" under Perception, etc.).

REBELLIOUS —Unruly— Refractory—Antagonistic—Contrary—Hostile—♂ is the author of rebellion, hostility, and of antagonism, war, etc. Caused by ☿ ill-dignified at B., and afflicted by the ☽ and ♂; many planets in fixed signs at B., and with these signs upon the angles; ♉ on the Asc., and ♂ afflicted in ♉. (See Erring; "Fixed Signs" under Fixed; Intractable, Irascible, Irritable, Obstinate, Perverse, Rashness, Reactionary, Reformers, Refractory, Revolutionary, Sedition; "High Temper" under Temper; Ungovernable, Unruly, etc.).

RECEPTACLES—The ☽ governs all Receptacles in the body, and the fluids in them, as the Stomach, Bladder, Uterus, etc. (See Cavities).

RECEPTIVITY—Reception—Receptive—The principle of the ☽ is receptivity, and people born under the strong influence of the ☽, the ☽ as ruler, or who have many planets in the negative and feminine signs of the Zodiac, are more receptive and susceptible to external and outside influences, and to environment. (See Environment, External, Hyperaesthesia, Influenced; "Influence Of" under Moon; Mutable, Negative, Susceptibility, etc.).

Semen—The Seed—The receptivity of the semen into the womb is ruled by the ☽. (See Fecundation, Fertile, Semen).

RECKLESSNESS — Wild — Hasty—Desperate—Foolhardy—Impulsive—Indiscreet, etc. — Caused principally by ♂ influences and afflictions; ♂ elevated above, and in evil asp. to the ruling planet; ♂ progressed to the ☌ or ill-asp. ♄, ♀, or ☿, or vice versa; ♂ afflicted in ♌, or afflicting the ☉, ☽, or Asc. from this sign; ♂ to the cusp the 11th H.; the ☉ in ♑ and afflicted by ♂, hasty and reckless at times; the ☉ to the ☌ or ill-asp. ♂ by dir.; the Prog. ☉ or ☽ to the ☌ or ill-asp. ♂; ♅ by transit to the ☌ ♂, ☿, or the ☽ in the radical map, or vice versa; ♃ to the ill-asps. ♂ by dir.; ♀ in ♌ and afflicted by ♂, hasty and reckless at times; ♀ afflicted at B., and to the ☌ or ill-asp. the Asc. by dir.; ☿ afflicted in ♈; ☿ ☌ or ill-asp. ♂ at B., or by dir.; the 4° ♋ or ♐, or 3° ♓ on the Asc. at B. (See Anger, Choleric, Erratic, Erring, Excitable, Explosive, Foolhardy; "Lack Of" under Forethought; Fury, Hasty, Imprudent, Impulsive, Indiscreet, Irascible, Judgment, Perverse, Precipitate, Quarrelsome, Rashness, Reactionary, Riotous; "High Temper" under Temper; Vicious, Violent, etc.).

RECLUSE — Secretive — Solitariness — Fond of Seclusion—Aversion to Society — Reserved — Retiring — Separateness, etc.—Caused by ♄, ♆, and the 12th H. influences; ♄ or ♆ in the 4th H., a recluse in old age, and usually ends life in seclusion; ♄ in the 1st H., shy and fond of solitude; ♄ ruler of the Asc., or horoscope, and afflicted; ♄ strong at B., and rising, a confederate in secrecy; ♄ afflicted in ♉; ♄ in the 12th H. leads to a secluded life; ♄ is the author of solitariness; born under ♄; ♄ □ or ☍ ☿ at B., and by dir.; the ☉ in the 4th H., and afflicted by ♄, inclined to secrecy; ☿ rising in ♍, contemplative, fond of retirement, and to dwell alone; ☿ □ or ☍ ♄; strong ☿ influence at B.; ruler of the Asc. in the 12th H.; the 15° ♉, the 13th and 30° ♎, the 12th and 21° ♑, or the 2nd and 3° ♒ on the Asc. at B.; the 1st Decan. of ♍, ruled by the ☉, on the Asc. (See Aversions, Backwardness, Bashfulness, Celibacy, Miserly, Mistrustful, Misunderstood, Modesty; "Asylum" under Old Age; "Free from Passion" under Passion; Renunciation, Reserved, Retiring, Saturn, Seclusion, Secretive, Self-Denying, Shy, Solitude, Suspicious, Twelfth House, etc.).

RECOLLECTION—(See Memory).

RECONDENSATION — (See Sublimation).

RECOVERY—Recovery from Disease—Convalescence — Recuperation — Pros-

pects of Recovery, etc. — See the following subjects in the alphabetical arrangement when not considered here—

Amelioration—The Abatement of the Disease — (See Amelioration; "Better" under Disease; Moderation).

Better—The Disease Changes for the Better—(See "Better" under Disease).

Certain—Recovery Is Certain—If at decumbiture the ☽ is applying to the ☉, or to benefics, and with small affliction to the hyleg from malefics, recovery is certain. (See "Rapid" under Recuperation; "Good" under Resistance, Vitality; "Will Recover" in this section).

Child Will Recover—The Child Sickly But Will Recover—(See "Sickly" under Children).

Complications; Continuity of Disease —(See Continuity).

Convalescence — (See Amelioration, Better, Moderation, Patient Will Recover, Resolution, in this section).

Crises In Disease—(See Crises).

Curable Diseases—(See Curable).

Cured, But Has Relapse — (See Relapse).

Dangerous Maladies — (See Dangerous).

Decrease—The Disease Will Decrease —The Disease Will Remove Shortly— Lord of the Asc. stronger than lord of the 6th; a malefic leaving the 6th H., the disease will remove shortly, in so many days or weeks, according to the nature of the sign; the ☽ sepr. from a malefic and applying to a benefic. (See Amelioration; "Better" under Disease; Moderation, Resolution).

Delayed Recovery—(See "Disease Delayed" under Delays; "Worse" under Disease; "Disease" under Increase; "Delayed" under Pneumonia; Relapse).

Denoted — Recovery Denoted — (See "Patient Will Recover" in this section).

Difficult to Cure—(See "Difficult" under Cure; Incurable, Obstinate).

Doubtful Recovery — The Illness Is Not Without Peril—Little Hope of Recovery—The ☽ at decumbiture under the Sun's beams, or ☌ ♄ or ♂, and with no assistance of the benefics to the ☽; lord of the Asc., or the ☽, combust, and applying to the ☉, and if not applying at the same time to a benefic, the danger is imminent (Hor'y); lord of the Asc., or the ☽, in ☌ lord of the 8th; lord of the Asc., or the ☽, applying by evil asp. to lord of the 8th, and if the latter be a malefic, death is considered certain; lord of the 1st in the 4th or 8th, and afflicted; lord of the 8th in an angle, and lord of the 1st cadent and afflicted; lord of the 8th in the 10th, or lord of the 1st in the 4th, 6th, or 7th H.; lord of the Asc., or the ☽, with violent fixed stars; an evil application to lord of the 8th is considered a fatal symptom; a malefic in the 6th H. (See "Arguments for Death", "Certain Death", under Death; Fatal).

Duration of Disease—(See Duration).

End of the Disease—(See "End of the Disease" under Disease, End; "Disease" under Termination).

Expected—Recovery Expected — (See "Patient Will Recover" in this section).

Hard to Cure — (See Chronic; "Difficult" under Cure; Incurable, Lingering, Long Diseases, Slow Diseases, Tedious, etc.).

Health Better — (See "Better" under Health).

Hopes of Recovery—(See "Doubtful", "Patient Will Recover", in this section; "Certain Death" under Death; Fatal, Incurable).

How Long Before Recovery? Used in Hor'y Questions—Observe the lord of the Asc. Observe what benefic planet is applying to an aspect of the lord of the Asc. Note what Signs and Houses they are in, whether in angles, moveable Signs, etc., and then frame the measure of time according to the quality of the disease. If the planet be angular, and the sign moveable, judge the time of recovery as many days as there are degrees to complete the aspect. If the planet be succedent, and the sign common, judge recovery in as many weeks as there are degrees to complete the aspect. If the planet be cadent, and the sign fixed, judge recovery to take place in as many months as there are degrees to complete the aspect. If the sign be common in which the application is, use discretion, according to the nature of the disease, and not by any fast rule of days, weeks, or months. The quick or slow motion of the ☽, the sign she is in, and her situation as to angles, often tends to hasten or retard the progress towards recovery. The patient often recovers very quickly when the lord of the Asc. quits the sign he is in, and enters one in which he has dignities. If a common sign be 28° on the cusp of the 6th H., judge that the disease will vary, or resolve itself in two weeks. (See Acute, Chronic, Continuity, Course, Crises, Curable; "Arguments for Death", "Certain Death", under Death; Duration, Fatal, Incurable, Lingering; "Long Diseases" under Long; "Short Diseases" under Short; Slow, Tedious, etc.).

Important — The Disease Is Not Important—(See "The Disease Will Soon End" under End; Mild, Slight).

Impossible—Recovery Almost Impossible—♄ afflicted in the 6th H. (See "Certain Death" under Death; "The Sick Will Hardly Escape" under Escape; Fatal, Incurable, Invalids, Wastings; "Doubtful" in this section).

Improved—The Sick Improved—(See Amelioration; "Better" under Disease; "Disease" under Improved; Moderation; "Rapid" under Recuperation; Resolution).

Increase — The Disease Will Increase —(See Crises; "Worse" under Disease; "Disease" under Increase).

Incurable; Little Hope of Recovery—(See Doubtful, Impossible, in this section).

Long Diseases — (See Chronic; "Diseases" under Lingering, Long, Prolonged, Slow, Tedious, etc.).

Moderation of Disease — The Disease Will Moderate—(See Amelioration, Crises; "Better" under Disease; Improved, Moderation, Modification).

Modification of Disease—(See Amelioration, Complications, Crises; "Better", "Worse", under Disease; Moderation, Modification, Relapse, etc.).

Old Diseases Return—(See Return).

Patient Will Recover—Testimonies of Recovery—Signs of Recovery—The ☽ leaving the ☍ the ☉, and applying to the ✶ or △ ♃ or ♀; the ☽ sepr. from malefics and applying to benefics, and without prohibition or frustration; the ☽ applying to a benefic in power, the former health is restored; the ☽ in the houses of ♃ or ♀, or in her own house, and free from the affliction of malefics; the ☽ applying to ♃ or ♀ by good aspect, or to the good asp. the ☉; the ☽ ☌ ♃ denotes recovery, but slower when in ♑; the ☽ incr. in light, in a good house, and applying to the good asp. the lord of the Asc.; the ☽ well-dignified, or in the Asc., or in ✶ or △ the Asc.; the ☽ applying to the lord of the Asc. by good asp., and not afflicted by lords of the 6th or 8th; the ☽ void of course at the beginning of the sickness, but at her next crisis forming a ✶ or △ to ♃ or ♀ in the exact degree which forms the perfect critical aspect; the ☉ or ☽ ruler of the Asc. at the beginning of a disease, and free from the evil asps. of malefics, or lord of the 8th; the ☉, ♃, or ♀ in the Asc., and in no way afflicted by the lord of the 6th or 8th, and especially if in the houses of the ☉, ☽, or benefics; lord of the Asc. a benefic, or the benefics angular and well-aspected; the lord of the Asc., or of the 6th, in good asp. or reception with the Lights, or with one of them, or if wholly free from affliction; reception by house and triplicity between the lords of the Asc. and 8th, and the benefics in good asp. to the degree ascending, or to the cusp of the 6th H., or in ☌, ✶, or △ the ☽, the sick will perfectly recover; lord of the 8th applying to the good asp. the benefics; fixed signs on the angles, and the ☉ and ♂ strong and well-aspected at B., and the ☉ ✶ or △ ♂. (See Curable; "Disease Not Dangerous" under Dangerous; "Disease Will Soon End" under End; Mild, Slight; "Rapid" under Recuperation; "Good" under Resistance; Resources, Vitality; "Certain" in this section).

Peril — Danger — The Illness Is Not Without Peril—(See Doubtful, Impossible, in this section).

Prognosis; Prolonged — The Disease Will Be Prolonged — (See Chronic, Lingering, Long, Prolonged, Slow, Tedious, etc.).

Quick Recovery—(See Immunity, Mild; "Rapid" under Recuperation; "Good" under Resistance; Slight).

Rapid Recovery—(See "Quick" in this section; "Recovery" under Quick).

Recuperation—(See "Rapid", "Slow", and the various paragraphs under Recuperation).

Readaptation; Relapses; Remission—The Remission of Disease — (See Remission).

Resolution — The Resolution of the Disease—(See Resolution).

Return — Old Maladies Return— (See Return).

Shifting—Of the Disease—(See "Shifting" under Disease).

Short Diseases — (See Acute; "High Fever" under Fever; Fierce, Mild, Quick, Rapid, Sharp, Short, etc.).

Signs of Recovery — (See "Patient Will Recover" in this section).

Slight Ailments — (See Colds, Mild, Slight).

Slow Recovery—(See Chronic, Lingering, Long Diseases, Prolonged, Slow, Tedious, etc.).

Solution of Disease—(See Amelioration, Moderation, Resolution, Solution).

Succumbs Easily to Disease — (See "Succumbs" under Disease).

Will Recover—(See "Patient Will Recover" in this section).

Worse — Patient Gets Worse — (See "Worse" under Disease).

RECREATIONS — Amusements — Sports —Exercise—Play, etc.

Death or Injury — Accident, Injury, or Death While Seeking Recreation, or Engaging In Sports — Caused principally by afflictions in the 5th H., and in the ♐ sign. (See Amusements, Athletics, Bathings, Exercise, Horses, Hunting, Play, Pleasures, Riding, Sports, Theatres, Travel, etc.).

Honest Recreations—Fond of—The ☉ Sig. in ♍; ♀ Sig. in ♐, fond of honest and innocent recreations.

Moderate—In Recreations—♃ Sig. in ♒. (See Moderate, Temperate).

Partial To—Partial to Recreation and Exercise—♃ Sig. in ♎ or ♐. (See "Fond Of" under Exercise).

Travel—(See "Love of Travel" under Travel).

RECTIFICATION — Of the Birth Hour and Moment of Birth—It is important in health matters to know, or determine, the exact moment of birth, as each degree rising upon the Eastern horizon at B. has a different meaning. Also the house positions of the planets at B. should be accurately known to give a proper prognosis or delineation. There are certain laws and rules, which if properly applied, make the science of Rectification practically certain and absolute, and the student should become familiar with these rules. Rectification is quite thoroughly discussed, and the principles given, in the various Textbooks and Dictionaries of Astrology. See the Articles on Rectification in Wilson's Dictionary of Astrology, and in Alan Leo's Dictionary of Astrology. Also the time of birth can be rectified by the Prenatal Epoch Method, as given in the book, "The Prenatal Epoch", by Mr. E. H. Bailey. When the time of birth is approximately known, the Prenatal Method is considered very accurate, as the Ascendant at conception is the degree and sign of the ☽ at B., and the place of the ☽ at conception is the sign and degree of the Asc. or Descendant at B. (See Prenatal Epoch).

RECTUM—The Lower Part of the Large Intestine—The Rectum is ruled by ♂, ♏, and the 6th and 8th H. The 6th H. denotes the Rectum. The Anus and the Meso-Colon are ruled by ♏. See the following subjects in the alphabetical arrangement when not considered here.

All Diseases In—In Hor'y Q., signified by the 8th H., and afflictions in the ♏ sign. (See "Diseases" in this section).

Anus — Disorders of — (See Anus; "Sphincter Ani" in this section).

Aphthae; Cancer Of—♄ afflicted in ♏; ♄ ☌ ♅ in ♏; Subs at LPP (4, 5L), and also at KP. (See Carcinoma).

Circulation Obstructed In—♄ afflicted in ♏; ♄ ☌ ♃ or ♀ in ♏.

Cloaca—A Common Outlet to the Rectum and Bladder—(See Cloaca).

Condyloma—(See Anus).

Contraction — Of the Anus Muscle — (See "Inbreathing" under Anus; "Sphincter" in this section).

Diseases In Rectum — Malefics in ♏, the 6th or 8th H., and afflicted; the ☽ in ♏, ☌, or ill-asp. ♄ (or ☿ if he be of the nature of ♄) at the beginning of an illness, or at decumbiture (Hor'y); ♄ or ♂ afflicted in ♏; Subs at PP, LPP. (See Fundament; the various paragraphs in this section).

Elimination—Rectal Elimination Obstructed—♄ afflicted in ♏; malefics in ♉ or ♏. (See "Rectal" under Elimination).

Fissure—(See Anus).

Fistula; Flux—Too Much Flux of the Hemorrhoids—(See Hemorrhoids).

Fundament—Disorders of—(See Fundament).

Hemorrhoids; Imperforate Anus—(See Anus).

Inbreathing—Thru the Rectum—(See Anus).

Inflammatory Diseases — Of the Rectum—♂ afflicted in ♉ or ♏; ♀ in ♉, ☌, □, or ☍ ♂. (See Hemorrhoids).

Meso-Rectum — Meso-Colon — (See Colon).

Nervous Trouble — In the Rectal Region—☿ afflicted in ♏.

Neuralgia In—Pains In—♄, ♂, or ☿ afflicted in ♏; ♅ ☌ ☿ in ♏; Subs at KP and LPP. (See Neuralgia).

No Rectum—Absence of—Case—See "Twins", No. 241, in 1001 N.N.

Obstructions—Obstructed Rectal Region—♄ afflicted in ♉ or ♏; Subs at PP and LLP (See Anus, Constipation, Faeces; Circulation, Elimination, in this section).

One Passage — (See "Cloaca" in this section; Hermaphrodites).

Opening—A Common Opening to the Bladder and Rectum—(See Cloaca, One Passage, in this section).

Piles—(See Hemorrhoids).

Right Side — Rectum On the Right Side — Case — See "Heart", No. 981, in 1001 N.N.

Spasmodic Action—Of the Sphincter Ani—(See "Sphincter" in this section).

Sphincter Ani — The Anus Muscle — Contraction and Spasmodic Action of—

♄ in ♏ ☌ ♅; the ☽ in ♏ and afflicted by ♄. (See "Inbreathing" under Anus).

Syphilis Of—♂ ☌ ♀ in ♏; ♀ afflicted in ♏; Subs at KP and LPP. (See Syphilis).

Tumor In—♄ ☌ ♃ or ♀ in ♏; ♄ or ♂ afflicted in ♏. (See Tumors).

Ulcer In—♂ in ♏, and afflicted by ♄. (See Ulcers).

Wart-Like Growths — (See "Condyloma" under Anus).

RECUPERATION — The Recuperative Powers—

Augmented—The Recuperative Powers Augmented and Increased—The ☉ in the Asc. at B., and well-aspected; the ☉ well-aspected in ♈ or ♌; the ☉ ⚹ or △ the ☽; ♃ or ♀ ☌, ⚹, or △ the Asc.; ♈ or ♌ upon the Asc. at B. (See Augmented, Endurance; "Good Health" under Health; Immunity, Increased; "Good" under Resistance, Vitality; "Good", "Rapid", in this section).

Below Average—The Recuperative Powers Below Average — Arrested — Hindered—Low—The ☉ or ☽ in the 6th or 12th H., in a weak sign, and afflicted by malefics; a weak sign on the Asc., and a malefic in the rising sign; ♋, ♑, or ♓ on the Asc.; ♐ on the Asc., due to an over-active body, and using up the vital force too fast. (See Feeble; "Low" under Resistance, Vitality; "Weak Body" under Weak).

Fair Recuperative Powers — Medium —The ☽ hyleg in ♒ with females; the airy signs on the Asc., not as strong as the fiery signs for vitality. (See "Medium" under Vitality).

Functional Disorders — Well Able to Fight Against—(See "Resistance" under Functions).

Good Recuperative Powers — Resistance to Disease Strong—Good Vitality —Throws Off Disease Quickly—The ☉ well-aspected in the Asc.; the ☉ ⚹ or △ the ☽; the ☉ rising in ♌, and not afflicted; the ☉ ⚹ ♄ at B. gives persistence and tenacity of life; the ☉ ☌, P., ⚹ or △ ♃; the greater the power of the ☉ at B., and the less the ☉ is afflicted, the stronger are the recuperative powers, and especially with males, and the ☽ likewise with females, but as the ☉ is the source of vital power, the resistance to disease is stronger in both sexes when the ☉ is strong and well-aspected at B.; the ☽ hyleg in ♍ or ♎ with females; the ☽ in the Asc. or M.C., well-aspected by benefics, and free from too much affliction of malefics; ♃ ascending at B., and well-aspected by the ☉ or ☽; ♃ or ♀ in the 6th H., and well-aspected; ♂ ☌, or in any aspect to the ☉ or ☽; ♂ in good asp. to the ☉ at B. especially tends to give a good store of vitality to draw upon when sick; ♈ or ♌ upon the Asc.; ♍ upon the Asc. if not too much afflicted, or containing malefics; lord of the 6th in the 6th, and well-aspected; a strong map of birth, and the hyleg well-aspected, good powers of recuperation, no matter how evil the directions, except in old age; fiery signs upon the Asc.; the airy signs upon the Asc. at B. are next in power to the fiery signs for good powers of recuperation; of the earthy

signs, the 3° ♑ is stronger for recuperation when on the Asc. at B. (See Endurance; "Abundance", "Good Health", under Health; Immunity; "Good" under Resistance, Vitality; "Rapid" in this section).

Inability to Throw Off Disease—The ☉ afflicted in ♍, or ♍ on the Asc., as it is said the ♍ people court disease, and spend much time in thinking of disease and the condition of their health; common signs on the angles at B. (See "Low" under Resistance, Vitality; Virgo; "Low", "Slow", in this section).

Increased — Powers of Recuperation Increased — (See Augmented, Good, Rapid, in this section).

Less Power to Throw Off Disease—(See Inability, Low, Slow, in this section).

Little Recuperative Power—(See Below Average, Inability, Low, Slow, in this section; Debility, Emaciation, Feeble; "Low" under Resistance, Vitality; "Weak Body" under Weak).

Lives Thru Disease — (See "Spared" under Life; "Lives" under Serious; "Good" under Resistance; "Good", "Rapid", in this section).

Low—Recuperative Powers Low—Inability to Throw Off Disease — Little Recuperative Power—Little Power to Throw Off Disease — Less Power to Throw Off Disease — Throws Off Disease With Difficulty — Resistance to Disease Low, etc. — The ☉ ☌ ♄ in a fixed sign; the ☉ afflicted in ♎, the sign of his fall; weak signs on the angles, as ♋, ♑, or ♓, and with the ☉ in a weak sign, and the ☉ in no aspect to ♂; ♄ afflicted in the 6th H.; many planets in fixed signs, or fixed signs on the angles, and especially the ♌ sign predominant; common signs on the angles, the patient is more passive, and hard to arouse from sickness; many afflictions in angles, and with common signs on the angles; ♋, ♑, or ♓ on the Asc.; afflictions in fixed signs, and mutable signs on the angles, succumbs easily to disease. (See Below Average, Inability, Less, Little, Slow, in this section; Diminished; "Gives Up Easily" under Disease; "Disease" under Inability; "Mutable Signs" under Mutable; "Slow" under Recovery; "Low" under Resistance, Vitality; "Weak Body" under Weak).

Makes Effort to Throw Off Disease—(See "Overcoming Disease" under Disease).

Males—Recuperative Powers Good In —The ☉ strong and well-aspected at B.; the ☉ rising and elevated in ♌; the ☉ in ♌ in the Asc., and with ♌ rising, strong recuperative powers. These powers tend to be weak in males when the ☉ is weak at B., and afflicted by ♄ and other malefics, and also when the ☉ is ☌ ♄ in common signs. (See Augmented, Below Average, in this section; "Health" under Males).

Medium Powers—Of Recuperation—(See "Fair" in this section).

Moderation of Disease—Recuperation Is Taking Place — (See Amelioration; "Better" under Disease; Moderation, Resolution, Solution).

Much Recuperative Power—(See Augmented, Good, Rapid, in this section).

Overcomes Disease—(See "Overcoming Disease" under Disease; "Good Health" under Health; Immunity; "Good", "Lives Thru Disease", "Rapid", in this section).

Poor Recuperative Powers—(See Below Average, Inability, Less, Little, Low, Slow, in this section).

Quickly Throws Off Disease — (See "Rapid" in this section).

Rapid Recuperation—Throws Off Disease Quickly—Strong Powers of Recuperation—Good Powers of Resistance to Disease—The ☉ or ♂ in the Asc. at B., and well-aspected; the ☉ well-aspected in ♈ or ♌, and especially when rising, or in the Asc. or M.C.; the ☉ in ♌, and with ♈ on the Asc.; the ☉ ✱ or △ ♂; ♅ ✱ or △ ♄ and ♂; ♂ ✱ or △ the ☉; ♂ in the 6th H., as ♂ by fever burns out the poisons quickly when in this house; ♂ well-aspected in ♍; taken sick in a ♃ hour, the patient soon recovers; born with fiery signs on the Asc., and with benefics in the 6th H., and the hyleg not badly afflicted; airy signs upon the Asc., as the airy signs tend to rapid recuperation thru mental rest and change of scenery; born under positive signs, and with many planets rising and elevated in positive, or masculine signs; positive signs on the Asc. at B.; cardinal signs on angles, and especially with a cardinal and positive sign on the Asc.; with the afflictions in common signs, and with fixed signs on the angles, the native overcomes disease. (See Augmented, Good, in this section; "Good" under Constitution, Resistance, Vitality; Immunity; "Body" under Strong).

Reserve Forces Large — (See Augmented, Good, Rapid, in this section).

Resistance to Disease—Good—Low—(See the paragraphs under Resistance).

Restoration to Health — (See "Lives Thru Disease" in this section).

Sickly, But Will Recover—(See "Sickly But Recovers" under Infancy).

Slow Recuperation — The Powers of Recuperation Low—The Recuperative Power Lessened — Resistance to Disease Low — Throws Off Disease with Difficulty—Little Power to Throw Off Disease—The Vitality Low, etc.—The ☉ or ☽ afflicted by malefics, and the malefics elevated above the Lights; the ☉ or ☽ afflicted in the 6th H. at B.; the ☉ □ ☽ at B.; the Prog. ☉ or ☽ to the ☌ or ill-asp. ♄ in the radix; the ☉ ☌ ♄ in a fixed sign; the ☽ hyleg in ♑ in a female nativity; ♄ ruler of the 6th H., or in the 6th H. at B., and afflicted; ♄ passing thru the 6th H. by transit or progression; ♄ ☌ ☿ in the 6th H.; ♄ rising at B., and afflicting the ☉ or ☽, and the ☉ badly aspected by the ☽; the ♄ sign ♑ upon the Asc. at B., weak during early years; the earthy signs on the Asc. at B., unless well aspected, tend to slow recovery or recuperation; ♋, ♑, or ♓ on the Asc.; many planets in fixed signs at B., or afflictions from fixed signs at the time of illness, the disease is prolonged. (See Below Average, Inability, Little, Low, in this section; Chronic, Consumptions, Emaciation, Feeble, Invalids, Lingering, Long Diseases, Prolonged; "Low" under Resistance, Vitality; Slow, Tuberculosis, Wastings; "Weak Body" under Weak).

Strong Powers of Recuperation—(See Augmented, Good, Rapid, in this section).

Throwing Off Disease — Much Power to Throw Off Disease—Little Power—(See "Throwing Off Disease" under Disease; the various paragraphs in this section).

Vitality—Good Vitality—Low Vitality—(See Vitality).

Weak—The Powers of Recuperation Weak—(See Below Average, Inability, Low, Slow, in this section).

Will Soon Recover—(See "Rapid" in this section; "Quick", "Rapid", under Recovery).

RECURRENT DISEASES—(See "Periods of Bad Health" under Health; Periodical; "Old Maladies Return" under Return).

RED — Red Color — Reddened — Reddish — Reddening — Red is the color ruled by ♂ in the Solar Spectrum. Red is ruled by ♂, the 3rd, 4th, and 10th Houses. The fiery red of ♂ is the result of intemperate heat and dryness. Red mixed with green is denoted by ♃. Aries denotes red and white; ♉ denotes red mixed with **citrine**; ♊, red and white mixed; ♌, red or green; ♎, dark crimson. (See Colors).

Beard—(See "Red" under Beard).

Blood—The Red Blood—The Arterial Blood — Red Blood Corpuscles — The Haemoglobin—Alterations In the Red Blood—Changes In the Blood Particles—The Red Blood Particles Defective—Red Blood Corpuscles Deficient, etc.—The afflictions of ♃ tend to cause alterations in the red blood, and such are considered ♃ diseases. Defects, deficiencies in the red blood corpuscles, or particles, are classed as ☽ diseases. Also such deficiency often exists in people born with the Lymphatic Temperament. For increase in the red blood corpuscles see "Red Blood Corpuscles" in this section. (See Anaemia, Arteries, Blood, Circulation, Haemoglobin, Iron, Jupiter Diseases; "Temperament" under Lymphatic; "Red Blood" in this section).

Body—Red Marks On— Given by ♂. (See "Red" under Marks).

Cheeks—Red Cheeks—♀ Sig. in ♋, in the Asc., and in the terms of ♂, a tinge of red color in the cheeks. (See Cheeks; "Red" under Complexion, Face).

Citrine and Red—♉ colors.

Color—Red Color and Combinations—(See the Introduction to this Article).

Complexion — (See "Red", "Ruddy", under Complexion, Face).

Enthusiasm — Red-Hot Enthusiasm — (See Enthusiasm).

Eyes—(See Fiery, Inflamed, Ophthalmia, Red Cast, under Eyes).

Face—Red Face—Morbid Red Face—(See "Red" under Complexion, Face, Nose; "Cheeks" in this section).

Gravel—Red Gravel—Voiding of Red Gravel—(See Gravel).

Haemoglobin — The Coloring Matter of Red Corpuscles—(See Haemoglobin, Iron; "Blood", "Red Blood", in this section).

Hair—(See "Red" under Hair).

Iron—The Red Metal of ♂—(See Iron; "Metal" under Mars).

Lips—(See "Red" under Lips).

Marks — Red Marks On the Body — (See "Red" under Marks).

Mars—Red is the Color of ♂, the Red Planet. (See "Color", "Red Planet", under Mars).

Nose—Red Nose—Morbid Red Nose—(See "Red" under Face, Nose). For the Toper's Red Nose see the influences under Drink, Drunkenness, Intoxication.

Red Blood Corpuscles—Increase of—Decrease of—♂ action increases them; ♂ ✱ or △ ♃. The afflictions of ♃ and the ☽ tend to decrease them. (See Blood, Haemoglobin, in this section; "Coloring Matter" under Blood; Corpuscles, Haemoglobin, Iron).

Red Pepper—(See Capsicum).

Reddening — Local Irritants — (See Rubefacients).

Rubefacients—An Agent that Reddens the Skin—(See Rubefacients).

Ruddy Complexion—(See Red, Ruddy, under Complexion).

Sandy Red Hair—(See "Sandy" under Hair).

Skin — Red Skin — (See "Red" under Cheeks, Complexion, Face; Pimples, Ruddy).

Treatment — The Treatment of Diseases by the Use of Red Color, Red Surroundings — Red Color is a tonic. Red color is used in the treatment of Inflammatory Skin Diseases, and Inflammatory Diseases of all kinds, and in the treatment of Lupus, Smallpox, Hypochondria, etc., and patients confined in a red room where all the colorings are red benefit when suffering with such diseases. The Herbs of ♂ are also used in the treatment and cure of diseases caused by ♂, on the basis of treatment by Sympathy. (See Antipathy; "Therapy", "Vibration", under Colors; "Mars Group" under Herbs; Hypochondria, Lupus; "Therapeutic Qualities" under Mars; Opposites, Skin, Smallpox, Sympathy, Tonic).

White and Red Colors — Ruled by ♈. (See the Introduction to this Article).

White and Red Complexion — (See "Red" under Complexion).

REDUCING — Reduced — Reducing Disorders are generally the work of ♄. The ☉ ☌ ♄ at B. tends to reduce males, and bring ill-health. The ☽ ☌ or P. asp. ♄ at B., and by dir. tends to reduce the system in females. (See Atrophy, Consumptions, Decay, Degeneration, Deterioration, Diminished, Emaciation; "Mal-Nutrition" under Nutrition; Phthisis, Tabes, Tuberculosis, Wastings, etc.).

REDUNDANT—Excessive—Overflowing —♀ in quality is redundant, excessive, and overflowing. Also ♃ is overflowing, and an afflicted ♃ or ♀ tend to excesses, gluttony, dissipation, surfeits, etc. (See Dissipation, Excessive, Gluttony, Jupiter Influence, Overflowing, Surfeits, Venus Influence, etc.).

REFINED — Refinement—Elegant—Excellent—

Refined Body — The ☉ in airy signs, refined mind and body; airy signs on the Asc. at B. (See Beautiful, Comely, Elegant, Handsome; "Pure Skin" under Skin).

Refined Expression — (See "Intellectual Look" under Look).

Refined Manners—(See "Elegant" under Manners).

Refined Mind — An Elegant Mind — (See "Elegant Mind" under Elegant).

Refined Tastes—(See Tastes).

Unrefined Manners—And Body—(See Unrefined).

REFLECTED — Reflection — Reflexes — Reflex Action — Reflex Action is principally the work of ☿. Reflected Excitement is a ☿ disease and affliction. Planets and Signs of the Zodiac have a reflex, or supplemental action, upon each other. Opposite Signs of the Zodiac have an especially strong reflex action upon each other. (See Ablation, Action, Antipathy, Aspects, Excitement, Opposites, Planets, Signs of the Zodiac, Sympathy, etc.).

REFORMERS — The desire to reform Social, Civic, Political, or Religious conditions is usually due to the strong influences of ♅ in the map of birth, and especially when in ☌ ♃ strongly placed, as in the Asc. or M.C. An afflicted ♅ may lead to violence, rebelliousness, and indiscreet methods in working Reforms. (See Anarchists, Destructiveness, Fanatical, Hygiene, Ideals, Independent, Judgment, Misunderstood, Persecution, Quarrelsome, Rashness, Reactionary, Recklessness, Religion, Revolutionary, Riotous, Socialism, Uranus, Violent, etc.).

REFRACTORY—Rebellious—Unruly—Ungovernable, etc.—♂ influence; ♂ afflicted in the Asc. or M.C.; born under ♂, and with ♂ in the 10th H., and afflicted by ♄. (See Anger, Choleric, Erratic, Perverse; "Unreasonable" under Reason; "High Temper" under Temper; Ungovernable, Unruly, Vicious; "Tendency To" under Violence).

REFRESHMENT—Rest—Sleep—Illness from Lack of Rest or Sleep—The ☽ in ♒, ☌, or ill-asp. ♄ (or ☿ if he be of the nature of ♄) at the beginning of an illness, or at decumbiture (Hor'y). (See "Brain Fag" under Brain; Fatigue, Rest; "Insomnia" under Sleep; Weariness).

REFRIGERANT — Cooling — A Therapeutic Property of ♄ and ♄ Remedies. Aconite, a ♄ remedy, is used to combat and cool down the high fevers produced by ♂. (See Cold, Cooling; "Treatment" under Fevers; Saturn).

REFUSE—The Refuse, or Wastes of the System — The Elimination of — (See Cleansing, Elimination, Excretion, Faeces, Fevers, Inflammation, Mars Influence, Sweat, Urine, Wastes, etc.).

REGENERATION — The Organs of — The Regenerative Organs—The Reproductive System — The Generative Organs—(See Generation, Genitals, Genito-Urinary, Privates, Reproduction, Secrets, Sex Organs, Womb, etc.).

REGRETFUL — Murmuring — Repining—♄ influence. (See Anguish, Anxiety, Brooding, Complaining, Dejected, Depressed, Despondent, Discontentment, Ennui, Exhibitionism, Fears, Grief, Hypochondria, Imaginations, Lamentations, Low Spirits, Melancholy; "No Peace of Mind" under Mind; Obsessions, Peevish, Repining, Retrospective, Sadness, Sorrow, Worry, etc.).

REGULAR—Regularity—

Bowels—The Bowels Should Be Kept Regular—(See "Open" under Bowels).

Features — (See "Regular" under Features).

Females—Regular Functions In—The ☽ hyleg in ♍ tends to give good regularity of the system and functions in females. The ☽ weak and afflicted, or in a fiery sign, tends to irregular and disturbed functions. The regularity of the female system and health after puberty depends almost entirely upon the conditions, positions, and affections of the ☽ and ♀. (See "Functions" under Females; "Irregular", "Regular", under Functions; Menses, Puberty).

Habits — Regular Habits Should Be Cultivated — (See "Regular" under Habits).

Health—Regularity of the Health In Females—(See "Functions" under Females; "Females" in this section). See Irregular, Periodical, Recurrent, Return.

REGULUS — Cor Leo — Cor Leonis — Lion's Heart—A violent fixed star of the nature of ♂, in the 28° ♌. Some Authors also say of the nature of H. It is said principally to give Military Honours, but to eventually end in ruin, disgrace, or a violent death, and especially if joined to either of the Luminaries. The influence of Regulus enters into many of the afflictions of life, and which have been listed and referred to under various subjects in this book. See the following subjects for the various influences of this Star— Accidents (Causes, Death By); Acute Disease (see "Hot Diseases" under Acute); Apoplexy (Cerebral); Blindness (Total, One Eye); Danger (Many Dangers); Death (see "Death by Accident" under Accidents); Disease (Threatened); Disgrace; Exercise (Eyes Injured); Extreme Sickness (see "Extreme" under Sickness); Eyes (see "Total", "One Eye", under Blindness); Father (Violent Diseases To); Fevers (see "Fevers" under Putrid); Gunshot (Gunshot Wounds); Head — Rush of Blood To—(see "Blood" under Head); Health (Periods of Bad Health); Hot Diseases (see "Hot Diseases" under Heat); Ill-Health (Signs of); Inflammation (Causes of); Injuries (Danger of); Medicines (Care In Taking); Mother Suffers (see "Danger", "Disease", under Mother); Parents (Afflicted); Pirates (Death By); Putrid (Fevers); Ruin; Sickness (Extreme);

Total Blindness (see Blindness); Violence—Violent (Danger By, Death By, Diseases).

REGURGITATION — (See this subject under Heart, Nose).

REINCARNATION—Rebirth—Metempsychosis — The Doctrine that the Soul lives many times in a physical body upon the Earth Plane—This Doctrine is believed in by three-fourths of the people of the World today. In the New Testament, the doctrine is rather veiled, but is there. The Occult Masters teach the doctrine of Reincarnation, and that each life on Earth is but a day in School, and to gain experience, knowledge, and Soul-Growth. One life in a physical body is but a small time to learn, and to gain wisdom, and also one life would not account for the various inequalities between people, their many diseases, deformities, malformations, monsters, limitations, missing members, idiocy, deafness; born blind, deaf, or dumb, etc., or the death of children in infancy. Every Soul, in its Evolution, must travel in a Cycle, and alternately in the upper half of the Circle, which is the Heaven, or Astral World, and then again in the lower half of the Circle, which is the Physical, or Material World, and it takes repeated experiences in both Worlds to perfect the Soul, as well as to reach a more perfect body, and one which can be free from disease, suffering, and death. These matters, and the Secret Mysteries in general, are taught in the Theosophical and Rosicrucian Doctrines. Also in the books, "Cosmo-Conception", by Max Heindel; "The Key of Destiny", by Dr. and Mrs. Homer Curtiss, of the Order of Christian Mystics, and by many others. This subject would be too long to go into fully here, but if you are interested to know the Truth, you can find it. (See Baptism, Character, Conception, External; "Ripe Fate" under Fate; Heliocentric, Heredity; "Moment of Birth" under Birth, Moment; Nativity, Prenatal Epoch).

REINS—Inward Parts—Loins—Region of the Kidneys—The Seat of the Feelings, Affections, and Passions are sometimes referred to as being in the Reins. "I am He which searcheth the Reins and Hearts" (Revelation 2:23). There are a number of references to the Reins in the Bible, and in the various books and textbooks they are referred to sometimes in a spiritual way, but mostly in a physical and material way, and as having reference to the body. The following subjects refer to Diseases and Afflictions in the Reins. In Astrology, the Reins are ruled by ♃, ♂, ♀, ♎, the 7th H., and also affected by all the cardinal signs. (See Kidneys, Loins).

Abscesses In — Imposthumes—Ulcers — A ♎ disease, and afflictions in ♎. (See Abscesses, Ulcers).

Affected — The Reins are affected when the ☉ is in ♒; ☽ in ♑; ♄ ♋, ♌; ♃ ♊, ♍; ♂ ♉, ♎; ♀ ♈, ♏; ☿ ♐, ♓. (See "Affected" under Head. Also see Table 196, in Simmonite's Arcana).

All Diseases In—Signified by the 6th H., the House of Health, and also by the conditions of the 7th H. and the ♎ sign.

Back — Reins of the Back — All Diseases In—♎ diseases, and afflictions in ♎. (See Back, Kidneys, Stone).

Blood In—Inflammation and Obstructions In the Reins Thru Bad Blood—♃ affl. in ♎. (See "Impure Blood" under Impure).

Consumption—Of the Inward Parts—♄ in ♌ when ♄ is the afflictor in the disease. (See Consumption).

Diseases Of—Disordered Reins—Distempers In—Infirmities In—The ☉ afflicted in ♎ or ♒; the ☽ afflicted in ♎; the ☽ in ♉ and afflicted by the ☉ or ♂ when taken ill (Hor'y); the ☽ in ♋, ☌, or ill-asp. ♄ (or ☿ if he be of the nature of ♄) at the beginning of an illness, or at decumb., and if the ☽ be decr., and near the body of ♄, the disease may continue a long time; the ☽ afflicted in ♑; ♄ afflicted in ♋, ♌, or ♎; ♃ afflicted in ♊ or ♍; ♂ affl. in ♎; ♀ affl. in ♈, ♎, or ♏; caused by afflictions to ♀; ☿ affl. in ♎, ♐, or ♓; afflictions in ♎, and a ♎ disease; Subs at KP. (See the paragraphs in this section).

Distempers In—(See "Diseases Of" in this section).

Heat In—Heats In—The ☽ in ♊, and afflicted by the ☉ or ♂ when taken ill (Hor'y). (See "Heats" under Buttocks, Heat, Loins).

Imposthumes — (See "Abscesses" in this section).

Infirmities In—(See "Diseases" in this section).

Inflammation In—(See "Blood" in this section).

Inward Parts—(See "Consumption Of" in this section).

Kidneys—Reins of the Kidneys—All Diseases In — (See "All Diseases Of" under Kidneys).

Loins — (See the paragraphs under Loins).

Moles On — (See "Location Of" under Moles).

Obstructions In—(See "Blood" in this section).

Pain In—The ☽ in ♉, and assisted by the ☉ or ♂ when taken ill (Hor'y).

Passions — Disorders of — (See the paragraphs under Desire, Passion).

Running of the Reins — (See Gonorrhoea).

Stone In — (See "Kidneys" under Stone).

Tumors In—♃ afflicted in ♎; ♃ in ♎ in the 6th H., and afflicted; ♃ in ♎, and afflicting the ☽ or Asc. (See Tumors).

Ulcers In — (See "Abscesses" in this section; Ulcers).

RELAPSES — Relapsing — Relapse In Disease—Relapsing Fevers—Relapses tend to occur when the Significator of the disease at decumbiture is in a double-bodied sign, as in ♊, the first half of ♐, or in ♓. If there is not a relapse, the disease may, under such conditions, change into some other form of disease, or disorder. The lord of the 1st H. in the 4th or 8th, ℞ or combust, the disease may be cured but afterwards relapse. (See Chronic, Complications, Continuity, Course, Crises; "Worse" under Disease; "Relapsing" under Fevers; Intermittent, Periodical, Prolonged, Remittent, Remote, Return, Sympathy).

RELATIVES — Relations — Brethren — Kindred—The 3rd, 6th, 7th, 9th, and 12th Houses rule Kindred and Brethren, according to the relationship. Note the various paragraphs in this section for these rulerships. Male relatives are ruled by ♂, and the ☽ and ♀ rule female relatives. Also ♅ rules Relatives in general. The following subjects have to do with Relatives, which see in the alphabetical arrangement when only listed here—

Aged Female—Death of In the Family—(See Aunts, Grandparents).

Aunts—Death of—(See Aunts).

Brethren—(See the paragraphs under Brethren).

Brothers; Children; Cousins — (See Cousins, Third House).

Cursed By—(See Execrated).

Danger To—An eclipse of the ☉ falling on the place of the radical ♄; ♅ stationary, and near the place of the ☉ or ☽ at B., or in evil asp. to either.

Daughter; Death Among—The ☉ or ☽ to the ill-aspects ♅ by dir.; the ☉ by dir. to the ill-asps. the ☽, Asc., or M.C., or to the ill-asps. his own place; the ☉ hyleg, and to the ☌ or ill-asps. ♄; the ☽ to the ill-asp. the ☉ or ♅ by dir.; the ☽ by periodic revolution to the ill-asp. the radical ♂; the ☽ at a Solar Rev. passing the place of the radical ♅; ♅ sta. near the place of the ☉ or ☽ at B., or in evil asp. to either; ♄ to the ill-asps. the ☉, ☽, ♀, or the M.C. by dir.; ♄ in the 3rd H. at B., and by dir. in evil asp. to the Asc.; ♄ in the 3rd H. at B., or ruler of the 3rd; the periodic direction of ♄ to the radical ☽; the ill-asps. of ♄ or ♂ to the hyleg, or to the ☉, ☽, Asc., or M.C.; ♄ to the ill-asps. ♀ by dir.; the Asc. to the bad asps. the ☽ by dir.; the M.C. to the bad asps. ♀ by dir.; malefics in the 8th H. at a Solar Rev.; the transit of malefics thru the 8th H., and especially if they afflict the 8th H. at B., or lord of the 8th; lord of the 12th a malefic, in the 3rd H., and afflicted. (See "Death Of" under Loved Ones, and also under the various subjects listed in this Article).

Deceitful Relatives—Injured By—(See Deceitful; "Enemies" in this section).

Distant Relatives—Death Of—The ☉ or ♂ by Periodic Rev. to the ☌, □, or ☍ ♅ in the radix.

Early Death Of—(See "Sickly" in this section).

Enemies Among—♄ or ♂ in the 3rd, 6th, or 12th H., or malefics as rulers of these houses. (See Deceitful; "Secret Enemies" under Enemies; "Plots" under Prison; Treachery; "Significators" in this section).

Execrated By—(See Execrated).

Family—(See the subjects under Family).

Father—Relatives on the father's side are ruled by the 6th H., and on the mother's side by the 12th H. Also the father's relatives are ruled by ♃, and those of the mother by ☿. (See "Relatives", and the various paragraphs under Father; "Aunts and Uncles" under Maternal).

Female Relatives — Death of — Death of an Aged Female Relative — Ill-Health of—The ☽ and ♀ rule female relatives, and afflictions to these planets by direction in the map of the native tend to the death of a female relative, or their illness, as the wife, mother, sister, or daughter; the ☽ hyleg in a female nativity, and to the ☌ or ill-asp. ♄ by dir.; the ☽ afflicted at B., and to the evil asps. the Asc. by dir.; ♅ or ♄ passing the place of the ☽ or ♀ at B. by transit, or ☌ the ☽ or ♀ at a Solar Rev.; ♂ passing the place of the radical ☽ at a Solar Rev. (See "Death", "Ill-Health", or "Sickness", under Aunts, Daughter, Females, Grandparents, Mother, Sister, Wife).

Few Brethren — (See "Few" under Brothers, Children).

Godfathers; Grandparents; Guardians;

Hated by Relatives—(See "Enemies" in this section; Hatred).

Husband—(See the paragraphs under Husband).

Ill-Health Of — (See Death, Female Relatives, Sickly, and the various paragraphs in this section).

Imprisoned By — (See "Plots" under Prison).

Long Life For—(See "Long Life" under Brothers, Father, Life, Mother, Sister).

Love Affairs—(See the paragraphs under Love Affairs).

Loved Ones — Death of — (See Loved Ones).

Male Relatives—Ruled by ♂.

Marriage — (See the subjects under Fiance, Husband, Love Affairs, Marriage, Marriage Partner, Wife).

Maternal—Maternal Aunts and Uncles —(See Maternal).

Mother—Mother-In-Law—Relatives of the Mother—(See Maternal; the paragraphs under Mother; "Father" in this section).

Near Relatives—

(1) Die Early In Life—Lord of the 6th in the 3rd, 6th, or 12th H. of the native. (See "Sickly" in this section).

(2) Have Poor Health — Lord of the 6th in the 3rd H. of the native. (See "Sickly" in this section).

(3) Danger To—Death of—The ☉ or ☽ to the ill-asps. ♅ by dir.; ♅ passing over the place of ♄ at B. by transit; lord of the 6th, 8th, or 12th, a malefic, and in the 3rd, 4th, 5th, 7th, or 10th H., and afflicted. (See "Danger", "Death", under Brothers, Children, Father, Husband, Mother, Wife, Sister; "Danger To", "Death Among", and the various paragraphs in this section).

Nephews—Nieces—(See Nieces).

Old Age—Brethren Do Not Live To—Lord of the 3rd in the 8th or 10th; lord of the 6th, 8th, or 12th a malefic in the 3rd, 6th, or 9th H., and afflicted. (See "Short Life" under Life; "Death At Middle Life" under Middle Life; Death, Early Death, Sickly, in this section).

Outlives Relatives—(See "Death Among", "Sickly", in this section).

Paternal Aunts and Uncles—(See "Paternal" under Aunts; "Relatives" under Father; Uncles; "Father" in this section).

Plots—The Victim of Plots of Relatives—(See "Enemies" in this section).

Quarrels with Relatives—(See "Relatives" under Quarrels; "Enemies", "Significators", in this section).

Short Life Of—Death, Old Age, Sickly, in this section).

Sickly and Short-Lived—The malefics afflicting the ☽ or ♀ in map of the native; malefics in the 3rd H., and afflicting or over-powering the benefics, or surrounding the ☉; malefics afflicting the M.C. and the maternal places in the map, as afflicting ♀ by day, or the ☽ by night, or the paternal places, as the ☉ by day, or ♄ by night. Afflictions to the ☉, ♄, or ♂ in the map of the native tend to sickness, and ill-health to his male relatives, and afflictions to the ☽ and ♀, to his female relations. (See "Death", and the various paragraphs in this section).

Significators Of—The 3rd H. and its lord are considered Significators of Brethren, Brothers, and Sisters. Venus by day, and the ☽ by night, are also Sigs. of Brethren, and if the ☽ and ♀ be in dignities, well-aspected by many planets, and also in favorable asp. to each other, the brethren will love each other, but if in signs inconjunct, or in evil familiarity, they will hate or injure each other. (See Antipathy, Compatibility, Execrated, Sympathy; "Enemies", "Quarrels", in this section).

Sisters; Social Relations; Sons;

Terror to Relatives—(See Execrated).

Treachery Of — (See Enemies, Hated, Quarrels, Significators, in this section).

Uncles—(See Aunts, Maternal, Paternal, Uncles).

Wife; Woman's Horoscope — The Father and Mother In—The Father-In-Law, etc.—(See Father, Fourth House, Mother, Tenth House).

RELAXATION — Relaxed — Relaxing — Laxity — Laxness — Prolapse — Relaxation of Animal Bodies, etc.—♆ and ♀ tend to relaxation of the tissues. Neptune is more relaxing than ♀, and is more elusive, protean, formless, and changeable. Moisture and Moist Diseases, as given by ♆ and ♀, tend to relaxation of tissues. (See "Damp Vapors", "Relaxation", under Moisture; "Animal Bodies" under Putrefaction).

Cutis Relaxed—(See Derma).

Drooping Body—(See Limp).

Dull — (See Dull, Ease, Idle, Inertia, Labor, Lassitude, Lazy).

Energy — (See "Lack Of" under Energy; Feeble, Inactive, Inertia; "Weak Body" under Body).

Feeble — (See Debility, Dull, Feeble, Inactive, Inertia, Infirm, etc.).

Fiber—(See "Laxity" under Fiber).

Flabby—(See Flabby, Soft Tissues).

General Relaxation—A ♀ disease, and due to an afflicted ♀; ♓ on the Asc., or with the ☉, ☽, and many planets in this sign, as ♓ has a relaxing influence on the tissues. (See Dull; "Lack Of" under Energy; Lethargy; "Low" under Vitality; "Weak Body" under Weak).

Heat—Heat is relaxing, and cold is contracting. The heat of ♂ tends to relax the cutis and veins which have been contracted by the cold of ♄. (See Heat).

Lassitude—(See Lassitude, Listless).

Laxity—(See Laxity; the various paragraphs in this section).

Limp—Drooping—(See Limp).

Moisture—Moist Diseases—Moisture is relaxing. (See "Damp Vapors", "Relaxation", under Moisture).

Muscular Tissues—Laxity of—(See "Laxity" under Muscles).

Prolapse—(See the paragraphs under Prolapse).

Stimulus—Loss of—(See Dull; "Lack Of" under Energy; Lassitude, Lethargy; "General Relaxation" in this section).

Throat—Relaxed Throat—(See "Relaxed" under Throat).

Tissues—Relaxed Tissues—Softening of the Tissues—♆ and ♀ diseases; the ☽ in ♓, and ♓ influence; ♓ on the Asc. (See Emollient, Flabby, Malacia, Softening, Tissues; "General Relaxation" in this section).

Veins Relaxed—(See "Relaxation" under Veins; "Heat" in this section).

Viscera Relaxed—(See Viscera).

Weak and Relaxed Body—(See Debility, Feeble, Flabby, Infirm, Invalids; "Depletion" under Vital; "Low" under Vitality; "Weak Body" under Weak).

RELIABLE—Trustworthy—Honest—(See Character, Honest, Honorable, Humane; "Manly and Sober" under Manners; "Good Morals" under Morals; Noble, Religion, Responsibility, Sincere, etc.).

RELIEF IN DISEASE—(See Amelioration, Crises; "Better" under Disease; Ease, Moderation, Modification, Recovery, Recuperation, Resolution, etc.).

RELIGION—Piety—Devotion—Veneration—Adoration—Beliefs—Ecclesiastical Matters—Spiritual Matters—The Clergy—The Churches—The State of the Mind and the Relation of the Native to Such Matters, etc.—The Ninth House, the house of the Higher Mind, is classed as the House of Religion and Philosophy, and rules such matters, and also the ♐ sign, the 9th Sign, which Sign affiliates with the 9th H. Also ♃, the ruler of the ♐ Sign, rules Religion, along with ♐ and the 9th H. A powerful ♃ at B., and the 9th H. occupied by benefics at B., or ruled by a benefic, and free from the affliction of malefics, tend to make one very religious, pious, conscientious, honest, just, noble, sincere, generous, faithful, and to be more of the Orthodox type. The influence of ♅ in the 9th H., or afflicting ♃, tends to advanced, independent, occult, and metaphysical views of Truth, and with a desire to know the Mysteries and the Inner Truths of all Religions, and such Uranus characters are usually termed "Unorthodox." The following subjects have to do with Religion, Religious Views of the native, and the effects of such upon his mind, character, conduct, actions, and health, etc. See these subjects in the alphabetical arrangement when only listed here—

Advocates—Advocates Some Unpopular Religious Dogma—(See "Unpopular" in this section).

Anarchists; Anchorites—(See Celibacy; "Anchorite" under Husband).

Argumentative—In Religious and Other Matters—♂ and ♅ in ♊, and especially when in the 3rd H., and afflicting ☿. (See Quarrelsome).

Ascetic—(See Self-Denying).

Atheistical—The ☽ separating from the ☉ and applying to ☿ in a day geniture; ♆ ☌ ♂; ♅ or ♂ in ♐, and afflicted; ♂ afflicted in the 9th H., and with frankness and freedom of expression. (See "Irreligious" in this section).

Awakening—Religious Awakening—(See "Exaltation" under Emotions).

Awe and Fear—(See "Religious" under Fears).

Banished—On Account of His Religion or Political Views—(See Banishment, Execrated, Exile, Imprisonment; "Unpopular" in this section).

Beside Oneself—(See Excitable).

Bigoted In Religion—♂ Sig. ⚹ or △ ♄; ♂ afflicted in the 9th H. (See Fanatical, Hypocritical, Intolerance, in this section).

Blasphemy—Usually occurs in a coarse map, with many afflictions, and planets weak and out of dignity; ♂ afflicted in the 9th H., or ♂ ☌ ♃ in the 9th, and with ♃ also otherwise weak by sign, and afflicted by the ☉, ☽, and malefics. (See Atheistical, Bigoted, Intolerance, Irreligious, Scornful, in this section).

Cares Nothing for Religion—(See "Irreligious" in this section).

Ceremoniousness—Religious Ritualism—Fond of—Mania For—♃ strong at B., and well aspected, or in the 9th H.; the water signs predominant at B.; ♅ entering into the configuration gives desire for more show and ceremony where there is an occult purpose or meaning; ♄ and ☿ strong at B., little desire for ceremoniousness unless it be along the more stately and solemn lines; ♂ likes military ceremony; ♌, ♏, ♑ characteristics. Case—Mania for Religious Ceremony—See "Marriage", No. 834, in 1001 N.N. (See Magic).

Changeable—Inconstant In Religion—The ☽ afflicted in the 9th H. (See Credulity, Easy of Belief, in this section).

Chaotic Religious Mania—Chaotic Mind—(See "Mental Chaos" under Chaotic; "Religious Mania" under Mania).

Church Affairs—Fortunate In—Unfortunate In—(See Clergymen, Fortunate, Preferment, Unfortunate, in this section; Clergymen).

Churches—Cathedrals—Monasteries—Profanation of—An eclipse of the ☉ in the 3rd Decan. of ♌, ruled by ♂.

Clergymen—Ministers—Priests—

(1) Anxiety and Sadness To — (See Clergymen).

(2) Enemies Among—Hated or Execrated by the Clergy — Trouble Thru the Clergy—♄ Sig. □ or ☍ ♃; ♄ ☌ ♂ in the 9th H.; ♂ Sig. □ or ☍ ♃, on account of Theological opinions; ♀ Sig. □ or ☍ ♃, many enemies among the Clergy. (See Atheistical, Banished, Unfortunate, Unorthodox, Unpopular, in this section).

(3) Success As a Clergyman — Gains by Preaching—♄ Sig. ☌ ♃; ♃ Sig. ☌ ☿, a good Divine; ♂ Sig. ☌ ♃, success in the Church, and at Law. (See Fortunate, Pious, Preferment, in this section).

Contempt for Religion — Comets appearing in ♑, contempt for religion prevalent. (See Anarchists, Atheistical, Blasphemy, Irreligious, Scornful, in this section).

Cranks—Religious Cranks—(See Anarchists, Fanatical, Intolerance, Radicalism, Reformers, Unorthodox, and the various paragraphs in this section).

Credulity—Easy of Belief On Slight Evidence or Thought—(See Influenced; "Shallow" under Mentality; "Light in Mind" under Mind; "Mutable Disposition" under Mutable; Negative Nature, Receptive, Susceptible; "Changeable" in this section).

Curious Beliefs—♄ in the 9th H. at B., and afflicted, curious beliefs and superstitions.

Daring — In Expressing Religious Views—♂ in the 9th H.

Death — By Religious Persecution — (See Persecution).

Delusions; Desperate Sectarian—(See "Sectarian" in this section).

Destructiveness — (See "Iconoclasm" in this section).

Devils—Demons—Possessed of—(See Demoniac, Obsessions, Spirit Controls).

Devotion — Devout In Religion — ♃ governs devotion; ♃ well-aspected in ♐ or the 9th H.; ♃ in the Asc. or M.C. in ♐; the 2nd face of ♐ on the Asc. (See Emotions, Honest, Humane, Kind, Sincere, Spiritual; "Pious" in ths section).

Disease—Caused by Religion—♃ afflicting the ☽, Asc., and dispositors of the Lights, and especially if ♃ is lord of an evil house. (See "Disorders Of" under Emotions; Fears, Insanity, Madness; "Religious" under Mania; Obsessions, Spirit Controls).

Dishonest—In Religion—(See Deceitful, Dishonest, Dual, Hypocritical; "False" in this section).

Dogma — Advocates Some Unpopular Religious Dogma — (See "Unpopular" in this section).

Dreads—Religious Dreads and Fears —(See Dreads, Fears).

Easy of Belief — ☿ ill-dignified at B. (See "Changeable", "Credulity", in this section).

Ecstasy—Religious Ecstasy—A ♆ disease and affliction; caused by ♆ afflictions at B., and the result of religious excitement, and predominance of the psychic and spiritual powers. Also produced by the Ether, or Luminous Gas in the Spinal Canal, vibrating the Pineal Gland, and the greater the rate of vibration the more the native sees. A high rate of supernormal vibration of the Pineal Gland tends to religious ecstasy. (See "Exaltation" under Emotions; "Beside Oneself", "Religious Excitement" under Excitable; Happiness, Neptune, Pineal).

Egotistical Religious Notions — ♆ afflicted in the 9th H. (See Ego).

Elation — (See "Exaltation" under Emotions).

Emotionalism—(See Emotions).

Enemy To the Church — ♄ influence; ♄ ill-dignified and badly aspected in the 9th H. (See Contempt, Irreligious, in this section).

Established Religion — Fanatically Against—In Favor of — (See Atheistical, Contempt, Devotion, Faith, Fanatical, Fundamentalist, Irreligious, Orthodox, Unorthodox, and the various paragraphs in this section).

Enthusiasts—(See Fanatical, Sectarian, in this section; Enthusiasm).

Evil Spirits — Obsessed By — (See "Devils" in this section).

Exaltation — (See "Exaltation" under Emotions).

Excitement—(See "Exaltation", "Uncontrolled", under Emotions; "Religious" under Excitement; Frenzy).

Excommunicated—(See Banished, Clergymen, Persecution, Unpopular, in this section).

Exiled — On Account of Religious or Political Beliefs — (See Banishment, Execrated, Exile).

Faith—Strong Religious Faith—Given by ♃, ♐, and the 9th H. well-aspected; benefics in the 9th H., and well-aspected. Also given by the fiery signs, and especially ♌ and ♐. Aquarius gives strong religious leaders, Mystics, and Occultists. (See Devotion, Pious, in this section).

False Religionists—The ☉ Sig. ☌ ♃, and ♃ ill-aspected and ill-dignified at B.; the ☽ ruler of the employment, in her decrease, in ♈, ♌, or ♎, and configurated with ☿, and with ♅ strong and aspected by ☿ or the ☽. (See Bigoted, Contempt, Cranks, Dishonest, Fanatical, Hypocritical, Iconoclasm, in this section).

Fanatical—Ranters—Intemperate or Irrational Zeal — The ☉ in ♑ in an angle, and afflicting ♂ and ☿; the ☉ Sig. ☌ ♃, and ♃ ill-aspected and ill-dignified at B.; the ☽ ruler of the employment, in her decrease, in ♈, ♌, or ♎, and with ♅ strong and aspected by ☿ or the ☽; ♆ or ♅ ☌, P., □ or ☍ ♂; ♅ ruler of the horoscope and afflicted; ♅ afflicted in the 9th H., fanatical in whatever Cause they espouse; ♅ or ♂ in ♐, and afflicted, fanatical against Established Religion and Society; ♅ □ or ☍ ☿, raving in public; ♅ afflicted in ♊ or ♐; ♅ □ or ☍ ♀; ♄ afflicted in the

9th H. tends to a sombre kind of intolerance or bigotry; ♅ or ♂ afflicted in the 9th H., or giving their evil aspects to this house, or to the lord of the 9th H., and ♀ and the ♎ sign are also usually involved in such afflictions; caused by the □ or ☍ aspects of ♅ to the 9th H., lord of the 9th, or planets in the 9th, or in ♐; ♂ ruler of the horoscope, and afflicted; ♂ afflicted in the 9th H.; ♂ afflicting ♃ tends to religious enthusiasm; ☿ in ♓, angular, and afflicted by the ☉ or ♂; ☿ ☌ or ☍ ♂. (See Anarchists, Enthusiasm, Fanatical, Genius, Prodigies, Radicalism, Reactionary, Reformers; Argumentative, Bigoted, Cranks, Iconoclasm, Property, Sectarian, in this section).

Fanciful—Indulges In Fanciful Speculations About Religion — ♃ Sig. ☌ ☉, and the ☉ ill-aspected and ill-dignified at B. (See Chaotic, Confusion; "Dreamy" under Dreams; Fancies; "Bad" under Judgment; "Light In Mind" under Mind).

Fatalism—(See Scepticism).

Fears—Religious Fears—Ruled by ♆. (See Awe, Chaotic, Dreads, Demoniac, Dreads, Forebodings, Insanity, Mania, Obsessions, Spirit Controls, Superstition, Veneration, in this section; "Religious" under Fears).

Feelings—Inclined to Religious Feelings—The 6th face of ♋ on the Asc. (See Devotion, Pious, in this section).

Forebodings; Forms — Fond of Religious Forms and Ceremonial — (See "Ceremoniousness" in this section).

Fortunate—In Church Affairs—♄, ♂, ♀, or the ☽ ☌ ♃. (See "Clergymen" in this section).

Freedom of Thought — (See Daring, Independent, Misunderstood, Modernists, Persecuted, in this section).

Frenzy — (See "Religious" under Frenzy).

Fundamentalist — ♃ well-aspected in the 9th H., and with no malefics in the 9th, or afflicting the 9th, or lord of the 9th. (See Clergymen, Devotion, Faith, Fortunate, Orthodox, Pious, in this section).

Hallucinations; Hated by Clergymen —(See "Clergymen" in this section).

Healers—(See "Divine Healers" under Healers).

Heretical—(See Atheistical, Contempt, False Religionists, Freedom, Independent, Irreligious, Misunderstood, Persecuted, in this section).

Hypocritical—Insincere—(See Deceitful, Dishonest, Dual, Hypocritical; "False" in this section).

Iconoclasm — Image-Breaking—Radicalism — ♅ and ♂ are the destructive planets in religious or political matters. Violent configurations in the 9th H. tend to Iconoclasm in religious matters, such as ♅ ☌ ♂ in the 9th. Also ♅ or ♂ □ ☉, and with ♄ obscurely placed. (See Anarchists, Destructiveness, Radicalism, Reactionary, Reformers; Fanatical, Lawless, in this section).

Ideals; Ideas; Illumination — No certain judgment can be made from the Chart of Birth as to the degree and nature of illumination which proceeds from a spiritual source. Religion is an inherent aspiration of the Soul, and not a Man-made Institution, but is capable of transcending all external interests and affections, and the planetary influences at B. However, ♆, the ruler of the Pineal Gland, strong at B., tends to greater vibration of the Pineal, and to ecstasy, exaltation, and greater spiritual sight and illumination. (See Character, Intuition, Pineal, Spiritual).

Illusions; Image-Breaking — (See "Iconoclasm" in this section).

Imaginations; Inclined to Religion— (See Devotion, Feelings, Pious, in this section).

Inconstant—In Religion—(See Changeable, Credulity, Easy of Belief, in this section).

Independent — In Religious Matters and Thinking—(See Independent, Metaphysical, Misunderstood, Occult, Science, Truth; "Freedom" in this section)

Infidels — (See Heretical, Scepticism, in this section).

Injured—On Account of His Religion —Caused by fixed stars of the nature of ♃ if joined to the Anareta, or mixed with those of the nature of ♄ or ♂. (See Persecution; Banished, Clergymen, Unpopular, in this section).

Insanity; Intolerance — Self-Opinionated In Religious Matters — Religious Intolerance — Afflictions in or to the 9th H.; ☿ and ♅ in fixed signs, and in □ or ☍; ☿ in a fixed sign and afflicted by ♄ or ♂ from fixed signs; ☿ and ♅ in ☍ asp. from ♉ and ♏; the ☉ and ☽ in fixed signs in □ or ☍ asp., and with ♃ and the 9th H. afflicted. (See "Religion" under Public; Bigoted, Fanatical, Sectarian, in this section).

Intuition; Irreligious—Cares Nothing for Religion—The ☽ incr., or at Full, in a day geniture, sepr. from ☿ and apply. to ♂; strong ♄ characters, or with ♄ ruler at B., or ♄ in the 9th H. and afflicting the ☉, ☽, ♃, or ☿; ♃ or ♂ afflicting ☿; ♀ ill-dignified at B., cares little for religion. (See Atheistical, Contempt, Enemy, Heretical, Perjured, Scepticism, in this section).

Lawless — In Religious Matters — Afflictions to ♃; ♂ ☌, P., □, or ☍ ♆. (See "Iconoclasm" in this section).

Leaders — Religious Leaders — (See Clergymen, Faith, Fortunate, in this section).

Magic; Mania—(See "Religious Mania" under Mania; "Ceremoniousness" in this section).

Mediumship; Melancholia—Case—See "Religious Melancholia", No. 976, in 1001 N.N.

Metaphysical—♆ and ♅ strong at B., and well-aspected. (See Metaphysics).

Ministers—Priests—(See "Clergymen" in this section).

Misunderstood—(See Independent, Metaphysics, Misunderstood, Occult, Opinions; Banished, Clergymen, Daring, Freedom, Heretical, Iconoclasm, Persecution, Unorthodox, Unpopular, in this section).

Mockery; Modernists—♅ or ♂ in the 9th H. (See Freedom, Independent, in this section).

Monasteries—(See "Churches" in this section).

Much Given to Religion—The ☉ Sig. ☌ ♃ if ♃ is strong and well-aspected at B. (See Devotion, Enthusiasts, Faith, Fanatical, Pious, in this section).

Mystics—Mysticism—(See Mystical).

Obsessions; Occultists—(See Occult).

Opinions—Beliefs—Persecuted On Account of — (See Banished, Clergymen, Execrated, Persecuted, Unpopular, in this section).

Orthodox—In Religious Views—(See Clergymen, Devotion, Faith, Fundamentalist, Pious, in this section).

Peculiar Beliefs—(See Anarchists, Atheistical, Cranks, Fanatical, Freedom, Heretical, Independent, Intolerance, Metaphysical, Misunderstood, Occult, and the various paragraphs in this section; Peculiar).

Perjured—The ☽ incr. or at full in a day geniture, sepr. from ☿ and apply. to ♂. (See Atheistical, Blasphemy, Dishonest, False Religionists, Hypocritical, Irreligious, in this section; Perjury).

Persecution — (See Banished, Clergymen, Death, Exiled, Metaphysical, Misunderstood, Occult, Opinions, Unpopular, in this section; Persecution).

Perversions—(See Perversions; "Perversions" under Spiritual).

Philosophical—(See Philosophy).

Pious — Piety — A Religious Disposition — Devotion — Veneration — Much Given to Religion and Worship—The ☉ Sig. ☌ ♃; the ☽ decr. in a day geniture, and applying to ♀ in the 10th H., tends to make Prelates, religious Leaders, builders of Churches, etc.; ♄ Sig. ⚹ or △ ♃; ♃ well-aspected in the 9th H., and especially with ♃ in ♐; ♃ in the Asc., M.C., or 9th H., and well-aspected; ♃ strong at B., in one of his own signs or houses, and well-aspected; ♃ well-aspected in ♐ or ♓; ♂, ♀, or ☿ Sig. ☌ ♃. (See Devotion, Faith, Feelings, Much Given, Spiritual, Veneration, in this section).

Popular In Religion — (See "Fortunate" in this section).

Preaching—Gains By—(See "Clergymen" in this section).

Preferment—Ecclesiastical Preferment—The ☽, ♄, ♂, or ♀ Sig. ☌ ♃. (See Clergymen, Fortunate, in this section).

Prelates — (See Clergymen, Pious, in this section).

Premonitions; Priests — (See Clergymen, Fortunate, Pious, in this section).

Profanation of Churches — (See "Churches" in this section).

Property — Property Is Impoverished by Hypocritical Fanatics—The ☽ Sig. □ or ☍ ♃. (See Property).

Prophetic; Psychic Powers — (See Psychic).

Rabid Sectarian—(See "Sectarian" in this section).

Radicalism; Ranters — (See "Fanatical" in this section).

Raving In Public — (See "Fanatical" in this section).

Reactionary; Reformers;

Renunciation; Revolutionary;

Ritualism — (See "Ceremoniousness" in this section; "Ceremonial Magic" under Magic).

Sanctimonious—Self-Righteousness—Caused by the afflictions of ♅ or ♄ to ☿; ♆ ☌ ♂ in ♓; ♄ in the 9th H., and especially in ♌; ♂ afflicted in ♉. (See Argumentative, Devotion, Pious, Self-Righteousness, in this section).

Scepticism — ♃ afflicted in ♊ or ♍. (See Argumentative, Atheistical, Heretical, in this section; Scepticism).

Scornful — (See Mockery, Scornful; Blasphemy, Contempt, Enemy, Iconoclasm, Irreligious, Profanation, in this section).

Sectarian—Rabid Sectarian—Desperate Sectarian—♄, ♂, or ☋ in the 9th H., a desperate Sectarian; ♂ afflicting ♃, and with other testimonies, a rabid Sectarian. (See Fanatical, Intolerance, in this section).

Seers—(See Prophetic, Seers).

Self-Exaltation—Of a Religious Kind —♆ or ♃ afflicting the ☉ or ☿. (See "Self-Righteousness" in this section).

Self-Opinionated — (See "Intolerance" in this section).

Self-Righteousness — Ego Exaltation —♓ influence; ♂ ☌ ♆ in ♓; ♌ influence; ♄ in ♌, and ruler of the 9th H.; ☿ affl. in ♓; many planets in □ asp. to the ♓ sign, and afflicting planets in ♓; ♂ in ♉ tends to obstinacy in religious matters, and a refusal to change beliefs, or admit one is wrong; ♄ and ♅ afflictions to ☿. (See Argumentative, Bigoted, Egotistical, Pious, Sanctimonious, Self-Exaltation, in this section).

Sincere—In Religion—(See Devotion, Faith, Pious, in this section).

Skepticism—(See Skepticism; "Unorthodox" in this section).

Socialism; Speculative—In Religion—(See Atheistical, Changeable, Credulity, Easy of Belief, Fanciful, Heretical, in this section).

Speech—Freedom of Speech In—(See Daring, Freedom, Hated, Independent, Intolerance, Misunderstood, Persecution, in this section).

Spirit Controls — (See Demoniac, Obsessions, Spirit Controls).

Spiritual Powers — (See Character, Ego, Individuality, Intuition; "Higher Mind" under Mind; Neptune, Pineal, Soul, Spirit, Spiritual, etc.).

Spiritualism—♆ strong at B. tends to the beliefs of Spiriualism, and to give the special powers and faculties for Spirit Communications, Mediumship, etc. (See Clairvoyance, Mediumship, Mystical, Psychic, Seances, Spirit Controls, Spiritualism).

Stoicism — Self-Abnegation — Given largely by the ♏ and ♒ Signs. Also indicated by the stubborn indifference of the ♉ sign, and especially when ♄ is strongly placed, and the negative signs predominant.

Strange Views—Strange and Chaotic Views Regarding Religion and the Higher Life—♆ in the 9th H. (See Chaotic, Fancies, Metaphysics, Mysterious, Mystical, Occult, Spiritual, Strange, Superstitious, Visionary, Weird).

Superstitious — (See Awe, Dreads, Fears, Veneration, in this section; Forebodings, Horrors, Premonitions, Superstitious, Terrors, Uncanny, Visions, Weird, etc.).

Theological Opinions—Popular or Unpopular On Account of — (See Clergymen, Excommunicated, Fortunate, Unorthodox, Unpopular, and the various paragraphs in this section).

Truth — A lover and Seeker After Truth In Religious Matters—♆ and ♅ influences strong and predominant at B. (See Knowledge, Learning, Metaphysics, Mysterious, Mystical, Neptune, Occult, Philosophy, Pineal, Psychic, Spiritual, Study, Truth, Uranus).

Unfortunate — In Religion or Church Work—Malefics in the 9th H., and afflicted, and especially ♄ or ♂ in this house. (See Banished, Clergymen, Execrated, Exile, Persecution, Unpopular, in this section).

Unorthodox — ♅ in the 9th H. (See Independent, Metaphysics, Misunderstood, Mystical, Occult, Skepticism, Science; Freedom, Truth, Unpopular, in this section).

Unpopular—Advocates Unpopular Religious Dogma — Lord of the 10th a malefic in the 12th H.; lord of the 12th H. a benefic in the 9th H.; ☿ Sig. □ or ☍ ♃, is persecuted because of his singular religious opinions. (See Unfortunate, Unorthodox, in this section).

Utopianism; Veneration — (See Awe, Fears, Pious, Superstititious, in this section).

Views — Beliefs — Opinions — (See Ideals, Ideas, Morals, Motives, Opinions, Principles, Purposes; the various paragraphs in this section).

Visions—Visionary—(See Visions).

Weird; Wicked—(See Evil, Wicked).

Zeal—(See Enthusiasts, Fanatical, Sectarian, in this section).

REMARKABLE — Unusual — Extraordinary—Singular—Sudden, etc.—

Remarkable Death — ♅ as the afflicting planet tends to death in some remarkable, extraordinary, sudden, unusual, or violent manner; ♄ and ♂ both in evil aspect to the ☉ and ☽, or even only one, and at the same time the Asc. be afflicted; the malefics in ☌ or ☍, and lords of the anaretic places, and if one or more malefics attack the ☉ or ☽. (See "Death" under Accidents, Extraordinary, Mysterious, Peculiar, Sudden, Untimely, Unusual, Violent).

Remarkable Misfortunes — (See Calamity, Disgrace, Dishonour, Events, Evils, Fortune, Misfortune, Prison, Property, Reputation, Reverses, Riches, Ruin, etc.).

Remarkable Persons — Remarkable Individuals represent a climax, or the greatest altitude in the family line, from whence the pendulum turns and moves in the opposite direction. (See Genius, Great, Heredity, Mathematician, Prodigies, etc.).

Remarkable Sickness — (See "Diseases" under Extraordinary).

REMEDIES—Remedy—Palliatives—The Modification, Cure, and Relief of Physical, Mental, or Spiritual Ailments—Therapeutics — Treatment, etc. — The main object of a remedy, as related to the human mind and body, is to counteract an undesirable condition. This can be done in manifold ways, and where spiritual, mental, and material means are used. Articles on the Therapeutic Properties of Remedies are listed in this book in the alphabetical arrangement. Also, in the Article on "Drugs", you will find quite a complete list of Remedies, and their Therapeutic actions, and this list will not be repeated here. Only the more abstract conditions about Remedies will be included in this Article. See the following subjects in the alphabetical arrangement—

Acid Conditions — In the Body — Require An Alkaline Remedy to Neutralize — A good remedy to use as a drink several times a day is the Granular Effervescent Citrocarbonate put up by Upjohn, which is alkaline, and tends to relieve Acidosis, Hyperacidity, Gout, Rheumatism, etc. (See Acids, Alkaline, Antipathy, Hyperacidity).

Alkalinity—(See "Acid Conditions" in this section; Acids, Alkalinity).

Antidotes; Antipathy—Remedies Which Oppose the Condition—(See Antipathy, Opposites, Polarity, Sympathy).

Colors As Remedies—(See Colors).

Cooling Remedies—Refrigerants—(See Cooling).

Cosmetics — Beautifying Remedies — (See Cosmetics).

Curable Diseases—Diseases Which Have a Remedy—(See Curable, Incurable).

Drugs As Remedies — Remedies by Drugs should be chosen according to the Temperament. Mars remedies should be used for ♂ people; ♄ remedies for ♄ people; ☉ remedies for ☉ people. This would be treating by Sympathy, or the Homeopathic principle. (See Homeopathy, Sympathy). By antipathy, ♂ people should use ♄ remedies, as ♄ opposes the diseases of ♂. This is the Allopathic Principle of treating by Opposites. (See the list of Therapeutic Properties of Drugs under Drugs. Also see Antipathy, Opposites). In every region of the Earth, and where the various maladies originate, there is also in that Region a Remedy, an Antidote, an Herb, a Metal, a Mineral, etc., all found in Nature, which has been placed there to relieve and combat the diseases of that locality, and the Native Medicine Men in the most obscure places are familiar with such remedies, and remedies which have been imported from other places, or Countries, may not be as efficacious as local ones. (See Drugs, Medicines, Praeincipients, Treatment).

Exciting Remedies—The remedies of ♂ are exciting, such as Aphrodisiacs,

Caustics, Rubefacients, Stimulants, Tonics. etc. (See these subjects. Also see Depressants; "Therapeutics Qualities" under Mars).

Healers—The Various Forms of Healing, and the Use of Remedies — (See the paragraphs under Healers).

Herbs As Remedies—(See Herbs).

Hurts—Hurts and Injuries Which Are Incapable of Remedy — Malefics in angles, well fortified, and preferably in fixed signs, elevated above the Luminaries and the Benefics, and the latter in weak signs, and in ♂, □, or 8 the malefics. Such configurations in the Chart of Birth tend to permanent defects, and to make the effects of disease, hurts, and injuries more lasting, or to result in death. (See Events; "Remedy" under Hurts, Injuries; Incurable, Permanent).

Incapable of Remedy — (See "Hurts" in this section).

Incurable—(See "Hurts" in this section).

Injuries—Incapable of Remedy—(See "Hurts" in this section).

Medicines As Remedies—(See Drugs, Herbs, Medicines, Roots, Therapeutics, Treatment).

Mental Remedies—(See Healers, Hypnotism, Magic, Magnetic, Psychic, Spiritual, Suggestion).

Periodic Remedies—(See Periodic).

Planetary Remedies—(See Antipathy, Herbs, Medicines, Metals, Minerals, Opposites, Planets, Polarity, Praecipients, Sympathy, Treatment, etc. Also see "Metal", "Remedies", "Therapeutical Qualities", "Typical Drugs", under each of the Planets).

Poisons As Remedies — (See "Remedies" under Poison).

Polycrest Remedies—(See "Polycrest" under Zodiac).

Proper Remedy Used—(See "Moderation of Disease" under Moderation). For the influences where improper remedies may be used see "Compatibility", "Death", "Poisoned", under Healers; "Care Taken", "Improper Medicines", under Medicines).

Quieting Remedies — (See Anaesthetics, Anaphrodisiac; "Quieting Remedies" under Quiet: Sedatives, Soothing, etc.).

Suggestion—Suggestive Therapeutics —Easily Affected by Suggestion—(See Environment, External, Influenced, Negative, Receptive, Suggestion, Susceptibility).

Sympathy—Remedies by Sympathy— (See Sympathy).

Therapeutics; Tissue Remedies—(See "Zodiac Salts" under Healers).

Treatment of Disease — (See Antipathy, Cure, Drugs, Events, Healers, Hygiene, Medicines, Opposites, Praecipients, Prevention, Sanitation, Sympathy, Treatment, etc.).

Zodiac Remedies—(See Zodiac).

REMISSION—The Remission of Disease — Abatement — Amelioration — The period of abatement in fevers is under the rule of ♀. The remission of dis-

ease is associated with the common signs, and disease tends to fall off, and to be alleviated, as the afflicting planets leave the cardinal signs and pass into the mutable signs. Cardinal signs show the intensity of the disease. (See Abatement, Amelioration, Cataphora, Continuity, Course, Crises; "Better" under Disease; Duration, Ease, Intermittent, Moderation, Modification, Recovery, Recuperation, Remittent, Resolution, Solution, etc.).

REMITS — The Pulse Remits — (See "Slow" under Pulse).

REMITTENT—Alternately Abating and Returning — Remittent Fevers — The Daily Return of Fever—Intermittent—Irregular, etc. — These influences are discussed and given under the following subjects. (See Ague, Amelioration, Complications, Course, Crises, Ease, Epilepsy, Fever, Insanity, Intermittent, Irregular, Malaria, Moderation, Peculiar, Periodical, Quality, Quartan, Quotidian, Remission, Return, Semi-Tertian, Tertian, Various, etc.).

REMORSE — Remorselessness — (See Cruel, Gloom, Low Spirits, Merciless, Worry, etc.).

REMOTE ORGANS — A close relationship exists between the opposite signs of the Zodiac, as between ♈ and ♎, between 8 and ♏, etc. Thus a disease in the Reproductive System, or the Genito-Urinary System, ruled by ♏, will be apt to affect the throat, voice, or neck, ruled by 8. This is the cause of the shifting of disease. (See Ablation, Complications, Course, Crises; "Shifting" under Disease; "Ablation" under Ovaries, Tonsils; Relapse, Removal, Suppressions).

REMOVAL—Of Organs or Parts of the Body — Ablation — Suppression, etc.— Such organs as the Tonsils, Ovaries, or the Mammae, may be removed, suppressed, shrunken, or absorbed, by the influences in opposite signs of the Zodiac, and known as pairs of signs, such as 8 and ♏, ♋ and ♑, etc. Afflictions in ♏ tend to affect the tonsils, throat, voice, and to cause defects in, loss of voice, abnormal changes in the voice, the shrinking up or loss of the tonsils, etc. Afflictions in ♑, by reflex action, may cause the shrinking up, ablation, loss of, or loss of function of the Mammae, the Milk Glands of the Breasts. Also afflictions in ♏, when not causing ablation, or removal of organs or parts ruled by 8, may cause diseases in the parts ruled by 8. Dr. Duz, the French Astrologer, in his book, "Astral Medicine", on page 80, discusses the theories of Ablation, and Removal of Organs by opposite sign influences. (See Remote, Suppression).

Operations — Removal of Organs or Parts by Surgical Operations, and Rules for Time of Operations, etc. — (See Operations).

REMOVALS—Changes of Residence or Location—(See Abroad, Foreign Lands, Location; "Native Land" under Native; "Place of Birth" under Place; Residence, Travel, Wanderer, etc.).

RENAL — Pertaining to the Kidneys — (See "Renal" under Kidneys).

RENDING OF PARTS — (See Bursting, Lacerations; "Accelerated" under Motion; Rupture).

RENEWALS—In the System—(See Conservation, Glycogen, Preservation, Readaptation, Recovery, Recuperation, Restoration, Revitalization).

RENOWN—Fame—Desire for Eminence and Distinction — Becomes Renowned —The ☉ Sig. in ♈, becomes famous; the ☉ strong at B., rising and elevated in the East, or in the M.C., and well-aspected; the ☉ Sig. in ♐, often becomes ennobled, or receives titles or honorary distinctions; ♃ approaching the Meridian at B., unless evil aspects counteract, the native becomes wealthy, and comes to distinction; ♃ Sig. □ or ☍ ☉, has a great desire to be distinguished, but rarely atains it; ♂ in ♐ tends to distinction; the ♊ and ♑ influences strong at B. (See Commanding, Famous; "The Great" under Great; Kings, Nobles, President, Princes, Rulers).

RENUNCIATION—Retirement from the World—Seclusion—Forsaking the World—A Recluse—The motive for renunciation should be considered. The afflictions of ♄ would cause retirement from a deep philosophical ambition, or disappointed ambitions. The influences of ♆ and the ♓ sign would tend to renunciation for religious reasons. Venus may cause retirement and seclusion because of failure to combat successfully with the trials or social conditions of life, or because of disappointment in love. The afflictions and influences of ♅ and ♂ tend to sudden retirement. Saturn afflicted in the 10th H. tends to downfall in business, loss of honour, and to seclusion and fondness for solitude. Scorpio influence tends to renunciation of the world due to some deep sorrow, or for emotional reasons, or in order to think deeply upon philosophical matters, and get at the root of things, and the truth about life and destiny. (See Aversions, Celibacy; "Anchorite" under Husband; "Recluse" under Old Age; Recluse, Reserved, Resignation, Retiring, Seclusion, Secretive, Solitude; "Release From" under Sorrow).

REPETITION — Habits Formed By — (See Automatic, Habits).

REPINING—Complaining—Murmuring —The ☉ or ☽ Sig. □ or ☍ ♄; the ☉ to the ☌, P. □, or ☍ ♄ by dir.; ♄ to the ill-asps. his own place by tr. or dir.; ♄ Sig. □ or ☍ the ☉ or ☽; ☿ Sig. in ♓; ☿ in ♓ in partile asp. the Asc.; the 3rd face of ♊, or the 3rd decan. of ♒ on the Asc. (See Anguish, Brooding, Complaining, Dejected, Discontentment, Exhibitionism, Fretful, Gloom, Grief; "Low Spirits" under Low; Melancholy; "No Peace of Mind" under Mind; Morbid, Miserable, Murmuring, Patience, Peevish, Regretful, Restlessness, Retrospective, Sadness, Sorrowful, Suffering, Trouble, Unhappy, Worry, Wretched).

REPLETION—The Condition of Being Full—(See Full, Gluttony).

REPRESSIONS—(See Confinements, Hindrances, Inhibitions, Limitations, Restraints, Retardation, Saturn Influence, Stoppages, Suppressions, Twelfth House).

REPRODUCTION—Reproductive Organs—Sex Organs—Secrets—Privates —Genitals—Generative System—Reins —Res Venereae—Procreative Organs— Members of Generation, etc.—This subject is largely considered in the Articles on Conception, Fecundation, Fertile, Foetus, Fruitful, Generative System, Genitals, Genito-Urinary, Gestation, Prenatal Epoch, Privates, Procreation, Proliferation, Secrets, Sex Organs. (See these subjects). The Reproductive Organs are ruled by ♂ and the ♏ sign. Also the ♌ sign and the 5th H. conditions show the power of reproduction, and the necessity for survival, and for offspring. The female reproductive organs, and especially the womb, are strongly influenced and ruled by the ♍, ♎, and ♏ signs. The external sex organs of males are ruled by ♂. The following subjects are related to the reproductive organs, which see in the alphabetical arrangement when not considered here—

Abscesses In — (See "Abscess" under Secrets).

Adolescence—(See Puberty).

All Diseases Of—(See "All Diseases" under Generative).

Barrenness; Castration—(See Testes).

Cell Reproduction — (See "Reproduction" under Cells).

Chancre—Hard Chancre—(See Syphilis).

Chancroid—(See Gonorrhoea).

Change of Life — In Women — (See "Menopause" under Menses).

Clitoris; Cohabitation; Conception;

Death—From Disorders of the Generative System—(See "Death" under Generation).

Deformities—Of the Sex Organs—(See "Deformities" under Generative).

Diseases In — (1) Diseases Incident To the Generative System—(See "Diseases" under Genitals; "Private Diseases" under Private; Venereal, Womb, etc.). (2) Diseases of the Reproductive Organs Prevalent — Comets appearing in ♏.

Fallopian Tubes—(See Fallopian).

Fecundation; Female Functions—(See "Functions" under Females).

Foetus; Fruitful; Gemmation — (See Cells, Gemmation, Proliferation).

Generative Organs — (See Generative, Genitals, Sex Organs).

Genitals; Genito-Urinary; Gestation;

Glands—Gonads—(See "Reproductive" under Glands).

Hermaphrodites; Impotent;

Injured In Privates — (See "Injuries" under Genitals; Maimed, Mutilated).

Intercourse; Leucorrhoea; Maimed;

Male Organs — (See "Mens' Genitals" under Genitals; "Male Organ" under Male).

Members of Generation—Disorders of — (See Generative, Genitals, Secret Parts, Sex. Also note the various paragraphs in this section).

Menses; Monsters; Offspring — (See Children).

Ovaries—Ovum—(See Ovaries).

Pain In—(See "Pain" under Genitals, Secrets).

Parturition; Passion; Penis;

Perversions; Pregnancy; Prevalent — Diseases of Reproductive Organs Prevalent—(See "Diseases" in this section).

Private Diseases—(See Genitals, Private, Scandalous, Venereal).

Privates — Privy Parts — (See Privates).

Processes — Reproductive Processes—Ruled by ♏. (See "Reproductive Processes" under Processes).

Procreation—Ruled by the ☽ and ♀. (See Procreation).

Proliferation; Prolific; Puberty;

Puerperal; Scandalous Diseases—(See Scandalous, Private, Venereal).

Secret Parts—(See Genitals, Privates, Secrets, Sex Organs).

Semen; Sex Organs—(See Sex).

Shameless Practices—(See Exhibition, Perversions, Rape, Shameless, Unnatural).

Sores—On Genitals—(See "Chancroid" under Gonorrhoea; "Abscesses" under Secrets; "Chancre" under Syphilis; "Genitals" under Ulcers).

Spermatic Cord—(See Spermatic).

Syphilis; Testes; Tubes—(See Fallopian: "Seminal Vesicles" under Semen).

Ulcers—(See "Genitals" under Ulcers).

Urethra; Uterus—(See Womb).

Vagina; Venereal; Voice—Changes In At Puberty — (See "Voice" under Puberty).

Vulva; Weakness—Of the Generative Organs—(See "Weakness" under Generative).

Whites—(See Leucorrhoea).

Womb — (See the paragraphs under Womb).

REPTILES — Reptilian — Serpents — Snakes—The Reptilian, or Dumb Signs of the Zodiac, are ♋, ♏, and ♓. (See Dumb, Mute).

Death or Injury By—The ☉ or ♂ with Fomahaut tends to bites by venomous animals; ♄ and ♂ in Terrestrial Signs, with ☿ concurring, and malefics afflicting the Luminaries; ♄ near the Constellation of the Serpent in the 4th face of ♏, configurated with ☿, and with ♄ in the 1st H. in ☍ to the ☉ or ☽ setting. (See Adder; "Journeys" under Bites; Fomahaut; "Bites To" under Kings; Obnoxious, Quadrupeds, Serpents, Stings, Terrestrial; "Danger" under Travel; Venomous).

REPULSIONS — Repulsive — (See Antipathy, Compatibility, Enemies, Hatred, Incompatibility, Opposites).

Repulsive Diseases — (See "Catarrh" under Head; Fetid, Foul, Gangrene, Odors, Offensive, Putrid, Rotten, Scandalous, Sores; "Fetid" under Sweat; Ulcers, Venereal).

REPUTATION—Public Estimation—

Abilities — Gains a Great Reputation from His Abilities—The ☽ Sig. ☌ ☿. (See Genius; "Great Ability" under Great; "Abilities" under Mental; "Good Mind" under Mind; Prodigies).

Bad Reputation—Of No Repute—Held In Low Esteem — Unpopular — The ☽ Sig. in ♑; ♀ ill-dignified at B. (See Banished, Conduct, Criminal, Debauched, Disgrace, Dishonest, Drink, Drunkenness; "Many" under Enemies; Execrated, Execution, Exile, Harlots; "Hated by Others" under Hatred; "Loss Of" under Honour; Infamous; "Low and Base" under Low; Loose Morals" under Morals; "Imprisonment" under Prison; Scandalous, Shameless; Unfortunate; "Vile Wretch" under Vile).

Good Reputation—(See "Popular" in this section).

Hated by Others—(See Hatred).

Loss of Reputation — (See Disgrace, Downfall; "Loss Of" under Honour; Sentence of Law (see "Death" under Judges; Prisons); Ruin, Scandal, etc.).

No Regard for Reputation—♀ ill-dignified at B.

Of No Repute — (See "Bad" in this section).

Popular — A General Favorite — Beloved and Esteemed—Highly Respected, etc.—The ☉ Sig. ⚹ or △ ♃, always respected; the ☽ Sig. in ♉, gains in esteem and much respect; the ☽ Sig. in ♋, well-beloved; the ☽ Sig. in ♎ or ♐; ♃ rising at B., and well-aspected, held in high esteem; ♃ Sig. in ♎; ♃ Sig. ☌ ♀, admired and respected; ♀ Sig. in ♎, generally beloved; ♀ Sig. in ♐ or ♒; ♀ Sig. ☌ ♃. (See Pleasant, Popular).

Unpopular — (See "Bad Reputation" in this section).

REQUIREMENTS — Nature's Requirements—(See "Requirements" under Nature).

RES VENEREAE — Sex Diseases — (See "Diseases" under Generative, Genitals, Genito-Urinary, Private, Reproductive Organs, Sex, Venereal, etc.).

RESCUE WORK—Hazards His Life to Rescue Others—♄ in ♎, ☌, □, or ☍ the Asc. by dir., and ♄ ruling the 1st H., rescues others from impending danger. (See Danger).

RESEARCH — Fond of Study and Research Work—(See Knowledge, Learning, Metaphysics, Occult, Philosophy, Reading, Science, Study, Truth, etc.).

RESENTFUL—Indignant Displeasure—♄ Sig. ⚹ or △ ♂, more open in resentment. (See Antipathy, Hatred, Jealousy, Offended, Revenge, Sensitive, Treachery, etc.).

RESERVATION — Of Cell Substances— (See "Substance" under Cells).

RESERVE FORCES — The Reserve Forces of the Body Strong or Weak—Reserve Forces Good — (See "Good" under Constitution, Health, Immunity, Recovery, Recuperation, Resistance, Stamina, Strength, Tone, Vitality).

Reserve Forces Low — (See Debility, Feeble, Infirm, Invalids; "Much Sickness" under Sickness; "Weak Body" under Weak).

RESERVED — Retiring—Quiet—Serious — Thoughtful — R e t i c e n t — Seclusive, etc. — The ☽ Sig. in ♍; ♄ influence strong at B.; ♄ in ♎, reserved and unsociable; ♄ Sig. in ♍ (Hor'y); ☿ strong at B.; ☿ Sig. ✶ or △ the ☽; ♏ on the Asc.; ♏ influence tends to make one thoughtful and reserved. (See Bashfulness, Grave, Mistrustful, Modesty, Mystical, Recluse, Retiring, Seclusion, Secretive, Serious, Shy, Solitude, Suspicious, etc.).

RESIDENCE—Place of Residence—Location—The Place of Residence is governed by the ☽ and the 4th H. The following subjects have to do with Residence, changes of, conditions over, its benefits or evils, etc. See the following subjects in the alphabetical arrangement when not considered here—

Abroad — Residence Abroad — Should Live Abroad — Should Not Live or Travel Abroad—The 9th H. containing benefics, and free from the affliction of malefics, is favorable for residence Abroad. If there are malefics in the 9th H. at B., in weak signs, and afflicted, avoid foreign residence or travel. In choosing a location Abroad for the best of health, or to benefit the health, if the map indicates life Abroad, choose a Country ruled by the Signs of the Zodiac containing ♃ or ♀ at birth if such signs are free from the presence, or severe affliction of the malefics. The native should live Abroad, or away from the Native Place or Land, if at birth the ☉, ☽, ♃, or ♀ were in the 1st, 9th, 10th, or 12th H., or if the ☉ or ☽ were afflicted in the 4th H., or malefics in the 4th. Malefics ruling the 4th H., or malefics in the 4th, always make it advisable for the native to remove from his place of birth. (See Abroad, Foreign Lands, Fourth House; "Native Land" under Native; Ninth House; "Place of Birth" under Place; Travel, Voyages).

Air Sign People — When the map of birth predominates with the airy sign influences, and with an air sign on the Asc., frequent changes of scenery or residence are good for such natives, and also to live in a high altitude where the air is lighter. The Air Signs tend to rapid recuperation thru mental rest and change of scenery. (See "Signs" under Air; Altitude).

Altitude — Should Reside In a High Altitude — (See Altitude; "Air Sign People" in this section).

Bad Time for Changes—Of Residence —The ☉ to the ☌, P, □, or ☍ ♅ by dir.; the ☉ to the ☌ or ill-asp. the ☽; the ☽ to the ill-asps. her own place by dir. (See "Bad Time" under Journeys, Travel; "Avoid" under Voyages).

Birthplace — Should Remain There — Should Remove—(See "Place of Birth" under Place; "Abroad" in this section).

Changes—Many Changes of Residence —Few Changes—People born under the strong influence of the Fixed Signs, and with the ☉, ☽, and many planets in these signs, or fixed signs on the Asc. or angles at B., are not given much to change, and often remain in one location for a lifetime. The Common Sign influences strong at B. tend to many changes, and inconstacy. The evil directions of ♅ tend to make one restless, notionate, and under this influence sudden and unwise changes of residence are apt to occur. (See Changes; "Fixed Habits", "Fixed Signs", under Fixed; Restlessness, Roaming; "Many Changes", "One Place", in this section).

Colds Taken—By Living In Cold and Damp Places — (See "Colds" under Moisture).

Comfort — Changes Which Interfere with Health and Comfort—♅ in the 6th H. at B. (See Comforts).

Constant In No Place—(See Changes, Many Changes, in this section).

Countries—Countries and Nations In Which To Reside—(See Countries, Location, Nations; Abroad, Prospers Anywhere, Where Not To Locate, and the various paragraphs in this section).

Damp Places — Living In, and Ill-Health From — (See "Colds" under Moisture).

Desire for Changes — (See Changes; "Inability" under Concentration; Discontentment, Patience, Restlessness, Roaming, Scattering, Vacillating, Vagabond, Wanderer; Discontentment, Many Changes, and the various paragraphs in this section).

Discontentment—Changes Due To—☿ to the good asps. the ☽ by Periodic Rev. tends to changes of residence if unsettled or discontented. (See Discontentment; "Instability", "No Peace of Mind", under Mind; Restless; the various paragraphs in this section).

Fixed In Habits — And Opinions, and Not Given To Change—(See "Fixed In Habits" under Fixed; "Change", "One Place", in this section).

Foreign Lands—Residence Abroad— (See "Abroad" in this section).

Fortunate Locations—(See "Abroad", "Friends", in this section; "Native Land" under Native; "Place of Birth" under Place; "Directions To Travel" under Travel).

Friends — The Best Locations for Friends and Prosperity — Parts of the World Where To Meet the Most Friends —Signs containing ♃ and ♀, or the angles containing them, show the best directions and locations for the best prosperity, true, and helpful friends. (See Abroad, Birthplace, Native Land, Place of Birth, in this section).

Good Time To Remove—The ☽ to her own good aspects by dir. (See "Good Time" under Journeys, Voyages).

Health—The Best Location for Health —When Health is the object of travel, or a change of location, follow the lord of the Ascendant and the ☽. Also locate in places ruled by the signs which contain the Benefics at B., or in the direction of the Benefics. (See Abroad, Fortunate, Location, Friends, Where Not To Locate, in this section; "Location" under Health).

Home or Abroad — Whether To Live At Home or Abroad — (See Abroad, Liberty, in this section).

Ill-Health — Due To Location — (See Abroad, Altitude, Places to Avoid, Should Remove, Where Not to Locate, in this section).

Inconstant—(See Changes, Desire for Changes, Many Changes, in this section; Inconstant).

Leads Unsettled Life—(See Changes, Inconstant, Many Changes, Roamer, Unsettled, Wanderer, in this section).

Liberty — Can Travel or Locate Anywhere — (See "Prospers Anywhere" in this section; "Home or Abroad" under Travel).

Lives In One Place — (See Changes, One Place, in this section).

Location—Where To Locate—(See Location; "Native Land" under Native; "Place of Birth" under Place; "Direction To Travel" under Travel; Fortunate, Health, Ill-Health, Where Not To Locate, and the various paragraphs in this section).

Low Altitudes—Should Live In—(See Altitude).

Many Changes—Of Residence—Constant In No Place—Removes Constantly—Continually Shifting Their Situations—The ☉ Sig. ☌ ☽; the ☽ in the Asc., or ruler at B.; the ☽ in the 4th H.; ♄ or ♃ Sig. ☌ ☽; ♂ Sig. in ♊; ♂ Sig. ☌ ☽; ☿ ill-dignified at B.; ☿ Sig. □ or ☍ ☽, and especially if ☿ be in a movable sign; several planets conjoined with ☿, and also in configuration with the ☽; ☿ Sig. ☌ ☽, unsteady in his pursuits; a common sign on the cusp the 2nd H. at B., and ♄ in the 2nd by dir. (See Air Sign People, Changes, Desire for Changes, Discontentment, Inconstant, Mutable, in this section).

Military Life—Changes Caused By—(See Military, War).

Moisture — Colds and Ill-Health by Living In Moist and Damp Places — (See "Colds" under Moisture; "Ill-Health" in this section).

Mutable Signs — Their influence predominant at B. tends to many changes of residence. (See "Mutable Signs" under Mutable; "Many Changes" in this section).

Nations—The Rulerships of the Nations—(See Nations).

Native Land — Should Remain In — Should Leave—(See "Native Land" under Native; "Place of Birth" under Place; "Abroad" in this section).

Not Given To Changes—(See Changes, Fixed, One Place, in this section).

One Place—Lives In One Place for a Lifetime—Many influences in the fixed signs at B.; the ☉, ☽, and ☿ well-aspected by ♄; ♄ a strong ruler at B., may spend a lifetime in one place, and in one employment; ♄ afflicted in the 4th H. tends to tie the native down to one place to his detriment. (See Changes, Fixed, in this section; "Fixed Signs" under Fixed).

Place of Birth—Should Remain In—Should Remove — (See Fourth House, Nadir; "Native Land" under Native; "Place of Birth" under Place; "Abroad" in this section).

Places To Avoid—During the Current Year—When the ☉ or ☽ are hyleg, and the hyleg falls in the 8th H. at a Solar Rev., places and Countries ruled by the sign containing the hyleg at B. should be avoided, or ill-health, accident, or death might result. (See "Where Not To Locate" in this section; "Bad Time", "Current Year", under Travel). For places to avoid generally see Abroad; "Native Land" under Native; "Place of Birth" under Place).

Prosperity—Best Location For—(See "Friends" in this section).

Prospers Anywhere — At Home or Abroad — The ☉, ☽, ♃, or ♀ well-aspected in the Asc. (See Liberty, Prosperity).

Removals — Removes Constantly — Should Remain—Should Remove—(See Changes, Desire for Changes, Discontentment, Inconstant, Should Remain, Should Remove, in this section).

Roamer — (See Roamer, Vagabond, Wanderer; Changes, Desire for Changes, Many Changes, in this section).

Sailor — Travels About As a Sailor — (See Maritime, Navigation, Sailor, Sea, Ships).

Scenery—Change of Scenery Good—(See "Air Sign People" in this section).

Sea Level—Should Live At Sea Level —(See Altitude).

Shifting Here and There—(See Many Changes, Removals, in this section).

Should Remain—Should Not Move—A malefic in the 7th H., or the ☽ or lord of the 1st sepr. from a benefic, remain; lord of the Asc. and planets in the 1st stronger than the lord of the 7th, or planets in the 7th, should remain (Hor'y). (See Abroad, Nadir; "Native Land" under Native; "Place of Birth" under Place; "Abroad" in this section).

Should Remove—Caused by ♅ and his afflictions; the ☽ sepr. from a malefic, or ☋, or a benefic in the 7th H., should remove. (See "Should Remain" in this section).

Soldiers—Changes of Residence For, and For Sailors—(See Maritime, Military, Sailors, Ships, Soldiers, War).

Sudden Changes—Of Residence—♅ influence. (See "Sudden" under Changes).

Tied to One Place — (See Changes, Fixed, One Place, in this section).

Time—Best Time for Changes—Bad Time For—(See Bad Time, Good Time, in this section).

Travel — Good or Bad Time For — Travels Much—(See the various paragraphs under Travel; Vagabond, Wanderer; "Many Changes" in this section).

Unfortunate Locations — (See Places to Avoid, Where Not to Locate, and the various paragraphs in this section).

Unsettled Life—(See Changes, Desire For Changes, Discontentment, Inconstant, Many Changes, Removals, Roamer, Vagabond, Wanderer, in this section).

Vagabond — (See Roamer, Vagabond, Wanderer).

Wanderer—(See "Travels Much" under Travel; Vagabond, Wanderer; "Many Changes" in this section).

War—Causing Changes of Location or Residence—(See Army, Military, Ships, Soldiers, War).

Wet and Damp Locations—Colds and Illness From—(See "Colds" under Moisture).

Where Not to Locate—Signs containing malefics, and places and directions ruled by such signs, show the places and directions to avoid, and where the native would be apt to meet with inveterate opposition from public and private enemies, or suffer accident, ill-health, downfall, etc., unless the malefic itself be Significator, or the malefic well-aspected in his own sign, as ♄ in ♑, ♂ in ♈ or ♏, etc., and the malefic not ℞, combust, or badly afflicted. Avoid the direction of planets much afflicted, even though they be a benefic, as such afflictions tend to ill-health, misfortune, delays, execration, sorrows, suffering, enemies, downfall, losses, isolation, reversals, trouble, plots, treachery by others, loss of friends, etc. (See Abroad, Ill-Health, Location, Native Land, Place of Birth, Places to Avoid, in this section; "Countries to Avoid" under Travel).

RESIGNATION—

Resigned to Disease—Characteristic of the ♍ people. (See "Does Not Complain" under Complaining; Patience, Renunciation; the Introduction under Virgo).

Resigned to Fate—(See "Resigned" under Fate; Limitations, Recluse, Seclusion, Secretive, Solitude, Twelfth House).

RESINS—A Vegetable Exudate Soluble in Alcohol and Oils, but Insoluble in Water—Ruled mostly by ♅. (See Amber, Herbs, Shellac, Xylan).

RESISTANCE TO DISEASE—The degree of resistance, the vitality, and the powers of recuperation, vary in different individuals according to the conditions existing in the map of birth, or according to the degree of education, self-control, spiritual attainment, etc. The following subjects have to do with the powers to resist disease, which powers may be strong, medium, or weak. See these subjects in the alphabetical arrangement when not considered here—

Ascendant—Fiery signs on the Asc. give greater vitality, while the watery signs on the Asc. at B., and especially ♋ and ♓, tend to lower the resistance, and give a weaker body. (See Ascendant; "Fire Signs" under Fire; First House; "Body" under Strong; "Good", "Low", under Vitality).

Childhood—(See "Danger", "Death", "Fevers", under Childhood).

Children—Resistance to Disease Good In—A strong sign upon the Asc. at B., as ♈, ♌, or ♐, and the ruler of the Asc. well-placed and free from affliction. (See "Strong" under Children, Infancy).

Chronic Diseases—Poor Resistance—(See Chronic).

Debility Greater—(See "Chronic" under Debility).

Directions—(1) Overcomes Evil Directions—♃ rising at B. in power and dignity, and well-aspected. (See "Overcoming Directions" under Directions; Immunity; "Good" under Vitality; "Good" in this section). (2) Succumbs Easily Under Evil Directions—(See "Evil Directions" under Directions; "Directions Kill" under Infancy; "Low" in this section).

Early Death—(See "Death During Childhood" under Childhood; Early; "Death In Infancy" under Infancy; "Short Life" under Life).

Endurance; Feeble; Functions—Good, Strong, or Weak—(See Functions).

Gives Up Easily—To Disease—(See "Gives Up Easily" under Disease).

Good Powers of Resistance—The Resistance to Disease Increased—Throws Off Disease Easily—The ☉ ☌ or P. asp. ☿ increases and strengthens the Will, and gives the mind more power to resist disease, and to act against disorders; the ☉ or ☽ to the good asps. ♂ by dir.; the ☉ or ♂ ⚹ or △ the Asc., much organic resistance; the ☉ ☌, P., ⚹ or △ ♃ enables to overcome disease; the ☉ in a fire sign; the ☉ in the Asc. or M.C. at B., in a strong or fiery sign; the ☉ angular and diurnal at B.; the less the ☉ is afflicted at B. the greater is the vitality, and the more certain to ward off disease; the ☉ in ♈ or ♌, and well-aspected; the ☉ in ♌, and with ♈ on the Asc.; the ☽ free from affliction at B., and well-aspected by the benefics, and the Asc. free from the affliction of malefics; the ☽ hyleg in ♉ with females; ♄ on the Asc. at B. gives good resistance to disease, tenacity of life, and persistence against disease; ♃ and ♀ rising at B., and in good asp. to the ☉ and ☽; ♃ in the 6th H., and free from affliction, wards off disease easily; ♃ in the Asc. at B., and in good asp. to the ☉ and ☽; ♃ and ♀ in the Asc. at B., and free from the affliction of malefics; ♂ ⚹ or △ the ☉ at B.; ♂ in good asp. to the ☉ or ☽ at B.; fiery signs on the Asc. at B.; the 2° ♍ on the Asc. at B.; fixed signs on the angles, and the afflicting planets in common signs; many planets in fixed signs at B. give greater resistance and endurance, but tend to prolong the disease; born under the positive and masculine signs, and with many planets in such signs, will overcome, resist, and fight off disease; ♊ on the Asc., which is the strongest of the common signs to control illness. (See "Active Body" under Active; Defensive, Directions, Endurance; "Good Health" under Health; Immunity, Majority, Physical, Recovery, Recuperation, Resources, Stamina, Strength; "Body" under Strong; Tone; "Good" under Vitality, etc.).

Immunity from Disease—(See Immunity).

Inability—To Throw Off Disease—(See "Overcoming Disease", "Throwing Off Disease", under Disease; "Disease" under Inability; "Low" in this section).

Increased Resistance—To Disease—(See "Good" in this section).

Infancy—Powers of Resistance In—(See the paragraphs under Infancy).

Infirm; Invalids;

Less Liable to Disease—Proof Against Disease—(See "Less Liable" under Disease).

Less Power—To Throw Off Disease—(See "Less Power", "Overcoming", under Disease; "Low" in this section).

Lives Thru Sickness—(See "Good" under Recuperation; "Lives Thru Serious Illnesses" under Serious; "Good" in this section).

Long Illnesses—(See Chronic, Invalids; "Diseases" under Long; Prolonged; "Slow" under Recuperation; Tedious).

Long Life—(See "Long" under Life).

Low—Resistance Low—The ☉, ☽, or ♄ in the 6th H., and afflicted; the ☉ ☌ or P. ♄, and especially in common signs; the ☽ hyleg in ♏ and afflicted in female nativities; ♄ rising, and the ☉ afflicted by the ☽; a malefic afflicting the ☉ or ☽, and elevated above the Luminary; ♒, ♑, or ♓ on the Asc. (See "Low" under Recuperation, Vitality; "Weak Body" under Weak).

Majority—The majority of the planets rising, or rising and elevated at B., give greater resistance to disease. (See Elevated, Majority, Rising).

Makes Effort—To Throw Off Disease—(See "Overcoming" under Disease).

Middle Life—Dies Before or At Middle Life—(See Middle Life).

Offspring—(See "Children" in this section).

Old Age—Dies In Old Age—(See "Long Life" under Life; Old Age).

Organic Resistance—Has Much Organic Resistance—(See "Organic Resistance" under Organic; "Good" in this section).

Overcomes Disease—(See "Overcoming" under Disease; "Good" in this section).

Physical Resistance—(See "Resistance" under Physical; "Good", "Low", in this section).

Proof Against Disease—(See "Less Liable" under Disease; Immunity).

Protective Influences—(See Protection).

Receptive—More Open to Disease—(See Receptive, Susceptibility; "Inability", "Less Power", in this section).

Recovery Rapid—(See "Rapid" under Recovery).

Recuperative Powers—(See Defensive, Phagocytes, Protection, Recuperation, Vitality).

Rising Planets—Give Greater Resistance. (See Elevated, Majority, Rising, Setting).

Robust; Sickly; Sickness—(See "Much Sickness", and the various paragraphs under Sickness).

Stamina; Strong Resistance—To Disease—(See Immunity; "Good" under Recuperation, Vitality; "Good" in this section).

Stubborn Diseases—(See Chronic, Consumptions, Lingering; "Long Diseases" under Long; Prolonged, Slow, Tedious, Wastings; "Low" in this section).

Succumbs Easily—To Disease—(See "Succumbs Easily" under Disease; "Early Death" under Early; "Short Life" under Life; "Low" under Recuperation, Vitality; Sickly; "Weak Body" under Weak; Inability, Low, in this section).

Susceptibility—(See Contagions, Environment, External, Infections, Negative, Passive, Receptive, Susceptibility).

Tedious Diseases—(See Chronic, Long, Slow, Tedious, etc.).

Throwing Off Disease—(See this subject under Disease; Good, Inability, Low, Strong, in this section).

Tone; Treatment—Disease Resists Treatment Stubbornly—(See "Stubborn" in this section).

Vital Signs—Of the Zodiac—(See "Signs" under Vital).

Vitality—(See "Good", "Low", under Vitality).

Wards Off Disease Easily—(See "Over-coming", "Throwing Off", under Disease; Immunity; "Rapid" under Recovery; "Good" under Recuperation, Vitality; Strength, Strong, etc.).

Weak Constitution—(See Constitution, Feeble, Sickly; "Weak Body" under Weak).

Weak Will—Makes Little Effort to Resist Disease—(See "Overcoming" under Disease; Negative, Passive, Receptive, Susceptibility; "Weak" under Will, etc.).

Wear and Tear—Ability to Withstand—(See Wear).

Will-Power—Weak Will—Strong Will—(See "Weak Will" in this section; Positive, Power, Resolute, Will).

RESOLUTE—Resolution—Firmness—Determined—Daring—Resourceful—Valiant—Brave—Self-Reliant—Resolution of Disease or Tissues, etc.—Mars is the giver of resolution, resourcefulness, courage, boldness, daring, etc. In Hor'y Questions resolution, or a resolute temper, is denoted by ♄ Sig. in ♈, or ♃ Sig. in ♏; ♂ ruler of the horoscope, a resolute temper; the good aspects of ♂ to the ☉, ☽, or ☿; ♂ in ♈ or ♏; the ☉ strong at B.; the ♌ sign on the Asc. (See "Active Mind" under Active; Ambition; "Abundance", "Great", under Energy; Persevering, Positive, Rule, Self-Reliant; "Strong Will" under Will, etc.).

Lacking In Resolution—The ☉ Sig. in ♊; ♂ weak and ill-dignified at B.; born under the strong influence of ♀. (See Dull, Fears, Idle, Inactive, Indifferent, Indolent, Lassitude; "Mutable Disposition" under Mutable; "Negative Nature" under Negative; "Weak Ill" under Will).

Pneumonia—Delayed Resolution In—(See "Delayed" under Pneumonia).

Resolution of Disease—The Solution of Continuity In Disease—Abatement of Disease, etc.—(See Abatement, Amelioration, Cataphora, Continuity, Course, Crises; "Degree Of" under Disturbed; Duration; "Disease" under Force; Improved, Minimizing, Moderation, Modification, Prognosis, Recovery, Recuperation, Remission, Retrograde, Solution, etc.).

Resolution of the Nerves—Dissolving—Absorption, etc.—A ♄ disease; ☿ afflicted by ♄. (See "Resolution" under Nerves).

Resolution of Tissues — The Resolution, Absorption, or Analysis of Tissue Into Its Elements—The work of ♄, and a ♄ disease. (See Absorption, Dissolution, Solution; "Absorption" under Tissues).

RESOLVENT—That Which Causes Solution of Tissue — An Agent Removing Swelling or Effusion — Discutients — A Therapeutic Property of ♂. A Poultice of the fresh root of Bryonia Dioica is considered good to remove swellings from external injuries, to soften and promote absorption of oedematous and hard tumors, and to relieve rheumatic pains, etc. (See Absorption, Bryonia, Discutients, Emollient; "Remedies" under Inflammation; "Sugar of Lead" under Lead; "Therapeutic Properties" under Mars; Solution).

RESOURCE—Resourcefulness—

Lacking In Resourcefulness — (See Backwardness, Dull, Fears, Helplessness, Idle, Imprudent, Indifferent, Indolent, Inert, Inferior; "Bad" under Judgment; Lack Of; "Light In Mind" under Mind; Mutable, Negative, Purposes, Receptive, Resolution, Susceptibility, Timidity, Void Of, etc.).

Readiness Of — (See "Active Mind" under Active; Genius; "Good" under Judgment; "Inventive Mind" under Learning; "Abilities", "Quickened", under Mentality; "Good" under Mind; Positive, Resolute, Self-Reliant, etc.).

RESOURCES — Assets — Money — Property, etc.—The husbanding of financial and property resources is signified by ♄ and the ♑ sign. (See Property, Riches).

Bodily Resources — The resources, or strength of the human body, its vitality, recuperative powers, resistance to disease, etc., are strengthened and built up by the good influences of the ☉, ♂, ♃, and ♀, and also by a strong and powerful sign upon the Asc. at B. The influences of ♄, when afflicting, tend to tear down, retard, and hinder bodily processes. (See Immunity, Recuperation, Resistance, Strength; "Body" under Strong; Tone, Vitality).

RESPECT—Consideration For Others—♂ Sig. □ or ☍ ♃, or ♂ Sig. ☌ ☿, has little respect for the persons or possessions of others when advantage can be gained by sacrificing them to his own interests. (See Cheating, Cruel, Deceitful, Dishonest, Liars, Plots, Thieves, Treachery, etc.).

Respect For Others—Has Respect and High Regard for the Rights of Others —(See Honest, Humane, Kind, Sincere, Sympathetic, etc.).

RESPIRATORY SYSTEM — Respiration —Breathing—Organs of Respiration—Respiratory Tract—The Breathing Organs, etc. — (See Breath, Breathing, Bronchial, Lungs, Pulmonary).

RESPONSE — The Degree of Response Against Disease — (See "Response Against Disease" under Degree).

RESPONSIBILITY — The Sense of Responsibility—♄ strong and well-placed at B. gives a grave, serious, and thoughtful nature, and with a strong sense of responsibility, and indicates that many great responsibilities will be encountered along thru life. As to whether the native will be able to cope with them successfully and wisely, and overcome obstacles, will depend largely upon the strength of the horoscope as a whole, the judgment, the mental qualities, the spiritual sight and force, the state of the health, etc. (See Ambitions, Anxieties, Carelessness, Character, Destiny, Fate, Fortune, Honesty, Honour, Improvident, Indifferent, Irresponsible, Judgment, Morals, Motives, Purposes, Reliable, Reputation, etc.).

REST — Relaxation — Recuperation — Restoration — Sleep, etc. — Rest is signified by the 4th H., decay, death, and the end of things.

Mental Rest—The airy signs tend to rapid recuperation thru mental rest and change of scenery. (See "Signs" under Air; "Air Sign People" under Residence).

Sickness—Patient Has Very Little, or No Rest In Sickness—The ☽ in ♎, afflicted by the ☉ or ♂ when taken ill, and which is generally caused by too much blood (Hor'y); ♂ in ♈ when taken ill, and ♂ the afflictor in the disease. (See Aches; "Too Much Blood" under Blood; Delirium, Discomfort, Fatigue, Malaise, Pain, Plethora, Refreshment, Restlessness; "Insomnia" under Sleep; Suffering, Weariness, etc.).

Want of Rest — (See "Sickness" in this section).

RESTLESSNESS — Restless — Unsettled — Fretful — Discontented, etc. — The SUN ill-dignified at B., and afflicted; the ☉ Sig. ☌ ☽; the ☉ to the ☌ or P. asp. the ☽; the ☉ to the ill-asps. ♅ by dir., restless and unsettled; the MOON afflicted at B., and to the ☌ the M.C. by dir.; the ☽ ill-aspected by ♅ at B., and by dir.; the ☽ ☌ or P. asp. ♂; the ☽ to the ☌ or ill-asp. ♂ by dir., and ♂ in a sign or house of the ☽; the ☽ in the 3rd H. at B., perpetual restlessness; the ☽ in the 1st or 10th H.; the ☽ ruler of the horoscope and afflicted by malefics; the ☽ ascending at B.; the ☽ in ♊; the ☽ in ♑ unless well-aspected; the Progressed ☽ (or ☉) in ⚹ or △ asp. the radical ♂; the ☽ and ☿ configurated with several planets, restless, unsettled, and unstable; the ☽ afflicted in ♈; the ☽ in ♈, and afflicted by the ☉ or ♂ when taken ill (Hor'y); the ☽ ☌ the Asc. or M.C. by Secondary Direction, restless and unsettled; the ☽ to the ill aspects the Asc. or M.C., a restless and anxious time; the ☽ to the ☌ or ill-asp. ☿ by dir., and ☿ not dignified at B.; the ☽ to the ☌ or ill-asp. ♅ by dir.; the ☽ hyleg in ♈, and afflicted, and especially with females, and tends to ailments from restlessness; NEPTUNE afflicted in ♊; ♆ in transit over the place of the radical ☿; URANUS strong and ascending at B.; ♅ in the 1st, 3rd, or 9th H.; the place of the radical ♅, ☽, or ☿ ascending at a Solar Rev.; ♅ afflicting the ☽; SATURN Sig. □ or ☍ ☽, unsettled, wandering, and changeable; JUPITER Sig. ☌ ☽; ♃ afflicted in ♒; MARS Sig. in ♊; ♂ in a mutable sign; ♂ afflicted in ♈, extreme restlessness; ♂ Sig. ☌, ✱, or △ ☽; ♂ in the 6th H. in ♉, ♌, or ♏, and afflicted by the ☉ or ☽; ♂ to the cusp the 1st H. by dir.; VENUS Sig. □ or ☍ ☽, an unsettled and changeable life; MERCURY ☌ ♂ or ♀ in ♈, and otherwise afflicted by □ or ☍ aspects of other planets; ☿ in the Asc. at B., and in no aspect with any planet, great restlessness and desire for change; ☿ afflicted at B., weak, and ill-dignified; ☿ progressed in ☌, P., □, or ☍ the radical ♅, and vice versa; ☿ configurated with several planets; ☿ afflicted in the 1st or 10th H., a restless spirit; a ☿ disease, and afflictions to ☿; ☿ Sig. □ or ☍ ☽; the Asc. or M.C. to the ☌ ☽ by dir.; the ASCENDANT to the □ or ☍ ☿ by dir.; characteristic of the nervous temperament, ruled by ♅, ♄, ☿, and the earthy signs; a common sign on the cusp of 2nd H. at B., and ♄ therein by dir.; ♊ on the Asc. at B. tends to nervous disorders brought on by restlessness and discontentment; the 3rd decan. of ♊ on the Asc., ruled by the ☉, a restless and anxious life; cardinal signs on angles, and many planets in them; an ♈ influence. (See Active, Anxiety, Cardinal, Changes, Crime, Dejected, Depressed, Despondent, Discontentment, Fretful, Influenced, Instability, Journeys, Love Affairs, Low Spirits, Marriage, Mutable, Negative, Novelties, Patience, Peevish, Receptive, Recklessness, Regretful, Removals, Repining, Residence, Roaming, Scattering, Travel, Vacillating, Vagabond, Wanderer, Worry, etc.).

RESTORATION — To Health — (See Crises, Cure; "Better" under Disease; "Spared" under Life; Recovery, Recuperation, Rest; "Good" under Vitality).

Restoratives—(See Analeptic, Drugs, Healers, Medicines, Recreations, Remedies, Rest, Sleep, Stimulants, Tonics, Treatment, etc.).

RESTRAINTS — Restrictions — Limitations—To Hold In Check—Hindrances, etc. — Caused generally by the influences and afflictions of ♄.

Bodily Restraints—Physical Restrictions — The influence of ♄ over the body is confining, restrictive, hindering and retarding. Also the 12th H. influences tend to confinement, limitations and restrictions. Saturn tends to restrain the action of the nerves, circulation, stop bodily functions, and retard and obstruct the proper action of the organs of the body, hinder elimination, excretion, secretion, etc. For the details and influences, aspects, etc., causing these restrictions and disturbances, note carefully the paragraphs under each of the organs, and parts of the body, as given in the alphabetical arrangement of this book. Also the various evil aspects between the planets at birth and at conception, the house positions of planets, the influences of the fixed stars and Constellations at birth, and the Prenatal influences during gestation, play their important part in bringing restrictions over both mind and body. (See Birth, Blindness, Circulation, Conception, Confinement, Congenital, Crystallization, Deafness, Deformities, Elimination, Excretion, Fluids, Foetus, Functions, Hardening, Hearing, Hindrances, Limitations, Malformations, Missing, Monsters, Mutes, Nerves, Obstructions, Organs, Parts, Prenatal Epoch, Prison, Retardation, Retentions, Saturn, Secretions, Senses, Stoppages, Suppressions, Twelfth House, etc.).

Lack of Restraint — The Evil Tendencies of the Temperament Unrestrained — The ☽ sepr. from ♀ and applying to ☿; ♆ rising, or in the 3rd or 9th H., and afflicted; ♂ ☌, P., □, or ☍ ♆, lack of restraint in almost everything. (See Anger, Conduct, Cruel, Debauched, Depraved, Drink, Drunkenness, Eating, Excesses, Free, Gluttony, Habits, High Living, Indiscretions, Indulgences, Lascivious, Lewd, Licentious, Loose, Love Affairs; "Low and Base" under Low; "Loose Morals" under Morals; Luxuries, Narcotics; "Passional Excesses" under Passion; Perversions, Pleasures, Rashness, Recklessness, Riotous, Self-Control, Sex; "High Temper" under Temper; Uncontrolled, Venery, Vices, etc.).

Mental Restraints—Restrictions Over the Mind — These are caused principally by afflictions to ☿ at birth, or before birth, the evil aspects to ☿, the house position of ☿, etc., as this planet is the general ruler of the mind. The afflictions of ♄ to ☿ tend to dull and retard the mind, and the afflictions of each of the planets to ☿ tend to affect the mind according to the nature of the afflicting planet. Also, ☿ weak and ill-dignified at B., and with no relation to the ☽ or Asc., tends to impair the acton of the mind. (For influences along this line, see Chaotic, Confusion, Dull, Faculties, Fears, Foolish, Forethought, Idiocy, Imbecile, Insanity, Intellect, Judgment, Memory, Mentality, Mind, Obsessions, Perception, Reason, Understanding, etc. Especially note the paragraphs and subjects under Mental, Mind).

RESTRICTIVE—Restraining—Retarding—(See Restraints, Retardation).

RETAINS—Retains Anger—Retains a Wrong or Injury—Unforgiving—(See Anger, Enemies, Enmity, Hatred, Jealousy, Malevolent, Malice, Murderous, Plots, Revenge, Treachery, Vicious, Violent, etc.).

RETARDATION — Retarded — Retarding—

Retarded Action—Due to ♄ influence and affliction. (See "Lack Of" under Action; Arrested, Decrease, Diminished, Dull, Energy, Feeble, Functions, Growth, Hindrances, Inactive, Inertia, Lassitude, Lazy, Lethargy, Motion, Movement, Obstructions, Restraint, Slow, Stoppages, Suppression, etc.).

Retarded Mental Powers — (See Arrested; "Fails In" under Examinations; Foolish, Growth, Idiocy, Imbecile, Impediments, Inhibitions; "Arrested" under Mental; "Weak Mind" under Mind; "Mental Restraints" under Restraints; "Void Of" under Reason).

RETENTION—Retentive—Holding Back—Stoppage—In the body ♄ is the planet of retention, and rules the retentive faculty. By nature, ♄ is frigid, dry, and intropulsive, tending to retain and drive inward the wastes of the body. (See "Influences of Saturn", Qualities", under Saturn).

Faeces—Retention of—(See "Hardening" under Faeces).

Food — Retention of Difficult — (See "Retention" under Food).

Memory — (See "Retentive Memory" under Memory).

Poisons of the Body—Retention of—Retention of Wastes — Caused principally by the afflictions of ♄, the planet of retention; ♄ ☌ the ☉ or ☽ in ♏; ♅ in ♎, ☌, P., □, or ☍ ♂, due to spasmodic kidney action; caused by ♀ when the dominion of death is vested in her. (See Accumulative, Crystallization, Deposits, Elimination, Excretion, Filth, Gout, Hardening, Hyperacidity, Lameness, Local Parts; "Deposits Of" under Minerals; Poisons, Rheumatism, Stone, Stoppages, Suppression; "Lessened" under Sweat; Uric, Wastes, etc.).

Urea—Retention of—(See Gout, Urea).

Uric Acid Deposits—(See Uric).

Urine—(See "Retention" under Urine).

Wastes of Body—Retention of—(See "Poisons" in this section).

RETINA—The Expansion of the Optic Nerve, and the Internal Membrane of the Eye—Ruled by the ☉ and the ♈ Sign. The etheric vibrations sensed by the retina are often interfered with by the afflicted stellar rays from certain parts of the Zodiac, as from Nebulous Spots, the ☉ or ☽ in ☌ with Nebulous Stars and Clusters at B., and tend to blindness, or to impair the physical sight. (See Blindness; "Retina" under Eyes; Nebulous; "Optic Nerve" under Optic; Pleiades, Sight).

Blind Spot Of—This is blind because it is not responsive to the etheric Mercurial vibrations. However, the spiritual ray of ♆ makes this spot sensitive, and one who may be blind physically, or have weak sight, may have great spiritual sight under the influence of ♆. (See Neptune, Spiritual).

RETIRING—Retirement—Quiet—Modest—

Retirement—The ☽ P. ♄ at B., with females.

Retiring Nature — Reserved — Quiet — ♄ and ☿ influence strong at B.; ☿ rising in ♍; ♀ Sig. ⚹ or △ ♄, retiring in manner. (See Grave; "Retiring" under Manner; Quiet, Recluse, Renunciation, Reserved, Serious, Thoughtful, etc.).

RETRACTION—Retractive—Shortening—Drawing Backward—The retractive forces over the body are ruled by ♄. (See Contractions; "Retraction" under Eyeballs; Opisthotonos, Rigidity, Saturn Influences).

RETROGRADE PLANETS—A planet is retrograde (℞) when it appears to be moving backward in the Zodiac, as seen from the Earth. In Astrology, this condition of a planet is considered a debility, and to weaken the action of the planet over disease and human affairs. This is because it denotes a solution of continuity, interrupted sequence, the same as the direct motion of a planet indicates continuty of influence. In health matters, a planet turning ℞ indicates a change in the disease, a possible breaking up and disorganization of the disease, while the disease may continue strong as long as the afflicting planet remains direct and rapid in motion. Planets are not as forceful over the life when ℞ at B., and a person born with many planets ℞ usually has a weaker constitution, more trouble in life, less energy, etc. It is said, however, that planets ℞ at B. have a direct spiritual effect upon the life, which, in the end, often leads to greater success by Soul Growth than when the nature is more dominated by merely materialistic ambitions. Planets ℞ tend to give the Intuitional Powers greater rule, rather than Reason and the Intellect. The ☉ and ☽ are never ℞ in motion, as seen from the Earth, but the ☽ is said to be equivalent to a ℞ planet when she is slow in motion, and moving less than 13° in the 24 hours. By some Authors planets ℞ at B. are said to bring poverty and sickness. (See Continuity, Direct; "Degree Of" under Disturbed; Interrupted, Poverty, Resolution, Sequence, Sickness, Solution, Stationary).

RETROGRESSIVE—The Cellular Retrogressive Metamorphosis is presided over by ♀. (See "Alterations" under Cells; Metamorphosis).

RETROPHARYNGEAL ABSCESS—(See "Abscess" under Pharynx).

RETROSPECTIVE—Retrospection—Brooding—Living In the Past—A special trait of the ♋, or mother sign, and to be much given to the memories of childhood; ♄ in ♋, or afflicting ♋ and ☿, unpleasant memories, brooding over the mistakes of life, repining, regrets, etc. (See Brooding, Introspection, Melancholy, Morbid, Regretful, Repining, etc.).

RETURN—Returning—Returning Diseases—The Return of Disease After a Time—Old Maladies Return, etc.—The ☽ causes diseases which return after a time, such as Epilepsy, Fits, Spasms, Vertigo, etc.; the evil directions of ♄ to the hyleg; ♂ rising at B., and again at a Solar Rev.; the Asc. to the ☌ or ill-asp. ♄ by dir. (See Complications, Course, Epilepsy, Insanity, Intermittent, Irregular, Periodic, Recurrent, Regular, Relapses, Vertigo, etc.).

REVENGEFUL — Revenge — Spiteful — Vindictive — Unforgiving — Malice, etc. —The ☉ □ or ☍ ♂; the ☉ Sig. □ or ☍ ♄, spiteful; the ☽ in ♍ and afflicted by ♂; ♄ as Sig. denotes such a person in Hor'y Q.; a strong ♄ characteristic; ♄ □ or ☍ ☿, and attended with secret revenge; ♂ Sig. □ or ☍ ♄, given to secret revenge; ♂ Sig. in ♍ or ♏; the evil aspects of ♂ to the Significators; the 28° ♏ on the Asc. (See Anger, Cruel; "Secret" under Enemies; Enmity, Feuds, Hatred, Jealousy, Knavish, Malevolent, Malice, Mean, Mischief, Murderous, Plots, Poison Death, Resentful, Suicide, Treachery, Unforgiving).

REVERSES — Reversals — Failure In Business — Misfortune — Bankruptcy — Discredit — Disgrace — Dishonour — Trouble — Miseries — Downfall — Failure of Desires, etc. — The ☽ to the ☌ or P. Dec. the ☉, if the ☽ be hyleg, and the ☉ afflicted at B.; the ☽ in the 2nd H. at B., and to the ☌ or ill-asp. ♄ by dir.; ♂ Sig. ☌ ☉, sudden failures and downfall. For other influences along this line see Ambitions, Ascelli, Calamity, Cares, Castor, Catstrophies; "Failure" under Desires; Disgrace, Downfall; "Own Worst Enemy" under Enemies; Evils, Failure, Fate; "Ill-Fortune" under Fortune; "Loss Of" under Honour; Inheritance, Loss Of, Mischief, Miseries, Misfortune, Plots, Pollux, Poverty. Prison, Property; "Diseases" under Psychic; Reputation, Riches, Ruin, Scandal, Sorrow, Treachery, Trials, Trouble, Unfortunate, Wretched, etc.).

Reversing Your Stars — (See Character, Fate, Nadir; "Free Will" under Will).

REVITALIZATION — Of Fluids and Functions — (See "First Quarter" under Moon).

REVOLUTION —

Civil Revolution — Civil War — (See Revolutionary; "Civil" under War).

Periodic Revolution — Of the Planets — (See Periodic).

Planets — Revolution of — (See Climacteric; "Metonic Cycle" under Moon; "Periods of the Planets" under Periods).

Solar Revolution — (See Solar).

REVOLUTIONARY —

Revolutionary Figure — (See "Planetary Periods" under Periods; "Solar Revolution" under Solar).

Revolutionary Ideas — ♃ afflicted in ♒. (See Anarchists, Destructiveness, Radicalism, Reactionary, Reformers, Riotous, Sedition; "Civil War" under War).

Revolutions — Political Revolutions and Upheavals — Revolutionary — Civil War, etc. — ☿ elevated above, and configurated with ♄ at a Solar Ingress or Eclipse. (See "Much Misery Everywhere" under Misery; "Public Discord" under Quarrels; Riotous, Riots; "Civil War" under War).

RHEUM — Any Watery Flux or Catarrhal Discharge — A Watery Discharge from the Mucous Membranes, Nose, Skin, etc. — Signified by ♄ in ♈ when ♄ is the afflictor in the disease; a ♉ disease. (See Catarrh, Colds, Defluxions, Discharges, Fluxes, Humours; "Watery Humours" under Watery).

Defluxions of Rheum — The ☽ afflicted in ♈; ♄ in ♓; a ♉ and ♓ disease. (See Defluxions; "Rheum" under Head).

Discharges of Rheum — ♈ and ♉ diseases. (See Catarrh, Colds, Defluxions; "Rheum" under Head; "Discharges" under Nose; "Humours", "Rheum", under Throat).

Distillation — Of Rheum — ☿ afflicted in ♋.

Eyes — (See "Rheum" under Eyes).

Head — (See "Rheum" under Head).

Much Rheum — The ☉ in a water sign, and ☌ the Asc. by direction

Salt Rheum — A Form of Chronic Eczema — (See Eczema).

Throat — (See "Rheum" under Throat).

RHEUMATISM — Rheumatic — Rheumatism is caused by ♄, and ♄ afflicting the ☉ and ☽, and is caused by the retention of the wastes and poisons of the body, by the deposit of mineral wastes, or the deposit of Urates, Uric Acid, Urea, etc. (See Precipitation). Rheumatism is also brought on by worry, lowered vitality and nerve force, by over-eating, irregular habits, excesses, surfeits, and by breaking the laws of health. (For further influences causing this disease see "Causes", "Tendency To", and the various paragraphs in this section. Also see Saturn).

Acute Rheumatism — ♂ in the 6th H. in a cardinal sign, and afflicted by the ☉ or ☽.

Arms — Hands — Legs — Feet — ♄ or ♂ in signs which rule the arms, hands, legs, and feet tend to rheumatism in these parts. (See "Rheumatism" under Arms, Feet, Hands, Legs).

Arthritis — (See Joints).

Articular Rheumatism — (See "Rheumatism" under Joints).

Back — (See "Muscular Rheumatism" under Back; Lumbago).

Bones — (See "Rheumatism" under Bones).

Cases of Rheumatism — Birth Data, etc. — See Figures 11G and 11H, in the book, "Astro-Diagnosis" by the Heindels).

Causes of Rheumatism — A ☽ disease, and by the afflictions of ♄ to the ☽; ♄ or ♂ ☌ ☽; ♄ afflicted in ♋ or ♑; a ☿ disease; a ♐, ♑, and ♒ disease; malefics angular, occi. to the ☽, and in the last degrees of ♊ or ♐, and if the benefics are with the malefics, or ori. or angular, and cast any ray to the Lights, the disease will be cured, and the rapidity and the certainty of the cure will be proportionate to their strength. If the benefics are weak, and do not assist, it will tend to be incurable, or greatly prolonged. (See the Introduction to this Article," Tendency To", and the various paragraphs in this section; Hyperacidity; "Impure Blood" under Impure).

Chronic Deformans — (See Ankylosis, Arthritis, Rheumatism, under Joints).

Chronic Rheumatism — ♄ in the 6th H. at B., in a fixed sign, and afflicted by the ☉ or ☽.

Cold, Rheumatic Diseases — A ☽ disease, and afflictions to the ☽; the ☽ afflicted by ♄, and especially in earthy signs.

Continued and Promoted — ♄ or ☿ holding dominion at B., and in familiarity with each other; ♄ angular and elevated above the Lights, and in familiarity with ☿. (See "Tendency" in this section).

Curable — (See "Causes" in this section).

Death by Rheumatism — Death from Rheumatic Fever — ♄ occi, and afflicting the hyleg by dir.; ♄ holding the dominion of death, and afflicting the hyleg by dir.; ♄ in the 8th H. at a Solar Rev. into ♈, and afflicting the ☽ or planet ascending, tends to be very fatal according to the sign occupied by ♄. (See Fever, Tendency, in this section).

Deformities From—(See "Ankylosis", and the various paragraphs under Joints).

Dengue — (See "Fever" in this section).

Deposits—Mineral and Waste Deposits Causing Rheumatism — (See Bile, Deposits, Minerals, Poisons, Uric, Wastes).

Extremities — Rheumatism In — (See "Rheumatism" under Arms, Extremities, Feet, Hands, Legs, Limbs).

Feet—(See "Rheumatism" under Feet).

Fever — Rheumatic Fever — Also Resembles Dengue—The ☽ hyleg, and to the ☌, P., □, or ☍ ♄ by dir.; ♂ afflicted in ♑; ♂ in ♑ in the 6th H.; ♂ in ♑, and afflicting the ☽ or Asc.; Subs. at CP, KP. (See Dengue; "Death" in this section).

Gall Disturbances—(See Bile).

Gout—Rheumatic Gout—(See Gout).

Hands—(See "Arms" in this section).

Headaches—(See "Rheumatic" under Headaches).

Heart — (See "Rheumatic" under Heart).

Hips and Thighs—(See "Rheumatism" under Hips).

Incurable—(See "Causes" in this section).

Joints — (See Ankylosis, Arthritis, Rheumatism, under Joints).

Knees—(See "Rheumatism" under Knees).

Legs — (See "Arms" in this section; "Rheumatism" under Extremities, Legs).

Limbs—Rheumatism In—(See Arms, Extremities, Legs, in this section).

Melancholy—(See "Rheumatism" under Melancholy).

Mineral Deposits—(See Deposits, Minerals).

Muscular Rheumatism — (See "Rheumatism" under Muscles).

Pains — Rheumatic Pains — (See "Pains", "Rheumatism", under Arms, Extremities, Feet, Hands, Hips, Knees, Legs, Thighs; Gout, Resolvent).

Promoted and Continued—(See "Continued" in this section).

Remedy For—(See "Acid Conditions" under Remedies; Resolvent).

Rheumatic Fever — (See "Fever" in this section).

Rheumatoid Arthritis—(See "Arthritis" under Joints).

Shoulders—(See "Rheumatism" under Arms; "Pains", "Rheumatism", under Shoulders).

Tendency to Rheumatism — ♄ influence and affliction at B., and by dir., is the principal cause. Saturn deposits Urea and Gall over the body as Uric Acid, which is one of the principal causes of Rheumatism. (See Bile, Uric Acid). Caused by ♄, and especially when the dominion of death is vested in him; ♄ in an angle, occi. of the ☉, and ori. of the ☽, tends to promote the continuance of rheumatism, and especially if he is also in familiarity with ☿; ♄ afflicting the hyleg or Asc.; ♄ in ♎, ♑, or ♓, occi., and afflicting the ☉, ☽, or Asc.; ♄, ♅, or ♆ in ♒, and afflicting the ☉ or ☽; ♄ afflicted in the 6th H. in cardinal signs; a ♑ disease, the sign of ♄; afflictions in ♐ or ♑; afflictions in ♒, also the sign of ♄; ♑ on the Asc. or 6th H.; ♄ sole ruler of a Solar Eclipse; ♄ to the ☌ or ill-asps. the ☽ if the ☽ be hyleg, or ruler of the 6th or 8th H.; an ♒ disease, the day sign of ♄; ♄ afflicted in ♒; the ☉ to the ☌, P., □, or ☍ ♄ by dir.; the ☉ to the ☌ ☋ by dir.; the ☉, ♄, ♂, or ☿ afflicted in ♑; the ☉, ♄, or ♂ in the 6th H., afflicted, and in a cardinal sign; the ☉ in ♋ and afflicted by ♄; the parallel or ☌ of ♄ and the ☉ in ♋, ♑, or ♒; the ☉ to the ☌ or ill-asp. ♄ by dir., and the ☉ and ♄ in ♋, ♑, or ♒ at B.; the ☽ hyleg, and to the ☌, P., □, or ☍ ♄ by dir.; the ☽ hyleg in ♑, and afflicted, and especially with females; the ☽ sign ♋ upon the Asc., and afflicted by ♄; the ☽ ☌, □, or ☍ ♄ at a Solar Rev.; ♆ in ♓ and afflicting the ☉; ♆ in ♒ and afflicting the ☉ or ☽; ♅ in ♒ and afflicting the ☉ or ☽; ♃ afflicted in ♐; a ♐ disease, and caused by afflictions in ♐; ♃ afflicted in ♉, ♋, or in the 6th H., and usually from over-eating and surfeits; ♂ and ♄ in signs which rule the arms, hands, legs and feet tend to rheumatism in these parts; ♂ in the 6th H. in cardinal signs, and afflicting the ☉ or ☽, tends to acute rheumatism; ☿ in ♏ or ♒, ☌, or ill-asp. any of the malefics as Promittors, tends to touches of rheumatism; a ♓ disease, and caused by afflictions in ♓. (For other influences see the various paragraphs in this Article).

Thighs — (See "Rheumatism" under Hips).

Treatment For — (See "Remedy" in this section).

Urea—Retention of—(See Urea).

Uric Acid Deposits—(See Uric). For collateral study, see such subjects as "Pressure", "Too Much Blood", under Blood; Diet, Eating, Excesses, Gluttony, Habits, Hyperacidity, Plethora, Surfeits, etc.

RHINITIS—Cold In the Head—Coryza —(See "Rhinitis" under Nose).

RHUS TOXICODENDRON—Poison Ivy —(See Ivy).

RHYTHM—Rhythmical—Symmetric Movement—

Arhythmia Cordis — (See "Rhythm" under Heart).

Breathing—Interference With Rhythmic Breathing — (See "Rhythmic Breathing" under Breath).

Diaphragm—Rhythmic Action of Disturbed—(See "Rhythm" under Diaphragm).

Heart — Rhythm of Disturbed — (See "Rhythm" under Heart).

Operations — The Rhythmical Operations In the Body — These depend largely upon the vital points in the Cranium and Encephalon, and ruled over by the first zone, or node of ♈. The ☉ in ♈ in this zone, and influenced by ☿, excites the nervous cell. The ☉ incites organic rhythm. The ☽ also excites the organismic rhythm according to the Zodiac zones she passes through, and gives way to Zymotic Periodicity. Venus also largely influences the harmony and rhythm in the system. In Nature, there is a rhythmic movement throughout the Universe, and everything moves in cycles of more or less regularity, and the pendulum swings back and forth in human, and other matters, in rhythmic order. The Planets also have their rhythm. The student should make a study of the subject of Rhythm in the Occult and Metaphysical books, as such books go into various details as to the rhythm in the Universe. (See Balance, Coalition, Coordination, Dexterity, Equilibrium, Harmony, Nature, Sympathy, Vibration, etc.).

RIBES—Ganglion of—(See "Ribes" under Ganglion).

RIBS—Costal—The Ribs are under the structural rulership of the ♋ sign. Gemini also rules over the upper Ribs. Also ♃ rules the ribs. Saturn in ♉, ♊, and ♋ rules and affects the ribs and bones connected with the Respiratory System. There are 24 Ribs, with 12 on each side, and their attachments to the vertebrae are given under the subject of Vertebrae.

All Diseases In—In and Around the Ribs—♌ diseases, and afflictions in ♌; diseases of ♃.

Broken Ribs—Fractures of—Caused generally by ♄ or ♂ afflicted in ♊ or ♋.

Shooting Pains—Under the Ribs—The ☽ in ♍, ☌, P., □, or ☍ ♄ (or ☿ if he be of the nature of ♄) at the beginning of an illness, or at decumb., and under this affliction the patient is generally ailing a long time (Hor'y).

Upper Ribs—The True Ribs—Ruled by ♊. The Lower, or False Ribs, are ruled by ♊ and the ♋ sign. (See Chest, Flanks, Intercostal, Sides, Sternum, Thorax, Vertebrae).

RICH—Abundant—Copious—

Blood Too Rich — Gross Blood — (See Gross, Rich, under Blood).

Food Too Rich—Love of Rich Food—(See "Rich" under Food). See Riches.

RICHES—Wealth—Property Interests—Real Estate—Lands—Fortune—Material Prosperity, etc.—

Accumulates Great Riches — The ☽ Sig. ☌ ♃, but is apt to lose it thru many impositions upon his kindness and generosity; ♃ aspecting the Meridian at B., unless evil aspects counteract, becomes extremely wealthy, and comes to distinction; ☿ Sig. ☌ ♃. (See "Confers", and the various paragraphs in this section.

Acquires Property—(See Property).

Bankruptcy — And Reverses — (See Failure, Loss Of, Reverses, Ruin).

Benevolent — Gives Money Freely — The ☽ ☌ ♃; ♃ in the Asc. or M.C., in ♐ or ♓, and well-aspected. (See Generous; "Accumulates" in this section).

Betting—(See "Gambling" in this section).

Buildings and Real Estate—Gains By—The ☽ on the Meridian at B., or coming to it, and well-aspected by ♄, and ♄ strong and dignified. (See Property).

Confers Riches—The ☉ Sig. ⚹ or △ ♃, gains money rapidly; the ☉ Sig. ⚹ or △ ☽, confers riches and honours; the ☽ on the Meridian at B., or coming to, and well-aspected by ♃; ♃ Sig. ☌, ⚹, or △ ♀; ♀ Sig. ☌ ♃; fixed stars of a fortunate nature ascending, culminating, or with the ☉ or ☽, such as Arista, North Scale, Rigel, etc. (See "Accumulates", and the various paragraphs in this section).

Death — Thru Worry from Loss of Property—(See Property).

Disgrace—And Loss of Riches—(See Disgrace, Honour, Reverses, Ruin, Scandal; "Losses" in this section).

Duped of His Property — (See Property).

Extravagant—(See Expense, Extravagance, Luxuries, Prodigal, etc.).

Failure — In Business — (See Failure, Property, Reverses, Ruin).

Free Living — High Living — (See "Free Living" under Free; "Living" under High).

Gains Property—Often Gains Considerable Property, Although Unstable In Disposition—♀ Sig. ⚹ or △ the ☽. (See Accumulates, Confers, in this section; Property).

Gambling—Losses By—Fond of Betting—♃ afflicted at B., and ♃ to the ill-asps. ♂ by dir. (See Gambling).

Generous With Money—(See "Benevolent" in this section; Money).

Great Riches—(See "Accumulates" in this section).

Honors Conferred — Confers Honors and Riches—The ☉ Sig. ⚹ or △ the ☽ or ♃; ♃ strong, dignified, and well-aspected in the 10th H.; ♀ Sig. ☌ ♃. (See "Confers" in this section).

Hypocritical Fanatics — Impoverished By—(See "Impoverished" in this section).

Impoverished—Property Impoverished by Hypocritical Fanatics—The ☽ Sig. □ or ☍ ♃.

Indigent—(See Apathy, Dull, Indifferent, Indigent, Lazy, Poor, Poverty, Property).

Lawsuits — Losses By — Brings Lawsuits Over Money Matters — Lawsuits are ruled by the 7th H., and malefics passing thru this house by transit or direction tend to lawsuits; the ☉ to the ☌ or ill-asp. ♂ by dir.; the ☽ to the □ or ☍ ☿ by dir.; the ☽ hyleg, and ☿ afflicted at B.; ♃ Sig. □ or ☍ ☿, becomes indigent and poor; ☿ Sig. □ or ☍ ♄. (See Law, Libel; "Lawsuits" under Public; Quarrelsome).

Losses—Suffers Losses—The ☉ Sig. □ or ☍ the ☽ or ♃; ♄ in the 2nd H. at B., in a weak sign, and afflicted. (See Misfortune, Property, Reverses, Ruin; the various paragraphs in this section).

Luxuries—Waste of Fortune By—(See "Extravagant" in this section).

Merchandise—Gains a Fortune By—♄ Sig. ♂ ♃.

Mines—Riches From—(See Mines).

Miserly—(See Miserly, Penurious).

Misfortune—(See Fate, Fortune, Misery, Misfortune, Wretched).

Money—Makes Money—Loses Money — (See Money, Property, Reverses, Ruin, Wealth; the various paragraphs in this section).

Poverty and Indigence — (See "Indigent" in this section).

Preaching — Gains Riches By — (See "Clergymen" under Religion).

Profession—Gains Riches By—Loses By — (See Confers, Losses, and the various paragraphs in this section; "Fortunate" under Fortune; Prosperity).

Property—Gains Property—Losses of — (See Property; the various paragraphs in this section).

Prosperity — (See "Degrees", "Fortunate", under Fortune; Prosperity; "Confers" in this section).

Rapidly—Gains Money Rapidly—(See "Confers" in this section).

Real Estate—Gains By—(See "Buildings" in this section).

Reverses—(See Failure; "Ill-Fortune" under Fortune; Misfortune, Reverses, Ruin, etc.).

Rich—Becomes Rich—(See Accumulates, Confers, in this section).

Riotous Living—Wastes Riches By—(See Drink, Expense, Extravagant, Free, Loose, Luxuries, Prodigal, Riotous).

Ruined — Financial Ruin — (See Disgrace, Drink, Excesses, Failure, Free Living, Gambling, High Living, Honour, Loose Living, Prodigal, Ruin, Thieving, etc.).

Speculation—Loses By—The ☉ Sig. ♂ ♄; malefics afflicted in the 5th H., or a malefic lord of the 5th, and afflicted, and with no fortunate influences over the 5th H. (See Gambling).

Uncharitable — (See Cruel, Miserly, Mistrustful, Penurious, Pity, Selfish, Suspicious).

Unsettled—Not Settled Long Enough to Gain Wealth — ♃ Sig. ♂ ☽. (See Changes, Residence, Restless, Travel, Vacillating, etc.).

Vocation — Many Changes In — (See Vocation).

Waste of Fortune—(See "Riotous" in this section).

Wealth—Gains Wealth—Loses Wealth (See Accumulates, Confers, Losses, Reverses, Riotous, and the various paragraphs in this section).

RICKETS—Rachitis—A ♄ disease; ♄ afflicted in ♓; the ☉ afflicted by ♄ at B. This is a disease of childhood, and with increased cell growth of the bones, softening of the bones, lack of earthy matter, with deformity, and changes in the liver and spleen.

Case of Rickets—(See Fig. 13G in the book, "Astro-Diagnosis", by the Heindels).

Foetal Rickets — Due to Improper Formation of Cartilage — (See Cartilage).

Mineral Salts—Lack of In the Blood, Causing Rickets—(See "Blood" under Minerals).

RIDING—Horseback Riding—Fond of—(See "Riding" under Horses; "Outdoor" under Sports).

Injury By—(See "Injury", "Thrown", under Horses).

RIGEL—Orion's Foot—A star of the 1st magnitude in the 3rd face of ♊, and of the nature of ♃ and ♂. When rising or culminating at B. tends to bring honors, riches, and happiness. The ☉ to the place of gives boldness, and also tends to loss of blood. The ☽ to the place of brings danger of sickness, death of the wife or mother, or an aged female relative. The Asc. to the place of causes melancholy and timidity. (See "Death Of" under Aunts; Mechanical; "Tendency To" under Melancholy; "Death Of" under Mother, Wife, Timidity).

RIGHT—Right Side of the Body—Taken as a whole the ☉ is said to rule the right side of the body. It is also ruled by heat, and the hot and dry elements, and has more heat than the left side, and the left side is ruled by cold, and cold and moisture. The even, negative, and feminine signs of the Zodiac correspond to the right side of the body in the male, and the odd, positive, and masculine signs to the right side of the body in the female. Thus in the male the right side is ruled by the 2nd, 4th, 6th, 8th, 10th, and 12th Houses, corresponding also to the ♉, ♎, ♍, ♏, ♑, and ♓ signs. These influences would rule the left side of the female. In the female the right side is ruled by the positive signs and houses, as the 1st, 3rd, 5th, 7th, 9th, and 11th Houses, and by ♈, ♊, ♌, ♎, ♐, and ♒, etc. However, the ☉ and the masculine signs are said to rule the right side as a whole, regardless of sex, and the ☽ and feminine signs over the left side as a whole. However, in determining the degree of heat and cold in the different organs and parts of the right side of the body, it is well to be governed by the rules according to the sex of the nativity. (See "Houses", "Signs", under Feminine, Masculine, Negative, Odd, Positive; Houses; "Left Side of Body" under Left; Signs of the Zodiac).

Accidents to Right Side — Hurts and Injuries To—Malefics, and especially ♄ and ♂ in feminine signs. Thus ♄ in ♑ at B. tends to injuries to the right knee in a male, and to the left knee in a female, etc.

Auricle—Right Auricles of the Heart —(See "Auricles", "Right Side", under Heart).

Cerebral Hemisphere — The Right Cerebral Hemisphere—(See Cerebral).

Coronary Plexus—The Right Coronary Plexus—(See "Middle Cervical" under Ganglion).

Eyes — The Right Eye in a male is ruled by the ☉, and by the ☽ in a female. The ☉ afflicted by malefics, Nebulous Stars, or the ☉ afflicted in ♈

or the 1st H., or the ☉ to the evil asp. a malefic by dir., tends especially to accidents, blindness, impediments, marks, scars, diseases, or injuries to the right eye of a male, and the ☽ under similar conditions to the right eye of a female. Hurts, Blows, and Injuries to the right eye of a male are caused also by the ☉ afflicted at B., and to the ☌, P., or ill-asp. the Asc. by dir., and especially if the ☉ be in an airy sign. The ☉ to the ☌ ♄ by dir., or the ☉ to the place of Antares, tends to hurts to the right eye of a male by blows, injuries, or falls. The ☽ when afflicted under similar conditions tends to the same kind of afflictions, marks, or injuries to the right eye of a female. In Hindu Astrology the 2nd House rules the right eye. (See "Right Eye" under Eyes, Females, Males, Scars; "Eyes" under Left, Marks).

Face—Marks on Right Side of—(See "Marks" under Face).

Females—Right Eye In — Right Side of—(See the Introduction, and "Eyes" in this section).

Foot — Mark or Mole on the Right Foot—(See "Marks" under Feet).

Heat—The Right Side of the body is ruled by heat, and heat is the elemental quality. (See Heat; Introduction to this Article).

Injuries—To Right Side—(See "Accidents", "Eyes", and the Introduction in this section).

Lungs — (See "Right Lung" under Lungs).

Males — Right Side of — (See "Accidents", "Eyes", and the Introduction in this section; "Right Eye" under Males).

Marks—Moles—On Right Side of the Body—(See "Right Side" under Marks; the various paragraphs, and the Introduction in this section).

Right-Handedness—(See Dexterity).

RIGHTS OF OTHERS — Little Regard For — (See Cruel, Improvident, Indifferent, Respect).

RIGIDITY — Rigid—Stiffness—Immobility — Inflexible — Spastic, etc. — Caused by ♄, and the hardening of the synovial membranes. (See Contortions, Contractions, Crystallization, Deposits, Gout, Hardening, Immobility, Inflexible, Joints, Limbs, Minerals, Muscles, Opisthotonos, Retraction, Rheumatism, Spasmodic, Spine, Stiffness, Synovial, Tetanus, Tonic Spasm, etc.).

Rigid Parts — Contortion of — ♄ ☌ or ill-asp. ♅. (See Contortions, Distortions, Twistings).

Rigid Self-Denial — (See Miserly, Penurious, Recluse, Renunciation, Self-Denial, Selfishness).

Rigors—(See Rigors).

Testicle—Right Testicle—(See Testes).

RIGORS—Coldness—Stiffness—Rigidity —♄ ☌ or ill-asp. the ☉. (See "Body" under Cold; Rigidity, Stiffness).

Rigor Mortis — The Rigidity of the Body After Death — Ruled over and produced by ♄. (See Death).

RINGWORM — The Circling Tinea or Herpes—Tetter—Ringworm is a ♀ disease, and results from Gormandizing and Gluttony, as a rule; a ♂ disease, and caused by ♂ afflictions; an ♈ disease when malefics are in this sign; ♂ afflicted in ♈, or ♂ in ♈ in the 6th H., and afflicted; the ☽ afflicted in ♋, ♌, or ♍; ♃ afflicted in ♉. (See "Barber's Itch" under Barbers; Eczema, Herpes, Tetter).

RIOTOUS — A Turbulent Mind — A ♂ quality; ♂ ☌ or ill-asp. ☿; ♂ ill-dignified at B., and afflicted; ♂ to the ill-asps. ☿ by dir.; ♂ □ or ☍ ☿, a sharp and turbulent mind; ♂ Sig. in ♒; the ☽ in ♋, and afflicted by ♂ or the ☉; ♄ Sig. ☌ ♂, rash and turbulent; ♀ ill-dignified at B.; Part of Fortune (⊕) to the ill-asps. ♀ by dir.; the M.C. to the place of Algol or Hydra's Heart; strong ♋ and ♑ influence at B. (See Anarchists, Destructiveness, Erratic, Foolhardy; "Impractical" under Ideals; Malevolent, Mischief, Quarrelsome, Radicalism, Rashness, Reactionary, Recklessness, Reformers; "High Temper" under Temper; Turbulent, Vicious, Violent, etc.).

Death—A Riotous Death—Death In a Riotous Manner—♆ and ♂ predispose to when they are Anareta, and holding the dominion of death. (See Anareta, Lynching, Mobs; "Death" under Neptune, Violent; Riots, etc.).

Fancies—Turbulent and Riotous Fancies—(See "Turbulent" under Fancies).

Riotous Living—The ☉ Sig. □ or ☍ ♃; ♀ diseases, and afflictions to ♀. (See Debauchery, Dissipation, Dissolute, Drunkenness; "Free Living" under Free; "High Living" under High; Living; "Loose Morals" under Morals).

Stomach Disordered — By Drink and Riotous Living—(See "Stomach" under Drink).

RIOTS—Danger of—Danger of Death In —♂ in the Asc. at the Vernal, lord of the year, and afflicted. (See Hanging, Lynching, Mobs; "Death" under Riotous, Violent; "Flying Stones" under Stones; Trampled, Tumults, War).

RIPE—Ripening—Maturation—

Ripe Fate—(See Fate).

Ripe Old Age—Lives To—(See "Long Life" under Life).

Ripening — (See Fruit, Maturation, Tubercle).

RISING — Rising Planets—Rising Sign —Risings—

A Rising—(See Abscesses, Boils, Carbuncles, Swellings, Tumors, etc.).

Rising Planets—Planets when rising at B., between Midnight and Noon, are more powerful for good or ill over the native than when setting between the time of Noon and Midnight. Children born in the morning hours, with the ☉ rising, tend to be leaders in the World, and have better health and vitality, while those born in the afternoon hours, with the ☉ setting in the West, tend, as a rule, to be followers, and especially if other conditions and majorities of the planets concur. (See Elevated, Majority; "Above the Earth" under Moon; Occidental, Oriental, Quarters, Setting, etc.).

Rising Sign—The Sign rising on the cusp of the First House at Birth—The

Ascendant—The Degree Rising on the Eastern Horizon at Birth—The Rising Sign rules largely over the life and the health. The most vital and sensitive part of the body is ruled by the Rising Sign, and when this part of the body is weakened, long illnesses often result. Also the Sign upon the Ascendant at B. shows the nature of the diseases the native is subject to during life. (See Ascendant; "Zodiac" under Degrees; First House).

RISKS — Perils — Has Endured Many Dangers — (See Dangers, Perils, Rescue).

RITUAL—Ritualism—(See "Ritualism" under Religion).

RIVERS—Streams—Running Water—

Corruption Of—Eclipses of the ☉ or ☽ in ♍ or ♓. (See Corruption, Fishes, Moisture, Waters).

Rivers Fail — Eclipses of ☉ in 1st Decan. of ♓. (See Drought; "Fountains" under Dry; Famine, Fountains; "Extreme Heat" under Heat).

ROAMING NATURE — A Roving and Wandering Nature—A ☽ influence; the ☽ in the Asc. or M.C. at B. (See Changes, Instability, Location, Novelties, Residence, Restlessness; "Travels Much" under Travel; Vacillating; Vagabond, Wanderer, etc.).

ROBBERS — Bandits — Robberies — Thieves—

A Robber—♂ and ☿ together lords of the employment; ♂ stronger, and in ill-asp. to the ☽; ☿ Sig. ☌ ♂. (See Cheating, Deceitful, Dishonest, Gambling, Highwaymen, Murderous, Pirates, Thieves, etc.).

Accidents—In Attacks by Robbers—(See "Death by Burns" under Burns).

Attacks By — Attacks or Injury by Robbers, Bandits, or Burglars — The malefics in the M.C., and elevated above the Lights, and ♂ holding dominion and afflicting the hyleg; ♅ afflicted in the 12th H.; ♄ and ♂ in human signs and controlling the Luminaries; ♂ afflicted in ♊ or ♍, and ☌, □, or ☍ the Asc. by dir.; ♂ in the 12th H., and afflicted by ♅ or ♄. (See Distortions, Excrescences, Highwaymen; "Dangers" under Travel; the various paragraphs in this section).

Burned to Death—During Attack by Robbers—(See "Death by Burns" under Burns).

Danger by Robbers—Or Thieves—Injury By—The ☽ passing over the place of the radical ♂ at a Solar Rev.; eclipse of ☽ in 3rd dec. ♓; the Periodic Rev. of ♄ on the place of the radical ♂; the ⊕ to the ☌, P, or ill-asp. ♂ by dir.; the cusp of the 2nd H., or its ruler, to the ☌, P, or evil asp. ♂ by dir.; the ☉ to the ☌ ♂ by dir.; ♂ ☌ the Asc. by dir. (See the various paragraphs in this section).

Death by Robbers—Violent Death by Robbers, Highwaymen or Thieves — The ☽ passing over the place of the radical ♂ at a Solar Rev.; ♅ afflicted in the 12th H.; ♄ and ♂ in ♊, ♍, ♐, or ♒, and in □ or ☍ the ☉ or ☽, and ☿ also evilly configurated with ♂; ♃ Sig. □ or ☍ ♂; ♂ in signs of human form, □ or ☍ the ☉ or ☽, and contrary in condition, and ☿ also configurated with them; ♂ by Periodic Rev. to the evil asps. ♅; ♂, (or ☿ afflicted by ♂), and either of them ruler of the 12th H. at B., and be found on the cusp the 7th H. in a Solar Rev., danger during the ensuing year; ♂ badly aspected at B., and ♄ passing over the place of ♂ by transit, or at a Solar Rev.; ♂ ori. in fixed signs, and □ or ☍ the ☉ at B., or ♂ occi., □ or ☍ the ☽ at B.; ♂ Sig. □ or ☍ ☉ if ☉ be lord of 7th H.; ☿ afflicted at B. by ♄ or ♂, and ♂ afflicting the hyleg by dir., and ☿ holding the dominion of death; ☿ occi. at B., ☌, □, or ☍ ♄ or ♂, and afflicting the hyleg by dir., and in a train of fatal directions; ☿ afflicting the hyleg, or giver of life, by dir. (See Bandits, Highwaymen, Murdered, Pirates, Thieves; "Danger" under Travel).

Distortions — Excrescences — The Result of Attacks by Robbers—(See Distortions, Excrescences).

Excrescences — (See "Distortions" in this section).

Eyes — Injury To by Robbers — (See "Robbers" under Eyes).

Gunshot Wounds By—(See Gunshot).

Highwaymen—Death or Injury By—(See Death, Prevalent, in this section; Highwaymen).

Hurts By—Injury By—(See "Attacks", and the various paragraphs in this section).

Injury By—(See Attacks, Distortions, and the various paragraphs in this section).

Journey—Hurts By On a Journey—♂ or ☋ in the 3rd H. in a fiery sign. (See "Accidents" under Journeys).

Killed By — (See "Death" in this section).

Many Robberies—(See Highwaymen, Prevalent, in this section).

Prevalent — Many Robberies Prevalent—An eclipse of the ☉ in 2nd decan. of ♊ or ♒; eclipse of ☽ in 2nd decan. ♑; ♂ in ♏ at the Vernal, and lord of the year. (See Crime, Highwaymen, Rapine, Thieves).

Rapine Prevalent — Plundering — (See Rapine, Thefts).

Thieves — Injury or Death By — (See Attacks, Death, and the various paragraphs in this section).

Travel—Attacks by Robbers or Highwaymen During Travel—The afflictor to the Sig. of travel being in the 12th H., and in ♊ or ♍, and especially if ♂ or ☿ be the afflictor. (See Highwaymen, Pirates; "Danger" under Travel; "Journey" in this section).

Violent Death By — (See "Death" in this section).

ROBUST—Robust Body—Strong Body—Wiry Body — Robust Constitution — Rugged—Ruddy—Hardy—Sturdy—Enduring Health and Strength, etc.—

Complexion—Robust and Ruddy Complexion—(See Complexion, Ruddy).

Constitution—Robust Constitution—♂ people tend to have a strong, robust, sturdy body; ♂ ascending at B.; born under the strong rule of ♂, and ♂ ruler; the ♂ signs ♈ or ♏ upon the Asc. at B.; the ☽ or ♃ in ♌; ♃ strong at B.; ♃ well-aspected in ♏; born under ♃; fiery signs on the Asc. at B.; born under the whole signs ♊, ♎, and ♒, strong and robust; ♏ on the Asc., strong, robust, and corpulent, and of middle size; ♒ on the Asc., robust, strong, well-set, healthy, plump, but usually not tall; the 19° ♍ on the Asc. at B. (See "Good" under Constitution; "Abundance", "Good", under Health; Immunity, Invigoration; "Great Physical Powers" under Physical; Ruddy, Stamina, Strength; "Body" under Strong; Tone; "Good" under Vitality).

Females Robust—(See "Robust" under Females).

Frame Strengthened—(See "Strengthening" under Bones).

Health Good—(See "Good" under Health).

Less Robust—(See Debility, Feeble, Ill-Health, Infirm, Invalids; "Much Sickness" under Sickness; "Low" under Vitality; "Weak Body" under Weak).

Men More Robust—(See "Good Health", "Robust", under Males).

Not Robust—(See "Bad Health" under Health; "Ill-Health" All Thru Life" under Ill-Health; Pale, Sickly; "Weakened" under Strength; "Not Strong" under Strong; "Less Robust" in this section).

Sports—Fond of Robust Sports—(See "Robust" under Sports).

Tone—(See "Good Tone" under Tone).

Vitality Good—(See "Good" under Vitality).

Weak Body—(See "Weak Body" under Weak).

ROCKS—Rocky—(See Metals, Minerals).

Rocky Mountain Fever—(See Mountain).

ROLLING STOCK—Accidents, Injuries, or Death By—(See Journeys, Railroads, Travel, Vehicles).

Rolling Eyes—(See "Rolling" under Eyes).

ROMAN EMPEROR—Should be Careful of Assassination by a Stab—♂ in ♑, Ruler of the Year at the Vernal Equi., and ori., and especially if the ☽ is in the 8th H., or with the lord of the 8th, or with ♂ in an angle, and with no good aspect from ♃. (See Kings, Nobles, Princes, Rulers).

ROMANCE—Romantic—Love of Romance—Romantic Disposition—Given by ♆ and ♅; ♆ ☌ ☽ in ♓; ♅ strong and rising at B.; the 2° ♉ on the Asc., ruled by the ☽. The watery signs are also strongly connected with romance and emotionalism, and also the ♌ sign. (See Emotions, Feelings, Leo Sign; "Romance" under Love Affairs; Mental, Neptune, Temperament, Uranus, Watery Signs).

ROOTS—Root Vegetables which grow under the ground, such as carrots, turnips, potatoes, etc, are not as nourishing and life-giving as the leafy vegetables and fruits which grow above the ground, as the latter are Sun-kissed, and contain more of the vital power of the ☉. Roots are more governed by ♄, and grow in the dark and cold, as ♄ rules the ground. In illness, fruit juices are more vitalizing than roots. (See Drugs, Herbs, Medicines, Remedies, Treatment, Vegetables, etc.).

ROSE COLD—(See "Hay Fever" under Nose).

ROSE-COLORED—Rosy—

Rose-Colored Vital Fluid—(See "Fluid" under Vital). See Roseola.

Rosy Complexion—(See "Rosy" under Complexion).

ROSEOLA—A Rose-Colored Efflorescence on the Skin—A ♄ and ♑ disease; ♄ afflicted in ♑, or in the Asc.; ♑ on the Asc.; afflictions in ♑. (See Efflorescence, Skin).

ROTTEN—Rottenness—Putrid—Corruption—See the following subjects—

Abscesses; Breath—Rotten and Putrid Breath—(See "Foul" under Breath).

Corrupt; Coughs—(See "Rotten" under Cough).

Death—♀ denotes death from diseases arising from rottenness and putrefaction, and such as arise from too much moisture. (See "Death" under Moisture, Putrid).

Diseases—Arising from Rottenness—Death From—(See "Death" in this section).

Disintegration; Fetid; Food—(See "Rottenness" under Food).

Foul; Fruit; Gangrene; Herbs—Rottenness of—(See "Seeds" in this section).

Impure—Impurities—(See Corrupt, Impure).

Moisture—Moisture and Dampness are associated with rottenness. (See "Moist Warmth" under Moisture; "Physiological Action" under Moon; Vapors).

Mortification; Pus; Putrid;

Seeds and Herbs—Rottenness of—An eclipse of the ☉ or ☽ in ♎; an eclipse of the ☽ in ♒, seeds are injured; Comets appearing in ♑, detriment to seeds of the Earth. (See Comets, Eclipses, Fruit, Grain, Herbs, Putrefaction, Seeds, Vegetation, etc.).

Sores; Teeth—(See "Rotten" under Teeth).

Ulcers; Vegetation.

ROUGH—Not Smooth—Harsh—Rugged—Uncouth—Coarse—

Carriage—Rough In Carriage—(See "Rough" under Gait).

Gait—(See "Rough" under Gait).

Hair—(See "Coarse", "Rough", under Hair).

Manner—Rough In Manner—Rude—Unrefined—Vulgar—Coarse—The ☽ Sig. ☌ ♄; caused by the undesirable aspects and afflictions of ♄ and ♂ to the ☉, ☽, ☿, or Asc.; ♄ ☍ ♂ in angles. The signs of ☿ also tend to a lack of polish and refinement if ♀ is not strong and well-placed, but the strong and good aspects of ♃ and ♀ tend to counteract this. Neptune and the ☽ when well-aspected do not tend to roughness of manner, but give more refinement. (See Awkwardness, Coarse, Cruel, Gross; "Rough" under Manners; Merciless, Pity, Profane, Refined, Rugged, Unrefined, Vulgar, etc.).

Skin — Rough and Hard Skin — (See "Skin" under Hard; Scales; "Rough", "Thick", under Skin).

Voice—(See Hoarseness; "Rough" under Voice).

ROUND—Circular—(See "Round" under Eyes, Face, Head, Shoulders, Upper).

ROUSE—Arouse—Hard to Arouse—Difficult to Excite to Action — The occidental positions of the planets at B. tend to make the native less active, and difficult to arouse to action. Also, ♄ influence strong at B. tends to heaviness and moroseness. (See "Degree Of" under Activity; Apathy, Careless, Dull; "Lack Of" under Energy; Enervation, Heavy, Idle, Improvident, Inactive, Indifferent, Inertia, Labor, Lassitude, Lazy, Lethargy, Listless, Morose, Negative, Neglectful, Occidental, Procrastination, Sickly; "Arouse" under Sickness; "Low" under Vitality; "Weak Body" under Weak, etc.).

ROVING NATURE — A Roamer — A Wanderer — Many Changes of Residence, etc. — (See Changes, Location, Residence, Restlessness, Roaming, Travel, Vagabond, Wanderer).

ROYAL—Royalty—

Royal Disposition—The ☉ Sig. in ♌. (See Leo, Noble, Sincere, Temperament).

Royalty — (See Kings, Monarchs, Princes, Queens, Roman, Rulers).

RUBBING—Friction—Fremitus—Irritation—(See Friction).

RUBEFACIENT — Counter-Irritants — An Agent Which Reddens the Skin— The action of ♂ is rubefacient and reddening. Cantharides, a ♂ drug, is used as a rubefacient, and for blistering. Capsicum (Red Pepper) is used in strong Pain Liniments, a ♂ remedy. Sinapis Nigra and Alba (Mustard), ☉ remedies, are also strong rubefacients. (See Applications, Blisters, Cantharides, Capsicum, Caustics, Efflorescent, Liniments, Lotions, Mustard, Rashes, Sinapis, Stimulant, Tar, Vesicant).

RUBEOLA—(See Measles).

RUDDY—Healthy Appearance—

Ruddy Complexion—Florid Complexion—Ruddy Countenance—Ruddy Face —The ☉ and ♂ make the complexion more florid; the ☉ strong at B.; the ☉ Sig. in ♎; the ☉ rising in the Asc.; the ☽ in ♍, dark and ruddy; the ☽ Sig. in ♎, ♐, or ♒; ♄ in ♈ in Hor'y Q.; ♄ in ♈ in partile asp. the Asc., and in good aspect to the Asc.; ♃ ascending; ♃ Sig. in ♌ or ♐; ♃ in ♌ or ♐, partile asp. the Asc.; ♃ Sig. in ♍, ruddy but not clear or fair; ♂ occidental; characteristic of ♂ people; ♂ ascending; ♂ in the Asc. tends to increase the iron in the system, giving a ruddy color, red hair, etc.; in Hor'y Q., ♂ Sig. of the person; ♂ Sig. in ♉, or ♂ in ♉ in partile asp. the Asc., ruddy, but never fair; ♂ Sig. in ♈ or ♏, ruddy and smooth countenance if ♂ be ori.; ♂ in ♌; ♂ strong at B., and ruler; ♀ Sig., ruddy but not fair; ☿ Sig. in ♎, or ♐; ☿ in ♐ in partile asp. the Asc.; ♌, ♍, and ♐ on the Asc.; ♍ on the Asc., a dark, ruddy complexion; ♌ on the Asc., a ruddy, oval countenance; ♎ on the Asc., a ruddy complexion in youth, but with pimples in middle life and old age. (See "Ruddy Constitution" in this section; Beautiful; "Good" under Complexion, Constitution, Health, Vitality; "Red Face" under Face; Fresh, Handsome, Robust; "Body" under Strong; "Complexion" under Youth, etc.).

Ruddy Constitution—The ☉ rising in the Asc.; the ⚹ and △ aspects of the ☉ to ♂ and the planets; the ☽ in ♍ in partile asp. the Asc., tall and rather ruddy; born under ♃; ♂ ruler of the Asc., and ori.; ♂ in ♈, partile the Asc. if ♂ be occi., the native will be more ruddy and smooth, but if ♂ be ori., tall and less swarthy; ♐ on the Asc., ruddy and handsome. (See "Good" under Constitution; "Abundance" under Health; Immunity, Resistance, Robust, Strong; "Good" under Vitality).

Ruddy Countenance — Ruddy Face — (See "Ruddy Complexion" in this section).

Ruddy Face — (See "Ruddy Complexion" in this section).

RUDE—In Manner—(See Rough).

RUFFIANS — Assaults By — The 15° ♑ on the Asc. at B. (See Assaults).

RUGGED—Rough—Unkempt—Sturdy—Robust, etc.—

Rugged Disposition — Overbearing — The ☉ afflicted in ♍; ♄ Sig. □ or ☍ the ☉. (See "Manner" under Rough).

Rugged Hair — (See "Rugged" under Hair).

Rugged Health — Rugged Stature — (See Robust, Ruddy).

RUIN—Ruined—

Ruined In Business—Reverses—Bankruptcy — In Hor'y Questions, ♄ is the Significator of Ruin and Disgrace; ♄ afflicted in the 2nd or 10th H., danger of periodical downfall, loss of position, and of the favor of employer; ♄ in the 10th H., in detriment or fall, and afflicted, almost irretrievable ruin to the average native so born, and difficult to get a permanent foothold in business until he finds his real place in life, and a master of his destiny; the ☉ to the □ ♀ by dir., thru marriage, love affairs, and women; the ☉ directed to Antares, Aldebaran, Deneb, Regulus, Betelguese, Bellatrix, South Scale, Frons Scorpio, threatens ultimate ruin; the ☉ or ☽ joined to the Whale's Jaw; the ☽ directed to Deneb, ultimate ruin and disgrace; the ☽ to the ☌ Cor Hydra, Bellatrix, Left Shoulder of Bootes; ♃ Sig. □ or ☍ ♄; ♂ afflicted in the 10th or 11th H.; the Asc. or M.C. to the □ or ☍ the ☉ or ♄ by dir.; the M.C. directed to Nebulous Stars, the Pleiades, Praesepe, Hyades, Shoulders of Orion, and the Twins, causes ruin and disgrace; the Hyades rising or setting with ☉; the M.C. directed to the Ascelli, Caput Hercules, Markab, Auriga's Right Shoulder, and Medusa's Head; lord of the 10th H. in the 12th; lord of the 12th in the 1st, 9th, or 10th; lord of the 12th in the 2nd, poverty and ruin; lord of the 12th in the 10th, ruin by envy. In order to prevent reverses, business failure, bankruptcy, etc., every person should early in life have their horoscope, and see what their limitations are, find out what their proper vocation is, whether they are calculated for leadership, or to be a follower in life, and then live within their means, and always be saving in times of prosperity, and be ready for the financial emergencies of life, and not be too much given over to the pleasures of this World. The pendulum is ever swinging back and forth, and unusual prosperity comes in cycles, and we must pass thru the Spring, Summer, Autumn, and Winter Periods of life. Seek balance, poise, self-control, and be prepared. (See Business, Disgrace, Downfall; "Own Worst Enemy" under Enemies; Evils, Fate; "Ill-Fortune", "Malice of Fortune", under Fortune; "Loss Of" under Honour; "Ill-Fortune" under Ill; Infamous; "Ruins Himself" under Intemperance; "Ruined" under Love Affairs, Women; Miseries, Misfortune, Neglect, Privation, Poverty, Property, Reputation, Restless, Reverses, Riches, Scandal, Unfortunate).

Ruined by Disgrace — By Dishonour, etc.—(See Disgrace, Dishonour; "Loss Of" under Honour; Scandal, etc.).

Ruined by Love Affairs—And Women —(See "Ruined" under Love Affairs; "Injured Thru Women" under Men).

RULE—Ruling—Ruling Nature—Fond of Rule and Authority—The ☉ Sig. in ♌ or ♒; the ☉ Sig. ☌ ♂ in ♈ or ♌, autocratic; the ☽ Sig. in ♌, and abhors servitude and dependence; ♃ Sig. in ♏, desirous to bear rule over his equals. (See Austere, Commanding, Cruel, Dynamic; "Abundance" under Energy; "Fearless" under Fears; Kings, Merciless; "Shows No Pity" under Pity; "Positive Nature" under Positive; Power, Self-Assertive, Self-Confidence, Self-Reliant; "Disposition" under Severe; "Strong Will" under Will, etc.).

RULERS—Kings—Monarchs—Princes— Death by the Wrath of Rulers—Death of, etc.—Rulers are ruled by the ☉, the ♌ sign, and also denoted by the 10th H. (See Famous; "Great Men", "The Great", under Great; Kings, Nobles, President, Princes, Queens, Roman).

RUMBLING—Noises—

Bowels — Rumbling In the Bowels — (See "Rumbling" under Bowels).

Head—A Rumbling Noise In the Head —(See "Noises" under Head).

RUMINANT SIGNS — Of the Zodiac — Symbolic of an animal which chews the cud, as ♈, ♉, and ♑. Medicines should not be given when the ☽ is passing thru one of these signs, as they tend to produce vomiting or nausea at such a time, and to have an emetic influence. The best time to give an emetic is when the ☽ is in one of these signs. (See Emetics, Nausea, Vomiting).

RUMP — Haunches — Buttocks — (See Buttocks).

RUNNING—

Running of the Reins — (See Gonorrhœa).

Running Pains — Shooting Pains — Flying Pains—Wandering Pains—(See "Running Pains" under Arms, Shoulders; "Flying Pains" under Flying; "Shooting Pains" under Shooting; "Pains" under Whole Body).

Running Sores — (See Discharges, Sores, Ulcers).

RUPTURE—Hernia—Bursting of Parts —Rending—Lacerations—A ♂ and ♏ disorder, and afflictions in ♏. Also caused by the tonic action of ♅, and ♂ ☌ ♅, and the exaggerated action of ♂. See the following subjects in the alphabetical arrangement—

Abdominal Rupture — (See "Abdominal", "Inguinal", "Umbilical", under Hernia).

Aneurysm — (See Aneurysm; "Aneurysm" under Hernia).

Blood Vessels—Rupture of—(See Apoplexy; "Rupture" under Vessels).

Brain—Rupture of Blood Vessels In— Hernia of the Brain — (See Apoplexy, Cerebral; "Brain" under Hernia).

Burstings; Death — By Rupture, and by Rupture of Blood Vessels — (See Apoplexy; "Death" under Hernia).

Exaggerated Action—Of the Planets, and Causing Rupture — The tonic action of ♅ and ♂. (See Exaggerated).

Groin—Rupture In—(See Groins; "Inguinal" under Hernia).

Head — Rupture of Vessels In — (See Apoplexy).

Hemorrhages—From Ruptures—(See Apoplexy; "Rupture" under Hemorrhage, Vessels).

Hernia—(See the various paragraphs under Hernia).

Inguinal Rupture — (See "Inguinal" under Hernia).

Lacerations; Motion — (See "Accelerated" under Motion).

Organs—Rupture of—(See "Accelerated" under Motion; Organs).

Peritoneum — (See "Rupture" under Peritoneum).

Rending — (See Bursting; "Exaggerated Action" under Exaggerated; Lacerations; "Accelerated" under Motion).

Scrotum—Rupture In—(See "Hernia" under Scrotum).

Strangulation—Of a Part Due to Rupture—(See the paragraphs under Hernia).

Tears—Tearing and Rending of Parts —(See "Rending" in this section).

Testicle—Rupture of—(See Testes).

Umbilical Rupture — (See "Hernia" under Navel).

Ventral Hernia — (See "Ventral" under Hernia).

Vessels — Rupture of — (See "Blood Vessels" in this section).

RUSH—Rush of Blood—Determination of Blood To a Part—Flow of Blood—

Head—Rush of Blood To the Head— (See "Blood" under Head).

Part—Rush of Blood To a Part—♂ influence. (See Centrifugal, Determination, Flow, Rubefacient).

RUSSET COLOR—Ruled by the ♋ and ♑ Signs. (See Colors).

RUTHLESSNESS — (See Cruel, Merciless, Pity).

S

SACRUM — Sacral Region — Sacral — Os Sacrum—Sacral Nerves—Sacral Plexus — Sacral Region of the Spine — Ruled by ♏ and ♐. The Bones of the Sacrum are under the structural rulership of the ♏ Sign, and also of ♄, as ♄ rules all the bones. The Sacral Region as a whole is said to be ruled by ♐. The Sacral Plexus is ruled by ♏. The Sacrum includes the large triangular bone above the Coccyx. (See Coccyx, Pelvis, Spine, Subluxations; "Sacrum" under Vertebrae).

Circulation Obstructed—In the Sacral Region—♄ afflicted in ♐; ♄ in ♐, ☌, □, or ☍ ♃ or ♀. (See "Nerves" in this section).

Disorders—In the Sacrum and Sacral Region—Afflictions in ♏ and ♐; ♄ afflicted in ♐; ♄ ☌ ♂ in ♐, and afflicted by ♆; ♂ afflicted in ♐, danger of inflammations and hurts to.

Nerves—The Sacral Nerves Obstructed —♄ afflicted in ♐, and in □ ♃; ♅ or ☿ afflicted in ♏ or ♐.

Obstruction — In the Sacral Circulation and Nerves — (See Circulation, Nerves, in this section).

Pelvis—Formed Partly by the Sacrum —(See Pelvis).

Spina Bifida—Cleft of the Spine Over the Sacrum—Case—(See "Spina Bifida" under Spine).

SACS — Pouch — (See Cavities, Cysts, Follicles, Pouch, Receptacles, Scrotum, Vesicles).

SAD — Sadness — Sad Expression — Sad Hair—Grief—Doleful—Pensive—Lugubrious — Sorrowful — Sad Appearance, etc.—The following subjects have to do with Sadness, which see in the alphabetical arrangement—

Appearance — A Sad Appearance — A Sad Countenance—Thoughtful Expression—A Pensive Aspect—♄ in ♋ gives a thoughtful and sad expression; ♀ afflicted in ♈, a pensive aspect. (See "Sadness" in this section).

Aspect—A Pensive Aspect—(See "Appearance" in this section).

Complexion — (See "Sad Brown" under Complexion).

Countenance — (See "Appearance" in this section).

Death — A Sad Death — Death from Sadness—The 23° ♓ on the Asc. (See the various paragraphs under Death).

Dejected; Depressed; Despondency;

Disgrace — Sad Disgrace—Lord of the 12th in the 10th H., sad disgrace. (See Disgrace).

Expression—(See Appearance" in this section).

Fears; Gloom; Grave; Grief — (See "Public Grief" under Grief).

Hair—Sad Black or Sad Brown Hair —(See "Sad" under Hair).

Hypochondria; Imaginations — (See Doubts, Fears, Imagination).

Low Spirits—(See Low, Melancholy).

Melancholy; Mournful;

Much Sadness Generally — ♄ Lord of the Year at the Vernal, and afflicted; Comets appearing in ♏ or ♎; an eclipse of the ☉ in the 3rd decan. of ♈. (See "Public Grief" under Grief; Highwaymen).

Old Age — (See "Sad Old Age" under Old Age).

Pensive Aspect — (See "Appearance" in this section).

Prevalent — (See the subjects under Prevalent).

Public Sadness — (See "Much Sadness" in this section).

Reserved; Sadism—(See Sadism).

Sadness — A Sad Disposition — A Sad Countenance and Expression—Caused principally by ♄ influence and afflictions, and by the signs of ♄ on the Asc. at B., or with ♄ in his own signs and afflicting the ☉, ☽, ☿, or the Asc.; ♄ in ♋; ♄ in the Asc. or M.C., and afflicting ☿, the mental ruler, or in evil asp. to the ☉ or ☽; ♄ ☌ the Asc. at B.; the ☉, ☽, or ☿ ☌ or ill-asp. ♄ at B., and by dir. or transit; the ☽ at a Solar Rev. passing over the place of ♄ at B.; ♀ Sig. in ♈, a pensive aspect; ☿ Sig. ☌ ♄; ☿ in ♑ and afflicted by ♄; ♑ or ♒ on the Asc., and with ♄ as ruler, and afflicted; lord of the 12th in the 10th, sad disgrace; the 3rd decan. of ♒ on the Asc., inclined to be lugubrious; the 4th face of ♋ on the Asc. at B. (See "Appearance", and the various paragraphs in this section).

Sickness—Sad and Heavy Sickness— (See "Heavy and Sad Sickness" under Heavy).

SADISM—Sex Gratification Attended by Violence — ♂ configurated with ♀. (See "Violent" under Men; "Violence" under Passion; Perversions).

SAFFRON — A Deep Orange Color— Ruled by the ☉ and the 11th H. (See Colors; "Saffron" under Complexion; Eleventh House, Orange).

SAGACIOUS—Sagacity—Shrewdness— Quick Discernment — Wisdom — (See Discernment; "Good" under Judgment; Shrewdness, Wisdom).

SAGITTARIUS — (♐). The Ninth Sign of the Zodiac, ruled by ♃, and is the day sign or house of ♃, and the joy of ♃. This is a fiery, hot, dry, positive, masculine, choleric, common, mutable, changeable, obeying, bicorporeal, quadrupedal, four-footed, autumnal, southern, half human and half mute, speaking, religious, philosophical, restless, adventurous, venturesome, motive, mental sign, and of long ascension. This Sign is affiliated with the Ninth House, the house of Religion, Philosophy, and of Foreign Residence or Travel. It is a rather fruitful sign because of its ♃ influence. The Symbol of this Sign is the Centaur, the Archer. Its influence is strongly for Sports and outdoor life, horseback riding, hunting, etc. When upon the Asc. at

B. it tends to enlarge the body, make the native tall, and many Giants have this sign rising at B. The sign when strong, or ruling at B., tends to give a ruddy complexion, oval face, fine clear eyes, chestnut colored hair, but apt to be bald, and especially about the temples, and with a high forehead. The native of this sign is usually strong, active, intrepid, and with plenty of motive force. Jupiter, the ruler of this sign, when in the Asc. at B., tends to give strong and well-proportioned hips, thighs, and legs. The Colors ruled by this sign are Light Green or Olive, Light Olive, Sanguine, Light Green and Blue, Yellow. For Countries and Nations ruled by this sign see "Sagittarius Rules" under Nations. The Hebrew Letter Samech (S) is connected with ♐, and also with the sense of Smell and Perception. Mercury (Mercurius) is the typical Polycrest Remedy assigned to this sign. (See "Polycrest" under Zodiac). The Pathological Qualities of this sign tend to cause accidents, fractures, restlessness, and venturesomeness. The following Qualities are assigned to this sign—Active, Autumnal, Bicorporeal, Bitter, Changeable, Choleric, Common, Confiding, Conscientious, Diurnal, Double-Bodied, Dry, Eastern, Excitable, Feral (the 2nd half); Fiery, Foolhardy, Fortunate, Frank, Fruitful, Hasty, Heedless, Honest, Hot, Intrepid, Masculine, Mental, Mutable, Obeying, Open-Minded, Philosophical, Pleasure-Loving, Quick, Receptive, Reckless, Religious, Restless, Southern, Speaking, Strong, Susceptible, (being a Common and Mutable Sign); Trusting, Venturesome, etc.

SAGITTARIUS RULES — Arterial System, and especially the Iliac Arteries; Bones (the Coccygeal and Sacral Bones, Pelvis); Buttocks; Coccygeal Region of the Spine, and Coccygeal Vertebrae; Colors — Light Green and Olive or Blue, Sanguine, Yellow; Externally, rules the Hips and Thighs; Femur; Fractures of the Hip and Thigh Bones; Gluteus Muscles; Green Color—Light Green; Hams; Haunches; Hips—Region around the Hips—Locomotor Muscles of the Hips and Thighs; Iliac Arteries and Veins; Ilium; Internally, rules Arterial System and Sciatic Nerve; Ischium; Light Green and Light Olive Colors; Liver; Lungs; Motive Force; Mind—The Higher Mind, a 9th H. influence; Muscles—Gluteus, Sartorius, Rectus Muscles, the Locomotor Muscles of the Hips and Thighs, and also considerable influence over the Muscular System generally; Nerves —The Sciatic Nerve, and has some rule over the Nervous System generally, along with the ☐ Sign; Olive Color (Light Olive); Os Sacrum; Pelvis; Physical Strength, and especially with ♐ on the Asc. at B.; Quartz; Rectus Muscles; Sacrum—The Os Sacrum — The Sacral Bones and Coccygeal Region of the Spine; Sanguine and Green Color; Sartorius Muscles; Sciatic Nerves; Silica; Spine—The Sacral and Coccygeal Region of; Structurally rules the Thigh Bone and Femur; Thighs — The Locomotor Muscles of Hips and Thighs; Veins — The Iliac

Arteries and Veins; Yellow Color. (See Coccyx; "Fire Signs" under Fire; Jupiter; Mutable Signs (see Mutable); Ninth House, Pelvis, Philosophy, Religion, Sacrum, Spine, Vertebrae).

SAGITTARIUS DISEASES—And Afflictions—The ♐ people are usually easily cured of disease because of their confiding, trusting, frank, and open natures if good and positive suggestions are made, but evil and negative suggestions are also equally powerful with them in health matters. The ♐ sign belongs to the Mutable Cross, made up of ☐, ♍, ♐, and ♓, and afflictions and malefics in ♐, or any of these signs, tend to afflict the parts of the body ruled by ♐. The ☐ sign is in 8 to ♐, and supplemental, and afflictions in either sign tend to affect the lungs, hips, thighs, and sacral region. The diseases of ♐ are caused principally, however, by afflictions in ♐, or with ♐ on the Asc., afflicted, and containing malefics; caused by the ☉, ☽, or other planets afflicted in ♐; afflictions in the common, or mutable signs, and with such signs on the angles, and containing malefics. The following diseases and afflictions are ruled over, or influenced by the ♐ sign.

Accidents — Hurts or Injuries to the Hips or Thighs — The principal accidents of this sign are fractures, broken hips or thighs, femurs, etc., and caused by ♄ or ♂ afflicted in ♐, and especially with ♐ on the Asc., and malefics in ♐ in the 1st H. (See Femur, Fractures; "Accidents", "Hurts", under Hips; Thighs).

Aches — In Hips or Thighs — (See "Aches" under Hips).

All Diseases — In Hips or Thighs — (See "All Diseases" under Hips, Thighs).

Baldness—(See Baldness).

Bees Destroyed—(See Bees).

Blood (See "Over-Heated" under Blood).

Bones—Broken Bones—Fractures of the Hip, Femur, and Bones of the Lower Extremities—(See Fractures).

Bowel Disorders—Enteric Diseases—(See "Disorders Of" under Bowels).

Broken Bones—(See Accidents, Bones, in this section).

Bronchitis—(See Bronchial).

Buttocks—Diseases In—Injuries To—(See Buttocks, Haunches).

Consumptive Pains—In the Thighs—(See Thighs).

Coxalgia—(See "Pain" under Hips).

Deformities — Of Hips and Thighs — (See "Deformity" under Thighs).

Dislocation—Of the Hip Joint—(See "Dislocation" under Hips).

Endemic Diseases—(See Endemic).

Enteric Diseases—(See "Disorders Of", and the various paragraphs under Bowels).

Eye—Loss of One Eye—The ☽ with the Arrow Head of ♐ tends to blindness in one eye. (See Arrow Head; "One Eye" under Blindness; Nebulous).

Falls from Horses—(See Horses).

Femur — Dislocation of—Fracture of (See Femur).

Fevers—(See "High Fevers", "Liable To", under Fever).

Fire — Danger or Injury By — (See Fire).

Fistulous Tumors — (See "Buttocks", "Thighs", under Fistula).

Four-Footed Beasts—Hurts By—(See Quadrupeds).

Fractures—Of the Hips or Thighs— (See Fractures).

Gout — In Hips and Thighs — (See "Hips" under Gout).

Gunshot Wounds—(See Gunshot).

Haunches—Disorders In—Injuries To —(See Buttocks, Haunches).

Heat—Fire—Danger or Prejudice By —(See Fire, Heat).

Heated Blood — (See "Over-Heated" under Blood).

Hemorrhoids — Piles — (See Hemorrhoids).

Hips—All Diseases In—Injuries To— (See the various paragraphs under Hips).

Horses—Hurts By—Falls From—(See Horses).

Hot Humours — (See "Hot" under Hips).

Humours—(See "Hot Humours", "Humours In", under Hips).

Hunting — Riding — Injuries In — (See "Riding" under Horses; Hunting).

Hurts—By Horses and Quadrupeds— (See Horses. Quadrupeds).

Injuries — (See Femur, Fractures; "Accidents", "Hurts", "Injuries", under Hips, Thighs).

Intemperateness—In Sports—(See Exercise; "Intemperate" under Sports).

Ischium—Disorders of—(See Ischium).

Itching — In Thighs — (See "Itching" under Thighs).

Knees—Pains In—(See Knees).

Legs—Disorders In—Fractures—(See Extremities, Femur, Fractures, Legs, Limbs, Thighs).

Locomotor Ataxia—Tabes Dorsalis— (See Locomotor).

Lower Extremities — Disorders In — Fractures In — (See Extremities, Femur, Fractures, Legs, Limbs, Lower, Thighs).

Lumbago; Lungs—Disorders of—(See Lungs).

Muscles—Disorders of—(See Muscles).

Nerve Power—(See "Loss Of" under Nerves).

Over-Heated Blood — (See "Over-Heated" under Blood).

Pains — (See "Pains" under Hips, Thighs).

Pestilence; Piles—(See Hemorrhoids).

Prejudice by Fire — (See "Danger", "Injury", under Fire; "Injuries By" under Heat).

Quadrupeds—Injuries By—(See Horses, Quadrupeds).

Respiratory Troubles — (See Breath, Bronchial. Lungs).

Rheumatism; Riding—Injured In Horseback Riding — (See "Riding", "Thrown", under Horses; Hunting).

Sciatica; Sports—Injuries In—Intemperate In—(See Exercise, Sports).

Tabes Dorsalis — (See Locomotor Ataxia).

Thighs—All Diseases In—Injuries To —(See Femur, Fractures, Hips, Thighs).

Tumors—(See "Tumors" under Hips, Thighs).

Ulcers — (See "Ulcers" under Hips, Thighs).

Volition—(See "Loss Of" under Volition).

Weakness — (See "Weakness" under Hips, Thighs).

SAILORS—The ☽ indicates, represents, and rules Sailors. For influences which indicate Injury to, or Death of, see Maritime, Military, Navigation, Seas, Ships, Shipwreck, Soldiers).

SAINT ANTHONY'S FIRE — (See Erysipelas).

SAINT VITUS DANCE—Chorea—Involuntary Muscular Twitchings — Spasmodic Muscular Contractions — An Irregular Minor Spasm — Involuntary Twitchings of Muscles—Incoordination — Caused by Incoordination, and the reflex influence of ♅ in ♉, in which sign the Organ of Coordination is situated. Also due to non-adjustment between the Vital Body and the Physical Body. In this disease, and also in Idiocy, the nerve centers are not properly adjusted, and there is mal-adjustment between the mind, brain, and body, which prevents the Ego from having full and proper control of its instrument, the human body. The general causes of this disorder are as follows—♆ in ♈, and □ ♅, and both afflicted by ♄ or ♂, and the progressed ☽ passing a radical malefic in this case, tends to attacks; ♅ afflicted in ♉; ♅ in ♏ tends, by reflex action, to afflict the ♉ sign, or planets in ♉; ♅ afflicted in the 6th H.; ♅ ☌, P, □, or ☍ the ☉; ♅ and ♃ afflicting ♀; ♄ or ♂ afflicting ♀; ☿ ☌ or P. ♂ in fixed signs, and with ☿ and the ☽ in mutual affliction at the same time; Subs at AT and AX. (See Contractions, Coordination; "Movements" under Erratic; Idiocy, Incoordination, Jerkings; "Contractions", "Involuntary", under Muscles; Spasmodic. Tics, Tremors, Twitchings; "Body" under Vital). Cases of Saint Vitus Dance, Map, Birth Data, etc.—See Figures 12, 13, and 15, in the book, "Message of the Stars", by the Heindels).

SALACIOUS—Lustful—Lecherous—Impure — (See Effeminate, Lewd, Licentious, Lust; "Loose Morals" under Morals; Shameless, Wanton, etc.).

SALICYLATE OF SODA—(See Sodium).

SALIVA — Spittle — Salivary Glands — Parotid Gland — The Parotid Gland, ruled by ♉, yields saliva. The Salivary Glands are ruled by the ♉ sign. The Saliva is ruled by the ☽ and ♋ sign. (See Parotid).

Inflammation—Of the Salivary Glands — Mumps — (See "Mumps" under Parotid).

Pellitory — An Agent increasing the flow of Saliva—(See Pellitory).

Salivation—Too Much Saliva—Ptyalism—Great Abundance of Spittle—A ♀ disease, and ☿ afflicted shows salivation; the ☽ in ♋, ☌, P, □, or ☍ ♄ (or ☿ if he be of the nature of ♄) at the beginning of an illness, or at decumb. (Hor'y); the ☽ afflicted in ♈ affects and disturbs the saliva; ♀ afflicted in ♉; Subs at LCP and SP. (See "Frothing" under Mouth).

Too Little—Dry Mouth—(See Fauces).

SALLOW—Sallow Complexion—A Jaundiced Look—Yellow Complexion—(See "Sallow" under Complexion; Pale, Sickly).

SALOONS—Frequenter of Taverns and Saloons—Saloons are ruled by the 5th H., the house of pleasures and dissipations. Venus afflicted in the 5th H. tends to such dissipations. (See Drunkenness, Taverns).

SALPINGITIS—(See Fallopian).

SALT — Salts — Sodium Chloride — The Salts of the Body—Zodiac Salts—

Salts of the Body—Are connected with the earthy signs and ♄. The Salts in Milk are ruled by ♄. (See "Earthy Signs" under Earth; Milk, Minerals, Saturn; "Salts" under Zodiac).

Salt Phlegm—Salt Rheum—(See "Salt Phlegm" under Phlegm).

Salt Rheum — (See "Salt Phlegm" in this section).

Salt Water—The Oceans—(See Ocean).

Sodium Chloride — Common Salt — Ruled by ♒. (See Sodium; "Salts" under Zodiac).

Zodiac Salts—(See Zodiac).

SANCTIMONIOUS — Self-Righteous — (See "Sanctimonious" under Religion).

SAND—Sandy—Gravel—Concretions—

Kidney and Bladder—Sand In—Urinary Sand — These deposits are the work of ♄, being the retention and crystallization of waste products, and also gravel; a ♄ disease; ♄ in ♎ or ♏; the ☽ to the ☌ or ill-asp. ♂ by dir.; the ☽ in ♎, and afflicted by the ☉ or ♂ when taken ill (Hor'y); ♂ in ♌ or ♏; a ♏ disease, and afflictions in ♏. (See Crystallization, Deposits, Elimination, Gravel, Retentions, Stone, Suppressions, etc.).

Sandy Hair—(See Hair).

SANE—Sanity—(See "Sound Mind" under Mind; Sanity).

SANGUINARY — Bloodthirsty — Generally a ♂ and ♏ influence, and of the fiery signs. (See Assassins, Cruel, Merciless, Murderous, Pity, Revengeful, Treachery, etc.).

Sanguinary Fevers—♃ in fiery signs, and the ☉ weak and afflicted, causes them at decumbiture in Hor'y Q. (See "Blood", "Sanguinary", under Fever).

SANGUINE — Buoyant — Hopeful — Sanguineous—

Sanguine Color—Ruled by ♐ and the 5th H.

Sanguine Complexion—The ☉ strong at B., more sanguine than otherwise; the ☉ Sig. in ♊, ♌, or ♐; the ☉ or ☽ in ♈, ♉, or ♊; the ☉ in ♊, ♌, or ♐ in partile asp. the Asc.; the ☉ as Sig. in Hor'y Q.; the ☽ Sig. in ♈, ♉, ♊, ♌, ♎, ♐, or ♒, or in these signs in partile the Asc.; ☽ in ♒ partile Asc., clear sanguine; ♄ in ♊, a dark sanguine; ♄ Sig. in ♊ in Hor'y Q.; ♄ in ♑ or ♒; ♃ strong at B.; born under ♃; ♃ oriental; ♃ Sig. in ♊, ♌, ♍, or ♐; ♃ in ♊, partile the Asc., sanguine, but of dusky complexion; ♂ Sig. in ♊, ♌, ♎, or ♐; ♂ in ♊, ♎, or ♐, partile the Asc.; ♀ Sig. in ♉, ♍, ♎, ♐, or ♒; ♀ in ♎, partile the Asc., a beautiful sanguine; ♀ in ♐, partile the Asc., fair sanguine; ☿ Sig. in ♎ or ♐; ☿ in ♎, partile the Asc.; ☿ ori., but if occi., lean and sallow; ☿ orientally posited as regards the ☉, except when ☿ is in ♊; ♊ or ♍ on the Asc., a dark sanguine; ♈, ♉, ♊, ♌, ♎, ♐, or ♒ on the Asc.; ♌ on the Asc., a ruddy, high sanguine; ♎ on the Asc., a fine sanguine complexion in youth, but with pimples in middle life and old age; given by the 5th H. influences strong at B., as this house rules sanguine color; ♐ and ♒ on the Asc., a clear sanguine, and especially when ♀ is rising in these signs; ♓ on Asc., sometimes sanguine if the ☉ be rising in ♓. (See "Red", "Rosy", under Complexion; "Ruddy" under Face; Robust, Ruddy; "Good" under Vitality).

Sanguine Signs—The Airy Signs ♊, ♎, and ♒. Also the fiery signs, and especially ♌ and ♐ when on the Asc.

Sanguine Temperament—Artistic Temperament—The Ardent, Buoyant, Confident, Enthusiastic, Hopeful, Optimistic Temperament or Disposition — Ruled by ♃ and the Airy Signs. This Temperament is moist in general, and not a hot and dry temperament. (See Air Signs, Moisture). The Choleric and Sanguine Temperament act, while the Lymphatic and Nervous Temperaments think and feel. This temperament gives a plump body, good circulation, fine complexion, jovial nature, good cheer, hopefulness, etc. The people of this temperament benefit by fasting. (See Cheerfulness, Fasting; "Diathesis" under Hemorrhage; "Hot and Moist Body" under Moisture; Optimistic, Plump).

Sanguineous Discharges—(See Blood, Discharges, Hemorrhage, Menses; "Epistaxis" under Nose).

Sanguineous System — The Blood — Blood Vessels—Arteries—Veins, etc.— Ruled principally by ♃ and ♀, and also greatly affected by the ♒ sign. (See Arteries, Blood, Capillaries, Circulation, Lymph, Veins, Vessels).

SANITARIUMS—(See "Sanitariums" under Healers; Hospitals).

SANITATION—Hygiene—Cleanly—Prevention of Disease — Sanitary, etc. — These matters are associated largely with the ♍ sign, the sign which rules over health matters. Mars well aspected in ♍ tends to give good success as a Sanitary Worker. (See Cleanly, Healers, Hygiene, Nurses, Prevention).

Neglects Sanitation—Unsanitary— Filthy In Habits and Surroundings—♄ afflicted in ♉; ♄ ☌ ♆ or ☋ in ♉. (See Careless, Cleanly, Filthy; "Careless" under Habits; Improvident, Knavish, Laxity, Neglect, Untidy, etc.).

SANITY—Sane—Insane—(See Insanity; "Sound Mind" under Mind).

SARCASM—Sarcastic—Bitter In Temper —Ironical — Vituperative — A strong characteristic of the ♏ sign, and ♂, its ruler; ♂ strong at B., and afflicting ☿; ♂ Sig. ☌ ☿, an acute, sarcastic wit; ♂ or ♅ to the ☌ or ill-asp. ☿ by dir.; ☿ in ♏ and afflicted by ♂; many planets in mutable signs. (See Anger, Choleric, Imprudent, Rashness, Satire; "High Temper", "Nasty", under Temper).

SARCOMA—A Fleshy Tumor—A Tumor of Modified and Embryonic Connective Tissue—

Adipose Sarcoma — A Fatty Tumor — Caused by ♃ and afflictions to ♃; ♂ ☌ or ill-asp. ♃. (See "Tumors" under Fat, Fleshy; "Fatty" under Tumors).

SARDONIC — Derisive — Sneering — Mocking—Unnatural—♆ rising in the Asc., a sardonic look. (See Mockery).

SARSAPARILLA—A Typical Drug of ♂. Is Alterative, Diuretic, Tonic.

SATIRE—Irony—Ridicule—Derisive—Sarcasm — A characteristic of the ♏ and ♐ signs. Also ♍ when strong at B. tends to satire and criticism. The Mercurial signs ♊ and ♍, and especially when afflicted, or joined with ♄ or ♂ influences, tend to satire, and along the lines of making fun, or light of people and things, or making lamentations over the evils and dengeneracy of the Times, etc. The ♒ and ♑ signs are also given to satire. (See Sarcasm).

SATISFACTION OF MIND—(See Cheerfulness, Contentment; "Peace of Mind" under Mind).

SATURDAY — The day of ♄. For the significance of the Days of the Week see Week. (See Saturn; "Saturday" under Week).

SATURN — The Planet Saturn — Also known as Kronos, or Cronos—Known as a malefic, and "The Greater Infortune." However, Saturn, in himself, is not evil, but is chastening, corrective, and untiring in his efforts to arouse Humanity to better and right living, and by bringing sorrow, suffering, sickness, trials, and tribulations upon people that they may learn by their experiences, and reap what they sow. To the Angel of Saturn has been given the great task of the Redemption of Humanity, and He was one of the first of the Hierarchies upon the field at the Creation, the "Serpent" of Eden, and He will be at his work until the last human Soul is redeemed and perfected, and able to master all Earth and material conditions when in physical incarnation. Saturn is a masculine planet, and of a cold, dry, and barren nature, and his influence is of a steadying nature, and to restore the balance with those who need it. The afflictions of ♄ usually force people on, and out of ruts in life, and to a better environment if they are living in the wrong place, or engaging in a wrong and illegitimate business, or are much tortured by the aggressions of enemies, relatives, or business associates. Such changes usually conduce to greater happiness and usefulness in life, greater success, and better health. Saturn is known as "The Reaper", "The Tester", "The Chastener", "The Initiator", and also as the Planet of Death. (See "Periods of Bad Health" under Health). This Planet is much written about in the Textbooks of Astrology, and I have spent considerable time gathering up, and arranging these influences so that they will be more readily available to students. This Article will be arranged into three Sections, as follows: Section One —General Influences of Saturn; Section Two—Saturn Rules; Section Three —The Diseases of Saturn, and the Afflictions of Saturn. In any of these three Sections, when subjects are listed without comment, see the subject in the alphabetical arrangement.

— SECTION ONE —

THE INFLUENCES OF SATURN—

Action of Saturn—His action is principally binding, chastening, chronic, cold, crystallizing, denuding, hardening, depleting, hindering, limiting, magnetic, obstructing, retarding, suppressing, etc. Also centripetal, driving the blood inwards from the surface, thru chill and cold. To those who have the New Birth, his action is also very helpful, spiritual, and leads to attainment and advancement. (Note the various paragraphs in this Article).

Afflictions—♄ afflicts by the ☌, P, □, and ☍ aspects. He afflicts any part of the map of birth, or by transit or direction, in which he may be located, and even when in his own signs ♑ and ♒, or in his exaltation sign ♎, but to a less extent when in signs of his debility, as in ♈, ♋, or ♌. His afflictions seem to be inimicable to the great masses of people of the Earth, due to their lack of self-control, spiritual sight and development, and materialistic tendencies, as they are as yet unable to respond to his higher vibrations. (See "Aspects" in this section).

Ameliorated—His afflictions are ameliorated and moderated when the benefics are favorably configurated with him, or when the progressed ☽ forms good aspects to him, or to ♃.

Angel Of—Casiel is known as the Angel of ♄. Also Orifiel is mentioned by some Authors. Mikael is said to be the Regent of Saturn. Also by some Satan is said to represent ♄, and to try the hearts of men, discover their weak points, bring temptations and testings, which, if the native can successfully meet, makes him all the stronger in the end.

Ascending at Birth—Makes the native liable to falls, bruises, blows, accidents, fractures, debility, catarrh, rheumatism, nervous affections, melancholy, etc.

Aspects — ♄ well-aspected and fortified in a map tends to have a beneficial influence over the planets he aspects, but afflicts the sign he is in, and the parts, or organs, ruled by such sign. The good aspects of ♄ are physically inimicable, but may help mentally and spiritually. The evil aspects of ♄ deplete and denude. (See Afflictions, Earth, Evil, Good, Jupiter, Mars, Moon, Sun, Venus, in this section).

Barren — ♄ is a barren planet, and tends to barrenness, and to deny children when in the houses of children at B. (See Barrenness).

Body—In the human body ♄ crystallizes, and makes bone, cartilage and the tendons.

Causes—♄ Causes—(See the various paragraphs and subjects in this Article).

Chaos—♄ is said to be the "Door to Chaos", and especially if you appropriate his afflicting vibrations and influences, and are not living a proper moral and balanced life.

Characteristics — His typical characteristics are coldness, gravity, and concretion. His influence is also depressing, cachectic, clotting, coagulating, etc. (See "Qualities", and the various paragraphs in this section).

Cheer—♄ takes the cheer out of life to many, and especially when rising at B., and afflicted, or afflicting ☿, the mental ruler. (See Cheerfulness).

Children — ♄ being a barren planet denies children when in the houses of children at B., and to cause their death if born, or to be less fortunate in life until awakened and spiritualized. (See Barrenness; "Death Of" under Children).

Chronic—♄ is chronic, enduring, and the principal cause of chronic diseases.

Church—♄ evilly aspected at B. tends to an evil mind, and to make one an enemy of Society, the Church, and the State.

Cold — ♄ produces dryness and cold, being remote from the ☉ and the vapors of the Earth, but he is more effective in producing cold than dryness. He causes excess of cold and dryness, and is malevolent. (See Cold, Dryness).

Colors — Black, Indigo, Green, Lead Color, Gray. In the Solar Spectrum ♄ rules Indigo. (See Colors).

Day and Night—♄ is less malignant by day, as his cold is modified by the heat of the ☉, but he is more malignant at night, and adds his cold influence to that of the cold, dampness, and moisture of the night. (See Day, Night).

Death — ♄ Causes Death By — (See "Death" in Sec. 3 of this Article).

Decay and Decrepitude — ♄ is the planet of. (See Decay, Decrepitude).

Delights In — ♄ delights in the 12th H., the house of self-undoing, prisons, imprisonment, confinement, limitations, hospitals, secret enemies, plots, treachery, chronic diseases, etc. (See Twelfth House).

Denotes—(See the various paragraphs and subjects in this Article).

Denudes and Depletes — (See these subjects. Also see "Aspects" in this section).

Depression of Mind—(See Depression).

Destructive—His influence in the human body is destructive, and he afflicts any part of the map he is in at B., or by transit or direction. (See Destructive; "Afflictions" in this section).

Diathesis—♄ adds or subtracts to the Splenic Diathesis, or the Splenic Process. (See the Introductions under Knees, Lymph).

Directions—The evil directions of ♄ tend to bring fears, jealousies, and mistrust. His good directions to the hyleg favor better health for the time, and more peace of mind, a better fate, etc. His evil directions are more pernicious and evil during old age, or during the period ruled by ♄, as from the 63rd to 77th years of life, when afflicting the hyleg. (See Directions).

Distress—♄ causes distress by colds, bruises, falls, and chronic diseases.

Dragon's Tail—And ♄—(See Dragon).

Drugs—Typical Drugs of ♄ are Aconite, Antimony, Astringents, Belladonna, Conium (Hemlock), Helleborus, Hyoscyamus, Hydrocyanic Acid, Indian Hemp, Lead, Mullein, Rhus Toxicodendron, Salicylate of Soda, Tincture Saturnina (see "Hectic Fever" under Fever); Styptics, Verbascum, etc. (See "Saturn Group" under Herbs; Lead).

Dry—♄ is dry and cold by nature, and his afflictions over the body tend to dry up the fluids and tissues. (See Cold, Dry).

Earth—His evil aspects and afflictions seem to be inimical to the inhabitants of the Earth, as the Earth is said to be the lowest in Materialism in our Solar System, and also the only planet where the sexes are separated, and where the Sex Problem, its control, and proper uses, are the great issues. (See "Afflictions" in this section).

Ends Life—♄ tends by his afflictions to end life in the physical body, to weaken and lower vitality, and opposes the life-giving ☉. (See Opposites).

Endurance — A principal of ♄, and strong ♄ people cling to life tenaciously in sickness, trouble, and adversity. (See Endurance).

Environment—♄ being a negative and magnetic planet renders the native more receptive and susceptible to external influences and environment. (See Environment, External, Negative, Receptive, Susceptibility).

Evil Lessened—The influence of ♄ for evil is lessened when he is occi. of the ☉ at B., and increased when ori., and rising before the ☉.

External Influences — (See "Environment" in this section).

Fears—Creates Fears—(See Fears).

Febrifuge — (See Antipyretic, Febrifuge).

Fixed Signs—♄ in a fixed sign tends to be a very evil afflictor, and to tend to chronic and lingering diseases. (See Fixed Signs).

Fluids of the Body—♄ adds the Salts to the Milk and Fluids of the body. (See Fluids).

Foetus — The physical plasm of the foetus is developed under ♄. (See Foetus).

Gall—♄ forms the Gall—(See Bile).

Gases—(See Hydrogen).

Gloom—♄ brings gloom and death by his afflictions. (See Gloom).

God — (See "Will of Providence" in this section).

Good Aspects—The good aspects of ♄ tend to obstruct when applying to other planets. (See "Aspects" in this section).

Gravity — A ♄ characteristic. (See Grave).

Hard—His influence is hard, hardening, and barren. (See Hard).

Health—♄ and Health—(See Health; the various paragraphs in this Article).

Heat—♄ is cold, of little heat, and with low caloric. The cold of ♄ is opposed to the heat of the ☉ and ♂. (See "Cold" in this section).

Herbs Of—(See "Saturn Group" under Herbs).

Hinders—♄ contracts, binds, hinders, restricts, while ♂ accelerates and burns up the wastes of the body by fevers and inflammations. (See Hindrances).

Hour—♄ Hour—(See "Hours" under Planets).

Husbanding—One great influence of ♄ is the husbanding of resources, and even to hoarding and miserliness. (See Miserly).

Hypocrites — In religious, and other matters, ♄ tends to breed hypocrites. (See Hypocritical).

Ills of Life—The ills of life are ascribed to ♄ and his afflictions, and to his chastenings. Saturn allows people to pursue their wicked courses, but calls them severely to account under his evil aspects, and to bring suffering, sorrows, disease, or death to those who are not living right. (See Affliction; "Afflictions" in this section; "Diseases" in Sec. 3 of this Article).

Infortune — ♄ is classed as "The Greater Infortune", due to his severe and prolonged periods of affliction, while Mars is known as "The Lesser Infortune". However, ♄ is not an Infortune to those who are living right, and striving to rule their lower natures, and the evils of life. The Planetary Hierarch which rules over ♄, is one of the Elohim, one of the "Seven Spirits Before the Throne", a Messenger of God, and assigned to the work of uplifting humanity, and working out their ultimate salvation and perfection. No planet is evil, but only seems evil from our viewpoint when we come under his afflictions and chastenings, which are not given as punishments or retribution, but only to make humanity better. (See Benefics, Malefics).

Intropulsive — ♄ is intropulsive, and tends to retain and drive inward the poisons and wastes of the body. By chilling the surface he drives the blood inward, causing internal congestions. His action is centripetal, towards the center, while the action of ♂ is centrifugal, away from the center. (See Centripetal, Intropulsion).

Jealousy—(See Jealousy; "Directions" in this section).

Joy—♄ tends to suppress life and joy, and take the cheer out of life in the ordinary, unawakened, and unspiritualized person. (See Cheer, Joy).

Jupiter and Saturn—In the treatment of ♄ diseases, the good aspects of ♃, or the remedies, herbs, or roots of ♃, help more than those of ♀. (See "Jupiter Group" under Herbs; Jupiter).

Keynote — The keynote of ♄ is obstruction. (See Obstruction).

Lasting Influence—The influence of ♄ by his aspects is the most lasting and malignant of all the planets.

Life—♄ suppresses life and joy. (See Suppressions).

Limitation — The Principle of ♄ is limitation, and he, therefore, rules the skin and bones, as these tend to define and limit the corporature. (See Limitations).

Liver—♄ forms Uric Acid, Urea, and Gall in the Liver, and during muscular activity these are deposited over the body and cause Gout and Rheumatism. Saturn is chronic and causes torpid liver and constipation. (See Bile, Constipation, Gout, Liver, Rheumatism, Urea, Uric).

Low Caloric—(See Cold, Dry, Heat, in this section).

Magnetic—♄ is a negative and magnetic planet. (See "Environment" in this section; Magnetic; "Negative Planets" under Negative).

Malefic — ♄ is considered malefic, or chastening in his influence. (See "Infortune" in this section).

Malevolent — ♄ is malevolent in his action upon the human body in that he produces an excess of cold and dryness. (See Cold, Dry, Malevolent).

Malignant — (See Malignant; "Lasting" in this section).

Mars and Saturn—♄ is the negative of ♂, and the opposite of ♂ action. Saturn is centripetal, and ♂ is centrifugal; ♄ is restrained, and ♂ is intensive. Together ♄ and ♂ act as heat and cold, acute and chronic. Saturn tends to offset the active life given by ♂, and to check, delay, repress, and smother the fiery spirit of ♂. Saturn tends to depress, and ♂ to enhance. What is given by ♂ is overcome by ♄. One is sudden, and the other is tardy. Saturn draws from the circumference to a center, along lines of radii, drawing the blood inward, contracting, crystallizing, restricting, binding, hampering, consolidating, etc., while the action of ♂ is the opposite. Saturn opposes the heat, life, energy, courage, and vital power given by ♂ and the ☉. The mind is considerably improved by the good aspects of ♂ to ♄. (See Mars).

Mercury and Saturn—(See the Introduction under Mercury).

Metals of Saturn — Lead is the principal Metal of ♄. (See Lead, Therapeutics; "Mineral" in this section).

Milk—♄ adds the Salts to Milk. (See Milk).

Mind—The afflictions of ♄ tend to afflict the mind, cause depression and melancholy, jealousy, hatred, revenge, and an evil mind. (See Mind; "Church" in this section).

Mineral World—Minerals of—In the mineral world ♄ crystallizes, such as coal, rock, lead, etc. Graphite and Lead are principal minerals of ♄.

Mischief—♄ is said to be the author of mischief, and especially when he is afflicted in the 12th H. (See Mischief).

Mistrusts — (See Mistrustful; "Directions" in this section).

Moon and Saturn—♄ is antagonistic to the ☽, and tends to aggravate all ☽ diseases by his ☌ and evil aspects to the ☽. The ☽, ruler of ♋, opposes ♄, ruler of ♑. (See Moon, Opposites).

Muscular Activity—The Action of ♄ During—(See "Liver" in this section).

Nature of Saturn—Cold and dry, contracting, obstructing, etc. (See "Qualities", and the various paragraphs in this Article).

Negation—♄ is the planet of negation.

Negative—♄ is a negative and magnetic planet and gives negative qualities, such as fear, worry, timidity, cowardice, pessimism, revenge, etc.

Nervous—♄ influence is nervous. (See Nerves).

Night — ♄ influence by Night — (See "Day" in this section).

Obstruction—Obstruction is the keynote, and the most salient characteristic of ♄. (See Obstructions).

Occidental and Oriental — (See "Evil Lessened" in this section).

Old Age—♄ is the planet of, and rules old age. (See Old Age).

Oriental—(See "Evil Lessened" in this section).

Part of Body—The Parts Afflicted by ♄—(See "Afflictions" in this section).

Pathological Action — ♄ is a pathological planet, and especially in his afflictions and lower vibrations. The pathological action of ♄ Herbs, Minerals, and Metals, and his own direct action over the body by his afflictions, is to disturb the Peripheral Nerves, the Connective Tissues, the Osseous, Mucous, and Cutaneous Systems, to cause the degeneration of tissues, and disturbances of vaso-constriction.

Period Of—(See "Planetary Periods" under Periods).

People — Saturn people are secretive, fond of solitude, melancholic, pessimistic, penurious, hypochondriac, but capable of great endurance; are strong in enmity, are austere, grave, often ascetic, and very stupid if ♄ afflict ☿. (See "Saturn Persons" in this section).

Places Ruled By—Graveyards, churchyards, the Desert, woods, obscure places, dens, caves, holes, mountains, coal mines, stinking and dirty places, sinks, cess pools, stagnant ponds, etc. For Places and Countries ruled by ♄ see "Capricorn Rules", "Aquarius Rules", under Nations.

Plants, Herbs, Roots — Of ♄ — (See "Saturn Group" under Herbs).

Principle Of—Limitation. (See Limitations).

Punishment — Chastisement — ♄ chastens and punishes our wayward natures, but what seem to be his evils are only good in the making. (See Punishment; "Afflictions", "Infortune", in this section).

Qualities—Qualities Given and Ruled Over by Saturn—These are here listed alphabetically, the most of which you can find in the alphabetical arrangement of this book—Abnormal, Abortive, Absorbing, Accumulative, Acquisitive, Afflicting, Anaphrodisiac, Antiperistaltic, Antiphlogistic, Antipyretic, Ascetic, Asphyxiating, Astringent, Atrophying, Austere, Avaricious, Barren, Beggarly, Binding, Blighting, Brooding, Cachetic, Careful, Catabolic, Cautious, Centripetal, Chaotic, Chastening, Checking, Checkmating, Cheerlessness, Chilling, Chronic, Clotting, Coagulating, Cold, Cold and Dry, Cold and Moist when Oriental, Compressing, Concretive, Condensing, Confining, Congealing, Consolidating, Constant, Constricting, Consumptive, Contemptous, Contentious, Contracting, Corrupting, Covetous, Cowardly, Cruel, Crushing, Crystallizing, Death-Dealing, Deathly, Debilitating, Decaying, Deceitful, Decrepitating, Defective, Defensive, Deforming, Degenerating, Dejecting, Delaying, Deluding, Delusive, Denuding, Depleting, Depressing, Deprivating, Despairing, Despondent, Destructive, Deteriorating, Devitalizing, Diminishing, Disagreeable, Dissoluting, Dissolving, Distressing, Distributing, Disturbing, Diuretic, Diurnal, Dry, Dull, Earth-bound, Earthy, Emaciating, Enduring, Enervating, Enlarging, Enmity, Envious, Eruptive, Evil, Excessive, Fearful, Fear-Producing, Febrifuge, Fretful, Frigid, Frugal, Gloomy, Granulating, Grasping, Grave, Greedy, Habit-Forming, Haemostatic, Hallucinating, Hampering, Hard, Hardening, Heaviness, Hindering, Hopelessness, Husbanding of Resources, Hypochondriac, Hypocritical, Ill (Evil); Illusive, Imaginative, Impairing, Impeding, Imposing, Induration, Inflaming, Ingenious, Inhibiting, Injurious, Intropulsive, Invalidating, Jealous, Lasting, Lessening, Limiting, Lingering, Long-Enduring, Lowering, Lumpy (Lump-forming); Lying, Maddening, Magnetic, Malefic, Malevolent, Malicious, Malignant, Malnutritive, Maniacal, Masculine, Materialistic, Melancholic, Miscarrying, Mischievous, Miserly, Mistrustful, Moody, Moping, Morbid, Mortifying, Motive, Mournful, Mystical, Mystifying, Narrowing, Nauseating, Negative, Neglectful, Nervous, Neurotic, Nodular (Node-forming); Nucleolating, Obsessing, Obstinate, Obstructing, Ossifying, Painful, Paralyzing, Pathological, Patient, Paucity, Penurious, Permanency, Pernicious, Persevering, Perverse, Perverting, Pessimistic, Petrifactive, Petulant, Phlegmatic, Pitiless, Poisonous, Privative, Procrastinating, Prolonging, Proud, Pus-forming, Quarrelsome, Reclusive, Reducing, Refrigerant, Regretful, Repining, Repressive, Resentful, Reserved, Resolving, Restraining, Restrictive, Retarding, Retentive, Retractive, Revengeful, Rheumatic, Rigid, Ruinous, Rupturing, Sad, Saddening, Scolding, Scybalous, Secretive, Sedate, Sedative, Sedentary, Selfish, Self-Undoing, Serious, Servile, Serving, Severe, Shrinking, Sickening, Skeptical, Slavish, Slow, Smothering, Sober, Solitary, Sorrowful, Souring, Speculative, Stagnating, Stenotic, Stiffening, Stopping, Strangulating, Styptic, Subduing, Subtle, Suffering, Suffocating, Suicidal, Sullen, Suppressing, Suspicious, Taciturn, Tactful, Tardy in Action, Tedious, Testing, Thickening, Thrifty, Timid, Tissue-Destroying, Torpid, Torturing, Toughening, Tremulous, Troublesome, Tuberculous, Tumorous, Ulcerating, Unmerciful, Unsociable, Vain, Vapourous, Visionary, Wasting, Wayward, Weakening, Wicked, Worrisome, Wrinkling, etc.

Recluse—(See Recluse, Reserved, Secretive, Solitude).

Remedies Of — (See Drugs, Herbs, Metals, Minerals, Therapeutic, Treatment, in this section. Also see Antipathy, Opposites, Remedies, Sympathy, Treatment).

Resources—Husbanding of—(See Resources).

Restraint — ♄ influence tends to restraints, confinements, and limitations. (See Restraints).

Roots and Herbs—(See "Saturn Group" under Herbs).

Ruin and Disgrace—♄ in the M.C. at B., and afflicted, danger of. (See Disgrace, Ruin).

Salts Of—(See Salts; "Fluids" in this section).

Saturday—Saturn's Day—(See Week).

Saturn Persons—The unawakened and drifting ♄ person frets, mopes, and worries, and thereby renders himself liable to suicidal mania, melancholia, liver disease, and chronic ailments in general, and to an earlier death. (See "People" in this section).

Senses and Saturn—♄ is not a builder to the Senses, but rather exerts a strong psychological and intellectual power. (See Senses).

Signifies—♄ signifies servitude, limitation, husbanding of resources, nucleolation, induration, etc.

Signs — ♄ rules the ♑ and ♒ signs. He is considered an affliction in any sign, and even in his own signs afflicts the knees, lower limbs, and ankles. (See "Afflictions", "Aspects" in this section).

Sixth House — ♄ when in the 6th H., or afflicting the hyleg or Asc., produces cold, lingering and chronic complaints.

Skin — ♄ rules the skin. (See Skin; "Limitation" in this section).

Society—An Enemy To—(See "Church" in this section).

Sours People — ♄ afflictions tend to sour people upon the World, and to make recluses and pessimists. (See Pessimistic, Recluse).

Spirituality — The good aspects of ♄ tend to help spirituality. (See Spiritual; "Aspects" in this section).

Splenic Diathesis — (See "Diathesis" in this section).

Stagnation—♄ is the planet of. (See Stagnation).

State—(See "Church" in this section).

Suicide — ♄ afflictions tend to — (See Suicide).

Sun — Relation of ♄ to — (See Cold, Evil, Heat, in this section; Opposites, Sun).

Suppresses Life—And Joy—(See Joy, Life, in this section).

Suppression — The planet of — (See Hindrances, Retarding, Retentions, Stagnation, Stoppages, Suppressions).

Symbol Of — The Reaper with his Scythe and Hour Glass in hand. Also the Black Vulture, or Raven.

Sympathizes With—In disease ♄ sympathizes with the ☽, and aggravates all diseases of the ☽. He also adds his sympathy to the other malefics in bringing oppression, suffering, and evils upon humanity in order to teach self-control thru varied experiences.

Temperament — ♄ gives the Nervous Temperament, and also the Melancholic Disposition, the Sad, Grave, Gloomy, and Pessimistic nature, and with reserve, suspicion, and selfishness. (See "Temperament" under Nerves).

Therapeutic Qualities—Antiphlogistic, Antipyretic, Astringent, Diuretic, Febrifuge, Refrigerant, Sedative, Styptic. (See Drugs, Remedies, in this section).

Treatment — In the treatment of ♄ diseases, the Herbs and Remedies ruled by Signs in 8 to the signs of ♄ are best, as the ☉ and ☽ remedies of the ♋ and ♌ signs. Also, ♂ remedies oppose ♄, being opposite in effect, one cold, and the other hot, etc. (See Antipathy, Opposites, Remedies, Sympathy, Treatment).

Twelfth House — ♄ delights in this house, as he is the Author of Mischief. (See Mischief, Twelfth House).

Typical Drugs Of—(See "Drugs" in this section).

Urea—♄ forms Urea. (See Urea).

Uric Acid — ♄ forms Uric Acid and deposits it over the body. (See Uric).

Venus and Saturn — ♄ with ♀ at B. tends to lower and debauch the good influences of ♀. (See Love Affairs, Passion, Perversions, Venus; "Jupiter" in this section).

Victims of Saturn—The victims of ♄ are hard to reach, as they are usually full of fears, worries, are pessimistic, skeptical of a cure, and lack joy and cheer when unawakened and living in their lower minds.

Vocations of Saturn — Undertakers, Gravediggers, Dealers in Lead, Mines, Minerals; Agriculture, Building, etc.

Vulnerable Spots — (See "Weak" in this section).

Wastes of the Body — The afflictions of ♄ tend to retain the wastes and poisons of the body, and to deposit them over the system in the form of urea and uric acid, causing Gout, Rheumatism, etc. (See Deposits, Minerals, Wastes, etc.).

Waywardness—♄ tends to subdue our wayward natures, to correct the evils of our lives, and to "Punish", or chastise, for our sins, to restore our balance, and make us better. (See "Punishment" in this section).

Weak Spots—The position of ♄ at B., by transit, by direction, progression, shows the weak and vulnerable spots in our horoscope, and the parts or faculties under affliction along thru life.

Well-Aspected — (See Aspects, Good, Spirituality, in this section).

Wickedness — (See "Ills of Life" in this section).

Will of Providence—♄ is the cause of the greater part of human suffering, but subservient to the Will of Providence.

Worry—Tends To—(See Worry).

— SECTION TWO —

SATURN RULES—These subjects are merely listed here, and the most of them you will find in the alphabetical arrangement of this book — Abortion; Accumulations; Acquisitiveness; Afflictions; Aged People (see Old Age); Agnostics; Anaphrodisiacs; Animals (Small); Antiphlogistics; Antipyretics; Apoplexies; Aquarius Sign; Articulations (see Joints); Ash; Ashes; Astringents; Atheists; Atrophies; Auditory Organs (especially the Right Ear); Auricle (Left Auricle of Heart when ♄ is in ♌); Barrenness; Bindings, Black —Black Clothing—Black Color, Black Hair, the Black Raven; Bladder; Blood —The Composition of the Blood, and the Circulation of the Blood in the Tissues; Blows; Bones—The Bones in all Parts of the Body, and the Joints; Bruises; Burial Alive; Cachexia; Calcarea (Lime); Calces (Calcium); Caloric (Low Caloric); Calves of Legs; Capricorn Sign; Carbon; Cartilage; Cartilaginous Tissue Building; Catabolism; Catalysis; Caves; Centripetal Action; Cervical Vertebrae (♄ in ♉ rules and affects them); Cesspools; Chalk; Chaos; Chastisement; Checkmates; Chronic Diseases; Chyle; Chylification; Chylopoiesis; Circulation of the Blood in the Tissues; Clothing (Black); Clots; Clotting; Coagulation; Coal and Coal Mines; Cold (Intemperate Cold); Colds; Colors—Black, Lead, Green, Gray, Indigo; Composition of the Blood; Compressions; Concretions; Condensation; Confinements; Congelation; Consolidation; Constrictor Nerves; Consumptions; Contractions; Contusions; Covetousness; Cowardice; Cramps; Crushings (Death By); Crystallization; Cube (The Geometrical Cube); Cutaneous Capillary Vaso-Contrictor Nerves; Darkness; Death; Debility; Decay; Decomposition; Decrepitude; Defensiveness; Deficiencies; Degeneration; Dejection; Delays; Denuding; Depletions; Deposits; Depression; Deprivations; Desert (The Desert); Despair; Destruction; Dirty Places; Disease (Chronic); Dissolution; Distribution and Circulation of the Blood in the Tissues; Dross of Metals; Drugs (Narcotic); Dryness and Cold; Ear (Right Ear); Earthy Minerals Carried by the Blood; East Wind; Emaciations; End of Life (Old Age); Endocardium; Endurance; Enemies (Secret); Envy; Evils; Excretions; Faculty — The Retentive Faculty throughout the Body; Faeces;

Falls; Father (the Father); Fears; Febrifuges; Foetus (the Physical Plasm of); Foul Odors; Fractures; Fretfulness; Friendships and Long Ties; Frigidity; Frost and Snow (Atmospherically); Gall and the Gall Bladder; Genito-Urinary Organs (Bones of); Gloom; Grandfathers; Graphite; Grave (the Grave); Graveyards; Grave Diggers; Gravity (Grave Disposition); Green Color in the Solar Spectrum; Gristle; Habits; Hair (Black Hair); Hangings; Hardening and Hardness; Heart (Left Auricle and Endocardium); Heaviness; Hermits; Hindrances in Life; Holes (Holes in the Ground, Cesspools, etc.); Hopelessness, Humours; Husbanding of Resources; Hydrogen; Hypochondria; Hypocrites; Ice; Ills of Life; Impediments; Imprisonment; Indigo Color; Indurations; Intellectual Power; Intropulsion; Introspection; Invalidism; Jealousy; Joints; Knees; Lead and Lead Color; Left Auricle of the Heart; Leukocytes; Life from 56 to 70 Years; Ligaments; Lime; Limitations; Lingering Diseases and Lingering Death; Liver; Long Ties and Friendships; Low Caloric; Lower Mind; Lower Strata, as Coal and the Deposits in the Earth; Lumpy Faeces (Scybalum); Magnetism; Malignant Conditions; Melancholy; Memory; Metal — Lead; Metals (Dross of); Minerals (Earthy Carried by the Blood, and also Minerals in General; Mines; Mischief; Misers; Misfortunes; Mistrusts; Moping; Morbid Conditions and Morbid States of the Mind and Body; Mortification; Motive Temperament; Mountains; Mourning; Narcotic Drugs; Neck (Bones of); Negation; Negative Qualities; Neglect and Privation; Nerves— The Cutaneous Capillary Vaso-Constrictor Nerves—The Peripheral Sympathetic Nerves — The Pneumogastric Nerve; Nervous Temperament; Nucleolation; Obstacles; Obstructions; Old Age (and especially Decrepit Old Men); Onions; Ossification; Pathological Conditions; Peripheral Nerves and the Peripheral Sympathetic Nerves; Permanency; Pernicious Actions; Pessimism; Petrifactions; Phlegm; Plots; Plumbago (Lead); Pneumogastric Nerve; Poverty; Privation; Psychological Powers; Punishments (Chastisements); Putrefactions; Raven (the Black Raven, or Black Vulture); Recluses; Reducing Agencies and Drugs; Refrigerants; Regrets; Religious Hypocrites; Repining; Repression; Reserve; Resources (Husbanding of); Respiratory System (when ♄ is in ♉, ♊, or ♋); Restrictions; Retentions (and the Faculty of Retention in the Body); Retraction; Revenge; Reverses; Ribs; Right Ear; Rigidity; Rigors; Rocks; Ruin; Sand (in Kidneys or Bladder); Saturday; Scybalous Agencies and Matter; Secret Enemies; Secretive System Generally; Secretiveness; Sedatives; Sedentary Habits; Selfishness; Senility and Senile Feebleness; Servitude; Shrinkings; Sigmoid Flexure; Signs of the Zodiac—♑ and ♒; Shameless Practices; Skeptics; Skin; Skull (♄ in ♈); Slavery; Small Animals; Snow and Frost (Atmospherically); Solitudes; Soot; Soured Disposition; Spine (Vertebrae); Spleen; Splenic Diathesis and Splenic Process;

Stagnation and Stagnant Waters; Stiffness of Joints and Muscles, and Stiff and Rigid Conditions in the Body in General; Stinking Places (Foul Odors); Stones; Strata (Lower Strata in the Earth, as Coal, etc.); Strifes; Styptics; Subduings; Suffering; Suffocation; Suicides; Sullenness; Suppressions; Suspicions; Sympathetic Nerve and the Sympathetic Peripheral Nerves; Tabefaction; Teeth; Temperament (the Nervous Temperament); Tendons and their Crystallization; Throat (Bones of with ♄ in ♉); Ties (Long Ties and Friendships); Time (the Reaper); Timidity; Tissue Building (Cartilaginous); Tissues (the Blood Circulation In); Tortures; Treachery; Troubles; Urea; Uric Acid; Urinary Organs; Vagus Nerve; Vaso-Constrictor Cutaneous Nerves; Veneral Desire (Drugs which Lessen — Anaphrodisiacs); Vertebrae; Vulture (Black Vulture or Black Raven); Want and Neglect; Waste Products of the Body; Weakness; Wickedness; Woods; Worry, etc.

— SECTION THREE —

THE DISEASES OF SATURN — The Afflictions of Saturn—Diseases Ruled by ♄—Diseases which proceed from ♄ are more permanent, and are generally regulated by the motion of the ☉. His influence is destructive in the human body, and he tends to afflict any sign he is in, and to disturb the organs or parts ruled by such sign. He especially causes distress by bruises, colds, chronic diseases, by mineral deposits, urea, and uric acid over the system. He causes hindrances, disturbances of function, stoppages, retentions, suppressions, suspensions, stagnations, lowered vitality, melancholy, etc., and finally death of the physical body. In normal conditions he furnishes the lime, minerals, earthy salts for the body, and in the proper proportions, but as age creeps on, the minerals and wastes of the body are deposited more unevenly, retained, not properly eliminated, until the body becomes acid, hardened, crystallized, and unable to further carry on its work, and death results. The three score and ten years are assigned to man, and it is the work of ♄ to see to it that people do not live too long on the Earth at one time. When in a fixed sign at B., and by dir., ♄ tends to be a very evil afflictor, and to lead to long, lingering, chronic and tedious diseases. Saturn is depressing, antipyretic, and opposed to the action of ♂ and the Luminaries over the body. The most of his diseases are brought on by cold, exposure to cold, chill, and he specializes in cold and dry diseases, which are more destructive to the body. His influence over the mind is worrisome, pessimistic, depressing, melancholic, etc., which states of mind tend to lowered vitality, and earlier death. Saturn in the Signs and Houses at B. shows the weak spots in our map, and where we are liable to go wrong, and what parts of the body are more subject to disease and permanent affliction, the vulnerable parts of the body. Saturn afflicted in the 6th H., or afflicting the ☉, ☽, Asc., M.C., or Hyleg therefrom, is very

evil in health matters. Also ♄ posited in the 12th H. tends to confinements, restraints, bodily defects, limitation of the five senses, and to chronic diseases. As it takes ♄ about 2½ years to pass thru one Sign or House, his afflictions tend to be prolonged, and people ignorant of Astrology, and of what vibration is working over them, causing worry and anxiety, fears, etc., usually begin to lose weight, vitality, and have no peace of mind, and to eventually go into some form of chronic disease until ♄ changes signs, and turns his affliction to other classes of people. It need not be so, however, if people knew of ♄ and his working, and the times of his increased afflictions over their lives, and then could relax, avoid worry, and go right along, and at the same time try to gain in Wisdom, Knowledge, and Spiritual Power.

Many of the influences of Saturn along the lines of disease and his afflictions are listed in Sec. 1 of this Article. The diseases and afflictions of ♄ are, perhaps, more numerous than those of any other planet, and more spoken of in the Textbooks of Astrology. In order to handle the great mass of material gathered about the afflictions of this planet, these subjects have been placed in the alphabetical arrangement of this book for quick reference, rather than to deal with them more fully here in this Article. Therefore, this Section is mostly an alphabetical Summary of the Saturn Diseases and Afflictions, to bring them to your attention, and you are requested to follow them up throughout the book. See the following subjects in the alphabetical arrangement—

Abeyance; Ablation; Abortion; Absorption; Accidents; Aches; Acute Nervous Diseases—(See "Acute Nervous" under Nerves).

Adynamia; Ague; Analysis of Tissues —(See Absorption, Tissues).

Antiperistalsis; Apoplexies; Arms — Infirmities In—(See Arms).

Arterio-Sclerosis—(See Arteries, Hardening).

Arthritis—(See Joints, Synovial).

Articular Rheumatism — (See Gout, Joints).

Articulations — Hardening of — (See Joints).

Asphyxia — Cutaneous — (See Asphyxia).

Assimilation—Imperfect—(See Assimilation).

Asthenia; Asthma; Ataxia; Atrophy; Auricular Disease—(See "Auricles" under Heart).

Back—Disorders In—(See Back).

Barrenness; Bellyache—Dry Bellyache —(See Belly).

Berberi—(See Anaemia, Dropsy).

Black Jaundice—(See "Black" under Jaundice).

Bladder Disorders; Blemishes; Blight; Blindness—By Cataracts, Colds, Decay of the Optic Nerve, and by Specks, Gutta Serena, etc.—(See Blindness).

Blood—Disorders of—Impure Blood— Blood Driven Inwards — Congestion —

Impeded Circulation—Blood Tumors—Blood Vessels—Constrictions, etc.—(See Blood, Centripetal, Circulation, Constrictions, Haematoma, Impeded, Impure. Vessels, etc.).

Blows; Bodily Energies—Bodily Fluids—Bodily Functions—Disorders of—(See Abeyance, Energy, Fluids, Functions, Impairments, Impeded, Suppressions, etc.).

Body—Debility of—Depressions In—(See Body, Debility, Depressions).

Bones—All Diseases In—Fractures—Pains In—(See Bones).

Bowels—Gripings In—Obstructions In—Peristaltic Action Impeded—Pains In—(See Bowels).

Breakings Out—(See Eruptions, Pimples).

Breasts—Bruises In—Cancer of—Obstructions In — Suppressions—(See Breast).

Breath—Foul Breath—(See Breath).

Breathing—Cutaneous Breathing Suppressed—(See "Cutaneous" under Asphyxia).

Bright's Disease—(See Bright's).

Broken Bones — Fractures—(See the various parts and subjects under Fracture).

Bronchitis — (See "Chronic" under Bronchial; Lungs, Pulmonary).

Bruises; Bunions; Cachexia; Calamity—Fear of—(See Calamity).

Calculus; Cancer Disease—(See Carcinoma).

Carcinoma; Caries; Cataract; Catarrh; Cavities—Pus In—Disorders of—(See Cavities, Pus, Receptacles, Sacs).

Celibacy; Cells — Disorders of — (See the various paragraphs under Cells).

Centripetal Action; Cerebral Disorders; Cessations; Chalk Stones—(See Calculus, Chalk, Lime, Stone).

Chest Disorders; Chilblain; Childhood—Disorders of—(See Childhood, Children, Infancy).

Childless—(See Barrenness, Impotent; "Unfruitful" under Wife).

Children—Afflictions To—Hurts To—Early Death of—(See Childhood, Children. Infancy).

Chill; Chlorosis; Chronic Diseases; Chyle Disordered; Circulation Disordered; Cirrhosis; Claw Hand; Cloaca; Clogging; Clots; Clouded Mind—Clouded Sight—(See Clouded).

Club Feet; Coagulation; Cold — Diseases Arising From — Cold and Dry Diseases—(See Cold, Dry).

Colds; Colic; Colon Disordered; Compressions; Concretions; Concussions; Condensations; Confinements; Congelation; Congenital Defects; Congestions; Consolidations; Constant Diseases; Constipation; Constitutional Disorders; Constrictions; Consumptions; Contractions; Contusions; Cord — Maladies of the Spinal Cord—(See "Cord" under Spine).

Corns—Bunions—(See Bunions).

Corrosions; Corruption; Costiveness; Coughs; Cramps; Cravings; Criminals; Crippled; Crooked Body; Crushings;

Crusts; Crystallization; Curvature—Of Spine—(See Spine).

Cutaneous Diseases—(See Cutaneous, Skin).

Cuticle (Thickening of); **Cutis**—Contraction of—(See Derma).

Cyanosis; Dead Tissue—(See Crusts; "Tissue" under Dead; Scales).

Deafness; Death—ʰ causes death by Agues, Blows, Bruises, Chronic Diseases, Cold, Colds, Consumptions, Crushings, Dropsies, Drowning, Epilepsy, Falls, Fears, Fluxes, Fractures, Hysterics, Ileac Passion, Lingering Diseases, Melancholy, Phthisis, Slow Diseases, Suffocation, etc. (See these subjects, and also the paragraphs under Death).

Debauchery; Debility; Decay; Declines; Decreased Motility—(See Decrease).

Decrepitude; Deep-Seated Diseases; Defects; Deficiencies; Defluxions; Deformities; Degeneracy; Degeneration; Dejection; Delays; Delicacy; Delusions; Demoniac; Density; Dental Disorders—(See Dental, Teeth).

Denuding; Depletion; Deposits; Depravity; Depressed—Depressions—(See Depressed).

Derangements; Derma Disordered; Desires Abnormal; Despondency; Destructive Processes — (See Atrophy, Consumptions. Emaciations; "Low Fever" under Low; "Malnutrition" under Nutrition; Tabes, Tuberculosis, Wastings, etc.).

Deteriorations; Detriments; Deviations; Devitalization; Diarrhoea (Chronic); **Difficulties; Digestion** (Disorders of); **Dilatations; Diminishments; Disabilities; Disagreeable; Disaster; Discharges; Discolorations; Discomposed; Discontentment; Disease** (Chronic); **Disfigurements; Disgrace; Dishonesty; Disintegration; Dislocations; Disorders; Disorganization; Dispersions; Displacements; Disproportionate Body; Disputes; Dissipations; Dissolution; Distempers; Distortions; Distraction; Distress; Disturbances; Dizziness; Doubts; Downcast; Downfall**—(See Disgrace, Dishonour, Losses, Property, Reputation, Reverses, Ruin).

Dreads — (See Anxieties, Dreads, Fears).

Driving Blood Inwards—(See Centripetal, Chill, Cold).

Drooping; Dropsy; Drought; Drowning; Drowsiness—(See Sleep).

Drug Habit—(See Narcotics).

Dry and Cold Diseases — (See Cold, Dry).

Dullness—Dull Pains and Aches—(See Dull).

Durable Diseases—(See Chronic, Duration, Lingering, Long, Prolonged, Slow, Tedious).

Dwarfed; Dysmenorrhoea — (See Menses).

Dyspepsia; Dyspnoea; Ears—Impediments In—(See Ears; "Right Ear" under Right).

Eczema; Elimination (Disorders of); **Emaciation; Embolism; Emotions** (Disorders of); **Endocarditis**—(See Heart).

Enemies (Secret);

Energy (Abeyance of); **Enervation; Enlargements; Enmities; Ennui; Enteralgia; Enteric Fever** — (See Bowels, Typhoid).

Epidemics; Epilepsy; Epithelioma; Erratic; Eructations—(See Belching).

Eruptions; Erysipelas; Evil—Evils—King's Evil, Scrofula).

Excesses — Excessive Deposits — Excess of Urea and Uric Acid—(See Deposits, Minerals, Poisons, Urea, Uric, Wastes).

Excoriations; Excrescences; Excretion (Disorders of); **Exercise** (Lack of); **Exertion**—Lack of—(See "Sickly" under Exertion).

Exhaustion; Exposure; External Disorders — (See Eruptions, External, Pimples, Skin).

Extremities (Disorders of); **Eyes** — (See "Blindness" in this section; Eyeballs, Eyes).

Face (Disorders of—Red Face); **Faculties Inhibited**—(See Inhibitions).

Fading; Faeces (Disorders of); **Fag; Faint; Fainting; Falls; Family**—Death In — Sickness In — (See Family, Relatives).

Famine; Fancies (Distempered); **Fatal Illness; Fate** (Bad Fate); **Father** (Death or Illness of); **Fatigue; Fauces** (Dryness of); **Fears; Feeble; Feelings** (Disorders of); **Feet** (Distempered — Gout In); **Female Disorders** — (See Female, Menses, Ovaries, Womb, Women, etc.).

Festerings; Fetid Conditions; Fevers (Hectic, Low); **Fibrous Tumors; Filth; Fissure; Fistula; Fixed Habits** — (See "Habits" under Fixed).

Flesh (Loss of); **Fluids** (Disturbances of); **Fluxes**—(See Flux, Hemorrhoids).

Foetus (Disorders of); **Food**—Errors In Diet—(See Diet, Eating, Food).

Fools; Forebodings; Fortune (Ill-Fortune); **Foul Conditions; Fractures; Frail; Freaks; Fretfulness; Frictions; Friends** (Death of—Illness of); **Frigidity; Functions** (Atrophy of—Suppression of); **Fury** (Fits of); **Gait** (Disorders of); **Gall Disorders**—Gall Stones (See Bile).

Gangrene; Gas (In Stomach or Bowels); **Gastric Disorders; General Debility**—(See Debility).

Generative Organs — Disorders of — (See Generation, Genitals, Genito-Urinary).

Gestation (Disorders of); **Ghastly Look**—(See Pale, Sickly).

Giddiness; Glaucoma; Gloom; Goiter; Gout; Grandparents (Afflictions To — Death of); **Gravel; Grief; Grievous Diseases; Gripings; Gristle**—Disorders of—(See Cartilage).

Groins (Disorders In); **Growth** (Disorders of); **Growths** (Morbid, Obstructing); **Gutta Serena; Habits** (Fixed Habits, Evil Habits, Habitual Disorders); **Haematoma; Hair** (Little Hair); **Halitosis** — (See "Foul" under Breath).

Hallucinations; Hands (Gout In); **Hard; Hardening; Hatred; Head** (Colds In, Pains In); **Headaches; Health** (Bad Health, Periods of Bad Health); **Hearing** (Deafness, Impaired); **Heart** (Afflicted with Grief, Afflicted with Poison,

Action Impeded, Left Auricle Disordered); **Heavy Aches** — And Pains — (See Aches, Heavy).

Heights (Falls From); **Hematochromatosis; Hemiplegia; Hemorrhoids** (Too Much Flux of); **Hernia; Herpes; Hip Diseases** (Hip Joint); **Hoarseness; Homicide; Hopelessness; Horny Growths; Hospitals** (Death In); **Houses** —Death by Fall of—(See Buildings).

Humours (Gouty, Offensive); **Humpback**—(See "Curvature", "Humpback", under Spine).

Hunger; Hurts; Husband (Death of); **Hypochondria; Hysterics; Ignoble Death; Ileac Passion; Ileum** (Obstructions In); **Ill-Formed; Ill-Health; Imaginations; Imbecility; Impairments; Impediments; Impending Disaster** — Fear of—(See Calamity).

Imperfections; Imperforations; Impotency; Impoverishments; Imprisonment—(See Prison).

Impure Blood—(See "Corrupt" under Impure).

Inabilities; Inactive; Incapable; Incomplete; Increases (Dryness and Disease Increased); **Incurable Diseases; Incurvating Body; Indifference; Indigestion; Indisposition; Indurations; Infamous; Infancy** (Death In); **Infarcts; Inferiority Complex; Infirmities; Inflammation** (Chronic, and Lungs Inflamed); **Inflexibility; Inherent Diseases; Inhibitions; Inhuman Shape; Injuries** (By Blows, Depressions in Skull or Body, by Falls, Crushings, Fractures, but with no loss of Blood).

Insufficiencies; Internal Disorders (Congestions, Intropulsion); **Intestines** —Disorders of—(See Bowels).

Intropulsion; Invalidism; Inward — Blood Driven Inward — (See Centripetal, Chill).

Inward Parts — Disorders of — (See Reins).

Irregularities; Irremediable Diseases —(See Incurable, Permanent, Remedy).

Irritations; Ischium (Disorders of); **Ischuria**—(See Urine).

Itch; Ivy Poison; Jaundice (Black); **Jealousy; Jejunum** (Obstructions In); **Joints** (Disorders of); **Journeys** (Death During, Delays, Fatigue, Illness); **Joy** (Life Robbed of); **Judges** (Death by Sentence of); **Judgment Bad; Kidneys** (Bright's Disease, Distempered, Renal Colic, Stone In, etc.); **Killed** (By Blows, Falls, etc.); **King's Evil** — (See Scrofula).

Knees (Disorders of); **Knuckles** — Swollen—Enlarged—(See Fingers).

Lack Of—(See subjects under "Lack Of").

Lameness; Lamenting; Languid; Lapses; Larynx (Disorders of); **Lassitude; Latent Diseases; Lazy; Leakages; Leanness; Leathery Skin; Legs** (Crooked, Gout In); **Leprosy; Less**—Lessened—(See Less).

Lethargy; Leucorrhoea; Leukocytes (Increased); **Lewd; Liars; Life** (Short Life); **Ligaments** (Disorders of); **Limbs** (Disorders of); **Limitations; Limp Body; Limping; Lingering Diseases; Lisping; Listless; Lithemia; Little**—(See subjects under Little).

Liver (Disorders of); **Local Parts** (Disorders of); **Lock-Jaw; Locomotion** (Disorders of); **Locomotor Ataxia; Loneliness; Long Diseases; Longings; Look** (Downward Look); **Loose Morals;** —(See "Loose" under Morals).

Loss Of — (See subjects under "Loss Of").

Love Affairs (Troubles In); **Loved Ones** (Death of); **Low Fevers** — (See "Low" under Fever).

Lower Parts — Disorders In — (See Lower).

Lowered—Lowering—(See these subjects).

Lubrication (Disorders of); **Luck** (Bad Luck); **Lumbago; Lumbar Disorders; Lumps; Lungs** (Congestions, Consumption, Disorders of); **Lupus; Luxations**—(See Dislocations).

Lymph (Disorders of); **Lynching; Maiming; Maladies; Malaise; Males** Disorders In); **Malice; Malignant Diseases; Malnutrition**—(See Nutrition).

Mammae—Disorders of—(See Breasts).

Mania (Suicidal); **Marasmus; Marks; Marriage** (Disturbances In); **Marriage Partner** (Death of — Illness of); **Mastoid Abscess; Masturbation** — (See "Solitary" under Vice).

Materialism; Matrix—Disorders of—(See Womb).

Matter (Decay of); **Maturity** (Death Before); **Meagre Body; Mean Stature**—Mean-Spirited—(See Mean).

Meat (Ill-Digested); **Medicines** (Cooling); **Medium Vitality**—(See Vitality).

Medulla (Bulbar Paralysis); **Melancholy; Members of Body** (Disorders of); **Membranes** (Disorders of); **Memory** (Disorders of); **Men** (Disability To); **Menses** (Disorders of); **Mental Disorders** — (See Intellect, Mental, Mind).

Merciless; Metabolism (Disorders of); **Metamorphosis** (Disorders of); **Micturition** — Disorders of — (See "Strangury" under Urine).

Middle Life (Disorders of, Death At); **Milk** (Disorders of); **Mind** (Disorders of); **Mineral Deposits**—(See Deposits, Minerals, Wastes).

Misanthropic; Miscarriages; Mischief; Miseries; Miserly; Misfortunes; Misshaped Body; Mistrustful; Mitral Diseases—(See Heart).

Mobs (Death By); **Moist and Cold Diseases**—(See "Cold and Moist" under Humours).

Moles; Monsters; Moods; Moping; Morals (Loose); **Morbid Diseases; Moroseness; Mortal Illness; Mortality** (Increased); **Mortification; Mother** (Death of, Affliction To); **Motion In Body** (Impeded); **Mournful; Mouth** (Disorders of); **Movement** (Slow); **Moving Parts** (Impediments In); **Much Sickness**—(See Sickness).

Mucous Membranes (Disorders of); **Muddling Creature**—(See "Ill-Formed" under Ill).

Mumps—(See Parotid).

Murderous; Murmuring; Muscles (Stiffness of, Contraction of); **Mutes; Mutilations; Mydriasis**—(See Iris).

Myopia—(See Accommodation, Sight).

Mystical; Nakedness — Wandering In —(See "Outrageous" under Insanity).

Narcotic Habit; Narrowing (Of Parts); **Nasal Diseases**—(See Catarrh, Nose).

Nasty Temper—(See Temper).

Nature (Nature of the Death — Disposition Ill-Natured); **Nausea; Navigation** (Dangers In); **Near** (Near Some Danger); **Neck** (Disorders In); **Necrosis; Negative Nature; Neglect and Privation** (Diseases Arising From); **Nerves** (Disorders of); **Neuralgia; Night Diseases**—(See Day, Night).

Night Sweats—(See Phthisis).

Nipples (Disorders of); **Nobles** (Infirmities To—Death of); **Nodules; Nose** (Disorders of); **Nourishment** — Disorders of—(See Nutrition).

Noxious Diseases; Numbness; Nutrition (Disorders of); **Obnoxious Diseases; Obscenity; Obsessions; Obstinate Diseases; Obstructions; Occlusions; Odors** (Foul); **Oesophagus** (Disorders of); **Offensive Diseases; Offspring**—Disorders of—Death of—(See Children).

Often Ailing—(See Often).

Old Age (Disorders of — Senility); **Operations** (Rules and Times for Surgical); **Ophthalmia**—(See Conjunctiva).

Opinions (Distorted); **Opposite Sex** (Aversions To); **Oppressions; Organic Diseases; Organs** (Diseases of); **Orifices** (Disorders of); **Orphans; Osseous Deposits; Ovaries** (Diseases of); **Own Death**—Fears Own Death—(See "Fears" under Death).

Oxygenation (Disorders of); **Pains** (Dull Pains and Aches); **Pale; Palsy; Paraesthesia; Paralysis; Parasitic Diseases; Parents** (Afflictions to, and especially to the Father or Grandfather); **Parotid Gland** (Disorders of); **Parts of the Body**—Afflictions To—(See Parts).

Parturition (Disturbances of); **Passages** (Narrowing of); **Passion**—Disorders of—Lack of—Perversion of—(See Apathy, Passion, Perversions).

Paternal Afflictions — (See Father, Paternal).

Pathological Conditions; Patricide —(See Father).

Peace of Mind—(See "No Peace" under Mind).

Peccant Humours—(See Humours).

Pectoral Affections; Peevishness; Pensiveness; Penurious; Perils; Periodic Diseases—The diseases of ♄ tend to return about every seven years, when ♄ afflicts his place in the radix, and tend to become chronic, due to the long period of ♄ in one sign, or house. (See Periodic, Returning).

Peripheral Nerves (Disorders of); **Peristalsis** (Impeded); **Permanent Diseases; Perplexities; Perversions; Perversity; Pessimism; Petrifaction; Pettifogging; Petulant; Phantasies; Phlegmatic Diseases; Phobias** — (See Fears).

Phthisis; Physical Disorders — (See "Ailments" under Physical).

Piles—(See Hemorrhoids).

Pimples; Pity (Without Pity); **Place** — Place of Birth Unfortunate — Place of Death In the Map of Birth — (See Anareta; "Place of Birth" under Place).

Plague; Planets—The Afflictions of ♄ as a Planet—(See "Afflictions Of" under Planets).

Pleasure (Aversion To); **Plodding**—(See "Laborious" under Labor).

Plots; Plugs; Pneumogastric Nerve (Disorders of); **Pneumonia** (Consolidation In); **Podagra**—(See "Feet" under Gout).

Poison (Heart Afflicted By—Retained Poisons); **Pollutions; Poor**—(See "Poor" under Circulation, Health; Poverty).

Posture (Defects of); **Poverty; Power** (Loss of); **Practices** (Evil); **Praecipients; Precipitation; Predispositions; Pregnancy** (Disorders of); **Prejudice; Premature** (Premature Birth—Death); **Premonitions; Presentiments; Pressure; Pretenders; Preventions** (Functions Prevented); **Prison** (Imprisonment); **Private** (Private Enemies—Private Sex Practices); **Processes** (Disturbances of); **Prodigal; Profligate; Prohibitions; Prolapsus; Prolonged Diseases; Promoted** (Rheumatism Promoted); **Prostrations; Protracted Diseases; Provisions** (Scarcity of); **Prudery; Psoriasis; Psychic Disturbances; Ptosis**—(See Eyelids, Prolapsus).

Public (Public Calamity—Public Sorrow); **Puerperal Disorders; Pulmonary Diseases; Pulse** (Feeble); **Punishments; Pupils Dilated**—(See Iris).

Pupura; Pus Diseases; Putrid Diseases; Pyorrhoea; Pyrosis—(See Belching).

Quadrupeds (Hurts By); **Quarrels; Quartan Ague; Rape; Rashes; Raw-Boned Body; Reason** (Disorders of); **Receptacles** (Disorders of); **Recklessness; Recluse; Recovery Slow; Rectum** (Disorders of); **Recuperation Slow; Recurrent Diseases; Red Face**—Morbid—(See Face).

Reducing Disorders; Refrigerant; Refuse of Body—Retention of—(See Elimination, Retention, Wastes).

Regeneration (Organs of Diseased); **Regretful; Reins** (Disorders of); **Relapses; Relatives** (Illness or Death of); **Relaxation; Religion** (Hypocrites In); **Remarkable** (Remarkable Misfortunes); **Remedy** (Incapable of); **Remorse; Remote Organs** (Disorders of); **Removal of Organs**—By Ablation—(See Remote, Removal).

Renal Disorders—(See Kidneys).

Rending of Parts—(See Rupture).

Renunciation; Repining; Repressions; Reptiles (Death or Injury By); **Reputation** (Loss of); **Resentful; Reserved; Residence** (Place of Unfortunate); **Resignation** (To Fate); **Resistance Low; Resolution** (Of Tissues); **Resources** (Husbanding of—Loss of); **Respiratory Organs**—Disorders of—(See Breath, Bronchial, Lungs).

Rest (Lack of); **Restlessness; Restraints; Restrictions; Retardations; Retentions; Retiring; Retractions; Retrospective; Returning Diseases; Revengeful; Reverses; Rheum; Rheumatism; Rhythm In Body** (Disturbed Rhythm); **Ribs** (Fractures of); **Riches** (Loss of); **Rickets; Right Side of Body**—Disorders In—Right Ear Disordered—(See Right).

Rigidity; Rigors; Riotous; Robbers; Roseola; Rottenness; Rough (Rough Skin); **Rouse** (Hard to Arouse); **Ruin; Rupture; Sadness; Sailors** (Death or Injury To); **Saliva**—Too Little—(See Fauces, Saliva).

Sallow; Salts of Body (Disturbances of); **Sand** (In Kidneys); **Satire; Saturnine**—(See Melancholy).

Sciatica; Sclerosis; Scrofula; Scurvy; Scybalum—Hard Faeces—(See Faeces).

Secret Parts—Disorders In—(See Secrets).

Secretions (Disorders of); **Sedentary Habits; Selfishness; Self-Undoing; Senility**—(See Old Age).

Sensibility (Diminished); **Severe Diseases; Sex**—Disorders of Sex Organs—Sex Perversions—(See Perversions, Sex).

Shoulders (Infirmities In); **Shrinkages; Sickly; Sickness**—(See Chronic, Lingering, Long Diseases, Sickness, Tedious).

Signs—The Diseases of ♄ in the Signs of the Zodiac—♄ in any sign tends to hinder and restrict the functions and circulation in the part ruled by the sign he is in at B., or by direction, progression, or transit. For classified lists of the diseases of ♄ in the Signs, see the various Textbooks and Dictionaries of Astrology. (See the paragraph, "Pathological Qualities" in Sec. 1 of this Article).

Skin (Disorders of); **Skull** (Depressions In); **Slow Diseases; Sluggishness; Solitary Vice**—(See Vice).

Solitude (Fond of); **Sore Throat**—(See Throat).

Sorrow; Spare Body; Spasmodic Pains (In Bowels); **Specks Over Eyes**—(See Eyes, Specks).

Speech (Impediments In); **Spinal Cord**—Spine (Disorders of); **Spleen** (Disorders of); **Sprains; Stagnations; Stamina** (Low); **Stammering**—(See Speech).

Starvation; Stature Limited—(See Dwarfed, Growth, Limitations).

Stenosis; Stiffness; Stomach (Disorders of—Indigestion); **Stone In Kidneys**—Chalk Stones of Gout—(See Stone).

Stools—Lumpy and Hard—(See Faeces).

Stoppages; Strangulation; Strangury—(See Urine).

Strictures; Subluxations; Subnormalities; Suffocation; Suicidal Mania—(See Suicide).

Suppressions; Surface of Body—Chilling of—(See Centripetal, Chill, Constrictions).

Suspensions; Suspicious; Sweat (Disorders of); **Swellings** (In Joints, Neck, Secret Parts, Throat).

Swindler; Syncope; Synovial Membranes—And Fluids (Disorders of); **System Disordered**—(See System).

Tabefaction; Tabes; Tedious Diseases; Teeth (Decay of—Disorders of); **Tetter; Thickenings; Thighs** (Disorders of); **Thin Body; Throat** (Disorders of); **Thrombus; Thyroid Gland** (Disturbed); **Tidal Air** (Lack of in Lungs); **Tissues**

(Disorders of); **Tone** (Lack of); **Tongue** (Foul); **Tonsils** (Ablation of — Tonsilitis); **Toothache**—(See Teeth).

Torpidity; **Toughening**; **Toxaemia**; **Travel** (Dangers or Death In); **Treachery**; **Treatment**—Of ♄ Diseases—(See "Jupiter", "Treatment", in Sec. 1 of this Article).

Tremors; **Trials**; **Trouble**; **Tubercles**; **Tuberculosis**; **Tumors**; **Typhus Fever**; **Ugly Body**; **Ulcers**; **Uncleanly**; **Uncles** (Death or Illness of); **Undersized Body**; **Unfortunate**; **Ungainly**; **Unhappy**; **Unhealthy**; **Unrefined**; **Untimely Death**; **Urea** (Deposits of); **Uremia**; **Urethra** (Stricture of); **Uric Acid** (Deposits of); **Urine** (Disorders of); **Uterus**—Disorders of—(See Womb).

Vain Fears—(See Fears).

Valves (Disorders of); **Vapors** (Foul — Low Spirits); **Varicose Veins**; **Vaso-Constrictor Nerves** (Disorders of); **Veins**; (Disorders of); **Venereal Diseases**; **Vertebrae** (Subluxations of); **Vessels** (Disorders of); **Vexations**; **Vices** (Addicted To); **Vigor** (Lack of); **Violent Tendencies** — (See Revenge, Treachery, Violent).

Virulent Disorders; **Vision**—Disorders of—(See Sight).

Vital Activity (Lack of); **Vitality** (Lessened, Low); **Vitiated**; **Vocal Organs**—Voice (Disorders of); **Voluntary Power** (Diseased); **Vomiting**; **Voyages** (Danger On); **Vulnerable Parts** — (See "Weak Spots" in Sec. 1 of this Article).

Vultures (Body Devoured By); **Walk** (Disorders of); **Walls of Cells**—Thickening of—(See Cells).

Waning of Forces; **Want** (In Want); **Warts**; **Wastes of Body** (Retention of); **Wasting Diseases**; **Weak** — (Weak Body, Weak Back, Debility, Feeble); **Weariness**; **Weight** (Loss of); **Wife** (Danger To)—Death of); **Womb** (Disorders of); **Women** (Diseases of — Female Weaknesses — Womb Disorders); **Worms**; **Worry**; **Wretched**; **Wrinkles**; **Wrists** (Fracture of); **Wrong Habits**—(See Habits).

Xanthanuria. For subjects, diseases, and afflictions which may involve the ♄ influences, and not listed or included in this Article, look in the alphabetical arrangement for the subject you have in mind.

SAUCY—Impudent—Independent—Disrespectful—Insolent—Insulting—♂ Sig. ♂ ☿; ♂ Sig. □ or ☍ ♃; the ☽ in good aspect to ♂, but ♂ evilly aspected by other planets, and especially by ♅ or ♄, tends to make the native bold and impudent. (See Bold, Impudent, Independent, Respect).

SAVAGE—Savages—Wild— Indocile— Savage Disposition—(See "Beastly Form" under Beasts; Brutish; Cannibals; "Dogs" under Children; Cruel; Destructiveness, Fierce, Indocile, Inhuman, Merciless; "Animal Forms" under Monsters; "Shows No Pity" under Pity; Prenatal Epoch, Vicious, Violent, Wild, etc.).

SAVED — Life Will Be Saved — (See "Saved" under Life).

SAYINGS — Mysterious Sayings — (See Delirium, Demoniac, Dreams).

SCABS—Scabies—Scabs may be the result of Abrasions, Injuries, or from Sores, Pus conditions, Eruptions, etc. Scabs are more bursting at the Full ☽. (See Chickenpox, Crusts, Eruptions, Favus, Sloughings, Smallpox, etc.).

Scabbed Lips—(See Lips).

Scabies — The Itch — A Contagious, Parasitic Disease—A ♑ and ♓ disease, and caused by afflictions in these signs; ♂ afflicted in ♉, ♍, ♑, or ♓; ♂ afflicted in ♓, and ♂, □, or ☍ the Asc. by dir.; ♂ in ♍ when ♂ is the afflictor in the disease. (See Itch, Parasites).

SCALDS—Scalding — Scald — Burns by Hot Water or Hot Liquids—

Death by Scalds—The ☉ to the ♂ or ill-asp. ♂ by dir.; ♂ ori. at B., and afflicting the hyleg by dir.; ♂ afflictions dispose to; ♂ the afflicting planet, in violent signs, and afflicting the hyleg; ♂ in ♉ or ♏, and afflicting the hyleg; cardinal signs show. (See "Death" under Burns, Liquids; "Hot Liquids" under Heat; "Fire" under Home).

Liable to Scalds—Danger of—Caused by the ☉ and ♂, the positive, electric, and heat-producing planets; the ☉ or ☽ to the ♂ or ill-asp. ♂ by dir.; the ☉ hyleg, and the ☉ to the ♂ or ill-asp. ♂ by dir.; the progressed ☉ to the ♂ or ill-asp. ♂; the ☽ in water signs, and to the ♂ or ill-asp. ♂ by dir.; the ☽ Sig. ♂ the ☉, subject to; the ☽ Sig. ♂, □, or ☍ the ☉, and especially if ♂ aspects the ☉; the ☽ ♂ ♂ in the M.C., and in evil asp. to Antares; ♂ afflictions predispose to, and born under ♂; ♂ diseases and afflictions; ♂ afflicted in ♈; ♂ in the 6th H., in a cardinal sign; ♂ afflicted in the 1st H.; ♂ afflicted in water signs, and ♂ or ill-asp. the Asc. by dir.; ♂ □ or ☍ the ☉; ☿ Sig. ♂ the ☉, and the ☉ ill-dignified at B.; the Asc. to the place of the Ascelli or Capricornus. (See "Danger Of" under Burns; "Hot Liquids" under Heat).

Scald-Head—(See Favus).

Urine—(See "Scalding" under Urine).

SCALES—Scale Formation — Scaling— Desquamation — Scale Tetter—Caused principally by ♄. May also be caused by excess dryness of the skin, and due to the heat of the ☉ and ♂. (See Bunions, Crusts; "Body" under Dry; Eczema, Exudations; "Skin" under Hard; "Body" under Heat; Herpes, Horny; "Desquamative Nephritis" under Kidneys; Parched, Psoriasis; "Dry Skin" under Skin; Tetter, Xeransis, Xeroderma). See North Scale, South Scale.

SCALP — The Skin Over the Skull — Ruled by ♈, and the ☉ in ♈ tends to dry up the scalp, and cause Baldness. (See Baldness; "Loss of Hair" under Hair).

Favus of Scalp — Scald-Head — (See Favus).

Wounds To — ♂ afflicted in ♈. (See "Accidents","Hurts",under Head; Skull).

SCANDAL—Scandalous Diseases—

Danger of Scandal—Loss of Honour— Disrepute — Loss of Reputation—Disgraced — Dishonoured, etc. — The ☉ by Periodic Rev. to the ill-asps. the radical ♅; the ☉ to his own ill-asps. by dir.; the ☉ to the bad aspects ♀; the ☽ to the P. Dec. South Scale; the ☽ to the bad asps. ♀ by dir., or transit; the ☽ decr. in light, and be carried or conjoined with ♀; ♅ or ♂ to the ill-asps. ♀ by dir.; ♄ to the ☌ ☋ by dir.; ♄ or ♂ passing over the place of ♀ at B., or by transit, or at a Solar Rev.; ♃ to the place of ☋; ♂ to the ☌ or ill-asp. ♀; ♂ by periodic rev. to the ill-asps. the ☉ tends to infamy; ♀ afflicted by malefics at B.; the M.C. to the □ or ☍ the ☽ or ♀ by dir. (See Disgrace; "Own Worst Enemy" under Enemies; Evils, Execrated, Harlots; "Loss Of" under Honour, Reputation; Infamous, Love Affairs, Misfortune, Passion, Reverses, Ruin, Sex, Shame, Sorrow, Trouble, Vile, Wanton; "Ruined" under Women, etc.).

Scandalmongers—Loves to Defame, Gossip, and Slander Others—Afflictions to the ☽ or ☿, and with ♂ entering into the configuration; ♆ and ♏ afflictions tend to the most treacherous attacks; the ☽ and the ♒ sign afflicted tend to domestic gossip. (See "Secret Enemies" under Enemies; Liars, Libelers; "Injured" under Men; Revenge, Treachery, etc.).

Scandalous Diseases—Danger of—Suspicion of—The ☽ in ♏ and afflicted by the ☉ or ♂ when taken ill, and especially if ♀ afflict the ☽ (Hor'y); ♀ or ☿ afflicted in ♏. (See Genitals, Gonorrhoea, Private Diseases, Syphilis, Venereal).

Women Openly Scandalous—The ☽ Sig. in ♏, infamous, obscene, and openly scandalous, and if the ☽ also be in □ or ☍ ♄ or ♂. (See Infamous, Lewd, Licentiousness, Obscene, Shameless, etc.).

SCANTY—

Scanty Hair On Head—(See Baldness).

Scanty Menses—(See Menses).

SCAPULA—The Shoulder Blade—Ruled by ♊. (See Shoulders).

SCAR—Scars—Scar Tissue—Scarred—Scarified Sores—Cicatrix—Dents—Blemishes—Marks, etc.—Scars on any part of the body are usually the result of ♂ affliction to that part of the body, and from wounds or injury. There tend to be scars on the right side of the body when masculine signs are upon the Asc., and a masculine planet in the Asc., or sign indicated, and on the left side of the body when feminine, etc. Mars on the Asc. tends to a scar or mark on that part of the body ruled by the sign ♂ is in at B. This does not indicate that the scar exists at B., but it may happen after birth from an accident or injury. (See "Scars" under Arms, Back, Breasts, Eyes, Face, Feet, Forehead, Head, Knees, Legs, Neck, Skin, Throat; Blemishes, Cuts, Dents, Left Side; "Organs" under Lower, Middle, Upper; Marks, Moles, Pitted, Right Side, Scarlet Fever; "Face" under Smallpox; Stabs, Wounds, etc.).

Scarified Sores—♄ and ♂ in an angle, occi. of the ☉, and ori. of the ☽, and ☿ in familiarity with ♂. (See "Face" under Smallpox).

SCARCITY—Lack of—Diminished Supply—

Corn Destroyed—An eclipse of the ☉ or ☽ in the earthy signs ♉, ♍, or ♑, and loss to grains such as are sown annually; an eclipse of the ☉ in ♎, and especially the 1st decan. of ♎; an eclipse of the ☉ in the 1st decan. of ♌, scarcity of corn and bread; ♄ in a fixed sign at the Vernal, and during the year, scarcity of grains and crops; Comets appearing in ♉; Comets in ♌ tend to worms and vermin, destroying grains and crops; Comets appearing in ♏. (See Drought, Earth, Famine, Fountains; "Extreme Heat" under Heat; Grain).

Famine—(See Famine).

Food—Scarcity of—(See Drought, Famine; "Scarcity" under Food).

Fruits—Scarcity of—(See Fruit).

Rain—Scarcity of—(See Drought; "Air", "Fountains", under Dry; Famine, Fountains, Rain, Rivers).

Seeds—(See "Scarcity" under Seeds).

Waters—(See "Scarcity" under Waters).

Wheat—(See "Scarcity" under Wheat; "Corn" in this section).

SCARF SKIN—The Cuticle—Epidermis—(See Cuticle, Epidermis, Skin).

SCARLET FEVER—Scarlatina—A Contagious, Epidemic, Exanthematous Disease, with Fever and a Scarlet Eruption—Caused by ♂ afflictions to the hyleg at B., and in such cases often proves quickly fatal. Those free from ♂ affliction to the hyleg at B., or ♂ in power at B., are usually immune to the disease, and also immune to smallpox. In such cases of natural immunity vaccination is unnecessary. (See "Immunity" under Smallpox). Mars afflicting the hyleg at B. tends to leave malignant scars resulting from this disease, or smallpox. Mars alone, his afflictions at B., and by transit or direction to the hyleg, and to the Asc., is said to be the cause of this disease. Mars rising at a Solar Eclipse; ♂ ☌ ♄ and ♃ at a Solar Eclipse; ♂ supreme at the Equinoxes or Solstices; ♂ is supreme in years of Scarlatina epidemics, afflicts the hyleg in those who succumb, or are attacked; ♂ in ♏ and afflicting the hyleg; ♂ coming to the ☌ or ill-asp. the Asc. early in life usually causes scarlet fever, scarlatina, smallpox, or measles; ♂ in ♉ at B., occi., and lord of the year at the Vernal E., many children die from scarlatina and smallpox; ♂ lord of the year at the Vernal, in ♈, and afflicted by ♄; ♂ predominating at a ☌ of three or four of the superior planets tends to epidemics of Scarlatina or Smallpox, and severe in type, with many deaths, but milder in form when ♂ is in ☌ or ☍ only one other superior planet, and ♂ holding power; ♂ in power at B., and to the ☌ or ill-asp. ♄ by dir., and especially liable to the disease in childhood; the ☉, ☽, or Asc. to the ☌, P, □, or ☍ ♂ by dir., and ♂ in power, and afflicting the hyleg at B.; the ☉ and ☽ □ the radical ♂ at a Solar eclipse; the ☉ at the Vernal ☌ or ill-asp. ♂; the ☉ or ☽ ☌ ♄ and ♂ at an eclipse of the ☽; the ill-asps. of the ☉ to the hyleg by tr. or dir. if the ☉ be afflicted by ♂ at B.; the ill-asps. of the ☉ or ♂ to the Asc. early in life; the ☉ or ☽ hyleg and afflicted by ♂; the ☽ sepr. from the ☉ and applying to ♂ at a Solar Ingress; the hyleg much afflicted at B. by ♂; the Asc. to the □ or ☍ ♃ by dir., and ♃ afflicted by ♂ at B.; the Asc. to the ☌ or ill-asp. ♂ by dir. if ♂ is in power at B., or afflicting the Asc. or hyleg; especially identified with the fixed signs, and especially ♉ and ♏, and also causes Diphtheria under these fixed sign afflictions; Comets appearing in ♊ tend to much mortality from scarlet fever; Subs at MCP, CP, SP, and KP. (See Chickenpox; "Mortality Great" under Children; Contagious, Diphtheria, Epidemics, Eruptive Fevers, Infections. Measles; "Mumps" under Parotid; Smallpox). Cases of Scarlet Fever—See Chap. XIII in Daath's Medical Astrology.

SCARS—(See Scar. Also see Blemishes, Marks, Moles, Naevus).

SCATTERING—Scattered—Dissipation of Mental and Bodily Forces—(See Changes, Chaotic, Concentration, Confusion, Diffusiveness, Dispersions, Dissipation, Dull, Effervescent; "Scattered" under Energy; Improvident, Indifferent, Influenced; "Shallow" under Mentality; Mutable, Negative, Receptive, Restless, Susceptibility, Vacillating, Vagabond, Wanderer, etc.).

SCENERY—Changes of Scenery Good for the Health—(See "Rapid" under Recuperation).

SCEPTICISM—Sceptical—Skeptic—Doubt—Indifference to Orthodox Religion—Caused principally by ♃ weak and afflicted at B.; ♃ afflicted in signs of his detriment, debility, or fall, as in ♊, ♍, or ♑, incline to indifference, a more superficial and sceptical nature along religious and philosophical lines, and to selfishness, covetousness, and a more self-centered nature. The strong afflictions of ♄ at B., and especially to ☿, tend to indifference, fatalism, doubt, materialism, etc. Also ☿ prominent at B., and afflicted, or malefics in the signs of ☿. The 9th H. afflicted by malefics, and especially with ♄ there. (See Doubts, Fears, Independent, Materialism, Metaphysical, Occult; "Mind" under Prejudice; "Irreligious" under Religion; Science, etc.).

SCHEAT PEGASI—A Star of the 2nd magnitude, of the nature of ♄, in the last face of ♓, and produces danger of death by drowning. (See Drowning).

SCHEMES—Scheming—Calculating—(See Artifice, Cheating, Deceitful, Dishonest; "Secret Enemies" under Enemies; Evil, Feuds, Mischief, Plots, Poison Death, Quarrelsome, Revenge, Secret, Shrewdness, Treachery, etc.).

SCHOLAR—Scholarly—Studious—Smart In Books and Learning—Obtains Profound Knowledge—The ☽ Sig. ☌, ⚹, or △ ☿; the good aspects of ♅ or ♄ to the 9th H., and lord of the 9th, or ♄ well-aspected in the 9th H., a deep desire to get at the philosophy of life, go into profound things, and get at ultimates; ♃ Sig. ⚹ or △ ☿, gives great learning; ♂ Sig. ⚹ or △ ☿; ☿ Sig. in ♍ and free from affliction; ♀ Sig. ⚹ or △ the ☽; ♍ influence, and this sign on the Asc. at B.; the Asc. favorably aspected by the ☽ and ♀. (See Genius; "Great Ability" under Great; Intellect; "Good" under Judgment; Knowledge, Learning; "Abilities", "Quickened", under Mental; Metaphysical; "Cultivation", "Deep and Profound", "Good", under Mind; Occult, Perception, Philosophy, Prodigies, Reading, Science, Study; "Good" under Understanding).

SCIATIC NERVES—Are under the internal rulership of the ♐ sign.

Fear of Sciatica—The ☽ in ♎, ☌, or ill-asp. ♄ (or ☿ if he be of the nature of ♄) at the beginning of an illness or at decumbiture (Hor'y). (See Fears).

Sciatica—Pains In the Sciatic Nerves—Principally a ♐ disease, and with afflictions in this sign and in the opposite sign ♊; the ☉ afflicted in ♐; the ☽ afflicted in ♐, or afflicting the hyleg therefrom; the ☽ hyleg in ♐, and afflicted, and especially with females; a ☽ disease, and afflictions to the ☽; the ☽ hyleg, and to the ☌ or ill-asp. ♄ by dir.; ♆, ♅, or ♄ in ♎ or ♐, and afflicting the ☉ or ☽; ♅ in ♐ and afflicting the ☉, ☽, or Asc.; ♅ in ♐; ♅ in ♐ in the 6th H.; ♄ in ♊ by reflex action; ♄ in ♐, occi., and afflicting the ☉, ☽, or Asc.; ♄ afflicted in ♐; ♄ in ♊, ♎, or ♐ and afflicting the ☉, ☽, or Asc.; ♄ in ♐ in the 6th H., and afflicted; ♃ afflicted in ♐, and especially in the 6th H.; ♂ in ♊ or ♐; ♂ in ♐ and afflicting the ☽; ♂ in ♐ in the 6th H., and afflicting the hyleg; ☿ afflicted in ♐; ♐ on the Asc.; afflictions in common signs. Subs at LLP (4, 5L). (See "Pains In" under Thighs).

SCIENCE—A Scientific Mind—The Applied Sciences—

Arts and Sciences—Proficient In—Fond of—(See "Arts and Sciences" under Learning).

Astrology—Studious of—♅ strong at B., rising, or in the M.C., and in favorable aspect to ☿; ♆ □ or ☍ ♅ at B. inclines to the study of Astrology, but in a more superficial way, and to make bogus Astrologers, or Charlatans; ☿ Sig. in any aspect of ♅, and if the ☽ assist ☿, tends to make a good, studious, honest and sincere Astrologer; the ♒ and ♑ influences strong at B. (See "Occult Study" in this section; "Metaphysics" under Learning; Metaphysics, Mystical, Occult, Philosophy, Reading, Study).

Learns Science Easily—(See "Learns Easily" under Learning).

Little Ability For Science—(See "Void Of" under Learning; "Shallow" under Mentality; "Light in Mind", "Weak Mind", under Mind; "Scientific Mind" in this section).

Occult Science—Fond of—♅ strong at B.; ♅ and ♄ conjoined with ☿; the ☽ Sig. in ♒, lover of the Curious and Scientific studies. (See "Astrology" in this section; Intuition, Perception, Psychic Powers, Spiritual Sight, Truth, Understanding).

Scientific Mind—The ♊, ♍, and ♒ Signs are highly scientific; the ☉ or ☿ in ♍

or ♒; ♅ ⚹ or △ ♃, ♀, or ☿; ♃ Sig. in ♒; ☿ in ♊, ♍, or ♒, well-aspected, and especially by ♅. There is little ability for scientific learning when ☿ is combust and close to the ☉ at B. (See Genius; "Inventive Mind" under Learning, Prodigies; Mathematical, Mechanical).

Scientific Signs — Of the Zodiac — ♊, ♍, ♒.

SCIRRHUS—A Hard Form of Carcinoma —(See "Scirrhus" under Axillae, Tumors; "Breasts" under Carcinoma).

SCLEROSIS—Hardening of Tissue—Induration, Over-growth, and Hardening of the connective tissue of an organ, are the work of ♄ deposits. Also a ♋ and ♑ disease. (See "Thickening" under Cells; Cirrhosis, Congelation, Deposits, Hardening, Hypertrophy, Minerals; "Over-Growth" under Organs; Thickening).

Arteries—Hardening of—(See "Arterio—Sclerosis" under Arteries).

Lungs — (See "Hardening" under Lungs).

Spinal Cord—(See "Spinal Cord" under Hardening).

See "Earth Signs" under Earth; "Salts of the Body" under Salts; Saturn.

SCOLDING — Rebuking — Reproving — Fault-Finding—Critical—A ♄ characteristic. Also the ♍ people are given to much criticism, scolding, and fault-finding. (See Fretful, Noisy, Peevish, Petulant; "Mind" under Prejudice; Virgo, Worry, etc.).

SCOPE—Scope of the Disease Enlarged —(See "Scope" under Enlarged).

SCORNFUL—Contemptuous—Disdainful — Given To Mockery and Scoffing — ♂ ruler at B., and afflicted. In Hor'y Q. ♂ Sig. of the person. (See Mars Influence, Mockery; "Scornful" under Religion).

SCORPIO—The Scorpio Sign (♏)—The Eighth Sign of the Zodiac, and ruled by ♂. This Sign is affiliated with the 8th H., the House of Death. Scorpio is symbolized by both the Scorpion and the Eagle. Scorpio gives the death sting, and then the Soul soars away like an eagle into its airy home. This sign also gives features resembling an eagle. The Scorpion is the symbol of the lower mind, and the Eagle of the Higher Mind. This sign is the night sign, or house, of ♂, the exaltation of ♅, and the fall of the ☽, and the ☽ is most unfortunate in this sign, and especially with females, and tends to disturbed and irregular female functions. This sign belongs to the Fixed Cross, made up of ♉, ♌, ♏, and ♒, and is sympathetic with all the fixed signs, and planets in these signs tend to influence or afflict the parts, or organs ruled by all the fixed signs, and this thru sympathy or reflex action. Scorpio is a sign of long ascension and is classed as a cold, watery, feminine, fixed, negative, nocturnal, moist, fruitful, magnetic, vital, nervous, broken, hurtful, imperfect, mute, phlegmatic, unfortunate, obeying, southern, autumnal sign. The Scorpio people are said to be "The Salt of the Earth" when awakened, spiritualized, and living in their Higher Minds, but when living in the lower mind, its influence is to make the natives of the sign more treacherous, deceptive, jealous, murderous, passionate, revengeful, deliberate in crime and evil, and to be selfish, and especially when the ♆ influence is involved. Taurus and ♏ are the strongest of the negative and feminine signs, and these signs when on the Asc. at B. give considerable vitality, and more strength than the other earthy or watery signs. Scorpio is known as the "Genital Pole of Paracelsus", while the other ♂ sign, ♈, is called the "Cerebral Pole of Paracelsus". This sign has to do with Procreation, Readaptation, and the Reproductive and Destructive Processes of Life. Scorpio tends to give an excess of magnetic power, and to attract disease, and especially infectious complaints, contagious diseases, and to fall easy victims to Epidemics. (See External). The ☽ in ♏ at B. gives the ♏ and ♂ personality, and often a very troublesome, warlike and combative nature, and if afflicted, to center the mind more upon passion and sex matters. Being a strong occult sign, and the exaltation of ♅, this sign when on the Asc. at B., or containing the ☉, ☿, and other planets, tends to make the native very fond of the Occult, Mystical, Metaphysical, and Astrological Sciences. The Sex Organs are ruled by ♏, and in the early stages of humanity, the opposite and complemental sign ♉ is said to have drawn the larynx and vocal organs from ♏, and this is the reason the larynx, throat, and vocal cords are so intimately related, and why the voice changes at puberty in males. (See Larynx). Scorpio has special affinity with the Nose, Nasal Bones, and the Bladder. When on the Asc. at B., ♏ gives a strong constitution, and the strongest of the watery signs. Excretion is a function of ♏ and ♂, and to burn out the wastes and poisons of the system by fevers and inflammation. This is a fruitful sign, but the least fruitful of the watery signs because of its ♂ influence. The Hebrew Letter "Nun", or "N", is connected with the ♏ sign, which rules the Generative Organs. The Pathological Qualities of this sign are Destructiveness, Reproduction, Tyranny, Worry. The Places denoted by ♏ are Drains, Sinks, Kitchens, Washhouses, Stinking Pools, Quagmires, Muddy Swamps, Marshes, Ruins near Water, and places where Reptiles and Vermin breed. Brown is the Color of ♏, and also red, and a reddish brown, as red is the color of ♂. Also rules dark brown color. People born with the ☉ in ♏, and especially if this sign, or ♂, are not in the Asc., often have very black eyes and black hair, and some of our most beautiful brunettes were born with the ☉ in this sign. (See "Black Hair" under Hair). The Star Antares, also known as "Cor Scorpio", or Scorpion's Heart, partakes of the nature of ♂ and ♃, and some Writers say of the nature of ♂ and ☿. (See Antares). Frons Scorpio is a fixed star in ♐. (See Frons Scorpio). The Zodiac Salt ruled by the ♏ sign is Calcium

Sulphate. The following are some of the principal Qualities assigned to this sign—Autumnal, Bold, Broken, Burning, Caustic, Cleansing, Cold, Combative, Constructive, Courageous, Crooked, Deceptive, Destructive, Excitable, Feminine, Feverish, Fiery in Temper, Fixed, Foolhardy, Fruitful, Harmful, Hasty, Hot-Tempered, Hurtful, Imperfect, Impetuous, Incisive, Irritable, Jealous, Lustful, Malicious, Military, Moist, Murderous, Mute, Negative, Nervous, Nocturnal, Obeying, Obstinate, Occult, Passionate, Phlegmatic, Pungent, Quarrelsome, Rash, Rebellious, Reckless, Red, Reproductive, Revengeful, Ruinous, Southern, Strong, Stubborn, Treacherous, Tyrannical, Unfortunate, Vicious, Violent, Vital, Warlike, Watery, Worrisome.

SCORPIO RULES—See the following subjects in the alphabetical arrangement—Anus (the Sphincter Ani Muscle); Appendix Vermiformis; Bladder—The Sphincter of—Stone in Bladder —Elimination of Urine Thru the Bladder; Blood (Red Coloring Matter of); Bones—the Nasal Bones—Brim of Pelvis—Pubic Bone; Bronchials; Brown Color; Calcium Sulphate; Calculi; Canal (the Inguinal); Capsules (Supra-Renal); Cervix of Uterus and the Glandular Portion of Cervix; Clitoris; Coccyx (the Os Coccyx); Colon (the Descending Colon, the Meso-Colon, and probably the whole of the Colon); Colors (Brown, Dark Brown, Red); Cowper's Gland; Descending Colon; Destructive Processes of Life; Ductless Glands; Elimination of Urine Thru the Bladder and Urethra; Excrementitious Fluids; Excretion (Excretory Bowels—Excretory System—Excretory Organs — The Lower Bowels — Excretory Vessels of the Testicles—Internal Excretory System—Excretion in the Kidneys); External Humoural Secretions; Female Functions (Menses); Fluids (Excrementitious); Functions (of Excretion, Reproduction, and the Female Functions); Fundament; Gall; Ganglia (the Intestinal); Generative Organs; Genitals; Genito-Urinary System; Glands (Cowper's Glands—Ductless Glands—Glans Clitoris—Glans Penis — Muciparous Glands—Glandular Portion of the Prostates — Glandular Portion of the Uterine Cervix — Thymus Gland—Thyroid Gland); Gravel; Groins; Healers (Magnetic); Humoural Secretions (the External and Internal); Iliac Region; Inguinal Canal and Region; Internally ♏ rules the Internal Generative and Excretory Systems, the Bladder, Appendix, and the Internal Humoural Secretions; Intestines (Large Intestine—Lower Excretory Bowels—Descending Colon); Ischium (Tuberosity of); Kidneys (Excretion In—Lower Portion of the Pelvis or Sinus); Large Intestine; Lime Sulphate; Liver; Lower Excretory Bowels; Magnetic Healers; Menses; Meso-Colon; Muciparous Glands of the Generative System; Nasal Bones and Nasal Orifice; Nose; Organs (Organs of Excretion — Sex and Reproductive Organs); Orifice (of Nose, Penis, and Rectum); Os Coccyx; Ovaries; Pasty Complexion; Pelvis (Pelvic Bones — Brim of Pelvis—Pelvis of Kidneys);

Penis (Glans Penis); Perineum; Pituitary Gland (or Body); Plexus (the Intestinal Ganglia and Plexus ruling the Internal and External Humoural Secretions—the Sacral Plexus); Private Members and Privy Parts; Procreation; Prostate Gland; Pubes and Pubic Bone; Pulsatilla; Readaptation; Rectum (the Anus and the Meso-Rectum); Red Coloring Matter of the Blood; Renal Capsules (Supra-Renals); Reproduction and Reproductive Organs; Sacrum and Sacral Plexus; Sand (in Kidneys and Bladder); Scrotum; Secret Parts (Stone In, and Disorders of); Secretions (the External and Internal Humoural Secretions); Sex Organs; Sigmoid Flexure; Sinus of Kidneys; Spermatic Cord; Sphincter Muscle (of Bladder and Anus); Spleen; Stone (in Bladder, Kidneys, or Secret Parts); Structurally ♏ rules the Nasal Bones, the Sacrum, Ischium, and Os Coccyx; Supra-Renal Capsules; Sweat; Symphysis Pubis; Testicles (Excretory Vessels of); Thymus Gland; Thyroid Gland; Tuberosity of the Ischium; Ureters, Urethra; Urine (Urinary Organs and the Elimination of Urine); Uro-Genital Orifice; Uterus (Glandular Portion of the Uterine Cervix); Vessels (Excretory Vessels of the Testicles); Womb, etc.

SCORPIO DISEASES—The Afflictions of Scorpio — Scorpio attracts disease, and especially contagious and infectious diseases. Scorpio has special affinity with the Nose and Bladder. The principal causes of diseases ruled by ♏ are afflictions in the ♏ sign, the presence of malefics in this sign, or with ♏ upon the Asc. at B., or on the cusp of the 6th H., and afflicted. Planets in ♉, the opposite sign, also tend to increase and aggravate ♏ diseases, as well as planets in ♌ and ♒, in evil aspect to ♏. The Fixed Signs, or the Fixed Sign Cross, when containing a preponderance of planets at B. tends to afflict all parts and organs ruled by the fixed signs, and the afflictions are even greater, and more lasting, when the fixed signs are found upon the four angles of the map at B. The following is an Alphabetical Summary of Diseases and Afflictions caused and ruled by the Scorpio Sign. See these subjects in the alphabetical arrangement—

Anus (Disorders of—Contraction of); **Appendicitis; Back** (Disorders of); **Bladder** (Diseases of—Stone In); **Blood** —Disorders of Red Coloring Matter of — (see Haemoglobin, Iron; "Blood" under Red); **Bow Legs** — (see Legs); **Bowels**—Disorders In the Lower, Excretory Bowels, In the Colon and Descending Colon — (see Bowels, Colon, Excretion, Faeces); **Bubo; Calculus; Caries**—Of the Cartilage of the Nose— (see "Caries" under Nose); **Catamenial Disorders** — (see Menses); **Cecum** —Inflammation of—(see Caecum); **Chronic** —Chronic Exanthematous Sore Throat —(see Throat); **Colon**—Disorders of—Colitis—(see Colon); **Contagions; Discharges** (Unnatural); **Drunkenness; Ductless Glands** (Disorders of); **Elimination** (Disorders of); **Emissions**—(see Semen); **Enlarged Prostate**—(see Prostate); **Epidemics; Exanthema; Excess; Excesses; Excretion** (Disorders of);

Falling of Womb—(see Womb); **Fissure**—(see Anus); **Fistula; Fluids**—Disorders of the Excrementitious Fluids—(see "Fluids" under Excretion); **Fossae of Nose**—Disorders of—(see Nose); **Functions**—Female Functions Irregular—(see Menses); **Fundament** (Disorders of); **Gall**—Disorders of—(see Bile, Gall); **Generative System** (Disorders of); **Genitals** (Disorders of); **Genito-Urinary System** (Disorders of); **Glands**—(see Parotid; "Cervix" under Womb); **Goiter; Gonorrhoea; Gout; Gravel; Groins** (Diseases In); **Heart** (Disorders of); **Hemorrhoids; Hernia** (Inguinal); **Humoural Secretions**—Disorders of—(see "External" under Humours); **Hydrocele; Infections** (Infectious Diseases); **Inflammations**—(see Genitals, Parotid, Secret Parts, Womb); **Inguinal Hernia**—(see Hernia); **Injuries**—To Sex Organs—(see Genitals, Maimed, Penis, Secret Parts, Sex Organs, Spermatic Cord, Testes, Womb); **Irregular Menses**—(see Menses); **Kidneys**—Stone In—(see "Kidneys" under Stone); **Larynx** (Disorders of); **Legs** (Ill-Formed); **Leucorrhoea; Liver** (Disorders of); **Lues**—(see Syphilis); **Magnetic Power** (Excess of); **Matrix**—Defects In—(see Womb); **Menses** (Disorders of); **Mucous Membranes**—Of the Nose—Disorders of—(see Nose); **Mumps**—(see Parotid); **Natural Powers**—Lowered In Females—(see "Natural Forces" under Natural); **Nose**—Disorders of—(see Catarrh, Colds, Nose); **Obstruction**—Of Urine—(see Urine); **Ovaries** (Diseases of); **Pain**—Pain In Groins—Painful Menses—(see Groins, Menses); **Parotid Gland** (Swelling of); **Parturition** (Disorders In); **Penis** (Diseases and Injury); **Perityphlitis**—(see Caecum); **Piles**—(see Hemorrhoids); **Prevalent**—Scorpio Diseases Prevalent—♂ in ♏, ori., and lord of the year at the Vernal. (See "Public Health Bad" under Public); **Priapism**—(see Penis); **Private Diseases; Prostate Gland** (Disorders of); **Puerperal Disorders; Rectum** (Disorders of); **Regenerative Organs** (Disorders of); **Renal Stone**—(see "Kidneys" under Stone); **Reproductive Organs** (Disorders of); **Retention**—Of Poisons—Of Urine—(see Poisons, Retention, Urine); **Rupture**—In Groins—(see "Inguinal" under Hernia); **Sand** (In Kidneys); **Scandalous Diseases; Scrotum** (Disorders of); **Scurvy; Secret Parts** (Distempers In—Stone In); **Secretions** (Disorders of); **Semen** (Emissions); **Sex Organs** (Disorders of—Injuries to); **Sigmoid Flexure** (Disorders of); **Sore Throat**—Exanthematous and Syphilitic—(see Throat); **Spasm** (of Bladder and Urethra); **Spermatic Cord** (Injuries To); **Sphincter Ani**—Contractions of—(see Anus); **Spleen** (Derangements of); **Stone**—In Bladder, Kidneys, or Secret Parts—(see Stone); **Strangury** (see Urine); **Stricture** (of Urethra); **Syphilis; Testicles** (Disorders of); **Throat** (Chronic Exanthematous Sore Throat—Syphilitic—Ulcerated); **Thyroid Gland** (Disorders of); **Ulceration** (Of the Throat In Syphilis); **Unnatural Discharges** (see Discharges); **Urethra** (Disorders of—Stricture—Urethritis); **Urine** (Disorders of—Retention—Obstructions); **Uterus**—Disorders of—(see Womb); **Vagina** (Disorders of); **Venereal Diseases; Vitality Lowered** (see Vitality); **Vulva** (Disorders of); **Womb** (Disorders of). For subjects which may have been overlooked for this list, and which you have in mind, look for them in the alphabetical arrangement.

SCOURGE—Punished by the Lash or Whip—Death or Injury By—(See Assaults, Blows; "Beaten In Prison" under Prison).

SCROFULA—King's Evil—Struma—Scrofulous Tumors—A Constitutional Disease with Glandular Tumors, and a Tuberculous Tendency—A ☉ disease, and afflictions to the ☉; a ☽ disease, and afflictions to the ☽; the ☽ afflicted in ♌, or afflicting the hyleg therefrom; the ☽ hyleg in ♌, and afflicted, and especially among females; ♆, ♅, or ♄ in ♋ and afflicting the ☉ or ☽; ♄ afflicted in ♉ or ♓; ♄ in ♉, ♊, or ♓, occi., and afflicting the ☉, ☽, or Asc., and with a strong tubercular and wasting tendency; ♄ or ♂ in the Asc. or M.C., in ♋, ♑, or ♓, and signs ascribed to animals or fishes; ♄ in ♉ when Sig. of the disease; ♄ in ♋ and afflicting the ☉, ☽, or Asc.; ♄ and ♂ joined anywhere in the figure, and especially in angles, or in their own nodes, or in the Lunar nodes; a ♃ disease; ♂ afflicted in ♉; ♀ afflicted in ♊; a ♉ disease when malefics are in ♉ at B., and the disease appears in the neck; a ♊ disease; ♋ on the Asc.; a ♏ disease; malefics in ♋, ♑, and ♓, angular, ori. of the ☉ and occi. of the ☽, tend to scurvy or scrofula, and if the malefics be in the 1st or 7th H. tends to add putridity; ♉, ♏, and ♀ rulers of the 4th and 10th Houses, the houses of the parents, bring the danger of inheriting scrofulous blood; airy signs on the Asc. and 6th H. at B., or at decumb., or Sigs. at the beginning of an illness, indicate scrofula in Hor'y Q.; signified by the 2nd H. influences. (See Adenoma, Glands; "Scrofula" under Neck; Scurvy, Tuberculosis).

SCROTUM—The Pouch Containing the Testes—Ruled by ♏.

Hernia—Scrotal Hernia—The ☉ in ♏ in the 6th H., and afflicted by ♅ or ♂; the ☉ ☌ ☿ in ♏ in the 6th H., and afflicted by ♅, ♄, and the ☽; ♂ afflicted in ♏; ♂ in ♏ in the 6th H., and afflicted. Case of Scrotal Hernia—See Chap. XIII in Daath's Medical Astrology. (See Hernia, Rupture).

Hydrocele—(See this subject).

Varicocele—Dilated Veins In Scrotum—(See Testes, Varicocele).

SCRUPLES—Motives—Conduct, etc.—(See Cheating, Conduct, Deceitful, Dishonest, Gamblers, Honest, Liars, Libelers, Motives, Purposes, Sincere, Thieves, etc.).

SCURVY—A Form of Purpura Due to Deficient and Improper Diet—The ☉ afflicted in ♊; the ☽ afflicted in ♎, ♏, or ♐, the autumnal signs; ♄ in ♉ when ♄ is the afflictor in the disease; ♄ afflicted in ♋, due to improper and deficient diet; ♄ in an angle, occi. of the ☉ and ori. of the ☽; ♄ Sig. of the party in Hor'y Q., a scurvy face and countenance; ♃ affl. in ♋; ♃ in an earthy sign, peregrine, and ☌ the Asc.

by dir.; caused by ♀ when the dominion of death is vested in her; a ♏ disease, and afflictions in ♏; malefics in ♋, ♑, or ♓, angular, ori. to the ☉, and occi. to the ☽, and especially if the malefics be in the 1st or 7th H., which tends to putridity; Subs at CP, SP, and KP. (See Diet, Food, Purpura, Putrid, Scrofula).

SCYBALUM — Scybalous Matter — Hard and Lumpy Faeces—(See Faeces).

SEA—Seas—The Oceans—Salt Water—The Seas are ruled by the ☽, ♆, and the ♓ Sign. The ♋ Sign rules Rivers, Lakes, Fresh Water, and Running Streams. The ☽ and planets in the watery signs ♋, ♏, and ♓ at B. tend to bring events affecting Waters, Seas, Lakes and Rivers. The ☉, ☽, or ♂ cadent dispose to Sea Voyages. (See Voyages).

Accidents At Sea — (See Ships, Shipwreck).

Aground — (See "Foundering" under Ships).

Avalanches — Danger From On Voyages—(See Avalanches).

Bathing—Bathing In Sea Dangerous — (See Bathing; "Perils By" under Water).

Bites—Bitten by Animal On Sea Voyage—(See "Bites" under Voyages).

Burns—Suffers Burns On Sea Voyage —(See "Journeys" under Burns).

Calamities At Sea—(See Ships, Shipwreck; the various paragraphs in this section).

Corruption of the Seas—Death of Fish —(See Fish).

Cuts On Voyages—(See "Travel" under Cuts).

Danger By—Danger In Navigation—Peril by Waters — (See Drowning, Maritime, Navigation, Ships, Shipwreck; "Danger" under Travel; "Peril By" under Waters).

Death At Sea—Drowning At Sea—The ☽ afflicted in the 8th H.; ♄ or ♂ afflicted in the 9th H. at B., and by dir.; planets in ♋, ♏, or ♓, and afflicting the ☽ or hyleg. (See Drowning; "Death" under Shipwreck, Waters).

Drowning At Sea — (See "Death" in this section).

Events — Events On the Waters and Seas—(See "Nature Of" under Events).

Explosion At Sea—(See "Ships" under Explosions).

Falls On Voyages—(See "Travel" under Falls).

Famine On Voyages—(See Famine).

Fevers At Sea—(See "Health" under Journeys; "Fever" under Voyages).

Fire At Sea—(See "Ships" under Fire).

Fish — Death of In the Seas — (See Fish).

Foreign Travel—(See Abroad; "Long Journeys" under Journeys; Ocean; "Foreign Travel" under Travel; Voyages).

Fortunate Upon the Seas—Successful In Maritime Pursuits — Fond of the Water—The ☉ Sig. in ♏; ♃ Sig. in ♋, ♏, or ♓, or ☌ ☽; ♃ Sig. in ♓ if the ☽ is not afflicted. (See Maritime; "Fortunate" under Travel, Water).

Foundering of Ship—(See "Foundering" under Ships).

Good Time For Voyages—(See "Good Time" under Voyages).

Injury At Sea—Losses At Sea—♄ or ♂ afflicted in the 9th H. (See "Death", and the various paragraphs in this section).

Journeys by Sea—(See Abroad, Journeys, Maritime, Navigation, Sailors, Ships, Voyages).

Lightning At Sea — Death or Injury By—(See "Voyages" under Lightning).

Long Journeys—By Sea—(See Abroad; "Long Journeys" under Journeys; "Foreign Travel" under Travel; Voyages).

Losses At Sea—(See "Injury" in this section).

Maritime Affairs — (See Maritime, Navigation, Ships).

Misfortunes At Sea—An eclipse of the ☉ in the 1st decan. of ♓. (See Calamity, Danger, and the various paragraphs in this section; Shipwreck; "Danger" under Voyages; "Perils" under Water).

Navigation — (See Maritime, Navigation, Sailors, Ships, Voyages).

Near Water — Danger to Go Near Water—(See Bathing; "Petrils" under Water).

Ocean—(See Ocean).

Peril by Waters — (See Bathing, Drowning, Maritime, Navigation, Pirates, Ships, Shipwreck; "Danger" under Voyages; "Perils" under Waters).

Piracy; Privations — On Journeys or Voyages—Malefics in the 3rd or 9th H., in earthy signs, and afflicting the ☉ or ☽ at B., or by dir. (See Famine, Privation).

Sailing—Good Time For—(See "Good Time" under Voyages).

Sailors—Dangers To—(See Sailors).

Sea Level—Should Live There—(See Altitude).

Sea Sickness—(See "Sickness" under Voyages).

Sea Travel — (See "Long Journeys" under Journeys; Ships, Voyages).

Ships—Shipping—(See Ships).

Shipwreck—(See Ships, Shipwreck).

Sickness At Sea—(See "Sickness" under Voyages).

Stabs At Sea — (See "Travel" under Cuts).

Successful On the Sea — (See "Fortunate" in this section).

Tempests At Sea—Hurricanes—Lightning — (See "Fountains" under Dryness; "Voyages" under Lightning; Shipwreck; "Storms", "Tornadoes", under Wind).

Tidal Waves — (See "Tidal" under Water).

Travel — Sea Travel — (See Maritime, Navigation, Voyages).

Troubles by Sea—Danger In Navigation—Malefics in the 9th H. in water signs, weak and afflicted; an eclipse of the ☉ or ☽ in ♓; an eclipse of the ☽ in the 3rd decan. of ♓; Comets appearing in ♓. (See "Danger", and the various paragraphs in this section).

Unfortunate—On the Sea—Malefics in water signs in the 9th H., and afflicted. (See "Misfortunes", and the various paragraphs in this section; "Danger", "Death", under Voyages).

Voyages—(See the various paragraphs under Voyages).

Water Signs—♋, ♏, ♓.

Waters — Water — (See the subjects under Water).

SEANCES—(See Clairvoyance, Mediumship, Negative, Psychic, Spirit Controls, Spiritualism).

SEARING BURNS—(See "Burning" under Blindness; "Searing" under Burns).

SEASONS — The Four Seasons — (See Autumnal, Equinoxes, Ingresses, Solstices, Spring, Summer, Tropical, Vernal, Winter; "Lord of the Year" under Year, etc.).

Cold Winter—Much Suffering From— (See Snow; "Cold" under Weather; Winter).

Sickly Summer—(See "Extreme Heat" under Heat; Summer).

SEBACEOUS—Pertaining To Fat or Suet — Sebaceous Glands — Sebaceous Ducts—

Comedo — Blackheads — Sebaceous Ducts Obstructed — Afflictions to ♃ at B.; ♃ afflicted in ♈; ♃ ill-aspected by ♄; ♀ in signs which rule the arms, hands, legs and feet tends to blackheads in these parts due to wrong habits of living; Subs at CP and KP (11D). (See Fat, Sweat).

Cysts—Sebaceous Cysts—Steatoma— (See Wens).

Inflammation — Of the Sebaceous Glands—(See Acne).

Tumor — Sebaceous, Encysted Tumor —(See Wen).

SECLUSION—Secluded—Seclusiveness—

Ends Life In Seclusion—(See "Seclusion" under Old Age; Recluse).

Fond of Seclusion—♄ influence. (See Loneliness, Misanthropic, Miserly, Mistrustful, Recluse, Renunciation, Reserved, Retiring, Secretive, Shy, Solitude, Suspicious, Twelfth House).

Secluded by Law — (See Banishment, Exile; "Imprisonment" under Prison).

SECOND—

Second Death—(See the Introduction under Twelfth House).

Second Half of Life — (See Fourth House, Middle Life, Old Age).

Second House—This House is related to the ♉ Sign, the second sign of the Zodiac. This is a feminine and succedent house. Is known as the House of Finance. It rules the Neck, the back part of the Neck down to the Shoulders; the Vocal Organs; Throat, etc. It denotes the Throat and Ears. In material matters, rules Property, Wealth, and the Financial Condition of the Native. The Benefics in this house at B., and well-aspected, denote wealth and good business success. The Malefics here tend to losses, reversals of fortune, poverty, etc. Rules the Color Green. In Hindu Astrology, the Second House rules the Eyes. This House signifies all diseases in the throat and neck, quinsy, glandular swellings, sore throat, scrofula, etc., and malefics in this house at B. tend to affect adversely the neck and throat, the eyes, and to cause diseases in these parts. (See Finance, Neck, Poverty, Property, Riches, Taurus, Throat, Wealth).

SECONDARY DIRECTIONS—These are the Progressed Moon directions, counting each day after birth as a year of life, and the aspects the ☽ forms to the radical planets on each day after birth are very important to study in connection with health matters. Ill-health, and other dangers, are apt to attend the native when the progressed ☽ thus forms evil aspects to the radical planets. An evil secondary direction, when combined with an evil periodic direction, may frustrate the good of a fortunate primary direction. Directions, Transits, or Solar Revolutions, cannot bring anything to pass not shown in the radical map. The subjects of Primary and Secondary Directions are discussed, and the methods of calculation given, in the various Textbooks of Astrology. See Lilly's Astrology, Sepharial's Manual of Astrology, Pearce's Textbook of Astrology, Simmonite's Arcana of Astral Philosophy, and others. (See Directions, Lunations, Periodic, Primary Directions, Prognosis, Progression, Transits).

SECRET—Secretly—Secrecy—Secretive —Secrets of Life, etc.—

Secret Bad Habits—The ☽ afflicted in ♏; ♄ in the 1st H.; ♄ ☌ or ill-asp. ♀, addicted to secret and unnatural practices; ♀ in bad aspect to ♄, secret and evil practices; ☿ in bad asp. to ♄. (See Habits, Perversions, Unnatural; "Solitary" under Vice, etc.).

Secret Dangers — (See "Secret Dangers" under Danger; "Secret Enemies" under Enemies; Plots, Poison Death, Treachery, etc.).

Secret Enemies—(See "Secret" under Enemies).

Secret Parts — Private Parts — (See Secrets).

Secret Revenge—(See Revengeful).

Secret Societies—Are ruled by ♆.

Secret Sorrow — (See "Secret" under Sorrow).

Secret Treachery—(See Ambushes; "Secret Enemies" under Enemies; Plots, Poison Death, Treachery).

Secret Vices—(See Perversions; "Solitary" under Vice).

Secretive—Secrecy—♄ people are very secretive; ♄ strong at B., and rising, a confederate in secrecy; ♄ in ♉; a quality of ♆; ♏ on the Asc. (See Recluse, Renunciation, Reserved, Retiring, Seclusion, Solitude, etc.).

Secretly Lascivious— (See Lascivious).

Secretly Vicious — (See Artifice, Lascivious, Malice, Plots, Poison Death, Revenge, Treachery, Vicious).

Secrets of Life — Are under the rule of ♆. (See Neptune).

SECRETIONS—Secretion—Secretory System—Secretory Organs—Glands—The Secretive System generally is ruled by ♄, and also the ☽ has influence over the secretions of the body. Also ♏ rules the Secretory Organs. The Secretory Nerves are ruled by ♏. The Bronchials, which are secretory organs, are ruled by the ♏ sign. (See Bronchial). Interferences, stoppages, diminishing, morbid conditions, stoppages, suppressions, and hindrances over the secretory organs and system, are under the general rule of ♄ and his afflictions. (See Tumors). For the Secretions of the various parts and organs of the body, and the influences controlling or disturbing them, look in the alphabetical arrangement for the part, or organ, you have in mind. A few subjects concerning the Secretions will be listed here. See the following subjects in the alphabetical arrangement—

Augmented; Bronchial Secretions—(See Bronchial).

Diminished; Discharges; Elimination; Excretion; Fluids; Follicles; Functions; Glands; Hindrances;

Humoural Secretions—(See Humours).

Increased; Interferences; Interrupted; Irregular; Juices;

Lack Of—(See the various paragraphs under "Lack Of").

Milk; Morbid Secretions—(See Morbid).

Mucous Membranes—Secretions of—(See Mucous).

Normal Secretions—The ☽ in the airy signs tends to normal and regular secretions, but liable to skin, blood, and kidney disorders. (See Abnormal, Augmented, Decreased, Diminished, Increased, Irregular, Normal, Regular).

Obstructions; Organs—The Secreting Structure of Organs—(See Parenchyma).

Over-Secretion—(See Abundance, Augmented, Excess, Flow, Increased, Over-Flowing, etc.).

Phlegm; Regular—(See Regular; "Normal" in this section).

Serum; Skin; Stomach—(See Glands, Secretions, under Stomach).

Stoppages; Suppressions; Sweat;

Synovial; Urates (Over-Secretion of); **Urine** (Secretion of Obstructed).

SECRETIVE—Inclined to Secrecy—(See "Secretive" under Secret).

Secretive System—(See Secretions).

SECRETS—Secret Parts—Private Parts—Sex Organs, etc.—This subject is largely considered in the Articles on Generative System, Genitals, Genito-Urinary System, Privates, Reins, Reproduction, Sex Organs, etc. However, in the Textbooks of Astrology the Sex Organs are often spoken of as the "Secret Parts", and for convenience of reference, such subjects are again listed alphabetically in this present Article. The Secret Parts are ruled in general by the ♏ sign and the 8th House, and also by ♂, the ruler of the ♏ sign. See the following subjects in the alphabetical arrangement when only listed here—

Abscess—In the Secret Parts—In the Private Parts—♃ afflicted in ♏; ♃ in ♏ and afflicting the ☽ or Asc.; ♃ in ♏ in the 6th H., and afflicted. (See Abscesses).

Affected—The Secret Parts are affected when the ☽ is in ♒; ♅ in ♍; ♄ in ♌ or ♍; ♃ in ♎; ♂ in ♊ or ♏; ♀ in ♉; ☿ in ♈ or ♑. (See Table 196 in Simmonite's Arcana).

Afflicted—In the Secret Parts—(See "Distempers", and the various paragraphs in this section).

All Diseases In—♏ diseases and afflictions in ♏, either in men or women; ☽ diseases and caused by afflictions to the ☽ at B.; the ☽ afflicted in ♏; ♂ diseases, and caused by afflictions of ♂ in either sex; ♂, and other malefics, afflicted in ♏; signified by the 7th H. (See "All Diseases In" under Generative System).

Channels and Vents—Lack of Proper Sex Channels—(See "Channels" under Genitals).

Death—Arising from Diseases of the Secret Parts—(See "Death" under Generative).

Diseases In—(See "Distempers" in this section).

Distempers—In Secret Parts—Diseases In—Infirmities In—The ☉ or ☽ afflicted in ♏ or ♓, ☌, or ill-asp. any of the malefics as promittors; the ☉ afflicted in ♒; ☽ diseases; the ☽ afflicted in ♏, ♒, or ♓; ♄ affl. in ♋, ♌, ♍, or ♏; ♃ affl. in ♊, ♋, or ♎; ♂ diseases; ♂ afflicted in ♊, ♎, or ♏; ♂ in ♏, ☌, or ill-asp. the ☉; ☿ affl. in ♎ or ♏. (See "Diseases" under Generative, Genitals, Genito-Urinary, Reproduction, Sex, and also note the various paragraphs in this section).

Eunuchs; Eruptions—(See "Eruptions" under Generative).

Functional Disorders—(See "Functions" under Females; "Female Functions" under Functions; Menses).

Generation—Disorders of Organs of—(See Generative System).

Genitals—Disorders of—(See Genitals).

Hermaphrodites; Impotency;

Infirmities In—(See "Distempers" in this section).

Inflammatory Diseases—♂ afflicted in ♏, and especially in the Asc., 6th, or 8th H. (See "Inflammatory" under Generative; "Inflammation" under Genitals).

Injuries To—(See "Men's Genitals" under Genitals; Maimed).

Maimed; Matrix—Disorders of—(See Womb).

Members of Generation—Disorders of—(See the paragraphs under Generative, Genitals, Genito-Urinary, Ovaries, Penis, Privates, Reproduction, Sex Organs, Testes, Womb, etc.).

Mens' Genitals—Disorders of—Injury To—(See "Mens' Genitals" under Genitals; Penis, Scrotum, Testes).

Nerves—Of the Privy Parts—Disorders of—♅ or ☿ afflicted in ♏. (See Nerves).

Ovaries—Disorders of—(See Ovaries, Fallopian).

Pains In—Neuralgia In—The ☉ in ♓ when the afflictor in the disease, violent pains in; the ☽ afflicted in ♒; ♄ afflicted in ♓, violent pains in; ♂ in ♏, ☌, or ill-asp. the ☉; ♀ afflicted in ♉ or ♏; ☿ affl. in ♏. (See "Pain In" under Genitals).

Penis — Disorders of — (See Genitals, Gonorrhoea, Penis, Urethra).

Private Parts—Privy Parts—Privates — Disorders In — Injuries To — (See Genitals, Maimed, Penis, Privates, Reproduction, Sex Organs, Vagina, Womb).

Regenerative Organs—Disorders of—(See Regeneration).

Reins—Disorders of—(See the paragraphs under Reins).

Scandalous Diseases — (See Genitals, Gonorrhoea, Private, Scandalous, Syphilis, Venereal).

Scrotum—Disorders of—(See Scrotum).

Secret Enemy—Secret Diseases of—(See "Secret Enemies" under Enemies).

Sensitive — Sensitive Generative Organs—♏ on the Asc. (See Sensitive).

Sex Organs—Disorders of—(See the various paragraphs in this section, and under Sex Organs).

Spermatic Cord — Disorders of — (See Spermatic).

Stone In—(See "Secret Parts" under Stone).

Swellings In—The ☽ and ♂ afflicted in ♏; the ☽ afflicted in ♒; ♄ in ♏ when ♄ is the afflictor in the disease; ♃ afflicted in ♏. See "Swellings" under Generative; Hydrocele, Varicocele; "Swellings" under Womb).

Syphilis; Testicles — Disorders of — (See Testes).

Ulcers In — (See "Genitals" under Ulcers).

Urethra—Disorders of—(See Urethra).

Uterus—Disorders of—(See Womb).

Vagina—Disorders of—(See Vagina).

Violent Pains In — (See "Pains" in this section).

Vulva—Disorders of—(See Vulva).

Womb—Disorders of—(See Womb).

SEDATE—Sober—(See Harmless, Quiet, Reserved, Retiring, Serious, Sober, Thoughtful, etc.).

SEDATIVE — Sedatives— Soothing—Depressants — Quieting Remedies — A Therapeutic quality of ♄ and ♄ remedies. Also the ☽ has sedative and sleep-inducing influences. Sedatives do little good during the increase of the ☽, are weakest in effect then, and the dose should be increased. During the decrease of the ☽ sedatives work more rapidly, and can be given in smaller doses. (See Aconite, Anaesthetics, Anaphrodisiacs, Anodyne; "Sedative" under Heart; "Saturn Group" under Herbs; Narcotics; "Nervine" under Nerves; "Quieting Remedies" under Quiet; "Soporifics" under Sleep; Soothing, etc.).

SEDENTARY HABITS — A characteristic of ♄ people, and with ♄ ruler, or strong at B. Also ruled by the ☽, and caused by afflictions to the ☽. Mars weak and ill-dig. at B. tends to less activity in the nature, and more liable to seek a life of ease. Also caused by ♀ weak and afflicted at B. (See "Of No Ambition" under Ambition; Apathy; "Lack Of" under Exercise; Inactive, Indifferent, Inertia, Lazy, Lethargy, Listless, Negative Nature, Obesity, Tumors, etc.).

SEDIMENTS — (See Deposits, Gravel, Minerals, Sand, Stone; "Brick Dust Deposits" under Urine).

SEDITION — Opposition to the Government — Treason — A Promoter of Sedition—

Deadly Sedition—An eclipse of the ☉ in ♈; an eclipse of the ☉ or ☽ in watery signs; an eclipse of the ☉ or ☽ in airy signs, and especially in Regions under such signs; a solar eclipse in the 2nd decan. of ♍, and enduring as many years as the eclipse lasted in hours, and especially with People and Countries under the rule of ♍; an eclipse of the ☉ in the 2nd decan. of ♎, or the 3rd decan. of ♓; an eclipse of the ☽ in ♍, ♏, or ♑, and affecting Countries ruled by these Signs; an eclipse of the ☽ in the 3rd decan. of ♏ or ♑; ♂ ill-dignified at B., and afflicted, tends to make one seditious and rebellious to established Laws, Government, and Social customs. (See Anarchists, Reactionary, Rebellious, Reformers, Revolutionary, etc.).

SEDUCTION—Danger of—Liable to Seductive Influences—Liable to Be Led Astray—The ☽ Sig. ☌ ♂, if a female; ♆ afflicted in the 5th H.; ♅ in aspect to ♀; ♅ in ♉ or ♏, □ ♂, or ♂ in ♉ or ♏ in □ to ♅, escape from seduction almost impossible unless warned, or the early training is good and restraining; ♅ □ ♂ in a woman's horoscope when occurring in any part of the map; ♄ ☌ the ☽, or afflicting the ☽, and ♂ also in bad aspect to the ☽; ♂ ☌ or bad asp. the ☽; ♀ with ♂ alone at B., and afflicted, women liable to be led astray. (See "Chaste", "Unchaste", "Virtue", under Females; "Free Love" under Free; Kidnapped; "Liaisons" under Love Affairs; Rape; "Clandestine" under Sex).

Seductive — The influence of ♆ is seductive, and under his evil aspects the moral nature tends to suffer. (See "Free Living" under Free; "Loose Morals" under Morals; Neptune).

SEED — Seeds — Seminal — The Seed is ruled by ♃. Earth and Plant Seeds are ruled by the ☽. The Semen is ruled by ♀. (See Semen).

Rottenness — Of Seeds and Herbs — (See "Seeds" under Rottenness).

Scarcity Of—An eclipse of the ☽ in the 2nd decan. of ♉, or in the 2nd decan. of ♒, the seeds of the Earth are hurt. (See Drought, Famine, Grain, Scarcity).

Seed Atom—(See Barren, Conception).

SEERS — Prophets — One Who Foresees the Future—The ♆ influence strong at B. tends to enhance this Faculty. Also the ♅ influence strong at B. gives a desire to study the laws of the Mental, Psychic, and Spiritual Worlds, and to develop Spiritual Faculties, and to know the Truth. (See Clairvoyance,

Magic, Mediumship, Metaphysical, Mystical, Occult, Prophetic, Religion, Spiritual, Visions).

SEGMENTS — Motor Segment of the Spinal Cord — (See "Cord", "Lesions", "Motor", under Spine).

SELDOM—Rare—Infrequent—

Seldom Healthy—(See "Ill-Health All Thru Life" under Ill-Health; "Much Sickness" under Sickness).

Seldom Ill—(See "Strong" under Constitution; "Good Health" under Health; Immunity; "Good" under Recuperation, Resistance, Vitality; Robust, Ruddy; "Increased" under Strength; "Body" under Strong).

SELECTION — Selection of Cell Substances—(See "Substance" under Cells).

SELENITE—A Mineral ruled by the ☽.

SELF—All words beginning with "Self" are listed in this section.

Self-Absorbed — Self-Contained — ☿ in the 12th H.

Self-Abuse—(See "Solitary" under Vice).

Self-Approbation — Excessive Vanity —Principally ♀ influence, and the ♎ and ♓ signs prominent. Also ♌ is proud, vain at times, and fond of flattery. (See Vain).

Self-Assertive — Dogged — Fond of Rule and Authority—Positive—The ☉, ♅, and ♂ are all self-assertive; the ☉ Sig. in ♌, fond of rule and authority; ☿ Sig. in ♌; ♌ qualities. (See Commanding, Independent, Obstinate, Opinions, Positive Nature, Ruling).

Self-Centered — (See "Selfishness" in this section; Misanthropic, Penurious).

Self-Confidence — ♂ rising at B.; ♂ Sig. in ♈; the good asps. of ♂ to the ☉, ☽, or ☿; ♂ Sig. ✱ or △ ☿, extremely self-confident; the ☽, ♀, and ♆ influences tend to a lack of self-confidence. (See "Self-Reliant" in this section; "Inferiority Complex" under Inferior).

Self-Consciousness — The Airy Signs are Self-Conscious. (See "Signs" under Air; Egotistical).

Self-Contained—(See "Self-Absorbed" in this section).

Self-Control — Has good self-control when ♄ is strong at B., and in a fixed sign; ♄ well-aspected by ♅; ♄ in ♏ and well-aspected by ♅. In this matter, however, the star map of birth as a whole should be studied. The influences tending to lack of self-control are—♆ rising at B., or in the 3rd or 9th H., and afflicted; ♆ ☌ or ill-asp. ♂; the ☽ sepr. from ♀ and applying to ☿. (See Anger, Control, Disorderly, Harmless, Hasty, Immoderate, Impulsive, Inoffensive, Inordinate, Intemperance; "Command" under Passion; Restraints, Temperance, Uncontrolled, Violent).

Self-Debasement—♄ ☌ or ill-asp. ♀; the 11° ♌ on the Asc. (See Debauched, Depraved, Lewd, Obscene, Perversions, Profligate, Shameless, Wanton, etc.).

Self-Denying—Ascetic—Abstemious—Hermits — Reclusive — Reserved — ♄ ruler of the horoscope, and of the Asc. at B.; ♄ ruler of the 12th H., and ♄ in the 12th and afflicted; ♄ people, and born under ♄, often ascetic; ♄ in any aspect to ☿, and configurated with ♃; a strong ♄ influence in the 5th H., or ♄ afflicting the lord of the 5th. (See Celibacy, Misanthropic, Miserly, Penurious; "Averse To" under Pleasure; Recluse, Renunciation, Reserved, Retiring, Seclusion, Secretive, Solitude; "Selfishness" in this section).

Self-Esteem — Self-Approval — The ☉ and ♃ strong at B., but afflicted; ♃ afflicted by ♆; the ♌ sign prominent at B. (See Egotistical, Pretender, Pride; "Self-Approbation", "Self-Righteous", in this section).

Self-Exaltation—(See this subject under Religion).

Self-Flattery — (See Egotistical, Erratic; "Bad" under Judgment; "Light In Mind" under Mind; Pretender; "Self-Approbation", "Self-Esteem", in this section).

Self-Glorifying — (See "Self-Esteem" in this section).

Self-Indulgent — Hedonism — The ☉ afflicted in ♓; the ☽ afflicted in ♏ or ♐; ♆ ruler of the horoscope, and afflicted; ♆ afflicted in ♋; ♆ afflicted in the 6th H., self-indulgent manner of living; ♆ ☌ or ill-asp. ♂; due to the □ and ☍ aspects of ♆ to planets; ♆ in the 3rd or 9th H. in asp. to the ☽ or ☿; ♃ in the Asc. in ♋, and afflicted; ♃ afflicted in ♏, diseases arising from self-indulgence; afflictions to ♃; ♃ □ or ☍ the ☉ or ♀; ♃ afflicted in the 7th H., a self-indulgent marriage partner; ☿ Sig., and to the ☌ ♀, and ♀ ill-dignified at B.; ♂ afflicted in ♋ in the 1st H.; ♀ afflicted by ♂; ♀ affl. in ♎; the 10° ♉, the 8° ♋, the 11° ♌, or the 15° ♎ on the Asc. at B. Cases of Self-Indulgence—See "Self-Indulgence", No. 229, in 1001 N.N. Also Fig. 35 in the book, "Message of the Stars" by the Heindels. (See Conduct, Debauched, Diet, Drink, Drunkenness, Eating, Epicureans, Excesses, Feasting, Food, Gluttony, Habits, Indulgent; "Passional Excesses" under Passion; Pleasures, Vices, etc.).

Self-Inflicted Wounds — (See Demoniac, Suicide, Superstitious).

Selfishness—Careful of Own Interests — Not Easily Imposed Upon — Niggardly—Penurious—Frugal, etc.—A ♄ characteristic; ♄ strong at B., rising in the Asc. or M.C., and afflicting ♃; ♄ afflicted in the 6th H., ill-health thru selfish aims; ♄ afflicted in ♊; the ☽ or ☿ afflicted by ♄; ♃ Sig. ☌ ♄; ♃ or ♀ in ♑; ♃ Sig. in ♍, careful of own interests, and not easily imposed upon; ♃ Sig. in ♏; ☿ ori. at B., all for own interests; ☿ Sig. in ♊, understands own interests, and not easily deluded by the most cunning knave; ☿ Sig. in ♏, careful of own interests; many planets in ♑ at B.; ♑ influence; the 3rd decan. of ♑ on the Asc.; the 5th Face of ♒ on the Asc.; selfishness comes principally under ♈, ♍, and ♑. (See Misanthropic, Miserly, Mistrustful, Penurious, Scepticism, Secretive, Suspicious).

Self-Laudation—Self-Praise—The ☉ □ ♃ in fixed signs. (See "Self-Esteem", "Self-Flattery", in this section).

Self-Motivated Acts—Diseases or Injury From—(See "Disease or Injury" under Rashness).

Self-Opinionated— (See "Intolerance" under Religion).

Self-Preservation — The ♄ influence strong at B. gives tenacity to hold onto life, and to husband the resources, and for self-preservation. (See Careful, Miserly, Prudent; "Selfishness" in this section).

Self-Reliant—The ☉, ♅, and ♂ are all self-reliant; the ☉ Sig. in ♉; the ☉ well-aspected by ♂; ♂ Sig. in ♈; the good asps. of ♂ to the ☉, ☽, or ☿; ♂ Sig. ⚹ or △ ☿; ♂ in ♐; the ♈ people usually have much self-reliance. (See Self-Assertive, Self-Confidence, in this section; Ambition; "Positive Nature" under Positive; Ruling).

Self-Righteous—(See "Sanctimonious" under Religion).

Self-Satisfaction—The ☉ weak in ♓, and afflicted; the ☽ weak in ♌, and ill-dignified; mutable signs on angles. (See "Of No Ambition" under Ambition; Contentment, Dull; "Fond of Ease" under Ease; Idle, Lassitude, Negative Nature, etc.).

Self-Sufficient—♅, ♏, and ♍ influence. (See "Self-Absorbed" in this section).

Self-Torture — Usually from a Religious Cause or Belief — Usually caused by afflictions to ♆ in the map of birth, and especially if ♆ is weak and ill-dignified, and due to spiritual causes, obsessions, narrow religious views, hallucinations, etc.; ♆ afflicted by ♅, ♄, or ♂; afflictions in the 12th H. at B. (See Obsessions, Religion, Spirit Controls; "Self-Denying" in this secton).

Self-Undoing—Ruled by the 12th H., its afflictions and influences; also largely characteristic of the ♓ sign, the 12th sign; the ☉ or ☽ ☌ ♄ in the 12th H., and espec. if in ♓; ♆ or ♄ afflicted in ♓ or the 12th H.; ♂ afflicted in the 12th H.; lord of the 12th H. a malefic, and in the 12th, and afflicting the lord of the Asc.; malefics afflicted in the 12th H.; the 12° ♋ on the Asc. at B. (See Disgrace; "Own Worst Enemy" under Enemies; Fate, Folly, Grief, Honour, Misery, Misfortune, Rashness, Recklessness; "Loss Of" under Reputation; Reverses, Ruin, Scandal, Sorrow, Trouble, Unfortunate).

Self-Willed—The 30° ♓ on the Asc. at B. (See Obstinate, Stubborn; "Strong Will" under Will).

SEMEN — Seminal — Seminal Fluid — Vital Fluid—The Seed—Spermatozoa—Seminal Vesicles, etc.—The Semen is ruled by ♃ and ♀, and also the seminal vesicles and their contents. The reception of semen into the womb is ruled by the ☽. The seminal tubes, the Tubuli Seminiferi, or Vesicles, are ruled by ♀. (See "Fluid" under Vital).

Emissions — Loss of Seed — Involuntary Discharges of Semen — Night Losses—Wet Dreams—♆ afflicted in ♏; ♀ diseases, and afflictions to ♀; ♃ in ♏ and afflicted by ♂; Subs at PP (2, 3, 4L).

Seminal Complaints—♃ afflicted in ♏; ♃ in ♏ in the 6th H., and afflicted; ♃ in ♏ and afflicting the ☉ or ☽; ♀ diseases, and afflictions to ♀. (See Barrenness).

Seminal Signs—The Fruitful Signs—The watery signs, ♋, ♏, and ♓ are called the fruitful, or seminal signs. (See "Fruitful Signs" under Fruitful).

SEMI—

Semi-Lunar Ganglion — (See "Semi-Lunar" under Ganglion).

Semi-Spiritual — The abstract influence of ♆. (See Spiritual).

Semi-Square Aspect—The 45° aspect, or one-half of the □ aspect. Partakes of the nature of the □ aspect, but is milder. However, the ∠ aspect is evil in health, and other matters, and the ∠ asp. of the ☉ to ♀ tends to Intemperance and Indiscretions. (See Aspects).

Semi-Tertian Fevers—Have the characteristics of both a Tertian and Quaternary Fever. Caused by ♂ when the dominion of death is vested in him. (See Ague, Quartan, Tertian).

SEMINAL—(See Semen).

SENILITY — (See "Senility" under Old Age).

SENSATION—Sensations—Corporeal Feeling — Sensorial — Sensory—The Physical Sense of Feeling—The Sense of Touch, etc. — The Sensations are ruled by the ☽, ☿, and the Asc.

Altered Sensations — (See Paraesthesia).

Animal Sensations — Love of — ♆ rising, or in the 3rd or 9th H., and afflicted. (See "Animal Instincts" under Animal; Appetites, Astral Body, Cravings; "Desire Body" under Desire; Hunger, Passion, Thirst, etc.).

Burning Sensations—Burning Pains— (See Belching; "Heartburn" under Heart; "Hot Flashes" under Heat; Paraesthesia).

Crawling Sensations — Creeping Sensations — (See Hyperaemia, Hyperaesthesia, Paraesthesia).

Disorders Of—(See Senses; the various paragraphs in this section).

Easily Moved by Sensation—The 5th face of ♋ on the Asc. at B., very impressionable, and often reflecting others. (See Influenced, Negative Nature, Receptive, Susceptible, etc.).

Functions — The Sensorial Functions Impaired—♄ ☌ or ill-asp. the ☽. (See Functions, Senses).

Hot and Cold Sensations—Hot Flashes —Chill, etc.—(See Chill, Cold, Congestions, Fever, Heat, Paraesthesia, Rigors, etc.).

Hyperaesthesia; Morbid Sensations—(See Paraesthesia).

Numbness; Paraesthesia;

Physical Sensation — Represented by the watery signs, and as brought on by contact with, and stimulation from the external world, and such as give comfort, ease, or distress to the physical body. (See External, Physical).

Prickling Sensations—(See Prickling).

Senses—(See the various paragraphs under Senses).

Sensory Nerves — Ruled by ☿. (See "Elimination" under Urine).

Tingling—(See Numbness, Tingling). See Sensibility, Sensitive.

Touch—Sense of—Ruled by ☿. (See Touch, Senses).

SENSATIONAL—Sensationalism—Sensations—Along emotional and sensational lines the watery signs are excitable and sensational. Also the fiery signs love sensation, and in a positive way. The ♏ sign gives a love of sensationalism along lines of crime, adventure, and the Occult. Pisces along lines of trouble, sorrow, bereavement, etc. (See Astral Body; "Desire Body" under Desire; Emotions; Excitement).

SENSE NATURE—(See Amorous, Emotions, Feelings, Passion, Sensuality).

SENSES—The Five Senses—Sensorium—Sense Organs—☿ is the originator of the sense vibrations, and also rules all sense perceptions, as seeing, hearing, smelling, feeling, tasting, etc. Saturn is not a builder to the senses, but exerts rather a strong psychological and intellectual power. In the Hindu System the five physical Senses are attributed to the First House.

Acute—The Senses Made Acute—☿ elevated and well-aspected, and the mind is keen. (See "Active Mind" under Active; "Quickened" under Mentality).

Animal Instincts—(See Animal).

Color—Sense of—(See Color).

Dulling of the Senses—Hebetude—Non-Sensitive—☿ afflicted at B.; ♄ influence; ♄ ☌ ☿, the mind is dull and heavy. (See "Mind" under Dull, Heavy; Hebetude, Hyperaesthesia, Inertia, Lassitude, Lethargy, etc.).

Feeling—(See Sensation, Sensibility, Touch).

Functions—The Sensorial Functions Impaired—(See "Functions" under Sensation).

Gratification—Of the Senses—(See Appetites, Conduct, Desires, Drink, Excesses, Food, Gluttony, Habits, Passion, etc.).

Hypersensitive—(See Hyperaesthesia).

Impaired Senses—(See "Dulling" in this section; "Functions" under Sensation).

Intuition—(See Intuition).

Limitations—Upon the Senses—(See Blindness, Deafness, Dull, Hearing, Hindrances, Impairments, Impediments, Limitations, Sight, Smell, Suppressions, Touch, Twelfth House, etc.).

Passion—(See the paragraphs under Passion).

Perception—(See the paragraphs under Perception).

Physical Sensations—(See "Physical" under Sensation).

Saturn and the Senses—(See the Introduction to this Article).

Sensation—Disorders of—(See Sensation).

Sense Mind—(See Personality).

Sensibility—(See this subject).

Sensory Nerves—(See "Sensory" under Sensation).

Sight—Sense of—(See Accommodation, Blindness, Eyes, Sight).

Sixth Sense—(See Pineal Gland).

Taste—(See paragraphs under Taste).

Touch—(See Sensation, Touch).

Vibrations—Sense Vibrations—(See Introduction to this Article; Vibration).

Vision—(See Sight).

SENSIBILITY—Susceptibility of Feeling—

Augmented Sensibility—Excessive Sensibility—A ♂ disease, and due to the tonic action of ♂. Also caused by afflictions to ☿. (See Hyperaesthesia).

Diminished Sensibility—A ♄ disease. (See Diminished).

Insensibility—(See this subject).

Sensible—(See "Good" under Judgment; "Sound" under Mind). See Sensation, Senses, Sensitive.

SENSITIVE—Sensitives—Sensitiveness—Sensibility—The part of the body ruled by the sign containing the ☽ at B. is always a very sensitive spot, and any part of the body ruled by the sign thru which the ☽ is passing for the time is made more sensitive, and operations should not be performed upon such a part, or parts, until the ☽ has passed into the next sign, or several signs further along. (See "Rules" under Operations). The Sensitive, or Irrational Faculties, are ruled by the ☽.

Augmented Sensibility—(See Sensibility).

Body—A Sensitive Body—♆ ☌ the Asc.

Chart of Birth—Sensitive Places In—The parts or organs ruled by the Signs, Houses, and Degrees in which the ☉, ☽, and planets are found at B., and especially the ☉, ☽, and malefics, and also the parts ruled by the Asc., the Midheaven, the 4th, 6th, 8th, and 12th Houses, the cusps of these houses, or their lords, tend to be the sensitive parts of the body, and more subject to disease and affliction. (See Map, Nativity, Star Map).

Constitution—A Sensitive Constitution—The ☉ in ♍; ♍ on the Asc., and also very sensitive to suggestions of ill-health. (See Constitution; "Zodiac" under Degrees).

Degrees—Sensitive Degrees of the Zodiac—(See "Sensitive" under Zodiac).

Deviations—(See "Faculties" in this section).

Diminished Sensitiveness—A ♄ disease and affliction. (See Diminished).

Disposition—The ♋ sign influences give a sensitive disposition; the ☉ or ☽ in ♋ at B., or this sign on the Asc. (See "Sensitiveness" in this section).

Excessive Sensitiveness—(See Hyperaesthesia; "Augmented" under Sensibility).

Faculties—Deviation of the Sensitive Faculties—(See Deviations, Faculties).

Fright—Easily Frightened—(See Fright).

Generative Organs—Sensitive Generative Organs—♏ on the Asc.

High Strung—(See "Strung" under High).

Hypersensitive—(See "Excessive" in this section).

Ill-Health — Sensitive to Suggestions of Ill-Health—The ☉ in ♍, or ♍ on the Asc. at B. (See Virgo).

Mind—A Sensitive and Acute Mind—(See "Active Mind" under Active; "Quickened" under Mentality).

Nerves—Sensitive Nerves—High Strung—♅ ☌ ☿. (See "Strung" under High; "High Tension", "Neurasthenia", under Nerves).

Non-Sensitive—(See "Dulling" under Senses).

Organs—Sensitive Organs—Sensitive Parts—The more sensitive organs, or parts of the body, are those ruled by the sign upon the Asc. at B. Thus ♏ on the Asc. tends to make the Generative Organs, and the Excretory System more sensitive; ♊ on the Asc., the lungs sensitive; ♎ on the Asc., the kidneys sensitive, and more liable to disturbances, etc. (See Organs, Parts).

Psychic Conditions — Sensitive To — (See "Sensitive" under Psychic).

Sensitive Degrees — Of the Zodiac — (See Zodiac).

Sensitiveness—Highly Sensitive—Sensitives—The ☉ or ☽ afflicted in the ♋ sign tend to give a sensitive nature, to take offense easily, and to be greatly disturbed by adverse environment; the ☉ in ♍, a sensitive constitution; the ☽ in the 1st H. in ♋ or ♓, and afflicted; the ☽ in the 1st H.; the ☽ ruler of the Asc. or M.C., and not strongly supported by aspects; the aspects of ♆ tend to greatly affect the native for good or ill, but only the sensitive people in the World today feel the rays of ♆ and ♅; ♆ has the most effect upon sensitives; ♆ ☌ ☿; ♅ in ♋; ♄ afflicting ♀; ♀ in ♈, ♍, or ♐; many cross, or □ aspects to a planet, or planets ascending at B.; ♑ on the Asc.; the 3rd decan. of ♉ on the Asc., ruled by ♄; common to all the watery signs, and especially to ♋, which sign makes the native more susceptible to external influences and environment; a ♓ influence; the negative, or feminine signs, are negative and receptive, with the exception of ♉; ♍ is rather sensitive, critical, and quickly resents slights or injury; ♎ is quickly offended, and over-sensitive, but does not retain the memory of insult very long; ♊, ♌, ♐, and ♒ do not feel injury, slight, or insult as easily, as they are more mental than emotional. (See Augmented, Emotions, Environment, External, Feelings; "High Strung" under High; Hyperaesthesia, Negative Nature; "Sensitive" under Psychic; Receptive; "Augmented" under Sensibility; Susceptibility, etc.).

Sensitives — (See "Sensitiveness" in this section).

Skin—(See "Sensitive" under Skin).

Slights—Sensitive to Real or Fancied Slights — The ☽ afflicted in ♑. (See Imaginations, Offended).

Spirit Controls — Sensitive To — (See Clairvoyant, Mediumistic, Spirit Controls).

Suggestion — Sensitive To — (See "Ill-Health" in this section; Hypnotism, Influenced, Negative Nature, Receptive, Suggestion, Susceptible).

Super-Sensitive—♄ influence; a ♑ and ♒ disease, and afflictions in these signs. (See Hyperaesthesia).

Troubles and Worries — Sensitive to the Conditions of Others, etc.—☿ afflicted in the 6th H. (See Brooding, Despondency, Environment, External, Hyperaesthesia, Hypochondria, Servants, Suicide, Worry, etc.).

Zodiac — Sensitive Degrees of — (See "Sensitive Degrees" under Zodiac).

SENSORIAL—Sensory—

Functions—Sensorial Functions—(See "Functions" under Sensation).

Sensory Nerves — (See "Sensory Nerves" under Sensation). See Senses, Sensibility, Sensitive.

SENSUALITY — Sensuous — Sensuous Mind—Sensuous Appetites—Sense Nature—The Passional Nature Predominant—The ☽ rules the sensual faculties. Also ♆, ♂, and ♀ when configurated together, or with ♆ or ♂ ☌, or afflicting ♀ and the ☽, licentiousness is increased. In a general way ♂ is king and ruler of the sense nature, and of the passions and emotions. See the following subjects in the alphabetical arrangement when only listed here—

Amorous; Amours — (See "Amours" under Love Affairs).

Animal Instincts—(See Animal).

Death — Early Death from Passional Excesses — (See "Dies Before Middle Life" under Middle Life).

Debauched; Depraved; Diseases — From Sensuality—♀ afflicted at B., and by dir. (See Venery; "Death" in this section).

Dissolute; Early Death—From Excessive Sensuality—(See "Death" in this section).

Emotions; Energies Wasted — Thru the Opposite Sex—(See "Injured" under Men; "Health Suffers" under Opposite Sex; "Unfortunate Pleasures" under Pleasure).

Enjoyments—Given to Sensuous Enjoyments—All Sensuous Enjoyments—Denoted by the 5th H.; ♆ afflicted in the 5th H.; ♂ ☌ ♀ in the 5th H. (See Energies, Sensuous, in this section; "Sensuous" under Pleasures).

Excesses—(See "Passional Excesses" under Passion).

Fits — Fits of Sensuality or Drink — (See "Fits" under Drink).

Gratification—Sensual Gratification—(See "Sensuous", and the various paragraphs in this section; Gratification).

Harlots; Highly Sensuous—♆ afflicted in ♌, the 5th H., or afflicting the ☽ or ♀. (See Lewd, Licentious, Nymphomania, Passion, Perversions, Sex, etc.).

Imaginations—(See "Sensuous" under Imagination).

Lascivious; Lewd; Liaisons — (See "Liaisons" under Love Affairs).

Licentiousness; Low Pleasures—Given To—(See "Low" under Pleasures).

Lust; Men—Sensuous Gratifications In —(See "Licentious", "Violent", under Men).

Opposite Sex—Wastes Vital Energies On—(See "Energies" in this section).

Passion — (See "Passional Excesses" under Passion).

Perversions; Pleasures — Given to Sensuous Pleasures — (See Amorous, Excesses, Passion; "Unfortunate" under Pleasure; Venery, etc.).

Profligate; Prostitutes—(See Harlots).

Puberty—Sensuous At Time of—(See "Imaginations" under Puberty).

Self-Indulgent; Sensualist—(See "Sensuous" in this section).

Sensuous—A Sensuous Mind—A Sensualist — Sensuous Gratification — Sex Addict—Sensuality—Sensual Appetites —A Passionate Nature—Voluptuous—Given to Sensuous Pleasures and Enjoyments, etc.—The ☽ to the ill-asps. ♀ by dir.; the ☽ Sig. in ♎; the ☽ in ♓, danger of a sensuous mind if afflicted by ♄ or ♀; ♆ afflicted in the 5th or 6th H.; ♆ afflicted in ♌, supersensual; ♆ afflicted in ♉ or ♏; ♆ ☌ or ill-asp. ♂, coarse and sensual; ♆ progressed to the ☌ or ill-asps. the radical ♀, or vice versa; ♅ ruler of the horoscope and afflicted; ♃ afflicted in ♌; ♃ in the Asc. in ♏, and afflicted; afflictions to ♃; ♂ ☌ or ill-asp. the ☽ or ♀; ♂ afflicted in ♎, voluptuous; ♂ □ or ☍ ♀; ♀ weak at B., and afflicted by ♄; ♀ in the Asc. and afflicted by ♄ or ♂; ♀ afflicted at B., weak, and ill-dignified; ♀ afflicted by the □ or ☍ ♆, ♅, ♄, ♂, and the ☽; ♀ □ or ☍ ☽; ♀ ruler of the horoscope and afflicted by malefics; ♀ afflicted at B., and to the ☌ or evil asp. the Asc. by dir., voluptuous; ☿ affl. in ♌; the transit of malefics thru the 5th H. if they afflict the 5th at B., and other indications show sensuality; the 1st decan. of ♏ on the Asc., ruled by ♂; the 4° ♋ on the Asc.; 22nd and 29° ♍ on the Asc.; the 3rd dec. of ♏ on the Asc., ruled by ♀; the 17° ♏ on the Asc.; ♓ on the Asc.; the 9° ♓ on the Asc., apt to die young thru passional excesses. (See Amorous, Licentious; "Passional Excesses" under Passion; the various paragraphs in this section).

Sex Addict—(See Amorous, Lewd, Licentious; "Unbridled" under Passion; "Sensuous" in this section).

Supersensual—♆ afflicted in ♌. (See Highly Sensuous, Sensuous, in this section).

Voluptuous—(See "Sensuous" in this section).

Wanton; Wench; Women—Sensuality In—(See "Sex Gratification" under Females; Nymphomania, Women).

SENTENCE OF LAW—Death By—(See Judges).

SENTIENT FACULTIES—The Faculties of Consciousness, Feeling, Knowing, Perception, Sensation, etc. — Ruled by the ☽, ☿, and the Asc. Also the ☉, his positions and aspects, are essential factors in our conscious life. (See Consciousness, Emotions, Faculties, Feeling, Feelings, Intellect, Knowledge, Learning, Mental, Mind, Perception, Sensation, Senses, Sensibility, Understanding, Volition, Will, etc.).

SENTIMENTS—Sentimental—(See Effeminate, Emotions, Feelings, Ideas, Motives, Notions, Philosophy, Principles, Purposes, Religion, Truth, etc.).

SEPARATION—Separations—Separateness—Separating—

Aspects — In health matters the aspects of planets when separating from the exact aspect are less evil, and indicate some relief and amelioration of the disease. (See Aspects).

Family—Separation In—(See "Separation of Parents" under Parents).

Parents — Separation of Parents — Separation from Parents—(See Adoption, Orphans, Parents).

Separateness—♄ influence. (See Loneliness, Recluse, Renunciation, Reserved, Retiring, Secretive, Solitude).

Sexes—Separation of—(See "Separation" under Sex).

SEPTIC—Septic Poisoning—Relating to Putrefaction—Septicaemia—

Blood Poisoning—Septicaemia—(See "Impure Blood" under Impure; "Blood Poisoning" under Poison).

Pyemia—Septicaemia with Abcess Formations—(See Pyemia).

Septic Fevers — Septic Poisoning — ♂ in ♏; ♂ in ♏ in the 6th H.; ♂ in ♏ and afflicting the ☽ or Asc. (See "Fevers" under Putrid).

Septicemia — (See "Blood Poisoning" under Poison).

Throat — Septic Poisoning In — (See "Septic" under Throat). See Abscesses, Festering, Infections, Odors, Poison, Pus, Putrid, Sloughings, Suppuration, Toxaemia.

SEPTUM—Nasal Septum—(See Nose).

SEQUENCE — Interrupted Sequence In Disease—Sequence of Progression In Disease—Planets ℞ tend to interrupted sequence in disease, and solution of continuity, just as planets direct, swift, and rapid in motion denote continuity and sequence of progression. (See Amelioration, Constancy, Continuity, Course, Direct, Duration, Interrupted, Moderation, Modification, Resolution, Retrograde, Solution, Stationary).

SERIOUS — Dangerous — Severe — Important—Serious-Minded—

Accidents — Serious Accidents — (See "Dangerous" under Accidents).

Constitutional Diseases—Serious Constitutional Disorders and Defects—(See "Constitutional Diseases" under Constitution).

Lives Thru Serious Illnesses — The fiery and airy signs, or with ♍ or ♏ upon the Asc. at B., and with the hyleg favorably aspected, the native will live thru serious illnesses which would prove fatal to those born under the weaker signs, as ♋ and ♓; born with strong signs upon the Asc., and especially the fiery signs ♈ or ♌; ♃ or ♀ in the Asc., in good aspect to the hyleg, and the lord of the Asc. well-placed and free from affliction. (See "Good" under Constitution, Recuperation, Resistance, Stamina, Strength, Tone, Vitality; "Body" under Strong).

Organic Diseases — Serious Organic, Constitutional, and Structural Diseases —(See Chronic, Congenital; "Constitutional Diseases" under Constitution; Consumptions, Hereditary; "Organic Diseases" under Organic; Structural, Tuberculosis, Wastings, etc.).

Serious Illnesses—Long and Tedious Diseases — Difficult to Cure — Apt to Prove Fatal — (See Chronic; "Arguments for Death", "Sure Death", under Death; "The Sick Will Hardly Escape" under Escape; Fatal; "High" under Fever; Fierce, Fulminating, Grievous; "Bad Health" under Health; "Heavy and Sad Sickness" under Heavy; Incurable, Invalids, Lingering, Long Diseases, Pernicious, Quick, Severe, Sharp, Slow Diseases, Swift Diseases, Tedious Diseases, Vehement, Violent Diseases, etc.).

Serious Mind—♄ strong at B.; ♄ ☌ ☿; the ☉, ☽, or ☿ in ♑ and afflicted by ♄; the 4th face of ♏ on the Asc.; ♑ on the Asc. (See Dejected, Depressed, Despondency, Gloom, Grave, Hypochondria; "Low Spirits" under Low; Melancholy, Recluse, Regretful, Renunciation, Repining, Reserved, Responsibility, Retiring, Sad, Secretive, Solitude, Sorrowful, Taciturn, Thoughtful, etc.).

Suffering—Forebodes Serious Suffering—(See Grievous; "Painful Diseases" under Painful; Severe, Sharp, Violent Diseases, etc.).

SEROUS—Serous Membranes—(See Serum).

SERPENTS—Venomous Creatures—Obnoxious Creatures—Snakes—Death or Wounds from Bites of — (See Adder; "Journeys", "Venomous", under Bites; Obnoxious, Reptiles, Stings, Venomous).

Cruelty On Serpents—Prevalence of—An eclipse of the ☽ in the 3rd decan. of ♉.

SERUM—Serous—Serous Membranes—The Serum, the fluid constituent of the blood, is ruled principally by the ☽. The Serous Membranes, Surfaces, and Fluids are under the rule of the ☽. Also the Serum of the Blood is ruled by the ♋ sign. (See Blood). The Pericardium, Peritoneum, Pleura, Synovial Membranes, Tunica Vaginalis, etc., are classed as Serous Membranes. (See these subjects).

Serous Circulation—(See Circulation).

Serous Collections — Serous Effusions — In Various Parts of the Body — ☽ diseases, and afflictions to the ☽. Connected with the watery signs, and the ☽ afflicted in such signs, and especially in ♓. (See Blisters, Blood, Circulation, Cysts, Dropsy, Effusions, Fluids, Hydrocele, Hydrocephalus, Hydrothorax, Infiltration, Oedema, Osmosis, Peritoneum, Puffing, Synovial, Vesicles, Watery, etc.).

Serous Discharges — And Effusions — ☽ diseases, and afflictions to the ☽, and are especially characteristic of the Lymphatic Temperament.

Serous Diseases—☽ diseases, and afflictions to the ☽ at B., and by dir. The inherent disposition to serous diseases is characteristic of the Lymphatic Temperament. (See Lymphatic).

Serous Infiltrations — Infiltration of Serum—A ☽ disease. (See Dropsy, Osmosis).

Serous Stools — (See "Serous" under Faeces).

SERVANTS—Subordinates—Dependents —Ruled by ☿. Also the 6th H. is the house of Servants. Benefics in the 6th H. at B. make the relations and dealings with servants pleasant and fortunate. The malefics in this house the servants are rebellious, insubordinate, and tend to bring misfortune to the master. (See Sixth House).

Hurts By—Danger of Being Killed by a Servant—Lord of the 8th H. a malefic, and afflicted by lord of the 6th or 12th, and especially if the hyleg, or lord of the Asc. are also afflicted.

Sickness Of — Disability or Sickness Among—The ☽ in the 6th H., or in ☍ to the lord of the 6th (Hor'y); ♄ ruler of the year at the Vernal E., in ♎, and ℞ planets in the 6th H., afflicted, or themselves afflicting the Significators, the ☉, ☽, Asc., or M.C.

Worries Thru Servants—Or Subordinates—Malefics in the 6th H. at B., or lord of the 6th a malefic, and with no favorable influences over the 6th H.; ☿ afflicted in the 6th H., and tending to mental stress and ill-health thru worries brought on by servants.

SERVILE — Dependent — Enslaved — ♃ Sig. ☌ the ☉; ♂ Sig. in ♋; ♂ Sig. ⚹ or △ the ☽; ♂ weak and ill-dignified at B. (See Dull, Energy (Lack of); Fears, Inactive, Indifferent, Indolent, Inertia, Labor (Fear of); Languid, Lassitude, Lazy, Lethargy, Limitations, Mean (Mean Creature); Resolution (Lack of); Servitude, Timidity; "Weak Will" under Will, etc.).

SERVITUDE — Bondage — Subjection — Limitations, etc.—Servitude is signified by ♄, the ♑ sign, and the 12th H. conditions. The ☽ decr. in light, sepr. from ♃, and applying to ♄; the ☉, ☽, or ♄ afflicted in the 12th H., and in a negative horoscope; lord of the Asc. in the 12th H., and afflicted; ♂ weak, afflicted, and ill-dignified at B. Uranus, ♂, and the ☉ are courageous, and never servile. (See Confinements, Fears, Limitations, Negative, Prison, Rule, Servile, Twelfth House).

SETTING PLANETS—Planets setting in the West are less powerful than when rising, as a rule. Planets setting in an occidental quarter show disease, but setting in an oriental quarter indicates accidents and injuries. The health is not as good when the ☉ and many planets are setting in the West, and also the nature is less forceful, and not as capable of leadership. Mercury setting also somewhat impairs the mind for hard study and school life, but tends to enhance the mind for success in commercial enterprises, and where the native learns in the school of experience rather than out of books. When the hyleg sets on the Western horizon, death usually results. (See Elevated, Majority, Occidental, Oriental, Rising).

SEVEN—Seven-Year Periods of Life—Seven Months Children—Life from the cradle to the grave is divided into periods of seven years, and certain and definite changes come into the life at every 7th year, as the 7th, 14th, 21st, 28th, 35th, etc. Every 7th year tends to be a more critical year, and especially in health and other matters, as every 7th year begins a new cycle in life. More deaths occur in these cycle years, as a rule, than during the years in between them in the life of the native. The cycle of ♅ is 84 years, and every seven years he changes signs of the Zodiac, thus tending to changes in the life of the native. Also every seven years the planet ♄ is at the quarter points in his journey thru his orbit from the place where he was at the birth of the native, and at these seven-year places he forms the ∠, □, ☍, and ⛢ aspects to his place in the radical map, and tends to bring on disease, worries, sorrows, anxieties, and to chasten the native who is not living right, and who may be living a life of sin and wickedness, until thru worry, disgrace, financial disaster, etc., he may weaken and go into some form of chronic disease, or even meet with death of the physical body. It is said also that the particles of the body are entirely changed and renewed once in every seven years. These 7th year places in life also correspond to the Quarters of the ☽, and are years of affliction, and correspond to the □ aspect and its divisions. The number 7 is said to be the number of Perfection, and is mentioned many times in the Bible, and in Occult Literature. There are the Seven Days of the Week, the Seven Planetary Angels, the Seven Churches in Asia, the Seven Spirits Before the Throne, etc. Read about the number "7" in the book, "The Key To the Universe" by Dr. and Mrs. Homer Curtiss. Also see the Seventh Card in the Tarot of the Bohemians. (See Cycles, Periods).

Seven Months Children—Born At the Seventh Month—(See "Seven Months Children" under Children).

SEVENTH HOUSE—Known as the Descendant, or Angle of the West. (See Descendant). This House is closely affiliated with the ♎ Sign, the 7th Sign of the Zodiac, and also with ♀, the ruler of this sign. It is known as the House of Marriage, Partnerships, Agreements, Disagreements, Contracts, Litigation, Public and Open Enemies, the Marriage Partner, Sweetheart, Fiance or Fiancee, the Husband in a female nativity, the Wife in a male horoscope. It denotes the Physician or Healer in health matters; gives the description, shape, and condition of the Sweetheart or Marriage Partner; indicates quarrels, contests, thieves, thefts, separations, divorce, losses thru business partners, the aggression of open and public enemies if afflicted by malefics. The Ingress of the ☉ into this house may be indicative of War, if War is threatened, or of Peace, if War is raging. This is a masculine house, and positive. The ☉ in this house is indicative of good health, but gives a good and honorable wife. Saturn in this house at B. tends to short life. Mars here, a bad wife and sickness.

Color—The Colors ruled by this house are Blue, Brown, Black, or Dark Black.

Diseases Ruled By—This house signifies all diseases in the Hams, Flanks, Bladder, Small Intestines, Members of Generation, the Kidneys, Lower Part of the Back, in the Reins, Haunches, Loins, Navel, Diseases of the Womb or Matrix; Diseases and afflictions in any parts of the body ruled by this house or the ♎ sign; diseases and afflictions of the Marriage Partner, or of Public Enemies, etc.

Seventh House Rules—Agreements; Back (Lower Part of); Bladder; Business Partners; Buttocks (the Haunches to the Buttocks); Colors (Blue, Brown, Black, and Dark Black); Contests; Contracts, Duels, Enemies (Open and Public); Flanks; Generation (Members of); Grandfather; Hams, Haunches (Down to the Buttocks); Healers; Husband; Kidneys; Law (the Law); Lawsuits; Litigation; Loins; Marriage; Marriage Partner; Matrix of the Womb; Navel; Paternal Love and Affection; Partners; Physician in the Case; Public Affairs and Public Enemies; Quarrels; Reins; Small Intestines; Sweethearts; Theft; Thieves; Veins; Wife; Womb, etc. (See Libra Sign).

SEVERE—Severity—Severely—

Accidents — (See "Dangerous" under Accidents).

Blows—(See "Severe" under Blows).

Bruises — (See "Death By" under Bruises).

Cuts—(See "Severe" under Cuts).

Disease—The Disease More Severe—Severe Illness — The Severity of the Disease—The severity and intensity of the disease depend upon the power of the aspecting bodies, aspect configurations, and other impressions of celestial influences. Intensity and severity are associated with the cardinal signs, while remission is related to the mutable signs. The motion of the ☽ indicates the duration and severity of the disease by the nature of the critical days which accompany every attack. The afflictions of the major planets cause the disease to be more severe and fulminating, while the minor planets tend to milder and slight disorders. (See Major). The following aspects and influences indicate severity of the disease—The SUN and ☽ afflicted by malefics at B., and the malefics elevated above them; the ☉ and ☽ cadent, and their dispositors unfortunate; the ☉ and ☽ with malefics, or in ☌ with them at the beginning of an illness, the sick will hardly escape; the ☉ and ☽ afflicting each other at B., or by dir., long and severe illness; the ☉ in fiery signs with males, but it is soon over; the ☉ causes death by slow and severe illnesses, and feverish disorders in females; the ☉ or ♄ in the 6th H., in ☌, □, or ☍ asp. to each other, heavy and serious illness; to be taken sick in a ☉ Hour, the disease tends to be severe (see "Hours" under Planets); the ☉ or ☽ to the ☌ or ill-asps. ♄ by dir.; the ☉ hyleg, and to the ☌ or ill-asp. ♄ by dir.; the ☉ to the ill-asps. the ☽ by dir., and the ☽ hyleg or afflicted at B., according to the sign the ☉ is in; the ☉ hyleg, and the ☉ to the ☌ or P. asp. ☿ by dir., and ☿ afflicted and unfortunate at B.; the MOON at decumbiture, or first taking sick, be under the beams of the ☉, or ☌ ♅, ♄, or ♂ if the party be old, or even her ☌ with ♃, ♀, or ☿, the disease is not without peril; if the ☽ is in a sign occupied by a malefic at B. at the beginning of an illness, is apt to prove severe and dangerous; the ☽ to the ☌ or P. dec. the ☉ at B. if the ☽ be hyleg, and the ☉ afflicted at B.; the ☽ to the ☌ or ill-asp. ♄ or ♂ by dir., or in their place at the beginning of an illness; the ☽ decr. in light, and apply. to the ☌, □, or ☍ ♄, very dangerous unless the disease is already leaving the patient; the ☽ in the Asc., ☌, □, or ☍ ♄, ♂, ♅, or ♆, severe, and with danger unless in mutual reception with the afflicting planet; URANUS ☌ ♄ in the 6th H., and afflicting the hyleg, heavy and prolonged illness; SATURN in the 6th H., and afflicted, or afflicting the hyleg, sad and heavy sickness; ♄ and ♂ between the 10th and 7th H. at B., or in the 7th, and afflicted, heavy and prolonged illness; MARS in the 6th H., and afflicting the ☉ or ☽; malefics in the 1st or 7th H., or near the cusps of other angles, and more severe if the Lights be angular; the fiery sign ♌ on the Asc., suffers severely when ill; earthy signs give long and severe illnesses; the Asc. to the ☌ or P. Dec. ☿ by dir. if ☿ be much afflicted at B. (See Acute, Angles, Cardinal, Consumptions, Course, Crises, Dangerous; "Arguments For" under Death; Destructive, Diathesis, Direct Motion, Directions, Escape, Fatal; "High" under Fever; Fierce, Force, Fulminating, Grievous, Heavy, Increase, Incurable, Intensity, Invalids, Killing, Malignant; "Moon" under Motion; Mortal; "Disease" under Nature; Painful, Pernicious, Prognosis, Quick, Rapid, Serious, Sharp, Sudden, Swift, Terrible, Vehement, Violent, Virulent, Wastings, Worse, etc.).

Disposition—The Disposition Severe, Stern, and Austere—The ☉ Sig. in ♐; ♄ in ♈ or ♊, austere; characteristic of ♄ people; ♄ ruler of the Asc. and horoscope, and afflicted; ♄ Sig. ✶ or △ the ☉, austere in behavior; ♄ well-dignified in ♎, ♑, or ♒; ♂ influence is sudden, severe, and fulminating. (See Austere).

Epidemics—(See "Severe" under Epidemics).

Fevers — Severe Fevers — (See "High Fever" under Fever).

Fulminating—Sudden Severity of Disease—(See Fulminating).

Headaches—Severe Headaches—(See "Shooting Pains", "Violent", under Headaches).

Illnesses—Severe Illness—(See "Disease" in this section).

Injuries—Severe Injuries—(See Accidents, Cuts, Blows, in this section; "Serious" under Injuries).

Punishment — Severe Punishments — (See Punishment).

Sudden Severity of Disease — (See Fulminating).

Temper—Severe In Temper and Disposition — (See Anger, Cruel, Fierce, Merciless, Pity; "High Temper" under Temper; "Tendency To" under Violence; "Disposition" in this section).

Women—Fevers, Severe and Painful Diseases To — (See "Females" under Fever).

SEX — Sex Organs—Sex Diseases—Sexual — Sex Deformities — Sex Desires — Sex Functions — Sex Relations — Sex Powers — Sex Perversions — Sex Passions—Sexual Instincts—Sex Abuses—Sexual Deportment—Sex Excesses, etc. —The subject of Sex is also considered under the subjects of Generative Organs, Genitals, Genito-Urinary, Privates, Reproduction, and Secrets. The Sex Organs are ruled principally by the Scorpio Sign. The Hebrew Letter "Nun", or "N", is connected with the ♏ sign, the sign which rules the Sex Organs and Nature. The following subjects have to do with Sex, the Sex Nature, Sex Diseases, the Uses of Sex, the Sex Organs, etc., which subjects see in the alphabetical arrangement when only listed here—

Abandoned Persons—(See Profligate).

Abnormalities—(See Abnormal, Apathy, Aversions, Celibacy, Deformities, Desire, Deviations, Genitals; "Anchorite" under Husband; Passages, Passion, Perversions, Unnatural, etc.).

Abortion; Abuses Of — (See Amorous, Excesses; "Passional Excesses" under Passion; Perversions, Venery, Vices).

Addicts—Sex Addicts—(See Amorous, Excesses; "Sex Addict" under Marriage Partner; "Licentious" under Men; Nymphomania, "Passional Excesses" under Passion; Perversions, etc.).

Adolescence—Disorders At Time of—(See Puberty).

Adulterous—(See Love Affairs).

Affections—Disorders of—(See Affections).

Amorous; Amours — (See Love Affairs).

Anaphrodisiacs; Animal Propensities —(See Animal).

Apathy; Aphrodisiacs; Appetites — (See "Sexual Appetites" under Appetites).

Ardent—(See Love Affairs).

Aversions; Bachelors; Barrenness;

Bashful; Bisexual—(See Hermaphrodites).

Bohemian Pleasures—(See Pleasure).

Bubo; Cancer of Sex Organs — (See "Generative Organs" under Carcinoma).

Cases of Sex Disorders—See "Sexual", No. 285 in 1001 N.N.; Fig. 34 in the book, "Message of the Stars" by the Heindels; Figures 8A, 8B, 8C, 8D, 8F, 8G, 8H, 8I, 8J, in the book, "Astro-Diagnosis" by the Heindels. Also see Cases under Nymphomania.

Castration—(See Testes).

Celibacy; Chancre—(See Syphilis).

Chancroid—(See Gonorrhoea).

Channels and Vents—(See "Channels" under Genitals).

Chaotic Sex Relations — (See "Adultery", "Liaisons", under Love Affairs; "Clandestine", "Relations", in this section).

Chaste — (See "Chaste" under Females).

Childbirth—(See Parturition).

Children; Clandestine Relations—Love Intrigues—Fornication—Unlawful Intercourse — Adultery — Promiscuity —

The ☉ to the ☌ ♀ by dir. if ♀ be weak and afflicted at B.; the ☽ in any aspect to ♅; the ☽ afflicted in the 12th H.; the ☽ to the ☌ or ill-asps. ♀ or ♅ by dir.; ♆ or ♅ □ or ☍ ♀; ♆ afflicted in ≏, or in the 7th or 12th H.; ♅ afflicted in ♌ or ≏; the strong afflictions of ♅ tend to, and to perversion of the generative function; ♅ to the ill-asps. ♀ by dir.; ♅ afflicted in the 5th or 7th H.; ♅ ☌ or P. the ☽; ♂ afflicted in ♓; ♀ in the 7th H. in ♏ or ♑, and afflicted; in a male horoscope ♀ in a masculine sign, and ♂ in a feminine sign; ♀ ☌ ♄ or ♂ in ♏. (See "Free Love" under Free; Harlots, Lewd, Licentious; "Adultery", "Amours", "Liaisons", under Love Affairs; Lust; "Loose Morals" under Morals; Obscene, Perversions, Scandalous, Shameless, Venery, etc.).

Cohabitation—Little or No Desire For —Excessive Cohabitation—(See Cohabitation, Intercourse; "Married Women", "Single Persons", in this section).

Conception; Confinement—(See Parturition, Puerperal).

Conscious—Sex-Conscious—(See Amative; "Erotic" under Mania; Nymphomania; "Solitary" under Vice; "Sex-Conscious" in this section).

Control—Good Control Over the Passions and Sex Nature—Little Control Over—(See "Command", "Unbridled", under Passion).

Conventions—Disregard of Sex Conventions—Unconventional—♆ afflicted in ≏; ♅ afflicted in ♌ or ≏, or in the 5th or 7th H.; the ☽ ☌ ♂ in ♏; ♀ afflicted in ♒. (See "Free Love" under Free; "Liaisons" under Love Affairs; "Clandestine" in this section).

Creative Force—The Sex Force—Is ruled over by the Anterior Lobe of the Pituitary Body, ruled by ♅. (See Creative, Pituitary).

Criminal Intercourse—(See Intercourse; "Adultery" under Love Affairs; Rape; "Clandestine" in this section).

Death—From Sex Disorders and Dissipations—(See "Causes His Own Death" under Death; "Brings Disease Upon Himself" under Disease; "His Own Worst Enemy" under Enemies; "Death" under Generative, Syphilis, Womb, etc.).

Debauched; Deformities—Sex Deformities—(See "Channels" under Genitals; Hermaphrodites; "Deformity" under Womb).

Degeneracy; Deportment—Sex Deportment—(See the various paragraphs in this Article).

Depraved; Depressant—A Sex Depressant—(See Anaphrodisiacs).

Desires—Sex Desires—(See Amorous, Desire, Love Affairs, Passion, Perversions, Venery; the various paragraphs in this section).

Development Of—Sex Organs Not Fully Developed—(See "Undeveloped" in this section).

Deviations; Diseases—Sex Diseases—Are caused principally by afflictions in ♏, which sign rules the Sex Organs and Genitals. Uranus, said to be exalted in ♏, tends to produce Venereal Diseases, Sex Disorders, and deep-seated when in ♏ at B., or afflicting that sign. Also caused by many planets, a Stellium, in ♏ or the 8th H. Diseases from inordinate lust and sex excesses are caused by ♀. Comets appearing in ♏ tend to a prevalence of sex diseases. (See Excesses, Generation, Genitals, Genito-Urinary; "Health Injured" under Men; Opposite Sex, Passion, Private, Scandalous, Venereal, etc.; "Cases" in this section).

Early Death—From Sex Excesses and Venery—(See Early; "Dies Before Middle Life" under Middle Life).

Emissions—(See Semen).

Emotions; Enjoyments—Given to Sex Enjoyments—(See Amorous, Excesses, Harlots, Licentiousness, Love Affairs, Lust, Passion, Venery, etc.).

Entanglements—(See "Free Love" under Free; Love Affairs; "Clandestine" in this section).

Erections—Painful—(See Penis).

Erotic Mania—(See Mania).

Erratic—In Sex Life—(See Amorous, Free Love, Love Affairs, Passion, Venery; "Clandestine", and the various paragraphs in this section).

Eunuchs; Excesses—(See "Sex Excesses" under Excesses; Passion; the various paragraphs in this section).

Exhibitionism; Expression—Sex Expression—(See "Freedom" in this section).

Fallopian Tubes—(See Fallopian).

Fecundation; Feelings—Sex Feelings —(See Control, Regulated, Restraint, and the various paragraphs in this section).

Females—Female Sex Organs—Sex Gratification In—(See "Sex Gratification" under Females; Ovaries, Vagina, Womb, etc.).

Foetus; Force—Sex Force—(See "Creative" in this section).

Fornication—(See "Clandestine" in this section).

Free from Passion—(See "Free From" under Passion).

Free Love—(See Free).

Freedom of Sex Expression—♂ ☌ or ill-asp. ♀, or ♀ in a ♂ sign. (See Amorous; "Free Love" under Free; "Unwomanly Freedom" under Morals; "Passional Excesses" under Passion).

Fruitful; Generation—Organs and Members of—(See Generative).

Generative Function—Abuse of—(See "Clandestine" in this section; Perversions; "Passional Excesses" under Passion).

Genitals; Genito-Urinary System;

Gestation; Glands—(See "Sex Glands" under Glands).

Gonorrhoea; Gratification;

Great Command—Of the Passions—(See "Control" in this section).

Habits—Sex Habits—(See Amorous; "Licentious" under Men; "Unbridled", "Violence", under Passion; Perversions, Sadism; "Solitary" under Vice; the various paragraphs in this section).

Harlots; Hermaphrodites;

Highly Sexed—♂ in the 5th H. in any aspect to ♀. (See "Strong" under Passion).

Homosexuality; Husband; Hydrocele;

Illegitimate Sex Relations—(See "Free Love" under Free; "Adultery", "Liaisons", under Love Affairs; "Clandestine" in this section).

Illicit Amours — (See "Amours", "Adultery", "Liaisons", under Love Affairs; "Clandestine" in this section).

Immodest; Immorality — (See "Loose Morals" under Morals).

Impotent; Impurity—In Sex Relations —(See Illegitimate, Illicit, Immorality, in this section).

Incest—(See Perversions).

Indecent; Indiscretions — (See "Sex Life" under Indiscretions).

Indulgences; Infamous;

Inflamed with Passion — (See "Inflamed With" under Passion).

Intemperate — (See "Sex Life" under Intemperance).

Intercourse; Lack of Passion — (See "Free From" under Passion).

Larynx — The Larynx As Related to the Sex Force—(See Larynx).

Lascivious; Leucorrhoea; Lewd;

Liaisons—(See Love Affairs).

Libidinous—(See Lewd).

Licentiousness; Life Force — (See Life).

Little Sex Desire—(See Apathy, Celibacy, Indifferent; "Free From" under Passion).

Loose Morals—(See Morals).

Loss of Sex Desire—(See "Little Sex Desire" in this section).

Love Affairs; Love Passion—(See this subject under Love Affairs).

Low and Base — Low Women — Fond of Low Company—Low Public Houses —(See Harlots, Low).

Lower Passions—Carried Away By—(See "Lower Passions" under Passion; Venery, etc.).

Lues—(See Syphilis).

Lust; Male Sex Organs — (See "Sex" under Male; Penis, Scrotum, Testes).

Mania—Sex Mania—(See "Erotic" under Mania; "Licentious" under Men; Nymphomania).

Marriage; Marriage Partner;

Married Women—Cohabits With—The ☽ ☌, □, or ☍ ♅. (See "Adultery" under Love Affairs; "Single Persons" in this section).

Masochism; Masturbation—(See "Solitary" under Vice).

Maternity; Men — (See Genitals, Licentious, Sex, under Men).

Menses; Middle Life — (See "Early Death" in this section).

Mind—The Mind Absorbed with Passion—(See "Mind" under Passion).

Miscarriages; Mixture of Sex — (See Hermaphrodite, Virile).

Modesty; Monsters; Morals — (See "Loose" under Morals).

Morbid Sex Desires — (See "Desires" under Morbid).

Mother—Motherhood—(See Maternity, Mother, Parturition).

Nakedness — Wandering In — (See "Outrageous" under Insanity).

Necrophilia—Sexual Congress with a Dead Body—(See Necrophilism).

Neurotic—A Sexual Neurotic—Case—See "Sexual Neurotic", No. 285, in 1001 N.N.

Notoriety — Of the Passions — (See Notoriety).

Nymphomania; Obscene; Obsessions—Sexual Obsessions—(See "Erotic" under Mania; Nymphomania, Perversions).

Obstructions — In the Sex Organs — (See "Obstructions" under Generative).

Offspring—(See Children).

Opposite Sex; Outbursts—Of Passion —(See Outbursts, Storms, under Passion).

Outrages Nature's Laws — (See "Nature's Laws" under Nature; Obscene, Perversions, Shameless).

Ovaries; Over-Indulgence—Of the Sex Passion—(See Amorous, Excesses, Indulgence, Licentiousness; "Passional Excesses" under Passion; Venery).

Ovum; Pain — In Sex Organs — (See "Pain" under Generative, Genitals, Penis, Secrets).

Parturition; Passion — (See "Free From", "Passional Excesses", and the various paragraphs under Passion).

Penis; Perverse; Perversions;

Pleasures—Sex Pleasures—(See Amorous, Lewd, Licentious, Passion, Sensuality; the various paragraphs in this section).

Powers—The Sex Powers—(See Control, Creative, Highly Sexed, Strong, Weak, and the various paragraphs in this section; Barrenness, Fruitfulness, Generative, Impotent, Reproduction).

Predetermination—Of the Sex Before Birth — (See "First-Born Child" under Children; Predetermination).

Pregnancy; Prenatal Epoch;

Prevalent—Sex Diseases Prevalent—(See "Diseases" in this section).

Privates — Private Diseases — (See Privates, Venereal).

Profligate; Promiscuity—(See "Clandestine" in this section).

Prostitutes—(See Harlots).

Prudery; Puberty—Sex Activity At—(See Puberty).

Puerperal; Rape; Regeneration;

Regulated — The sex feeling is regulated, moderated, and better controlled by the good aspects of ♄ or ♃ to the ☽ and ♀. (See "Control" in this section).

Relations — The Sex Relations — Legitimate — Illegitimate — Controlled — Uncontrolled, etc. — (See the various paragraphs in this section).

Reproduction; Restraint — Unnatural Sex Restraint — Lack of Restraint — (See "Passional Excesses", "Restraint", under Passion).

Sadism; Salacious—(See Lust).

Same Sex — Unnatural Sex Relations With—(See Homosexuality).

Scandalous Diseases; Scheming—Underhanded In Measures to Gratify Passion—(See "Scheming" under Passion).

Scorpio Sign—The Sex Sign—Diseases Ruled By—(See Scorpio).

Scrotum; Secret Vices — (See Secret, Solitary, under Vices).

Secrets (Secret Parts); **Seduction;**

Self-Abuse—(See "Solitary" under Vice).

Semen — Seminal Vesicles — (See Semen).

Senility—(See Old Age).

Sensuality; Separation of the Sexes—The First Two Races of Mankind are said to have been Bisexual, or Androgynous, Hermaphroditic, but during the Third, or Lemurian Race, the sexes were separated into two bodies, male and female, and Adam and Eve are considered the first types of the separated sexes. The separation of the sexes was not sudden, but took place gradually over a long period of time. It is said that the ♍ and ♏ signs were separated at the time of the separation of the sexes, and the ♎ sign inserted between them. This subject is considered, and its history given, in the books, "Cosmo-Conception", by the Heindels; in the "Key of Destiny", by Dr. and Mrs. Homer Curtiss. Also see the subject of "Scales" in Sepharial's New Dictionary of Astrology.

Sex Addicts—(See "Addicts" in this section).

Sex Appetites — (See "Sexual" under Appetites).

Sex Channels — (See "Channels" under Genitals).

Sex-Conscious — ♂ in the 5th H. in aspect to ♀, and especially if ♀ is in ♉ or ♑. (See "Conscious" in this section).

Sex Desires — (See "Desires" in this section).

Sex Excesses—(See "Excesses" in this section).

Sex Expression—(See "Freedom" in this section).

Sex Feelings—(See "Feelings" in this section).

Sex Force—(See "Creative Force" in this section).

Sex Gratification—(See Gratification, Indulgent, Love Affairs, Marriage, Passion, Self-Indulgent, Venery; the various paragraphs in this section).

Sex Indiscretions — (See "Sex Life" under Indiscretions; the various paragraphs in this section).

Sex Organs — (See Generative, Genitals, Ovaries, Penis, Privates, Reproduction, Secrets, Testes, Vagina, Womb; the various paragraphs in this section).

Sex Passion—(See Amorous, Love Affairs, Passion; the various paragraphs in this section).

Sex Perversions—(See Perversions).

Sex Powers—(See Apathy, Aversions, Imbecile, Impotent, Passion; "Powers" in this section).

Sex Relations — (See Adultery, Clandestine, Illegitimate, Illicit, Intemperate, Relations, Trouble, Unfaithful, and the various paragraphs in this section; Husband, Love Affairs, Marriage, Marriage Partner, Men, Passion, Venery, Wife, Women, etc.).

Shameless; Single Persons—Cohabits With—♅ ☌, □, or ☍ ♀. (See "Married Women" in this section).

Social Relations—(See Social).

Society—Aversions To—(See Celibacy, Recluse, Renunciation, Reserved, Retiring, Secretive, Solitude).

Sodomy—(See Homesexuality).

Solitary Vice — (See "Solitary" under Vice).

Spermatic Cord—(See Spermatic).

Spermatozoon—(See Semen).

Spinsters; Sterility—(See Barren).

Stimulated—The Sex Feelings Stimulated—(See Aphrodisiacs).

Storms—Sudden Storms of Passion—(See "Outbursts" in this section).

Strangury—(See Urine).

Strengthened—The Passional Nature Strengthened — (See "Strong" under Passion).

Stricture — Of the Urethra — (See Stricture, Urethra).

Strong Passions — (See "Strong" under Passion).

Strong Sex Powers — (See Fruitful; Highly Sexed, Powers, in this section).

Sudden Storms — Of Passion — (See "Outbursts" in this section).

Syphilis; Testes; Trouble—Thru Sex Relations—♆ or ♅ □ or ☍ ♀. (See "Adultery", "Liaisons", under Love Affairs; "Health Injured" under Men; Opposite Sex; "Clandestine" in this section).

Unbridled Passion — Uncontrolled — (See Nymphomania; "Unbridled" under Passion).

Unconventional—In Sex Relations—(See "Free Love" under Free; "Amours", "Liaisons", under Love Affairs; Clandestine, Conventions, Illicit, in this section).

Undersized — The Sex Organs Undersized and Undeveloped—(See "Sex Organs" under Undersized, Undeveloped).

Undeveloped Sex Organs—(See Undersized, Undevloped).

Unfaithful—In Sex Relations—♆ afflicted in ♎; ♅ afflicted in ♌ or ♎. (See Adulterous, Clandestine, Conventions, Illegitimate, Illicit, Sex Relations, in this section).

Unnatural Desires—Unnatural Restraint Over the Sex Nature—Unnatural Sex Desires — (See Chaotic, Depraved, Desires; "Restraint" under Passion; Perversions, Unnatural).

Unwise Entanglements — (See "Entanglements" in this section).

Urethra; Uterus—(See Womb).

Vagina; Varicocele; Varicose;

Vehement Passion — (See Outbursts, Storms, Unbridled, Violence, under Passion; Vehement, Venery).

Venereal Diseases; Venery;

Vents and Channels—(See "Channels" under Genitals).

Vices — Sex Vices — (See Lewd, Obscene, Perversions, Shameless; "Solitary" under Vice).

Violence—(See "Violence" under Passion).

Virile Members—(See Virile).

Virtue — Virtuous — Not Virtuous — (See "Chaste" under Females; Modesty, Nymphomania; "Unbridled" under Passion; "Unchaste" under Women).

Vital Fluid—(See "Fluid" under Vital; "Creative Force" in this section).

Vitality—Depletion of Thru Sex Excesses — (See "Health Injured" under Men; Opposite Sex; "Lessened", "Wasted", under Vitality).

Voice—The Voice and the Sex Force —(See Larynx, Puberty).

Voluptuous; Vulva; Wanton;

Wastes Energies—On Opposite Sex— (See Amorous, Harlots; "Health Injured" under Men; Opposite Sex; "Passional Excesses" under Passion; "Wasted" under Vitality).

Weak Sex Powers — ♄ afflicted in ♏ usually tends to an earlier breakdown sexually, and especially if the native has been given over to sexual excesses. (See Impotent; "Senility" under Old Age).

Wench; Wife; Womb; Women—(See "Women" under Passion; "Sex Gratification" under Women).

SEXTILE ASPECT—The 60 degree aspect (✳). This aspect is based upon the trine (△) aspect and is very fortunate in health, and other matters. (See Aspects).

SHAGGY—Bushy—(See "Bushy" under Eyebrows, Hair).

SHAKING — (See Chill, Concussion, Palsy, Paralysis, Spasmodic, Tremors).

SHALLOW—Not Deep—

Shallow Breathing — (See "Shallow" under Breath).

Shallow Mind — Shallow Intellect — (See "Shallow" under Intellect, Mentality, Mind; "Bad" under Judgment; "Void Of" under Learning; Pretender).

SHAME—Shameless—

Sense of Shame—And Bashfulness— ♄ strong and well-dignified tends to give a sense of shame and bashfulness; ♄ to the ♂ ☊. (See Bashful, Blushing, Modesty, Reserved, Shy).

Shameless Practices — Shameless and Immodest Sex Practices—

(1) **In Men**—♂ in a female sign, and ♀ in a masculine sign, and ♄ configurated with them, makes men more prone to violence, unnatural desires, impurity, and obsenity. Mercury adds to their lusts and gives a greater variety of contrivances to give vent to lasciviousness and shameless practices. Jupiter taking part in the configuration tends to moderate the desires and make either sex more circumspect, and less vicious or open in their practices. The ☽ sepr. from ♀ and applying to ☿, and the ☽ decreasing, tends to shameless viciousness. (See "Licentious" under Men; Obscene; "Violence" under Passion; Perversions, etc.).

(2) **In Females**—The ☽ afflicted in ♏; ♀ ♂ ♂ in ♏; ♀ Sig. □ or ☍ ♂, and often becomes a harlot. (See Harlots, Immodest, Nymphomania, Virile).

Sickness from Shame—Or Disgrace— Lord of the 6th H. in the 10th. (See

Disgrace, Downfall; "Ruined by Women" under Love Affairs; Reputation, Reverses, Ruin, Scandal). See Debased, Depraved; "Sex Organs" under Exhibition; Infamous, Lascivious, Lewd, Licentiousness; "Loose Morals" under Morals; "Notoriety of the Passions" under Passion; Profligate, Wanton, Wench).

SHANKS—Shin Bone—(See Tibia).

SHAPE OF THE BODY — For the description of the form, shape, and appearance of the various parts of the body, see in the alphabetical arrangement the part, or organ, you have in mind. Thus see such subjects as Abdomen, Arms, Cheeks, Chest, Chin, Ears, Extremities, Eyes, Face, Feet, Forehead, Hands, Head, Hips, Jaws, Knees, Legs, Limbs, Lips, Mouth, Nails, Neck, Nose, Shoulders, Thighs, etc. Also under the following subjects you will find lists of the descriptions of the form and shape of the body— Appearance, Beautiful, Body, Coarse, Comely, Compact, Corpulent, Decanates, Deformities, Diminished, Dwarfed, Elegant, Enlarged, Fat, Features, Figure, Fleshy, Form, Frame, Freaks, Full, Good, Handsome, Height, Ill-Formed, Large, Lean, Long, Malformations, Mean, Medium, Members, Middle, Misshaped, Missing, Monsters, Oval, Posture, Rough, Round, Short, Size, Skeleton, Slender, Small, Smooth, Square, Stature, Stooping, Stout, Tall, Thick, Thin, Ugly, Weight, Well-Formed, Well-Proportioned, Wide, etc. Nearly all the adjectives describing the form and shape of the body are listed in the alphabetical arrangement of this book, and with the planetary influences causing them. Look for the subject you have in mind.

SHARP—

Diseases—Sharp Diseases—Sharp, Sudden, Violent, and Short Attacks of Sicknesses—Caused by ♂. (See Acute, Dangerous; "High" under Fever; Fierce; Fulminating, Painful, Pernicious, Poignant, Quick, Rapid, Sudden, Swift, Vehement, Violent, etc.).

Eyes — Sharp Eyes — Sharp Sight — Quick Sight — (See "Sharp" under Eyes).

Face—Sharp Face—Sharp Features— (See "Sharp" under Face).

Features — Sharp Features — (See "Sharp" under Face).

Fevers—(See "Sharp" under Fever).

Instruments — Sharp Instruments — Cuts and Injury By—(See Cuts, Instruments).

Look—Sharp Look—(See Look).

Males — Sharp Illnesses for Males — (See "Sharp Illnesses" under Males).

Mind — A Sharp, Active, and Acute Mind—(See "Active Mind" under Active; "Good" under Intellect; "Quickened" under Mentality; "Sharpened" under Mind; "Good" under Understanding).

Nose—(See "Sharp" under Nose).

Pains—Sharp Pains—Denoted by ♂, and are ♂ diseases and afflictions. (See "Sharp" under Pains; Poignant).

Sicknesses — Short and Sharp Sicknesses—(See "Diseases" in this section).

Sight — Sharp Sight — Sharp Eyes — (See "Eyes" in this section).

Violent—And Sharp Affections—(See "Diseases" in this section).

SHEATHS — The Nerve Sheaths — (See "Sheaths" under Nerves).

Synovial Sheaths—(See Synovial).

SHEDDING—Sheds—

Shedding of Blood—Bloodshed—Loss of Blood—♂ is the planet of Bloodshed, and of War. Injuries with the loss of blood are caused by ♂, while ♄ rules hurts and injuries without loss of blood. Compound injuries, with possible fracture and loss of blood, are caused by the combined influences of ♄ and ♂ in the configuration. (See Assassins; "Loss Of", "Shedding", under Blood; Criminals, Cuts, Duels, Effusions; "Patricide" under Father; Feuds, Gunshot, Hemorrhage, Homicide, Hurts, Incised, Injuries, Instruments, Menses; "Depopulation" under Mortality; Murder; "Epistaxis" under Nose; Rigel, Slaughter, Stabs, Suicide, Sword, War, Weapons, Wounds, etc.).

Sheds Tears Easily—(See Tears).

SHEEP—Rams—Lambs—Ruled by the ♈ Sign, the sign of "The Ram". (See Aries). Also ruled by the 6th H., the house of Small Animals.

Diseases Among — Many Will Die — Afflictions or eclipses in ♈ at a Solar Ingress; Comets appearing in ♈. (See "Small Animals" under Animals; "Small Cattle" under Cattle; Goats).

Epidemics Among—Sheep and Cattle Will Die—The ☽ in the 6th H. at the Vernal E., lady of the year, and afflicted; ♄ Lord of the Year at the Vernal, and afflicted by ♂; ♂ in ♉, ♒, ♌, or ♐, direct in motion, ori., Lord of the Year, and afflicted, many cattle, oxen, and sheep die. Many eclipses occurring in the same year tend to the death of many small animals, small cattle, sheep, goats, etc., and especially if they occur in four-footed signs, and in the territory afflicted by the eclipse. (See "Small" under Animals, Cattle; Comets, Eclipses, Epidemics, Horses, Oxen; "Virus" under Pestilence; Pets, Swine, Virus; "Cold" under Weather).

SHELLAC—A Resinous Substance ruled by ♅. (See Resins).

SHIFTING — Of the Disease — (See "Shifting" under Complications).

SHIN BONE—Shins—(See Tibia).

SHINGLES — Herpes Zoster — (See "Herpes Zoster" under Herpes).

SHINY—Shining—Glossy—

Shiny Face—(See "Shiny" under Face).

Shining Hair — (See "Glossy" under Hair).

Shiny Skin—Oily Skin—♃ gives. (See "Oily" under Face; Glossy, Oils).

SHIPS — Shipping — Shipwreck — Maritime Affairs—Navigation, etc.—The ☽ in general rules Ships, Shipping, the Ocean and Seas. Also these matters are influenced by ♆, the ♓ sign, and 9th H., the house of Foreign Travel and Long Journeys. The following subjects have to do with Ships, Shipping, Ocean Voyages, etc., and the dangers or benefits which may attend them.

Abroad — Journeys Abroad — (See Abroad).

Accidents On Ships — Or To Ships — (See Fire, Foundering, and the various paragraphs in this section). Case—An Accident On Trial Trip—See "Launching", No. 852, in 1001 N.N.

Best Time to Sail—When ♃ or ♀ are in the Asc., the M.C., 2nd or 9th H., and no malefics in the angles. (See "Good Time" under Journeys, Voyages; "Fortunate" under Travel).

Burning of Ship—(See "Ships" under Fire).

Collide — Ships Collide — Case — 300 drowned. See "Launching", No. 711, in 1001 N.N.

Crew Sickly — Sickness On Board — Lord of the Asc., or the ☽ combust, or if they be in the 6th or 12th H., and in evil aspect their lords, denotes sickness, or great calamity (Hor'y); if the Asc. and ☽ be fortunate, and lord of the Asc. unfortunate, the ship is safe, but the crew sickly (Hor'y). See Death, Sickness, in this section).

Death On Ship — Danger of — (See "Long Journeys" under Journeys; "Death At Sea" under Sea; Shipwreck; "Death" under Voyages, Water).

Drowning At Sea — (See Drowning). Case — Fell Overboard and Was Drowned—See "Died In Harness", No. 802, in 1001 N.N.

Explosion On Ship—(See "Ships" under Explosions).

Fell from Ship—And Was Drowned—(See "Drowning" in this section).

Fire On Ship — (See "Ships" under Fire).

Foreign Travel — (See Abroad, Foreign; "Long Journeys" under Journeys; Travel, Voyages).

Foundering — Danger of Running Aground — Malefics in the 9th H., afflicting the ☉ or ☽ at time of sailing, or during the voyage, and especially if the configurations are in earthy signs. (See Shipwreck).

Hurricanes At Sea—(See "Fountains" under Dry; "Voyages" under Lightning; Shipwreck; "Storms" under Travel).

Launching of Ships — Good Time For —The ☽ in ♓ and free from affliction. The ☽ should not be afflicted by malefics. (See "Best Time to Sail" in this section). Cases of Launchings — See "Launching", No. 711, and No. 852, in 1001 N.N.

Lightning — Ships At Sea Injured or Burned By—♂ in a fiery sign on cusp the 10th H., and near violent fixed stars. (See "Sea", "Voyages", under Lightning).

Long Journeys — (See "Long" under Journeys; Maritime, Navigation, Travel, Voyages).

Lost — The Ship Is Probably Lost — Lord of the Asc. or the ☽ combust (Hor'y); lord of the 8th in the 1st H., or lord of the 1st in the 8th in evil asp. with its lord; or lord of the 1st in the 4th H. in evil asp. with its lord, or with lord of the 8th if the aspect be separating, and if the lords of the 4th are malefics the danger is more imminent (Hor'y). (See "Sunk", in this section; Shipwreck).

Maritime Affairs — (See Maritime, Navigation, Ocean, Sailors, Sea, Voyages; "Shipping" in this section).

Murder On Ship — Danger of — ♂ afflicted in ♏, ♐, or ♒ denotes in Hor'y Questions.

Navigation—(See Navigation).

Navy—The Army and Navy—Attains Considerable Rank In—The ☉ Sig. ☌ ♂; ♂ Sig. ☌ ♃ or ☿, or ⚹ or △ the ☉. (See Army, Sailors, War).

Officer — Death of a Principal Officer of Ship—Lord of the Asc. only in the 8th H., or in evil asp. with its lord (Hor'y).

Runs Aground—(See "Foundering" in this section).

Sailing Time — (See "Best Time" in this section).

Sailors — Seamen — (See Maritime, Sailors).

Sea—(See the paragraphs under Sea).

Shipping—Successful In—♃ Sig. ☌ ☽. (See Maritime).

Shipwreck—(See Shipwreck).

Sickness On Ship—(See Crew, Death, in this section).

Submersion of Ship — (See Burning, Lightning, Sunk, in this section; Shipwreck).

Successful—In Maritime Affairs—(See Maritime; "Shipping" in this section).

Sunk—The Ship Has Sunk—Lord of the Asc. under the Earth, and in the 4th H. (Hor'y).

Travel — (See the paragraphs under Travel).

Trial Trip—Accident On—Case—See "Launching", No. 852, in 1001 N.N.

Voyages—(See the paragraphs under Voyages).

Waters—(See Danger, Death, Fortunate, Perils, and the various paragraphs under Water).

"One ship sails East, and another sails
  West
 With the selfsame winds that blow,
'Tis the set of the sail,
And not the gale,
 Which determines the way they go.

"Like the winds of the Sea are the ways
  of Fate,
 As we voyage along through life,
'Tis the act of the Soul
That determines the goal,
 And not the calm or the strife."

SHIPWRECK—Calamities At Sea—

Danger of Shipwreck—The following influences may exist in the chart of birth of the individual; have reference to the time of launching or sailing, and also exist at the time of the calamity. The following influences tend to cause shipwreck, or involve the native in such a misfortune. Good influences in the 9th H. at B., such as ♃ or ♀, or both benefics in this house, and in ☌, even though there may also be malefics in this house at B., usually save the native from death of injury, or bring about his escape and rescue. The general influences causing shipwreck are — The SUN afflicted at B., and the ☉ by dir. in evil asp. the Asc.; the ☉ hyleg, and to the ☌, P., □ or ☍ ♄ by dir.; the ☉ to the cusp the 9th H., and if any of the malefics afflict this house at B., and by dir.; the ☉ to the ☌ or ill-asp. ♄ by dir. in water signs; the ☉ near Argo; the ☉ joined with the Ascelli, Castor, Pollux, Hyades, Pleiades, or Praesepe, and danger of death by; an eclipse of the ☉ or ☽ in ♓, the sign which rules the Ocean; an eclipse of the ☉ or ☽ in ♑, shipwreck and submersion of ships, and especially in places ruled by ♑; the MOON in ♋, ♏, or ♓ in the 3rd or 9th H., and afflicted by malefics; the ☽ to the □ or ☍ ♂ by dir.; the ☽ afflicted at B., and to the evil asp. the Asc. by dir.; NEPTUNE in tr. over the radical ♂, or ♆ ☌ ♂ at a Solar Rev.; ♆ in ♓ in the 9th H., and afflicted by malefics; URANUS or ♄ in ♋, ♍, ♏, or ♓, and afflicting the ☽, and if ♅ or ♄ be near Argo; ♅, ♄, or ♂ afflicted in the 9th H.; SATURN ascending at B., and the ☉ to the ☌ or ill-asp. ♄ by dir.; ♄ near Argo, and afflicting the ☽ hyleg; ♄ in ♋ at B., and afflicted by ♂ at the Vernal E., and ♄ Lord of the Year; ♄ afflicted in the 10th H.; ♄ afflicting the Asc. and the ☽; ♄ sole ruler at an eclipse of the ☉; ♄ Lord of the Year at the Vernal, and occi., destruction of ships and loss of life of sailors; ♄ ascending in ♓ at departure; ♄ in the Asc. when the ship leaves port, or a fiery sign on the Asc., which usually places a watery sign on the 8th H.; ♄ and ♂ in watery signs, controlling the Lights, and when ♄ and ♂ are distant from each other, and not active in concert; ♄ in water signs, or in ♍, configurated with the ☽, and near Argo; ♄ angular at B., and holding dominion, and elevated above the Lights; JUPITER in ♏ and afflicted or ℞, and lord of the year at the Vernal; MARS sole ruler at an eclipse of the ☉; ♂ in power and lord of the year at the Equinoxes or Solstices; ♂ in ♋ and lord of the year at the Vernal; ♂ in the Asc. when the ship sails, and also danger of fire on ship; ♂ in the 9th H. in a water sign, and afflicted; planets in ♋, ♏, or ♓, and afflicting the ☽, or afflicting the Sigs. of travel; lord of the ASC. in the 9th H., and afflicted; malefics in the 9th H. in water signs, afflicted, or afflicting the ☉ or ☽; the Asc. to the □ or ☍ the ☉ by dir.; malefics in the M.C., elevated above the Luminaries, and ♄ holding dominion; lord of the 12th H. in the 9th; the 11° ♋ on the Asc.; common signs show. (See "Long Journeys" under Journeys; Maritime, Navigation, Ocean, Sea, Ships; "Danger" under Travel; Voyages, Waters; the various paragraphs in this section).

Death At Sea—Death In Shipwreck—The ☽ in the 9th H. at the Vernal, lady of the year, and afflicted; ♆ in the 8th H., and afflicting the hyleg by dir.; ♅ in the 8th H., and afflicting the hyleg by dir., and other testimonies concurring; ♅ or ♄ in ♋, ♍, ♏, or ♓, and afflicting the ☽, and if ♅ or ♄ be near Argo; planets in ♋, ♏, or ♓, and afflicting the ☽ and hyleg. (See "Fountains" under Dry; "Death" under Sea, Ships, Voyages, Waters).

Distortions — From Injury In Shipwreck—(See Distortions).

Drowning At Sea — By Shipwreck — (See Drowning; "Death" in this section).

Explosion — Shipwreck By — (See "Ships" under Explosion).

Fire At Sea—(See "Ships" under Fire).

Foundering — (See "Foundering" under Ships).

Hurricanes — Shipwreck By — (See "Hurricanes" under Ships).

Injury — In Shipwreck — (See Distortions).

Lightning — Shipwreck By — (See "Ships" under Fire; "Lightning" under Ships).

Long Journeys — Ocean Voyages — Danger of Shipwreck On—(See "Danger" in this section; "Long" under Journeys; "Danger" under Voyages).

Maritime—Much Loss of Life Among Maritime People by Shipwreck — (See Maritime, Navigation, Ocean, Sailors, Sea, Ships; "Danger" under Travel, Voyages, Water).

Misfortunes At Sea — (See "Misfortunes" under Sea).

Navigation—Danger In—(See Navigation).

Ocean—Much Danger On—(See Ocean, Sea, Ships, Voyages).

Paralysis—From Injury In Shipwreck —(See Distortions).

Prevalent—Shipwrecks Prevalent—♄ lord of the year at the Vernal, and occi.; ♃ in ♏, and afflicted or ℞, and lord of the year at the Vernal; ♂ in ♋ and lord of the year at the Vernal; ☿ in ♋ and afflicted by ♂ at the Vernal, and ☿ lord of the year; ☿ in ♓ at the Vernal, afflicted, and lord of the year or Quarter; ☿ in an angle at an Equinox or Solstice; an eclipse of the ☉ or ☽ in ♓.

Runs Aground — (See "Foundering" under Ships).

Sailors—Seamen—Loss of Life Among by Shipwreck—(See "Maritime" in this section).

Sea — Troubles by Sea — (See Ocean; "Troubles" under Sea; Ships, Voyages; the various paragraphs in this section).

Ships — Loss of by Shipwreck — (See Ships; the various paragraphs in this section).

Storms At Sea—Shipwreck By—(See Hurricanes, Lightning, in this section).

Travel — Danger In Ocean Travel — (See "Danger" under Travel; the various paragraphs in this section).

Troubles by Sea—(See "Sea" in this section).

Voyages—Danger In—(See "Danger" under Voyages; the various paragraphs in this section).

Water — Accidents and Dangers On the Water—(See the paragraphs under Ocean, Voyages, Water, and in this section).

Wind Storms — Danger of Shipwreck By — (See "Hurricanes" under Ships; "Storms" under Wind).

SHOCK — Shocks — Shocks from any cause are usually due to ♅ influence and affliction. (See Ether). Uranus afflicted in ♌ tends to make shocks very harmful to the system due to disturbance of the heart action, circulation, and nerves. Saturn in ♌ tends to make sudden shocks harmful. Mars tends to shock by cuts, hurts, and injuries.

Brain Disorders—From Shock — (See "Shocks" under Brain).

Childbirth—Nervous Shock In—(See "Nervous Shock" under Parturition).

Died from Shock — Due to Fire and Loss of Family—Case—See "Leland", No. 813 in 1001 N.N.

Electricity—Shocks By—Death By— Caused by ♅; ♅ ☌ or ill-asp. the ☉; ♅ afflicted by ♂; the Asc. afflicted by ♅. (See Electricity, Lightning).

Fright—Shocks By—(See Fright).

Lightning — Shock By — (See Lightning).

Nervous Shock — (See "Shock and Strain" under Nerves; "Childbirth" in this section).

Violent Shocks—The work of ♂ or ♅, or their combined influences. Death or serious injury may result from shocks according to the degree and power of the shock, and the planetary influences operating at the time. (See Accidents, Blows, Bruises, Concussion, Employment, Exaggerated Action, Explosions, Extraordinary, Falls, Hurts, Injuries, Lightning, Machinery, Railroads, Sudden, Uranus, etc.).

SHOOTING—

Fond of Shooting—Fond of Hunting, Riding, Robust Sports, etc.—♂ Sig. in ♌. (See Hunting, Sports).

Shooting Pains — Darting Pains — Sharp Pains—Flying Pains, etc.—Denoted by ♂; ☿ afflicted in ♒; common signs on the cusp of 6th H., sharp, shooting pains generally. (See Acute, Fierce, Flying, Gnawing, Headaches, Pain, Poignant; "Shooting Pains" under Ribs; Sharp, Violent; "Pains" under Whole Body).

SHORT—Shortened—Shortening—

Arms—(See "Short" under Arms).

Ascension—Signs of Short Ascension —♑, ♒, ♓, ♈, ♉, ♊.

Body — Short Body — The ☽ in ♉ in partile asp. the Asc., rather short and well-set; ♄ in ♏, partile the Asc.; ♄ in ♑, partile the Asc., rather short than otherwise; ♄ in S. Lat. makes the body shorter; ♄ occi., a shorter body than when oriental; born under ♃, and ♃ occi., the body is somewhat shorter; ♂ in ♉, partile the Asc., rather short, compact, well-set, corpulent, but rather ugly; born under ♂, short, strong, and well-set; ♀ or ☿ in their signs of fall or detriment causes shortness; ♀ Sig. in Hor'y Q., rather short than tall; ♉,

♋, ♏, ♑, or ♓ on the Asc.; ♉ on the Asc., short and well-set; ♏ on the Asc., short, strong, corpulent, able body; ♓ on the Asc., short or medium, and usually crooked and stooped. (See Diminished, Dwarfed, Low, Mean, Medium, Middle, Small, Squab, Stature).

Breath—(See "Short" under Breath).

Chest—(See "Short and Wide" under Chest).

Chin—(See "Short" under Chin).

Coarse—Coarse, Short, and Hairy Body —♏ on the Asc. (See Coarse; "Body" under Hairy).

Compact—Short, Corpulent, and Compact—♂ in ♉, partile the Asc. (See Compact, Corpulent).

Corpulent — Corpulent, Short, and Compact—(See "Compact" in this section).

Crooked — Short, Crooked, and Ill-Made—(See Crooked).

Diseases — Short Diseases — (See "Illnesses" in this section).

Face—Short, Small, and Round Face —(See "Short" under Face).

Fat—Short, Mean, Fat, Plump Stature —(See "Body" under Fat).

Father—Short Life For—(See "Short Life" under Father).

Feet—(See "Short and Fleshy" under Feet).

Fleshy — Short and Fleshy — (See "Fleshy Body" under Fleshy).

Full and Short — (See "Body" under Full).

Hair—(See "Short and Thick" under Hair).

Hairy Body — Short, Coarse, Hairy Body—(See "Body" under Hair).

Hands—(See "Short" under Hands).

Ill-Formed — Ill-Formed, Lean and Short—(See "Ill-Formed Body" under Ill).

Illnesses — Short Diseases and Illnesses—Signs of a Short Disease—The Disease Is of Short Duration — The Disease Terminates Quickly — Brief Diseases — Short and Sudden — Quick Diseases — The Disease Is Curtailed — The Disease Will Remove Shortly — Will the Disease Be Short?, etc.—Diseases beginning in the Summer are usually shorter than those beginning in Winter. The ☉, ♃, and ♂ cause short diseases. Hot and Dry diseases brought on by the ☉ and ♂ are usually short, and regulated by the motion of the ☽. Long and chronic diseases brought on by ♄ are regulated by the motion of the ☉. (See Chronic; "Diseases" under Long). The predominance of diseases is usually attended with a fever, and acute in nature, and many of the influences which tend to cause short illnesses are considered in the Articles on Acute Diseases, Fevers, Fierce, Fulminating, Rapid, Swift, etc. The following are general influences which tend to cause Short Diseases—The ☉, ♃, and ♂ cause short diseases, but ♂ is the most acute of all; the ☽ in a fiery sign, or a fire sign on the Asc. or 6th H. at decumbiture; the ☽ ☌ an oriental planet which is direct and swift in motion; the ☽ swift in motion and aspecting the lord of the Asc.; the ☽ applying to the ☌, P, ⚹ or △ a benefic at decumb.; the ☽ in a common sign, and a common sign on the cusp of 6th H.; the ☽ or cusp of the 6th H. in a moveable sign, the disease terminates quickly either in recovery or death; the ☽ in a movable sign; in sickness when the ☽ applies to a planet contrary to the nature of the disease, and especially if it be a benefic, the disease will soon be changed for the better; ♆ in the 8th H. at B. tends to short illnesses, and of a watery nature; ♄ lord of the Asc., strong and well-qualified, not ℞, and fast in motion; ♂ ☌, □, or ☍ the ☉, short but sharp attacks of sickness; ♂ afflictions tend to death after a short or sudden illness; planets oriental signify short attacks of sickness; afflictions from cardinal signs, the disease is more acute, transient, and more quickly broken; malefics in ori. quarters, the illness will be acute, short, and painful; afflictions from common signs are more amenable to treatment; a benefic in the 6th H., judge that the disease will be short; the last degrees of a sign on the cusp of 6th H., the disease is almost at an end; lord of the Asc. swift in motion, and going out of his own sign or house into another, except into the sign of the 6th or 12th H.; lord of the Asc. or 6th, or the ☽, be in ☌, ⚹, or △ a benefic, or with the lord of the 10th, or the last degree of a sign be on the cusp the 6th H., the disease is not of long duration; a movable sign, or ♓, on the cusp the 6th H.; lord of the 6th a benefic in the 6th; lord of the Asc. stronger than lord of the 6th; a malefic leaving the 6th, the disease will remove shortly, and in so many days, weeks, or months, according to the nature of the sign; lord of the 6th H. cadent; lords of the 1st and 6th H., and the cusp of the 6th and the ☽ in movable signs. (For further influences along this line see Acute, Cardinal, Course, Crises, Curtailed; "Arguments For" under Death; Duration, Fatal; "High" under Fever; Fierce, Fulminating, Grievous, Mars Diseases, Mild, Painful Diseases, Pernicious, Quick Diseases, Rapid Diseases; "Rapid" under Recovery, Recuperation; "Good" under Resistance; Severe Diseases, Sharp Diseases, Slight, Sudden Diseases, Swift, Termination, Transient, Vehement, Violent Diseases, etc.).

Journeys — (See "Short" under Journeys).

Lean—Lean, Short, and Ill-Formed—(See "Ill-Formed" under Ill).

Legs—(See "Short" under Legs).

Life—Short Life—Early Death—(See "Short Life" under Life).

Long or Short Diseases—Will the Disease Be Long or Short?—Indicated by the 6th H. conditions at B., and at decumbiture. Diseases beginning in Summer are shorter than those which start in the Winter. (See "Illnesses" in this section).

Low—Low, Short and Squat Stature —(See "Low Stature" under Low).

Lower Parts—Short and Small—(See "Parts" under Lower).

Mean, Short Stature — (See "Short Stature" under Mean).

Medium Stature—(See Medium).

Members—(See "Brevity" under Members).

Middle-Sized—Short, Thick, and Strong Body — (See "Middle Stature" under Middle).

Mother — (See "Short Life" under Mother).

Neck—(See "Short" under Neck).

Nose—(See "Short" under Nose).

Pale—Sickly, Pale, Short, and Fleshy —♓ on the Asc. (See Pale).

Plump — Short, Mean, Plump, Fat Stature—(See Plump).

Rather Short Body — (See "Body" in this section).

Short Body — Short Stature — (See "Body" in this section).

Shortened—The Disease Is Shortened — (See Curtailed; "Illnesses" in this section).

Sickly—Sickly, Pale, and Short—(See "Pale" in this section).

Sight—Short-Sighted—(See "Myopia" under Sight).

Slender — Short and Slender — (See Slender).

Squab—Short, Squab Figure—☿ in ♋ in partile asp. the Asc., short, squab stature. (See "Low Stature" under Low; "Parts" under Lower; Plump, Squab, Squatty).

Squat—Short, Low, and Squat Body— (See "Low Stature" under Low; Squab, Squat).

Stature—Short Stature—(See "Body" in this section; Fat; "Low Stature" under Low; Mean, Plump, Squab, Squatty).

Strong — Short, Strong, Middle-Sized, Thick Body—♉ on the Asc. (See "Middle Stature" under Middle).

Temper — A Short Temper — (See "Short" under Temper).

Thick — Thick, Short Body — (See "Fleshy Body" under Fleshy; "Middle Stature" under Middle; Thick).

Well-Set and Short — Born under ♂. (See Well-Set).

SHOTGUN WOUNDS—Shot To Death—Injury by Gunshot — Danger by Fire Arms—(See Gunshot).

SHOULDERS — Shoulder Joint — The Arms and Shoulders are ruled by ☿, ♊, and the 3rd H.. The Shoulders are under the external rulership of ♊. The Scapula, or Shoulder Blade, is under the internal rulership of the ♊ Sign. The hinder part of the Shoulders is ruled by the 5th H. Many of the influences mentioned in this Article also apply to the Arms. (See Arms).

Accidents — All Accidents and Hurts To—♊ signifies; ♂ afflicted in ♊. (See "Accidents" under Arms).

Affected—According to Table 196 in Simmonite's Arcana, the shoulders are affected when the ☉ is in ♎; the ☽ in ♊, ♌, ♍; ♄ in ♓; ♃ in ♉; ♂ in ♑; ♀ in ♋ or ♐.

All Diseases In—Signified by the 3rd H. All diseases in the hinder part of the shoulders are signified by the 5th H.

Arms — (See the various paragraphs under Arms).

Auriga's Right Shoulder — (See Auriga).

Bent Forward—(See Stooping).

Broad Shoulders—Strong Shoulders—Thick and Powerful Shoulders — ♈ gives; ♈ on the Asc., thick, broad, and powerful; ♉ gives, and with ♉ on the Asc.; ♌ on the Asc., broad and well-set, and powerful; ♏ on the Asc.; ♄ ascending at B.; ♄ Sig. in ♌ or ♏ in Hor'y Q.; ♄ in ♏ in partile asp. the Asc.; ♄ in ♌, partile the Asc., broad, round shoulders; ♃ in the Asc.; ♂ Sig. of the person in Hor'y Q.; characteristic of ♂ people; ☿ Sig. in ♏. (See "Large" in this section).

Clavicle—(See the paragraphs under Clavicle).

Cramp In—♅ in ♊. (See Cramps).

Crooked Shoulders—♄ ascending at B. (See Crooked).

Cuts To—(See "Arms" under Cuts).

Diseases In — (See "All Diseases In", "Diseases Of", under Arms; "All Diseases In", and the various paragraphs in this section).

Dislocation — ♄ afflicted in ♊. (See Dislocations).

Eruptions On—♂ afflicted in ♊ in the 6th H. (See Eruptions).

Gout In — (See "Shoulders" under Gout).

Granulations — In Shoulder Joint — ♄ afflicted in ♊ or ♐. (See Granulations; "Hardening" under Joints; Synovial).

Hardening—In Shoulder Joint—(See "Hardening" under Joints; "Granulations" in this section).

Hinder Part — Of the Shoulders — All Diseases In—Signified by the 5th H.

Hurts To — (See "Accidents" in this section).

Infirmities In—(See "Diseases In" in this section).

Joint—Shoulder Joint—(See Dislocation, Gout, Granulations, Pain, in this section).

Lameness In—♄ afflicted in ♊ or the 3rd H. (See Gout, Rheumatism, in this section).

Large Shoulders — Large and Uncomely — ♉ on the Asc. gives large shoulders; ♊ gives large and uncomely shoulders if ♄ or ♃ also be setting. (See "Broad" in this section).

Marks On—Moles On—Malefics in ♊ or the 3rd H. (See Marks, Moles).

Muscles Of — Disorders In — (See "Muscles" under Arms; Pains, Rheumatic, in this section).

Nerve Pains In—☿ afflicted in ♊. (See "Pains" under Arms; "Nerves", "Pains", under Hands).

Orion—Shoulders of—(See Orion).

Pains In—☉ ☌ ♂ in ♊; ♄ or ♂ in ♊; ☿ afflicted in ♊, nerve pains in. (See Gout, Granulations, Joint, Lameness, Nerve Pains, Rheumatic, Stiffness, in this section).

Rheumatic Pains In—(See "Rheumatism" under Arms).

Round Shoulders — ♓ influence tends to unless the ☉ be rising; ♓ on the Asc.; 1st face of ♊ on the Asc.; in Hor'y Q. ♄ Sig. in ♌, broad and round. (See "Downward Look" under Look; Stooping; "Stoop" in this section).

Running Pains—(See "Running" under Arms; "Flying Pains" under Flying).

Scapula—Fracture of—♂ afflicted in ♊.

Scars On—(See "Marks" in this section).

Stiffness In—Stiffness and Pain—♄ or ♂ afflicted in ♊.

Stoop Shoulders — Stooping Body — ♄ ascending at B., and afflicted, the head and shoulders stooping; ♄ Sig. in ♌ Hor'y); the ✱ or △ aspects to the ☉ tend to round shoulders and stooping; the 2nd face of ♉ on the Asc.; ♓ influence tends to a stooping gait, and to hold the head downward when walking; ♓ on the Asc., round and stooped, with crooked body, head bent forward, the shoulders thick and round, and with an ill figure. (See "Round" in this section).

Strong Shoulders — (See "Broad" in this section).

Thick Shoulders — Thick and Powerful—Broad—♈ on the Asc., thick and powerful; ♓ on the Asc., thick and round. (See Broad, Round, in this section).

Uncomely — Large and Uncomely — (See Broad, Large, Round, Stoop, in this section).

Warts On—(See "Arms" under Warts).

Weakness In—The ☽ afflicted in ♊ or ♍. (See "Weakness" under Arms).

Well-Set — (See "Broad" in this section).

SHREWDNESS—Shrewd—Sagacious—Artful—Cunning—Sly, etc.—Are strong characteristics of the ♋ sign, and ☿, and often used for all purposes when ♋ and ☿ are sorely afflicted by malefics at B., and by dir.; the ☽ Sig. in ♊, crafty and subtle to excess; the ☽ Sig. □ or ☍ ☿, a low cunning, and often applied to dishonest purposes; ♄ Sig. □ or ☍ ♀ or ☿; ♄ Sig. ☌ ☿, subtle and crafty; ♂ Sig. ☌, □, or ☍ ♄; ♂ Sig. in ♑; ♂ Sig. in ♓, sly and artful if in terms of ☿; ♂ Sig. ✱ or △ ☿, crafty; ♀ Sig. ☌, □, or ☍ ♄; ☿ Sig. in ♊, cunning; ☿ Sig. in ♈; ♂ Sig. ☌ ♄, calculating and covetous; ☿ in the 12th H., active in schemes, plots, and intrigues; ☿ Sig. □ or ☍ ♄; ☿ or ♂ afflicted in ♊. (See Cheating, Deceitful, Dishonest, Gambling, Pettifogging, Plots, Schemes, Thieves, Treachery, etc.).

SHRINKAGE — Shrinking — Due to the atonic action of ♄. Also caused by ♆.

Arms—♆ or ♄ in signs which rule the Arms, Hands, and Legs tends to shrinking and withering of these parts. (See Withering).

Brain — (See "Shrinkage" under Brain).

Limbs—Withering and Shrinkage of —(See "Arms" in this section; "Arms" under Limbs).

Organs or Tissues — Shrinkage of — ♄ influences and afflictions, and with ♄ in the sign or house ruling such parts. (See Atrophy, Contractions, Diminished, Emaciation, Hardening, Old Age, Remote, Removal, Undersized, Undeveloped, Wasting, Withering, Wrinkles, etc.).

SHUFFLING GAIT—(See Gait, Walk).

SHY—Bashful—A ♄ influence; ♄ in the 1st H. at B. (See Bashfulness).

SIALAGOG—(See Pellitory, Saliva).

SICCATION—Drying Up—Lack of Moisture—(See Xeransis).

SICK—The Sick—

Care and Cure Of — Success In — ♃ well-aspected by the ☽; ♃ well-aspected in ♓; lord of the employment in ♏, and well-aspected; the 6th face of ♋ culminating on the M.C. (See the various paragraphs under Healers).

Escape—The Sick Will Hardly Escape —(See "Sick" under Escape).

Headaches — (See "Sick Headache" under Headache).

Improved—The Sick Improved—(See Amelioration; "Better" under Disease; Moderation, Recovery, Recuperation).

Industries — Success In Industries Connected with the Sick — ♂ well-aspected in ♍. (See "Health Foods" under Food; "Specialties" under Healers; Hospitals, Hygiene, Sanitation).

Sick Bed — Confined In — (See "Sick Bed" under Confinement).

Sickly—(See Invalids, Sickly).

Sickness—(See Disease, Sickness).

State of the Sick — The nature and state of the planet from which the ☽ is separating at decumbiture shows the cause and nature of the disease, and the state of the sick. (See Acute, Chronic, Curable, Grievous; "Heavy and Sad Sickness" under Heavy; Incurable, Long Diseases, Quality, Recovery, Relapse, Resolution, Short Diseases, Worse, etc.).

Worse — The Sick Become Worse — (See Worse).

SICKLY — Sickly Looking — Pale — Debilitated and Wan Look—An Unhealthy Aspect — Sickly Persons — Vitality Low, etc.—

Body—Sickly Body—(See "Constitution" in this section).

Brothers Sickly—(See "Health Poor" under Brothers).

Children — (See "Sickly" under Children).

Complexion — (See "Sickly" under Complexion).

Constitution — Sickly Constitution — Sickly Body—Weak Body—Low Vitality—Debilitated Look—Ill-Health All Thru Life — The Quadrant from the Autumnal Equinox to the Winter Solstice, tends to produce weak and sickly persons; the ☉ or ☽ in the Autumnal Signs ♎, ♏, or ♐, or with these signs upon the Asc., the constitution is inclined to be weak and sickly; the ☉ or ☽ □ or ☍ ♄ at B., and by dir.; the ☉ or ☽ Sig. to the ☌ or ill-asps. ♄ by dir.; the ☉ Sig. □ or ☍ ♄ and ♄ in the Asc.; the ☉ afflicted by ♄ in a male horoscope; the ☉ ☌ ♄ in the 1st H. in ♋ or ♑ with males; the ☉ afflicted in the 6th H.; the ☉ Sig. in ♋, an unhealthy aspect; the ☉ Sig. in ♑; the ☽ Sig. ☌ ☉; the ☽ combust, applying to the ☌ ☉, sickly and short-lived; the ☽ Sig. □ or ☍ ☉, and especially if the ☽ be sepr. from the ☍; the ☽ Sig. □ or ☍ ♄ at B.; the ☽ carried to, or conjoined with the ☉ at B. in any part of the horoscope; the ☽ decr. in light, sepr. from ♄ and applying to ♀; ☽ sepr. from ♃ and applying to ♂ in a nocturnal nativity, and the ☽ incr. in light; ☽ decreasing, separating from ♂ and apply. to ♃; the ☽ afflicted in ♋; the ☽ or ☉ ☌ ♄ or ♂ in the 8th H., and the hyleg afflicted by malefics; ♄ in the 10th H., and afflicting the hyleg; ♄ Sig. ☌ ☉ or ☽ at B.; ♄ Sig. in ♋; ♄ in ♋, partile asp. the Asc., thin, pale face; ♄ in an angle, occi. of the ☉ and ori. of the ☽; ♃ Sig. in ♋ or ♑; ♃ in ♑, partile Asc., weak, small and sickly; ♀ Sig. to the ☌ ☉ and the ☉ ill-dignified at B.; born under ♀ influence the constitution is usually not strong, and the habits of living tend to ill-health and short life; ♀ Sig. in ♋ or ♑; ♀ Sig. ☌ ☉, too sickly to make much exertion; ♀ in ♑ in partile the Asc., pale, sickly, and thin visage; ☿ Sig. in ♑, sickly and feeble due to worry and melancholy; ☿ in ♑ or ♓ in partile asp. the Asc.; ♋ on the Asc., and the ☽ in her fall; ♋, ♎, ♐, ♑, or ♓ on the Asc.; a ♓ disease, as ♓ is classed as a sickly sign; lord of the 1st H. applying to the ☌, □, or ☍ a malefic (Hor'y); lords of the 1st and 6th being in each other's houses, or afflicting each other, or if lord of the 1st be disposed of by lord of the 6th, or be in □ or ☍ ♄ or ♂, or be combust in the 6th, 7th, or 12th houses; malefics elevated above, and in evil asp. to the ruling planet. (See Anaemia; "Poor Blood" under Blood; Consumptions, Debility, Delicate; "Early Death" under Early; Emaciated, Feeble, Fragile, Frail; "Bad Health" under Health; "Ill-Favored Body" under Ill; "Ill-Health All Thru Life" under Ill-Health; "Short Life" under Life; "Malnutrition" under Nutrition; Pale; "Low" under Recuperation, Resistance, Vitality; "Red Blood" under Red; "Much Sickness" under Sickness; Unhealthy, Wastings; "Weak Body" under Weak; "Complexion" under White).

Face — Sickly Looking Face — (See "Sickly" under Face; Pale; "Complexion" under White).

Father—(See "Sickly" under Father).

Females Sickly — (See "Ill-Health", "Short Life", under Females).

Fleshy and Sickly Looking—♓ on the Asc. at B. (See Fleshy, Pale).

Males Sickly—(See "Bad Health For" under Males).

Men Sickly—(See "Ill-Health" under Men).

Mother—(See "Sickly" under Mother).

Pale and Sickly — (See Complexion, Constitution, in this section; Pale).

Relatives—(See "Sickly" under Relatives).

Secret Enemy Sickly — (See "Secret Enemies" under Enemies).

Short, Pale, and Sickly — ♓ on the Asc. at B. (See "Pale" under Short).

Sickly But Recovers — (See "Reared with Difficulty" under Children; "Sickly But Recovers" under Infancy).

Sister Sickly—(See Sister).

Summer—Sickly Summer—(See Summer).

Thin, Pale, and Sickly — ♀ in ♑ in partile asp. the Asc. (See "Thin Face" under Face; Pale, Thin).

Visage—Sickly Visage—(See "Face" in this section).

Women Sickly—(See "Ill Health" under Women).

Youth — Sickly In Youth — (See "Sickly" under Youth).

SICKNESS — Illness — Maladies — Ill-Health — Disease — Bodily Disorders, etc.—Sickness and health are largely determined by the conditions of the 4th, 6th, 8th and 12th houses and the planets therein at B., and the aspects to the ☉, ☽, Asc., M.C., and hyleg. The 6th H. and its lord signify the sickness, its nature, and the part, or parts of the body afflicted. Sickness, or accidents, usually come, or begin, when the ☉ or ☽ are transiting the place of the radical ♄ or ♂, or when ♄ or ♂ are on the places of the radical ☉, ☽, Asc., or in □ or ☍ to them by transit, or when a malefic is transiting the 6th H., and at these times more care and caution are necessary, and especially if the hyleg was afflicted at the previous New or Full ☽. A Total Eclipse of the ☉ falling on the place of the ☉ at B. is indicative of sickness. (See the paragraphs under Acute, Chronic, Disease, Distempers, Health, Ill-Health, Infirmities, etc.). The following subjects have to do with sickness, which see in the alphabetical arrangement when not considered here—

Abroad—(See "Sickness Abroad" under Abroad).

Absent Party—(See "Sick" under Absent Party).

Ailments; Amelioration; Animals — (See "Sickness Of" under Animals).

Appetites — Sickness from Over-Indulgence of — (See "Sickness" under Eating; "Disease" under Excesses; Indulgences; "Health Injured" under Men; "Passional Excesses" under Passion, etc.).

Arouse — Difficult to Arouse from Sickness — Many planets in common signs, or such signs on the angles at B. (See Rouse).

Begins—Sickness Begins When, etc.—(See the Introduction to this Article; "Time of the Disease" under Disease).

Better—(See "Better" under Disease).

Blood — Sickness from Corrupt Blood —(See "Sickness" under Impure).

Body—The Body Alone Is Afflicted—(See "Afflicted" under Body).

Causes of Sickness — (See "Causes" under Disease).

Changes — Changes To Another Disease—(See "Changes" under Disease).

Children — Sickness of — Sickness Caused By — (See Parents, Sickness, Unhealthy, Worries, under Children).

Chronic Sickness — (See Chronic, Incurable, Invalids, Lingering Diseases, Long Diseases, Prolonged, Slow, Tedious, etc.).

Colds—Sickness From—(See Colds).

Complications; Continued Sickness — (See Chronic, Consumptions, Continuity, Course, Duration; "Low Fevers" under Fever; Incurable, Invalids, Long Diseases, Permanent, Tedious, Wastings, etc.).

Course of the Disease—(See Course).

Crises; Curable; Danger of Sickness — Liable To — Sickness Threatened — Weak Body—Vitality Low—The ☉ to the mundane ☌ ♄ may cause great sickness, and especially with males; the ☉ to the ☌ ♄ by dir. in the Zodiac, or mundane; the ☉ to the ☌, □, or ☍ the ☽ by dir.; the ☉ joined with Antares, Aldebaran, Bellatrix, Caput Algol, Hercules, Regulus, South Scale, or any eminent star of the nature of ♂, extreme sickness; the ☉ directed to stars in the Lion, Goat's Back, the South Scale, Knee and Right Leg of Ophiucus, Left Shoulder and Right Arm of Aquaries causes sickness; the ☉ ☌ the Asc. by dir.; malefics elevated above the ☉ or ☽ (see Elevated); the ☽ to the □ or ☍ ☉ in Zodiac or mundane; the ☽ weak and afflicted at B., and ☌ the Asc. by dir.; the ☽ to the □ or ☍ ♂ by dir., all kinds of sickness; the ☽ to the ☌ the ☉ or Asc. by dir.; the ☽ to the place of Hercules; the ☽ to the □ or ☍ the ☉, ♄, or ♂ by dir.; the Lights joined to the Whale's Jaw; ♄ ☌ ♃ at B.; ♄ ☌ the Asc. by dir.; ♄ afflicted in the 6th H.; ♃ Sig. ☌ the ☉, and ♃ combust, is an evil familiarity and denotes sickness; ♂ and ☿ both ℞ are a mark of sickness, says Placidus; ♂ afflicted in the 7th H.; denoted by the 6th H.; lord of the 5th in the 6th, thru worries by children; lord of the 6th in the 2nd, sickness thru financial losses and waste of property; lord of the 6th by transit over the cusp the Asc.; the Pleiades rising, or with the ☉ or ☽, or directed to the Asc.; Pleiades, Hyades, Praesepe, Castor, Pollux, or The Ascelli directed to the Asc. or Lights; Antares, Aldebaran, Regulus, Frons Scorpio, Deneb, and the Shoulders of Orion, when directed to the ☉, ☽, or Asc., tend to sickness, trouble, and danger of violence; the Asc. to the □ or ☍ the ☉ or ♄ by dir. (See "Danger", "Liable To", "Threatened", under Disease; "Liable To" under Ill-Health; "Much Sickness" in this section).

Dangerous Sickness—(See Dangerous; "Arguments for Death" under Death; Fatal; "High Fever" under Fever; Grievous, Pernicious, Severe, Vehement, Violent, etc.).

Death—Death Averted—Illness Ends In Death — (See Averted; "Certain Death" under Death; Fatal).

Debility — (See "Sickness" under Debility).

Delirium; Disease—(See the various paragraphs under Disease).

Disgrace—Sickness From—(See Disgrace).

Disordered System—(See Disordered; "Disordered" under System).

Distempers; Distressful Sicknesses—(See Distress).

Duration; Eating — (See "Sickness" under Eating).

Elevated Planets—And Sickness—(See Elevated).

Endures Sickness — Does Not Complain—(See Complaining, Endures).

Enemy—Sickness of Secret Enemy—(See "Secret Enemies" under Enemies).

Escape—Little Escape from the Sickness — (See Escape, Fatal, Grievous, Prolonged, Tedious, etc.).

Excesses—Sickness From—(See "Sickness" under Excesses).

Exposure—Sickness From—(See Exposure).

Extraordinary Sickness — (See Extarordinary, Mysterious, Obscure, Peculiar, Strange, Unusual, etc.).

Extreme Sickness — The ☉ joined with Antares, Aldebaran, Bellatrix, Caput Algol, Hercules, Regulus, or any eminent star of the nature of ♂. (See Extreme).

Falling Sickness—(See Fainting).

Fatal Sickness—(See Fatal).

Father — (See "Sickness To" under Father).

Fatigue — Sickness From — (See Fatigue).

Feeble; Females — Sickness of — (See "Ill-Health" under Females).

Fevers; Fighting — Sickness From — (See Fighting).

Food — Sickness From — (See "Sickness" under Eating; "Rich Food" under Food).

Friends — Sickness On Account of — (See "Sickness" under Friends).

Fruit—Sickness from Eating Corrupt Fruit—(See Fruit).

Gluttony—Sickness From—(See Gluttony).

Great — The Great — Much Sickness Among — (See "The Great" under Great).

Greatness — Sickness by Aiming At and Striving For — (See "Greatness" under Great).

Grievous Sickness—(See Grievous).

Habits — Sickness From — (See "Bad Habits", "Diseases", under Habits).

Headache—(See "Sick Headache" under Headaches).

Health Bad — (See "Bad Health", "Periods of Bad Health", under Health).

Heavy Sickness—(See Heavy).

Humours; Hurts—Incurable Hurts—(See Incurable, Permanent).

Husband — (See "Sickness Of" under Husband).

Ill-Health — (See the paragraphs under Ill-Health).

Ill Treatment—Sickness From—Lord of the 6th in the 11th H. (See Cruel; "Poisoned" under Healers; "Beaten" under Prison).

Immunity from Sickness — (See Immunity).

Impairments; Imprisonment — Sickness From—Lord of the 6th in the 12th H. (See "Imprisonment" under Prison).

Increase — Sickness Will Increase — (See "Disease" under Increase).

Incurable; Indiscretions — Sickness From—(See Indiscretions).

Indisposition; Infirmities; Inheritance — Sickness from Loss of — (See Inheritance. Also for Hereditary Sicknesses see Heredity).

Invalids; Irregularities — (See "Sickness" under Irregularities).

Journeys — Sickness On — (See "Sickness" under Journeys, Travel, Voyages).

Less Liable — To Sickness — The ☉ angular, free from affliction, and also the hyleg not afflicted by malefics at B. (See Angles, Immunity; "Good" under Resistance, Vitality).

Life Spared — (See "Spared" under Life).

Lingering Sickness—(See Chronic, Lingering, Long Diseases, Prolonged, Slow Diseases, Tedious, Wastings).

Little Sickness — (See "Abundance", "Good Health", under Health; Immunity; "Good" under Resistance, Vitality).

Location — Sickness Due To — (See "Ill-Health" under Residence).

Long Sicknesses — (See "Lingering" in this section).

Long or Short Illnesses—(See "Long or Short" under Short).

Many Sicknesses—Lord of the Asc. in the 6th H., afflicted by lord of the 6th, and coming to combust, which will be apt to cling until death. Death will be more certain if the ☽ and lords of the 1st and 8th be in the 6th H. (See "Ill-Health All Thru Life" under Ill-Health; "Much Sickness" in this section).

Medicines — The Medicines Given In Sickness—(See "Sickness" under Medicines).

Melancholy — Sickness From — (See "Death By", "Diseases", under Melancholy).

Mental Disturbances—Sickness From —(See Anguish, Cares, Despondency, Disgrace, Distress, Melancholy; "Irritations" under Mental; Reverses, Ruin, Vexations, Worry, etc.).

Moderation; Mortal Illness — (See "Certain Death" under Death; Fatal).

Mortality — (See "Death Rate Augmented" under Mortality).

Mother—Sickness of—(See Mother).

Much Sickness — Much Sickness All Thru Life — Much Sickness Generally — Frequent Sicknesses — Many Sicknesses—The ☉ in ♋ or ♌ and much afflicted, and not well-placed in the houses in the map; the ☉ afflicted in the 6th H., and the ☽ afflicted in ♋ at the same time; the ☉ or ☽ □ ♄ at B.; the ☉ or ☽ Sig. □ or ☍ ♄ and ♄ be in the Asc.; the ☉ joined with Hercules, Antares, Hyades, Regulus, Aldebaran, or any eminent star of the nature of ♂; the ☉ or ☽ in the 6th or 12th H. in weak signs, and afflicted by malefics; the ☽ afflicted in ♑; the ☽ sepr. from ♄ and applying to ♂; the ☽ decr. and sepr. from ♃ and apply. to ♄; the ☽ sepr. from the ☉ and apply. to ♄ in a nocturnal geniture; ♅ afflicted in the 6th or 12th H.; ♄ afflicted in the 6th H., or afflicting the hyleg from this house; the Knee of Castor and Pollux, the Whale's Jaw, Little Bear, or Cynosura, joined with the ☉ in an angle, much sickness, disgrace, and great affliction and trouble; lord of the 1st in the 6th; lord of the 6th in the 1st, by the native's irregularities; lord of the 12th in the 6th; lord of the 6th ℞, combust, in ☌, □, or ☍ ♄ or ♂, or the lord of the 4th or 8th, there will be much sickness and great danger. (See Chronic; "Bad Health" under Health; "Ill-Health All Thru Life" under Ill-Health; Infirmities, Invalids; "Public Health Bad" under Public; Sickly; "Low" under Recuperation, Resistance, Vitality; "Weak Body" under Weak; "Many Sicknesses" in this section).

Nature of the Sickness — (See "Disease" under Nature; "Quality" in this section).

Nausea — Sickness At Stomach — (See Nausea).

Nobles—(See "Sickness" under Nobles).

Old Age — Dangerous Sickness In — (See "Dangerous" under Old Age).

Old Maladies Return—(See Return).

Over-Eating — Sickness From — (See "Sickness" under Eating).

Over-Indulgence—Of the Appetites—Sickness From — (See "Over-Indulgence" under Appetites; "Diseases" under Excesses; Indulgences).

Painful Sickness—(See "Diseases" under Pain).

Passional Nature — Sickness from Over-Indulgence of — (See Amorous; "Health Injured" under Men; "Health Suffers" under Opposite Sex; "Passional Excesses" under Passion; "Diseases" under Sex; Venery, etc.).

Past Sicknesses — The times of possible past sicknesses, or great affliction, can be obtained by looking back thru the Planetary Tables, and noting the times when the vital centers of the map, such as the ☉, ☽, Asc., M.C., Hyleg, or 6th H., were under the serious afflictions of the malefics by transit, direction, or progression, and also by noting the general strength or weakness of the radix. (See "Judgment of the Disease", "Time of the Disease", under Disease; "Periods of Bad Health" under Health).

Peculiar Sicknesses—(See Peculiar).

Periodic Sicknesses—(See Periodic).

Periods of Bad Health—(See this subject under Health).

Pleasure — Sickness by Excess of — (See "Disease", "Sickness", under Pleasure).

Poison—Sickness From—(See Poison).

Prolonged Sickness — (See Chronic, Heavy, Lingering, Prolonged, Tedious).

Property — Waste and Loss of Property, and Sickness By—(See "Sickness" under Property).

Public Health Bad — (See this subject under Public).

Quality of the Sickness — Nature of the Disease — Indicated by the 6th H.

and its conditions. In Hor'y Q. the Significators in fiery signs, and a fire sign on the Asc. and 6th H., indicate feverish and hot complaints, hectic fevers, erysipelas, etc. The Sigs. in earthy signs, and an earthy sign on the Asc. and 6th H., signify chronic, tedious and long diseases, intermittent fevers, ague, and such diseases as proceed from consumptions or melancholy. Airy signs on the Asc. and 6th H. at B., or decumb., or the Sigs. in airy signs, indicate cutaneous diseases, gout, corrupt blood, scrofula, etc. Water signs on the Asc. and 6th H. at B., or at decumb., or with the Sigs. in watery signs at the beginning of an illness, show coughs, stomach disorders, and diseases which proceed from moisture and cold. The planet from which the ☽ is sepr. at decumb. shows the nature and quality of the disease, the state of the sick, and also the cause of the sickness. The sign descending at B., or on the cusp the 6th H., shows the nature and quality of the disease. Thus if the sign be ♈, the head is affected; if ♉, the neck and throat, etc. The 6th H., its lord, and planets in the 6th H. at B., if any, describe the nature of the disease, and especially if they afflict the ☉, ☽, or lord of the Asc. The lord of the 6th H. afflicted indicates the nature of the disease. (See "Causes" under Disease; Directions, Events, First House, Hyleg, Malefics; "Disease" under Nature; Quality, Sixth House, Transits, Type, Virgo, etc.).

Quarrels—Sickness From—(See "Sickness" under Quarrels).

Raving During Sickness — (See Raving).

Recovery — Will Recover — Will Not Recover—(See Recovery).

Recuperation; Relapses;

Remarkable Features — Of the Sickness—(See "Diseases" under Extraordinary).

Resistance; Rest — Has No Rest In Sickness—(See Rest).

Sad and Heavy Sickness—(See "Heavy and Sad" under Heavy).

Sea — Sickness At Sea — (See "Sickness" under Voyages).

Secret Enemy — Sickness of — (See "Secret Enemies" under Enemies).

Serious Sickness—(See Serious).

Servants — Sickness of — (See Servants).

Severe Sickness—(See Severe).

Shame and Disgrace—Sickness From —(See Disgrace).

Short Sicknesses — Short or Long Sicknesses — Sickness On Short Journeys—(See "Sickness" under Journeys; "Illnesses", "Long or Short", under Short).

Sick—The Sick—State of the Sick—(See Sick).

Sick Bed — Confined In — (See "Sick Bed" under Confinement; Invalids).

Sick Headache—(See Headaches).

Sickly — Pale — Weak — (See Feeble, Sickly, Pale; "Weak Body" under Weak).

Significators of Sickness — The ☉, ☽, Asc., lord of the Asc., and lords of the 6th and 12th Houses. The lords of the 4th and 8th H. are more the Sigs. of Death. In Hor'y Q. in rendering judgment as to the disease, its nature, etc., the 1st and 6th Houses, their lords, the Lights and their disposition, are to be taken. (See "Significators" under Disease).

Signs of Sickness—(See "Signs of Ill-Health" under Ill-Health).

Stomach—Sickness At—(See Nausea; "Sickness" under Stomach; Vomiting).

Strange Sicknesses—(See Strange).

Succumbs Easily—To Disease—♍, ♑, or ♓ on the Asc. at B., and the hyleg severely afflicted by malefics. (See Feeble, Frail; "Low" under Recuperation, Resistance, Vitality; Succumbs; "Weak Body" under Weak).

Suffers Much—In Sickness—♌ on the Asc. at B. (See Anguish; "High Fever" under Fever; Fierce, Painful Disease, Poignant, Sharp, Severe, Suffering, Violent Diseases, etc.).

Sure to Come — The Sickness Almost Sure to Come — The ☽ hyleg, and to the ☌, P., ☐, or ☍ ♄ by dir., and especially if the direction fall in the 6th H. (See Directions; "Certain", "Time Of", under Disease; Events; "Periods of Bad Health" under Health; "Periods of Ill-Health" under Ill-Health).

Tedious Sickness — (See Chronic, Lingering, Long Diseases, Prolonged, Slow, Tedious, Wastings, etc.).

Terminates Quickly — (See "Disease Will Soon End" under End; Quick Diseases, Short Diseases, Termination).

Threatened — Sickness Threatened — (See "Threatened" under Disease; "Danger Of" in this section).

Thrives and Lives — Thru Serious Sickness—(See "Stamina Good" under Infancy; "Good" under Recuperation, Resistance, Vitality; "Lives Thru" under Serious).

Time of the Sickness — (See Directions; "Time Of" under Disease).

Travel — Sickness During — Sickness Resulting From — (See Fatigue; "Health" under Journeys; "Sickness" under Ships, Travel, Voyages).

Treatment—Of Sickness—(See Antipathy, Cure; "Treatment" under Disease; Drugs, Healers, Ill-Health, Incurable, Medicines, Operations, Remedies, Subluxations, Sympathy, Treatment, etc.).

Uncommon Sicknesses—(See Extraordinary, Mysterious, Obscure, Peculiar; "Diseases" under Psychic; Strange, Uncommon).

Vehement Sickness—(See Vehement).

Vexations—Sickness From—(See Vexations).

Violent Sickness—(See "High Fevers" under Fever; Fierce, Fulminating, Painful Diseases, Severe, Sharp, Swift, Vehement, Violent, etc.).

Vitality Low—Sickness From — (See Anaemia, Debility, Emaciation, Feeble, Infirm, Invalids, Malignant, Morbid; "Malnutrition" under Nutrition; "Low" under Recuperation, Resistance, Stamina, Vitality; "Weakened" under Strength; "Lack Of" under Tone; Wastings; "Weak Body" under Weak).

Vulnerable Spots—Parts Predisposed to Disease—(See Vulnerable).

War—Much Sickness and Want In—(See War).

Weak Body—(See "Weak Body" under Weak).

Wife—(See "Sickness" under Wife).

Women—Sickness of—Sickness Caused By—(See "Sickness" under Women).

Worry—Sickness Caused By—(See Worry).

Worse—The Sickness Worse—(See Worse).

Young Men—Sickness of Prevalent—(See "Young Men" under Young; "Death" under Youth).

SIDEREAL BODY—The Astral Body—Paracelsus says "Man is related to the Stars by reason of his Sidereal Body", called the Astral Body by Modern Astro-Psychologists. (See Astral Body; "Desire Body" under Desire).

SIDES—Sides of the Body—Strongly ruled by ♌ and the 5th H. The Sides are denoted by the 5th H. Dr. Broughton says the Sides are ruled by ♃.

All Diseases In—Afflictions in ♌, the 5th H., and are signified by the 5th H.; ♌ diseases.

Narrow Sides—♌ gives. (See Ribs, Trunk).

SIGHING—Yawning—A Prolonged Deep Inspiration—(See "Sighs" under Breathing).

SIGHT—Eyesight—Vision—The Sense of Vision—The Sight is ruled by the ☉, ☽, ♅, ♄, ♀ and ☿, and is also under the internal rulership of the ♒ sign. The ether, thru which light is transmitted, is ruled by ♅ and ♒. The vibrations which give sight are originated by ☿, and the Blind Spot in the eye is blind because it is not responsive to the etheric Mercurial vibrations. The ♒ sign has affinity with the sense of Sight, and it is the sign which corresponds to the etheric vibrations, and this sign when on the Asc. at B. is especially closely connected with Sight. The Nebulous Areas greatly afflict the Sight of Man, and the influence of ♆ is said to be largely with these Areas, as his vibration is very ethereal. The Pleiades especially are a Nebulous Cluster which tend to blindness, and many disorders of Sight, when with the ☉ or ☽ at B., or by dir. In the Hindu System of Astrology the 2nd H. rules the Eyes and Sight. (See Aquarius, Ether, Eyes; "Rays" under Light; Nebulous, Neptune, Uranus). The following subjects have to do with Sight, or Disorders of Sight, which see in the alphabetical arrangement when not more fully considered here—

Accommodation—Errors of—(See Accommodation, Hyperopia, Myopia, Presbyopia, in this section).

Affliction to Sight—The ☽ to the ☌ or ill-asp. ♂, and ♂ in ♌ aspected by the ☉ or ♄, or ♂ be near Cor Scorpio. (See the various paragraphs in this section).

Artifice—Blindness By—(See "Artifice" under Blindness).

Asthenopia—(See "Painful", "Weak", in this section).

Astigmatism; Bad Eyes—(See "Bad Eyes" under Eyes).

Blepharitis—(See Eyelids).

Blindness; Both Eyes—Loss of—Injury To—(See "Both Eyes" under Eyes).

Bloodshot Eyes—(See "Bloodshot" under Eyes).

Cataracts; Clouded Sight—The ☉ or ☽ with Nebulous Stars and Clusters at B. (See "Film" under Blindness; Cataracts; "Cornea" under Eyes; Specks; the various paragraphs in this section).

Cornea—Disorders of—(See Cornea).

Crossed Eyes—(See "Strabismus" under Eyes).

Crystallization—Of the Muscles and Nerves of the Eyes—The ☉ or ☽ ☌ Nebulous Stars, and at the same time in □ or ☍ ♄, tends to, and to destroy the sight. (See Crystallization).

Danger to Sight—The ☉ and ☽ with Nebulous Stars at B., and especially in ☌ or ☍ Antares, Aldebaran, The Ascelli, or the Pleiades. The central degrees of the mutable signs afflicted, and when the Lights, or those areas are much involved by malefics, or with Nebulous Stars, and especially in angles, there is much danger to the sight. Afflictions to ☿ tend to endanger the sight, as ☿ is ruler of the nervous system, and also ☿ originates the vibrations which give sight. The ♒ sign on the Asc., and when the ruler of the Decan. on the Asc. is in the 2nd H. and afflicted by malefics. In the Hindu System of Astrology, the 2nd H. rules the eyes and sight. (See the various paragraphs in this section).

Day Blindness—Nyctalopia—Vision Best At Night—Caused by ♆. (See "Day Blindness" under Blindness).

Defective Sight—Or Vision—Bad Vision—The ☉ and ☽ in signs of their fall, as the ☉ in ♎, and the ☽ in ♏, and afflicted; the ☉ or ☽ with, or near the Pleiades, Ascelli, or Antares, and afflicted by any planet, the cause differing according to the afflicting planet; the ☽ unfortunate, and with Nebulous Stars; the ☽ to the place of Praesepe, great defect in the sight, and often blindness, and especially if the Lights are with Nebulous Stars. Defects in sight are especially ☽ diseases. Case of Defective Sight—See "Sight Defective", No. 684, in 1001 N.N. (See the various paragraphs in this section).

Destroyed—Sight Destroyed—(See Blindness; "Decay Of" under Optic; "Crystallization" in this section).

Dim Sight—Dim Vision—Nearly Blind—(See "Nearly Blind" under Blind; "Dim Eyes" under Eyes).

Diplopia—Double Vision—May be caused by afflictions in ♋, and due to indigestion. Caused by Subluxations at SP (7D). Also caused by Crossed Eyes. (See "Muscae", "Strabismus", under Eyes).

Disordered Sight—(See Affliction To, Defective, and the various paragraphs in this section).

Disturbances—Visual Disturbances—(See Migraine; "Diplopia" and the various paragraphs in this section).

Dots and Specks—Before the Eyes—(See "Muscae Volitantes" under Eyes).

Double Vision—(See "Diplopia" in this section).

Effective Sight—(See "Good" in this section).

Eyelids — Eyelashes — Sight Injured by Inverted Lashes—(See "Blepharitis" under Eyelids).

Eyes—(See "Sight", and the various paragraphs under Eyes).

Eyestrain — Tending to Blindness —(See "Eyestrain" under Eyes).

Far-Sighted — (See "Hyperopia" in this section).

Father — Injury To Sight of — (See "Eyes" under Father).

Feeble Vision — (See "Weak" in this section).

Film—Blindness from White Film—(See "Film" under Blindness).

Focus — Defect of Focus — Usually caused by ♊ influence. (See Accommodation, Unequal, and the various paragraphs in this section).

Glaucoma—Blindness By—(See Glaucoma).

Good Sight — Effective Sight — Keen Vision—Perfect Sight—A Quick Eye—Sharp Eyes, etc.—♊, ♒, or ♑ on the Asc. (See "Good Eyes" under Eyes).

Hemianopia — Blindness of One-Half the Visual Field—Defective Vision In the Outer Half of the Eyes—Afflictions in ♈ and ♉, and with subluxations at MCP (4C).

Hyperopia—Hypermetropia—Far-Sighted—A ☽ disease; the ☽ afflicted in ♈; ♅ and ♀ afflictions to the ☉ or ☽, a relaxing action on the tissues, tendons and muscles, tending to a flattened crystalline lens, relaxed Ciliary muscles, and a distant focus. Myopia is the opposite condition to this. (See "Myopia" in this section).

Infants—Sight of—(See "Sight" under Infancy).

Infirmities of Sight — (See Defective, Weak, and the various paragraphs in this section).

Injury to Sight — (See Accidents, Artifice, Burning, under Blindness; "Accidents To" under Eyes).

Keen Vision — ♊ gives when on the Asc., and not afflicted. (See "Good" in this section).

Left Eye — Sight of Affected — (See "Left Eye" under Eyes).

Loss of Sight—Danger of—The ☽ to the ☌ ♂ by dir. (See Blindness; "Accidents" under Eyes; "Decay" under Optic; Crystallization, Danger, and various paragraphs in this section).

Migraine—Causing Visual Disturbances—(See Migraine).

Muscae Volitantes—Specks or Threads Before the Eyes—(See "Muscae" under Eyes).

Muscles of Eyes—Crystallization of, and Impairing the Sight—(See "Crystallization" in this section).

Myopia—Short Sight—Near-Sighted—The ☉ in any part of the heavens conjoined with the Pleiades; the ☉ rising in the Asc. in ♉ ☽ decreasing in the 7th H., and in the ♒ and ♑ signs; the ☽ in ♈ or ♉, and afflicted by ♆; a ☽ disease; the ☽ Sig. ☌ ☉, myopia from too much reading; the ☽ rising in ♍, □ the ☉ and ♂, and applying to ☌ ♅, existed in a case; ♆ in ♈; ♆ in ♈ in the 6th H.; ♆ in ♈, and afflicting the ☽, Asc., or hyleg; strong afflictions to ☿, the ruler of the nervous system; many planets in ♒ and ♑ in ☌ or ☍, and these signs on the Asc. and Desc., tends to extreme myopia and astigmatism. Also caused by Subs at MCP (4C). Cases of Myopia — See "Sight Defective", No. 684, and "Spinal Curvature", No. 838, in 1001 N.N. Case No. 684 is Myopic in one eye, and Hyperopic in the other. Also see Cases in Chap. XIII in Daath's Medical Astrology.

Near-Sighted—(See "Myopia" in this section).

Nearly Blind — (See "Nearly Blind" under Blindness; Cataracts; "Defects In", "Dim Eyes", under Eyes).

Nebulous Stars—Sight Impaired By—(See Nebulous).

Nerves of Eyes—Sight Affected By—(See "Decay" under Optic; Retina; "Crystallization" in this section).

Night Vision—Vision Best At Night—(See "Day Blindness" under Blindness).

Nyctalopia — (See "Day Blindness" under Blindness).

Obstructions To Sight — (See "Film" under Blindness; Cataracts; "Growths", "Obstructions", under Eyes; Glaucoma; Crystallization, Muscae, and the various paragraphs in this section).

Old Age Vision — (See "Presbyopia" in this section).

One Eye—Blindness In—Myopia In—(See "One Eye" under Blindness; "Myopia" in this section).

One-Half Vision—(See "Hemianopia" in this section).

Ophthalmia—(See Conjunctivitis; "Ophthalmia" under Infancy).

Optic Nerve—Decay of—(See Optic).

Painful Vision — Asthenopia — Afflictions in ♉; Subs at MCP (4C). (See "Weak" in this section).

Peculiarity of Vision—Caused by ♆; ♆ afflicting the ☉ or ☽; ♆ with one of the Nebulous Clusters and afflicting the ☉ or ☽.

Penetrating Sight — (See "Penetrating" under Eyes).

Perfect Sight—(See "Good Sight" in this section).

Pleiades — Sight Affected By — (See Pleiades).

Presbyopia — Old Age Vision — Lack of the Power of Accommodation — Failure of the Ciliary Muscle to Contract for Accommodation—♄ influence, and due to the deposits and crystallizing influences of ♄, which take place over the whole body with age; ♄ afflicted in ♈, especially aggravated cases, and require a strong convex glass. Presbyopia may be considered an aggravated condition of Hyperopia, and the conditions tending to cause Hyperopia will also apply here. (See Crystallization, Hyperopia, in this section).

Quick Sight — (See "Good Eyes", "Quick Eye", under Eyes; "Good Sight" in this section).

Reading—Sight Disordered By—(See "Reading and Study" under Blindness; "Eyestrain" under Eyes).

Retina—Disorders of—(See Retina).

Right Eye—Sight of Impaired—Loss of—(See "Right Eye" under Right).

Sharp Sight—(See "Sharp Eyes" under Eyes).

Short Sight — (See "Myopia" in this section).

Specks Over Eyes — (See "Muscae" under Eyes; Specks).

Squint — Crossed Eyes — (See "Strabismus" under Eyes).

Stomach — Disturbances of Vision from Stomach Disorders—(See "Muscae" under Eyes; "Diplopia" in this section).

Strabismus — Crossed Eyes — (See "Strabismus" under Eyes).

Study—Sight Impaired by Too Much Reading and Study — (See "Reading" in this section).

Threads Before Eyes — Dots and Specks—(See "Muscae Volitantes" under Eyes).

Total Blindness — (See "Total" under Blindness).

Unequal Sight—Caused by the ☉ and ☽ in strong mutual affliction to each other. Also as the right and left eyes are under different planetary rulership, the planetary afflictions to these rulers may cause inequalities in the sight so that the two eyes do not focus in harmony. Thus there may be myopia in one eye, and hyperopia in the other. Case—See "Myopia" in this section. This is also caused by Strabismus, and where one eye loses its power for want of proper use. Can also be caused by decay of optic nerve, and various disease conditions which may affect only one side of the body. (See "Strabismus" under Eyes; "Eyes" under Left, Right; "Decay" under Optic).

Weak Sight—Weak Vision—Asthenopia—Feeble Vision—Weak or Painful Vision—A ☉ disease, and caused by afflictions to the ☉; the ☉ or ☽ with Nebulous Stars at B., and afflicted by malefics or ☋; the ☉ or ☽ in the Western Angle, and conjoined with the Pleiades, or the ☉ in any part of the heavens conjoined with the Pleiades; the ☉ and ☽ in signs of their fall, as the ☉ in ♎, and the ☽ in ♏; the ☉ afflicted in ♎ or ♒; the ☉ ☌ ♄ in ♒; the ☉ ☌ ☋ in ♐ near Antares; the ☉ or ☽ afflicted by ♄, and at the same time the ☉ and ☽ afflict each other; the ☉ in ♎, and ♄ in ♈, weak eyes; one or both Lights afflicted by Nebulous Stars or malefics; the affliction of the ☉ or ☽ from angles by the malefics, and especially if the ☉ or ☽ be near the Pleiades; the ☉ or ☽ in □ or

☍ each other from angles; the ☉ and ☽ in ☍ from ♈ and ♎; the ☉ or ☽ in ♈, and afflicted by ♂; the ☽ occi. at B., and in evil asp. to ♂; the ☽ sepr. from the ☉ and applying to ♂ in a day nativity; the ☽ afflicted in ♈, or afflicting the hyleg therefrom; the ☽ afflicted in ♏; the Full ☽ rising at B.; ♅ ☌ Nebulous Stars, and in □ or ☍ the ☉ or ☽; ♅ afflicted in ♈; ♄ to the ☌ or ill-asps. the ☉ by dir.; the periodic direction of ♄ to the radical ☉; Fixed Stars of the nature of ♂ and the ☽ ascending at B.; malefics with Nebulous Stars in the 6th or 12th H., and afflicting the ☉ or ☽; in Hor'y Q., the Sig. with Nebulous Stars; the 3rd Decan. of ♒ on the Asc., ruled by the ☽; afflictions in ♉, and Subs at MCP (4C). (See Defective, Dim, Painful, and the various paragraphs in this section; Blindness; "Bad Eyes", "Weak Eyes", under Eyes).

Yellow Vision—(See Xanthopsia).

SIGMOID FLEXURE — The S-shaped portion of the Colon above the Rectum —Ruled by ♏. Some Authors also say it is ruled by ♄.

Disorders Of — ♄ or ♂ afflicted in ♏; Subs at PP (3, 4L). (See Colon).

SIGNATURE — Correspondences — The Law of—There are many resemblances in the Material World to parts and shapes in the human body, and also affinity between herbs, roots, minerals, metals, etc., and parts of the body. Thus the kidney-bean resembles the kidneys in shape. The convolutions of nuts resemble the convolutions of the brain. The coffee seed resembles the two cerebral lobes, etc. The bitterness of Nux Vomica is a good remedy in bile disorders. The subject of Signatures is considered quite fully in the book, "Astral Medicine", by Dr. Duz. (See Antipathy, Opposites, Remedies, Sympathy, Treatment, etc.).

SIGNIFICATORS—In the horoscope of birth the ☉, ☽, Asc., and Midheaven, are called Significators, as they are the vital points, or centers of the map, and afflictions to them mean more than to other places, and in the diagnosis and prognosis of disease the Significators should be examined first as to their strength or weakness. (See "Significators" under Disease, Form, Health. Also see Indicators).

SIGNS—Indicators—Symbols—

Children — Signs of — (See "Signs Of" under Children; Fruitful).

Death — Signs of — (See "Arguments For", "Certain Death", under Death).

Health—Signs of Good or Bad Health —(See "Bad Health", "Good Health", under Health).

Long Diseases—Signs of—(See "Diseases" under Long).

Pregnancy — Signs of—(See Conception, Pregnancy).

Recovery—Signs of—(See "Signs Of" under Recovery).

Short Diseases—Signs of—(See "Illnesses" under Short).

Zodiac—Signs of—(See the next Article).

SIGNS OF THE ZODIAC — There are twelve Signs of the Zodiac, as listed and divided today. In the early stages of Humanity, before the separation of the sexes, the ♍ and ♏ signs were united into one sign, but when the sexes were separated, these signs were separated and ♎ inserted between them. (See "Separation of the Sexes" under Sex). Each Sign of the Zodiac has a certain influence on the Mental and Physical Constitution of Man, and each sign rules a certain part, parts, or organs of the body, and with chief attention to the Sign rising upon the Eastern Horizon at B., which is called the Rising Sign. (See Ascendant, First House). The Signs are also closely affiliated with their corresponding Houses. Thus ♈ is in close sympathy with the First House; ♉ with the 2nd H.; ♊ with the 3rd H., etc. The following is a classified list of the Signs, showing their different qualities, characteristics, functions, and their various classifications, etc. Each Sign of the Zodiac is considered in an Article in the alphabetical arrangement of this book. See the following subjects in the alphabetical arrangement when they are only listed here—

Acid Signs — (See Acids; "Negative Signs" under Negative).

Air Signs—(See "Signs" under Air).

Alkaline Signs—(See Alkaline; "Positive Signs" under Positive).

Animal Signs — (See "Animal Signs" under Animal; Quadrupeds).

Aquarius Sign; Aries Sign;

Articulate Signs—(See Articulate).

Autumnal Signs—(See Autumnal).

Barren Signs — (See "Barren Signs" under Barrenness).

Bestial Signs—(See Beasts).

Bicorporeal Signs — (See Double-Bodied).

Bilious Signs—(See Bile).

Birds—Signs Which Give Forms Resembling Birds or Animals—(See "Animal Forms" under Monsters).

Bitter Signs—(See Bitter).

Brevity—Signs of—♋, ♑, and ♓, and when on the Asc. at B. tend to make the body shorter. (See Brevity).

Broken Signs—(See Broken).

Brutish Signs — (See Brutish; "Human Signs" under Human).

Cancer Sign; Capricorn Sign;

Cardinal Signs—(See Cardinal).

Changeable Signs—♊, ♌, ♍, ♎, ♐. (See Changeable; "Mutable Signs" under Mutable).

Choleric Signs—(See Choleric).

Cold Signs—The Earthy and Watery Signs—(See Cold).

Colors—The Colors ruled by the Signs are given under each Sign. (See "Colors" under Aries, Taurus, etc. Also see Colors).

Commanding Signs—(See Commanding).

Common Signs—(See "Mutable Signs" under Mutable).

Conditional Signs — (See "Constitutional" in this section).

Constitutional Signs — Conditional Signs — (See the Introduction under Constitution).

Crooked Signs—(See Broken, Crooked).

Cud-Chewing Signs—(See Ruminant).

Debility — Signs of Debility of the Planets—A Planet is in debility and detriment when in the opposite sign to its home sign at B. (See Lists of Debilities and Dignities of the Planets in the various Textbooks of Astrology. See "Debilities" under Planets in this book).

Decanates of Signs—(See Decanates).

Deformed Signs—Broken Signs—Imperfect Signs—(See Broken, Deformities, Imperfect).

Detriment — Planets In Detriment In Signs—(See "Detriment" under Planets).

Dignities—Of the Planets In the Signs —(See "Dignities" under Planets).

Distorted Signs — (See Broken, Crooked, Distortions).

Diurnal Signs—(See "Nocturnal Signs" under Night).

Domestic Signs—♋ and ♑. (See Cancer, Capricorn).

Double-Bodied Signs; Dry Signs—(See "Signs" under Dry).

Dumb Signs — Mute Signs — (See Dumb).

Earth Signs—(See "Earthy Signs" under Earth).

Eastern Signs—(See Eastern).

Effeminate Signs—(See "Signs" under Effeminate).

Electro-Negative Signs—Electro-Positive Signs — The masculine signs are electro-positive, and alkaline. The feminine signs are acid, and electro-negative.

Elemental Signs—Temperamental Signs—(See Elements).

Equinoctial Signs—(See Equinoxes).

Estival Signs—(See Summer).

Even Signs — The Feminine Signs — (See "Signs" under Female).

Exaltation—Planets Exalted In Signs — (See "Planets" under Exaltation; "Debilities" under Planets).

External Rulership—Of Signs—Each Sign of the Zodiac exerts an external, internal, and structural rulership over the part, or parts of the body ruled by such sign. Thus ♈ rules the head and face externally, the brain internally, and the cranium and facial bones structurally, and so on with each of the signs. These rulerships are given in each of the Articles on the Signs in this book. (See "Aries Rules" under Aries; "Taurus Rules" under Taurus).

Faces of Signs—There are six Faces of five degrees in each sign. (See Chap. IV, on "Faces of the Signs", in Simmonite's Arcana).

Fall of Planets—In Signs—(See "Debilities", "Fall of Planets", under Planets).

Feminine Signs—(See "Signs" under Female).

Feral Signs — Bestial Signs — (See Beasts).

Fire Signs—(See "Fire Signs" under Fire).

Fixed Signs—(See "Fixed Signs" under Fixed).

Flexed Signs — (See "Mutable Signs" under Mutable).

Food — The Food Adapted to People Born Under Each Sign—(See "Signs of Zodiac" under Food).

Fortunate Signs—(See "Signs of Zodiac" under Fortune).

Foundation Signs—(See "Fixed Signs" under Fixed).

Four-Footed Signs — (See Quadrupeds).

Fowls — Resembling Fowls — (See "Birds" in this section).

Fruitful Signs—(See Fruitful).

Gemini Sign; Half Feral Sign—♊.

Hoarse Signs—(See Hoarseness).

Horas — The Positive and Negative Halves of Signs—(See Horas).

Hot Signs—The fiery signs. Also the airy signs are classed as moist and warm. (See "Signs" under Heat).

Human Form—Signs of—(See Articulate; "Human Form" under Human).

Human Signs — (See "Human Signs" under Human).

Humane Signs—The Airy Signs, and especially ♒. (See Humane).

Hurtful Signs—(See Hurtful).

Hyemal Signs — Winter Signs — (See Winter).

Idle Sign—♓ is classed as an idle and dull sign. (See Idle).

Imperfect Signs—(See Imperfect).

Inarticulate Signs—(See Inarticulate).

Indifferent Signs—Neither Fruitful nor Barren—♎, ♑, and ♒.

Internal Rulership — Of Signs — (See "External" in this section. Also see Internal).

Jacob—The 12 Sons of Jacob—Each son is said to have been born with the ☉ in a different Sign of the Zodiac, and being typical of the 12 fundamental classes of Humanity. See the book, "Bible Astrology" by Lyman Stowe. To get this book, address Mildred K. Stowe, 1325 Madison Ave., Detroit, Michigan, U. S. A. Lyman Stowe was one of the great Writers of his day on Biblical and Medical Astrology, and gave the World many new interpretations of the Bible, and also did much to help explain the causes of disease, and the Philosophy of Life, and every student should have a copy of this book.

Leo Sign; Libra Sign;

Life-Giving Signs — The fiery signs, and especially ♌.

Long Ascension—Signs of—(See "Ascension" under Long).

Luxuriant Sign—(See Luxuriant).

Lymphatic Signs—(See Lymphatic).

Magnetic Sign — (See "Signs" under Magnetic).

Masculine Signs—The positive signs, the odd signs, as ♈, ♊, ♌, ♎, ♐, ♒. The ☉ rules the first half of masculine

signs, and the ☽ the second half. (See "Odd Signs" under Odd).

Melancholic Signs—(See "Signs" under Melancholy).

Members of Body—Members ruled by Signs—(See each Sign in the alphabetical arrangement).

Mental Signs — (See "Signs" under Mental).

Mineral Signs—(See Earth, Signs).

Moderately Strong Signs — ♉, ♊, ♍, ♏, ♒.

Moist Signs — (See "Signs" under Moisture).

Motive Signs—(See Motive).

Movable Signs—(See Cardinal Signs).

Mutable Signs — (See Common, Mutable).

Mute Signs—(See Dumb, Mute).

Mutilated Signs—(See Mutilated).

Navamsa—Navamsa Division of Signs —(See Navamsa).

Negative Signs—(See Negative; "Electro-Negative" in this section).

Nervous Signs — (See "Signs" under Nerves).

Nocturnal Signs—(See "Signs" under Night).

Northern Signs—(See Northern).

Obeying Signs—Southern Signs—(See "Northern Signs" under North).

Obnoxious Signs—(See "Hurtful Signs" under Hurtful).

Odd Signs—(See Odd, Positive).

Opposite Signs—(See Opposite).

Organs Ruled by Signs—(See the Introduction under Organs).

Parts of the Body—Ruled by Signs—(See Parts).

Pestilential Signs—(See Pestilence).

Phlegmatic Signs—(See Phlegm).

Pisces Sign; Planets and Signs—(See "Signs Ruled By" under Planets).

Positive Signs—(See Positive; "Electro-Negative" in this section).

Psychic Signs—(See the Introduction under Psychic).

Quadrupedal Signs — (See Quadrupeds).

Rational Signs—(See Rational).

Receptive Signs—(See Receptivity).

Reptilian Signs—(See Reptiles).

Right Side of Body—And the Signs—(See Left, Right).

Rising Sign—(See Ascendant, Rising).

Ruminant Signs—(See Ruminant).

Sagittarius Sign; Sanguine Signs — (See Sanguine).

Scientific Signs—(See Science).

Scorpio Sign; Seminal Signs — (See Semen).

Short Ascension—Signs of—(See "Ascension" under Long, Short).

Sickly Signs—♒ and ♓, and especially when upon the Asc. at B. (See Sickly; "Low" under Vitality).

Slow of Voice—Signs of—(See "Slow of Voice" under Voice).

Southern Signs—(See Northern, Southern).

Speaking Signs—(See Speaking).

Strong Signs—(See "Fixed Signs" under Fixed).

Structural Rulership—Of Signs—(See "External" in this section).

Sub-Divisions of Signs — (See Decanates, Faces, Horas, Navamsa).

Summer Signs—(See Summer).

Sweet Signs—Air Signs—(See Sweet).

Symbols of the Signs — (See the Introduction under each of the Signs, as Aries, Taurus, etc.).

Sympathetic Signs—Signs in Sympathy with Each Other—(See Sympathy). Aquarius is said to be the most sympathetic and humane sign.

Taurus Sign; Temperamental Signs—(See "Elemental" in this section).

Terminal Signs—(See Terminal).

Terrestrial Signs—(See Quadrupeds).

Torpid Sign—(See Pisces, Torpid).

Tropical Signs—(See Tropical).

Unfortunate Signs — (See Unfortunate).

Vernal Equinox Sign—(See Vernal).

Violent Signs — (See "Signs" under Violent).

Virgo Sign; Vital Signs—(See "Signs" under Vital).

Voice—Signs of—(See "Signs" under Voice).

Warm and Moist Signs—(See "Signs" under Moisture).

Water Signs — (See "Signs" under Water).

Weak Signs — ♋, ♑, and ♓ are considered the weak signs when upon the Asc. at B., and tend to lower vitality, and ♋ and ♓ especially, as they correspond to the terminal houses, the 4th and 12th houses. (See "Low" under Recuperation, Resistance, Vitality; "Weak Body" under Weak).

Western Signs—(See Western).

Whole Signs — (See "Signs" under Whole).

Winter Signs—(See Winter).

Zodiac—Signs of—Zodiac Salts—(See Zodiac).

SILENT — (See Dumb, Hermaphrodites, Mutes; "Silent" under Speech).

SILICA—Quartz—Ruled by ♐. Silica is called "The Surgeon of the Body".

SILVER — Argentum — Ruled by the ☽, and is a typical drug and metal of the ☽. (See Metals, Therapeutics).

Silver Cord—The Cord which connects the Soul to the body. When this Cord is snapped, disintegration of the physical body begins. This happens usually about 3½ days after the apparent death of the body, and during that time there is hope that the body may be revived. Therefore, the body should not be embalmed, disturbed, buried, or cremated until this period has elapsed. Saturn and ♂ cut the Cord. (See Death). What we call the death of the body is not death, as the body becomes more alive than ever when its Captain and Leader, the Ego, has left it, as the atoms and particles then begin their disorganized battle in earnest to free themselves in order to enter into new combinations. Cremation sets the particles free immediately, and without the long period of decay and disintegration. The physical body is but a wrapping for the Soul, a physical vehicle to work with and through on the Earth Plane, and when we have finished our "Day in School" here, we are thru with this body, and should forget it, burn it up, the same as we would do to some old worn out cloak or garment. By setting the particles of the body free by fire, the Soul also is more free to depart to the Heaven World, and to have nothing to hold it back, or worry about except the loved ones and relatives left behind. Graveyards are a menace to the health of a Community, and constantly give off foul vapors, and a stench of decaying bodies, and the Astral Shell, or counterpart of the physical body, haunts the grave about its corpse, and appears to those who are psychic enough to see them as an Apparition, or "Ghost", at times until the body is finally disposed of. The questions of the Silver Cord, of Cremation, and other subjects about Death, etc., are quite fully considered in the book, "Cosmo-Conception", by Max Heindel. In the Bible the Silver Cord is spoken of in Eccl. 12:6. (See "Astral Shells" under Astral).

SIMILAR — Similars — Treatment By — (See Homeopathy, Sympathy).

SIMPLE—

Simple Fevers — (See "Non-Contagious" under Fevers).

Simple Fractures—(See "Simple" under Fractures).

Simple-Minded—(See Foolish, Idiocy, Imbecility, Insanity; "Weak Mind" under Mind, etc.).

SIMULATION—Simulated—

Simulated Death — (See Catalepsy, Trance).

Simulation of Disease—A ♍ trait. (See Virgo).

SINAPSIS NIGRA — Mustard — Sinapsis Alba—Typical Plants of the ☉. (See Mustard).

SINCERE — Honest — Conscientious — ♅ and ♂ influences tend to sincerity unless they are badly afflicted. Aries and ♌ are sincere and open-minded, and also the ♒ people. Sagittarius is sincere unless ♃, its ruler, is ill-aspected by malefics. Also the 5th face of ♌, the 1st face of ♏, or the 6th face of ♐, when on the Asc. at B. tend to make the nature sincere. The afflictions of ♆ and ♄ to the mental rulers tend to Deception and Hypocrisy. (See Character, Cheating, Deceitful, Dishonest, Gambling, Honest, Hypocritical, Motives, Noble, Purposes, Reputation).

SINEWS — Tendons — Ligamentous Tissues—(See Achilles, Fiber, Ligaments, Muscles; "Sinews" under Nerves; Tendons).

SINGING—(See "Speech" under Breath; Humming, Larynx; "Singers" under Music; "Injudicious Use", "Speaking Signs", under Speech; "Melodious", "Musical", under Voice).

SINGLE—

Single Births — (See "Single Births" under Children).

Single People—(See Aversions, Bachelors, Celibacy, Deviations; "Aversion" under Marriage; Spinsters).

SINGULAR—

Singular Death—(See "Death" under Extraordinary, Murder, Mysterious, Notorious, Peculiar, Poison, Public, Remarkable, Strange, Sudden, Suicide, Tragical, Uncommon, Untimely, Unusual, Violent, etc.).

SINISTER — Situated on the Left Side, or Left Hand — Evil — Perverse — Wicked, etc.—

Aspects — Sinister Aspects—Evil Aspects—(See Aspects).

Left-Handed—(See "Left-Handed" under Left).

Perverse—(See Conduct, Evil, Morals, Perverse, Prodigal, Wanton, Wicked).

SINKING—Sunken—

Sinking of Parts—Of the Body—Depressions, etc.—Caused by ♄ afflictions. (See "Sunken" under Chest; Compression, Contractions, Depressions, Eyeballs; "Sunken" under Face; Hollow; Saturn Influence, Skull, Sunken).

Sinking Spells—(See Collapse, Fainting; "Faintings" under Heart; Prostration, Weak, etc.).

SINUS—Sinuses—(See Fossae, Frontal).

Sinus of Kidneys—(See Kidneys).

SIRIUS—The Dog Star—Of the nature of ♃ and ♂, and situated in 12° ♋. Produces glory, renown, and great wealth. The Asc. to the place of tends to good health. Sirius also tends to bring some evils when with the ☽, and the danger of death by Soldiers or Wild Beasts. Also Dog Days were originally named after Sirius. (See "Corrupt Air" under Air; "Dog Days" under Dogs; "Death" under Soldiers; "Wild Animals" under Wild).

SISTER—Sisters—Are ruled by the 3rd H., and also indicated by the ☽ and ♀. Happenings to them, dangers, ill-health, death, etc., are indicated by afflictions to the ☽, ♀, or 3rd H. (See Brethren).

Danger To—Accident or Injury To—The ☽ hyleg and to the ☌, P., □ or ☍ ♅ by dir.; the M.C. to the ill-aspects the ☽ or ♀ by dir.; an eclipse falling on ♀ in a child's map.

Death or Illness Of—The ☽ to the □ or ☍ the ☉ or ♀ by dir.; ♄ passing over the place of the ☽ or ♀ at B., by transit, or at a Solar Rev., and the ☽ or ♀ afflicted at B., or at a Solar Rev. by malefics; the M.C. to the □ or ☍ the ☽ or ♀ by dir.; the M.C. to the ☌, P., □, or ☍ the ☽ or ♀ if either be weak or afflicted at B.; the Asc. to the □ or ☍ the ☽ or ♀ by dir.; the Asc. to the ☌ ♂ by dir. (See "Sickness Among" under Brethren).

Long Life For — And Good Relations With—Benefics in, or ruling, the 3rd H., and no malefic influences over this house at B.; the ☽ and ♀ well-aspected at B., and free from affliction in the map of a brother. (See "Long Life" under Females, Mother).

Short Life For—Evil Relations With —Malefics in or ruling the 3rd H. of the native; the ☽ and ♀ badly afflicted at B., and by dir., and with no good influences over the 3rd H.; the Asc. to the □ or ☍ the ☽ or ♀ by dir., and the ☽ and ♀ sorely afflicted at B. (See "Short Life" under Females, Mother, Relatives).

Sisters Indicated — Stars femininely constituted, which promise brethren, indicate sisters. (See Brothers Indicated" under Brothers; "First-Born Child", "Many Children", under Children).

SITUATION IN LIFE—Location, etc.— (See Abroad, Altitude, Changes, Foreign Lands, Journeys, Location; "Native Land" under Native; "Place of Birth" under Place; Residence, Travel, Voyages, etc.).

SITUATIONS—(See Ambition, Business, Employment, Fortune, Idle; "Ill-Fortune" under Ill; Improvident, Poverty, Reputation, Riches, Vocation, etc.).

SIXTH HOUSE — This is a feminine house, and is known as the House of Health, and also of Sickness, and is affiliated with the 6th Sign, Virgo. The 6th H. and ♍ are indicators of disease, and the Sign on the cusp of this house indicates the part of the body more liable to disease and affliction. (See "Action of the Mind" under Mind; Virgo; "Principal" under Vital). Disease is apt to come from the 6th H. conditions, and this house shows the natural and ordinary state of the health. Benefic influences in and ruling this house show better health, while malefics in the 6th H. at B. tend to ill-health, and also indicate the nature of the disease most liable to afflict the body or mind. Malefics in the 6th H. indicate an evil end to the disease. This house shows disease, its cause and quality; it shows the principal humour or disease offending, and whether curable or incurable, and whether the disease will be long or short. The 6th H., in a broad sense, governs disease, and especially if there are planets in this house at B. (See Majority). Diagnosis is more remote, and less accurate, when considering only the lord of the 6th. Wilson in his Dictionary says, "Not to depend too much upon the 6th H. to judge of the disease unless it is very conspicuous in influence." The ☉ in this house at B. tends to lower the vitality, and to cause mental diseases. The ☽ here tends to diseases of the head. Jupiter, ♂, or ♀ here denote a good Physician. Also ♀ afflicted in this house at B. tends to Venereal Diseases. Mercury here tends to bad breath, and a disordered brain. Mars here tends to fevers, evil servants, and destruction of cattle.

Colors Ruled By—Dark, or Black.

Denotes — This house denotes the Lower Belly, the Solar Plexus, the Intestines, and the Rectum.

Diseases Ruled By—Signifies all diseases in the lower part of the Abdomen, in the Intestines, Liver, and Reins. Also tends to General Ailments. Rules the sicknesses of Servants, Dependents, and also malefic influences over this house tend to the destruction of the small cattle, and small animals of the native.

Rules — The Sixth House Rules the Abdomen, Belly, the inferior part of the Belly and the Intestines, even to the Rectum; the Womb; the Climatic and other conditions affecting the health; Food; Clothing; Ritual; the Colors Black or Dark; the physical Comforts of Life; the Common People and the relation of the native to them; the Mother's brothers and sisters in a male horoscope; Aunts and Uncles, and Kindred on the father's side; Aunts and Uncles in a female nativity, or the Father's brothers and sisters; Enemies (in the Hindu System); General Ailments; Healers; Physicians; Sickness, and the nature of the Sickness; rules the Health; Servants, Slaves, Dependents, Persons in employ; Small Animals, such as Ponies, small Cattle, Sheep, Hogs, Goats, Rabbits, etc. The Sixth House influences are referred to many times throughout his Book, and under the various diseases and conditions. See the Sixth House influences in the paragraph "Arguments for Death" under Death; "Indicators of Health", "Judging the Health", under Health; "Signs of Ill-Health" under Ill-Health; "Judgment of the Disease" under Judgment; "Nature of the Disease" under Nature; "Quality of the Sickness" under Sickness; the subjects and diseases under Virgo.

SIXTH RACE — Sixth Sub-Race — (See Neptune, Pineal Gland).

SIXTH SENSE—(See Pineal Gland).

SIZE—Measurements—Volume, etc.—

Body—Size and Weight of the Physical Body — (See Body, Commanding, Corpulent, Diminished, Dwarfed, Enlarged, Fat, Figure, Fleshy, Form, Frame, Full, Giants, Growth, Heavy, Height, High, Large, Lean, Little, Low, Mean, Medium, Middle, Moderate, Portly, Round, Shape, Short, Skeleton, Small, Stature, Stout, Tall, Thin, Undersized, Undeveloped, Weight, etc.).

Brain—Size and Weight of the Brain —(See the Introduction under Brain).

Good Habit and Size — (See "Good Habit" under Habit).

SKELETON — The Framework of the Body—The Bones—Ruled by ♄. The skeletone is built up by deposits formed by ♄, and from earthy minerals carried by the blood. (See Bones, Deposits, Minerals).

A Living Skeleton — Case — See "Living Skeleton", No. 053 in 1001 N.N.

Well-Framed Body—The ☽ Sig. in ♊; ♀ Sig. in ♒; ☿ Sig. in ♊ or ♐; the ♍ influences give a neat, well-formed, and well-framed body; ♐ gives a tall, well-formed, and well-framed body. (See "Large" under Bones; Well-Proportioned, Well-Shaped).

Whole Frame Disordered — (See "Frame" under Whole).

SKEPTICISM—Doubt In Religious Matters—Unorthodox—Due usually to ☿ and the ☿ signs ♊ and ♍ prominent at B.; caused by ♄ affliction; ♄ in the 9th H.; ♃ afflicted in ♊; malefics in ♊ and ♍ in □ asp. to each other; ♅ afflicted in the 9th H. (See Independent, Misunderstood, Occult, Metaphysical; "Unorthodox" under Religion; Science).

SKIN — Cutis — Derma — The External Covering of the Body—The Cuanteous Surface — Epidermis — Cuticle—Corium — The True Skin — Epithelium, etc. — The Skin is under the external rulership of the ♑ sign, and also ruled by ♄. The Skin is also largely influenced by the ♎ sign, the exalted sign of ♄. By internal government the skin is influenced by all the cardinal signs, and planets in these signs. Cardinal signs denote the skin. The external layer of the skin is called the Epithelium, the Epidermis, the Cuticle, or Scarf Skin. The Derma is the deep layer of the Skin, known as the Corium, Cutis, or True Skin. (See Cutis, Derma). The principle of ♄ is Limitation, and he, therefore, rules the skin and bones, as these tend to define and limit the corporature. (See Capricorn, Saturn Influence). The planets tend to affect the skin according to their nature. Venus tends especially to affect the complexion, and the skin of the face, and to cause disorders thru the wrong use of Cosmetics. Mars causes inflammations of the skin. The afflictions of ♅ and ☿, disorders of the nerves of the skin. Saturn tends to hardening, thickening, scaling, dryness, and chilling of the skin, etc. (See Centripetal). This Article is divided into Two Sections. Section One—Characteristics of the Skin. Section Two—Diseases of the Skin.

— SECTION ONE —

CHARACTERISTICS OF THE SKIN— These are also largely considered in the Articles on Appearance, Blemishes, Complexion, Face, Marks, Moles, Scars.

Black Skin—Black Personal Figure— (See "Dark Complexion" under Complexion; "Figure" under Dark; Races).

Brown Skin—(See "Complexion" under Brown).

Chalky and White—♓ gives, and especially when on the Asc. at B.; ♅ or ☿ rising in the Asc., white skin. (See Pale, Sickly; "Complexion" under White).

Clear Skin — Clear and Lucid — (See "Clear" under Complexion).

Color of the Skin—The First House has signification of the color of the skin, the complexion, form, shape, etc. (See the various paragraphs in this section, and under Color, Complexion, Face, Races).

Complexion—(See the paragraphs under Complexion).

Dark Skin—(See "Dark" under Complexion; "Figure" under Dark).

Delicate Skin—♍, ♒, and ♓ give when on the Asc. at B. (See "Delicate" under Complexion).

Face—Skin of—(See the various paragraphs under Face).

Fair Skin—(See "Fair", "Light", under Complexion; "Degrees" under Light).

Flabby Skin—(See Flabby, Wrinkles).

Glossy Skin — Oily — Shiny — (See Shiny).

Hard and Rough Skin—Denoted by ♄. (See "Skin" under Hard; "Thick" in this section).

Negro Race—(See Negro, Races).

Oily Skin—(See Oils, Shiny).

Pigment In—(See Sulphur; "Pigmentation" in Sec. 2 of this Article).

Pure Skin—♒ gives. (See "Pure" under Complexion).

Race Color—(See "Color" in this section).

Rough and Hard—(See "Hard" in this section; "Rough" in Section Two of this Article).

Shiny and Oily—(See Oils, Shiny).

Soft Skin — ♍ gives a soft, velvety skin, and pure, delicate, thin, and easily broken or injured. (See "Delicate" in this section).

Sulphur Pigment—(See Sulphur).

Tender Skin—White and Tender Skin —The ☉ strong at B., and produced by the ☉ influence.

Thick Skin—♄ gives; ♄ ascending at B. (See "Skin" under Hard).

Thin Skin — (See "Soft" in this section).

Vaso-Constrictor Nerves—Of the Skin —(See "Vaso-Constrictor" under Vaso).

White and Chalky—(See "Chalky" in this section).

White and Tender—(See Chalky, Delicate, Tender, in this section).

Yellow Skin — (See "Yellow" under Complexion, Face; "Jaundiced Look" under Jaundice).

— SECTION TWO —

DISEASES OF THE SKIN—See "Tendency to Skin Diseases" in this section for the general influences which make one more liable to skin diseases. The following subjects have to do with the diseases, afflictions, hurts and injuries to the skin. See these subjects in the alphabetical arrangement when only listed here—

Abrasions; Abscesses; Acne;

Acute Diseases Of — Acute Pustular Inflammation — (See Eruptions; Impetigo; "Inflammation" in this section).

All Cutaneous Diseases—♑ diseases.

Anthrax—(See Carbuncles).

Arms — ♀ in signs which rule the arms, hands, legs, and feet tends to skin eruptions of these parts, and skin affections due to wrong habits of living, and also tends to blackheads. Mars in signs which rule these parts tends to skin diseases of an inflammatory nature. Saturn in such signs tends to chill the skin, disturbances of the capillary circulation, the nerves of the skin, and to dryness, shrinking, hardening, contractions, defects, and various impediments. These influences also may apply to the skin of any part of the body. (See "Eruptions" under Arms).

Asphyxia—Cutaneous Asphyxia—(See "Cutaneous" under Asphyxia).

Barber's Itch—(See Barbers).

Bathing; Birthmarks—(See Naevus).

Blackheads — (See "Comedo" under Sebaceous; "Arms" in this section).

Bleeding; Blemishes; Blisters; Blood —(See "Skin" under Blood).

Blotches; Blows; Blue Discolorations— (See Cyanosis; "Bluish" under Marks).

Boils; Breakings Out—(See Breakings Out, Eruptions, Pimples).

Breathing—Skin Breathing Interfered With—(See "Cutaneous" under Asphyxia).

Bruises; Bunions; Burns; Cancer— (See Carcinoma).

Capillaries — Disturbances of — (See Capillaries, Centripetal, Constrictions; "Vaso-Constrictor" under Vaso; "Arms" in this section).

Carbuncles; Carcinoma; Chickenpox;

Chilblain; Chill—The Surface Chilled —(See Capillaries, Centripetal, Chill, Constrictions; "Vaso-Constrictor" under Vaso).

Chloasma — (See "Pigmentation" in this section).

Chlorosis — Greenish Discoloration— (See Chlorosis).

Chronic Skin Trouble—(See Psoriasis).

Coarse and Rough Skin—(See "Rough" in this section).

Cold Skin—♄ in ♑. (See "Chill" in this section; the Introduction under Cold; Hemachromatosis).

Color Of — Discolorations — (See Discolorations, Pigmentation, Red, White, Yellow, in this section; "Color" in Sec. 1 of this Article).

Comedo — (See "Blackheads" in this section).

Complexion—Disorders of—(See Complexion, Cosmetics; "Lotions" under Face).

Compound Fractures—Breaking Thru the Skin—(See Fractures).

Congestions—Caused by Chill of the Skin—(See "Chill" in this section; Congestions).

Constrictions — Due to Chill — (See "Chill" in this section).

Contractions—Due to Cold and Chill —(See Centripetal, Chill, Constrictions, Contractions; Arms, Chill, in this section).

Contusions—(See Bruises).

Cornification; Corns; Cosmetics—Disorders from Wrong Use of—(See Cosmetics).

Crusts; Cutaneous Disorders—All Cutaneous Diseases—♑ diseases, and afflictions in ♑. (See "Tendency To", and the various subjects in this section).

Cuticle—Epidermis—Scarf Skin—Epithelium—Disorders of—♑ diseases, and afflictions in ♑; ♄ diseases, causing hardening, thickening, etc.; ♂ causes inflammatory conditions of. (See the various paragraphs in this section).

Cutis — Derma — Corium — The True Skin—Disorders of—♄ and ♑ diseases; ♂ diseases, with inflammations, abscesses, etc. (See the various paragraphs in this section).

Cuts; Cyanosis Discolorations—(See Cyanosis).

Dead Tissue—(See Crusts, Scales, Sloughing; "Dry" in this section).

Defects—(See Blemishes, Blotches, Defects, Marks, Moles, Naevus, Scars; "Arms" in this section).

Dermatitis—(See "Cutis", "Inflammation", in this section).

Discharges; Discolorations—(See Chlorosis, Cyanosis, Marks, Moles, Naevus, Scabs, Scars; Pigmentation, Red, Yellow, in this section).

Dry Skin—♄ the afflicting planet; ♄ ✳ or △ the Asc.; ♑ on the Asc. (See Crusts; "Body" under Dry; Hardening, Hemachromatosis, Psoriasis, Scales, Shrinkage, Tetter, Withering, Wrinkles, Xeransis, etc.).

Ducts—(See Ducts, Follicles, Sebaceous).

Eczema; Efflorescence; Elephantiasis; Ephemeral Skin Eruption—(See Urticaria).

Epidermis—Disorders of—(See "Cuticle", and the various paragraphs in this section).

Epithelioma; Eruptions; Erysipelas; Exanthema; Excoriations—(See Abrasions).

Excrescences; Exudations; Face—Skin Disorders of — (See Acne, Cosmetics; "Lotions" under Face; Pimples).

Favus; Feet—Skin Disorders of—(See "Eruptions", and the various paragraphs under Feet; "Arms" in this section).

Flabby; Fluids—(See Elimination, Excretion; "Skin" under Fluids; Osmosis, Sebaceous, Sweat).

Follicles; Freckles; Gangrene; Glands—(See "Skin" under Glands).

Glossy Skin—(See Oils, Shiny).

Greenish Discoloration—(See Chlorosis).

Growths; Gunshot Wounds—(See Gunshot).

Habits—Skin Diseases from Wrong Habits of Living—(See Cosmetics; "Eruptions" under Face; Pimples; "Arms" in this section).

Hair—Hairy Body—(See "Body" under Hair).

Hands—(See "Skin" under Hands; "Arms" in this section).

Hardening—(See "Skin" under Hard; Hemachromatosis; Rough, Thick, in this section).

Hemorrhage—Into the Skin—(See Purpura, Scurvy).

Herpes; Hives; Horny; Hot Skin—(See Fevers; "Body" under Heat).

Hurts To—(See Blows, Bruises, Burns, Cuts, Hurts, Injuries, Instruments, Stabs, Weapons, Wounds, etc.).

Hyperaemia; Hypertrophy; Icthyosis—(See Xeroderma).

Impediments—(See Impediments; "Arms", and the various paragraphs in this section).

Impetigo; Incised Wounds—(See Cuts, Instruments, Stabs).

Indurations; Infections; Inflammation—Inflammatory Skin Complaints—Dermatitis—Cutaneous Inflammations—Caused by ♂; ♂ afflicted in ♑. Mars in any sign tends to inflammation of the skin of the part ruled by such sign. Red color, red rays, or to be confined in a red room, are good in the treatment of inflammatory skin diseases. Chilblains are cutaneous inflammation due to cold. (See Chilblain, Impetigo, Inflammation, Psoriasis; "Treatment" under Red; Swellings, etc.).

Injuries to Skin—(See "Hurts" in this section).

Itch; Ivy Poisoning—(See Ivy).

Jaundiced Skin—(See "Yellow" under Complexion; Jaundice).

King's Evil—(See Scurvy).

Lead Color—(See Lead).

Leathery Skin—(See Hemachromatosis; Hardened, Rough, Thick, in this section).

Legs—(See "Skin Diseases" under Legs; "Arms" in this section).

Leprosy; Lips—(See "Scabbed" under Lips).

Liver Spots—(See "Spots" under Liver).

Lotions—Bad Effects of Face Lotions—(See Cosmetics; "Lotions" under Face).

Lupus; Marks; Measles; Membranes; Moisture—Of the Skin—(See Exudations, Oils, Sweat).

Moles; Naevus; Nails; Nerves of Skin—(See Peripheral; "Arms" in this section).

Nettle Rash—(See Hives, Itch, Urticaria).

Nodules—(See "Nodules" under Nodes).

Nose—Morbid Red Nose—(See "Morbid Red" under Face; "Capillaries" under Nose).

Numbness; Obstructions—In the Skin—(See Comedo, Elimination, Eruptions, Excretion, Growths, Hardening, Inflammations, Pores, Swellings, and the various paragraphs in this section).

Oedema; Oily Skin—(See Oils, Shiny).

Oozing of Fluids—(See Oozing).

Operations—Surgical Incision—Best Time For—(See "Rules" under Operations).

Pale Skin—(See Pale, Sickly).

Papilloma; Papules; Paraesthesia; Parched; Pigmentation—Chloasma—The color of the pigment in the skin, as in the different Races, is largely regulated by climatic conditions and the heat of the ☉. In the hottest Countries the pigment is dark, or black, as black does not absorb the heat as readily, and gives a cooler body. (See Races). Saturn contributes Sulphur for the pigment of the skin. (See Sulphur). People born under ♄, and with ♑ or ♒ on the Asc., or the ☉ and many planets in the signs of ♄, tend to white hair earlier in life, and due to the influence of ♄ in withdrawing the pigment, and also due to lower vitality. Various colorings of the skin are also caused by deposits from disease, as in Jaundice, or Chlorosis, Green Sickness.

(See Chlorosis; "Yellow Complexion" under Complexion; "Figure" under Dark; Yellow; Red, Yellow, in this section).

Pimples; Poison Ivy—Skin Susceptible To—(See Ivy).

Pores—(See Ducts, Glands; "Comedo" under Sebaceous; Sweat).

Porrigo—Scald-Head—(See Favus).

Prevalent—Skin Diseases Prevalent—♂ in ♊, ori., lord of the year at the Vernal).

Prickling Sensations—(See Prickling).

Pruritis—Intense Itching—(See Itch).

Psoriasis; Purpura; Pus—Pustules—Pustular Inflammation—(See "Pustular Diseases" under Pus).

Putrefaction—(See Putrid).

Rashes; Reddish Color—(See "Red Complexion" under Complexion; "Red" under Face; "Cheeks" under Red; "Ruddy Complexion" under Ruddy).

Remedies—Skin Remedies—(See Collyria, Lead, Lotions, Ointments, Zinc).

Rheum; Ringworm; Rose-Colored Skin—(See "Rosy" under Complexion).

Roseola; Rough Skin—Denoted by ♄; ♄ in ♉; ♄ in ♑, partile asp. the Asc., rough and coarse. (See Hardening, Thick, in this section; Hemachromatosis, Psoriasis, Scales).

Rubefacients; Rubeola—(See Measles).

Ruddy Looking—(See "Reddish" in this section).

Rush of Blood—To the Skin—♂ influence. (See Caustic, Centrifugal; "Action of Mars" under Mars; Rubefacient).

Saint Anthony's Fire—(See Erysipelas).

Sarcoma; Scabbed Lips—(See Lips).

Scabs—Scabies—(See Scabs).

Scald-Head—Porrigo—(See Favus).

Scalds; Scales; Scalp; Scarlatina;

Scarlet Fever; Scars; Scrofula;

Scurvy; Searing—(See "Searing" under Burns).

Sebaceous Glands—Of Skin—(See Sebaceous).

Sensation; Senses—Sense of Touch—(See Feeling, Sensation, Sensibility, Touch).

Sensitive Skin—♒ gives. Extreme sensitiveness of the skin is an ♒ disease, and afflictions in ♒. (See "Delicate" in Sec. 1 of this Article).

Shingles—(See "Herpes Zoster" under Herpes).

Shiny Skin—(See Oils, Shiny).

Shrinkage; Sickly Looking—(See Pale, Sickly; "Complexion" under White).

Sloughings; Smallpox; Soft Skin—(See Delicate, Soft, in Sec. 1 of this Article; Flabby, Laxity, Soft).

Sores; Stabs; Subcutaneous Diseases—(See Abscesses, Boils, Carbuncles).

Sudorifics; Suppressions—Suppression of Skin Breathing, or Elimination, Excretion, Sweat, etc.—(See "Cutaneous" under Asphyxiation; "Hindered" under Elimination; "Obstructions" under Excretion; Suppressions; "Lessened" under Sweat).

Surface Chilled—(See "Chill" in this section).

Sweat; Swellings; Syphilis;

Tendency to Skin Diseases—Liable to Cutaneous Disorders—The ☉ afflicted in ♎ or ♑; the ☽ hyleg in ♌, ♍, or ♑, and especially with females; the ☽ afflicted in airy signs; ☽ diseases, and the ☽ afflicted at B.; the ☽ in ♊ or ♏, afflicted by the ☉ or ♂ when taken ill, or the ☽ in ♑ (Hor'y); ♆ in ♑; ♆ in ♑ in the 6th H., and especially when afflicting the Asc. or hyleg; ♄ in ♒ or ♑, and especially when afflicting the ☉, ☽, Asc., or hyleg; ♃ afflicted in ♑, from indiscretions; ♃ afflicted in ♑ in the 6th H.; ♃ afflicted in ♒; ♂ afflicted in ♓, and ☌, P., □, or ☍ the Asc. by dir.; ♂ in ♑; ♀ afflicted in ♈, ♎, or ♑ in the 6th H., or afflicting the ☽ or Asc.; ☿ affl. in ♑; ☿ afflicted at B., and to the evil asp. the Asc. by dir.; the Asc. to the ill-asps. ☿ by dir., and ☿ afflicted at B.; ♎ or ♑ on the Asc.; a ♎ and ♑ disease; cardinal signs show, and especially afflictions in ♑; the malefics, or afflicting planets in cardinal signs; afflictions in ♌ or ♒, due to blood disorders; airy signs on the Asc. and 6th H. at B., or at decumb., or the ☽ in an airy sign at such times, indicate corrupt blood, gout, or cutaneous diseases. (See the various paragraphs in this section).

Tetters; Thickening—Of the Cuticle—♄ influence; a ♄ disease and affliction. (See "Skin" under Hard; Hemachromatosis, Thickening).

Tinea—(See Ringworm, Worms).

Tingling; Tissues; Touch—Disorders of Sense of—(See "Senses" in this section).

Toughening—Of the Skin—Caused by ♄, and brought about gradually with age. (See "Thickening" in this section).

Transudations—(See Exudations, Oozing, Osmosis).

Treatment—Of Skin Diseases—Red color, red rooms, red rays, red clothing, etc., are beneficial, as ♂ rules red, and ♂ color and remedies oppose the influence of ♄ in skin disorders. The acute and inflammatory skin conditions caused by ♂ are treated and opposed by the remedies of ♄, as Lead Ointments or solutions. (See Remedies, Water, in this section; Antipathy, Remedies, Treatment).

Tubercles; Tubercular Skin Diseases—(See Lupus, Scrofula).

Tumors; Ulcers; Urticaria;

Varicose Ulcers—(See Varicose).

Various Forms—Of Skin Diseases—(See "Tendency To", and the various paragraphs in this section).

Venereal Eruptions—(See "Chancroid" under Gonorrhoea; "Chancre" under Syphilis; Venereal).

Warts; Water—Water on the skin is Man's best friend to keep the skin clean, and prevent skin diseases. Hydrant water is good for external use, but after middle life, distilled water should be used exclusively for drinking purposes, as it is free from minerals, and helps to take up and absorb the excess of mineral deposits laid down by ♄, and to aid the kidneys in elimination, and prevent skin disorders. Max Heindel says, in the book, "Cosmo-Conception", — "Undistilled water, taken internally, is Man's worst enemy, but used externally on the skin, is his best friend." (See Bathing; "Mineral Waters" under Healers).

Wens; White Skin—(See "Chalky and White" in Sec. 1 of this Article).

Withering; Women — The Skin and Complexion In — (See "Skin" under Women).

Wounds; Wrinkles; Yellow Skin — Yellow Discoloration — (See "Yellow" under Complexion; "Yellow" under Face; "Jaundiced Look" under Jaundice; "Complexion" under Yellow; "Pigmentation" in this section).

Zoster — (See "Herpes Zoster" under Herpes). For subjects which may have been overlooked in this Article, look in the alphabetical arrangement for what you have in mind.

SKIPPISH MANNER — Jumps Forward When Speaking — Nods Head to One Side—(See "Nodding" in Sec. 1 under Head).

SKULL — Cranium — The Cranial Bones —The Bony Framework of the Head— The Bones of the skull are ruled by ♄, as ♄ rules the bones in general. Also the bones of the skull are under the structural rulership of the ♈ sign. Saturn in ♈ tends to especially affect the bones of the skull, and also the teeth and left ear. The Base of the Skull, or the Occipital Region, is ruled by the ♉ sign. (See Cranium, Occipital).

Depression In—Malformation—The ☉ or ☽ in the Asc., ill-aspected by ♅ or other malefics; malefics in the Asc.; ♈ on the Asc. and containing malefics, and especially ♄ or ♅. (See "Skull" under Excrescences; "Deformities", "Malformations", under Head; Idiocy).

Excrescences—Hemispherical Excrescences on the Skull — Case — (See "Skull" under Excrescences).

Fontanelles — Slow Closure of — (See "Fontanelles" under Head).

Fracture—♄ or ♂ afflicted in ♈ in the Asc.; a ♊ affliction, and afflictions in ♊. Case—See "Run Over", No. 853, in 1001 N.N. (See "Accidents To" under Head).

Longitudinal Depression—In Central Part of Head — (See "Malformation" under Head).

Malformation — (See "Skull" under Excrescences; "Deformities", "Malformation", under Head; Hydrocephalus, Idiocy).

Pressure — Upon the Brain — (See "Nerves" under Pressure).

Skin Over Skull — (See Forehead, Scalp, Temples).

Soft Water Excrescences — Of the Skull — (See "Skull" under Excrescences).

SLANDEROUS—Slander—(See Disgrace, Libel; "Scandalmongers" under Scandal).

SLAUGHTER — Bloodshed — Murders— Killed In Battle and War—

A Lover of Slaughter—♂ ill-dignified at B., and afflicted. (See "Shedding of Blood" under Blood; Cruel; "Murderous" under Murder; Vicious, Violent).

Great Men—Slaughter of—(See Assassination, Famous; "Great Men" under Great; "Assassination" under Kings; President).

Much Slaughter Everywhere—Slaughter Prevalent—An eclipse of the ☉ in ♏; an eclipse of the ☉ in the 2nd decan. of ♊, the 3rd dec. of ♌ or ♍, or in the 1st dec. of ♏; ♄ ☌ ♂ in the first three degrees of ♋; ♃ ☌ ♂ in the Asc. at the Vernal, and ♂ ℞ and in perigee; ♂ elevated above, and configurated with ☿ at a Solar Ingress or Eclipse; Comets appearing in ♈, ♊, ♋, ♌, ♎, ♏, ♐, ♒, or ♓. (See "Shedding of Blood" under Blood; "Blood" under Effusions; "Many Murders Prevalent" under Murder; "War and Bloodshed" under War).

Slaughter's Disease—(See "Knee Cap" under Knees).

War — Slaughter In — (See "War and Bloodshed" under War).

SLAVISH — Enslaved — Servile — (See "Morbid Fears" under Fears; "Negative Nature" under Negative; Servile, Servitude, etc.).

SLEEP — Drowsiness — Stupor — Soporifics — Sleeping Sickness — Insomnia, etc.—The Twelfth House rules and governs Sleep. (See Twelfth House). The following paragraphs and subjects have to do with Sleep, and Disorders of Sleep, or Consciousness, which see in the alphabetical arrangement when only listed here—

Anaesthetics; Analgesia; Anodynes; Brain Fag—(See Brain).

Broken Sleep — Sleep Disturbed — Sleeps Unquietly — Wakefulness — Insomnia, etc.—The ☽ in ♉, and afflicted by ♂ or the ☉ when taken ill, or the ☽ ☌ ♂ in the Asc. when taken ill (Hor'y). (See Illness, Insomnia, Refreshment, Rest, in this section).

Catalepsy; Cold Feet — Wakefulness By—(See "Cold Feet" under Feet).

Coma; Consciousness; Deep Sleep — (See Catalepsy, Coma, Trance).

Died During Sleep — Case — See "Sarasto", No. 329, in 1001 N.N.

Disorders of Sleep—Caused especially by afflictions in ♓. (See the various paragraphs in this section).

Disturbed Sleep — (See Broken, Cold Feet, Coma, Insomnia, Rest, and the various paragraphs in this section).

Dreams; Drowsiness—Inclined to Sleep — Somnolence — Sleepiness — Stupor— The ☽ in ♌ and afflicted by the ☉ or ♂ when taken ill (Hor'y); a ♆ disease; ♄ ☌ the Asc. by dir., a lethargic drowsiness; ♃ afflicted in ♈. (See "Brain Fag" under Brain; "Mind" under Dull; "Sleepy Eyes" under Eyes; Fatigue, Lassitude, Lethargy, Narcotics, Refreshment, Rest; "Heaviness of Mind" in this section).

Drugs — Sleep-Producing Drugs — Soporifics—Narcotics—Ruled by the ☽ and ♆. (See Narcotics; "Sleep-inducing" in this section).

Epilepsy; Eyes — (See "Sleepy Eyes" under Eyes).

Fainting; Fatigue; Heart Action — Sleeping Potions Harmful To — (See "Sleeping Potions" under Heart).

Heaviness of Mind Dull Drowsiness —The ☽ in ♈, □ or ☍ ♄ (or ☿ if he be of the nature of ♄) when taken ill, or at decumbiture(Hor'y). (See "Mind" under Heavy; "Drowsiness" in this section).

Horrors During Sleep—(See Dreams; "Nightmare" in this section).

Hypnotic Sleep—(See Hypnotism).

Illness—From Want of Sleep or Due Refreshment—(See Refreshment, Rest, "Insomnia" in this section).

Inclined to Sleep—(See "Drowsiness" in this section).

Insensibility; Insomnia—Inability to Sleep — Broken Sleep — Nervous Disorders of Sleep—Wakefulness—Sleeplessness — The ☽ afflicted in ♈ or ♎; the ☽ hyleg in ♈, and afflicted, and especially with females; any ill-aspects to the ☽ or ☿ tend to by affecting the emotions, but the evil is less when the cadent houses are not involved; ♆ ☌ the ☽ in ♈, and afflicted by the □ or ☍ of ♅ and ♂; ♅ or ☿ afflicted in ♈; ♂ in ♈, and especially when in ☌ or ill-asp. the ☉; denoted by ☿; a ☿ disease; ☿ afflicted in ♈; ☿ ☌ ♂ in ♈; ☿ ☌ ♀ in ♈, and in □ or ☍ ♆, ♃, or the ☽; an ♈ and ♎ disease, and especially when these signs are on angles, or strongly occupied at B.; many planets in ♈ at B.; a 12th H. influence, and planets therein; afflictions to the 12th H. from other cadent houses; afflictions in ♓, and especially ♄ in ♓, tends to Insomnia from cold feet. (See "Cold Feet" under Feet; Refreshment, Rest; Broken Sleep, Wakefulness, in this section).

Lack of Sleep—(See "Diseases" under Pain; Refreshment, Rest; "Suffers Much" under Sickness; Broken Sleep, Insomnia, Wakefulness, in this section).

Mind — Heavy Drowsiness of Mind — (See "Brain Fag" under Brain; "Mind" under Dull, Heavy; Drowsiness, Heaviness, in this section).

Moonlight and Sleep — (See "Sleep" under Moon; "Sleep-Inducing" in this section).

Narcotics; Neptune — (See "Influence Of" under Neptune).

Nervous Disorders — Of Sleep — (See Insomnia, Wakefulness, in this section).

Nightmare—Horrible Dreams During Sleep—♆ in ♈, □ or ☍ the ☽ at B., and ♆ afflicted by dir. (See Dreams, Obsessions, Spirit Controls). Nightmare occurs mostly about 48 hours before the Moon's perigee, and when the ☽ is about an hour high.

Potions — Sleeping Potions — (See "Sleeping Potions" under Heart; Potions).

Quiet — Sleep tends to be more quiet during the Last Quarter of the ☽. (See "Last Quarter" under Moon).

Refreshment — Illness from Lack of Refreshing Sleep—(See Refreshment, Rest).

Rest — Sickness from Lack of Rest and Sleep — (See Refreshment; "Sickness" under Rest; "Insomnia" in this section).

Restoring Sleep — Sleep is more restoring from midnight to sunrise. (See "Quiet" in this section).

Sedatives; Sleep-Inducing Drugs — (See Drugs, Potions, in this section; Anaesthetics, Narcotics, Sedatives, Soothing). Moonlight has a soothing, sleep-inducing effect, but tends to decay in the vegetable kingdom. It is advised that people do not sleep with the moonlight directly upon them, as it is depleting and weakening. (See Decay; "Sleep" under Moon).

Sleep-Walking Somnambulism—The ☽ rising at B., and afflicted by ♆; the ☽ in the 1st H., and afflicted, and especially afflicted by ♆ at B., and by dir.; caused by planets in the 6th and 12th H., and in ☍ aspect, and especially where the ☽, ☿, and ♆ are involved; a ♆ disease, and caused primarily by ♆ afflictions to the ☽ or ☿ at B., and by dir., and occurs at times of such evil directions. Also caused by Subs at AT and AX. (See Hypnotism, Neptune, Obsessions, Spirit Controls).

Sleepiness—(See "Drowsiness" in this section).

Sleeping Dropsy—(See "Sleeping Sickness" in this section).

Sleeping Potions — (See Drugs, Potions, in this section).

Sleeping Sickness—Also called Sleeping Dropsy—Lethargic Encephalitis— A Peculiar Disease of West Africa, and characterized by increasing Drowsiness—A ♆ disease; afflictions of ♆ to the ☉, ☽, Asc. or hyleg at B., and by dir., and especially if ☿ is also involved in the configuration; ♆ ☌, □, or ☍ the ☉; ♆ afflicted in the 8th H. (See "Encephalitis" under Encephalon; Epidemics, Influenza, La Grippe, Lethargy; "Drowsiness" in this section).

Sleeplessness—(See Broken Sleep, Insomnia, Wakefulness, in this section).

Sleepy Eyes — (See "Sleepy" under Eyes; "Drowsiness" in this section).

Snoring — (See "Snoring" under Breathing).

Somnambulism—(See "Sleep Walking" in this section).

Somnolence — (See "Drowsiness" in this section).

Soothing Drugs — (See "Sleep-Inducing" in this section; Soothing).

Soporifics — (See "Sleep-Inducing" in this section; "Soporifics" under Narcotics; Soothing).

Stupor—Caused by ♆ afflictions; Subs at AT and AX. (See "Drowsiness" in this section; Analgesia, Anodyne, Coma, Consciousness, Delirium; "Mind" under Dull; Lethargy).

Swoonings—(See Fainting).

Trance; Unconsciousness — (See Consciousness).

Unquietly — Sleeps Unquietly — (See Broken, Insomnia, Wakefulness, in this section).

Walking In Sleep—(See "Sleep-Walking" in this section).

Wakefulness—The 3rd H. is said to rule wakefulness, and caused especially by malefics in this house afflicting the ☽, ☿, the hyleg, or Asc. at B., and by dir. (See Broken, Insomnia, in this section; "Cold Feet" under Feet; Refreshment, Rest).

Want of Sleep — Illness From — (See Refreshment, Rest; Broken, Insomnia, Wakefulness, in this section).

SLENDER—Thin Body—Lean Make—

Body—Slender Body—Slender Make—The ☉ in ♍; ♅ and ☿ make tall and thin, tall and slender; ♅ on the Asc., or in close aspect thereto, tends to give a slender body and long limbs; ♀ in ♈ or ♊; a ☿ person; ♍ on the Asc., slender, well-made, and of medium stature, but with females tends to give a slender little body; ♑ on the Asc., slender make, and with long, thin visage; the Autumnal Signs ♎, ♏, and ♐ on the Asc., or the ☉ or ☽ in these signs, the body is inclined to be lean and slender, and especially if ☿ is also oriental; the Quadrant from the Autumnal Equinox to the Winter Solstice makes slender. (See Lean, Tall, Thin).

Extremities—(See "Long and Slender" under Extremities).

Face—(See "Slender" under Face).

Graceful and Slender—(See Graceful).

Legs—(See "Slender" under Legs).

Limbs—(See "Slender" under Limbs).

Little, Slender Body — ♍ on the Asc., and especially with females.

Make—Slender Make, and with Long, Thin Visage—♑ on the Asc.

Medium Stature—Slender, Medium, and Well-Made—♍ on the Asc. (See Medium).

Middle Stature—And Slender—♀ in ♈ in partile asp. the Asc. (See Middle).

Short and Slender—♑ on the Asc., and tending to be ill-formed.

Tall and Slender — The ☉ or ☿ in ♍, partile the Asc.; the ☉ Sig. in ♎; ♅ and ☿ make tall and slender; ♀ in ♊, partile the Asc., tall, slender, and well-made; ♍ on the Asc., tall, slender, and well-proportioned; ♎ on the Asc., tall, slender, and graceful. (See Tall).

Thin, Tall, and Slender—The ☉, ♄, or ☿ in ♍, partile asp. the Asc.; indicated by ☿, and characteristic of ☿ people. (See Tall, Thin).

Upright and Slender—♃ in ♎ in partile asp. the Asc. (See Erect, Upright).

Visage—Slender Visage—(See "Slender" under Face).

Well-Proportioned — And Slender — The ☉ or ☿ in ♍, partile the Asc.; ♍ on the Asc. (See Well-Proportioned).

Youth—Slender In Youth—♍ or ♎ on the Asc.

SLIGHT—

Slight Build—(See "Little Body" under Little; "Body" under Small).

Slight Cuts—(See Cuts).

Slight Deafness—(See "Slight" under Hearing).

Slight Deformities — A Little Deformed In Body—♄ or ☋ in the Asc.; ♑ on the Asc. (See Deformities).

Slight Disorders—(See Colds, Ephemeral; "Slight" under Excesses, Fevers, Indiscretions; Indisposition, Mild, Minor, Transient).

Slight Fevers — (See "Slight" under Fever).

Slight Indisposition — (See Indisposition; "Quick Recovery" under Recovery).

Slights—Sensitive To—(See "Slights" under Sensitive). For further influences, such as slight cuts or injury to the face, head, and hands see "Cuts To" under Hands; "Accidents To" under Head).

SLIMY MATTER—The Breast Affected By—(See "Slimy" under Breast).

SLOTHFUL — ♂ weak and ill-dignified at B.; ♓ influence, and ♂ afflicted in ♓. (See Apathy, Careless, Dull, Idle, Indifferent, Indolent, Inertia, Labor, Lassitude, Lazy, Procrastination, Rouse, Slovenly, Uncleanly, etc.).

SLOUGHING — Dry Slough — Eschar — Ruled by ♂. (See Crusts; "Eschar" under Escharotic; "Crusts" under Tissue).

Sloughings — Denoted by ♀, those arising from weakness and poison. (See "Vascular Tissues" under Vascular).

Sloughing Sores—Denoted by ♀, such as arise from pustular diseases, as smallpox, measles, etc. (See Pus, Scabs, Smallpox, Sores, Ulcers, etc.).

SLOVENLY—Generally caused by ♄ influence, and ♄ afflicting ☿. (See Careless, Dirty, Dress, Filth; "Bad Habits" under Habits; Improvident, Indifferent, Knavish, Lazy, Neglectful, Slothful, Sluggish, Uncleanly, Untidy, etc.).

SLOW— Retarded — Hindered—Sluggish — Impeded — Arrested, etc. The influence of ♄ is to slow up conditions and functions in the body, and to hinder and retard. (See Hindrances, Impediments, Limitations, Obstructions, Retarded, Saturn, Stoppages, Suppressions, etc.).

Slow Death—(See "Lingering" under Death).

Slow Diseases—Are diseases of the ☉ and ♄. The course of chronic and permanent diseases is regulated by the motion of the ☉. (See Carcinoma, Chronic, Consumptions, Continuity, Duration; "Fixed Signs" under Fixed; Incurable, Inhibitions, Invalids, Lingering Diseases, Long Diseases, Low Fevers, Permanent Diseases, Phthisis, Prognosis, Prolonged, Saturn Influences, Tabes, Tedious, Tuberculosis, Wastings, etc.).

Slow Fevers—(See 'Slow" under Fevers).

Slow Functions — In Females — (See "Functions" under Females; "Slow" under Functions).

Slow Growth — (See "Arrested", "Retarded", under Growth).

Slow Mental Development—(See "Arrested", "Retarded", under Mentality; "Contracted", "Weak", under Mind).

Slow Motion—(See "Slow" under Gait, Motion, Movement, Planets; Impediments, Locomotion, Retarded, Sluggish, Stoppages, Suppressions).

Slow Pulse—(See "Slow" under Heart, Pulse).

Slow Recovery—Slow Recuperation—(See "Slow" under Recovery, Recuperation).

Slow of Speech — (See Halting, Impediment, Slow, Stammering, under Speech; "Slow of Voice" under Voice).

Slow of Voice—(See "Slow of Speech" in this section).

SLUGGISH—Slow—Inactive—Torpid—Dull—♄ influence.

Blood — (See "Sluggish Circulation" under Circulation).

Body—Sluggish Body—♄ afflicted in ♎. Also given by the water signs, and especially ♋ or ♓ on the Asc. Those parts of the body tend to be more sluggish which are ruled by the signs containing ♃ and ♀ at B. (See Dull, Idle, Inactive, Indifferent, Inertia, Lassitude, Lethargy, Listless, etc.).

Bowels — (See "Sluggish" under Bowels).

Circulation — (See "Sluggish" under Circulation).

Ears—Sluggish Circulation In—(See "Circulation" under Ears).

Eczema — Skin Diseases and Eczema from Sluggish Circulation—♃ afflicted in ♑. (See Eczema, Skin).

Fluids of the Body—Sluggish Condition of — (See "Restricted", and the various paragraphs under Fluids).

Gastric Juices — Sluggish Production of—(See "Juices" under Gastric).

Heart — Sluggish Action of — (See "Slow Action" under Heart).

Kidneys—(See "Sluggish" under Kidneys).

Liver—(See "Sluggish" under Liver).

Oesophagus — Sluggish Action of — (See Oesophagus).

Parts of the Body — The Sluggish Parts—(See "Blood" in this section).

Peristaltic Action—Sluggish and Impeded—(See Peristalsis).

Persons — Sluggish Persons — Dull People—The ☽ separating from ♂ and applying to ♄. (See Dull, Heavy, Inactive, Inertia, Labor, Lassitude, Lazy, Lethargy, Slothful, Slovenly, etc.).

Secretions Sluggish—(See Secretions).

Skin Diseases—From Sluggish Circulation—(See "Eczema" in this section).

Spinal Fluids — Sluggish and Obstructed — (See "Obstruction" under Spine).

Stomach — Sluggish Action of — (See "Peristaltic Action", "Sluggish", under Stomach). For further study see Hindrances, Retarded, Retention, Stagnant, Stoppages, Suppressions.

SLY — (See Cheating, Deceitful, Dishonest, Hypocritical, Petifogging, Shrewdness, etc.).

SMALL—Diminutive—Little—

Animals — (See "Small" under Animals).

Body—Small Body—♄ influence tends to a small body and small features; ♄ rising in ♑ tends to reduce the stature; ♄ lord of the Asc. and occi., as between the Nadir and Asc., or between the M.C. and Descendant, gives a small, thin body, and with dark complexion; ♋ on the Asc. gives short, small persons; the second half of ♌ on Asc., smaller than when first half is rising; ♑ on the Asc., short, slender, and ill-formed. (See "Body" under Diminished; Dwarfed; "Mean Stature" under Mean; "Body" under Short) .

Bones — (See "Small" under Bones; "Body" in this section).

Bowels — The Small Intestines — (See "Small Intestines" under Bowels).

Eyes—(See "Small" under Eyes).

Face—(See "Narrow", "Small", under Face).

Features — (See "Small", "Thin", under Features).

Fever — (See "Small Fevers" under Fever).

Finger Nails—(See "Small Nails" under Nails).

Head — (See "Little", "Small", under Head).

Hips—(See "Small" under Hips).

Intestines — (See "Small" under Bowels).

Lean, Small and Thin — (See "Small" under Lean).

Legs—(See "Small" under Legs).

Mean, Small Figure — (See "Mean Stature" under Mean).

Mind—A Small Mind—(See "Light In Mind" under Mind).

Neck—(See "Small" under Neck).

Shrill, Small Voice—(See Voice).

Slender, Small Body—Slender, Small Legs — (See "Slender" under Legs; "Little" under Slender).

Smaller and Weaker Bodies—Planets oriental, and in their second orientality, cause smaller and weaker bodies. (See "Weak Body" under Weak).

Smallpox; Thighs — Small Hips and Thighs — (See "Small" under Hips, Thighs).

Thin, Small and Lean—(See "Small" under Lean; Thin).

Voice—(See "Small" under Voice).

Weak, Small Figure — (See "Mean Stature" under Mean).

Weaker and Smaller Bodies — (See "Smaller and Weaker" in this section).

Weakly, Small and Sickly — ♃ in ♑, partile the Asc. (See "Constitution" under Sickly).

SMALLPOX — Variola — Varioloid Diseases—Caused principally by ♂, and ♂ too much in evidence at B.; ♂ afflicted in the Asc. at B., and ♂ in the Asc. tends to precipitate the disease when ♂ reaches the ☌ the rising degree at B.; ♂ ☌ the Asc. by dir.; ♂ in ♈ or ♑; ♂ afflicted in ♈ tends to blindness by smallpox; ♂ in ♈ in the 6th H.; ♂ exactly rising or setting at B., and especially in ♈, ♉, or ♍; ♂ afflicted in ♊ or ♍, and ♂ ☌, P., or evil asp. the Asc. by dir.; ♂ afflicted in ♓, and ☌, P., □, or ☍ the Asc. by dir.; this disease is peculiar to ♂, and often happens when ♂ is □ the Asc. in the

Zodiac; the ☉ afflicted in ♒; the ☉ to the □ or ☍ the ☽ by dir., and the ☽ afflicted by ♂ at B.; the ill-asps. of the ☉ to the hyleg or Asc. by transit or dir. tend to if the ☉ be afflicted by ♂ at B.; the ☉, ☽, or Asc. to the ☌, P., □, or ☍ ♂ by dir.; a ☽ disease; the ☽ afflicted in ♒ or ♏; the ☽ afflicted in ♏, and afflicting the hyleg therefrom; the ☽ in an earthy sign, and to the ☌, P., or ill-asp. ♂ by dir., and the ☽ hyleg; the ☽ afflicted in a watery sign, and to the ill-asps. ♀ by dir.; caused by afflictions to the ☽; the ☽ to the ill-asps. ♀ by dir., and ♀ in a watery sign at B.; ♄ in ♒, ♏, or ♓, and ☌, P., or evil asp. the Asc. by dir.; ♃ in an airy or watery sign, peregrine, and ☌ the Asc. by dir.; a pustular disease denoted by ♀; the Asc. to the ☌ or ill-asp. ♂ by dir., and ♂ in ♉ at B.; the Asc. to the □ or ☍ ♃ by dir., and ♃ afflicted by ♂ at B.; attacks are liable when the ☉, ☽, Asc., or hyleg, come to the ☌, P., or ill-asps. ♂ by dir.; the Asc. to the place of ☋ by dir.; the hyleg much afflicted at B. by ♂; an ♈ disease when malefic planets are in ♈ at B.; a ♌ disease, and caused by afflictions in ♌; the 6th face of ♉ on the Asc., and with the Pleiades in the Asc.; Subs at MCP 4, 5C), and at CP, or KP (11D). (See Chickenpox, Measles, Scabs, Scarlatina; Face, Pitted, Pock-Marked, and the various paragraphs in this section).

Blindness By—(See "Smallpox" under Blindness).

Children Die—From Smallpox—(See "Mortality Great" under Children).

Children Suffer—From Smallpox, but May Not Die—♂ coming to the ☌ or ill-asp. the Asc. early in life tends to smallpox, measles, or scarlatina. The ☽ to the □ or ☍ ♀ by dir. tends to smallpox in children.

Death by Smallpox—Great Danger of—♂ afflicting the ☉, ☽, Asc., or hyleg by dir.; ♂ in ♉ or ♏, and afflicting the hyleg; ♂ denotes. Case of Death By—See "Prince", No. 651, in 1001 N.N. (See Measles, Scarlet Fever).

Epidemic of Smallpox—Smallpox Prevalent—♂ is supreme in years of smallpox epidemics, and afflicts the hyleg in those affected; ♂ supreme at the Equinoxes and Solstices; ♂ ☍ the ☉ at the Vernal; ♂ predominating at a ☌ of three or four superior planets, and severe in type, but milder when ♂ is in ☌ or ☍ only one other superior planet, and ♂ holding power; ♂ in the 8th H. at a Solar Ingress into ♈, and afflicting the ☽ or planet ascending; ♃ in perigee tends to a great epidemic of smallpox, and which spreads and proves fatal in spite of vaccination. (See Epidemics).

Eyes—Blindness In by Smallpox—(See "Smallpox" under Blindness).

Face—Smallpox In—Pock-Marked—Pitted Face—A ♂ affliction; ♂ in ♈, and especially in the Asc.; caused by ♆ afflictions, and with ♆ in ♈ or the 1st H., and configurated with ♂ at B.; ♆ ☌ ♂ at B., and especially in the Asc.; in Hor'y Q. indicated by the ☽ with ♄ in ♈; ♀ Sig. in ♈, and especially if ♀ is afflicted by ♂; the 5° ♊ on the Asc.; the first face of ♓ on the Asc., and ♂ therein; the Asc. or its lord in one of the pitted degrees of the Zodiac at B. (See Pitted, Scars).

Immunity from Smallpox—There is little danger of taking smallpox unless ♂ afflicts the ☉, ☽, or Asc. at B., or in a train of evil directions. Vaccination is not needed in cases immune from this disease from birth. Also, in cases destined to fatality by the afflictions of ♂ to the ☉, ☽, Asc., or hyleg at B. vaccination is of little, or no avail. (See Immunity; "Epidemic" in this section).

Pitted Degrees—Of the Zodiac—The Asc., or its lord, in one of these degrees at B. tends to leave pitted scars on the face. (See Pitted; "Face" in this section).

Pock-Marked—(See "Face" in this section).

Prevalent—Smallpox Prevalent—(See "Epidemic" in this section).

Treatment—Of Smallpox—Red color, the color ruled by ♂, and to be confined in a red room, or have red rays and lights about the patient, is said to help alleviate the severity of the disease. This is on the theory of treatment by Similars and Sympathy. Also on this basis Vaccination often proves beneficial and preventive, which is the introduction of the lymph from the cow-pox vesicle into the human body, which lymph is under the rule of ♂, the same as ♂ rules the vesicle in the human. There is also a tablet remedy, known as "Double Sulphide", discovered and advocated by Dr. William Burgess, of the New Field Laboratory, Chattanooga, Tenn. Dr. Burgess is now deceased, and the address of this Laboratory is now P. O. Box 52, Lawrence, Long Island, New York. This remedy is a combination of Lime, Sulphur, and Magnesia, and quickly raises the resistance of the body, and overcomes the disease in a short time. Also, it is claimed, if these tablets are taken immediately after exposure to smallpox, the disease does not develop in the patient. Every family should have a box of these tablets in the house for emergencies in Chickenpox, Measles, Smallpox, Rashes, and Epidemic Diseases. This tablet is made up of materials ruled by ♄, ♂, and ♑, and represents a combination of both Antipathy and Sympathy in the treatment. The remedies of ♄ oppose the diseases of ♂. (See Antipathy, Opposites, Red, Remedies, Sympathy, Treatment).

Vaccination—(See "Immunity" in this section).

Varioloid Diseases—♂ afflicted in ♑.

Vascular Tissues—Affected by Smallpox—(See "Vascular Tissues" under Vascular).

Young People—Many Die of Smallpox—(See "Mortality Great" under Children).

SMART—

Smart Appearance—Smart and Active Appearance—♊ on the Asc. at B. (See "Body" under Active; Brisk, Energetic, Quick, etc.).

Smart In Learning—(See Learning; "Quickened" under Mentality; "Good Mind" under Mind; Reading, Scholar, Study, etc.).

Smart and Quick Step—(See "Energetic" under Gait).

SMELL—The Sense of Smell—Olfaction—Olfactory Nerves—The etheric vibrations of ☿ give Smell. Also ruled by ♂. Wilson, in his Dictionary, says the Olfactory Nerves are ruled by ♀. Smell is also influenced by the ♏ sign, which sign rules the nose, and ♄ or ♂ afflicted in this sign tend to affect the smell, and cause various disorders of smell. Loss of Smell (Anosmia), and Perversions of Smell (Parosmia), are caused by ♄ afflicted in ♏, and also by Subs at AT, AX, and MCP (3, 4C). (See Nose). The Hebrew Letter Samech (S) is connected with the sense of Smell.

SMILES—Smiling Face—Pleasing Smiles—♀ in the Asc., or ruler of the Asc., well-aspected and dignified, gives dimples, and a pleasing, smiling face; ♀ Sig. in ♎, pleasing smiles; in Hor'y Q., ♀ Sig. of the person. Also, the ☽ Sig. in ♒, gives a smiling, cheerful, kind, humane, and benevolent countenance. People born under ♄ are not much given to smiles, as they are of a more serious, melancholic and taciturn nature. (See Cheerfulness, Contentment, Countenance, Dimples, Expression; "Smiling" under Face; Happiness, Humane, Joyful, Kind, Laughter; "Peace of Mind" under Mind; Mirth, Optimistic, Pleasant; "Sanguine Temperament" under Sanguine).

SMOKING—(See "Drug Heart" under Heart; Narcotics, Tobacco).

SMOKY—The Smoky Degrees of the Zodiac—If the Asc., or its lord, are in any of these degrees at B., the native is more dun and swarthy of complexion, and with a dull intellect. These degrees are as follows—0° ♈; 0° ♉; 0° ♊; 20° ♋; 20° ♌; 22° ♍; 0° ♎; 24° ♏; 23° ♐; 15° ♑; 4° ♒; 0° ♓. (See "Swarthy" under Complexion; "Mind" under Dull).

SMOOTH—

Body—Smooth Body—The ☽ gives a smooth, corpulent, and phlegmatic body; the ☽, when oriental, gives a smooth, corpulent, and tall body; ♄ in S. Lat. tends to a smooth and fleshy body, but in N. Lat. to one more lean, hairy, and bony; ♂ in ♈, partile the Asc., and occi., the native will be more ruddy and smooth, but if ♂ be ori., tall and less swarthy.

Face—(See "Smooth" under Face).

Hair—(See "Smooth" under Hair).

SMOTHERED—Smothering—Smothering Sensation—Danger of Being Smothered—(See Angina, Asphyxia, Cyanosis, Fainting; "Faintings" under Heart; "Non-Oxygenation" under Oxygen; Strangulation, Suffocation).

SNAKES—(See Reptiles, Serpents).

SNEEZING—(See "Hay Fever", "Sneezing", under Nose).

SNORING—(See "Snoring" under Breathing).

SNOW—Snow is ruled by ♄.

Suffering From—Extremes of Snow—♃ ☌ ♂, mischief by snow. The ♉ sign ascending at the Vernal E., and ♀ afflicted, and especially in Countries ruled by ♉. (See Blizzards, Cold, Frost, Hail, Ice, Saturn, Storms, Weather, Wind, Winter).

SNUFF—(See "Snuff" under Narcotics).

SNUFFLES—Snuffling—Snaffling—(See "Snuffling" under Nose).

SOBER—Well-Balanced—Self-Possessed—Dispassionate—Even-Tempered—Grave—Seriously Thoughtful, etc.—

Sober and Commanding—Born under ♃. (See Commanding).

Sober and Manly—(See "Manly" under Manner).

Sober and Serious—(See Despondent, Grave, Melancholic; "Serious Mind" under Serious, etc.).

SOCIAL RELATIONS—Social Life—Society—Social Diseases, etc.—The following subjects have to do with the Social Life, and the Social Relations of the native, his dealings with others, etc., and also with the dealings of the Social Classes with each other. The position, strength, power, weakness, and afflictions to the planet ♀ in the map of birth indicate to a large degree the kind and nature of the dealings of the native with the World socially, and his fate in such matters. A strong ♃ at B. also will help the native to be fortunate and well-received by the people. Each of the planets in their own sphere, and their positions, aspects, and strength in the radical map, will play their part in the conduct of the native, for better or worse, and in accordance with the character, attainments, conduct, morals, motives, purposes, and self-control manifested. Many of the subjects in this book have a bearing upon social relations, and which would be too numerous to list here, but the following are a few of the more important ones. See the following subjects in the alphabetical arrangement when only listed here—

Amusements; Anarchists;

Aversion to Society—(See Aversions, Recluse, Renunciation, Seclusion, Secretive, Solitude, etc.).

Banishment; Busy-Body—(See Meddlers).

Character; Classes of Society—Much Discord Between—(See "Discord" under Quarrels).

Common People—Injured By—(See Common).

Companions—Companionships—(See Companions).

Conduct; Crime—Criminal Tendencies—(See Crime).

Dangerous; Deception; Destiny;

Destructiveness; Discord—Discord Between the Classes of Society—(See "Discord" under Quarrels).

Diseases—Social Diseases—(See "Scandalous Diseases" under Scandal; Venereal).

Enemies; Environment; Execrated;

Exile; External Influences—Reaction of the Native To—(See Environment, External, Influenced, Negative, Positive, Receptive, Ruling, Susceptibility).

Family Life—(See Family).

Fanatical—Fanatical Against Established Religion and Society—(See "Fanatical" under Religion).

Fate; Friends; Government — Rebellious Against the Government — (See Anarchists, Mutiny, Sedition).

Hand of Man—Injury or Death By—(See Hand of Man).

Hatreds; Honesty; Humanity—Every Evil Upon—(See Humanity).

Hypocrisy; Ideals; Imprisoned — (See Prison).

Jealousies; Judge — Sentenced By — (See Judges).

Laws—Disregard for Social or Moral Laws—(See "Moral Laws" under Love Affairs; "Loose Morals" under Morals).

Libelers; Love Affairs — (Note the various paragraphs under Love Affairs).

Marriage — (See the subjects under Husband, Marriage, Marriage Partner, Wife).

Men—The Many Conditions Affecting Men—(See the subjects under Men).

Mistrustful; Misunderstood;

Mob Violence—Victim of—(See Lynching, Mobs; "Flying Stones" under Stones; Trampled).

Money—Reckless In Use of—(See Expense, Money, Prodigal).

Morals — (See "Good", "Loose", and the various paragraphs under Morals).

Murderers; Neighbors; Outcaste — A Social Outcaste—♂ afflicted in the 12th H. (See Disgrace, Execrated; "Hated by Others" under Hatred; "Loss Of" under Reputation).

Pest to Society—(See Execrated).

Pleasures; Politics; Popularity;

Prattlers—(See Meddlers).

Property; Public — The Public — (See Public).

Quarrelsome; Radicalism;

Reactionary; Rebellious; Recluse;

Reformers; Relatives; Religion;

Renunciation; Reputation; Reserved;

Residence; Reverses; Revolutionary;

Riches; Riotous; Roamer; Ruin;

Secret Societies—(See Secret).

Secretive; Sedition; Sex Relations — (See Amorous, Cohabitation, Intercourse; "Adultery", "Liaisons", under Love Affairs; Marriage, Morals, Opposite Sex; "Passional Excesses" under Passion; Sensuality; "Clandestine" under Sex; Wanton, Wench, etc.).

Socialism; Suspicious;

Terror to Society—(See Execrated).

Thieves; Treachery; Treason — (See Sedition).

Unruly; Vagabond; Violent;

Wanderer; Wealth; Women — Conditions Affecting Women Socially—(See the various paragraphs under Women). For other subjects along this line, which may not be listed in this Article, look in the alphabetical arrangement for the subject you have in mind.

SOCIALISM—Socialism is said to be under the rule of ♅ and the ♒ sign, and is one of the New Movements now being brought into manifestation for the establishment of the Aquarian Age, Fraternity, and Justice, and the overthrow of the old Political Bosses. The Movement seems to be peculiar, and somewhat misunderstood, due to its Uranian character. Some of the influences in the radical map which indicate Socialistic tendencies are the ☉ ☌ or ill-asp. ♅; ♅ ☌ or ill-asp. ♂; ♅ afflicted in the 9th H.; lord of the 10th a malefic, and afflicted in the 12th H. Mars strong at B., rising and elevated, and configurated with ♅ and ☿, tends to make Extremists in any Cause of Reformation. (See Ideals, Ideas, Independent, Misunderstood, Politics, Radicalism, Reactionary, Rebellious, Reformers; "Fanatical" under Religion; Revolutionary).

SOCIETY—(See Social Relations).

SODIUM—Soda—Sodium is an alkaline metal, and the base of Salt. Being alkaline it is used internally to counteract over-acidity in the system, caused by the deposits, retentions, and suppressions of ♄. The Alkaline Salts in the body also help to keep the balance between acidity and alkalinity when they are normal. (See Acidity). Alkaline substances are under the rule of the positive planets, and the positive Signs of the Zodiac. The planet ♂ is, therefore, a strong ruler over Sodium, and tends to counteract the diseases of ♄ in the system, and to restore the balance of alkalinity in the body. The ☉, ♅, and ♃, being positive planets, also have a strong influence over Sodium, and its various forms. (See Alkalinity).

Sodium Chloride — Common Salt — Ruled by the ♒ sign, and is connected with the control of water in the system.

Sodium Hydrate — Caustic Soda — Is said to be strongly ruled by ♂, due to its caustic and escharotic qualities. (See Caustic).

Sodium Phosphate—The Salt ruled by the ♎ Sign, and is said to be connected with the acids of the body, and is a combination of Sodium and Phosphoric Acid. Libra is the exalted sign of ♄, and Sodium Phosphate is partly ruled by ♄, and also by ♀, negative planets which rule the acids in the body.

Sodium Salicylate—Partly ruled by ♄, due to the combination of Sodium with Salicylic Acid, and is strongly antipyretic, and opposes the fevers of ♂ when given internally in large doses. Also, due to its positive qualities, it is cholagogue and diaphoretic.

Sodium Sulphate — The Salt ruled by the ♉ Sign, and is connected with the elimination of water in the system. Internally Sodium Sulphate stimulates the liver, pancreas, and also the intestinal secretions, and acts as a purgative. (See "Salts" under Zodiac).

SODOMY — (See Homosexuality, Perversions).

SOFT—Softening—

Agents — Softening Agents — (See Emollient, Ointments, Resolvent).

Body—A Soft Body—(See Flabby).

Bones—Softening of—(See Rickets).

Brain—(See "Softening" under Brain).

Cellular Tissue—Soft Cellular Tissue —(See Parenchyma).

Chancre—Soft Chancre—Chancroid— (See Gonorrhoea).

Complexion—(See "Soft" under Complexion).

Effeminate and Soft — (See Effeminate).

Excrescences Soft, Watery Excrescences—(See Excrescences).

Glandular Tissues — Softening of — (See "Softening" under Glands).

Hair—(See "Soft" under Hair).

Nature—Soft and Effeminate Nature —(See Effeminate).

Nerve Tissue — Softening of — (See "Softening" under Nerves).

Parts—Soft Parts—Enlargement and Thickening of — Acromegaly— (See "Acromegaly" under Enlargements; "Enlargements" under Extremities).

Skin—(See "Soft" under Skin).

Thickening — Of Soft Parts — (See "Parts" in this section).

Tissues—The Soft Tissues—Disorders of—(See Elephantiasis, Fiber, Flabby, Gangrene; "Softening" under Glands; Hypertrophy, Malacia, Mortification, Muscles, Parenchyma, Relaxation, Thickening; "Soft Tissues" under Tissues; Wastings; "Agents" in this section).

Tubercles — Softening of — (See Tubercles).

SOLANOID CANCER — (See "Solanoid" under Carcinoma).

SOLAR—Pertaining to the Sun—

Solar Eclipse—(See Eclipse).

Solar Forces—The Spleen is the gateway to the Solar Forces. (See "Forces" under Sun).

Solar Horas—(See Horas).

Solar Ingresses—(See Ingresses).

Solar Life Currents—The Vital Fluid —(See "Fluid" under Vital).

Solar-Lunar Activities—The combined influences of the ☉ and ☽ at B. represent the constitution and the health, and according to the harmony or adverse aspects existing between the ☉ and ☽ at B., so will the vitality, the efficiency of the functions, and the general health be. Dr. Duz. in his book, "Astral Medicine", discusses the Solar-Lunar System, and the Solar-Lunar Chart, from quite a new and advanced standpoint, and somewhat different from anything seen in the regular Textbooks of Astrology, and every student should read this book by Dr. Duz. (See Constitution, Functions, Health; "Quarters of the Moon" under Moon; "Moon and the Sun" under Sun; "Depletion", "Force", under Vital; "Good", "Low", under Vitality).

Solar Orb—(See "Forces" under Sun).

Solar Periodicity—(See "Periodicity" under Sun).

Solar Plexus — (See "Solar" under Plexus).

Solar Revolution—This is the return of the ☉ each year to the same degree of Longitude as in at B. These times are important to note in connection with health matters, as the malefics falling upon the places of the radical (☉, ☽, Asc., or hyleg, at the Solar Revolution tend to many evils, disturbances in the constitution or mind, and in the general affairs of the native, according to the nature of the afflicting planet, or planets. Solar Revolutions, Transits, or Directions cannot bring anything to pass which is not shown in the map of birth. Chapter XXXVI in Pearce's Textbook of Astrology gives a good Treatise on Solar Revolutions, their various influences and aspects, and as related to disease. (See "Birthday" under Birth). The influences of Solar Revolutions are mentioned many times under the various diseases and afflictions in this book. The following are some of the subjects in which the Solar Rev. influence is mentioned. See these subjects in the alphabetical arrangement — Abroad; Anguish; "Causes" under Chronic; Contentment; "Causes" under Disease; Disgrace; Dissipation; Eclipses; "Conduct" under Evil; "Accidents To", "Eye Trouble", under Eyes; "Death In" under Family; "Danger To" under Father; "Death Of" under Friends; "Periods of Bad Health" under Health; Imbecility; Influenza; "Abroad" under Journeys; "Danger To" under Life; "Chronic Diseases" under Malignant; "Affliction Of", "Peace of Mind", under Mind; "Liable To" under Misfortune; "Danger To" under Mother; "Death Of" under Parents; "Periodic Revolution" under Periodic; "Danger of Imprisonment" under Prison; "Death By" under Rheumatism; "Birth Of" under Son).

Solar Spectrum — (See "Planets and Color" under Colors).

SOLDIERS—Military People—

Assaults By — Prevalence of — An eclipse of the ☽ in the 2nd decan. of ♑.

Bloodshed — Many Soldiers Killed — (See "Shedding" under Blood; "Shedding of Blood" under Shedding; Slaughter; "War and Bloodshed" under War).

Cruelty Of—Inhumanity of—Furiousness of—An eclipse of the ☉ in the 3rd decan. of ♓.

Danger To—The ☽ to the ☌ Aldebaran by dir. (See Army, Military; "Navy" under Ships; War).

Death by Soldiers—The ☽ with Sirius or ♄, or with Markab and ♂.

Death In the Service — (See "Battle" under Abroad; Military Life; "Death" under War).

Injury by Soldiers—The ☉ to the ☌ ♂ by dir. (See Assaults, Cruelty, Death By, in this section).

Killed In Battle—(See "Death In War" under War).

Officer Killed — (See "Officer Killed" under Military).

Slaughter — (See "Much Slaughter Everywhere" under Slaughter).

War—Death or Injury In—(See War).

Wounded In Battle—The ☉ Sig. ☌ ♂; the ☉ to the ☌ ♂ by dir. if ♂ afflict the

⊙ or hyleg at B.; ♂ in the Asc. at B., and ill-dignified, may be dangerously wounded; ♂ □ or ☍ the Asc., and if he is also in ☍ to the ⊙ or ☽, danger of a violent death, and if applying and near the exact ☍, killed on the spot. (See "Death or Injury In" under War).

SOLID—

Solid Constitution—Given by the earthy signs, and able to withstand much wear and tear. (See "Good" under Constitution; Endurance, Wear and Tear).

Solid Countenance—(See "Solid Countenance" under Face).

Solid Intellect—(See "Solidarity" under Intellect).

Solid Judgment—Void Of—(See "Bad Judgment" under Judgment).

Solid Learning—Void of—(See "Void Of" under Learning).

Solid Sense — (See "Good Judgment" under Judgment).

Solidification—Of the Body—(See Cirrhosis, Crystallization, Density, Deposits, Hardening, Lime, Minerals, Precipitation, Sclerosis, Stone, etc.).

SOLITARY VICE — Self-Abuse — (See "Solitary" under Vice).

SOLITUDE—

Fear and Dread Of — (See Darkness; "Solitude" under Fear).

Fond Of—Propensity to Solitude and Retirement—The ☽ P ♄ at B., and especially with females; ♄ inclines to solitude, and retirement from the World, which they equally fear and detest. (See Misanthropic, Mistrustful, Recluse, Renunciation, Reserved, Resignation, Retiring, Saturn, Seclusive, Secretive, Serious, Shy, Suspicious, Twelfth House, etc.).

SOLSTICES — The Summer and Winter Solstices—The Summer Solstice is when the ⊙ passes into the ♋ sign, usually on June 21st. At the Winter Solstice the ⊙ passes into the ♑ sign, usually on Dec. 21st or 22nd. These Solstice Points constitute the beginning of Angles in the map, and the cusps of the 4th and 10th Houses, and have an important bearing in health matters over the World in General, and also over the individual whose map of birth they may strongly affect. The influences of the configurations at the time of the Solstices are mentioned quite a number of times in this book under various diseases and conditions, and the following are a few of them. Also read the Chapter on "Equinoxes and Solstices" in Pearce's Textbook of Astrology, Chapter 2, of Book 2. The times of the Solstices are also Ingresses of the ⊙ into the ♋ and ♑ signs, known as the Tropical Signs. (See Equinoxes, Ingresses, Tropical, Vernal. Also see Angles, Cancer Sign, Capricorn Sign, Cardinal, Crime; "Air" under Dryness; "Dog Days" under Dogs; Epidemics; "Prevalent" under Fluxes; Fourth House, Hail; "Nil" under Mars Diseases; "Minor Disorders" under Minor; "Death" under Mutilated; "Great Pestilence" under Pestilence; "Sickly Summer" under Summer; Tenth House; "Dry" under Winter).

SOLUTION — Disintegration—The Termination of a Disease—A Crisis—Resolution In Disease, etc.

Disease — The Solution of Continuity In Disease—(See the Introduction under Continuity. Also see Abatement, Amelioration, Course, Crises; "Better" under Disease; "Degree of Disturbance" under Disturbed; Duration, Interrupted, Moderation, Modification, Recovery, Recuperation, Resolution, Retrograde, Sequence, etc.).

Tissue—Solution of—(See Decay, Disintegration, Resolution, Resolvent; "Solution" under Tissues).

SOMNAMBULISM — (See "Sleep-Walking" under Sleep).

SON—Sons—

Birth of a Son — The ⊙ to the ☌ or good aspect ♃ by dir.; the ☽, lords of the Asc. and 5th H., and the signs on the Asc. and 5th H. being masculine, denote a male, but female if such conditions are feminine; the ☽ to the ⚹ or △ ♂ by dir.; ♃ at a Solar Rev. ☌ the place of the radical ⊙; the M.C. to the ☌ or good asp. the ⊙ in a female nativity; the M.C. to the good asp. the ☽, as the ☽ may be aspected; the Asc. to the ⚹ or △ the ⊙ or ♂ by dir.; the majority of the planets in masculine signs and houses, and with the Asc. and sign on the 5th H. masculine. (See "Female Children", "First-Born Child", "Male Children Born", under Children; "Births" under Male; Predetermination).

Death of a Son — (See "First-Born Child", "Son Born May Die", under Children; Eclipses; "Death of a Male" under Males).

Health of Sons—(See "Good Health", "Ill-Health", under Males).

SOOTHING—Mitigating—Calming — Blue is a soothing color in the treatment of the sick.

Disease Soothed — (See Amelioration, Calm, Convalescence, Ease; "Disease" under Improved, Solution; Moderation, Recovery, Recuperation).

Soothing Drugs—The drugs of ♆ are especially soothing, as Opiates and Narcotics. Also ♄ remedies are soothing, and act as sedatives, and tend to relieve the excitement and irritability of ♂ diseases. (See Anaesthetics, Anodyne, Narcotics, Sedatives; "Soporifics" under Sleep).

Soothing Influences—Over the Body—The Adrenal Secretions, under the rule of ♃, when scattered over the body, tend to exert a soothing, quieting, and peaceful effect when the nature is disturbed by the evil aspects of the malefics, and especially by ♄ and ♂. The influence of ♀ is also soothing. The benefics, ♃ and ♀, are both soothing and beneficent in their action upon the body. Moonlight has a soothing influence over the body. Blue color is soothing. (See Blue, Calm; "Moonlight" under Moon; Sedatives; "Soothing Drugs" in this section).

SOPORIFIC DRUGS—Ruled by ♆. (See Narcotics, Neptune; "Soporifics" under Sleep).

SORCERY—Witchcraft—Black Magic—(See "Practices Hypnotism" under Hypnotism; "Black Magic" under Magic; Pretender, Witchcraft).

SORDES—(See "Sordes" under Teeth).

SORDID — (See Depraved; "Low and Base" under Low; Vile).

SORE—Soreness—Inflamed—

Eyes—Sore Eyes—(See "Inflamed" under Eyes).

Sore Gums — (See "Inflamed" under Gums).

Sore Mouth—(See "Sore" under Mouth).

Sore Nipples—(See Nipples).

Sore Throat — (See "Sore" under Throat).

For further influences along this line see the various paragraphs under Blows, Bruises, Burns, Cuts, Hurts, Inflammation, Injuries, Swellings, Wounds, etc.).

SORES—Any Ulcer, Chafe, or Wound—Sores resulting from feverish disturbances, epidemics, violence, or an injury, are denoted by ♂, and brought on by ♂ in an angle, occi. of the ☉, and ori. of the ☽. Sores from impure blood, plethora, surfeits, etc., are usually the result of ♃ afflictions. Venereal sores are brought on by ♀. Sores caused by deposits, retention of poisons and wastes in the system, etc., are ruled by ♄. The ☽ also rules sores brought on by disturbance of the fluids and functions of the body. Sores are also considered ♎ diseases, and by afflictions in ♎, due to disturbed kidneys, and improper elimination. Also the ♓ sign tends to sores and ulcers. The ☉ and ♂, the fiery and electric planets, tend to bring on sores by excess of heat in a part, as bed sores, etc. For the general influences along this line see the following subjects — Abscesses, Apthae, Boils, Canker, Carbuncles, Carcinoma; "Offensive" under Discharges; Eruptions; "Chancroid" under Gonorrhoea; "Sores On" under Face, Legs; Foul, Gangrene, Impure, Malignant, Pimples; "Plague Sores" under Plague; Pus Sores, Putrid Sores, Scabs; "Scarified Sores" under Scars; Skin Disorders, Sloughing, Smallpox; "Chancre" under Syphilis; Ulcers, Venereal, etc. For other subjects which may have to do with Sores, and which are not listed here, look in the alphabetical arrangement for the subject you have in mind.

SORREL COLOR — Ruled by the Third House. (See Colors).

SORROW — Grief — Miseries — Afflictions — Anxieties — Losses, etc. Saturn is generally looked upon as the planet which brings sorrows into our lives, chastenings, afflictions, etc., but for our own good, in the end, and to test us, and burn the dross from our natures. Also ♂ brings sorrow thru violence, injuries, fevers, quarrels, disputes, etc. The 12th H. is called the House of Sorrows and Self-Undoing. All of the malefic planets by their afflictions tend to bring more or less of sorrow, affliction, disappointment, anxiety, and grief into our lives until we learn to transcend them, become spiritualized, and live more in our Higher Minds. For the general influences which tend to bring sorrows see "Much Sorrow" in this section.

Abundance of Sorrow — (See "Many Sorrows" in this section).

Aries—Sorrow to People Under Aries —(See "Sorrow" under Aries).

Dies of Sorrow—And a Broken Heart —The 29° ♑ on the Asc. at B. (See "Broken Heart" under Broken).

Face — Sorrowful Face — (See "Sad Face" under Face).

Life Robbed of Its Joy — (See Joy, Melancholy, Sadness).

Many Sorrows — Has Much Sorrow — The ☉ or ☽ afflicted by ♄ at B., and to the ☌ ♄ by dir.; the ☉ to the ill-asps. the ☽ by dir., and the ☉ afflicted by the ☽ at B.; the ☽ to the ☌ or ill-asps. ♄ or ♂ by dir.; the ☽ to the cusp the 12th H. by dir.; ♆ afflicted in ♓; ♆ □ or ☍ ♀; ♅ afflicted in ♎, ♑, ♒, or in the 10th H.; ♄ in the 1st H. at B., much sorrow and melancholy; ♄ ruler of the 12th H. at B., and to the ☌ or ill-asp. the Asc. by dir.; ♄ to his own ill-asps. by dir.; given by the □ and ☍ aspects of ♄ to the planets at B., and by dir., and also by his ☌ with the Lights; ♄ in ♎, ☌, □, or ☍ the Asc. by dir., and ♄ ruler of the 1st H. at B.; in Hor'y Q. ♄ afflicting the Significator of the person; ♄ to the ☌, or ill-asps. the ☉, ☽, or Asc. by dir.; ♃ ruler of the 1st H., and to the ill-asps. ♄ by dir.; ♃ by periodic revolution to the ☌ ♄ in the radix; ♂ to the ☌ or ill-asp. ♄ by dir.; ♂ afflicted in the 12th H.; ♀ by periodic rev. to the ill-asps. the ☽ or M.C. in the radix, and produced by previous pleasures; ♀ progressed in ☌, P, □, or ☍ ♄ in the radix, or vice versa; lord of the Asc. in the 12th H., and afflicted at B., and by dir.; the M.C. to the cusp the 12th H. by dir.; the 2nd H., or its ruler, to the ☌, P, □, or ☍ ♄ by dir.; the 2nd face of ♉ on the Asc. at B.; the 2nd decan. of ♐ on the Asc. shows afflictions, distress of mind, suspicion, woe, mistrust, and sorrow. (See Affliction, Anguish, Anxiety, Brooding, Cares, Dejected, Depressed, Despair, Despondent, Discontentment, Disgrace, Distress; "Own Worst Enemy" under Enemies; Evils, Fate, Fears; "Ill-Fortune" under Fortune; Gloom, Grief; "Hopes Cut Off" under Hope; "Low Spirits" under Low; Melancholy; "No Peace of Mind" under Mind; Miserable, Regretful, Renunciation, Repining; "Loss Of" under Reputation; Reverses, Ruin, Sadness, Scandal, Self-Undoing, Suffering, Trouble, Twelfth House, Worry, etc.).

Periods of Sorrow—The ☉ or ☽ to the ☌, P, □, or ☍ ♄ or ♂ by dir. (See "Periods of Bad Health" under Health).

Prevalent—Much Sorrow Prevalent—(See "Public Grief" under Grief).

Public Sorrow — Public Sorrow and Grief—Much Sorrow Generally—♄ lord of the year, and afflicted at the Vernal Equinox; ☿ in ♑ at the Vernal, lord of the year, and afflicted, and especially to Peoples and Countries under the rule of ♑. (See Casualties; "Much Grief Generally", "Public Grief", under

Grief; "Much Misery Everywhere" under Misery; "Much Misfortune Generally" under Misfortune; Prevalent, Public).

Release from Sorrow—Through Resignation and Atonement—The ☉ or ☽ to the ☌, or ill-asps. ♄ by dir. (See Renunciation).

Secret Sorrows—The ☽ in the 12th H., and to the ☌ or ill-asp. ♅ or ♄ by dir.; ♄ ruler of, or in the 12th H. at B., and afflicted; ♃ to the ill-asps. ♄ by dir., and the direction falling in the 12th H.; ruler of the Asc. in the 12th H.; the Asc. or M.C. to the cusp the 12th H. by dir.

Sorrowful Spirit — ♄ afflicting the ☉, ☽, ☿, Asc., or hyleg at B., and by dir. (See Sad).

Suffering — A Life of Suffering and Sorrow—(See "Life of Suffering" under Suffering; "Many Sorrows" in this section).

Women — Much Sorrow To — (See "Women" under Misfortune).

SOTTISHNESS — Dull — Stupid—Foolish — Senseless — Danger of Excesses In Drink, etc.—The ☽ afflicted in ♑, ♏, or ♓; ♂ Sig. in ♋ or ♓; ♂ Sig. in water signs unless well-aspected by the ☉, ☽, or ♃; ♀ Sig. ☌ ♂; ♀ afflicted in ♓; ☿ afflicted in ♋ or ♓; a ♓ influence, and with the ☉, ☽, ♂, or ☿ afflicted in ♓, or with ♓ on the Asc. at B.; many planets in watery signs at B., and especially in ♓. (See "Habitual Drunkard" under Drunkenness; "Mind" under Dull; "Lack Of" under Energy; Idle, Improvident, Inactive, Indifferent, Inertia, Lazy, Taverns, etc.).

SOUL—The Soul is said to be governed by the 5th H., and corresponds to the ♌ Sign. (See Ego, Heliocentric, Pineal Gland, Spirit).

Physical Being — The Soul of — (See "Being" under Physical).

SOUND—

Sound Constitution—(See "Sound" under Constitution).

Sound Intellect—(See "Sound" under Intellect, Mind).

Sound Judgment—(See "Good" under Judgment).

Sound Mind—(See "Sound" under Intellect, Mind).

SOURCE—The ☉ is the chief source and regulator of the life forces. (See "Life Force" under Life; Sun; "Fluid", "Force", under Vital).

SOUTH SCALE—A Star of the nature of ♄ and ♀, in the 13° ♏, violent in nature, and productive of every species of disease and misfortune when rising or with the Lights, and especially in female nativities. The ☉ with at B. is indicative of trouble and disgrace. The ☉ or ☽ to the ☌ of tends to scandal, disgrace, misfortune, and ill-health. The influences of this star are listed a number of times in the various Articles in this book. The following are some of them—See "Threatened With" under Disease; Disgrace; "Every Evil" under Evil; "Liable To" under Misfortune; Ruin; "Danger Of" under Sickness; "Disease" under Species.

SOUTHERN SIGNS — (See "Northern Signs" under North).

SPACES — Intercellular Spaces — (See "Intercellular" under Cells).

SPARE BODY—Indicated by ♄; ☿ in ♐, partile the Asc., spare, tall, well-shaped, and large-boned; born under ♈, spare, dry, strong, moderate-sized body, as with ♈ on the Asc.; ♍ on the Asc., spare, tall, well-made, but compact body; the first half of ♐ rising, a spare body; the second half of ♒ on the Asc., spare and thin body. (See "Raw-Boned" under Bones; Lean, Slender, Thin).

SPARED — The Life Spared — (See "Spared" under Life; "Patient Will Recover" under Recovery; "Good Powers of Resistance" under Resistance; "Good" under Vitality).

SPASMODIC DISEASES — Spasms — Spasmodic Movements — Convulsive Movements — Erratic Movements — Increased Motility — Paroxysms — Motor Neuroses—Jerky and Irregular Movements—Involuntary Movements—Tonic Action—Spastic Action—Rigidity, etc. The planet ♅ is spasmodic, and spasmodic action is largely ruled by this planet, and also by the ♒ sign, the strong sign of ♅. Uranus in any sign tends to spasmodic action over that part of the body, and its opposite. Both ♅ and ♆, when afflicted, indicate spasmodic action. Uranus in signs which rule the arms, hands, legs, and feet tends to spasm and cramps in these parts. Spasmodic diseases are further caused by ♅ in the 6th H., or afflicting the ☉, ☽, Asc., or hyleg from this house; the ☉ afflicted in ♒; ☿ afflicted in ♒, spasmodic action arising from debility, and called "Wind in the Blood" by the Ancients; ♒ diseases, and afflictions in ♒; ♒ on the Asc. or 6th H. Also caused especially by Subs at the Atlas, the 1st Cervical Vertebra. The following subjects have to do with Spasmodic Diseases, which see in the alphabetical arrangement when only listed here—

Abdomen — Spasm of Muscles of — Spasmodic Pains In — (See "Colic", "Cramps", "Pain", under Bowels; Ileac Passion; "Abdominal" under Muscles).

Acute and Spasmodic Pains — In the Head—(See "Pains" under Head).

Alternating Spasm — (See "Clonic" in this section).

Angina Pectoris—(See Angina).

Antispasmodic Remedies—(See Antispasmodic).

Aorta — Spasmodic Gushing of Blood Thru—(See Aorta).

Arms — (See "Cramps", "Spasm", under Arms).

Arterial Circulation—Spasmodic Disturbance of — (See "Arterial" under Circulation).

Asthma — (See "Spasmodic" under Asthma).

Bladder — (See "Spasm" under Bladder).

Blood—Spasmodic Gushing of—(See "Aorta" in this section).

Bowels—(See "Spasm" under Bowels).

Brain—(See "Spasmodic Diseases" under Brain).

Breathing — (See "Spasmodic" under Breath).

Ceaseless Motion — (See Excitable, Motion).

Cheyne-Stokes Breathing—(See "Cheyne-Stokes" under Breathing).

Chorea—(See Saint Vitus Dance).

Clonic Spasm—Spasm with Alternating Relaxations — Myoclonus — Paramyoclonus Multiplex — Involuntary Muscular Contractions — A H disease and affliction: Subs at AT and AX. Uranus in any sign tends to cause clonic spasms in the part, or parts, ruled by such sign. (See "Myoclonia" under Arms; Contractions, Epilepsy; "Movements" under Erratic; "Nystagmus" under Eyeballs; Incoordination; "Contractions" under Involuntary, Muscles; "Clonic Spasm" under Iris; Jerkings; "Paramyoclonus" under Muscles; Quivering; Saint Vitus Dance, Tremors, Twitching; "Tonic" in this section).

Colic; Constrictions; Continued Spasm —(See "Tonic" in this section).

Contortions; Contractions — Involuntary Muscular Contractions — Caused by the afflictions of H in the sign which rules the part. (See Contractions, Coordination, Hyperkinesia; "Contractions" under Involuntary, Muscles; Tetanus, Twitchings; "Clonic", "Tonic", and the various paragraphs in this section).

Convulsions; Convulsive Movements—(See "Movements" under Convulsions).

Coordination; Cough; Cramps;

Dancing Spasm—(See "Saltatory" in this section).

Death by Spasms — (See "Death" under Fits).

Diaphragm—(See "Spasmodic" under Diaphragm).

Diseases — Spasmodic Diseases — (See the Introduction, and the various paragraphs in this Article).

Distortions; Dsypnoea; Eclampsia — (See Eclampsia, Epilepsy).

Emotions — (See "Spasmodic" under Emotions).

Epilepsy; Erratic Movements — (See "Movements" under Erratic).

Exaggerated Action; Eyeballs — (See "Clonic Spasm", "Nystagmus", under Eyeballs).

Face—(See "Spasmodic Diseases" under Face).

Feet—(See "Spasms In" under Feet).

Fits; Fluttering — (See "Fluttering" under Heart).

Gait—The Peculiar Walk of Paralysis Agitans — (See "Festination" under Walk).

Glottis—Involuntary Closure of—(See Glottis).

Gripings; Hands — (See "Cramps", "Spasms", under Hands).

Head — (See "Spasmodic Pains", "Spasms In", under Head).

Headache — (See "Spasmodic" under Headache).

Heart—(See "Spasm" under Heart).

Hiccough; Hippus — (See "Clonic Spasm" under Eyeballs).

Hyperkinesia—(See Muscles).

Hysteria; Ilcac Passion;

Incoordination; Infancy—(See "Colic", "Cramps", "Convulsions", "Paralysis", "Paroxysms", under Infancy).

Inspiration—(See "Spasmodic" under Breath).

Intermittent; Interrupted; Intestines —(See "Spasm" under Bowels)

Introversion; Involuntary; Iris—(See "Clonic Spasm" under Iris).

Irregular Spasm—(See Colic, Cramps, Saint Vitus Dance; "Clonic" in this section).

Jerkings; Jumping Spasm — (See "Saltatory" in this section).

Kidney Action—(See "Spasmodic" under Kidneys).

Larynx — (See "Spasmodic" under Larynx).

Leaping Spasm—(See "Saltatory" in this section).

Legs—(See "Spasms In" under Legs).

Lock-Jaw; Lumbago — Spasmodic Lumbago—(See Lumbago).

Lungs — (See "Spasmodic" under Lungs).

Minor Spasm—(See Saint Vitus Dance, Twitchings).

Motion — (See "Spasmodic" under Motion).

Motor Disturbances — (See "Arms", "Disturbances", "Neuroses", and the various paragraphs under Motor).

Movements—Spasmodic Movements— (See the various paragraphs in this section).

Muscles — (See "Spasm Of" under Muscles).

Myoclonia — (See "Myoclonia" under Arms; "Paramyoclonus" under Muscles; "Clonic" in this section).

Nerves — (See "Spasmodic Diseases" under Nerves).

Neuralgia—Spasmodic Neuralgia— (See "Neuralgia" under Face; Neuralgia).

Nodding Spasm—(See "Nodding" under Head).

Oesophagus—(See "Stricture Of" under Oesophagus).

Opisthotonos; Organs—Spasmodic Action of—Note the various Organs in this section. Also see Erratic, Intermittent, Irregular, Organs, Palpitation, etc.).

Oscillation—(See Eyeballs).

Oxygenation—Spasmodic Oxygenation —(See "Non-Oxygenation" under Oxygen).

Pains—(See "Spasmodic" under Pain).

Palpitations; Paralysis;

Paramyoclonus Multiplex — (See "Paramyoclonus" under Muscles; "Clonic" in this section).

Paroxysms; Prickling;

Puerperal Convulsions — (See Puerperal).

Quiverings; Reflexes; Remedies—(See Antispasmodic).

Remittent; Respiration — (See "Spasmodic" under Breathing).

Retraction; Rhythm — Interferences With—(See Rhythm).

Rigidity; Saint Vitus Dance;

Saltatory Spasm — Dancing Spasm — Jumping Spasm — Leaping Spasm — ♅ afflicted in signs which rule the lower extremities; Subs at PP (2, 3, 4L). (See "Clonic" in this section).

Shaking; Sneezing—(See Nose).

Spasms — Spasm — Spasms are due to incoordination, and afflictions of ♅ to the Organ of Coordination in the ♉ sign; ♅ influence by reflex from the ♏ sign, in which sign he is exalted. The afflictions of ♅ tend to cause spasms, and in the part of the body ruled by the sign he is in at B., or the part ruled by the opposite sign; ♅ in the 6th H.; ♄ angular, holding dominion, elevated above the Lights, and afflicting the hyleg; caused by ♃ when the dominion of death is vested in him; ♃ afflicted in ♉; ☿ afflicted in ♎. For Death by Spasms see "Death" under Fits. Spasms and muscular contractions are directly the result of nervous disturbances, and dominated by ♅. A clonic spasm is alternating, while a tonic spasm is continued. Case of Spasms—See Fig. 20A in "Astro-Diagnosis" by the Heindels. (See "Spasm" under Bladder, Heart, Urethra; Convulsions, Epilepsy; "Death" under Fits; "Clonic", "Tonic", and the various paragraphs in this section).

Spastic Action — Spasmodic Action — Rigidity — (See Rigidity; the various paragraphs in this section).

Squint—Crossed Eyes—(See "Strabismus" under Eyes).

Stomach—(See "Pains", "Spasm", under Eyes).

Strictures—Spasmodic Stricture of the Bladder or Urethra—(See "Stricture" under Bladder, Urethra; Stricture).

Subluxations; Subsultus — Morbid Tremors or Twitching—(See Subsultus, Tremors, Twitching).

Suffocation—Spasmodic Suffocating Attacks—(See Angina Pectoris, Cyanosis, Dyspnoea; "Non-Oxygenation" under Oxygen; Suffocation).

Tetanus; Throat — (See "Spasmodic Disorders" under Throat).

Tics—Tic Dourouleux—(See Tics).

Tonic Spasm—A Continued Rigid Muscular Spasm — This form of Spasm occurs in the more serious and chronic cases, and where ♅ is configurated with other malefics, as ♄ and ♂, and also when the subluxations of vertebrae may be more severe. The occasional, or alternating form of spasm, the clonic spasm, may be only temporary, and more easily remedied, as in twitchings, Saint Vitus Dance, etc. Also, in tonic spasm, the organ of coordination in ♉ is more permanently afflicted, and which may be caused by ♅ or ♄ badly afflicted in ♉. Epilepsy and Tetanus are typical forms of tonic spasm. (See Contractions, Convulsions, Epilepsy, Incoordination, Rigidity, Tetanus, Tonic; "Clonic" in this section).

Torsion; Torticollis—(See "Wry Neck" under Neck).

Tremblings; Tremors; Trismus—(See Lock-Jaw).

Twistings; Twitching;

Uranus Diseases—(See Uranus).

Uremia; Urethra — (See "Spasmodic", "Stricture", under Urethra).

Venous Circulation — Spasmodic Disturbance of — (See "Spasmodic" under Veins).

Vomiting; Walk — (See "Incoordinated", "Twisted", under Walk).

Will — Spasmodic Will — (See "Weak Will" under Will).

Wind Spasm — (See "Spasm" under Wind).

Winking—(See Eyelids).

Writer's Cramp — (See "Cramps" under Hands).

Wry Neck — (See "Wry Neck" under Neck). For subjects along this line which may have been omitted in this Article, look in the alphabetical arrangement for the subject you have in mind.

SPASTIC ACTION—(See Rigidity, Spasmodic).

SPEAKING—

Loud Speaking—Should be Avoided—(See "Loud" under Speech; "Injudicious Use" under Voice).

Speaking Signs—Human Signs—Signs of Voice—♊, ♍, ♎, ♐, ♒. (See "Human Signs" under Human; "Signs Of" under Voice).

SPECIES — Kind — Nature of — Quality of—

Death — Species of the Death — This depends upon the one malefic planet which occupies an Anaretic Place. The quality of the death is indicated by the nature of the least prominent, or least powerful directions, in a train of directions to the hyleg, and by the nature of the sign, or signs containing them. These directions, even though benevolent, show the quality, and when acting with the major killing directions. (See Anareta; "Immediate Cause Of", "Quality Of", under Death; Directions; Dominion; Events; "Death" under Nature, Quality).

Disease — Species of Disease — Causes Every Species of Disease — Species of the Disease—The South Scale, a violent star, when joined to the ☉ or ☽, or afflicting the vital places of the map, is said to cause every species of disease. (See South Scale). For the influences which tend to define the Species, Type, and Quality of the disease, see "Disease" under Nature, Quality; "Quality Of" under Sickness; Type).

SPECKS—Specks Over the Eyes—Blindness By—Vision Impaired By—The ☉ directed to Praesepe, Hyades, Castor and Pollux, and other stars of the nature of ♂ and the ☽ combined, and especially if Praesepe be on the Asc., or with the ☉ or ☽ in an angle, which tends to certain blindness. Specks are also caused by ♄, and with ♄ the afflicting planet. (See Cataract; "Defects", "Film", "Total", under Blindness; "Muscae", "Specks", under Eyes).

SPECTRUM — Solar Spectrum — (See "Planets and Color" under Colors).

SPECULATION — Speculative — Visionary—

Mind — A Speculative Mind — A Promoter—♄, ♃, or ☿ in ♍; ♒ and ♑ influence. (See Gambling).

Property — Loses Property by Speculation—The ☉ Sig. ☌ ♄. (See Expense, Property, Riches).

Religion—Fanciful Speculations About Religion and Other Matters—(See "Fanciful" under Religion).

SPEECH—Utterance—Talk—Language — Sound — Communication — Words — Tone—Conversation—Phonation—Voice —Delivery—Signs—Gesticulation, etc. The planet ☿ rules Speech, and the nerves of Speech. Also ruled by the ♈, ♉, and ♊ Signs. Uranus rules the motor nerves of speech. Mercury in ♉ especially rules and affects the nerves of speech, and ♅ in ♉ rules and affects the motor nerves of speech. The Hebrew letter "He" (E) is connected with speech, and the ♈ sign, which sign rules the intellectual faculties, of which speech is the natural expression. The ♉ sign is closely connected with speech, as the center where thought is transformed into speech is under the rule of ♉. The following subjects have to do with speech, its normal and abnormal expression, defects in, suppression of, etc.

Amnesia—Loss of Memory for Words —(See "Amnesia" under Memory).

Aphasia—Loss of Power of Speech—The ☉ afflicted in ♈; Subs at Atlas. (See "Loss of Speech" in this section).

Aphonia — (See "Aphonia" under Voice).

Articulation Bad—(See "Impediment", "Inarticulate", "Stammering", in this section; Articulation, Inarticulate).

Backwardness of Speech — ☿ afflicted in the 6th or 12th H., and if also afflicted by the ☽, ♄, or ♂, there may be an impediment of speech. Under these conditions if ☿ be in a mute sign, and afflicted by ♄, the native may be born dumb. (See Dumb, Mutes; "Impediment" in this section).

Breathing—Improper Breathing In Speaking or Singing — (See "Speech" under Breath).

Cannot Talk — Case — A Dwarf and Hunchback — See Chap. 8 in Daath's Medical Astrology.

Clear Voice — (See "Clear" under Voice).

Coarse Voice — In Women — (See "Coarse" under Voice).

Coprolalia — (See "Obscene" in this section).

Deaf Mute — (See "Deaf and Dumb" under Hearing).

Deep Voice — (See "Deep" under Voice).

Defects In Speech—Caused principally by afflictions to ☿; the ☽ Sig. □ or ☍ ☿; the ☉ in an angle, ☌ ♄ and ☿, especially if ☿ be occi., and both ♄ and ☿ configurated with the ☽. The defect in the tongue, or speech, may be removed if ♂ be found with them, after the ☽ by direction or progression passes her ☌ with ♂, or completes her approach to him. (See "Impediments", "Stuttering", and the various paragraphs in this section).

Disconnected Speech—(See Dysphasia, Halting, Incoordination, Stammering, in this section).

Disorders of Speech—Afflictions to ☿ at B.; ☿ diseases; ☿ in the 6th H., ☌ ☉ and afflicted by ♄ or ♂; ☿ in any of the first six degrees of ♏, and in ☍ the ☽; afflictions in or to the ♈, ♉, or ♏ signs. (See the various paragraphs in this section).

Drawling Speech — The 3rd face of ♒ on the Asc.; ♎ influence.

Dumb—(See Dumb, Hearing, Mute).

Dysphasia—Disconnected speech from loss of words, or faulty arrangement of words — This is due to a ♄ limitation over the mind, a mind slow to think, and can be caused by ♄ ☌ the ☽ or ☿ in the 12th H., and otherwise afflicted by malefics; ♄ and the ☽ disconnected, and also having no relation to the Asc. (See "Bad Judgment" under Judgment; "Amnesia" under Memory; "Weaknesses" under Mental; "Weak Mind" under Mind; "Halting", "Rambling", "Stammering", in this section).

Dysphonia—Difficulty In Phonation—(See "Hoarseness" under Larynx).

Easy and Gentle Address—The ☽ Sig. ☌ ♀.

Effeminate Voice In Men — (See Effeminate).

Eloquent of Speech — A Good Orator and Linguist—♀ in ♍; ♀ Sig. in ♍; ☿ ⚹ ♃ and ♀; ☿ ascending at B., and free from affliction, and especially when ☿ is in ♍, a great orator. (See "Fluency" in this section; "Gifted Vocally", "Great Voice", under Voice).

Esperanto—Inventor of—See "Zamenhof", No. 432 in 1001 N.N.

Excited Manner—In Speaking—(See "Excitable" under Excitement; "Rapid", "Speaking", in this section).

Expression Good—(See "Expression" under Voice).

Fluency of Speech—Oratorical Ability —☿ angular at B., in the 1st, 7th, or 10th H., well-aspected, or in ♈, ♎, or ♑, signs corresponding to these houses. The 16° ♉ and ♏ are closely associated with voice control and tone. The 17° ♈ and ♎, and 7° ♑ and ♓ give fluency of expression. Power to sway the masses is given by ♒. Aries incites to anger and martial action, and ♏ excites powerful emotions. (See "Eloquent" in this section).

Functional Disorders — Of Speech — Caused by afflictions to ☿.

Gentle and Easy Address — (See "Easy" in this section).

Gestures—(See Gesticulation).

Gifted Vocally — (See "Eloquent", "Fluency", in this section).

Good Voice Expression — (See "Expression" under Voice; "Eloquent" in this section).

Great Orator—(See "Eloquent", "Fluency", in this section).

Halting—Hesitating Speech—♄ in ♎, a sign of voice, and ☿ in ♌, a bestial sign, tend to, and to obstruct perfect vocalization; many planets in mutable signs. (See "Dysphasia", "Impediment", "Stammering", in this section).

Has Never Talked—Case—See "Defective Mentality", No. 670, in 1001 N.N.

Head — Nods Head to One Side In Speaking — (See "Nodding" in Sec. 1 under Head).

Hearing and the Speech—(See "Deaf and Dumb" under Hearing).

High Voice—Tenor Voice—(See "Men" under Effeminate).

Hoarseness — (See "Hoarseness" under Larynx).

Humming—Droning—(See Humming).

Hurried Speech — (See "Excited" "Rapid", in this section).

Impediment In Speech — Defects In Utterance — Slow of Speech — Speaks with Difficulty — Impediment On the Tongue—The ☉ ☌ ♄ and ☿ in the 1st or 7th H., and especially when in the 7th, and ☿ P., □, or ☍ the ☽, and the impediment is worse when ☿ is in a mute sign, as in ♋, ♏, or ♓. If ♂ be with them the speech becomes better when the ☽ by dir. leaves the aspect to ☿; the ☽ decr., and sepr. from ♄, and applying to ☿; the ☽ □ or ☍ ♄ if the ☽ is otherwise much afflicted; the ☽ incr. in a day geniture, sepr. from ☿, and applying to ♄; the ☽ sepr. from ☿ and applying to the ☉; the ☽ Sig. □ or ☍ ☿; ♅ afflicted in ♉, the organ of coordination; ☿ diseases; ☿ Sig. ☌ ♄; ☿ ruler of the 6th H., in a watery sign, and afflicted by ♄ or ♂; ☿ afflicted in ♓; ☿ and the ☽ afflicted, and ☌, P., □, or ☍ ♄; ♄ ☌ or ill-asp. ☿; ♄ ☌ ☿ in ♈; ♄ ascending in a bestial sign, as ♈, ♉, ♌, or ♑, or in a mute sign, as ♋, ♏, or ♓; the native of ♄ usually has an impediment of speech; ♄ afflicting ☿, and the ☽ also afflicted; ♃ Sig. in a water sign, and in □ or ☍ ☿; ☿ ill-dignified, and ☌ ♄; ☿ in ♉, □ ♄ in ♌; caused by the □ or ☍ aspects of ☿; ruler of the Asc. in a mute sign; ♑ on the Asc. (See Articulation, Inarticulate, Lisping; "Pitted Degrees" under Pitted; "Defects" under Tongue; Backwardness, Defects, Dumb, Halting, Incoordination, Slow, Stammering, and the various paragraphs in this section).

Imperfections of Speech — (See Defects, Impediment, and the various paragraphs in this section; "Defects" under Tongue).

Inarticulate Speaking—Planets, or ☿ in the inarticulate signs ♈, ♉, ♌, or ♑. (See Inarticulate, Mute; "Defects" under Tongue; "Impediment In", and the various paragraphs in this section).

Incoordination of Speech — (See Dysphasia, Impediment, Stammering, in this section; Incoordination).

Injudicious Use—Of the Voice—Loud Speaking or Singing should be avoided when ☿ is in ♉ and afflicted by malefics. (See "Hoarseness" under Larynx; "Injudicious" under Voice).

Jumps Forward — When Addressing or Speaking — Skippish Manner — (See "Nodding" in Sec. 1 under Head).

Larynx—Disorders of—(See "Hoarseness", and the various paragraphs under Larynx).

Linguist — (See "Eloquent" in this section).

Lisping—(See Lisping).

Logorrhoea — (See "Rapid" in this section).

Loss of Speech — Inability to Talk — Unable to Talk — Loss of the Power of Speech — Loss of Voice — Aphasia — The ☉ afflicted in ♈; ♆ in ♊ in ☍ ♄ and ☿; ♅ ☌ ♄ in ♉ or ♏; ♅ or ♄ afflicted in ♉ or ♏; ♄ afflicted in ♉ tends to loss of voice, and usually due to some chronic laryngeal and throat trouble, hoarseness, etc.; ☿ afflicted in ♉; afflictions to ☿, to a ☿ sign, or the ☉ in the ☿ signs ♊ or ♍, and afflicted by malefics; Subs at Atlas. (See "Hoarseness" under Larynx; Mute, Removal; "Aphonia" under Voice; Aphasia. Cannot Talk, Has Never Talked, in this section). Cases of Loss of Speech — See Fig. 3G in the book, "Astro-Diagnosis", and Fig. 1 in "Message of the Stars", by the Heindels.

Loud Speaking — Should Avoid Loud Speaking or Singing—(See "Injudicious Use" in this section).

Manner — Skippish Manner In Speaking — Jumps Forward — Nods Head to One Side—(See "Nodding" in Sec. 1 under Head).

Men—Effeminate Voice In—(See Effeminate; Bass, High, Low, Tenor, under Voice).

Moans — Unable to Articulate — (See "Deaf and Dumb" under Hearing; Idiocy, Inarticulate, Insanity, Mute).

Motor Nerves of Speech — Disorders of — ♅ afflicted in ♉. (See "Motor Nerves" under Motor).

Musical Voice—(See "Singers" under Music; "Musical" under Voice).

Mutes—(See Dumb; "Deaf and Dumb" under Hearing; Mute).

Nerves of Speech — Ruled by ☿, and are especially affected and disturbed by ☿ or ♅ afflicted in ♉.

Nervous Manner—In Speaking—Quick and Nervous Speech—(See Jumps Forward, Quick and Nervous, Rapid, in this section).

Obscene Use of Words—Coprolalia—Caused by the afflictions of ♄ and ♂ to ♀ and ☿; Subs at AT. (See Obscene, Profane).

Orator — A Good Orator — (See Eloquent, Fluency, in this section).

Paralysis of Speech — Danger of — ♅ afflicted in ♉, ♏, or the 2nd H.; ♅ □ or ☍ ☿. (See "Speech" under Paralysis; Cannot Talk, Has Never Talked, Loss of Speech, in this section).

Peculiarities of Speech—(See the various paragraphs in this section. For the peculiarities of speech, as given by each Sign of the Zodiac, see the subject of "Speech" in Carter's Encyclopaedia of Psychological Astrology.

Phonation—Difficulty In—(See Articulation, Inarticulate; "Hoarseness" under Larynx; Lisping, Mute; Defects, Impediment, Imperfections, Stammering, in this section).

Pitted Degrees — Of the Zodiac — Effects of Upon Speech — (See "Pitted Degrees" under Pitted).

Pleasing Address — The ☉ Sig. ☌ ♀. (See "Easy Address" in this section).

Power to Sway Masses — The ♒ sign strong and well-occupied at B. (See "Eloquent" in this section).

Quick and Nervous Speech—☿ in the 1st H., and afflicted by ♅. (See "Rapid" in this section).

Rambling Speech — Afflictions in ♓, and involving the 3rd H., the ♊ sign, and ☿. (See "Mind" under Chaotic; "Inability" under Concentration; Confusion; "Light In Mind" under Mind).

Rapid Speech — Logorrhoea — Speaks Rapidly and Hastily—Rattle-Brained—The ☽ in a fiery sign, and ☌ or ill-asp. ☿; ♅ or ♂ in ♈ at B., and ♅ □ or ☍ ♂, rattle-brained. (See Excited, Quick and Nervous, in this section). Case of Curiously Rapid Utterance — See "Puzzle Horoscopes", No. 347, in 1001 N.N.

Refuses to Talk—Prefers Silence—In the radix of such a case, ☿ was in ♉, □ ♄ in a fixed sign. Birth Data not available.

Shrill, Small Voice—(See "Shrill" under Voice).

Signs of Voice — Speaking Signs — (See "Speaking Signs" under Speaking; "Signs of Voice" under Voice).

Silent — Refuses to Talk — (See "Refuses to Talk" in this section).

Singing—(See "Singers" under Music; Singing; "Singing" under Voice; "Injudicious Use" in this section).

Skippish Manner—In Speaking—(See "Nodding" in Sec. 1 under Head).

Slow of Speech — (See Halting, Impediment, Stammering, in this section; "Slow of Voice" under Voice).

Small, Shrill Voice—(See "Shrill" under Voice).

Speaking—Manner of Speaking—(See the various paragraphs in this section).

Speaking Signs — (See "Signs of Voice" in this section).

Speechless — (See Dumb; "Deaf and Dumb" under Hearing; Mute; Cannot Talk, Has Never Talked, Loss of Speech, Refuses to Talk, in this section).

Stammering — Stuttering — Hesitating Speech — Slow of Speech — Halting — Impediment In Speech—Bad Articulation—The ☉ in an angle, ☌ ♄ and ☿, especially if ☿ be occi., and both ♄ and ☿ configurated with the ☽; the ☽ incr. in a day geniture, sepr. from ☿ and applying to ♄; the ☽ and ☿ afflicted, and P., ☌, □, or ☍ ♄; caused by the □ and ☍ aspects of the ☽; ♄ gives the stammer and ♂ the lisp; ♄ ☌ ☿, and in □ or ☍ the ☽; a ☿ disease; ☿ afflicted at B.; ☿ in a weak sign, as in ♋, ♐, or ♓, and afflicted by ♄; ☿ afflicted in ♉ or ♏; ☿ in the 1st H., and afflicted by ♄; ☿ ruler of the 6th H., in a water sign, and afflicted by ♄ or ♂; ☿ in a water sign anywhere in the map; ☿ afflicted by ♄ or ♂, and with the ♐ sign involved, and with one of the planets in the 12th H.; a mute sign, as ♋, ♏, or ♓ on the Asc., or the ☽ or lord of the Asc. in one of these signs; many planets afflicted in mute signs. (See Halting, Impediment, in this section; "Pitted Degrees" under Pitted; "Defects" under Tongue).

Straining the Voice—Should Avoid—(See "Injudicious Use" in this section; "Singers" under Music).

Strong Voice — (See "Strong" under Voice; "Eloquent" in this section).

Stuttering — (See Impediment, Stammering, in this section).

Taciturn—Not Inclined to Converse—Quiet—Silent—Reserved—Born under ♄, and with ♄ rising in the Asc.; ♄ ☌ or ill-asp. ☿. (See Grave; "Taciturn" under Manner; Recluse, Renunciation, Reserved, Secretive, Taciturn).

Talk—(See Cannot Talk, Has Never Talked, Refuses to Talk, in this section).

Talking to Oneself — A ♆ influence, and ♆ strong at B.; ♆ in ♈; ♆ ☌ ☿. (See Humming).

Tenor Voice — (See "Men" under Effeminate).

Tone and Voice Control—(See "Fluency" in this section; "Control" under Throat).

Tongue — Imperfections In — (See Impediment, Stammering, in this section; "Defects" under Tongue).

Unable to Talk — (See Cannot Talk, Has Never Talked, Loss of Speech, in this section; Dumb; "Deaf and Dumb" under Hearing; Mute).

Utterance—(See Rapid, Slow, and the various paragraphs in this section).

Vertical Larynx — And Speech — (See "Vertical" under Spine).

Vocal Cords — Disorders of — (See Larynx; "Vocal Cords" under Voice).

Vocalization—(See Lisping; Articulation, Defects, Impediment, Inarticulate, Stammering, in this section).

Voice — Disorders of — Signs of Voice —(See "Disorders", "Signs of Voice", and the various paragraphs under Voice).

Weak Voice — (See "Weak" under Voice).

Whispering Voice — (See "Aphonia" under Voice).

Whistling — Whistling Sound to the Voice—(See Whistling).

Women — Coarse Voice In — (See "Coarse", "Deep", under Voice; "Masculine Women" under Women).

Words—Loss of Memory for Words—(See "Amnesia" under Memory).

SPENDTHRIFT—Wastefully Lavish of Money — (See Expense, Improvident, Money, Prodigal).

SPERMATIC CORD—

Injuries To — ♏ diseases, and afflictions in ♏; ♂ afflicted in ♏. (See Testes).

Spermatic Plexus — (See "Ductless Glands" under Ductless).

SPHENOID BONE—Is under the structural rulership of the ♈ Sign. It is through this bone that food odors, and other impressions, reach the Pituitary Body, and start the Uranus Alchemistry. For a discussion of this subject see the Chapter on "Ductless Glands" in the book, "The Message of the Stars" by the Heindels.

SPHINCTER ANI MUSCLE—(See Anus, Rectum).

SPICA VIRGO—A Star. (See Arista).

SPICE—

A Spice of Gout — (See "Feet" under Gout).

Spices — Ruled by ♀. (See "Condiments" under Food).

SPINE — Spinal Cord — Spinal Canal — Backbone — Spinal Vertebrae — The Spine is ruled by the ☉, ♆, and the ♌ sign. The vertebrae of the Spine are ruled and influenced by the Signs of the Zodiac, according to the distribution of the nerves to the various parts and organs of the body. The Spinal Cord, taken as a whole, is said to be ruled by the ☉ and the ♌ Sign. The Cord is also strongly influenced by ♆ and ♀. The Motor Segment of the Spinal Cord is ruled by ♂. Some Writers say by ☿. The membranes of the Cord are ruled by ♅. The Spinal Canal is ruled by ♆, and this canal is filled with a force called "Spinal Spirit Fire." The Spinal Fluid, called "The River of Life", is ruled by ♆ and the ♌ sign, and connects the organs ruled by ♉ and ♏. The different parts of the Spine, and their rulerships, are considered under the subject of Vertebrae. (See Vertebrae). The Cerebro-Spinal Nervous system is ruled by ☿. The following subjects have to do with the Spine, its Divisions, functions, anatomy, defects, disorders, injuries to, etc.

Accidents To—Injuries To—The ☉ afflicted by malefics at B., and by dir.; malefics afflicted in ♌, and especially ♄ and ♂; malefics in the 5th H. and afflicting the ☉, and especially if in ♌ in this house; malefics in ♍, injuries to the lower part of the spine, and the lumbar region. (See "Injuries To" under Back).

Adjustments Of — (See Subluxations).

All Diseases In—Signified by the 8th H. in Hor'y Q.

Ankylosis — (See Adhesions, Ankylosis, Joints).

Arm Place—In the Spine—(See "First Dorsal", "Seventh Cervical", under Vertebrae).

Atlas Vertebra — (See Atlas; "First Cervical" under Vertebrae).

Atrophy of Cord — ♄ afflicted in ♌. (See Atrophy; "Inability to Walk" under Walk).

Axis Vertebra — (See "Second Cervical" under Vertebrae).

Azoth — In the Spinal Canal — (See Azoth).

Backbone—(See Ankylosis, Curvature, Humpback, Malformed, Pains In, Rigid, Spina Bifida, Subluxations, in this section).

Bifida — (See "Spina Bifida" in this section).

Bulbar Paralysis—(See Medulla).

Canal—The Spinal Canal—Is ruled by ♆. Is said to be filled with Ether during life, which becomes fluid when exposed to the air. The Spinal Spirit Fire which fills the Canal is a luminous gas. (See "Azoth", "Fluids", "Obstruction", "Spinal Spirit Fire", in this section). The theories about the Canal, the Spinal Spirit Fire, etc., are discussed in the book, "The Message of the Stars", by Max Heindel.

Caries—Of the Spine—♄ afflicted in ♌ or ♒.

Cases of Spinal Trouble — (See Deformed, Diseases of Spine, Potts, Spina Bifida, Weakness, in this section).

Centers—The Spinal Centers Affected and Weakenetd—♄ ☌ or ill-asp. the ☉.

Central Place — In the Spine — (See "Fifth Dorsal" under Vertebrae).

Cerebro-Spinal System — Disorders of —(See Cebro-Spinal).

Cervical Region—Of the Spine—Cervical Vertebrae — (See Cervical; "Cervical Vertebrae" under Vertebrae).

Cleft In—(See "Spina Bifida" in this section).

Coccyx—Coccygeal Region—(See Coccyx; "Coccyx" under Vertebrae).

Columns — (See "Motor" in this section).

Compression — Of the Cord — (See "Spinal Cord" under Compressed).

Cord—The Spinal Cord—Ruled by the ♌ Sign. Salt, Sulphur, Mercury, and Azoth are found in the spinal cord. Azoth is ruled by ♆. The Motor Segment of the Cord is ruled by ♂, and ♂ afflicted in ♌ tends to disorders of this part of the Cord. Some Writers say the Motor Segment is ruled by ☿. Maladies of the Cord are frequent when ♄ afflicts the ☉, or when ♄ is afflicted in ♌, or when there are malefics in ♌ at B. For the various afflictions to the Cord see Atrophy, Compression, Dura Mater, Inflammation, Leptomeningitis, Lesions, Motor, Myelitis, Sclerosis, Spinal Meningitis, Tabes, and other paragraphs in this section).

Crevice — (See "Spina Bifida" in this section).

Curvature of Spine—Malformed Spine — Pott's Curvature — Pott's Disease — (See "Pott's Curvature" in this section). See Case — "Spinal Curvature", No. 838, in 1001 N.N.

Death — From Spinal Complaints — ☉ diseases; the ☉ badly afflicted in ♌ or ♒, and especially when in the 5th, 6th, or 12th H. at B. Fixed Signs dispose to, and many planets in such signs, and especially in ♌ or ♒.

Defects In Spine — The ☉ afflicted in ♌ or ♒; ♄ in ♌ on the cusp of the 12th H., and in □ asp. the ☉, and both in fixed signs. (See the various paragraphs in this section).

Deformed Spine—Afflictions in ♌, and especially ♄ in ♌. Case—See "Deformed", No. 689, in 1001 N.N. (See Humpback, Pott's Curvature, Spina Bifida, in this section).

Diseases of Spine—Diseased Spine—Spinal Complaints—Spinal Trouble—Spinal Affections—♌ diseases, and afflictions in ♌; ♌ on the Asc., and afflicted; the ☉ afflicted in ♌ or ♒; the ☉ ☌ ♄ or ♆ in ♌ or ♒; a ☉ disease; the ☉ afflicted in ♐ sometimes affects the spine; malefics in ♌ and the hyleg much afflicted at B.; the ☽ afflicted in ♌, or afflicting the hyleg therefrom; a ♆ affliction; ♆ in ♊ in ☍ to ♃ or ♂; ♆ afflicted in ♌; ♆ □ or ☍ ♅, ♄, or ♂; ♆ ☌ ♄ in ♌; caused by ♄ and ♄ afflictions at B., and by dir.; ♄ afflicted in ♌ or ♒, and afflicting the hyleg therefrom; ♄ in ♌, occi., and afflicting the ☉, ☽, or Asc.; ♄ afflicting the hyleg or Asc. at B., and by dir.; ♄ afflicted in the 6th H., and especially when in ♌, and also afflicting the hyleg; ♀ diseases; ♀ afflicted in ♌. Cases of Spinal Trouble—See Figures 9A, 9B, 9C, 9D, 18G, in the book, "Astro-Diagnosis", by the Heindels. Also see Chap. 13, in Daath's Medical Astrology. See Case under "Deformed" in this section. (See the various paragraphs in this Article for other influences along this line).

Dislocations—Partial Dislocation of Vertebrae—(See Subluxations).

Dorsal Region—Of the Spine—(See Dorsal. Also see "Dorsal Vertebrae" under Vertebrae).

Dura Mater—Of the Cord—(See Dura Mater).

Dwarfed Hunchback—(See "Humpback" in this section).

End of Backbone—Disorders in Region of—(See Buttocks, Coccyx, Lumbar, Sacrum).

Ether—In Spinal Canal—(See Azoth, Ether).

Fire—The Spinal Spirit Fire—(See "Spirit Fire" in this section).

Fissure—Of the Spine—(See "Spina Bifida" in this section).

Fluids—The Spinal Fluids—Obstruction of—Lack of—(See Canal, Obstruction, Synovial, in this section; the Introduction to this Article).

Ganglion—(See "Spinal" under Ganglion).

Gas—The Spinal Gas—The Spinal Fluid—The Spinal Spirit Fire—(See Canal, Obstruction, Spirit Fire, in this section; Azoth, Ether).

Gray Matter—Of the Cord—Inflammation of—(See Inflammation, Myelitis, Poliomyelitis, in this section).

Haematomyelia—Hemorrhage Into the Cord—(See "Spine" under Hemorrhage).

Hardening—Of the Cord—(See "Sclerosis" in this section).

Heart Place—In the Spine—(See "Second Dorsal" under Vertebrae).

Hemorrhage—Into the Cord—(See "Spine" under Hemorrhage).

Humpback—Hunchback—Kyphosis—Curvature of the Spine—Dwarfed Hunchback—Deformed Spine—The ☉ in ♌ or ♒ on the cusp the 6th or 12th H., and □ ♆; the ☉ and ☽ in the 6th or 12th H., and afflicted by malefics; ♅, ♄, and ♂ in fixed signs in ☌ or ☍; the bodies or rays of ♅, ♄, and ♂ in, or directed upon, the 5th, 6th, or 12th H., or cusps of these houses, or the cusp of the Asc.; ♄ afflicted in ♌; ♂ in ♌, □ the Asc.; ♂ or the ☽ ☌ ☊ or ☋ in the 12th H., and the ☉ and ♃ in the 4th H.; ♉ on the Asc., and the rising degree □ ♂ in ♌; ♉, ♏, or ♑ on the Asc.; many planets in ♍ in the 6th or 12th H. Cases of Humpback—See "Hunchback", No. 685; "Spinal Curvature", No. 838, both in 1001 N.N. See Chap. 8, Case of a Female, in Daath's Medical Astrology. See Fig. 20 in the book, "Message of the Stars", by Max Heindel. (See Defects, Deformed, Pott's Curvature, in this section; "Arrested Mental Powers" under Mental).

Incomplete Spine—(See "Deformed", "Spina Bifida", in this section).

Infantile Paralysis—Accompanied by Poliomyelitis, or Inflammation of the Gray Matter of the Spine—(See "Infantile Paralysis" under Paralysis; Inflammation, Poliomyelitis, in this section).

Inflammation—Of the Spinal Cord—Myelitis—Leptomeningitis—Poliomyelitis—♂ afflicted in ♌ or the 5th H.; Subs at AT, AX, CP. (See "Infantile Paralysis" in this section).

Kidney Place—In the Spine—(See "Eleventh Dorsal", "Tenth Dorsal", "Twelfth Dorsal", under Vertebrae).

Kyphosis—(See "Humpback" in this section).

Leptomeningitis—Inflammation of the Pia and Arachnoid Membranes of the Brain and Cord—(See this subject under Meninges).

Lesions—Lesions of the Motory Columns Within the Spine—♄ ☌ or ill-asp. the ☉; ♅, ♄, or ♂ afflicted in ♌. (See Lesions, Locomotor Ataxia; "Motor Nerves" under Nerves; "Lesions" under Paralysis).

Ligaments—Of the Spine—Loss of Strength In—♄ afflicted in ♌. (See Ligaments).

Liver Place—In the Spine—(See "Fourth Dorsal" under Vertebrae).

Lumbar Region—Of the Spine—(See Lumbar; "Lumbar Vertebrae" under Vertebrae).

Lung Place—In the Spine—(See "Third Dorsal" under Vertebrae).

Luxations—(See Dislocations, Subluxations).

Malformed Spine—(See Defects, Humpback, Pott's Curvature, Spina Bifida, in this section).

Marrow—Spinal Marrow Diseased—♀ afflicted in ♌. (See Marrow).

Medulla Oblongata—Disorders of—(See Medulla).

Meningitis—Spinal—(See Meninges).

Motor Segment—Motory Columns of the Cord—Disorders of—(See Cord, Lesions, in this section).

Myelitis—Inflammation of the Cord—(See "Inflammation" in this section).

Nerves—Pain In the Spinal Nerves—☿ afflicted in ♌; ☿ affl. in ♊, pains in the upper spinal nerves. (See "Pain In Nerve" under Nerves; "Pain", and the Introduction in this Article).

Obstruction — Of the Spinal Fluids — Of the Spinal Gas—The Vital Fluids of the Spine Obstructed—The Spinal Fluid Sluggish and Restricted—The ☉ in ♌ or ♒, ☌ or ☍ ♄; the ☉ ☌ ♆ or ♄ in ♌; ♆ ☌ ♄ in ♌, ♒, or the 5th H.; ♆ ☌, □, or ☍ the ☉ or ♄; ♆ in ♊, ☌, □, or ☍ the ☉ or ♄; ♅ in ♌ or ♒, □, or ☍ the ☉ and ♄, the functions of the spinal canal are interfered with. (See Canal, Fluids, Gas, Spirit Fire, Synovial, in this section; the Introduction to this Article).

Operations—Avoid surgical operations on the spine when the ☽ is in ♌. (See "Rules" under Operations).

Os Coccyx—(See "Coccyx" in this section).

Pain — In the Spine — Pains In the Backbone—A ♃ disease. (See "Nerves" in this section).

Paralysis — Bulbar Paralysis — (See Medulla).

Poliomyelitis — Inflammation of the Gray Matter of the Cord — Occurs in Infantile Paralysis. (See "Inflammation" in this section; "Infantile Paralysis" under Paralysis).

Pott's Curvature — Of the Spine — Pott's Disease—Spondylitis—Tubercular Spine — Vertebral Arthritis Deformans—The ☉ or ♄ afflicted in ♌; the ☉ or ☽ in the 6th H. in ♌, or other fixed signs, and afflicted by several malefics; ♄ afflicted in ♌, tubercular spine; malefics conjoined in the 5th H., and afflicted by others from the 11th H.; ♌ and ♒ are signs which greatly affect the heart and spine, and especially when afflicted, or containing the Lights or malefics, or when on angles, or on the cusps of the 5th or 6th H. Cases—See "Pott's Disease", No. 224 in 1001 N.N. See Fig. 9C in "Astro-Diagnosis" by the Heindels. See Case in Chap. 8 in Daath's Medical Astrology. (See "Humpback", "Tubercular", in this section).

Private Place — In the Spine — The Lumbar Vertebrae — (See Lumbar; "Lumbar Vertebrae" under Vertebrae).

Rigid Spine — Stiff Spine — Caused by ♄, and the hardening of the synovial membranes by ♄ influence; ♄ afflicted in ♌ tends to restrict and to dry up the synovial fluids in the joints of the spine. (See Joints, Rigidity, Synovial).

Sacrum — The Sacral Region of the Spine — (See Sacrum; "Sacrum" under Vertebrae; "Spina Bifida" in this section).

Sclerosis—Of the Cord—(See "Spinal Cord" under Hardening).

Segment—Motor Segment of the Cord —(See "Motor Segment" in this section).

Spina Bifida—Cleft of the Spine Over Sacrum — Crevice — Fissure — The ☉ or ☽ in ♌, and afflicted by malefics; the ☽ in ♌, □ or ☍ ♅ and ♀, and applying to, or afflicted by ♄. Case — Male, born Nov. 22, 1853, 5:40 p.m., in Lat. 53° 23′ N., and 10′ 12″ W. L. Also see case under "Deformed" in this section).

Spinal Canal — (See "Canal" in this section).

Spinal Centers—(See "Centers" in this section).

Spinal Cord—(See "Cord" in this section).

Spinal Diseases—(See "Diseases", and the various paragraphs in this section).

Spinal Marrow — (See "Marrow" in this section).

Spinal Meningitis—(See Meninges).

Spinal Nerves—(See "Nerves" in this section).

Spinal Spirit Fire—(See "Spirit Fire" in this section).

Spinal Trouble — (See "Diseases" in this section).

Spirit Fire — Spinal Spirit Fire — The Force which fills the Spinal Canal, and called by the Heindels, "The Life of the Father". Also this Force is said to be ruled by ♆, and spoken of as "The Spinal Spirit Fires of Neptune", which represent the Will. The Spinal Spirit Fire, by vibrating the Pineal Gland, produces Spiritual Sight. See Chap. 29, on "The Pathogenic Effects of Neptune", in the book, "Message of the Stars", where this matter is discussed. The Spinal Spirit Fire tends to be obstructed when the ☉ is in ♌ or ♒ in ☌ or ☍ ♄. (See Canal, Obstructions, in this section; Pineal Gland).

Spleen Place — In the Spine — (See Spleen; "Ninth Dorsal" under Vertebrae).

Spondylitis—(See "Tubercular" in this section).

Stiff Spine—(See "Rigid" in this section).

Stomach Place — In the Spine — (See "Sixth Dorsal" under Vertebrae).

Subluxations — (See Subluxations, Vertebrae).

Synovial Fluid—Lack of In Joints of Spine—(See "Rigid" in this section).

Tabes Dorsalis — Progressive Degeneration of the Posterior Columns of the Cord—(See Tabes).

Tubercular Spine—Spondylitis—♄ afflicted in ♌. Case — See Fig. 9C in "Astro-Diagnosis", by the Heindels. (See "Pott's Curvature" in this section).

Upper Spinal Nerves—Are ruled by ♊, and affected when there are malefics afflicted in ♊, or pains in with ☿ afflicted in ♊.

Vertebrae—Disorders of—(See "Backbone" in this section; Subluxations, Vertebrae).

Vertical Spine—Vertical Larynx and Spine In Man—The Ego can work only thru a vertical spine, as in Man. The animals, with a horizontal spine, are under the direction of Group Spirits, and are subject to the horizontal currents of the Desire World. See Chap. X in the book, "Cosmo-Conception", by Max Heindel, in which chapter the Evolution of the Spine in Man is discussed. The vertical larynx, as in man, is the only larynx capable of speech. The Parrot has a vertical larynx, and can utter and imitate human speech.

Vital Fluids — Obstruction of In the Spine—(See "Obstruction" in this section).

Weakness—Case of Spinal Weakness —See "Seventeen Years in Bed", No. 843 in 1001 N.N.

SPINSTERS—Women Who Have Never Married—Unmarried Elderly Women— The ☉ ☌ or ill-asp. ♄ at B.; the ☉ in ♏, ☌, P, □, or ☍ ♄; ♄ afflicted in ♏. (See Bachelors, Celibacy; "Aversion from Marriage", "Delayed", "Denied", under Marriage).

SPIRIT — The Spirit. The Soul. The Ego—The ☉ is typical of Spirit, and the ☽ of Matter. The Spirit is especially ruled by the ☉, the ♌ sign, and the 5th H., the house of the ☉ and the ♌ Sign. Also the Fiery Signs predominate in Spirit. The Pineal Gland is said to be the Seat of the Soul in the body, and the direct point of contact of the Ego. (See Astral Body, Aura, Character, Ego, Intuition, Pineal Gland, Soul, Will). Planets ℞ at B. are conducive to more rapid Soul Growth. (See Retrograde). The Spiritual Faculties are especially ruled over by ♆, the ruler of the Pineal Gland. (See Neptune, Spirit Controls, Spiritual).

SPIRIT CONTROLS—Obsessions—Controlled by Elemental Spirits—Demoniacal Obsession—Caused principally by ♆ and his afflictions; ♆ ☌ the ☉ or ☽ in the 9th H., and afflicted; ♆ ☌ ♄ in the 8th H., and afflicted by the □ aspect of ☿; ♆ afflicted in the 12th H., liable to be preyed upon by Spirit Controls, and assuming demoniacal shapes; ♆ ruler of the horoscope, and afflicted; ♆ ☌ the Asc., or afflicted in the 1st H., spirit obsessions; ♆ afflicted in the 6th H., or in ♍ or ♓, or in a watery sign; ♆ □ or ☍ ♄; ♆ ☌, P, □ or ☍ ♂; ♆ ☌ the ☽, and in □ ♅; ♆ ☍ Antares; ♆ □ ♅ at B., and the Prog. ☽, or Lunations, forming a □ aspect to them; caused by the evil aspects of ♆; the ☽ in the 9th H., □ or ☍ ♅; the ☽ in ♓, □ or ☍ ♆; ♅ ☌ the ☽ in the 9th H., and in □ or ☍ ♆ and ♂; ♓ on the Asc., the tool of low spirits; the 27° ♓ on the Asc. The subject of Spirit Controls is discussed quite fully in the book, "The Message of the Stars", by Max Heindel. Cases of Spirit Controls—See Fig. 16A, 16B, in "Astro-Diagnosis"; Fig. 2 in "Message of the Stars", both books by the Heindels. (See Antares, Astral Body; "Involuntary" under Clairvoyance; Demoniac, Fears, Horrors, Insanity; "Black Magic" under Magic; Mania; "Dangers" under Mediumship; Obsessions, Sensitives; "Terrors" under Strange; Visions).

SPIRITED—Animated—Full of Life—Vigorous—Active—Lively—Given by the fiery signs, many planets in a fiery sign, or a fiery sign on the Asc. and angles. Also ♂ rising in ♈ or ♏, and well-aspected by the ☉; many planets elevated in the East in positive, or fiery signs at B. (See Active, Brisk, Energetic; "Fire Signs" under Fire; Lively, Quick; "Good" under Vitality).

SPIRITS — Obsessed by Evil Spirits — (See Demoniac, Obsessions, Spirit Controls).

SPIRITUAL — Spirituality—Spiritual Faculties—Spiritual Sight—The Religious Faculties — Religion, Philosophy, and the Spiritual Faculties, are ruled by ♃ and the 9th H. Also by the ☉, ♆, ♅, ♄, and the ♐ and ♒ Signs. In fact, all of the Planets by their higher vibrations, have to do with the Evolution and Spiritual advancement of the Race, and the Seven Planetary Angels, or the Seven Spirits Before The Throne, are ever on the alert to help the individual who wants help, and it is only those who are living in their lower minds, and are dominated by personality, materialism, and the lower things of this Earth, who do not progress under the various planetary influences, but become stragglers and laggards in the scheme of life. The following subjects have to do with the Spiritual Side of Man, his Spiritual Faculties, his Higher Mind, and with Spiritual Forces and Influences in the Universe which affect Man. See these subjects in the alphabetical arrangement when only listed here—

Aquarius Sign — Considered the most spiritual of all the Signs. (See Aquarius).

Astral Body—(See Astral).

Aura; Aversions; Beside Oneself—(See Excitable).

Calm—Lack of Spiritual Calm—☿ afflicted by ♄ or ♆. (See Despondent, Fears; "Low Spirits" under Low; Melancholy; "No Peace of Mind" under Mind; Worry, etc.).

Centers—The Spiritual Centers of the Body — (See Pineal Gland, Pituitary Body).

Chaotic Mind — (See "Mind" under Chaotic).

Character; Clairaudience;

Clairvoyance; Color — The Spiritual Color—Indigo. (See Blue, Indigo).

Confusion of Mind—(See "Mind" under Chaotic, Confusion, Ideas).

Contentment; Death—Spiritual Causes of—♆ influences; ♆ in the 8th H. at B. (See Catalepsy, Catalysis, Coma, Delirium, Demoniac, Insanity, Madness, Mania, Obsessions, Spirit Controls, Trance).

Desires—Desire Body—(See Desire).

Deviations; Dreams; Ecstasy; Ego;

Emotions; Exaltation — Emotional Exaltation—(See Exaltation).

Excitement — (See "Religious" under Excitement).

Faculties—The Spiritual Faculties are ruled by ♅ and ♆, and thru the centers of the Pineal Gland and the Pituitary Body. (See Neptune, Pineal, Pituitary, Uranus).

Fanaticism — (See "Fanatical" under Religion).

Fate; Fears — (See "Religious" under Fears).

Feelings; Forebodings; Free-Will — (See Will).

Genius; Good — Good and Evil — (See Good, Evil).

Hallucinations; Happiness; Healing— (See "Spiritual Healers" under Healers).

Health — Good Health Thru Spiritual Power—♆ and ♅ strong at B., dignified, and well-aspected, and by attainment, and knowledge of the great Truths of the Universe, the Plan of Things, and the Destiny of the Soul.

Higher Mind—(See Ego, Soul, Spirit).

Honesty; Honor; Hope, Humane;

Hypocrisy; Ideals; Ideas;

Illumination—(See this subject under Religion).

Indigo Color — The Spiritual Color — (See Indigo).

Individuality; Insanity; Intuition;

Joy; Jupiter — (See the influences of this planet).

Justice; Kind; Lower Mind — (See "Mind" under Lower).

Mathematical; Mediumship;

Mentality — (See the various paragraphs under Mentality).

Mind—The Spiritual Mind—Indigo is the Color of the Spiritual Mind. (See Ego; "Higher Mind" under Mind; Soul, Spirit).

Morals; Motives; Negative — (See "Negative Nature" under Negative).

Neptune — (See the influences under Neptune).

New Birth — (See "Exaltation" under Emotion; "Ecstasy" under Religion).

Ninth House—The House of Religion and the Higher Mind — (See Ninth House).

Noble; Obsessions; Opinions;

Optimism; Peace of Mind — (See this subject under Mind).

Personality; Perversions—Spiritual Perversions — Usually caused by the afflictions and lower vibrations of ♆. (See "Mind" under Chaotic; "Involuntary" under Clairvoyance; Delusions, Fears, Hallucinations, Hypnotism, Illusions, Insanity, Magic, Mediumship; "No Peace of Mind" under Mind; Obsessions, Perversions; "Fanatical", "Intolerance", under Religion; Spirit Controls).

Pineal Gland — The Spiritual Center in the Body—(See Pineal).

Pituitary Body—(See Pituitary).

Positive — (See Individuality; "Positive Nature" under Positive; Ruling).

Power—Spiritual Power—Given especially by the higher vibrations of ♆ and ♅, and through the Pineal Gland and Pituitary Body. (See Pineal, Pituitary, Retrograde, Soul, Spirit, Will).

Prana; Premonitions; Pretender;

Pretenses; Principles; Prophetic;

Psychic; Purposes; Qualities—Spiritual Qualities—(See the various paragraphs in this section; "Desirable Mental Traits" under Mind).

Radicalism; Ranters — (See "Fanatical" under Religion).

Rationalism; Reactionary; Rebellious;

Reformers; Religion — (See the various paragraphs under Religion).

Renunciation; Resignation;

Revolutionary; Ruling; Sagittarius—(See the Influences under Pisces, Sagittarius, the Signs of ♃).

Seers; Sensitive—Sensitive To Psychic and Spiritual Influences — (See Clairvoyance, Mediumship, Obsessions; "Sensitive" under Psychic; Receptive, Sensitive, Spirit Controls, Susceptibility).

Sensitives — (See this subject under Sensitive).

Sincere; Sleep—(See "Nightmare", "Somnambulism", under Sleep).

Soul; Spirit; Spirit Controls;

Spiritual Sight — (See Antares, Neptune, Pineal Gland).

Spirituality — The Different Degrees of—(See the various paragraphs in this section, and also under Religion).

Sun—(See the Influences under Sun).

Sympathetic; Truth — Lover of—(See Truth).

Twelfth House — (See the influences under Twelfth House).

Uncanny Feelings—(See Uncanny).

Uranus — (See the influences under Uranus).

Veneration; Visions; Weird. Look in the alphabetical arrangement for subjects along this line, and which may not be listed here.

SPIRITUOUS LIQUORS—Excessive Use of—(See Dipsomania, Drink, Intoxication).

SPITEFUL — (See Revengeful, Treachery).

SPITTING—Spittle—

Spitting of Blood—(See Haemoptysis).

Spittle—(See Expectoration, Saliva).

SPLANCHNIC — Pertaining to the Viscera — (See "Splanchnic Ganglia" under Ganglion; Viscera).

SPLAY FOOT—Flat Foot—(See "Splay Foot" under Feet).

SPLEEN—Splenic—Milt—The Spleen is under the internal rulership of the ♏ sign. Also ruled by the ☉, ♄, and the ♏ sign. Saturn in ♏ especially rules and affects the activities of the Spleen. The Solar Forces enter the body thru the Spleen, and are then circulated thru the body as the Vital Etheric Fluid, which fluid is ruled by the ☉. The Spleen is called the Gateway of the Solar Forces. (See "Fluid" under Vital). The focal point of the Astral Body in the physical body is in the Spleen, and the Spleen contains the center which connects the physical body with the Astral World, and to coordinate with its activities requires much balanced power of understanding. (See Astral Body). The Liver is the great central vortex of the Desire Body. (See "Desire Body" under Desire). The Spleen Place in the Spine is the 9th Dorsal Vertebra. (See "Ninth Dorsal" under Vertebrae).

Afflicted with Spleen—(See Anger).

Calculi of Spleen — (See "Stone" in this section; Stone).

Cancer Of—Carcinoma—♄ afflicted in ♏; ♄ ☌ ♃ or ♀ in ♏; Subs at Spl.P., and at KP. (See Carcinoma).

Catarrh Of — The ☉, ☽, or ♄ afflicted in ♏; ♄ ☌ the ☉ or ☽ in ♏; Subs at SP, Spl.P., and KP. (See Catarrh).

Death— By Disordered Spleen—Caused by ♄ when the dominion of death is vested in him: ♄ afflicted in ♍ at B., and afflicting the hyleg therefrom.

Diseases Of—Disorders of—The ☉ and ♄ diseases; the ☉ afflicted in ♌, or ♌ on the Asc.; the ☉ or ♄ afflicted in ♍; afflictions in ♌, ♍, or ♏; Subs at Spl.P. (See the various paragraphs in this section).

Enlarged Spleen— Weil's Disease, and attended with Jaundice or Malaria Fever—A ♄ disease; ♄ and ♂ afflicted in ♍, and especially in the 6th H.: ♄ ☌ ♃ in ♍; Subs at CP, Spl.P., and KP. (See Ague, Jaundice, Malaria).

Flexure—Of the Spleen—Splenic Flexure—A ♄ disease; ♄ afflicted in ♍, and due to weakening of the supports and attachments; ♄ afflicted in ♏; Subs at PP. (See Flexure).

Hyperaemia — Of the Spleen, and usually attended with Fever — The ☉ or ♂ afflicted in ♍; ♂ ☌ the ☉ or ♃ in ♍; Subs at SP (8D). (See Hyperaemia).

Hypertrophy — ♃ or ♂ afflicted in ♍; Subs at SP (8D), and at Spl.P. (See Hypertrophy).

Inflammation Of—♂ afflicted in ♍; ♂ ☌ the ☉ in ♍; Subs at SP (8D), and Spl.P.

Leukemia—(See Leukocytes).

Malaria Fever—Enlarged Spleen In—(See "Enlarged" in this section).

Prolapsus—Splenoptosis—♅ or ♄ afflicted in ♍; Subs at Spl.P. (See Prolapse).

Rickets — Due to Changes in the Spleen—(See Rickets).

Right Side—The Spleen On the Right Side — Case — See "Heart", No. 981, in 1001 N.N.

Splenic Diathesis—(See the Introductions under Knees, Lymph).

Splenic Humour—The Splenic Humour has dominion from 3 P.M. to 9 P.M. of each day, and is more active during this time. (See "Astral Medicine", by Dr. Duz, page 74. Also see Humours).

Splenic Plexus—(See "Fifth Thoracic" under Ganglion).

Splenic Process—♄ adds or subtracts to the Splenic Process. (See "Alterations" under Cells; Metamorphosis. Also see Chap. VI in "Astral Medicine", by Dr. Duz).

Splenoptosis—(See "Prolapsus" in this section).

Stone In—Calculi—A ♄ affliction; ♄ afflicted in ♍; Subs at SP and Spl.P. (See Stone).

Symptoms of Spleen — (See "Symptoms Of" under Consumption).

Treatment—By Sympathy diseases of the Spleen are treated by ♄ remedies. By Antipathy, use the remedies and Herbs of ♂. (See Antipathy, Opposites, Sympathy). Also the Spleen Place in the Spine (Spl.P.) should be adjusted, to see that the nerve forces thru the spine to the Spleen are not impinged. (See Treatment).

Tuberculosis—Of the Spleen—A ♄ disease; ♄ afflicted in ♍; ♄ in ♍ in the 6th H.; Subs at SP and Spl.P. (See Tuberculosis).

Upper Spleen—Disorders of—The ☉, ♄, or ♂ afflicted in the first degrees of the ♍ sign; Subs at SP (8D).

Weil's Disease — (See "Enlarged" in this section).

White Blood Corpuscles—Excess of—(See Leukocytes).

SPONGES — Ruled by ♆. (See Fungus; "Vegetable Growths" under Vegetable).

Spongy Gums—(See Gums).

SPONTANEOUS—Sudden—♅ and ♂ influences tend to sudden and spontaneous events. (See Accidents, Events, Explosions, Hurts, Injuries, Sudden, Unexpected, Untimely; "Spontaneous" under Wounds).

SPORADIC CHOLERA — (See "Cholera Morbus" under Cholera).

SPORTS—Athletics— Exercise—Recreations—Pastimes—Amusements—Play—Games—Muscular Exercises—Hunting —Fishing, etc. There are many dangers in connection with Sports, and attended with accidents, disease, death, injuries, etc., and some of these conditions, and their planetary causes, are listed here.

Amusements — Death or Injury In — ♂ in the 5th H., □ or ☍ the ☉. (See Amusements; "Blindness" in this section).

Athletics—Injury or Death In—(See Athletics; "Death", "Injury", under Exercise; "Death", "Injuries", in this section).

Blindness—From Injury in Sports or Amusements — (See Amusements; "Amusements" under Blindness; "Eyes" under Exercise).

Blood — Over-Heated Blood Thru Sports and Violent Exercise — (See "Blood Over-Heated" under Exercise).

Burned to Death — From Accident During Sports—(See "Death by Burns" under Burns).

Care—Lack of Care In Sports—♂ in ♐.

Colds—From Over-Exercise and Over-Exertion — (See "Colds" under Exercise).

Dancing—The ☉ Sig. in ♎, spends his time in Sports, Pastimes, and Dancing.

Death by Sports—By Accidents or Injuries In Sports—The ☉ afflicted in ♐; ☿ afflicted by ♄ or ♂ at B., and ☿ holding the dominion of death; ☿ afflicting the hyleg by dir., and ☿ or the hyleg badly afflicted by malefics at B. (See Amusements; "Death" under Exercise).

Exercise — Excesses In — Injury or Death In — Hurts to Eyes During — (See the paragraphs under Exercise; "Amusements" in this section).

Falls During Sports—The ☉ afflicted in ♐.

Fatigue—Fatigue from Sports or Exercise—(See "Exercise" under Fatigue).

Fishing—Fond of—The ☉ or ☽ in ♓ at B.; ♓ upon the Asc.; many planets in watery signs at B.; the ♃ signs ♐ or ♓ strong at B. (See "Outdoor Exercise" in this section).

Fond of Sports—♃ Sig. in ♎ or ♐.

Horses—Injury by Horseback Riding —(See "Riding" under Horses).

Hunting — Injury or Death In — (See Gunshot, Hunting, Shooting).

Hurts—And Injuries During Sports—The ☉, ☽, ♅, or ♂ afflicted in ♐; afflictions in ♐. (See the various paragraphs in this section).

Indiscretions — In Sports, and Warning Against—♂ or ♀ afflicted in ♐, and especially with females. (See "Intemperate" under Exercise).

Injuries — Hurts or Accidents In Sports—The ☉, ♄, ♂, or ♅ afflicted in ♐; afflictions in ♐. (See Amusements, Death, Injury, and the various paragraphs in this section).

Inordinate Exercise — Fatigue or Illness From — (See "Inordinate" under Exercise; Fatigue).

Intemperate — In Sports — The ☉ afflicted in ♐; a ♐ disorder, and afflictions in ♐. (See "Intemperate" under Exercise; Intemperance).

Lack of Exercise — (See "Lack Of" under Exercise; Obesity, Sedentary).

Muscular Body—Athletic Body—(See Athletics; "Body" under Muscles, Strong).

Outdoor Exercise—And Sports—Fond of—♐ is primarily the Sportsman Sign, and the ☉, ☽, ♃, ♂, and ☿ in this sign favor outdoor sports, riding, hunting, fishing, etc.; ♃ in ♐ makes one fond of horses, riding, hunting, etc.; ♂ in ♌, fond of robust sports. (See "Riding" under Horses, Hunting; "Fishing" in this section).

Over-Exercise — Over-Exertion — Disease, Illness, Fatigue, or Colds From—(See "Colds", "Inordinate", under Exercise; Fatigue).

Pleasure—(See "Abnormally Fond Of" under Pleasure).

Rash Actions—In Sports, and Warns Against Injury By — ♂ afflicted in ♐. (See Hasty; "Sudden Impulses" under Impulses; "Painful Complaints" under Rashness).

Recreations — Death or Injury In — (See Recreations).

Riding—(See "Riding" under Horses; "Outdoor Exercise" in this section).

Robust Sports—(See "Outdoor" in this section).

Shooting — (See Gunshot, Hunting, Shooting).

Theatres—Death or Injury In — (See Theatres).

Travel — (See "Love of Travel", and the various paragraphs under Travel).

Vicious Pleasures — Vicious Sports — Fond of—♀ Sig. in ♋. (See Pleasures).

Wrestling — (See "Pugilist", "Wrestler", under Athletics).

SPOTS—Spotted—

Nebulous Spots—(See Nebulous).

Skin Spots—(See Blemishes, Blotches; "Spots" under Liver; Marks, Moles, Naevus, Scars; "Pock-Marked" under Smallpox. Also note the various paragraphs under Skin).

Sun Spots — A number of Spots appear upon the Sun when ♃ is in perihelion, and disappear when ♃ is in aphelion. They tend to affect the Nervous System, make men irritable, quarrelsome, and given to War. These spots disturb the gases of our atmosphere, and tend to epidemics, tornadoes, cyclones, cloudbursts, and atmospheric disturbances. (See Epidemics, Perihelion; "Tornadoes" under Wind).

SPOTTED—

Spotted Colors — Mixed Colors — (See "Mixed" under Colors).

Spotted Fever—Cerebro-Spinal Fever —Cerebro-Spinal Meningitis with Fever and Eruption — The ☉ afflicted in ♌; the ☉ in ♌ when the afflictor in the disease. Coincident with the appearance of Comets. Halley's Comet has brought it, and been followed by Plague. It very frequently accompanies Cerebro-Spinal Meningitis, and also Herpes. (See "Cerebro-Spinal Meningitis" under Cerebro-Spinal; Comets, Herpes, Plague).

SPRAINS—Strains—The accidents of ♑ are Sprains, Dislocations, and Broken Limbs. Caused by ♑ on the Asc. at B. Also caused by ♄, the ruler of the ♑ Sign.

Ankles — Sprains In — (See "Sprains" under Ankles).

Knees — (See "Strains In" under Knees).

Lower Parts—Sprains In—The ☽ afflicted in ♑; ♄ in ♑ or ♒. (See "Parts" under Lower).

Wrists — Sprains In — (See "Sprains" under Wrists). See Strains.

SPREAD OF DISEASE — (See "Corrupt Air" under Air; Cholera, Comets, Endemic, Epidemics, Noxious, Obnoxious, Pandemics, Perihelion, Pestilence, Plague; "Sun Spots" under Spots).

SPRING EQUINOX—The Vernal Equinox—(See Equinoxes, Vernal).

SPRINGS DRY UP — (See Drought; "Fountains Dry Up" under Dry; Famine, Fountains; "Extreme Heat" under Heat; "Hot Blasting Winds" under Wind).

SPURIOUS ISCHURIA — (See this subject under Urine. Also see False).

SPUTUM — (See Expectoration, Mucus, Phlegm, Saliva, Spitting, etc.).

SQUAB BODY — Fat and Short — Low and Bulky — Lumpish — Plump — Well-Trussed — Squat — Short and Thick — The ☽ in her decrease causes a short, low, squat stature; ♄ Sig. in ♏ in Hor'y Q.; ☿ in ♋ or ♓; ☿ Sig. in ♋, short, squab body; ☿ in ♓, partile the Asc., a short squab figure, but some Authorities say thin; ♋, ♏, or ♓ on the Asc.; some Authorities say that ♒ on the Asc. gives a squab figure, and especially if there are many planets in watery signs. (See "Body" under Fat; "Fleshy Body" under Fleshy; Lumpish; "Low Stature" under Low; Plump; "Body" under Short, Thick; Well-Trussed, etc.).

SQUARE—

Aspect—The Square Aspect (□)—The 90° Aspect, and very evil and afflicting. This is the cross aspect of crucifixion, and many of these aspects between the planets at B. tend to a life of trouble, sorrow, and ill-health for the native, and a more turbulent career. (See Aspects).

Body — Square-Built Body — Square Make—The ☉ in ♍, square and fleshy; the ☉ or ☽ in ♑, ♒, or ♓, or these signs upon the Asc., square make; ♄ in ♈ in good aspect the Asc.; ♃ Sig. in a fiery sign, the body is square made and strong. (See "Body" under Fat; "Fleshy Body" under Fleshy; Squab).

Face—(See "Square" under Face).

Head—(See "Square" under Head).

SQUAT STATURE—(See Fat, Squab).

SQUINTING — Squint Eyes — Crossed Eyes—(See "Strabismus" under Eyes).

STABS — Cuts — Wounds by Knife or Sword—Caused by ♂, as ♂ is the instigator of quarrels, disputes, contests, and violence; ♂ ☐ or ☍ the ☉ at B., and by dir.; ♂ afflicted in the 1st H. at B.; born under ♂, and with ♂ ruler of the Asc., and afflicted; ♂ in the 1st or 10th H., and afflicting the hyleg; ♂ afflicting the ☉, ☽, or hyleg at B., and elevated above them in a violent map; ♂ with Aldebaran, and especially in angles, and afflicting the ☽; the ☉ or ☽ to the ☌ or ill-asps. ♂ by dir.; the ☉ joined with the Ascelli, Castor, Pollux, Hyades, Praesepe, or the Pleiades; the ☽ directed to Capella; the Asc. to the ☌ or evil asp. ♂ by dir., and especially if ♂ be in a fiery sign; the M.C. to the place of Pollux or the Pleiades; the Ascelli, Pleiades, Hyades, Castor, Praesepe, directed to the Asc. or Lights. (See Blows, Cuts, Duels, Instruments, Sword).

Contests—Killed or Injured In—(See Chartering, Contests, Duels, Quarrels).

Cuts — (See the various paragraphs under Cuts).

Death by Stabs—♂ causes death by; ♂ with Aldebaran, and ♂ in ☐ or ☍ the ☉, and ♂ just setting at B.; ♂ the afflicting planet, in a violent sign, and afflicting the hyleg; ♂ in the 10th H., and ☐ the Asc., and the ☉ afflicted; the ☽ to the ☌ or ill-asp. ♂ by dir.; the ☽ directed to Capella, danger of death by stabs or blows; the ☽ Sig. ☌, ☐, or ☍ ♂; the ☉ to the place of Praesepe. Case of Death by Stabs—See "Terris", No. 789, in 1001 N.N. (See Assassination; "Death" under Blows, Cuts, Duels, Sword; Roman Emperor).

Distortions — Lameness, or Paralysis Resulting from Stabs — (See Distortions).

Duels — Death or Injury In — (See Duels).

Incised Wounds—(See Cuts, Incised).

Instruments—Stabs by Sharp Instruments, and Edged Tools — (See Cuts, Duels, Instruments, Iron, Sword; the various paragraphs in this section).

Journeys — Stabs or Cuts During — (See "Travel" under Cuts).

Lameness—From Stabs—(See Distortions; "Lameness" under Cuts; "Stabs" under Lameness).

Paralysis—From Stabs—(See Distortions).

Quarrels—(See "Death", "Injury", under Quarrels).

Sharp Instruments — Stabs By — (See Cuts, Duels, Instruments, Sword; the various paragraphs in this section).

Spinal Curvature—From Stabs—Case —See "Spinal Curvature", No. 838, in 1001 N.N.

Travel—Journeys—Voyages—Stabs or Cuts During — (See "Travel" under Cuts).

Violent Death—By Cuts or Stabs—In a violent map, ♂ elevated above, and afflicting the ☉, ☽, or hyleg at B., and by dir. (See "Death" in this section).

Voyages — Stabs or Cuts On — (See "Travel" under Cuts).

War — Stabs In — Death In — (See "Death or Injury In" under War).

Weapons — Stabs by Sharp Weapons —(See Cuts, Duels, Instruments, Sword; the various paragraphs in this section).

STAGES OF LIFE—(See Childhood, Infancy, Middle Life, Old Age; "Life" under Periods; Youth).

STAGGERING WALK — (See Drunkenness; "Staggering" under Gait; Intoxication).

STAGNATION—Stagnant—

Air — Stagnant Air — (See "Corrupt" under Air).

Blood—(See "Stagnant" under Blood).

Functions — (See "Stagnation" under Functions).

Pools—Stagnant Pools—(See Pools).

STAKE—Burned At Stake—Case—(See "Stake" under Burns).

STAMINA—Vital Stamina—Tone—Vitality, etc. The bodily Stamina is ruled by the Asc. The Fiery Signs on the Asc. at B. give the best stamina, and next to these the Airy Signs, and the Watery Signs ♋ and ♓ give the least stamina. Of the earthy and watery signs the ♉, ♍, and ♏ signs give good stamina when on the Asc. at B. The ☽ has much to do with the stamina of the constitution at all times, and the health will not be as good if the ☽ is badly afflicted in a female nativity, or the ☉ weak and afflicted in a male nativity, and also the fate and fortune of the native is less favorable.

Stamina Good—The Stamina Increased —The ☉ ✶ or △ ♂ or the Asc., and also the organic resistance is increased; ♈, ♌, ♎, or ♐ upon the Asc. at B. (See "Good" under Resistance, Tone, Vitality; "Increased" under Strength; "Body" under Strong).

Stamina In Infancy—(See "Stamina" under Infancy).

Stamina Low — The ☉ in ♑; ♋, ♑, or ♓ on the Asc. at B. (See "Low" under Recuperation, Resistance, Vitality).

Stamina Reduced — (See "Stamina Low" in this section; "Lessened" under Vitality; "Weak Body" under Weak).

Stamina Strengthened — Increased — (See "Stamina Good" in this section).

Void of Stamina — The ☉ or ☽ in an angle at B., and ☌ a malefic. (See "Weakest Constitution" under Constitution; "Early Death" under Early; Feeble, Infirm, Invalids; Sickly; "Low" under Resistance, Vitality).

STAMMERING—(See "Stammering" under Speech).

STANDING — Standing On the Feet — (See "Standing" under Feet).

STANNUM—Tin—A Typical Metal of ♃. (See Metals).

STARCH—Starches—Amylum—Starch-Like—Amyloid—Starches are ruled by ♃, and are the physiological action of ♃. (See Hydrocarbonates, Jupiter, Sugar).

Animal Starch—This is the Glycogen found in the Blood and Liver, and is ruled by ♃. (See Glycogen).

Desire for Starches—Tendency to Excess of Starches In the Food — (See "Starches", "Sweets", under Food).

Kidneys—(See "Amyloid Kidney" under Kidneys).

STARING EYES—(See "Large", "Staring" under Eyes).

STAR MAP OF BIRTH—(See Map, Nativity, Radix, Will).

STARS—Fixed Stars—Constellations—The Stars outside of our Solar System, and which are not our Planets, are called Fixed Stars. Only the Stars near the Ecliptic will be considered here. (See Planets). The Constellations make up a Group of Stars. These stars have much effect upon Humanity when in the Asc. or Angles at B., when near the ☉ or ☽, and also when directed to the Angles. Fixed Stars operate only by ☌, P., or ☍ aspects in the Zodiac, or Mundane, and not by ⚹, □, or △. The Fixed Stars have various natures after the order of our Planets, and tend to cause good fortune, calamity, sickness, disease, pestilence, misfortune, accidents, injuries, blindness, eye troubles, drowning, disgrace, imprisonment, violent death, etc., according to their nature. Some Fixed Stars are of the nature of ♂, or of ♂ and the ☽ combined, of ♂ and ♀, or of ♂ and ☿ combined, etc. Other stars are of the nature of ♅, ♄, ♃, ♀, and ☿, and their various combined influences. Fixed stars of the nature of ♂ tend to fevers, accidents, injuries, violent death, etc. Those of the nature of ♄, chronic disorders, and ill-fortune. Those of the nature of ♃ and ♀, good fortune, etc. The violent fixed stars are of the nature of ♂ and ♂ combinations, and are the most dangerous to Humanity, and when joined with the ☉ at B., threaten a violent death or extreme sickness. (See "Violent Stars" in this section). Stars of the nature of ♃ and ♀, or ♃ and ♀ combined influences, are more fortunate in their influences, and tend to bring good fortune, good health, honors, renown, happiness, etc. Arista, of the nature of ♂ and ♀, is said to be one of the most fortunate of the fixed stars. Algol is said to be the most evil of all the Fixed Stars. Lists of the Fixed Stars are to be found in the various Textbooks and Dictionaries of Astrology. In this Article you will find an alphabetical list of the Fixed Stars referred to in the various Textbooks, as related to, and causing disease, and other conditions over Humanity. See these Stars in the alphabetical arrangement for further information about them, their position, influences, etc. Also in this Article the various Groups of Fixed Stars are given.

Fixed Stars—Alphabetical List of the Fixed Stars mentioned in the Textbooks in relation to Disease, Accidents, Misfortunes, Violence, etc. — Acquirius, Aldebaran, Algenib, Algol, Alphard, Altair, Andromeda, Antares, Aquaries, Arcturus, Argo, Arista, Ascelli, Auriga (Capella); Bellatrix, Betelgeuse, Bootes, Bull's Eyes and Horns, Canis Majoris, Capella (Auriga); Capricornus, Caput Algol, Caput Andromeda, Caput Hercules (Pollux); Castor, Cauda Lucida (Deneb, Lion's Tail); Cepheus, Ceti, Cor Hydra (Alphard, Hydra's Heart); Cor Leonis (Regulus, Lion's Heart); Cor Scorpio (Antares); Cratch (Ascelli); Crater, Cynosura (Little Bear, Ursa Minor); Deneb (Lion's Tail); Dorsa Leonis (Lion's Back); Eagle (Attair, Scorpio); Fomahaut, Frons Scorpio, Gemini (Twins); Goat (Capricorn); Gorgon's Head (Algol); Hercules (Pollux); Hircus, Hyades, Hydra's Heart (Alphard, Cor Hydra); Lion (Cor Leonis, Dorsa Leonis, Mane of Leo, etc. — See Lion); Little Bear (Cynosura); Lucida Maxilla (Ceti, Menkar, Whale's Jaw); Lucida Pleiadum (Pleiades); Markab, Medusa's Head (Algol); Menkar (Ceti, Whale's Jaw); Nebulous Spots (see Nebulous); North Scale; Oculus Taurus (Bull's Eye); Ophiucus, Orion, Pleiades, Pollux (Hercules); Praesepe, Procyon, Propus, Regulus, Rigel, Scales (North and South Scale); Scheat Pegasi, Scorpion's Heart (Cor Scorpio, Antares); Sirius, Twins (Castor and Pollux, Gemini); Urn of Aquarius, Ursa Minor (Little Bear, Cynosura); Vega, Vindemiatrix, Virgin's Spixe (Arista); Vulture (Altair); Whale's Jaw — Whale's Belly (Ceti, Menkar); Zona Andromeda (Andromeda).

Fortunate Stars — Arista (Spica Virginus), of the nature of ♂ and ♀, is said to be the most fortunate in influence of the Fixed Stars. Also the stars of the ♃ and ♀ Group in this section.

Jupiter and Mars Group — Arcturus, Antares, North Scale, Rigel, Sirius. Fixed Stars of the nature of ♃, or of ♃ and ♂, when joined to the Anareta, denote injuries to arise from Religion, or some one in Power.

Jupiter and Venus Group—Caput Andromedae, Crater. Stars of the nature of ♃ and ♀ can do little injury unless mixed with those of ♄ and ♂.

Mars Group—The principal group of ♂ stars, listed as purely of ♂ influence, are Aldebaran, Bull's North and South Horns, Cor Leo (Regulus), Propus, and Pollux. Fixed stars of the ♂ nature denote sudden fevers, accidents, or murders. (See "Stars of Mars Nature" under Mars).

Mars and Mercury Group — Algenib, Antares (Cor Scorpio), Bellatrix (Orion's Left Shoulder); Betelgeuse (Orion's Right Shoulder); Capella (In Auriga's Left Shoulder); Hircus, Procyon.

Mars and Moon Group — Ascelli, Hyades, Nebulous Spots and Clusters, Pleiades, Praesepe. This group also acts like the ♂ group, but especially on the eyes, and to cause eye troubles, blindness, and also fevers, accidents, injuries, and violent death. (See Hyades, Nebulous, Pleiades, etc.).

Mars and Venus Group—Arista (Virgin's Spixe); Markab, Serpentis.

Moon Group—The Constellation Argo is typical of the ☽ group, and tends to drowning. Fixed stars of the nature of the ☽ tend to drowning, colic, cold and watery diseases. There are practically no stars listed in the Textbooks of Astrology as being distinctly of a ☽ nature, but those referred to in Astrology are the ♂ and ☽ combination, such as the Nebulous Clusters, Pleiades, etc. (See "Mars and Moon Group" in this section. Also see Argo, Drowning, Shipwreck).

Ruling Your Stars — (See Character, Fate, Hospitals, Map, Medical Astrology; "Treatment" under Melancholy; Occult, Science, Spiritual, etc.).

Saturn Group—Cauda Lucida (Lion's Tail, Deneb); Scheat Pegasi, Ceti (Menkar, Whale's Jaw); Whale's Belly, Whale's Tail, Capricornus. Afflictions of the ♄ group tend to Agues, Cold Diseases, Palsies, and denote Falls.

Saturn and Jupiter Group — Algol, Orion's Belt (Orion). Algol is considered the most evil and malign of all the fixed stars. (See Algol).

Saturn and Mars Group — Left Hand of Ophiucus, Ram's Head, Frons Scorpio. Wilson, in his Dictionary of Astrology, gives Frons Scorpio as of the nature of ♄ and ♀. Simmonite gives it as of the nature of ♄ and ♂.

Saturn, Mars and Venus—Castor.

Saturn, Mercury, and Venus — Lion's Tail (Deneb); Vindemiatrix, both as given in Wilson's Dictionary of Astrology.

Saturn and Venus — Dorsa Leonis (Lion's Back); Hydra's Heart, Frons Scorpio, Right Knee of Ophiucus, South Scale, Vindemiatrix.

Sun and Mars Group — The Ascelli, Capricornus. Tend to Blindness, Eye Disorders, Fevers, etc.

Unfortunate Stars—The principal unfortunate stars are Aldebaran (♂); Algol (♄ and ♃); Antares (♂ and ☿); Castor (♄, ♂, ♀); Deneb (♅); Dorsa Leonis (♄ and ♀); Hyades (♂ and ☽); Pleiades (♂ and ☽); Praesepe (♂ and ☽); Whale's Jaw (♄). Fixed Stars of the nature of the malefics ♅, ♄, and ♂, and some of the combinations with these malefics, are very unfortunate over human affairs when found with the ☉ or ☽ at B.

Uranus Group — Acquirius, Aquaries, Altair, Deneb (Lion's Tail, listed as of ♅ influence in Simmonite). These stars tend to sudden mishaps, sudden death, and violence.

Venus Group—Bull's South Eye (Oculus Taurus), Canis Majoris, Zona Andromeda. In the lists of Fixed Stars in the Textbooks Wilson gives the Bull's North Eye as Oculus Taurus, and of the nature of ♀. Wilson gives the Bull's South Eye as Aldebaran, and of the nature of ♂. Simmonite gives the Bull's South Eye as of ♀, and the North Eye (Aldebaran) as of ♂. Pearce gives Oculus Taurus as of ♀, and Aldebaran as of ♂. Alan Leo's Dictionary of Astrology gives the same as in Pearce's Textbook, and Wilson's Dictionary seems to stand alone in giving Aldebaran as the Bull's South Eye.

Violent Fixed Stars — Fixed Stars of the nature of ♂, and of ♂ combinations, tend to be violent in their nature and effects. Also some stars of ♄ influence are violent in nature. In addition to those stars listed in the Mars Group in this section, the following stars are considered violent in nature: Aldebaran (♂); Algenib (♂ and ☿); Algol (♄ and ♃); Antares (♂ and ☿); Bellatrix (♂ and ☿); Castor (♄, ♂, and ♀); Markab (♂ and ♀); Procyon (♂ and ☿); South Scale (♄ and ♀). (See "Mars Group" in this section).

STARVATION—Want of Food—Famine —♄ and ♂ in ☍ aspect, in Equinoctial Signs, and controlling the Luminaries. (See "Lost In" under Desert; Drought, Famine, Neglect, Poverty; "Dangers" under Travel).

Desert — Danger of Starvation In — (See Desert).

Starved to Death—Case—See "Popejoy", No. 771 in 1001 N.N.

Tissues—Starvation of—(See Emaciation; "Incapable Of", "Malnutrition", under Nutrition; Wastings).

STATIONARY PLANETS — The afflicting planet in disease when stationary in the Zodiac tends to prolong the disease, make it more constant and enduring in its effects. (See Constancy, Continuity, Course, Direct Motion; "Degree Of" under Disturbed; Duration, Lingering Diseases, Prolonged, Retrograde, etc.).

STATURE—Form—Shape of the Body—Figure—Height—Weight, etc. The Sign ascending, and the First House, have significance of the Stature of Man. The matter of determining the stature from the horoscope is not an easy task, and it requires considerable knowledge of the nature and qualities of the Planets, Signs, Houses, Aspects, etc., and of Synthesis, to form a reasonable judgment of the appearance, build, complexion, height, weight, etc., without seeing the native. However, the influences given in connection with the following subjects have proven very accurate along these lines. Planets ascending, the sign ascending, the degree ascending at B., the Ascendant, lord of the Ascendant, the nature and position of the majorities of the planets, the dignities of the planets, planets rising, setting, elevated, below the Earth, the combinations and aspects of the planets, and the general synthesis of the map, have to be carefully examined in order to form a judgment about the appearance of the native. These rules are further set forth in the Articles on Appearance, Complexion, Form, Height, Shape, Weight, etc. When the ☉ or ☽ are ascending at B., judge from the quality of the sign they are in. When ☿ is ascending he gives a stature according to the lord of the Ascendant. In the Articles on each of the planets something is said about the kind of a form and stature such planet tends to give when predominant at B. By making a study of the following subjects the student will get a very good idea of the various causes and influences which tend to produce the different types of body and physique. See these subjects in the alphabetical arrangement when they are only listed here—

Abdomen Prominent — (See "Prominent" under Abdomen).

Abnormally Tall — (See Enlarged, Giants, Height, Tall).

Above Average Height—(See Giants, Height, Tall).

Above Middle Height — (See Height, Middle).

Advantageous Stature — (See "Good Constitution" under Constitution).

Appearance — (See the various subjects and references under Appearance).

Arms — (See "Long", "Short", under Arms).

Awkward; Badly Made — And Ugly — (See Crooked; "Not Handsome" under Handsome; "Ill-Formed" under Ill; Ugly).

Beautiful; Bent Forward—(See "Body Bent Forward" under Bending).

Best-Formed Body — ♌ on the Asc. (See Beautiful, Form, Handsome, Well-Formed).

Big Head and Face—(See "Big" under Face; "Large" under Head; "Body" under Large).

Body—(See the various subjects and references under Body).

Broad; Build; Chest — (See Hollow, Narrow, Wide, and the various descriptions under Chest).

Coarse; Comely; Commanding;

Compact; Conformity of Members — (See Well-Proportioned).

Constitution — (See Good, Strong, Weak, and the various paragraphs under Constitution).

Contracted Body—Small—(See Diminished, Dwarfed, Small Body).

Corpulent; Crooked;

Decent-Made and Compact—(See Compact).

Deformed; Diminished — (See Diminished, Dwarfed, Low, Short Body, Small).

Discomposed; Disproportioned;

Distorted; Dwarfed; Elegant;

Enlarged; Erect; Face—(See Angular, Broad, Long, Oval, Round, Thin, and the various descriptions under Face).

Fair; Fat; Fine; Fleshy; Form of Body —(See Form).

Full Stature—(See Full).

Giants; Good Stature—(See Beautiful, Comely, Elegant, Fine, Good, Handsome, Well-Proportioned).

Hands — (See Broad, Fleshy, Long, Short, and the various descriptions under Hands).

Handsome; Harmonious; Head—(See Large, Round, Small, and the various descriptions under Head).

Healthy Make—(See Healthy).

Height—(See the various paragraphs and references under Height).

Hips—(See Narrow, Small, Well-Proportioned, under Hips).

Hooked Forward — (See Bending; "Downward" under Look; "Stoop Shoulders" under Shoulders; Stooping).

Horary Questions—Stature In—Indicated by the Sign ascending.

Ill-Formed Body—(See Crooked, Deformed; "Ill-Formed" under Ill; Incurvating, Malformations, Misshaped, Ugly).

Incurvating—Crooked—Not Straight —(See Incurvating).

Indifferent Stature — (See "Stature" under Indifferent).

Knees—(See Crooked, Ill-Made, Knock-Knees, under Knees).

Large Stature — (See Full, Giants, Large).

Lean; Legs—(See the descriptions under Legs).

Limbs — (See Crooked, Large, Long, Short, Small, Stout, and the various paragraphs under Limbs).

Little Stature — (See Diminished, Dwarfed, Short, Small).

Low Stature—(See "Low Stature" under Low).

Lumpish; Mean Stature—(See Mean).

Medium Stature—(See Medium).

Members — (See Brevity Of, Long, Missing, under Members).

Middle-Sized—(See Medium, Middle).

Misshaped; Moderate Stature — (See Moderate).

Monsters; Muscular Body—(See Athletic; "Body" under Muscles).

Not High — (See Diminished, Dwarf, Low, Short, Small).

Not Well-Made—(See "Ill-Formed" in this section).

Obesity; Physique—(See Physical).

Plump; Positive Form — (See Positive).

Posture; Prepossessing Stature—(See Commanding).

Proper Stature—(See Proper).

Proportionate — (See "Fair Proportions" under Fair).

Raw-Boned — (See "Raw-Boned" under Bones).

Robust Looking—(See Robust).

Rugged; Shape — (See the references under Shape).

Shapely—(See Beautiful, Handsome).

Short Body—(See "Body" under Short).

Shoulders—(See Broad, Round, Stoop, Thick, under Shoulders).

Sickly Looking—(See Sickly).

Size; Skeleton; Slender; Small Body—(See "Body" under Small).

Squab Body—(See Squab).

Square-Built—(See Square).

Squatty—(See Fat, Squab; "Short and Thick" under Thick).

Stooped—(See "Hooked Forward" in this section).

Stout; Straight—(See Erect, Straight, Upright).

Strong Body — (See "Body" under Strong).

Sturdy—(See Robust, Rugged).

Tall; Thick Body—(See Thick).

Thighs — (See Long, Short, Small, Strong, under Thighs).

Thin Body—(See Lean, Slender, Thin).

Trunk; Ugly; Undersized;

Undeveloped; Ungainly; Unrefined;

Upright; Weak and Small — (See "Smaller and Weaker" under Small).

Weight; Well-Built; Well-Favored;

Well-Formed; Well-Framed;

Well-Made; Well-Proportioned;

Well-Set; Well-Shaped; Well-Trussed;

Youthful Looking — (See "Youthfulness" under Youth). For other subjects along this line, and which may be omitted here, look in the alphabetical arrangement for what you have in mind.

STEALING — (See Kleptomaniac, Robbers, Thieves).

STEATOMA — Steatomatous Tumor — (See Cysts, Fat, Sebaceous, Wen).

STEEL—The Metal Steel is ruled by ♂.

Wounds By—(See Iron).

STELLAR BAPTISM — (See "Planetary Baptism" under Baptism; "Moment of Birth" under Moment).

STELLIUM—An Over-Cargo of Planets in a Sign or House. A Stellium, or group of Stars, in a house, tends to cause disease, and corresponding to the Sign ordinarily ruling the House. Thus many planets in the 2nd H. denote throat trouble. A Stellium in ♌ or the 5th H., heart disturbances. A Stellium in ♓ or the 12th H., humours in the feet, etc. A Stellium in ♊ or the 3rd H., Lung and Nervous Disorders. (See Majority).

STENOSIS—A Narrowing or Constriction—A Contraction—Stenosis is presided over by ♄. Cold, ruled by ♄, is a strong factor in contractions.

Bile Ducts—Stenosis of—(See "Ducts" under Bile).

Blood Vessels—Stenosis of—(See Constrictions).

Cells—(See "Stenosis" under Cells).

Mitral Stenosis—(See "Mitral" under Heart).

Nose—Nares—(See "Stenosis" under Nose).

Pulmonary Stenosis—(See "Stenosis" under Lungs).

Pylorus—Stenosis of—(See "Pylorus" under Stomach).

Vaso-Constriction — (See Constrictions, Vaso).

Vessels—Stenosis of Blood Vessels—(See Constrictions, Vaso, Vessels). See Capillaries, Centripetal, Cold, Colds, Congestions, Constrictions, Contractions, Spasmodic Diseases, Stricture).

STEP—Gait—Walk—For the different variations in Step see Gait, Walk).

Step Children — (See "Step Children" under Children).

STERILITY—(See Barren, Impotent).

Sterilization — Forcible Castration — Danger of—(See Maimed; "Violent Castration" under Testes).

STERN — Stern Expression — (See Austere).

STERNUM—The Flat Bone of the Breast — Manubrium — Ensiform Cartilage — Xiphisternum—Is under the structural rulership of the ♋ Sign. (See "Breast bone" under Breast).

Pain In—(See Xiphodynia).

Sterno-Mastoid Region—Sterno-Mastoid Muscle—Disorders of—(See Mastoid).

STERTOROUS — Sonorous — Stertorous Breathing — (See "Snoring", "Stertorous", under Breathing).

STHENIA—Sthenic—Strong—Active—

Sthenic Inflammation—(See "Sthenic" under Inflammation).

Sthenic Plethora—(See "Sthenic" under Plethora).

Sthenic Process—Is presided over by ♂. (See "Active Body" under Active; Asthenic, Dynamic, Energetic, Mars, Strength, Strong).

STIFFNESS — Stiff — Rigid — Stiff and rigid conditions in the body are caused by ♄, and by Cold, which is ruled by ♄. They also occur during Spasmodic conditions. (See Cold, Rigidity, Saturn, Spasmodic).

Stiff Body—Caused by ♄ deposits, retention of the wastes of the body, excess of Uric Acid, etc. (See Crystallization, Deposits, Gout, Hardening, Retentions, Rheumatism, Sand, Stone, Wastes, etc.).

Stiff Hair—(See "Stiff" under Hair).

Stiff Joints—(See Adhesions, Ankylosis; "Stiff" under Joints; Rheumatism).

Stiff Muscles — (See "Contractions" under Muscles; Rigidity, Rigors).

Stiff Neck—(See "Stiff" under Neck).

Stiff Shoulder Joint—(See "Stiffness" under Shoulders).

Stiff Spine—(See "Stiff" under Spine).

STILLBORN — Stillbirth — Born Dead — Child Dies In the Womb — Child Thought Born Dead—♅ afflicted in ♏ in the map of the mother; all of the Significators afflicted, as the ☉, ☽, Asc., lord of the Asc., and with no assistance from Benefics; the Benefics in the 1st, 5th, or 11th H., and sorely afflicted by malefics; ♄ exactly on the cusp of the 1st or 7th H., born dead, or breathes only a few times and dies. (See Abortion; "Death at Birth" under Children; "Mutilation Of" under Foetus; Miscarriage). Cases of Stillbirth — See "Breech Presentation", No. 075 in 1001 N.N. Case — Thought Born Dead, and does not breathe until two hours after birth—See "Foot", No. 106 in 1001 N.N. Prenatal conditions, and afflictions to the ☽ during Gestation, are usually the causes of a stillbirth, and which kill the foetus in utero. (See Prenatal Epoch).

STIMULANTS — Stimulant —Stimulation —Tonics—Stimulus—Mars is stimulant, and the drugs of ♂ are used in Tonics and Stimulant Remedies. The ☉ Group of Plants are stimulant. Neptune is associated with Drugs, and especially Narcotic Stimulants, as Opiates, Tobacco, etc. The Adrenals, ruled by ♃, are the organs which stimulate the body. The Glycogen in the liver is drawn upon by ♂ for fuel during muscular activity. (See Adrenals, Glycogen).

Avoid Stimulants—Stimulants should be avoided when the ☽ is ☌ ♂, and especially ♂ in ♈, the Asc., or strong at B. Also avoid stimulants during the decrease of the ☽. (See "Best Time to Give Medicine" under Medicines).

Digestive Stimulants — (See "Stimulated" under Digestion).

Disordered Stimulation—In the Body —Caused by afflictions to ♃, and interference with the Adrenal Secretions. (See "Diminished Secretion" under Adrenals).

Dosage of Stimulants — Should be smaller during the increase of the ☽, and larger dosage during the decrease of the ☽. (See "Decrease", "Increase", under Moon).

Given to Stimulants — To Liquors or Narcotics—The ☉, ☽, and many planets in watery signs at B., more desire for drink; ♆ in a watery sign; ♆ afflicted in the 6th H., or in ♍; ♄ in the Asc., and afflicted by ♆. (See Drink, Drunkenness; "Sugar" under Food; Intoxicants, Narcotics, Wine).

Greatest Effect—Stimulants have the greatest effect when the ☽ is increasing in light, and sedatives do little good. The ☽ ☌ ♄ causes stimulants to have little effect. (See Sedatives).

Heart Stimulants—Cautions In Using —(See "Stimulants" under Heart).

Of Little Effect — See Avoid, Dosage, Greatest Effect, in this section).

Rubefacients — Local Stimulants— Caustics — External Stimulants — The remedies of ♂ are stimulant when applied to the skin, and may cause blistering, and are used to stimulate the local circulation which has been impeded by ♄. Cantharides is a typical ♂ rubefacient and caustic. The remedies of the ☉, such as Mustard, are stimulant locally on the skin. (See Applications, Cantharides, Caustics, Mustard, Rubefacients, Sinapis, Vesicant).

Stimulus—Incentive—Ambition—Energy—Lack of—Loss of—(See "Of No Ambition" under Ambition; Apathy, Dull; "Lack Of" under Energy; "Mind" under Heaviness; Inactive, Indifferent, Inertia, Languid, Lassitude. Lazy, Lethargy, Listless, Malaise, Morose, Relaxation, Rouse; "Drowsiness" under Sleep; Slothful, Slovenly, Torpid, etc.).

Tonic Medicines — (See "Liquids", "Stimulants", under Drink; Narcotics, Poisons; "Medicines" under Tonic; Wine, etc.).

STINGS—Venomous Stings—Wounds or Death By Obnoxious Creatures—♄ or ♂ in the Terrestrial, or Quadrupedal Signs (see Quadrupeds); ♄ near the Constellation of the Serpent, and with ♄ in the 1st H., configurated with ☿, and in ♉ the ☉ or ☽ setting, and also tends to death from such; ♄ and ♂ conjoined in ♏; ♂ causes bites and stings, and with swellings and eruptions; the star Fomahaut conjoined with ♂. (See Adder, Bites, Insects, Obnoxious, Reptiles, Serpents, Venomous).

STINKING — Foul — Offensive — Loathsome—Obnoxious—Unpleasant Odors— (See "Foul" under Breath; Corruption, Decay, Decomposition, Fetid, Foul, Odors, Offensive; "Stagnant" under Pools; Putrefaction; "Fetid" under Sweat).

STOCK BODY—Stocky and Short—The ☉ in ♉, or ♉ on the Asc. at B. (See Corpulent, Fat Body, Fleshy; "Body" under Short).

STOICISM — Self-Abnegation—(See "Stoicism" under Religion).

STOMACH—Gastric—The Chief Digestive Organ of the Body—The stomach is under the internal rulership of the ♋ sign. Also ruled by the ☽ and the 4th H. The 5th H. denotes the stomach. The Cardinal Signs influence and affect the stomach, and especially ♋ and ♑.

— SECTION ONE —

GENERAL CONSIDERATIONS — Organs and Matters Related to the Stomach—See the following subjects in the alphabetical arrangement—

Abdomen; Acids — Of the Stomach — (See Gastric, Juices; "Juices" in this section).

Alimentation—Alimentary Canal— (See Alimentary).

Appetite; Arteries—Of the Stomach— Ruled by ♃, and ♃ in ♋.

Assimilation; Cardinal Signs — The cardinal signs denote the Head, Stomach, Kidneys, and Skin. (See Cardinal).

Diet; Digestion; Drink; Duodenum; Eating; Emetics; Epigastrium;

External Lining—Of the Stomach—Is ruled by ♋, and ♄ in ♋.

Fluids Of—(See Acids; "Fluids" under Digestion; Gastric, Hydrochloric, Juices, etc.).

Food; Functions — Of the Stomach — Ruled by the ☽ and the ☽ in ♋. (See Assimilation, Digestion; "Functions" under Stomach).

Gastric — Gastronomical — Gastro-Abdominal—(See Gastric).

Glands — The Glands of the Stomach are ruled by the ☽, and the ☽ in ♋. Also the glands and secretions in the stomach are ruled by ♆, and ♆ in ♋.

Gustativeness; Hydrochloric Acid — (See Hydrochloric).

Juices — The Juices of the Stomach are under the rule of the ☽. (See Fluids, Glands, in this section).

Lining — Of the Stomach — (See "External" in this section).

Lower Part—Of the Stomach—Ruled by ♍. (See "Splanchnic" under Ganglion).

Membranes—Of the Stomach—Ruled, and largely influenced by ♅, and ♅ in ♋.

Muscles—Of the Stomach—Ruled by ♂, and ♂ in ♋. (See Muscles).

Nerves—Of the Stomach—Ruled by ☿, and ☿ in ♋. (See Nerves).

Oesophagus; Pepsin; Peristalsis — In the Stomach—Ruled by ♋. (See Peristalsis).

Pylorus—Pyloric Valve—Ruled by ♍, the sign which rules the lower part of the Stomach.

Receptacle—The Stomach as a receptacle is ruled by the ☽ and the ♋ sign.

Secretions — Of the Stomach — (See Acids, Fluids, Glands, Hydrochloric, Juices, Pepsin, in this section).

Stomach Place—In the Spine—Known as "S.P.", and consists of the 6th, 7th, and 8th Dorsal Vertebrae. (See Subluxations; "Dorsal Vertebrae" under Vertebrae).

Structure—Of the Stomach—Ruled by the ☉, and the ☉ in ♋. (See Organic, Structural).

Tunics—The Gastro-Intestinal Tunics —(See "Impar" under Ganglion).

Upper Part—Of the Stomach—Ruled by the ♌ sign. (See the Introduction under Heart).

Veins—Of the Stomach—Ruled by ♀ and ♀ in ♋.

— SECTION TWO —

DISEASES OF THE STOMACH — See these subjects in the alphabetical arrangement when only listed here—

Abnormal Functioning—Of the Stomach—♆ afflicted in ♋ or the 4th H.

Abscess—(See "Ulcer" under Gastric).

Ache—Stomachache—A ☽ disease; the ☽ afflicted in ♋. (See Aches; Neuralgia, Pain, in this section).

Acidity — (See "Gastric Acidity" under Acids).

Acute Catarrh—Of the Stomach—(See "Gastritis" under Gastric; "Inflammation" in this section).

Affected — The Stomach tends to be affected when the ☽ is in ♋ or ♏; ♀ in ♍, or ☿ in ♎ or ♑. See Table 196 in Simmonite's Arcana.

Alimentation — Alimentary Canal — Disorders of—(See Alimentary).

Antiperistalsis — (See Antiperistalsis, Nausea, Peristalsis, Vomiting; "Peristalsis" in this section).

Anxiety—Stomach Disorders Due To —(See "Anxiety" under Digestion).

Appetite — Excess or Lack of — (See "Abnormal", "Loss Of", under Appetite).

Arteries of Stomach — Disorders of — ♃ afflicted in ♋. (See Arteries).

Assimilation—Disorders of—(See Assimilation).

Asthma—(See "Stomach Asthma" under Asthma).

Belching; Bilious Vomiting — (See Nausea, Vomiting).

Bloating; Blood — Stomach Disorders from Corrupt Blood—The ☉, ♄, ♃, or ♀ afflicted in ♋. (See "Impure Blood" under Impure). For the influences which cause vomiting of blood see Haemoptysis; "Blood" under Vomiting).

Cancer—Of the Stomach—(See "Stomach" under Carcinoma).

Carcinoma — (See "Stomach" under Carcinoma).

Cases—Of Stomach Disorders—Maps and Birth Data — See Figures 6A, 6B, 6C, 6D, in "Astro-Diagnosis", and also Figures 17 and 18 in "Message of the Stars", by the Heindels. Also see Seventeen Years in Bed", No. 843 in 1001 N.N., Case of Weak Stomach.

Catarrh — Of the Stomach — Gastric Catarrh—A ♋ disease, and afflictions in ♋; ♄ afflicted in ♋; the ☽ afflicted in ♋ or ♍; Subs at SP (7D), and at KP. (See "Gastritis" under Gastric; "Inflammation" in this section).

Cestode—(See "Worms" in this section).

Chronic Disorders—Of the Stomach—Chronic Gastritis — Chronic Catarrh — Chronic Indigestion—The ☉ hyleg, and to the ☌, P, □, or ☍ ♄ by dir., according to the sign ♄ is in at B.; ♄ afflicted in ♋ tends to chronic stomach troubles, chronic catarrh, and chronic indigestion. (See "Gastritis" under Gastric; "Chronic" under Indigestion; "Catarrh" in this section).

Circulation—Of the Stomach Impeded —♄ in ♋ or ♑, ☌, □, or ☍ ♃ or ♀; ♃ or ♀ in ♋, ☌, □, or ☍ ♄; ♀ in ♋, □, or ☍ ♄ or ♂; Subs at SP. (See "Impeded" under Circulation).

Cold Stomach—Cold Humours In—Indigestion from Taking Cold — (See "Cold", "Raw Humours", under Indigestion).

Colic In Stomach—Due to Worry and Anxiety—The ☽, ♅, or ☿ afflicted in ♋. (See Colic; Cramps, Pain, Wind, in this section).

Congestion—In Stomach—♄ afflicted in ♋. (See Congestion).

Contraction — Of the Pylorus — (See "Pylorus" in this section).

Corrupt Blood — Stomach Trouble From—(See "Blood" in this section).

Cough — Stomach Cough — (See "Dry, Hard Cough", "Stomach Cough", under Cough).

Cramps In — ♅ afflicted in ♋ or the 4th H. (See Cramps).

Death — By Stomach Trouble — ♃ causes death by foul stomach and foul blood; ♀ afflicted at B., and afflicting the hyleg in a train of fatal directions; denoted by ☿; cardinal signs dispose to.

Defects In — Born under ♃, some defect in digestion.

Deglutition; Deranged Stomach—(See "Disordered", and the various paragraphs in this section).

Diet—Ailments Due to Wrong Diet—(See "Ailments", "Excesses", under Diet).

Digestion—Disorders of—(See Digestion, Indigestion).

Dilatation—Of the Stomach—♃ or ♀ afflicted in ♋. (See Dilatations, Distentions, Flatulence; "Distended" in this section).

Diseased Stomach—(See "Disordered", and the various paragraphs in this section).

Disordered Stomach—Diseased Stomach—Stomach Trouble—Gastric Disorders—The Stomach Offended—Digestive Disorders, etc.—Afflictions in ♋, ♑, in the cardinal signs, or in the 4th H.; ♋ on the Asc., and afflicted; Subs at SP. (See the various paragraphs in this section, and under Gastric. Also see Digestion, Indigestion).

Distended Stomach — ♃, ♂, or ♀ afflicted in ♋; ♂ afflictions to the stomach. (See Belching, Dilatations, Distentions, Flatulence; "Stomach" under Gas; Inflation, Tympanites; Fermentation, Wind, in this section).

Dizziness — From Stomach Trouble — Afflictions in ♈ and ♋; a ☽ disease; the ☽ afflicted in ♋; ♃ or ♀ afflicted in ♋; Subs at SP (7D), and at KP. (See Dizziness, Vertigo).

Drink — Stomach Trouble from Too Much Drink and Riotous Living—(See "Stomach" under Drink).

Dry Stomach Cough—(See "Cough" in this section).

Dyspepsia; Dystrophia—(See "Defective Nutrition" under Nutrition).

Eating—(See the various paragraphs under Eating).

Eats Nails—Eats Glass, etc.—Case—(See "Human Ostrich" under Human).

Emetics; Enlarged Stomach—(See Dilated, Distended, in this section).

Epicureans; Epigastrium;

Eructations—(See Belching).

External Lining — Of the Stomach — Disorders of—♄ afflicted in ♋.

Eyes — Floating Specks Before the Eyes from Stomach Trouble — (See "Muscae" under Eyes).

Faecal Vomiting—(See Ileac Passion).

Feasting; Fermentation—In the Stomach—♋ influence; ♋ sign on the cusp the 6th H.; the ☽ hyleg in ♋ with females. (See "Putrid Matter" under Bowels; "Stomach" under Gas).

Fever In Stomach — Gastric Fever — (See "Fever" under Gastric; "Hot" in this section).

Flatulence; Fluids—Of the Stomach—Disordered and Retarded — ♄ afflicted in ♋ or ♑. (See "Fluids" under Gastric; Hydrochloric).

Food — Retention of Difficult — (See "Retention", and the various paragraphs under Food).

Foul Stomach—♃ afflicted in ♋; ♃ ☌ ♄ in ♋. Also ♃ causes death by foul stomach. (See "Foul" under Breath; "Raw Humours" under Indigestion).

Fullness—At the Stomach—(See Flatulence; "Stomach" under Gas).

Functions Disordered — Functional Weakness of the Stomach—Digestive Functions Disturbed—♄, ♅, or ♆ afflicted in ♋; the ☽ afflicted in ♋ with females; the ☽ afflicted by ♄; ♃ afflicted in ♋ or ♑; Subs at SP. (See "Functions" under Digestion; "Juices" under Gastric; Abnormal, Impeded, Obstructions, Stopped, in this section).

Gas In Stomach — (See Belching; "Stomach" under Gas).

Gastralgia—(See Neuralgia, Pains, in this section).

Gastric Disorders — (See Digestion; "Stomach" under Gas; "Disorders" under Gastric; Indigestion; the various paragraphs in this section).

Gastritis—(See "Inflammation" in this section).

Gastro-Abdominal Disorders — (See "Gastro-Abdominal" under Gastric).

Gastronomical Indiscretions—(See "Indiscretions" under Gastric).

Gastroenteritis—(See this subject under Gastric).

Glands—Glands of the Stomach Disordered—(See "Stomach" under Glands; Fluids, Functions, Sluggish, Spasmodic, Undersized, in this section).

Glass — Eats Glass and Nails — (See "Eats Nails" in this section).

Gluttony; Gormandizing; Gripings—☿ afflicted in ♋. (See Gripings; "Cramps" in this section).

Haematemesis — (See "Blood" under Vomiting).

Haemoptysis — (See "Blood" in this section).

Hard and Dry Cough—(See "Cough" in this section).

Head Affected—By Stomach Disorders —(See "Noises In", "Stomach", under Head; Headaches).

Heated Stomach—(See Fever, Hot, in this section).

Heaviness—Of the Stomach—The ☽ ☌ or ill-asp. ♄ (or ☿ if he be of the nature of ♄) at the beginning of an illness, or at decumbiture. (See Heaviness).

Hemorrhage—♂ afflicted in ♋; ♂ in ♋ in the 6th H. (See Haemoptysis; "Blood" under Vomiting).

Hiccough; High Living — Disorders From—(See "Living" under High).

Hindered — The Stomach Fluids Hindered — (See Fluids, Obstructions, Stopped, in this section).

Hot Stomach — Over-Heated Stomach —Feverish Stomach—The ☉ ☌ ♂ in ♋, and ♋ on the Asc., tends to degeneration of the stomach walls, ulceration, and an over-heated stomach if over-eating is indulged in. (See Fever, Irritable, Ulcer, in this section).

Human Ostrich—Eats Nails and Glass —Case—(See "Human Ostrich" under Human).

Humours—(See "Raw Humours" under Indigestion).

Hydrochloric Acid — (See Hydrochloric).

Hypochondria; Illnesses—Arising from Indigestion, Anxiety, and Worry —(See "Anxiety" under Digestion; Indigestion).

Impeded—Functions of the Stomach Impeded — Peristaltic Action Impeded —(See Fluids, Functions, Obstructions, Peristaltic Action, in this section).

Imperfections—In Stomach—♋ gives when afflicted; a ♋ disease, and afflictions in ♋; the malefics afflicted in ♋; Subs at SP. (See Imperfections).

Imposthumes — Abscess — Ulcer — (See "Ulcer" under Gastric; "Hot Stomach" in this section).

Impurities of System — Stomach Diseases Arising From—The ☉ afflicted in ♓; the ☽ affl. in ♓ with females. (See "Blood" in this section).

Indigestion; Indiscretions—In Diet—Diseases From—(See "Evil Diet" under Diet; Starches, Sugar, Sweets, under Food; Gluttony; "Living" under High; Obesity, Plethora, Surfeits, etc.).

Inflammation — Of the Stomach — The ☉ or ♂ afflicted in ♋; ☉ ☌ ♂ in ♋. (See "Gastritis" under Gastric; "Hot Stomach" in this section). The Mucous Membranes of the stomach tend to become inflamed when the ☽ is in ♋ and afflicted by ♂. (See "Irritations" in this section).

Injuries—To the Stomach—Afflictions in ♋; ♂ afflicted in ♋.

Interfered With—(See Fluids, Functions, Impeded, Obstructions, Stopped, and the various paragraphs in this section).

Intestinal Indigestion—(See "Intestinal" under Indigestion).

Irregularities—Stomach Irregularities—Afflictions in ♋; the ☽ afflicted in ♋. (See Fluids, Functions, Impeded, Obstructions, and the various paragraphs in this section).

Irritable Stomach—Irritable Stomach Walls—The ☉ and ♂ action in ♋; the ☉ ☌ ♂ in ♋; ♂ afflicted in ♋. These influences also tend to difficulty in retaining food, and to hemorrhage and acute gastritis. (See "Retention" under Food; "Gastritis" under Gastric; Nausea).

Irritations — Of the Stomach — ♄ afflicted in ♋ or ♑; the ♄ and ♑ influences, and with ♄ or afflictions in ♑, tend to irritate the nervous terminations of the mucous membranes of the stomach by their action on the peripheral nerves, and afflicting the ♋ sign by reflex action, and tending to nausea or vomiting. (See Nausea, Vomiting; "Peristaltic Action" in this section).

Juices Retarded—(See "Fluids" under Digestion; "Juices" under Gastric; Hydrochloric; Fluids, Obstructions, in this section).

Lining of Stomach — Irritation of — (See External Lining, Inflammation, Irritable, Irritations, in this section; Nausea, Vomiting).

Liver—Enlarged Liver Resulting from Indiscretions In Diet—(See "Enlarged" under Liver).

Lower Part—Of the Stomach Affected—Afflictions in ♍. (See "Splanchnic" under Ganglion; "Pylorus" in this section).

Malnutrition—(See Nutrition).

Meat—Ill-Digested Meat—(See "Raw Humours" under Indigestion; Meat).

Membranes—Of the Stomach—Disorders of—♅ afflicted in ♋. (See Lining, Mucous Membranes, in this section).

Menstruation — Vicarious Thru the Stomach — (See "Vicarious" under Menses).

Mucous Membranes—Of the Stomach—Irritation and Inflammation of—(See Inflammation, Irritations, Lining, Mucus, Phlegm, in this section).

Mucus In Stomach—Phlegm In—The Stomach Obstructed By—(See Catarrh, Irritations, Mucous, Obstructions, Phlegm, in this section).

Muscae Volitantes—(See "Muscae" under Eyes).

Muscles Disordered—♂ afflicted in ♋ tends to afflict and disorder the muscles of the stomach.

Nails — Swallows Nails — Case — (See "Human Ostrich" under Human).

Nausea; Nerves of Stomach — Nerves of Disordered—Nerve Terminations Irritated—Nerve Pains In—Nervous Indigestion—Neuroses — (See Irritations, Neuralgia, Neuroses, Pains, in this section; "Nervous Indigestion" under Indigestion).

Neuralgia—Of Stomach—Nerve Pains In—☿ afflicted in ♋. (See Neuralgia).

Neuroses—Of Stomach—Gastric Neuroses—☿ afflicted in ♋.

Nutrition Faulty — (See "Defective" under Nutrition).

Obesity; Obstructions—In Stomach—Stoppages At the Stomach—The ☉ afflicted in ♋, ♍, or ♏; the ☽ afflicted in ♋, ♎, or ♑; ♄ afflicted in ♋ or ♑; ☿ afflicted in ♐; Subs at SP. (See "Stopped" under Digestion; "Juices" under Gastric; Fluids, Functions, Impeded, Peristaltic, Phlegm, Pylorus, in this section).

Oesophagus— Disorders of —Stricture of—(See Oesophagus).

Offended — The Stomach Offended — (See "Disordered Stomach" in this section).

Operations — Avoid Surgical Operations upon the Stomach when the ☽ is in ♋, and also when ♂ is in ♋, or afflicting the ☽ in ♋. (See "Rules" under Operation).

Organic Disease — Of the Stomach — Structural Defects—The ☉ afflicted in ♋. (See Organic, Structural).

Ostrich — The Human Ostrich — Eats Nails and Glass—(See "Eats Nails" in this section).

Over-Activity—Of the Stomach—The ☽ afflicted in ♐, and especially if the ☽ is coming to the ☍ of ♃ in ♊, which tends to over-activity of the stomach, lungs, and nerves. (See Over-Activity).

Over-Indulgence—Of Food—(See "Excesses In Eating" under Eating; Gluttony, Gormandizing, Over-Indulgence, Self-Indulgent).

Over-Loaded Stomach — (See "Over-Indulgence" in this section).

Pains In—Nerve Pains In—Neuralgia—Burning Pains In—Spasmodic Pains In—☿ in ♋, nerve pains and neuralgia in stomach; ♅ and ☿ afflicted in ♋, spasmodic pains in; ♂ afflicted in ♋, eructations, belching, and burning pains in stomach; ♂ in ♋ when ♂ is the afflictor in the disease, or ♂ in ♋, ☌ or ill-asp. the ☉ or ☽. (See Belching; "Gastralgia" under Gastric).

Pepsin—Lack of—♄ afflicted in ♋ or ♑. (See Pepsin).

Periodic Vomiting—(See Vomiting).

Peristaltic Action—Peristalsis Interrupted, Impeded, and Obstructed—Antiperistaltic Action of the Stomach — The peristaltic action of the stomach is ruled by the ♋ sign, and afflictions in ♋ or ♑ tend to interfere with this action; the ☽ afflicted in ♑ tends to antiperistaltic action in the stomach, as ♑, the sign in ☍ to ♋, tends to reverse and oppose the stomach processes, and to cause nausea or vomiting; also caused by ♄ afflicted in ♋ or ♑. (See Antiperistalsis, Nausea, Peristalsis, Vomiting; "Obstructions" in this section).

Phlegm — In the Stomach — Mucus — Stomach Obstructed By—♄ afflicted in ♋; ☿ afflicted in ♋, and especially when ☿ partakes of the nature of ♄. (See Catarrh, Inflammation, Mucous Membranes, Obstructions, in this section).

Plethora; Poor Digestion—(See "Poor" under Digestion).

Pylorus—Constriction of—Contraction of—Stenosis of—Undersized—♄ in the latter degrees of ♋, or the first degrees of ♍, and in □ or ☍ ♆, the pylorus tends to be constricted, or undersized, so that the food cannot pass, but is vomited; ♆ afflicted in ♋; Subs at SP (7D). Case—See Fig. 6C in "Astro-Diagnosis" by the Heindels. (See Pylorus; Obstructions, Undersized, in this section).

Pyrosis—(See Belching).

Raw Humours—In the Stomach—(See "Raw Humours" under Indigestion).

Retarded—Retarded Fluids and Juices —Retarded Functions—Peristalsis Retarded—♄ afflicted in ♋ or ♑. (See Fluids, Functions, Impeded, Obstructions, Peristalsis, Pylorus, Stopped, in this section).

Retention of Food—Difficulty In Retaining Food—(See "Retention" under Food; Nausea, Vomiting; "Pylorus" in this section).

Secretions Disordered—The ☽, ♄, or ♅ afflicted in ♋. (See "Stopped" under Digestion; "Juices" under Gastric; Hydrochloric; Fluids, Impeded, Obstructions, in this section).

Sickness at Stomach—The ☽ afflicted in ♑. (See Nausea, Vomiting; Peristaltic Action, Pylorus, in this section).

Sluggish Action—Of the Glands of the Stomach—♄ afflicted in ♋ or ♑; ♆ in ♋, □, or ☍ ♄. (See Fluids, Glands, in this section).

Spasmodic Action—In the Stomach—Wind Spasm — Spasmodic Pains In — Spasmodic Action of the Glands—♅ afflicted in ♋ or ♑, wind spasm in, and spasmodic action; ♅ and ☿ afflicted in ♋, spasmodic pains in. (See Colic, Cramps, Gas, Gripings, Pains, Wind, in this section).

Spitting of Blood—(See Haemoptysis; "Blood" under Vomiting).

Spots and Specks — Before the Eyes from Stomach Trouble—(See "Muscae Volitantes" under Eyes).

Stenosis—Of the Pylorus—(See "Pylorus" in this section).

Stomachache—(See "Ache" in this section).

Stomach Trouble — (See "Disordered Stomach", and the various paragraphs in this section).

Stomatitis—(See "Mouth" under Aphthae).

Stopped — Digestion Stopped — Stoppages At the Stomach—♄ afflicted in ♋ or ♑. (See "Stopped" under Digestion; Fluids, Functions, Impeded, Obstructions, in this section).

Structural Disorders—(See "Organic" in this section).

Surfeits — From Over-Eating — ♃ afflicted in ♋. (See "Excesses" under Eating; Obesity, Plethora, Surfeits).

Swallowing—Difficulty In—(See Deglutition).

Swollen Stomach—(See Dilatation, Distended, in this section).

Trouble — Stomach Trouble — (See "Disordered", and the various paragraphs in this section).

Tumor — In Stomach — (See "Tumor" under Gastric; Tumors).

Tympanites; Ulcer—(See "Ulcer" under Gastric; "Hot Stomach" in this section).

Undersized Stomach — Undersized Glands — The Pylorus Undersized and Contracted — ♆ and ♄ influence, and with these planets afflicted in ♋; ♆ in ♋ and in □ or ☍ ♄ and H. (See "Pylorus" in this section; Undersized).

Undigested Humours — In Stomach — (See "Raw Humours" under Indigestion).

Upper Part — Of Stomach — Affected and Disordered when there are afflictions in the latter degrees of ♌, and the first face of ♋; Subs at SP (6D). (See "Upper Part" in the first part of this Article).

Veins of Stomach — Tend to be disordered when ♀ is afflicted in ♋. (See Veins).

Vertigo — From Stomach Trouble — The afflicting planets in the cardinal signs, and especially with ♈ and ♋ involved. (See Dizziness, Vertigo).

Vomiting — (See Nausea, Vomiting; "Pylorus" in this section).

Walls of Stomach — (See Irritable, Irritations, Lining, in this section).

Water Brash — Pyrosis — Belching — (See Belching, Pyrosis).

Weak Stomach—The Digestion Weak —(See "Weak", "Weakest", under Digestion; "Cases" in this section).

Wind In Stomach—♅, ☿, or the ☽ afflicted in ♋; ♅ afflicted in ♋, wind spasm in stomach. (See Colic, Cramps, Distended, Gas, Gripings, Spasmodic, in this section; Belching, Flatulence, Indigestion, Tympanites).

Women—Stomach Disorders In—(See "Women" under Digestion).

Worms In—Cestode—☿ afflicted in ♋; Subs at SP (7D). (See Worms).

Worry — Stomach Trouble Due To — (See "Anxiety" under Digestion).

Wrong Diet — Stomach Disorders From — (See "Ailments Due to Diet", "Evil Diet", "Excesses in Diet", under Diet; "Dainty Foods", "Rich Food", "Starches", "Sweets", under Food; Gluttony).

STOMATITIS — (See "Mouth" under Aphthae).

STONE—Stones—Concretions—Calculus — Lithiasis — Osseous Deposits — Mineral Deposits In the Body—Calcareous Matter—Gravel—Sand—Chalk—Lime—Stone Blindness — Birth Stones — Violence with Stones, etc.—The following subjects have to do with the various forms of Concretions and Stone in the body, and also in some of the other senses in which the word Stone is used, as "Assaults by Stones", "Stone Blind", etc.

Assaults by Stones—Injuries by Flying Stones — (See "Flying Stones" in this section).

Back—Stone In the Reins of the Back —A ♎ disease, and afflictions in ♎; ♅ or ♄ afflicted in ♎. (See "Kidneys" in this section).

Biliary Calculi — (See "Gall Stones" under Bile).

Birth Stones — The following are the Birthstones of the various Signs of the Zodiac when these signs are rising upon the Ascendant at birth. This does not especially apply to the ☉ in Signs unless you are born at Sunrise, and with the ☉ in the rising sign. It is said that a birthstone which vibrates in harmony with your ruling planet, and when worn as a Talisman, is favorable for good health, good fortune, peace of mind, and also protection against dangers. The Birthstones of the Signs are as follows—♈, Diamond and Amethyst; ♉, Emerald and Moss Agate; ♊, the Aqua Marine and Crystal; ♋, the Emerald and Black Onyx; ♌, the Diamond and Ruby; ♍, the Hyacinth and Pink Jasper; ♎, the Opal and Diamond; ♏, the Topaz and Malachite; ♐, the Turquoise and Carbuncle; ♑, the Moonstone and White Onyx; ♒, the Opal and Sapphire; ♓, the Chrysolite and Moonstone. (See Amulets). Considerable valuable information is given about Birthstones, Amulets, and Talismans, in the book, "Message of the Stars", by Max Heindel.

Bladder—Stone In—Gravel In—Death from Stone In—The ☉, ☽, ♄, or ♂ in the 6th H., and afflicted, in fixed signs; the ☉ afflicted in ♏; the ☽ to the ill-asps. ♂ by dir.; the ☽ in ♏, and to the ☌, P., □, or ☍ ♄ (or ☿ if he be of the nature of ♄) at the beginning of an illness, or at decumbiture, is an indication of stone or gravel existing in the bladder; ♆, ♅, or ♄ in ♍, and afflicting the ☉ or ☽; ♄ in ♏ in the 6th H., and afflicted; a ♄ disease; caused by ♂ afflictions; ♂ in ♏ and afflicting the ☽ or Asc.; ♂ denotes death from; ♂ in ♉ or ♏ in the 6th H., and afflicted; a ♎ disease, and afflictions in ♎; a ♏ disease, and with afflictions in ♏; ♏ on the Asc. and the ☽ in ♒ (Hor'y). People of the melancholic type, and who suffer from Hypochondria, a ♄ disease, are more subject to Stone or Gravel, as ♄ tends to crystallize and deposit the solid substances of the urine in such subjects. Cases—Of Stone In the Bladder — See Chap. XIII in Daath's Medical Astrology. (See Gravel; the various paragraphs in this section).

Body Turns Into Stone—(See "Petrifaction" in this section).

Calces—(See Chalk).

Calculus—A stone-like concretion in the body, and usually formed by the mineral deposits of the body as thrown down, deposited, and accumulated by the work of ♄. (See Concretions; the various paragraphs in this section).

Causes of Stone—In the Body—Stone, Sand, Gravel, and Concretions in the body, are principally the work of ♄, and his afflictions to the ☉ and ☽, or to both at the same time, and where the signs of ♄ may also be strongly occupied, or many planets in the earthy signs at B.; ♄ afflicted in ♏; the ☽ to the □ or ☍ ♂ by dir. tends to the formation of stone if other conditions in the radical map concur. Also the afflictions of ♅ to the ☉ and ☽, from a ♄ sign, tend to stone formation. Stone in the kidney is usuauly the result of afflictions from cardinal signs. In Gall Stones, the afflictions are from mutable signs. Lilly says Stones in the body are mostly limited to diurnal maps. These Causes are further discussed in the Articles on Concretions, Deposits, Minerals, and also in the different paragraphs of this Article.

Chalk—(See Chalk, Lime).

Chololithiasis—(See "Gall Stones" under Bile).

Cold—Cold As a Cause of Stone—(See Cold, Concretions).

Concretions—Osseous Deposits—Stone —(See Concretions; the various paragraphs in this section).

Crystallization — Hardening In the Body — (See Crystallization, Hardening).

Death from Stone—In the Kidneys or Bladder—Denoted by ♂, and especially when ♂ is afflicted in the 6th H. in a fixed sign, as in ♏; fixed signs, and many planets in these signs, and especially in the 6th H., dispose to death from stone, sand, or gravel in the bladder; many planets in cardinal signs, to death from stone in the kidneys, and many planets in mutable signs to death from Gall Stones.

Deposits — Calcareous Deposits—♄ in ♏ tends to stone by obstructing the elimination of urine, and causing calcareous deposits. (See Chalk, Concretions, Deposits, Minerals).

Ductless Glands—As Related to Stone —(See "Petrifaction" in this section).

Elimination—Faulty Elimination As a Cause of Stone—(See "Faulty" under Elimination).

Excretion—Obstructions of, and Tending to Stone—(See "Obstructions" under Excretion).

Fixed Signs—Many afflictions in these signs at B. tend to stone, sand, or gravel in the bladder, and death by such disorders. (See "Fixed Signs" under Fixed; "Death" in this section).

Flying Stones — Injury or Death by Flying Stones In Mob Violence—♂ afflicted in ♊ or ♍, and ☌, P., □, or ☍ the Asc. by dir. (See Mobs). Wounds by wood or stones are indicated in Hor'y Q. when ♄ is in the 1st H. at B., and a malefic planet with the lord of the 1st. When ♂ is lord of the year at the

Vernal, and afflicted, many people tend to be injured by flying stones and mob violence.

Gall Stones — (See "Gall Stones" under Bile).

Goiter—This disease is a Crystallization. (See Goiter).

Gout—Chalk Stones of—(See Chalk).

Gravel — Gravel In the Kidneys or Bladder—Voiding of Red Gravel—(See Gravel).

Hardening — (See Cirrhosis, Crystallization, Hardening, Sclerosis; the various paragraphs in this section).

Injury by Stones — (See "Flying Stones" in this section).

Kidneys—Stone, Sand, or Gravel In—Renal Stones—Nephrolithiasis—Stone In the Reins of the Back—Death from Stone In Kidneys — Gravel and Renal Stones are formed in the peduncles, or pelvis of the kidneys, which part is ruled by ♏, and the ♏ sign has more to do with stone in the kidneys than the ♎ sign for this reason. However, the ♎ influence is also responsible, as the stone is crystallized in the kidney by ♄, and by virtue of his exalted power in ♎. Stone in the kidney is ruled principally, or fundamentally, by ♏ and the 8th H. Is caused by the ☉ afflicted in ♏; the ☉ or ☽ afflicted by ♄ or ♅ from a ♄ sign; the ☉ afflicted in ♌, ♎, or ♒; the ☽ afflicted in ♏ or ♐, or afflicting the hyleg therefrom; the ☽ afflicted in ♑; the ☽ to the ☌, P., □, or ☍ ♂ by dir.; the ☽ in ♌, ☌, P., or ill-asp. ♄ (or ☿ if he be of the nature of ♄) at the beginning of an illness, or at decumbiture, and the patient may die when the ☽ comes to the ☍ aspect of ♄, and if no good aspect prevent it (Hor'y); the ☽ in ♎, and afflicted by the ☉ or ♂ when taken ill (Hor'y); ♆, ♅, or ☿ in ♍, ♎, or ♏, and especially in the 6th or 8th H., and afflicting the ☉ or ☽; ♄ afflicted in the 6th H. in a fixed sign; ♄ afflicted in ♈, ♍, ♎, or ♏; ♄ in ♏ tends to stone by obstructing the elimination of urine, and causing calcareous deposits; ♄ in the Asc. in ♎; ♂ in ♉ or ♏, and afflicting the hyleg at B.; caused by ♂ afflictions; ♂ afflicted in ♈, ♉, ♎, or ♏; ♂ in the 6th H. in a fixed sign, and afflicted, and this influence also denotes death by stone; a ♎ and ♏ disease, and afflictions in these signs; Subs at KP (11D). (See Deposits, Elimination; Back, Bladder, and the various paragraphs in this section).

Lime — Limestone Deposits — ♄ afflicted in ♓ tends to lime deposits, and to petrifaction, crystallization, and hardening of the body, or ♄ in ♍ by reflex action. Also caused by ♄ afflicted in ♒. (See Chalk, Deposits, Lime, Minerals; "Petrifaction" in this section).

Lithiasis — The Formation of a Calculus, or Stone in the Body. For causes, see Calculus, Chalk, Concretions, Crystallization, Deposits, Hardening, Minerals, etc. Also note the various paragraphs in this section).

Liver—In Cirrhosis of the liver there is a hardening and thickening process, the work of ♄, and which is along the same lines as the forming of stones. (See "Hardening", "Hobnail Liver", under Liver).

Mineral Deposits — Tending to the Formation of Stone—(See Chalk, Concretions, Deposits, Gravel, Lime, Minerals, Osseous, Sand; the various paragraphs in this section).

Nephrolithiasis — (See "Kidneys" in this section).

Obstructions—Stone in the Body is an Obstruction, and caused by ♄. (See Impediments, Obstructions, Retentions, Saturn Influence, Suppressions).

Osseous Deposits—(See Osseous).

Pelvis of Kidneys — Stone In — (See "Kidneys" in this section).

Petrifaction — Turning of the Body Into Stone—♄ afflicted in ♒, and especially in the 6th or 8th H., and with many planets in fixed signs, have been recorded as existing in a case; ♄ afflicted in ♍ or ♓. Also the earthy and mineral signs, as ♉, ♍, and ♑, when well-filled with planets at B., and such a sign on the Asc. also, may cause, and with other stone-forming conditions concurring. Some Physicians attribute Petrifaction to disorders of the Ductless Glands, which are largely ruled by the ♏ sign. (See Ductless Glands; "Earthy Signs" under Earth; Hardening, Lime, Minerals; "Lime", and the various paragraphs in this section).

Red Gravel—Voiding of—(See Gravel).

Reins—Stone In Reins—In Reins of the Back—(See "Kidneys" in this section).

Remedy for Stone—Docoction of Geranium Robertianum (Daath).

Renal Stone — Renal Calculi — (See "Kidneys" in this section).

Retentions — (See "Poisons of the Body" under Retention).

Sand—Sand In Kidneys—(See Sand).

Secret Parts—Stone In—A ♏ disease, and afflictions in ♏; ♏ on the Asc., and the ☽ in ♒ (Hor'y). (See Bladder, Kidneys, in this section).

Spleen—(See "Stone In" under Spleen).

Stone—The Stone—The following influences indicate Stone in Hor'y Q., and that Stone may exist at the beginning of an illness, and at decumbiture. The ☉ afflicted in ♒; the ☉ in ♌ when the afflictor in the disease; the ☽ in ♑ signifies the Stone when the afflictor in the disease; the ☽ in ♉ and afflicted by the ☉ or ♂ when taken ill. (See the various paragraphs in this section).

Stone Blind — (See "Total" under Blindness).

Stones — Injury by Flying Stones — (See "Flying Stones" in this section).

Suppressions — Tending to Stone — (See Concretions, Deposits, Hindrances, Impediments, Retentions, Suppressions, Wastes, etc.).

Thickening — (See Cirrhosis, Hardening, Thickening).

Touch of Stone—The ☽ to the ill-asps. ♂ by dir.

Urea — Urates — Uric Acid — Excess of —Retention of—(See these subjects).

Urinary Calculi—(See "Calculi" under Urine).

Wastes—Retention of—(See Deposits; "Faulty", "Hindered", under Elimination; Retention, Suppression, Wastes).

Xanthic Calculus—(See Xanthic).

STOOLS — Bowel Discharges — (See Faeces).

STOOPING — Stooping Posture — Body Hooked Forward—Body Bent Forward —♓ gives a stooping, heavy gait, and holding the head downward when walking, and especially with ♓ on the Asc. at B.; ♄ ascending at B., and afflicted; ♄ Sig. in ♌; ♄ in ♌, partile the Asc.; ♄ Sig. in ♑, a stooping, awkward posture in walking; ♄ Sig. □ or ☍ ☽. (See Bending; "Crooked Body" under Crooked; Limp; "Downward" under Look; "General Relaxation" under Relaxation; "Stoop Shoulders" under Shoulders).

STOPPAGES—Obstructions—Impediments—Inhibitions—Hindrances—

Bowels—Stoppages In—(See "Intussusception", "Obstructions", under Bowels; Constipation; "Hardening" under Faeces).

Circulation—Stoppages In—(See "Interferred With", "Sluggish", under Circulation; Clots, Embolus, Infarct, Thrombus, etc.).

Digestion Stopped—(See "Stopped" under Digestion).

Elimination — (See "Hindered" under Elimination).

Functions — (See "Stoppage" under Functions).

Gait—(See "Stoppage Gait" under Gait).

Gall Ducts — Stoppage In — (See "Ducts", "Gall Stones", under Bile).

Growth — (See "Arrested" under Growth).

Head—(See "Stoppages" under Head).

Heart—(See "Stoppage" under Heart).

Menses—(See "Suppressed" under Menses).

Nose—(See "Stoppage" under Nose).

Secretions Stopped—(See Secretions).

Speech—(See "Halting" under Speech).

Stomach — Stoppages In — (See "Pylorus", "Stopped", under Stomach).

Throat — (See "Stoppages", "Swellings", under Throat; "Swollen" under Tonsils).

Urethra — (See "Stricture" under Urethra).

Urine—(See "Stoppage" under Urine).

Vibration—Mental Vibrations Stopped —(See Vibration). For further study along this line see Arrested, Clogging, Congestions, Constrictions, Contractions, Crystallization, Dropsy, Growth, Hardening, Hindrances, Hyperacidity, Impediments, Impure, Inflammation, Inhibitions, Interrupted; "Obstructive" under Jaundice; Limitations, Obstructions, Retarded, Retentions, Slow, Stenosis, Stone, Strictures, Suppressions, Suspensions, Swellings, Thickening, Tumors, etc.

STORING — Storing Functions of the Body—(See Conservation).

STORMS—

Brain Storms — (See "Brain Storms" under Brain; "Psychic Storms" under Psychic).

Hail Storms—(See Hail).

Rain Storms—(See Rain, Storms).

Snow Storms—(See Blizzards, Snow).

Thunder Storms — (See Lightning, Thunder).

Wind Storms — (See "Storms" under Wind).

STOUT — Stoutness—A Stout Person— Corpulent—Fleshy—Lords of Nativity of stout people have great Latitude as a rule. Oriental planets in their first orientation cause large, stout bodies. The Quadrants from the Summer Tropic to the Autumnal Equinox, and from the Winter Tropic to the Vernal Equinox, tend to give stout bodies, and with the ☉, ☽, and many planets in these Quarters at B.; ♄ ori. at B. makes the body more stout, tall and hairy than when he is occi., and also gives a stout chest; ♃ Sig. in ♉, ♏, ♒, or ♓; ♃ in ♉, partile the Asc., stout, well-set, but not handsome; ♃ Sig. in ♉, compact and well-set; ♃ in ♏, partile the Asc., or ♃ Sig. in ♏, stout and compact, ♃ in the Asc., stout, and with a stout chest; ♃ in ♒, partile the Asc., stout, compact, and of middle stature; ♂ in ♌, partile the Asc., stout limbs; ♀ Sig. in ♏; ♀ in ♏, partile the Asc., stout, corpulent, and well-set; ♉, ♏, or ♒ on the Asc.; the last few degrees of ♎ on the Asc. give a shorter and stouter body, but the most of the sign tends to a tall, graceful, and slender body; ♐ on the Asc., a stout, athletic frame. Case — Stout In Build — See "Jaaskelainen", No. 213, in 1001 N.N. (See Athletic, Compact, Corpulent, Fat Body, Fleshy, Muscular, Portly; "Body" under Strong; Thick Body, Well-Set).

STRABISMUS — Crossed Eyes — (See "Strabismus" under Eyes).

STRAIGHT—Straight Body—Erect and Upright Body—The ☉ in ♎, partile the Asc., tall, straight, and upright; the ☽ in ♊, partile the Asc., tall, straight, upright, comely, and well-made; born under strong ♃ influence, tall, fine, straight, and well-made; ♃ in ♐, partile the Asc., tall, straight, fine, and well-made; born under ♀, and ♀ ori., tall, straight, and upright; ☿ in ♊, partile the Asc., tall, straight, and well-made; ♊ on the Asc., tall, fine, and straight; ♎ on the Asc., straight, tall, and handsome if ♀ is also oriental. (See Erect, Tall, Upright).

Forehead — The Forehead Straight, Deep, and Tall — (See "Deep" under Forehead).

Nose—(See "Straight" under Nose).

STRAIN—Stress and Strain—Tension—

Body—The Constitution—Over-Straining of — Physical Strain — Muscular Strain — Stress and strain of the body are caused by ♂ activities, and often from anger, which stress is relieved by the release of Glycogn in greater quantity by the Adrenals to restore the equilibrium. Physical strain is harmful when ♄ is in ♌ at B., and afflicting the ☉, ☽, Asc., or hyleg, due to weakened heart action at times, and unsustained circulation of the blood during severe exercise. When the airy signs are upon the Asc. at B. the constitution becomes easily run down under strain, and subject to nervous disorders. (See Adrenals, Anger, Excitable; "Inordinate" under Exercise; "Over-Exertion" under Exertion; Fatigue, Glycogen; "Intemperate" under Sports).

Excretory System—(See "Strain" under Excretion).

Eyestrain — (See "Eyestrain" under Eyes).

Headaches — From Nervous Strain — (See "Nervous Headaches" under Headaches).

Heart Strain — (See "Strain" under Heart).

Knees — (See "Strains In" under Knees).

Mental Strain — (See "Strain" under Mental, Mind).

Muscular Strain — And of Ligaments and Tendons—(See Exercise, Exertion, Ligaments, Sports, Tendons, Tension; "Body" in this section).

Nervous Strain—(See "Strain" under Nerves).

Over-Strain—Of Mind and Body—(See Over-Strain; the various paragraphs in this section).

Physical Strain—(See Body, Muscular, in this section).

Sprains—(See Sprains).

STRANGE — Unusual — Extraordinary—Mysterious, etc. — The influences of ♆ and ♅ in a configuration tend to produce strange, extraordinary, mysterious, obscure, unusual, and curious events, which would be unexplainable to the ordinary mind, and without a knowledge of Astrology. (See Neptune, Uranus).

Accidents — Strange Accidents—♅ afflicted by ♂, or ♂ ill-aspected by ♅. (See "Extraordinary" under Accidents).

Ailments—Strange Ailments—Strange Diseases—♅ afflicted in ♍; ♅ afflicted in the Asc.; ♅ ☌, □, or ☍ the Asc.; ♆ diseases, and of a psychic origin. (See "Diseases" under Extraordinary, Mysterious, Obscure, Peculiar, Psychic, Sudden, Uncommon; "Imaginary Diseases" under Imagination; Incurable, Praeincipients, Pseudo, Remarkable, Unusual).

Anxieties — Strange Anxieties — (See Anxiety; "Impending Calamity" under Calamity; "Fears; "Low Spirits" under Low; Worry, etc.).

Calamities — Strange Calamities or Catastrophies — (See "Strange" under Calamity).

Conduct—Strange Conduct—The ☉ by dir. to the ☌ or P. aspect ♅.

Death—Death from Strange Causes—♆ the afflicting planet. (See "Mysterious Death" under Mysterious).

Diseases — Strange Diseases — (See "Ailments" in this section).

Dreams — Strange Dreams — (See Dreams).

Events—(See "Strange" under Events).

Fancies — (See "Distempered" under Fancies).

Fears—Strange Fears—(See "Morbid", "Solitude", under Fears; Forebodings, Spirit Controls; Terrors, Visions, in this section).

Growth — Strange and Abnormal Growth — (See "Abnormal" under Growth).

Hurts—(See "Strange" under Hurts).

Imaginations — (See "Strange" under Imagination).

Injuries—Strange Injuries—(See Accidents, Hurts, in this section).

Land — Death In a Strange Land — (See "Accidents" under Abroad).

Mysterious—(See the paragraphs under Mysterious).

Occupations — Strange Occupational Diseases—(See Occupation).

Premonitions — (See Dreams, Forebodings, Premonitions).

Sayings—Strange Sayings—(See Demoniac, Insanity).

Sicknesses — (See "Ailments" in this section).

Spirit Controls—The Strange Terrors of—(See Obsessions, Spirit Controls).

Tastes—Strange Tastes—(See Tastes).

Terrors — Strange Terrors of Mind — The 3rd decan. of ♒ on the Asc. (See Obsessions, Spirit Controls, Terrors, Visions).

Vagaries—(See "Peculiar" under Vagaries).

Views—Strange Views — (See Eccentric, Ideals, Ideas, Independent, Metaphysical, Misunderstood, Occult, Reformers; "Fanatical" under Religion).

Visions — Strange Visions — (See Dreams, Forebodings, Horrors, Obsessions, Premonitions; "Nightmare" under Sleep; Spirit Controls, Visions).

STRANGERS — Death In the Presence of Strangers—The ☽ in the 8th H. at B. (See "Public Death" under Public).

STRANGULATION—Strangulated—Suffocated—A ♉ disease and affliction.

Birth—Strangled At Birth—Cases—(See "Birth" under Asphyxia).

Death By—Death by Strangulation or Suffocation—♄ exactly on the Asc. at B., danger of at B.; ♄ in a fixed sign, □ or ☍ the ☉, and contrary in condition, or ♄ be occidental, and the ☽ be succedent to him; ♄ in ♉. and evil fixed stars and ♄ afflicting the hyleg; ♄ to the ☌ or ill-asp. ♂ by dir.; ♄ and many planets in fixed signs show; earthy signs strong, prominent, and well-occupied at B. tend to; malefics in ♉. Cases—See "Beach Murder", No. 134; "Morrison", No. 188; "Child Strangled", No. 252; "Strangled", No. 922, all in 1001 N.N. (See Asphyxia, Drowning, Execution, Halter, Hanging; "Death" under Suffocation).

Hernia — (See "Strangulated Hernia" under Hernia).

Wife—Strangles His Wife—Case—See "Beach Murder", No. 134, in 1001 N.N.

STRANGURY—Painful Urination—(See "Strangury" under Urine).

STRATEGY—Injury or Death By—(See Artifice; "Death By" under Enemies; Plots, Poison Death, Treachery, etc.).

STREETS—Public Death In the Streets —(See "Public Death" under Public).

STRENGTH—Power—Force—Activity —Energy—The Asc. rules the physical strength, the body, and the organic force. The strength of the body, and the organic resistance to disease, are largely shown and revealed by the sign rising upon the Asc. at B. Mars in any aspect to the ☉ produces strength, and a stronger constitution. Also ♂, known as the planet of dynamic power and energy, is the planet of courage, boldness, and physical prowess. The Mind and Mental Faculties are strengthened when ☿ is strong and well-fortified at B., as ☿ is the ruler of the mind, the planet of mental power, and especially when rising in the Asc. at B., well-aspected, and not combust with the ☉. The following subjects have to do with the strength of the Mind and Body, which subjects see in the alphabetical arrangement when only listed here—

Active—Active Mind—Active and Strong Body—(See "Full of Action" under Action; "Active Body", "Active Mind", under Active; Dynamic; "Quickened" under Mentality; "Strong Mind" under Mind; "Strength" under Muscles; "Activity" under Physical; "Body" under Strong).

Adynamia—Loss of Vital Power— (See Adynamia).

Asthenia—Loss of Strength—(See Asthenia; "Weakened" in this section).

Athletic—Pugilist—Wrestler—(See Athletics).

Body—Strong Body—The Body Strengthened—Great Physical Powers —The body is strengthened when ♃ is ✶ or △ the Asc. The fiery signs rising on the Asc. give a strong body, and especially ♈ or ♌ on the Asc. at B. (See Endurance; "Abundance" under Energy; Immunity; "Good" under Resistance; Robust, Ruddy, Stamina; "Body" under Strong; Tone; "Good" under Vitality).

Bones Strengthened—(See "Strengthening Of" under Bones).

Collapse; Constitution—(See Strength, Strong, Weak, under Constitution; "Good", "Low", under Vitality).

Debility; Degree of Strength—(See Degree).

Depletion; Diminished Strength— (See Diminished, Lessened).

Dissipated—The Strength Dissipated —The ☉ in ♌ in the Asc., ✶ or △ ♂ gives great energy, but a tendency to dissipate it; the ☉ and ♀ in the Asc. in ♑, and afflicted by ♅, ♃, or ♂, the strength is dissipated; ♂ in ♌ in the Asc., and afflicted by ♃ or ♀; ♂ in ♌ on the Asc., and the ☉ ruler of the Asc., and afflicted; weak signs on the Asc., and containing afflicting planets. (See "Energy Dissipated" under Dissipation; "Wasted" under Energy; "Health Suffers" under Opposite Sex).

Early Years—Little Strength In—(See "Early Years of Life" under Early).

Emaciation; Endurance; Energy;

Exhaustion; Fatigue; Feeble; Force;

Functions Strengthened—Or Weakened—(See Functions).

Health—(See "Bad Health", "Good Health", under Health).

Immunity from Disease—(See Immunity; "Abundance of Health" under Health; "Good" under Vitality).

Increased—The Strength Increased— The upper and anterior parts of ♈, ♉, and ♌ increase the strength, and also the posterior parts of ♊, ♏, and ♐; ♃ or ♀ in the Asc., or the ☉, ☽, ♃, ♀ in the Asc. or M.C., and well-aspected; ♃ and ♀ ☌ or good aspect the Asc.; ♂ in good aspect to the ☉ assists the bodily strength. (See "Strength" under Increased; "Improved" under Health; Robust, Ruddy; "Increased" under Vitality).

Infancy—(See "Strength Increased", "Vitality", under Infancy).

Infirm; Injured—The Strength of the Constitution Injured—(See "Weakened" in this section).

Intellect—Strength of Intellect—(See the paragraphs under Intellect).

Invalids; Less Muscular Strength— (See "Strength" under Muscles).

Life Force—(See "Life Force" under Force).

Little Sickness—Rarely Ill—(See "Little Sickness" under Sickness).

Loss of Strength—(See Diminished, Lessened, Loss Of; "Lessened" under Vitality; "Dissipated" in this section).

Males—The Strength of—(See "Males Nearly Impotent", "Strength", and the various paragraphs under Males).

Mind—Strength of Mind—(See the various paragraphs under Intellect, Mental, Mind, Perception, Understanding).

Muscular Strength—(See Muscles).

Not Very Strong—(See Debility, Feeble; "Bad Health" under Health; Infirm, Invalids, Sickly; "Much Sickness" under Sickness; "Low" under Resistance, Vitality; "Weak Body" under Weak).

Physical Strength—Degree of—(See Action, Active, Degree, Feeble, Muscles, Physical, Stamina, Strong, Tone, Vitality, Weak; the various paragraphs in this section).

Powerful—Powerful Body—Powerful Mind—(See "Powerful" under Intellect; "Strong" under Mind; Power; "Body" under Strong).

Prostration; Proud—Proud of His Physical Strength—(See Proud).

Pugilist—(See Athletics).

Recuperative Power—Strong—Weak —(See Recuperation).

Resistance—Powers of Resistance to Disease—(See Endurance, Feeble, Immunity, Resistance; "Body" under Strong; "Good", "Low", under Vitality; "Weak Body" under Weak).

Restoratives—Of Health and Strength —(See Analeptic, Restoratives).

Robust; Ruddy; Stamina;

Strong Body — (See "Body" under Strong).

Tone; Vital Force—(See "Force" under Vital).

Vitality—(See "Good", "Low", and the various paragraphs under Vitality).

Wasting of the Body — (See Tabes, Wasting).

Weak Body—(See "Weak Body" under Weak).

Weakened — Strength of the Body Weakened—Loss of Strength—Asthenia—The lower and posterior parts of ♈, ♉, and ♌ tend to make the body weaker, and also the anterior parts of ♊, ♍, and ♐; the ☉ or ☽ ☌ a malefic planet tends to injure and weaken the constitution; the ☉ or ☽ in weak signs and afflicted; the ☉ or ☽ to the ☌ or ill-asps. ♄ by dir.; the ☉ to the evil aspects ♃ by dir.; ♄ in the 6th H., and conjoined with the ☉; ♄ afflicted in ♒; ♃ afflicting the ☉; the Asc. ruled by ♄; the 3rd decan. of ♉ on the Asc. (See Adynamia, Asthenia, Dissipation, Dull, Emaciation, Feeble; "Bad Health" under Health; Inactive, Inertia, Languishing, Lassitude, Lethargy, Listless, Loss Of; "Low" under Resistance, Vitality; "Weakened" under Vitality; "Weak Body" under Weak).

Wrestler—(See Athletics). For subjects along this line which may have been overlooked, and not included in this Article, see the alphabetical arrangement.

STRESS AND STRAIN — (See "Strain" under Nerves; Strain, Tension).

STRICTURE — A Narrowing — Contraction—Stenosis—A ♅ disease, and due to the tonic action of ♅; ♅ in the 6th H.; a ♄ disease; ♄ ☌ or ill-asp. ♅. (See Adhesions, Constrictions, Contractions, Obstructions, Spasmodic, Stenosis).

Bladder—(See "Stricture" under Bladder).

Nose—Nares—(See "Stricture" under Nose).

Oesophagus — (See "Stricture" under Oesophagus).

Prostatic Stricture — (See Prostate Gland).

Pylorus—Constriction of—(See "Pylorus" under Stomach).

Throat — (See "Stricture" under Throat).

Urethra — Spasmodic Stricture of — (See Urethra).

Womb—Stricture of the Neck of the Womb—(See "Stricture" under Womb).

STRIFE — Injuries or Death By — (See Contests, Duels, Enemies, Feuds, Hatred, Jealousy, Murdered, Plots, Poison Death, Quarrels, Revenge, Sword, Treachery, War, etc.).

STROKES — Blows — (See Assaults; "Strokes" under Blindness; Blows, Stabs, Sword, etc.).

Paralytic Strokes—(See Paralysis).

STRONG — Active — Sthenic — Strong Body and Mind—Good Powers of Resistance and Vitality—Stronger—Strongest—Strength—Virile, etc.—

Body—Strong and Active Body—Able Body — Strong Constitution — Healthy Appearance—Robust—Vigorous, etc.—The SUN rising at B., and especially in a fiery or airy sign, or in ♉ or ♏, and well aspected, and more so if the ☉ be hyleg; the ☉ strong and well-dignified at B.; the ☉ in ♉ if not afflicted; the ☉ gives a large, strong, and bony body; the ☉ in ♈ or ♌, partile the Asc., strong and well-made; the ☉ in ♐ unless the hyleg be afflicted; the ☉, ☽, and Asc. well-aspected by benefics, and free from the affliction of malefics; the ☉ in the Asc. or M.C. at B., and well-aspected; the ☉ in good asp. to ♃, ♂, or the ☽, and especially if the ☉ be rising, or in any house except the 6th, or 8th; the ☉ or ☽ in ♋, ♌, or ♍, signs of the Summer Quarter, or with these signs upon the Asc. at B. if the ☉ is in them and free from affliction; the ☉ in the signs of the Winter Quarter, in ♑, ♒, or ♓, tend to give a square and strong make, or with these signs upon the Asc. if the ☉ is in them and well-aspected; the ☉ in signs of the Spring months, in ♈, ♉, ♊, tend to give a strong constitution, and stronger than when the ☉ is in the Winter signs; the MOON in ♉, partile the Asc., strong, corpulent, and well-set; the ☽ Sig. in ♉, strong and well-set; the ☽ in ♌, partile the Asc., tall, strong, and large-boned; the ☽ well-aspected in ♌, strong and robust; the ☽ in ♑, partile the Asc., never strong; the ☽ in the Asc., and well-aspected by the ☉, ♃, and ♀, and free from the affliction of malefics; the ☽ angular, and the Lights nearly free from affliction, tolerably healthy and strong; SATURN in N. Lat. makes the body more strong, corpulent and bony; ♄ ✱ or △ ♂; ♄ in ♏, partile asp. the Asc., strong, well-set, but short; ♄ well-aspected in ♒; JUPITER rising in the Asc. or M.C., in an airy sign, and well-aspected; ♃ Sig. in airy signs denotes the body is more strong and corpulent in Hor'y Q.; ♃ in ♉, partile the Asc., strong and compact; ♃ well-aspected in ♉; ♃ Sig. in ♌; ♃ in ♌, partile the Asc., strong, tall, large, and well-made; ♃ Sig. in a fiery sign, the body is strong and square-made; ♃ and ♀ in good asp. the hyleg, and free from the affliction of malefics; ♃ well-aspected in ♎, good and strong nature; ♃ rising at B. confers strength of constitution, and the power to overcome very evil directions; born under ♂ the body is strong, well-set, but short or medium-sized; MARS ✱ or △ the ☉, ☽, ♅, or ♄; ♂ in good asp. the ☉ gives great strength of constitution; ♂ ☌ or any asp. the ☉, the native is usually strong and healthy; the ♂ signs ♈ and ♏ upon the Asc. at B. tend to give great strength and vitality; ♂ rising at B., and well-aspected; ♂ in the Asc., and well-aspected in a fiery sign, or in ♑, or if evilly aspected in the Asc., tends to strengthen the constitution; ♂ well-aspected in the 4th H.; in Hor'y Q., ♂ Sig. of the person; ♂ rising in the Asc. in ♌; ♂ in ♌, partile the Asc., strong, large, and tall; given by the ✱ or △ aspects of ♂; VENUS when ☌ ♃ adds power to ♃, but ♀ of herself does not tend to give muscular power, or any very great physical strength; MERCURY rising and well-aspected in ♉, or Sig. in ♉, tends to make the native strong, thick and well-set; the ☿ sign ♊ when upon the Asc. at B. tends to give a strong and active body; the ☿ sign ♍ when on the Asc. gives fair vitality and endurance; many planets rising at B., well-aspected, and in their strong signs, give a strong body; fiery signs upon the Asc. at B. give the strongest constitutions, and the airy signs, along with ♉ and ♏, are the next in strength, while the watery signs ♋ and ♓ when upon the Asc. at B. give the weakest constitutions; fixed signs give a strong constitution when on the Asc., and many planets in them, and give stamina and endurance; many planets in succedent houses, corresponding to the fixed signs, give a strong constitution; ♉ on the Asc. gives a strong, thick, short, or middle-sized body; ♈ on the Asc., a strong, spare, dry, bony, moderate-sized body; born under ♈ tends to a strong body; ♌ on the Asc., a strong, large, athletic, ruddy body, and with broad shoulders; the first half of ♌ on the Asc. gives a stronger body than the second half when rising; ♏ on the Asc., a strong, able, athletic, heavy, corpulent, robust, middle-sized or short body; ♐ on the Asc., a strong, intrepid, well-formed, well-made, tall body; ♒ on the Asc., strong, athletic, robust, healthy, plump, well-set body, but not tall; born under the whole signs ♊, ♎, or ♒, strong and robust. (See "Full of Action" under Action; "Active Body" under Active; "Good" under Constitution; Corpulent, Dynamic, Endurance, Energy, Exertion, Force; "Abundance", "Good", under Health; Healthy, Immunity, Muscles, Physical, Power; "Good" under Recuperation, Resistance, Stamina, Tone, Vitality; Resources, Robust, Ruddy, Rugged, Stout, Strength, Vigor; "Force" under Vital).

Constitution—(See "Strong" under Constitution; "Body" in this section).

Drink—Given to Strong Drink—(See "Strong Drink" under Drink).

Fairly Strong—(See "Medium Vitality" under Vitality).

Females—Strong Constitution In—(See "Constitution", "Health Good", under Females).

Fits—Strong Fits—(See "Strong" under Fits).

Functions—(See "Strong" under Functions).

Health—The Health Stronger—(See "Abundance", "Good", "Stronger", under Health).

Hips—(See "Strong" under Hips).

Imagination—(See "Strong" under Imagination).

Intellect—(See "Strong" under Intellect, Mind).

Legs—(See "Strong" under Legs).

Limbs—(See "Strong" under Limbs).

Liquors—Strong Liquors—Craving For—(See "Strong Drink" under Drink; "Strong Intoxicants" under Intoxication).

Males—Men—(See "Strong Constitution" under Males, Men).

Medium Strong—(See "Medium" under Vitality).

Men—(See "Strong Constitution" under Men).

Mind—(See "Strong" under Mind).

Moderately Strong—(See "Tolerably Healthy" under Health; "Medium" under Vitality).

Never Strong—The ☽ in ♑, in partile aspect the Asc. (See Emaciated; Feeble; "Ill-Health All Thru Life" under Ill-Health; Infirm, Invalids; "Short Life" under Life; Pale, Sickly; "Much Sickness" under Sickness; "Low" under Resistance, Stamina, Tone, Vitality; "Weak Body" under Weak).

Not Strong—The Constitution Not Very Strong—The ☉ or ☽ to the ☌ or ill-asp. the malefics by dir.; born at the time of an eclipse of the ☉ or ☽; the ☽ nearly in ☌ with the ☉ tends to weaken the constitution; the ☽ applying to ♂, or conjoined with him in a day nativity; the ☽ in ♑ in partile the Asc.; the ☽ Sig. in ♑, thin, feeble, weak, and sickly; ♄ in ♌ unless the energies are conserved; ♃ or ♀ ☌ the ☉ when the ☉ is hyleg, as all planets combust are weakened; ♃ Sig. in ♑, a weakly person; ♂ weak and ill-dignified at B.; ♀ in the 6th H. tends to good health, and a harmonious constitution, as long as excesses are avoided, and good habits adhered to; ☿ Sig. in ♑; ♋ or ♓ on the Asc.; the ♋ influence tends to a weakly constitution. (See "Weak" under Constitution; Eclipses, Feeble; "Bad Health" under Health; "Ill-Health All Thru Life" under Ill-Health; Infirm, Invalids; "Short Life" under Life; Pale, Sickly; "Much Sickness" under Sickness; "Low" under Resistance, Vitality; "Weakened" under Strength; "Weak Body" under Weak).

Passions—(See "Strong" under Passion).

Plethora—(See "Sthenic" under Plethora).

Recuperative Powers—(See "Strong" under Recuperation).

Resistance—(See "Strong Resistance to Disease" under Resistance).

Robust—(See "Robust Constitution" under Robust).

Shoulders—(See "Strong" under Shoulders).

Signs of Zodiac—The Strong Signs—(See "Fixed Signs" under Fixed).

Sthenic Process—(See Sthenic).

Stronger—The Health Stronger—(See "Health" in this section).

Strongest Body—The strongest body is given by ♌ on the Asc., and with the ☉ hyleg, and many planets elevated in the East at B., and preferably in fiery signs.

Thighs—(See "Strong" under Thighs).

Very Strong Body—(See Athletic; "Body", "Strength", under Muscles; "Body" under Strength; "Body" in this section).

Vigorous Body—(See Vigor).

Voice—(See "Strong" under Voice).

Will Power—(See "Strong" under Will).

Women—Strong Constitution In—(See "Constitution" under Females).

STRUCTURAL— Organic—The ☉ rules the structural organization of the parts and organs of the body, while the ☽ rules the functions, habits, and general health. The ☉ afflicted, therefore, tends to structural deterioration, and to inherent, hereditary, and constitutional diseases. The Sign on the Asc. at B. rules the structure of the part, or organ signified, both internally and externally. The nature of structural and functional disorders can be inferred from the combination of Sign, Planet, House, and Aspects. The bones of each part of the body come under the structural rulership of the Sign ruling such part. Thus ♈, in a structural way, would rule the Cranium, the Facial Bones, bones of the skull, etc. Externally ♈ would rule the skin, face, muscles, hair of the head, etc. Internally ♈ rules the Brain, and the contents of the skull, etc. The structural rulership is given under each of the Signs. The question of Structural Influences is further considered in the Article on Organic. (See Organic).

Brain— Structural Defects In — (See "Defects" under Brain).

Cells— Structural Changes In — (See "Structural" under Cells; Metabolism, Metamorphosis, Transformation).

Changes— Structural changes are brought about principally by the ☉, and an afflicted ☉, while functional changes and disorders are due to ☽ influence.

Defects—Structural Defects—(See Defects; "Organic Weakness" under Organic).

Degeneration — Structural Deterioration of Tissues — (See Decay, Degeneration; "Degeneration" under Tissues).

Disorders — Structural Disorders — (See "Organic Diseases" under Organic).

Eyes — Structural Defects In — (See "Defects In" under Eyes).

Heart — (See "Structural Disorders" under Heart).

Lumbar Region — Organic and Structural Weakness In — (See "Organic" under Lumbar).

Lungs—(See "Structural Defects" under Lungs).

Metabolism — Metamorphosis — (See these subjects. Also see "Cells" in this section).

Organic Diseases — (See "Constitutional Diseases" under Constitution; "Organic Diseases" under Organic; the various paragraphs in this section).

Respiratory Organs — (See "Structural Defects" under Breathing, Lungs, Throat).

Stomach—(See "Structural Disorders" under Stomach).

Throat—(See "Structural Defects" under Throat).

Tissues — (See "Structural Defects" under Tissues). For further study along this line see Acquired, Chronic, Congenital, Diathesis, Directions, Heredity, Hexis, Idiosyncrasies, Organic, Praeincipients, Sun Influence. For a list of typical structural diseases see "Constitutional Diseases" under Constitution, and also note the paragraphs under Organic.

STRUMA—(See Scrofula).

STRUTTING GAIT — (See "Strutting" under Gait).

STRYCHNINE—Strychnin—Strychnia— An Alkaloid of Nux Vomica. (See Nux Vomica).

STUBBORN—Stubborn Diseases—Stubborn Nature — Obstinate — (See Obstinate).

STUDY—Mental Exertion — Reading— Studious—

Active Mind—(See "Active Mind" under Active; "Quickened" under Mentality; "Good Mind" under Mind).

Aversion to Study—The ☽ to the □ or ☍ ☿ by dir., and ☿ weak and afflicted at B.; ☿ setting in the West, and following after the ☉; ☿ ☌ ♄, and also afflicted by the ☽, and in no relation to the Asc. (See "Mental Chaos" under Chaotic; "Inability" under Concentration; "Mind" under Dull; "Fails In" under Examinations; Flightiness; "Mind" under Heavy; Idle; "Bad" under Judgment; "Incapable", "Void Of", under Learning; "Shallow" under Mentality; "Light In Mind" under Mind; Pretender; "Weak" under Understanding, etc.).

Blindness — From Too Much Reading and Study—(See "Reading and Study" under Blindness; "Eyestrain" under Eyes).

Disease — From Too Much Reading and Study—(See "Disease" under Reading).

Educational Mind—(See "Educational Mind" under Mind).

Examinations—Fails In—(See Examinations).

Fatigue—Mental Fatigue from Over-Study—(See "Brain Fag" under Brain; "Mind" under Fatigue).

Genius — (See Genius, Mathematical, Scholar).

Good Student — Scholar — Studious Mind—☿ rising, dignified, well-aspected by the ☽ and Asc., and ☿ in one of his own signs, as in ♊ or ♍, and not combust; ♍ on the Asc. at B. (See "Active Mind" under Active; Education, Genius; "Good", "Sound", under Intellect; "Good" under Judgment; Knowledge, Learning, Mathematical; "Quickened" under Mentality; Metaphysics; "Deep", "Educational", "Good", "Sound", under Mind; Occult, Perception, Philosophy, Scholar, Science; "Great Love Of" under Truth; "Good" under Understanding, etc.).

Learning—(See "Fond Of", "Incapable Of", and the various paragraphs under Learning).

Loses Interest — In Studies — (See "Fails In" under Examinations; "Mind" under Indifferent; "Aversion" in this section).

Mathematics—Fond of—(See Mathematical).

Mind Quickened— (See "Quickened" under Mentality; "Good", "Penetrating", under Mind; "Good Student" in this section).

Night Study—Avoid when ☿ is afflicted in ♈ at B.

Occult Study—Fond of—(See Occult; "Astrology", "Occult Science", under Science).

Over-Study—Injury From—☿ afflicted in ♈, and too much reading, study, and night study, should be avoided. (See "Brain Fag" under Brain; Cares; "Mind" under Fatigue; "Strain" under Mental; Blindness, Disease, in this section).

Poor Student—(See Aversion, Loses Interest, in this section).

Renowned—Becomes Famous by His Studies—Takes Degrees—(See Renown).

Scholar—(See Scholar; "Good Student" in this section).

Science—Fond of Scientific Study—(See Science).

Studious Mind—(See "Learns Easily", "Studious Mind", under Learning; "Good Student" in this section).

Unqualified—For Study—(See "Mental Abilities" under Impaired; "Shallow" under Mentality; "Light" under Mind; Aversion, Loses Interest, in this section).

STUPIDITY—Stupid—Slow of Wit—(See "Mind" under Dull, Heavy; Foolish, Idle, Improvident, Indifferent; "Bad" under Judgment; "Weak Mind" under Mind; "Disorders" under Perception; "Stupor" under Sleep; "Persons" under Sluggish; "Slow Mental Development" under Slow; Sottish; "Weak" under Understanding).

STUPOR—A Condition of Insensibility—(See Catalepsy, Coma, Consciousness, Delirium, Insensibility; "Stupor" under Sleep; Trance, Unconsciousness).

STURDY—Robust—Hardy—Enduring—(See "Good" under Constitution: Robust, Ruddy, Rugged; "Body" under Strong; "Good" under Vitality, etc.).

STUTTERING—(See "Stammering" under Speech).

STYPTIC—(See Haemostatics).

SUB-ACUTE DISEASES—(See Chronic).

SUBCONSCIOUS MIND—Corresponds to the ☽. (See "Subconscious" under Mind; Reason, Superconscious).

SUBCUTANEOUS DISEASES—(See Abscesses, Boils, Carbuncles; "Subcutaneous" under Skin).

SUBDUING—Repression—Suppression—A ♄ quality. (See Repressions, Suppression).

SUBJECTIVITY—(See Introspection).

SUBLIMATION—Vaporization and Recondensation—Implied by the ♎ sign. (See Distillation, Filtration, Libra, Vapor).

Urine—Sublimation of—(See Filtration" under Urine).

SUBLUXATIONS—A Partial Dislocation of a Vertebra, or a Partial Dislocation in a Joint in any Part of the Body. Under the pull and pressure of the planetary vibrations and afflictions, the vertebrae are easily diverted from their normal positions, become partially dislocated, and impinge upon the nerves passing thru them, tending to shut off the nerve supply to the various organs and parts of the body, and leading to disease and discomfort in the body. The Spine is the central keyboard of the body, and if the nerve currents to the different parts of the body are to be kept free, open, and unimpeded, the vertebrae must be kept in proper line. Palpation and X-Ray examinations discover these deviations, but there are other ways also of knowing when and in what part of the spine these subluxations exist, and that is by Astrology, as each vertebra is ruled by a Sign of the Zodiac, and the planets in the various Signs at B., and along thru life, tend to afflict the vertebra, or vertebrae, ruled by such sign, and to cause it to deviate. Thus, these subluxations are coming and going constantly in every human being, and many of the partial dislocations adjust themselves at night during sleep. Some subluxations are more serious and prolonged, and especially the vertebra ruled by the Sign in which ♄ is found at B., and if ♄ is also afflicting this sign by direction and his position in the Zodac at the time of a chronic illness, and which also may involve and cause a major subluxation. Such subluxation tends to be the major one throughout life, and occurs about every seven years, and may endure for two years at a time. The ♎ sign rules the Kidneys, and if ♄ is in ♎ at B. the kidneys become the weakest and most afflicted organs of the body, and are subject to severe affliction when ♄ along thru life is passing thru any of the cardinal signs, for a period of 2½ years to a sign, as thru ♈, ♋, ♎, and ♑, but the most severe when ♄ is again passing thru the kidney sign ♎ in the 28th and 29th years of life, and again in the 56th, 57th, and 58th years of life when ♄ finishes his second cycle, and is back in the ♎ sign again, and considering that he was in ♎ at B. Thus we know in what years of life the Kidney Place (KP) in the spine is under affliction by ♄, and we know this without palpation or examination of the patient if we have his birth data. Also the ☉ in ♎ at B., or ♂, tend to afflict the kidneys, and the vertebrae thru which the nerves pass to the kidneys, and you can usually set it down that a person born with the ☉, ♄, ♂, ♆, or any planet in ♎ at B., or with ♎ rising upon the Eastern horizon, the Ascendant, that they are a kidney subject, and that from the standpoint of the vertebrae, the kidney place in the spine should be the first place to be adjusted. This rather lengthy illustration can be applied to any sign of the Zodiac. The ☉, ♄, or ♂ in the ♋ sign at B. would affect the stomach, and SP in the spine. If the ☉ and malefics are in ♊, the lungs would be affected, and the Lung Place (Lu.P.), the 3rd Dorsal vertebra, would be the major subluxation, and need constant attention for a time, and during the time the afflicting planet is afflicting the Lung vertebrae. The major subluxations tend to be brought on by the major planets, as ♆, ♅, ♄, and ♂, and also the ☉, and with several planets afflicting one vertebrae at the same time. The minor subluxations are caused usually by the minor planets, ♀ and ☿, and also by the less severe aspects of the other planets. Every Physician, Chiropractor, Osteopath, or Healer, who would understand his patients, what vertebrae and parts of the body, or organs, are afflicted, should understand Astrology, and how to erect a star map of birth, and to know the planetary influences that are working over his patient at birth, and at the time of illness. The subluxations caused by the slower moving planets are more prolonged. It takes ♄ over two years to pass thru one Sign of the Zodiac, and his afflictions last longer, and tend to a chronic disease. Mars will pass thru one sign usually in about six weeks, and tend to bring on an acute disease, or high fever during this period if the afflicted vertebra is not adjusted frequently. The ☉ passes thru one sign in about one month, and his afflictions tend to last for a month, by his transits. It takes ♅ seven years to pass thru one sign, and during this period he may cause frequent subluxations of the vertebra he is afflicting. By knowing these laws, the Physician, Chiropractor, or Healer, can have a proper knowledge of what vertebrae are afflicted, when they began to be afflicted, and when to stop giving adjustments. This subject is further discussed in the Article on Vertebrae, and each of the Vertebrae given, the parts and organs they supply, etc. At the end of the various Articles on the diseases throughout this book, the subluxations tending to cause the disease have been listed as an aid to Chiropractors who may be using this book. The writer of this Encyclopaedia is a graduate Chiropractor, with the degree of D.C., having taken a resident course at the Palmer School of Chiropractic, at Davenport, Iowa. Also later, in recognition of his Writings, and research work along the lines of Chiropractic, and the Spine, as related to Astrology, he was given the Honorary Degree of Ph.C. by the Mecca College of Chiropractic, located at 143 Roseville Ave., Newark, New Jersey, of which Dr. Frederick W. Collins, A.M., M.D., is the Dean and President. Also the Mecca College of Chiropractic has had a chair of Medical Astrology for some years now, and instructs its students in the Astrological Analysis of the Spine. (See Anatomical, Cervical, Coccyx, Compressed, Dorsal, Healers, Lumbar, Medical Astrology, Numbness, Pressure, Ribs, Sacrum, Spine, Vertebrae; "Fluid" under Vital, etc.).

SUBNORMAL—Subnormalities of the Mind and Body—Below Normal—Almost every subject in this book is dealing with some subnormal, or abnormal condition of the mind, or body, and will ask you to look in the alphabetical arrangement for the subject you have in mind. The planet ♄ tends principally to subnormal conditions by his inhibitions, retentions, and suppressions. Also the afflictions of ♆ tend to subnormal conditions, as lack of development, undersized body, or organs. The ☉, ♃, ♂, and ♀ tend, by their good aspects, to keep the body and mind at normal. Afflictions during Gestation tend to subnormal conditions, and defective births. See the following subjects, which are suggestive along the lines of subnormalities, and the weaknesses and defects of body and mind. See Abeyance, Abnormal, Adynamia, Anaemia, Apathy, Arrested, Asthenia, Atonic, Atrophy, Aversions, Birth, Blemishes, Body, Congenital, Defects, Deficient, Deformities, Deviations, Diminished, Disease, Dull, Dwarfed, Enervation, Feeble, Foolish, Heredity, Idiocy, Ill-Health, Imbecile, Impairments, Imperfections, Impotent, Inactive, Inertia, Infirm, Insanity, Intellect, Lack Of, Lethargy, Listless, Loss Of, Malformations, Mind, Missing, Monsters, Perversions, Prenatal Epoch, Sickness; "Subnormal" under Temperature; Undersized, Understanding, Unnatural, Void Of, Weak, etc.

SUBSTANCE—Matter—(See "Substance" under Brain, Cells; Matter; "Medullary Substance" under Medulla).

SUBSULTUS—Any Morbid Tremor or Twitching—A ♅ disease. (See "Movements" under Erratic; Jerkings, Saint Vitus Dance, Spasmodic, Tremors, Twitchings).

SUCCEDENT HOUSES—The Houses Between the Cardinal and Cadent Houses—The Succedent Houses correspond to the Fixed Sign influence, and many planets in them tend to give a strong constitution. The qualities of these houses are much the same as those of the Fixed Signs. (See "Fixed Signs" under Fixed; "Succedent" under Houses).

SUCCESS—The benefic planets ♃ and ♀ when rising, strong, and well-aspected at B. tend to bring material success, honors, and good health, and especially when in the M.C. in an otherwise fortunate map. (See Ambition, Famous, Fate; "Fortunate" under Fortune; "Good Health" under Health; Optimism, Power, Prosperity, Renown, Reputation, Riches, etc.).

SUCCUMBS—

Disease—Succumbs Easily to Disease—♋, ♑, or ♓ on the Asc., and the hyleg heavily afflicted by malefics; afflictions in fixed signs, and with mutable signs on the angles. The ☽ people become easy subjects to contagions and infectious diseases. The ♍ people court disease, and give up easily to it, and bad suggestions along health lines should not be made to the ♍ people. The ♏ people, by their excess of magnetic power, attract disease, and especially contagious and infectious diseases, and fall easy victims in epidemics. (See Contagions, Directions; "Succumbs Easily" under Disease, Sickness; "Ill-Health All Thru Life" under Ill-Health; Infectious Diseases, Influenced; "Negative Nature" under Negative; Receptive; "Low" under Recuperation, Resistance, Vitality; "Much Sickness" under Sickness; Susceptibility, Virgo; "Weak Body" under Weak).

Does Not Succumb—Strong Resistance to Disease—(See "Abundance", "Good", under Health; Immunity; "Good" under Resistance, Stamina, Tone, Vitality; "Body" under Strong).

SUDDEN—Spontaneous—Unexpected—Untimely—Sudden Events, etc.—The action of ♂ is sudden, intense, fulminating, and severe. Also the action and influence of ♅ tends to sudden and unexpected diseases and events in the life of the native. See the following subjects in the alphabetical arrangement when only listed here—

Accidents—(See the various paragraphs under Accidents).

Blows; Burns; Calamities—(See "Sudden" under Calamity).

Casualties; Catastrophies; Chances;

Changes—(See "Sudden" under Changes).

Child—Sudden Death of—(See "Sudden Death Of" under Children).

Collapse—(See "Sudden" under Collapse).

Cramps; Cuts; Danger—Sudden Danger—The ☉ hyleg, ♅ in the 8th H. and Anareta, and the ☉ to the ☌ or ill-asp. ♅ by dir. (See the paragraphs under Danger).

Death—Sudden Death—Unexpected—Sudden and Extraordinary Death—Quick Death by Violence—The ☉ or ☽ afflicted by the □ or ☍ ♂, and ♂ elevated above the Lights; the ☉ in the 8th H., ☌, □, or ☍ ♂; the ☉ much afflicted in ♉; the ☉ hyleg, and with ♅ in the 8th H., and Anareta, and the ☉ to the ☌, P, □, or ☍ ♅; the ☉ to the ill-asps. ♂ or ♅ by dir.; the ☽ at Full, or increasing, sepr. from ♀, and applying to ♂ in a day geniture, sudden death thru a love affair; the ☽ sepr. from the ☉, and applying to ♂ in a day nativity; the ☽ in the 8th H., and afflicted by ♅, ♄, or ♂; the ☽ to the place of Caput Algol; ♅ afflicted in ♌, ♏, or in the 4th or 8th H.; ♅ and ♂ afflicted in the 8th H.; ♅ afflicted in ♏ in the 8th H.; ♅ and ♂ cause sudden deaths, and especially when in the 8th H., and afflicting the hyleg by dir.; ♅ does not kill by himself, but assists in destroying life by his evil espects, and when they concur in afflicting the hyleg is usually sudden, singular, and of an extraordinary nature; ♆ afflicted at B., and to the ☌ or ill-asp. the hyleg by dir., and it may be by drowning or suffocation; ♄, ♂, or ☋ in the 8th H.; ♂ afflicted in the 1st, 4th, or 8th H.; ♂ lord of the 1st, and in the 8th H.; ♂ in the 8th H., and afflicting the hyleg, death may be sudden and violent; ♂ ☌ or ill-asp. the ☉ at B., and by dir.; ♂ ☌ the ☉ or ☽ in the 1st, 6th, 8th, or 10th H., and especially if ♅ and ♄ add their evil testimony to ♂. There are many ways to meet with a sudden death, too numerous to list here. Look in the alphabetical arrangement for the subject, cause, and kind of death you have in mind. Especially see the following subjects—Accidents, Blows, Contests, Death, Drowning, Duels, Earthquake, Electricity, Enemies, Explosion, Extraordinary, Falls, Flood, Gases, Gunshot, Highwaymen, Hurts, Injury, Killed, Lightning, Murdered, Mysterious, Peculiar, Poison, Quarrels, Quick, Railroads, Remarkable, Shipwreck, Singular, Stabs, Storms, Strange, Suicide, Sword, Thieves, Tornadoes, Tragical, Travel, Treachery, Uncommon, Unexpected, Untimely, Unusual, Vehicles, Violent, Wind, Wounds, etc.).

Diseases—Sudden and Unexpected Diseases—Sudden Distempers—Mad and Sudden Diseases—Severe, Sharp, and Fulminating—♅ rules all sudden diseases, and afflicts the part of the body ♅ is in at B.; ♅ afflicted in the 6th H.; ♅ afflictions and influences show sudden attacks of disease, as by cramps, spasms, ruptures, shocks, etc.; ♅ □, ☍, or P. the ☉, sudden and incurable diseases; ♂ also shows sudden diseases, and death from them; ♂ in the 6th H., and afflicting the ☉ or ☽; ♂ diseases are sudden, and caused by an over-abundance of animal heat. (See Acute; "High" under Fever; Fierce, Fulminating; "Sudden Distempers" under Head; "Animal" under Heat; Painful Diseases, Pernicious, Quick Diseases, Severe, Sharp, Short Diseases, Swift, Vehement, Violent Diseases).

Disgrace—Sudden Disgrace—(See "Causes" under Disgrace).

Distempers—Sudden Distempers—Mad and Sudden—(See "Diseases in this section; "Sudden" under Distempers, Head; "Distempers" under Mad).

Downfall—Sudden Downfall—(See Downfall).

Drowning; Enthusiasms—(See "Sudden" under Enthusiasm).

Escapes; Events—(See "Sudden" under Events).

Evils—(See "Sudden" under Evils).

Explosions; Exposure—Illness from Sudden Exposure—(See Exposure).

Extraordinary—Sudden and Extraordinary Diseases—(See Extraordinary).

Failure—Sudden Failure—(See Disgrace, Downfall, Reverses, Ruin).

Fainting—(See "Sudden Swoonings" under Fainting).

Falls; Family—Sudden Death In—(See "Sudden Death" under Family).

Father—Sudden Death of—(See "Sudden Death" under Father).

Fever—(See "High", "Sudden", under Fever).

Fulminating; Good—Sudden Good or Ill—(See "Sudden Good" under Good).

Head—Sudden Distempers In—Sudden Headaches—(See "Sudden" under Head, Headache).

Heart—Sudden Death from Heart Trouble—(See "Sudden Death" under Heart).

Homicide; Hurts—(See "Strange", "Sudden", under Hurts).

Ill—Sudden Good or Ill—(See "Good" in this section).

Illnesses—Short and Sudden Illnesses—(See Acute; "High Fever" under Fever; Fierce Maladies, Pernicious; "Illnesses" under Short; "Diseases" in this section).

Impulses—(See "Sudden" under Impulses).

Incurable—(See "Sudden and Incurable Diseases" under Incurable).

Injuries—(See the various paragraphs under Injuries; "Accidents" in this section).

Journeys—(See "Sudden" under Journeys).

Lightning — Sudden Death By — (See Electricity, Lightning).

Mad Distempers—Mad and Sudden—(See "Distempers" in this section).

Marriage Partner — (See "Sudden Death Of" under Marriage Partner).

Mischief — Some Sudden Mischief — (See "Danger From" under Mischief).

Mother — (See "Sudden Death Of", "Sudden Sickness Of", under Mother).

Murder; Mysterious and Sudden—(See "Mysterious and Sudden Death" under Mysterious).

Paroxysms—Sudden Paroxysms—(See Convulsions, Epilepsy, Fainting, Fits, Paroxysms, Spasmodic Diseases).

Passion — (See "Sudden Storms Of" under Passion).

Peculiar and Sudden—(See "Extraordinary Accidents" under Accidents; "Death" under Extraordinary; Peculiar).

Perils; Remarkable and Sudden—(See Remarkable).

Reputation — (See "Loss Of" under Reputation).

Reverses; Ruin; Ruptures;

Severe and Sudden—Sudden Severity of Disease—(See Fulminating, Severe, Sharp; "Diseases" in this section).

Sharp and Sudden—(See Sharp).

Shocks; Short Diseases — Short and Sudden — (See Acute, Quick Diseases; "Illnesses" under Short).

Sickness — (See "Diseases" in this section).

Singular; Spontaneous; Stabs;

Strange and Sudden—(See Strange).

Strokes; Suffocation; Suicide;

Swoonings — (See "Fainting" in this secton).

Tragical Death—(See Tragical).

Troubles — Sudden Troubles — (See "Causes" under Trouble; the various paragraphs in this section).

Uncommon and Sudden — (See Uncommon).

Unexpected and Sudden — (See Unexpected).

Unlooked-For and Sudden — (See the various paragraphs in this section).

Untimely; Unusual and Sudden—(See Unusual).

Violent and Sudden — (See "Death", and the various paragraphs under Violence).

Wounds. If the subject you have in mind has been omitted in this Article, look for it in the alphabetical arrangement.

SUDORIFIC — Sudorifics—Diaphoretics—Remedies which Increase the Sweat—A Therapeutic Property of the ☉ remedies. (See Sweat).

SUFFERING — Suffers—Distress—Painful Experiences—Pains In the Body—Anguish of Mind—Anxiety—Sorrow—Trouble, etc. — Suffering is produced principally by the 12th H. influences, as this is the house of sorrow and self-undoing, of hindrances, limita-

tions, and confinements. Suffering is also brought on by the ☐ and 8 aspects of ♄, as ♄ is known as "The Chastener", and the Angel of Saturn is ever working with Humanity to right the wrongs, establish justice, and it is often necessary for the Gods Above to bring many afflictions, troubles, sorrows, suffering, or even death, to awaken and arouse the individual to a better life, more spiritual discernment, and to attainment. (See Punishment). The greater part of the suffering brought upon mankind is due to the abuse and improper use of the sex forces, and to use them for sensuous gratifications, lust, and venery, which brings on disease, and an earlier death. (See Passion, Sex). Nearly every subject in this book deals with the sufferings of Humanity in one form and another, and it will not be advisable to list in this Article all these subjects, but you can find them in the alphabetical arrangement. The following subjects will be listed here, however, which see in the alphabetical arrangement when not more fully considered here—

Abroad — Suffering and Distress Abroad — (See "Suffering" under Abroad).

Affliction; Anguish; Anxiety; Body — Suffering In—Physical Suffering—(See Disease; "Bad Health" under Health; Ill-Health, Infirm, Invalids, Sickness).

Death — Little Suffering At Death — (See "Easy Death" under Death).

Detriment; Disease—Suffers Much In Disease — The afflictions of ♄ tend to prolonged and chronic suffering, dull aches, weakness, and depression. Mars tends to high fevers, sharp pains, etc. (See Aches, Acute, Chronic; "High Fevers" under Fever; Fierce, Fulminating, Grievous; "Heavy and Sad Sickness" under Heavy; "Diseases" under Pain; Pernicious, Poignant; "Serious Illnesses" under Serious; "Disease" under Severe; "Diseases" under Sharp; Vehement, Violent Diseases, etc.).

Disgrace; Distress; Evils; Grief;

Illness—Suffers Severely When Ill— ♌ on the Asc. at B.

Ill-Health—(See "Ill-Health All Thru Life", and the various paragraphs under Ill-Health; "Much Sickness" under Sickness).

Life of Suffering—♄ ♂ the ☉ or ☽ in the 6th H.; ♄ afflicted in the 6th or 12th H.; malefic planets in the 12th H., and afflicting the hyleg; a weak sign on the Asc., and a malefic planet in the rising sign. (See "Many Afflictions" under Affliction; "Malice of Fortune" under Fortune; Miseries, Misfortune, Self-Undoing, Sorrow, Trouble, Twelfth House).

Mind — Suffering In — (See Anguish, Anxiety, Dejected, Despondent, Doubts, Fears; "Low Spirits" under Low; Melancholy; "No Peace of Mind" under Mind; Renunciation, Worry, etc.).

Miseries; Moderated — Suffering and Pain Alleviated — Moderation In Disease—(See Amelioration, Ease, Moderation; "Alleviated" under Pain; Recovery).

Much Suffering—The ☽ to the ☐ or ☍ the ☉ by dir.; the ☽ to the place of Antares; ♃ Sig. ☐ or ☍ ♄, ruin, disgrace, misery, and suffering; ♂ Sig. ☐ or ☍ ♄, and especially if ♄ be stronger than ♂; lord of the 11th in the 12th H. (See "Every Evil" under Evil; "Much Misery Everywhere" under Misery; "Much Sickness" under Sickness; "Many Sorrows" under Sorrow; Trouble).

Pain—(See "Suffers Much Pain", and the various paragraphs under Pain).

Patience—Has Much Patience In Suffering—(See "Does Not Complain" under Complaining; Patience).

Plots — Suffers Much by Plots — (See "Secret Enemies" under Enemies; Plots, Treachery).

Poverty—Suffers From—(See Neglect, Poverty, Privation).

Quarrels—Suffers By—(See Quarrels).

Rash Actions—Suffers By—(See Rashness).

Religion—Suffers Because of His Religion—(See Persecution).

Rest—Has No Rest In Sickness—Suffers Much — (See "Sickness" under Rest).

Reverses; Ruin; Sadness;

Scandal — Suffers From — (See Scandal).

Serious Suffering—Forebodes Serious Suffering—(See Grievous; "Heavy and Sad Sickness" under Heavy; "Suffers Much Pain" under Pain; "Serious Illnesses" under Serious; "Disease" under Severe; Vehement, etc.).

Sickness—Suffers Much In—(See Disease, Illness, Pain, in this section).

Sorrow; Treachery—Suffers By—(See "Female Treachery", "Injury By", under Treachery).

Trouble; Vehicles—Suffers Injury or Death By — (See Railroads, Travel, Vehicles).

Wounds — Injury and Suffering By — (See Cuts, Hurts, Injuries, Instruments, Iron, Mobs, Stabs, Violence, Wounds, etc.).

SUFFOCATION—Suffocated—Stoppage of Respiration—Smothered—Strangulation—Asphyxiation—See the following subjects—

Angina—A Sense of Suffocation—(See Angina).

Asphyxiation—(See Asphyxiation; "Delayed Births" under Children; "Non-Oxygenation" under Oxygen).

Birth — Danger of Suffocation At Birth—(See "Asphyxiation", "Delayed Births", under Children).

Buried Alive—(See Burial).

Choking — (See Asphyxiation, Choking, Drowning, Hanging, Strangulation; "Stricture" under Throat).

Cutaneous Asphyxiation — (See "Cutaneous" under Asphyxia).

Danger of Suffocation—♄ in bad asp. the ☉; the Asc. to the ☌ or ill-asp. ♂ by dir., and ♂ in an earthy sign at B.; the Asc. to the ☌ or ill-asp. ♄ by dir., and ♄ in ♍ at B.

Death by Suffocation—Danger of—If the ☽ be with Antares in ☍ to ♂ with Hercules or Arcturus, and especially in ♂ from angles, threatens death by suffocation; ♄ ☐ or ☍ the ☉ from a fixed sign, and ori., or when occi. in a fixed sign and ☐ or ☍ the ☽, produces death by hanging, suffocation, or by being trodden or crushed to death in a tumult; ♄ in the M.C., or close to the Asc. at B., and afflicting the hyleg by dir.; ♄ afflicting the hyleg by dir., and holding the dominion of death, and especially with ♄ in ♍; ♄ in ♉, and evil fixed stars and ♄ afflicting the hyleg, and are in mutual ☐ or ☍; ♄ or ♅ in ♎, ♍, ♏, or ♓, and afflicting the ☽; ♄ in ♍ and afflicting the hyleg; ♄ ☌ or ill-asp. the ☉ in fixed signs; ♄ influences tend to; ♂ with Hercules or Arcturus, in angles, and afflicting the ☽; fixed signs dispose to. (See Asphyxia, Burial, Choking, Drowning; "Death" under Gas; Halter, Hanging, Strangulation).

Drowning; Dyspnoea; Gas—Death by Escaping Gas — (See "Death" under Gas).

Halter; Hanging; Hysterical Fits — Danger of Suffocation In — (See Hysteria).

Non-Oxygenation — Of the Blood — (See Oxygen).

Phlegm — Almost Suffocated With — (See "Great Expectoration" under Phlegm).

Smothering Sensation — (See Angina, Asphyxia, Cyanosis, Dyspnoea; "Non-Oxygenation" under Oxygen; Smothered).

Spasmodic Suffocation—(See Angina, Dyspnoea; "Non-Oxygenation" under Oxygen).

Strangulation — (See the paragraphs under Strangulation).

Trampled by Mob — Suffocation By — (See Trampled).

SUGAR—Sweets—Candies—Pastries—Preserves—Sugar is the physiological action of ♃. Sugar is also ruled by ♀, as strong ♀ influence at B. inclines to the use of sweets. (See Hydrocarbonates).

Abnormal Desire For — Heavy Sugar Eaters — (See "Pastries", "Starches", "Sugar", "Sweets", under Food; Starches).

Blood—Sugar In—A ♃ disease.

Pyorrhoea — From Eating Excess of Sugar—(See Pyorrhoea).

Urine—Sugar In—Diabetes Mellitus—(See Diabetes).

Xylan—Xylose—Wood Sugar—Wood Gum—(See Xylan, Xylose).

SUGGESTION—Easily Affected By—The ☉ in ♍, or with ♍ on the Asc.; characteristic of the ♍ people, and especially along health lines, as this is the sign which rules over the health. (See Virgo). The planet ♆ is suggestive, and people born under the very strong influence of this planet are very susceptible to suggestion, and especially along passional lines. (See "Attracts Disease" under Attracts; Contagions, Environment, External; "Hypnotic Subject" under Hypnotism; Infections,

Influenced, Magic, Magnetic, Mesmerism; "Mutable Disposition" under Mutable; "Negative Nature" under Negative; Neptune, Obsessions; "Morbid Passional Desires" under Passion; Passive, Receptive, Susceptible, Sympathy, Telepathy, Virgo).

SUICIDE — Suicidal Tendency — Suicide is ruled principally by the 12th House.

Cases of Suicide — Birth Data, etc. — See "Suicide", No. 137, and No. 171; "Husband", No. 162; "Schauman", No. 209; "Puzzle Horoscopes", No. 672; "Prince", No. 744; "Haydon", No. 818; "Allonby", and "Bavaria", No. 823, all in 1001 N.N. Also see Figures 12, 13, and 14 in "Message of the Stars" by the Heindels.

Causes of Suicide—Any of the planets may cause suicide when such planet is under the heavy affliction of malefics, and from causes due to the nature of the afflicting planet. The ☉ and ♂ tend to suicide thru haste, excitement, sudden impulses, and from quarrels. Saturn tends to suicide from worry, brooding, despondency, moping, etc., and to bring on Suicidal Mania. General Causes are—the SUN, ☽, and malefics in the 8th H. in common signs; the ☉ hyleg, and to the ☌ or ill-asp. ♄ by dir.; the ☉ and ☽ afflicted by malefics; the □ and ☍ aspects of the ☉ tend to cause; the ☉ or ☽ ☌ ♄ or ♂ in the M.C., may commit suicide to escape public execution; the MOON to the ☌ or ill-asp. ♅ by dir., and ♅ afflicting the ☽ at B., and especially thru intrigues with the opposite sex; the ☽ in ♏, □ ♄, and ☿ or ♀ □ ♅; the ☽ ☌ ♅, and in □ or ☍ ♄ or ♂, and with ♄ ☌ ☿; NEPTUNE □ or ☍ ♄ or ☿; ♆ afflicted in ♏; ♆ in and about the 16° or cardinal signs, and afflicting ☿; the afflictions of URANUS tend to; ♅ afflicting the Significators, the ☉, ☽, Asc., or M.C. when other indications point to mental derangement; ♅ afflicted in ♓; the transit of ♅ thru the 3rd or 9th H. if afflicting these houses at B.; in violent deaths ♅ disposes to; ♅ afflicting the hyleg; ♅ afflicted in the 8th H.; SATURN ruler of the 12th H. at B., and ♄ ☌ or ill-asp. the Asc. by dir.; ♄ in the Asc., and afflicted by cross aspects; ♄ people are often driven to suicide thru moroseness; ♄ and ♂ in ♊, ♍, ♐, or ♒, and in □ or ☍ the ☉ or ☽; the ♄ sign ♑ on the Asc., and with ♄ as ruler, and afflictions to the Asc. when ♄ is in the 8th H.; ♄ afflicted in the 12th H. at B., has thoughts of suicide; ♄ ☌ or ☍ ☿, and afflicting the hyleg; ♄ in the 3rd or 9th H., and afflicting the ☉, ☽, ☿, or the hyleg; JUPITER weak and afflicted by malefics at B., and especially if ♃ is afflicting the hyleg; ♃ ☌ ♄ and ♂, and otherwise afflicted, or afflicting the hyleg, and thru financial losses or bankruptcy, and the 2nd H. also badly afflicted at B.; MARS ori., □ or ☍ the ☉ from fixed signs, or ♂ occi., □ or ☍ the ☽ from fixed signs, and caused by women if ♀ be with ♂; ♂ ☌ ☿, and also □ or ☍ ♄; ♂ in signs of human form, and □ or ☍ the ☉ or ☽, and contrary in condition; ♂ Sig. □ or ☍ ♄, addicted to suicide or secret revenge; ♂ Sig. □ or ☍ ♄ if either be in the Asc., or ♄ in the M.C.; ♂ afflicting the hyleg by dir., and holding the dominion of death, and especially when the radical map shows a violent death; ♂ in the Asc. in evil asp. to ♄ often leads to times of misfortune, or false accusation, and to suicide; ♂ ☌ the Lights in the 3rd or 9th H., and afflicted by ♄, and also afflicting the hyleg by dir.; VENUS ☌ ♄ or ♂, and ♀ badly afflicted by malefics by dir., it may be thru jealousy, or some love affair; MERCURY, the mental ruler, in the 8th H., and afflicted by the ☽ or malefics, gives some tendency to suicide, and especially when ☿ and the ☽ are in fixed signs; ☿ in the 6th H., and afflicted by ♅, ♄, or ♂; ☿ weak, afflicted, and unfortunate at B., and afflicted by the evil directions of one or more malefics, and especially by ♄, threatens to do away with himself, and especially with the mad or insane; ☿ in an earthy sign at decumbiture, and ♂ afflicting ☿, danger of suicide (Hor'y); many planets in common signs show, and with these signs on the angles, and containing malefics; lord of the Asc. in the 8th H., with lord of the 6th in the 8th, and especially if the lord of the Asc. apply to the □ or ☍ lord of the 6th; lord of the 8th in the 1st H., and from irregularities; lord of the 8th in the 7th, and usually due to mental troubles, or thru quarrels; lord of the 1st in the 8th, and lord of the 8th in the 1st H.; lord of the 1st H. also being lord of the 8th, and lord of the 8th also lord of the 1st; people born under ♎ are said to be prone to suicide, for with ♎ on the Asc., ♉, also ruled by ♀, is on the cusp of the 8th, or near it, which makes the lady of the Asc. also the lady of the 8th H., and such people usually cause their own death; also when ♈ is on the Asc. at B., ♏ is on cusp of the 8th, which may lead to self-destruction under evil aspects to ♂, or evil directions falling in the 8th H., and afflicting lord of the 1st and 8th; afflictions in the 8th H.; planets or malefics in and around the 15° of cardinal signs, the 25° of fixed signs, and the 26° of common signs, known as the more violent areas, or degrees, give suicidal tendencies. (See "Causes His Own Death" under Death).

Cutting the Throat—Suicide By—(See "Cuts His Own Throat" under Throat).

Drowning—Suicide By—(See Drowning).

Fire Arms—Suicide By—(See "Death By" under Gunshot).

Husband—(See "Suicide" under Husband).

Insane — Commits Suicide While Insane—(See "Cases Of" under Insanity).

Poison—(See "Suicide By" under Poison).

Shot Himself—(See Nos. 209, 672, 818, under "Cases" in this section; "Death by Gunshot" under Gunshot).

Suicidal Mania — Caused by ♄; ♄ in the 3rd or 9th H., and afflicting the hyleg; ♄ ☌ ☿ in the 8th H., and afflicting the hyleg or the Asc.; ♄ ruler at B., and afflicting ☿ and the hyleg. (See "Of No Ambition" under Ambition;

Brooding, Dejection, Depressed, Despair, Despondent, Gloom; "Hopes Cut Off" under Hope; Hyperacidity, Hypochondria, Insanity; "Low Spirits" under Low; Melancholy; "No Peace of Mind" under Mind; Morose, Twelfth House; "Death" under Violent; Worry).

SULPHATES—Calcium Sulphate (Lime Sulphate) — Potassium Sulphate — Sodium Sulphate—(See Lime, Potassium, Sodium).

SULPHUR — Brimstone — Is one of the Twelve Polycrest Remedies, and corresponding to the ♑ sign. It is ruled by both ♄ and ♂. Daath mentions sulphur as a typical drug of ♂. The ♑ sign is the sign of ♄, and also ♂ has his exaltation in this sign. The hair is darkened by sulphur, and ♄ rising at B. tends to produce dark and black hair. (See Hair). When in aspect to the ascending degree ♄ contributes sulphur pigment to the skin, and makes the complexion dark and sombre. (See Complexion, Mucous; "Pigmentation" under Skin; "Polycrest" under Zodiac).

SUMMER—

Sickly Summer—♄ or ♂ in power at the Summer Solstice, in the 6th or 8th H., and afflicting the ☽. (See Drought; "Extreme Heat" under Heat; "Death Rate High" under Mortality; "Winds" under Pestilence; "Hot Blasting Winds" under Wind).

Summer Signs—Of the Zodiac—♋, ♌, ♍. Diseases which begin when the ☉ is in these signs are usually short, more fierce, sharp and severe for the time. (See "Illnesses" under Short).

Summer Solstices—(See Solstices).

Warm Summers — (See Drought; "Fountains Dry Up" under Dry; Famine, Fountains; "Extreme Heat" under Heat; Scarcity; "Sickly" in this section).

SUN—The Sun (☉)—Solar Influences— The ☉ is the central body of our Solar System, and around which the planets move. The ☉ is the source of the vital power, and is the regulator and principal source of the life forces. The ☉ stands at the head of the Vital Group. The ♌ Sign is the home Sign, and the only Sign of the ☉, and the ☉ and the ♌ Sign are closely affiliated with the 5th House, as ♌ is the 5th Sign of the Zodiac. The ☉ when strong and powerful at B. tends to make the life and general fate of the native much more favorable, and when weak, ill-dignified, and badly aspected, the health, vitality, fate and destiny of the individual are very trying, and unfavorable. The ☉ is typical of Spirit, and the ☽ of Matter. The ☉ is hot, dry, fiery, inflammatory, electric, positive, barren, masculine, diurnal, life-giving, constructive, expansive, tonic, variable, and vital in action. Much has been written in the Textbooks of Astrology about the various influences of the ☉, and in order that the student may have quicker and more systematic access to these influences, this Article will be arranged into three Sections, as follows: Section One—Influences of the Sun. Section Two—The Sun Rules. Section Three—Diseases Ruled by the Sun.

— SECTION ONE —

INFLUENCES OF THE SUN—The ☉ is a physiological planet (classed as a Planet in Astrology), and is called "The Light of Time". He gives principally the Brain and Heart in Man.

Above the Earth — The ☉ is more powerful in health matters when above the Earth, or horizon at B., and weaker when below, as the ☉ rules by day, and the ☽ by night. (See Elevated, Majority, Rising).

Action Of — The ☉ is hot, electric, vital, and positive in action, and acts upon the whole substance of the Globe, and not upon just any one part or element. (See "Qualities", and the various paragraphs in this section and Article).

Affinity—The ☉ has affinity with all the Planets.

Afflictions Of — Tend to Fevers and Inflammations.

Anareta—The ☉ may become Anareta when the ☽ or Asc. are hyleg. (See Anareta).

Angel Of—Michael.

Angular and Diurnal—The ☉ angular and diurnal exerts his strongest influence in health and other matters.

Ascendant — The ☉ tends to cause death by his evil aspects to the Asc. or ☽ if they are hyleg, in which case he acts like ♂, and produces death by fire if other testimonies concur.

Aspects—Aspects to the ☉ are necessary to give zest to life, and bad aspects are better than none at all. Planets in ☌ the ☉ are known as in Combust, and the ☉ in such an aspect tends to destroy the nature and influence of such planet, and appropriate its qualities to himself. In other aspects the ☉ afflicts only by his □ and ☍.

Beams Of — (See "Rays" in this section).

Below the Earth — (See "Above" in this section).

Benefic—The ☉ is reckoned as benefic, and a Fortune, when with, or in good aspect the Benefics, and not afflicted by malefics.

Blood—The ☉ supplies oxygen to the blood, and also presides over Blood Making. (See Haematopoiesis).

Body—In the body the ☉ concerns itself with the Brain, Heart, Circulation of the Blood, and the Vitality.

Bondage — The ☉ influence is ever clamoring for deliverance and freedom from the thraldom of matter and the flesh, the opposite to the ☽ influence, which gives bondage.

Brain — The rays of the ☉ feed the nerves of the Brain.

Caloric—(See "Heat" in this section).

Capricorn — The ☉ in the ♄ sign ♑ tends to give longevity, and great tenacity of life. (See Endurance).

Cellular Excitation — The ☉ presides over. (See "Excitation" under Cells).

Center — The ☉ is one of the vital centers in a star map, along with the ☽, Asc., M.C., and hyleg.

Chief Index Of — (See "Organic" in this section).

Chronic Type—The inflammatory action of the ☉ is of the chronic type. Also the motion of the ☉ regulates Chronic Diseases. (See Chronic).

Circulation of Blood—(See "Body" in this section).

Circumferential—The influence of the ☉ is circumferential, in circles, like the ripples on water when a stone is thrown into a pond.

Colors—Gold, Orange, Saffron, Golden Yellow, and inclined to Purple. (See Colors).

Combust Planets—(See "Aspects" in this section).

Combustion—A physical action of the ☉. (See Combustion).

Complexion—The ☉ gives a sunburnt complexion. (See Complexion).

Conjunction Aspect — (See "Aspects" in this section).

Constitution—The ☉ has strong rule over the constitution, and the strength of the constitution is at full when the ☉ is above the horizon at B., and hyleg. (See "Strongest Constitution" under Constitution).

Constructiveness — The Principle of the ☉.

Contains In Itself—The ☉ contains in itself all the inherent powers and qualities specialized in the other planets, and the planets abstract from the ☉ certain properties, and transmit them to the Earth Sphere in modified form. (See "Forces", "Phenomena", in this section).

Corresponds To — The ☉ corresponds to the heart and the right eye of a man. The ☉ in nature and action corresponds closely to ♂. (See Mars, Left, Right).

Crucified—The ☉ is crucified in the ♑ sign. (See "Saturn" in this section).

Cycle—The Cycle of the ☉ is 28 years.

Denotes—The ☉ denotes Hysterics in women; Fevers and Sunstroke when afflicting the Asc., arising from excess of heat. The ☉ denotes inherent tendencies, and hereditary transmissions, organic diseases, constitutional and structural defects, etc. (See Organic, Structural).

Detriment Of — (See "Dignities" in this section).

Dignities Of—The ☉ is at home and strongest in his own sign ♌; has his exaltation in ♈, his fall in ♎, and his detriment in ♒. (See Antipathy, Opposites).

Directions—The evil directions of the ☉ are more critical during the ☉ period of life, from the 18th to 37th years of life. (See "Life" under Periods). When the ☉ is afflicted at B. he becomes a malefic in nature, and his evil directions to the ☽ or Asc., if they be hyleg, tend to destroy life. (See "Anareta" in this section; Directions).

Disease — The ☉ is an Indicator of Disease, and his position, strength, and aspects should always be noted when forming a judgment of disease. (See

"Significators" under Disease; "Indicators of Health" under Health).

Diurnal—(See "Angular" in this section).

Drugs—Of the ☉—The general action of Drugs and Herbs ruled by the ☉ are Stimulant, Tonic, and Preservative. By their physiological action they act upon the Cerebral-Spinal Nervous System, the Circulatory System, the Tonicity, and the Vital Force. Typical Drugs of the ☉ are Aurum (Gold), Chamomilla, and the Sun Flower (Helianthus). The Therapeutic Properties of ☉ Remedies are Anticachectic, Cardiac, and Sudorific. (See Gold; "Sun Group" under Herbs, and the other subjects mentioned in this paragraph).

Dryness — The ☉ produces heat and moderate dryness. The ☉ is classed as dry and hot.

Earth and Sun — The ☉ is the sole vital agent of the Earth, and therefore of our organism. (See "Action Of" in this section).

Ease In Disease—During the daytime the electric force of the ☉ tends to diminish fevers and ease disease. (See Magnetic).

Eclipses—Of the ☉—(See Eclipses).

Electric—The ☉ is identified with the positive, masculine, electric, active, and constructive forces of Nature. The ☉ is a positive and electric body, and tends to heat and expansion in the body, and a confident, forceful, and positive mind. The ☉ influence is electric, strong, fearless, inflammatory, vital, fiery, sanguine, dry, hot, and the rays rather fruitful. (See Electric).

Electricity—The energy of the ☉ is partly represented by electricity, which is ☉ force reflected thru the planet ♅. (See Electricity).

Energy Of—(See "Electricity" in this section).

Equinoxes—(See Equinoxes).

Exaltation Of — (See "Dignities" in this section).

Expansive—The influence of the ☉ is expansive, expanding, and circumferential, as denoted by the dot in the circle in its symbol. (See "Electric" in this section).

Experience—(See "Expressive Of" in this section).

Expressive Of — The ☉ is expressive of Infinity, Continuity, Life, and Enlargement of Experience.

Fall Of—(See "Dignities" in this section).

Father — The ☉ signifies the father and his affairs. (See Father).

First House—The ☉ well-aspected in the 1st H., and especially when in a fiery sign, gives a strong constitution. (See Constitution).

Foetus—(See Quickening).

Force—The ☉ in the Solar System has to do with the renewal and interchange of Force, Circulation, and the Conservation of Matter.

Forces—Of the ☉—The Forces of the ☉ are made of use to us by the reflective and refractive powers of the encircling planets, and the rays of the planets are combined in the Solar Orb, the same as white contains all the colors of the Solar Spectrum. The Spleen is the gateway of the Solar Forces which enter the body. The ☉ in the 4th H. at B. tends to deprive the native of the Solar Forces during a greater part of life, but is good for old age. The Solar Life Currents in the body are diminished when the ☉ is in ♂ ♄ at B. (See Forces, Solar; "Force" under Vital).

Fortune—A Benefic—The ☉ is equal to one of the Benefics for good when well-dignified at B. (See "Benefic" in this section).

Friendly To — The ☉ is said to be friendly to all the planets except ♄.

Haematopoiesis—Blood-Making—(See "Blood" in this section).

Health—The ☉ is general Significator of Health, and especially in a male nativity. (See "Indicators" under Health).

Heart—In Man the ☉ corresponds to the heart.

Heat—The ☉ is hot and dry by nature, and tends to produce dry and hot diseases. The ☉ is caloric, and heat-producing, but is also vitalizing and constructive. The ☉ is vital heat and energy. The rays of the ☉ are dry, hot, and rather fruitful, and sunlight is beneficial to growth, health, and vitality. Without sunlight and Solar Forces none could live. The ☉ and ♂, being hot by nature, tend to fevers and inflammations by their afflictions. The ☉ disseminates heat over the body, and gives heat to the part of the body ruled by the sign he is in at B. (See Dry, Electric, Sunlight, in this section).

Heliocentric—(See this subject).

Herbs of the Sun—(See "Sun Group" under Herbs).

Heredity — The ☉ is the Significator of Hereditary Transmissions—(See Heredity, Organic, Structural; "Organic" in this section).

Hot and Dry—(See Dryness, Heat, in this section).

Hour—☉ Hour—(See "Hours" under Planets).

Hyleg—The ☉ as Hyleg—(See Hyleg).

Identified With — (See "Electric" in this section).

Incites — (See "Rhythm" in this section).

Indicator Of—(See Disease, Health, in this section).

Infinity—(See "Expressive Of" in this section).

Ingresses—(See Ingresses).

Inherent Powers — (See "Contains In Itself" in this section).

Joined to Planets—(See "Aspects" in this section).

Jupiter and the Sun—Give Short Diseases. The ☉ is friendly to ♃, and the ☉ is equivalent to a Benefic in influence when dignified, and well-aspected at B. (See "Benefic" in this section).

Leo Sign—Ruled by the ☉. (See Leo).

Life—Life Forces—The ☉ is life and motion. The ☉ is the Life Giver, and the Regulator of the Life Forces. (See Hyleg). The ☉ tends to destroy life when malefic. (See "Directions" in this section). The ☉ is Significator of life and health. (See "Health" in this section). The ☉ maintains life. The most salient characteristic of the ☉ is life, and the giving of life. The Life Forces are governed by the aspects and position of the ☉. (See "Life Force" under Force; "Force" under Vital).

Magnetic and Negative — When setting and occidental, the ☉ has a magnetic and negative influence. (See Magnetic; "Oriental" in this section).

Male Nativities — The ☉ is Sig. of Health in, and also taken as hyleg, when the ☉ is strong at B., and in a hylegiacal place. (See Hyleg; "Health" in this section).

Malefic—Malefics and the ☉—When in ♂ or evil asp. the malefics, the ☉ acquires their nature and operates as a malefic. Planets combust transfer their power to the ☉, good or evil. (See "Aspects" in this section).

Mars and the Sun — (See "Action of Mars", "Sun and Mars", under Mars; "Ascendant", "Corresponds To", in this section). The ☉ ♂ ♂ causes the same diseases as ♂ in the Asc. at B.

Masculine — The ☉ is classed as a masculine planet, positive and electric.

Matter — (See "Bondage", "Force", in this section. Also see Matter).

Mentality—Mentally, the ☉ gives stability, firmness, perseverance, and strong will power, and especially when strong, rising, and well-aspected at B.

Metals and Minerals—Ruled by the ☉ —Carbuncle, Chrysolite, Gold, Hyacinth.

Mind — (See "Electric", "Mental", in this section).

Minerals — (See "Metals" in this section).

Moon and the Sun — The ☉ is malignant to the ☽ when ♂ or ☍ the ☽. The ☉ is stronger during the decrease and waning of the ☽. (See Moon; "Ascendant", "Directions", in this section).

Motion of the Sun — (See "Chronic", "Life", in this section). The motion of the ☉ is always direct, and never retrograde.

Negative — (See "Magnetic" in this section).

Nerves—(See "Brain" in this section).

Occidental—(See "Magnetic", "Oriental", in this section).

Orb Of—(See Orbs).

Organic—The ☉ is organic, and the ☽ functional. The ☉ is the chief index of the organic constitution. The ☉, its position and influence, is looked to for structural, organic, and hereditary troubles, and the vital physiological history of the native's constitution. (See Heredity, Organic, Structural; "Denotes", "Earth", "Rhythm", in this section).

Oriental—The ☉ when rising and oriental, has a positive, or electric influence upon the mind and body.

Oxygen—(See "Blood" in this section).

Pathological Action — Pathologically, the ☉ by his afflictions tends to feverish conditions, hemorrhage, plethora, superfluous nutriment, and syncope.

Periodicity — Many diseases follow a Solar Periodicity, such as Tumors, Pains and Fluxions, and increase in proportion to the Declination of the ☉ towards the West. (See Periodicity).

Phenomena — The ☉ is the Soul of Physical Being, and contains in itself every form of manifestation of Phenomena. (See "Contains In Itself" in this section).

Physical Being — (See "Phenomena" in this section).

Physiological Action—Of the ☉ Plants, Herbs, and Remedies, tend to the generation of heat in the body, and to build up the Tone and Vital Force. They also act upon the Cerebro-Spinal Nervous System, and the Circulatory System. (See "Drugs" in this section).

Planets and the Sun — (See Aspects, Contains In Itself, Forces, Jupiter, Mars, Moon, Saturn, in this section).

Plant Remedies Of — (See Drugs, Physiological Action, in this section).

Plexus — The Solar Plexus — (See "Solar" under Plexus).

Positive — (See Electric, Oriental, in this section).

Powers of the Sun—(See "Contains In Itself", "Forces", "Phenomena", and the various paragraphs in this section).

Presides Over—(See "Cellular" in this section).

Principle Of—Constructiveness.

Produces—(See Electricity, Foetus, Force, Heat, Motion, and the various paragraphs in this section).

Qualities—Action of the ☉—The most of these subjects appear in the alphabetical arrangement — Active, Anticachectic, Ardent, Autocratic, Barren, Benefic (when well-aspected and dignified), Caloric-Producing, Cardiac, Chronic, Circumferential, Combustive, Commanding, Confident, Constitutional, Constructive, Courageous, Destructive (when malefic), Diurnal, Dry, Dynamic, Electric, Enlarging, Eruptive, Expanding, Fearless, Feverish, Fiery, Forceful, Fruitful (rather fruitful), Hemorrhagic, Hot, Inflamatory, Kinetic, Life-Giving, Magnetic (when occidental), Malefic (when ill-dignified), Masculine, Muscular, Organic, Pernicious, Physiological, Positive, Preservative, Quickening, Ruling, Rhythmic, Sanguine, Spiritual, Strong, Structural, Sudorific, Supporting, Temperate, Tonic, Variable, Vital, Vitalizing, Vivifying, etc.

Quickened—The Foetus is quickened by the ☉. (See Quickening).

Rays of the Sun—The Rays of the ☉ are dry, hot, and fruitful. (See Brain, Electric, Heat, in this section).

Regulator Of—The Life Forces. (See "Life" in this section).

Resistance to Disease — Is stronger when the ☉ is angular and diurnal. (See "Good" under Resistance).

Revolution — Solar Revolution — (See Solar).

Rhythm — The ☉ incites organic rhythm. (See Rhythm).

Right Eye—(See "Corresponds To" in this section).

Rising — (See "Oriental" in this section).

Salient Characteristic—(See "Life" in this section).

Saturn and the Sun—The ☉ is crucified in ♑, the sign ruled by ♄, and which is the exalted sign of ♂, and thus the ☉ is crucified "Between the Two Thieves" of the Heavens in this sign. The ☉ is opposed to ♄.

Sensitive Part — Of the Body — The Sign in which the ☉ is posited at B. indicates an internal part of the body which is very sensitive, and if the ☉ is also much afflicted, complaints of such organ, or part, usually result, and according to the sign and nature of the afflicting planet.

Setting—(See "Magnetic" in this section; Setting).

Seventh House—The ☉ well-aspected in the 7th H. gives a strong constitution, and is also favorable for marriage.

Sign In At Birth — (See "Sensitive Part" in this section).

Significator Of — The ☉ is Sig. of Honor, Credit, and accidentally of Health and Life. (See "Male Nativities" in this section).

Signifies—The ☉ signifies the Father. (See Father). The ☉ also signifies diseases of the Brain, and also Fevers and Sunstroke.

Solar—Solar Eclipse—Solar Forces—Solar Ingresses — Solar-Lunar Activities—Solar Orb—Solar Plexus—Solar Periodicity — Solar Revolution—Solar Spectrum—(See Eclipses, Ingresses, Orbs, Periodicity, Plexus, Revolution, Solar, Spectrum; "Forces" in this section).

Solstices—(See this subject.

Soul of Physical Being — (See "Phenomena" in this section).

Source Of—The ☉ is the source of the Life Forces and the Vital Powers. (See Vital, Vitality; "Forces", "Life" in this section).

Spleen — The Gateway of the Solar Forces—(See Spleen; "Forces" in this section).

Spots—Sun Spots—(See Spots).

Strength—Of the ☉ At Birth—Great care should be taken in judging of the strength of the ☉ at B., as the physical powers, the constitution, the vitality, and the entire life, depend upon its aspects and position in the Signs and Houses. (See "Judging the Health" under Health).

Structural Rulership—(See "Organic" in this section).

Sunburnt Complexion — The ☉ gives. (See "Sunburnt" under Complexion).

Sunday—(See Week).

Sunlight—People born under the fiery signs need more sunlight for the best of health. (See "Heat" in this section).

Sunrise and Sunset — Sunrise is the best time of the day to be born for a strong constitution. The ☉ in the 7th H. just before sunset also gives a strong constitution, but the ☉ becomes weaker for health and strength when he passes into the 6th H., after sunset, and especially if afflicted by, or ♂ a malefic. (See Ascendant, First House, Sixth House).

Sun Spots—(See Spots).

Symbol Of — The Dot within the Circle (☉). Chapter V in the book, "The Key To the Universe", by Dr. and Mrs. Homer Curtiss, is devoted to the Occult and Spiritual meaning of this symbol.

Tenth House — The Midheaven — The ☉ well-aspected in this house, and in a strong sign for the ☉, tends to give a strong constitution, honors, and good fortune in life. (See Tenth House).

Therapeutic Properties—(See "Drugs Of" in this section).

Typical Drugs Of — (See "Drugs" in this section).

Vital — The Vital Powers — Ptolemy says the ☉ is the source of Vital Power, and there would be no life without the ☉. The ☉ rules over the Vital Powers, the Constitution, and the Prana, no matter in what part of the map he is in at birth. The ☉ is one of the vital centers of the map, along with the ☽, Asc., M.C., and hyleg. The Vital Fluid, ruled by the ☉, enters the body thru the Spleen. The ☉ stands at the head of the Vital Group. The Vital Powers are at full when the ☉ is above the horizon at B., and hyleg. (See Center, Constitution, Forces, Life, Source Of, Strength, in this section; "Life Force" under Force; Prana; "Fluid", "Force", and the various paragraphs under Vital; "Life Force" under Vitality).

Weather and the Sun—(See Drought, Famine; "Extreme Heat" under Heat; "Winds" under Pestilence; "Warm Weather" under Weather; "Storms" under Wind).

Winter Solstice — Entrance of the ☉ into ♑. (See Equinoxes, Solstices).

Zest—(See "Aspects" in this section; Zest).

— SECTION TWO —

THE SUN RULES — Look for these subjects in the alphabetical arrangement — Ardency; Arms — The Blood in the Arms, Hands, Legs and Feet when the ☉ is in Signs ruling these parts; Arteries; Back; Barrenness; Bilious Temperament (see Choleric); Blood—Blood-Making—The Blood—Oxygen in the Blood (see Blood, Haematopoiesis, Oxygen); Brain (the Structure of); Casein; Cellular Excitation (see Cells); Choleric Temperament (see Choleric); Chronic Diseases (motion of the ☉ regulates); Circulation of the Blood (see Circulation); Colors (see "Colors" in Sec. 1 of this Article); Constitution and Constitutional Diseases; Constructive Energy; Creative Powers; Daytime (see Day); Diamonds; Dorsal Region of Spine (see Dorsal); Drugs (see "Drugs" in Sec. 1 of this Article); Emotional Nature in Women (see Emotions); Energy (see Constructive, Vital,

under Energy); Etheric Fluid (see "Fluid" under Vital); Eyes — Right Eye of Male and Left Eye of Female; Faculties (see "Physical" under Faculties); Father (the Father); Feet — (Blood in when ☉ is in ♓); Feminine Signs of Zodiac—Second Half of (see "Signs" under Female); Fires of Life (see "Fires" under Life); Gold; Grape (Vinus Vinifera); Hands (Blood in when ☉ is in Sign which rules Hands); Health Matters in Males; Heart (Structure of when ☉ is in ♌); Heat (Distribution of in the Body—Excess Heat in the Body—Heat in the Parts or Organs ruled by the Sign ☉ is in at birth); Herbs (see "Sun Group" under Herbs); Hereditary Complaints; Hot and Dry Diseases (see "Dry and Hot" under Heat); Hyleg in the Male (see Hyleg); Internal Diseases (and especially in the part or organs ruled by the Sign the ☉ is in at birth); Kings; Left Eye in Females; Legs (Blood in when ☉ is in Signs ruling the Legs); Leo Sign; Life Force (see "Life Force" under Force); Males (Health Matters in); Man (the Heart and Brain in); Masculine Signs of the Zodiac—First Half of—(see "Masculine Signs" under Signs); Memory; Mustard; Nobles; Nucleus of Cells; Orange Color; Organic Conditions in the Body—Organic Diseases—Organic and Structural Disorders — Organismic Rhythm; Ovary (the Right Ovary); Oxygen in the Blood and Body; Physical Faculties (see "Physical" under Faculties); Plant Remedies (see "Sun Group" under Herbs; "Herbs" in Sec. 1 of this Article); Pons Varolii; Prana; Proteids; Protoplasm; Remedies (see "Drugs" in Sec. 1 of this Article); Retentive Faculties (see Memory); Right Side of Body—Right Eye in the Male — Right Ovary — Right Testicle (see Right); Rulers; Rhythm (Organic); Saffron Color; Second Half of Life (see "Second Half" under Life); Sinews (see "Sinews" under Nerves); Solar Spectrum — Orange In (see Colors); Spine—Dorsal Region of (see Dorsal); Spleen (the Vital Etheric Fluid entering thru the Spleen); Stomach (the ☉ in ♋ rules the Structure of); Strength of Youth (see Youth); Structural and Organic Diseases — Structure of the Body; Sunday; Sun Flower; Sympathetic Nervous System (see Sympathetic); System (the Physical System in the Male); Temperament — Bilious Temperament (see Choleric); Testicle (Right); Vital Energy—Vital Force—Vital Body—Vital Etheric Fluid—Vital Parts—Vital Powers—Vital Principle—Vital Spirit in Women—Vital Group (see Vital; "Vital" in Sec. 1 of this Article); Vitality; Women—Emotional Nature In—Left Eye In—Vital Spirit In (see Women); Yellow Color; Youth—The Strength of Youth (see Youth).

— SECTION THREE —

DISEASES RULED BY THE SUN — Afflictions and Disturbances Caused by the Adverse Aspects and Influences of the Sun—Here are a few axioms, or concise statements, about the influences of the ☉ as related to health and disease, which the student and Diagnostician should keep in mind when forming judgment. The diseases of the ⊙ are organic, constitutional, and structural. The chief diseases of the ⊙ are of the Brain, Eyes, and Heart, and the ⊙ has special affinity with the Eyes. The ⊙ especially rules health matters in the male. The ⊙ is more powerful in health matters when above the horizon, or hyleg, and weaker when below the horizon, and not hyleg, or dignified by sign and aspect, as the ⊙ rules the day, and the ☽ the night. The sign the ⊙ is in at B. indicates an internal part of the body which is very sensitive, and if the ⊙ is also afflicted, complaints of such organ, or part, usually result, and according to the sign and nature of the afflicting planet. The ⊙ angular and diurnal exerts his strongest influence in health matters, and gives greater resistance to disease. Chronic diseases are regulated by the motion of the ⊙. Fevers and Inflammations produced by the ⊙ are slow, but severe, while those of ♂ are quick, destructive, and contagious. The ⊙ in whatever part of the map largely determines the strength of the constitution in both males and females. The ⊙ joined with ♂ causes the same diseases as ♂ in the Asc. at B. In judging of the importance of the disease, note whether the ⊙ is weak by sign and house. The ⊙ cadent, and in a common sign, tends especially to ⊙ diseases, but less so when the ⊙ is in the 9th H., or in the ♐ sign. There is less liability to sickness and disease when the ⊙ is angular, and the powers of immunity and resistance to disease are greater. As the ⊙ is the source of the vital powers, his position, aspects, house position, and dignities in the map should be looked to first in determining the nature and prognosis of the disease, as a weak ⊙ at B. usually means an earlier death, short life, while a strong and dignified ⊙ at B. promises long life, stronger vitality, and good health. The following are classed as diseases of the ⊙. See these subjects in the alphabetical arrangement when they are merely listed here—

Acne; Acute Fever — (See "Fevers" under Acute).

Apoplexy; Appendicitis; Arms—Pains In—(See Arms).

Arteries—Diseases of—(See Arteries).

Augmented Vitality — A Morbid Condition—(See "Augmented" under Vitality).

Back — Pains In — Weak Back — (See Back).

Barrenness; Bilious Affections — (See Bile).

Blood Disorders — Inflamed Blood — Disorders of the Blood in the Arms, Hands, Legs, and Feet — Blood Disorders — Blood Impurities — Blood Poisoning—(See Blood, Impure).

Bloody Flux—(See Flux).

Bowel Disorders— Cancer of—Inflammation of — Organic Diseases of — Humours In—(See Bowels).

Brain—Diseases of—Disordered Brain —Brain Fever—Organic Brain Trouble —Structural Defects of—(See Brain).

Breakings Out—On the Body—On the Face—In the Throat—(See Eruptions, Face, Pimples, Skin Diseases, Throat).

Breath—(See "Foul" under Breath).

Cancer—Carcinoma of the Bowels or Stomach—(See Carcinoma).

Cataract; Catarrhs; Choroiditis—(See Choroid).

Chronic Inflammation—(See "Chronic" under Inflammation).

Circulation—Of the Blood—Disorders of—(See Circulation).

Cold—Diseases Arising From—The ⊙ afflicting the Asc. at B., and by dir. (See "Diseases Arising From" under Cold).

Combustion; Conjunctivitis—(See Conjunctiva).

Constitutional Diseases—(See Constitution, Organic, Structural).

Cramps; Cuts; Death — The ⊙ causes death by Pleurisy, or some obstruction in the Viscera. Also death by fire if other testimonies concur. (See "Death" under Fire, Pleura; "Obstruction" under Viscera).

Defects—The ⊙ causes structural defects, and with attending diseases. (See Defects; "Defects" under Eyes; Structural).

Defluxions; Deprived — Of the Solar Forces—(See "Forces" in Sec. 1 of this Article).

Destroys Life — (See "Anareta", "Ascendant", in Sec. 1 of this Article; "Death" in this section).

Diphtheria; Distempers — In Secret Parts — Venereal — (See "Distempers" under Secrets; Venereal).

Dizziness; Dropsy;

Dry and Hot Diseases—(See "Dry and Hot" under Heat).

Ease In Disease—(See "Ease" in Sec. 1 of this Article).

Epidemic Fevers—(See Epidemics).

Eruptions; Eyes—All Infirmities In—Defects—Disorders — Hurts To—Sore Eyes—Structural Disorders—The Right Eye In Males and the Left Eye In Females Affected—(See Eyes).

Face—Breakings Out—Pimples—(See "Eruptions" under Face; Pimples).

Faintings; Feet—Swellings In—Blood Disorders In—(See Feet).

Fevers—Acute Fevers—Epidemic Fevers — Fevers Generally — Putrid Fevers—Spotted Fever—The fevers produced by the ⊙ are slow, but severe. (See "Fevers" under Acute; "Epidemic Fevers" under Epidemics; "Generally" under Fevers; "Fevers" under Putrid; Spotted).

Fire—Death By—(See "Death" under Fire).

Fistula; Flushings — Heated Flushings — Hot Flashes — (See Flushings; "Flushings" under Heat).

Fluxes; Foul Breath — (See "Foul" under Breath).

Fullness—Of the System—(See "System" under Fullness; Plethora).

Giddiness—In the Head—(See Dizziness).

Glaucoma; Gravel; Growths—Fungus, or Vegetable Growths In the Body — (See Fungus; "Growths" under Vegetable).

Head — Giddiness In — Headaches — Violent Pains In — (See "Dizziness; "Pains" under Head; Headaches).

Heart — Diseases of — Palpitations — Organic Heart Trouble—Trembling of —Weak Heart—(See Heart).

Heat—Diseases Arising from Excess of Heat, as Fever and Sunstroke—(See Fever; Flushings; "Extreme Heat", "Flushings", under Heat; "Sunstroke" in this section).

Heated Flushings — (See Flushings; "Heat" in this section).

Hemorrhage; Hereditary Diseases — (See Constitutional, Heredity, Organic, Structural).

Hips — Hot Humours In — (See "Hot Humours" under Hips).

Hoarseness—(See Larynx).

Hot and Dry Diseases—Hot Humours —(See "Dry and Hot Diseases" under Heat; "Hot Humours" under Hips; "Heat" in this section).

Hot Flashes — (See "Flushings" in this section).

Hour—The ☉ Hour—A critical hour to fall ill, as the sickness is liable to be violent and dangerous. (See "Hours" under Planets).

Humours — In the Bowels — Hot Humours In the Hips — (See "Hot Humours" under Hips; "Bowels" under Humours).

Hurts to Eyes — (See "Hurts To", "Left", "Right", under Eyes).

Hyperaemia; Hysteria; Impure — Impurities — Impure Blood — Impure Breath — (See "Foul" under Breath; Impure).

Inflammation—Of All Kinds—Chronic Inflammation — Inflamed Blood — Inflammation of the Lungs and Stomach —(See "Inflamed" under Blood; "All Kinds", "Chronic", under Inflammation; "Pulmonitis" under Lungs; "Inflammation" under Stomach).

Inherent Diseases—Innate Diseases— (See Constitutional, Heredity, Innate, Organic, Structural).

Internal Diseases—(See Internal).

Iritis—(See Iris).

Judgment of Sun Diseases — Rules For—(See the Introduction to this section).

Keratitis—(See "Cornea" under Eyes).

Knees—Lameness In—Tumors In— (See Knees).

Lameness — (See "Lameness" under Knees).

Left Eye — Defects In — Hurts To — (See "Left Eye" under Eyes; "Eyes" under Left).

Legs—Impure Blood In—Milk Leg— Pains In—Weakness In—(See Legs).

Life — Tends to Destroy Life When, etc.—(See Anareta, Ascendant, Directions, Life, in Sec. 1 of this Article; "Death" in this section).

Life Forces — Disorders of — Obstruc-

tion of—(See "Life Force" under Life; "Obstructed" under Vital; "Forces of the Sun" in Sec. 1 of this Article).

Lungs — (See "Hyperaemia", "Inflammation", under Lungs).

Mania — May be caused by afflictions to the ☉ at a Solar Ingress into ♈. (See Mania).

Measles; Megrims — Migraine — (See Migraine).

Milk Leg—(See Legs).

Mouth—All Diseases of—(See "Affections" under Mouth).

Neck — (See "Swellings In" under Neck).

Nervousness—Nervous Prostration— Neurasthenia—(See Nerves).

Nutriment—(See "Superfluous" under Nutrition).

Obstructions—In the Stomach—(See "Poor Digestion" under Digestion; "Obstructions" under Stomach).

Ophthalmia — (See "Conjunctivitis" under Conjunctiva).

Organic Diseases—Organic Defects— (See Organic, Structural; "Defects", "Eyes", in this section).

Pains—In the Arms, Back, Head, and Legs — (See "Pain" under these subjects; Headaches; "Periodicity" in Sec. 1 of this Article).

Palpitation—(See Heart).

Periodicity — Many Diseases Follow a Solar Periodicity—(See "Periodicity" in Sec. 1 of this Article).

Phlegmatic Dolens—(See "Milk Leg" under Legs).

Physical Disorders — (See Physical; "Disordered System" under System; the various paragraphs in this section).

Pimples; Plague; Plethora; Polypus; Prostration — (See "Prostration" under Nerves).

Putrid Fevers—(See Putrid).

Quinsy—(See "Quinsy" under Tonsils).

Reins Disordered—(See Reins).

Remedies — Sun Remedies — (See "Drugs" in Sec. 1 of this Article; "Treatment" in this section).

Respiratory Troubles—(See the various paragraphs under Breathing, Bronchial; "Diseased", "Pulmonitis", under Lungs).

Right Eye—Disorders and Defects of In Males—Hurts To—(See "Right Eye" under Eyes; "Eyes" under Right).

Scrofula; Scurvy; Secret Parts—Distempers In — Violent Pains In — (See Secrets).

Sharpness of Urine—(See Urine).

Short Diseases—(See "Illnesses" under Short).

Shoulders — (See "Pains In" under Shoulders).

Sight—Weak Sight—Disorders of Vision—(See Sight).

Slow Diseases—(See "Slow Diseases" under Slow).

Smallpox; Solar Forces—Deprived of —(See "Forces" in Sec. 1 of this Article).

Sore Eyes — Sore Throat — (See Conjunctiva; "Inflamed" under Eyes; "Sore" under Throat).

Spine—Disorders of—(See Spine).

Spotted Fever—(See Spotted).

Stomach — Disorders of — Structural Defects of — Obstructions In — (See Stomach).

Stone; Strangury — (See this subject under Urine).

Structural Diseases — And Defects — (See Organic, Structural).

Sudden Swoonings—(See Fainting).

Sun Spots — As Causes of Disease — (See Spots).

Sunstroke—Heat Prostration—The ☉ denotes; the ☉ afflicting the Asc.; the ☉ or ♂ afflicted in ♈; a fiery sign on the Asc. at B., and many planets in a fiery sign; Subs at AT, AX, and KP. (See "Excessive Bodily Heat" under Heat; "Sunstroke" under Voyages; "Denotes", "Signifies", in Sec. 1 of this Article).

Superfluous Nutriment — An afflicted ☉ inclines to excesses in eating. (See Gluttony; "Superfluous" under Nutrition).

Swellings—In the Neck or Feet—(See "Dropsy" under Feet; "Swellings" under Neck).

Swoonings — (See "Falling Fits" under Fainting).

Syncope—(See Fainting).

Thighs — (See "Hot Humours" under Hips).

Throat — Breakings Out In — Sore Throat—Swellings In—All Diseases In —Organic Defects of—(See Throat).

Tissues—Combustion of—(See "Combustion" under Tissues).

Treatment—The diseases of the ☉ are combatted by ♄ remedies, as ♄ opposes the ☉. (See Antipathy, Opposites).

Tremblings — (See "Palpitation" under Heart; Tremblings).

Tumors—(See "Tumors" under Knees; "Periodicity" in Sec. 1 of this Article).

Tympanites; Urine — Sharpness of — Strangury—(See Urine).

Venereal Distempers—(See Venereal).

Violent Pains—In the Head—In the Secrets — (See "Violent Pains" under Head, Secrets).

Vision—Disorders of—(See Sight).

Vital Force—Vital Powers—Vitality —Disturbances of—Obstructions To— (See the various paragraphs under Vital, Vitality).

Vitality Augmented — A Morbid Plus Condition — (See "Augmented" under Vitality).

Weak — Weak Back — Weak Sight — (See "Weak" under Back, Sight).

Weakness—In the Heart—In the Legs —(See "Weakness" under Heart; "Weak Legs" under Legs).

Women — Hysterics In — (See Hysteria).

SUBCONSCIOUS MIND—Corresponds to the ☉. (See "Subconscious" under Mind).

SUNBURNT COMPLEXION—(See "Sunburnt" under Complexion).

SUNDAY—Ruled by the ☉. (See Week).

SUNKEN—Hollow—(See "Sunken" under Chest, Eyeballs, Face; "Falling In Of" under Cheeks; Hollow).

SUNRISE AND SUNSET—Effects of In Health Matters—(See "Sunrise" under Sun).

SUNSTROKE—Heat Prostration—(See "Sunstroke" under Sun).

SUPERABUNDANCE—Over-Abundance —Excessive—

Air — Death or Disease from Superabundance of Air—(See "Superabundance" under Air).

Animal Heat — Superabundance of — (See "Animal Heat" under Heat).

Blood—(See "Too Much Blood" under Blood; Plethora).

Cold — Disease or Death from Too Much Cold, or a Cold Body — (See "Superabundance" under Cold; "Cold" under Weather).

Energy — Superabundance of Energy, and of Vital Energy — (See "Superabundance" under Energy; "Energy" under Vital).

Heat — (See "Superabundance" under Heat; "High Fever" under Fever; "Sunstroke" under Sun).

Moisture—(See "Superabundance" under Moisture).

Passion — (See "Excess of Passion" under Passion).

Rain — (See "Too Much Rain" under Rain). See the subjects under Exaggerated, Excess, Excesses, Hyper, Increased, Over, Too Much).

SUPERFICIAL MIND — (See "Superficial" under Mind).

SUPERFLUOUS — (See "Superfluous" under Nutrition).

SUPERIOR—

Ganglion — The Superior Cervical Ganglion — (See "Cervical Ganglion" under Cervical).

Jaw—Superior Maxillary Bone—(See "Upper Jaw" under Jaws).

Superior Planets—The Major Planets —♆, ♅, ♄, ♃, ♂. Called Superior because their orbs are beyond those of ☿ and ♀, the Inferior Planets, and because they are more powerful in their effects. (See "Major Planets" under Major).

Superior Vena Cava—(See Veins).

SUPERSENSITIVE — (See Hyperaesthesia; "Supersensitive" under Sensitive).

SUPERSENSUAL—(See "Excess Of" under Passion; "Supersensuality" under Sensual).

SUPERSTITIOUS — (See Fears, Forebodings, Horrors, Obsessions, Premonitions; "Superstitious" under Religion; Spirit Controls, Strange, Terrors, Visions, etc.).

SUPPORTING — The Constitution Supported—A ♃ quality. Also the ☉ supports by giving the Vital Life Forces. Mars supports by giving energy, dynamic power, and also is constructive by helping to cleanse the body of impurities by fevers and inflammations. (See Conservation, Preservation).

SUPPRESSIONS—Inhibitions—Restrictions—Ablation or Removal of Organs or a Part of the Body—Suppressions are caused principally by ♄, and also by ☋. (See Dragon's Tail, Saturn).

Ablation of Organs — By Suppression —(See Removal).

Cutaneous Breathing—Suppression of —(See "Cutaneous" under Asphyxia).

Faeces — (See "Suppression" under Faeces).

Functions—(See "Suppressed" under Functions).

Gastric Juices — (See "Stopped" under Digestion; "Ailments Of" under Fluids; "Obstructions" under Stomach).

Growth Suppressed—(See "Arrested" under Growth).

Mammae — (See "Ablation" under Breasts).

Mental Powers — Mind — Suppression of—(See Idiocy, Imbecility; "Arrested Mental Powers", "Retarded", under Mentality; "Weak Mind" under Mind).

Nervous Energy — Suppression of — (See "Nervous Energy" under Nerves).

Organs — Suppression of — (See Remote, Removal; "Ablation" under Tonsils).

Ovaries — Ablation or Suppression of —(See "Ablation" under Ovaries).

Stools—(See "Faeces" in this section).

Sweat—(See "Lessened" under Sweat).

Tonsils—(See "Ablation" under Tonsils).

Urine — (See "Suppression" under Urine). For further study along this line see Ablation, Arrested, Atrophy, Cirrhosis, Clots, Concretions, Congelation, Congestions, Crystallization, Deafness, Decrease, Delayed, Diminished, Dropsy; "Hindered" under Elimination; "Arrested" under Emotions; Hardening, Hindrances, Hyperacidity, Impediments, Impure, Incurable, Inhibitions, Interrupted, Irregular, Lessened, Lethargy, Morbid, Mutes, Obstructions; "Osseous Deposits" under Osseous; Prevented, Restraints, Retarded, Rigidity, Sclerosis, Slow, Sluggish, Stone, Stoppages, Suspensions, Thickening, Tumors, Twelfth House.

SUPPURATION—The Formation of Pus —Pus Diseases—Festering Diseases—(See Pus).

SUPRA-RENAL CAPSULES — Supra-Renal Plexus—(See Adrenals).

SURE—

Sickness Sure — (See "Sure to Come" under Sickness).

Sure Death — (See "Certain" under Death; Fatal; "Death" under Immediate; "Time of Death" under Time).

SURFACE—Constrictions of the Blood Vessels of the Surface—(See Centripetal, Chill, Constrictions, External; "Chill" under Skin).

Rubbing of Surfaces—Fremitus—(See Friction).

Serous Surfaces—Mucous Surfaces—(See Mucous, Serum).

SURFEITS—A Surfeit—Excess—A Surplus—More Than Enough—Congestion —♃ denotes diseases arising from surfeits, congestion, over-functional activity of a part, parts, or organ ruled by the sign he is in at B., or by dir. Also caused by ♃ afflicted in ♋; ♃ afflicted in ♎, from too much blood; ♃, ♂, and ♀ cause degeneration thru excesses and surfeits; ♃ afflicted in ♉, ♋, or ♑, surfeits from wrong and evil diet; the ☉ afflicted in ♉, and especially by ♃; a disease of the ☽, and afflictions to the ☽ at B., and by dir.; the ☽ afflicted in ♋ or ♎; the ☽ afflicted in ♊, or afflicting the hyleg therefrom; the ☽ in ♉ or ♎, ☌, or ill-asp. ♄ (or ☿ if he be of the nature of ♄) when first taken ill, or at decumbiture, and occasioned by high living and surfeits; ♄ afflicted in ♋; ♂ afflicted in ♊ or ♒; ♂ by periodic revolution to the ☌ or ill-asps. ♃ or the ☽; ♀ afflicted in ♋ or ♐; ♀ afflicted in ♎, from too much eating and drinking; ♀ afflicted at B., and to the ☌, P, or evil asp. the Asc. by dir.; ♀ in ♋ in the 6th H., afflicted, or afflicting the ☽ or Asc.; the Asc. to the ill-asps. ♀ by dir. (See Appetite, Degeneration; "Evil Diet" under Diet; Drink; "Excesses In" under Eating; Epicureans, Feasting; "Excesses In", "Rich Food", under Food; Gluttony; "High Living" under High; Intoxication, Over-Indulgence, Plethora, Redundant).

Blood—Surfeit Arising from Too Much Blood—♃ afflicted in ♎. (See "Too Much Blood" under Blood).

Congestion — Surfeits From — (See Congestion).

Death from Surfeits—The ☽ occi. at B., and afflicting the hyleg by dir., and according to her familiarity with the malefics. (See "Death" under Indiscretions).

Degeneration — Thru Surfeits — (See Degeneration).

Diet — Surfeits Arising from Wrong and Evil Diet—(See "Evil Diet" under Diet; "Excesses In", "Rich Food", "Sweets", under Food).

Disease — Arising from Surfeit — Denoted by ♃. (See Jupiter, Toxaemia, Tumors).

Drinking and Eating—Surfeits From —(See Diet, Drink, Eating, Food, Wine).

Dropsy from Surfeits — (See the Introduction under Dropsy).

Eating — Surfeits by Excesses In — (See "Excesses" under Eating).

Excess—Excesses—Surfeits and Diseases From—(See "Excesses In" under Eating, Food; Excess, Excesses, Gluttony).

Fevers—From Surfeits—(See "Fever" under Heart, Liver; "Feverish" under Lungs).

Food — Surfeits from Excesses In — (See "Excesses In" under Food).

Fullness — From Surfeits — (See "Engorgement" under Fullness; Plethora).

Functions—The Functions Disordered by Surfeits—(See "Over-Activity" under Functions).

Gluttony—(See "Big Appetite" under Appetite; Gluttony).

Gout—From Surfeits—The ☉ or ♃ afflicted in ♉, and usually from over-eating, and excess of rich food. (See "Rich Food" under Food; Gout).

Impure Blood—Caused by Surfeits—(See "Too Much Blood" under Blood; Impure).

Over-Functional Activity—From Surfeits—(See "Over-Activity" under Functions).

Plethora—From Surfeit—(See Plethora).

Puffing—Of the Body—(See Inflation, Plethora, Puffing).

Rheumatism—From Surfeits—(See "Tendency To" under Rheumatsm).

Rich Foods—Surfeits From—(See "Dainty", "Rich", under Food).

Stomach—Afflicted with Surfeits—(See "Surfeits" under Stomach).

Wine—Surfeits from Excessive Use of—(See Wine).

SURGEONS—Surgical—Surgery—♂ rules Surgeons and Surgical Operations.

Danger to Surgeons—The ☽ to the ☌ or P. Dec. Aldebaran by dir.; the M.C. to the ☌ ♂ if ♂ be afflicted at B.

Dealing with Surgeons—Good Time For—When the ☽ is applying to the good aspects ♂, but this is not a good time for a surgical operation. (See "Rules" under Operations).

Dishonest Surgeons—Tricky In Diagnosis—♅ or ♂ in ♏ or ♓, and especially if ♅ and ♂ form an evil asp. to each other at B.

Fame As Surgeon—♂ ✶ or △ the ☉ at B., and the stronger the position of ♂ the greater will be the success. (See "Honors" in this section).

Fortunate—As Surgeons—The ☉ Sig. in ♏; the ☽ Sig. ☌ ♂, and ♂ well-aspected by ♃; ♆ in good aspect ♂; ♃ Sig. ☌, ✶, or △ ♂; the 29° ♐ on the Asc. at B.; many planets in fiery signs, and especially if ♂ be strong, dignified, and well-aspected by the ☉, ☽, or ♃. (See "Good Surgeon", "Honors", in this section).

Good Surgeon—Makes a Good Surgeon—The ☉, ☽, or ♂ well-aspected in ♏; the ☽ Sig. ☌ ♂ and ♂ well-dignified; the ☽ on the Meridian, or coming to, and well-aspected by ♂; ♆ or ♅ in good aspect to ♂; ♃ Sig. ☌ ♂; ♃ in ♏, and especially when in ☌ or good asp. to ♂; ♂ strong at B., and well-dignified; ♂ in the 6th or 10th H., and well-aspected; ♂ well-aspected in ♍, ♏, or ♓; ♂ ruler of the horoscope; ♂ and ☿ together lords of the employment; ♂ ✶ or △ the ☉ at B., and especially when ♂ is otherwise strong; surgeons should have good aspects between the ☉, ♂, and ☿ to make good surgeons and be successful; ♂ ☌ ☿; ♂ in ♏ in the 10th H.; ♂ well-aspected in ♓, or ♂ in the 12th H., and especially in hospitals, prisons, or asylums; the ✶ or △ aspects of ♂, skillful in surgery; any aspect of ♂ to the ☽ or ☿; ♂ in good aspect to ♅; ♀ Sig. ☌ ♂ and ♂ well-dignified; ☿ and the Lights configurated with ♂; ☿ ☌ or good asp. ♂ at B.; ☿ joined with ♂ makes good surgeons; in Hor'y Q. ♂ Sig. of the party, or the Sig. in a fiery sign, or in ♏; born under ♏; the 6th face of ♎, the 1st face of ♌, or the 6th face of ♐ culminating on the M.C.; ruler of the employment in ♏, strong and well-aspected; the majority of planets in fiery signs at B. (See Barbers, Chemists; "Physicians" under Healers).

Honours—Promotion and Honours for Surgeons—Periods of Success for Surgeons—The ☉, ☽, or ♃ Sig., and to the good asps. ♂ by dir.; the ☉ to the ☌ or P. Dec. Aldebaran, surgeons gain distinction for a time; the ☉ in the 11th H. in ♈, well-aspected by ♂ at the Vernal, and lord of the year; the Prog. ☽ ✶ or △ ♂ if ♂ is well-aspected at B.; ♂ ✶ or △ the Asc. or M.C. by dir.; lord of the Asc. in his own dignities if he apply to ♂ exalted, and in an angle.

Horary Questions—In Hor'y Q. ♂ Sig. of the party, or the Sig. in a fiery sign, or in ♏, denotes a Surgeon, Chemist, or Physician..

Hospitals—Prisons and Asylums—Successful as Surgeon In—♂ well-aspected in ♓ or the 12th H. (See Hospitals; "Asylums" under Insanity; Prisons, Twelfth House).

Operations—The Best Time for Surgical Operations—(See "Rules" under Operations).

Periods of Success—For Surgeons—(See "Honours" in this section).

Study of Surgery—Inclined To—Any aspect of ♂ to the ☽ or ☿ inclines to the study of Medicine or Surgery.

Surgeon of the Body—(See Silica).

Unfeeling Surgeons—Cruel—♅ in ♉ or ♏ and □ ♂, or ♂ in ♉ or ♏ and □ ♅.

Unfortunate as Surgeons—♂ in a weak sign at B., and sorely afflicted by the ☉, ☽, and malefics, and tends to downfall or disgrace under the evil directions of ♂ to the Asc., M.C., ☉ or ☽ along thru life; an absence of the ☉, ☽, ♃, or ♂ in the ♏ sign at B., or strong ♂ influence in ♍, the 1st, 6th, 8th, or 12th H. at B. (See "Unfortunate" under Healers).

Vivisectionists—(See this subject).

SURLY—(See "Gruff" under Manners).

SURROUNDINGS—Much Affected By—The 4th face of ♎ on the Asc. (See Environment, External, Influenced, Negative Nature, Receptive, Susceptible).

SUSCEPTIBILITY—Susceptible—Idiosyncrasies—Predisposition—Receptivity—Sensitiveness, etc.—

Climate—Susceptibility to Changes In—(See Climate).

Cold or Colds—Susceptible To—(See Cold, Colds).

Contagious Diseases—Infectious Diseases—Susceptible To—(See Contagions, Epidemics, Infectious Diseases, Magnetism, Scorpio).

Disease—Susceptibility To—Predisposition To—(See Attracts; "Susceptibility" under Disease; Magnetism, Predisposed, Propensities; "Much Sickness" under Sickness; "Low" under Vitality; "Weak Body" under Weak).

External Influences—Susceptible To—(See Environment, External, Influenced; "Negative Nature" under Negative; Passive, Receptive).

Fever—(See "Susceptibility" under Fever).

Inflammation — (See "Susceptibility" under Inflammation).

Nervous Susceptibility—(See "Susceptibility" under Nerves).

Psychic Susceptibility — (See Clairvoyance, Emotions, Feelings, Hyperaesthesia, Hynotism, Magnetism, Mediumship, Psychic, Sensitives, Suggestion).

Women—More Susceptible to Disease and Outside Influences—(See "External Influences" under Women). For further study along this line see Diathesis, Flexible, Heredity, Idiopathy, Idiosyncrasies, Organic, Plastic, Structural.

SUSPENSIONS—

Animation — Suspended Animation — (See "Buried Alive" under Burial; "Suppressed" under Functions; Trance).

Breathing—(See "Suspension" under Breathing).

Digestion—(See "Stopped" under Digestion).

Functions—(See "Suppressed" under Functions).

Heart Action—(See "Stoppage" under Heart).

Stomach—(See "Stopped" under Digestion; "Obstructions" under Stomach). See Interrupted, Irregular, Obstructions, Retentions, Stoppages, Suppressions.

SUSPICION—Of Some Venereal Disease —(See Venereal).

SUSPICIOUS—♄ strong at B. tends to give a suspicious mind. (See Jealousy, Mistrustful; Scepticism; "Many Sorrows" under Sorrow).

SWALLOWING—Deglutition—Difficulty In—(See Deglutition).

Swallows Glass—Nails, etc.—Case—(See "Human Ostrich" under Human).

SWAMPS — Marshes — Ruled by the ☽. (See Dampness, Moisture, Moon).

SWARTHY — Swarthy Complexion — Swarthy Brown—(See "Swarthy" under Brown, Complexion).

SWEAT—Sudor—Sweating—Perspiration—Sweat is an excrementitious fluid and ruled by the ♏ sign. (See Excrement). It is also the work of the ☽, as the ☽ influences the fluids of the body. The ☉ exerts a sudorific action.

Anhidrosis — Anidrosis — (See "Lessened" in this section).

Axillae—Fetid Perspiration In—(See Axillae).

Bloody Sweat — (See Haematidrosis" in this section).

Bromidrosis — Fetid Perspiration — Caused by ♂ in signs; ♂ in ♎, fetid perspiration in axillae; ♂ in ♓, in feet. (See "Excessive" in this section; Axillae; "Bromidrosis" under Feet).

Chromidrosis — Colored Sweat — Observed in the attacks of Hysteria when the sweat may be blue, brown, yellow or red. Also in Jaundice the sweat may be yellow. (See Hysteria, Jaundice).

Colliquative Sweats—(See Phthisis).

Deficiency Of — (See "Lessened" in this section).

Diaphoretics — (See "Sudorifics" in this section).

Dysidrosis—Impaired Perspiration In Hands or Feet ♂ afflicted in ♍ or ♓. (See Dysidrosis; "Bromidrosis" in this section).

Excessive Sweating—Hyperidrosis—♂, a hot planet, in any sign, tends to more heat and sweating in the part of the body ruled by such sign, and the perspiration to be more fetid if confined. (See "Bromidrosis" in this section; "Night Sweats" under Phthisis).

Excrement—Sweat is an excrementitious fluid, ruled by the ♏ sign. The Menses and Urine also belong to this class. (See Excrement).

Feet — Fetid Perspiration In — (See "Bromidrosis", "Excessive", in this section).

Fetid Perspiration — (See "Bromidrosis", "Excessive", in this section).

Frequent Perspirings — The ☽ in ♊ under the Sun's beams, or ☌ ♅, ♄, or ♂ at decumbiture, or at the beginning of an illness, tends to frequent attacks of perspiration (Hor'y).

Haematidrosis — Menidrosis — Bloody Sweat — Caused by the extravasation of blood into the cells and ducts of the sweat glands, capillary hemorrhages of nervous origin, or may be a species of vicarious menstruation known as Menidrosis. The ♒ sign rules strongly over the nerves and blood, and ♅, ♄, or ♂ badly afflicted in this sign, and also afflictions in ♑, the sign which rules the surface, are causes of these conditions, and along with other influences which tend to great nervousness, anxiety, stress or strain.

Hands—(See "Dysidrosis" in this section).

Hyperidrosis — (See "Excessive" in this section).

Impaired Sweating—(See the various paragraphs in this section).

Lessened—Anidrosis—Diminuation or Absence of—Occurs during the high fevers of ♂. Also ♄ in ♏ may cause it by hindering the excretion of sweat in a chronic condition. (See "Obstructions" under Excretion; "High Fever" under Fever).

Menidrosis — (See Haematidrosis" in this section).

Night Sweats—(See Phthisis).

Profuse Sweating—(See "Excessive", "Night Sweats", in this section).

Sudorifics — Diaphoretics—Agents Inducing Sweating — ☉ remedies. (See Sudorific).

Suppression Of — (See "Lessened" in this section).

Vicarious—Vicarious Menses Thru the Sweat Glands — (See "Haematidrosis" in this section).

Violent Sweating—Unseasonable—The ☽ in ♈, □ or ☍ ♄ (or ☿ if he be of the nature of ♄) when first taken ill, or at decumbiture (Hor'y).

SWEET—

Sweetbread—(See Pancreas).

Sweet Signs—Of the Zodiac—The Airy Signs, ♊, ♎, ♒, and are said to give a sweet disposition. (See "Amiable" under Manner).

Sweet Things — Sweets — Comfits — Ruled by ♃, and ♃ rules all sweet things in merchandise. Also ruled by ♀, and especially in their use, and afflictions to ♃ and ♀ tend to over-indulgence in sweets, sugars, and pastries. (See "Sugar", "Sweets", under Food).

SWELLINGS — Swelling — Swollen — Tumefactions—Morbid Enlargements — Various planetary influences may cause swellings, according to causes, habits, inherent tendencies, and the parts of the body afflicted. The following subjects have to do with swellings, which see in the alphabetical arrangement when only listed here—

Abdominal Swellings — (See "Swellings" under Abdomen).

Abscesses; Ankles — (See "Swollen" under Ankles).

Arms — ♃ in signs which rule the Arms, Hands, Legs and Feet tends to swellings in these parts. (See "Swelling Of" under Feet; "Swelling In" under Hands; "Swellings In" under Legs).

Blisters; Bloating; Body Swollen — Puffy Body—The ☽ in ♓ and afflicted by the ☉ or ♂ when taken ill (Hor'y). (See Puffing; "Fleshy" in this section).

Boils; Carbuncles; Carcinoma; Cysts;

Death By—Caused by ♃.

Discutients — Resolvents — Agents Which Remove Swellings—♂ remedies. (See Discutients, Resolvents).

Distentions; Dropsy; Effusions;

Emphysema; Enlargements;

Extravasations—(See Effusions).

Face—(See "Bloated", "Swellings", under Face).

Feet—(See "Dropsy", "Swelling", under Feet; "Arms" in this section).

Fixed Points — Swellings At — ♀ diseases.

Flatulence; Fleshy—Fleshy and Swelling—♃ in watery signs; ♏ on the Asc.; ♓ on the Asc., fleshy and swelling. (See Bloating, Puffing; "Body Swollen" in this section).

Fluids — Swellings from Accumulations of — (See Accumulative, Cysts, Dropsy, Hydrocephalus, etc.).

Gas—Swellings By—(See Flatulence, Gas, Tympanites, etc.).

Glands — (See "Swellings" under Glands).

Gout; Hands — (See "Arms" in this section).

Head—(See "Swells" under Head).

Hips and Thighs — (See "Swellings" under Hips).

Hydrocele; Hydrocephalus;

Hydrothorax; Hyperaemia;

Incurable Swellings — Those Arising from Structural Defects and Incurable Diseases — (See Aneurysm, Apoplexy; "Tumor" under Brain; "Valves" under Heart; Incurable, Inflation, Malignant, Morbid, Ruptures, etc.).

Inflammations; Inflation; Jaws—(See "Swollen" under Jaws).

Knees — (See "Swellings In" under Knees).

Knots; Larynx—(See "Swollen" under Larynx).

Legs—(See "Arms" in this section).

Localized Swellings—(See Local).

Lower Parts — Swellings In — The ☽ afflicted in ♑, ♒, or ♓. (See "Swellings" under Ankles, Feet, Knees, Legs).

Neck — (See "Swellings In" under Neck; "Glandular Swellings" under Throat).

Nodules; Painful Swellings—(See Abscesses, Boils, Carbuncles; the subjects under Pain; "Mumps" under Parotid; Sore, Sores, Testes, Throat, Tonsils, etc.).

Plethora; Puffing Up—Of the Sinews of the Nerves — (See "Puffing" under Nerves; Puffing).

Puffy Body—(See "Body Swollen" in this section).

Remedy—For Swellings—(See Discutients, Resolvents).

Resolvents — An Agent to Reduce Swelling — (See Discutients, Resolvents).

Ruptures; Scrotum — Swelling In — (See Hydrocele, Scrotum, Testes, Varicocele, Varicose).

Secret Parts—(See "Swellings" under Secrets).

Sharp Pains By—Caused by ♂. (See "Pains" under Sharp).

Sinews — (See "Puffing Up" in this section).

Skin — (See Eruptions, Inflammation, Rashes; the various paragraphs under Skin).

Sore Parts—(See Sore).

Sores; Testes — (See "Swollen" under Testes).

Thighs—(See "Hips" in this section).

Throat — (See Diphtheria, Neck; "Glandular", "Swellings", under Throat; Tonsils).

Tonsils—(See "Tonsilitis" under Tonsils).

Treatment Of — (See Discutients, Resolvents).

Tubercles; Tumors; Ulcers;

Varicocele; Varicose Veins—(See Varicose).

Wind—In Stomach and Bowels—(See "Gas", "Wind", under Bowels; Flatulence; "Wind" under Stomach; Tympanites).

SWIFT DISEASES—Swift, Rapid, and Violent Fevers — Diseases tend to be swift and violent when ♂ is in the Asc., and death may follow if the ☉ and ☽, and their dispositors, be afflicted. (See Acute, Directions; "High" under Fever; Fierce, Fulminating, Pernicious, Quick, Rapid, Sharp, Severe, Vehement, Violent Diseases).

SWIMMING—

In the Head — (See Dizziness, Fainting, Vertigo).

In Water — Dangerous to Go Near Water—(See Bathing, Drowning).

SWINDLER—♄ Sig. □ or ☍ ☿, a swindler, cheat, or thief; ♂ Sig. in ♊, a mere swindler, but the good aspects of the ☉, ♃, or ♀ mitigate the evil; ☿ Sig. ☌

♂. (See Cheating, Deceitful, Dishonest, Forgers, Gambling, Liars, Pettifogging, Shrewd, Thieves, etc.).

SWINE—Pigs—Hogs—The interest of the native in hogs, swine, sheep, small animals, etc., for good or ill, profit or loss, is denoted by the 6th H. (See "Small Animals" under Animals; Hogs, Sheep, Sixth House).

Performing Pig—(See Hogs).

Resembles Swine—(See "Animal Forms" under Monsters).

SWOLLEN—(See Swellings).

SWOONINGS—Faintings—Sudden Swoonings—(See "Falling Fits" under Fainting).

SWORD—

Death By—Injury By—Severe Stabs or Cuts—The ☉ or ☽ ori., and afflicted by ♄ or ♂; ♂ disposes to; ♂ afflicting the hyleg by dir., and holding the dominion of death, and especially when the radical map shows a violent death; the ☽ Sig. □ or ☍ ♂; in Hor'y Q. lord of the 1st H., or the ☽ in ♉ or ♌, and ☍ ♂, slain by the sword, or in a quarrel; the 5° ♎ on the Asc. (See Contests, Cuts, Duels, Murdered, Quarrels, War).

Eyes—Injury to the Eyes by a Stroke, Blow, the Sword, or Burning—The ☉ in the Asc. or M.C., ♂ rising before him, and the ☉ ☌ or ☍ the ☽, and may cause blindness; the ☉ in an angle, in the same sign with the ☽, or in ☍, and with ♄ and ♂ ori. to the ☉, ascending before him, and ♄ and ♂ occi. of the ☽; the ☉ or ☽ afflicted by ♂ by dir., and the Lights with Nebulous Stars at B.; the ☽ to the ☌, P., or evil asp. ♂ by dir., and the ☽ afflicted at B. (See "Burning" under Blindness; "Hurts", "Injuries", under Eyes).

SYBARITES—(See Epicureans).

SYCOSIS—(See "Barber's Itch" under Barbers).

SYMBOLS—Signs—

Children—(See "Symbols Of" under Children).

Death—(See "Symbols Of" under Death).

Disease—(See "Indicators Of" under Disease).

Health—Signs of Good or Bad Health—(See "Signs Of" under Health).

Signs of Zodiac—Symbols of—(See each of the Signs in the alphabetical arrangement, as Aries, Taurus, etc.).

SYMMETRY OF FORM—(See Beautiful, Comely, Handsome, Harmonious, Well-Formed, Well-Proportioned, etc.).

SYMPATHY—Sympathetic—

Cured by Sympathy—Paracelsus was the first Physician to suggest giving Similars, and drugs to produce symptoms similar to those of the malady. Hahnemann afterwards demonstrated this principle in Homeopathy. Hippocrates also observed that diseases were sometimes cured by similars. The Astrological selection of remedies was based principally upon Sympathy and Antipathy. The diseases of ♄ were treated by the remedies of ♂, which is by sympathy, or ♂ diseases by ♄ remedies, as ♄ and ♂, both being malefics, work together in greater sympathy. Also ♄ diseases are treated by ♄ remedies; ♂ diseases by ♂ remedies; ♃ diseases by ♃ or ♀ remedies, etc., which is treatment by sympathy. It was also believed by the Ancients that every planet was capable of curing its own diseases, and by its own remedies. Thus remedies of the ☉ and ☽ were used to cure Eye Diseases. Diseases of the Spleen were cured by ♄ remedies; of the Liver, by ♃ remedies, etc. Dr. Broughton, in his book, "The Elements of Astrology", on page 241, gives a Table of the Friendships and Enmities of the Planets. Planets which rule opposite Signs of the Zodiac are not in sympathy. Thus ♌, ruled by the ☉, is in ☍ to ♒, ruled by ♄; the ♒ sign, ruled by the ☽, is in ☍ to ♑, ruled by ♄, and by this rule we can know that ♄ is opposed to the ☉ and ☽, and not sympathetic with them, and that the diseases of ♄ can be mitigated by remedies of the ☉ or ☽. The ♈ and ♌ signs are in △ aspect, and in harmony, and ♂, the ruler of ♈, is friendly with the ☉, and the ☉ has his exaltation in ♈, the sign of ♂, etc. Thus when the diseases of the ☉ are treated by ♂ remedies, it is by sympathy, or vice versa. (For further influences along this line see Antipathy, Colors, Cure, Drugs, Harmony, Herbs, Hippocrates, Homeopathy, Medicines, Ointments, Opposites, Paracelsus, Polarity, Praeincipients, Remedies, Rhythm, Signature, Treatment, etc.).

Disease—Disease Caused by Sympathy—There is an analogy and sympathy between each Sign of the Zodiac and some definite zone of the body. If the afflicting planet governs the part diseased or afflicted, it is caused by sympathy. If the disease is in the bones, and ♄ is the cause of it, it is by sympathy, as ♄ rules the bones. If the disease is in the Arteries, Veins, and Circulation, it is usually caused by ♃ or ♀, the rulers of these matters, etc. If by the ☉, diseases of the Brain, Eyes, or Heart, with which the ☉ has affinity. (See Attracts, Complications; "Complications" under Disease; Magnetic, Polarity, Relapses, Zones).

Disposition—Sympathetic Disposition—(See "Nature" in this section).

Expression—A Sympathetic Expression On the Face—Born under ♃. (See Honest, Humane, Kind, Sincere, Smiling, etc.).

Irritation—Sympathetic Irritation—A ☿ disease and affliction.

Lactation—Case of Sympathetic Lactation—(See Lactation).

Narrow Sympathies—Cruel—Not Humane—(See Narrow).

Nature—A Sympathetic Nature and Disposition—Born under ♃ and ♃ strong at B.; the 5th face of ♌ on the Asc.; ♒ on the Asc., and with the ☉, ☽, and several planets in ♒. (See "Expression" in this section).

Signs of Zodiac—The Signs In Sympathy with Each Other—The Signs in ⚹ and △ relation to each other are in sympathy, or harmony. In matters of health and disease all the fixed signs are in sympathy, and form the Fixed Cross of ♉, ♌, ♏, and ♒, and afflictions in any of these signs tend to affect by sympathy all the parts, or organs, ruled by these signs, which is the fundamental cause of complications in disease. Thus afflictions in ♉ or ♏ tend to affect the throat and sex organs. So with the Cardinal and Common Signs. Afflictions in ♈, ♋, ♎, and ♑ tend to affect the Head, Stomach, Kidneys, and Skin. Afflictions in the Common Sign Cross, ♊, ♍, ♐, and ♓, to affect the Lungs, Bowels, Thighs and Feet. (See Complications).

Sympathetic Nervous System — This System is ruled by the ☽, ♄, ♂, and the ♍ Sign. It automatically takes care of the process of digestion ruled by ♍, and also pertains to the care of indvidual preservation. It begins with ♈, the Cerebral Pole of Paracelsus, and ends with ♏, the Genital Pole of Paracelsus. The Peripheral Sympathetic Nerves are ruled by ♄ and ♑. (See Cerebral, Genitals; "Pathological Action" under Mars). The ☽ Group of Herbs, by their physiological action, tend to act upon, and to especially affect the Sympathetic Nervous System. This system is also called the Involuntary Nervous System, and rules over the involuntary functions and actions of the body, such as Digestion, the Heart Action, etc. (See Cardia).

SYMPTOMS — Symptoms In Disease — The word "Symptoms" is not mentioned much in the Textbooks of Astrology, as Astrology deals more with the Causes and Philosophy of Disease rather than Symptoms. However, I have run across the following influences, which have been referred to as Symptoms—

Consumption — (See "Symptoms Of" under Consumption).

Peculiar Symptoms—In Disease—The ☽ ☌, □, or ☍ ♄, ♅, or ♂, or passing their place at B., or at the beginning of an illness, and especially when the ☽ is afflicted by ♅. (See "Course of Disease" under Peculiar).

Symptoms of Spleen—(See "Symptoms Of" under Consumption). For the symptoms which may attend the various diseases, and which may be caused by the planetary aspects and afflictions, see in the alphabetical arrangement the subject you have in mind.

SYNCOPE—Swooning or Fainting—(See Fainting).

SYNOCHA—(See "Continuous Fevers" under Fever).

SYNOVIAL—Synovial Fluid—Synovial Membrane—The Synovial Fluid is ruled by the ☽, and is also under the internal rulership of the ♓ Sign, and lubricates the joints. The Synovial Serum is connected with the ♓ Sign, and the ☉ and ☽ acting thru ♓ tend to affect the Synovial System. (See Ligaments).

Bursitis — In the Knee Joint — (See Bursa).

Hardening — Of the Synovial Membrane—Caused by ♄, and making the joints, limbs, and spine rigid. (See "Hardening" under Joints).

Hips and Thighs—Drying Up of Synovial Fluid In Joints of—♄ afflicted in ♐. (See "Synovial" under Hips; Lubrication).

Inflammation—Of the Synovial Membrane—Synovitis—Caused by ♂, and in the part of the body ruled by the sign he is in at B.; ♂ in ♐, in hips and thighs; ♂ in ♑, in the knees, etc.

Joints — Lack of Synovial Fluid In Joints — Drying Up of — ♄ influence. (See "Hardening" under Joints; Lubrication).

Knees—Bursitis In—Inflammation In —(See Bursa; "Inflammation", "Joint", "Synovitis", under Knees).

Lack of Synovial Fluid—In the Joints —Drying Up of—The ☽ afflicted in ♑; the work of ♄, as ♄ tends to dry up the bodily fluids. (See "Drying Up" under Fluids; Lubrication).

Synovial Troubles—The ☽ afflicted in ♑.

Synovitis — (See "Inflammation" in this section).

Thickening—Of the Synovial Membrane—A ♄ disease, and caused by retention of wastes. (See Hardening, Retention, Thickening).

Vertebrae — Lack of Synovial Fluid Between the Vertebrae—♄ afflicted in ♌. (See "Diseases" under Vertebrae).

SYPHILIS — Lues — Syphilitic Blood — Pox—A ♀ disease, and caused by afflictions to ♀; ♀ denotes death by; ♀ afflicted in ♏; the ☽ in ♏ and afflicted by the ☉ or ♂ when taken ill (Hor'y); the ☽ in the 6th H., and afflicting ♀ in ♏; the ☽ to the ☌ or □ ♂ by dir.; ♅ in ♎, and with venereal eruptions on the skin; ♅ in ♏ and in □ or ☍ ♀; ♂ in ♎ when ♂ is the afflictor in the disease, Lues may be suspected; a ♎ disease and afflictions in ♎; when on the Asc., ♎ gives a milder form of syphilis; a ♏ disease and afflictions in ♏, and affecting also the throat (♉) by reflex action, and causing syphilitic ulcers of the throat; ♏ on the Asc. tends to the worst form of syphilis; a ♓ disease and afflictions in ♓, and tends to affect the Matrix and Secrets where syphilitic contagion is involved; caused by Fixed Stars of the nature of ♀; Subs at KP and PP.

Chancre — Called "Hard Chancre" to distinguish it from the Soft Chancre of Gonorrhoea. The Chancre is the primary sore, or ulcer, which may appear on the Privates, or other parts of the body in syphilis, and is caused by the foregoing influences.

Death by Syphilis — ♂ afflicting the hyleg, or Giver of Life, by dir.; ♀ denotes death by; ♀ afflicted in ♏ in the 8th H., holding the dominion of death, and afflicting the hyleg. (See Gonorrhoea, Private Diseases, Scandalous Diseases, Venereal).

Eruptions — Syphilitic Eruptions On the Skin — H afflicted in ♎, and also afflictions in ♎, and due to greater disturbance of the action of the kidneys.

Rectum — (See "Syphilis" under Rectum).

Throat — Syphilitc Ulcers In — ♂ afflicted in ♏; afflictions in ♉ or ♏.

SYSTEM—The System—Systemic—The Constitution—The Physical Body—

Arterial System—(See Arteries, Blood, Circulation).

Assimilative System—(See Assimilation).

Cleansing—Of the System—(See Cleansing).

Clogging—Of the System—(See Clogging, Retentions, Suppressions, Wastes).

Cold—The System Affected Generally with Cold—(See "Body" under Cold).

Decayed System—(See "Death" under Decay).

Deranged System—(See "Disordered" in this section).

Digestive System—(See Digestion, Gastric, Indigestion, Stomach, etc.).

Disordered System—Deranged System—Physical Disorders—The ☉ in the 6th H. in cardinal signs, and afflicted by the ☽ or ♄; the ☉ to the ill-aspects ♄, ♃, or the ☽ in the radix; the ☽ to the bad aspects ♄, ♃, or ♀ by dir.; ♄, ♅, or ♆ in ♍, and afflicting the ☉ or ☽; ♄ or ♃ in tne 6th H. in a cardinal sign, and afflicted by the ☉ or ☽; the appearance of Comets tends to a deranged system and many evils upon Mankind. (See Deranged, Disease, Disordered; "Bad" under Health; Ill-Health; "Much Sickness" under Sickness; "Low" under Vitality; "Weak Body" under Weak).

Dry System—(See "Body" under Dry).

Excretory System—(See Elimination, Excretion).

Females—Regularity of the System In—(See "Functions In" under Females; "Females" under Regularity).

Fluidic System—(See Fluids).

Fullness—Of the System—(See "System" under Fullness).

Functional System—(See Functions).

Glandular System—(See Glands).

Hot System—(See "Animal Heat", "Excessive Bodily Heat", under Heat).

Impurities—Of the System—(See Elimination, Excretion, Faeces, Impure, Sweat, Urine, Wastes, etc.).

Inactive State—Of the System—(See Apathy, Dull, Inactive, Inertia, Lassitude, Lethargy, Listless, etc.).

Invigorated System—Strong System—(See "Active Body" under Active; "Abundance of Energy" under Energy; "Abundance of Health" under Health; Invigoration; "Good" under Resistance, Stamina, Tone, Vitality; Robust, Ruddy, Rugged; "Body" under Strength, Strong; "Vigorous Body" under Vigor).

Irregularities—Systemic Irregularities—(See Irregularities).

Lymphatic System—(See Lymphatic).

Moist System—(See "Bodily Temperament" under Moisture).

Muscular System—(See Muscles).

Nervous System—(See Nerves).

Preservation—Of the System—(See Conservation, Nutrition, Preservation).

Readaptation—In the System—(See Readaptation).

Regularity—Of the System—(See Regularity).

Relaxation—In the System—(See Relaxation).

Vascular System—(See Arteries, Blood, Capillaries, Vascular, Vaso, Veins, Vessels).

Venous System—(See Veins).

Vitality—Of the System—(See Vitality).

Wastes—Of the System—(See "Impurities" in this section).

Wasting—Of the System—(See Consumptions, Emaciation; "Malnutrition" under Nutrition; Phthisis, Tabes, Tuberculosis, Wasting, etc.).

Weak System—(See Weak). For other subjects along this line, and not listed here, look in the alphabetical arrangement for what you have in mind.

SYSTOLE—The New Moon is the Lunar Systole. (See "New Moon" under Moon).

SYZYGES—The Times of the ☌ and ☍ of Planets. Also the New and Full Moon, or the ☌ and ☍ of the ☉ and ☽.

T

TABES—Tabefactions—Gradual and Progressive Emaciation—The ☽ afflicted in ♓; Subs at SP and KP. (See Atrophy, Consumptions, Emaciation, Lean; "Progressive Muscular Atrophy" under Muscles; "Malnutrition" under Nutrition; "A Living Skeleton" under Skeleton; Thin, Wasting, etc.).

TACHYCARDIA—(See this subject under Heart).

TACITURN—Habitually Silent and Reserved—Not Inclined to Converse—♄ influence, and ♄ strong at B. (See Grave; "Taciturn" under Manner, Speech; Melancholic, Recluse, Renunciation, Reserved, Retiring, Seclusive, Serious, Solitude; "Refuses to Talk", "Taciturn", under Speech).

TACT—Tactful—(See "Good Judgment" under Judgment).

TAENIA—Tenia—A Parasitic Worm—Cestode—(See Cestode, Parasites, Tapeworm, Worms).

TAKING COLD—(See "Taking Cold" under Colds).

TALENTS—

Good Talents—Talented—(See Genius; "Great Ability" under Great).

Perverted Talents—(See Cheating, Criminal, Dishonest, Gambling, Pettifogging, Thieves, etc.).

Unused Talents—(See Dull, Idle, Improvident, Inactive, Indifferent, Lazy, Listless, Negative Nature, Passive, Procrastination, Slovenly, Vagabond, Wanderer, etc.).

TALIPES—Talipes Varus—Club Foot—(See "Club Feet" under Feet).

TALISMANS—(See Amulets).

TALK—Speech—(See "Talk", "Talking to Oneself", under Speech; Tongue, Voice).

TALL BODY—High Stature—♅ and ☿ lengthen the body, and make taller, and especially when rising in the Sign they rule. Uranus on the Asc. tends to tallness and the true Uranians are usually very tall people. The tallest people, and Giants, usually have the ♐ sign upon the Asc. at B. The ♌ sign rising is the next tallest. The fiery and airy signs upon the Asc. give a tall person, while the earthy and watery signs produce short people. For the general influences producing a tall body see "Tall Body" in this section.

Abnormally Tall—(See Giants; "Abnormal Growth" under Growth; "Above Average Height" under Height).

Bones — Large-Boned — (See "Large" under Bones).

Commanding and Tall — (See Commanding).

Compact and Tall—(See Compact).

Corpulent and Tall—(See Corpulent).

Elegant and Tall — (See "Tall and Elegant" under Elegant).

Enlarged Body — (See "Body" under Enlarged).

Erect and Tall—(See Erect).

Fair and Tall—(See Fair).

Fat and Tall — (See "Tall and Fat" under Fat).

Fine and Tall — (See "Body" under Fine).

Fleshy and Tall—(See "Fleshy Body" under Fleshy).

Forehead — A Deep and Tall Forehead—(See "Deep" under Forehead).

Full-Bodied and Tall — (See "Body" under Full).

Giants; Graceful and Tall — (See Graceful).

Growth — (See "Abnormal" under Growth).

Hairy and Tall — (See "Body" under Hair).

Handsome and Tall—(See "Tall and Handsome" under Handsome).

Height—(See "Above Average" under Height).

High Stature — (See Giants; "Tall Body" in this section).

Inclined to be Tall — ♍ influence; ♍ on the Asc.

Large and Tall—(See "Large Bones" under Bones; "Tall, Large and Strong" under Large).

Large-Boned and Tall—(See "Large" under Bones).

Long Body—(See "Body" under Long; "Tall" in this section).

Plump and Tall—(See Plump).

Rather Tall — ♒ influence; ♒ on the Asc., rather tall, and never short.

Slender and Tall — (See "Tall and Slender" under Slender).

Smooth, Tall Body—(See Smooth).

Spare and Tall—(See Spare).

Stature Above Average—(See "Above Average" under Height).

Stout and Tall—(See Stout).

Straight and Tall—(See Straight).

Strong and Tall — ♃ or the ☽ in ♌, partile the Asc. (See "Body" under Strong).

Swarthy and Tall — ♂ in ♈, partile the Asc. (See "Swarthy" under Complexion).

Tall Body — High Stature — In this paragraph is given a summary of the influences causing tallness, and with the accompanying characteristics — The SUN in ♊ or ♐, tall and well-proportioned; the ☉ strong and dignified, tall, fleshy, strong, and of large frame; the ☉ in ♍, partile the Asc., tall, slender, and well-proportioned; the ☉ in ♎, partile the Asc., tall, erect, straight, and upright; the MOON in ♊, partile the Asc., tall, well-made, well-formed, comely, and upright; the ☽ in ♌ in the Asc., or partile the Asc., tall, of fine proportions, strong, and large-boned; the ☽ in ♍, partile the Asc., tall and rather ruddy; the ☽ in ♎, partile the Asc., tall and of pleasing form; the ☽ in her increase gives a tall, fat, plump, and full body; the ☽ ori. gives a body more tall, corpulent, and smooth; URANUS on the Asc.; SATURN in ♊, in good asp. the Asc., tall and well-proportioned; ♄ in ♍, partile the Asc., tall and thin; ♄ in ♎, partile the Asc.; ♄ ori. makes the body taller than when he is occidental, and also with a stout and hairy body; born under JUPITER, tall, well-made, and upright; ♃ indicates a tall and commanding body; ♃ in ♊, partile the Asc., rather tall; ♃ in ♌, partile the Asc., tall, strong, well-made, and large-boned; ♃ in ♎, partile the Asc., tall, elegant, and handsome; ♃ in ♐, partile the Asc., tall, fine, upright, and well-made; MARS in ♈, partile the Asc., and ori., tall and less swarthy; ♂ in ♊, partile the Asc., tall, well-made, and well-formed; ♂ in ♎, partile the Asc., tall, commanding, and well-proportioned; ♂ in ♐, partile the Asc., tall, compact, and well-made; ♂ in ♒; partile the Asc., tall, well-set, and corpulent; VENUS or ☿ in their own signs or exaltation give tallness; the ⚹ and △ aspects of ♀ give a tall and elegantly made body; ♀ in ♊, partile the Asc., tall, slender, but well-made; ♀ in ♌, partile the Asc., tall, well-boned; the ☽ in ♍, partile the Asc. tall made, and well-formed; ♀ in ♍, partile the Asc., tall and well-proportioned; ♀ in ♐, partile the Asc., well-made, tall, and well-formed; born under ♀ and ♀ ori., tall, handsome, elegantly made, erect, straight, and upright; MERCURY indicates tall and thin persons; ☿ in ♊, partile the Asc., tall, well-made and upright; ☿ in ♎, partile the Asc., tall, handsome, and not thin; ☿ in ♐, partile the Asc., tall, well-shaped, but rather spare and large-boned; ♊ on the Asc., tall, erect, straight, fair, well-formed; ♌ on the Asc., commanding and tall; ♍ on the Asc., compact, well-made, well-proportioned, rather slender, and inclined to be tall; ♎ on the Asc., tall, beautiful, graceful, handsome, elegantly made, well-framed; ♎ on the Asc. and ♀ ori., tall, straight, upright, and elegantly made; the last few degrees of ♎ rising tend to a shorter and stouter body due to the nearness of the ♏ influence; ♐ on the Asc., tall, strong, well-made, well-formed, and this sign on the Asc. produces the tallest people of all signs, as a rule; ♒ on the Asc., strong, healthy, robust, well-set, and rather tall. (See the various paragraphs in this article).

Tallest People—♐ on the Asc.

Thin and Tall—(See "Thin and Tall" under Thin).

Upright and Tall — (See Erect, Straight, Upright).

Well-Formed and Tall — (See Well-Formed).

Well-Made and Tall — (See Well-Made).

Well-Proportioned and Tall — (See Well-Proportioned).

Well-Set and Tall—(See Well-Set).

Well-Shaped and Tall — (See Well-Shaped).

TAN COMPLEXION —Tanned —Tawny — Bronzed — Brownish Color — (See "Tan" under Complexion).

TAPEWORM—One of the Cestoda—A Parasitic Worm In the Bowels—♀ or ☿ afflicted in ♍; afflictions in ♍; Subs at SP (8D), and at PP (2L). (See Worms).

TAR — Pix Liquida — Obtained by the destructive distillation of the wood of the Pine Tree. Pine Trees, Cone-bearing Trees, are ruled by ♂. Turpentine is also procured from the Yellow Pine, and other varities of Pine. The blistering, caustic, counter-irritant, and penetrating qualities of Tar Preparations, and of Turpentine, are qualities of Mars Remedies. (See Rubefacients).

Coal Tar—(See Xylene).

TARSUS — The Bones of the Instep of the Feet — Are under the structural rulership of the ♓ Sign, and correspond to the Carpal Bones in the Hands, ruled by ♍. (See Feet, Hands, Wrists).

TARTAR—On the Teeth—(See "Tartar" under Teeth).

TASTE—Gustatory—The Sense of Taste —The Sense by which Savors are Perceived — Ruled by ♂ and the ♉ sign. The Gustatory Process is ruled by ♉. The Hebrew Letter "Tzaddi", which is connected with the ♒ Sign, is also connected with the Sense of Taste. (See Gustativeness).

TASTES—

Abnormal Tastes—Along Food Lines — (See "Tastes", "Unnatural", under Food).

Appetites—Peculiar Tastes and Appetites — (See Appetites; "Peculiar" under Food; "Appetites" under Peculiar).

Clothing — Dress — Peculiar Tastes In —(See "Peculiar" under Dress).

Food—(See "Peculiar Tastes", "Sugar", "Sweets", under Food).

Perverted Tastes — ♆ afflicted in the 1st or 12th H.; ♅ ruler of the horoscope, and afflicted; ♀ ruler of the horoscope, and afflicted by malefics. (See Cravings, Depraved, Drink; "Per-

verted Tastes" under Food; Narcotics, Perversions).

Refined Tastes—Born under the Airy Signs. (See Genteel; "Elegant" under Manner; "Elegant Mind" under Mind; Refined).

Strange Tastes — And Fancies — (See "Distempered Fancies" under Fancies).

TAURUS—The Second Sign of the Zodiac, and ruled by ♀, and also affiliated with the 2nd H. This is the night Sign of ♀, and ♎ is the day Sign of ♀. The ☽ has her exaltation in ♉, and ♂ his detriment. Taurus is the Sign opposite to ♏, and is supplemental to the ♏ sign, and for this reason planets in either of these signs tend to affect the throat and sex organs, as this sign represents the sex organs, along with the ♏ sign. Taurus is the sign of "The Bull", and is symbolized by the Bull, and the sign partakes much of the animal nature of the Bull, being stubborn, obstinate, and easily maddened, as a rule. Also being the sign of ♀, the ♉ people have their artistic and musical side, and also strong desires for pleasure, gluttony, and excesses, which makes this the sign for Gout, Rheumatism, and earlier death thru over-eating, and the excessive use of rich foods. Statistics show that ♉ people are averse to taking baths, and cold baths especially. Taurus is a fixed sign, feminine, negative, cold, dry, bestial, brutish, hurtful, four-footed, animal, commanding, crooked, earthy, even, fruitful, hoarse, luxurious, melancholic, nocturnal, northern, vernal, vital, unfortunate, and a sign of short ascension. It is rather fruitful, belonging to ♀, one of the Givers of Children. The ♉ and ♏ signs are the strongest of the negative signs, and these signs upon the Asc. at B. give considerable vitality, and are next to the fiery and airy signs in degree of vitility. Being cold and dry the ♉ sign requires some energizing from without. Taurus is influenced by all the Fixed Signs, and belongs to the Fixed Sign Cross of ♉, ♌, ♏, and ♒, and planets in these signs at B. tend to affect all the organs and parts ruled by these signs, as the Throat, Heart, Sex Organs and Nature, and the Blood. Planets in these signs also tend to make disease more stubborn, enduring and permanent, and an afflicting planet in one of these signs at the beginning of an illness tends to keep the disease going until the planet changes signs, and enters a common sign. The ♉ people have a great fear of disease, and should never be told anything discouraging about their case when sick, as they are very susceptible to suggestion. They hold onto disease, and also tend to bring disease upon themselves due to their strong animal appetites, and tendency to excesses, and to suffer from Impure Blood, Gout, Rheumatism, and end with Paralysis or Heart Trouble. They are usually a materialistic class of people, earth-bound, covetous, of good business abilities, and the wealth of the world is largely in their hands. The ☽ well-aspected in ♉ is strong, and tends to regular functions, methodical habits, and good health. This sign has affinity with the Ears, Tongue, Bladder, and Sex Organs. The body given by ♉ is much like that of the ♍ sign. Taurus gives a strong neck and shoulders, and often stooped; full nostrils and thick lips, pensive brows, wavy or curling hair, dark eyes, full and broad forehead, heavy jaws, and a thick neck. The Colors ruled by this sign are red, and red mixed with citrine, and white mixed with lemon. For Countries ruled by this sign see "Taurus Sign" under Nations. The Pathological Qualities of this sign are anger, brooding, love of luxury, excessive stubbornness, and uncontrolled emotions. The Organ of Coordination is situated in ♉. (See Coordination). Also the Larynx, situated in ♉, was originally built up by the ♍ sign, and taken from ♍, and this is the reason why the voice and throat are so quickly affected by sex changes, as at puberty, or by sex diseases, as in the throat ulcers of syphilis. (See Larynx, Puberty, Voice).

TAURUS RULES—See the following subjects in the alphabetical arrangement—Arbor Vitae; Arteries and Veins of the Neck and Throat; Atlas Vertebra; Axis Vertebra; Base of the Brain; Beard; Belladonna; Bladder (has affinity with); Blood Vessels (Minor Blood Vessels of the Neck); Bones of the Neck; Brain (Base of); Carotid Arteries; Cerebellum; Cervical Nerves and Vertebrae; Chin, and Beard of Chin; Colors — White mixed with Lemon — Red mixed with Citrine; Coordinated Action (Organ of); Countries (see Nations); Drugs (Belladonna, Sodium Sulphate); Ears (has special affinity with); Eustachian Tubes; External Carotid Arteries; Externally rules the neck, throat, and lower back part of the head, the occipital region; Fear of Sickness; Functions, and Disorders of the Functions when the ☽ is afflicted in ♉; Generative Organs (♉ represents these organs, along with ♍); Glands (the Parotids and Salivary Glands); Gullet; Gustatory Process; Head (lower back part of, and Occiput); Internally rules the Gullet, Larynx and Cerebellum; Jaw (Lower Jaw); Jugular Veins; Larynx; Lower Jaw and Lower Teeth; Neck (Bones of, Region of, Cervical Nerves of, Blood Vessels of, Carotid Arteries, Jugular Veins, Cervical Vertebrae); Nerves (the Cervical Nerves); Occipital Region; Occiput; Oesophagus (upper part of); Palate; Parotids; Passages Thru the Throat; Pharynx; Process (the Gustatory Process); Region of the Neck; Salivary Glands; Sex Organs (by reflex action to ♍); Sodium Sulphate; Structurally Rules the Cervical Vertebrae; Taste (Sense of); Teeth (Lower Teeth); Throat and All Passages Thru the Throat); Thyroid Gland and Cartilage; Tissues of the Throat; Tongue (has affinity with); Tonsils; Trachea; Tubes (Eustachian); Uvula; Veins of the Throat; Vertebrae (Cervical); Vessels (the Blood Vessels of the Neck, Carotid Arteries, Jugular Veins, Minor Blood Vessels, etc.); Vocal Cords and Vocal Organs; Windpipe.

TAURUS DISEASES—And Afflictions —The ☽ and the Benefics when in ♉, and well-aspected, tend to give greater immunity against diseases of the throat and neck, but the presence of malefics, or any planet afflicted in this sign, and also afflicted in the 2nd H., tend to disorders of the throat, neck, larynx, vocal cords, etc. The following subjects have to do with the diseases and afflictions presided over by the Taurus Sign. See these subjects in the alphabetical arrangement when only listed here—

Abscess — Of the Throat or Neck — (See "Abscess" under Neck, Throat).

Angina; Aphonia — (See this subject under Voice).

Apoplexy; Bladder Disorders — (See Bladder).

Bronchial Consumption — (See Bronchial).

Bronchocele—(See Goiter).

Collapse—Sudden Collapse—(See Collapse).

Constipation; Consumption—Bronchial and Laryngeal — (See Bronchial, Larynx).

Coordination—Disorders of Organ of —(See Coordination, Incoordination).

Cough; Countries under Taurus—Afflictions to People and Countries under the Rule of Taurus — Comets appearing in ♉; total eclipses of the ☉ or ☽ in ♉. (See Comets, Eclipses; "Taurus Rules" under Nations).

Croup; Death—♉ denotes death from Putrid Sore Throat. (See "Putrid" under Throat).

Defluxions of Rheum — Discharges of Rheum—(See Rheum; "Rheum" under Throat).

Diet—Disease from Erroneous Diet—(See "Evil Diet" under Diet).

Discharges—Of Phlegm—Of Rheum—(See Phlegm, Rheum).

Diphtheria; Ear Disorders — (See Ears).

Epistaxis — (See this subject under Nose).

Erratic Movements — (See "Movements" under Erratic; Incoordination).

Fluxes of Rheum — Falling Into the Throat—(See "Rheum" under Throat).

Functions — (See "Irregular" under Functions).

Glandular Swelling — In the Neck — (See "Glands" under Neck).

Goiter; Gout; Guillotine—Death By— (See Guillotine).

Halter—Death By—(See Halter).

Hanging—Death By—(See Hanging).

Heart Trouble—(See "Heart Trouble" under Heart).

Hoarseness—(See Larynx).

Impure Blood—(See Impure).

Incoordination; Inflammation—Of the Throat — (See "Inflammation" under Throat).

Irregular Functions—(See "Irregular" under Functions).

King's Evil—(See Scrofula).

Laryngitis—(See Larynx).

Melancholy; Menses Irregular — (See Menses).

Mumps—(See Parotid).

Neck — Various Disorders of — (See Neck).

Nose Bleed—(See "Epistaxis" under Nose).

Obscure Diseases—(See Obscure).

Occipital Region—Occiput—Disorders of—(See Occipital).

Pains—In the Neck and Throat—(See "Pains In" under Neck).

Palate—Disorders of—(See Palate).

Paralysis; Parotiditis—(See "Mumps" under Parotid).

Pharyngitis—(See Pharynx).

Phlegm—Discharges of—(See Phlegm).

Poisonings—Septic Poisoning In the Throat—(See "Septic" under Throat).

Polypus; Putrid Sore Throat — (See "Putrid" under Throat).

Quinsy—(See "Quinsy" under Tonsils).

Rheum — Discharges of — Fluxes of — Defluxions of—Rheum In the Throat— (See Rheum; "Rheum" under Throat).

Rheumatism; Scrofula — Of the Neck —(See "Scrofula" under Neck).

Septic Poisonings—(See "Septic" under Throat).

Sore Throat — (See "Purtid", "Sore Throat", under Throat).

Strangulation; Sudden Collapse—(See Collapse).

Suffocation; Swellings—(See "Glandular", "Swellings", under Throat; "Tonsilitis" under Tonsils).

Syphilis — In the Throat — (See "Throat" under Syphilis).

Throat — Various Disorders of — (See Throat).

Tonsilitis—(See Tonsils).

Tumors — Of the Neck or Throat — (See "Tumors" under Neck, Throat).

Ulcerated Throat — (See "Ulcerated" under Throat).

Venereal Diseases—(See Venereal).

Vocal Cords — Voice — Disorders of — (See Larynx, Voice).

Wens — In the Neck — (See Wens). See the Articles on Fixed Signs, Scorpio, Second House).

TAVERNS — Saloons — Ruled by the Fifth House.

Brawling In—♀ Sig. ☌ ♂; ♀ ill-dignified at B.; ♀ afflicted in the 5th H. If a female, ♀ afflicted in ♋ or ♏. (See Drink, Drunkenness, Harlots, Intoxication; "Low Character" under Low; Saloons, Sottishness).

TAWNY COMPLEXION — (See "Tan" under Complexion; "Tawny" under Hair).

TEARING OF PARTS — Tears — (See Bursting, Laceration, Rupture).

TEARS — The Lachrymal Apparatus — Lachrymal Canal — The Nasal Duct — The ☽ rules the Tears and Lachrymal Apparatus, and its diseases. Tears are the physiological action of the ☽. Tears are also ruled by ♆, which planet is strong in ♓ and the 12th H., the House of Sorrows.

Crying Spells — Due to Despondency, Sorrow, or Worry — Caused by ♄; ♄ afflicted in the 12th H., and also with many planets in watery signs; ♄ or ♆ afflicted in ♓ in the 12th H.; ♆ afflicted in the 12th H. (See Anguish, Bereavement, Despondency, Emotions, Gloom, Grief, Sad, Sorrow, Worry).

Ducts — The Nasal Ducts — The Tear Ducts — Disorders of — Stoppage In — Obstruction In Tumor In—♄ afflicted in ♈; Subs at MCP (4C).

Epiphora — (See "Watery Eyes" in this section).

Excessive Flow of Tears — (See "Watery" in this section).

Hay Fever—The Lacrimation of—(See "Hay Fever" under Nose).

Humours — Lachrymal Humours — ♀ afflicted in ♈.

Obstruction—Of the Tear Ducts—(See "Ducts" in this section).

Overflow of Tears — (See "Watery Eyes" in this section).

Sheds Tears Easily—Many planets in watery signs at B., and the ☽ especially in such a sign, as in ♋ or ♓, and afflicted by malefics. (See "Intensified Emotions" under Emotions; "Acute Feelings" under Feeling; "Sensitiveness" under Sensitive).

Stoppage — Of the Tear Ducts — (See "Ducts" in this section).

Tumor — Of the Tear Duct — (See "Ducts" in this section).

Watery Eyes — Epiphora — Excessive Flow of Tears — Overflow of Tears — The ☽ on ♀ afflicted in ♈; ♄ afflicted in ♈, due to stoppage of the Nasal Duct to drain away the tears; Subs at MCP (4C), and at KP (11D).

TEDIOUS — Slow — Lingering — Prolonged—

Tedious Death — (See "Lingering Death" under Death, Lingering).

Tedious Diseases — The ☉ occi., and afflicted by ♄: taken sick when the ☉, ☽, and many planets are in fixed signs; the ☉ in the 6th H. unless well-aspected; lord of the Asc. in the 6th H., afflicted by lord of the 6th, and coming to combust, and the disease will be apt to cling until death, and death be more certain if the ☽ and lords of the 1st and 8th are in the 6th H. (See Chronic; "Many Diseases" under Complications; "Disease" under Constancy; Consumption; "Continued Sickness" under Continuity; "Low Fevers" under Fever; "Long Siege" under Ill-Health; Incurable, Invalids, Lingering; "Diseases" under Long; Permanent Diseases, Phthisis, Prolonged, Relapses; "Incapable of Remedy" under Remedy; Slow Diseases, Tuberculosis, Wastings, etc.).

TEETH — Dentition — The Organs of Mastication—The Teeth are ruled by ♄, which planet rules the bones of the body. The upper teeth are ruled by the ♈ Sign, and ♉ rules the lower teeth and the lower jaw. (See Jaws). Also ♃ has influence over the teeth. Saturn affects the teeth, the skull, and the left ear. The teeth are concerned also with the ♋ Sign, and Calcium Fluoride, the ♋ Sign Salt, which supplies the calcium and lime to the teeth. (See Lime). The following subjects have to do with the teeth, which see in the alphabetical arrangement when not more fully considered here—

Absence of Teeth—No Teeth—Cannot Talk—Case—See Chap. IX in Daath's Medical Astrology.

Accidents To—Injuries To—♂ in ♈ or ♉, and afflicted, and especially with ♂ in the Asc.; ♄ in ♈ or ♉, and in the Asc., causes injuries to the teeth from blows or falls, knocking the teeth out, etc. (See "Accidents" under Head, Jaws).

Ailments Of—(See the various paragraphs in this section).

Alveolus—The Bony Socket of the Teeth—Necrosis, Decay, and Disorders of—♄ afflicted in ♈ or ♉. (See Necrosis, Pyorrhoea).

Bad Teeth—Rotten—Caries of—Erosions of—Decayed—Broken and Decayed—Indifferent Teeth—Those born under the rule of ♄ tend to, and earlier loss of the teeth; ♄ in ♈, decay of the upper teeth; ♄ in ♉, of the lower teeth; ♄ rising at B.; ♄ in the 1st H.; ♄ always gives bad teeth, decay of, and toothache, and ♄ as Sig. in Hor'y Q. indicates a party with bad and decayed teeth, or if an elderly party, one with false teeth; ♄ afflicted in ♓; the ☉ afflicted in ♏, or with this sign on the Asc. (See the various paragraphs in this section).

Beautiful Teeth—(See "Small" in this section).

Black and Rotten—Discolored—♃ Sig. in a watery sign, and especially if he be with ☋, or ill-aspected by ♄ or ♂, the teeth grow black and rotten, and tend to sudden decay; ♃ Sig. in an earthy sign tends to discoloration of the teeth. (See "Decayed" in this section).

Bony Sockets—Decay of—(See "Alveolus" in this section).

Broad Teeth—Well-Set—♃ strong at B. (See "Fore-Teeth" in this section).

Broken and Decayed—(See "Bad Teeth" in this section). Case—See "Unfortunate Case", No. 351 in 1001 N.N.

Carious Teeth—Erosion of—Ulcerous Inflammation of the Bony Structure—(See "Bad Teeth", "Toothache", in this section).

Convulsions—During Dentition—(See "Dentition" in this section).

Crooked Teeth—♄ in ♑ or ♒; ♃ Sig. in a fiery sign.

Death During Dentition—(See "Dentition" in this section).

Decay Of—Early Decay of—The ☉ afflicted in ♏, or this sign on the Asc. and afflicted; ♄ afflicted in ♈, ♉, or ♓; the 5th face of ♈ on the Asc.; the 3rd face of ♊ on the Asc. (See Alveolus, Bad, Black, Treatment, and the various paragraphs in this section; Acidity, Decay).

Defects—Dental Defects—♄ in ♌ on the cusp the 12th H., and □ the ☉, and both in fixed signs. (See the various paragraphs in this section).

Dental Maladies—(See "Diseases", and the various paragraphs in this section).

Dentated—If the edges of the teeth are dentated or furrowed it is an indication of malnutrition or scrofula. (See "Malnutrition" under Nutrition; Scrofula).

Dentist—Makes a Good Dentist—(See "Dentist" under Dental).

Dentition—Teething—Disorders of—Fits During—Convulsions During—Death From—Difficult Dentition—Paroxysms In—♉ on the Asc., with ♄ or ♂ therein tends to fits during dentition, and difficult dentition, and if the ☉ or ☽ be afflicted in a fixed sign, and the figure be a weak one generally, the child may die in a paroxysm. (See Fits).

Difficult Dentition—(See "Dentition" in this section).

Discolored—(See "Black" in this section).

Diseases Of—Dental Maladies—♄ and ♃ diseases; ♄ afflicted in ♈ affects the upper teeth and jaw, and ♄ in ♉, the lower teeth and lower jaw; ♄ afflicted in ♑, ♒, or ♓; ♄ rising at B., and especially when afflicted in the Asc. (See the subjects in this section).

Distorted Teeth—Irregular—Caused by the ☉ influence; ♄ afflicted in ♒ or ♓; ♄ Sig. in ♓ indicates such a person in Hor'y Q.; ♂ and the ♏ sign Significators of the party (Hor'y); the ♒ sign gives distorted teeth if ♄ also be ascending; the 5th and 6th faces of ♈ on the Asc.; the 2nd face of ♉, ♊, or ♌ on the Asc. Also in inherited syphilitic conditions, known as "Hutchinson's Teeth", "Screw Driver Teeth", etc., the teeth may be notched, widely separated, tapering, pointed, peg-like, and especially the two front upper incisors. (See Syphilis).

Early Decay Of—(See "Decay" in this section).

Erosion Of—(See "Bad", "Carious", in this section).

Evenly Set—(See "Regular" in this section).

Extraction Of—Avoid when the ☽ is passing thru ♈ or ♉. (See "Rules" under Operations).

Fits During Dentition—(See "Dentition" in this section).

Fore-Teeth—The Two Front Upper Teeth—The Incisors—In Hor'y Q. ♃ Sig. of the party, and in an airy sign, denotes broad upper front teeth. Also ♃ Sig. denotes some defect in the two upper front teeth, a mark of difference between them, either standing awry, or some imperfection or blackness in them. (See "Black", "Distorted", in this section).

Front Teeth—(See "Fore-Teeth" in this section).

Furrowed—(See "Dentated" in this section).

Good Teeth—Well-Preserved—♃ rising at B.; ♃ in the 1st H.; ♃ as Sig. of the party (Hor'y); ♎ gives, and with this sign on the Asc.

Grinding the Teeth—A Symptom of Worms in Children. (See Worms).

Gums—Disorders of—(See Gums).

Hutchinson's Teeth—(See "Distorted" in this section).

Ill-Placed Teeth—♄ afflicted in ♓; ♄ in ♓ in partile asp. the Asc. (See Crooked, Distorted, Fore-Teeth, in this section).

Impediments In—♄ in ♈ or ♉; a ♄ disease and affliction.

Incisors — (See "Fore-Teeth" in this section).

Indifferent Teeth—(See "Bad Teeth" in this section).

Irregular — (See "Distorted" in this section).

Jaws — (See the paragraphs under Jaws).

Knocked Out—(See "Accidents To" in this section).

Large Teeth—♏ gives; the ☉ in ♏, or this sign on the Asc.

Lime—The Lime Supply to the Teeth —(See the Introduction to this Article).

Lock-Jaw; Loosened—(See "Alveolus" in this section; Pyorrhoea).

Lower Teeth—Ruled by the ♉ sign, and ♄ afflicted in ♉ tends to decay and disorders of the lower teeth and lower gums.

Malnutrition Of—(See "Dentated" in this section).

Marks On — (See Distorted, Fore-Teeth, in this section).

Mastication; Mouth — Disorders of — (See Gums; "Affections" under Mouth).

Necrosis—(See "Alveolus" in this section).

Neuralgia Of — (See "Toothache" in this section).

No Teeth or Hair — Case — (See "No Hair" under Hair).

Notched—(See "Distorted" in this section).

Nutrition — Interfered With — (See "Dentated" in this section).

Obliquely Set—Caused by ☉ influence; the ☉ in ♈, ♉, or ♏, and afflicted by ♄.

Pain In — (See "Toothache" in this section).

Paroxysm — During Dentition — (See "Dentition" in this section).

Peg-Like — (See "Distorted" in this section).

Pitted Teeth—Caused by an Inflamed Mouth, or Stomatitis conditions. (See "Mouth" under Aphthae).

Pointed—(See "Distorted" in this section).

Projecting Teeth — (See "Prominent" in this section).

Prominent—Projecting—Given by ♒; the ☉ or ♄ afflicted in ♒; ♒ on the Asc. Also people conceived while the ☉ was in ♒ often have this defect.

Pulling Teeth—(See "Extraction" in this section).

Pyorrhoea; Regularly Set — Even Teeth—♃ strong at B., well-aspected, or in the Asc., and free from ♄ affliction.

Rotten and Black — (See "Black" in this section).

Screw Driver Teeth—(See "Distorted" in this section).

Scrofulous — (See "Dentated" in this section).

Separated — Widely Separated — (See "Distorted" in this section).

Small Teeth—Beautiful—Even—Given by ♃ strong and well-aspected at B.

Sockets—(See "Alveolus" in this section).

Sordes — Fetid Accumulations About the Teeth—Increased by ♄ in ♈ or ♉, and the teeth should be brushed after each meal.

Sudden Decay Of — (See "Black" in this section).

Syphilitic Teeth—(See "Distorted" in this section).

Tapering — (See "Distorted" in this section).

Tartar On—Caused by ♄, and with ♄ in ♈ or ♉.

Teething — (See "Dentition" in this section).

Toothache — Neuralgia of Teeth — Caused by ♄. Those born under the rule of ♄ suffer much with toothache and decayed teeth; ♄ occi. in ♈, ♉, or ♒, and afflicting the ☉, ☽, or Asc.; ♄ in ♈ or ♉ when he is the afflictor in the disease; ♆, ♅, or ♄ in ♈, and afflicting the ☉ or ☽; ♄ afflicted in ♓; ♄ in ♈ or ♎; ♄ in asp. the Asc., or in ill-asp. the lord of the Asc.; an ♈ and ♉ disease, and with malefics in these signs. (See "Bad Teeth" in this section).

Treatment—The decay of the teeth is due to the over-acid conditions in the body, due to ♄ influence. (See Acidity, Decay, Hyperacidity). A diet which keeps the body more alkaline tends to preserve the teeth, or to take an alkaline preparation daily, such as Upjohn's Citrocarbonate Effervescent drink. Natives on Islands, or in Countries where the drinking water is largely dominated with Lime and Alkali, usually have good teeth to old age, and rarely ever see or use a toothbrush. The cure for decaying teeth must be from within, and keeping down the acidity of the system, and tooth pastes and mouth washes do not remedy the trouble, altho they assist in keeping the mouth in a more antiseptic and clean condition, and to prevent Sordes. The planetary influences at birth largely determine the nature and life of the teeth regardless of treatment. People who have the positive Signs of the Zodiac prominent at birth, and well-filled with planets, are more alkaline, and have better teeth. (See Alkalinity).

Ulceration Of—Erosion of—(See "Carious" in this section).

Upper Teeth—Ruled by ♈. Disorders and decay of are caused by ♄ and other malefics afflicted in ♈. (See "Bad Teeth" in this section).

Well-Preserved—(See "Good", "Treatment", in this section).

Well-Set and Broad—(See "Broad" in this section).

Widely Separated — (See "Distorted", "Fore-Teeth", in this section).

TELEPATHY—The Telepathic and Psychometric Functions are ruled by ♆. The Telepathic Functions are also influenced by ♅, and especially in a pathological way. (See Psychic, Suggestion, Thought).

TELLURIC INFLUENCES—(See Earth).

TEMPER—Heat of Mind or Passion—Disposition to Become Angry—The Nature and Disposition—

Even Temper—Mild Temper—♎ gives, and with this sign on the Asc. at B., if the mental rulers are not otherwise badly afflicted. (See Excellent, Gentle, Harmless, Inoffensive, Kind; "Amiable" under Manner; Mild; "Lover of Peace" under Peace; Quiet, Sober).

Furious Temper — (See Cruel, Furious).

High Temper—Choleric—Excitable—Quick Temper—Goes to Mental Extremes of Anger and Fury—The ☉ or ☽ afflicted by ♂; ♄ and ♂ in angles, and in ☌ or ☍ each other; ♂ ☌ or ill-asp. ☿ at B.; due to the afflictions of ♂ at B., as ♂ is the planet of anger, fury, passion, and violence; ♂ in the 6th H. in ☍ ☿ in the 12th H.; ♌ on the Asc. (See Anger; "Choleric Temperament" under Choleric; "Destructiveness, Excitable; "Manner" under Explosive; Fury, Hasty, Impulsiveness, Irascible, Murderous, Profane, Quarrelsome, Rashness; "Tendency to Violence" under Violence, etc.).

Ill-Disposed—Ill-Tempered—A Mean Disposition—The ☽ Sig. in ♈, ♍, ♏, or ♓; the ☽ Sig. □ or ☍ ♄; in Hor'y Q. ♄ Sig. in ♈; ☿ afflicted at B., and in evil asp. the Asc. by dir.; ☿ Sig. in ♈, ♒, ♌, ♏, ♑, or ♓. (See Anger, Choleric, Cruel, Deceitful, Dishonest, Hatred; "Ill-Disposed", "Ill-Natured", under Ill; Irritable, Jealousy, Liars, Libelers, Malevolent, Malicious; "Abrupt", "Disagreeable", under Manner; "Mean Spirited" under Mean; "Active to Do Mischief" under Mischief; Revengeful, Selfish, Thieves, Vicious, etc.).

Mild Temper—(See "Even Temper" in this section).

Nasty Temper—Bitter—Short Temper—Sarcastic—♅ to the ill-aspects ☿ by dir.; ♄ ☌ or ill-asp. ♂, and especially in the 1st, 3rd, 9th, or 10th Houses. (See "Abrupt", "Disagreeable", under Manner; Sarcasm).

Quick Temper—(See "Temper" under Quick; "High" in this section).

Short Temper — (See "Nasty" in this section).

Surly Temper—(See "Gruff", "Rough", "Rude", under Manner; "Manner" under Rough).

Violent Temper — Terrible Temper When Enraged—The ☉ Sig. ☌ ♂; the ☽ ☌ ♂ in ♏; ♆ afflicted in ♏; ♅ ☌ ♄ in ♈, ♉, ♒, or ♌; ♅ ☌, P., □, or ☍ ♂; ♅ □ or ☍ ♄; ♂ afflicted in ♈, ♉, or ♌; ♂ Sig. ☌, □, or ☍ ♄, and especially in angles. (See Cruel, Fury, Madness; "Shows No Pity" under Pity; Raving; "Tendency to Violence" under Violence).

TEMPERAMENT—Temperaments—The Bodily Temperaments—In the matter of health, and in the diagnosis of disease, the subject of Temperament is an important one, as people born with a predominance of planets in the different Signs of the Zodiac, as in the fiery, airy, earthy, and watery signs, the cardinal, fixed, or mutable signs, etc., are subject to different classes of diseases, and each temperament tends to furnish its own list of diseases. Temperament is judged according to the grouping of the planets in the Chart of Birth. The four fundamental Temperaments are determined by the predominance of the planets at birth in the Temperamental Signs, the Fiery, Airy, Earthy, and Watery signs, and known as the Choleric, Sanguine, Nervous, and Lymphatic Temperaments respectively. The Constitutional, or Conditional Temperament, is determined by the predominance of planets in the Constitutional Signs, the Cardinal, Fixed, or Common Signs at birth. The Natural, or Bodily Temperaments, are determined by the Decanate of the Sign rising upon the Ascendant at birth. If the ☉, ☽, and ☿ were in ♌ at birth, ♃ and ♂ in ♈, ♅ and ♄ in ♐, and with a fiery sign on the Asc. at B., the predominating influences would be fiery, and indicate the Choleric, or Bilious Temperament. If the planets predominated in the earthy signs, and also with an earthy sign on the Asc., the temperament produced would be the Nervous Temperament, etc. If the majorities of the planets at B. were in the fiery and fixed signs, the temperament would be that of the Fixed-Fire Combination. If the majorities of planets at B. were in the cardinal and earthy signs, the combination would be Cardinal-Earth, etc. It is very difficult to determine the Temperament from any one group of Signs, but the majorities and combinations of the Temperamental and Constitutional Signs must be considered, along with the nature of the Sign and Decanate rising on the Ascendant at birth. The Ascendant, the sign on the Asc. at birth, rule and determine largely the nature of the physical body, and whether it is hot or cold, cold and dry, cold and moist, hot and dry, hot and moist, etc., and each of the four fundamental temperaments correspond to one of the bodily temperaments. Thus the Choleric Temperament has a hot and dry body. The Nervous Temperament, a cold and dry body. The Sanguine Temperament, a hot and moist body. The Lymphatic, or Phlegmatic Temperament, a cold and moist body, etc. The best balanced temperaments are those wherein the planets at birth are more equally divided between the different groups of signs, as to have all the planets in fiery signs at birth, would greatly unbalance the native. Thus the ☉ in a fiery sign, and the ☽ in a watery sign, help to balance the nature, and avoid extremes, as the fiery and watery elements oppose each other, etc. The Choleric Temperament produces anger, excitement, haste, fevers, etc., and is fiery. The Nervous Temperament leads to increased nervousness, neurasthenia, but with good mental abilities. The Sanguine Temperament is refined, artistic, intellectual, and also known as the Artistic

Temperament. The Lymphatic Temperament is dull, idle, lethargic, slow, slovenly, and with less vitality. (See "Air Signs" under Air; Ascendant, Cardinal; the Introduction under Constitution; Decanates; "Earthy Signs" under Earth; "Fire Signs" under Fire; First House; "Fixed Signs" under Fixed; "Mutable Signs" under Mutable; "Signs" under Water). The following paragraphs on the Temperaments are here arranged alphabetically for quicker reference—

Bilious Temperament—(See "Choleric Temperament" under Choleric).

Bodily Temperaments—Natural Temperaments—Physical Temperaments—(See Cold, Cold and Dry, Cold and Moist, Hot, Hot and Dry, Hot and Moist, in this section).

Choleric Temperament — (See "Choleric Temperament" under Choleric; "Hot and Dry Body" in this section).

Cold Bodily Temperament — (See "Body", "Temperament", under Cold).

Cold and Dry Body — (See "Cold and Dry Body" under Dry; "Nervous Temperament" in this section).

Cold and Moist Body—(See "Cold and Moist Body" under Moisture; "Temperament" under Lymphatic, Phlegmatic).

Constitutional Temperaments—Conditional Temperaments—(See the Introduction to this Article; the Introduction under Constitution).

Dry Bodily Temperament — (See "Body" under Dry).

Dry and Cold Body — (See "Cold and Dry Body" under Dry; "Nervous Temperament" in this section).

Dry and Hot Body — (See "Hot and Dry Body" in this section).

Hot Bodily Temperament — (See this subject under Heat).

Hot and Dry Body — (See "Choleric Temperament" under Choleric; "Heat and Dryness" under Dry; "Hot and Dry Body" under Heat).

Hot and Moist Body—(See "Hot and Moist Body" under Moisture; "Sanguine Temperament" under Sanguine).

Lymphatic Temperament—(See "Cold and Moist Body" under Moisture; "Temperament" under Lymphatic, Phlegmatic).

Melancholic Temperament — (See "Nervous Temperament" in this section).

Mental Temperament — (See Decanates; "Temperament" under Mental).

Moist Bodily Temperament — (See "Bodily Temperament" under Moisture).

Moist and Cold Body—(See "Cold and Moist Body" in this section).

Moist and Hot Body—(See "Hot and Moist" in this section).

Motive Temperament—(See Decanates, Motive).

Natural Temperaments—The Physical Temperaments — (See "Natural Temperament" under Natural; "Bodily Temperaments" in this section).

Nervous Temperament — The Melancholic Temperament—(See "Cold and Dry Body" under Dry; "Disposition" under Melancholy; "Temperament" under Nerves).

Phlegmatic Temperament—(See "Lymphatic" in this section).

Physical Temperament — (See "Natural" in this section).

Sanguine Temperament — (See "Hot and Moist Body" in this section).

Vital Temperament—(See Decanates; "Fixed Signs" under Fixed; the Introduction under Life).

Well-Balanced Temperament — (See Well-Balanced).

TEMPERANCE — Temperate — ♃ is the author of Temperance, and this planet is also mild and temperate in nature.

Eating and Drinking—Temperate In —(See "Moderate" under Drink, Eating).

Habits—Temperate In—♃ in the Asc., and well-aspected; ♃ ☌ ☿; ♃ Sig. in ♒; the ☽ to the ☌ ♀, the mind is more temperate. (See Control, Self-Control).

Intemperance—(See Intemperance).

Pleasure—Should be Temperate In—(See "Temperate" under Pleasure; "Moderate" under Recreations).

TEMPERATURE—

High Temperature—(See "High Fevers" under Fever).

Increase—Of Temperature—Due to the ☉ and ♂ influences. (See "Increased" under Fever).

Rapid Extremes — Of Temperature — ♂ with ♄, and both the afflictors at the same time.

Subnormal Temperature—(See "Body" under Cold; "Lack of Animal Heat" under Heat. As a pathological condition, persistent subnormal temperature may be present in cases of Consumption, Wasting Diseases, Tuberculosis, during convalescence from Fevers, in cases of Acute Alcoholism, poisoning from Carbolic Acid, or some other drug, Opiate, or Intoxicant; from loss of blood in Hemorrhage; from Melancholy, Cretinism, or Myxoedema; occurs during the intervals in Intermittent Fevers, and occurs in some cases of Starvation. See these subjects, and note the planetary influences causing them. The influence of ♄ tends to depress and suppress the heat of the body, and in most cases of subnormal temperature the ♄ afflictions are the fundamental causes of the disorder.

TEMPESTS—Danger, Injury, or Death In—(See Blizzards; "Tempests at Sea" under Sea; "Storms at Sea" under Shipwreck; Storms; "Tornadoes" under Wind).

TEMPLES — The Temporal Region — The Temples are ruled by ♃, and much affected by ♃ in ♐.

Bald About Temples—(See "Temples" under Baldness).

Hair — Light Brown Hair Near the Temples and Forehead—Born under ♃, and ♃ occidental. (See "Light Hair" under Hair).

Head—The Head Wide at the Temples —(See Decanates).

Headaches — (See "Temporal" under Headaches).

Temporal Bones—The Mastoid Bones are the protruding parts of the Temporal Bone, and subject to Mastoid Abscess. (See "Mastoid Abscess" under Mastoid).

TEMPORARY—Of Brief Duration—

Deafness—(See "Temporary Deafness" under Hearing).

Diseases—Temporary Diseases—(See Acute, Colds, Indisposition, Mild, Short Diseases, Slight).

Insanity—(See "Temporary Insanity", "Violent Forms", under Insanity).

Mental Derangement—(See "Temporary" under Mental).

TEMPTATIONS—

Many Temptations—Subject to Many Temptations to Do Wrong—Caused by the afflictions of ♂ and ♀, or of ♂ to ♀, and especially along moral and passional lines; ♂ ☌, P, □, or ☍ ♀ at B., and by dir. Also the ♂ afflictions to the ☉, ☽, ♄, ☿, or the Asc. tend to criminal acts. The afflictions of ♄ and ♂ to ☿ tend to dishonesty. The afflictions of ♆ tend to deceit. (See Cheating, Criminal, Deceitful, Dishonest, Evil, Forgers, Gambling, Liars; "Illicit" under Love Affairs; "Loose Morals" under Morals; "Clandestine" under Sex; Thieves, etc.).

Resists Evil Temptations—(See Honest; "Good Morals" under Morals; Noble; "Popular" under Reputation; Sincere, etc.).

Yields to Temptation—(See Amorous, Debauched, Dissipated, Drink, Drunkenness, Excesses, Gluttony, Harlots, Lewd; "Promiscuity" under Love Affairs; Lust; "Immoral" under Morals; Opposite Sex, Prodigal, Recklessness; "Many Temptations" in this section).

TENACITY—

Tenacity of Life — (See Endurance; "Good Powers of Resistance" under Resistance; "Good" under Vitality; Wear and Tear).

Tenacious Nature—(See Obstinate).

TENDENCIES—The tendencies of each individual are largely shown and indicated by the Map of Birth, and also the Prenatal Epoch Map for the time of Conception. The tendencies of the Mind, the talents and abilities of the native, and the line of work most fitted for, and the various relationships he will have with the World, are indicated by the map of birth. The real inner character is indicated more by the map for the time of conception. The radical map also indicates the tendencies to disease, what diseases, and what parts of the body are more subject to affliction. The influence of the ☉ in the map shows the innate, hereditary, organic, and structural disorders to which the native is subject. The ☽ influence denotes acquired tendencies. It would take too much space here to list all the tendencies of mind and body, for good or ill, which are mentioned in this book, but will give a few suggestive subjects, and for other subjects not listed, look for it in the alphabetical arrangement. See Acquired, Animal Instincts, Attracts, Character, Conduct, Congenital, Constitution, Criminal, Depravity, Desires, Diathesis; "Tendency To" under Disease; Dishonest, Evil, Good, Habits, Health, Heredity, Honest, Idiosyncrasies, Inclined, Innate, Instincts; "Low and Base" under Low; Magnetism, Melancholic, Mind, Morals, Motives, Murderous, Nativity, Natural, Nature, Noble, Organic, Predisposition, Prenatal, Propensities, Purposes, Sickness, Sincere, Spiritual, Strong, Structural, Susceptibility, Temper, Temperaments, Violent, Vitality, Weak, Wicked, etc.

TENDER—Tenderness—

Axillae—Tenderness In—(See Axillae).

Feet—(See "Tender" under Feet).

Skin — (See "Delicate", "Tender", under Skin).

TENDONS — The Attachments of Muscles—Ruled by ♂. Are also ruled by ♄, as ♄ tends to harden, strengthen and solidify them, but ♂ brings them into action in connection with muscular activity. The Tendons are crystallized by ♄. The tendons and sinews should not be strained when ♅ is in ♎ at B. (See Achilles, Cartilage, Fiber, Ligaments, Muscles, Sinews).

TENIA—(See Taenia, Worms).

TENOR VOICE — (See "Tenor" under Voice).

TENSION—Tensity—Strain—

Body — Tension In — Produced by ♂ during muscular activity. (See "Activity", "Strength", "Tensity", under Muscles).

Eyes — Intraocular Tension — (See Glaucoma).

Fluids and Liquids — High tension with the fluids and liquids of the body is reached at the time of the Full Moon. (See "Full Moon" under Moon).

Mind—Mental Strain—The influences of ♅ and ☿ tend to bring the mind and nervous forces under greater tension. (See "Strain" under Mental, Mind; "Strain", "Stress and Strain", "Tension", under Nerves).

Muscular Strain—(See "Body" in this section; "Body", "Muscular Strain", under Strain).

Nervous Tension—High Nervous Tension—(See "High Strung", "High Tension", under Nerves; "Mind" in this section).

TENTH HOUSE — The House of the Midheaven—The M.C.—The Meridian—Medium Coeli—The Zenith, etc.—This House corresponds to the ♑ Sign, and is a feminine house, and is also the house of ♄. Planets culminate in this house, and are strong by accidental dignity if not otherwise in a strong sign, or dignified. This House rules the Knees, Hams, and Thighs, and signifies all diseases in the knees, and the upper part of the leg behind the knees. Planets in this house have a powerful influence in matters of health and disease, and especially malefic planets here, and which may be elevated above the Lights, or afflicting the hyleg from this position. This house signifies Kings, Rulers, Presidents, Princes, Judges, Magistrates, the Profession, the Employment, Vocation, Business, Honors, Preferment, Fame, Renown. Also signifies the Medicine given in sickness, the credit and honor of the native, and his business standing. In a male nativity, it rules the father, and in a female nativity, the mother, and the affairs of the mother. It also governs the hidden and Occult side of life. Saturn afflicted in this house at birth, or ruler of this house, tends to bring ruin, disgrace, self-undoing, sudden downfall, imprisonment, or an ignominious death. Also ♄ or ☋ here bring disgrace and ruin to Great Men. Mars afflicted in this house, or ruler of, tends to bring trouble with Judges, Magistrates, great misery, and also causes sickness, danger of accidents, a violent death, and much evil to a parent, according to the sex of the nativity. The malefic planets when coming to the ☌ the M.C., or the cusp of this house, and especially ♄ or ♂, indicate the danger of death, violence to the native, falls, blows, injury, or the death of a parent, as the cusp of this house is one of the very sensitive places of the map of birth, along with the Ascendant, and the ☉, ☽, and the Hyleg. The M.C. and the Ascendant are considered passive points in the map, and very strong for good or evil according to the aspects formed with them at birth and by direction. The Colors ruled by this house are Red and White. (See Nadir). For a list of the various influences of the Planets in this House, see Chapter VI in Sepharial's Manual of Astrology.

TERATOLOGY — The Science of Monsters—(See Monsters).

TERMINAL HOUSES — Terminal Signs —The Terminal Triangle—The triangle formed by the Fourth, Eighth, and Twelfth Houses have a close relation to death, the cause of death, the manner of death, the end of life in the physical body, and to old age. The 8th and 12th Houses have no affinity with the Ascendant. The Fourth House, which is affiliated with the ♋ sign, shows the death of the physical body, the end of life, and the fate in old age. (See Cancer Sign, Fourth House). The Eighth House, known as the House of Death, and which is affiliated with the ♏ sign, shows the transition from the physical body to the spiritual. (See Eighth House, Scorpio). The Twelfth House, the last of the Houses, and affiliated with the ♓ sign, and last of the 12 Signs, is the house of privation, suffering, and limitation, and shows the death of the psychic nature. (See "Arguments For Death", "Certain Death", under Death; "End of Life" under Life; "Kind of Death" under Old Age; Pisces Sign; "Death" under Psychic; Twelfth House).

Terminal Signs—♋, ♏, ♓.

TERMINATION—The End—

Disease—Termination of the Disease —The last degrees of a sign on the cusp of the 6th H. during a sickness denote that the disease will soon end, and when the sign on the cusp changes. The lord of the Asc. changing signs, and entering a sign in which he has dignity, also indicates the speedy termination of the disease. Benefics in the 6th H. help to end the disease, if they are free from affliction, and also not afflicting the hyleg. Malefics in the 6th H. tend to prolong the disease, or bring an evil ending to the disease. The lord of the 6th H. in the Asc., or lord of the Asc. in the 6th, the disease will continue until one of the Significators changes signs. When the ☽, or cusp of the 6th H., are in a cardinal sign, the disease tends to terminate quickly. When the afflictor is in a cardinal sign, the disease is severe, but soon over. (See Acute, Amelioration, Chronic, Complications, Continuity, Crises, Curable; "Certain Death" under Death; "Better", "Worse", under Disease; Duration, Ease, End, Fatal; "Disease" under Force; Increase, Incurable, Lingering, Long Diseases, Minimizing, Moderation, Modification, Prognosis, Prolonged, Quick Diseases, Recovery, Recuperation, Relapse, Resolution, Short Diseases, Tedious, Worse).

Life—Termination of In the Physical Body—The Terminus Vitae—(See "Arguments for Death", "Certain Death", "Time of Death", under Death; Fatal; "Terminal Houses" under Terminal).

TERMINUS VITAE—(See Death; "Life" under Termination).

TERMS — There are certain degrees of the Zodiac, which are supposed to alter the nature of planets when they are in these degrees. Thus, a malefic in the terms of ♃ or ♀ is modified for good, and the evil of the malefic mitigated. The word "Term" is mentioned much in Astrological Literature, and the student should be familiar with the subject. In the Article on "Terms" in Alan Leo's New Dictionary of Astrology, and also in Wilson's Dictionary of Astrology, there are Tables of these Terms, and showing in what degrees each planet is more powerful. A study of this subject will help students to understand better why a malefic in a sign does not always act in the same way in disease. (See Degrees).

TERRESTRIAL — Of the Earth—Pertaining to the Earth—

Terrestrial Magnetism — Is ruled by ♅. (See Magnetism).

Terrestrial Signs—(See "Signs" under Quadrupeds).

TERRIBLE—Dreadful—Horrible—

Terrible Death — (See "Dreadful Death" under Death; Execution, Guillotine, Hanging, Judges, etc.).

Terrible Diseases Prevail—If ♄ and ♃ be in ☌, and ♄ have higher Latitude than ♃, terrible diseases, and Influenza prevail, but if the Lat. of ♃ be more Northern, the evil will be mitigated. (See Carcinoma, Cholera, Dreadful, Epidemics; "Portentous" under Fever; Influenza, Leprosy, Malignant, Outrageous, Pestilence, Plague, Smallpox, Sores, Syphilis, Ulcers, etc.).

Terribly Wounded — In Battle — (See War).

TERRORS—Extreme Fright or Fear—

Strange Terrors—(See Forebodings, Horrors, Obsessions, Premonitions, Spirit Controls; "Terrors", "Visions", under Strange; Visions).

Terror to Society—(See Execrated).

TERTIAN FEVERS—(See "Tertian" under Ague).

TESTES—Testicles—The Testicles, and the Sac, or Scrotum, containing them, are ruled by ♂, as a unit. The Excretory Vessels of the Testes are ruled by the ♏ sign. The ☉ rules the right testicle, and the ☽ the left one. The Serum of the Tunica Vaginalis is ruled by the ☽. (See Serum).

Castration—Should not be done when the ☽ is passing through the ♍, ♎, or ♏ signs. The ♉ and ♏ signs, being opposite and supplemental, castration affects the voice, and tends to make the voice effeminate, or into a tenor. (See Effeminate, Eunuchs, Voice).

Hydrocele—A Collection of Serum in the Tunica Vaginalis—(See Hydrocele).

Infirmities In—A ♍ disease, and afflictions in ♍; Subs at PP.

Injuries To—Accidents To—Afflictions in ♏; ♂ afflicted in ♏. (See Scrotum, Spermatic).

Rupture Of—Case—See "Imperfectly Formed", No. 303, in 1001 N.N.

Scrotum—The Pouch Containing the Testes—Disorders of—(See Scrotum).

Seminal Tubes—Tubuli Seminiferi—(See Semen).

Spermatic Cord—Injuries To—(See Spermatic).

Swollen Testes—(See "Mumps" under Parotid). See Generation, Genitals, Privates, Reproduction, Sex Organs, Varicocele, Varicose.

TETANUS—Tetany—Tonic Spasm—Tetanilla—A Disease with Spasmodic and Continuous Contractions of the Muscles—Caused by ♅ afflictions, and causing Incoordination. Also caused by Subs at AT, AX, MCP, and CP. This disease sometimes occurs as a result of a deficiency of the Mineral Salts in the Blood, and caused by ♄ afflicted in ♍, obstructing intestinal digestion and assimilation. Case of Tetanus—See Fig. 13G in the book, "Astro-Diagnosis", by the Heindels. (See Incoordination; "Blood" under Minerals; "Tonic Spasm" under Spasmodic).

Fingers and Toes—Tetanic Spasm In—Tetanilla—♅ afflicted in ♍ or ♓.

TETTER—Tetters—A form of Ringworm, Herpes, Eczema—Dry Tetter—Scaly Tetter—Caused by the ☽ in the sign of the Summer Tropic at birth; the ☽ in ♋, ♌, or ♍; ♄ and ♂ in an angle, occi. of the ☉, and ori. of the ☽, and ☿ in familiarity with ♂; ♄ or ♂ in the 1st or 7th H. in ♋, ♑, or ♓, and signs ascribed to animals and fishes; ♂ or ☿ holding dominion at birth, and in familiarity with each other, and ♂ afflicting the hyleg, and elevated above the Luminaries, Tetters are increased. The Dry and Scaly forms of Tetter are caused more by ♄ and the earthy sign influences, and the moisture forms where the ☽ and moist signs are involved. (See Eczema, Herpes, Psoriasis, Ringworm, Scales; "Dry Skin" under Skin).

TEXTURE—Of the Tissues of the Body—Ruled by ☿. (See Tissues).

Textural Nutrition—Changes In the Processes of—(See "Textural" under Nutrition).

THEATRES—Music Halls—Places of Amusement—Ruled by the 5th H.

Death or Injury In—Malefics in the 5th H.; ♂ in the 5th H., in □ or ☍ the ☉ or ☽. (See Amusements; "Music Halls" under Music; Pleasure, Recreations, Sports, Taverns).

Loves the Theatre—♀ in ♌ or the 5th H.

Theatre Fire—Case—188 Lives Lost—See "Exeter", No. 717, in 1001 N.N. Also see Case under "Music Halls" under Music).

THEFTS—Thefts Prevalent—Rapine—Robberies—An eclipse of the ☉ in the 2nd Dec. of ♊, thefts and robberies; an eclipse of the ☉ in the 2nd Decan. of ♒, public thefts, robberies, and rapines; an eclipse of the ☽ in the 1st Dec. of ♐, thefts and rapines; an eclipse of the ☽ in the 2nd dec. of ♑; an eclipse of the ☽ in the 3rd dec. of ♓, rapines, robberies, and piracies. (See Highwaymen, Piracy, Rapine, Robbers, Thieves).

THERAPEUTICS—The Science of the Application of Remedies and the Treatment of Disease. The word Therapeutics means literally, "The Worship of the Gods, or Cure by Faith in the Divinities of Certain Planets." The seven Therapeutical Pioneers for the treatment of disease are Gold (☉), Silver (☽), Lead (♄), Tin (♃), Iron (♂), Copper (♀), and Mercury or Quicksilver (☿). For the Therapeutic Properties of the Planets see "Therapeutic Properties" under each of the Planets. (See Antipathy, Colors, Cure, Drugs, Healers, Herbs, Medicines, Metals, Minerals, Opposites, Poisons, Remedies, Sympathy, Treatment, Vibration).

THICK—Thick Body—

Beard—(See "Thick" under Beard).

Body—Thick Body—The ☉ Sig. in ♉, thick and well-set; the ☽ Sig. in ♉ or ♏; the ☽ Sig. in ♏, thick, short, well-set, ill-made; the ☽ in ♏, partile the Asc., thick, short, fleshy, ill-made; ♄ Sig. in ♏, thick, squat, well-trussed; ♄ in ♏, partile the Asc.; ♄ Sig. in ♒; ♂ in ♏, partile the Asc., thick and well-set; ♀ in ♋, partile the Asc., thick and short; ☿ Sig. in ♉, thick, strong, and well-set; ☿ Sig. in ♋, thick, squat, and well-trussed; ☿ in ♏, partile the Asc., thick and well-set; ♉ on the Asc., thick, well-set, strong, middle-sized, or short; ♏ on the Asc., thick, well-set, fleshy, middle stature. (See Corpulent, Fat, Fleshy, Full, Lumpish, Obesity, Plump, Short Body, Squat, Well-Set, Well-Trussed).

Feet—(See "Thick" under Feet).

Fleshy and Thick—(See Fleshy; "Body" in this section).

Hair—(See "Thick" under Hair).

Hands—(See "Thick" under Hands).

Ill-Made and Thick—(See "Ill-Formed" under Ill; "Body" in this section).

Legs—(See "Thick" under Legs).

Lips—(See "Thick" under Lips).

Middle-Sized and Thick—(See "Middle Stature" under Middle; "Body" in this section).

Neck—(See "Thick" under Neck).

Nose—Nostrils—(See "Thick" under Nose).

Short and Thick—(See "Thick" under Short; "Body" in this section).

Shoulders—(See "Thick" under Shoulders).

Skin—(See "Thick", "Thickening", under Skin).

Strong and Thick—(See "Body" in this section; "Body" under Strong).

Thick-Trussed—Well-Trussed—(See "Body" in this section; "Well-Trussed" under Well).

Thickening—(See the next Article after this one).

Well-Set and Thick—(See "Body" in this section; "Well-Set" under Well).

Well-Trussed and Thick—(See "Thick-Trussed" in this section).

THICKENING—Thickening of the Tissues—Saturn by his deposits tends to thickening of the cell walls and tissues.

Acromegaly—Enlargements by Thickening—(See "Acromegaly" under Enlargements, Extremities).

Cell Walls—(See "Thickening" under Cells).

Cirrhosis—Thickening of Connective Tissue—(See Cirrhosis, Connective).

Connective Tissue—(See "Cirrhosis" in this section).

Enlargements—(See "Acromegaly" in this section; Hypertrophy).

Extremities—(See "Enlargements" under Extremities).

Hypertrophy—(See this subject).

Kidneys—(See "Thickening" under Kidneys).

Liver—(See "Thickening" under Liver).

Sclerosis—Hardening and Thickening of Tissues—(See Sclerosis).

Skin—(See "Thickening" under Skin).

Soft Parts—Thickening of—(See "Parts" under Soft; "Acromegaly" in this section).

THIEVES—Thieving—The Seventh House rules Thieves, and is the Sig. of Thieves in Hor'y Q.

A Thief—The afflictions to ♂ and ☿ tend to make thieves; ♂ ill-dignified, Significator, and ☌ ♄; ♂ Sig. □ or ☍ ☽; ♂ Sig. □ or ☍ ☿, a thief and swindler; ♂ afflicted in ♊; ♀ Sig. □ or ☍ ♃, often a secret thief or murderer; ☿ Sig. in ♋; ☿ afflicted by ♄ and ♂. Case—See "Marriage", No. 425 in 1001 N.N. (See Cheating, Criminal, Deceitful, Dishonest, Forgers, Gambling, Kleptomaniac, Liars, Peregrine, Swindlers, etc.).

Danger by Thieves—Death or Injury By—The ☽ directed to the Whale's Jaw, Knees of Castor and Pollux, Belly of the Twins, or Cynosura; ♂ ori. in fixed signs, □ or ☍ the ☉ at B., or ♂ occi., □ or ☍ the ☽. (See Highwaymen, Murdered, Piracy, Rapine, Robbers, Thefts).

THIGHS—Hams—Hamstrings—The Thighs are under the external rulership of the ♐ sign. The Thigh Bones are under the structural rulership of ♐. (See Sagittarius). The Thighs are also ruled by the 9th H. (See Ninth House). Also ruled by ♃, and influenced by the 10th H. The Hams are ruled by ♃ and ♐. The Hamstrings are ruled by ♑ and the 10th H.

Accidents To—♅, ♄, or ♂ afflicted in ♐; ♄ ☌ ♂ in ♐; afflictions in ♐; ♐ on the Asc. (See "Accidents" under Hips, Legs).

Aches In—(See "Aches" under Hips).

Affected—The thighs are affected when the ☉ is in ♈ or ♓; the ☽ in ♊, ♐, ♑, ♓; ♅ in ♎; ♄ in ♍ or ♎; ♃ in ♋, ♌, or ♏; ♂ in ♏; ♀ in ♊ or ♐; ☿ in ♉ or ♓. (See Table 196 in Simmonite's Arcana).

All Diseases In—Signified by the 9th H. (See "All Diseases In" under Hips).

Broken Femur—(See Femur).

Bruises To—Contusions—♄ in ♐.

Chill and Cold In—♄ in ♐.

Circulation Poor—♄ in ♐, ☌, □, or ☍ ♃ or ♀.

Cold and Moist Humours—(See "Cold and Moist" under Hips).

Consumptive Pains In—♄ in ♎ or ♐ when ♄ is the afflictor in the disease.

Contusions—(See "Bruises" in this section).

Cramps In—♅ in ♐. (See Cramps).

Cuts To—(See "Cuts" under Hips).

Deformity—The ☽ in ♐, □ ♄ or ♅; ♄ in ♐ in the 6th H.

Diseases In—The ☉ afflicted in ♈ or ♓; the ☽ afflicted in ♊, ♐, ♑, or ♓; signified by ♄ in ♍, ♎, or ♓; ♃ afflicted in ♋, ♌, ♏, ♐, or ♓; ♂ afflicted in ♏ or ♓; ♀ afflicted in ♊, ♐, or ♑; ☿ afflicted in ♊, ♐, ♑, or ♓; ♐, ♑ and ♓ diseases. (See "Impar" under Ganglion; "Diseases In" under Hips).

Dislocation—Of the Femur—(See Femur).

Feverish Ailments In—♂ in ♐; ♂ in ♐ in the Asc. or 6th H.; ♐ on the Asc. (See "Feverish", "Hot Humours", under Hips).

Fistulous Tumor In—(See "Thighs" under Fistula).

Fracture—(See "Accidents To" under Femur; "Fracture" under Hips).

Gout In—(See "Hips and Thighs" under Gout).

Hamstrings—All Diseases In—Signified by afflictions in ♑, and in the 7th and 10th H.

Heats In—(See "Heats In" under Hips).

Hips—Many of the influences given in the subjects under Hips will also apply to the Thighs. (See the various subjects under Hips).

Hot Humours In—(See "Hot Humours" under Hips).

Humours In—(See "Humours" under Hips).

Hurts To—Injuries or Wounds—(See "Accidents To" under Femur, and in this section; "Hurts", "Injuries", under Hips).

Injuries To—(See "Accidents" "Hurts", in this section).

Itching—In the Thighs—The ☽ in ♎, ☌, P., □ or ☍ ♄ (or ☿ if he be of the nature of ♄) at the beginning of an illness, or at decumbiture (Hor'y).

Lameness In—(See "Lameness" under Hips).

Lean Thighs—Thin—♄ gives; ♄ ascending at B.

Legs—(See the various subjects under Legs).

Lightning—The Thigh Injured By—Case—See "Child" under Lightning.

Locomotor Ataxia—(See this subject).

Long Thighs—(See "Long" under Legs).

Men—Men Suffer With Thigh Diseases—(See "Men Suffer" under Hips).

Moist and Cold Humours—(See "Cold and Moist" under Hips).

Mole On—(See "Location of Moles" under Moles).

Muscles Of—Disorders of—Afflictions in ♐, ♑, the 9th and 10th H.; Subs at PP and Sacrum.

Neuralgia In—(See "Pains" in this section).

Old Aches In—(See "Aches" under Hips).

Operations On—Surgical—Avoid when the ☽ is passing thru the ♐ sign. (See "Rules" under Operations).

Pains In—Neuralgia In—Malefics in ♐ and afflicting the ☉ or ☽; ♄ afflicted in ♐, rheumatic pains in; ♃ afflicted in ♐, and especially with ♃ in the 6th H.; ♂ in ♐, pain or ulcers in the hips or thighs by humours settled in those parts; ☿ afflicted in ♐. (See "Pain" under Hips; "Consumptive", "Gout", "Rheumatism", in this section).

Restrictions—In Region of—♄ afflicted in ♐.

Rheumatism In—(See "Rheumatism" under Hips).

Sciatica—(See Sciatic).

Short Thighs—(See "Short" under Legs).

Shorter—Left Leg Shorter—Case—(See "Leg" under Left).

Small and Lean—(See "Slender" under Legs).

Strong—And Well-Proportioned Legs and Thighs—(See "Strong" under Hips).

Swellings In—(See "Swellings" under Hips).

Thick and Short—(See "Thick" under Legs).

Thin—(See "Lean" in this section).

Tumors In—(See "Thighs" under Fistula; "Tumors" under Hips).

Ulcers—(See "Ulcers" under Hips; "Pains" in this section).

Weakness In—(See "Weakness" under Hips).

Well-Formed—♐ on the Asc.

Well-Proportioned—♃ in the Asc.; ♐ on the Asc.

Wounds To—(See "Hurts" in this section).

THIN—Thinness—

Beard—(See "Thin" under Beard).

Blood—(See "Thin" under Blood).

Body—Thin Body—The Quadrant from the Autumnal Equinox to the Winter Solstice tends to produce thin, weak, and sickly people. Lords of thin people have little or no Latitude. The ☉ in ♍, partile the Asc., thin, tall and slender; the ☽ occi., and decr. at B.; the ☽ in ♑, partile the Asc., thin body and face; ♄ in ♑, partile the Asc., thin, raw-boned, and ungainly; ♄ occi., thin and small; ♄ lord of the Asc. and occi., as between the M.C. and Desc., and between the Nadir and Asc., a thin, small body; ♄ in So. Lat. makes the body thinner, and more corpulent when in N. Lat.; ♄ ascending at B.; ♄ in ♍, partile the Asc., thin and tall; ♂ in ♑, partile the Asc., thin, small, lean body; ☿ ascending at B., and free from the rays of other planets; ☿ indicates tall and thin persons; ☿ posited occidentally as regards the ☉ except when ☿ is in ♊; ☿ in ♈, partile the Asc., thin, mean stature; ☿ ruler of the Asc., and occidental; ☿ in ♌, partile the Asc., rather lean and thin, and not tall; ☿ in ♓, partile the Asc., thin and small, say some Writers; ♈ on the Asc.; the latter parts of ♈, ♉, ♌, or ♒ ascending, and the foreparts of ♊ or ♏, cause thinness; ♍ on the Asc., tall, well-made, and rather thin and slender; ♑ on the Asc. (See "Raw-Boned" under Bones; Lean, Slender, Spare; "Noted Thin Man" in this section).

Chin—(See "Thin" under Chin).

Face—(See "Thin" under Face).

Lean and Thin—(See Lean; "Body" in this section).

Legs—(See "Thin" under Legs).

Lips—(See "Thin" under Lips).

Living Skeleton—(See Skeleton).

Mean and Thin—(See "Mean Stature" under Mean; "Body" in this section).

Noted Thin Man—Case—(See "A Living Skeleton" under Skeleton).

Pale and Thin—(See "Thin Face" under Face; Pale, Sickly).

Raw-Boned and Thin—(See "Raw-Boned" under Bones).

Sickly and Thin—(See Emaciated; "Thin Face" under Face; Pale, Sickly, Wastings).

Skeleton—(See "Living Skeleton" under Skeleton).

Skin—(See "Thin" under Skin).

Slender and Thin—(See "Body" under Slender).

Small and Thin—(See "Body" under Small, and in this section; "Small" under Lean).

Spare and Thin—(See Spare).

Tall and Thin—♅ and ☿ make more tall and thin; the ☉ in ♍, partile the

Asc.; ♄ in ♍, partile the Asc.; ♍ on the Asc.; ♍ on the Asc., tall, well-made, and rather slender. (See "Body" under Slender, and in this section; "Tall Body" under Tall).

Thighs—(See "Lean" under Thighs).

Ungainly and Thin — (See "Raw-Boned" under Bones; Crooked; "Ill-Formed" under Ill; Ugly, Ungainly).

Visage—(See "Face", "Pale", "Sickly", in this section).

THINKING—Thought—Thoughts—

Disorders Of—(See Aversions, Dejected, Delusions, Depressed, Despondent, Deviations, Evils, Fears, Hallucinations, Ideals, Ideas, Illusions, Insanity; "Low Spirits" under Low; Melancholy, Negative, Obsessions, Opinions, Rashness, Spirit Controls, Temper, Uncontrolled, Worry, etc.).

Good Thinking—Right Thinking—A Good Thinker — (See Cheerfulness, Contentment, Gentle, Happiness, Honest, Humane, Joy, Kind; "Peace of Mind" under Mind; Noble, Optimistic, Positive, Sanguine, Sincere, etc.).

Thought—Little Depth of Thought or Mind — (See "Light In Mind" under Mind; "Thought" under Reason). For the opposite influences see "Deep and Profound" under Mind).

Thoughtful Expression — (See "Appearance" under Sadness). See Thought.

THIRD EYE—(See Pineal).

THIRD HOUSE — The House of Brethren, Brothers, Sisters, Cousins, Neighbors, Short Inland Journeys. This is a masculine and cadent house, and is affiliated with ☿ and the ♊ Sign. Denotes and rules the Neck, Arms, Shoulders, Hands, Fingers, Chest, Lungs, the Lower Mind, Wakefulness or Waking. It governs also the Mental Capacity, and the Educational Mind. The Third and Ninth Houses are the Houses of Mind, and malefics in these Houses tend to disturb and unbalance the Mind. Benefics and ☿ well-aspected and dignified in this house give a good mind. In the Hindu System of Astrology, this house rules the Ears. Its Colors are Red, Yellow, and Sorrel. For a Horoscope Example of a Stellium in this House at birth see "Pasteur", No. 950, in 1001 N.N. (See the subjects mentioned in this Article).

THIRST—Thirsty—

Craving for Liquids — The ☽ afflicted in ♓; the ☽ in water signs. (See Cravings).

Drinks — Desire for Strong Drinks, Strong Coffee, Hot Drinks, etc.—The ☽ afflicted in ♓; ♄ ☌ ♀ in ♋, and also afflicted by the ☽. (See Dipsomania, Drink, Drunkenness, Intoxication, Liquors, Wine, etc.).

Extreme Thirst — The ☽ in ♓ or ♈, and afflicted by the ☉ or ♂ when taken ill; ♂ ☌ or ill-asp. ☿. People born under the Hot and Dry Bodily Temperament often suffer from extreme thirst, and need to drink plenty of water to help keep the fluids of the body replenished. (See "Hot and Dry Body" under Heat).

Unquenchable Thirst — Many planets in fiery signs at B., and with a fire sign upon the Asc.; the ☉ and ♂ in the Asc. at B. Also occurs in the high fevers of ♂. (See "High Fever" under Fever; "Excessive Bodily Heat" under Heat; "Extreme" in this section).

Vehement Thirst — A Violent Thirst and Craving, and Especially for Spirituous Liquors—(See Dipsomania). See Appetites, Bloodthirsty (see "A Murderer" under Murder); Drought, Eating, Epicureans, Excesses, Famine, Feasting, Food, Gluttony, Starvation.

THORAX — Thoracic — The Chest — The Cavity Above the Abdomen—Ruled by the ☽ and the ♋ Sign.

Diathesis — The Thoracic Diathesis — (See Fiber; "Impar" under Ganglion; Ligaments).

Dropsy Of — (See "Hydrothorax" under Chest).

Duct — Thoracic Duct — Ruled by the ♋ Sign. (See Lymph).

Ganglia — Thoracic Ganglia — (See "Fifth Thoracic", "Middle Cervical", under Ganglion).

Hydrothorax—Dropsy In Chest—(See "Dropsy" under Chest).

Mediastinum—Septum of the Thoracic Cavity—Tumor of—(See "Mediastinal" under Tumors).

Process — Thoracic Process — ♃ adds or subtracts to the Thoracic Process. (See "Alterations" under Cells; Metabolism, Metamorphosis).

Tumor — In Thoracic Cavity — (See "Mediastinum" in this section).

THORIUM — A Metal ruled by ♅. (See Uranus).

THOUGHT — Thoughts — Thoughtful — Thoughtless—

Evil Thoughts—(See Evil).

Expression — Thoughtful Expression —(See "Appearance" under Sad).

Little Depth — Of Thought — (See "Thought" under Thinking).

Thoughtful — Sober — Serious — ♄ influence; the 4th face of ♏ on the Asc. (See Austere, Grave, Melancholy, Reserved, Responsibility; "Sadness" under Sad; Serious, Sober).

Thoughtless — (See Excitable, Foolhardy; "Lack Of" under Forethought; Hasty; "Sudden Impulses" under Impulses; Rashness, Recklessness, etc.).

THREADS—Threads and Specks Before the Eyes—(See "Threads" under Eyes).

THREATS—Threatened—

Danger Threatened—(See "Near Some Danger" under Danger).

Death Threatened — (See "Threatened" under Death; "Death Imminent" under Imminent).

Disease Threatened—(See "Threatened" under Disease).

Misfortune Threatened — (See "Some Misfortune Near" under Misfortune).

THRILLS—(See "Thrills" under Heart).

THRIVES—And Lives Thru Serious Illness — (See Immunity; "Good" under Recuperation, Resistance, Vitality; "Lives Thru Serious Illnesses" under Serious).

THROAT—The Fauces—Larynx—Pharynx—The Throat is under the external rulership of the ♉ Sign. Also ruled by ♀, the 2nd H., and influenced by all the Fixed Signs. (See Fixed Signs, Second House, Taurus, Venus). Planets when in signs immediately following their own home signs affect the throat, and influence the ♉ sign. The ☉ is at home in ♌, and thus when he is in ♍ he affects the throat, and so on with all the planets. The ☉ also in ♉, ♌, ♏, or ♒, the fixed signs, affects the throat, in addition to his other sign influences, according to this rule. Table 196 in Simmonite's Arcana is worked out along this line. The following subjects have to do with the diseases and afflictions of the throat, which see in the alphabetical arrangement when only listed here—

Abscesses—Of the Throat or Neck—(See "Abscesses" under Neck).

Adenoids; Affected—The Throat or Neck Affected—The ☉ in ♍ and the fixed signs; the ☽ in ♌ and fixed signs; ♄ in ♒ or ♓; ♃ in ♑, ♈, and fixed signs; ♂ in ♉, ♐, and fixed signs; ♀ in ♊, ♏, and fixed signs; ☿ in ♋, ♎, and fixed signs. (See "Affected" under Head; the Introduction to this Article, and Table 196 in Simmonite's Arcana).

All Diseases Of—☉ diseases; signified by afflictions in ♉, the 2nd H., and the fixed signs, and especially ♉ and ♏.

Aphasia—(See "Aphasia" under Speech).

Arteries and Veins—Of the Throat—Ruled by ♃ and ♀, and these planets afflicted in ♉ tend to affect the blood vessels of the throat and neck.

Blood—Excess of Blood In the Throat—♆ in ♉, ☌ the ☉ or ♂.

Breaking Out—In the Throat—The ☉ afflicted in ♉ when the ☉ is the afflictor in the disease; ♂ in ♏, by reflex action to ♉, as in Lues; a ♏ disease.

Breath Affected—By Catarrh In the Throat—♄ afflicted in ♉. (See "Foul Breath" under Breath; "Catarrh" in this section).

Cases of Throat Diseases—(See Figures 3A, 3B, 3C, 3D, 3E, 3F, 3G, 8A, 8B, 16B, in the book, "Astro-Diagnosis" by the Heindels; Figures 9, 10, 11, and 34, in "Message of the Stars", by the Heindels; Chap. XIII in Daath's Medical Astrology.

Catarrh Of—♄ afflicted in ♉; ♄ ☌ ☽ in ♉; the ☉ in ♉ and afflicted by ♄; Subs at MCP.

Cervical Region—Disorders In—(See Cervical).

Choking—♄ afflicted in ♉. (See Choking).

Chronic Distempers—About the Throat—♄ in ♉ when ♄ is the afflictor in the disease.

Circulation—The Circulation About the Throat Impaired—♄ ☌ ♃ or ♀ in ♉; ♃ or ♀ in ♉, □, or ☍ the ☉ or ♄. (See "Restricted" in this section).

Colds In—♄ afflicted in ♉.

Constrictions In—♅ or ♄ afflicted in ♉. (See Constrictions).

Contractions In—Spasmodic Contractions of—Constrictions—♅ afflicted in ♉; ♄ or ☋ in ♉, and especially in the 6th H. (See Constrictions, Contractions, Spasmodic).

Control—Loss of Nervous Control of the Throat—Swallowing Difficult—(See Deglutition; "Nerves" in this section).

Cough—(See "Throat Cough" under Cough).

Croup; Crystallization—(See Goiter).

Cuts His Own Throat—Suicide By—♂ afflicted in ♉, and with the Pleiades at B.; ♂ elevated above, and afflicting the hyleg. (See Suicide).

Death—By Throat Disorders—By Putrid Sore Throat—♄ afflicted in ♉; ♀ afflicted in ♉, by putrid sore throat; afflictions in the fixed signs, and especially in ♉ or ♏.

Defects—In the Throat—The ☉, ♄, or ☿ afflicted in ♉. (See "Structural" in this section).

Deglutition Difficult—Swallowing Difficult—(See Deglutition; "Nerves" in this section).

Diphtheria; Diseased Throat—Distempers In—Throat Trouble—Disordered Throat—Afflictions in ♉, ♏, and the fixed signs; the ☉ or ☽ afflicted in ♉ or ♏, and ☌ malefics in these signs; the ☉ afflicted in ♏, throat trouble of a violent and inflammatory nature; the ☽ hyleg in ♉, and afflicted, throat trouble in females; ♆, ♅, ♄, ♃, ♂, ♀, or ☿ afflicted in ♉ or ♏; a Stellium of planets in ♉, ♏, or the 2nd H., and afflicted, or containing malefics; planets in ♉ or ♏ in the Asc., 2nd, 6th, 8th, or 12th H., and afflicted; planets in fixed signs in the 6th H., and afflicted; malefics in ♉ and afflicting the hyleg; ♉ on the cusp the Asc. or 6th H., and afflicted by malefics; born under ♀ and ♀ badly afflicted at B., and by dir.; ♀ in ♉ in the 6th H., afflicted, or afflicting the ☽ or Asc.; ♏ on the cusp the Asc. or 6th H., and containing malefics; any planet afflicted in the 6th H. in a fixed sign; fixed signs on the cusp the 6th H., and afflicted, or containing malefics. The ♉ and ♏ signs are opposite and supplemental signs, and planets and afflictions in either of these signs tend to especially affect the throat and sex organs. This relationship is more fully explained in the Article on Larynx. Thus Syphilis, a ♏ disease, produces the ulcerated throat by reflex action in ♉. Also Subluxations of the Cervical Vertebrae, or MCP, and LCP, and at SP (7D), and at PP, tend to affect the throat. (See the various paragraphs in this section).

Distempers In—(See "Chronic", "Diseased Throat", in this section).

Dress—The Throat Disordered by Improper Dress—♀ afflicted in ♉. (See Dress).

Dryness—Dry and Feverish Throat—Dryness of the Throat Increased—Dry Fauces—♂ in ♉. (See Fauces).

Dysphonia—(See "Hoarseness" under Larynx).

Enlarged Tonsils—(See Tonsils).

Exanthematous Sore Throat—Afflictions in ♏. (See "Sore Throat" in this section).

Excess of Blood In—(See "Blood" in this section).

Expectoration — Great Expectoration of Phlegm—The ☽ afflicted in ♉, excess of mucus and phlegm in the throat; ♄ afflicted in ♈, much falling of mucus into the throat. (See "Great Expectoration" under Phlegm; "Humours", "Phlegm", in this section).

Exudations — Membranous Exudation In the Throat—(See Diphtheria, Exudations).

Fauces—Dryness of—(See "Dryness" in this section).

Fluids of Throat—Disorders of—Disturbance of—Restriction of—♄ afflicted in ♉ or ♏. (See "Ailments Of" under Fluids; "Dryness", "Restricted", in this section).

Fluxes — Of Rheum In the Throat — (See "Rheum" in this section).

Glandular Swellings — In Throat and Neck—A ♉ disease; afflictions in ♉ or ♏, and fixed signs; ♄ ☌ ♅ in ♉ or ♏; ♀ afflicted in ♉; signified by the 2nd H.; Subs at CP and KP. (See "Glands" under Neck; "Swellings" in this section).

Goiter; Heat — Extreme Heat In the Throat and Mouth—♂ in ♐ when ♂ is the afflictor in the disease; ♂ in ♐, ☌, or ill-asp. the ☉, and with ♂ as Promittor. (See "Heats" under Heat).

Hoarseness—(See Larynx).

Humours—Falling Into the Throat—The ☽ in ♈, □, or ☍ ♄ (or ☿ if he be of the nature of ♄) when first taken ill, or at decumbiture. (See "Expectoration", "Rheum", in this section).

Inflammation — All Inflammatory Action In the Throat — ♂ afflicted in ♉; ♉ diseases. (See "Sore Throat" in this section; Diphtheria; "Inflammation" under Larynx; "Pharyngitis" under Pharynx; "Tonsilitis" under Tonsils).

Influenza — Involving the Throat — (See Influenza).

Irritations — ♅, and other bodies afflicted in ♉. (See "Cough", "Spasmodic", in this section).

Larynx — Disorders of — (See Larynx; "Vocal Cords" under Voice).

Lymphatic Vessels Of—(See "Throat" under Lymphatic).

Membranes—Membranous Exudations—Membranous Deposits — (See Croup, Diphtheria, Exudations; "Mucous Membranes" in this section).

Minor Diseases—Of the Throat—The benefics in ♉; ♉ on the cusp of the Asc. or 6th H., and not severely afflicted; few planets in fixed signs at B.

Mole—Mole On the Throat or Neck—Malefics in ♉ or the 2nd H. (See "Moles" under Neck).

Motor Nerves — Of the Throat — Disorders of—♅ afflicted in ♉. (See Incoordination).

Mucous Membranes — Mucous Surfaces—Mucus—Mucus Falling Into the Throat—Exudations—Expectoration of Mucus and Phlegm, etc.—(See Croup, Diphtheria, Exudations; Expectoration, Humours, Phlegm, Rheum, in this section).

Mumps—(See Parotid).

Neck — (See the various paragraphs under Neck).

Nerves—Of the Throat—Disorders of—♅ afflicted in ♉, disturbances of the motor nerves of the throat; ☿ afflicted in ♉. (See "Control", "Deglutition", in this section; "Nervous Disorders" under Neck).

Obscure Diseases—Of the Throat and Neck—♆ afflicted in ♉. (See Obscure).

Obstructions In — The Throat Obstructed—♄ afflicted in ♉ or ♏; ♃ afflicted in ♑ when the afflictor in the disease. (See Stoppages, Swellings, Tumors, in this section; "Hoarseness" under Larynx; Tonsils).

Operations — Avoid surgical operations upon the throat when the ☽ is passing thru the ♈, ♉, or ♊ signs, and when the ☽ is in a fixed sign, if possible. (See "Rules" under Operations).

Pains In — (See "Pains In" under Neck).

Palate; Pertussis — (See "Convulsive" under Cough; Whooping).

Pharynx—(See the paragraphs under Pharynx).

Phlegm—An Excess of Phlegm In the Throat—The ☽ in ♉, ☌, P., □, or ☍ ♄ (or ☿ if he be of the nature of ♄) at the beginning of an illness, or at decumbiture; ♄ afflicted in ♉ or ♏. (See Expectoration, Humours, Mucous, Rheum, in this section; Phlegm).

Poisonings In — (See "Septic" in this section).

Polypus; Prevalent—Throat Disorders Prevalent—♂ in ♉ or ♋ at the Vernal Equinox, and lord of the year.

Putrid Sore Throat—The ☽ in ♉, and afflicted by the ☉ or ♂ when taken ill (Hor'y); ♀ afflicted in ♉, and denotes death by. (See "Death", "Septic", "Sore Throat", in this section).

Quinsy—(See Tonsils).

Relaxed Throat — A ♀ disease; ♀ afflicted in ♉; the ☽ and ♀ afflicted in ♉. (See Relaxation).

Restricted—The Circulation or Fluids of the Throat Restricted — ♄ afflicted in ♉ or ♏. (See "Circulation", "Fluids", in this section).

Rheum — Fluxes of Rheum Into the Throat — A ♉ disease, and afflictions in ♉; ♄ in ♈ when ♄ is the afflictor in the disease. (See Rheum; Expectoration, Humours, Mucous, Phlegm, in this section).

Scar—In the Throat, or On the Neck — Malefics in ♉ or the 2nd H. (See "Mole" in this section; Marks, Moles, Scars).

Septic Poisonings—Of the Throat—♆ afflicted in ♉. (See "Putrid", "Sore Throat", in this section).

Singing — Avoid Loud Singing—(See "Singers" under Music).

Sore Throat—Putrid Sore Throat—♉ diseases, and afflictions in ♉; malefics afflicted in ♉; ♀ afflicted in ♉, putrid sore throat and death by; afflictions in ♏; ♉ or ♏ on the Asc. or cusp the 6th H., and containing afflictions; afflictions in ♏ tend to exanthematous sore throat; the ☉ in ♉ or ♍, ☌, or ill-asp. any of the malefics as Promittors; the ☽ in ♉, ♏, or any of the fixed signs, and ☌ or ill-asp. ♄ (or ☿ if he be of the nature of ♄) at the beginning of an illness, or at decumbiture (Hor'y); ♆, ♅, or ♄ in ♒, and afflicting the ☉ or ☽; ♃ or ♀ ☌ ♄ in ♉, due to congestion and poor circulation; ♂ afflicted in ♉; ♂ in ♉ or fixed signs in the 6th H., and afflicted; signified by the 2nd H., and by malefics in this house at B. (See Hoarseness, Inflammation, Putrid, Quinsy, Septic, Swellings, Syphilitic, Tonsils, Ulcerated, and the various paragraphs in this section).

Spasmodic Disorders — In the Throat —♅ afflicted in ♉. (See Spasmodic; "Contractions" in this section).

Stoppages In—The ☽ or ♄ afflicted in ♉; ♄ ☌ the ☽ in ♉. (See "Obstructions" in this section).

Stricture Of — ♅ or ♄ afflicted in ♉. (See Stricture; "Contractions" in this section).

Structural Defects—The ☉ afflicted in ♉. (See Structural).

Suppurations — (See Exudations, Putrid, Septic, Sore, Tonsils, Ulcerated, in this section).

Swallowing Difficult — (See Control, Deglutition, Nerves, in this section).

Swellings In—The ☉, ☽, ♄, or ♃ afflicted in ♉; ♃ afflicted in ♈, and caused by ill-blood in the veins of the head. (See Glandular, Inflammation, Obstructions, Sore, Tumors, in this section).

Syphilitic Throat—Syphilitic Ulcers—(See "Throat" under Syphilis; "Ulcerated" in this section).

Taurus—(See "Diseases" under Taurus).

Throat Complaints Generally—The ☉ afflicted in ♉. (See "Prevalent" in this section).

Throat Trouble— (See "Diseased Throat", and the various paragraphs in this section).

Tissues—♆ has special rule over the tissues of the throat, and ♆ afflicted in ♉ or the 2nd H. tends to disorders, septic poisonings, and wastings of the tissues of the throat. (See "Wasting" under Tissues).

Tonsils—Disorders of—(See Tonsils).

Tubercular Throat—♄ affl. in ♉. (See "Consumption" under Larynx).

Tumors—(See "Tumors" under Neck).

Ulcerated Throat—A ♉ and ♏ disease; the ☽ afflicted in ♉; ♀ afflicted in ♉, ulceration and disorders due to improper protection of the throat, and indiscretions in dress; ♂ afflicted in ♏ tends to ulcerated throat, and the Venereal Ulcers of Lues, or Syphilis. (See Ulcers; "Sore Throat" in this section).

Veins—(See "Arteries" in this section).

Venereal Ulcers — In Throat — (See "Ulcerated" in this section).

Voice—Vocal Cords—Disorders of—(See Larynx, Speech, Voice).

Wasting — Of the Tissues of the Throat—(See "Tissues" in this section).

Whooping Cough—(See Whooping).

THROBBING—Pulsating—Beating—Throbbing in the different parts of the body may be caused by various planetary influences. Palpitation of the heart is usually caused by ♅ in the heart sign ♌. The throbbing from the fullness of blood vessels, and high blood pressure, is usually caused by ♃, and due to plethoric conditions. The ♂ influence over a part tends to draw too much blood to the part, due to his heating influence, and cause throbbing. The deposits and obstructions of ♄ often cause throbbing, pain, and aches in a part. For these various influences see "Throbbing" under Aches, Ears, Heart, Limbs; "Fullness of Blood", "High Blood Pressure", under Blood; "Rush of Blood" under Head; Pain, Plethora, Pulse, Surfeits, Tremors; "Beating" under Vessels).

THROMBUS—A Blood Clot In a Vessel —Embolism—Infarct—The influence of ♄ is clotting and obstructing; ♄ ☌ ♃ or ♀, rulers of the circulation, and affecting the part containing the affliction.

Brain—Thrombus In—(See "Clot On Brain" under Brain). See Clots, Embolism, Infarcts, Obstructions.

THRUSH — Aphthae — (See Aphthae; "Thrush" under Mouth).

THRUSTS — Thrusts with Weapons — Kicks by Animals, etc. — (See Duels, Instruments, Kicks, Stabs, Sword, War).

THUMBS — (See "Thumb" under Fingers).

THUNDER—Ruled by ♃.

Deaths—Many Deaths from Thunder and Lightning Storms—♄ in ♊, direct in motion, and angular at the Vernal Equinox; ♂ in ♊ and lord of the year at the Vernal; Eclipses of the ☽ in ♏; Comets appearing in ♊ or ♒. (See Clouds, Lightning, Storms, Wind).

Much Thunder—And Lightning—An eclipse of the ☽ in the 1st Decan. of ♏.

THURSDAY—Day of the Week. Ruled by ♃. (See "Days of the Week" under Week).

THYMUS GLANDS—A Glandular Organ at the Base of the Tongue—Ruled by ♀. Some Authors say it is also ruled by ♊ and ♍.

Disorders Of—♀ afflicted by malefics. Case—See Fig. 17C in the book, "Astro-Diagnosis", by the Heindels.

THYROID GLAND — Thyroid Cartilage —Ruled by ☿, and also by the ♉ and ♍ Signs. The ☽ when in ♉ rules and affects this Gland. The Thyroid Gland acts as a connecting link between the Pineal Gland and the Pituitary Body. (See Pineal, Pituitary). The Thyroid Cartilage is ruled by ♄ and the ♉ sign. Brain Balance is also under the rule of the Thyroid Gland, and is controlled largely by the secretions of this Gland.

Brain Balance—Disturbances of—Afflictions to ☿. (See "Unbalanced Mentality" under Mental).

Circulation Disturbed—Circulation and Functions of the Thyroid Disturbed—♆ afflicted by ♄; ♆ in ♉, ☌, □, or ☍ ♄; Subs at LCP (6C). Case—See Fig. 17B in "Astro-Diagnosis", by the Heindels.

Disturbed Thyroid — ♆ or H afflicted in ♉; malefics in ♉; H ☌ ♄ in ♉ or ♏.

Enlarged Thyroid — Goiter — ♆ in ♉, and afflicted by ♄; ♆ ☌ the ☉ and ♂ in ♉; ♀ afflicted in ♉. Case—See Fig. 17A in "Astro-Diagnosis", by the Heindels. (See Goiter).

Functions Disturbed — (See "Circulation" in this section).

Goiter — Enlarged Thyroid — (See Goiter; "Enlarged" in this section).

Mental Growth Retarded — Arrested Mental and Physical Growth — Caused by afflictions to ☿, the ruler of this Gland. (See Backwardness, Cretinism, Dwarfed, Idiocy, Imbecile, Myxoedema).

Physical Disorders—Diseases Which Often Accompany Disturbed Thyroid—(See Cretinism, Goiter; "Arrested" under Growth; Leprosy, Myxoedema; the various paragraphs in this section).

Thyroid Cartilage — Adam's Apple — Prominent Adam's Apple—(See "Long" under Neck).

TIBIA—The Shin Bone—Shank—Under the structural rulership of the ♒ Sign. Is opposite to, and corresponds to the Radius in the arm, ruled by ♌. All diseases in, infirmities or accidents to, fracture, etc., are signified by the 11th H., and also caused by afflictions in ♒. Dislocation of the head of the Tibia is caused by afflictions in ♑. (See Ankles, Fibula, Knees, Legs, Radius).

TICS—Spasmodic Twitchings—

Tic Dourouleux—Spasmodic Facial Neuralgia — (See "Movements" under Erratic; "Neuralgia", "Spasmodic", under Face; Jerkings, Saint Vitus Dance, Spasmodic Diseases, Tremors, Twitchings).

TIDAL AIR — In the Lungs — Ruled by the ☽.

Lack of In Lungs—Insufficient—♄ in ♊ and ☍ the ☽ tends to insufficient tidal air in the lungs, and lack of oxygenation. The tidal air in the lungs is almost stopped by ♄ or ☋ in ♊, and other afflictions in ♊; the ☉ in ♊ or ♐, interferences with the tidal air; ♄ afflicted in ♏, the tidal air in the bowels is disturbed, causing a weakened action of the diaphragm, and disturbed breathing. (See "Inbreathing" under Anus; "Labored" under Breathing; "Carbonic Acid Poisoning" under Carbon; "Non-Oxygenation" under Oxygen).

TIDES—(See "Tides" under Moon).

Tidal Waves — (See this subject under Water).

TIGHT—Tightness—

Tightness of Chest—(See "Tightness" under Chest).

Tightness of Feature — (See "Tightness" under Features).

Tight Lacing — Causing Respiratory Troubles — (See "Indiscretions" under Dress).

TIME—The Time Factor In Life—"To Everything There Is a Season, and a Time to Every Purpose under the Heaven; a Time to be Born, and a Time to Die." Eccl. 3:1, 2. These Times are governed by the Planetary movements, as the Planets are but the visible material bodies, or vehicles, thru which the Archangels of God work to carry out His Orders, and to administer, direct, and supervise Human Affairs on our Earth, and in other parts of our Solar System. The ☽ is the Time Marker in Human Affairs and World Conditions, the minute hand on the Clock of Destiny, and the ☉ is the Hour Hand. (See "Aspects" under Moon).

Accidents—(See "Time of Accidents" under Accidents).

Acute Diseases—The Time When Apt to Come—(See "Periods of Acute Disease" under Acute).

Birth—Time of—The Time of Birth is a fixed quantity, if not interfered with, and the child will be born when the heavens form the star map predetermined. Delivery, therefore, should not be hastened by drugs or instruments, except in emergencies to save the life of the mother or child, or both, and where abnormalities exist. (See "Causes of Birth", "Delayed Birth", "Moment of Birth", "Premature Birth", "Time of Birth", under Birth; "Birth of a Child", "Born", "Delayed Births", "Time of Advent", under Children; "Moment of Birth" under Moment; Premature, Prenatal Epoch).

Child Promised — (See "Birth of a Child" under Children).

Conception — (See "Time of Conception" under Conception).

Crises In Disease — Time of — (See Crises).

Death—Time of Death—In the ordinary course of events in the life of an individual, the planetary influences and directions, or progressions, reach a point where there is a checkmate, and when the game of life in the physical body must cease. This time can be ascertained if the student cares to work long enough, and hard enough to determine all the influences which may be afflicting the Hyleg in the train of fatal directions. However, it is unwise, and unethical for Astrologers to predict the time of death of people, even if they know, or to state openly when noted and famous people will die, due to the worry it might cause. The time of death, or what may seem to us to be the apparent time of death, can sometimes be put off, or prevented for the time, by right living, right thinking, spiritual attainment, and by obtaining wisdom and knowledge of the plan of things. However, most people die on scheduled time, and fit right into the scheme of things by drifting along with their stars, and by following their natural, or evil tendencies. The only proper way of discovering the probable time of death is by directing the Hyleg to the Anareta, and this can only be done when the true hour and moment of birth are known. One fatal direction to the Hyleg ordinarily dose not kill, and death by disease is usually the result of the afflictions of a train of evil directions to the hyleg. When the hour of birth is not known a Horary Figure may be erected at the strong desire of the Querent, which figure tends to answer the purpose of a true map of birth for judgment in the matter. These rules for working out the time of death in Hor'y Questions would be too lengthy to list here, but they are given quite fully in Lilly's Astrology. Also a smaller and handy book is "Raphael's Horary Astrology." There are a number of standard books on Horary Astrology, and the student should own them, and make a study of this subject. For further rules and influences along this line in this book, see Anareta; "Death During Childhood" under Childhood; "Death of Children" under Children; Crises; "Arguments for Death", "Certain Death", "Day of Death", "Hour of Death", under Death; Directions; "Early Death" under Early; Events, Fatal, Hyleg; "Death In Infancy" under Infancy; "Long Life", "Probable Length of Life", "Short Life", under Life; "Death At Middle Life" under Middle Life; "Dies In Old Age" under Old Age; "Death In Youth" under Youth, etc.

Disease—Illness—Sickness—The Time When Due In the Ordinary Course of Life—(See "Time of the Disease" under Disease; "Periods of Bad Health" under Health; "Type of the Disease" under Type).

Energy—A Time of Great Energy—(See "Great Energy" under Energy).

Events—The Time of Events of Various Kinds—(See Events).

Evil—An Evil Time for the Native—(See "Time" under Evil).

Hurts—(See "Time Of" under Hurts).

Imprisonment—(See "Time Of" under Prison).

Injuries — (See "Time Of" under Injuries).

Life—The Time Factor In Life—(See Childhood, Climacteric; "Critical Days", "Critical Periods", under Critical; Cycles, Infancy, Middle Life, Old Age, Periodic; "Life", "Seven Year Periods", under Periods; Youth).

Misfortune — (See Disgrace, Dishonour; "Time Of" under Misfortune; "Loss Of" under Reputation; Reverses, Ruin, Scandal, Sorrow, Trouble, etc.).

Public Grief—A Time of—(See "Public Grief" under Public).

Recovery—The Time of—(See Amelioration; "Better" under Disease; Moderation; "How Long Before Recovery", "Signs of Recovery", under Recovery).

Sorrow—A Time of—(See Sorrow).

Travel—Good and Bad Times For—(See Travel).

Trouble—A Time of—(See Trouble). For other subjects along this line not listed here look in the alphabetical arrangement for the subject you have in mind.

TIMIDITY—A ☽ and ♋ Sign influence. Also caused by the afflictions of ♆. (See Backwardness, Bashfulness; "Mind" under Dull; Fears, Mistrustful, Modesty, Recluse, Reserved, Retiring, Rigel, Secretive, Sensitiveness, Shy, Solitude, Suspicious, etc.).

TIN—Stannum—A Typical Metal of ♃. (See Jupiter, Metals, Therapeutics).

TINEA—A Skin Disease from Fungi—(See "Barber's Itch" under Barbers; Herpes, Itch, Ringworm, Tetter, Worms).

TINGLING — Of the Nerves — Tingling Sensations—Numbness In a Nerve—♄ ☌ or ill-asp. ☿; ♅ ☌ ☿, and in the part ruled by the sign ♅ is in at B. (See Numbness, Paraesthesia).

TINNITUS AURIUM — (See "Ringing" under Ears).

TIRED FEELING—The ☽ afflicted in ♑; ♃ in ♑; ♑ or ♋ on the Asc. at B. (See Apathy, Dull, Fatigue, Inactive, Indifferent, Inertia, Lassitude, Lazy, Lethargy, Listless; "Low" under Vitality; "Weak Body" under Weak).

TISSUES—The Modern Writers say that ♆ has strong rule over the Tissues, and that ♆ afflicted in any sign tends to wasting of the tissues of the part involved. All of the planets affect the tissues in their own way. The ☉ and ♂ supply heat and force to the tissues, and also help to burn up wastes. Decay and disintegration, and the death of tissue, are the work of ♄ and the ☽. The conservation and preservation of tissue are the work of the benefics ♃ and ♀. The nerve tissues are supported by ☿. The following subjects have to do with the tissues, which subjects see in the alphabetical arrangement when only listed here—

Absorption of Tissue — Analysis of Tissue — Resolution of — A ♄ disease. (See Absorption).

Adipose Tissue—(See Fat).

Alterations In — (See "Alterations" under Cells).

Analysis Of — (See "Absorption" in this section).

Animal Tissue — The Animal Tissues are connected with the ♊ Sign, and the ♊ Salt, Potassium Chloride. (See Potassium; "Salts" under Zodiac).

Areolar Tissue—Connective, or Cellular Tissue—Inflammation of—Combustion of—(See Phlegmon; Cellular, Combustion, Connective, in this section).

Arms—Wasting of the Tissues of—♆ afflicted in signs which rule the arms, hands, legs, and feet tends to wasting of the tissues of these parts. (See "Wasting" in this section).

Atrophy Of—(See Atrophy).

Blood Circulation — And Distribution In the Tissues — Ruled and presided over by the ♒ Sign. (See Circulation).

Blood Vessels—Of the Tissues—(See "Blood Vessels" under Blood).

Bony Tissue—(See Bones).

Building—Cellular Tissue Building—(See "Tissue Building" under Cells).

Capillaries; Cartilage—Cartilaginous Tissue Building—The work of ♄. (See Cartilage).

Cells—Cellular Tissue Building—(See Cells).

Changes—Structural Changes In the Tissues—(See Lesions, Structural).

Circulation — In the Tissues — (See Circulation).

Cirrhosis; Cleansing—Of the Tissues —(See Cleansing).

Combustion — Of the Tissues — (See Combustion).

Connective Tissue (See Connective).

Conservation Of —(See Conservation).

Contraction Of (See Contractions).

Corrosion; Crusts—Of Dead Tissue— ♂ diseases. (See Crusts).

Crystallization; Dead Tissue — (See "Crusts" in this section).

Decay Of — Decomposition of — The work of ♄ and the ☽. Urea is the principal nitrogenous product of tissue decomposition. (See "Tissues" under Decay; Decomposition, Urea).

Decomposition Of — (See "Decay" in this section).

Defects In — Structural Defects are caused by afflictions to the ☉. Defects in the bony structure are ♄ afflictions. (See Bones, Defects, Organic, Structural).

Degeneration — Of the Tissues — Deterioration of — Presided over by ♄. (See Decay, Degeneration, Deterioration, Emaciation, Fatigue, Softening, Wasting, etc.).

Depletion—(See "Constitution" under Depletion).

Development—Of the Tissues—Is assisted greatly when ♆ is △ or ⚹ the Asc. (See Assimilation, Nutrition).

Dissolution Of—(See Dissolution).

Drying Up — Of Tissues — ♄ diseases and afflictions. (See Atrophy, Crystallization; "Dry Diseases" under Dry; Scales, Shrinking, Withering).

Effusions Into—(See Effusions).

Elephantiasis; Emollients — Agents Which Soften the Tissues—(See Emollients).

Epithelioma; Expansion Of—(See Expansion).

Extravasations—(See Effusions).

Face—(See "Tissues" under Face).

Feet — (See "Tissues" under Feet; "Wasting" in this section).

Fibers — Fibrous Tissue Building — The work of ♂. (See Fiber).

Glandular Tissue—(See "Tissues" under Glands).

Hands—(See "Wasting" under Hands, and in this section).

Hardening; Hypertrophy; Induration; Inflammation Of—(See "Tissues" under Inflammation).

Intercellular Spaces—(See "Intercellular" under Cells).

Interstitial Tissues—(See "Intercellular" under Cells; Connective, Interstitial).

Laxity Of—(See Laxity, Relaxation).

Legs — Wasting of the Tissues of — (See "Arms" in this section).

Lesions; Ligaments; Lymphatics;

Malacia — Softening of Tissue — (See Malacia, Softening).

Metabolism; Metamorphosis; Muscles;

Nerves—Nerve Tissue Building—The work of ♅ and ☿. Wasting of the Nerve Tissues is a ♆ disease and affliction. (See "Neurotic", "Tissues", under Nerves; "Wasting" in this section).

Nutrition—(See "Tissues" under Nutrition).

Obstruction — Of Tissues —(See Hindrances, Obstructions, Retarded, Stoppages. Suppressions).

Oedema; Organic Defects—(See Congenital, Organic, Structural).

Parenchyma—Soft Cellular Tissue— (See Parenchyma).

Polarity Of—(See Polarity).

Preservation Of — (See Conservation, Preservation).

Relaxed Tissues — (See Emollient, Laxity, Relaxation).

Resolution Of—(See "Absorption" in this section; "Resolution Of" under Resolution).

Resolvents — Agents Reducing the Swelling of Tissue—(See Resolvent).

Respiratory System — Tissues of Affected—(See "Tissues Affected" under Breathing).

Sclerosis—(See Hardening, Sclerosis).

Serum Collections—(See Serum).

Shrinking; Sinews; Soft Tissues—The Soft Tissues, taken as a whole, are under the rule of the ☽, and the ☽ afflicted tends to disorders of these tissues. (See Decay, Gangrene, Glands, Muscles, Parenchyma; "Tissues" under Soft).

Softening Agents — (See Emollients, Resolvent).

Softening of Tissues—♓ and ♀ influence. (See Malacia, Softening).

Solution of Tissue — (See Resolvent; "Tissue" under Solution; "Absorption", "Degeneration", in this section).

Structural Defects — (See Congenital, Defects, Hereditary, Innate, Organic, Structural).

Suppressions—Of Tissues—(See Ablation, Remote, Removal, Suppressions).

Suppurations — (See Phlegmon, Pus, Putrid).

Tendons; Texture—Of the Tissues— Ruled by ☿. (See Texture).

Thickening; Throat—Wasting of the Tissues of — (See "Tissues" under Throat).

Tissue Building — (See "Building" in this section).

Tissue Remedies—(See "Zodiac Salts" under Healers).

Tubes—Tubules—(See Tubes).

Vascular Tissues—(See Arteries, Capillaries, Vascular, Vaso, Veins, Vessels).

Vessels; Warmth — Of the Tissues — (See Electric, Heat).

Wasting — Of the Tissues — ♆ and ♄ influence. (See Atrophy, Consumptions, Emaciation; "Malnutrition" under Nutrition; Phthisis, Tabes, Tuberculosis, Wasting; "Arms", "Nerves", in this section).

Withering Of — (See Atrophy, Emaciation, Hardening, Infirm, Old Age, Scales, Shrinkage, Tabes, Withering, Wrinkles). For other subjects which have to do with the Tissues, and which may have been overlooked for this Article, look for the subject in the alphabetical arrangement.

TOBACCO — Tabacum — Nicotine — The Dried Leaves of Nicotiana Tabacum, and is a powerful Depressant. Tobacco is classed as an Herb of Mars. (See Mars Group under Herbs). The Herbs of ♂ are generally stimulant. Tobacco stimulates at first, but later, if its use is persisted in, it becomes a depressant, and paralyzes the motor nerves of the involuntary muscles, and of the secreting nerves of the glands, and also of the Spinal Cord, and the Vagus Nerve. It is also sedative and narcotic, and undoubtedly comes under the rulership of ♆ under its persistent and habitual use. The moderate use of tobacco, if it does not debilitate the system, is said to be a protection against infection. (See Infections).

Drug Heart — Tobacco Heart — (See "Drug Heart", "Tobacco Heart", under Heart).

Snuff Habit—(See "Snuff" under Narcotics).

Tobacco Habit—Smoking—Chewing—Cigarette Habit, etc.—♆ influence; ♆ afflicted in the 6th or 12th H.; ♆ ☌ ♄ in the 6th or 12th H.; ♆ afflicted in ♌ or the 5th H., tobacco heart. (See "Cigarettes", "Tobacco Habit" under Narcotics). Case—Addicted to the Use of Tobacco—See "Self-Indulgent", No. 229, in 1001 N.N.

TOES — Digits of the Feet — The Toes are under the structural rulership of the ♓ Sign, and are opposite to the fingers, which are ruled by the ♍ Sign. The Toes are also ruled by the 12th H.

Accidents To — Hurts, Injuries, or Wounds To—♄ or ♂ afflicted in ♓ or the 12th H. (See "Accidents", "Hurts", "Injuries", under Feet).

All Diseases In — Signified by afflictions in the 12th H., and in the ♓ Sign; the malefics afflicted in ♓.

Athetosis—Inability to Hold the Fingers or Toes in One Position—A Nervous and Spasmodic Affliction — ♅ afflicted in ♓ or the 12th H.; Subs at LPP. (See "Athetosis" under Fingers).

Coldness Of—Coldness and Whiteness of — (See "Raynaud's Disease" under Fingers).

Corns — Corns and Bunions — (See Bunions).

Cramps In — ♅ afflicted in ♓. (See "Cramps" under Feet).

Deformed Toes — Afflictions in ♓ or the 12th H.; ♄ or ♂ afflicted in ♓.

Diseases Of — Distempers In — Afflictions in ♍ or ♓; ♄ or ♂ afflicted in ♓; malefics in ♓. (See "Diseases In", "Distempers", under Feet).

Feet — (See the various subjects under Feet).

Fingers—(See the paragraphs under Fingers).

Gout In—(See "Feet" under Gout).

Ingrowing Nails — (See "Ingrowing" under Nails).

Joints — Gout In — (See "Feet" under Gout).

Left Foot — Two Toes Missing On — Case—See "Born Incomplete", No. 281, in 1001 N.N.

Missing—Two Toes Missing on Left Foot—(See "Left Foot" in this section).

Nails—Suppuration and Phlegmonous Inflammation About the Nails—Panaris — Whitlows — Falling Out of the Nails — ♆ afflicted in ♍, ♓, or in the Signs in the 6th or 12th H., and affecting the nails of the fingers or toes. (See "Felons" under Fingers; Phlegmon, Pus).

Raynaud's Disease — (See "Coldness" in this section).

Tetanic Spasm In—(See "Fingers and Toes" under Tetanus).

Two Toes Missing—On the Left Foot —(See "Left Foot" in this section).

Whitlows—(See "Nails" in this section).

Writes with Toes—Case—See "Armless Wonder", No. 054, in 1001 N.N.

TOMBOYISHNESS — (See this subject under Females).

TONE — Tonicity of the Body — Vital Tonicity—The Normal Activity or Vigor —The Pressure or Resistance of the Body to Disease, Wear and Tear—The Stamina and Vitality—

Good Tone—The ☉ or ☽ ☌, ⚹, or △ the Asc. at B.; the ☉ well-aspected by ♂ at B.; the ☽ to the ☌ or good aspect ♃ by dir. (See "Good" under Constitution, Health, Resistance, Recuperation, Stamina, Vitality; Invigoration, Robust; "Body" under Strong; Vigor, Zest).

Lack of Tone—The Tone Lowered—Atony—The ☉ or ☽ weak and afflicted at B.; the ☽ afflicted in ♑, lowers the tone and vitality thru worry and depression; the ☽ afflicted in ♏ lowers the whole tone and the vital and natural powers of the body; the ☽ to the ☌ or ill-asp. ♄ by dir., the health suffers from want of tone; the Asc. afflicted by the ☉ or ☽; afflictions in ♎ show disturbance in the system, causing want of tone; characteristic of the Lymphatic Temperament. (See Atony, Debility, Feeble, Infirm, Invalids, Lymphatic, Pale; "Low" under Resistance, Stamina, Vitality; Sickly; "Much Sickness" under Sickness; "Weak Body" under Weak).

TONGUE—Glossa—The Organ of Taste and Speech—Ruled by ☿. The ♉ sign and ☿ have special affinity with the tongue, and the papillae of the tongue. Dr. Duz says the tongue is ruled by the ♎ sign. When in ♈ the planet ☿ has strong rule over the tongue, and greatly affects the tongue for good or ill, according to his aspects.

Chronic Glossitis—(See "Glossitis" in this section).

Cystic Tumor — Under the Tongue — Epulis — Ranula — ♀ affl. in ♉. (See "Tumor" under Gums).

Defects In — Imperfections — Impediment On—The ☉ ☌ ☿ in angles. However, if ♂ is also with them, the defect will tend to be removed when the ☽ by progression reaches the place of ♂; the ☽ Sig. □ or ☍ ☿; a ☿ disease; ☿ afflicted at B.; ☿ affl. in ♓, an impediment in the tongue. (See Dumb, Inarticulate, Mute; "Impediment", "Stammering", under Speech; "Tongue-Tied" in this section).

Epulis—(See "Cystic" in this section).

Foul Tongue—Foul and Diseased—A ☿ disease, and afflictions to ☿ at B.; ♄ ☌ or ill-asp. ☿ at B., and by dir.; the ☽ in ♈, and afflicted by the ☉ or ♂ when taken ill (Hor'y); Subs at MCP and SP. (See "Foul" under Breath).

Glossitis—Inflammation of the Tongue—Swollen Tongue—♂ afflicted in ♉; Subs at MCP and SP (7D). The chronic form is caused by ♄ affl. in ♉. or ♄ ☌ ♂ in ♉ at B. (See Aphthae; "Inflamed" under Gums).

Impediment On—(See "Defects" in this section).

Imperfections In—(See "Defects" in this section).

Paralysis Of—♅ or ☿ affl. in ♉; ♅ ☌ ☿ in ♉, and otherwise afflicted by malefics. (See Coordination, Incoordination, Paralysis).

Ranula—(See "Cystic" in this section).

Stammering—Stuttering—(See "Stammering" under Speech).

Tongue-Tied—Case—See "Born Incomplete", No. 281 in 1001 N.N. This defect is caused by afflictions to ☿ at B.; ☿ affl. by ♄; born under ☿; a ☿ sign rising on the Asc. at B., and ☿ badly afflicted.

Tumor Of—(See "Cystic" in this section).

Writes—With Aid of the Tongue—Case—See "Tunison", No. 113, in 1001 N.N.

TONIC—Tonic Action—Tonics—The ☉ and ♂ have a tonic influence over the body. (See Constructive, Electric, Energy, Exaggerated; "Life Force" under Force; Mars, Sun).

Color—Red is a tonic color, and to wear red colors, be confined in a red room, or be treated with red lights and rays, are stimulating and bracing to the weak. Red Color is ruled by ♂. (See Colors; "Treatment" under Red; Stimulant).

Disorders—Tonic Disorders—Perverted Tonic Action—The ☉ and ♂ weak and affl. at B., or afflicting each other.

Fibers—Over-Braced Tonic Fibers—A ♂ disease. (See Fiber).

Hair Tonics—Injury From—(See Cosmetics; "Tonics" under Hair).

Medicines—Tonic Drugs—The ☉ and ♂ drugs and plants are tonic. Tonic medicines are ruled by ♂. Medicinally ♂ is tonic, and rules Iron and iron tonics. The tonic remedies of ♂ relieve neuralgia from a weak circulation caused by ♄. (See "Drugs" under Mars, Sun; Medicines, Stimulants, Treatment).

Perverted Tonic Action—(See "Disorders" in this section).

Planets—Tonic Action of—Each planet in the map of birth, according to position and aspects, is intrinsically tonic or atonic, electric or magnetic, positive or negative, and exerts a normal, natural, unnatural, or perverted influence, a plus or minus influence over the body. Planets in great conflict with each other at B. by evil aspects, and being situated contrary to their natural influences, tend to perverted tonic disorders, such as enlargements, exaggerated action, hypertrophy, overactivity, tumors, growths, etc. (See these subjects. Also see "Perverted Action" under Planets). The Tonic Planets are the ☉, ♅, ♃ and ♂. The Atonic Planets are ♆, ♄, ☽, and ♀. (See Atonic). The planet ♅ exerts an alternate, or clonic action, as in spasms, spasmodic diseases, contractions, convulsions, etc. (See Aspects, Clonic; "Organs" under Enlargement; Exaggerated, Hyperactivity, Hypertrophy; "Action Of", "Tonic Action", under Mars; Motion; "Clonic", "Tonic", under Spasmodic; "Action Of" under Sun).

Spasms—Tonic Spasms—(See Convulsions, Epilepsy; "Spasms", "Tonic", under Spasmodic).

Stimulants—Tonic Medicines—(See "Medicines" in this section; Drugs, Medicines, Poisons, Rubefacients, Stimulants).

TONSILS—The Glandular Organ on Each Side of the Fauces—Ruled by the ♉ Sign. Also strongly influenced by the opposite sign ♏, and especially at the time of Adolescence. (See "Disturbed" under Puberty). The ☽ when in ♉ strongly rules over, and affects the tonsils for good or ill, according to her aspects.

Ablation—Suppression of the Tonsils—Removal by Suppression—♄ afflicted in ♉ or ♏. Case—Of Removal of the Tonsils by Ablation—See Chap. XIII in Daath's Medical Astrology. (See Ablation, Remote, Removal, Suppression).

Amygdalitis—(See "Tonsilitis" in this section).

Cases—Of Tonsils Affected—See Figures 3A, 3B, 3C, 3D, 16B, in the book, "Astro-Diagnosis" by the Heindels; Chap. XIII in Daath's Medical Astrology.

Diseased Tonsils—Afflictions in ♉; Subs at LCP (6C), and at SP (7D). (See the various paragraphs in this section).

Enlarged Tonsils—♂ affl. in ♉ or ♏; a ♀ disease, and caused by afflictions to ♀; ♀ afflicted in ♉. (See "Swollen", "Tonsilitis", in this section; Enlargements).

Exudation On—(See Diphtheria, Exudations).

Fauces—(See the paragraphs under Fauces).

Follicular Tonsilitis—(See "Tonsilitis" in this section).

Inflamed Tonsils—♂ afflicted in ♉. (See "Tonsilitis" in this section).

Operations—For Removal of Tonsils—Do not operate when the ☽ is passing thru the ♈, ♉, or ♊ Signs. Removal of the Tonsils by an operation tends to affect the voice, and to interfere with the proper modulation and tone of the voice. Also as the ♉ and ♏ signs are opposite and supplemental signs, removal of the tonsils adversely affects the sex functions, disturbs the puberty, and also makes child-bearing more difficult. In reality, the tonsils should never be removed, but can be shrunken, diminished, and rendered of little trouble, by the application of strong nitrate of silver solution, or the nitrate of silver stick as a cautery. It is better to snare and pinch them off with a wire snare, than to cut them off suddenly, as extreme and dangerous hemorrhage often results, or even death, from the sudden severing of the blood vessels which supply the tonsils. (See "Rules" under Operations; "Disturbed" under Puberty).

Quinsy—An Acute, Severe Inflammation of the Tonsils, and with Fever—Suppurative Tonsilitis—A ♉ and ♏ disease; ♉ or ♏ on the cusp of the Asc. or 6th H., and containing malefics; the ☉ affl. in ♉; the ☉ in ♉, ☌, or ill-asp. any of the malefics; the ☉ ☌ ♂ in the 6th H., in fixed signs, and espec. in ♉ or ♏; the ☽ affl. in ♉ or ♌, or afflicting the hyleg therefrom; the ☽ hyleg in ♉, and afflicted, and espec. with females; the ☽ in the 1st face of ♉ on the Asc., and ☌ any of the malefics; ♄ or ♂ affl. in ♉ or ♏, and espec. when afflicted in the 6th H.; ♄ ☌ ♆ in ♉; ♄ in ♒, occi., and affl. the ☉, ☽, or Asc.; a ♃ disease; ♃ affl. in ♈, and chiefly from ill-blood in the head; ♃ affl. in ♉; ♃ ☌ ♄ or ♂ in ♉, due to disturbed and restricted circulation in the tonsils; ♃ causes death by Quinsy when he is the afflictor in the disease, holding the dominion of death, and affl. the hyleg by dir.; ♂ affl. in ♉; ♀ affl. in ♉ or ♏; ♀ in ♉ in the 6th H., and affl. the ☽ or Asc. (See "Tonsilitis" in this section).

Removal of Tonsils—(See "Ablation", "Operations", in this section).

Suppuration—Of the Tonsils—Suppurative Tonsilitis—♆ affl. in ♉; ♆ ☌ ♄ in ♉. (See "Quinsy", "Tonsilitis", in this section).

Swollen Tonsils—Enlarged—Bulky—♆ in ♉, and affl. by ♄; ♆ in ♉, and between the ☉ and ♀, gives bulk to the tonsils; ♂ in ♉. (See Enlarged, Quinsy, Tonsilitis, in this section).

Throat—(See "Sore Throat", and the various paragraphs under Throat).

Tonsilitis — Amygdalitis — Inflamed Tonsils—Follicular Tonsilitis—Suppurative Tonsilitis — Many of the influences under Quinsy in this section will also apply here. The ☉, ♄, ♂, or ♀ affl. in ♉ or ♏; ♆ ☌ ♄ or ♃ in ♉; ♆ ☌ ♄ in ♉, inflamed and suppurative; ♂ ☌ ♄ in ♉, inflamed, and follicular tonsilitis; ♂ in ♉ in the 6th H. (See Quinsy, Suppuration, Swollen, in this section; Putrid, Sore Throat, Swellings, under Throat).

Trouble with Tonsils—Caused mostly by afflictions in the ♉ and ♏ zones; ♎ or ♐ on the Asc., which ordinarily places ♉ on the cusp the 6th or 8th Houses; ♉ or ♏ upon the Asc. at B.; ♂ in ♉, and with the ☽ or ♀ in ♏. Also the nasal obstructions caused by afflictions in ♏ tend to disturb the throat and tonsils. In cases of Adenoids the tonsils often become involved. (See Adenoids, Nose, Throat; the various paragraphs in this section).

TOO MUCH — Excessive — Superabundance—(See "Too Much" under Blood, Drink, Moisture, Passion, Pleasure, Rain. Also see Abundance, Excess, Excesses, Fullness; "Too Full a Habit" under Habit; Hyperactivity, Over-Abundance, Plethora, Superabundance, Surfeits, etc.).

TOOLS—Sharp Tools—Injury or Death By—(See Cuts, Duels, Incised, Instruments, Iron, Stabs, Sword, Weapons).

TOOTHACHE—(See this subject under Teeth).

TOPHUS—Nodes—Nodules—(See "Nodules" under Nodes).

TORMENTED—In Mind and Body—(See Anguish, Dejection, Fears, Grief, Grievous; "Hopes Cut Off" under Hope; Insanity; "Low Spirits" under Low; Melancholic; "No Peace" under Mind; Misfortune, Obsessions, Pain, Reverses, Ruin, Suffering, Trouble, Worry, etc.).

TORN — Mangled — Lacerations — (See "Wild Animals" under Animals; Explosions, Lacerations, Machinery, Mangled, Rupture, etc.).

TORNADOES — Injury or Death By — (See "High Winds", "Hurricanes", "Tornadoes", under Wind).

TORPID—Torpidity—Torpor—The principal torpid Sign is ♓, and this sign is low in vitality. (See Pisces). Torpor is also a ♄ influence, as ♄ by his afflictions tends to hinder and suppress the functions of the body, and also to dull the mind. (See Apathy, Dull, Idle, Inactive, Indifferent, Inertia, Lassitude, Lethargy, Malaise; "Drowsiness" under Sleep; Sluggish, Stupidity; "Low" under Vitality, etc.).

TORSALGIA — Painful Torsions — (See "Torsalgia" under Torsion).

TORSION — Twistings — Contortions — ♅ influence; ♅ afflicted in signs which rule the part afflicted. (See Spasmodic, Twistings).

Torsalgia—Painful Torsion or Twisting—♅ ☌ ♂ or ☿ in the sign ruling the afflicted part. (See Contortions, Contractions, Cramps; "Twistings" under Feet, Legs; "Spasmodic" under Pain; Spasmodic).

Torticollis — (See "Wry Neck" under Neck; Torticollis).

TORTICOLLIS—Contraction and Twisting of the Muscles of the Neck, and with Bending of the Head—Wry Neck —♅ afflicted in ♉. (See Contortions, Contractions, Cramps, Distortions; "Wry Neck" under Neck; Torsion, Twistings).

TORTURE — Tortured — Tortured to Death—(See "Burned At Stake" under Burning; Execution, Hanging, Lynched, Mobs).

TOTAL—

Total Blindness—(See "Total" under Blindness; Cataracts; "Both Eyes" under Eyes; Gutta Serena; "Loss Of" under Sight).

Total Depravity — (See Degenerate, Depraved, Infamous, Lewd, Licentiousness; "Low and Base" under Low; Obscene, Perversions, Shameless, Sottishness, Vile, Wench, etc.).

Total Disability — (See Deformities, Disabilities, Helplessness, Incurable, Infirm, Insanity, Invalids, Paralysis; "Weakly Person" under Weak, etc.).

TOUCH—The Sense of Touch—Feeling—Sensation—Ruled by ♉. (See Feeling; "Chiropractors" under Healers; Sensation).

Disorders Of—(See Feeling, Hyperaesthesia, Insensibility, Numbness, Paraesthesia, Paralysis, Sensation, Senses, Sensibility, etc.).

TOUGH—Toughening—

Phlegm—Tough Phlegm—(See "Breast" under Phlegm).

Skin—Toughening of—(See "Toughening" under Skin). See Hardening, Thickening.

TOXAEMIA—Toxic—Toxins—A Poisonous State of the Blood—

Auto-Toxic Psychoses—Caused by afflictions in ♎, and usually due to disordered kidneys. (See "Psychoses" in this section).

Blood—Toxic Blood—Poisonous Blood—(See Impure; "Blood Poisoning" under Poison; Urea, Uremia, Uric Acid).

Gastritis—The Toxic Form from Swallowing Poison—(See "Gastritis" under Gastric).

Headache—(See "Toxaemia" under Headaches).

Jaundice—(See "Toxaemic" under Jaundice).

Psychoses—Auto-Toxic Psychoses—Toxic Psychoses—(See Autointoxication, Diabetes; "Psychoses" under Psychic; Uremia).

Toxaemia—A Poisoned State of the Blood—Caused by ♄, due to the retention of the wastes of the system. Also the pathological action of ♃, due to excesses in diet, over-eating, plethora, etc. Also caused by afflictions in ♎, improper kidney action, and the accumulation of too much Urea in the blood. (See "Blood" in this section; Deposits; "Excesses" under Diet, Eating; Elimination, Excretion, Fatigue; "Diseased" under Kidneys; Plethora, Septic, Surfeits, Uremia, Wastes).

Toxins—(See "Offensive" under Humours).

Uremia—Toxic Blood from Urea—(See Uremia).

TRACHEA—Windpipe—Under the internal rulership of the ♉ sign. Also ruled by ♊. Also ☿ in ♉, ♊, or ♋ rules and affects the windpipe, the air cells, breath, and nerves of the Respiratory System.

Nervous Contraction Of—♄ in ♌, and affl. by the ☍ of ☿ in ♒.

Obstructed—The Trachea Obstructed with Phlegm—(See "Breast" under Phlegm).

Phlegm In—(See "Obstructed" in this section). Subluxations at LCP (7C) tend to disorders of the Trachea.

TRACHOMA—(See "Granulated Lids" under Eyelids).

TRACT—A Canal or Passage—

Alimentary Tract—(See Alimentary).

Genito-Urinary Tract—(See Genito-Urinary).

Respiratory Tract—(See Breathing, Bronchial, Lungs, Pulmonary).

TRADE—The Business—The Occupation—The Employment—Accidents, Injury, Illness, or Death In—(See Business, Employment, Machinery, Vocation).

TRAFFIC—Killed or Injured In—(See Journeys, Railroads, Travel, Vehicles).

TRAGEDIES—Tragical—The planet ♅ rules Tragedies, Sudden Events, Calamities, Catastrophies, Explosions, Accidents by Electricity, Machinery, etc. (See these subjects).

Tragical Death—(See "Tragical" under Death).

TRAMPLED—Trodden—Crushed—

Trampled to Death—Trampled by a Mob—Crushed By—Danger of—♄ ori. in a fixed sign, □ or ☍ the ☉ at B., or ♄ occi. in a fixed sign, and □ or ☍ the ☽, and ♄ in a contrary condition. (See Crushed, Mobs, Riots; "Death" under Suffocation; Tumults).

TRANCE—A Form of Catalepsy—Protracted Syncope—

Trance Conditions—Involuntary Trance—A ♆ disease and affliction, and afflictions to ♆; ♆ □ or ☍ ♃; ♆ afflicted in the 8th H., danger of premature burial, or being buried alive, due to trance conditions simulating death; ♆ the afflicting planet tends to trance, or simulated death, and ending in coma or death; ♆ afflicted in ♈, and espec. in the 8th H.; an ♈ disease, and afflictions in ♈. (See "Buried Alive" under Burial; Catalepsy, Coma, Dreams, Emotions, Fainting, Sleep).

TRANQUILITY—A Tranquil Mind and Nature—(See Balance, Calm, Cheerfulness, Contentment, Equilibrium, Gentle, Happiness, Joy, Kind, Mild; "Peace of Mind" under Mind; Peaceful, Poise, Quiet; "Even Temper" under Temper).

TRANSFORMATION—Transforming—Metamorphosis—Structural Changes—Metabolism, etc.—

Cell Substance—Transformation of—(See "Substance" under Cells; Metabolism, Metamorphosis, Structural).

Functions—The Transforming Functions In the Body—(See "Substance" under Cells; Conservation).

Liver—Fatty Transformation of—Fatty Degeneration of—(See Liver).

TRANSFUSION—Of Blood—(See Bleeding).

TRANSIENT DISEASES—(See Acute, Colds; "Temporary" under Insanity; "Transitory" under Mania; Mild, Quick Diseases, Slight, Temporary, Transitory, etc.).

Transient Disposition—In Disease—(See Diathesis, Directions).

TRANSITORY—Of Short Duration—

Transitory Diseases—(See Cholera, Epidemics, Pestilence, Transient).

Transitory Experiences—Are represented by the ☽. (See Events; "Represents" under Moon).

Transitory Mania—(See Mania).

TRANSITS—Of the Planets—The transits of the planets are not, in themselves, as dangerous as the Progressed influences, or Primary Directions, but transits assist in bringing an evil direction into action. It is important to watch the evil transits of the malefics. especially in passing judgment upon a disease, and when it will tend to be worse, or get better, according to the nature of the transiting planet, whether it be benefic or malefic. When there are some very evil directions culminating over a person, the transit of ♄ or ♂, or other malefics, which may add their evil force to the directions, can usually be depended upon as causing a time of misfortune, accident, disaster, or ill-health in the life of the native, even though the life seemed to be moving along quietly until the transit came upon the scene. Also the transit of a malefic over a Stellium of planets in a sign is bound to cause considerable disturbance for the time, and also a transit by □ or ☍ is evil in its effects, and helps to intensify other evils which may be culminating over the native, if a malefic, or to bring some great good if the transit of a benefic unites its force to that of good directions, or progressions. The transit of ♄ thru any sign tends to bring disease, lowered functions, and suppressions in the part ruled by the sign he is in for the time, and especially if he is passing his own radical place, or in signs in □ or ☍ to his place in the map of birth. The transit of ♂ thru the signs tends to bring injury, fever, or inflammation to the part ruled by the sign he is transiting, and to draw more heat to that part for the time. And so on with each of the planets, as they all tend to carry their special benefits or afflictions along with them, according to their nature, and aspects for the time, and to affect each sign they pass thru for good or ill. Chap. XXXIX, in Pearce's Textbook of Astrology is devoted entirely to Transits, and the effects of each planet by transit. (See Directions, Primary Directions, Secondary Directions).

TRANSMISSION—Hereditary Transmission—(See Diathesis, Heredity, Innate, Organic, Structural).

TRANSUDATION—Of Fluids—☽ disorders. (See Dropsy, Exudations, Fluids, Oedema, Osmosis).

TRANSVERSE COLON—(See Colon).

TRAP ROCKS—Minerals ruled by ♂.

TRAUMATISM—(See Injuries, Wounds).

TRAVEL—The 3rd H. rules Short Journeys, Inland Journeys, as by Rail, Automobile, Bus, or Vehicle. The 9th H. rules Long Journeys, Ocean Voyages, and Travel Abroad. The conditions ruling these two houses in the map of birth, and also how the present planetary positions affect these radical houses and the hyleg by transit, direction, or progression, should be consulted before engaging in travel, and to know whether the native would be fortunate or unfortunate in these matters. It is better for the health and general affairs for some people to travel and seek change of location, while others should keep quiet, remain in one locality, or at their place of birth, and avoid travel. This subject of Travel is largely considered in the Articles on Abroad, Journeys, Rail-

roads, Ships, Vehicles, and Voyages, and will be further considered here. See the following subjects, and the paragraphs under them, when only listed here—

Abroad — Travel Abroad — Fortunate or Unfortunate—(See the various paragraphs under Abroad, Foreign Lands, Sea, Ships, Shipwreck, Voyages).

Accidents In—Malefics in the 3rd or 9th H. at B., and by tr. or dir., or the lords of these houses afflicted; malefics in the 3rd or 9th H. at a Solar Rev., travel should be avoided during the following year; the ☽ to the ☌ ♂ by dir., and either the ☽ or ♂ in the 3rd or 9th H. at B., or by dir. (See "Accidents" under Abroad, Journeys, Railroads, Ships, Vehicles, Voyages; Maritime, Navigation, Shipwreck. For Sickness from an Accident in Travel see "Sickness" in this section).

Altitude — Whether to Travel In a High or Low Altitude—(See Altitude).

Assassinated — During Travel — (See "Assassinated Abroad" under Assassination).

Avalanches — Hurt By — (See Avalanches).

Avoid Travel—When the malefics are in the 3rd or 9th H. at B., or the lords of these houses are seriously afflicted by malefics at B., and by dir. (See "Avoid" under Journeys, Voyages; Bad Time For, Current Year, Danger In, Death During, and the various paragraphs in this section).

Bad Time for Travel—Dangerous to Travel — When malefics are passing thru the 3rd or 9th H. of the radix by tr., dir., or progression, and espec. if these houses contained malefics at B.; do not travel at a time when the lords of the 3rd or 9th H. at B. are under severe affliction; ♂ to the cusp of the 3rd or 9th H. by dir. (See "Bad Time For" under Journeys; Avoid, Current Year, Danger, Death, and the various paragraphs in this section).

Bandits—Injured by During Travel—(See Bandits).

Beasts—Attacks by Wild Beasts During Travel—(See "Wild Beasts" in this section).

Beneficial—Travel Safe and Beneficial —Good Time For — ♃ and ♀ in good asp. to the ☽; ♃ or ♀ in the 3rd or 9th H. at B., and no malefics therein, and the benefics not affl., and the benefics well-aspected by dir.; lords of the 3rd and 9th H. at B. being benefics, and with no malefics in these houses, and the benefics well-aspected by dir. (See Fortunate, Good Time For, Health, in this section).

Bites During Travel—(See "Journeys" under Bites).

Burns—(See "Journeys" under Burns).

Cannibals — Attacks By — (See "Savages" in this section).

Captivity—Held In Captivity During Travel—(See Captivity).

Cattle—Attacks by During Travel—(See "Travel" under Cattle).

Change of Scenery—Good for the Health—(See "Air Sign People" under Residence).

Countries to Avoid—Places Unfavorable for Travel—Avoid Countries ruled by the Sign containing ♄ or ♂ at B.; avoid those ruled by ♃ and ♀ if they be lords of evil houses, as of the 6th, 8th, or 12th H.; avoid those Quarters and directions in the map of birth containing malefics unless the malefics be essentially dignified and strong, or lords of the 1st, 2nd, 10th, or 4th H. (See Countries, Location, Nations; "Native Land" under Native; "Place of Birth" under Place; "Abroad" under Residence; "Direction" in this section).

Current Year — Dangerous to Travel During—♅, ♄, or ♂ on the cusp of the 3rd or 9th H. at B., and these degrees of the malefics ascending at a Solar Rev. (See Accidents, Danger, Death, Drowned, Fire, and the various paragraphs in this section).

Cuts—(See "Travel" under Cuts).

Danger In Travel — Dangerous to Travel—The ☉ hyleg at B., and to the ☌ or ill-asp. ♄ or ♂ by dir., or other malefic, if such malefic were in the 3rd or 9th H. at B.; the ☉ to the ☌ or ill-asp. ♅ or ♂ by dir.; the ☉ to the ☌ ♄ by dir., either by Land or Sea, and if ♄ and ♂ govern the Lights, or oppose them, travel will be dangerous and unprofitable, and if these planets be in watery signs there is great danger of shipwreck or being lost in the Desert and uninhabitable places — if in fixed signs they tend to death or injury climbing precipices—if in cardinal signs, to be sickly and in want of food — if in human signs, to suffer danger from injury by robbers and bandits—if in earthy signs, to suffer injury or death in an earthquake, or by wild beasts, and if ☿ have dignity there also, there is danger of injury by venomous reptiles; the ☽ in the 3rd or 9th H. at B., and to the ☌ or ill-asp. ♅, ♄, or ♂ by dir.; the ☽ to the ☌ or ill-asps. the Asc. or M.C. by dir.; the ☽ to the □ or ☍ ☿ by dir., and the ☽ hyleg, and ☿ affl. at B.; the ☽ to the ☌ ♂ by tr. or dir.; ♆, ♅, ♄, or ♂ affl. in ♊ or ♐ at B., or in the 3rd or 9th H.; ♄ by tr., prog., or dir., or at a Solar Rev., affl. the places of the ☽ or ☿ at B., and espec. if ♄ affl. these planets at B.; ♄ ascending at B., and the ☉ to the ☌ or ill-asp. ♄ by dir.; ♃ affl. in ♊ or ♐, or in the 3rd or 9th H.; ♃ in ♐, R and afflicted, and lord of the year at the Vernal, danger in travel generally; ♂ to the ☌ or ill-asp. ♄ by dir., and espec. if either rule the 3rd or 9th H. at B.; ☿ affl. in the 8th H. at B., and by dir.; the Asc. to the place of ♄ or ☋ in the 3rd H. at B.; the 2nd decan. of ♊ on the Asc. at B., ruled by ♂; malefics in the 3rd or 9th H. at B., and affl. the ☉ or ☽; the Sig. of travel in evil asp. to the ☉, ♅, ♄, or ♂, and these widely separated from each other, or ascend after the other Significators. (See Abroad, Bandits; "Lost In" under Desert; Foreign Lands, Highwaymen; "Danger" under Journeys, Voyages; Maritime, Navigation, Ocean, Pirates, Railroads, Robbers, Sea, Ships, Shipwreck, Vehicles; "Perils By" under Waters; the various paragraphs in this Article).

Death During Travel — Sickness or Death During Travel—Any of the malefics in the 3rd or 9th H. at B., and afflicted; ♄ ruler of the 3rd or 9th H. at B., and ♄ ☌ or evil asp. the Asc. by dir.; ☿ in the 8th H. and afflicted; malefics in the 3rd or 9th H., and affl. the ☉ or ☽; the afflictor to the Sig. of Travel being in the 12th H., and afflicted in ♈, ♎, or ♑; lord of the 6th H. in the 8th H., and afflicted. (See "Death" under Abroad, Falls, Heights, Journeys, Railroads, Sea, Ships, Voyages).

Desert — Lost In the Desert — In the Wilderness, or In Inaccessible Places —(See Desert).

Direction to Travel — For the Best Health and Success — Travel in the direction of the Benefics at B. if they are not rulers of evil houses, or severely afflicted by malefics at B., or by dir. Travel to Countries ruled by the Signs containing the Benefics at B. if they are not evilly disposed. (See "Friends" under Residence; the references in the paragraph, "Countries to Avoid", in this section).

Drowned During Travel—(See Drowning; "Drowning" under Sea; Ships, Shipwreck).

Earthquake—Injured by In Travel— (See "Danger" in this section).

Escapes — Has Narrow Escapes from Death or Injury During Travel—♃ in ♊ or the 3rd H., and afflicted, may be in wrecks, but escapes injury; ♃ in ♐ or the 9th H., and afflicted, may be in a shipwreck, or in railroad wrecks Abroad, but usually escapes injury, and is saved, and espec. if the ⚹ or △ aspects of ♃ intervene, or the Benefics are elevated above the malefics or afflicting planet at the time. (See Escapes, Railroads).

Evil Time for Travel — (See "Bad Time" in this section).

Exposure In Travel — Health Suffers From—(See "Travel" under Exposure; Weather, Wet, in this section).

Falls — (See "Travel" under Falls, Heights; Accidents, Danger, Sickness, in this section).

Famine—Danger of During Travel— (See Famine; "Food" in this section).

Fatigue—Sickness From—(See "Sickness" in this section).

Fevers — (See "Health" under Journeys; "Sickness" in this section).

Fire — Danger From — (See "Ships" under Fire).

Food—Lack of—Danger of Starvation and Privation During Travel—Malefics in the 3rd or 9th H. in earthy signs, and afflicting the ☉ or ☽; the afflictor to the Sig. of Travel in the 12th H., and in ♈, ♎, or ♑. (See Desert, Famine).

Foreign Travel—Will prove favorable and benefit the health when there are benefics in the 9th H. at B., and not afflicted, and when the radix indicates that the Native Land is not beneficial. Malefics in the 9th H., and afflicted, and with a benefic in the 4th H., the native should remain in his Native Land. (See Abroad, Foreign, Nadir;

"Native Land" under Native; "Place of Birth" under Place; Countries to Avoid, Health, and the various paragraphs in this section).

Fortunate In Travel—Benefics in the 3rd or 9th H. at B., well-aspected, and with no malefics in these houses, and with many planets in watery signs; lords of the 3rd and 9th H. well-placed and aspected, and with fortunate signs upon the cusps of the 3rd or 9th H.

Good Time For — (See "Good Time" under Journeys, Voyages; "Beneficial" in this section).

Health — Travels for Health — ☿ affl. in the 6th H., and usually on account of nervousness, nervous breakdown, overwork, worries and troubles. (See "Travel" under Health). For influences which tend to impair the health during travel see Exposure, Sickness, Wet Journeys, in this section.

Heights — Falls from During Travel —(See "Falls" in this section).

High Altitudes — Should Travel In — (See Altitude).

Home or Abroad—Travel Where You Will, At Home or Abroad—The ☉ or lord of the Asc. in no way unfortunate, and not afflicted by any planet. (See "Native Land" under Native; "Prospers Anywhere" under Residence).

Hurts—Or Injuries During Travel—Malefics in the 3rd or 9th H., and affl. the ☉ or ☽; ♄, ♂, and the ☽ conjoined in ♒; the 2nd decan. of ♊ on the Asc., ruled by ♂; ♂ afflicting the cusp of the 3rd or 9th H. by dir. The time of possible injury during travel is shown by the arcs of directions to the Sigs. of Travel. (See "Time Of" under Accidents; Accidents, Avalanches, Danger, Falls, Heights, Robbers, Stabs, and the various paragraphs in this section).

Illness — During Travel, or Due to Travel—(See Exposure, Fevers, Health, Sickness, and the various paragraphs in this section).

Imprisonment — During Travel — (See Captivity; "Travel" under Prison).

Inconveniences — Incommodities During Travel — An eclipse of the ☉ in the 2nd decan. of ♉.

Injuries—(See Accidents, Escapes, Falls, Fire, Hurts, Sickness, and the various paragraphs in this section).

Inland Travel — (See "Inland" under Journeys; Railroads, Vehicles).

Journeys — (See the subjects under Journeys).

Kicks—During Travel—(See Kicks).

Land Travel—Danger In—(See "Land Journeys" under Journeys; Railroads, Vehicles).

Location—Travel As Related To—(See Abroad, Location, Native Land, Place of Birth, Residence; Countries to Avoid, Direction, in this section).

Long Journeys — (See Abroad, Journeys, Ships, Voyages).

Losses — (See Bad Time, Robbers, Weather, and the various paragraphs in this section).

Love of Travel—♃ and ♐ prominent at B.; the ☉ in a cardinal sign in the 3rd or 9th H., and with a card. sign on the cusp of these houses. (See "Wanderer" in this section).

Low Altitudes—Should Live, or Travel In—(See Altitude).

Misfortunes — In Travel — (See Accidents, Danger, Death, Falls, Hurts, Imprisonment, Robbers, Sickness, and the various paragraphs in this section. Also see the subjects under Abroad, Foreign Lands, Journeys, Navigation, Railroads, Sea, Ships, Shipwreck, Vehicles, Voyages).

Much Travel — Travels Much — (See Love of Travel, Wanderer, in this section).

Murdered — During Travel — (See "Journey" under Murder).

Narrow Escapes—(See "Escapes" in this section).

Native Land — Should Remain In — Should Remove — (See "Native Land" under Native).

Ocean Travel — ♆ prominent at B. leads to. (See "Disposes To" under Voyages).

Parts of World—Fortunate and Unfortunate Parts for Travel—(See Countries to Avoid, Direction, in this section).

Pirates—Danger From—(See Pirates).

Place of Birth — Travel As Related To — (See "Place of Birth" under Place).

Poisoning—(See "Travel" under Poison).

Precipices—Falls From—(See "Travel" under Heights).

Privations—(See Desert, Food, Losses, Starvation, and the various paragraphs in this section).

Railroad Travel—(See Railroads).

Remains In One Place—The ☉, ☽, and many planets in fixed signs at B., or fixed signs upon the angles, not inclined to travel much, and such people often spend their entire lives in the community of their birth. (See "Good Powers Of" under Concentration; "Fixed Signs" under Fixed; Recluse; "Travels Little" in this section).

Removals; Reptiles—Injured by During Travel — (See Reptiles; "Danger" in this section).

Residence — (See the subjects under Residence).

Robbers — Attacks by During Travel —(See Robbers; "Danger" in this section).

Safe — Travel Safe and Beneficial — (See Beneficial, Fortunate, Good Time, in this section).

Savages — Attacks By — (See Cannibals).

Sea Travel — (See Abroad, Foreign Lands, Maritime, Navigation, Ocean, Sailors, Sea, Ships, Shipwreck, Voyages).

Shipwreck; Short Journeys — (See "Short" under Journeys; Railroads, Vehicles).

Should Never Travel—(See Avoid, Remains In One Place, in this section; "Place of Birth" under Place).

Sickness — During Travel — Sickly — Fatigue — Lord of the 6th H. in the 9th, and afflicted; ♄ or ♂ ruler of the 6th H. at B., and in the 3rd or 9th H. at a Solar Rev., or in the 3rd or 9th by tr. or dir., sickness from an accident, injury, fall, or misfortune; ♄ affl. in ♌ or ♐ tends to sickness from fatigue in travel. (See "Sickness" under Abroad, Ships, Voyages; "Ill-Health" under Foreign Lands; "Health" under Journeys; Danger, Death, Fevers, and the various paragraphs in this section).

Stabs and Cuts—(See "Travel" under Cuts).

Starvation—(See "Food" in this section; "Privations" under Sea).

Stings—(See "Journeys" under Bites; Stings).

Storms at Sea—(See "Tempests" under Sea; Shipwreck).

Thirst — May Suffer From — (See "Food" in this section; "Lost In" under Desert).

Time to Travel—Good and Bad Times —Time of Injury In—(See Accidents, Bad Time, Good Time, Hurts, Sickness, and the various paragraphs in this section).

Travel Where You Will—(See "Home or Abroad" in this section).

Travels Little—The ☽ cadent, and in a fixed sign, except when in ♏; the ☽ and ☿ in fixed signs, in angles, little disposition to travel; many planets in fixed signs, or fixed signs upon the angles. (See "Remains In One Place" in this section).

Travels Much — (See Love of Travel, Wanderer, in this section; "Many Changes" under Residence).

Trouble—In Travel—(See "Weather", and the various paragraphs in this section).

Unfortunate—In Travel—(See "Should Never Travel", and the various paragraphs in this section).

Vehicles—(See the subjects under Vehicles).

Venomous Creatures — Injured By — (See "Journeys" under Bites; Venomous; "Danger" in this section).

Voyages — (See the various subjects under Voyages).

Wanderer — Travels Much — Love of Travel—♅ strong and ascending at B.; ♄ or ♂ Sig. □ or ☍ ☽; ♂ Sig. ☌ ☽; the ☽ ascending at B.; the ☽ cadent in the 3rd or 9th H.; the ☽ ruler at B.; ♃ Sig. ☌ ☽; the 21° ♒ on the Asc. (See "Love Of" in this section; Roaming, Wanderer).

Water Travel — (See "Sea Travel" in this section; Voyages).

Weather—Meets with Losses, Trouble, or Bad Weather In Travel—The ☽ in the 3rd or 9th H. at B., and affl. by malefics; the malefics in evil asp. the ☽ at B. (See "Wet" under Journeys; "Tempests" under Sea; "Exposure", "Winds", in this section).

Wet Journeys — Health Suffers By — (See "Wet" under Journeys).

Wild Beasts — Attacks by During Travel — (See "Wild Animals" under Animals; "Danger" in this section).

Wilderness—Lost In—(See Desert).

Winds — Meets with Contrary Winds and Storms — (See "Weather" in this section; "Storms" under Wind).

TREACHERY—Treacherous—The ♆, ♓, and 12th H. influences tend to secret treachery. Deliberate treachery, and with malice, is usually ♏ influence. Treachery thru greed, covetousness, or for revenge, is ♄ influence. Also the ♂ element is usually configurated with the influences which lead to violent treachery. When ♀ adds her influence, women are usually involved, or a poison death. The ♆ and ♏ influences usually lead to the most treacherous attacks. Ambush attacks, plots, and the work of secret enemies, are denoted by the 12th H. The 8th H. shows the influences working over, and the fate of secret enemies. The Signs containing malefics at B. show the types and locations of the worst enemies. Private and secret enemies are ruled and indicated by the 12th H. and its conditions.

Blindness By—(See "Treachery" under Blindness).

Death or Injury By—Denoted by the 12th H., and malefics in the 12th, afflicting the 12th, or lord of the 12th a malefic, and afflicted; the ☉ to the ☌ ♂ by dir., and especially involving the 12th H.; the ☉ to the place of Antares, threatened with treachery; the ☽, ♄, or ♂ to the cusp the 12th H. by dir.; the ☽ to the ☌ or ill-asp. ♂ by dir.; the ☽ in the 12th H. at the Vernal, lady of the year, and afflicted, and with no gd. asp. of ♃ or ♀; ♆ the afflicting planet; ♆ affl. in the 1st or 12th H.; ♄ in ♏, ☌, or evil asp. the Asc. by dir.; ♄ and ♂ in signs of human form, and afflicting the Luminaries; lord of the 8th H. a malefic, in the 8th, and affl. by the lord of the 6th or 12th H.; lord of the 7th H. a malefic, and in the 12th H., and afflicted; lord of the 8th in the 12th, and affl. the hyleg or lord of the Asc., and with no benefics in the 12th H.; ruler of the 12th afflicting the Significator; the 20° ♍ on the Asc. (See Ambushes, Assassination; "Secret Enemies" under Enemies; Feuds, Jealousy; "Mischief at Hand" under Mischief; Murdered, Plots; "Death by Poison" under Poison; Revenge, Twelfth House; "Death" under Violence; the various paragraphs in this section).

Female Treachery—Death or Injury By—The ☽ hyleg, and to the ☌ or ill-asp. ♂ by dir., and ♀ throwing an ill aspect; ♄ in the Asc., ☍ the ☉ or ☽, and ♀ also be evilly configurated with both ♄ and ☿; ♄ in a brutal sign, ori., and □ or ☍ the ☉ at B., or occi., □ or ☍ the ☽ at B., and ♀ give testimony, and by poison; ♂ just setting in □ or ☍ the ☉ or ☽, and ♀ adding her testimony to ♂; ♀ and ☿ conjoined with ♄, and ♄ affl. the hyleg; the M.C. to the place of the Pleiades or Pollux. (See "Tragical Death" under Death; "Injured Thru Women" under Men; "Women" under Poison).

Imprisonment—By Treachery of Relatives or Enemies—(See "Plots" under Prison).

Insane Asylum — Confined In by the Work of an Enemy—(See "Asylums" under Insanity).

Treacherous — Given to Treachery — The ☉ Sig. □ or ☍ ♄; the ☽ Sig. in ♏: the ☽, ♀, or ☿ Sig. □ or ☍ ♂; ♅ □ or ☍ ♄; ♄ Sig. □ or ☍ ♂ or ☿; ♂ ill-dignified at B., and afflicted; ♂ Sig. in ♉, and afflicted; ♂ Sig. □ or ☍ ♄; ☿ Sig. ☌ ♂, a treacherous miscreant; the 28° ♏, or the 13° ♓ on the Asc. (See Cheating, Deceitful, Dishonest, Forgers, Gambling, Liars, Libelers; "Low and Base" under Low; Malevolent, Malicious; "Active to Do Mischief" under Mischief; Pettifogging, Revengeful, Shrewd, Thieves; "Vile Wretch" under Vile; Wicked, etc.).

TREAD — The Step — Treading Walk — (See "Awry" under Gait. Note the various paragraphs under Gait, Walk).

TREASON—(See Sedition).

TREATMENT—The Treatment of Disease—This book is not intended to be a Treatise on the Treatment or Cure of Disease, but rather to go into the Planetary Causes of Disease. However, the true treatment of disease is based upon the planetary influences, and upon the Antipathy and Sympathy between the Planets, and what they rule. The Planets cause disease by their afflicting aspects, and according to their nature, and the diseases of one planet are combatted by the forces, herbs, and remedies of an opposing planet, or by the remedies of the afflicting planet itself. Thus arose the theories of Antipathy and Sympathy in the treatment of disease. The Allopathic School is based upon Antipathy, or contrary influences, in the treatment of disease. The Homeopathic School is based upon Sympathy, and Similars, in the treatment of disease. These Principles are discussed in the Articles on Antipathy, Cure, Healers, Homeopathy, Medicines, Opposites, Polarity, Praecipients, Remedies, Sympathy, Therapeutics, etc. While there is in Nature a remedy for every disease in its locality, an Herb, Mineral, Root, or Plant, there are also various ways and means which Man has discovered to combat disease, and neutralize the afflicting forces. These are represented in the various Schools of Healing, and all are good, have their strong points, and their place in the cure and treatment of disease. This book is not intended to go into the merits of any School of Healing, but rather to give to all a Scientific explanation of the Philosophy and Causes of Disease, and they are left free to apply whatever treatment they desire, and in which they have faith, and in which the Patient also has faith. Wrong thinking and adverse mental states, are also the cause of many diseases, due to the afflictions in the Map of Birth, which often lead to Imaginary Diseases at first, and then to real ones, and lower the vital forces of the body. These can be combatted by the Mental, Psychic, and Spiritual Schools of Healing, to a large extent, for when the Mind is once set right, many of the evils of ill-health soon take their exit. (See "Treatment" under Melan-

choly). Good Health should be Man's heritage, and he should be taught to think in terms of perfect heatlh, and avoid thinking in terms of disease. In Ancient Times all Physicians were required to be Astrologers before they were allowed to Practice Medicine, or the Healing Art. They were required to know the Philosophy of each case, and how to go at the treatment on a planetary basis, and to properly combat the disease with the remedies at hand. But in the Middle Ages the Science of Medical Astrology was more or less suppressed by those in Authority, and this knowledge became a Lost Science, but it is now being revived, and soon should be a required study in the Curriculum of every School which teaches the Art of Healing. Each Physician, or Healer, should know something of the Elements of Astrology, and how to draw up a Star Map of Birth for his patients, or at least look up the Signs in which the planets were at birth, to know what parts of the body are most afflicted, and the vulnerable parts, or organs, be sure of your diagnosis, and then proceed with the treatment intelligently. The Temperament of the patient also should be studied from the star map of birth, as every patient is under one of the fundamental Temperaments, the Choleric, Nervous, Sanguine, or Lymphatic, and each of these Temperaments requires a different handling. Also Location plays an important part in treatment, and the Map of Birth shows the proper location, whether it should be in a high or low altitude, at the birthplace, in the Native Land, or to go Abroad, and in what direction to travel, and which Nation or Country will give the patient the best vibrations for healing. Also the compatibility, or incompatibility between Healer and Patient should be looked into, and the Radical Maps of each show this, as the wrong Healer often unknowingly kills his patient, and the right Healer sees him get well. Also the Map of Birth should be studied to know what the nature of the trials of the patient are, his peculiar weaknesses, his besetting sins, his wrong tendencies, which may be causing the disease, so as to give proper advice. A volume in itself could be written along these lines as to how to treat patients Scientifically, and according to the leadings and indications of Astrology, which shows God's Plan over each individual, and the relation of every one to Nature.

For further study along this line, see the following subjects in this book—Abroad, Acquired Diseases, Altitude, Antipathy, Aspects, Attraction, Character, Colors; "Compatibility" under Healers; Correspondences, Course of Disease, Crises in Disease; Death (Arguments For); Diagnosis, Diathesis, Directions, Disease, Drugs, Duration of Disease, Electricity (Healing By); Environment, Events, External Influences, Fate, Galen, Habits, Harmony, Healers, Health, Herbs, Heredity, Hippocrates, Homeopathy, Horoscope, Hypnotism, Idiosyncrasies, Ill-Health; "Incompatibility", "Injured By", under

Healers; Kepler, Location, Long Diseases, Magic, Magnetism, Map of Birth, Medical Astrology, Mind, Nations; "Native Land" under Native; Nativity; "Negative Nature" under Negative; Newton (Sir Isaac); Operations (Rules For); Opposites, Organic Diseases, Paracelsus, Parts of the Body; Physicians (see Healers); "Place of Birth" under Place; Planets, Polarity, Positive Nature, Pracincipients, Predisposition, Prevention of Disease; Prognosis, Psychic Diseases, Radix, Receptive, Remedies, Repulsions, Residence, Short Diseases, Sickness, Signature, Spiritual, Structural Diseases, Subluxations, Suggestion, Surgeons, Susceptibility, Sympathy, Temperaments, Tendencies, Therapeutics, Travel, Typical Drugs, Vertebrae, Vibration; "Days of the Week" under Week; Zodiac Salts, etc. These, and many other subjects listed in this book, have their place in a knowledge of the patient, the disease in hand, and its treatment. If the subject you have in mind is not mentioned in this Article, look for it in the alphabetical arrangement.

TREES—Corruption of the Fruit of—(See Corruption, Fig Trees, Fruit, Herbs, Plants, Roots, Rottenness, Seeds, Vegetation, Vines, etc.).

TREMBLINGS—(See Tremors).

TREMORS — Tremblings — Quivering — Twitching—Thrills—A ♅ affliction to ♉, which Sign rules the Organ of Coordination, and due to Incoordination and impeded nerve force to a part, or organ; a ♅ disease; ♅ affl. in ♉; ♅ afflicted in the 6th H.; a ☉ disease; a ♄ disease, due to deposits, hardening, and impaired functions; ♄ affl. in ♊, nervous trembling; a ☿ disease, and caused by afflictions to ☿. (See Contractions, Coordination; "Movements" under Erratic; Incoordination, Jerky, Motor, Palsy, Saint Vitus Dance, Spasmodic, Tics, Twitchings).

Eyeballs—Trembling of—(See "Nystagmus" under Eyeballs).

Heart — Trembling of — (See "Trembling" under Heart).

Morbid Tremors—(See Subsultus).

Muscles — Trembling of — (See "Tensity" under Muscles).

Subsultus — Morbid Tremors — (See Subsultus).

TRIALS — Tribulations — Troubles — Trouble and Sorrow are ruled by the 12th H.

Has Many Trials—And Tribulations—A total eclipse falling on the place of the ☉ at B.; ♄ Sig. □ or ☍ the ☽; the ☽ Sig. □ or ☍ ♄ or ♂. (See Fortune, Miseries, Misfortune, Renunciation, Reverses, Ruin, Self-Undoing, Sorrow, Trouble, Twelfth House, Vexations).

TRIANGLE — The Terminal Triangle — The Terminal Houses—(See Terminal). The Triangle is also the symbol of the Trine Aspect, one of the very fortunate aspects between the planets. (See Aspects, Trine, Triplicities).

TRIBULATIONS—(See Trials, Trouble).

TRICHIASIS—(See Eyelids).

TRICKY — (See Deceitful, Dishonest, Liars, Pettifogging, Shrewd).

TRINE ASPECT—(△)—The 120° Aspect between the planets, and one of the very fortunate aspects for harmony and good health. (See Aspects, Sextile, Triplicities).

TRIPLE PERSONALITY—(See Personality).

TRIPLETS—

Three Born—♃, ♀, or ☊ in a fruitful sign on the cusp of the 1st or 5th H., three may be born, and espec. if the ☽ have good aspect. Also ♃ or ♀ in the 10th or 11th H., in a watery sign, or in the 4th or 5th H. if there are no benefics in the 10th or 11th, there may be two or three children at one confinement, and espec. if in bicorporeal signs, but if in other places, only one child. (See "Single Births" under Children; Double Bodied Signs, Fruitful, Predetermination, Quadruplets, Twins). Cases of Triplets Born—See "Triplets", Numbers 333, 334, 335, in 1001 N.N.

Three Females—If the ☽, ♀, and ☿ at conception behold the ☉, ☽, or Asc. from bicorporeal signs, there will be three females conceived.

Three Males—If ♄, ♃, and ♂ behold the ☉, ☽, or Asc. at conception, from bicorporeal signs, there will be three males conceived. Also when ♄, ♃, and ♂ are in ♊, ♐, or ♓, and configurated with the ☉, ☽, Asc., or 1st H. Such conceptions very often are not complete, and children so born have deformities or imperfections.

Two Females, One Male—If two feminine planets, and one masculine planet at conception behold the ☉, ☽, or Asc. from bicorporeal signs, as ♊, ♐, ♓, two females and one male will be conceived.

Two Males, One Female—If two masculine planets, and one feminine planet at conception, as ♄, ♃, and ♀, behold the ☉, ☽, or Asc. from bicorporeal signs, two males and one female will be conceived. (See Conception, Congenital; "Predetermination of Sex" under Predetermination; Prenatal Epoch).

TRIPLICITY — Triplicities — These are the Fiery, Airy, Earthy, and Watery Signs, and there are three signs in each class. In the Fiery signs there are ♈, ♌, ♐. In the Airy Signs, ♊, ♎, ♒. In the Earthy Triplicity, ♉, ♍, ♑, and in the Watery triangle, ♋, ♏, ♓. The signs in each triplicity are in △ aspect, and in great harmony. People born with the majority of the planets in any one of these Triplicities, as many planets in ♈, ♌, and ♐, have better balance, a more even temper, whereas a mixture of planets, and occupying several of the Triplicities at B., tend to unbalance the native, cause more discord, strife, inharmony, and ill-health, as such mixtures involve the □ and ☍ aspects in the Map of Birth. (See "Airy Signs" under Air; Aspects; "Earthy Signs" under Earth; "Fire Signs" under Fire; Heredity; "Signs" under Water).

TRISMUS—(See Lock-Jaw).

TRODDEN—(See Crushed, Mobs, Trampled).

TROPICAL SIGNS—♋ and ♑. (See Angles, Blemishes, Cancer, Capricorn,

Cardinal, Equinoxes, Fourth House, Ingresses, Minor Ailments, Solstices, Tenth House).

TROUBLE — Troubled — Troublesome — Trials—Vexations—

A Time of Trouble—Causes of Trouble In the Life of the Native—Has Much Trouble—The SUN to the ☌ ♄ by dir.; the ☉ to the ill-asps. the ☽ by dir.; the ☉ or ☽ to the ☌ or ill-asp. the malefics; the ☉ □ or ☍ the ☽ at B., and by dir.; the ☉ with South Scale, or the Knee of Ophiucus at B.; an eclipse of the ☉ or ☽ falling close to the places of the ☉ or ☽ at B., or in ☍ thereto, or near the ☌ or ☍ a malefic, and espec. if such eclipse is visible at the birthplace, or falls on the place of the hyleg, there will tend to be much trouble or ill-health; the ☉ or ☽ in weak signs in the 3rd or 6th H., and afflicted; the MOON □ or ☍ ♄ at B., and by dir.; the ☽ hyleg, and afflicted, and to the ☌ or ill-asp. the ☉ by dir.; the ☽ to the ☌ or ill-asp. any of the malefics by dir.; the ☽ weak and afflicted at B., and to the ☌ the Asc. by dir., much trouble in mind and body; the ☽ directed to the Pleiades, Hyades, Praesepe, Deneb, or The Twins; the ☽ to the □ or ☍ the ☉ by dir.; the ☽ Sig. □ or ☍ ♄; the ☽ sepr. from ♀ and apply. to the ☉; the ☽ at a Solar Rev. passing over the place of ♄ or ♂ at B.; the Prog. ☽ ☌, P., or ill-asp. the place of ♄ at B.; the Prog. ☽ □ or ☍ the Asc. or M.C.; NEPTUNE □ or ☍ ♀ at B., much trouble all thru life, and espec. in love affairs; URANUS passing the place of ♄ at B. by tr., sudden troubles; ♅ affl. the ☉ or ☽ at B., and by dir.; ♅ afflicted in the 10th H.; ♅ affl. in ♎ or ♑; SATURN by tr. or dir. ☌ or ill-asp. the ☉, ☽, or any of the radical planets; ♄ in the 10th H. at a Solar Rev., and elevated above the Lights; ♄ ruler of the 12th H. at B., and ♄ ☌ or evil asp. the Asc. by dir.; ♄ elevated above, and in evil asp. the ruling planet; ♄ on the Meridian, or coming to it at B., perpetual trouble or disgrace; JUPITER Sig. □ or ☍ ☿; ♃ prog., and in □ or ☍ ♀, or vice versa; MARS affl. in the 12th H.; ♂ prog. ☌, □, or ☍ ☿, or vice versa, much trouble thru recklessness; ♂ at a Solar Rev. passing the places of the radical ☉, ☽, or planets; VENUS prog. ☌, P., □, or ☍ ♄ at B., or vice versa; ♀ ☌ the ☉ at a Solar Rev., and ☿ affl. by malefics at the same time; ♀ by periodic rev. to the ill-asps. the ☉ at B.; ♀ to the ☌ or ill-asp. ♄ by dir.; MERCURY affl. at B., and the ☽ to the ill-asps. ☿ by dir.; ☿ at a Solar Rev. passing the place of ♄ or ♂ at B.; ☿ affl. in the 7th, 10th, or 11th H., many worries and vexations; the ASC. to the place of Deneb; the Asc. to the ☌ or ill-asp. ♄ by dir.; the M.C. to the ☌ or P. the ☽, and espec. if the ☽ is affl. at B.; the M.C. to the ill-asps. the ☉ by dir.; the M.C. to the place of Algol or Hydra's Heart; a Lunation falling on the place of the malefics, and espec. if it occurs with evil primary directions; the 2nd decan. of ♊ on the Asc., ruled by ♂, tends to much grief, anxiety, and trouble; Fixed Stars of the nature of ♄ culminating at B.; an evil direction to the ☉, ☽, Hyleg, or Asc. signifies trouble or illness; Antares, Aldebaran, Frons Scorpio, Deneb, and the Shoulders of Orion, when directed to the ☉, ☽, or Asc. tend to trouble and sickness. (For further influences along this line see Accidents, Affliction, Anguish, Anxiety, Cares, Dejected, Delays, Depressed, Despondency, Disgrace, Dishonor, Distress, Enemies (Secret); Evils, Fears, Females (Injuries by); Foolhardy, Fortune (Malice of); Gloom, Grief, Honor (Loss of); Imprudent, Indiscretions, Injury, Judgment Bad, Low Spirits (see Low); Melancholy, Men (Injured Thru Women); Miseries, Misfortune, Mind (No Peace of); Own Worst Enemy (see "His Own Worst Enemy" under Enemies); Plots, Poverty, Rashness, Recklessness, Reputation (Loss of); Reverses, Ruin, Scandal, Self-Undoing, Sickness, Sorrows, Suffering, Tears (Crying Spells); Trials, Twelfth House, Vexations, Women (Injuries by); Worries, etc.).

Appearance—Troubled Appearance—♄ Sig. □ or ☍ the ☽, or vice versa.

Mind—Troubled Mind—(See Anguish, Anxiety, Dejected, Despondency, Distress, Doubts, Fears, Gloom, Grief, Hope (Hopes Cut Off); Lamenting; Low Spirits, Melancholy, Mournful, Recluse, Renunciation, Sad, Worry, etc.).

Person—A Troublesome Person—(See Anarchist, Assassin, Criminal, Destructiveness, Forgers, Gambler, Knavish; "Full of Mischief" under Mischief; Murderous, Newsmonger, Reactionary, Reformer; "Intolerance" under Religion; Revolutionary, Riotous, Thief, Violent, etc.).

Prevalent—Trouble Prevalent—Much Trouble Generally—An eclipse of the ☽ in the 3rd decan. of ♏; ♄ lord of the year at the Vernal, much trouble and tribulation generally; Comets appearing in ♎ or ♑, much trouble and distress generally. (For the various kinds of Troubles which may be prevalent, see the subjects and references under Humanity, Mankind, Prevalent, Public).

Pulse—(See "Troubled" under Pulse).

Women—Trouble To—(See "Women" under Misfortune). This Encyclopaedia is full of subjects and influences which deal with the Troubles of Humanity, which would be too numerous to list here. Look in the alphabetical arrangement for the subject you have in mind.

TRUE—

True Moment of Birth—(See "Moment of Birth" under Birth).

True Motives — And Purposes — (See Honest).

True Ribs—(See "Upper" under Ribs).

True Skin—(See Derma).

TRUNK — The Body Except the Head and Limbs — Ruled and influenced by the Fixed Signs. For Disorders of the Trunk, or parts thereof, see Bowels, Chest, Heart, Kidneys, Liver, Lungs, Pelvis, Ribs, Sides, Stomach, Thorax, and the various organs of the Trunk. Also see "Opisthotonos", a spasmodic disorder in which there is rigidity of the upper body, and the trunk is thrown backward and arched upward. (See "Fixed Signs" under Fixed).

TRUSTWORTHY (See Honest, Honorable, Humane, Kind, Noble, Reliable, Responsibility, Sincere, etc.).

TRUTH—

Lover of Truth — Born under the strong influence of ♅. (See "Treatment" under Melancholy; Metaphysics, Occult, Philosophy; "Reasonableness" under Reason; "Truth" under Religion; "Astrology" under Science).

Truthful—(See Honest, Trustworthy).

Untruthful—(See Cheating, Deceitful, Dishonest, Liars, etc.). Case — See "Nymphomania", No. 306, in 1001 N.N.

TUBERCLES — A Small Eminence, or Nodule — Nodes — A ♄ disease. (See "Nodules" under Nodes).

Ears — Tubercles In — (See "Nodes" under Ears).

Fat — Tubercles In — (See "Adiposa Dolorosa" under Fat).

Maturation—And Softening of Tubercle—♄ ☌ or ill-asp. the ☽. (See Excrescences).

Xanthoma — Yellowish Tubercles On the Skin—(See Xanthoma).

TUBERCULOSIS—Tubercular Tendency —Tuberculosis is a wasting and depleting disease, and is classed fundamentally as a disease of ♄. It may occur in any part of the body, but is generally circumscribed, or limited to certain parts, or organs, altho the entire system feels its effects. Note the following subjects of Tuberculosis in the various parts of the body, and also see these subjects in the alphabetical arrangement when they are not more fully set forth here—

Addison's Disease—(See Adrenals).

Adrenals—Tuberculosis of—(See "Addison's Disease" under Adrenals).

Bladder — (See "Tuberculosis Of" under Bladder).

Bones—(See "Tuberculosis" under Bones).

Bowels — (See "Tuberculosis" under Bowels; "Abdomen" under Phthisis).

Brain — (See "Tuberculosis" under Brain).

Bronchial — (See "Consumption" under Bronchial).

Cases — Of Tuberculosis — Birth Data, etc.—See Figures 4A, 4B, 4C, 6A, 9C, 19C, in the book, "Astro-Diagnosis", by the Heindels. See Figures 15, 16, 25, 26, 35, in "Message of the Stars", by the Heindels. See Cases in Chap. XIV, in Daath's Medical Astrology. Also for other Cases see "Consumptive" under Consumption.

Consumptive—(See "Consumptive" under Consumption).

Death By—And Cases—(See "Death" under Consumption, Phthisis).

Foci — Tubercular Foci In the Lungs —♄ in ♊, ☌ or ill-asp. the ☉ or ☽.

Kidneys — (See "Tuberculosis" under Kidneys).

Larynx — (See "Consumption Of" under Larynx).

Liver—(See "Tuberculosis" under Liver).

Lungs — Tuberculosis of — Consumption of Lungs—The ☉ ☌ ♄ in ♊ or ♐, or the ☉ ☍ ♄ in these signs; the ☉ ☌ or P. ♄ in ♊; the ☉ in ♊ or ♐, □ or P. ♄; the ☉ rising at B., and affl. by ♄; the ☉ or ☽ in the 6th H. in common signs, and afflicted; the ☉ or ☽ in common signs, in cadent houses, and espec. in the 6th or 12th H., and affl. by malefics; the ☽ in ♊ or ♓ in the 8th H., and affl. by malefics; ♆ in ♊ in the 12th H., and affl. by malefics; ♄ or ☋ in ♊, and due to hardening of the lungs; ♄ affl. in ♊ or ♐; ♄ ☌ ♆ in ♉, ♊, or ♋; ♄ in ♊, and affl. by both ♃ and ♀; ♄ and ☋ ☌ ♃ or ♀ in ♊; a ♄ disease; ♄ in ♋, occi., and affl. the ☉, ☽, Asc., or hyleg; ♄ people become an easy prey to tuberculosis from catching cold from drafts or wettings; ♄ in ♊ when ♄ is the afflictor in the disease; ♄ affl. in ♓, and due to cold and wet feet; ♄ in ♓, occi., and affl. the ☉, ☽, Asc., or hyleg; ♃ in ♊ or ♐, and affl. by ♄ and ♀; caused by ♀ when the dominion of death is vested in her; ☿ affl. in ♓; the Asc. ☌, P., □, or ☍ ♄ by dir., and ♄ occi. at B.; ☋ in ♊, and espec. when ♄ is also in ♊, ♐, or ♓; a ♉ disease when there are malefics in ♉; a ♊ and ♋ disease, and afflictions in these signs; planets in ♊ in ☍ to planets in ♐; afflictions in ♓, the result of colds in the feet; many planets afflicted in common signs; the 6th face of ♒ on the Asc. if ♄ be there; the 6th face of ♓ on the Asc.; Subs at Lu.P. (See "Consumptive" under Consumption; "Pulmonary Phthisis" under Phthisis; Wastings; "Cases" in this section).

Lupus — Tubercular Skin Disease — (See Lupus).

Phthisis — Pulmonary Consumption — (See "Pulmonary" under Phthisis).

Reins—(See "Consumption" under Reins).

Scrofula — Tubercular Tendency In — (See Scrofula).

Skin—Tubercular Skin Disease—(See Lupus).

Spine — (See "Tubercular" under Spine).

Spleen — (See "Tuberculosis" under Spleen).

Supra-Renals — Tuberculosis of—(See "Addison's Disease" under Adrenals).

Tuberculosis—Tubercular Tendency— (See "Lungs", and the various paragraphs in this section). For further study along this line see Asthma, Atrophy, Crystallization, Deposits, Emaciation, Hardening, Saturn, Tabes, Wastings.

TUBES — Tubules — The Tubes and Canals of the body are ruled by the different Signs of the Zodiac, according to their location, and also by the various planets which may rule their special function. (See "Blood Vessels" under Blood; "Tubes" under Bronchial; Canals, Capillaries, Eustachian, Oesophagus, Receptacles, Trachea (Windpipe); Tubuli Seminiferi (see Semen); Ureters, Urethra, Vessels).

TUESDAY—The Day of the Week ruled by ♂. (See "Days of the Week" under Week).

TUMEFACTIONS—(See Swellings).

TUMORS— A Swelling—Abnormal Enlargement—Lumps—Neoplasm—A New Growth Not the Result of Inflammation—Tumors are mostly the work of ♃ and ♀, and result from excesses of various kinds, over-eating, sedentary habits, lack of exercise, poor circulation, stomach disorders, indiscretions, dissolute living, kidney trouble, etc., and are diseases resulting from an ill-dignified, weak, and afflicted ♃ or ♀ at birth. Tumors are of various kinds and types, and may occur in any part of the body wherever there is weakness, deposits, accumulations, and increase of leukocytes. The ♃ and ♀ afflictions pile up the excesses and accumulations, and then ♄ takes them up and does his work by impeding elimination, stopping of functions and secretions, and excess of mineral deposits in the weak and afflicted parts of the body, as shown by the Chart of Birth. Tumors are also a ☽ disease, a ♃, ♋, and ♓ disease. Recent Writers also say that ♆ causes tumors. The action of ♃ conduces to blood changes, and the accumulation of fluids, either in the form of a tumor, or obesity. Tumors follow a Solar Periodicity, and increase in size in proportion to the Sun's Declination towards the West. (See "Periodicity" under Sun). Tumors tend to decrease in size during the decrease of the ☽. (See "Decrease" under Moon. Also see Deposits, Excesses, Hardening, Leukocytes, Retentions, Stoppages, Suppressions, Wastes, etc.). The following subjects have to do with Tumors and Enlargements in the body, which see in the alphabetical arrangement when only listed here—

Abdomen — Tumors In — ♀ affl. in ♍, and usually due to bad habits, feasting, over-eating, etc. (See "Aqueous" in this section).

Abscesses; Adenoma; Aqueous Tumor — In the Abdomen — ♅ in ♍, and affl. by ♀. Case—See "Aqueous", No. 120, in 1001 N.N. (See Abdomen, Fluids, in this section).

Bag-Like Tumor—(See Cysts).

Blood Tumor—(See Haematoma).

Boils; Bowels—(See "Tumors" under Bowels).

Brain—(See "Tumor" under Brain).

Breast—(See "Tumors" under Breast).

Bubo—Inguinal Tumor—(See Bubo).

Cancer—(See Carcinoma).

Carbuncles; Carcinoma;

Cartilaginous Tumor — (See "Chondroma" under Cartilage).

Cysts; Death by Tumor — Caused by ♄ and ♃. (See "Malignant" in this section).

Elastic Tumor—(See "Tumor" under Gums).

Encysted Tumors—Steatoma—Encysted Sebaceous Tumors—(See Steatoma, Wens).

Enlargements; Epithelioma; Epulis—(See "Tumor" under Gums).

Fatty Tumor—(See Degeneration; "Tumors" under Fat; Lipoma).

Fibroid Tumor—Fibroma—(See "Fibroma" under Fiber).

Fibroma — (See "Fibroma" under Fiber).

Fistulous Tumor—(See Fistula).

Fleshy Tumors—(See Caruncle; "Tumors" under Fat, Fleshy; Sarcoma).

Fluids — Watery Tumors — (See "Tumors" under Fluids; "Aqueous" in this section).

Fungus Growths—(See Fungus).

Gastric Tumor—Tumor In the Stomach—(See "Tumor" under Gastric).

Generative Organs—(See "Tumors In" under Generative).

Glandular Tumor — (See Adenoma, Scrofula).

Goiter; Groins—(See Bubo; "Tumors" under Groins).

Gums—(See "Tumor" under Gums).

Haematoma; Hard Tumor — Scirrhus—Ruled and caused by ♄ when ♄ is the afflictor in the disease. Also caused by the mineral deposits of ♄. (See "Scirrhus" under Carcinoma; Deposits, Hard, Resolvent, Scirrhus).

Head — Tumorous Growth In — (See "Growths In" under Head).

Hips and Thighs—(See "Tumors" under Hips, Thighs).

Hollow Tumors — (See "Hollow" under Cysts).

Hypertrophy; Inguinal Tumor—(See Bubo).

Intestines — (See "Tumors" under Bowels).

Kidneys — (See "Tumor" under Kidneys).

Knees — (See "Tumors In" under Knees).

Larynx — (See "Tumors Of" under Larynx).

Legs—(See "Tumors In" under Legs).

Lipoma — (See "Fatty" in this section).

Lumps; Malignant Tumors — Deadly—Fatal—Caused when the ♄ influence enters into the configuration; ♄ ☌ ♃ or ♀. (See Carcinoma, Malignant).

Mediastinal — Tumor In the Chest or Thorax—♃ or ♀ affl. in ♋; Subs at SP. (See Chest, Thorax).

Neck — And Throat — (See "Tumors In" under Neck).

Neoplasm; Nerve Tumor—Neuroma—. (See "Neuroma" under Nerves).

New Growths—Neoplasm—(See Neoplasm, Warts, Wens).

Obesity — ♃ causes Obesity and Tumors. (See Obesity).

Oedematous Tumors — (See Oedema, Resolvent).

Pedunculated Tumor—(See Polypus).

Polypus; Reins — (See "Tumors" under Reins).

Remedy for Tumors—(See Resolvent).

Resolvents — Remedies to Dissolve Tumors—(See Resolvents).

Sarcoma; Scirrhus Tumors—The Hard Form—♄ and ☿ diseases. (See Scirrhus; "Hard" in this section).

Scrofulous Tumors—(See Scrofula).

Sebaceous Tumors—Steatoma—Containing Fat or Suet — Lipoma — (See "Sebaceous", "Tumors", under Fat; Lipoma, Sebaceous, Steatoma, Wens).

Steatoma—(See Encysted, Sebaceous, in this section).

Stomach — (See "Tumor" under Gastric).

Thighs—(See "Thighs" under Fistula; "Tumors" under Hips).

Thorax — (See "Mediastinal" in this section).

Throat—(See "Tumors" under Neck).

Tongue—(See "Cystic Tumor" under Tongue).

Treatment Of—(See Resolvents).

Tumourous Complaints—(See the Introduction, and the various subjects in this Article).

Ulcers; Uterine Tumor—(See "Fibroid", "Tumors", under Womb).

Womb—(See "Tumors" under Womb).

TUMULTS—Injury or Death by Popular Tumult—The ☽ to the bad asps. the ☉ or ☿. (See Hanging, Lynching, Mobs, Riots; "Death" under Suffocation; Trampled). An eclipse of the ☉ in the 1st decan. of ♏ tends to stir up Tumults, War, and Slaughter. (See Riots, Slaughter, War).

TUNICS — An Enveloping or Lining Membrane—Tunica—

Gastro-Intestinal Tunics — (See "Impar" under Ganglion).

Tunica Vaginalis — (See Serum, Testes). Also for other membranes which are classed as Tunics, see Arteries, Conjunctiva, Membranes, Peritoneum).

TURBINATED BONES—(See Nose).

TURBULENT MIND—(See Anarchists; "Turbulent" under Fancies; Perverse, Quarrelsome, Rashness, Reactionary, Rebellious, Recklessness, Reformers, Revolutionary, Riotous; "High Temper" under Temper; Ungovernable, Vicious, Violent).

TURPENTINE—Tar—Pix Cones—Pine Tree—Ruled by ♂. (See Tar).

TURPITUDE—(See Debased, Depraved, Indecent, Lewd; "Low and Base" under Low; "Loose Morals" under Morals; Obscene, Perversions, Shameless, Unnatural, Vile, etc.).

TUSSIS—(See Cough).

Pertussis—(See Whooping Cough).

TWELFTH HOUSE—This is the last of the 12 Houses, and is affiliated with ♓, the 12th Sign of the Zodiac, and also with ♆. This house is a part of the Terminal Triangle, and is a terminal house, showing the end of life, the death of the Psychic Nature, and refers to the sundering of Soul and Spirit, and is what is called the "Second Death". The 8th and 12th Houses are bases of the Occult Triangle, with the 4th H. as the apex. (See Pisces, Terminal). This House was formerly supposed to be connected with the Elementals, the Evil Spirits, and obsessions by them, and is said to be the House of Witchcraft. The confining influences of life, the restraints, limitations, and restrictions, are ruled and represented by this house, and its influences tend to bring trouble, sorrow, privation, confinement, self-undoing, folly, grief, anxiety, suffering, impaired senses, anguish, affliction, mis-

ery, misfortune, distress of every kind, persecution, imprisonment, secret enemies, malice, assassination, suicide, treason, sedition, and every evil that can befall humanity, and especially when there are afflictions and malefics in this house at birth. Saturn delights in this house, and has his joy here, being the Author of Mischief. Saturn and ♂ in this house tend to bring every evil, except death, that Mankind can suffer. The planet ♆ also delights in this house, and when afflicted here tends to Obsessions, Spirit Controls, Involuntary Mediumship, and to unusual and detrimental Psychic and Spiritual conditions, unless the native is awakened, and can respond to the higher influences of ♆. The ☉ ♂ ☿ in this house tends to deafness, and to hinder and limit the Soul in its manifestations in the physical body, by deprivation or destruction of the five Senses, thus thwarting the Soul in its search for knowledge. This is one of the evil houses, along with the 6th and 8th H., and people born with many planets in these houses at B., or the lord of the Asc. in them, and afflicted, are considered quite unfortunate in life, and subject to many diseases and troubles, and to have a less favorable fate. Being an evil house, evil in a human sense, this house is also a favorable place for the Anareta, or killing planet, and the 12th H. also, when badly afflicted, can act as Anareta. (See Anareta). This is a feminine and passive house, and its conditions at B., and especially when malefic, tend to greatly affect negative and passive people, and to cause much worry and brooding, and often resulting in suicide in a moment of despair and despondency. This house denotes the feet, ankles, and toes, and all hurts and diseases incident to them.

Color — Green is the Color ruled by this house.

Denotes — The 12th H. denotes the ankles, feet, and toes, and all diseases and hurts incident to them.

Diseases Of—Diseases, Hurts, Injury, and Affliction to the Ankles, Feet, Toes, and also to impaired Senses, as Deafness, and other physical and mental limitations. Also Chronic Diseases in general are ruled by this house.

Rules — The 12th House rules Afflictions, Anarchists, Anguish of Mind, Animals (Large); Ankles, Anxieties, Assassinations, Asylums, Aunts and Uncles (On the father's side in a male nativity, and on the mother's side in a female nativity); Backbiters, Banishment, Bondage, Captivity, Cattle (Great and Large); Chronic Diseases, Clairvoyance, Color (Green); Confinements, Desert (The); Desolate Places, Distress, Enemies (Secret and Private); Envy, Exile, Feet, Folly, Great Cattle, Green Color, Hermits, Hospitals, Imprisonment, Insane Asylums, Institutions where people are confined; Invalids (Bed-ridden); Kidnappings, Large Animals, Limitations, Mediumship, Miseries, Misfortunes, Morgues, Obsessions, Oxen, Persecutions, Plots,

Prisons, Private Enemies, Psychic Powers and Experiences, Recluses, Relatives (see "Aunts and Uncles" in this paragraph); Revenge, Secret Enemies, Sedition, Seduction, Self - Undoing, Servitude, Sleep, Solitary Vice, Solitude (Desire for); Spiritual Powers and Experiences, Suffering, Suicide, Toes, Treachery, Treason, Trouble, Wilderness (The); Witchcraft, etc.

Stellium — In the 12th H. at birth — Case—Six Planets in ♍ in the 12th H. —See "Idiot from Birth", No. 742, in 1001 N.N.

TWINS—Double Births—Multiple Births — Triplets — Quadruplets — Twins are especially produced and given by the ♊ Sign influences, a double-bodied sign, and which is also known as the Sign of "The Twins", and of Castor and Pollux. When Twins are conceived, the bicorporeal Signs ♊, ♐, or ♓, are prominent at conception, and also usually at B., and contain the ☽, and planets dominant in the giving of children. A study of the Prenatal Epoch Map, the map for the time of conception, is very important to understand the causes of multiple conceptions, and to determine the facts as to sex and number, etc. (See Predetermination, Prenatal Epoch, Triplets). The Planets at B. are in harmony with Prenatal conditions, normally, and help to account for single or multiple births, but it must be understood that it is not altogether the positions of the planets at B. which produce children, but those at conception also play their part. There is a close dependency between the time of conception and the moment of birth, and when one of these times is known, the time of the other can be mathematically calculated, as is proven in the Prenatal Epoch work. The influences at the time of conception work with, and concur with the influences in the natal map, and that is why there is often much similarity in the planetary positions at conception, and at birth. The influences in the radix bring the child into the world at the time predetermined at conception, and concur with those at conception under normal conditions. Twins may be conceived near the same time, or as much as a month apart. When conceived several weeks apart, the older twin, being at maturity, forces the younger twin away, which may be only at eight months. In such a case the last one born is considered the older of the two, and for this reason it was the belief of the Ancients that Jacob was older than Esau, altho born after him, and this is, no doubt, the Occult reason why the father Isaac bestowed the blessing upon Jacob instead of the first-born Esau. Twins are very much alike in appearance when the same Sign is rising upon the Eastern Horizon, or Ascendant, but if the rising Signs differ, as when the first twin is born with ♓ upon the Asc., and the second one with ♈ rising, they will be under different rulerships, and differ much in form and disposition. The one born under Pisces will be shorter, and of less vitality, and if either of them die soon after birth, or in infancy or childhood, it will be apt to be the ♓ one, as ♈ rising is one of the very strong and vital signs, and also produces a taller body than ♓. Thus one of these twins may be short, fleshy, and flabby in early life and youth, while the other will be tall, thin, and wiry, and possibly not as plump and handsome as the first-born, or ♓-born child. (See Appearance). Noting the influences at the time of conception, the planet which is connected with the ruling places indicates the number generated, and the planets which are configurated with the ☉, ☽, or Asc., determine the sex, or sexes. This subject of the number and sex of multiple conceptions is discussed in the Article on Predetermination, and also in the Article on Triplets. (See these Articles). The following are the general influences which tend to produce Twins, influences which predominate at conception, and also those which are known to exist at birth in cases of multiple births.

Birth of Twins — Twins Conceived — When only two of the Significators of children behold the ☉, ☽, or Asc. at conception, only two are conceived. If these Sigs. both be masculine planets, two males will be conceived. If they both be feminine planets, two females will be conceived. If one of the Sigs. be masculine, and the other feminine, one male and one female will be conceived. The masculine Significators are the masculine planets ♄, ♃, and ♂. The feminine Sigs. are the ☽, ♀, and ☿, if they behold the ☉, ☽, or Asc. at conception. (See "Three Males", "Three Females", and the other paragraphs in the Article on Triplets). If the planets which promise progeny be in feminine, or bicorporeal signs, double offspring is granted, and if in the prolific and seminal signs, as ♋, ♏, or ♓, they will grant twins, and even more. If the ☉, ☽, or Asc., or planet aspecting them, be in bicorporeal signs at conception, there will be twins, or more, and the same if both the ☉ and ☽ are in the South Angle; the ☉, ☽, and Asc. occupied by double-bodied signs, as ♊, ♐, or ♓, or many prolific stars cast a good aspect to them; twins occur when both the ☉ and ☽ are in the Midheaven in a bicorporeal sign; the ☉ and ☽ in bicorporeal signs, or lords of the Asc. or 5th H., in such signs; the ☽ in the 5th H. in ♓; ♃, ♀, or the ☽ in the 10th, 11th, 4th, or 5th H. in double-bodied or feminine signs; ☊ with ♃, ♀, or the ☽, and all of them in double-bodied signs; a double-bodied sign on the Asc. or 7th H., or their lords, or the ☽, in these signs, as in ♊, ♓, or the first half of ♐; if the 1st or 5th H., or their lords, be in bicorporeal signs, twins are denoted in Hor'y Questions; a fruitful planet, or planets, in the 10th, 11th, 4th, or 5th H. in fruitful, feminine, bicorporeal, or water signs, there are two, or more, at a birth; a double-bodied sign on the Asc. or 5th H., and with ♃ or ♀ therein. (See "Single Births" in Sec. 1 in the Article on Children. Also see Birth, Conception, Foetus, Fruitful, Gestation, Parturition, Pregnancy, Prenatal Epoch).

Cases of Twin Births—See "Twins", Numbers 215, 216, 236, 241, 324, 325, 326, 327, 638, 639, 675, 676, 680, 681, 682, 683, 715, 716, 740, 955, all in 1001 N.N.

Had Twins Three Times—See "Twins", No. 740, in 1001 N.N.

One Male, One Female — (See "Birth of Twins" in this section).

Siamese Twins — United Twins — See "Twins", No. 236, 241, in 1001 N.N.

Two Females—(See "Birth of Twins" in this section).

Two Males—(See "Birth of Twins" in this section).

United Twins—(See "Siamese" in this section; Xyphodymus).

TWISTINGS—Torsion—A ♅ disease and affliction, and due to incoordination, or lack of proper nerve supply to a part, or organ. Twisting may occur in any part of the body, and especially in the part ruled by the sign ♅ is in at B. This is classed as a Spasmodic disorder. If the contraction and twisting become chronic, a deformity may result, lameness, or disability. (See Contortions, Contractions, Deformities, Distortions; "Wry Neck" under Neck; Spasmodic Diseases, Torsion, Torticollis).

TWITCHING—An Irregular Minor Spasm—A ♅ disease and affliction, and where ♅ may not be as severely afflicted as in twistings. Twitchings are an indication that the nerves are being overworked, or affected by systemic disorders, and are a signal that something is wrong, and that habits, or the manner of living are wrong, and that it is time to slow up a bit before the vital forces become lowered or dissipated. (See Contractions; "Movements" under Erratic; Jerkings, Saint Vitus Dance, Spasmodic Diseases, Tics, Tremors, etc.).

TYMPANIES—Tympanites—Gaseous Distention of the Abdomen—Caused by the ☉ afflicted; the ☽ affl. in ♎ or ♍; also a ♂ disease. (See "Gas" under Bowels; Distentions, Flatulence; "Abdomen" under Gas; Inflation).

TYMPANUM—Tympanitis—(See "Drum" under Ears).

TYPE OF THE DISEASE—The Time and Type of the disease are indicated by the nature of the Direction, or Directions, operating at the time, and the nature of the afflicting planet, or planets, but only such disease can be predicted, or consummated, as is contained, or foreshadowed in the radical map. (See "Disease" under Nature, Quality, Species).

TYPHLITIS—Inflammation of the Caecum—(See Caecum).

TYPHOID FEVER—Enteric Fever—Intestinal Lesions and Eruptions—A ♍ disease, and caused by afflictions in ♍; the ☉ afflicted in ♍ or the opposite sign ♓; a ♂ disease, and ♂ is usually the afflictor; ♂ affl. in ♍, and especialy in the 6th H.; ♂ affl. in ♋ in the 6th H.; ☿ affl. in ♍; afflictions in ♐; occurs mostly when ♍, ♎, or ♏ are on the Asc. (See "Fever" under Bowels; "Epidemics" under Cholera; Epidemics). Case—Death by Typhoid Fever—See "De", No. 226, in 1001 N.N.

Typhoid Pneumonia—(See "Typhoid" under Pneumonia).

TYPHUS FEVER—Camp Fever—This fever is more prevalent when the major planets, and especially ♄ and ♃, are in perihelion. Is caused by the vitiated and disturbed atmospheric conditions by planetary influence. Caused by ♂ and ♀. Venus denotes death by when the afflictor in the disease. (See "Corrupt Air" under Air; Epidemics, La Grippe, Perihelion).

Typhomania—The Delirium of Typhus—Caused by ♆, and ♆ afflicted at B., or afflicting the hyleg.

TYPICAL DRUGS—Of Each Planet—(See "Typical Drugs" under each of the Planets).

TYRANTS—(See Cruel; "Shows No Pity" under Pity).

U

UGLY—An Ugly Person—Not Handsome—Not Attractive—Ugliness is usually caused by malefics afflicting the Asc., causing defects in the features, complexion, and form of the body, and according to the nature of the planets and signs involved. The signs ♋ and ♑, when prominent at B., or upon the Asc., are said to give the least beauty of all the signs, and especially ♑. The ♑ sign especially causes a crooked, raw-boned, ill-shaped body, knock-knees, bow legs, and usually a pale and swarthy complexion. The ♎ and ♒ influences, and the ♀ influences, tend to give the most beautiful and comely bodies when upon the Asc. at B., or ♀ dignified in the Asc.

Ugly Disposition—Given especially by the afflictions of the malefics ♄ and ♂, and when these planets are prominent at B., in angles, and afflicting each other. (See Cruel; "Cross", "Rough", under Manners; "High Temper" under Temper).

Ugly Face—(See "Ugly" under Face).

Ugly In Person—Ugly Body—Not Handsome—The ☉ Sig. in ♉, a rather ugly person; the ☉ in ♉ in partile asp. the Asc., short, well-set, and rather ugly; the ☽ ill-dignified at B., not handsome, but a muddling creature; the □ and ☍ aspects of the ☽ tend to give an ugly, crooked, and badly made body; ♄ Sig. in ♉, in no wise comely; in Hor'y Q. ♄ Sig. in ♉, ♋, ♑, or ♓; ♄ Sig. in ♑, thin and ungainly; in Hor'y Q. ♄ denotes a person of a lean, crooked, and ill-made body; ♄ indicates a person of a black, earthy, brown complexion; ♄ Sig. in ♉ or ♓; ♄ in ♓, partile the Asc., generally very ugly; ♄ Sig. □ or ☍ ☿, not of a genteel form; ♂ Sig. in ♓, far from handsome;

♂ in ♓, partile the Asc., generally ugly; ♀ Sig. □ or ☍ ♄, not very handsome; ☿ Sig. in ♏, not in any way elegant or pleasing; ♑ on the Asc., a crooked body. Also note the influences in the Introduction to this Article. (See Awkwardness, Bloated; "Raw-Boned" under Bones; "Bad" under Complexion; Commonplace, Crooked, Deformed, Distortions; "Ugly" under Face; Freckles; Ill-Formed" under Ill; Lean, Lumpish, Marks, Pimples, Scars; "Pock-Marked" under Smallpox; Spare, Thin, etc.).

ULCERS—Ulceration—Ulcerous Sores—Open Sores — Erosions — Suppuration Upon a Free Surface — Ulcerous Growths — For the main influences causing Ulcer see "Tendency To" in this section. The following subjects have to do with Ulcer in its various forms and manifestations. See these subjects in the alphabetical arrangement when only listed here—

Abscesses; Aneurysm; Anus — (See "Ulceration" under Anus).

Aphthous Ulcers—Of the Mouth—(See Aphthae).

Arms — Ulcers In the Arms, Hands, Legs and Feet — The ☽ affl. in signs which rule these parts. (See Aneurysm).

Bladder — (See "Ulcers" under Bladder).

Blood — Ulcers Proceeding from Corrupt Blood — A ♓ disease, and afflictions in ♓. (See Impure).

Bone—Ulcerous Inflammation of—(See "Ulcerous" under Bones).

Bowels—(See "Ulcers" under Bowels).

Breast—(See "Ulcers" under Breast).

Cancer—(See Carcinoma).

Cancrum Oris — (See "Mouth" under Gangrene).

Caries; Chancroid—(See Gonorrhoea).

Corrupt Blood—(See "Blood" in this section).

Crusts; Duodenum—(See "Ulcer" under Duodenum).

Dysentery—Ulcer of Bowels In—(See Dysentery).

Eyes—(See "Ulcer" under Eyes).

Face—(See "Ulcers" under Face).

Feet—(See "Ulcers" under Feet).

Forehead — (See "Ulceration" under Forehead).

Gangrene; Gastric Ulcer—(See "Ulcer" under Gastric).

Generally Some Ulcer—The ☽ in ♏, and affl. by the ☉ or ♂ when taken ill, patients generally have some ulcer (Hor'y).

Genitals—Ulcer of—♂ affl. in ♏ tends to ulcer in the Genitals, Secret Parts, Urethra, Vagina, Womb, Vulva, and to the Chancroid accompanying Gonorrhoea. (See "Ulceration" under Womb).

Growths — Ulcerous Growths — (See "Tendency To" in this section).

Gums—(See "Ulcerated" under Gums).

Hands—(See "Ulcers" under Hands).

Head—(See "Ulceration" under Head).

Hips and Thighs—(See "Ulcers" under Hips).

Imposthumes—(See Abscesses).

Increased — Ulcers Increased — ♄ and ♂ in an angle, occi. of the ☉, and ori. of the ☽, and ☿ in familiarity with ♂; ♂ or ☿ holding dominion at B., and in familiarity with each other, and ♂ affl. the hyleg.

Inflamed Ulcers—(See "Phlegmonous" in this section).

Jaws — (See Gums, Necrosis, Pyorrhoea; "Ulceration" under Teeth).

Kidneys — (See "Ulceration" under Kidneys).

Legs—(See "Ulcers" under Legs).

Liver—(See "Ulcerated" under Liver).

Loins—(See "Ulcers" under Loins).

Lower Jaw—Ulcerated Gums of—(See Gums).

Lungs — (See "Ulceration" under Lungs).

Milk Leg — (See this subject under Legs).

Mortification—(See Gangrene, Granulations, Mortification).

Mouth—Ulcers In—(See Aphthae).

Nose—(See "Ulcers" under Nose).

Ovaries—(See "Ulceration" under Ovaries).

Phlegmonous Ulcer — Inflamed Ulcer — Putrefying Ulcer — ♂ in an angle, occi. of the ☉, and ori. of the ☽. (See "Pus" in this section).

Pus — Ulcers with Pus — (See "Phlegmon" under Pus; "Phlegmonous" in this section).

Putrefying Ulcers — (See Phlegmonous, Pus, in this section).

Pyorrhoea; Rectum—(See "Ulcer" under Rectum).

Reins—(See "Ulcers" under Reins).

Remedy for Ulcer — Lead Ointment. (See Lead).

Secret Parts—(See "Genitals" in this section).

Sloughing; Sores—Ulcerous Sores—A ♓ disease, and afflictions in ♓. (See Sores).

Stomach — (See "Ulcer" under Stomach).

Suppurative Ulcer—Ulcer with Pus—(See "Pus" in this section).

Syphilitic Ulcer—Sores of Syphilis—Throat Ulcer of—(See Syphilis).

Tendency to Ulcer — Afflictions in ♓; a ♓ disease; a ♋, ♎, and ♓ disease, and afflictions in these signs; the ☽ affl. in ♒; a ♄ disease; ♄, ♅, or ♆ in ♋, and affl. the ☉ or ☽; ♄ and ♃ in ♍, and affl. the ☉ and ♅ in ♊; a ♂ disease; ♂ in ♏ or ♐, ☌, or ill-asp. the ☉. (See Leukocytes; the various paragraphs in this section).

Thighs—(See "Ulcers" under Thighs).

Throat — (See "Ulcerated" under Throat).

Thrush—(See Aphthae).

Treatment Of—(See "Remedy" in this section).

Ulcerous Growths — (See "Tendency To", and the various paragraphs in this section).

Upper Jaw—Ulcerated Gums of—(See Gums).

Urethra—(See "Genitals" in this section; Urethra).

Vagina—(See "Genitals" in this section; Vagina).

Varicose; Venereal Ulcers—♂ afflicted in ♏. (See "Ulcers" under Venereal).

Vulva — (See "Genitals" in this section; Vulva).

Womb — (See "Ulceration" under Womb).

ULNA — The Large Bone of the Forearm — Under the structural rulership of the ♌ Sign. Is opposite to, and corresponds to the Fibula in the leg, ruled by the ♒ Sign. Mars afflicted in ♌ tends to fracture of the Ulna. (See Forearm, Radius).

UMBILICUS—(See Navel).

UNBALANCED MIND — (See "Unbalanced" under Mentality, Reason).

UNBRIDLED PASSION—(See Nymphomania; "Passional Excesses", "Unbridled", under Passion).

UNCANNY FEELINGS — (See Dreams, Fears, Forebodings, Mysterious, Premonitions, Strange, Superstitious, Visions, Weird, etc.).

UNCERTAIN—

Uncertain Action — To the Body — ♓ on the Asc.

Uncertain Health — (See "Uncertain" under Health).

Uncertain Mind — (See "Uncertain" under Mind).

UNCHARITABLE — ♄ influence. (See Miserly).

UNCHASTE — (See "Chaste" under Females; "Adultery", "Liaisons", under Love Affairs; "Loose Morals" under Morals; "Unbridled" under Passion; "Clandestine" under Sex; "Unchaste" under Women).

UNCLEANLY — Filthy Habits of Body and Mind — Dirty—Slovenly—Untidy—Careless About the Body—The ☽ affl. ♀ at B.; ♄ ill-dignified at B., and affl.; in Horary Questions ♄ Sig. denotes a dirty person; ♄ ☌ ♀; ♄ and ♂ in the Asc., and affl. the ☽ and ♀; ♂ prominent at B., with many planets in earthy and watery signs, and ♂ without the strong support of the ☉, ♃ or ♀; ♂ affl. in ♓, slovenly in habits; ♀ weak and ill-dignified at B.; ♀ affl. the ☽; ♀ to the bad asps. ☿ by dir.; ♀ ☌ ☽ ♎, and □ ♂ ♋; ♓ on cusp 6th, or in the 6th H., tends to carelessness in personal cleanliness; ♓ when afflicted produces ailments thru carelessness and forgetfulness. These afflictions existing at B., often tend to ill-health thru lack of proper care of the body. (See Carelessness, Cleanliness, Filthy, Habits, Knavish, Leprosy, Neglect, Slovenly, Untidy, etc.).

Unclean Mind — (See Lewd, Lust; "Loose Morals" under Morals; Obscene, Profane, Shameless, Vile, Wanton, etc.).

UNCLES—The Aunts and Uncles on the father's side, when considering a female nativity, are ruled by the 6th H., but in a male nativity, they are ruled by the 12th H. The Aunts and Uncles on the mother's side, in a female nativity, are ruled by the 12th H., and in a male nativity, by the 6th H. By noting these distinctions, and the nature of the planets in, or influences affecting the 6th and 12th houses at birth, the native can get some idea of the events, destiny, health, illness, early or late death, etc., which are apt to overtake an Aunt or Uncle on either side of the house. The Uncles on the father's side are ruled by ♄, and on the mother's side, by ☿. Thus ♄ badly afflicted at B., and by direction, tends to affliction or trouble to an Uncle, on one side of the house, according to the sex of the native, and the transits, progressions, and arcs of direction of afflictions to ♄ will give the time of the events and afflictions. Also ☿ is to be treated in the same way to determine the time and nature of events and afflictions to Aunts and Uncles on the mother's side. (See Aunts, Brethren, Sixth House, Twelfth House).

Maternal Uncles—And Aunts—Death or Suffering To — (See "Aunts and Uncles" under Maternal).

Paternal Uncles—And Aunts—Death or Suffering To—♄ ruler of the 6th or 12th H. at B., and ♄ ☌ or ill-asp. the Asc. by dir., according to the sex of the native, and especially as related to the aunts and uncles on the father's side. On the mother's side, if ☿ should rule the 6th, or be in the 6th, and be much affl. at B., and by direction by ♄, and other malefics, or by an Eclipse, then judge that the affliction will occur to an aunt or uncle on the mother's side, and according to the sex of the native, as to whether the affliction is to be judged as from the 6th or 12th H. Some Authors ignore these finer distinctions, and others lay great stress upon them, the same as in the finer distinctions concerning the 10th and 4th houses, in the cases of the father and mother in a male or female nativity. Most Writers just take the general rule that the 6th H. rules the aunts and uncles on the father's side, in either a male or female nativity, and the 12th H. on the mother's side, and that afflictions in these houses, or to the Asc. by dir., whether they be of ♄, ☿, or any planet, tend to afflict an Uncle or Aunt accordingly. (See Aunts; "Relatives" under Father; Grandparents, Maternal, Mother, Parents, Paternal, Relatives).

UNCOMELY PERSON—♄ in ♉, partile the Asc. (See Crooked; "Ill-Formed" under Ill; Stooping, Ugly, etc.).

UNCOMMON—Unusual—

Uncommon Death—(See "Uncommon" under Death).

Uncommon Diseases — Unusual Diseases—Peculiar—Extraordinary—Strange—Mysterious—Caused by ♅. If there is also a mysterious element in them, ♆ helps to cause them, or may be the direct afflictor. (See Extraordinary, Mysterious, Obscure Diseases, Peculiar Diseases; "Diseases" under Psychic; Strange Diseases, Unusual).

Uncommon Occurrences — (See Phenomena).

Uncommon Persons—Born under the strong influence of ♅. (See Eccentric, Independent, Metaphysics, Misunderstood, Occult, Philosophy; "Truth" under Religion; "Astrology" under Science; "Lover of Truth" under Truth, etc.).

UNCOMPROMISING—Fixed Sign influence, and caused by many planets in these signs, or with fixed signs upon the Asc. and angles at birth. (See "Fixed Signs" under Fixed"; Inflexible, Obstinate).

UNCONSCIOUSNESS—Unconscious—(See Anaesthetics, Catalepsy, Coma, Consciousness, Delirium, Dreams, Epilepsy, Fainting, Fits, Hypnotism; "Sleep Walking" under Sleep; Trance).

Unconscious Behavior — (See the Introduction under Habits).

UNCONTROLLED—Unrestrained—

Emotions—(See "Uncontrolled" under Emotions).

Impulses—(See "Uncontrolled" under Impulses).

Passion — (See Nymphomania; "Unbridled" under Passion).

Thinking — Uncontrolled and Rash Thinking — Indicated by ♂ and the ♂ afflictions to the ☽, ♄, ☿, and the Asc. at B., and by dir. (See Anger; "Brain Storms" under Brain; Brutish, Control, Criminal, Cruel, Dejected, Despondency, Depressed, Excitable, Fear, Folly, Foolhardy, Fury, Hasty, Hatred, Insanity, Involuntary, Jealousy, Liars; "Low Spirits" under Low; Madness, Melancholy; "Thinking" under Mind; Murderous, Perverse, Prodigal, Quarrelsome, Rashness, Recklessness, Revenge, Suicide; "High Temper" under Temper; Unbalanced, Vicious, Violent, Worry, etc.).

UNDER—(See Lower).

UNDERMINED HEALTH — (See Excesses; "Undermined" under Health; "Health Injured" under Men; "Health Suffers" under Opposite Sex; "Passional Excesses" under Passion; "Thinking" under Uncontrolled; Venery; "Lessened" under Vitality).

UNDERSIZED BODY — Undersized Organs or Parts—Dwarfed—Undeveloped — Malformed — ♆ influence; ♆ affl. by ♄, and in the part of the body ruled by the sign containing ♆; ♆ □ or ☍ ♄; ♆ the afflictor, and assisted by ♄, tends to undersized or misshaped organs in the part, or parts afflicted; ♆ affl. in ♋ tends to an undersized stomach; ♆ affl. in ♏, to undersized sex organs, etc. (See Atrophy, Diminished, Dwarfed, Misshaped, Undeveloped).

UNDERSTANDING — Apprehension — Comprehension — Discernment — Perception — Reason — The Understanding of every one depends much upon the strength, and distance of ☿ from the ☉ at B., and the further ☿ is from the ☉, the better the understanding. Also ☿ rising or setting before the ☉ gives a better mind and understanding, and greater depth of thought. When ☿ is combust, the understanding is impaired.

Good Understanding — ♊ gives, and with ♊ on the Asc.; ♅ strong and well-aspected at B.; ☿ in ♍, and with the ☽ in ♋; ☿ well-aspected by the ☽, and also the ☽ and ☿ in good relation to the Asc. (See "Good" under Comprehension, Intellect, Judgment, Mind; "Quickened" under Mentality; "Clear and Incisive", "Sound Mind", under Mind).

Weak Understanding—Comprehension Dull—The ☽ sepr. from ☿ and applying to the ☉; the ☽ □ or ☍ ☿, and the ☽ or ☿ afflicting the Asc.; ♃ Sig. □ or ☍ ☿; ♂ afflicted in ♓, a dull and stupid understanding; ☿ Sig. □ or ☍ ♃. (See "Mental Chaos" under Chaotic; "Mind" under Dull; "Bad" under Judgment; "Weak" under Mentality, Mind; "Disorders Of" under Perception; "Void Of" under Reason; "Smoky Degrees of the Zodiac" under Smoky).

UNDERTAKERS—Embalmers—Morticians—Good Influences For—♂ and ♀ joint rulers of the Profession, and ♄ also give testimony; ♄ joined with ♂ and ♀. (See "Silver Cord" under Silver).

UNDEVELOPED—Undevelopment—Undersized—♆ influence tends to lack of development of any part or organ.

Undeveloped Body—(See Diminished, Dwarfed, Malformations, Myxoedema, Undersized).

Undeveloped Mind — (See Foolish, Idiocy, Imbecility; "Undeveloped" under Mentality). Case—See "Never Grew Up", No. 720, in 1001 N.N.

UNDIGESTED HUMOURS — (See "Raw Humours" under Indigestion).

UNDOING — Self-Undoing — (See Debauched, Disgrace, Dissipation, Drunkenness; "His Own Worst Enemy" under Enemies; "Ruined by Women" under Love Affairs; "Loss Of" under Reputation; Self-Undoing).

UNEASINESS — A Feeling of Uneasiness and Discomfort — (See Discomfort, Malaise).

Old Age—Uneasy Mind In Old Age—(See "Mind" under Old Age).

UNEQUAL—Unequal Sight of the Eyes —(See "Unequal Sight" under Sight).

UNEXPECTED — Unlooked For — Sudden—♅ causes unexpected and sudden disorders, accidents, events, and disasters.

Death—Unexpected and Sudden Death —(See Extraordinary; "Death" under Sudden; Untimely).

Diseases—Unexpected Diseases—(See "Diseases" under Sudden).

Events — Unexpected, Strange and Sudden Events—(See Events).

Wounds — Unexpected and Spontaneous — (See Accidents, Explosions, Hurts, Spontaneous, Wounds).

UNFAVORABLE—Detriments—

Crises—Unfavorable Crisis in Disease —(See Crisis).

Journeys — Unfavorable Journeys — (See Journeys).

Prognosis — Unfavorable — (See Prognosis).

UNFORGIVING — Malefics in the Fixed Signs in angles, retains anger. (See Anger, Jealousy, Revengeful).

UNFORTUNATE—Unfortunate In Life—

Extremely Unfortunate — The ☉ affl. in □ or ♑; the ☉ with South Scale at B.; the ☉ Sig. ☌ ♄; the ☽ carried to, or conjoined with the ☉ at B.; the ☽ Sig. ☌ ♄ or the ☉, or the ☽ □ or ☍ ♄, extremely unfortunate; the ☽ decr. and sepr. from ♃, and applying to ♄; the ☽ sepr. from ♄ and apply. to the ☉; the ☽ Sig. in ♈, ♌, or ♍, generally unfortunate; the ☽ Sig. in ♊, ♏, ♑, or ♓; the ☽ Sig. in ♎ unless ♀ be strong and well-aspected; the ☽ to Hydra's Heart or Ceti; ♅ ascending at B., or with the chief Significator; ♅ or ♆ affl. the Asc.; ♄ in the 10th or 4th H., and affl. the ☉ or ☽, malice of fortune is certain; signified by ♄ and his afflictions; ♄ to ☌ ☋ by dir.; ♄ Sig. ☌ ☽ or ♂; ♃ ♑; ♃ Sig. □, ☍ ♄; ♂ Sig. in ♉ near Pleiades; ♂ ♊, thru many changes in work or residence; ♂ Sig. in ♊, ♋, ♍, ♒ or ♓; ♂ Sig. ☌ ♄, and especially if the Significators be under the Earth; ♂ Sig. □ or ☍ the ☉ or ☽; ♀ Sig. ☌ the ☉ or ♄; ♀ Sig. in ♈ unless ♀ have the good asp. of ♃; ♀ Sig. in ♍ or ♑; ♀ Sig. □ or ☍ the ☽ or ♄; ☿ Sig. in ♈, ♉, ♋, ♐, ♑, or ♓; ♑ on the Asc.; the Sig. in ♍ in Hor'y Q. (See Disgrace, Fate; "Ill-Fortune", "Malice of Fortune", under Fortune; Misfortune, Poverty, Reverses, Ruin; "Much Sickness" under Sickness; Sorrow, Trouble, etc.).

Unfortunate Signs — Of the Zodiac — The Feminine Signs, the Even Signs, as ♉, ♋, ♍, ♏, ♑, and ♓. These are also the Negative Signs. People born under these Signs tend to worry and brood more, invite ill-health, and the general events of their lives tend to be more unfortunate than is the case with the positive, and more individualized classes of people. The ♑ sign is said to be the most unfortunate of all the Signs, being the Sign of ♄. (See "Negative Signs" under Negative).

Unfortunate Star Maps — Those having many □ and ☍ aspects; the malefic planets strong, rising, and elevated above the Lights; many planets out of dignity, in weak signs, cadent, setting, or under the Earth at B.; the hyleg severely afflicted by malefics at B.; ♄ rising in the 1st or 10th H., and afflicted, or ruler of these houses; ♑ upon the Asc. Such maps are considered unfortunate with the average person who is not awakened or spiritualized, as such maps usually tend to more sorrow, trouble, and ill-health, or an earlier death, and often result in crime, murder, suicide, and an untimely or tragical end. (See Character, Fate, Horoscope, Map, Nativity).

UNFRUITFUL — Unprolific — (See Barrenness; "Cold and Dry Body" under Dry; "Anchorite" under Husband; Impotent; "Woman Is Not With Child" under Pregnancy; "Unfruitful" under Wife).

UNGAINLY BODY — ♄ Sig. in ♑, thin and ungainly; ♄ in ♑, partile the Asc.; ♑ on the Asc. (See Awkward; "Raw-Boned" under Bones; Crooked; "Ill-Formed" under Ill; Thin, Ugly).

UNGOVERNABLE — Unmanageable — ♂ rising and elevated at B., and afflicted by malefics. Also in irrational states of mind, a patient may become ungovernable. In cases of defective, or monstrous births, the offspring may be ungovernable. (See Anger; "Beastly Form" under Beasts; Brutish; "Dogs" under Children; Cruel, Dangerous, Demoniac, Indocile, Insanity, Irrational, Irresponsible, Madness, Mania; "Animal Forms" under Monsters; Murderous; "Void Of" under Reason; Rebellious, Riotous, Savage; "High Temper" under Temper; Vicious, Violent, Wild).

UNGUENTS—(See Ointments).

UNHAPPY—Unhappiness—The 12th H. influences strong and malefic at B.; born under ♄, and with ♄ afflicted in the 12th H.; lord of the 1st H. in the 12th H.; the star Dorsa Leonis (Lion's Tail), when directed to the ☉, ☽, or Asc., tends to bring unhappiness and discontentment. (See Anguish, Anxiety, Cares, Contentment, Dejected, Depressed, Despair, Despondency, Discontentment, Fears, Fortune, Gloom, Grief, Happiness; "Hopes Cut Off" under Hope; Hypochondria; "Ill-Health All Thru Life" under Ill-Health; Introspection, Invalids; "Lion's Tail" under Lion; "Low Spirits" under Low; Melancholy; "Morbid" under Mind; Miseries, Misfortune, Restlessness, Sadness, Sorrow, Suicide, Trouble, Twelfth House, Unfortunate, Worry, Wretched, etc.).

Unhappy Time—(See Disgrace, Events; "Periods of Bad Health" under Health; "Loss Of" under Honour, Reputation; Misery, Reverses, Ruin, Scandal, Self-Undoing; "Much Sickness" under Sickness; Sorrow, Trouble, etc.).

UNHEALTHY— Pale—Sickly—Cadaverous — People who live in covered places, as in houses in the woods, where the sunshine does not enter, or in mines, caves, etc., tend to be unhealthy, and in places where vegetation does not grow, as all vegetation points to the Midheaven, or Zenith. The ♋ and ♑ signs are the weakest signs when upon the Asc. at B., and tend to the weakest bodies, and to be pale, sickly, and unhealthy. Also the ☉ in ♋, in partile asp. the Asc. tends to give an unhealthy countenance, pale and white. (See "Unhealthy" under Complexion; "Weak" under Constitution; Emaciated, Feeble; "Bad" under Health; "Ill-Health All Thru Life" under Ill-Health; Infirm, Invalids, Pale, Sickly; "Much Sickness" under Sickness; "Low" under Vitality; "Weak Body" under Weak).

Air—Unhealthy Air—(See "Corrupt" under Air).

Body—Unhealthy Body and Constitution—(See the first part of this Article).

Countenance—Unhealthy Countenance —(See "Unhealthy" under Complexion; "Unhealthy Aspect" under Face; Pale, Sickly; "Complexion" under White).

Imagination — (See "Unhealthy" under Imagination).

Mind—(See "Unhealthy" under Mind).

UNILATERAL—Affecting But One Side of the Body—

Ears — Deafness In One Ear — (See "One Ear" under Hearing).

Eyes — Blindness In One Eye — (See "One Eye" under Blindness, Eyes; "Eyes" under Left, Right).

Headache — Unilateral Headache — (See "Hemicrania" under Head; Migraine).

Hemianopia — Blindness In One-Half of the Visual Field — (See "Hemianopia" under Sight).

Hemicrania — Neuralgia of One-Half of the Head — (See "Hemicrania" under Head; Migraine).

Hemiplegia — Paralysis In One Side of the Body — (See "Hemiplegia" under Paralysis).

Neuralgia—In One Side of the Head —(See "Hemicrania" in this section).

Nutrition—Impaired Nutrition of One Side of the Face—(See "Hemiatrophy" under Face).

Paralysis—In One Side of the Body—(See "Hemiplegia" under Paralysis).

Vision—Blindness In One-Half of the Visual Field—(See "Hemianopia" under Sight).

UNION OF PARTS — (See Adhesions, Coalition).

UNKNOWN — Has Fears of An Unknown Danger—(See "Danger" under Fears).

UNLOOKED FOR—(See Extraordinary, Sudden, Unexpected, Untimely).

UNMANAGEABLE — (See "Outrageous" under Insanity; Ungovernable).

UNNATURAL—Abnormal—Contrary to the Laws of Nature—

Acts — Unnatural Acts — (See Aversions, Deviations, Perversions).

Appetites—Unnatural Appetites—The ☽ or ♀ afflicted by ♆. (See Appetites, Cravings, Drink, Eating, Excesses, Food, Gluttony, Passion, Perversions).

Chaotic Acts—Chaotic and Unnatural Acts—♆ influence; ♆ afflicting the ☽ or ♀; ♆ afflicted in the 5th H.; ♆ affl. in the 7th H., immoral and unnatural practices with others of the same sex. (See Chaotic, Deviations, Homesexuality, Perversions, Vices).

Conformations—Unnatural Conformations — Defective Births — (See "Beastly Form" under Beasts; "Defective" under Births; "Dogs" under Children; Cloaca, Cyclops, Inhuman, Malformations, Missing, Monsters, Virile).

Desires — Unnatural Desires — ♆ afflicted at B.; ♆ affl. in the 5th H.; ♄ ☌ or ill-asp. ♀. (See Chaotic, Depraved, Desires, Excesses, Gluttony; "Males Nearly Impotent" under Impotent; Nymphomania; "Passional Excesses" under Passion; Perversions).

Discharges — (See "Unnatural" under Discharges).

Foods—Desire for Unnatural Foods—(See "Unnatural" under Food).

Mind — Unnatural States of Mind — The ☽ or ☿ affl. by ♆. (See the various paragraphs in this section).

Secret Practices — Unnatural Secret Practices — (See Perversions; "Secret Bad Habits" under Secret; "Solitary" under Vice).

UNORTHODOX—(See Independent, Misunderstood, Ninth House, Occult; "Lover of Truth" under Truth).

UNPLEASANT—(See Fetid, Foul; "Unpleasant" under Manner; Odors, Offensive).

UNPRINCIPLED — (See Cheating, Deceitful, Dishonest, Forgers, Gamblers, Knavish, Liars, Libelers; "Low and Base" under Low; Pettifogging, Swindlers, Thieves, etc.).

UNPROLIFIC — (See Barrenness, Unfruitful).

UNREASONABLE — (See "Unreasonable" under Reason).

UNREFINED — A Coarse, Rough, Vulgar, and Unrefined Person—A Coarse Body and Mind—The ☽ ill-dignified at B.; the ☽ affl. in ♏, coarse, and often vulgar; the ☽ Sig. ☌ ♄; in Hor'y Q. the ☽ ill-dig. and afflicted, a very vulgar, coarse, and ill-mannered person; ♄ Sig. in ♊, unpolished; ♄ Sig. in ♉, rough in carriage (Hor'y); ♏ on the Asc., coarse body. (See Awkwardness, Coarse, Gross; "Unrefined" under Manners; Rough, Ugly).

UNRELIABLE—(See Deceitful, Dishonest, Irrational, Irresponsible, Liars, Swindlers, Thieves, Unprincipled, Vacillating, etc.).

UNRESTRAINED—(See Control, Debauched, Dissipation, Drink, Excesses, Gluttony, Inordinate; "Passional Excesses" under Passion; Prodigal, Profligate, Rebellious, Riotous, Self-Control, Self-Indulgent, Ungovernable, Vicous, Violent, etc.).

UNRULY—(See Erring, Perverse, Rebellious, Riotous, Sedition, Ungovernable, etc.).

UNSAVORY SUBJECTS—The Mind Morbid Upon—♆ affl. in the 5th H., along sex lines, and with passional cravings; ♆ in the 6th or 12th H., in ☍ ♅, and with ♉ or ♏ upon the cusps of the 6th and 12th H. (See Brooding; "Erotic" under Mania; "Morbid" under Mind; Nymphomania, Perversions).

UNSEASONABLE — Unseasonable Perspiration — (See "Violent" under Sweat).

UNSETTLED — (See Changes, Discontentment; "Unsettled" under Habits; Removals, Residence, Restlessness; "Unsettled" under Riches; Roaming, Travel, Vacillating, Vagabond, Wanderer, etc.).

UNSOUND—

Unsound Legs — (See "Unsound" under Legs).

Unsound Mind — (See Dementia, Demoniac, Foolish, Idiocy, Imbecile, Insanity; "Derangement" under Mental; "Unsound Mind", "Weak Mind", under Mind; "Unsound Mind" under Wife).

UNSTABLE—Common Signs on the Asc. and Angles at B.; many planets in the negative signs; ♍ on the Asc. (See Instability).

UNTIDY—Careless—Bad aspects to the ☽, ♀, or ☿, and espec. if they are in the Asc., or in cadent houses, but the good asps. to these planets so situated tend to tidiness. (See Carelessness, Cleanliness, Dress, Filthy, Habits, Improvident, Indifferent, Knavish, Slovenly, Uncleanly, etc.).

UNTIMELY DEATH—

Untimely End—A Premature Death—The ☉ or ☽ Sig. ☌ ♂, and ♂ ill-dignified at B.; the ☉ Sig. □ or ☍ ♄, may meet with a bad end; the ☉ or ☽ afflicted, and the ☽, or lord of the 1st, be near violent fixed stars, or a malefic or violent stars ascending, and danger of death Abroad; ☉ to the place of Aldebaran; the ☽ ill-dignified at B., and ☌ ♄, and ♂ in evil asp. the ☽, and the ☉ also ill-dig.; an eclipse of the ☽ in 1st decan. of ♑; ☽ to the ☌ Pleiades or Praesepe, and with the ☉ ☍ Asc. or ♂ at same time; Ψ, ♅, ♄, ♂ in violent signs at B., and affl. the hyleg; ♄ Sig. ☌ ☽, and the ☽ affl. by ♂, and ♂ ill-dig.; ♄ or ♂ affl. in the 4th H., danger of a bad end to life; ♂ Sig. □, ☍ ♄ if either be in the Asc., or ♄ in the M.C.; ♂ affl. by ♄ at B., and ♂ to the ☌ the M.C.; lord of the 6th in the 8th H.; ruler of the 8th, and the ☉ and ☽ affl. by malefics from angles; lord of the 12th in the 10th; the 29° ♋ on the Asc.; the 3rd Dec. ♑ on Asc., ruled by the ☉, premature death. There are many influences which tend to what we would call an untimely death, such as a high fever from contagion or infection; an accident, injury, wound, drowning, quarrels, duels, violence, murder, execution, hanging, tragedy, death in infancy or childhood, a bad end from drink or dissipation, immorality, etc. See these subjects in the alphabetical arrangement. For the various kinds of a premature and untimely death, note the lists in the Articles on Accidents, Death, Hurts, Injuries, Wounds. (See "Death" under Accidents, Childhood, Children, Fire, Infancy, Kings, Middle Life, Poison, Stabs, Storms, Tragical, Travel, Treachery, Violent, Voyages, Water, Wounds, Youth; also see Assassination, Drowning; "Early Death" under Early; Execution, Gunshot, Hanging, Highwaymen, Killed; "Short Life" under Life; Lightning, Murdered, Pirates; "Premature Death" under Premature; Robbers, Sea, Ships, Shipwreck, Vehicles, Weather, Wind, etc.).

UNTRUSTWORTHY—(See Unprincipled, Unreliable).

UNUSUAL—

Unusual Death—(See "Unusual" under Death; "Death" under Extraordinary, Mysterious, Peculiar, Strange, Untimely).

Unusual Diseases—(See "Unusual Diseases" under Children, Infancy; "Diseases" under Extraordinary, Mysterious, Obscure, Peculiar, Strange, Uncommon).

UNWHOLESOME—Unhealthy—

Unwholesome Air—(See "Corrupt", "Pestilential", under Air).

Unwholesome Complexion—(See "Unhealthy" under Complexion; Pale, Sickly, Unhealthy).

UPPER PARTS—Upper Parts of the Body—Upper Parts of Organs—The upper part of an organ is shown by the first degrees of a Sign, as the first face or decanate, and planets in this part of a sign tend to afflict the upper part of the organ; planets in the middle of a sign, the middle part of the organ; and planets in the last part of a sign, or the last part upon the cusp of an evil house, as on the 6th, 8th, or 12th, tend to affect the lower, or under part of an organ. Thus malefics in the first part of ♋ would tend to affect the oesophagus, the entrance and upper part of stomach. Planets in the middle of ♋ would affect more the main body of the stomach, its glands, juices, etc. Planets in the latter degrees of ♋, the lower end of the stomach, and the pylorus. (See "Parts of Body" under Accidents; "Organs" under Lower, Middle; "Upper Parts" under Organs). The following conditions have to do with the Upper Part of the body, the Upper, or Outer Part of Organs or Members.

Arms—The Upper Arms—(See "Upper Arm" under Arms).

Back Parts—Of the Body—(See Rear).

Blood—Too Much Blood In the Upper Parts—The majority of planets at B. in signs ruling the upper parts. (See "Too Much Blood" under Blood).

Body—Upper Part of—With ♋ on the Asc., the upper part, or upper half of the body, is rounder and larger than the lower part. With ♊ on the Asc., and many planets in ♊, the upper part of the body is longer than the lower part. (See "Parts" under Lower).

Diseases—In the Upper Parts of the Body—♂ in the Asc. at the beginning of an illness, or at decumbiture.

Dorsal Nerves—Upper Dorsal Nerves—(See Dorsal).

Ears—(See "Upper Ears" under Ears).

Extremities—Upper Extremities—(See Arms, Hands, Head).

Forehead—(See "Upper" under Forehead).

Front Part of Body—(See Front).

Jaw—(See "Upper" under Jaws).

Kidneys—(See "Upper Kidneys" under Kidneys).

Large Upper Part—Of the Body—(See "Body" in this section).

Legs—(See "Upper Parts Of" under Legs).

Lip—(See "Upper" under Lips).

Liver—Upper Lobes of—(See "Lobes" under Liver).

Lobes—Upper Lobes—(See "Lobes" under Liver, Lungs).

Long Upper Part—Of the Body—(See "Body" in this section).

Lower Parts—(See Lower).

Lungs—Upper Lobes of—(See "Lobes" under Lungs).

Marks and Moles—On the Upper Parts of the Body, or a Member—(See Marks, Moles, Scars).

Middle Parts—(See "Organs" under Middle).

Moles—On the Upper Parts of the Body, or Members—(See "Location" under Moles).

Organs—Upper Parts of—(See "Upper" under Organs; the Introduction to this section).

Ribs—(See "Upper" under Ribs).
Round Upper Body—(See "Body" in this section).
Scars—On the Upper Part of An Organ or Part—(See Marks, Moles, Scars, and especially read what is said under "Marks").
Spinal Nerves — The Upper Spinal Nerves—(See Spine).
Teeth—The Upper Teeth—(See Teeth).
Upper Half of Body — Larger and Longer Than Lower Half—(See "Body" in this section).

UPRIGHT—

Upright Body—Erect—Straight—The ☉ in ♎, in partile asp. the Asc., tall, straight, and upright; the ☽ in ♊, partile the Asc., tall, upright, well-made, and also comely; born under ♃ tends to give an erect, upright, tall, and well-made body; ♃ in ♎, partile the Asc., upright and slender; ♃ in ♐, partile the Asc., upright, tall, fine, and well-made; born under ♀, and ♀ ori., tall, straight, and upright; ☿ in ♊, partile the Asc., upright, tall, and well-made; ♊ on the Asc., tall, fair, erect, straight, and upright; ♎ on the Asc., and ori., tall and upright. (See Erect, Straight, Tall).

Upright Nature — And Disposition — (See Honest, Humane, Kind; "Good Morals" under Morals; Noble, Sincere).

URAEMIA—(See Urea, Uremia).

URANIUM—Uranite—Minerals ruled by ♅. (See Pitch-Blende, Radium).

URANUS — The planet ♅ — Also called "Herschel", in honor of its Discoverer. Also called Georgium Sidus. This planet was discovered on March 13th, 1781, by Sir William Herschel. By careful observation of the workings and effects of this planet over human affairs, much has been written about it, and especially in recent years. This Article will be arranged into three Sections, as follows: Section One—Influence of Uranus. Section Two —Uranus Rules. Section Three—Uranus Diseases and Afflictions. For the special Characteristics and Qualities of ♅, see "Qualities" in Sec. 1 of this Article.

— SECTION ONE —

INFLUENCE OF URANUS — Uranus is said to be a Ruler Among Planets. His influence is of a sudden and spasmodic nature, and fundamentally has been observed and determined to be more Psychic and Mental than Physical. In the Brain he rules the Pituitary Body, one of the Spiritual Centers, and closely associated with the Pineal Gland, ruled by ♆, in Spiritual and Psychic Development. (See Neptune, Pineal, Pituitary). Very few people as yet are able to respond to his higher vibrations, and it is asserted that the influences of ♅ and ♆ will be more positive over Races yet to come in the distant future, as the Sixth Sub-Race, and the Sixth Race itself. The Occult Significance of Uranus is well set forth in the book, "Message of the Stars", by the Heindels.

Affinity—♅ has affinity with the Eyes, as this planet rules the Ether, and transmits the rays of Light. Also ♅ has affinity with the ♒ sign, which is a strong sign of this planet.

Afflicts—♅ afflicts by his ☌, P., □ and ☍ aspects.

Alchemistry Of—(See Pituitary).

Anareta — ♅ may be Anareta, altho he does not kill by himself, but usually in with a train of evil directions to the hyleg. (See Anareta).

Aspects—(See "Afflicts" in this section). His favorable aspects to the ☉, ☽, ☿, and other planets, and to the Asc., tend to elevate the mind and nature, expand the Intuitions, make the native Altruistic and Humane, give a love of Truth, and to greatly increase the Spiritual Foresight and Perceptions.

Changes—The ♅ influence, and especially his afflictions, tend to many changes, removals, journeys, and to be restless and unsettled until the native becomes awakened to the Higher Things in life.

Colors—Deep Rich Blue.

Denotes — (See "Spasmodic" in this section).

Directions Of — (See "Directions" in Sec. Three of this Article).

Discovery Of—(See the Introduction to this Article).

Drugs Of—(See Metals, Typical Drugs of, in this section).

Ether — ♅ rules the Ether. (See Ether).

Events — Tends to sudden and unexpected events.

Evils — His evils come suddenly, as well as the good he brings.

Eyes—♅ has special affinity with the Eyes, as he rules the Ether, thru which Light Rays are transmitted. (See Blindness, Ether, Eyes; "Rays" under Light).

Free Love — (See "Free Love" under Free).

Higher Rays Of—Not many respond to the higher rays of ♅, and tend to be adversely affected by his vibrations.

Horoscope — ♅ affects the horoscope mostly by his influence upon the other planets, as he is a Ruler among Ruling Planets.

Impulses—(See "Sudden" in this section).

Indicates—♅ indicates eccentric and uncommon people, Bohemians, and those who are abrupt, original, and not of the ordinary type. (See Eccentric, Independent, Misunderstood, Occult).

Intuition — The Principle of ♅ is Intuition.

Journeys — Causes Many Journeys, Changes, and Removals. (See these subjects).

Laws of Society — ♅ people rebel against these Laws, and desire freedom. They also tend to chafe under the vows and restraints of marriage.

Love Affairs — The afflictions of ♅ to ♀, or with ♅ in the 5th or 7th H., tend to much trouble in love affairs and marriage, and to separations and estrangements.

Magnetism—♅ has influence over the Animal Magnetism, and the Impulses. (See Impulses, Magnetism).

Marriage Happiness—(See "Love Affairs" in this section).

Mental Effects—Mental and Psychic effects are shown by ♅ rather than physical.

Mental Qualities—Eccentric. Unconventional).

Metals and Minerals Of—(See Sec. 2 of this Article).

Metaphysics—Gives a great love for, and of the Occult, and of Truth, and especially by his Higher Vibrations, and to those who are awakened and ready for it. (See Metaphysics, Occult, Science).

Moral Lapses — His afflictions, and especially to ♀, tend to moral lapses, free love, clandestine love affairs, disregard of conventionalities, and to sex perversions.

Occult—His higher vibrations give a love of the Occult, the Metaphysical, and Truth.

Octave Of — Most Writers say he is the higher octave of ☿, but the Heindels, of the Rosicrucian Fellowship, say he is the higher octave of ♀.

Pathological Influence—Telepathic. (See Telepathy).

Physical Effects Of—The physical effects of this planet are not always shown, but rather a Mental and Psychic influence and effect. (See "Body", "Health", in Sec. 3 of this Article).

Principle Of—Intuition.

Province Of—The province of ♅ lies in his spasmodic, explosive, shock-producing, electric, and neuralgic influences.

Psychic — His influences are more Psychic and Mental than Physical.

Qualities—The following qualities are attributed to his higher and lower vibrations, and tend to affect the individual according to his degree of enlightenment and awakening. Some of these are also his abstract qualities—Abrupt, Accidental, Acute, Advanced, Afflicting, Airy, Alternating, Altruistic, Antiperistaltic, Arresting, Barren, Bereaving, Blinding, Bohemian, Breaking, Bursting, Cataclysmic, Changeable, Clandestine, Clonic, Cold, Compressing, Constructive, Contracting, Convertible, Convulsive, Corrosive, Cramping, Creative, Curious, Demoniacal, Disorganizing, Disruptive, Distorting, Distressing, Disturbing, Dry, Eccentric, Electric, Emotional, Enlarging, Erratic, Etheric, Exaggerating, Excitable, Explosive, Extraordinary, Fanatical, Fractious, Fracture-Producing, Freak-Producing, Free-Loving, Free-Thinking, Fretful, Gaseous, Hasty, Heedless, High-Strung, Hindering, Humane, Hurtful, Hysterical, Immoral, Impeding, Impulsive, Incoordinating, Independent, Injurious, Inquisitive, Intuitive, Inventive, Investigating, Involuntary, Irregular, Irresponsible, Irritating, Jeopardizing, Jerky, Lesional, Licentious, Lustful, Magnetic, Maniacal, Masculine, Mental, Metaphysical, Mis-

understood, Morbid, Motor-Disturbing, Murderous, Nauseating, Nervous, Neuralgic, Neurotic, Obscuring, Occult, Open-Minded, Original, Out-of-the Ordinary, Paroxysmal, Passional, Peculiar, Perverting, Phenomenal, Philosophical, Positive, Psychic, Quick in Action, Quivering, Radical, Radio-Active, Reactionary, Rebellious, Reckless, Reforming, Remarkable, Rending, Resisting, Resolute, Resourceful, Restless, Romantic, Ruling, Rupturing, Scientific, Shock-Producing, Spasmodic, Speculative, Stopping, Straining, Strange in Procedure, Strictural, Sudden, Suicidal, Tangential Action, Telepathic, Temperamental, Tempting, Tensional, Tragical, Trembling, Twisting, Twitching, Truth-Loving, Uncommon, Uncontrollable, Unconventional, Unexpected, Unordinary, Unorthodox, Unprejudiced, Unruly, Unusual, Variable, Vibratory, Violent, etc. (See these subjects).

Rays Of—(See "Higher Rays" in this section).

Removals — (See "Changes" in this section).

Romance — Gives Bohemian Tendencies and love of Romance.

Salient Characteristic—Altruism.

Sex—♅ being exalted in the sex sign ♏ has great influence over the sex nature and the sex organs, tending to great passion, unless controlled, and to perversions of the sex nature.

Sign—♅ has his home in the ♒ sign. Is exalted in ♏, and has his detriment in ♌.

Society—Disregard of Laws of—(See "Moral Laws" under Love Affairs).

Spasmodic—♅ is radio-active, and denotes spasmodic, tangential and eccentric action.

Strong—♅ is strong in ♒ and ♏.

Sudden—Sudden is the keynote to ♅ action. He tends to sudden impulses to do wrong; brings sudden good or ill, sudden diseases, accidents, explosions, shock, the unexpected, uncommon, the unusual, unlooked-for, etc.

Temptations — His afflictions to ♀ make the native very subject to many temptations, and especially along sex and passional lines, to free love, etc. (See "Free Love" under Free).

Therapeutic Action—Electric, Vibrational.

Typical Drugs — Croton Oil, Ether, Compressed Air and Gases.

Waves Of — The Waves of ♅ are neither continuous nor rounded, but broken and spasmodic.

— SECTION TWO —

URANUS RULES — The following is an alphabetical arrangement of the matters ruled over by ♅. See these subjects. Air (Compressed Air and Gases); Amber; Appendix; Aquarius Sign; Assimilation at Puberty and After; Aura (the Physical and Magnetic Aura); Bereavements; Blind Impulses; Brain (the Membranes of the Brain); Breathing (Respiratory Action); Catastrophies; Celluloid (Xylonite); Changes (Sudden Changes);

Circulation in the Kidneys; Compressed Air and Gases; Creative Force (Sex Force — see Pituitary); Dura Mater; Electricity; Erratic States of Mind; Ether (or Ethers); Etheric Body; Events (Sudden); Explosives (and tends to ignite them); Extraordinary Events; Eyes; Fluids of the Body—Nerve Fluids—(and acting thru the Pituitary Body); Gases; Genito-Urinary Organs (Nerves of); Growth (Abnormal); Heart (Valves of); Impulses (Animal and Blind Impulses); Jerky Movements; Kidneys (Circulation in); Lodestone; Magnetic Aura; Magnetism (Animal, and the Terrestrial Magnetism); Membranes (of the Brain and Stomach); Metals and Minerals (Amber, Actinium, Chalcolite, Lodestone, Pitch-Blende, Polonium, Radium, Shellac, Thorium, Uranite, Uranium, Zinc); Mind (Erratic States of); Motor Nerves of Speech; Murders; Nerves (of the Genito-Urinary Organs —the Nerve Fluids—Motor Nerves of Speech); Nervous Temperament; Nitrogen; Phenomena (Telepathic); Physical Aura; Pitch-Blende; Pituitary Body; Public Affairs; Radio Activity; Radium; Reformers; Resins; Respiratory Action; Romances; Sex Force (Creative Force); Shellac; Sky (Amber Color of); Spasmodic Movements; Speech (Motor Nerves of); Spinal Cord (Membranes of); Stomach (Membranes of); Sudden (Sudden Changes and Events); Suicides; Tall Body; Telepathic Phenomena; Temperament (the Nervous); Terrestrial Magnetism; Tragedies; Uncommon People; Understanding; Unusual Events; Uranium; Valves (of the Heart); Vibration; Xanthin; Xenon; X-Ray; Xyloidin, Xylonite; Zinc.

— SECTION THREE —

URANUS DISEASES, AFFLICTIONS —The Diseases and Complaints of ♅ are somewhat similar to the combined effects of ♄, ♀, and ☿ in the 12 Signs. His diseases are usually of a nervous origin, and difficult to understand, and often incurable. His afflictions tend to sudden and unexpected complaints, accidents, suicide, peculiar diseases, spasmodic disorders, and sometimes cause numbness and electrical pains, shooting pains, neuralgia, etc. His afflictions also tend to abnormal and strange growth, freaks of nature, etc. See the following subjects in the alphabetical arrangement when only listed here—

Abnormal Growth—(See "Abnormal" under Growth).

Accidents—♅ causes illness or death as a result of accidents. He causes accidents, injury, or death by Electricity, Machinery in the Employment, or by Violence. (See "Illness" under Accidents; Electricity, Employment, Lightning, Machinery, Violence).

Acute Pains — (See "Head" in this section).

Appendicitis—(See Appendix).

Arms—(See "Legs" in this section).

Asthma; Bathings—Death At, or Illness From — (See Bathing; "Bathing" under Demoniac).

Bladder—Spasm of—(See Bladder).

Blindness; Body — ♅ has a peculiar influence in relation to the human body, and his diseases are not usually of the ordinary character, but of a spasmodic and sudden nature. (See Spasmodic; "Diseases" under Sudden; "Health" in this section).

Bowels—Cramp In—Spasm In—Wind Colic In — (See these subjects under Bowels).

Brain — Peculiar Brain Affections — (See Brain).

Breathing—Spasmodic Breathing— (See Breathing).

Burstings—(See Apoplexy, Bursting, Hemorrhage, Laceration, Rupture).

Calamities—Sudden and Strange Calamities—(See Calamity).

Chorea—(See Saint Vitus Dance).

Claustrophobia; Clonic Spasm — (See "Clonic" under Spasmodic).

Cold and Dampness—Diseases Arising from Sudden Exposure To—(See "Cold and Dampness" under Exposure).

Cold and Dry Diseases — (See "Cold and Dry" under Dry).

Colic—(See "Wind" under Colic).

Contortions; Contractions; Cough;

Cramps—In Arms, Hands, Legs, Feet, Bowels, Stomach, etc.—♅ in the Signs which rule these parts. (See Cramps).

Dampness — (See "Cold and Dampness" in this section).

Death — ♅ does not kill by himself but assists by his evil aspects and directions. (See Death; "Death" under Sudden; "Accidents", "Sudden", "Tragical", in this section).

Demoniac; Directions—(See "Death", "Relatives", in this section).

Disruptions — (See Bursting, Laceration, Rupture).

Drink—(See "Death" under Intoxication).

Dry and Cold Diseases — (See "Cold and Dry" under Dry).

Electrical Pains — (See "Electric Pains" under Electric).

Electric Shocks — (See Electricity, Lightning).

Emphysema; Employment—Injury In by Machinery—(See Employment, Machinery).

Erratic Movements—(See Erratic).

Exaggerated Action—(See Exaggerated).

Explosions—Blindness, Death, or Injury By—(See Explosions).

Eyeballs—Quivering of — (See "Nystagmus" under Eyeballs).

Eyes—Disorders of—(See Blindness, Eyes).

Feet — Cramps In — (See "Legs" in this section).

Fits—(See Convulsions, Fits).

Floating Kidney — (See "Floating" under Kidneys).

Fractures; Freaks of Nature — (See Freaks, Genius, Giants, Prodigies).

Functions Suppressed — (See "Suppressed" under Functions).

Giants; Growth — (See Giants; "Abnormal" under Growth).

Hallucinations; Hands—Cramps In—(See "Cramps" under Hands; "Legs" in this section).

Head—Acute and Spasmodic Pains In—H affl. in ♈. (See Head).

Health — H has little influence over the health, except as reflected by psychic and mental states, or which is the result of accident, sudden and unexpected causes, etc. (See "Body" in this section).

Heart—Spasm of—Stoppage, Valvular Disease—Palpitation—(See Heart).

Hiccough; High Strung — And Nervous—(See High).

Homosexuality; Human Body—H influence over—(See "Body" in this section).

Hurts — Strange and Unexpected — (See Hurts).

Hysteria; Illness—Due to Accidents, Nervous Strain, etc.— ☽ affl. by H. (See "Nervous Strain" under Nerves).

Impediment—Of Speech—(See Speech).

Incoordination; Incurable Diseases—(See Incurable).

Injuries; Insanity—Violent Forms of —See "Outrageous", "Violent", under Insanity).

Intussusception — (See this subject under Bowels).

Involuntary Movements — (See Erratic, Involuntary, Spasmodic).

Irregular Action — (See Erratic, Irregular, Spasmodic).

Jerky Movements—(See Jerky).

Kidneys—(See "Floating" under Kidneys).

Killed — (See Electricity, Explosions, Lightning, Machinery; "Death" under Railroads, Sudden, Violent; Shock).

Legs — H in signs which rule the arms, hands, legs, feet, tends to cramps, spasms, paralysis, and disturbance of the motor nerves of these parts. (See Legs).

Lesions — Nerve Lesions — (See Lesions).

Lightning — Death or Injury By — (See Lightning).

Machinery—Death or Injury By—(See Machinery, Mangled).

Mobs — Death or Injury By — (See Mobs).

Monsters; Morals—Perverted Morals (See "Loose Morals" under Morals; "Moral Lapses" in Sec. 1 of this Article).

Morbid — Obscure Morbid Manifestations—(See "Obscure" under Morbid).

Motor Nerves—Disturbances of—(See Motor).

Muscular Action — (See Involuntary; "Involuntary Contractions" under Muscles).

Nausea; Neck — Motor Disturbances In—(See Neck).

Nerves—Various Disorders of—(See the subjects under Nerves. Also see Corrosion; "High Strung" under High; Lesions, Motor; "Nervous Strain" under Strain).

Neuralgia; Nodding Spasm — (See "Nodding" under Head).

Numbness; Nutrition—(See "Perverted" under Nutrition).

Nystagmus—(See Eyeballs).

Obscure Diseases — (See "Obscure" under Morbid; Obscure).

Opisthotonos; Pains — Acute and Spasmodic Pains In the Head—Electric Pains — (See "Electric Pains" under Electric; "Acute", "Darting", "Pains", "Spasmodic", under Head).

Palpitation — (See "Palpitation" under Heart; Palpitations).

Paralysis; Paroxysms;

Peculiar Diseases — (See "Peculiar" under Brain, Nerves; Peculiar).

Perversions; Physical Effects Of — See "Physical Effects" in Sec. 1 of this Article).

Pituitary Body — Disorders of — (See Pituitary).

Prolapsus; Ptosis; Quiverings;

Railroads—Death or Injury On—(See Railroads).

Relatives — Death of — (See "Death", "Distant", under Relations).

Remarkable Diseases—(See Extraordinary, Remarkable, Uncommon).

Rendings — (See Bursting, Lacerations, Rupture).

Respiratory Disorders—(See Asthma; "Spasmodic" under Breathing).

Rupture; Saint Vitus Dance;

Sex Disorders—(See Perversions, Sex, Venereal; "Sex" in Sec. 1 of this Article).

Shipwreck; Shock; Sight—Disorders of—(See Blindness, Sight).

Sodomy—(See Homesexuality).

Spasmodic Diseases—Spasms—Spasms In Arms, Hands, Legs, Feet—Spasm of Bladder—Spasmodic Breathing—Spasmodic Heart Action—Clonic Spasm—Nodding Spasm, etc.—(See "Spasmodic", or "Spasm", under Arms, Bladder, Breathing, Feet, Hands, Heart, Legs; "Nodding" under Head; "Clonic" under Spasmodic).

Speech—Impediment In—(See Speech).

Stomach—H ♎ tends to Cramp, Colic, and Wind Spasms of the Stomach. (See Stomach).

Stoppage—Of the Heart—(See Heart).

Strange Diseases — Strange Hurts — (See Strange, Unexpected).

Strictures; Subsultus;

Sudden Diseases—Sudden Death—(See Sudden).

Suicide; Suppressions — (See "Suppressed" under Functions; Suppressions).

Telepathy—Pathological Disturbances of—(See Telepathy).

Tetanus; Throat — (See "Spasmodic Disorders" under Throat).

Tics; Torticollis — (See "Wry Neck" under Neck).

Trade—Death or Injury In the Trade or Employment — (See Employment, Machinery).

Tragical Death—(See "Tragical" under Death).

Tremors; Twitchings;

Uncommon Diseases — (See Uncommon)

Uncontrolled Action — (See Control, Incoordination, Involuntary, Spasmodic, Uncontrolled).

Unexpected Disorders — (See Sudden, Unexpected).

Unusual Diseases—(See Uncommon).

Urethra — Spasm and Stricture of — (See Urethra).

Valvular Disease — Of the Heart — (See Heart).

Venereal Disease—(See Venereal).

Violent — Violent Accidents — Violent Forms of Insanity — (See "Hurts and Injuries" under Accidents; "Outrageous", "Violent", under Insanity).

Wind—Wind In Bowels—Wind Spasm of Stomach — (See "Wind" under Bowels, Colic, Stomach; "Bowels" under Wind).

Winking—(See Eyelids).

Wry Neck — (See "Wry Neck" under Neck).

URATES — Excess of — Over-Secretion of—♃ affl. in ♏. (See Urea, Uric Acid).

UREA—Urea is the chief solid constituent of the Urine, and the principal nitrogenous product of tissue decomposition. Urea is formed in the liver by ♄, and also deposited by ♄ over the body as Uric Acid, causing Gout, Rheumatism, Arthritis Deformans in the Joints, Toxaemia, etc. (See these subjects. Also see Uremia, Uric Acid).

Excess of Urea—Over-Secretion of—♀ affl. in ♎.

Retention Of — (See Deposits, Gout, Hyperacidity, Rheumatism, Toxaemia, Uremia).

UREMIA—Toxic Blood from Accumulation of Urea—Uremic Convulsions—An Auto-Toxic Psychoses—A ♎ disease; ♄ or ♀ affl. in ♎.

Uremic Coma—(See Coma).

Uremic Convulsions — (See the first part of this Article).

Uremic Headache — (See "Toxaemic" under Headache).

URETERS—Ruled by ♎ and ♏. Elimination of Urine thru the Ureters, Bladder, and Urethra is ruled by the ♏ sign.

Calculus In—Renal Colic—(See "Colic" under Kidneys).

Constriction Of — ♄ affl. in ♎. (See Constrictions).

Inflammation Of — Ureteritis—♂ affl. in ♎ or ♏.

URETHRA — Is ruled by the ♏ Sign. Elimination of Urine thru the Bladder and Urethra is ruled by ♏. Cowper's Glands are ruled by ♏.

Abscess Of—♂ affl. in ♏.

Chordee—♂ affl. in ♏. (See "Chordee" under Gonorrhoea).

Cloaca—A Common Outlet to the Bladder and Rectum—♄ affl. in ♏. (See Cloaca).

Contraction Of — (See "Stricture" in this section).

Gonorrhoea—Running of the Reins—(See Gonorrhoea).

Inflammation Of — Urethritis — Chordee—Gonorrhoea—♂ affl. in ♏ tends to, and to aggravated cases; a ♏ disease. (See Gonorrhoea).

Spasmodic Stricture Of—(See "Stricture" in this section).

Strangury — (See this subject under Urine).

Stricture — Contraction of — Obstruction of—A ♏ disease, and afflictions in ♏; ☿ affl. in ♉ or ♏; ♂ in ♏; H affl. in ♏, spasmodic stricture. Case of Stricture—See Chap. 13 in Daath's Medical Astrology. (See Constrictions, Contractions, Stricture).

Ulceration—♂ affl. in ♏.

Urethritis — (See "Inflammation" in this section).

URIC ACID—♄ forms Uric Acid in the liver, and also deposits Uric Acid over the body during muscular activity, causing Gout, Rheumatism, Enlarged Joints, etc.

Blood — Excess of Uric Acid In the Blood — Lithemia — ♄ influence. (See Lithemia).

Deposits—Excess Deposits of In Blood, and Over the Body—♄ influence; ♄ affl. in ♒ or ♑. (See Aches, Deposits, Gout, Lithemia, Pains, Rheumatism).

Lithemia — (See "Blood" in this section).

System—Uric Acid In—♂ affl. in ♎.

Urine—Excess of Uric Acid In—☿, H, or ♄ in ♍, and afflicting the ☉ or ☽. (For collateral study see Gall, Gout, Hyperacidity, Impure, Joints, Minerals; "Rheumatism" under Muscles; Rheumatism, Toxaemia, Urates, Urea, Uremia, Urine, Wastes).

URINE—Urinary Organs—Urinary System—Urinary Diseases—Are under the rule of the watery sign ♏. As a liquid, the ☽ rules the Urine. The Elimination of Urine thru the Ureters, Bladder and Urethra is under the rule of ♏. The Secretion of the Urine is under rule of ♎. (See Kidneys). Urine is an Excrementitious Fluid under the rule of ♏. The external Urinary Organs are under the external rule of ♎. Note the following subjects here, and in the alphabetical arrangement—

Absence of Urine — Anuria — (See "Suppression" in this section).

Acid Urine—(See Acidity).

Albuminuria; Alkaline Urine — (See Acidity, Alkalinity).

Anuria — (See "Suppression" in this section).

Bed-Wetting—(See "Incontinence" in this section).

Bladder — Bladder Troubles and the Urine—(See Bladder).

Blood In Urine—Haematuria—Occurs from Ulcerated and other conditions in Kidneys, Bladder or Urethra, or from passage of Gravel, etc. — (See Bladder, Gravel, Kidneys, Stone, Urethra, etc.).

Bright's Disease — (See this subject; "Nephritis" under Kidneys).

Calculi—Urinary Calculi—♄ ☌ or ill-asp. ♀. (See Calculus).

Cloudy Urine — (See "Milky" in this section).

Copious—Excessive Quantity—Polyuria—(See Diabetes).

Diabetes; Difficult Urination—(See "Painful" in this section).

Diseases—Of the Urinary Organs—Disorders of—(See "Disturbances" in this section).

Distillation—Of Urine—Disturbances of—Afflictions in ♎; ♄ affl. in ♎. (See Distillation).

Disturbances—Urinary Disturbances and Complaints—Urinary Troubles—The ☉ or ☽ affl. in ♏; ☉ ♏, and affl. by ♃; ☉ or ☽ ♏, ☌ or ill-asp. ♄, ♅, ♆ or ♂ as Promittors (Hor'y); ☉ affl. in ♓; ☽ affl. in ♏, or affl. the hyleg therefrom; ☽ hyleg in ♎ or ♏, with females; ☽ □ ☿; ♄ or ☋ in ♎ or ♏; ♄ ☌ or ill-asp. the ☉ in fixed signs; ♄ ♎ in the Asc.; ♃ affl. in ♏; ♃ ♏ in the 6th H., and affl.; ♃ ♏ and affl. the ☽ or Asc.; ♂ ♏; ♋, ♏ or ♓ on the Asc.; fixed signs show; a fixed sign on cusp the 6th H. (See the various paragraphs in this section).

Diuresis—Excessive Secretion of Urine—(See Diabetes; "Polyuria" in this section).

Diuretics—Medicines Increasing the Flow of Urine—(See Diuretics).

Drops—Passes Urine In Drops—(See "Strangury" in this section).

Dropsy—Renal Dropsy—(See "Dropsy" under Kidneys).

Dysuria—(See "Strangury" in this section).

Elimination—Of Urine—Retarded and Disturbed—Faulty Elimination—Suppression—The ☽ □ ☿, as ☿ rules the sensory nerves, and ♂ the motor nerves; the ☽ in ♎, □, or ☍ ☿; ♄ affl. in ♎ or ♏; ♃ in ♎, ☌ □, or ☍ ♄; ♂ in ♏ and affl. by ♄; ☋ in ♏. The elimination of urine thru the bladder and urethra is ruled by the ♏ sign. (See Elimination; "Over-worked" under Kidneys).

Enuresis—(See "Incontinence" in this section).

Excess of Urine—♃ affl. in ♎. (See Diabetes; "Polyuria" in this section).

Excretion Suppressed—(See Excretion, Expulsion; "Suppressed" in this section).

False Retention—Of Urine—False Suppression—False Ischuria—Spurious Ischuria—A ♎ disease and affliction; ♄ affl. in ♎.

Filtration of Urine—Sublimation of—Ruled by ♎ and ♀. Imperfect Filtration tends to result when ☿ is in ♑, ☌ or ill-asp. any of the malefics as Promittors.

Frequent Urination—(See Acid, Hot, Painful, and other subjects in this section).

Genito-Urinary Diseases—☽ affl. in ♏. (See Genito-Urinary).

Glycosuria—Sugar In Urine—Usually is found in Diabetes—(See Diabetes).

Haematuria—(See "Blood" in this section).

Highly Acid Urine—♂ ♎, and affl. by ♄ in ♋ or ♑. Occurs in cases of Scanty Urine, and in Rheumatism, Gout, Lithemia, Fevers, etc.

Highly Colored—☿ affl. in ♎. (See "Acid", "Scanty", in this section. Also occurs in Gout, Rheumatism, etc.).

Highly Loaded—♄ ☌ or ill-asp. ♀.

Hot Urine—(See "Scalding" in this section).

Impeded Passage—Impeded Excretion—(See "Stone" under Bladder; Gravel; "Suppressed" in this section).

Imperfect Filtration—(See "Filtration" in this section).

Incontinence—Involuntary Discharges of—Enuresis—Bed-Wetting—♂ in ♏; a ♀ disease, and caused by afflictions to ♀.

Insufficient Urine—(See "Scanty" in this section).

Involuntary Discharges of—(See "Incontinence" in this section).

Ischuria—Retention or Suppression of Urine—(See "False", "Retention", "Suppression", in this section).

Kidneys—The Kidneys and the Urine—(See Kidneys).

Micturition—The Act of Passing Urine—Disturbances of—(See False, Impeded, Obstructions, Painful, Retention, Strangury, in this section).

Milky Urine—Cloudy—Chyluria—Usually caused by pus in the urine, and may be due to Gonorrhoea, Chyle, Cystitis, Pyelitis, Abscesses or Ulcerations in the Kidneys, Bladder, or Urethra. (See these subjects; "Pus" in this section).

Mucus In—♄ affl. in ♎; ♃ in ♏, and affl. by ♂; ♃ in ♏ in the 6th H., and afflicted. (See Mucous).

Nervous Affections—Of the Urinary Organs—☿ affl. in ♉ or ♏.

Obstructions—To the Urine—A ♏ disease, and afflictions in ♏; ☉ or ☽ ♏, ☌ ♄ or ☋; ♄ affl. in ♎ or ♏; ☿ ♎, ☌ or ill-asp. any of the malefics as Promittors, urinal obstructions. (See "Painful", "Retention", "Stricture", "Suppression", in this section; "Stone" under Bladder; Gravel).

Painful Urination—Strangury—Dysuria—Difficult Urination, etc.—(See "Strangury" in this section).

Passage Impeded—(See "Obstructions" in this section).

Polyuria—Excessive Secretion of Urine—Caused by afflictions in ♎; ♂ ☌ or ill-asp. ♀; ♃ or ♀ affl. in ♎. (See Diabetes).

Prevalent—Urinary Diseases Prevalent—♄ or ♂ in ♎ at the Vernal Equi., and lords of the year; Comets appearing in ♏.

Pus In Urine—Pyuria—Milky Urine—Especially denoted by ♀ affl. in ♎. Other planets may cause pus in the urine, as from urethritis, ulcerated kidneys or urethra, cystitis of the bladder, etc. (See "Milky" in this section).

Retarded Elimination—(See "Elimination" in this section).

Retention of Urine—Ischuria—Retention is a ♏ disease, while Suppression is a ♎ disorder. Caused by ♄ or ☿ affl. in ♏; ♄ ♏ in the 6th H.; ♏ on cusp 6th H. (See "False", "Suppression", in this section).

Sand — Urinary Sand — Sand In the Kidneys—(See Sand).

Scalding Urine — Hot Urine — Sharpness of Urine—The ☉ affl. in ♏ when the afflictor in the disease; ♂ affl. in ♉ or ♏; ♂ in ♎ or ♏, and affl. by ♄; ♄ ♎, scanty and scalding.

Scanty Urine—Scarcity of—Anuria—♄ ♎; ☽ ♎, ☌ ♄; ☽ ♎ □ or ☍ ♅, ♃ and ☿.

Secretion Stopped — (See "Suppression" in this section).

Sediment In—Brick Dust Sediment—Deposits In—♂ affl. in ♎.

Sharpness — Of Urine — (See "Scalding" in this section).

Spurious Ischuria — (See "False" in this section).

Stoppage—Of Urine—(See "Suppression" in this section).

Strangury—Dysuria—Painful Urination In Drops—Painful Micturition—The ☉ in ♒ or ♓, ☌, or ill-asp. ♆, ♅, ♄, or ♂ as Promittors; the ☉ affl. in ♒; the ☽ in ♉ and affl. by the ☉ or ♂ when taken ill (Hor'y); the ☽ to the place of the Bull's Horns; ♃ affl. in ♏; a ♂ disease; ♂ affl. in ♉, ♊, or ♏; ♂ in ♊, ☌ or ill-asp. the ☉; ♏ on the Asc., and the ☽ in ♒ (Hor'y).

Sublimation—Of Urine—(See "Filtration" in this section).

Sugar In Urine — Glycosuria — ♃ affl. in ♎. (See Diabetes, Glycogen, Sugar).

Suppression — Of Urine — Anuria — Stoppage of—Ischuria—Faulty Secretion of — Suppression is a ♎ disease, while Retention is a ♏ disease. A ♎ affliction; the ☽ in ♎ ☌ ♄; ♄ affl. in ♎; Subs at KP. (See Elimination, False, Scanty, in this section).

Urates—(See Urates).

Uric Acid—Too Much In Urine—♄, ♅, or ♆ in ♍, and affl. the ☉ or ☽. (See Uric Acid).

Urinary Calculi — (See "Calculi" in this section; Stone).

Urinary Diseases — (See "Disturbances", and the various subjects in this Article).

Urinary Organs — Ruled by ♎ and ♏. (See the Introduction to this Article; Bladder, Kidneys, Ureters, Urethra).

Urination—Micturition—Disturbances of—(See "Micturition", "Strangury", in this section).

Xanthine—Excess of In Urine—(See Xanthin).

URN OF AQUARIUS — (See "One Eye" under Blindness).

URSA MINOR—(See Cynosura).

URTICARIA—Nettle Rash—Hives—An Ephemeral Skin Eruption with Itching—A Vesicular Cutaneous Eruption—A ♑ disease; ♑ on the Asc.; the ☽ hyleg, and afflicted in female nativities; ♂ affl. in ♑; Subs at KP (11D). (See Hives, Itch, Skin).

UTERUS—Disorders of—(See Womb).

UTOPIANISM — Impractical Ideals and Schemes—Caused by ♆ and his afflictions. The methods of attainment are more humanitarian when ♄ and ♂ are weak and obscurely placed at B., but if the malefics ♄ and ♂ are strong, and enter into the configuration, the native may become more radical, revolutionary, or violent in his methods to carry out his ideals. (See "Impractical" under Ideals; Radicalism, Reformers, Revolutionary, etc.).

UTTERANCE — (See Larynx, Speech, Tongue, Voice).

UVULA — Ruled by the ♉ sign, and is also much affected by the ☽ in ♉.

Inflammation Of—Uvulitis—The ☽ or ♂ affl. in ♉.

Long Uvula — (See "Snoring" under Breathing).

V

VACCINATION — (See "Immunity", "Treatment", under Smallpox).

VACILLATING — Unsteady — Wavering —Common Sign influence, and with these signs on the angles at B.; many planets in common signs, setting in the West, and out of dignity. (See Changes; "Mind" under Chaotic; Confusion; Influenced, Instability, Irresponsible, Location; "Light In Mind" under Mind; "Mutable Signs" under Mutable; "Negative Nature" under Negative; Receptive, Removals; "Many Changes" under Residence; Restlessness, Roamer, Susceptibility, Unstable, Wanderer, etc.).

VAGABOND — (See Degenerate; "No Home" under Home; Roamer, Wanderer).

VAGARIES—Peculiar Ideas—

Full Of—Wild Fancies—♅ in any asp. to the ☉, ☽, or ☿; ♅ affl. in ♊; ♅ affl. by ♀; the 28° ♊ on the Asc. (See "Wild" under Fancies).

Peculiar Vagaries—Strange Vagaries —♀ in bad asp. to ♅. (See Chaotic; "Dreamy" under Dreams; Extravagance, Fancies, Fears, Hallucinations, Ideals, Ideas, Imaginations, Notions, Peculiar, Uncanny, Vague, Visionary, Weird).

VAGINA—Ruled by the ♏ Sign.

Diseases Of — Afflictions in ♏; ♀ affl. in ♏; ♀ in ♏ in the 6th H., and afflicted; ♀ in ♏ and affl. the Asc. (See Gonorrhoea, Leucorrhoea).

Fluids Of — Secretions of — Fluids Passing Thru — (See Leucorrhoea, Menses).

Hymen—Imperforate Hymen—♄ in ♏, and to thickening of the hymen.

Inflammation Of — Vaginits — Ulceration of—♆ affl. in ♏.

Leucorrhoea—(See this subject).

Tunica Vaginalis — (See Serous, Testes).

Ulceration Of—♂ affl. in ♏.

Vulva—(See Vulva).

Whites—(See Leucorrhoea). See Clitoris, Hermaphrodites, Urethra).

VAGUE—Indistinct—

Vague Forebodings — (See Forebodings).

Vague Mental States — ♆ ♊. Caused also by the □ and ☍ aspects of ♆ to ☿, ☽ or Asc. (See "Mental Chaos" under Chaotic).

Vague and Obscure Diseases — (See "Diseases" under Obscure).

VAGUS NERVE—(See Pneumogastric).

VAIN—Vain Fears—Vain Imaginations —(See "Vain" under Fears, Imagination; Self-Approbation).

VALLEY — Should Live In a Valley — (See Altitude).

VALVES — ♄ tends to adversely affect the valves of the body, and when in, or afflicting the signs ruling the different valves. ♅ tends to cause spasmodic disturbances of the valves, and of the organs containing the valves. The valves of the heart are ruled by the ♌ sign. The Ileo-Caecal Valve is ruled by ♍, and ♄ in ♍ tends to obstruction of this valve.

Heart—Valves of—(See "Valves" under Heart).

Ileo-Caecal Valve — (See Caecum, Ileum).

VAPID—(See Dull, Listless).

VAPOR — Vapors — The Gaseous Form of a Substance—Aeriform—Airy—(See Air, Atmosphere, Gas, Miasma, Odors, Rain).

Damp Vapors — (See "Damp Vapors" under Moisture).

Foul Vapors — Danger of Sickness From—♄ and ♂ in watery signs, and afflicting the ☉ and ☽. (See Foul, Moisture).

Vaporization — Volatilization — Recondensation — (See "Operations" under Nature; Nitrogen, Sublimation, Volatilization).

VAPORS—Ennui—(See Ennui).

VARIABLE—

Variable Diseases — Caused by ☿, as ☿ is a variable planet. (See "Irregular Diseases" under Mercury; Various).

Variable Planets—The ☉, ☽, ☿. They tend to take on the nature of the planets with which they are in ☌, aspected, or configurated.

VARICELLA—(See Chicken Pox).

VARICOCELE—Dilatation of the Scrotal Veins—♄ affl. in ♏. (See Scrotum, Varicose).

VARICOSE VEINS—Varicosities — Enlarged Veins—Dilated Veins—Swollen and Knotted Veins—

Aneurysm—Varicose Aneurysm—(See Aneurysm).

Arms — Varicosities in the Arms, Hands, Legs, and Feet—The ☽ affl. in signs which rule these parts.

Legs—Varicose Veins In—An ♒ disease, and afflictions in ♒; the ☉, ☽, ♄, ♂, ♀, or ☿ affl. in ♒; the ☽ and ♀ affl. in ♒, and espec. if the ♂ influence is added; ♂ affl. in ♒ in the 6th H.; ♂ in ♒, and affl. the ☽ or Asc.; ♀ and ☿ in ♒, and affl. by the ☽ and ♂; ☿ in ♊, ☌, or ill-asp. any of the malefics as promittors (Hor'y); planets afflicted in ♒ in the 11th H.; a fixed sign affliction; a fixed sign on the cusp the 6th H.; Subs at PP (2L). Cases—See Fig. 11D in the book, "Astro-Diagnosis", and Fig. 7 in "Message of the Stars", by the Heindels. Also see the Case in Chap. 13 in Daath's Medical Astrology. (See Hemorrhoids, Varicocele, Veins).

VARIETY—Of Diseases—Causes Every Variety and Species of Disease—(See "Disease" under Species).

VARIOLA — Varioloid Diseases — (See Smallpox).

VARIOUS—Varied—

Consumption — Various Forms of — (See "Various" under Consumption).

Course of Disease—A Various Course In Disease, and Not Uniform—Diseases caused by ☿, and where ☿ is the principal afflictor in the disease. (See Complications, Course, Crises, Erratic, Intermittent, Irregular, Peculiar, Relapses, Spasmodic, Symptoms, Variable).

Functions—The Various Functions—(See "Harmony" under Functions).

Injuries — Various Injuries — (See "Various" under Injuries).

VASCULAR—Pertaining To Vessels—

Vascular Excitement — Of the Nerve Centers—(See Centers, Erethism).

Vascular Fullness—Vascular Congestion—♃ diseases. (See Arteries; "Pressure", "Too Much Blood", under Blood; Dilatations, Distentions, Engorgement, Fullness, Gluttony; "Epistaxis" under Nose; Plethora).

Vascular Tissues — ♀ influences the condition of the vascular tissues, and also the mucous membrane, thru such diseases as smallpox, measles, sloughings, pustular diseases, and diseases arising from blood impurities and poisoning of the system. (See Mucous Membranes, Tissues, Vaso, Vessels).

Want of Vascular Action — Characteristic of the Lymphatic Temperament. (See Lymphatic).

VASO—Vessels—

Vaso-Constrictor Nerves — The Cutaneous Capillary Vaso-Constrictor Nerves are influenced by, and under the rule of ♄ and his two signs ♑ and ♒, and also of ♃ and his two signs ♐ and ♓, and afflictions to ♄, ♃, and these signs tend to produce pathological conditions and disturbances, such as congestions, colds, etc. (See Centripetal, Congestion, Constrictions). Also the pathological action of the ♄ Group of Herbs tends to vaso-constriction.

Vaso-Dilator Action — Is under the rule of ♂, and his two signs ♈ and ♏, acting thru the central ganglia, and in an opposite manner to ♄ in his vaso-constrictor action. The Herbs of ♂ in their pathological action, also tend to vaso-dilation. The vaso-dilator action of ♂ and his signs tend to produce diseases acting from within outwards, and the vaso-constrictor action of ♄ tends to diseases operating from the surface of the body, and acting inwards, or towards the center, as by chilling the surface, etc. (See Centrifugal).

Vaso-Motor System—Ruled by the ♎ Sign. Disorders of are caused by ♅ affl. in ♎.

VEGETABLES —Vegetation— Herbs— Roots — Plants, etc. — All Vegetation points to the Zenith.

Blight—A ♄ affliction. (See Blight).

Cannot Eat Vegetables — Or Fruit — (See Fruit).

Crops—Destruction of—(See Crops).

Decay Of—Humus—Moonlight tends to decay in the Vegetable Kingdom. Also Moisture and Dampness, ruled by the ☽, tend to decay and rottenness of fruit and vegetation. Also the influence of ♄ tends to decay of vegetation, as he does in the human body, and especially when he is lord of the year at the Vernal Equinox, and afflicted. (See "Destruction" in this section).

Destruction To—Eclipses of the ☉ or ☽ in ♓. (See Blight, Drought, Famine, Fruit; "Virus" under Pestilence; Scarcity).

Exhalations—Of Vegetables—(See Carbon, Miasma; "Chemical Action" under Moon).

Fruit—Corruption of—(See Fruit).

Fungus Growths—(See "Growths" in this section).

Growths—Vegetable Growths—Fungus and Morbid Growths In the Body —Ruled by ♆, and afflictions to ♆; a ☉ disease; a ♄ disease; ♄ affl. in ♉ or ♏; afflictions in fixed signs. (See Adenoids, Fungus; "Morbid" under Growths).

Herbs—(See Herbs).

Humus — (See "Decay" in this section).

Life — Vegetable Life In the Body — The Cerebellum, ruled by the ☽ and the ♉ sign, is a type. (See Cerebellum).

Mosses—Ruled by ♆.

Plants—(See Plants, Vegetation).

Potato Blight—(See Potato).

Roots—(See Herbs, Roots).

Rottenness — Of Vegetation — (See "Seeds and Herbs" under Rotten).

Seeds—Rottenness of—Scarcity of— (See Seeds).

Sponges — Sponges, Mosses, Mushrooms, and Vegetable Fungus Growths, are ruled by ♆.

Trees—(See Fruit, Trees).

Vegetarians—An exclusive vegetable diet is said to be better for the body and health, and to increase spiritual power, and especially to eat those fruits and vegetables which grow above the ground, and which are Sun-kissed. Most Advanced Occult students are Vegetarians. The eating of Meat is said to be contrary to the real needs of the human body, as Man is not a carniverous animal. The best working animals, such as the Horse, Elephant, Camel, etc., are fed on grains and vegetation. Meat-eating animals do not work. A vegetable diet gives real strength and endurance. However, meat is said to contain the vegetable extracts, and the minerals, worked over by the animal, and made assimilable for man. (See "Meat Eating" under Meat). For further study see "Epidemics" under Cholera; Diet; "Fountains" under Dryness; Eating, Food.

VEHEMENT — Furious — Pernicious — Violent—

Vehement Diseases—(See "Vehement Maladies" in this section).

Vehement Fevers—(See "High", "Pernicious", "Violent", under Fever).

Vehement Maladies—Vehement Diseases and Pains — Violent Diseases — Caused by the ☉ and ♂, the positive, electric, and caloric-producing planets; ☉ affl. in ♏, disorders of a violent and vehement nature; taken sick in a ☉ hour; ☽ in ♐, and affl. by the ☉ or ♂ when taken ill, and usually the result of gluttony or repletion; ☽ in ♒ and affl. by the ☉ or ♂ when taken ill, and the ☽ slow in motion and decr. in light, tends to all violent, vehement and hot diseases caused by ♂; ♂ in the Asc. at an illness causes the disease to be vehement, violent and swift; the ill-asps. of ♂ to the hyleg by dir., or to the ☉, ☽, Asc., or M.C.; Comets appearing in ♉; ♌ on the Asc.; the ☌ of several superior planets in airy signs. (See Acute, Fierce, Inflammatory, Painful, Pernicious, Quick, Rapid, Sharp, Severe, Short Diseases, Sudden, Swift, Violent).

Vehement Pains — Violent Pains — Caused by ♂. (See "Pains" under Sharp).

Vehement Passion — And Diseases Arising From—☽ ♒ and affl. by ♄ or ♂ when taken ill, and the ☽ slow in motion, decr. in light (Hor'y). (See "Violence" under Passion).

Vehement Signs—Violent Signs of the Zodiac—♈, ♏ and ♑, being the signs of the exaltation of the malefics.

Vehement Thirst—(See Thirst).

VEHICLES—Conveyances—

Accidents—For the various causes of accidents or injuries by vehicles and conveyances, see the different subjects in this Article. Malefics in the 3rd house tend to accidents by vehicles, or on railroads on short journeys. Malefics in the 9th house tend to accidents on long journeys, and on voyages.

Aeroplanes — Injury or Death By — (See Aeroplanes).

Automobiles — Death or Injury By — ♅ or ♂ in the 3rd H., and afflicting the ☉, ☽, Asc., or hyleg, and especially if ♅ is here, as this planet has to do with gas, gasoline, and explosives. However, any malefic in this house may cause accidents in vehicles of any kind, as carriages, in automobiles, or on railroads. (See Railroads. Also see Fig. 21 in "Message of the Stars", by the Heindels).

Boarding a Car—Killed While Trying to Board a Street Car—♂ ruler 3rd H., and with ♄ in 3rd H. Case—See "Dey", Birth Data, No. 893, in 1001 Notable Nativities.

Danger By—(See "Falls" in this section).

Death By—(See the various parts of this Article; "Death" under Railroads).

Falls From — Danger By — ☽ to the place of Cor Scorpio by dir. (See Antares).

Injuries By — (See the various parts of this Article).

Journeys—Injuries or Death On—(See Journeys).

Man's Finer Vehicles — (See Desire Body, Vital Body).

Misfortune By — ☽ to the place of Deneb. (See "Lion's Tail" under Lion; Misfortune).

Motorcycle — Death By — Case — See "Foretold His Own Death", Birth Data, No. 979, in 1001 N.N.).

Railroads—Death or Injury On—(See Railroads; "Boarding a Car", "Run Over", in this section).

Ships — (See Ships, Shipwreck, Voyages).

Short Journeys—Death or Injury On —(See this subject under Journeys).

Street Railways—Street Cars—Street Accident—Cases—(1) Run Over—See "A Luckless Youth", Birth Data, No. 393. (2) "Run Over", Birth Data, No. 853. (3) "Lockjaw", Birth Data No. 913. (4) "Strafford", Birth Data No. 814. (5) "Died In Harness", Birth Data No. 801, all five cases in 1001 N.N. (See "Automobiles", "Boarding a Car", "Motorcycle", "Truck", in this section).

Traffic—(See "Street" in this section).

Train — Killed by Falling Under a Train — (See Case, "Strafford", Birth Data, No. 814, in 1001 N.N.).

Travel — Killed or Injured In — (See Travel).

Truck—Killed by a Truck Falling On Him — See Case, "Died in Harness", Birth Data, No. 801, in 1001 N.N.

Water — Killed or Injured On Water Vehicles—(See Ships, Shipwreck, Voyages).

VEINS — The Veins — The Venous System—The Venous Blood—The Venous Circulation—Ruled by ♀, the ♎ Sign, and the 7th H. Dr. Broughton says ♃ rules the Veins. Ptolemy says ♂ rules them. All three of these planets have their part to play in the activity and functioning of the Veins. The Airy Signs are also connected with the veins, and especially the ♒ Sign. However, ♀ bears strong rule over the veins in any part of the body. Thus ♀ in ♉ rules the veins of the throat. ♀ in ♍ rules the veins of the bowels, etc. In some instances, as will be noted in this article, ♃ rules both the arteries and veins of the part, and assumes a co-rulership along with ♀. It is to be noted that ♃ rules the blood, as a whole. Mars rules over blood-making, and fibrous tissue building, and thus has his part in building up the tissues of the veins, and giving strength and quality to the blood which flows thru them. Note the following Diseases and Afflictions of the Veins, the Venous System, the Venous Circulation, and the rulership of the more important Veins.

All Diseases In Veins — All diseases lying in the veins are classed as diseases of ♃ and ♀, the two planets which rule the circulation of the blood.

Blood Letting—(See Bleeding).

Bowels — ♀ in ♍ rules the veins of the bowels.

Contracted—♄ and cold tend to contract the veins and capillaries of the surface, driving the blood inward, and causing internal congestions, colds, etc, while the heat of ♂ tends to relax the veins and blood vessels, and drive the blood outward from the center to the surface. (See Centrifugal, Centripetal).

Dilated Veins—(See Varicose).

Diseases of the Veins — ♀ diseases; afflictions in ♎; caused by afflictions in ♒. (See the various subjects in this section).

Ears—Obstruction of the Venous Circulation In—(See "Venous Circulation" under Ears).

Enlarged Veins—Swollen—Knotted—(See "Varicocele" under Scrotum; Varicose).

Fullness Of—(See Plethora).

Gastric Vein—Ruled by ♋. (See Gastric).

Genito-Urinary System—♃ rules the veins and arteries of. (See Genito-Urinary).

Head — Ill-blood In Veins of — (See "Blood" under Head).

Heart—♀ in ♌ rules the veins of the heart.

Iliac Veins—And Arteries, ruled by ♐.

Inflammation of Vein — Phlebitis—♂ ☌ or ill-asp. ♀.

Jugular Veins—Ruled by ♉.

Knotted Veins—(See Varicocele, Varicose).

Legs — Venus rules the veins of the legs. For Obstruction of the Veins of the Leg, see "Milk Leg" under Legs).

Lungs—Veins of are ruled by ♀, and ♀ in ♊. (See "Obstruction", "Respiratory", in this section).

Milk Leg—Obstruction of the Venous Circulation In Leg — (See "Milk Leg" under Legs).

Neck—(See "Veins" under Neck).

Obstruction—Of the Venous Circulation—♄ ☌ ♀ in any sign, and especially in the parts ruled by the sign containing this ☌; ♄ ☌ ♀ in ♊, obstruction in lungs; ♄ ☌, P., □, ☍ ♀; ♄ or ♅ ☌ ♀. (See Ears, Legs, Poor Circulation, in this section).

Phlebitis—(See "Inflammation" in this section).

Plexus — A Network of Veins — (See Plexus).

Poor Circulation—Poor Circulation of the Venous Blood—☉ ☌ ♄ or ☋, and □ or ☍ ♀; ☽ □ or ☍ ♀; ♅ ☌, □, ☍ ♀, spasmodic disturbance of the Venous Circulation; ♄ ☌, □, ☍ ♀. (See "Obstruction" in this section).

Portal Vein—Ruled by ♍.

Relaxation — Of the Veins — ♂ influence, and by the heat of ♂. (See "Contracted" in this section).

Respiratory System — ♃ and ♀ in ♉, ♊ or ♋ rule and affect the veins of the Respiratory System. (See Breathing).

Scrotal Veins—Enlarged and Dilated Veins of Scrotum—(See Varicocele).

Spasmodic Disturbance — Of the Venous Circulation—♅ ☌, □, ☍ ♀.

Stomach — ♀ in ♋ rules the veins of stomach.

Swollen Veins—(See Varicocele, Varicose).

Throat—♃ and ♀ in ♉ rule and affect the veins of the throat and neck.

Varicocele—(See this subject).

Varicose Veins—(See Varicose).

Vena Cava — The Superior and Inferior Vena Cava Veins are ruled by ♌.

Windiness In Veins—□ signifies; a □ disease. (See Wind). For collateral study see Arteries, Blood, Capillaries, Circulation, Vascular, Venus; "Blood Vessels" under Vessels).

VENERATION — Awe — Dreads — Reverence—Adoration—(See Dreads, Fears; "Devotion", "Pious", "Superstitious", under Religion).

VENEREAL DISEASES—Venery—Diseases from Sexual Intercourse — Venereal Distemper — Suspicion of Some Venereal Distemper — The ☉ in ♎, ♏, or ♓, ☌ or ill-asp. any of the malefics as promittors; ☽ to the □ or ☍ ♀ by dir.; ☽ to Bull's Horns; ☽ to ☌ or ill-asp. ♂ by dir.; ☽ ♏ ☌ or ill-asp. any of the malefics as promittors; ☽ affl. in ♏; ♆ affl. in ♏; caused by ♆; ♅ affl. by ♂, and especially from ♉ or ♏; ♅ ♏, ☌, □, or ☍ ♀; ♅ ♏, □ or ☍ ♂ and the ☽; ♄ ♏, □ or ☍ ♂; ♃ affl. in ♏; ♂ ♏ when ♂ is the afflictor in the disease; ♂ ☌ ♀, and especially when in ♏; ♂ ☌ ♀ and also afflicted by the ☽; ♂ in ♏, ☌, or ill-asp. the ☉, ☽, or ♀; ♂ in ♏ in the 6th H.; ♂ in ♏ and affl. the ☽ or Asc.; ♀ affl. in ♏; ♀ ill-dig. at B., and ☌ ♂; ♀ affl. by ♂; ♀ in ♏ in the 6th H., and afflicted; ♀ in ♏, and affl. the ☽ or Asc.; ♀ affl. by evil aspects tends to venereal diseases in males; ♀ affl. in the 6th H.; ♀ in the Asc., and affl. by ♆, ♅, or ♂; ☿ affl. in ♏; a ♏ disease, and caused by afflictions in ♏; ♏ on the Asc.; the Asc. to the □ or ☍ ♀ by dir.; malefics in ♏; malefics in the 4th or 5th H., and affl. ♀; many afflictions in watery signs; ♌ on the Asc., and affl. by malefics in ♏. Leprosy may follow severe and malignant venereal diseases. (See Amorous, Bubo, Generation, Genitals, Genito-Urinary, Gonorrhoea, Leprosy; "Ulcers" under Nose; "Passional Excesses" under Passion; Penis, Private, Scandalous; "Distempers" under Secrets; "Diseases" under Sex; Testes, Vagina, Vulva, etc.).

Cases—Of Venereal Disease—See Figures 8F, and 8G, in the book, "Astro-Diagnosis", by the Heindels.

Excess of Venery — (See Amorous; "Women" under Men; "Health Suffers" under Opposite Sex; "Passional Excesses" under Passion).

Horny Venereal Growths — ♄ affl. in ♏. Case—See Fig. 36, in "Message of the Stars", by the Heindels. (See Horny).

Nose—Venereal Ulcers In—(See "Ulcers" under Nose).

Ulcers — Venereal Ulcers — In Nose, Throat, or Genitals—♂ ♏.

VENERY — Sex Indiscretions—(See Venereal).

VENOMOUS — Poisonous — Noxious — Venomous Creatures—Poisonous Animals and Insects—Reptiles—Scorpions—Serpents—Snakes, etc.—

Afflictions — By Storms of Venomous Creatures—♏ ascending at the Vernal Equi. tends to Floods, and afflictions by storms of venomous creatures. (See Floods).

Bites By—Fomahaut with the ☉ or ♂ tends to bites by venomous animals and creatures. (See Adder, Bites, "Bites" under Kings; Obnoxious, Reptiles, Serpents, Stings; "Danger" under Travel).

Fevers — Venomous Fevers — (See "High Fever" under Fever; Pernicious, Vehement).

Stings — Venomous Stings — (See Stings).

Swarms — Afflicted by Swarms of Venomous Creatures—(See "Afflictions" in this section).

Travel—Bites or Stings During—(See "Journeys" under Bites; Reptiles; "Danger" under Travel).

VENOUS BLOOD — Venous Circulation—Venous System—(See Veins).

VENTRAL HERNIA—(See Hernia).

VENTRICLES—

Cerebral Ventricles—Ruled by ♆. (See Cerebral).

Heart — (See "Ventricles" under Heart).

VENTS — Channels and Vents — (See "Channels" under Genitals).

VENUS—The Planet Venus—A Benefic and Fortunate planet, and called "The Lesser Fortune." This planet is feminine, fruitful, passive, negative, benign, benefic in her higher vibrations, nocturnal, and rules the signs ♉ and ♎. (See "Qualities" in this section). Much has been said about this beautiful planet in the Textbooks of Astrology, and in order to make the information I have gathered more convenient for reference, this Article will be made into three Sections, as follows: Section One, The Influences of Venus; Section Two, Venus Rules; Section Three, Diseases Ruled by Venus).

— SECTION ONE —

THE INFLUENCES OF VENUS—

Action Of — The action of ♀ is not rapid and tends to such results as proceed from Intemperance. (See Intemperance). The action of ♀ is also of a rotational or vortex motion.

Angel—Anael is the Angel of Venus.

Aspects Of—Her good aspects to the planets tend to greatly benefit the health, and also to enrich and ennoble the mind, to give a love of the beautiful, of harmony, and also to bring good fortune. The ☌ of ♀ with ♃ at B. tends to make the native very fortunate in life. Her ☌ with ♄, however, tends to vitiate her good influences in health matters. Venus afflicts only by her □ and ☍ aspects.

Atonic Action Of — (See "Asthenic Plethora" under Plethora).

Author Of—♀ is the author of mirth and cheerfulness.

Benefic — ♀ is classed as a Benefic, and is known as the "Lesser Fortune".

Body — ♀, and with ♀ in ♉, gives beauty of form and body, and as one Author says, "A Venus de Milo Figure." (See Beautiful, Handsome).

Coalition — This is the Salient Characteristic of ♀. (See Coalition).

Colors — Rules Blue, Sky Blue to Green; Yellow in the Solar Spectrum; Indigo; Purple and White. (See Colors).

Denotes — (See the Introduction to Sec. 3 of this Article).

Detriment — The home and strong signs of ♀ are ♉ and ♎. She has her exaltation in ♓; her fall in ♍, and her detriment in ♈ and ♏, signs opposite to her home signs. In judging of her power or weakness in connection with disease, it is well to bear these distinctions in mind.

Directions — The evil Directions of ♀ during the ♀ period of life are more critical, as from 10 to 18 years of age, according to Daath, or from the age of 14 to 28, according to others. (See "Life" in Sec. 2 of this Article).

Drugs Of — (See Herbs, Physiological Action, Typical Drugs, in this section).

Evil Aspects — (See "Aspects" in this section).

Evils — Her evils are shown mostly in General Debility, and general Relaxation of the System. (See Debility, Relaxation).

Exaltation — Her Sign of — (See "Detriment" in this section).

External Influences — Being a negative and magnetic planet, ♀ influence tends to render the mind more negative, timid and susceptible to external influences, and a variety of affections. (See External).

Fall Of — (See "Detriment" in this section).

Foetus — Sex distinction in the Foetus is effected by ♀. (See Foetus).

Form of Body — (See "Body" in this section).

Friendly To — ♀ is friendly to ♂, as ♂ rules strongly over the passions, and helps ♀ in forming alliances between the sexes, and to perpetuate the Race. The good aspects of ♂ to ♀ tend to a higher and truer form of love, while the ☌, ☐ and ☍ aspects of ♂ to ♀ tend to the lower forms of love, and to passional excesses, dissipation, etc.

Ganglion — (See "Pathological" under Ganglion).

Good Aspects Of — (See "Aspects" in this section).

Hair — ♀ gives light hair, and light complexion, and makes blondes. (See "Light" under Hair).

Harmony — (See "Influences" in this section).

Herbs Of — (See "Venus Group" under Herbs; "Physiological Action" in this section).

Hour Of — The Venus Hour — (See "Hours" under Planets).

House Of — ♀ is affiliated with the 2nd and 7th Houses, the houses corresponding to ♉ and ♎, the 2nd and 7th Signs.

Identified With — ♀ is especially identified with the Egg, Ovum, the Ovaries. (See Ovaries).

Influence Of — The influence of ♀ is to establish rhythm and harmony in the system, in whatever sign or house found, and to bring about Coalition. (See all the various paragraphs in this Article).

Jupiter and Venus — ♀ has more to do with Love and Social affairs, with Marriage, Sex Diseases, etc., than has ♃. In matters connected with the nutrition of cells, tissue building, etc., ♃ and ♀ both take part, and also ♆. (See Jupiter; "Cell", "Functions", "Nutrition", "Storing", "Tissue", "Transformation", in Sec. 2 of this Article; "Nourishing" in this section).

Love — ♀ when afflicted tends to lack of an uplifted love, to faulty desires, and to weakness of the Generative System.

Magnetic — (See "External Influences" in this section).

Mars and Venus — (See "Friendly" in this section).

Mental Qualities — Artistic, Amorous, Convivial.

Metal Ruled By — Copper. (See Copper, Therapeutics).

Moist and Warm — ♀ is moist and warm by nature. Some Authors say she is cold and moist.

Motion Of — (See "Action" in this section).

Nature Of — ♀ has a nutritive and relaxing nature. (See "Evils" in this section; Nutrition, Relaxation).

Negative — (See "External Influences" in this section).

Neptune and Venus — (See "Jupiter" in this section; Cells, Neptune).

Nourishing — ♃ and ♀ both have to do with the Nourishing, Conserving and Aphetic Processes, the storing of various cell substances, and with Selection, Transformation, Filtration and Reservation. (See Cells, Jupiter, Neptune, Nutrition, Tissues).

Octave — The Heindels say that ♅ is the higher octave of ♀, while others say ♆ is. The indications are that ♅ and ♀ form a pair in their workings, and ♆ and ☿ a pair.

Ovaries — Ovum — (See "Identified With" in this section).

Pathological Action — Cysts, Erotic, Laxity, Remission, Swellings. (See these subjects. Also see "Pathological" under Ganglion).

Physiological Action — The ☉, ☽, ♀ and ☿ are classed as Physiological Planets, and not necessarily pathological, as are ♄, ♃ and ♂. The general physiological actions of ♀ are fermentation, nutrition, and proliferation. In a physiological way, the Plants and Herbs of ♀ tend to affect, or modify and act upon the Humoural Secretions, the Kidneys or Renal System, and also the Glandular System. (See "Venus Group" under Herbs; "External" under Humours).

Plants Of—Plant Remedies of—(See "Physiological" in this section).

Presides Over— ♀ presides over the Cellular Retrogressive Metamorphosis. (See Metamorphosis).

Principle Of—Desire, Love, Sex.

Professions Of— ♀ as Ruler of the Profession disposes to dealing in Cordials, Medicines, Perfumes, Spices, Wines, etc., and if ♄ give testimony, to deal in Charms, Love Potions, Philtres, and Poisons.

Qualities— For the planetary influences concerning the most of these qualities, see the following subjects in the alphabetical arrangement — Amorous; Antinephritic; Aphetic; Artistic; Beautiful; Benefic; Benevolent; Benign; Careless; Cheerful; Clandestine; Clogging; Coalition; Cold and Moist (say some Authors); Comely; Congesting; Conserving; Convivial; Debilitating; Demulcent; Discontent; Dissolute; Diuretic; Emaciating; Emetic; Emotional; Enlarging; Erotic; Excessive; Feminine; Fertile; Folly-Loving; Free-Living; Fruitful; Gluttonous; Gormandizing; Graceful; Habit-Forming; Handsome; Harmonious; Hot and Moist; Hysterical; Immoral; Indiscreet; Indulgent; Inordinate; Intemperate; Irregular; Languid; Laxity; Lethargic; Lewd; Licentious; Lustful; Lymphatic; Magnetic; Mirthful; Moist and Hot (or Warm); Musical; Negative; Nocturnal; Non-Malignant; Nourishing; Nutritious; Nurturing; Overflowing; Pacific; Passional; Passive; Pleasure-Loving; Plethoric; Poisonous; Pustular; Putrid; Redundant; Relaxing; Rotational; Rhythmical; Sedentary; Sloughing; Softening; Soothing; Storing; Susceptible; Temperate (not cold); Timid; Transforming; Warm; Warm and Moist; Wasting. (For other Qualities not mentioned here, look for the subject in the alphabetical arrangement).

Remedies Of— (See Drugs, Herbs, Metal, Physiological Action, Typical Drugs, in this section).

Renal Process — ♀ adds or subtracts to. (See the Introduction under Kidneys; Process).

Salient Characteristic — Coalition— (See Coalition).

Saturn and Venus—(See "Aspects" in this section).

Signs Of— ♉ and ♎. (See Libra, Taurus).

Temperament—Lymphatic.

Tends To — Tends to Gormandizing Habits, and to Clogging of the System. (See Clogging, Gluttony).

Therapeutic Properties—Antinephritic, Demulcent, Diuretic, Emetic. (See these subjects).

Tonic Action Of—(See Plethora).

Typical Drugs Of—Copper (Cuprum), Pulsatilla. (See these subjects).

Unfriendly With— (See Antipathy, Opposites).

Uranus and Venus — H is the higher octave of ♀. The lower vibrations of H, and the ♂ and evil asps. of H to ♀, tend to Free Love, Clandestine Love Affairs, and the danger of Sex Excesses and Diseases from, and also to Sex Perversions. H and ♀ working together in their higher vibrations tend to a love of the Occult, a love of Truth and the Metaphysical, and to great Knowledge, Wisdom, and Spiritual Sight. (See Uranus; "Octave" in this section).

Warm and Moist — (See "Moist" in this section).

— SECTION TWO —

VENUS RULES — For the planetary influences concerning the majority of these subjects, see the subject in the alphabetical arrangement — Abdomen; Acephalocysts; Adornments; Amulets; Antinephritics; Aphetic Process (see Nutrition); Aphrodisiacs; Appetite — The Appetite; Arts—The Arts; Aural Ducts (see Ears); Beauty (see Beautiful); Bladder Worm (see Acephalocysts); Blood—The Venous Blood (see Veins); Blue—Blue Color in the Solar Spectrum; Breasts (of Women); Budding — The Process of — (see Gemmation); Cell Reproduction (see Cells, Gemmation); Cell Substances—Storing of—(see "Substance" under Cells); Cellular Retrogressive Metamorphosis—(see "Metamorphosis" under Cells; Metamorphosis); Cellular Tissue Building — (see "Tissue" under Cells); Charms (see Amulets); Cheeks; Cheerfulness; Chin; Chylification (see Chyle); Circulation — The Venous Circulation —(see Veins); Cohabitation; Coins (Money); Colors (see Sec. 1 of this Article); Comeliness; Complexion; Conserving Process in the Body—(see Conservation); Copper; Cordials; Cosmetics; Courtship; Cuprum; Demulcents; Dimples; Diuretics; Effeminate Matters; Egg (the Egg, or Ovum); Emetics; Eustachian Tubes; Exosmosis; Face; Fecundation; Female Relatives and Female Sex; Fermentation (see Fermentation, Nutrition); Fevers — The Period of Remission in Fevers; Filtration of Cell Substances— (see "Substance" under Cells); Flesh (the Flesh); Friday; Functions—The Nutritive Functions (see Nutrition); Gemmation; Generative Organs — Internal (see Generation); Gluttony; Growth; Gormandizing; Hair (Light Hair); Handsome Body; Harmony in the System; Herbs (see "Venus Group" under Herbs); Intercourse (Social and Sexual); Internal Generative Organs and System; Jewels; Kidneys; Learning; Libra Sign; Life—Life from 10 to 18 years (Daath)—Life from 15 to 24 years, or from 14 to 28 years, say other Authors; Light Hair and Complexion; Lip (Upper Lip); Liver; Love Affairs; Love Potions (Philtres); Lower Parts of the Body; Lymphatic Temperament; Marriage; Maternity; Medicines (Cordials, Lotions, Perfumes, Wines, etc.); Metal (Copper); Metamorphosis; Milk (The Milk); Mirth; Moisture—Excessive Atmospheric Moisture; Money (Coins); Mother (The Mother); Navel; Neck; Nerves (Olfactory); Nostrils; Nourishing Process (see Nutrition); Olfactory Nerve (see Smell); Ovaries; Ovum; Palate; Papillae (Renal); Pastries; Perfumes; Phenomena of Gemmation;

Philtres; Plants (see Venus Group under Herbs); Pleasures; Poisons; Processes of Nutrition (see Nutrition); Pulsatilla; Purple Color; Reins; Relatives (Female); Relaxation of Tissues (see Relaxation); Remedies — Venus Herbs — Cuprum (Copper), and Pulsatilla — (see "Therapeutic Properties", "Typical Drugs", in Sec. 1 of this Article); Remission (Periods of in Fevers); Renal Papillae; Renal Process; Reproduction by Gemmation (see Gemmation); Reproduction of the Species (see Reproduction); Res Venerae; Reservation (see "Substance" under Cells); Rhythm in the System; Selection of Cell Substance (see "Substance" under Cells); Semen; Seminal Vesicles (see Semen); Sensuality; Sex Desires; Sexual Intercourse (see Cohabitation, Intercourse); Sisters; Skin of Face (The Complexion); Spices; Spine; Stomach (Veins of); Storing Process (see "Substance" under Cells); Sugars; Sweets; Taurus Sign; Throat; Thymus Gland; Tissue Building—Cellular (see Cells); Tissue Relaxation (see Relaxation); Toilet Articles (see Cosmetics); Transformation of Cell Substance (see "Substance" under Cells); Tubuli Seminiferi (see Semen); Umbilicus (see Navel); Upper Lip; Uterus (see Womb); Veins—Venous Blood, Venous Circulation, Venous System (see Veins); Venery; White Color; Wines; Womb; Yellow Color; Youth—Periods of — (see "Life" in this section; Periods).

— SECTION THREE —

DISEASES RULED BY VENUS—Diseases and Afflictions of Venus — The diseases of ♀, when afflicted, are those affecting the Generative System, the Genitals, Matrix, Womb, Reins, Bladder, and Breasts. Also those arising from Excesses, Intemperance, Pleasures, Venery, Sensuality, etc. Also Smallpox, Measles, Sloughings, and diseases arising from Weakness, or injury by Poison. No aspect of ♃ or ♀ alone causes disease, but only as configurated with malefics. See the following Subjects and Diseases in the alphabetical arrangement when only listed here—

Abdomen — Disorders of — Pain In — Spasm of Abdominal Muscles — (See Abdomen).

Acephalocysts; Amorous Indulgence— Excess of, and Diseases From — (See Amorous).

Arms—(See "Eruptions" under Arms).

Asthenic Plethora—(See Plethora).

Atrophy — (See Atrophy, Emaciation, Wasting).

Back—Disorders of—(See Back).

Belly—Disorders of—(See Belly).

Bilious Flatulency—(See "Flatulency" under Bile).

Blackheads—Comedo—(See "Comedo" under Sebaceous).

Bladder Diseases — Bladder Worm — (See Bladder).

Blood—Corrupt and Impure, and Diseases Arising From — (See Blood, Impure).

Bowels — Distempers In — Flux In — Mucus In—(See Bowels).

Breasts—Disorders of—(See Breasts).

Breathing—The Breathing Distressed from Tight Lacing and Indiscretions In Dress—(See Lacing).

Brief Fevers—(See Ephemeral).

Bright's Disease—(See Bright's).

Cancer—Death By—(See Carcinoma).

Carelessness — Diseases and Irregularities From—(See Carelessness).

Cells—Cellular Congestion — Cellular Metamorphosis—(See Cells).

Chest — Burning Sensation In — (See "Heartburn" under Heart).

Chilblains; Children—Worms In—(See Worms).

Circulation — Of the Venous Blood Poor — (See "Poor Circulation" under Veins).

Clogging—Of the System—(See Clogging).

Cold — Head Disordered by Cold — Knees, Legs, or Stomach Affected by Cold—Cold and Moist Humours—(See "Cold" under these subjects).

Colds—In the Head—(See "Colds" under Head).

Comedo — Blackheads — (See Sebaceous).

Complexion—Disorders of by Wrong Use of Cosmetics—(See Cosmetics).

Congestion—Cellular—(See Cells).

Consumption—Caused by ♀ when the dominion of death is vested in her. (See Consumption, Tuberculosis, Wasting).

Contagious Diseases — (See Contagious, Venereal).

Corrupt Blood—(See Impure).

Cosmetics — Skin Eruptions From — (See Cosmetics).

Cysts; Death — ♀ denotes Death by Atrophy, Cancer, Diabetes, Dysentery; Epidemic Diseases such as proceed from too much Moisture; Fistulas, Flux, Gleets, Pestilential Diseases, Poisoning, Putrefaction, Putrid Diseases, Putrid Sore Throat, Rottenness and Diseases Arising from; Scurvy, Syphilis, Tabes Dorsalis, Typhus Fever, and Wasting Away.

Debility — General Debility of the System—(See Debility).

Desires—(See "Faulty", "Perverted", under Desires).

Diabetes; Diet—Indiscretions In, and Diseases From—(See "Evil Diet" under Diet).

Diphtheria; Discharges—Involuntary Discharge of Urine — Unnatural Discharges—(See Discharges, Gonorrhoea, Humours, Semen; "Incontinence" under Urine).

Discontentment; Displacements; Dissolute Living—(See Dissolute).

Distempers—In Bowels — Venereal — (See Bowels, Venereal).

Dress—Disorders from Improper Dress —(See Dress, Lacing; "Dress", "Ulcerated Throat", under Throat).

Drink—Drinking—Surfeits from Too Much Drinking, and Excess In Eating —(See Diet, Drink, Food, Surfeits).

Dropsy; Dysentery; Eating—Sickness from Over-Eating—(See Eating).

Effeminate; Emaciation—With a Consumption—(See Emaciation).

Emission—Of the Vital Fluids—(See Semen).

Emotions—Disorders of—(See Emotions).

Enlarged Tonsils—(See Tonsils).

Ennui; Ephemeral Fevers — (See Ephemeral).

Epidemics—From Too Much Moisture —(See Epidemics, Moisture).

Epigastrium—Disorders In—(See Epigastrium; "Heartburn" under Heart).

Erotic Disturbances; Eruptions—Skin Eruptions Due to Impure Blood, Wrong Habits of Living, Excessive Use of Cosmetics, etc.—(See Cosmetics, Habits, Impure Blood).

Excess—Of Amorous Indulgence, and Diseases From—(See Amorous).

Excesses — Passional, and Over-Eating, and Diseases From—(See Eating, Excesses, Passion; "Disease" under Pleasure; Venereal).

Exercise — Lack of — (See Exercise, Sedentary).

External Influences—Susceptible To, and Diseases Arising From—(See External).

Eyes—Humorous Discharges From— ♀ affl. in ♈. (See Eyes).

Faecal Vomiting—(See Ileac Passion).

Feet—Lameness In—Skin Eruptions and Diseases In Feet Due to Wrong Habits of Living — (See "Eruptions", "Lameness", under Feet).

Fevers—The Period of Remission In —(See Fevers).

Fibre—Laxity of—(See Fibre).

Fistula—Death By—(See Fistula).

Flatulency—Bilious—(See Bilious).

Fluids — Escape of the Vital Fluid — (See Semen, Vital Fluids).

Flux—In Bowels—Flux of Rheum— (See Bowels, Flux).

Folly — Moral Folly — (See Folly, Morals).

Free Living — And Diseases From — (See Free Living).

Gastronomical Indiscretions—(See Gastro).

General Debility—General Relaxation —(See Debility, Laxity, Relaxation).

Generation—Diseases of Members of —Impotency In—Diseases of the Generative Organs—Weakness of the Generative System — (See Generation, Genitals, Impotent, Reproduction).

Genitals — Diseases of—Any Disease of—(See Genitals).

Glandular Swellings—(See Glands).

Gleets—(See Gonorrhoea).

Gluttony; Goitre; Gonorrhoea;

Gormandizing; Gout—In Hips, Knees, Thighs—(See Gout).

Growths — Non-Malignant — (See Growths).

Habits — Bad Habits and Diseases From—Sedentary Habits—(See Habits, Sedentary).

Hands — Skin Eruptions On Due to Wrong Habits of Living—♀ affl. in ♍ or ♍. (See Hands).

Head—Affected by Cold—Colds In— Diseases In—Moist Humours In—Pains In—(See Head).

Heart — The Heart Afflicted or Ill-Affected—(See Heart).

Heartburn — (See this subject under Heart).

Hernia; Hip—Gout In—(See Gout).

Hollow Tumor—(See Cysts).

Humours — Moist Humours In Head —Cold and Moist Humours—Raw and Undigested Humours In Stomach—Humoural Discharges from Eyes — (See Humours).

Hysteria; Ileac Passion; Impotency;

Impure Blood; Incontinence — (See Urine).

Indiscretions—Diseases From—Wrong Diet and Habits — Gastronomical — Carelessness—Irregularities, etc.—(See Indiscretions).

Indulgences — Diseases from Excess of—(See Indulgence).

Inordinate Lust — Diseases From — (See Inordinate Lust).

Intemperance; Irregularities—In Food —In Habits, and Diseases From—(See Diet, Food, Habits, Indiscretions).

Involuntary Discharge — (See Emissions, Semen; "Incontinence" under Urine).

Kidneys — Diseased Kidneys — (See Kidneys).

King's Evil—(See Scrofula).

Knees—Cold In—Gout In—Pains In— Swellings In—(See Knees).

Lacing—Injury from Tight Lacing— (See Lacing).

Lameness—In Feet—(See Feet).

Languor—(See Dull, Inactive, Inertia, Lassitude, Lethargy, Listless).

Laxity—Of Fibre—Of Muscular Tissue — (See Fibre; "Laxity" under Muscles).

Legs—Cold In—Pains In—Skin Eruptions—Swellings—(See Legs).

Lethargy; Leucorrhoea; Liver — (See "Deranged" under Liver).

Loins—(See "Disorders" under Loins).

Lotions—Diseases from Wrong Use of —(See Cosmetics).

Lower Parts—Of the Body—Disorders of—(See "Lower Parts" under Lower).

Lues—(See Syphilis).

Lust — Any Disease Arising From — (See Lust).

Malacia; Matrix — Diseases of — (See Womb).

Measles; Mechanical Displacements— (See Displacements).

Members—Of Generation—Disorders of—(See "Generation" in this section).

Metamorphosis; Minor Disorders — (See Mild, Minor, Slight).

Moist — Moist and Cold Humours — Moist Humours In the Head — Moist and Warm Diseases—(See Head, Moisture).

Moisture—Diseases Arising from the Corruption of Moisture—Diseases Arising from Lack of Moisture—Diseases Arising from Superabundance of Moisture — (See "Corruption", "Lack of", "Superabundance", under Moisture).

Moral Folly—(See "Folly" under Morals).

Mucous Membranes — (See this subject under Mucous).

Mucus In Bowels—(See "Bowels" under Mucous).

Muscles—Spasm of Abdominal Muscles—Laxity of Muscular Tissue—(See Ileac Passion; "Laxity" under Muscles).

Navel—Disorders of—(See Navel).

Neck — Disorders of — Swellings In—(See Neck).

Night Losses — (See Emissions, Semen).

Non-Malignant Growths — (See Growths).

Nutrition—Disorders of—(See Nutrition).

Obesity; Ovaries—Disorders of—(See Ovaries).

Over-Eating — Sickness From — Surfeits From — (See Eating, Food, Surfeits).

Pain—In the Head, Knees, Legs, Private Parts, Secret Parts—(See "Pain" under these subjects. Also see these subjects, and the references, under Pain).

Passion — Passional Excesses—Erotic Disturbances — (See Erotic, Passion, Sex).

Pathological Action — Of ♀. (See "Pathological" in Sec. 1 of this Article).

Perversions — Sex Perversions — (See Perversions).

Plant Remedies of ♀—(See "Physiological Action" in Sec. 1 of this Article).

Pleasures — Excessive, and Diseases Arising From — (See "Disease" under Pleasure).

Plethora—Asthenic—(See Plethora).

Poisoning—Poison Death—(See "Blood Poisoning", "Body", "Death by Poison", under Poison).

Priapism—(See Erections).

Private Parts—Diseases In—Pains In — (See Generation, Genitals, Private Parts, Reproduction, Secrets).

Poor Circulation—Of the Venous Blood (See "Poor" under Veins).

Process—(See "Renal Process" in Sec. 1 of this Article).

Pustular Diseases—(See Pus).

Putrid Diseases — Putrefaction — (See "Death" under Putrid; "Putrid" under Throat).

Raw Humours — In Stomach — (See "Raw" under Indigestion).

Reins — The Reins Afflicted — Disordered — Running of the Reins — (See Gonorrhoea, Reins).

Relaxation—Laxity of the Tissues—Relaxed Throat—(See Relaxation).

Remedies—Plant Remedies of ♀. (See "Plant" in Sec. 1 of this Article).

Remission—♀ rules the period of Remission in Fevers.

Renal Disorders — Renal Process — (See Kidneys; "Renal Process" in Sec. 1 of this Article).

Respiration Bad—(See "Breathing" in this Section).

Rheum—Flux of—(See "Rheum" under Flux; Rheum).

Ringworm; Rottenness — Diseases Arising From—(See Rotten).

Running of Reins—(See Gonorrhoea, Reins).

Rupture—Hernia—Inguinal Hernia — (See Hernia, Rupture).

Scandalous Diseases — (See Scandalous).

Scrofula; Scurvy; Secret Parts—Diseases In—Pains In—(See Secrets).

Sedentary Habits—(See Sedentary).

Seminal Losses—(See Semen).

Sensuality—Diseases Arising From—(See Sensuality).

Sex Passion — Passional Excesses — Erotic Disturbances—(See Erotic, Love Affairs, Passion, Sex).

Signs—Diseases of ♀ in Signs—You will find classified lists of the diseases of ♀ in the Signs in the various Textbooks and Dictionaries of Astrology. Venus in any sign tends to disorders of the veins and circulation in the part ruled by such sign, and this is a good rule to follow.

Skin — Eruptions from Cosmetics — Eruptions On the Arms, Hands, Legs and Feet from Wrong Habits of Living — (See "Eruptions" under these subjects; Cosmetics; "Bad Habits" under Habits; Skin).

Sloughings; Smallpox; Softening—Of the Tissues—(See Malacia).

Sore Throat — (See "Putrid" under Throat).

Sores—Sloughing Sores—(See Sloughings).

Spasm—Of the Abdominal Muscles—(See Ileac Passion).

Spinal Disorders—(See Spine).

Sterility — Due to the Atonic Action of ♀. (See Barren, Impotent).

Stomach — Afflicted with Cold — Diseases of—Raw Humours In—(See Diet, Food; "Raw" under Indigestion; Stomach).

Surfeits — From Over-Eating and Wrong Diet — (See "Evil Diet" under Diet; Food, Surfeits).

Swellings — Glandular Swellings — Swellings In Knees, Legs, Neck, Thighs—(See "Swellings" under these subjects).

Syphilis; Tabes Dorsalis;

Textural Changes—In Nutrition—(See Nutrition).

Therapeutic Properties — Of ♀. (See "Therapeutic" in Sec. 1 of this Article).

Thighs—Gout In—Swellings In—(See Thighs).

Thorax — Disorders In — (See Chest; "Heartburn" under Heart).

Throat — Diseases of — Putrid Sore Throat — Relaxed Throat — Ulcerated — (See Throat).

Tight Lacing — Breathing Disturbed By — (See Lacing, Tight).

Tonsils — Enlarged, Tonsilitis — (See Tonsils).

Tuberculosis; Tumors — Hollow — (See Cysts, Tumors).

Typhus Fever; Typical Drugs — Of ♀. (See "Typical Drugs" in Sec. 1 of this Article).

Ulceration — Of the Throat — (See Throat).

Umbilicus — Disorders of — (See Navel).

Undigested Humours — In Stomach — (See "Raw" under Indigestion).

Unnatural Discharges — (See Discharges).

Uremia; Urine — Involuntary Discharges of — (See "Incontinence" under Urine).

Vascular Tissues — Disorders of — (See Vascular).

Veins — Disorders of — (See Veins).

Venereal Diseases; Venous Blood — Venous Circulation — Disorders of — (See Veins).

Venus Diseases — Suffers From — ⊙ to the ill-asps. ♀ by dir., according to the sign ♀ is in at B.; ☽ to the ill-asps. ♀ by dir.; ☽ ♏ and affl. by the ⊙ or ♂ when taken ill, and espec. if ♀ affl. the ☽ (Hor'y); the Asc. to the ☌ or ill-asps. ♀ by dir., and ♀ affl. at B.

Vital Fluids — Escape of — (See Emissions, Semen; "Fluids" under Vital).

Vomiting — Faecal Vomiting from Wrong Diet — (See Ileac Passion).

Warm and Moist Diseases — (See "Warm and Moist" under Moisture).

Wasting Away — Death By — (See Wasting).

Weariness — (See Ennui, Lassitude, Weariness).

Windy Disorders — (See Wind).

Womb — Disorders of — (See Womb).

Women — Minor Disorders of — (See Leucorrhoea, Menses, Mild, Minor, Slight, Women).

Worms — In Children — (See Worms).

VERATRUM — Veratrum Album — Ruled by ♓, and is one of the Twelve Typical Polycrest Remedies, as ruled by the 12 Signs of the Zodiac. (See "Polycrest" under Zodiac).

VERBASCUM — A Typical Drug of ♄. (See "Typical Drugs" under Saturn).

VERMIFORM APPENDIX — (See Appendix).

VERMIN — Pests, Insects, Rats, Mice, Noxious, Obnoxious Animals, Worms, etc. (See "Scarcity of Corn" under Scarcity).

VERNAL EQUINOX — The Spring Equinox — The entry of the ⊙ into the ♈ Sign. The Vernal Signs of the Zodiac are ♈, ♉, ♊. The entrance of the ⊙ into ♈ is a very sensitive time in World Affairs, and the planetary influences operating at the time tend to make the year a good, healthy, and fortunate one for the People, or for individuals who may be affected by it, or an unfortunate year, and tend to distress, evils, public ill-health, strife, etc. The Vernal Equinox is mentioned many times in this book, and in connection with various diseases, afflictions, the weather, World Conditions, etc. (See Air, Aries, Dry; "Inflammation" under Ears; Epidemics, Equinoxes; "Prevalent" under Eyes; "Eruptions" under Face; "Extreme Heat" under Heat; Ingresses, Lightning, Pestilence, Prevalent, Solstices, etc.).

VERSATILE — (See Genius, Learning, Metaphysics, Occult, Philosophy, Reading, Science, Study, etc.).

VERTEBRAE — The Bony Segments of the Spine. The Nerves which pass thru the Vertebrae supply the various Organs, and parts of the Body, from the Brain to the Feet. By making a study of the Signs of the Zodiac which rule the various Organs and Parts, and by knowing which Signs rule the different Vertebrae, it is a comparatively easy matter to know what Vertebrae, or Vertebra, are affected, or subluxated, when the symptoms of the various diseases of the Mind and Body manifest themselves. (See Subluxations). The Spinal Column is made up of seven Cervical Vertebrae, twelve Dorsal Vertebrae, and five Lumbar Vertebrae. The Sacrum is classed as No. 25, and the Coccyx as No. 26. (See Spine). The Vertebrae are also called the Zones of the Spine.

Abbreviations — For the Vertebrae —

At.P. — Atlas — 1st Cervical — Ruled by ♈, ♉.

Ax.P. — Axis — 2nd Cervical — ♈, ♉.

M.C.P. — 3rd, 4th, 5th Cervicals — All ruled by ♉, and influenced by ♈.

L.C.P. — 6th Cervical (♉) — 7th Cervical (♉, and 1st Dec. ♊).

A.P. — 7th Cervical (♉, first 10° ♊) — 1st Dorsal (♉, ♊).

H.P. — 2nd Dorsal (♌ and the ⊙) — 3rd Dorsal (♊, ♌).

Lu.P. — 3rd Dorsal (♊, ♌) — 4th Dorsal (♊, ♋, ♍, ♎, ♏).

Li.P. — 4th Dorsal (♊, ♋, ♍, ♎, ♏) — 5th Dorsal (♌).

C.P. — 5th Dorsal (♌).

S.P. — 6th Dorsal (♋) — 7th Dorsal (♋) — 8th Dorsal (♋, ♍).

Spl.P. — 9th Dorsal (♍, ♏).

K.P. — 10th Dorsal (♎) — 11th Dorsal (♎) — 12th Dorsal (♎, ♏).

U.P.P. — 1st Lumbar (♍, ♎, ♏) — 2nd Lumbar (♍, ♏, ♐, ♑, ♒).

P.P. — 2nd Lumbar (♍, ♏, ♐, ♑, ♒) — 3rd Lumbar (♍, ♏, ♐, ♑) — 4th Lumbar (♍, ♏, ♐, ♑, ♒, ♓).

L.P.P. — 4th Lumbar (♍, ♏, ♐, ♑, ♒, ♓) — 5th Lumbar (♎, ♏, ♐).

Sac. — Sacrum — (♎, ♏, ♐).

Coc. — Coccyx (♏, ♐).

Cervical Vertebrae — Taken as a whole, these Vertebrae are ruled by the ♉ Sign, the Sign which rules the throat and neck and the upper Cervicals, and are also strongly dominated by the ♈ Sign, the Sign which rules the Brain and Head. Also planets and afflictions in the opposite signs, ♏ and ♎, and also in any of the Fixed Signs, as in ♉, ♌, ♏ or ♒, tend to affect the Cervical Vertebrae. The ♉ and ♏ signs, being opposite and supplemental to each other, both strongly influence the throat and sex organs. The Larynx and the Sex Organs are so closely related that the voice in the male changes at Adolescence. (See Puberty). Any of the planets when in ♉, afflicted in this sign, or afflicting the ♉ sign by their evil aspects, tend to subluxations of these vertebrae. Planets when in the first third of the ♉ sign will afflict the upper Cervicals; when in the middle part of ♉, will afflict the middle Cervicals, and when in the latter third of ♉ at birth, or by direction, transit, or progression, will afflict the lower Cervicals. (See Cervical, Lower, Middle, Upper).

First Cervical — Atlas — Ruled by ♈ and ♉. The tissues and organs affected by the nerve supply passing thru this vertebra are the Brain, Scalp, Atlas, Optic Tract as far as the Commissure, the Cranial Bones, the Upper Ear, Ossicles, and the Upper Forehead. Subluxations at the Atlas tend to diseases which affect the substance of the brain; to diseases of the Brain which affect the Mind, the Motor Functions; to cause Spasmodic Diseases, diseases of the Head, Scalp, Ears, Eyes, Spinal Cord, etc. (See these subjects in the alphabetical arrangement).

Second Cervical—Also called the Axis. Ruled by ♈ and ♉. The nerves passing thru this vertebra supply the Brain, Ears, a part of the Face, and the back part of the Neck, and planetary afflictions in ♈ or ♉, or the opposite signs, ♎ or ♏, tend to disorders in these parts. (See these subjects. Also see "Diseases of Aries" under Aries; "Diseases of Taurus" under Taurus).

Third Cervical—The 3rd, 4th and 5th Cervicals are called The Middle Cervical Place (M.C.P.). Ruled by ♈ and ♉. The nerves which pass thru the 3rd Cervical vertebra supply the Retina, the Teeth, Cheeks, Nasal Passages, the Face, and planetary afflictions in ♈ and ♉ tend to subluxations of this vertebra, and to disease in these parts. (See these subjects).

Fourth Cervical—Ruled by ♈ and ♉. Nerves passing thru this vertebra pass to the Eyes, Cornea, Retina, Mouth, Gums, Teeth, Bones and Tissues of the Face; the Jaw, Eustachian Tubes, the Outer Ear, the Posterior Nares, Nasopharynx, and the Hyoid Bone, and afflictions in these signs at birth tend to subluxations of this vertebra, and to afflict these parts of the body. (See these subjects).

Fifth Cervical — Ruled by ♈ and ♉. Also strongly influenced by the ♏ sign. The nerves which pass thru this vertebra go to the Face, Nose, Eyes, Lower Jaw and Teeth; the Hyoid Bone, and to the Lateral and Posterior Muscles of the Neck, and planets afflicted in these signs tend to disturb these parts of the body, and cause subluxations of this vertebra. (See these subjects).

Sixth Cervical—Ruled by ♉, and especially affected by planets in the last Decanate of ♉. The 6th and 7th Cer-

vicals, taken together, are known as the Lower Cervical Place (L.C.P.). Nerves passing thru this vertebra supply the Larynx, Vocal Cords, and the surrounding tissues; the Thyroid Gland, Palate, Posterior part of the Mouth, Tonsils, upper parts of Shoulders, Anterior parts of the Arms, Lower parts of the Neck, Sterno-Mastoid Region, and Upper Parts of the Bronchii, and afflictions in ♉, ♏, and fixed signs, tend to subluxations of this vertebra, and to cause Throat, Sex, and Uterine Disorders. (See these subjects. Also see Puberty).

Seventh Cervical — Ruled by ♉, and also the first part of ♊. The 7th Cervical, and the 1st Dorsal, are called The Arm Place (A.P.). The Nerves passing thru the 7th Cervical vertebra pass to the Trachea (Windpipe), Radius, Upper Part of Arms, Muscles on back of Neck, and to Deltoid Muscles of the Shoulders, and afflicting planets in ♉ tend to subluxations of this vertebra, and to cause disorders in these parts. (See these subjects. Also see Cervical).

Coccyx—The Coccyx consists of four or five rudimentary vertebrae coalesced into one, and articulates with the apex of the Sacrum above. The Os Coccyx is ruled by the ♏ Sign, and the Coccygeal Region also influenced by the ♐ sign, and afflictions in these signs tend to Pain, Inflammation, or disease in this region, or to deviation of the Coccyx. (See Coccyx).

Diseases of the Vertebrae—Ankylosis, and the drying up of the Synovial Fluid, are the principal diseases of the vertebrae. Ankylosis is caused by the combined heat of the ☉ and ♂ in ♂ in the ♌ sign principally, as ♌ is also a hot sign. The Synovial Fluid is dried up by the presence of the cold and dry planet ♄, and especially ♄ affl. in ♌. (See Anatomical Changes, Ankylosis, Fractures; "Diseases of the Spine" under Spine; Synovial).

Dorsal Vertebrae—The ♌ Sign rules the Dorsal Region of the Spine. The Dorsal Vertebrae are under the structural rulership of ♌. They are also ruled by the ♊ Sign. However, as these Vertebrae cover a wide field of the vital organs, their range of rulership includes the last part of ♉, all of ♊, ♋, ♌, ♍, ♎, and the first degrees of ♏, according to the parts, or organs supplied by nerves passing thru these vertebrae.

First Dorsal—The 7th Cervical, and the 1st Dorsal are called the Arm Place (A.P.). The 1st Dorsal is ruled by ♉ and ♊. Nerves which pass thru this vertebra supply the Muscles of the Arms, the Humerus, Ulna, Bones of the Hands; the Clavicle, Scapula and Shoulders, the 1st Rib, the Manubrium, and the Upper Bronchii, and afflictions in the last degrees of ♉, and in ♊ tend to cause subluxations of this vertebra, and to bring diseases in these parts, and to tend to Aneurism of the Aorta, Asthma, Dyspnoea, Hay Fever, Bronchial Disorders, Disorders of the Sternum, and also Diseases in the Shoulders, Arms, Hands and Fingers. (See these subjects).

Second Dorsal—Ruled by ♌ and the ☉. The 2nd and 3rd Dorsals, taken together, are known as the Heart Place (H.P.). Nerves passing thru this vertebra supply the Heart, its Vessels and Covering, the Pericardium, the Aorta, the Bronchii, 2nd Rib, Hands, and Muscles of the Lower Arms, and planetary afflictions in ♌ at birth tend to subluxations of this vertebra, and to all Heart Disorders, Bronchial Disturbances, and to various diseases and afflictions to the Arms and Hands. (See these subjects).

Third Dorsal—Ruled by the last degrees of ♌, and by the □ Sign. The 3rd and 4th Dorsals taken together, are known as Lung Place (Lu.P.). Nerves passing thru this vertebra supply the Chest, Breast, Nipples, Lower Sternum, the 3rd Pair of Ribs, the lower Heart, the Lungs and Pleura, and subluxations at this vertebra tend to diseases in these parts, and to Consumption, Tuberculosis, Chest Deformities, and to various diseases of the Breasts, Heart and Lungs. (See these subjects).

Fourth Dorsal — Ruled by the last degrees of □, and by ♋, ♍, ♎ and ♏. This vertebra has a wide field of action, as the nerve supply passing thru it goes to the Lower Lungs, the 4th Pair of Ribs, and to the Liver, Gall Bladder and Bile Ducts. The 4th and 5th Dorsals are known as the Liver Place (Li.P.). Planets in these signs at birth tend to diseases in these parts and Organs, and to all Diseases of the Liver especially. (See these subjects).

Fifth Dorsal — A part of the Liver Place, and is also known as Center Place (C.P.). Under the strong rule of the ♌ Sign. Nerves passing thru this vertebra supply the 5th Pair of Ribs, and being the General Heat Center, subluxations of this vertebra tend to Diseases of the Brain and Spinal Cord, to Nervous Diseases, High and Burning Fevers, Impaired Nutrition, Cold Diseases, Cold Feet, Gout, Rheumatism, Dropsy, Influenza, Rashes, Scarlet Fever, Anaemia, Chills, Obesity, and a variety of Diseases. (See these subjects. Also see "Center" under Heat).

Sixth Dorsal — The 6th, 7th and 8th Dorsals are grouped together, and known as Stomach Place (S.P.). Is ruled principally by the ♋, or Stomach Sign, and also, in conjunction with the 7th and 8th Dorsals, influenced by the ♍ Sign. Subluxations at this vertebra tend to disorders in the upper part of the Stomach, and in the Oesophagus, in and about the 6th Pair of Ribs, and being nearly identical with the 7th Dorsal, tends to nearly all the same diseases as caused by subluxations at the 7th Dorsal. (See Oesophagus, Stomach).

Seventh Dorsal—Ruled principally by the ♋ Sign. The following Organs and Parts of the Body receive nerve supply and impetus thru the opening in this vertebra, namely, the Stomach, Oesophagus, the Mucous Membrane of the Mouth and Stomach; the Tonsils, Uvula, Pharynx, Palate, Throat,

Tongue, Gums, Salivary Glands, Glands of the Mouth and Stomach; the 7th Pair of Ribs; the Omentum, and also the Eyeballs, Pupils, Iris and Cornea of the Eyes, and afflictions in the ♋ Sign tend to subluxations of this vertebra, and to cause diseases in these parts and organs. (See these subjects).

Eighth Dorsal—A part of the Stomach Place in the Spine, and ruled by the ♋ sign, and also by ♍. The nerve supply thru this vertebra passes to the lower parts of the Stomach, the Pylorus, Duodenum, the Upper Spleen, the Pancreas, Diaphragm, and the 8th Pair of Ribs, and subluxations of this vertebra tend to diseases and ailments in these parts. (See these subjects).

Ninth Dorsal—Ruled by ♍ Sign, and also strongly influenced by the ♏ Sign. Is known as Spleen Place (Spl.P.). The nerve supply passing thru this vertebra goes to the Spleen, Omentum, Duodenum, and the 9th Pair of Ribs, and subluxations at this vertebra tend to diseases in these parts and organs, and also to Intestinal Worms. (See these subjects).

Tenth Dorsal — The 10th, 11th and 12th Dorsals are called the Kidney Place (K.P.). This vertebra is ruled by the ♎ Sign. The nerve supply passing thru this vertebra goes to the Upper Kidneys, the Supra-Renal Capsules, the 10th Pair of Ribs, and also to the Eyelids, and subluxations of this vertebra tend to diseases in these parts. (See these subjects).

Eleventh Dorsal — Ruled by the ♎ Sign. The nerve supply passing thru this vertebra is to the same parts and organs as mentioned under the 10th Dorsal, but this vertebra when subluxated, and being the middle one in the Kidney Place, tends to the more serious Kidney Diseases, and to a greater variety of them, such as Bright's Disease, Diabetes, Nephritis, Stone, Gravel, the Suppression of Urine, Uremia, Blepharitis, Granulated Lids, and also to Skin Rashes, Dropsy, Dysentery, Rheumatism, etc. (See these subjects).

Twelfth Dorsal — Ruled by ♎. Also the ♏ Sign influence begins to be felt at this vertebra. The nerve supply passing thru this vertebra goes to the lower portion of the Kidneys, the Ureters, the 12th Pair of Ribs, the end of the Spine, and also rules the Serous Circulation, and subluxations here tend to diseases and disorders of these parts and functions. (See these subjects. Also see Dorsal).

Lumbar Vertebrae—In the Astrological Textbooks, the ♎ Sign is given as general Ruler of the Lumbar Vertebrae, and Lumbar Region of the Spine. However, as the Sex Organs, the Reproductive Nature, the Bladder, Rectum, Lower Limbs, and Feet, get their nerve supply thru the Lumbar Vertebrae, the rest of the Signs of the Zodiac after ♎ must also have their influence over these vertebrae, and especially over those below the 1st Lumbar.

First Lumbar—This vertebra is ruled by the ♍, ♎ and ♏ Signs, and together with the 2nd Lumbar is known as the Upper Private Place (U.P.P.). The nerve supply thru this vertebra passes to the Ureters, Loins, Peritoneum, and to the Upper Small Intestines, and planetary afflictions in these Signs tend to subluxations of this vertebra, and to diseases in these parts. (See these subjects).

Second Lumbar — The 2nd, 3rd and 4th Lumbar Vertebrae, taken together as a unit, are known as the Private Place (P.P.). Considering the parts and organs supplied by nerves passing thru this vertebra, it is ruled by the middle third of the ♍ sign, and also by ♏, ♐, ♑, and the ♒ sign, as the nerve supply passing thru this opening goes to the Small Intestines, the Vermiform Appendix, the Ovaries, Caecum, Peritoneum, and the Muscles of the Legs, and subluxations of the vertebra must necessarily lead to diseases of these parts, and cause Abdominal Diseases, Bowel Disorders, Peritonitis, Varicose Veins in the Leg, Lameness, and various other disorders.

Third Lumbar—According to the organs supplied by nerves passing thru this vertebra, it is ruled by the latter third of ♍, and by ♏, ♐, and ♑, as the nerve supply goes to the Abdominal Muscles, to the lower Small Intestines, the Caecum, Colon, Appendix, the Hepatic and Splenic Flexures, the Ovaries and Broad Ligaments, the Bladder, Testicles, Sexual Organs, the Anterior Muscles of the Thighs, and to the Knees, and subluxations of this vertebra will tend to diseases and afflictions in these parts and organs. (See these subjects).

Fourth Lumbar — The 4th and 5th Lumbars, taken together, are known as the Lower Private Place (L.P.P.). This vertebra is ruled and influenced by the ♍, ♏, ♐, ♑, ♒ and ♓ Signs, as the nerve supply going thru it passes to the Womb, Vagina, Bladder, Prostate Gland, Large Intestines, Colon, Rectum, Pelvis, Hip Bone, Buttocks, Femur, Posterior Thighs, Tibia, Fibula, and the Feet, and subluxations of this vertebra tend to ailments and afflictions in these parts. (See these subjects).

Fifth Lumbar — Astrological writers give ♎ and ♐ as rulers of this vertebra, but ♏ should also be included, as the nerve supply thru this opening goes to the Uterus, Rectum, and the Buttocks, and planetary afflictions in these signs tend to subluxations of this vertebra, and to ailments and diseases in these parts, and in the lower abdominal region, and especially to Piles, Falling of the Womb, and Menstrual Disorders. (See these subjects. Also see Lumbar).

Sacrum—The nerve supply going out thru the foramen of the Sacrum passes to the Womb, Buttocks, the Posterior parts of the Thigh, and to the Anus and Rectum, and therefore this vertebra is ruled and influenced by the ♎, ♏ and ♐ Signs, and planets afflicted in these Signs tend to disorders in these parts and organs, and to deviations of the Sacrum. (See these subjects. Also see Sacrum).

VERTIGO — Giddiness — Dizziness — Lightness In the Brain—Swimming In the Head, etc.—The ☉ affl. in ♈; ☉ □, ☍ ☽ or Asc. at B., or by dir.; ☉ in 6th H. in a cardinal sign, and afflicted; a disease of the ☽, and afflictions to the ☽, as the ☽ causes diseases which return after a time, such as Vertigo; ♃ affl. in ♈ or ♎; ♂ affl. in ♊ or ♍, and ☌ or evil asp. the Asc. by dir.; a ☿ disease; ☿ affl. in ♈, and in ♎ by reflex action; ☿ in ♈, ☌, or ill-asp. any of the malefics as Promittors; ♄ ☌ ♃ in the Asc.; ♄ ☌ ♃ or ♀ in ♈; an ♈ disease; Subs at Li.P., SP. (7D), and at KP. (See Brain, Cerebral, Dizziness, Fainting).

Death from Vertigo — Afflictions in cardinal signs.

VESICA — Vesical — (See Bladder; "Jupiter Group" under Muscles).

VESICANT—An Agent Producing a Bleb or Blister—♂ influence and remedies. (See Blisters, Cantharides, Caustic, Mustard, Rubefacients).

VESICLES — Vesicle — A Small Sac — A Small Blister—The ☽ and ♃ in Signs which rule the Arms, Hands, Legs and Feet affect the Vesicles and Glands of these parts, causing Cysts, Ulcers, Aneurysm, and Varicose Veins. (See Aneurysm, Bladder, Blisters, Carbuncles, Cavities, Cysts; "Foot and Mouth Disease" under Feet; Herpes, Hives, Malignant, Pustules, Receptacles, Sacs, Seminal, Serum, Varicose, Vesicant).

VESSELS—Blood Vessels—Tubes—Sacs —Receptacles—Vascular—Vaso, etc. — See the following subjects in the alphabetical arrangement when only listed here. These subjects have to do with the vessels of the body, their contents, and disorders.

Absorbent Vessels—(See Absorption).

Action — Want of Vascular Action — Characteristic of the Lymphatic Temperament. (See Lymph).

Aneurysm; Aorta; Apoplexy; Arteries — Various Disorders of — (See Arteries).

Beating Of — Increased Beating and Throbbing of Blood Vessels—A ♃ disease. (See "Vascular Fullness" under Vascular).

Bile—(See "Ducts" under Bile).

Bladder; Blisters; Blood Vessels—Obstructions In—High Pressure In—Rupture of—Diseases of—(See Apoplexy; Arteries; "Pressure" under Blood; Capillaries, Clots, Embolism, Infarct, Rupture, Thrombus, Veins; "Rupture" in this section).

Bowels; Brain — Bursting of Blood Vessel In—(See Apoplexy).

Bursting — Of a Blood Vessel — (See "Blood Vessels" in this section).

Canals; Capillaries; Carotids;

Centrifugal; Centripetal; Cerebral;

Clots; Cold — The Action of Cold on Surface Blood Vessels—(See Centripetal).

Congestion; Constrictions—(See Constrictions, Contractions, Stenosis, Vaso).

Cysts; Dilatations — (See Aneurysm; "Pressure", "Too Much Blood", under Blood; Dilatation, Distentions, Varicose; "Vascular Fullness" under Vascular).

Ducts; Embolism; Fullness Of—(See Apoplexy; "Pressure", "Too Much Blood", under Blood; Dilatations, Distentions, Plethora; "Vascular Fullness" under Vascular).

Hardening; Heart; Hemorrhage;

High Blood Pressure—(See Apoplexy; "Pressure", "Too Much Blood", under Blood; Plethora; "Vascular Fullness" under Vascular).

Iliac Arteries—(See Ilium).

Infarcts; Inflammation Of—(See "Arteritis" under Arteries; "Phlebitis" under Veins).

Injuries To—(See "Hemorrhages" in this section).

Jugular; Lachrymal—(See Tears).

Lacteals—(See Breasts, Milk).

Low Blood Pressure—(See "Pressure" under Blood).

Lungs—Absorbent Vessels of—Other Vessels of — (See Absorption, Lungs, Lymph).

Lymphatic Vessels—(See Lymph; "Action" in this section).

Membranous Sacs—(See Cysts).

Mineral Deposits—(See Minerals).

Obstructions — (See Clots, Infarcts, Thrombus).

Peripheral—Vessels and Nerves—(See Peripheral).

Plethora; Plugs—(See Clots, Infarcts, Thrombus).

Portal Vein—(See Veins).

Pressure—High and Low Blood Pressure—(See "High Blood Pressure" in this section).

Pulse; Receptacles;

Respiratory System — Absorbent and Lymphatic Vessels of — (See Absorption, Breathing, Bronchial, Lungs, Lymph, Pulmonary).

Rupture—Of Blood Vessels—Bursting of — Caused by ♂, and apt to come when ♂ is exactly rising or setting; a ♂ disease; ♂ ☌ ♃ at B., and ♂ affl. the hyleg; ♂ ☌, □, or ☍ the ☽; ♂ affl. the ☉ or ☽ at B., and by dir., and also the ☉ or ☽ to the ☌ or ill-asp. ♂ by dir., or ♂ affl. the hyleg by dir., tend to death by the rupture of blood vessels; the ☉ to the ill-asps. ♃ by dir., and afflicted, and espec. if the ☉ or ☽ be affl. at B. by ♄ or ♂. The tonic action of ♂ tends to disruptions, rending, and bursting of parts or vessels. (See Apoplexy; "Pressure" under Blood; Bursting, Cerebral; "Accelerated" under Motion; Plethora, Rending; "Vascular Fullness" under Vascular).

Seminal Vesicles—(See Semen).

Stenosis — (See Constrictions, Stenosis).

Stomach; Surface Vessels—(See Centripetal, Constrictions).

Throat — Absorbent Vessels of — (See Absorbent, Lymphatic).

Throbbing — (See "Beating" in this section).

Thrombus; Too Much Blood — (See this subject under Blood).

Tumors; Valves; Varicocele; Varicose;

Vas Deferens—(See Testes).

Vascular Action — (See "Action" in this section).

Vascular Fullness—(See Vascular).

Vaso-Constriction — Vaso-Dilation — Vaso-Motor—(See Vaso).

Veins; Ventricles.

VETERINARY SURGEON — Makes a Good Veterinary—Ruler of the 10th H., or of the Employment, strong in ♈, or ♌, makes a good Veterinary, or Cow Doctor. The ♐ sign strong at B., and well-occupied, makes the native fortunate with horses and large animals, and if at the same time ♂ also be strong in ♏, or in ♏ in the 1st, 6th, or 12th H. at B., the native should make a successful Veterinary Surgeon; the ☉ or ☽ well-aspected in ♐; born under ♐, and with this sign on the Asc. (See Cattle, Horses, Surgeons).

VEXATIONS—A Time of Trouble, Sorrow, or Ill-Health—The ☉ or ☽ transiting the place of the malefics at B., and espec. if the ☉ and ☽ be □ their own place at the same time, or the preceding New ☽ be in an evil place; the ☉ ☍ a radical malefic, and the ☽ □ a radical malefic at same time; ☽ Sig. □, ☍ ♄; the ☽ at a Solar Rev. passing over her own place at B., and affl. by malefics, or the ☽ passing the place of the radical ♄ at such a time; ♄ Sig. □, ☍ ☽; ♃ Sig. □, ☍ ☿; caused by the evil directions of ♂ to the ☉, ☽, or asc.; ☿ affl. in 7th H.; Asc. to the □, ☍ ☿; lord of the 6th H. in the 12th H., sickness from deep vexation; lord of the 8th H. in the 4th, possible death from vexation over loss of property, or loss of inheritance; malefics in the 5th H., vexations and sorrows thru children; the Asc. to the □ or ☍ ☿; Fixed Stars of the nature of ♄ ascending. (See Anguish, Anxiety, Cares; "Parents", "Worries", under Children; Disgrace, Evil, Fate; "Vexations" under Females; Fortune, Honour, Inheritance, Love Affairs, Marriage, Mischief, Miseries, Misfortune, Perplexities, Property, Reputation, Reverses, Riches, Ruin, Sickness, Sorrow, Trouble, Twelfth House, Women, Worry, etc. Also look in the alphabetical arrangement for the subject you have in mind).

Death By—Lord of the 8th H. in the 4th H.

Sickness—From Deep Vexation—Lord of the 6th H. in the 12th H., and afflicted.

VIBRATION—Vibrational—Life manifests itself as Motion and Vibration. Vibration is a Therapeutic Property of ♅. (See Uranus). Also ☿ is vibrational, and the originator of vibratory movement, and afflictions to ☿ at B. tend to stop mental vibrations, and to dull the Senses. However, all the planets have their rate of vibration, and tend to cause disease when their vibrations reach the individual adversely, and as caused especially by the □, or ☍ aspects, which aspects and vibrations are contracting and afflicting, while the △ aspects to the Significators at B. tend to be benevolent and expanding. Disease and suffering are but rates of vibration, and a change to the proper vibrations in mind and body often cures the disease. (See Antipathy, Aspects, Attracts; "Vibration" under Colors; Compatibility, Discord, Ether, Harmony; "Compatibility", "Incompatibility", under Healers; Hearing, Hyperaesthesia, Lethargy, Life; "Rays" under Light; Motion, Movement, Opposites, Planets, Polarity, Repulsions, Rhythm, Sympathy, etc.).

Healing by Vibration—In disease, when the rates of vibration are weakening and detrimental, any means, or remedy, to restore the normal rate of vibration is beneficial. This may be done by the use of drugs, by suggestion, by diet, natural means and remedies, by massage, adjustments of the spine, by electricity, baths, and in a thousand various ways as used and practiced by the various Schools of Healing. From the planetary standpoint, when a patient is suffering from a ♂ disease, the remedies of ♄, which oppose the fiery action of ♂, tend to slow down the ♂ vibrations, and bring ease, relief, or a cure to the patient, and the vibration of the disease or affliction has been changed. (See Antipathy, Opposites, Sympathy). Also if the rates of vibration of the Healer blend with those of his patient, the patient will benefit, and make a quicker cure, but if the innate vibrations of the Healer antagonize and worry the patient, and their Star Maps of Birth are not in harmony, the patient may weaken, die, or make slow progress unless he changes Healers, and gets one who is fortunate for him. (See "Compatibility", "Death", "Enemies", "Incompatibility", "Poisoned", under Healers).

VICARIOUS—The Assumption of the Functions of One Organ by Another—(See "Vicarious" under Menses; "Blood" under Vomiting).

VICE—Vices—

Addicted to Vices—Given to Many Vices—Inclined to Vice—The ☉ ill-dig. at B., and afflicted, prone to many vices; the ☽ sepr. from the ☉, and apply. to ♀ in a day geniture; the ☽ to Capella, ruins himself by vices and with infamous women; the ☽ to the ☌ or ill-asp. ♂ by dir., addicted to vices, according to the sign ♂ is in; ♄ ☌ or ill-asp. ♀, secret and solitary vices; ♃ affl. in ♓; ♂ prog., ☌, or ill-asp. the radical ♄, or vice versa, all the vices of the character tend to be prominent and active; ♀ affl. by ♄; ♀ by Periodic Rev. to the ill-asps. the radical ☉; ♆ affl. in the 5th H., dissolute vices. (See Conduct, Debauched, Depraved, Dissolute, Drink, Gluttony, Habits, Homosexuality, Lascivious, Lewd, Lust, Narcotics, Obscene, Passion, Perversions, Self-Indulgent, Sex, Shameless, Tobacco, Women; "Solitary" in this section).

Solitary Vice—Secret Vice—Self-Abuse—Masturbation—Defilement—The ☉ in ♏, and affl. by ♆; principally a ♆ affliction; ♆ in the 12th H. in ☍ to the ☽ in ♏ in the 6th H., and espec. when ♆ is in ♉; ♆ affl. in ♏; ♆ affl. in the 6th or 12th H., sex activity and abuses during adolescence; ♆ afflicted at B.; ♅ ☌ ♄ in ♏, or these two planets otherwise afflicted in ♏; ♄ ☌ or ill-asp. ♀; ♂ ☌ ♀, an inflammatory sex condition; ♂ affl. in ♏; ♀ or ☿ in bad asp. to ♄; ♉ or ♏ on the cusp of the 6th or 12th H.; a 12th H. influence. (See Aversions, Deviations, Passion, Perversions; "Secret Bad Habits" under Secret; Self-Indulgence). Case of Insanity From Self-Abuse—(See "Self-Abuse" under Insanity).

VICIOUS—Depraved—Wicked, etc.—The influences of the malefic planets ♄ and ♂, when these planets are strong at B., rising in the Asc., or M.C., and afflicted, and espec. when ♄ is ☌ or ☍ ♂ in angles, tend to make the native vicious, high tempered, unruly, and violent at times, and apt to do some desperate things in life until he becomes awakened. (See Anarchists, Anger, Conduct, Dangerous, Depraved, Destructiveness, Evil, Hatred, Infamous, Irascible, Jealousy; "Low and Base" under Low; Malevolent, Malicious, Murderous, Plots; "Poisoner" under Poison; Rebellious, Revengeful, Riotous, Treachery, Unruly, Vile, Violent, Wicked, etc.).

Pleasures—Fond of Vicious Pleasures —♀ Sig. in ♋. (See Pleasure, Sports).

Secretly Vicious—Caused by ♄ afflictions. (See "Secret Enemies" under Enemy; Hatred, Malice, Plots; "Poisoner" under Poison; Revenge, Treachery).

VIEWS—(See Ideals, Ideas, Materialism, Metaphysics, Morals, Motives, Notions, Occult, Philosophy, Purposes, Religion, Science, Spiritual, Thinking).

VIGOR—Vim—Force—Energy—

Vigorous Body—The fiery signs ♈, ♌, or ♐ upon the Asc. tend to give the most vigorous bodies, and the greatest vitality; given by the ⚹ and △ aspects of ♂ to the ☉, hyleg and Asc.; the ☉ or ☽ in the signs of the Summer Quarter, as in ♋, ♌ or ♍, or when these signs are upon the Asc., and well-aspected, tend to give a vigorous body, but the ♋ sign on the Asc., if badly afflicted, and the map otherwise weak, would tend to a low vitality. The vigor and force of the constitution tend to become weakened and unbalanced when there are many evil aspects to the ☉, ☽, hyleg, or Asc., and the planets at birth at variance with each other by their □ and ☍ aspects. The △ aspects between the planets tend to give the best vigor, and espec. when the ☉ and ♂ favorably aspect each other. (See Action, Active; "Good Constitution" under Constitution, Females; "Abundance Of" under Energy; "Good Health" under Health, Males; Immunity; "Males Nearly Impotent" under Impotent; Invigorated; "Vigor and Strength" under Males; "Good" under Recuperation, Resistance, Stamina, Tone, Vitality; Robust, Ruddy; "Body" under Strong, etc.).

VILE—Sordid—Loathsome—Base—

Artifice—Blindness by Some Vile Artifice—(See "Blindness" in this section).

Blindness — By Some Vile Artifice — (See Artifice; "Total Blindness" under Blindness).

Diseases — Vile and Loathsome Diseases—(See Carcinoma, Leprosy, Private, Putrid, Sores, Syphilis, Ulcers, Venereal, etc.).

Vile Wretch—♂ Sig. □ or ☍ ☽; ♀ Sig. □ or ☍ ♂; ☿ Sig. ☌ ♂. (See Debased, Depraved, Infamous; "Low and Base" under Low; Obscene, Perversions, Shameless, Vagabond, Wanton, etc.).

VIM—Force—Energy—Spirit—(See Active, Energy, Force, Power, Stamina, Strong, Vigor, Vitality, Zest, etc.).

VINDEMIATRIX—A Star—(See "Fixed Stars" under Stars; Widows).

VINDICTIVE—(See Malice, Revenge).

VINES—Vineyards—(See Fruit, Trees, Vegetation).

VIOLENT—Violence—Forcible—Severe—Sharp—Fierce—Vehement—Furious, etc—Mars is the planet of violence. Also sudden violence, as in explosions, is caused by ♅. Violence by bruises, falls, etc., is caused by ♄. Any of the malefics, when afflicted, or even the ☉, and other planets, may cause violence, accidents, injuries, wounds, etc., by their evil aspects and directions, but ♂ is the principal planet causing violent diseases, violent, sharp and fierce fevers, or a violent death. See the following subjects in the alphabetical arrangement, which subjects have to do with violence in its various phases, whether it be violence and hurts to the body, or violent actions. Under these subjects look for such paragraphs as "Accidents", "Danger", "Death", "Hurts", "Injuries", Violent", "Wounds", etc.

Abroad; Accidents — The subject of Violence is largely dealt with in the Article on Accidents, and where Accidents are attended with Violence. (See the various paragraphs under Accidents).

Actions; Affections — Violent Affections and Diseases—(See "High" under Fever; Fierce, Painful Diseases, Pernicious, Poignant, Severe Diseases, Sharp Diseases, Vehement, etc.).

Ambushes; Anarchists; Anger;

Animals — Hurts By — (See Animals, Beasts, Bites, Cattle, Kicks, etc.).

Areas—Violent Areas In the Map of Birth—The 15° of cardinal signs; the 25° of fixed signs, and the 26° of the common signs, are known as violent degrees and areas, and people with the ☉ or ☽, or the malefics, in or very near these degrees at B., are more subject to violence in some form, or to commit suicide. (See "Causes" under Suicide).

Assassination; Assaults; Battle—(See War).

Becomes Violent—Given to Violence—♂ ☌ or ill-asp. ♄ at B., and espec. in the Asc., 10th H., and angles; the ☉ to the place of Antares; the 2nd decan. or face of ♉ on the Asc.; the 1st decan. of ♌ on the Asc., ruled by ♄; the 3rd decan. of ♌ on the Asc., ruled by ♂; the 1st decan. of ♏ on the Asc., ruled by ♂. (See "Tendency to Violence" in this section).

Beheaded; Bites; Blindness—By Violence—(See Artifice; "Total Blindness" under Blindness).

Blows; Bomb Plotters—(See Anarchists).

Brain Storms—(See Brain).

Bruises; Burning—Searings—(See the

Calamities; Catastrophies; Cattle;

Chances — Endures Many Violent Chances—(See Chances).

Conduct; Contractions — Violent In various paragarphs under Burns). voluntary Contractions—(See Convulsions).

Cough—(See "Violent" under Cough).

Countenance — (See "Violent Countenance" under Face).

Cruel; Crushed; Cuts;

Danger from Violence—☉ to the place of Antares; ♂ ☌ ☉, ☽, Asc. or hyleg at B., and by dir.; Aldebaran, Antares, Regulus, Frons Scorpio, Deneb, and the Shoulders of Orion when directed to the ☉, ☽, or Asc. (See Danger).

Dangerous — Dangerous Accidents — Dangerous Destructiveness—(See Accidents, Destructiveness).

Death—Violent Death—Death by Violence—Danger of Violent Death—Violent Death Threatened — In death by violence, observe the Genethliacal positions of the ☉ and ☽, how they are affected by the malefics, and how the ☉ and ☽ are concerned by Directions in the quality of death. In Countries where Wars and Violence are unknown, people born with maps indicating a violent death usually die a natural death, but in Countries where Wars and Violence predominate, they usually meet an untimely death, and even under slight afflictions. The most desperate men and worthless of people are generally the most anxious to engage in violent, hazardous, and dangerous enterprises. The □ and ☍ asps. of the ☉ to the Significators are the aspects of infamy and contempt, and lead often to a violent death, suicide, or public execution. The □ and ☍ asps. of the ☽, to a violent death by mobs, riots, etc. The following influences tend to a violent death—The SUN or ☽ to the ☌ or ill-asp. ♂ by dir., and the radix be a violent one, and the Lights affl. by ♂ at B.; the ☉ or ☽ to the ☌ or ill-asps. ♂ by dir., and affl. the hyleg, or ♂ affl. the ☉ or ☽ at B.; the ☉ or ☽ □ or ☍ ♂ from angles, and espec. from the 10th or 4th; the ☉ and ☽ affl. by a malefic, and with no assistance from ♃ or ♀; the ☉ affl. by one malefic, and the ☽ by another; the ☉ or ☽ in violent signs, as in ♈, ♏, or ♑, or the afflicting planets be in violent signs; the ☉ or ☽ alone affl. by more than one malefic, and no assistance from the benefics; ☉ Sig. ☌ ♄ or ♂, and these malefics ill-dig. at B.; ☉ Sig. □ or ☍ ♂; the ☉ near violent fixed stars, or having their declination, and affl. at same time by ♄ or ♂, great danger if the benefics do not interfere; the ☉ or ☽ affl. by malefics in the 1, 4, 6, 8, or 10th houses; the ☉ or ☽ affl. by one or more malefics, and one of the Luminaries, or one of the malefics be in a violent sign; both the ☉

and ☽ affl. by a malefic, and one Luminary oriental; ☉ Sig. □ ♂, and if ♄ or ♅ also add their testimony by disposing of the ☉ at the same time, the danger is greater, and almost certain death; the ☉ or ☽ affl. by ♂, and ♂ elevated above the Lights; the ☉ and ☽ affl. by anaretic bodies; the ☉ in the 8th H. ☌ or ill-asp. ♂; ☉ joined with Aldebaran, Antares, Ascelli, Bellatrix, Castor, Pollux, Caput Algol, Hercules, Hyades, Pleiades, Praesepe, or Regulus, or any eminent star of the nature of ♂, threatens a violent death, or extreme sickness; the MOON sepr. from ♂, and applying to the ☉; ☽ sepr. from the ☉, and applying to ♂ in a day geniture; ☽ decr., sepr. from ♂, and applying to ♄; ☽ decr., sepr. from ♃ and applying to ♄ or ♂, and espec. in a nocturnal nativity; ☽ applying to ♂ at B., or conjoined with him in a day nativity; ☽ Sig. ☌ ♂; ☽ Sig. □, ☍ ♄ or ♂; ☽ with Antares, and in ☍ ♄ and Aldebaran; the ☽ to the □ or ☍ the ☉ if the radix show a violent death; the ☽ in the 8th H., and affl. by ♅, ♄, or ♂; the ☽ conjoined with Antares, Aldebaran, Caput Algol, Cor Leo, Bellatrix, or Pollux; the full ☽ sepr. from ♂ and apply. to ☿ in a day nativity; NEPTUNE affl. in the 8th H., and may be by drowning or suffocation, or in a riotous manner if ♆ is Anareta; URANUS affl. in the 8th H., violent death, as by explosion, gas, machinery, lightning, or electricity; SATURN or ♂ in the 8th H., and affl. the ☉, ☽, or hyleg; ♄ Sig. to the ☌ or ill-asps. the ☉ or ♂ by dir.; ♄ with Regulus; ♄ and ♂, and evil or violent fixed stars affl. the hyleg; ♄ and ♂ in ♊, ♍, ♒, or ♐, and in □ or ☍ the ☉ or ☽; ♄ ☌ or ☍ the ☉ or ☽ from card. signs, and ♂ conjoined to ♄; ♄ Sig. □ or ☍ the ☉ or ♂; ♄ and ♂ having dignities in Anaretic Places, or □ or ☍ the ☉ or ☽ at B.; ♄ and ♂ both attacking the ☉ or ☽, or one of them, by dir., and at the same time the malefics or Asc. be afflicted, and with a malefic in the 8th H. as additional testimony; ♄ Sig., ill-dig., and ☌ ♂; ♄ or ♂ in the 4th or 10th H., and in □ or ☍ the ☉ or ☽; JUPITER Sig. □ or ☍ ♂, a violent death by blows, wounds, or resistance to robbers; MARS ☌ or ill-asp. the ☽, and ♄ in like asp. to the ☉ from angles; ♂ and ♄ in the 8th H., and affl. the hyleg; ♂ ☌, □, or ☍ ♄, and espec. when neither are essentially dignified; ♂ the ruling planet, or ruler of the Asc.; ♂ affl. in the 8th H.; ♂ sole ruler at a Solar Eclipse, many violent deaths generally; ♂ ☌, □, ☍ ☽, and at same time ♄ be in angle in ☌ or ill-asp. the ☉; ♂ affl. the ☉ or ☽, or one Light only, by ☌ or ill-asp., and be elevated above it; ♂ in a violent sign at B., and affl. the hyleg; ♂ ☌ or ill-asp. the ☉; ♂ ☌ the ☉ or ☽ in the 1st, 6th, 8th, or 10th H., and espec. if ♅ or ♄ add their evil testimony to ♂; ♂ with the Pleiades; ♂ on the Asc. at B., and affl.; ♂ in angles and affl. the ☉ or ☽, and espec. the ☉; ♂ and ♄ both having dignities in the Anaretic Place, or when □ or ☍ the ☉ and ☽ at B.; ♂ affl. the ☉, and the ☉ be weak and ill-dig.; MERCURY mixing his beams with ♂ is an argument for a violent death; lord of the Asc. affl. by ♄ or ♂ at B., or by dir.; ☋ in the 8th H.; the Asc. affl. by the □ or ☍ of ♄ and ♂ at B., or by dir., and espec. if the Asc. be hyleg; the M.C. to the ☌, P., □, or ☍ ♂, and espec. if ♂ be lord of the 8th H. at B., and the radix promotes it; the M.C. directed to Nebulous Stars, the Pleiades, Praesepe, the Ascelli, Hyades, The Twins, Shoulders of Orion, Auriga's Right Shoulder, Medusa's Head, Hercules, and Markab; Lion's Heart joined to the ☉ or ☽ at B.; Markab, a violent star, joined to the ☉, ☽, or ♂ at B.; eminent FIXED STARS of the nature of ♂ in an angle with the ☉ at B.; Aldebaran ☌ ♄, ♂, ☉, or ☽, and espec. in the Asc.; the MALEFICS in ☌ or ☍ lords of the anaretic places, and if one or more malefics attack the ☉ or ☽; a malefic being Anareta, and elevated above the Lights; a malefic planet in the 8th H. and afflicted; in Horary Questions, malefic planets lord of the 8th, or in the 8th, or affl. the cusp of the 8th by □, ☌, or ☍; a malefic on the cusp of the 7th, or in the 1st or 8th, and affl. the ☉ or ☽, or both; lord of the 8th a malefic, and in the 8th, or afflict cusp of 8th; malefics in ☍ asp. from angles, and in cardinal or violent signs; two malefics in ill-asp. to, and attacking the same Luminary; violent planets, as ♆, ♅, ♄ and ♂, in violent signs at B., and affl. the hyleg; malefics affl. the ☉ or ☽, and elevated above the Lights; lord of the 8th affl. by malefics; lord of the 8th a malefic, and in the 8th, and affl. by lord of the 6th or 12th, and espec. if the lord of the Asc. or the hyleg, are afflicted; lord of the 8th in the 10th, and lord of the 8th, a malefic, and lord of the 10th affl. by lord of the 8th; lord of the 8th in the 6th; the malefics having dignity in the anaretic places, or in □ or ☍ the ☉ or ☽ at B.; the hyleg affl. by planets angular, and elevated above them; the sign on cusp the 8th a violent sign, or if the ☉, ☽, or lord of the 8th be in a violent sign, or malefics in the 8th in evil asp. to lord of the Asc., the ☉ or ☽ from violent signs; malefics in the 10th H., or the Significators evilly disposed; lord of the 10th in the 8th; the 2nd Dec. of ☍ on the Asc. denotes violence; 28° ♐ on the Asc.; the 15° of cardinal signs, the 25° of fixed signs, and the 26° of mutable signs, are classed as violent areas, and malefics, or planets in these degrees at B. tend to a violent death, as by murder or suicide. (See "Causes His Own Death" under Death; "Own Worst Enemy" under Enemies; the various paragraphs in this section). Cases of Violent Death—See "Medici", No. 527; "Sebastian", No. 576; "Villiers", No. 647, all in 1001 N.N.

Decapitation; Deportment—(See Conduct).

Desires — Violent Desires — (See Impotent; "Violent" under Men; "Violence" under Passion; Virile).

Diseases — Violent Diseases — (See "High Fevers" under Fevers; Fierce, Painful, Quick, Sharp, Swift, Vehement).

Dislocations; Dispersals — (See "Violent" under Dispersions).

Disposition — Violent Nature — (See "Tendency to Violence" in this section; Inhuman, Savage).

Drowning; Duels; Effusions of Blood —(See Effusions).

Electricity; Enemies; Eruptions—(See "Violent" under Eruptions).

Evil; Excretory Sytsem—Violent Disorders of—(See "Disorders" under Excretion).

Execution—(See Execution, Hanging, Judges).

Exercise; Explosions; Extraordinary;

Falls; Famine; Father—Violent Diseases To—(See Father).

Females — Violently Libidinous—(See Lewd, Nymphomania, Virile).

Ferocious; Fevers—Violent and Burning — (See "High", "Violent", under Fevers).

Fierce — Violent and Fierce Maladies —Fierce Nature—(See Fierce, Savage, Sharp, Vehement, Wild).

Fire—(See Burns, Fire, Heat, Scalds).

Fixed Stars—The Violent Fixed Stars —(See Stars).

Fluxes; Foreign Lands — Danger of Violence In—(See Abroad).

Fractures; Frenzy; Gas;

Given to Violence — (See "Becomes Violent", "Tendency To", in this section).

Guillotine; Gunshot; Hand of Man — Death By—(See "Hand of Man" under Man).

Hanging; Head—(See "Pains" under Head).

Headaches — (See "Violent" under Headaches).

Heart — Violent Palpitation of — (See "Palpitation" under Heart).

Heat—(See "Extreme" under Heat).

Heights—Falls From—(See Heights).

Hemorrhages; High Fevers — High, Fierce and Violent—(See "High" under Fever).

Highwaymen; Hurts; Ignoble Death —(See Ignoble).

Incendiarism; Inflammation — Violent Inflammation—(See Inflammation).

Injuries; Insanity—(See "Violent" under Insanity).

Involuntary — (See "Contractions" in this section).

Iron—Or Steel—Hurts By—(See Iron).

Journeys—(See "Accidents" under Journeys).

Kicks; Killed; Libidinous — Violently Libidinous—(See Lewd, Virile).

Lightning; Lunatics — (See "Violent" under Insanity).

Lust; Lynching; Machinery; Maladies —(See "Violent" under Disease).

Man — Death by Hand of Man — (See Man).

Mania—(See "Violent" under Mania).

Manners—(See "Violent" under Manner).

Marriage Partner — (See "Violent Death" under Marriage Partner).

Men — Men Become Violent In Sex Gratification — (See "Violent" under Men; "Violence" under Passion; Shameless).

Mob Violence—(See Mobs).

Murder; Nature—A Violent Nature— (See "Given To", "Tendency To", in this section; Cruel; "Shows No Pity" under Pity; "High Temper" under Temper; Vicious).

Outbreaks of Violence — Generally — ♄ ☍ ☌ ♂, direct in motion and angular at the Vernal Equinox; ♂ in the 7th H. at a Solstice and Ingresses into ♋ or ♑.

Pains—(See "Violent" under Pain).

Palpitation — Violent — (See "Palpitation" under Heart).

Parents—Violent Death of—(See "Violent" under Parents).

Passion—(See "Violence" under Passion).

Perspiration — (See "Violent" under Sweat).

Planets — The Violent Planets — The Malefics, ♆, ♅, ♄, ♂.

Poison Death—(See Poison).

Prevalent—Violence Prevalent — (See Crime, Highwaymen, Pirates, Prevalent, Rapine, Robbers, Thieves).

Prison—(See "Beaten", "Injured", under Prison).

Public — (See "Public Death" under Public).

Quadrupeds; Quarrels; Railroads;

Rains—Violent Rains—(See Rain).

Rash; Reformers; Remarkable;

Reptiles; Riots; Robbers; Savage;

Scalds; Sex Passion—(See "Violence" under Passion).

Shedding of Blood—(See "Shedding" under Blood).

Shocks; Sicknesses — (See "Violent" under Disease, Sickness).

Signs—Violent Signs—♈, ♏, ♑.

Slaughter; Stabs; Stars — (See "Violent" under Stars).

Stings; Stones — (See "Assaults" under Stone).

Strangulation; Sudden — (See "Chances", "Death", "Diseases", "Hurts", "Severe", "Wounds", "Violent", and other paragraphs under Sudden).

Suffers from Violence — The ☉ hyleg, ruler of the 10th H., and to the ☌ or ill-asp. ♄, and espec. if an eclipse fall on the ☌ of the ☉ with ♄ by dir., and generally of a public nature; the evil directions of ♂ to the ☉, ☽, Asc., or hyleg, if ♂ be afflicted and strong at B. (See the various paragraphs in this section).

Suffocation; Suicide; Sweating—(See "Violent" under Sweat).

Swift; Sword; Temper—(See Furious, Temper).

Tendency to Violence—The ☉ and ♂ in the 1st H., in fiery or airy signs; the ☉ or ☽ to the ☌ or ill-asp. ♂ by dir., and ♂ affl. at B.; ☉ Sig. □, ☍ ♂; the ☉ in bestial or violent signs, and afflicted by malefics; ☽ applying to ♂, or conjoined with him in a nocturnal nativity; ☽ to the place of Medusa; ☽ sepr. from the ☉ and applying to ♂ in a nocturnal geniture; ☽ Sig. ☌ ☉; ♅ by transit ☌ the radical ♂; ♄ to the ill-asps. ♂ by dir.; ♄ Sig. in ♏, one who undertakes violent and dangerous actions; ♃ Sig. in ♊, with the Bull's North Horn, rash and violent; ♃ Sig. □, ☍ ♂ at B.; ♂ and ☿ together lords of the employment, and with ♂ stronger; ♂ ℞, and to the cusp the 11th H. by dir; the evil asps. of ♂ to the Significators; ♂ ill-dig. at B., and afll.; ♂ Sig. □, ☍ ☉; ♂ to the ill-asps. ♄ by dir.; ♂ in evil asp. ☿; ♂ to the ill-asps. ☿ by dir.; ♂ by tr. thru the Asc. or M.C. if in these houses at B.; ☿ ☌, □, ☍ ♂; ☿ afll. by ♅ or ♂, and espec. when ☿ is in the 12th H.; ☿ Sig. □ or ☍ ♂; the ♈ sign when afll. by malefics tends to give an angry disposition, and as violent as the Ram; ♉ on the Asc., and afflicted, violent and furious as the Bull when provoked; the M.C. to Algol or Hydra's Heart. (See Algol, Anarchists, Anger, Dangerous, Destructiveness, Fierce, Fury, Impulses; "A Murderer" under Murder; "Poisoner" under Poison; Profane, Rapacious, Rashness, Ravenous, Raving, Recklessness, Savage; "High Temper" under Temper; Vicious; "Becomes Violent", "Passion", and the various paragraphs in this section).

Thieves; Tragical; Trampled; Travel — Meets with Violence During — (See "Hurts", "Injuries", and the various paragraphs under Travel).

Untimely; Vehement; Vehicles;

Vicious; Violent Death—(See "Death" in this section).

War; Wild; Wounds.

VIOLET COLOR — Violet Rays — (See "Planets and Color", "Vibration", under Colors).

VIRGIN'S SPICA—(See Arista).

VIRGO — The sixth Sign of the Zodiac, and the second of the Common, or Mutable Signs. Ruled by ☿. This sign is affiliated with the 6th House, and is the sign which rules principally over Health Matters, Diet, Hygiene, Sanitation, and also over Servants, Small Animals, etc. (See Sixth House). This Sign is classed as a cold, dry, barren, earthy, feminine, common, mutable, nocturnal, mental, human, speaking, critical, melancholic, unfortunate, petulant, estival, northern, changeable, nervous, commanding sign, and a sign of long ascension. It is especially associated with the Bowels, Duodenum, Jejunum, Ileum, and Chylification. (See "Organic Functions" under Functions). Its functions are Assimilation, Absorption, Selection and Utilization of food products. The sign is commonly spoken of as the "Virgin Sign", and is considered a sign of great virtue and chastity. The Symbol of this sign is a Virgin. It is identified with Argo, the Ship, and with Zebulon, one of the sons of Jacob, of whom it was written in Scripture that he "Shall be a Haven for Ships". Being the sign of Health, the natives of this sign tend to center their minds much upon matters of health, diet, and disease, and even to court disease, and to give up more easily to disease, being a negative and susceptible sign. (See Mutable, Negative). They tend to take on the disease conditions of others, and for this reason should not be Physicians or Nurses. They often become chronic invalids, and imagine they have all kinds of diseases, and Healers, in dealing with them should avoid any adverse suggestions about their health, or impending crisis, as they are greatly weakened by fear. This sign acts strongly upon the mind and digestive organs. As a class, they seem to enjoy bad health, and to be always looking for sympathy, and to tell others of their many diseases. Simulation of disease is also a ♍ trait. (See "Unfortunate" under Healers). However, the ♍ people, as a class, should enjoy good health, if they will think properly, and it is said of them that they should never take medicines, and especially physics, as their bowels are more tender and susceptible to drugs. (See Eczema). When once sick, and in the grasp of disease, and poor thinking, they are usually very difficult to treat, or to see a cure effected. They should early be taught to think in terms of health, and not in terms of disease, and also to obey the laws of health. Virgo is said to be the most critical of all the Signs, and people born under ♍, with ♍ rising, or the ☉, ☽, and ☿ in this sign, are much given to criticism, fault-finding, and intolerance of the views and opinions of others, which often tends to adversely affect the health thru worry, fretfulness, and peevishness. This sign gives very thin, delicate and tender skin. The Colors ruled by this sign are Amber, Black or Brown Spotted with Blue. The Qualities of this sign are as follows—Barrenness, Changeableness, Chastity, Cold, Commanding, Common, Critical, Dry, Earthy, Fault-Finding, Feminine, Human, Intolerant, Long Ascension (one of the Signs of); Melancholy, Mental, Mutable, Negative, Nocturnal, Northern, Receptive, Selfishness, Speaking, Summer (a Summer Sign); Susceptibility, Unfortunate, Unsympathetic, Vituperative, etc.

VIRGO RULES — See the following subjects in the alphabetical arrangement — Abdomen, Abdominal Organs and Region; Absorption of Nourishment, Amber Color, Assimilation, Belly, Black Color speckled with Blue; Carpus Bones, Chastity; Chyle, Chylification, Chylopoiesis; Colors — Black spotted with Blue; Criticism, Diaphragm, Diet, Dorsal Nerves (the lower Dorsal); Duodenum; Externally ♍ rules the Abdominal Region, the Umbilicus and Hands; Food; Gastro-Abdominal System; Generative Organs, and especially when there is a malefic afflicted in this sign, and in the 6th House; Hands; Hygiene; Ileum; Internally ♍ rules the Bowels, Pyloris, Spleen, Solar Plexus, Duodenum, Jejunum, Ileum, Small Intestines, Mesenteric Glands, the Assimilative System; Intestinal Canal, Intestines—the Large and Small Intestines; Jejunum; Large Intestines; Liver (Lower Lobes of); Mesentery; Mesenteric Glands; Metacarpus; Nails; Nerves (the Lower Dorsal); Nutrition; Nux Vomica; Pancreas; Peristaltic Action of the Bowels; Peritoneum; Portal Veins; Potassium Sulphate Salt; Pylorus; Sanitation; Satire; Selection of Food; Selfishness; Servants; Sixth House (affiliated with); Small Animals; Small Intestines; Solar Plexus; Spine (part back of the ♍ Region); Spleen; Stone in Body; Sympathetic Nervous System; Umbilical Region (Externally); Uterus; Utilization of Food; Veins (Vena Portae); Virginity; Womb.

VIRGO DISEASES—Diseases and Afflictions of Virgo—The ☉ well-aspected in ♍ tends to natural habits. The ☽ is not as strong in ♍, and afflicted in this sign tends to digestive disorders, and irregularities of the bowels, and of the intestinal functions. See the following subjects in the alphabetical arrangement when only listed here—

Abdomen—Diseases and Injuries of—(See Abdomen).

Appendicitis; Assimilation—Disorders of—(See Assimilation).

Barrenness; Belly—Any Disease In—(See Belly).

Bowels — All Diseases, Disorders and Injuries of—(See Bowels).

Catarrh of Bowels — (See "Catarrh" under Bowels).

Cholera; Chronic Invalids — (See Invalids).

Chyle—Disorders of—(See Chyle).

Colic; Constipation; Cramps;

Croakings — (See "Croakings" under Bowels).

Diarrhoea; Digestion—Digestive Disorders — Intestinal Indigestion — (See Digestion, Indigestion).

Dysentery; Enteralgia — Pain In the Bowels — (See "Enteralgia", "Pain", under Bowels).

Enteric Fever — (See "Fever" under Bowels. Also see Typhoid).

Flatulence; Functions — Irregular Bowel Functions—(See "Irregular" under Bowels; "Organic" under Functions).

Generative Organs — Disorders of — (See the Introduction under Generation).

Hernia; Ileac Passion; Indigestion — Intestinal—(See Indigestion).

Infirmities—All Infirmities In the Intestines — (See "All Diseases" under Bowels).

Injuries—To Abdomen and Intestines — (See "Injuries" under Abdomen, Bowels).

Intestines — All Disorders In — (See "All Diseases" under Bowels).

Invalids—Chronic Invalids—(See Invalids).

Irregular Bowels — (See "Irregular" under Bowels).

Malnutrition; Melancholia; Neuralgia — Of Intestines — (See "Pain" under Bowels).

Obstructions In Bowels — (See "Obstructions" under Bowels).

Peritonitis—(See Peritoneum).

Simulation of Disease—A ♍ trait.

Spleen—Disorders of—(See Spleen).

Sterility—(See Barrenness).

Tapeworm; Testicles — Infirmities In —(See Testes).

Treatment — Of ♍ Diseases — (See Enema).

Tympanites; Typhoid; Wind In Bowels —(See "Colic" under Bowels; Colic, Wind).

Womb Disorders—(See Womb).

Worms—(See Cestode, Tinea, Worms).

VIRILE MEMBERS — Excessive Virile Members — Excessive In Males, and Hermaphrodites In Females — The ☉ and ☽ both in masculine signs, and configurated together, and both configurated with ♂ and ♀ in any way, males then born will have excessive virile members, and females be quite, or nearly, Hermaphrodites. If ♂ and ♀ be also in masculine signs, males will have a mixture of sex, and females be violently libidinous. If ♀ only be in a masculine sign, they will conceal their desires, and be more discreet. (See Eunuchs, Hermaphrodites, Lewd, Nymphomania).

VIRTUE—Virtuous—Chaste—

Females Virtuous—(See "Chaste" under Females; Honest; "Good" under Morals; "Popular" under Reputation; Sincere).

Void of Virtue—(See Harlots, Imprudent; "Adultery", "Liaisons", under Love Affairs; "Low and Base" under Low; Shameless, Unchaste; "Unchaste" under Women).

VIRULENT—Noxious—Malignant—(See Fatal, Malignant, Noxious, Poisonous).

VIRUS—A Morbid Product—A Pathogenic Microbe—

Pestiential Virus — (See "Virus" under Pestilence. Also see "Death" under Animals, Cattle, Fish, Fowls, Horses; Contagions, Eclipses, Epidemics; "Scarcity" under Fruit; Infections, Microbes, etc.).

VIS CONSERVATRIX — The Healing Powers of Nature — Are ruled by the ☉, ♂, ♃, and ♀. (See Absorption, Cleansing, Conservation, Cure, Defensive, Phagocytes, Preservation, Recuperation, Resistance, Restoration; "Good" under Vitality, etc.).

VISAGE — The Face — Countenance — Look — Expression—Aspect, etc.—This subject is mostly considered in the Article on Face. (See Appearance, Aspect, Cheeks, Chin, Complexion, Countenance, Cruel, Ears, Expression, Eyebrows, Eyes, Face, Forehead, Glances, Hair, Jaws, Lips, Look, Mouth, Nose, Pleasant, Profile, Smiling, Teeth, Temples, etc.).

VISCERA — The Contents of the Body Cavities—Splanchnic—Splanchnic Ganglia—♃ rules all the Viscera, and all diseases seated in these parts.

Death — By Some Obstruction In — (See "Obstruction" in this section).

Obstruction—Death by Some Obstruction In—Denoted by the ☉.

Prolapse Of — Splanchnoptosis — Relaxation of the Viscera—♆ and ♀ influence. (See Prolapse, Relaxation).

VISCUS — Organs Enclosed within the Cavities of the Body, as in the Cranium, Thorax, Abdomen, Pelvis, etc.— (See Abdomen, Bowels, Brain, Chest, Heart, Kidneys, Lungs, Pelvis, Stomach, Thorax, etc.).

Prolapse of a Viscus—(See Hernia).

VISION — Sight — Eyesight — The Sense of Vision—The Disorders of Vision are listed in the Article on Sight. See such subjects as Dim Vision, Double Vision, Feeble, Keen Vision, Night Vision, Old Age Vision, One-Half Vision, Painful Vision, Weak Vision, and the various paragraphs under Sight. Also see Accommodation, Blindness, Eyes.

VISIONS—Visionary—

A Dreamy Mind—(See "Dreamy Mind" under Dreams; "Visionary" in this section).

Hanging — Haunted by Visions of Hanging — (See "Fears of Hanging" under Hanging).

Visionary Mind — ♆ affl. at B.; ♆ affl. in ♊, or in the 1st, 9th, or 10th H. (See Chaotic, Concentration, Confusion; "Dreamy Mind" under Dreams; "Mind" under Erratic; Fancies; "Impractical" under Ideals; Imaginations, Vacillating, Vagaries, etc.).

Visions — Tendency to Visions — Visions are ruled by ♆ and the 9th H., and ♆ in one of the Houses of Mind, as in the 3rd or 9th H., tends to visions, and unusual psychic, clairvoyant, and mediumistic faculties; ♆ ⚹ or △ ☽, prophetic visions; ♆ ⚹, △ ♅, ♃, ☽; ♆ affl. in ♐, visions of distress; ♆ by tr. ☌ ☽ or ☿ in radical map; ♆ to the ☌, ☐ or ☍ Antares, may have visions, or hear spirit voices; the ☽ in the 9th H., and aspected by ♆; ☽ in ♒ and well-asp. by ☊; the Pr. ☽ ☌, P., ☐, ☍ the radical ♆ if ♆ affl. at B.; ♅ ♐; ♅ ⚹ or △ ♆, prophetic and inspirational nature; ♄ in the 9th H., and well-asp. by the ☽; the 3rd Dec. of ♒ on the Asc., ruled by the ☽. (See Clairvoyance, Delirium, Delusions, Demoniac, Dreams, Fancies, Fears, Forebodings, Hallucinations, Ideals, Ideas, Illusions, Imagination, Insanity, Intuition, Mediumship, Mind, Neptune, Ninth House, Notions, Obsessions, Premonitions, Prophetic, Psychic, Religion; "Sensitiveness" under Sensitive; "Nightmare" under Sleep; Spirit Controls, Third House, Vagaries, etc.).

VITAL — Vital Force — Vital Power — Vital Fluid—Vital Centers—Solar Life Currents — Pertaining to Life—Vitality, etc. — The subject of Vitality is considered in the next Article after this one. The ☉ is Vital, and stands at the head of the Vital Group. (See "Vital" under Sun). The ☉ rules the Vital Force, the Vital Body, the Vital Fluid, and has affinity with the Vital Centers in the body. The Vital Fluid in the Nerves is ruled by ☿. The Fixed Signs are Vital in Temperament. (See "Fixed Signs" under Fixed). The following subjects have to do with the Vital Power, Vital Force, etc.

Activity—Lowered Vital Activity—It

is lowered by ♄, and affecting the part ruled by the sign he is in at B., or in by Dir. or Tr. (See Activity; "Lowered" under Vitality).

Adynamia — Asthenia — Loss of Vital Power — (See Adynamia, Asthenia; "Lessened" under Vitality; "Weak Body" under Weak).

Asthenia — (See "Adynamia" in this section).

Augmented — The Vital Forces Augmented—The ☉ ⚹ or △ ☽, ♅ or ♂. (See Vitality).

Body—The Vital Body—Ruled by the ☉. The ☉ affl. at B. tends to diseases of the Vital Body. The Vital Body is one of Man's finer vehicles, and is made of Ether, and interpenetrates the physical body. The Blood and the Glands are the special manifestation of the Vital Body, and its function is to build up and restore the tone of the body when it is tired and worn thru its activities and from the emotions of the mind. (See Astral Body, Childhood, Desire Body).

Centres — The Vital Centres in the Star Map are the ☉, ☽, Asc., and Hyleg, and the ☉, ☽, or Asc. are usually taken as the Hyleg, or Life Giver, according to their strength, power, and aspects at B. (See Hyleg). The ☉ has special affinity with the Vital Centers. (See "Centers" under Nerves; Solar, Sun).

Currents — (See "Solar" in this section).

Deficiency — Of Vital Power — Vital Forces Depleted—Loss of Vital Power —The ☽ to the ☌ or ill-asps. ♆ by dir.; the circulation of the vital forces to the different organs is lowered and impeded by ♄, and that part suffers which is ruled by the sign containing ♄ at B., or temporarily by dir. or tr. (See Depletion, Lowered, Waste, Weak, in this section).

Depletion — Of the Vital Fluid and Vital Forces — Depletion of the Nerve Force—The evil asps. of the ☉ and ☽ to each other tend to deplete and lower the vital powers and forces, and also to disturb the organic functions ruled by the ☽; caused by the ☉ ☐ or ☍ ☽; ♆ ☐ or ☍ Asc. (See Energy, Vitality; "Deficiency" in this section).

Diminished — The Vital Solar Life Currents Diminished—The ☉ ☌ ♄ at B., and the ☉ affl. by ♄ by dir. (See Diminished).

Diseases—Vital Diseases—In all Vital Diseases the influence of the ☉ at B., and all afflictions to the ☉ by dir., should be carefully studied, to give a proper judgment, diagnosis, and prognosis upon the case, and the part of the body most afflicted.

Ears—Vital Fluid Lacking In—(See "Circulation" under Ears; Hearing).

Energy—Vital Power—Vital Heat— Vital Energy is connected with the ♓ Sign, and with Iron Phosphate, the ♓ Sign Salt. (See "Iron Phosphate" under Iron). For Increase of the Vital Energy, see "Augmented", "Force", in this section. For Decrease of, see Depletion, Diminished, Fluid, Nerves, in this section; "Lessened" under Vitality.

Etheric Fluid — The Vital Etheric Fluid—(See "Fluid" in this section).

Face — The Vital Type Face — (See Decanates).

Flow — The Vital Flow Along the Nerves Obstructed—(See "Vital Flow" under Nerves).

Fluid—The Vital Fluid—Prana—Vital Force — Nerve Force — Vital Etheric Fluid—The Vital Fluid is ruled by the ☉, and is made up of the Solar Force. It is concentrated and drawn in thru the Spleen, and passes from there to the Solar Plexus, and is distributed over the body. (See "Solar Plexus" under Plexus; Spleen). It is an invisible, rose-colored fluid, the vitalizing force of the body, and corresponds to the electric current going over the wires. Obstruction of this flow results in disease and disturbed functions. The Vital Fluid which flows in the Nerve Sheath is ruled by ☿. This flow of the Solar Life Currents is obstructed and diminished when the ☉ is afflicted by ♄; the ☉ ☌ ♄; the ☉ affl. by any of the malefics at B., and by dir.; the ☉ affl. in the 6th H.; ♆ in the Asc., or □ or ☍ the Asc., tends to a wasting away, depletion, escape of, loss of, or sapping of the Vital Fluids, causing premature decay, wrinkling, etc. (See the various paragraphs in this section. Also see Blood, Creative, Ears, Energy, Force; "Obstructed" under Nerves, Spine; Power, Prana, Semen; "Force" under Sex; Wrinkles).

Force—Vital Force—Vital Power—Prana—Nerve Force—Life Force—The ☉ rules the Vital Force, or the Prana, as it is called in the Hindu Philosophy. (See "Life Force" under Force; Prana). Also the planet Mars aids the Sun in giving Life Force, Energy, Zest, and Zeal to Humanity. (See Mars). The Sun Group of Plants also act on the Vital Force. (See "Sun Group" under Herbs). Plenty of Vital Force is given when the ☉ is in ♈, ♌ or ♏, and with females when the ☽ is hyleg in ♌. Aries on the Asc., and ♂ in ♈ in the Asc., tends to an excess of Life Force, and to augmented Vital Powers. These Powers are also augmented and increased, and with a superabundance of Vital Energy, when the planets ♅ and ♂ are in ✳ or △ asp. to the ☉, and espec. when the ☉ is in a fiery sign, or with such a sign upon the Asc. (See Augmented, Depleted, Fluid, Power, and the various paragraphs in this section).

Full—The Vital Powers and the Constitution are at their full, and greatest, when the ☉ is above the horizon at B., and espec. when the ☉ is rising in the East in the 1st or 10th H., or when in the 7th H., and in a Hylegiacal Place. (See "Good" under Recuperation, Resistance, Stamina, Tone, Vitality). The next strongest Vital Powers are given when the ☉ is in the 9th or 11th H., and the weakest when in the 4th, 6th, 8th, or 12th H., and afflicted.

Functions—The Vital Functions Suspended—(See "Vital Functions" under Functions).

Greatest — Vital Powers Greatest — (See "Full" in this section).

Heat—Vital Heat—Given when ♂ is in any asp. to the ☉ or ☽. Is also connected with the fiery signs, ♈, ♌, and ♐, and with these signs upon the Asc. at B. The ☉ and ♂ are the fiery, hot, and electric planets, and supply vital heat to the body. (See Electric; "Fire Signs" under Fire; "Energy" in this section).

Inhibition—Of Vital Power—♄ influence. (See Inhibition; Diminished, Depletion, in this section).

Iron Phosphate — The Vital Salt — Ruled by the ♓ Sign. (See Iron).

Knot — The Vital Knot — (See Pons Varolii).

Loss of Vital Power—(See Adynamia, Deficient, Depletion, Fluid, Force, Lowered, Obstructed, in this section).

Lowered—Vital Force Lowered—(See Activity, Depletion, Force, Loss Of, and the various paragraphs in this section).

Lowering — (See Depletion, Loss Of, in this section).

Lowest—(See "Lowest" under Vitality).

Medium Vital Power — The ☉ in the 9th or 11th H. at B. (See "Full" in this section).

Nerves—The Vital Fluid of the Nerves is ruled by ☿. The Vital Flow along the nerves is obstructed when the ☉ is affl. at B., and espec. when in ☌ ♄. (See Inhibition, Obstructed, in this section).

Obstructed — The Vital Forces and Vital Flow Obstructed — (See Fluid, Inhibition, Loss Of, Nerves, in this section).

Organs—The Vital Organs—(See Organs).

Part — The Most Vital Part of the Body — The Rising Sign, the Sign on the Eastern horizon at B., indicates the most vital and sensitive part of the body. (See "Weak Parts" under Parts; "Organs" under Sensitive; Vulnerable).

Perversion—Of the Vital Stimulus—(See "Stimulus" in this section).

Plenty—Of Vital Force—(See "Force" in this section).

Pons Varolii—The Vital Knot—(See Pons).

Power—The Vital Power—The ☉ and ♌ signify Vital Power. (See Augmented, Depletion, Diminished, Fluid, Force, Full, Heat, Loss Of, Obstructed, and the various paragraphs in this section; Vitality).

Prana — The Hindu Term for Vital Power and Vital Force—(See Prana).

Principle—The Vital Principle—Ruled by the ☉. The diseases of the body act upon the Mind thru the Vital Principle, and also the diseases of the mind act upon the body thru the same medium. This occurs largely thru the 6th House, known as the house of health, and ruled by ☿, a mental ruler, and it is thru this house that matter acts upon mind, and mind upon matter, thus tending in the unenlightened, and the unawakened native to generate diseases of both the mind and body. (See "Action of Mind" under Mind; Sixth House).

Processes — The Vital Processes of the body are ruled by the ☉, the Giver of Life, and are largely kept up by the power of the ☉, and aided by ♂ in giving iron and haemoglobin to the blood for fuel. The Vital Processes tend to be arrested when ♋, ♍, or ♑ are upon the Asc. at B., and thru fear of disease. (See "Disease" under Fear).

Salt—The Vital Salt—Iron Phosphate, the ♓ Salt. (See "Energy" in this section).

Signs—The Vital Signs of the Zodiac —The Fiery and Airy Signs, and also ♉ and ♏ are among the most vital of the signs when upon the Asc. at B., and well-aspected. The Fixed Signs are vital in temperament.

Solar — Solar Vital Life Currents — (See "Fluid" in this section; Solar).

Spark — The Vital Spark of Life is maintained by the ☉ and ♂, the ☉ as life-giver, and ♂ as giver of the iron and haemoglobin.

Spine — The Vital Flow Obstructed Through — (See "Obstruction" under Spine).

Spirit—The Vital Spirit in Women is ruled by the ☉, and denotes Hysterics. (See Hysteria).

Spleen—The Vital Fluid, ruled by the ☉, is drawn in thru the Spleen. (See Spleen).

Stamina—Vital Stamina—(See Stamina).

Stimulus — Perversion of the Vital Stimulus—A General Action of the ♃ Group of Herbs and Plants. (See "Jupiter Group" under Herbs).

Strength — The Vital Strength — (See Strength).

Sun—The ☉ is vital, and the source of Vital Power. (See Sun).

Superabundance — Of Vital Energy— (See Augmented, Energy, Force, in this section; "Excess", "Superabundance", under Vitality).

Suspended—The Vital Functions Suspended — (See "Suppressed" under Functions; "Processes" in this section).

Temperament — The Vital Temperament — When ♀ is strong at B., the Vital Temperament abounds; ♀ in the 1st H. (See Decanates; "Fixed Signs" under Fixed; the Introduction under Life; Temperament).

Tonicity—Vital Tonicity—(See Stamina, Tone, Vitality).

Vital Body—(See "Body" in this section).

Vital Type — Of Temperament — (See "Temperament" in this section).

Vitality—(See Vitality).

Waste — Of the Vital Force — The ☉ affl. in weak signs; the ☽ to the ill-asps. ♆ by dir.; the 1st Dec. of ♌ on the Asc., ruled by ♄; ♄ affl. in ♒; ♀ diseases. (See Adynamia, Depletion, Fluid, in this section; Debauched, Dissipated; "Passional Excesses" under Passion; "Wasted" under Vitality).

Weak Vital Powers—(See "Depleted" in this section; Impotent, Sickly; "Low", "Weak", under Vitality; "Weak Body" under Weak).

Weakened Vital Power—(See Activity, Adynamia, Depletion, Fluid, Force, Power, in this section; "Weakened" under Vitality).

Weaker — The Vital Powers tend to be weaker when the ☉ is in the 8th or 12th H.

Weakest—The Vital Powers are weakest when the ☉ is on the cusp of the 4th H. at B. (See Fourth House, Nadir).

VITALITY—Vital Tonicity—Vital Power —The Vital Principle of Life—Strength — Energy — The ☉ rules the Vitality, and is the source of vital energy. The Solar Force focussed thru the ☽ gives vitality. The less the ☉ is afflicted at B., the greater is the vitality. The ☉ is vitalizing, and concerns itself with the vitality in the human frame. The ☉ rules the vitality in both sexes. The vitality is governed by the aspects and position of the ☉. The vitality is not weakened by functional disorders and derangements when there is no aspect between the ☉ and ☽ at B. The following paragraphs have to do with the Vitality—See these subjects in the alphabetical arrangement when not considered here.

Abundance—Of Vitality—(See "Good", "Superabundance", in this section).

Active; Adynamia — Loss of Vital Power—(See Adynamia).

Amorous Indulgence—Vitality Sapped By—(See Amorous).

Arrested — (See "Lessened" in this section).

Ascendant—A Vital Center—(See Ascendant, First House).

Asthenia—Loss of Vital Power—(See Asthenia).

Atony — Low Vitality — (See Atony; "Low" in this section).

Augmented Vitality — A Morbid Plus Condition—A ☉ disease. In a normal way the vitality is increased and augmented when the ☉ at B. is well-asp. by ♅ and ♂. (See Excess, Good, Increased, Superabundance, in this section).

Bad Vitality—(See "Low" in this section).

Benefitted — (See Augmented, Good, Increased, in this section).

Better — The Vitality Better — The ☉ in ♈ or ♌; born in the increase of the ☽; fiery signs upon the Asc.; the majority of planets rising and elevated at B. (See "Increased" in this section).

Children — Vitality Bad In — (See "Sickly" under Children; "Early Years" under Early; "Vitality", "Weak", under Infancy).

Considerable Vitality — (See "Females", "Good", "Males", in this section).

Constitution Good—(See Constitution; "Good Health" under Health; "Body" under Strong).

Degree of Vitality — Of Physical Strength—Is largely determined by the rising sign in both sexes. (See Degree).

Depletion—Of the Vitality—Sapped— Undermined — (See "Lessened", "Wasted", in this section; Amorous; "Depletion" under Vital).

Devitalization—A ♄ disease. (See "Lessened" in this section).

Dissipation Of—(See "Wasted" in this section).

Dynamic Energy—(See Dynamic)

Early Death—(See Early).

Easily Weakened—By Illness or Excesses—The ☉ affl. by the ☽, ♄ and malefics at B.; the ☽ hyleg in ♏, and afflicted with females. (See Lessened, Low, Wasted, in this section).

Endurance; Energy—Vital Energy—(See Dynamic, Electric, Energy).

Excess of Vitality—A Morbid or Plus Condition—The ☉ □ or ☍ ♂, and tending to increased excitability and nervousness. (See "Augmented" in this section).

Excesses—Loss of Vitality By—(See Amorous; "Health Injured" under Men; "Health Suffers" under Opposite Sex; "Easily Weakened" in this section).

Fair Vitality—(See "Medium" in this section).

Females—(See "Vitality In" under Females; "Low", "Not Very Strong", in this section).

Force—Plenty of Vital Force—(See "Force" under Vital).

Good Vitality—Abundance—Considerable—Plenty—Fullness of—Much Vitality—Strong Vitality—The ☉ in the Asc., M.C., or 7th H. at B., and hyleg; the ☉ ⚹ or △ ♄ at B., good tenacity of life; the ☉ ☌ and good asp. ♂ at B.; the ☉ in a fiery sign, and espec. in ♈ or ♌; the ☉ in airy signs, but of more refined and mental nature than physical; the ☉ ☌ ♃ or ♀ in the Asc. at sunrise; the ☉ or ♂ in the Asc., and well-asp.; the ☉ rising in ♌ and not affl.; the ☉ ☌ or good asp. ♃; the ☉ in ♉ or ♏ in the Asc. at sunrise and not affl.; the ☉ ⚹ or △ ♃ at B., and the ☉ hyleg; the ☉ well-asp. in ♐ if the hyleg is not affl.; the ☉ or ☽ in good asp. ♂ at B., and by dir.; the ☉ strong by sign at B.; the ☉ well-asp. by ♂, ☽, or the benefics at B., and the ☉ essentially dignified, as exalted or elevated, in a male horoscope, and the ☽ similarly placed in a female nativity; the ☉ in ♈, plenty of vital force; the ☉ in ♌, and with ♈ on the Asc.; the ☉ above the horizon at B. gives the greatest vital power, and when in the 1st, 10th, or 7th houses, and the constitution and the vital powers are at their full when the ☉ at B. is in one of these places, a hylegiacal place, and the ☉ hyleg; the ☽ ⚹ or △ ♂ at B., and by dir.; the ☽ to the good asps. the ☉, ♃, ♂ or ♀ by dir.; the Pr. ☽ ⚹ or △ ♂ if ♂ is well-asp. at B.; the ☽ hyleg in ♉, ♒, ♌, ♎, or ♐ with females; ♃ in ♌, rising and well-asp., abundance of vitality; ♃ ascending at B., and in good asp. the ☉ and ☽; ♃ and ♀ both rising, and in good asp. the ☉ and ☽; ♂ ⚹ △ the ☉ or ☽; ♂ ☌ ☉; ♂ in good asp. the ☉ at B., the spark of vitality is not easily put out; ♈, ♉, ♌, ♏, or ♐ on the Asc.; the 3rd face of ♐ on the Asc.; the 3° ♑ on the Asc.; the 6th face of ♒ on the Asc. (For additional influences along this line see "Good" under Constitution, Health, Recuperation, Resistance, Stamina, Tone; Endurance, Hyleg, Immunity, Invigoration; "Long Life" under Life; Resources, Robust, Ruddy; "Little Sickness" under Sickness; "Increased" under Strength; "Body" under Strong; Vigor, etc.).

Hyleg; Immunity; Impaired;

Increased—The Vitality Increased—Benefitted—Augmented—Strengthened—The Health Improved—The Constitution Strengthened—The ☉ or ♂ in the 1st H., and well-asp.; the ☉ well-asp. in any sign; the ☉ rising in ♒; the ☉ rising and above the horizon in any sign; the ☉ ⚹ or △ ☽; the ☉ ☌ or good asp. ♂; the ☉ and ☽ to the good asps. ♂ by dir.; the ☉ rising in ♏; the ☉, ☽, and planets above the horizon; the ☉ ☌ and good asp. ♃; ☉ ⚹ or △ ♆, benefits the vitality and constitution psychically; good asps. to the ☉ in a male horo., and good asps. to the ☽ in a female horo.; ♃ in the Asc. increases the vitality and gives bulk to the body; ♂ ☌ and good asp. the ☉; ♂ in the 6th H., and well-asp.; ♂ Promittor to the good asps. the ☉ or ☽ by dir.; ♂ in good asp. the Asc., the system is invigorated; ♂ ☌ and good asp. ♃; the good asps. of ♃ and ♀ to the ☽; any asp. of the benefics, good or bad, to the hyleg at B. tend to strengthen the constitution rather than to weaken, but the good asps. are better. (See "Augmented", "Good", in this section; "Periods of Good Health" under Health; "Augmented", "Force", "Full", under Vital).

Infancy—Vitality Low In—(See "Vitality" under Infancy).

Invalids; Invigorated—(See Invigorated, Vigor).

Lack of Vitality—The ☉ ☌, □, ☍ ♄ at B.; ☉ ☌ ♄ in the 6th H.; ☉ □, ☍ ☽ at B.; ☉ in a weak sign and affl. by ♄; ♅ in ♑ or ♒ on the Asc.; ♄ affl. in the Asc. in a weak sign; ♄ the afflictor in disease and ♄ affl. the ☉, ☽, Asc. or hyleg at B.; ♃ □, ☍ ♄.; ruler of the Asc. in the 8th H. in a weak sign and afflicted. (See "Lessened", "Low", in this section; "Depletion", "Lowered", under Vital).

Large Body—Large and Strong—(See "Body" under Large, Strong).

Lessened—The Vitality Lessened—Lowered—Vitality Sapped—Wasted—Weakened—Impaired—Arrested—The ☉ in the 6th or 12th H., in a weak sign and affl.; the ☉ in the 6th H. ill-dig. and affl. by ♄ or ♂ at B.; the ☉ setting and below the horizon; the ☉, ☽ and many planets below the horizon at B.; the ☉ or ☽ hyleg, and to the ☌ or ill-asp. ♄ or ♂ by dir.; the ☽ affl. in 6th H., the vital forces depleted; the ☽ affl. in ♏, and hyleg with females; the ☽ to the ☌ or ill-asp. ♆ or ♄ by dir.; ♆, ♅, or ♄ in ♊, and affl. the ☉ or ☽; ♄ in 6th H. at B., and ☌ or ill-asp. the ☉ or ☽; ♄ ☌, P, □ or ☍ ☉; a ♄ disease, and ♄ affl. the ☉, ☽, Asc., or hyleg at B., and by dir.; a weak sign on the Asc. at B., and a malefic in the rising sign; ♀ ♏, ☌ ☽ or ♂, and thru sex excesses or abuses. (See Debauched, Depraved, Dissipation, Drink; "Wasted" under Energies; "Bad Habits" under Habits; Majority; "Health

Injured" under Men; "Health Suffers" under Opposite Sex; Excesses, Lack Of, Low, Wasted, Weakened, in this section).

Life Force—(1) Overabundance of—♈ on the Asc., and ♂ in ♈ in the Asc.; ♌ on the Asc. (See "Life Force" under Life; "Force" under Vital; Augmented, Excess, Superabundance, in this section). (2) Impeded and Obstructed—(See "Inhibition", "Obstructed", under Vital; Lessened, Low, Weakened, in this section).

Loss of Vitality—And Early Death From—(See "Early Death" under Early; "Easily Weakened", "Low", "Wasted", in this section).

Low Vitality—Weak Vitality—Poor Vitality—Vitality Bad—Weak Constitution—The Vitality Reduced—The ☉ or ☽ in the 6th H. in weak signs, and affl. by malefics; the ☉ in ♋, or ♋ on the Asc.; the ♋ person as a rule has the least vitality of any person; ♋, ♑, or ♓, the signs of low vitality, on the Asc.; the ☉ in ♑ and affl.; the ☉ affl. in the 1st, 4th, 6th, 8th or 12th houses; the ☉ in ♋ on the Nadir, and affl.; the ☉ ☌ ☽ if closer than three degrees; the ☉ affl. by ♄; the ☉ or ☽ to the ☌ or ill-asp. ♄ by dir.; the Pr. ☉ or ☽ to the ☌ or ill-asp. ♄ by dir.; the ☉ affl. in a sign of low vitality; the ☉ affl. in ♓, the vital powers are weak; the ☉ □, ☍ ☽, and at same time the hyleg affl. by malefics, and a weak sign on Asc.; the ☽ in bad asp. the ☉; the ☽ affl. in ♏; ☽ in 6th or 12th H., and affl. by malefics; the Pr. ☽ to the ☌ or ill-asps. ♆ if ♆ affl. at B.; the ☽ ♑, partile the Asc., never strong; the ☽ affl. in ♑; the ☽ hyleg in ♑ with females; ♄ ☌ or ill-asp. the ☉ or ☽; ♄ culminating and affl. the ☉ or ☽; ♄ by tr. in ☌ or bad asp. the ☉, ☽, ♃ or ♀; ♄ by dir. affl. the ☉, ☽, Asc. or hyleg; ♄ in the 6th H. and conjoined with the ☉; ♄ in evil asp. the ☉ from common signs; ♄ or ♂ affl. the ☉, ☽, or Asc. by body or asp.; ♄ in the 10th H., affl. the hyleg, and ♄ also rendered more evil by afflictions from ♅ and ♂; ♀ affl. in ♏; a weak sign on the Asc., and a malefic in the rising sign; bodies near the cusps of angles, and espec. in infancy; ♋ on the Asc. tends to give the least vitality unless containing the ☉ and benefics, and free from the affliction of malefics. (See Adynamia, Asthenia, Atonic; "Death" under Childhood, Children, Infancy, Middle Life, Youth; Consumptions, Debility; "Contracts Disease Easily" under Disease; "Early Death" under Early; Emaciation, Feeble; "Bad Health" under Health; "Offensive" under Humours; "Ill-Health All Thru Life" under Ill-Health; Infirm, Invalids; "Short Life" under Life; "Low" under Recuperation, Resistance, Stamina; Sickly; "Much Sickness" under Sickness; "Weakened" under Strength; "Lack Of" under Tone; Vitiated, Wasting; "Weak Body" under Weak).

Lowered Vitality—(See Lessened, Low, Wasted, Weakened, in this section; "Lowered" under Vital).

Lowest Vitality—The Vital Powers are at their lowest when the ☉ is on cusp the 4th H. at B., or in this house; the ☉ affl. in ♑, or with ♋, ♑, or ♓ on the Asc. (See "Low" in this section).

Males Vigorous—(See "Good Health" under Males; "Good", "Not Very Strong", in this section).

Mars Influence—(See Mars).

Medium Vitality—Vitality Fair—Moderately Vital—Fairly Strong—The Moderately Vital Signs are ♉, ♊, ♍, ♒ and ♏, and these signs on the Asc. at B. usually bring the native to mature life. The 3° ♑ on the Asc. is the strongest of the ♑ degrees, and usually gives fair vitality and recuperative powers. The ☽ hyleg in ♊, ♒, or ♓ gives fair vitality, and espec. with females. Earthy signs on the Asc. are classed as of medium vitality; the fiery signs the strongest, and the watery signs the weakest, and espec. ♋ and ♓, but ♏ on the Asc. is strongly vital. (See "Tolerably Healthy" under Health).

Mental Vitality—With the ♊ sign, the sign of ☿, the vitality is more mental than physical. (See Gemini).

Morbid Vitality—The ☉ and ♄ in the 6th H. at B. tend to give a lowered and morbid vitality all thru life, much sickness, and with slow powers of recuperation. (See Morbid; Lessened, Loss Of, Low, in this section).

Nerve Force—(See "Nerve Force" under Force; "Fluid", "Force", under Vital).

Not Very Strong—The Vitality Not Very Strong—The ☉ affl. in signs of low vitality with males; the ☽ affl. in ♈ or ♏ with females. (See Females, Low, Males, Medium, in this section).

Over-Abundance—Of Vitality and Life Force—(See "Superabundance" in this section, and under Vital).

Periods—Of Increased Vitality, and of Lowered Vitality—(See "Improved", "Loss of Health", "Periods of Bad Health", "Periods of Good Health", under Health).

Physical Vitality—(See "Mental" in this section).

Plenty of Vitality—(See Good, Superabundance, in this section; "Force" under Vital).

Poor Vitality—(See Low, Weakened, in this section).

Powers—The Vital Powers—Read carefully all the paragraphs under "Vital", and in this section).

Prodigal Of—(See "Wasted" in this section).

Recovery; Recuperation; Reduced—The Vitality Reduced—The ☉ or ♄ in the 6th H. (See Low, Lessened, Wasted, in this section; "Depletion" under Vital).

Resistance; Restored—The ☉ restores vitality by day. (See Day).

Revitalization; Robust, Sapped—(See "Depletion", "Lessened", "Reduced", "Wasted", in this section).

Signs—The Vital Signs—(See "Signs" under Vital; "Medium" in this section).

Stamina; Sthenic; Strength;

Strengthened Vitality—(See "Increased" in this section).

Strong; Strong Vitality—(See "Good" in this section; "Body" under Strong).

Sun Influence—(See Sun).

Superabundance—Of Vitality—The ☉ ☌ ♂ in ♈, and with ♈ on the Asc., but tends to burn up the body faster, and danger of breakdown earlier in life; ☉ ☌, P, ⚹, △ ♂; ♌ on the Asc.

System Invigorated — (See Invigorated, Vigor).

Tone; Undermined Vitality — (See "Wasted" in this section; Debauched, Dissipation, Drink, Habits; "Passional Excesses" under Passion).

Vigorous Body—(See Robust; "Strong Body" under Strong; Vigor; "Good Vitality" in this section).

Vital Fluid—(See "Fluid" under Vital).

Vital Force—(See "Force" under Vital).

Vital Stamina—(See Stamina).

Vitality Low—(See "Low" in this section).

Vitiated; Wasted Vitality — Waste of the Vital Forces—The ☉ or ☽ in weak signs at B., and affl.; the ☽ to the ill-asps. ♆ by dir., prodigal of the vitality; the ☉ or ☽ affl. in the 5th, 6th, or 12th H., the vitality wasted thru dissipation; ♂ affl. in ♌ or the 5th H., waste of thru prodigality, and with the opposite sex; ♂ ☌ ♀ in ♏; the 1st decan. of ♌ on the Asc. (See Amorous, Conduct, Debauched, Dissipation, Drink; "Wasted" under Energy; Excesses, Gluttony, Habits, Narcotics; "Passional Excesses" under Passion; Prodigal; "Easily Weakened", "Lessened", in this section).

Weak Vitality — (See "Low" in this section).

Weakened Vitality—The ☉ affl. by the ☽, ♄, and malefics at B.; the ☉ or ♄ in the 6th H., and tend to give a weakened vitality all thru life; the ☽ affl. in ♑ lowers the vital tonicity thru worry and mental depression; the evil asps. between the ☉ and ☽ at B., and by dir. act as a disturbing and retarding agent upon the functions and vital forces; ♄ ☌, P., □, or ☍ ☉. (See Depletion, Easily Weakened, Lessened, Low, Wasted, in this section; "Weakened" under Strength).

VITAMINES — (See "Vitamines" under Food).

VITIATED—In Mind and Body—♄ or ☋ in the Asc., and ♑ on the Asc.

Atmosphere — The Atmosphere Vitiated — (See "Corrupt Air" under Air; Cholera, Epidemics, Pestilence).

VITREOUS HUMOR — (See "Danger", "Muscae", "Vitreous", under Eyes).

VITUPERATIVE — (See Petulant, Sarcasm, Scolding; "Nasty Temper" under Temper; Virgo).

VIVACITY — Vivacious — Full of Life and Spirits—Lively—Active—(See Active, Buoyant; "Abundance" under Energy; "Full" under Expression; Lively, Quick, etc.).

VIVISECTIONISTS — Favored by Surgeons who have ♅ or ♂ in ♏ or ♓ at B., and these planets affl. each other; ☿ affl. by ♂, and with no good asps. from ♃ or ♀. (See Surgeons).

VOCAL ORGANS — Vocal Cords — The Voice—Larynx—Speech, etc.—This subject is considered in the Article on Voice. (See Voice. Also see Larynx, Speech).

VOCATION—The Business—The Occupation—The Employment—The Vocation—The Profession—Pursuits, etc.— The Vocation is ruled by the 10th H., and the Planets, or Planet in, or the ruler of this House, etc., determine the natural vocation, and where the native fits into the scheme of life. The indications of the 10th H. at B. show the natural Calling, and which, if the native follows it up, will tend to bring him success, happiness, and usefulness in life. For this reason every young person should have his, or her, horoscope cast early in life, to know what they are fitted for, and what the Higher Powers have ordained for them, so that they will not waste many years drifting, and trying to get into their right calling, after, perhaps, many failures and loss of time, effort and money. Many of the various Vocations are listed throughout this book, and the planetary influences which tend to bring success in them. See such subjects as Chemists, Healers, Nurses, Surgeons. Look in the alphabetical arrangement for the Vocation you have in mind. This subject is also considered in the Articles on Business, Employment, Occupation.

Accidents — In the Vocation — (See "Accidents" under Employment; Machinery, Pursuits).

Changes In—Makes Many Changes In Vocation — (See Changes, Instability, Restless, Unstable, Vacillating).

Death In — (See "Death" under Employment, Explosions, Machinery, Mines, Railroads).

Extraordinary Pursuits—Ruled by ♅; born under the strong influence of ♅, and with ♅ in the 10th H. (See Ideas; "Unusual" under Mental; Occult, Science, etc.).

Liquid Pursuits—Ruled and indicated by the ☽; many planets in watery signs at B., and espec. in the 10th H., or a watery sign upon the Asc.; the ♓ influence strong at B. (See "Pursuits" under Liquids).

Low Business — Follows Some Low Business—(See Crime, Gambling, Harlots, Highwaymen; "Low Business" under Low; Pettifogging, Robbers, Saloons, Taverns, Thieves, etc.).

Strange Diseases In — ♅ affl. in the 6th H. (See Occupation).

VOICE—The Voice—The Vocal Cords— The Larynx—Speech—The Vocal Organs, etc.—The Vocal Organs are ruled by ☿ and the ♉ sign. The larynx, as a whole, is ruled by ♉. The Vocal Cords are ruled by ☿, and ☿ rules the air which stirs the vocal cords into action. The vocal organs are also strongly ruled and influenced by the ♏ sign, as ♉ and ♏ are supplemental signs, and form a unit. The subjects concerning the Voice and Vocal Organs are also largely considered under Larynx, Speech, Tongue, and if the subject you have in mind is not listed here, look for it under these headings. The 2nd H., the house affiliated with ♉, also rules and influences the vocal organs, cords, voice, etc. Also influences in the 3rd H., the house of ☿, tend to influence and modify the speech and tones of the voice. See the following subjects in the alphabetical arrangement when not considered here—

Abused—The Voice Abused—(See "Injudicious" in this section).

Affections Of—(See "Disorders", and the various paragraphs in this section).

Aphasia—(See "Aphasia", "Loss of Speech" under Speech).

Aphonia—Loss of Voice—Whispering Voice—♅ or ☿ affl. in ♉; Subs at AT and LCP. (See "Hoarseness" under Larynx; Removal).

Articulation; Bass Voice—(See "Deep" in this section).

Beautiful Voice—(See "Melodious" in this section).

Breathing; Change of Voice—In Males At Puberty—(See Larynx, Puberty).

Clear Voice—The ☉ strong at B.; the ☉ well-asp. in ♉.

Coarse Voice — Rough — Strong — Coarse and Masculine Voice In Women — Contralto Voice — Afflictions in ♏, and due to debauchery or sex excesses; ♌ gives, and ♌ on the Asc.; ♑ on the Asc. The removal of any part of the sex organs in women tends to make the voice more masculine, and in men, more effeminate. (See Coarse, Deviations, Effeminate; "Hoarseness" under Larynx; "Deep" in this section).

Contralto Voice — (See Coarse, Deep, in this section).

Control — Tone and Voice Control — Largely influenced and controlled by the 16° of ♉ and ♏. (See "Fluency" under Speech; "Control" under Throat).

Cords — The Vocal Cords — Are ruled by the ♉ sign, and disorders of the Cords are caused by afflictions in ♉, and also by Subs at LCP (6C). (See Larynx; the various paragraphs in this section).

Cultivated Voice — Cultured — Refined — Pleasant — Given by ♒. (See Melodious, Musical, in this section).

Deep Voice — Bass Voice — ♄ in ♈ or ♉; ♏ influence, and espec. in women; ♌ on the Asc. tends to give a deep and strong voice. (See "Coarse" in this section).

Diaphragm; Disorders — Vocal Disorders—Afflictions in ♉; the ☽ hyleg in ♉ with females; ♅ affl. in ♉; ☿ affl. in ♉; afflictions to ☿; ☿ affl. in the 12th H. Cases—See Fig. 3F, 3G, in the book, "Astro-Diagnosis", by the Heindels. (See "Disorders" under Speech; the various paragraphs in this section).

Dumbness—Mutes—(See Dumb; "Deaf and Dumb" under Hearing; Mutes).

Effeminate Voice—Tenor Voice—(See Effeminate).

Expression—Good Voice Expression—☿ well-placed in a sign of voice. (See Larynx; "Signs" in this section).

Females—Masculine, or Coarse Voice In—(See "Coarse" in this section).

Feminine Voice—In Males—(See Effeminate).

Fluency In Speaking—(See "Fluency" under Speech).

Functions — Functional Disability of the Vocal Cords—☿ in a weak sign and affl., and espec. affl. by ♄.

Gifted Vocally — ♀ or ☿ in ♉, or the 2nd H., and free from affl., or if a sign of voice be on the cusp of the 2nd, as ♊, ♎, or ♒, then the native tends to be eloquent, a great singer, or endowed with some special vocal gift. (See "Eloquent", "Fluency", under Speech).

Great Voice—Good Orator—Eloquent —☿ ascending in ♍ and well-asp.; ☿ in ♊ or ♍; ☿ Sig. in ♍, a linguist; ☿ Sig. in ♊, a good orator; ☿ in the Asc., and well-dig.; a sign of voice on the Asc.; ♀ Sig. in ♍, eloquent. (See "Gifted", "Strong", and other paragraphs in this section).

Hears Voices—(See Clairaudience).

Hoarseness — (See Hoarseness; "Hoarseness" under Larynx).

Inarticulate; Injudicious Use—Of the Voice In Speaking or Singing—Danger of Injury to the Voice — ☿ in ♉, and affl. by malefics, and loud singing or speaking should be avoided. (See "Singers" under Music).

Larynx—Afflictions of—(See Larynx).

Linguist — (See "Gifted", "Great Voice", in this section; "Eloquent", "Fluency", under Speech).

Loss of Voice—(See "Aphonia" in this section; Ablation, Hoarseness, Removal, Remote; "Loss of Speech" under Speech).

Loud Speaking — Should Be Avoided —(See "Injudicious" in this section).

Masculine Voice In Women—(See Effeminate; "Coarse" in this section).

Melodious Voice—Beautiful Voice—A Sweet Voice—Born under ♀; ♀ in the Asc.; ♀ in ♉ in the Asc., and ☌ ☿; ♉ influence, and with ♉ on the Asc. (See "Musical" in this section; "Music" under Singers).

Men — Effeminate Voice In — Tenor Voice — Deep Voice — (See Effeminate; "Deep" in this section).

Musical Voice—♀ in the Asc. near the horizon; ♀ well-asp. in ♑. The ♍ sign gives an unmusical voice. (See Melodious" in this section; "Singers" under Music).

Mutes—(See Dumb; "Deaf and Dumb" under Hearing; Mutes).

Orator — A Good Orator — (See Fluency, Gifted, Great Voice, in this section).

Organic Afflictions — Of the Vocal Cords—The ♉ or ♏ signs afflicted by malefics at B., or by tr., dir., or progression; the ☉ affl. in ♉ or ♏, as the ☉ is organic. (See Organic, Structural).

Over-Straining—Of the Vocal Cords—(See "Injudicious" in this section).

Paralysis—Of the Vocal Cords—♅ or ♄ affl. in ♉.

Phonation Difficult — (See "Hoarseness" under Larynx; "Aphonia" in this section).

Puberty—Voice Changes At Puberty—(See Larynx, Puberty).

Refined Voice — (See "Cultivated" in this section).

Resonant Voice—♏ influence.

Ringing and Sharp Voice — ♈ infl; ♈ on the Asc.

Rough Voice—♑ on the Asc. tends to a weak voice, and with a kind of a whistling roughness. (See "Coarse" in this section; Hoarseness; "Hoarseness" under Larynx).

Sharp and Ringing—Incisive Voice—♈ influence.

Shrill Voice — Shrill and Small — ♍ produces; ♍ on the Asc.

Signs of Voice—Speaking Signs—♊, ♍, ♎, ♒, and the first half of ♐.

Singing—(See "Speech" under Breath; "Singers" under Music; "Gifted", "Melodious", "Musical", in this section).

Slow of Voice—Slow of Speech—Produced by the ☉ influence; in Hor'y Q. the ☉ as Sig.; ♄ in ♉; born under ♋, as ♋ is a mute sign, and slow of voice.

Small Voice—(See "Shrill" in this section).

Soprano Voice — High Voice — Born under ♀; the ☉, ☽, or ☿ well-aspected in ♉, and not afflicted by ♄; ♉ or ♎ on the Asc., and free from ♄ affliction, as ♄ tends to hamper, restrict, bind, and limit the vocal powers.

Sound—Tone Control—(See "Control", "Cords", in this section).

Speaking — Avoid Loud Speaking — (See "Injudicious" in this section; "Speaking" under Speech).

Speech—(See the various paragraphs under Speech).

Speechless—Mute—Cannot Talk—Refuses to Talk—(See "Deaf and Dumb" under Hearing; Mute; "Speechless" under Speech).

Stammering—(See Speech).

Straining the Voice — (See "Injudicious" in this section).

Strong Voice — Great Voice — Strong Vocal Organs — The ☉ in ♉ and not afflicted. (See Coarse, Deep, Great, Orator, in this section).

Stuttering—(See Speech).

Sways the Masses — (See Fluency; "Power to Sway" under Speech).

Sweet Voice—(See Gifted, Melodious, Musical, in this section).

Talk—Cannot Talk—Refuses to Talk—Mute—Dumb, etc. (See these subjects under Speech).

Tenor Voice—(See Effeminate, Testes).

Throat — Disorders of, and Affecting the Voice—(See the various paragraphs under Throat).

Tone Control—(See "Control" in this section).

Tongue — Impediments In — (See Tongue).

Unmusical Voice — (See "Musical" in this section).

Vocal Cords — Disorders of — (See Cords, Functions, Organic, Straining, and the Introduction to this section; Larynx).

Voice — (See the various paragraphs in this section).

Weak Voice—♋ gives; ♋ on the Asc.; ♑ on Asc. (See "Aphonia", "Rough", in this section; "Hoarseness" under Speech).

Weakness Of — Loss of Voice — Dysphonia — (See "Hoarseness" under Larynx; "Paralysis", "Speechless", in this section).

Whispering Voice — (See "Aphonia" in this section).

Whistling Sound — (See "Rough" in this section).

Women—Masculine Voice In—Coarse Voice In — (See Coarse, Deep, in this section; Deviations, Effeminate).

VOID—Void of—Devoid of—

Course—Planets Void of Course—A Planet is void of course when it forms no aspect to other planets during the remainder of its course thru the sign in which it is posited. This is considered a debility, and such a planet when the afflictor in the disease tends to have less effect upon the disease for the time, and the disease is more or less at a standstill, and lingers along, as it takes the aspects of the planets to the afflicting planet, for good or ill, to cause the disease to get better, worse, relapse, or resolve itself. (See Aspects, Course, Direct, Planets, Retrograde, Stationary).

Void Degrees — Of the Zodiac — The Asc., or its lord, in any of these degrees at B. tend to render the native empty and void of knowledge. The Void Degrees are ♈ 24°, 30°; ♉ 12°, 30°; ♊ 16°, 30°; ♋ 18°, 30°; ♌ 25°; ♍ 10°, 17°; ♎ 30°; ♏ 14°, 29°; ♐ 0°; ♑ 25°; ♒ 25°; ♓ 25°. (See Knowledge; "Void Of" under Learning; "Shallow" under Mentality).

Void Of—There are many things every individual is void of, or has a lack of, and such subjects would be too numerous to list here. Look in the alphabetical arrangement for the subject you have in mind. In the Articles on "Lack Of", "Loss Of", you will find many subjects listed along this line. Also see "Void Of" under Energy, Learning, Reason, Stamina. Also see such subjects as Aversions, Collapse, Depletion, Deviations, Diminished; "Fails In" under Examinations; Exhaustion, Idiocy, Irrational; "Free From" under Passion; "Shows No Pity" under Pity; Pretender; "Weak" under Understanding, etc.

VOLATILIZATION — (See "Operations" under Nature; Nitrogen, Sublimation, Vapor).

VOLCANOES—Volcanic Eruptions—Coincident with an eclipse of the ☉ in a watery sign; coincident with the appearance of Comets, and especially of Halley's Comet; due to major planets in perihelion. (See "Epidemics" under Cholera; "Earthquakes" under Earth).

VOLITION — The Will to Act—Willing—Ruled by ☿.

Loss of Volition—Indiscretions From —Denoted by ♐; ♆ affl. in ♐. (See "Mind" under Chaotic; Hypnotism, Influenced, Involuntary, Negative Nature (see Negative); Obsessions, Passive; "Negative Psychism" under Psychic; Self-Control, Spirit Controls, Suggestion, Voluntary; "Weak Will" under Will).

VOLUNTARY — Under the Control of the Will—The Voluntary Nervous System is under the rule of ☿.

Clonic Spasm — Of the Voluntary Muscles—(See "Paramyoclonus Multiplex", "Voluntary", under Muscles).

Diseased Voluntary Power — ♄ ☌ or ill-asp. the ☉. (See Volition).

Excessive Voluntary Power — Given by ♂, and is a ♂ disorder; the ☉ to the ☌ or ill-asp. ♂ by dir. It is relieved by the ♄ remedy, Antimony, and by the application of cold to the head.

Muscles — (See "Clonic" in this section).

Will—(See "Free Will" under Will).

VOLUPTUOUS—(See Amorous, Beautiful; "Voluptuous" under Face; "Sensuous" under Sensuality).

VOMITING—Antiperistalsis—Nausea—Sickness At the Stomach—

Billous Vomiting — ♂ affl. in ♋. (See Nausea).

Blood—Vomiting of—Haematemesis—The ☽ affl. in ♑; ♂ affl. in ♋, and also affl. the hyleg; ♂ ori. at B., and affl. the hyleg. (See "Ulcer" under Gastric; "Vicarious" under Menses).

Desire to Vomit—(See Nausea).

Diet — Vomiting from Wrong Diet — (See "Ailments" under Diet).

Emetics — Agents Producing Vomiting—(See Antiperistalsis, Emetic, Medicines, Ruminant).

Expulsion—(See Expulsion).

Faecal Vomiting — (See Faeces, Ileac Passion).

Haematemesis—(See "Blood" in this section).

Nausea — A Desire to Vomit — (See Nausea).

Periodic Vomiting — The ☽ affl. in ♋; the ☽ in ♋ and affl. by ♄; evil asps. of the ☽ to ♋ if the ☽ was in ♋ at B.; Subs at SP (7D), and at PP.

Pylorus Constricted—Causing Vomiting—(See "Pylorus" under Stomach).

Ruminant Signs — ♈, ♉, ♑. To give medicine when the ☽ is passing thru one of these signs tends to produce nausea or vomiting. (See Ruminant).

Stomach — (See "Peristalsis" under Stomach).

VORACIOUS—Voracity—Having An Insatiable Appetite—(See Appetite, Eating, Epicurean, Feasting, Food, Gluttony).

VOYAGES—Long Journeys by Water—Sea Travel—Are ruled by the 9th House, the house of Foreign Travel, or Foreign Residence. Are also ruled by the ☽. Long Voyages are also ruled and influenced by ♐, the 9th sign affiliated with the 9th H., and also by ♃, the ruler of this sign. The subject of Voyages is partly considered under such subjects as Journeys, Ships, Shipwreck, Travel, etc. The following subjects also have to do

with Voyages, which see in the alphabetical arrangement when not considered here—

Abroad — Avoid Journeys Abroad — (See Abroad).

Accidents—Accidents In Foreign Travel — (See "Accidents" under Abroad).

Advisability — Of Voyages — Benefic planets in the 9th H., and malefics in the 4th H. at B., make it advisable to go Abroad, take voyages, and leave the Native Land. (See Abroad; "Long Journeys" under Journeys; "Native Land" under Native; "Home or Abroad" under Travel).

Avoid Voyages—When there are malefics in the 9th H. at B., or the ruler of the 9th H. a malefic, and with no benefics in the 9th H. (See "Avoid" under Abroad; "Abroad" under Journeys; the various paragraphs under Travel).

Bad Time — For Voyages — (See "Avoid" under Journeys; "Bad Time" under Travel).

Bites, Kicks, or Fevers—On Journeys or Voyages—Fevers on Journeys—Malefics in the 3rd or 9th H., in fire signs, and affl. the ☉ or ☽. (See Bites).

Burns — On Journeys or Voyages — (See "Journeys" under Burns).

Calamities — At Sea — (See "Calamities" under Sea; Ships, Shipwreck).

Cuts — Stabs — On Voyages — (See "Travel" under Cuts).

Dampness—Suffers From on Voyages or Journeys — Malefics in the 3rd or 9th H., in watery signs, and affl. the ☉ or ☽. (See Moisture).

Danger On Voyages—Dangerous Voyages—Danger In Navigation—The ☉ to the ☌ ♄ by dir.; ☽ in the 9th H. at B., and to the ☌ or ill-asp. ♅ by dir.; ☽ affl. in the 8th H.; ♆, ♅, ♄, or ♂ in the 9th H., and affl.; ♄ affl. in ♏; ♄ or ♂ affl. in the 9th H., in watery signs; malefics in the 9th H., and affl. the ☉ or ☽; the transit of malefics thru the 9th H., if in the 9th at B., or affl. the lord of the 9th; the Asc. by dir. to the evil asps. the ☽ at B. (See Drowning, Journeys; "Dangers" under Navigation, Ocean; "Death At Sea" under Sea; Ships, Shipwreck; Travel; "Peril" under Waters; "Bad Time" in this section).

Death At Sea — (See Abroad, Drowning, Journeys; "Death" under Sea; Ships, Shipwreck, Travel, Water, etc.).

Directions — (See "Disposes To" in this section).

Disposes To Voyages—A Voyage Indicated—Primary Directions falling due in a watery sign; the ☉, ☽, or ♂ cadent, occidental, and in mutable signs at B. Many planets in fixed signs, or fixed signs on angles, do not dispose to travel or voyages. The passage of the ☽ or a benefic thru the 9th H. disposes to. (See "Good Time" in this section).

Drowning; Events — (See "Nature of Events" under Events).

Falls — On Voyages — (See "Travel" under Falls).

Famine On—(See Famine).

Fatal Voyages—(See "Bad Time", "Danger", "Death", in this section).

Fever—On a Voyage or Journey—(See "Bites" in this section).

Fire—On a Voyage—(See "Ships" under Fire).

Fixed Signs—(See "Disposes To" in this section).

Foreign Lands—Foreign Travel—(See "Advisability", "Avoid", in this section; Abroad).

Fortunate—Upon the Seas—(See "Fortunate" under Seas).

Foundering—(See Ships, Shipwreck).

Good Time—For Sea Voyage—The ☉ to the good asps. the 9th H. if the cusp of the 9th be ♋, ♏ or ♓, and the 9th be not affl. by malefics; the ☉ to the good asps. ♂, and the ☉ or ♂ ruler of the 9th; the ☽ to the good asps. the ☉, and espec. if the direction fall in the 9th H. and in a watery sign; the ☽ to the good asps. the Asc. by dir. if the ☽ was well-asp. at B.; the ☽ in the 9th H., and to the good asps. ♅ by dir.; the ☽ to the ☌ ☿ by dir., and ☿ in the 9th H. in ♋, or if the ☽ or ☿ be in the 3rd or 9th H. at B.; when the ☽, ♂, or ☿ are in the 9th H. at B. a voyage is usually made when the ☽, or planet, by primary dir. in mundo comes to the cusp of the 9th H.; when ♃ or ♀ are in the Asc., M.C., 2nd, or 9th houses, and malefics not in angles, a good time; M.C. to the ☌ ☽ if the ☽ rule the 9th H. at B.; M.C. to the good asps. the ☽; M.C. to the cusp the 9th, or to the good asps. ruler of the 9th H. (See "Good Times" under Journeys).

High Places—Falls From During Travel or Voyages—(See "Death" under Heights).

Indicated—A Voyage Indicated—(See "Disposes To" in this section).

Injury on Voyages—Malefics in the 9th H., and affl. the ☉ or ☽. (See Ships, Shipwreck; "Accidents", "Hurts", under Travel).

Journeys—Long Journeys—(See Abroad, Journeys; the various paragraphs in this section).

Kicks—On Voyages—(See "Bites" in this section; Kicks).

Lightning—Danger By On Voyages—(See "Voyages" under Lightning).

Long Journeys—(See Journeys, Ships, Travel; the various paragraphs in this section).

Maritime Affairs—(See Maritime, Navigation, Sailors, Sea; "Shipping" under Ships, Voyages, etc.).

Misfortunes At Sea—(See "Misfortunes" under Sea).

Moisture—Suffers From In Travel—(See "Dampness" in this section).

Nations—Where to Go On Voyages—(See Location, Nations, Native Land, Residence, Travel).

Native Land—Should Leave—Should Remain—(See Native Land).

Navigation; Ocean; Piracy;

Poisoning—During Travel—(See "Travel" under Poison).

Privations—(See Famine; "Privations" under Seas; "Food" under Travel).

Sailors; Sea Sickness—(See "Sickness" in this section).

Ships; Shipwreck; Sickness—On Voyages—Sea Sickness—☽ affl. in 8th H.; ♄ Sig. in the 9th H.; ♄ in 8th H. in a watery sign, and affl. the hyleg; the ship leaving Port in a ♄ hour, or with ♄ in the Asc., danger of, or some disaster; lord of the 6th in the 9th H., and affl.; malefics in the 9th H., or the tr. of malefics thru the 9th, if in the 9th at B., or affl. the lord of the 9th. (See "Health" under Journeys; "Sickness" under Travel). Seasickness is caused usually by ♄ in ♋, or in cardinal signs, and by the ☉, ☽, and many planets in card. signs; ♋ or card. signs upon angles, as the card. signs all afflict the stomach region. Also malefics in ♉ tend to disturb the organ of coordination.

Storms At Sea—(See "Voyages" under Lightning; Ships, Shipwreck; "Tempests" under Sea; Wind).

Sunstroke—During Travel, or At Sea—Malefics in the 3rd or 9th H., in fiery signs, and affl. the ☉ or ☽; the ☉ in ♌ in the 9th H., and ☌, or ill-asp. ♂ at B., and the ☉ affl. by ♂ by dir.

Tempests—(See "Tempests" under Sea).

Travel—Note the various subjects under Journeys, Maritime, Navigation, Sea, Ships, Travel, etc.).

Trouble by Sea—(See "Troubles" under Sea).

Unfortunate—On the Sea—(See "Unfortunate" under Sea).

Voyage Soon Follows—♆ ☌, or P. the ☉ at a Solar Rev., and the ☉ in a watery sign; the M.C. to the ⚹ or △ ♂. (See "Disposes To" in this section).

Water—Danger On—Danger By—(See Drowning, Sea, Water, etc.).

Where to Go—On Voyages—(See Abroad, Nations, Native Land, Residence).

Wind Storms—At Sea—(See Wind).

VULGAR—A Vulgar and Unrefined Body—(See Rough, Unrefined).

VULNERABLE—The vulnerable spots in the horoscope are the ☉, ☽, Asc. and Hyleg, when affl. by malefics. Also the degree and sign occupied by ♄ at B. denote a weak and vulnerable place, and the part of the body so ruled is always subject to more or less of affliction and weakness, in the ordinary course of life, and espec. when ♄ afflicts this degree by tr. or dir. All the malefics tend to weaken and afflict the part of the body ruled by the sign containing them at B. (See Malefics; "Weak Spots" under Saturn). With the Signs of the Zodiac, the ♋, ♑ and ♓ signs are the weakest and most vulnerable to bodily affliction and disease. (See "Vitality Low" under Vitality; "Weak Body" under Weak). The Nebulous Stars and Clusters are also quite dangerous and vulnerable when with the ☉ or ☽ at B. (See Nebulous).

VULTURES—Fowls—Birds of the Air—Vultures Eat the Body—The Body, or Corpse, may be devoured by beasts and birds if ♅, ♄ and ♂ all three occupy anaretic places, and be in signs similar in form to birds and beasts, and espec. if the benefics give no good asps. to the anaretic places or to the 4th H. (See "Birds of the Air" under Air; "Body Devoured" under Burial; Buzzards).

VULVA—Ruled by ♏.

Abscess Of—Ulceration of—♂ affl. in ♏; ♂ ☌ ♃ or ☽ in ♏; ♂ ☌ ♀ in ♏. (See Abscesses, Vagina). Subluxations of the Lumbar Vertebrae, at PP, tend to disorders of the Vulva, Vagina, and Sex Organs.

W

WADDLING GAIT—(See Gait).

WAKEFULNESS—(See "Cold Feet" under Feet; "Insomnia" under Sleep).

WALK—Gait—Carriage—Tread—Step—Locomotion, etc.—This subject is also considered in the Articles on Action, Gait, Locomotion, Motion, Movement. See these subjects, and also the following subjects in the alphabetical arrangement when not considered here—

Ankles Knock—When Walking—(See Ankles).

Awkward Walk—(See Gait).

Awry Walk—(See "Awry" under Gait).

Bad Gait—(See Gait).

Brisk Walk—(See Brisk; "Energetic" under Gait).

Carriage—Free In—Born under ♃. (See Carriage).

Child—Nine Years of Age Has Never Walked—Case—See "Defective Mentality, No. 670 in 1001 N.N.

Clumsy Walk—(See Clumsiness).

Commanding Walk—(See Commanding; "Majestic" under Gait).

Could Not Walk—Child Could Not Walk Before Six Years of Age—Case—See "Datas", No. 896 in 1001 N.N.

Defective Walk—The ☉ ☌ ♅ or ♄ in ♐; ♄ in the Asc. at B.; caused by ♄ afflictions; ♄ affl. in ♓; ♄ in ♑, □ or ☍ ♆. For Cases of Defective Walk see Figures 14C, 14D, in the book, "Astro-Diagnosis", by the Heindels. (See "Defective" under Gait).

Distorted Walk—(See "Distorted" under Gait).

Dragging Walk—(See "Dragging" under Gait).

Energetic Walk—(See "Energetic" under Gait).

Equilibrium Disturbed—Incoordinated Walk—Pitches Forward In Walking—♄ affl. in ♉; many planets, and malefics in ♉, afflicting the organ of Coordination. (See Balance, Coordination, Equilibrium, Incoordination).

Feet—(See "Club Feet", "Lameness In", and the various paragraphs under Feet; "Feet" under Gait).

Festination—The Peculiar Walk In Paralysis Agitans—♅ or ♄ affl. in ♓; Subs at LPP. (See "Shaking" under Palsy).

Firm Walk—Firm Step—♌ gives, and ♌ on the Asc. at B. (See "Commanding" under Gait).

Forward—Pitches Forward—(See "Equilibrium" in this section).

Free In Carriage—(See "Carriage" in this section).

Gait—(See the various paragraphs under Gait).

Genteel Walk—(See "Genteel" under Gait).

Has Never Walked—Case—(See "Child" in this section).

Heavy Walk—♓ influence; ♓ on the Asc. at B. (See Dull; "Heavy", "Stooping", under Gait; Heavy).

Inability to Walk—Unable to Walk or Stand—♆ in ♊ or ♌, and affl. by ♄, and due to obstruction of the spinal fluids; ♄ affl. in ♌, due to Spinal Sclerosis, and lack of synovial fluid in the vertebrae, and to atrophy of the spine; ♄ affl. in ♐, due to hip trouble; ♄ affl. in ♑, and espec. if ♄ afflict ♆ at the same time; ♄ affl. in ♓, due to chronic foot disorders, or deformed feet. Inability to walk is also due to afflictions to ☿, or a ☿ sign, or planets in a ☿ sign. Case—See Fig. 1 in "Message of the Stars", and Fig. 9D, in "Astro-Diagnosis", books by the Heindels. (See "Club Feet", "Paralysis", under Feet; "Hip Joint Disease" under Hips; "Paraplegia" under Legs; "Child", "Stand", in this section).

Incoordinated Walk—(See "Equilibrium" in this section).

Lameness; Legs—(See Club Feet, Crippled, Lameness, Missing, Paraplegia, under Legs).

Light Walk—Nimble—(See "Energetic" under Gait).

Limping—(See "Limping" under Gait).

Locomotion—Defects of—(See Gait, Locomotion, Motion, Movement; the various paragraphs in this section).

Lower Extremities—Disabilities In—(See "Extremities" under Lower).

Majestic Walk—Proud Walk—♌ gives, and with ♌ on the Asc. (See "Commanding" in this section).

Motion—Movement—(See "Motion" under Gait).

Nervous and Quick Walk—♅ or ☿ affl. by ♂. (See "Energetic" under Gait).

Paralysis of Legs—(See "Paralysis" under Legs, Limbs; "Festination" in this section).

Peculiar Walk—(See "Festination" in this section).

Pedestrianism; Pitches Forward—When Walking—(See "Equilibrium" in this section).

Proud Walk—♌ gives. (See "Majestic" in this section).

Quick Walk—Quick and Nervous Walk — (See "Nervous" in this section).

Rough Walk — (See "Rough" under Gait).

Shuffling Walk — Drags Feet — (See "Dragging" under Gait).

Six Years of Age — Could Not Walk Before this Age — Case — (See "Could Not Walk" in this section).

Smart and Quick Walk—(See "Energetic" under Gait).

Staggering Walk—Tottering—Swaying — (See "Staggering" under Gait; "Equilibrium" in this section).

Stand — Unable to Stand or Walk — See "Deformed", No. 689 in 1001 N.N. (See "Inability" in this section).

Step Firm and Majestic—(See "Firm", "Majestic", in this section).

Stooping Gait — (See "Stooping" under Gait; "Festination" in this section).

Strutting Walk—(See "Strutting" under Gait).

Swaying Walk—(See "Staggering" in this section).

Tottering Walk — (See "Staggering" under Gait; "Equilibrium" in this section).

Treading Walk — (See "Awry" under Gait).

Twisted Walk — (See "Awry" under Gait).

Unable to Walk — Or Stand — (See "Paralysis", "Stand", in this section).

Unsteady Walk — (See "Staggering" in this section).

Waddling Gait—(See "Waddling" under Gait).

Walking—Fondness For—(See Pedestrianism).

WALLS — Of the Stomach Irritable — (See "Irritable" under Stomach).

WAN FACE—(See Pale, Sickly).

WANDERER—Wandering—Roaming—Scattering—Vacillating—

Affections — Wandering Affections — (See "Fickle" under Love Affairs).

Diseases—Wandering Diseases—(See Flying; "Wandering" under Gout; "Whole Body" under Pain; Running, Whole Body).

Gout—Wandering Gout—(See "Wandering" under Gout).

Mind—Wandering Mind—(See "Mental" under Chaotic; "Inability" under Concentration; Confusion; "Dreamy" under Dreams; Vacillating, Vagaries, Weird).

Nature — A Wandering Nature — A Roamer — An Itinerant — (See "No Home" under Home; "Instability" under Mind; "Many Changes" under Residence; Restlessness, Roaming; "Wanderer" under Travel; Vacillating, Vagabond).

WANING FORCES — Brought on by ♄ influence and afflictions. (See Anaemia, Consumptions, Debility, Emaciation, Feeble, Ill-Health, Infirm, Invalids, Sickly; "Much Sickness" under Sickness; "Low" under Vitality; Wastings; "Weak Body" under Weak).

WANT — In Want and Misery — (See Miseries, Misfortune, Neglect, Poverty, Reverses, Ruin, Starvation, Wretched).

WANTON—Extravagant—Without Restraint—Libidinous—Lewd—Licentious—Loose, etc.—(See these subjects).

Destructiveness — Wanton Destructiveness—(See Destructiveness).

Disgrace — Thru Wantonness — (See Disgrace).

Wanton Look — ⊡ gives. (See Debauched, Depraved, Effeminate, Immodest; "Licentious" under Men; "Notoriety" under Passion; Perversions, Shameless, etc.).

WANT AND MISERY — (See Miseries, Misfortune, Neglect, Poverty, Wretched).

WANTS—Nature's Wants and Requirements — (See "Requirements" under Nature).

WAR—Battle—Strife—♂ is the planet of War and Bloodshed.

Battle—(See "Death" in this section).

Civil War—Danger of—♂ in the Asc. at the Vernal Equi., lord of the year, weak and afflicted; Comets appearing in the Ruling Sign of a Country. (See Politics; "Discord" under Quarrels; Revolutionary).

Death In Battle—Death or Injury In War — Killed In Battle — Wounded In Battle—Signs of Death In Battle—The ☉ Sig. to the ☌ ♂ by dir. if ♂ afflict the ☉ or hyleg at B., and the map be a violent one, or show a violent death, danger of being terribly wounded, or killed in battle; the ☉ in the 8th H., or with the lord of the 7th; the ☉ to the ☌ or P. Dec. Antares; the ☽ to the ☌ or P. Antares or Aldebaran; an eclipse of the ☉ or ☽ in a fiery sign, terrible slaughter in war; ♂ in signs of human form, and in □ or ☍ the ☉ or ☽, and contrary in condition; ♂ the afflicting planet, death in war; ♂ in the 8th H. at B., and afflicted; ♂ □ or ☍ the Asc., and if he is also in ☍ the ☉ or ☽, there is danger of a violent death, and if applying, and near the exact ☍, to be killed on the spot; ♂ in the Asc., afflicted, and ill-dignified, may be dangerously wounded in battle; leaving for war in a ♂ hour tends to death in battle; malefics affl. in the 8th H.; malefics in the 9th H. at B., danger of death in a Foreign War; lord of the Asc. in the 8th, or with lord of the 8th, or lord of the 8th in the Asc.; the Asc. to the ☌ or ill-asp. ♂ by dir., and ♂ in a sign of human form at B.; the 6th face of ♈, or the 5th face of ♋ culminating on the M.C. (See "Battle" under Abroad; Captivity, Contests, Duels, Feuds, Military, Shedding of Blood (see Shedding); Slaughter, Soldiers).

Excites and Stirs Up War—An eclipse of the ☽ in the 1st decan. of ♋. (See "Sun Spots" under Spots).

Fond of War — And Disputes — (See "Disputes" under Quarrels).

Killed In War—(See "Death" in this section).

Kings — Overthrow or Assassination of In War—(See Kings).

Military Officer—Death of—(See "Officer Killed" under Military).

Quarrels—Given To—(See "Discord", "Disputes", under Quarrels).

Radicalism; Reactionary; Rebellious;

Reformers; Revolutionary; Riotous;

Soldiers—Death By—(See Soldiers).

Stirs Up War—(See "Excites" in this section).

Sun Spots—Tending to Cause War—(See "Sun Spots" under Spots).

Terribly Wounded — In War — (See "Death" in this section).

Violent Death In — (See "Death" in this section).

War and Bloodshed—An eclipse of the ☉ in the 1st decan. of ♏ stirs up wars, tumults, and slaughter; coincident with the appearance of Comets; Comets appearing in the ♈ sign, and espec. in Countries under the rule of ♈; Comets appearing in ♈, ♊, ♋, ♌, ♏, ♐, ♑, ♒, or ♓, and espec. in Countries ruled by these signs. (See "Shedding" under Blood; "Blood" under Effusions; Public; "Discord" under Quarrels; Seventh House, Slaughter, Strife, etc.).

Warlike—(See "Disputes" under Quarrels; Revolutionary, Riotous, Violent).

Wounded In War—Injured In Battle —(See "Death" in this section).

WARDS OFF DISEASE — (See Immunity; "Good" under Recuperation, Resistance).

WARM—Warmth—Heat—♃ and ♀ are warm, and exert a warm influence over the body, but not hot. Libra and ♒ are warm and moist signs.

Air—(See "Warm" under Air).

Body — Warm Body — (See "Animal Heat", "Hot Bodily Temperament", under Heat).

Functions — Warmth and Expansion of—(See Electric).

Heat—(See "Warm", and the various paragraphs under Heat).

Moist and Warm Diseases—(See "Moist and Warm" under Heat).

Summers Warm—(See Summer).

Warm-Hearted—(See Good, Humane, Kind).

Warm Weather—(See "Warm" under Weather).

WARTS—Verruca—An Excrescence—

Anus—Wart-Like Growth On—Condyloma—♄ affl. in ♏; Subs at LPP (4, 5L). (See Anus, Rectum).

Arms — Hands or Shoulders — Warts On — Afflictions in signs which rule these parts; ♄ affl. in ♋, ♌, or ♍; Subs at AP (1D), and also at UHP (1D).

Eyelids—Warts On—♄ affl. in ♈; Subs at KP (11D). (See Eyelids).

Face—Warts On—(See "Marks" under Face).

Hands — Warts On—(See "Arms" in this section).

Head—(See "Warts" under Head).

Rectum—(See "Anus" in this section).

Shoulders—(See "Arms" in this section). See Blemishes, Marks, Moles, Naevus, Scars.

WASTE — Wastes — Waste Products of the Body—Retention of Wastes—Improper Elimination of—Wasted—Wasteful, etc.—The following subjects have to do with the Wastes of the body, their retention or excess in the body, and also of their elimination. See these subjects in the alphabetical arrangement when not considered here—

Accumulation of Wastes—(See Accumulative).

Acids — Over-Acidity of the Body — (See Acids, Hyperacidity).

Bathing—(See Bathing; "Water" under Skin).

Carbonic Acid Poisoning — (See Carbon).

Cleansing the Body — Of Wastes and Impurities—(See Cleansing, Elimination, Fever, Inflammation, Mars Action; "Bathing" in this section).

Crusts; Deposits; Dirty; Elimination —(See "Stopped" under Elimination).

Energies Wasted—(See Amorous; Debauched, Dissipation; "Wasted" under Energies; Excesses, Intemperate, Opposite Sex, Passion, Pleasure, Sports; "Sex Forces" in this section).

Eruptions; Excess; Excesses;

Excretion Disordered — (See Excretion).

Expulsion of Wastes — Carried on by the ☽ and ♂. The afflictions of ♄ to the ☽, and with ♄ affl. in ♍, ♎, ♏, or ♑, tend to disorders of expulsion and elimination. (See Elimination, Excretion, Expulsion, Faeces, Retention, Stoppages, Suppression, Sweat, Urine).

Exudations—(See Excretion, Exudations, Faeces, Sweat, Urine).

Faeces; Fevers — The fevers and inflammations of ♂ help to burn up and eliminate wastes, and in this regard are constructive and purifying forces if not too violent, and the life is saved. (See Fever; "Cleansing the Body" in this section).

Filth; Gout; Gravel; Hindered—Elimination of Wastes Hindered — (See Hindrances).

Hyperacidity; Impeded—(See the various paragraphs under Impeded).

Impurities—(See Excretions, Faeces, Hyperacidity, Impure; "Blood Poisoning" under Poison; Sweat, Urine, etc.).

Inflammation—A Cleanser of the Body from Impurities — (See "Cleansing", "Fevers", in this section).

Jaundice — (See "Obstructive" under Jaundice).

Leukocytes—As a Nucleus for Wastes —(See Leukocytes).

Menses; Mineral Deposits — (See Deposits, Gravel, Minerals, Sand, Stone).

Obstructions; Paralysis;

Poisons Retained—(See Impure, Poisons).

Portal Blood Stream—The Wastes of —(See Portal).

Retardations; Retention of Wastes—(See Hyperacidity, Retention).

Rheumatism; Sand; Secretions — The Secretions Hindered by Wastes — (See Secretion).

Sex Forces Wasted — (See Amorous; "Health Injured" under Men; "Health Suffers" under Opposite Sex; "Passional Excesses" under Passion).

Stone — Calculus — (See Gravel, Sand, Stone).

Stoppages; Suppressions; Sweat;

Toxaemia; Urea; Uric Acid; Urine — Suppression of—(See Urine).

Vital Fluid—Waste of—(See "Fluid", "Waste", under Vital).

Wasteful — (See Expense, Extravagant, Improvident, Luxuries, Money, Prodigal).

Wasting Diseases—(See Wasting).

WASTING DISEASES — Wasting Processes in the Body—Tabefaction—Marasmus—Consumptions, etc.—The influences and afflictions of ♆ and ♄ tend to wasting processes in the body. (See Neptune, Saturn). The following subjects have to do with the Wasting Processes in the body, which see in the alphabetical arrangement when not considered here—

Arms—Wasting of the Tissues of the Arms, Hands, Legs and Feet—Shrinking and Withering of the Limbs — ♆ influence, and caused by ♆ afflicted in the signs which rule these parts, and to cause shrinking and withering of such parts, and of the Limbs.

Assimilation — Wasting Due to Improper Assimilation of Food — (See "Imperfect" under Assimilation; "Incapable", "Malnutrition", under Nutrition).

Atrophy — Wasting of a Part — (See Atrophy; "Atrophy" under Feet, Hands).

Body—Wasting of the Body—Wasting Diseases—Tabefactions—A ♆ and ♄ disease; ♆ affl. in ♊; ♆ in ♊ in the 6th H., and affl. the Asc. or hyleg; the ☉ affl. by ♄; the ☽ in ♑, and affl. by the ☉ or ♂ when taken ill, the body extremely wasted (Hor'y); ♄ affl. the hyleg, and ♄ the afflictor in the disease; ♄ in ♓, occi., and affl. the ☉, ☽, or Asc. (See Atrophy, Consumption, Corrosion, Decay, Degeneration, Destructive, Emaciation, Marasmus, Phthisis, Tabes, Tuberculosis, etc.).

Bowels—♆ affl. in ♍, wasting of the glands of the bowels.

Chronic Low Fevers—(See "Chronic", "Hectic", under Fever).

Consumptions; Decay;

Destructive Processes—In the Body—(See "Destructive Processes" under Destructive).

Diabetes; Diseases—Wasting Diseases—These diseases are worse at sunset, and at night. They are caused principally by the afflictions of ♆ and ♄. (See the various paragraphs in this section).

Emaciation; Feet—Wasting of—(See "Arms" in this section).

Glands of Bowels—Wasting of—(See "Bowels" in this section).

Hands—Wasting of Tissues of—(See "Arms" in this section).

Hectic Fever—Low, Wasting Fevers—(See "Hectic" under Fever, Phthisis).

Legs — Wasting of — (See "Arms" in this section; "Wasting" under Legs).

Leprosy; Limbs—(See "Arms" in this section).

Liver—(See "Wasting" under Liver).

Locomotor Ataxia; Low Fevers—(See "Hectic", "Low", under Fever).

Malnutrition—(See Nutrition).

Marriage Partner—Neurotic Wasting of—(See Marriage Partner).

Neurotic Wasting — (See "Wasting" under Nerves).

Phthisis — Pulmonary Consumption—(See Phthisis).

Respiratory System — (See "Tissues Affected" under Breathing).

Scrofula — Tubercular and Wasting Tendency In—(See Scrofula).

Shrinking; Tabes; Throat — Wasting of Tissues of—♆ affl. in ♉.

Tissues—Wasting of—♆ □ or ☍ the Asc.; ♆ affl. in signs which rule the part; ♄ influence. (See "Wasting" under Tissues).

Tuberculosis; Wasting Away—Death By—Tabefaction—♄ affl. at B., holding the dominion of death, and affl. the ☉, ☽, Asc., or hyleg; ♀ affl. at B., holding the dominion of death, and affl. the hyleg by dir. (See Consumptions, Emaciation, Phthisis, Tabes, Tuberculosis).

Withering; Worse—Wasting diseases are worse at sunset, and at night. (For other diseases along this line, and which may not be listed here, look in the alphabetical arrangement for what you have in mind).

WATER — Waters — Watery — Fluids — Aqueous — Hydro, etc. — Waters and Fluids are ruled by the ☽, ♆, and the watery signs. (See "Operations" under Nature; "Signs" under Water). The following subjects have to do with Water, Waters, Liquids, and Fluids inside and outside the human body. See these subjects in the alphabetical arrangement when not considered here—

Accidents by Water—Injury By—☽ □, ☍ ♂; ♆ affl. in the 8th, 9th or 10th H.; ♆ affl. in ♏; ♂ affl. in watery signs and ☌ or ill-asp. the Asc. by dir. (See Bathing, Drowning, Navigation, Scalds, Shipwreck, Ships, Sea; the various paragraphs in this section).

Bathing; Blood—Watery Blood—(See "Thin" under Blood).

Brain—Water On—(See Hydrocephalus).

Brash—Water Brash—(See Belching).

Burns — By Hot Water — (See "Hot Liquids" under Heat; Scalds).

Chest—Water In—(See "Dropsy" under Chest).

Children—Watery Diseases In—(See "Watery" under Children).

Cold Water—Craving For In Illness—(See "Cold Water" under Cravings).

Cold, Watery Diseases — (See "Cold and Moist" under Humours).

Control of Water — In the System — (See "Sodium Chloride" under Sodium).

Corruption of Waters — (See Fish, Rivers).

Dampness — (See Linen, Moisture, Wet).

Danger by Water — (See Bathing, Drowning; "Hot Liquids" under Heat; Navigation, Scalds, Sea, Ships, Shipwreck, Voyages).

Death—By Means of Water—The ☉ to the ill-asps. ♄ by dir., and one or both in watery signs; the ☽ in a watery sign at B., and affl. by ♄, and affl. the hyleg by dir., or taking part in a fatal train of directions; ♆ affl. in the 8th H. at B., and also affl. the hyleg; ♅ or ♄ in ♋, ♍, ♏ or ♓ and affl. the ☽; ♄ ♍ and affl. the ☽ hyleg; ♄ in a watery sign and affl. the Asc. or hyleg by dir. (See Bathing, Drowning, Scalds, Ships, Shipwreck, Voyages, etc.).

Diarrhoea Profuse Watery — (See Diarrhoea).

Discharges — Watery Discharges — (See Discharges).

Distilled—(See "Water" under Skin).

Drinks Much Water—(See Cravings, Thirst).

Dropsies; Drowning;

Elimination of Water—From the System—Carried on by the ♉ sign, and the Sodium Sulphate Salt.

Epiphora—Watery Eyes—(See Tears).

Events—Affecting the Waters—(See "Nature" under Events; Navigation, Sea, Ships, Shipwreck, Voyages, etc.).

Excrescences — Watery Excrescences —(See "Skull" under Excrescences).

Eyes — Watery Eyes — Overflow of Tears—(See Tears).

Fallopian Tubes — Water In — (See Fallopian).

Fear of Water—(See Hydrophobia).

Fish—Destruction of In the Waters—(See Fish).

Fluids — Watery Fluid Collections — (See "Water" under Fluids; Serum).

Floods — (See Floods, Rain, Venomous).

Fond of the Water—The ☽ or ♆ in ♓; many planets in watery signs at B. (See "Fortunate" in this section).

Fortunate On the Water—Fond of the Water—♃ Sig. in ♋ or ♓, or ♃ ☌ ☽, fortunate on, and fond of the water, if the ☽ is not ill-asp.; the ☉ Sig. in ♏, and well-asp., fortunate on the Seas. (See "Fortunate" under Seas).

Fountains—Drying Up of—(See Fountains).

Fresh Water—(See "Running" in this section).

Head—Watery Excrescences of—(See "Excrescences" in this section; "Malformations" under Head).

Hot Water — Accidents and Injuries By — (See "Hot Liquids" under Heat; Scalds).

Humours—Watery Humours—☽ ☌ the Asc. by secondary dir.; ♆ in the 8th H.; ♄ sole ruler of a Solar Eclipse; ♃ affl. in ♍, and with possible discharges of blood; many planets in watery signs at B.; a water sign on the Asc. or 6th H. at B. The watery humours of the body are dried up by ♄ and ♂ as the native declines in life. Also the ☉ in the Asc. at B. tends to dry them up after middle life. (See Defluxions, Discharges; "Humours" under Father; Humours, Mucus, Phlegm, Rheum).

Hurts By — (See Bathing, Drowning; "Hot Liquids" under Heat; Scalds, Shipwreck; "Accidents" in this section).

Hydrocephalus; Hydrophobia;

Hydrosalpinx—(See Fallopian).

Hydrothorax — (See "Water" under Chest).

Injury — By Means of (See "Hurts" in this section).

Liquids; Maritime; Mineral Waters—(See this subject under Healers; "Distilled Water" under Skin).

Misfortune — By Water — (See Accidents, Death, Perils, in this section).

Moisture; Navigation; Neptune;

Ocean; Perils by Water—The ☽ in a watery sign, and to the ill-asps. the Asc. by dir.; ☽ to the ☌ or ill-asps. ♅ by dir., dangerous to go near bodies of water; ☽ to Deneb, misfortunes by water; ☽ at a Solar Rev. passing over the place of ♄ at B.; ♆ in tr. over the radical ♂, and ♂ in ♋, ♏, or ♓ at B.; ♆ and other malefics affl. in the 8th H., and espec. when in a watery sign, and also affl. the hyleg; ♂ affl. in watery signs, and to the ☌ or ill-asp. the Asc. by dir.; ♂ in evil asp. ♆, and ♆ in the 8th H. in a watery sign, and espec. in ♓; the Asc. to the ☌ or P. the ☽, and the ☽ affl. at B.; malefics in the 9th H. in water signs, and affl. (See "Accidents" in this section; Bathing, Sea, Ships, Shipwreck, Voyages).

Plastic; Pools; Pyrosis—Water Brash —(See Belching).

Rain; Running Water — Streams — Rivers—Fresh Water—Ruled by the ♋ sign. (See Rivers).

Sailors; Salt Water—(See Ocean, Sea).

Scalds; Scarcity of Waters — Comets appearing in ♏. (See Drought, Famine, Fountains, Scarcity).

Seas; Ships; Shipwreck; Signs — The Water Signs of the Zodiac—♋, ♏, ♓. The watery signs dispose to drowning, scalds, fluxes, colds, dropsy, catarrh, hydrocephalus, and to excess of fluid in the body. They give the Lymphatic, or Indolent Temperament. They rule and influence the Blood, and are connected with fluids, both in the body, and outside. The watery signs have much to do with the emotions, desires, romance, the physical sensations, self-protection, and self-preservation, and along emotional and sensational lines are excitable. (See Desires, Emotions, Excitable, Feelings, Imaginations, Romance, Sensation). They are also fruitful, and have much to do with reproduction, the sustaining and preservation of the Race. The ♋ sign has to do with the stomach, assimilation, and digestion. The ♏ sign with elimination, excretion, sex, and reproduction. The ♓ sign with the Lymphatics, and the Lymphatic Temperament. These signs are related to Hydrogen. (See Hydrogen). The ☉ in water signs tends to give a weak constitution, and lowered vitality, except when in ♏, or rising in the Asc. in a watery sign, and also tends to diseases of the glands, fluids, and Lymphatic System. Also the ♋ and ♓ signs when upon the Asc. tend to give low vitality. The ♏ sign gives both vitality and constitutional power, but attracts disease, and infectious diseases. When upon the Asc. at B., the ♏ sign gives the strongest vitality of the water signs, and a hardy and ruddy constitution. The ♏ sign is the worst position for the ☽, having her fall in this sign, which tends to painful and irregular functions, espec. in females, and to lower the natural powers, the vitality, and the whole tone of the body. The ☽ is very strong in ♋ and ♓, and in these signs tends to good and regular functions, and also the absorbent and lymphatic systems and vessels are regular in their respective functions and actions. These signs are also called the Dumb, or Mute Signs, and are said, under certain conditions, to cause impediments of speech, and espec. when ☿ is also afflicted at the same time. The Water Signs are also known as the Terminal Signs, being related to the 4th, 8th, and 12th Houses. (See Cancer, Events, External, Introspection, Lymphatic, Majority, Pisces, Pity, Plastic, Scorpio, Seas, Terminal; "Low" under Vitality. Also see the various subjects mentioned in this paragraph).

Springs — (See Fountains, Rivers, Springs).

Stagnant Pools—(See Pools).

Storms; Streams—(See Rivers; "Running" in this section).

Suffering by Water — (See Bathing, Drowning, Floods; "Hot Liquids" under Heat; Maritime, Navigation, Rain, Scalds, Sea, Ships, Shipwreck, Storms, Voyages, etc.; "Accidents", "Death", "Perils", in this section).

Superabundance of Waters — (See Floods, Rain).

Tears; Tidal Waves — An eclipse of the ☉ in watery signs, overflowing of the Sea banks; coincident with the appearance of Comets, and espec. Halley's Comet. (See "Tides" in this section).

Tides — (See "Tides" under Moon; "Tidal Waves" in this section).

Tumor—Watery Tumor—(See "Aqueous" under Tumor).

Urine; Voyages; Watery Diseases — Watery and Cold Diseases—(See Blood, Children, Cold, Diarrhoea, Discharges, Excrescences, Eyes, Fluids, Head, Humors, and the various paragraphs in this section).

Waves—(See "Tidal" in this section).

Wet Feet—(See Feet).

Wet Journeys — (See "Wet" under Journeys; Ships, Voyages).

Wetting—Bed Wetting—(See "Incontinence" under Urine).

WAXY—Fatty—

Ambergris—(See this subject).

Cancer—Waxy Cancer—(See "Fatty" under Carcinoma).

Fingers — (See "Raynaud's Disease" under Fingers).

Liver — (See "Waxy" under Liver). See Fat.

WAYWARD—(See Criminal, Debauched, Dissipated, Drink, Expense; "Free Living" under Free; "Loose Morals" under Morals; Perverse, Prodigal, Recklessness, etc.).

WEAK—Weaker—Weakest—Weakened — Weakening— Weakly— Weakness— Faint, etc.—Some parts of the human organism are usually weak from birth, and especially the part, or organ, ruled by the sign containing ♄ at B. Some charts of birth are considered weak and unfortunate while others may be termed strong and fortunate. Note the following subjects in the alphabetical arrangement when only listed here—

Action of the Body—Weak and Feeble—(See Action, Feeble; "Weak Body" in this section).

All Weaknesses—Of the Body—♄ diseases, and caused by ♄ afflictions.

Anæmia; Ankles—Weakness In—(See Ankles).

Arms—Weakness In—(See Arms).

Asthenia; Atrophy; Back—Weak Back —(See Back).

Beard—Weak and Thin—(See Beard).

Bladder — Weakness of — (See Bladder).

Blood — The Weakest Blood — Thin Blood—Blood Circulation Weak—(See Blood, Circulation, Rupture, Vessels).

Bodies — Weaker and Smaller Bodies — (See "Smaller", "Weaker", under Small).

Body—Weak Body—Feeble Action to the Body—Strength of the Body Rendered Weaker — (See Feeble; "Bad Health" under Health; "Much Sickness" under Sickness; Strength; "Low" under Vitality; "Weak Body" in this section).

Bones—Weak Bones—(See Bones).

Bowels—Weaknesses of—(See Bowels).

Breakdown; Chest—Weak Chest and Lungs—(See Chest, Lungs).

Children — Weak and Sickly — (See Children).

Chronic Diseases—Thru Weakness— ♄ diseases; ♄ affl. in the Asc. (See Chronic).

Circulation—Weak Circulation of the Blood—(See "Poor" under Circulation).

Collapse; Constitution—Weak Constitution—Frail—The Constitution Weakened — The Weakest Constitutions — The weakest constitutions are given by the water signs, except ♏. (See "Lessened" under Vitality; "Weak Body" in this section).

Consumptions; Death — Of the Frail and Weak—Caused by the evil asps. of the malefics to the ☉ at B., and by dir.; born under ♋, ♑, or ♓. (See "Aged People" under Old Age).

Debility; Decay; Decrepitude;

Degeneration; Degrees — The Weak and Lame Degrees of the Zodiac—(See Azimene).

Delicate; Digestion Weak—(See Digestion, Indigestion; "Weak" under Stomach).

Dull; Ears—The Hearing Weak—(See "Weak" under Hearing).

Emaciation; Energy—Lack of—(See Energy).

Enervation; Exhaustion; Eyes—Weak Eyes—Weak Sight—(See Eyes, Sight).

Faint; Feeble; Feet—Weakness In—(See Feet).

Females—Weaknesses In—(See Females).

Feminine Signs—Of the Zodiac—The Weaker Signs—(See "Signs" under Female).

Figure—Small and Weak Figure—(See "Mean Stature" under Mean; "Smaller and Weaker" under Small).

Frame—A Weak Frame—♋, ♑, or ♓ on the Asc. at B. (See Frame).

Functions—Impaired and Weakened—(See Functions).

General Weakness—(See Fatigue, Feeble; "General Ill-Health" under Ill-Health; "Much Sickness" under Sickness; "Low" under Vitality).

Generative System—Weakness of—(See Generation).

Health—Weak Health—(See "Bad Health" under Health; Invalids, Sickly; "Weak Body" in this section).

Hearing Weak—(See Hearing).

Heart Weak—(See Heart).

Hips—Weakness In—(See Hips).

Horoscope—A Weak Map of Birth—(See Aspects, Fate, Horoscope, Malefics, Map, Saturn, Vulnerable; "Free Will" under Will).

Inactive; Infirm; Infirmities; Insufficiency; Intellect Weak—(See Intellect, Mind, Understanding).

Intestines—Weaknesses In—(See Bowels, Intestines).

Invalidism; Kidneys—Weak Kidneys—Kidneys the Weakest Part—(See Kidneys).

Knees—Weakness In—(See Knees).

Lassitude; Laxity; Leakages; Legs—Weakness In—(See Legs).

Lessened; Lethargy; Limbs—Weak Limbs—(See Limbs).

Limitations; Limp; Listless; Loins—Weak Loins—(See Loins).

Low Vitality—(See Vitality).

Lowest; Lungs—Weak Lungs—(See Lungs).

Malacia; Malaise; Males—Health In Males Weak—(See Males).

Malefics—The Weakening Influences of—(See Malefics).

Map of Birth—Weak Map—(See "Horoscope" in this section).

Mean—Mean and Weak Stature—(See Mean, Stature).

Memory—Weak—(See Memory).

Men—Weaknesses In—(See Men).

Menses—Profuse and Weakening—(See Menses).

Mental Weakness—(See Intellect, Mental, Mind).

Middle Life—Death At—Weaknesses At—(See Middle Life).

Mind—Weak Mind—(See "Weak Mentality" under Mental; "Feeble", "Weak", under Mind).

Morals—Weak Morals—(See "Loose Morals" under Morals).

Much Weakness—Of Body—(See "Ill-Health All Thru Life" under Ill-Health; "Much Sickness" under Sickness).

Muscles—Weakened Condition of—(See Muscles).

Nature—Weak Nature—The 6th face of ♑ on the Asc. (See Influenced; "Negative Nature" under Negative; Passive, Vacillating).

Nerves—(See "Weakest Part", "Weakness", under Nerves).

Old Age—Weaknesses In—(See Old Age).

Organic Weakness—(See Organic).

Organs—Weak Organs—(See Organs).

Ovaries—Weaknesses In—(See Ovaries).

Pale; Parts of the Body—Weak Parts—Weakest Parts—(See Malefics, Organs, Parts, Saturn).

Passion—The Passions Weak—(See "Lack Of" under Passion).

Person—A Weakly Person—(See Feeble, Imbecility; "Weak Mind" under Mind; "Weak Body" in this section).

Peristaltic Action—Weakened—(See Peristaltic).

Physical Body—Weak—(See "Weak Body" in this section).

Poor—Poor Health—(See "Bad Health" under Health; Poor, Vitality Low; "Weak Body" in this section).

Prostration; Puberty Weakened—(See Puberty).

Pulse—Weak Pulse—(See Pulse).

Reason—The Reasoning Powers Weakened—(See Reason).

Recuperative Powers—Weak—(See Recuperation, Resistance, Vitality Low).

Regenerative Organs—(See "Weakness" under Generation).

Reins—Weakness and Disorders In—(See Reins).

Relaxation; Reproductive System—(See "Weakness" under Generation).

Resistance—To Disease—Low and Weak—(See "Low" under Resistance).

Respiratory System—Weakness of—(See the various paragraphs under Breathing, Lungs, Respiratory).

Ruptures; Saturn—(See "Influence of Saturn" under Saturn).

Secretory System—Weaknesses of—(See Secretions).

Sex Powers Weak—(See "Weak" under Sex).

Short Life—(See Short).

Shoulders—Weakness In—(See Shoulders).

Sickly; Sickness; Sight—Weak Sight—(See Sight).

Signs—Of the Zodiac—The Weak Signs—(See "Weak" under Signs).

Sloughings—From Weakness—(See Sloughing).

Slow—Slow and Weak Conditions In the Body—(See Slow).

Small — Small and Weak Body — (See Mean, Small).

Spine—Weaknesses of—(See Spine).

Stomach—Weak Stomach—(See Stomach).

Strength — (See "Weakened" under Strength).

Structure—The Structural Organization of the Body Weakened — (See Structural).

Suppressions; Suspensions; System—The System Weakened — (See Constitution, System, Vitality Lessened).

Thighs—Weakness In—(See Thighs).

Thin and Weak — (See Emaciated; "Thin Body" under Thin; Wasting).

Throat—Weak and Afflicted Throat—(See the various paragraphs under Throat).

Tone—The Tone of the Body Weak—(See Tone).

Trouble—Weakened Thru Trouble—(See Miseries, Misfortune, Reverses, Ruin, Sorrow, Trouble).

Understanding — (See "Weak" under Understanding).

Urinary Organs—Weaknesses of—(See Urine).

Valves—Weak Valves—(See Valves).

Vessels—Weakened Blood Vessels—(See Apoplexy, Hardening, Rupture, Vessels).

Vices—Weakened By—(See Vice).

Vigor — The Vigor Weakened — (See Vigor).

Vision—Weak Vision—(See Sight).

Vitality Weak—Weakened—(See Vitality).

Voice—(See "Weak Voice" under Voice).

Volition — The Powers of Volition Weakened—(See Volition, Will).

Wasting; Weak Body—Weak Constitution — Weakness — Feeble Constitution — Not Robust — The Constitution Not Very Strong, etc.—Vitality Low—The ☉ affl. in ♋, ♑, or ♓, or with these signs upon the Asc. at B.; the ☉ hyleg, and to the ☌ or ill-asp. ♄ by dir.; the ☉ or ☽ in the Asc., and hyleg, affl. by malefics in angles, and no good asps. from ♃ or ♀ to the hyleg, a weak constitution, and may die in infancy, or under the first train of evil directions, but the good asps. of the benefics to the hyleg will tend to prolong life under these conditions and strengthen the constitution; the ☉ or ☽ to the ☌ or ill-asps. ♄ or ♂, the constitution is weakened; the ☉ or ☽ in ☌ or ill-asp. the malefics; born at the time of a total eclipse of the ☉, and under its shadow, and males so born may die soon after birth; the ☽ decr. in light, sepr. from ♄ and applying to the ☉, ♂, or ☿; the ☽ nearly in ☌ with the ☉ at B., or at a total eclipse of the ☉; the ☽ affl. in ♑; ☽ ♑ partile Asc., never strong; the ☽ Sig. in ♑, thin, weak, feeble and sickly; the ☽ applying to ♂, or conjoined with him in a day nativity; ♄ affl. in ♋, a weak and infirm body; ♄ ascending at B.;

♄ in his second station at B.; ♄ in 6th H., and conjoined with the ☉ at B.; ♄ in S. Lat., the body weaker than when in N. Lat.; ♄ affl. in ♌ unless the energies are conserved; ♃ Sig. in ♑, a weakly person; ♃ or ♀ in ☌ with the ☉ when the ☉ is hyleg, as all planets combust are weakened; ♃ Sig. ☌ ☉; ♂ ♐; ♀ affl. in the 6th H., but the health may be good, and the constitution harmonious as long as excesses are avoided, and good habits adhered to; ☿ Sig. in ♑; many planets setting in weak signs or positions, and many evil asps. among them; ♎ on the Asc., the body weaker in old age; the lower and posterior parts of the ♈, ♉ and ♌ signs tend to make the body weaker, and also the anterior parts of ♊, ♍ and ♐; malefics in angles, and the ☉, ☽, and Asc. affl.; the Asc. hyleg, and ☌ or ill-asp. one or more malefics; the hyleg ☍ ♄ or ♂; the earthy and watery signs on the Asc., except ♉ or ♍, give a weaker body. (For other influences along this line see Debility; "Early Death" under Early; Emaciation, Enervation, Fatigue, Feeble, Infancy (Death In); "Health Bad" under Health; Malnutrition, Pale; "Much Sickness" under Sickness; "Low" under Resistance; "Short Life" under Short; Sickly; "Thin and Weak" under Thin; "Low" under Vitality, etc.).

Weak-Minded—(See Feeble, Impaired, Light, Shallow, Weak, Weakened, under Mind).

Weak Spots — In the Body and Star Map of Birth — (See "Horoscope" in this section; "Weak Parts" under Parts; Vulnerable).

Weakened — The Functions, Organs, and Vitality Weakened — The Disease Is Weakened—(See Diminished, Functions, Lessened, Minimizing, Moderation, Organs, Strength; "Lessened" under Vitality).

Weakening—Weakening Conditions and Diseases In the Mind and Body—(See Debauchery, Disease, Dissipation, Emaciation, Excesses, Habits, Hemorrhage; Insanity; "Profuse" under Menses; Passion, Venery, Vices, Waste, Wasting, Worry, etc.).

Weaker — The Strength of the Body Rendered Weaker — (See Breakdown, Collapse; "Weaker" under Constitution; "Wasted" under Energy; Exhaustion, Feeble, Prostration; "Weak" under Signs; "Weakened" under Strength; "Lessened" under Vitality; Worse, etc.).

Weakest—The Weakest Blood—The Weakest Constitution — The Weakest Organs—The Weakest Parts, etc.—The parts ruled by the signs containing the malefics at B. tend to be the weakest and most afflicted parts, and the part ruled by the sign containing ♄ at B. is always very sensitive to disease, weakness, breakdown, and affliction, whether ♄ is afflicted or not. (See "Weakest" under Blood, Constitution, Part; "Weak" under Organs; Saturn, Vulnerable; "Kidneys", "Parts", "Signs", in this section).

Weakly Person—(See Fatigue, Feeble; "Bad Health" under Health; "Ill-Health All Thru Life" under Ill-Health;

Infirm, Invalids; "Low" under Recuperation, Resistance, Vitality; Sickly; "Much Sickness" under Sickness; "Weak Body" in this section).

Weakness—Debility—Feeble—General Weakness—Female Weakness—Weakness In Children, Females, and Males, etc.—(See Childhood, Children, Debility, Females, Functions; "General Ill-Health" under Ill-Health; Infancy, Males, Men, Resistance, Sloughing, Stamina, Tone, Vitality, Women).

Will—A Weak Will—(See Influenced; "Negative Nature" under Negative; Passive, Vacillating, Volition; "Weak" under Will).

Women—Weakness In—(See Aunts, Daughter, Females, Functions, Menses, Mother, Sister, Wife, Women).

WEALTH—Money—Riches—Property—Assets—Wealth is ruled by the 2nd H., and benefics in this house at B., and fortunate conditions over this house, tend to the accumulation of wealth. (See Money, Property, Prosperity, Riches).

Loss of Wealth—A malefic ruling, or in the 2nd H. at B., and with no benefics in, or good influences, over this house at B. (See Disgrace, Expense, Extravagance, Honour, Loss Of, Luxuries, Miseries, Misfortune, Money, Pleasure, Poverty, Property; "Loss Of" under Reputation; Reverses; "Riotous Living" under Riotous; Ruin, Starvation, Wretched, etc.).

Promise of Wealth—♃ or ♀ in the 2nd H. at B., well-aspected, and with no malefic afflicting this house; ♃ well-aspected in the 8th H., thru legacy; ♃ well-aspected in the 4th or 10th H., thru inheritance. (See Money, Property, Prosperity, Riches, Success).

WEANING—Wean Infants after the ☽ has passed out of the ♏ sign. (See Breast, Infancy, Milk, Nursing).

WEAPONS—Injury or Death By—(See Cuts, Duels, Execution, Gun-Shot, Hurts, Injury, Instruments, Iron, Mobs, Sharp Instruments; "Flying Stones" under Stone; Sword, War, etc.).

WEAR AND TEAR—On the Body—The earthy signs, when strong, well-occupied, and well-aspected at B., and espec. ♉ on the Asc., give a solid constitution, and able to withstand much wear and tear on the physical body; the ☉ in an earthy sign at B., and well-aspected, gives much endurance to the constitution, and able to withstand much wear and tear; fiery signs on the Asc., great vitality, and resistance to disease. (See Endurance, Immunity; "Good" under Recuperation, Resistance, Stamina, Tone, Vitality; "Increased" under Strength; "Body" under Strong).

WEARINESS—Of Mind and Body—Ennui—Generally caused by ♄ influence. (See Apathy; "Brain Fag" under Brain; Dull, Ennui; "Dull" under Eyes; Fatigue, Inactive, Inertia, Languid, Lassitude, Lazy, Lethargy; "Low Spirits" under Low; Refreshment, Rest; "Drowsiness" under Sleep).

WEATHER—The Weather and atmospheric conditions are closely related to disease, suffering, as well as to human comforts and well-being. Millions have died, or been made sick thru weather conditions. See the following subjects in the alphabetical arrangement when only listed here—

Air—(See Air, Atmosphere).

Aqueous Vapors—(See Rain).

Blizzards; Changes—In the Weather—Susceptible To—People born when the Luminaries are afflicting each other. (See Colds).

Cold—Much Suffering from Extreme Cold—Severe Winters—The ☉ ☌ ♄ in ♑ at the Winter Solstice; ♅ in an angle at the Winter Solstice; ♅ or ♄ crossing the Equator in Winter; ♄ lord of the year at the Vernal, direct in motion, in an angle, and affl. by ♂ and the ☽, severe cold, and loss of cattle and sheep; ☿ in an angle at the Winter Solstice, and espec. when in asp. with ♅; an earthy sign, as ♉, ♍, or ♑, ascending at the Vernal, and the lord of the rising sign affl., tends to extremely cold weather, and much suffering from cold, diseases in the parts of the body ruled by such sign, and especially in Countries ruled by the sign rising. (See Cold).

Colds; Corrupt Air—(See Air).

Drought; Dry Weather—Dryness—Suffering From—(See Drought, Epidemics, Famine, Fountains, Heat, Pestilence, etc.).

Epidemics; Exposure—To the Elements—To Cold and Dampness, and Illness From—♄ affl. in the 6th H. (See Exposure).

Famine; Floods; Frost; Hailstorms—Furious and Tempestuous Hailstorms—(See Hail).

Heat—Extreme Heat and Suffering From—(See "Extreme Heat", "Warm", under Heat).

High Temperature—Hot Weather—♃ and ♂ act to produce higehr temperatures, being positive planets, while ♅ and ♄ produce a lower temperature.

High Winds—(See Winds).

Hot—Hot and Dry Air—Hot, Blasting Winds—Hot Weather—(See Drought; "Weather" under Heat; Winds).

Hurricanes—(See Winds).

Inundations—(See Floods, Rain).

Journeys—Wet Journeys—(See Journeys, Travel, Voyages).

Lightning; Low Temperatures—(See "Cold", "High", in this section).

Over-Moist Air—Suffering From—(See Rain).

Perihelion; Pestilential Air—(See "Corrupt" under Air).

Rain; Ships; Shipwreck; Snow;

Storms—(See Blizzards, Rain, Shipwreck, Snow, Storms, Wind).

Susceptible—To Changes In the Weather—(See "Changes" in this section).

Temperature—(See Cold, Heat, High, in this section).

Tempests—(See "Tempests" under Sea; Wind).

Thunder—(See Lightning, Thunder, Wind).

Travel—(See "Weather" under Travel).

Volcanic Eruptions—(See Volcanoes). Many of the same influences which tend to disturbed weather conditions, with suffering to humanity, also tend to Earthquakes, Volcanic Eruptions, Tidal Waves, Pestilence, Plague, etc., and to much destruction of property and human life.

Voyages—(See "Dampness" under Voyages).

Warm Weather—The ☉ ☌, or any asp. ♃ except when the ☉ is also in asp. with ♅ or ♄. (See "Fountains" under Dry; "Extreme", "Warm", under Heat; "Hot Winds" under Wind).

Wet Journeys—(See Journeys).

Wind Storms—(See Wind).

Winter—Severe and Cold Winters—(See "Cold" in this section). For further study of Astro-Meteorology, see Book III in Pearce's Text Book of Astrology; the Articles on "Weather" in Wilson's Dictionary of Astrology, and in Sepharial's New Dictionary of Astrology.

WEDNESDAY—The day of the week ruled by ☿. The first hour at sunrise on Wednesday is ruled by ☿. (See "Hours" under Planets; Weak).

WEEK—Days of the Week—In considering matters of health and disease, it is an advantage to know something of the planetary rulership of the days of the week, and of the planetary hours of each day.

Sunday—Ruled by the ☉. Patients suffering from slow and lingering ♄ diseases benefit most by treatments on Sunday, as the ☉ and ♄ rule opposite signs of the Zodiac, as ♌ and ♒. Sunday is named after the Sun, being "Sun's Day". The first hour at sunrise on Sunday is a ☉ hour, and treatment given in the three ☉ hours of Sunday are more beneficial than in other hours. (See "Hours" under Planets).

Monday—The day ruled by the ☽, being "Moon's Day". Monday is also a good day to treat ♄ diseases, and in the ☽ hours of this day, as the ☽ opposes ♄, the ☽ ruling ♋, and ♄ the opposite sign ♑. The ☽ moves fast, and people born on Monday tend to be restless, and fond of travel and change, and also to be more subject to ☽ diseases, and to be strongly affected at the Quarters of the ☽.

Tuesday—Ruled by ♂, and people born on Tuesday tend to be more hasty, excitable, and impetuous, and also to be more susceptible to accidents, injuries, wounds, fevers, inflammations, and to quarrels. Tuesday is a good day to give the remedies of ♂, as tonics and stimulants, and espec. in the three ♂ hours of the day, as at sunrise, the 8th and 16th hours after sunrise. Tuesday is a good day to apply poultices to draw out suppurations, or to draw boils to a head, as pus is a ♄ formation.

Wednesday—The day ruled by the planet ☿, the mental ruler. Wednesday people tend to be studious, and to suffer more from mental disorders, brain-fag, fatigue from over-study, or too much reading. They need periods of mental rest, and to relax the nerves. Mercury rules the ♊ and ♍ signs, and opposes the ♃ signs ♐ and ♓, and the diseases of ♃ tend to be benefitted on Wednesday, and to be treated by the Herbs and remedies of ☿, and to apply such in the ☿ hours of Wednesday. (See "Mercury Group" under Herbs).

Thursday—Ruled by ♃, and Thursday people tend to partake of the ♃ qualities, and to be more kindly and generous, or religiously inclined. Mental, nervous, and chronic disorders tend to rapid relief when treated on Thursday, in the ♃ hours of this day, and to be treated by the remedies of ♃ or the ☽, as the ♃ signs ♐ and ♓ oppose the ☿ signs ♊ and ♍, and also the ♋ sign, the exalted sign of ♃, opposes the ♄ sign ♑. Thursday is a good day for religious devotion, quietude, peace of mind, relaxation, etc.

Friday—The day ruled by ♀. A good day for pleasure, recreation, amusement, travel, etc. Also a good day to treat the diseases of ♂, as the ♂ and ♀ signs in the Zodiac are in ☍ aspect, as ♈ and ♎, or ♉ and ♏. Friday is a good day, and in the ♀ hours of Friday, to treat diseases of the head, ruled by ♈, and sex disorders, ruled by ♏ and ♂. The diseases of ♀ are apt to be more aggravated on Friday, or to have their incipiency thru dissipation, excesses, pleasures, or venery.

Saturday—Ruled by ♄, being "Saturn's Day". Is the day of rest in Nature, or the Sabbath Day. Is also the day of death, relaxation of tissue, of decay and degeneration. People born on Saturday tend to be more melancholic, serious, and grave, and to have delays, disappointments, and misfortunes in life. The inflammations and fevers of ♂ are greatly benefitted when treated on Saturday, and by the remedies of ♄, and by cold applications, as ♄ opposes ♂, one being cold by nature, and the other hot and inflammable. Poultices and applications to reduce a swelling, as from an injury caused by ♂, have greater effect when used on Saturday, and in a ♄ hour. (See the ♄ hour in the paragraph, "Hours" under Planets).

In prolonged and lingering diseases, the patient also tends to make more rapid progress when treated on the day, or days, ruled by the planets which have the best aspects in the map of birth, for to treat a patient on the days, or in the planetary hours, ruled by planets which are badly afflicted at B., not much progress is made, and even harm may be done, or a relapse occur. (See Antipathy, Opposites, Remedies, Treatment).

WEEPING—

Eczema—Weeping Eczema—(See Eczema). See Emotions, Tears.

WEIGHT—

Body—Weight of the Body—The body usually gains one or two pounds in the increase of the ☽, and falls off in weight during the decr. of ☽. The fluids of the body, and the weight, are at their height at Full ☽. The body tends to be lighter in weight, thin and small when ♑ is on the Asc. at B., and a watery sign on Asc. tends to a fleshy and corpulent body, and with less vitality, except ♏, which is a more vital sign. (See Corpulent, Fat, Fleshy, Giants, Mean, Short, Small, Thin, Emaciated, Wasted).

Brain — Weight of the Brain — (See "Weight" under Brain).

Gains Weight Rapidly—☽ in ♋ at B.

Loses Weight — (See Anaemia, Atrophy, Consumptions, Emaciation; "Malnutrition" under Nutrition; Tuberculosis, Wasting).

WEIL'S DISEASE—(See Spleen).

WEIRD—

Weird Mind — Weird Experiences — Uncanny Feelings—♆ affl. in the 3rd or 9th houses; the Pr. ☽ to the ☌ or ill-asp. ♆ if ♆ be affl. at B.; the 3rd decan. of ♒ on the Asc., strange terrors of mind. (See Chaotic, Confusion, Delirium, Delusions; "Dreamy Mind" under Dreams; Fears, Forebodings, Hallucinations, Illusions, Imagination, Insanity; "Low Spirits" under Low; Melancholy, Obsessions, Premonitions, Solitude, Spirit Controls, Visions).

WELL—Words beginning with "Well".

Well-Balanced — (1) Well-Balanced Body—(See Beautiful, Comely, Handsome, Harmony). (2) Well-Balanced Mind—(See "Well-Balanced" under Mind).

Well-Built Body—Well-Built Person —Indicated by ♂ and the ♌ sign; ♌ on the Asc.

Well-Composed Body—Good Make—The ☉ gives; the ☽ Sig. in ♎; ♄ Sig. in ♐; ♃ in ♐; ♃ Sig. in an earthy sign; in Hor'y Q., ♃ Sig. of the party; ♂ Sig. in ♒; ☿ ori. at B.; ♍ and ♒ give, and espec. when on the Asc. (See Beautiful, Handsome).

Well-Descended Body—♃ in an earthy sign; the ruler, or the Sig., in his own triplicity. (See Heredity).

Well-Disposed Mind—The 6th face of ♎ on the Asc. (See Humane, Kind, Noble; "Even Temper" under Temper).

Well-Favored Body — ♍ gives, and with ♍ on the Asc., but not necessarily beautiful or handsome.

Well-Formed Body — The ☉ or ☽ in ♒, in partile asp. the Asc., well-formed, middle-sized, and corpulent; the ☽ Sig. in ♊; the ☽ in ♊ or ♎, partile the Asc., well-formed and tall; ♄ ori. of the ☉; ♃ in ♊ or ♎; ♂ in ♊, partile the Asc., well-formed and tall; ♀ ori., or in the Asc.; ♀ in ♉, ♊, or ♎; ♀ in ♌ or ♐, partile the Asc., well-formed and tall; ♀ Sig. in ♒; ☿ Sig. in ♊ or ♐; ♍ on the Asc., well-formed, neat, and compact; ♊ or ♐ on the Asc., well-formed and tall; ♐ on the Asc., well-formed, rather tall and strong. (See Corpulent, Skeleton; "Well-Made" in this section).

Well-Framed Body — Tall and Elegantly Made — ♎ on the Asc. (See Skeleton).

Well-Jointed Body—(See Joints).

Well-Made Body — The ☉ gives; the ☉ as ruler; the ☉ in the Asc., rising, and well-aspected; the ☉ Sig. in ♈, ♌, or ♒; the ☉ in ♈ or ♌, partile the Asc., well-made and strong; the ☉ in ♑, partile the Asc., not very well made, and of mean stature; the ☉ or ☽ in ♒, partile the Asc., well-made, middle-sized, and corpulent; the ⚹ or △ asps. of the ☉ to the planets when the ☉ is strong and dignified at B., well-made, ruddy, and of good stature; the ☽ in ♊ or ♎, partile the Asc., well-made and tall; the ☽ in ♊, partile the Asc., well-made, tall, upright and erect; the ☽ Sig. in ♒; ♃ in ♊, ♌, ♍, or ♐; ♃ in ♌, partile the Asc., well-made, tall, and strong; ♃ in ♍, partile the Asc., well-made and handsome; ♃ in ♐, partile the Asc., well-made, fine, tall, and upright; born under strong ♃ influence, well-made, tall, and upright; ♂ ruler of the Asc., and ori.; ♂ Sig. in ♊, ♌, ♍, or ♐; ♂ in ♊, partile the Asc., well-made and tall; ♂ in ♐, partile the Asc., well-made, tall, and compact; ♀ Sig. in ♊, ♌, ♍, ♎, or ♐; ♀ in ♉, partile the Asc., well-made and fleshy; ♀ in ♊, partile the Asc., well-made, tall, and slender; ♀ in ♌ or ♐, partile the Asc., well-made and tall; ♀ in ♑, partile the Asc., well-made, handsome, and rather corpulent; ☿ in ♊, partile the Asc., well-made, tall, erect and upright; ☿ Sig. in ♎; ♊, ♍, ♎, or ♐ on the Asc.; ♍ on Asc., well-made, compact, but may be tall, slender, and of spare body; ♐ on the Asc., well-made, tall and strong. The body is usually not well-made when ♑ or ♓ are on the Asc. (See Comely, Corpulent, Crooked, Handsome, Ill-Formed; Well-Composed, Well-Favored, in this section).

Well-Preserved Body — Young Looking—Youthfulness—The ☉ hyleg, and ☌ or good asp. ♃. (See Juvenility, Preservation; "Youthfulness" under Youth).

Well-Proportioned Body—Conformity of Members—The ☉ or ☽ in the Summer Quarter Signs, as in ♋, ♌, or ♍, or these signs on the Asc.; the ☉ Sig. in ♊, ♌, ♍, ♐, or ♒; the ☉ or ☿ in ♍, partile the Asc., well-proportioned, tall, and slender; the ☽ in ♋, partile the Asc., fleshy, well-proportioned, and middle-sized; the ☽ Sig. in ♋, ♌, or ♐; ♄ ori. at B.; ♄ Sig. in ♊ or ♐, and in partile asp. the Asc.; ♄ in ♊, in good asp. the Asc., well-proportioned and tall; ♄ in ♐, partile the Asc.; ♃ in ♎, symmetry of form, and good stature; ♃ in the Asc.; ♃ Sig. in ♌; ♂ Sig. in ♊, ♌, ♍, ♎, or ♐; ♂ in ♎, partile the Asc., well-proportioned and tall; ♂ in ♍, partile the Asc., well-proportioned, middle-sized, but corpulent; ♂ in ♐, partile the Asc.; ♀ in the Asc., dignified, and well-aspected; ♀ Sig. in ♌, ♍, or ♒; ♀ in ♍, partile the Asc., well-proportioned and tall; ☿ Sig. in ♌ or ♍; ♌ on the Asc., well-proportioned and tall; ♍ on the Asc., well-proportioned, tall, slender, or compact; people born in temperate climates, with alternate heat and cold; the Quarters from the Summer Tropic to the Autumnal Equi., and from the Winter Tropic to the Vernal Equi., tend to give. (See Comely, Compact, Elegant, Handsome, Harmony; "Well-Proportioned" under Legs; "Proportioned" under Moderately; Proportionate; "Well-Shaped" in this section).

Well-Set Body — Thick Body—The ☉ or ☽ Sig. in ♉ or ♏, well-set, thick body; the ☉ in ♉, well-set, thick body; the ☉ in ♉, partile the Asc., well-set, short, and rather ugly; the ☽ in ♉, partile the Asc., well-set, strong, corpulent, and rather short; the ☽ Sig. in ♏, thick, stout, well-set, and rather ill-shaped; ♄ in ♏, partile the Asc., well-set and strong body; ♃ in ♉, partile the Asc., well-set, stout, but not handsome; ♃ in ♒, compact and well-set; born under ♂ gives a well-set, strong, short body; ♂ rising at B.; ♂ in ♈, partile the Asc., middle stature, with well-set body; ♂ in ♏, partile the Asc., well-set, middling stature; ♂ in ♐, partile the Asc., compact, well-set, and fleshy; ♂ in ♒, partile the Asc., well-set, middling, and corpulent, and some Authors say tall; ♀ Sig. in ♉ or ♏; ♀ in ♉, partile the Asc., well-set, corpulent, and of middling stature; ♀ in ♏, partile the Asc., well-set, stout, and corpulent; ☿ Sig. in ♉, thick, stout, and well-set; ☿ in ♉, partile the Asc., well-set, corpulent, and middle stature; ☿ in ♏, partile the Asc., full, well-set, and with broad shoulders; ♉ or ♏ on the Asc.; ♒ on the Asc., well-set, strong, robust, plump, and healthy make. (See Compact, Corpulent, Muscular, Stout, Thick; "Well-Trussed" in this section).

Well-Shaped Body — Good Shape — Handsome—♀ in the Asc., or ruler of the Asc.; ♀ Sig. in Hor'y Q.; ♀ Sig. ☌ ☿; ☿ in ♐, partile the Asc., well-shaped, tall, but spare and large-boned; the ⚹ or △ asps. of ☿, and ☿ well-dignified. Also ♄ lord of the Asc., and occi., as between the M.C. and Desc., or between the Nadir and Asc., is said to give a good shape. (See Handsome; "Well-Proportioned" in this section).

Well-Trussed — Squab — Squat — Fat and Short — Thick-Trussed — In Hor'y Q., ♄ Sig. in ♏, squat and well-trussed; ☿ Sig. in ♋, squab and well-trussed; ☿ Sig. in ♓, short, squab, well-trussed, and dumpy; ♏ and ♒ give. (See Corpulent, Fleshy, Lumpish, Plump, Stout; "Well-Set" in this section).

WENCH — (See Harlots, Lewd; "Low Company" under Low; "Harlots" under Men; Shameless).

WENS—A Sebaceous Cyst—Steatoma—A Sebaceous Encysted Tumor—♂ ☌ or ill-asp. ♃; ♂ ☌ ♃ in ♈, in the head; ♂ ☌ ♃ in ♉, in the neck; a ♉ disease. (See Cysts, Sebaceous).

WESTERN SIGNS — Of the Zodiac — ♊, ♎, ♒. (See Eastern, Northern, Signs of the Zodiac, Southern).

WET—Damp—Moist—

Bed Wetting — (See "Incontinence" under Urine).

Dreams — Wet Dreams — (See Emissions, Semen).

Feet—Wet Feet—(See "Bowel Complaints", "Cold Taken", "Damp", under Feet).

Journeys — (See "Wet" under Journeys).

Linen—Wet Linen or Clothing—Colds Taken By—The ☽ in ♓, ☌ or ill-asp. ♄ (or ☿ if he be of the nature of ♄) at the beginning of an illness, or at decumb., from wet feet or damp linen. (See "Colds Taken" under Feet; Linen; "Colds" under Moisture).

WHALE—

Sperm Whale—(See Ambergris).

Whale's Belly — Influences of — (See "Danger" under Blows; Falls).

Whale's Jaw — Ceti — Menkar — Influences of—(See Ceti, Disgrace; "Every Evil" under Evil; Menkar; "Much Sickness" under Sickness; Thieves).

WHEAT — Scarcity of — An eclipse of the ☉ in ♌; an eclipse of the ☉ or ☽ in earthy signs, and such grain as is sown Annually. (See Corn, Drought, Famine, Fruit, Grain; "Corn" under Scarcity; Vegetation).

WHEEZING—A Sibliant Respiration—(See "Labored" under Breathing).

WHIMS — Whimsical — Capricious — Eccentric—The ☽ affl. in ♒; ♀ ill-dig. at B.; ♑ influence tends to make the native whimsical, witty, and subtle; the 7° ♑ on the Asc., carried away with foolish whims. (See Eccentric; "Foolish Fancies" under Fancy).

WHISPERING — Whispering Voice—(See "Aphonia" under Voice).

Whistling Roughness — To the Voice —A Whistling Sound In the Voice—(See "Hoarseness" under Larynx; "Rough" under Voice).

WHITE — White is ruled by the ☽. White is the Symbol of the Full Moon, which is also the Symbol of Initiation. The 1st H. has signification of white, and espec. if a planet in the 1st at B. has signification of white, as the ☽. White is also ruled by the 5th, 9th and 10th houses. Ruled by ♀ and ♓. In Hor'y Q., ♀ rules white. All the colors are contained in white. White, the color signified by the ☽, has a passive power, and is the sign of radical moisture. The ☽ also denotes a white-spotted, or light mixed color. White and purple mixed are denoted by ♀. White and red are denoted by ♈. Also ♊ denotes white and red mixed. Pure white, or glistening white, is ruled by ♓. (See Colors).

Blindness—From White Film—(See "Film" under Blindness).

Blood—White Blood Corpuscles—(See Leukocytes).

Color—White Color—(See the Introduction to this section).

Complexion — A White Complexion — Clear—Fair—Pale, etc.—☉ strong at B., a white and tender skin; the ☉ generally denotes an obscure white color, mixed with red; ☉ Sig. in ♒, clear and white; ☽ Sig. in Hor'y Ques., face more white than red; the ☽ gives a whitely-colored stature; ☽ ascending at B., a whitish complexion; ☽ in Asc., pale and white; ☽ strong at B. gives a red and white mixed, but tending to paleness; ☽ Sig. in ♊, between a white and red complexion; ☽ Sig. in ♎, partile Asc., a fine, red and white complexion; ☽ Sig. in ♍, white skin; ☽ Sig. in ♒, clear and white; ♅ and ☿ rising in the Asc., a white skin; ♄ Sig. of the party, a pale and white complexion; ♃ strong at B., or ♃ Sig. of the person, a white and red mixture; ♃ ori., clear and white, or between a white and red complexion; ♃ ruler of the Asc., and ori., fair and white; ♂ ori. at B., and Martialists, some white mixed with red; ♀ ori., clear and white; ♀ in power at B., pale and white, but with a dark hue; ♀ Sig. in ♈, ♊, ♌, ♎, ♐, ♒, fair and white; ♀ Sig. in ♓ with females gives a clear, lucid skin, but very white; ☿ Sig. in ♒, clear and white; ♋ gives white and pale; ♎ infl. tends to neither excess of red nor white in youth, but pimpled or ruddy in old age; ♒ gives clear, white and delicate except when ♄ is in ♒; ♓ in females gives a clear, lucid and white, and ordinarily a chalky skin appearance; being born in cold climates, with alternating hot and cold Seasons, a whitish complexion. (For other influences see Cadaverous; "Good Complexion" under Complexion; Face, Fair, Light, Pale, Sickly, Skin).

Corpuscles — White Blood Corpuscles —(See Leukocytes).

Eyes—White Film Over—(See "Film" under Blindness; "Blindness" under Cold).

Face — White Face — (See "Complexion" in this section; Pale, Sickly).

Females—Complexion White and Lucid In—♓ gives. (See "Complexion" in this section).

Film — White Film Over Eyes — (See "Film" under Blindness).

Fingers—The Fingers Cold and White —(See "Raynaud" under Fingers).

Fluids—The White Fluids of the Body —The Body Oil—Ruled by the ☽. These fluids are obstructed when ♄ is in ☌ or ill-asp., the ☽ at B., and by dir.

Hair — The Hair Turns White In a Night—A Case Record—(See "White" under Hair).

Leprosy—White Leprosy—(See Leprosy).

Magic—White Magic—(See Magic).

Marks—White Marks On the Body—Indicated by the ☽, and the sign containing the ☽. (See Marks).

Nose — Whiteness of — (See "Cold Nose" under Nose).

Pale and White — (See Pale; "Complexion" under Poor; Sickly; "Complexion" in this section).

Red and White — A Mixed Red and White Complexion—(See "Complexion" in this section).

Skin—White Skin—(See "White" under Skin; "Complexion" in this section).

Toes—Whiteness of—(See "Raynaud" under Fingers).

WHITES — In Women — (See Leucorrhoea).

WHITLOWS — Panaris — Phlegmonous Inflammation About the Nails — (See "Whitlows" under Toes).

WHOLE—The Whole Body—The Entire Body—Whole Signs, etc.—

Abscesses—Over the Body, and Due to Bad Blood—♃ affl. in ♉. (See Abscesses).

Aches and Pains — Over the Entire Body—(See Aches; "Pains" in this section).

Disordered — The Whole Frame Disordered—The Disease Is Thru the Entire Body—The ☉, ☽, and Asc. afflicted; the ☽ in ♉, and affl. by the ☉ or ♂ when taken ill (Hor'y).

Dropsy — Over the Body — General Dropsy — (See "Anasarca" under Dropsy).

Entire Body Disordered — (See "Disordered" in this section).

Fever — In the Whole Body — The ☉ directed to Cor Scorpio. (See Fever).

Frame—The Whole Frame Disordered —(See "Disordered" in this section).

General—The Distemper Is General—Over the Whole Body—The ☽ affl. at B., and to the evil asps. the Asc. by dir. (See General).

Gnawing Pains — Over the Entire Body — (See "Pains" in this section; "Flying", "Gnawing", "Shooting", under Pain).

Heaviness — Over the Body — (See Aches, Dull, Feeble, Heavy Malaise).

Humours — The Whole Body Full of Gross Humours—(See Gross; "Gross" under Humours).

Imperfections — All Over the Body — Given by the ♋ sign, and afflictions in ♋. (See Imperfections).

Inflammation — All Over the Body — (See "All Over" under Inflammation).

Joints — Pain In the Joints All Over the Body—(See "Pain" under Joints).

Pains—Gnawing and Shooting Pains Over the Whole Body—The ☽ to the ☌ or ill-asp. ♄ by dir., the whole body suffers from aches and pains; the ☽ in ♊, and affl. by the ☉ or ♂ when taken ill (Hor'y); the ☽ ☌ ☉, combust, or the ☽ ☌ ♅, ♄, or ♂ at the beginning of an illness, or at decumb., and espec. if the party be old (Hor'y). (See "Gnawing" in this section).

Shooting Pains—Over the Body—(See "Pains" in this section).

Signs—The Whole Signs of the Zodiac —The Airy Signs, ♊, ♎, and ♒, and those born under these signs tend to be more robust, strong, and also more immune from accidents. (See "Air Signs" under Air).

Tone — The Tone of the Whole Body Lowered—The ☽ affl. in ♏. (See Tone).

WHOLESOME AIR—Pure and Good Air —(See Air).

WHOOPING COUGH—Pertussis—A Violent Convulsive Cough — A ♊ and ♐ disease; ♊ on cusp of 6th H.; ☿ affl. at B. by malefics, and the hyleg also afflicted; ☿ occi. at B., affl. by malefics, and ☿ affl. the hyleg by dir., and taking part in a train of fatal directions, tends to death by whooping cough; the Asc. to the □ or ☍ ☿ and ☿ affl. at B.; the hyleg much afflicted at B. Subs at LCP (6, 7C), and at SP. Coral Necklaces, or Amulets, are worn against Whooping Cough, and the drug, Corallium Rubrum, a Calcium Carbonate, Chalk, or Lime preparation, is useful in its cure. (See Amulets, Chalk; "Convulsive" under Cough; Talisman).

WICKED— Evil — Depraved — Vicious— Sinful—

Children — Wicked Children — (See Eleventh House; "Bad Children", "Injured", under Parents).

Countenance — Wicked and Cruel Countenance—♂ rising in the Asc. or M.C. at B., and afflicted by ♄. (See Abandoned, Cruel, Depraved, Evil; "Shows No Pity" under Pity; Profane, Vicious).

WIDE—Broad—

Chest—(See "Wide" under Chest).

Face — The Face Wide Across the Cheeks — (See Decanates; "Wide" under Face).

Head — The Head Wide Between the Temples—(See Decanates).

Mouth—(See "Wide" under Mouth).

Nose—(See "Wide" under Nose).

Shoulders—(See "Broad" under Shoulders).

WIDOWERS—The ☽ ori. in an angle in ♊, ♐, or ♓; the ☽ in this situation, and applying to several planets in oriental signs, indicates two or three marriages for men, by death of wife, or divorce. (See Fiancee; "Death" under Marriage Partner; "Death of Wife" under Wife).

WIDOWS—Often Becomes a Widow— The ☉ in an angle, ori., and in asp. to many planets oriental in ♊, ♐, or ♓; the ☽ incr. in light at B., and applying to ♄; the evil asps. of ♄ and malefics to the ☉, or ♄ in the 7th H. of the wife's horoscope; the 2nd face of ♍ on the Asc., which face contains the unfortunate star Vindemiatrix. Case — See "Princess", No. 851, in 1001 N.N. (See "Death of Husband" under Husband).

WIFE—The ☽ rules the wife in a male nativity, and afflictions to the ☽, and in the 7th H. in the husband's map of birth indicate her fate and the state of her health.

Accident To—♅ or ♂ affl. in ♎ or the 7th H. in a male nativity.

Afflicted — The Wife Afflicted — The directions of the ☽ in the husband's horoscope afflict and affect the wife for good or ill; ♄ in 7th H. of husband's map, and affl. by the ☉ or ☽; to marry when ♄ or ♂ are in the Asc. or 7th H., or the planet signifying the wife being combust in the husband's horo., indicates a life of affliction or sorrow to the wife. (See the various paragraphs in this section).

Barren—(See Barren).

Childbirth—The Wife Benefits By—♃ in the 11th H., and well-asp. (See Parturition).

Danger to Wife—☽ hyleg and to the ☌ or ill-asp. ♅ by dir.; ☽ to the place of Hercules by dir.; ☽ in 7th H., and eclipsed at a Solar Rev., and affl. by ♅, ♄, or ♂, and especially if the place of a malefic planet at B. ascends, or if ♄ ascends also at the time; ♄ in the 7th H. at B., and again in the 7th at a Solar Rev.; M.C. to the ill-asps. the ☽ or ♀ by dir.

Death of Wife—Death of Wife Threatened—These influences are to be noted in the husband's horoscope—The ☉ or

☽ to the ☌ or ill-asp. ♄, ♅, or ♂ by dir.; the ☉ to the ill-asps. the ☽ by dir.; the ☽ applying first to ♃, and then to ♅, and ♅ or ♄ be in the 7th H.; the ☽ to the ill-asps. the ☉ or ♀ by dir.; the ☽ to the place of Rigel or Cor Scorpio; ♅ or ♄ affl. in the 7th H. in husband's horo.; ♄ ruler of the 7th H. at B., and to the ☌ or ill-asp. the Asc. by dir.; ♄ passing over the place of the ☽ or ♀ at B. by tr. or at a Solar Rev.; ♄ to the ☌ or ill-asp. the ☽ or ♀ by dir.; the M.C. to the ill-asps. the ☽ or ♀ by dir.; lord of the 7th in the 2nd, wife does not live to be old. (See "Early Death" in this section; "Death" under Marriage Partner).

Dies Before Husband—Malefics in the 7th in husband's map, or lord of 7th a malefic, and with benefic influences over the 7th in the wife's horo. In Horary Questions, the lord of the 1st H. and the ☽ are taken for the man, and the lord of the 7th and the ☉ for the woman, and judge of the nature of the aspects to them. Another method is to measure the distance in degrees between the lords of the 1st and 7th, and the lord of the 8th, and then predict that the one will die first whose Sig. is nearer the lord of the 8th; the planet to which the ☽ first applies being a malefic; malefics affl. the ☽ in husband's horo.; the ruler of the 7th a malefic and R. (See Fiancee; "Dies Before Wife" under Husband; Widowers, Widows).

Directions — (See "Afflicted" in this section).

Dissolute Habits — Wife Given To — Profligate—☽ □ or ☍ ♀ in husband's horo. (See "Drink" in this section).

Drink—Given To—Influences in husband's map—☽ □, ☍ ♀; ♂ ☌ or ill-asp. ☽; ♂ in 7th H. in ♋, ♏, or ♓, and affl. the ☽.

Early Death—Wife May Die Soon After Marriage—Lord of the 6th in the 7th, and espec. if ♂ be in the 7th; malefics in the 7th H. in the husband's map. (See "Early Death" under Husband; "Death", "Early Death", under Marriage Partner).

Father—Wife's Father Afflicted—Lord of the 6th in the 10th H. (See Father).

Fiancee — Ill-Health, or Death of — (See Fiancee; "Ill-Health" in this section).

Fruitful—Wife Will Be Fruitful—♃ in the 11th H. of the husband's map if the map of the wife is also fruitful. (See Fruitful; "Fruitful" under Husband).

Grave and Morose—The ☽ apply. to ♄ in the husband's map of birth.

Habits—(See Dissolute, Drink, in this section).

Has Children — By Other Men — (See (Bastards; "Untrue" in this section).

Husband — Suffers Thru Wife — Sickness Caused by Wife—Lord of the 7th in the 6th, 8th, or 12th houses in husband's map.

Ill-Fortune To—☽ to the place of Hydra's Heart.

Ill-Health Of—Wife May Suffer—Illness of Wife or Fiancee — The Wife

Sickly—The ☽ applying to any asp. of
♄ in a man's horo., and ♄ be in the
7th H.; the ☽ or ♀ in the 7th H. at a
Solar Rev. and ☌ or ☍ ♅, ♄, or ♂; the
☽ at a Solar Rev. passing over the
place of ♄ at B.; ☽ to the □ or ☍ ☉ or
♀ by dir.; the ☽, or Pr. ☽, to the ☌
or ill-asp. ♄; ♄ passing over the place
of the ☽ or ♀ at B. by tr.; M.C. to the
☌ or ill-asp. the ☽ or ♀ if either be
weak and affl. at B. (See Improvident;
"Dissipated", "Drink", in this section).

Infamous—The Wife Infamous—The
☽ at Full, or incr. in a nocturnal sign,
sepr. from ♀, and apply. to ♄. (See
Infamous).

Jealous of Wife—(See "Jealousy" under Love Affairs).

Marriage Partner—(See this subject).

Mind Unsound — Has Nervous Disorders—☿ in 7th H. in husband's horo.,
and affl. by ♅ or ♂.

Murdered—By Husband—(See "Murders His Wife", "Strangles", under
Husband).

Nervous Disorders Of — (See "Mind
Unsound" in this section).

Plurality of Wives—(See "Plurality"
under Husband).

Relatives—The Wife's Relatives—Ill-
Health of — Lords of the 6th, 8th, or
12th a malefic, and in the 9th H., and
affl.; lord of the 9th a malefic and affl.;
malefics in the 9th H., and affl. (See
"Relatives" under Husband, Marriage
Partner).

Self-Indulgent—(See "Self-Indulgent"
under Marriage Partner; "Dissipation",
"Drink", in this section).

Seventh House—(See Marriage, Marriage Partner, Seventh House).

Several Wives—(See "Plurality" under Husband).

Sickness of Wife — (See "Ill-Health"
in this section).

Sterile—(See Barren).

Strangled—By Husband—(See "Murdered" in this section).

Sudden Death Of—♅ or ♂ affl. in the
7th H. in the husband's map. (See
"Death" in this section).

Suffers—Wife May Suffer—(See "Ill-
Health", and other paragraphs in this
section).

Time of Marriage—A Bad Time, and
Consequent Suffering—(See "Afflicted"
in this section).

Troublesome—The Wife Troublesome
—(See "Grave" in this section).

Unfruitful — The Wife May Be Unfruitful—♄ in the 11th H. (See Barren,
Maimed).

Unsound Mind — (See "Mind" in this
section).

Untrue — Wife Unfaithful — ♅ in the
7th H., □ or ☍ the ☽ in the husband's
map.

Widows—(See Widows).

WILD—Feral—Untamed—Savage—

Wild Animals—Attacks By—Death or
Injury By—The ☽ with ♄ and Sirius,
or with ♂ and Markab. (See "Wild
Animals" under Animals; Ferocious;
"Dangers" under Travel).

Wild Conduct — (See Conduct, Debauched, Dissipated, Evil, Loose, Low,
Morals, Perverse, Prodigal, Riotous).

Wild Delirium—(See Delirium).

Wild Fancies — (See Fancies, Vagaries).

Wild Nature—Indocile—Savage—(See
"Dogs" under Children; "Inhuman;
"Animal Forms" under Monsters; Sav-
age).

WILDERNESS—Lost In—(See Desert).

WILL — The Will — Will Power — Volition—The Power of Willing—The Stars
do not rule the Will, and the powers
of the Will, and what people will do,
is not always revealed in the horoscope. The Will is Divine, and by taking control of the life can, by the
proper efforts, largely change the limitations and afflictions indicated in the
map of birth, and the Will can be
asserted to such an extent as to
largely overcome the indications of the
birth map. However, it takes knowledge, and an increased consciousness
of power to do this, a realization of
your own Divinity, of your Higher
Self, of the God within you. Many
people are endowed with great powers,
but are unconscious of them, and drift
along thru life half asleep, and then
when awakened, the Will Power can
lead them on to new achievements, to
good health, to greater usefulness,
even tho they were passive and negative by birth. Astrology is a good
study to show and explain the causes
of things, the philosophy of life, but
it may not teach you how to think,
and for this you need Metaphysics,
Philosophy, Religion, Psychology, and
the Mental and Spiritual Sciences. We
are not here upon this Earth Plane
merely to hunt for happiness, worldly
pleasures, but to overcome the world,
to achieve, and to gain Soul Growth
from the experiences of life, and our
Will Power is given us to help us to
do these things, rather than to go thru
life as weaklings, sufferers, invalids,
failures, misfits, etc. The study of
your star map will show you your
natural fitness, your tendencies, the
lines of least resistance for you for
the best success, and then it is within
your power to follow up these leadings, and make a success of your life,
talents and powers.

Disorders of Volition — Affl. in ♐; ♆
affl. in ♐ or 9th H.

Free Will—The stars do not rule the
human Will, and Man is a free moral
agent to do and act according to his
degree of advancement, enlightenment,
knowledge, and self-control. Man is
held responsible for the influences
stamped upon him at B., and if his
Chart of Birth predominates in evil
aspects and tendencies, he is expected
to master the evils, transcend, and allow the good to predominate, and to
seek to perfect his nature and character, as perfection is the ultimate goal
of all life on Earth. We are all Gods
in the making, all Children of God at
various stages in our Evolution. Some
cannot keep up with the procession,
and fall out of line, become laggards,
stragglers, all because in the use of

their free will they have chosen the downward path of sin, wickedness, debauchery, and dissipation, instead of the upward path which leads to God. The Higher Mind is The God, or The Christ within us, and when this Super Mind is awakened, and we become conscious of our Inner Divine Powers, then we direct the Free Will within us to higher attainments, self-control, and the attainment of knowledge, wisdom, discretion, discrimination, spiritual power, and to conquer and overcome the World. Be careful how you use this gift of Free Will. The Animals do not have free will, but are under the power and direction of Group Spirits, and act according to Instinct. Man is above Instinct, and can be ruled by his own Spirit, his Higher and Divine Mind, when he allows his Mind and Body to be used for good and high purposes, and not to live just for the gratification of his animal nature, or to carry out selfish and unholy purposes. (See Character, Fate, Negative Nature, Positive Nature, Self-Control, Spiritual; "Positive", "Strong", "Weak", in this section).

Insistent Will — ♂ influence. (See Bold, Folly, Foolhardy, Quarrelsome, Recklessness, Riotous, Violent, etc.).

Loss of Volition—♐ influence, and afflictions in this sign; ♆ affl. in ♐. (See Catalepsy, Clairvoyance, Hypnotism, Influenced, Involuntary, Mediumship, Negative Nature, Obsessions, Passive, Spirit Controls, Volition, Voluntary; "Weak" in this section).

Negative — Passive — (See "Negative Nature" under Negative; "Weak" in this section).

Positive — A Positive and Strong-Willed Person—(See "Positive Nature" under Positive; "Strong" in this section).

Self-Willed — The 30° ♓ on the Asc. (See Obstinate, Rebellious, Stubborn).

Spasmodic Will—(See "Weak" in this section).

Spirit Fire—The Spinal Spirit Fires of ♆ are said to represent the Will. (See "Spirit Fire" under Spine).

Strengthened—The Will Strengthened — The ☉ ☌ or P ☿ increases and strengthens the Will, and gives the mind more power to resist disease, and act against disorders. (See "Strong" in this section).

Strong Will—Powerful Will—The Will Strengthened—The ☉, ♅, and ♄ tend to give strong will-power when strongly placed at birth; the ☉ ⚹ or △ ♂; the ☉ ☌ or P ☿; ♆ ⚹ or △ ♅; many planets in fixed signs, or in masculine signs at B.; many planets elevated in the east at B.; a Stellium in the Asc. or midheaven, in a masculine sign; cardinal or fixed signs on the angles, and with many planets in positive signs; the first face of ♏ on the Asc. (See Elevated, Majority; "Positive Nature" under Nature; Rising, Rule; "Strengthened" in this section).

Weak Will—Spasmodic Will—Planets in ♊, and opposed by malefics in ♐, the Will is weak or spasmodic; ♓ on the Asc., devoid of much will-power; the 3° of ♋ on Asc. The weakest-willed signs are ♎ and ♓. The mutable signs tend to indecision, and the watery signs to emotion, susceptible to external influences, to environment, and to be more easily influenced. Courage, self-confidence, and determination, are given by ♂ rising and strong at B. (See "Will-Power" under Drink; Influenced, Involuntary; "Weak Nature" under Nature; "Negative Nature" under Negative, Obsessions, Passive; "Lacking In" under Resolution; Spirit Controls, Vacillating; "Loss Of" in this section).

WIND—Winds—The following subjects have to do with Wind, Gas, or Air, both in the body and outside, and with Windy Diseases, and also Windy Weather. See these subjects in the alphabetical arrangement when only listed here—

Abdomen — Wind In — (See "Bowels" in this section).

Air; All Diseases—Arising from Wind In Bowels—♍ diseases, and afflictions in ♍; ♅ or ☿ affl. in ♍. (See Colic, Flatulence, Gas, Tympanites).

Atmosphere; Blasting Winds—Blasts of Wind — Death or Injury By — (See Air; "Fountains" under Dry; Heat; "Tempests", "Tornadoes", in this section).

Blizzards; Blood—Wind In the Blood —♃ affl. in ♉; ☿ affl. in ♊ or ♒. (See Flatulence; the Introduction under Spasmodic; "Windiness" under Veins).

Bowels—Wind In—Wind Colic—Flatulent Colic—Afflictions in ♍; a ♍ disease; ♍ on Asc.; a ☽ disease; ☽ ♍, and affl. by the ☉ or ♂ when taken ill; the ☽ or ♂ in ♍, and ♄ ruler of the 6th H. when taken ill; ♅ affl. in ♍, wind spasm, spasmodic pains and cramps from wind in bowels; ☿ lord of the Asc., and applying to the □ or ☍ a malefic; ☿ affl. in ♍, much wind in bowels; ☿ ♍ ☌ or ill-asp. any of the malefics as promittors; afflictions in ♒. (See "Cramps" under Bowels; Colic, Flatulence, Gas, Tympanites).

Cramps; Danger from Winds — (See the various paragraphs in this section).

Death or Injury — By Winds — (See "Storms", "Tornadoes", in this section).

Disorders — Windy Disorders — (See Blood, Bowels, Colic, Spasm, Stomach, in this section).

East Winds—Caused and ruled by ♄. (See Eastern).

Flatulence; Gas; Heart—Wind Around the Heart—☿ in ♌.

High Winds—Hurricanes—Tornadoes —Suffering From—♊ ascending at the Vernal Equi., and ☿ afflicted, and in places and Countries ruled by ♊; comets appearing in ♊; ☿ in an angle at an Equinox or Solstice; ☉ ☌ ☿; ♒ ascending at the Vernal Equinox, and places under ♒ suffer; ♂ in power at the Vernal, and lord of the year; ♂ in power at an Equinox or Solstice. (See "Corrupt Air" under Air; "Fountains" under Dry; "Storms", "Tornadoes", in this section).

Hot Blasting Winds — Parched and Hot — Much Suffering From — ♂ in power, and lord of the year at the

Vernal. (See Drought, Famine; "Excessive Heat" under Heat; "Winds" under Pestilence).

Hurricanes—(See "High Winds", "Tornadoes", in this section).

Loss of Life — From High Winds — (See High Winds, Storms, Tornadoes, in this section; Sea, Ships, Shipwreck, Voyages).

Pestilential Winds—(See "Winds" under Pestilence).

Shipwreck—(See "Hurricanes" under Shipwreck).

Snow Storms—(See Blizzards, Snow).

Spasm—Wind Spasms—(See Bowels, Stomach, in this section).

Stomach—Wind Spasm In—♅, ☿ or ☽ affl. in ♋. (See Colic, Flatulence; "Stomach" under Gas).

Storms—Danger from Wind Storms—An eclipse of the ☉ or ☽ in airy signs; ☉ hyleg, and to the ☌ or ill-asp. ♄ by dir.; ♄, ♂ and ☿ conjoined, great loss of life from wind storms and tempests; the afflictor to the Significators of travel in the 12th H. in a fixed sign, great danger from wind storms during travel; ♎ ascending at the Vernal, and ♀ also be afflicted; malefics in the 9th H., and affl. the ☉ or ☽ in airy signs, danger from wind storms on voyages and long journeys. (See "Tornadoes" in this section; Floods, Sea, Ships, Shipwreck, Travel, Voyages).

Strong Winds — (See "Tornadoes" in this section).

Tempests—(See "Storms" in this section; "Tempests" under Sea).

Tornadoes — Strong Winds — Hurricanes—♄ and ♂ in fixed signs, widely separated, and controlling the Luminaries. (See "Fountains" under Dry; "Sun Spots" under Spots; "High Winds", "Storms", in this section).

Travel—Suffers from Wind Storms In Travel—(See "Storms" in this section).

Tympanites; Veins — Windiness In — (See "Blood" in this section).

Voyages—Wind Storms—Tempests—(See "Storms" in this section).

Weather; Wind Colic—(See "Bowels" in this section).

WINDPIPE — Trachea—The Cartilaginous Tube extending from the Larynx to the Bronchi—Ruled by the ♉ and ♊ signs. For Disorders of, see Trachea.

WINE—

Addicted To — A Craving For — ☽ ♓; ☽ in ♉ or ♓, and affl. by the ☉ or ♂ when taken ill; ☿ Sig. in ♓. (See Drink, Food, Thirst).

Surfeit of Wine — Diseases Arising From—☽ ♎ ☌ ♄ (or ☿ if he be of the nature of ♄), at the beginning of an illness, or at decumbiture. (See "Excesses" under Diet).

WINKING—Spasmodic and Involuntary—(See Eyelids).

WINTER — Those born in the Winter months have a weaker constitution than those born in the Spring months. Diseases beginning in Winter are longer than those beginning in Summer, and are more apt to run into a chronic form.

Cold Winter — (See Blizzards, Frost, Ice, Snow; "Cold" under Weather).

Dry Winter — ♂ in ♌ at the Winter Solstice.

Winter Signs — Of the Zodiac — The Hyemal Signs—♑, ♒, ♓.

Winter Solstice—The time when the ☉ enters ♑. (See Solstice).

WIRY BODY—Wiry Constitution—♐ on the Asc. (See Endurance; "Good" under Resistance, Stamina, Tone, Vitality; "Body" under Strong).

Wiry Hair—Wiry and Rough—♈ on the Asc. (See Hair).

WISDOM—Discretion—Good Judgment — Understanding — Discrimination — Power, etc.—

Lacking In Wisdom—(See Foolhardy, Imprudent, Indiscreet; "Bad" under Judgment; Recklessness, etc.).

Seeker After Wisdom—(See Independent, Knowledge, Learning, Metaphysical, Misunderstood, Occult, Philosophy, Religion, Science, Spiritual, Truth).

WISHES — The Hopes, Wishes, Ambitions, Desires, are ruled by the 11th H. (See Ambition, Desire, Hope).

WIT—Comprehension—Reason—Judgment—

Acute Wit—Ready Wit—(See "Quickened" under Mentality).

Dull Wit—(See "Mind" under Dull).

WITCHCRAFT—Ruled and denoted by the 12th H.

Tendency To — ♆ ☌ ☿ in the 12th H. (See "Black Magic" under Magic; Sorcery, Spirit Controls).

WITCH-HAZEL — Ruled by ♂. (See "Mars Group" under Herbs).

WITHERING—Blight—Fading—Decay—Withered—(See Blight). ♆ in signs which rule the Arms, Hands, Legs, and Feet, tends to withering, shrinking, and wasting of these parts. (See Atrophy, Decay, Dry, Old Age, Shrinkage, Wasting, Wrinkles).

WOE — Affliction — Grief — Sorrow — Usually brought on by the afflictions and testings of ♄, and as a result of wrong living and thinking. (See Affliction, Disgrace, Grief, Miseries, Misfortune, Reputation, Reverses, Ruin, Sorrow, Suffering, Trouble, etc.).

WOMB—Uterus—Matrix—The Womb is ruled by the ☽ and ♀ among the planets. Ruled to some extent by the ♋ sign, the sign of the ☽. Ruled by the 6th H. and the ♍ sign. By their internal government, ruled by the ♊, ♋, ♍, ♏, ♐ and ♓ signs, and influenced by planets in these signs. The Matrix is under the rule of ♓, especially when Syphilitic contagion is involved. The Womb as a receptacle is ruled by the ♋ sign. The Cervix, the Glandular portion of the Womb, the Neck, is ruled by the ♏ sign. The following subjects have to do with the Womb, which see in the alphabetical arrangement when not considered here—

Abortions; All Diseases—Of the Womb—Signified by the 7th H.

Barren; Birth; Broad Ligaments — A fold of the Peritoneum—Ruled by ♍. Disorders of, affl. in ♍, and also caused by subluxations at PP, the 3rd lumbar vertebrae. (See Vertebrae).

Cancer Of—Carcinoma—(See "Generative System" under Carcinoma).

Catamenial Disorders—(See Menses).

Catarrh—Mucus In—The ☽ in ♎ or ♑, ☌, or ill-asp. any of the malefics as promittors; ♄ affl. in ♏; Subs at PP 2, 3, 4L), and at KP. (See Leucorrhoea).

Cervix — (See Cervix; "Contraction", "Neuralgia", in this section).

Change of Life — (See "Menopause" under Menses).

Child Dies In Womb—(See Stillborn).

Childbed Fever—(See Parturition).

Childbirth—(See Parturition).

Chronic — Chronic Womb Trouble—♄ affl. in ♋ or ♏ in the 8th H.

Conception; Contraction Of — Hour-Glass Contraction of — Case — (See "Hour-Glass", No. 240 in 1001 N.N.).

Death—Death by Womb Trouble—☽ occi., □ or ☍ ♄ in map of child; ♄ affl. in ♏ in map of the mother. Case of Sudden Death by Womb Trouble—See "Uterine", No. 985 in 1001 N.N. (See Abortion, Cancer Of, Hemorrhage, Tumors, in this section).

Death In the Womb—(See Stillborn).

Defects Of—Affl. in ♏, and ♏ diseases.

Deformity Of—♅ affl. in ♏.

Disordered Womb—Diseased—Uterine Affections — Matrix Disordered, etc. — The ☉ or ☽ affl. in ♏; ♏ diseases; afflictions in ♏; ☉ affl. in ♓; ☽ to the ill-asps. ♀ by dir., and espec. if the ☽ or ♀ be in the 5th H., or ruler of the 5th, or in ♉ or ♏; ☽ to the ill-asps. ♀ by dir., and ♀ in a water sign at B., and espec. in ♏; ☽ ♏ ☌ or ill-asp. ♄ (or ☿ if he be of the nature of ♄) at the beginning of an illness, or at decumbiture; the ☽ afflicted; ♅ affl. in ♏; ♄ ☌ ♆ and ♂ in ♉ or ♏; ♄ in an angle, occi. of the ☉ and ori. of the ☽; ♄ affl. in ♋ or ♏; ♂ affl. in ♏; ♀ affl. in ♈ or ♏; ♀ diseases are principally those of the matrix and members of generation, and espec. if ♀ be ruler of the 5th H., and throw an evil asp. to the ☽ or Asc.; ♀ affl. by evil aspects; ♀ in ♏ and affl. the ☽ or Asc.; ♀ in ♏ in the 6th H., and afflicted; ♀ affl. by ♄ or ♂; ☿ affl. in ♈; afflictions in ♍; ♍ diseases, and espec. when malefics are in ♍ in the 6th H. at B., and afflicted; malefics in ♉ or ♏; ♏ on the Asc.; Subs at PP (2, 3, 4L). Case of Disordered Womb—See Fig. 8H in the book, "Astro-Diagnosis" by the Heindels. (See the various paragraphs in this section).

Embryo—Disorders of—(See Foetus).

Excessive Menses—(See Menses).

Falling Of—Prolapsus—Afflictions in ♏; a ♏ disease; the ☽, ♄, ♂ or ♀ affl. in ♏; Subs at LPP (5L). (See Prolapsus).

Fallopian Tubes—(See Fallopian).

Fecundation; Fibroid Tumor—♄ affl. in ♏; ♄ ☌ ☽ in ♏; ♂ ☌ ♀ or ☿ in ♏; malefics in ♉ or ♏.

Flexion — Bending of the Uterus — ♄ affl. in ♏; Subs at PP (4, 5, 6L).

Flooding—(See Menses).

Fruitful; Generation—Disorders of—(See Generation, Reproduction, Sex).

Gestation; Hemorrhage—Of the Womb —♂ affl. in ♏; ♂ in ♏, and affl. the ☉, ☽, or Asc.; ♂ in ♏ in the 6th H. (See Abortion; "Childbirth" under Hemorrhage; "Flooding" under Menses; Miscarriage).

Hour-Glass Contraction — Irregular Contraction of the Womb—Contracted Cervix—♅ or ♄ affl. in ♉ or ♏. (See "Contraction" in this section).

Impregnation—(See Conception, Fecundation).

Inflammation — Metritis — The ☽ affl. by ♂ at the birth of child often tends to; ♄ or ♂ affl. in ♏; ♂ ♏ in 6th H.; ♂ ♏ and affl. the ☽ or Asc.; afflictions in ♏; a ♏ disease; a ♍ disease, and espec. when malefics in ♍ in the 6th H. at B., and afflicted.

Injuries To—A ♏ affliction; malefics in ♍ or ♏, and espec. when in the 6th H. at B., and afflicted; ♂ affl. in ♏ in 6th or 8th H. (See "Excision" under Foetus).

Leucorrhoea; Maternity; Matrix—Defects of—Disorders of—(See "Defects", "Disorders", and other subjects in this section).

Menopause; Menses; Metritis — (See "Inflammation" in this section).

Miscarriage; Mother—Womb Trouble In—(See "Womb" under Mother).

Mucous In — (See "Catarrh" in this section).

Neck Of—Cervix—Disorders of—Neuralgia of — (See Cervix, Hour-Glass, Neuralgia, Stricture, in this section).

Obstruction In—♄ in ♏. (See "Hour-Glass" in this section).

Operations On—Avoid when the ☽ is in ♍, ♎, or ♏. (See "Rules" under Operations).

Ovaries—Ovum—(See Ovaries).

Pains In—♅, ♄, ♂, or ☿ affl. in ♏.

Parturition; Placenta — Ruled by ♏. Abnormalities of, attachments, delayed delivery of, caused by ♄ affl. in ♏.

Pregnancy; Prenatal Epoch — (See Prenatal).

Prolapsus—(See "Falling" in this section).

Puberty; Regeneration; Reproduction;

Semen—Reception of—(See Semen).

Sex Disorders—(See Sex, Generation, Genitals, Reproduction).

Single Births—(See Children).

Sterility—(See Barren).

Stillborn; Stricture of Neck Of—♅ affl. in ♏. (See Cervix, Hour-Glass, in this section).

Swellings Of—(See Inflammation, Tumors, in this section).

Syphilis Of—Afflictions in ♓. (See the Introduction to this section).

Triplets; Tumors — Ulceration of — Fibroids — ♃ or ♀ affl. in ♏, tumors, and resulting from surfeits, too rich food, over-eating; ♄ affl. in ♏, fibroids; ♂ affl. in ♏, ulcers or ulceration. (See "Fibroid" in this section). The tumors are also caused by subluxations at PP (2, 3, 4L), and disturbances at KP. (See Swellings, Tumors).

Twins; Ulceration—(See "Tumors" in this section).

Uterine Disorders—(See "Disordered", and the various paragraphs in this section).

Vagina; Version — Of the Foetus — Caused by subluxations at PP, LPP, the 2, 3, 4, 5 lumbar vertebrae, and malefics in the signs which rule these vertebrae. (See Foetus).

Whites — In Women — (See Leucorrhoea).

WOMEN—Woman—Ladies—Females—This subject is partly considered in the Article on Females. In this section the subjects will be listed which apply more specifically to adult females. The ☽ and ♀ rule strongly over the health and affairs of women, and of females of all ages. The ☽ rules the adult female functions, such as the Menses, Maternity, Reproduction, etc. In a woman's horoscope, the ☽ is the Sig. of Health, and the ☉ in a male nativity. The ☽ is taken as hyleg in a woman's map, when possible, and the ☽ is favorably situated as hyleg. An afflicted ☽ in a woman's horoscope tends to disease, and disturbed functions. In female horoscopes, after puberty, the regulation of the health, the regularity of the system, and the function of maternity, depend upon the ☽ and ♀. The ☽ in the Asc. has much effect upon the health of the female sex, according to the aspects to the ☽. Women are denoted by the 5th H., and this is the house of women in the native's horoscope, and his relations to them. See the following subjects in the alphabetical arrangement, or under "Aunts", "Daughter", "Female", "Mother", "Sister", "Wife", when not considered here—

Abortion; Accidents To — Hurts To — The ☽ or ♀ to the ☌ or ill-asp. ♂ by dir.; malefics to the ☌ or ill-asp. the ☽ or ♀. (See "Children" under Hurts).

Active Mind and Body—(See "Active Body", "Active Mind", under Active).

Addicted to Women—(See "Addicted" under Men; "Addict" under Sex).

Aged Women—Illness or Death of—(See Aunts, Grandparents, Old Age).

Anaemia—(See Anaemia, Chlorosis).

Anxieties—Mental Anxieties—Mental Anxieties to Women—The ☽ to the ☌ the ☉ by dir.

Assaults By — Attacks By — Malefics in ♌ or the 5th H. in a man's map, or lord of the 5th a malefic, and placed in the 8th or 12th houses; lord of the 5th a malefic, and affl. by other malefics.

Astray — Women Liable To Be Led Astray—(See Seduction).

Attackers of Women—(See Rape).

Aunts; Bad Health For — (See "Ill-Health" under Females; "Health" in this section).

Bad Women — Loss and Waste of Property Thru — The M.C. to the evil asps. the ☽ by dir. (See "Free Living" under Free; Lewd; "Low Company" under Low; Riotous, etc.).

Barren; Beautiful; Bereavement;

Births To — (See Birth, Children, Fruitful).

Blind — In Left Eye — The ☉ to the evil asps. a malefic by dir. (See "Eyes", "Left Eye", under Left).

Blondes — (See "Light Complexion" under Light).

Blood—Irregular Circulation of—The Blood Corrupted — Dropsical Blood — The ☽ to the ill-asps. ♃ by dir.; the ☽ affl. in ♏, impurities in the blood and system; the ☽ hyleg in ♓, and afflicted, dropsical blood. (See Blood, Circulation, Impure).

Breasts In — Ruled by the ☽ and ♀. (See Breasts).

Brunettes — (See "Dark Complexion" under Dark; "Black Hair", "Brunettes", under Hair).

Cerebral Functions — Disorders of — (See Brain; "Cerebral Functions" under Cerebral).

Cervix—(See Cervix, Womb).

Change of Life — (See "Menopause" under Menses).

Chaste—The ☽ and ♀ free from the affl. of malefics.

Child — The Woman Is With Child — Is Not With Child—(See Pregnancy).

Childbed Fever—(See Parturition).

Childbirth—(See Parturition).

Children; Chills—Women Suffer With Fever from Chills and Cold — (See Chills).

Chlorosis; Chronic Diseases—Women Suffer By — Death By — (See "Death" under Chronic).

Circulation Irregular — (See "Blood" in this section).

Clitoris; Coarse — Coarse Body — Coarse Voice — (See Coarse; Effeminate; "Coarse" under Voice).

Cohabitation; Cold—Suffers from Cold and Chills—(See Chills).

Complexion; Conception—The Woman Will Conceive — Will Not Conceive — (See Barren, Conception, Fruitful).

Conduct—(See Conduct; "Chaste" under Females; Harlots, Immodest, Imprudent, Lewd, Loose; "Loose Morals" under Morals; Nymphomania, Shameless).

Constitution — Good Constitution—Strong Constitution—Constitution Deranged—(See "Constitution" under Females).

Courses—(See Menses).

Dangers to Women — (See Abortion, Births, Miscarriage, Parturition, Rape, Seduction).

Daughter Born—(See Daughter).

Death — Of a Female Friend — (See "Female Friend" under Friends).

Death — Of a Female Relative — (See "Female" under Relations).

Death—Of Women by Fevers and Severe Illnesses—(See "Females" under Fever).

Death by Women—By Female Treachery—(See "Women" under Poison; "Tragical Death" under Tragical; "Female" under Treachery).

Death of Women—Danger of Death To—The ☉ causes death to women by fevers and severe illnesses; the ☉ to the ☌ ☽ by dir., and the ☽ affl. at B.; ☽ to the ill-asps. ♅, ♄, or ♂ by dir.; the ☽ to the ☌ ☉ by dir., and espec. if in the 6th or 8th H. (See "Death" under Aunts, Females, Fever, Mother, Sister).

Debilitated—(See "Constitution" under Female).

Depraved; Deranged—(See Deranged; "Constitution" under Female).

Detriment To—The ☉ in the 5th H. at the Vernal, lord of the year and afflicted; ☽ to the ☌ ☉ by dir.; ♄, ♂, and ☿ conjoined in ♍.

Digestive Disorders—(See "Women" under Digestion).

Disappointments To—The ☽ to the ill-asps. ♀ by dir.; ♄ to the ☌ or ill-asps. the ☽ or ♀. (See Love Affairs, Marriage; "Women" under Misfortune; Wife).

Diseases of Women—(See the various paragraphs in this section, and under Females).

Disgrace For—(See "Women" under Disgrace; Harlots, Immodest, Scandalous, Seduction, Shameless; "Unchaste" in this section).

Dissolute Habits—The ☽ affl. in ♏. (See Dissolute; "Drink" in this section).

Drink—Fond of—Women Crave Drink—♄ to the ☌ or ill-asp. the ☽ by dir. (See Drink).

Dropsy—Dropsical Condition of the Blood—(See "Blood" in this section).

Eminent Lady—Death of Some Eminent and Prominent Woman—Comets appearing in ♒. (See Famous; "Great Women" under Great; Queens).

Emotions In—(See Emotions).

Evil—Sudden Evil For—♀ to the body of ♅ by dir.

Evil—Women Very Evil—Of Evil Qualities—The Asc., ☽, ♂, ♀ and ☿ in double-bodied signs. (See Evil).

External Influences—Susceptible To—The ☽ hyleg in ♏ or ♓. (See External).

Eyes—Fine and Beautiful—Left Eye Affected—(See "Fine", "Women", under Eyes; "Left Eye" under Left; "Blind" in this section).

Face—A Plump Face—♓ gives.

Father—Death of—(See "Death" under Father).

Female—Females—(See the various paragraphs under Females, which Article is supplemental to this one).

Female Child Promised—(See "Birth of a Female" under Female).

Female Complaints—Functional Disorders—(See the various paragraphs under Females, Functions, and in this Article).

Females—(See "Female" in this section).

Fever—Danger of—Death By—Suffers From—(See Chills; "Death", "Females", under Fever).

Fiancee—Death of—(See Fiancee).

Flooding—(See Menses).

Fluids—Of the System—(See "Ailments" under Fluids).

Foetus; Fond of Women—(See "Addicted" under Men).

Freedom—Unwomanly Freedom—(See "Unwomanly" under Morals).

Friend—Death of a Woman Friend—(See "Female" under Friend).

Fruitful; Functions—The Female Functions Disordered—(See "Female" under Functions).

Generation; Genitals; Gestation;

Good Constitution—Good Health For—(See "Good" under Constitution; "Health" under Females).

Grandmother—(See Grandparents).

Great Women—Death of—An eclipse of the ☉ in the 3rd decan. of ♈. (See Famous; "The Great" under Great; Queens).

Grief—Thru Women—(See "Females", "Grief", under Men). The ☽ to the ill-asps. ♀ by dir. tends to grief to women thru men. (See "Women" under Misfortune; Opposite Sex, Sorrow).

Habits—Dissolute Habits—(See "Dissolute", "Drink" in this section).

Hair; Harlots; Hatred of Women—Hated by Some Female—(See "Females" under Hatred).

Headaches In—(See "Pains" under Head; "Women" under Headaches).

Health—The ☽ is Sig. of health in women.

(1) Health Bad—(See "Ill-Health" under Females).

(2) Health Better—(See "Health" under Females).

(3) Health of the Female Sex—Is much affected when the ☽ is in the Asc., according to the aspects to the ☽.

(4) Health Good—(See "Health" under Females).

(5) Health Injured by Women—Sickness Caused by Women—Lord of the 6th in the 5th or 7th H.

(6) Health a Source of Trouble—(See "Constitution" under Female).

(7) Health Strengthened—(See "Health" under Females).

(8) Health Weaker—(See "Health" under Females).

Hermaphrodites; Hurts To—(See "Accidents" in this section).

Husband; Hyleg; Hysteria; Ill-Health—(See "Health", "Ill-Health", under Females; "Women" under Misfortune).

Impurities—Of the System—☽ affl. in ♏ tends to impurities in the female system. (See Impure).

Infamous—(See Harlots; "Women" under Scandal; Shameless).

Inflammations—(See "Females" under Inflammation).

Injuries To—(1) Injuries to Women—(See "Accidents" under Females, and in this section). (2) Injuries by Women—(See "Injured" under Men; Treachery).

Internal Complaints—(See "Women" under Internal).

Irregularities—Of the Functions, and of the System—☽ affl. in ♏. (See Functions, Irregularities).

Left—(1) Left Eye—Blind In—Hurts To — (See "Left Eye" under Left). (2) Left Side of the Body—(See Left).

Length of Life — (See "Length" "Long", "Short", under Females).

Leucorrhoea; Libidinous—Violently Libidinous—(See Lewd, Lust, Virile).

Licentious; Life—(See "Long", "Short", under Life; "Length of Life" in this section).

Liver Disordered—(See "Women" under Liver).

Long — (1) Long Diseases In and Death By — (See Chronic Diseases; "Death" under Females; "Females" under Fever). (2) Long Life — (See "Long" under Life).

Loose Morals In — (See "Unchaste" under Females; Harlots, Immodest; "Loose" under Morals; Shameless).

Lower Order of Women — (See Harlots).

Lust In—Unbridled Lust—(See Lewd, Lust, Nymphomania, Shameless, Virile).

Male Child Promised — (See "First-Born" under Children; "Births" under Male).

Marriage — (See the various paragraphs under Husband, Love Affairs, Marriage, Marriage Partner, Wife; "Free from Passion" under Passion; Spinsters, Widows).

Masculine Women — (See Deviations, Effeminate; "Coarse" under Voice; "Degrees" under Whole).

Maternity; Matrix—(See Womb).

Men Injured By—(See "Injured Thru Women" under Men; "Health Suffers" under Opposite Sex; Treachery).

Menopause; Menses; Midwives;

Minor Disorders—(See Colds, Leucorrhoea, Menses, Mild, Minor, Slight).

Miscarriage; Misfortune To—(See "Women" under Misfortune; Sorrow).

Moon — The Moon Influences Over Women — The Moon As Hyleg — (See "Female" under Functions; Hyleg, Menses, Moon).

Mortality — Much Mortality Among Women—The ☉, ☽, and ♃ conjoined in ♎; the ☽ or ♀ lady of the year at the Vernal, weak, and afflicted; ♂ in ♍ at the Vernal, and lord of the year. (See "Death" under Females; Mortality).

Mother; Murders — Many Murders of —(See "Women" under Murder).

Natural Functions Of—Ruled by the ☽. (See Functions, Maternity, Menses, Mother, Parturition).

Nervous Disorders — (See Emotions; "High Strung" under High; Hysteria; "Disordered" under Nerves).

Nurses; Nymphomania; Opposite Sex;

Ovaries; Painful Diseases—(See "Females" under Fever).

Parents — (See "Parents" under Females).

Parturition; Passion In—Ruled by ♀, and the afflictions of ♂ to ♀. (See "Passion" under Females; Lewd, Licentious, Nymphomania; "Passional Excesses", "Women", under Passion; Shameless, Virile).

Peace of Mind—(See Contentment, Happiness; "Peace of Mind" under Mind).

Periodic Illness—(See Menses).

Periods Of—(See Menses).

Poisoned By Treachery of Women—(See "Women" under Poison; "Female" under Treachery).

Pregnancy; Property—Waste of Thru Bad Women — (See "Bad Women" in this section).

Prostitutes—(See Harlots).

Puberty—Ill-Health at Time of—(See Puberty).

Puerperal Fever — (See Parturition, Puerperal).

Quarrels—With Women—M. C. to the □ or ☍ ♀ or the ☽ by dir. (See "Women" under Quarrels).

Rape; Regularity—Of the Health and Functions — (See "Females" under Regular).

Relatives — Female Relatives — (See "Female" under Relatives).

Reproduction; Right Eye—Defects In —Blindness In—Hurts To—(See "Right Eye" under Right).

Ruined by Women — Ruins Himself Among—(See "Ruined" under Love Affairs).

Salacious — (See Lust; "Masculine Women" under Masculine; Nymphomania).

Scandalous — (See "Women" under Scandal).

Seduction; Severe Diseases—(See "Females" under Fever; Severe).

Sex Diseases In—(See Venereal).

Sex Gratification In — (See Amorous, Cohabitation, Lewd, Lust, Nymphomania; "Women" under Passion; "Secret Bad Habits" under Secret; "Married Women" under Sex; Shameless, Virile).

Sex Organs Of—(See Fallopian, Ovaries, Vagina, Vulva, Womb, etc.).

Shameless; Sickness — Caused by Women—Much Sickness Among Women —(See "Ill-Health" under Females; "Health Injured" under Men; "Much Sickness" under Sickness).

Single Women—Not Inclined to Marry —(See Celibacy; "Aversion" under Marriage; "Free From Passion" under Passion; Spinsters).

Sister; Skin—The Skin and Complexion In — (See the various paragraphs under Complexion, Face, Skin).

Sorrows To — (See "Women" under Misfortune).

Spinsters; Sports—Indiscretions In— (See "Indiscretions" under Sports).

Sterility In — (See Barrenness; "Unfruitful" under Wife).

Stomach Disorders In—(See "Women" under Digestion; Gastric, Indigestion, Stomach).

Sudden Evil For—(See Disgrace, Rape, Scandal, Seduction; "Evil" in this section).

System—Disorders of—(See Functions; "Impurities", "Irregularities", in this section).

Tomboyishness—Caused by positive signs being prominent, and with the ☉, ☽, ♆, ♅, ♃, and ♀ obscurely placed.

Tragical Death—By Women—(See Tragical).

Treachery—Suffers by Treachery of—(See "Injured" under Men; "Women" under Poison; "Female" under Treachery).

Trouble—For Women—Through Women—(See "Women" under Misfortune; Poisoned, Tragical, Treachery, in this section).

Unbirdled Lust—(See Nymphomania; "Unbridled" under Passion).

Unchaste—♂ affl. in the 7th H. with females; ♄ or ♂ ☌ ♀ in ♏, danger of. (See "Chaste" under Females; Nymphomania; "Unbridled" under Passion).

Unmarried Women—(See Aversions, Celibacy; "Single Persons" under Sex; Single, Spinsters).

Unwomanly Freedom—(See Immodest; "Unwomanly" under Morals; "Unchaste" in this section).

Uterus—Disorders of—(See Womb).

Vagina; Venus Figure—(See "Brunettes" under Hair).

Vexations—Annoyances—

(1) By Women—☽ to place ☋ by dir. or tr.; ☽ Sig. □ or ☍ ♀; ♀ by periodic revolution to the ill-asps. the ☉ in the radix. (See "Women" under Men; Poisoned, Treachery, Trouble, in this section).

(2) To Women—(See "Women" under Misfortune; Sorrows, Trouble, Vexations).

Virgin—(See "Chaste" under Females).

Virile Members—(See Virile).

Virtue In—(See "Chaste" under Females; Harlots, Lewd, Immodest; "Good Morals", "Loose Morals", under Morals; Perversions, Shameless).

Vital Spirit In—Governed by the ☉. (See "Spirit" under Vital).

Vitality In—(See "Good" under Constitution; "Health" under Females; Vitality).

Voice In—(See Effeminate; "Coarse", "Deep", under Voice; "Masculine Women" in this section).

Vulva; Weak Constitution—(See "Constitution" under Females; "Weak Body" under Weak).

Whites—(See Leucorrhoea).

Widows; Wife; Woman With Child—Is Not With Child—(See "Woman" under Pregnancy).

Womanish—(See Effeminate).

Womanly—(See "Chaste" under Females; Modesty).

Womb; Young Women—(1) Chlorosis In—(See Chlorosis). (2) Weakness In at Puberty—(See Puberty).

WOOD—Hurts and Wounds by Wood or Flying Stones—(See "Flying Stones" under Stone).

WORDS—Loss of Memory for Words—(See "Amnesia" under Memory).

WORK—Labor—Exertion—

Fear of Work—Lazy—Not Inclined to Work—Ergophobia—(See Idle, Labor. Lazy).

Over-Work—Health Injured By—Fatigue From—(See "Brain Fag" under Brain; Exercise, Exertion, Fatigue, Reading, Study).

WORLDLINESS—Earth-Bound—Absorbed In Pleasure, Material Gains, and Selfish Purposes—The earthy signs strong and predominant at B., and espec. the ♑ sign, and with this sign upon the Asc.; ♄ influence; ♄ in the Asc. or M.C., and espec. when in ♑; ♂ rising and strong at B.; ♂ or ♀ affl. in the 5th H.; ♂ affl. in ♑, and in □ to the ☉ in ♈; ♀ influence, and with ♀ affl. by ♄ or ♂. The fiery and airy signs predominate more in spirit and intellect. The watery signs are more emotional, dreamy, scattering, and vacillating in seeking worldly gains and pleasures, and espec. ♋ and ♓. (See Amusements, Conduct, Excesses, Expense, Luxuries, Materialism, Passion, Pleasure, Prodigal, Riches, Sports).

WORMS—Cestode—Parasites—The ☉ to the evil asps. the ☽ by dir., and the ☽ affl. at B.; a ☽ disease, and the ☽ affl. in ♋ or ♍; ♂ affl. in ♍; a ♀ disease when ♀ is the afflictor in the disease, and espec. when affl. in ♍; ♀ in ♍ in the 6th H.; ♀ in ♍ or ♑, and affl. the ☽ or Asc.; ☿ affl. in ♍; a ♍ disease, and afflictions in ♍; Subs at SP (8D), and at PP (2L).

Anthelmintic—A Remedy Expelling Worms—A Therapeutic Property of ♃.

Bladder Worm—(See Acephalocyst).

Bowels—Worms In—♂, ♀, or ☿ affl. in ♍. (See Entozoons, Parasites, Tapeworm).

Children—Worms In—A ☽ disease, and afflictions to the ☽; the ☽ affl. in ♋ or ♍; ♂ affl. in ♍; ♂ in ♍, ☌ or ill-asp. the ☉; ♀ affl. in ♍; a ♍ disease.

Corn and Grain—Destroyed by Worms—(See "Corn Destroyed" under Scarcity).

Expulsion of Worms—(See "Anthelmintic" in this section).

Remedy for Worms—Anthelmintics—The Herbs and Remedies of ♃. (See "Jupiter Group" under Herbs).

Ringworm—(See Herpes, Ringworm).

Stomach—(See "Worms" under Stomach).

Tapeworm—(See Tapeworm).

WORRY—Fears—Fretfulness—Anxiety—Peevishness—The ☉ or ☽ affl. in ♑; the ☽ □ or ☍ ☿; the ☽ affl. in airy signs, and to cause irregularity of the functions thru worry, anxiety, and mental strain; ♄ strong and rising at B.; ♄ affl. in the Asc. or M.C.; ♄ ☌ or ill-asp. ☿; ♄ affl. in ♑; ☿ □ or ☍ ☽; ☿ ☌, □, or ☍ ♄; ☿ affl. in ♈, ♑, or ♓; ☿ ☌ ♄ in ♑; many planets in earthy signs at B., and with an earthy sign upon the Asc.; ♑ upon the Asc. (See Anxiety, Dejection, Depressed, Despondency, Downcast, Fears, Fretfulness, Gloom, Grief; "Life Robbed of Its

Joy" under Joy; "Low Spirits" under Low; Melancholy; "No Peace of Mind" under Mind; Misery, Peevishness, Sadness, Sorrow, Trouble, Vexations, etc.).

Business Cares—Many Worries By—(See Business, Cares, Property, Reverses, Riches, Ruin).

Children — Parents Worried Thru Children—(See "Parents" under Children; "Injured" under Parents).

Enemies—Worried By—(See "Secret Enemies" under Enemies; Plots, Treachery).

Females — Worries To and By — (See the various paragraphs under Females, Women; "Health Suffers", "Injured", under Men; Treachery).

Functions—The Functions Disturbed Thru Worry—The ☽ affl. in airy signs. (See Functions).

Gout from Worry—☿ in ♑, ♅, or ill-asp. any of the malefics as promittors. (See "Melancholy" under Gout).

Ill-Health from Worry—☿ affl. in the 6th H., and espec. when in ♑. (See Ill-Health).

Nervous Disorders—From Over-Work and Worry — (See "Worry" under Nerves).

Parents—Worries to Thru Children—(See "Children" in this section).

Servants — (See Hyperaesthesia; "Worries Thru Servants" under Servants).

Stomach Disorders—Due to Worry—(See "Anxiety" under Digestion).

Women — Worries Thru — (See the various paragraphs under Females, Husband, Jealousy, Love Affairs, Men, Treachery, Wife).

The diseases and disturbances of mind and body, which may be brought on by Worry, are legion, and too numerous to list here. Look in the alphabetical arrangement for the subject you have in mind. Especially see the following subjects, in addition to the references made in this Article—Anguish, Banishment, Bereavement, Brooding, Disease, Disgrace, Dishonour, Distress, Execrated, Exile, Family, Fortune, Imprisonment (see Prison); Injury, Judges, Marriage, Misfortune, Neglect, Neighbors, Obsessions, Poverty, Relatives, Reputation, Responsibility, Restraints, Scandal, Sickness, Spirit Controls, Suffering, Suicide, Terrors, Travel, Unfortunate, Vehicles, Visions, etc.

WORSE—Aggravated—Less Favorable—The Disease Worse, etc.—

Chronic Disease — A Turn for the Worse In—(See "Chronic Disease" under Crisis).

Crisis In Disease—The Disease Worse At—(See "Worse" under Crisis).

Disease Worse—The disease tends to be worse at crises days, as on the 7th, 14th, and 21st days after the beginning of the disease. Also when the planet which is the afflictor in the disease meets the evil aspect of a malefic, or of the ☉ or ☽, or when the afflictor changes from a common sign, and passes into a cardinal sign, the disease turns to run higher. Also the afflictor passing into the 4th, 6th, 8th, or 12th Houses, the disease may take a turn for the worse, or prove fatal. This subject is more fully discussed in paragraphs in the following Articles. (See "Worse" under Crises, Disease; "Arguments for Death", "Certain Death", under Death; Fatal; "High" under Fever; "Disease Will Increase" under Increase; "Disease Prolonged" under Prolonged; Relapse, etc.).

Dropsy Worse—(See "Increased" under Dropsy).

Epilepsy Worse—(See "Worse" under Epilepsy).

Eye Diseases Worse — Crisis Worse In—(See "Crisis" under Eyes).

Fever Worse—The Disease Runs High—Protracted Fever—(See Hectic, High, under Fever; "Fever" under Inflammation).

Fluxes Worse—Are worse at the Full Moon. (See "Bloody Flux" under Flux; "Full Moon" under Moon).

Health Worse—Health Weaker—Malefics elevated above the ☉ or ☽ tend to make the health worse than when the Lights are elevated above the malefics; the ☉ setting at B. (See Chronic, Complications, Consumptions; "Worse" under Disease; Emaciated; "Enlarged Scope" under Enlarged; Feeble; "Low Fever" under Fever; "Weakened" under Health; "Ill-Health All Thru Life" under Ill-Health; Infirm, Invalids, Relapses; "Much Sickness" under Sickness; "Low" under Vitality; "Weak Body" under Weak).

High—The Disease Runs High—(See "High Fever" under Fever; Poignant, Severe, Sharp, Swift, Violent Diseases).

Night—The Disease Worse at Night — (See "Diseases by Night" under Night; "Night Sweats" under Phthisis).

Relapse — The Disease Takes a Relapse — (See Complications, Increased, Prolonged, Relapse, Tedious). For further study see Continuity, Course; "Better" under Disease; "Degree" under Disturbance; Duration, Hospitals, Polarity, Praeincipients, Prevention, Remedies, Treatment, etc.

WOUNDS—Wounding—Hurts—Injuries—Traumatism—Wounds, such as Cuts, Stabs, Loss of Blood, and those due to violence against the person, Maiming, etc., are caused by ♂. The subject of Wounds is largely considered under Cuts, Hurts, Injuries, in this book, in which sections you will find subjects not listed here. The following subjects have to do with Wounds, and Wounds to the different parts of the body, which see in the alphabetical arrangement when not considered here. See "Accidents", "Hurts", "Injuries", "Wounds", under subjects which relate to Parts, Organs, or Members of the Body.

Abdomen; Abrasions; Accidents;

Ambushes; Animals — Hurts and Wounds By — (See Animals, Beasts, Bites, Kicks, Quadrupeds, Wild).

Arms; Assassins; Assaults; Battle — (See Bloodshed, War).

Beasts; Bites; Blindness; Blood—Loss of—(See Cuts, Effusions, Hemorrhage, Instruments, Iron, Menses, Shedding, Stabs, Sword, etc.).

Blows; Bones—(See Fractures).

Burns—(See Burns; "Hot Liquids" under Liquids; Scalds).

Buttocks—(See Haunches).

Chest; Contests; Cuts;

Danger of Wounds—Wounds Threatened—☉ affl. by ♂; ☉ hyleg, and ☉ to the ☌ or ill-asp. ♂ by dir.; the ☉ as Sig., or the Pr. ☉ to the ☌ or ill-asps. ♂; ☽ to the ☌ or ill-asps. ♂ by dir.; ☽ to the ☍ ♂ in mundo; ☽ to the ☌ or P. Dec. Aldebaran or Antares; ☽ to the ☌ Regulus if the ☽ be hyleg; ♅ to the ☌ or ill-asps. ☽ by dir. (See Electricity, Explosions, Machinery, Railroads); ♄, ♂, and ♀ conjoined in ♏ at B.; ♄ ascending at B., and the ☉ to the ☌ or ill-asp. ♄ by dir.; ♂ affl. in the Asc. at B.; ♂ ☌ or ill-asp. the ☉ or ☽ at B., and by dir.; a ♂ affliction, and liable to occur especially to ♂ people, those who have ♂ as ruler of the Asc., or ♂ in the Asc. or M.C.; ♂ in ♌ □ or ☍ ☉; ♂ in evil asp. ♄ at B.; ♂ affl. in ♊ or ♍, and to the ☌ or ill-asp. the Asc. by dir.; malefics in the M.C. elevated above the Luminaries, and ♂ holding dominion; fiery signs in the Asc. or 6th H., or the ☽ in a fiery sign at B., threatens wounds under the evil directions of ♂ to the Asc. or 6th H., or when ♂ is in the Asc. or 6th H. by tr. or dir.; ♂ coming to the Asc. early in life usually causes hurts and wounds; the 14° ♍, or the 1° ♎ on the Asc.; the Ascelli, Hyades, Castor, Pollux, Pleiades, Praesepe, directed to the Asc. or Lights; those born under the hurtful signs, ♈, ♉, ♋, ♏, or ♑, are more liable to wounds and hurts. (See the various paragraphs in this section, and under Hurts, Injuries).

Death by Wounds—Danger of—The ☉ to the ☌ or ill-asp. ♂ by dir. in a violent map; ☉ to the place of Praesepe; ☽ hyleg and to the ☌ or ill-asps. ♂ by dir.; ♃ Sig. □ or ☍ ♂; ♃ Sig. ☌ ♂, and ♂ ill-dig., and usually the result of folly; ♂ denotes death by; ♂ affl. the hyleg by dir., and ♂ holding the dominion of death, and espec. if ♂ be in the 8th H.; ♂ ori. at B., and affl. the hyleg by dir. (See "Death" under Hurts, Injuries, Violent; the various paragraphs in this section, as Cuts, Lightning, Machinery, Stabs, Sword).

Demoniacs—Wound Themselves—(See Demoniac).

Directions—Designate Events and Time of—(See Directions, Events).

Duels; Ears; Earthquakes;

Electricity; Enemies—Wounds or Death By—(See Enemies).

Events; Excoriations—(See Abrasions).

Explosions; Extremities; Eyes—(See Blindness; "Accidents" under Eyes).

Face; Falls; Father; Feet; Feuds;

Fire; Fire Arms—(See Gunshot).

Flying Stones—(See Stones).

Folly—(See "Death" in this section).

Fractures; Genitals—(See "Mens' Genitals" under Genitals).

Groins; Gunshot; Hands; Haunches;

Head; Heat; Heights; Hemorrhages;

Highwaymen; Himself—Brings Wounds Upon Himself—♂ people. (See Demoniac).

Hips; Hurts—Hurtful Signs—(See Hurts).

Incised Wounds—(See Cuts, Instruments, Iron, Stabs, Sword, etc.).

Injuries; Instruments; Iron; Kicks;

Kings; Knees; Lacerations; Legs;

Lightning; Limbs; Loins;

Loss of Blood—(See "Blood" in this section).

Machinery; Maiming; Mayhem—(See Maiming).

Mens' Genitals—(See Genitals, Penis).

Mobs; Mother; Mouth; Murder;

Muscles; Neck; Nose; Officers;

Parents; Pirates; Plots; Prison—Wounded In—(See Prison).

Privates—(See "Men's Genitals" under Genitals).

Quadrupeds; Quarrels; Railroads;

Reptiles; Revenge; Robbers, Ruffians;

Ruptures; Scalds; Scalp; Sea;

Secret Parts—(See "Injuries" under Secrets).

Self-Inflicted—(See Demoniac, Suicide; "Himself" in this section).

Serpents; Sharp Instruments—(See Instruments).

Ships; Shipwreck; Shoulders;

Soldiers; Skin—(See Abrasions, Bites, Blows, Cuts, Hurts, Injuries, Kicks, Stabs, Stings, Sword, etc.).

Sorely Wounded—But Will Not Die—(See "Badly Injured" under Injuries).

Spine—(See "Accidents" under Spine).

Spontaneous Wounds—Sudden—♂ causes when the dominion of death is vested in him. On the other hand, ♅ causes sudden accidents. (See Accidents, Sudden).

Sports; Stabs; Steel—(See Iron).

Stings; Stones—(See "Flying Stones" under Stones).

Storms—(See Weather, Wind).

Strokes—(See Blows, Stabs).

Sudden; Sword; Teeth—(See Gums; "Accidents" under Teeth).

Testicles; Thieves—(See Highwaymen, Robbers, Thieves).

Thighs; Thorax—(See Chest).

Threatened—(See "Danger Of" in this section).

Time Of—(See Directions, Events; "Time" under Hurts, Injuries).

Tornadoes—(See Wind).

Total Blindness—By Wounds—(See "Total" under Blindness).

Travel; Treachery; Venomous;

Violence; Voyages; War; Weapons;

Wild Animals—(See Wild).

Wind; Wood—(See "Assaults" under Stone).

Women—(See Assaults, Injuries, Tragical, Treachery, under Women).

WRANGLINGS — Suffering, Injury, or Death By—(See Contests, Duels, Feuds, Fighting, Quarrels, Revenge; "Shedding of Blood" under Shedding; War).

WRATH—Wrathful—

Death by a King—Death by Wrath of —(See Kings).

Wrathful—(See Anger, Hatred, Jealousy, Malice; "A Murderer" under Murder; Revengeful, Unforgiving, etc.).

WRESTLING—A Champion Wrestler—(See "Wrestler" under Athletics).

WRETCHED — Wretchedness — Miserable — Unhappy — Sunk In Dejection — The ☉ or ♃ Sig. ☐ or ☍ ♄; the ☉ directed to all Nebulous Clusters, and to Castor and Pollux; the 3rd Dec. of ♉ on the Asc., ruled by ♄, the face of poverty, slavery, and wretchedness. (See Dejected, Gloom, Misery, Unhappy).

WRINKLES—Wrinkled—Deep Lines In Skin—♆ in the 1st H. tends to premature wrinkling of the face, due to a wasting and sapping of the vital forces; ♄ influence and afflictions, and ♄ rising in the Asc., tends to dry up the skin and cause wrinkles; ♑ on the Asc. (See "Cold and Dry Body" under Dry; Juvenility, Old Age; "Dry Skin" under Skin; Withering).

WRISTS—Carpus—Carpal Bones—The Wrists in the upper extremities correspond to the ankles in the lower limbs, and are ruled by opposite Signs of the Zodiac. The ankles are ruled by ♒, and the wrists by ♌, the opposite sign. Writers also give the ♊ sign as ruler of the arms, wrists, and hands. (See Ankles).

Ankylosis In—Danger of—The ☉ ☌ ♂ in ♌. (See Ankylosis, Joints).

Dislocation Of — ♅ or ♄ affl. in ☐; malefics in ♌ or ♒; afflictions in fixed signs, and espec. with fixed signs on angles. Case—See "Wrist", No. 150, in 1001 N.N. (See Dislocations).

Fracture—Colles Fracture—♄ affl. in ☐, ♌, ♍, or ♒; malefics in ♌ or ♒. (See Fractures).

Gout In—The ☽ affl. in ☐, ♌, or ♍; a ☽ disease. (See "Arms", "Hands", under Gout).

WRITING—Transcribing—

Writer's Cramp—(See "Cramps" under Hands).

Writes With Toes — Case — (See "Writes With Toes" under Toes).

Writes With Tongue—Case and Birth Data—(See "Writes" under Tongue).

WRONG—Erratic—

Wrong Conduct — (See the various subjects under Conduct, Females, Habits, Love Affairs, Men, Morals, Passion, Sex, Women).

Wrong Diet—♃ and ♀ disorders. (See "Evil Diet" under Diet; "Wrong Diet" under Food).

Wrong Habits — (See "Bad Habits" under Habits).

Wrong Living — (See "Conduct" in this section; "Free Living" under Free; "High Living" under High; "Loose Living" under Loose; "Loose Morals" under Morals; "Passional Excesses" under Passion; "Riotous Living" under Riotous, etc.).

Wrong Thinking — (See "Mental Chaos" under Chaotic; "Mind" under Erratic; "Bad" under Judgment; "Shallow" under Mentality; "Light In Mind" under Mind; Perversions; "Disorders Of" under Thinking; Thought, Uncontrolled, etc.).

WRY NECK — Torticollis — (See Contortions; "Wry Neck" under Neck).

X

The subjects in "X" have been very much neglected in Astrological Literature, and in all my reading of the Textbooks of Astrology, I have not been able to record a single subject for the "X" Section of this book. However, by a careful research thru the Dictionaries, and the Medical Dictionaries, some very important subjects have been discovered which should be recorded in this book, and their Planetary relationships and correspondences given. This section of the book, therefore, is entirely original on my part, and if I make mistakes, or assign wrong planetary influences to any subject, the student will bear with me, and suggest the proper influences, and also further subjects, for later Editions of this Encyclopaedia. This Section of the book has not been correlated with the rest of the book, as it has only recently been prepared, and after the entire manuscript has been finished, and for this reason there will not be many references in the first half of this book to see subjects in the "X" Section, as the first half of the book at this writing has already been set up by the Linotyper. The following subjects are herewith submitted for your study.

XANTHALIN—Xanthaline—An Alkaloid from Opium — Ruled by ♆, and also may come under the rule partly of ♄, as Opium products are very depressing. (See Narcotics).

XANTHELASMA—(See Xanthoma).

XANTHIC — Yellow Color — Having a Yellow Color, and In Which Yellow Predominates — The Yellow Color is ruled by the ☉, and the Sun Fruits, such as the Orange, etc., have a yellow, or golden color, and are life-giving. Saturn also rules yellow in disease conditions, as in Jaundice, Stone, and the yellow skin of sickness, due to uric acid and urea deposits, hyperacidity, etc. In the Solar Spectrum the yellow ray is ruled by ☿. (See Yellow).

Xanthic Calculus — A Urinary Calculus composed of Xanthin—A ♄ disease and affliction. (See Stone, Xanthin).

Xanthic Oxide—(See Xanthin).

XANTHIN—Xanthine—Xanthinine—A thin, white, crystalline, nitrogenous compound, contained in blood, urine, and other secretions, and also present in the liver, spleen, pancreas, urinary calculi, and is closely related to uric acid. The nitrogenous element is ruled by ♅. (See Nitrogen). Also being a poisonous mineral deposit, when in excess, it also partakes of the ♄ nature. (See Uric).

XANTHINURIA — An Excess of Xanthine in the Urine—A ♄ disease and affliction. It is also undoubtedly true that the tonic action of ♅ in the ♎ sign, or ♅ ☌ ♂ in ♎, will tend to an excess of Xanthin in the urine, and to a pathological and unbalanced kidney action. (See "Calculi" under Urine; Xanthin).

XANTHOCHROIA — Xanthochroous — Xanthocroid—A Yellowness of the Skin —Under normal conditions the ☉ gives a yellowish tint to the skin, as in the Mongolian Races, as the Sun Color is yellow and golden, as indicated also in the fruits ruled by the ☉. In pathological and disease conditions a yellowish skin, and resembling Jaundice, is generally the result of ♄ action, and from hyperacidity, and excess deposits of Urea and Uric Acid. (See Jaundice, Yellow, Xanthin, Xanthochromia, Xanthoderma).

XANTHOCROID — Having a Yellowish or Fair Complexion, and with Xanthocroid Traits — (See Xanthic, Xanthocroia).

XANTHOCHROMIA—Yellowish Discoloration of the Skin, Resembling Jaundice—Also caused by a yellowish discoloration of the Cerebro-Spinal Fluid, from hemorrhage of the Spinal Cord. May be caused by ♄ and ♂ affl. in ♌, and espec. ♄ ☌ ♂ in this sign, or the ☌ of these planets in the 5th H., the house of ♌, the sign which rules the Spine, the Heart, and Circulation. (See "Spine" under Hemorrhage).

XANTHOCYANOPSIA—Color Blindness in which only Yellow and Blue can be distinguished. (See "Color Blindness" under Blindness).

XANTHODERMA — Xanthodermia — A Yellowness of the Skin, and no doubt a disease condition caused by the afflictions of ♄, and excess of mineral deposits, and espec. of the Xanthin variety. (See Xanthin).

XANTHODONT — Xanthodontous — Yellow discoloration of the teeth, and espec. of the Incisors—Caused by the afflictions of ♄ or ♃ in ♈ or ♉. The Incisors come especially under the rule of ♃, and ♃ afflicted by ♅ or ♄ may cause an excess of yellow mineral deposits in the teeth, of the yellow and Xanthic variety. (See "Fore-Teeth" under Teeth).

XANTHOMA—Xanthelasma— Xanthomatous—Yellow Tubercles of Neoplastic Growths — Yellowish Patches On the Skin and Eyelids—A Disease often associated with Diabetes Mellitus. On the Eyelids it may occur with ♄ affl. in ♈. When on the skin, or appearing as a tubercle, or neoplastic growth, ♄ is found strong at B., or affl. in a car-

dinal sign, and espec. in ♎ or ♑. (See Diabetes, Neoplasm, Tubercles, Xanthoderma).

XANTHOPATHY—A Morbid Yellowness of the Skin—Caused by ♄, and due to excess of mineral deposits, excess of Urea and Uric Acid over the body, torpid liver, and usually accompanied with lowered vitality. (See Deposits, Minerals, Saturn, Urea, Uric, Wastes, Xanthin, Xanthoderma).

XANTHOPICRINE—Berberine—A form of bitter yellow crystals from the root of the Barberry, Goldthread, and used as an antiperiodic and tonic, and is ruled by ♂. (See "Mars Group" under Herbs; Mars, Stimulant, Tonic).

XANTHOPSIA — Yellow Vision, as In Jaundice — Objects Appear Yellow—A ♄ disease and affliction; ♄ affl. in ♈. (See Jaundice).

XANTHOPSYDRACIA—A Skin Disease, and attended with small Yellow Pustules—♄ and the ♑ sign rule the skin, and skin diseases with yellow pustules are the work principally of ♄. Caused by ♄ in ♑, ♎, or in the Asc. or 6th H. in these signs; ♑ on cusp the Asc. or 6th H. Mars and ♀ also aid in causing pus, and pus diseases, and these planets entering into the configuration with ♄, or being with ♄ in ♑, would lend aid to the disease. (See Pus, Skin Diseases).

XANTHOSIS — Yellow Discoloration In Cancerous Tumors — Carcinoma (Cancer) tends to result in that part of the body ruled by the Sign ♄ is in at B., and the excess deposits of Urea, Uric Acid, and Xanthin, are brought to this part of the organism, tending to the yellowish discoloration which is so frequently seen in Carcinoma. Also ♄ ☌ ♃ or ♀, the rulers of the circulation, tends to such discolorations, and to cause stoppage of the circulation, lack of proper elimination, and unusual yellowish and poisonous deposits in the part ruled by the sign containing ♄ at B. (See Carcinoma).

XANTHOUS — Having a Yellow Skin — The Mongolian Races — People with Yellow, Red, Auburn, Blonde, or Brown Hair—Given principally by the ☉. If the ♂ influence is also strong at B., there is auburn, or red hair. (See Blondes, Light, Saffron, Yellow, under Complexion; "Light", "Yellow", under Hair; "Yellow" under Skin; "Complexion" under Yellow, Xanthochroia).

XANTHOXYLUM — Xanthoxylin — The Ash Tree—Prickly Ash—A Stimulant and Aromatic Bitter, and ruled by the ☉. Extracts from the Powdered Bark of this tree are used much by Physicians as a tonic, diuretic, and stimulant, and in the treatment of Chronic Rheumatism.

XENOGENESIS—Monsters—The Generation of Something Foreign—The Offspring Varying In Character and Life-Cycle from the Parents — Caused by Prenatal conditions, and afflictions to the ☽ at the monthly periods during Gestation. The afflictions of ♅, the ruler of the Pineal Gland, to the ☽ and other vital centers during the prenatal period, is assigned as a predominating cause. In such cases also, the past, the stage in Evolution, and many things, would have to be considered. (See Heredity, Inhuman, Monsters, Prenatal Epoch).

XENOMANIA — Attachment to Foreign Customs and Institutions—♅ well-aspected in the 9th H. at B., and also this house containing benefics, and free from the influences and afflictions of ♄ and ♂. (See Abroad, Foreign Lands, Location, Ninth House, Residence).

XENOMENIA — Xeromenia — Vicarious Menstruation—(See "Vicarious" under Menses).

XENON—A Heavy, Inert, Gaseous Element in the Atmosphere, discovered by Ramsay and Travers in 1898 — Ruled by ♅. (See Air, Atmosphere, Ether, Gases).

XENOPHOBIA—A Hatred of Foreigners — Malefics afflicted in the 9th H., and espec. ♄ or ♂. In such cases the native should also avoid Foreign Travel. (See Abroad, Foreign, Native Land; "Place of Birth" under Place; Residence, Travel).

XENOPHTHALMIA—Conjunctivitis Due to a Foreign Body In the Eye — Malefics afflicted in ♈, and espec. ♂ in ♈, which makes the eyes more susceptible to accident, injury, and the entrance of foreign and irritating bodies from without. (See Conjunctivitis, Xeroma).

XERANSIS—Xerantic—A Drying Up—Desiccation—Siccation—Lack of Moisture—Dry Skin and Body—A ♄ influence and affliction. Also caused by the ☉ and ♂, due to excessive heat in a part. (See "Body" under Dry; "Excessive Bodily Heat" under Heat; Parched, Scales; "Dry Skin" under Skin; Xeroderma, Xerosis, Xerotes, Xerotripsis).

XERASIA—Morbid Dryness of the Hair, and Cessation of Growth of—♄ affl. in ♈. (See Baldness; "Dry and Brittle" under Hair).

XEROCOLLYRIUM—A Dry Collyrium—An Eye-Salve — An Astringent Eye Remedy—Such preparations are ruled by ♄, and intended to allay the inflammations of ♂. Sugar of Lead, ruled by ♄, is usually the base of such preparations. (See Collyria, Lead).

XERODERMA — Dryness of the Skin — Roughness of, with Desquamation — A Mild Form of Ichthyosis — A ♄ disease and affliction. (See Scales; "Dry Skin" under Skin; Xeransis).

XEROMA—Xerophthalmia—Chronic Inflammation and Dryness of the Eyeball—Atrophy of the Conjunctiva—♄ affl. in ♈. (See Atrophy, Conjunctivitis, Eyeballs, Xenophthalmia).

XEROMENIA—(See Xenomenia).

XEROPHTHALMIA—(See Xeroma).

XEROSIS — Xerotic — Dryness—Marked by Dryness—Abnormal Dryness of the Skin or Eyes—Caused by ♄; ♄ affl. in cardinal signs; ♄ in ♈, of the eyes; ♄ in ♎ or ♑, of the skin. (See Xeransis, Xeroderma, Xeroma, Xerotes).

XEROSTOMA — Xerostomia — Abnormal Dryness of the Mouth, Due to Suppression of the Secretions—Dryness of the Mouth—(See Fauces).

XEROTES — Dryness — Dry Habit of Body — ♄ influence; many planets in earthy signs at B., and with an earth sign on the Asc. (See Xeransis, Xerosis).

XEROTIC—Dryness—(See Xerosis).

XEROTRIPSIS—Dry Friction—A Rubbing—Fremitus—Caused by ♄, and due to a suppression of the secretions, and espec. on the mucous surfaces. May also be caused by the ☉ and ♂, due to too much heat in a part, or by the afflictions of ♃, from lack of proper circulation. (See Friction, Xeransis).

XIPHICOSTAL—Relating to the Xiphoid Cartilage, and the Ribs — (See Ribs, Sternum, Xiphisternum, Xyphodynia, Xiphoid).

XIPHISTERNUM—The Metasternum, or Ensiform Cartilage — (See Sternum, Xiphicostal, Xiphodynia, Xiphoid).

XIPHODYMUS — A Double Monster, with United Pelvic and Thoracic Cavities, and Two Legs — This class of United Bodies comes under the same class of influences as given in the Article on Monsters. They are also due to irregular conceptions, and afflictions, and an unbalanced condition during the prenatal period. (See Conception, Monsters, Prenatal; "United" under Twins; Xiphopagus).

XIPHODYNIA — Pain In the Ensiform Cartilage—♅, ♄, ♂, or ☿ affl. in ♋. (See Sternum).

XIPHOID — Sword-Like — The Xiphoid Appendix, or Cartilage—The Third and Lowest Part of the Sternum — Ruled by the ♋ sign. (See Chest, Sternum, Thorax, Xiphicostal, Xiphisternum, Xiphodynia, Xiphopagus).

XIPHOPAGUS — A Double Monster United by the Xiphoid Cartilage, or the Epigastrium — (See Xiphodymus, Xiphoid).

X-RAYS—Röntgen Rays—Discovered in 1895 by Prof. Röntgen, of Würzburg. These Rays are produced by passing a high voltage of electricity thru a vacuum tube, and thru resisting substances, causing efflorescence. These Rays have the power of penetrating opaque substances, such as the bones and interior of the body, and from which Photographs, Shadowgrams, Skiagrams, etc., can be produced. These Rays are ruled by the planet Uranus, as ♅ rules Electricity, the Ether, Light, Rays, etc. (See Air, Atmosphere; "Vibration" under Colors; Electricity, Ether, Explosions, Light, Uranus, etc.).

XYLAN — Tree Gum — Wood Gum — A Gummy Substance of the Pentosan Class—A Gum which yields Xylose, a non-fermentable sugar, on hydrolysis. Pentose products, such as Xylan, Xylose, etc., and all Sugars and Sweets, are ruled by ♃. Xylan and Xylose contain five carbon atoms to the molecule, and being strong in carbon, which is ruled by ♄, they may also come strongly under the rule of ♄. Sugars, and substances of the Pentose class, are acid-forming in the system, if used to excess, and tend to the deposit of wastes, hyperacidity, etc., which matters are ruled by ♄. (See Carbon, Hydrocarbonates, Sugar, Xylite, Xylose).

XYLANTHRAX—Charcoal—Ash—Ruled by ♄. The Ash in the human body is also ruled by ♄. (See Ash).

XYLENE — Xylol — Xyloquinone — An Antiseptic Hydrocarbon from Coal Tar, and used in the treatment of Smallpox. Ruled by ♄, and opposes the diseases of ♂, such as Smallpox, and other Eruptive Diseases, Rashes, etc. Coal Tar Preparations, when taken internally, are very depressing, pain-killing, anodyne, and soothing for a time, and are generally used in Headache Tablets, and in Tablets to relieve pain, high fever, over-excitement, etc., matters ruled by ♂. The vegetable Tar taken from the Pine Tree, when applied externally, has a caustic and rubefacient effect, which qualities are ruled by ♂. (See Tar, Xylic Acid).

XYLIC ACID — A Tar and Petroleum Substance found in Coal and Wood Tar, and is obtained principally from Xylene. Ruled by ♄, as ♄ rules the mineral products of the ground. (See Xylene).

XYLITE—A Syrupy Liquid obtained by the reduction of Xylose — A Pentahydric Alcohol — Also contains five atoms of carbon to the molecule. Ruled by ♃. People born under the strong rule of ♃ tend to have a craving for alcohol, drink, intoxicants, sweets, etc., and especially those born under the ♃ sign ♓. (See Alcohol, Carbon, Drink, Jupiter, Sugar, Xylan, Xylose).

XYLOBALSAMUM — Balsamea Meccanensis—The Dried Twigs of the Balm of Gilead Tree — Balms and Balsams are ruled by ♃. (See "Jupiter Group" under Herbs). Also Balm (or Melissa)

is listed in the Mercury Group under Herbs.

XYLOIDIN—An Explosive Substance— Prepared by the action of Nitric Acid on Starch, or Wood Fiber. Ruled by ♅, as this planet rules explosive substances, and explosions. (See Explosions, Uranus, Xylonite).

XYLOL—(See Xylene).

XYLONITE—Celluloid—A Substance composed essentially of Camphor and Soluble Guncotton—Explosive and Inflammable. Ruled by ♅. (See Xyloidin).

XYLOPHONE — A Musical Instrument made up of a series of wooden bars, graduated in length to the musical scale, and sounded by striking with two wooden bars. Musical Instruments in general are ruled by ♀. (See Music, Venus).

XYLOQUINONE—(See Xylene).

XYLOSE — A Sugar obtained from Beechwood—Wood Sugar—A Non-fermentable Sugar of the Pentose Class. Ruled by ♃. (See Xylan, Xylite).

XYLOSTEIN—A Toxic Glucoside from the Berries of Lonicera Xylosteum — Honeysuckle — Ruled by the ☽. Is Emetic and Cathartic. (See Emetic; "Moon Group" under Herbs; "Therapeutic Qualities" under Moon; Physic).

XYLOTOMOUS — Having the Power of Boring, or Cutting into Wood—A quality possessed by many insects. A ♂ quality. (See Instruments, Mars).

XYSMA — Pseudo, or False Membrane, seen in the Stools of Diarrhoea—A ♍ disease, and afflictions in ♍; ♂ affl. in ♍. (See "Disorders Of" under Bowels; Cholera, Diarrhoea, Dysentery, False, Pseudo, Typhoid).

XYSTER—A Surgeon's Rasp. Surgeons, and the tools used by them, are ruled by ♂. (See Operations, Surgeons).

Y

YAWNING—(See "Sighs" under Breath).

YEARS—Year—

Critical Years — Critical Periods of Life—These are the years when the ☽ by progression finishes her first cycle, as at the 28th to 30th years of life, and also when by progression the ☽ is at her Quarters, or □ and ☍ aspects to her place at B. These times of the ☽ also nearly correspond to the evil aspects of ♄ every seven years over the life, and tend to be evil, critical, and changing years for the native, and also when ill-health may come, or some calamity, or misfortune, unless the native is forewarned, relaxes, keeps quiet, and avoids worry, anxiety, and despondency. (See Climateric, Crises, Critical; "Periods of Bad Health" under Health; Periodic, Periods, Square).

Favorable Years of Life—These years, or periods, are based upon the trine (△) aspects of the progressed ☽, and are multiples of the No. 9, as the 18th, 27th, 36th, 45th years, etc. Also the years in life when ♄, and other plan-

ets, form their △ aspects to their radical places tend to be fortunate years if not offset by a train of evil Directions to the Hyleg. (See Aspects, Climateric, Critical; "Periods of Good Health" under Health; Periods, Sextile, Trine).

Lord of the Year—The nature of the ruler of the year at the Vernal Equinox has much to do with the health of the Public during the year. Much mortality, and a prevalence of chronic diseases, are indicated when ♄ is lord of the year. When ♂ is lord of the year, many accidents, injuries, much bloodshed, and danger of War, and especially in Countries ruled by the Sign rising, etc. (See Vernal).

Public Health Good — Public Health Bad — Good and Bad Years for the Health of the People — (See "Public Health Bad", "Public Health Good", under Public. Also note the various paragraphs and subjects in the Article on Prevalent).

Quarters of the Year—Those born in the First Quarter of the year, between the times of the Vernal Equinox and the Summer Solstice, and especially in March, when the ☉ is passing thru his exalted sign ♈, have a stronger constitution, and are of longer life than those born in the Winter months when the ☉ is in the South and passing thru the ♄ Signs ♑ and ♒, and the 12th House sign ♓. The two Northern Quarters of the year, from the Vernal Equinox to the Autumnal Equinox, tend to give greater vitality when the ☉ is passing thru these Northern Signs, and especially if the fiery signs ♈ or ♌ are also upon the Asc. at B., while the Southern Signs, below the Equator, are not as strong for vitality unless there is a strong and vital sign rising on the Asc. at B., such as ♈, ♌, ♏, or ♐. (See Quarters).

YEAST—(See Fermentation, Zymosis).

YELLOW—Yellow Color—Yellowish—Xanthic—The ☉ denotes Yellow, or inclined to purple. Yellow color is ruled by the ☉, ♀, ☿, the 3rd H., and by the ♐ Sign. In the Solar Spectrum the Yellow Color is ruled by ☿. Deep Yellow, and Saffron, are ruled by the 11th H. (See Colors). The Sun-Kissed fruits, with the yellow, or golden yellow skin, such as the Orange, are ruled by the ☉, and denote strength, vitality, and health. In disease conditions the skin may have a yellow tinge due to the pathological action of ♄, and the deposits of poisons, wastes, minerals, Uric Acid, Urea, and Xanthin. Also in Jaundice, the skin may be yellow. (See Jaundice, Xanthin, Xanthoderma).

Bowel Disorders — The yellow color acts as an opening medicine in bowel disorders, and is somewhat of a Physic. Cathartic tablets should be coated with yellow color. (See Physic).

Complexion — Yellow Complexion — Yellowish — Sallow — Saffron — Mulatto — Unhealthy Yellowish Hue — The ☉ gives a yellowish, saffron complexion; ♄ in ♉; ♄ ♑, sallow; ♄ ori. at B.; ♂ Sig. in ♑; ♀ in ♈ in the 6th H., afflicted, or affl. the ☽ or Asc.; ☿ oriental at B.; a ☿ person is usually of a dark, yellow color, or a sad brown; ☿ posited occi. of the ☉, except when ☿ is in ♊; ♈ on the Asc.; the Quadrant from the Autumnal Equinox to the Winter Solstice causes a yellowish complexion. (See "Yellow" under Complexion; Jaundice, Xanthous).

Eyes — A Yellow Tinge — ♂ people — (See "Yellowish" under Eyes).

Face — Yellow Face — Face Yellowish In Sickness — (See "Yellow" under Face; Jaundice).

Fever — Yellow Fever — A ♌ disease, and afflictions in ♌. Also caused by vitiated and disturbed atmospheric conditions by planetary influences. Also contributed to by subluxations at CP, SP and KP. (See Epidemics, Immunity, Vertebrae).

Hair—Yellow—Yellowish—Yellowish Brown—(See "Yellow" under Hair).

Jaundice — (See "Yellow" under Jaundice).

Marks — Yellow Marks On Body — ♀ tends to give a yellow mark on the part of the body ruled by the sign she is in at B. (See Marks).

Opening Medicine — (See "Bowel Disorders" in this section).

Races—Yellow Races—Mulatto—Mongolian—(See Races, Xanthous; "Complexion" in this section).

Skin — Yellow Skin — (See "Yellow" under Complexion, Face, Jaundice, Skin; Xanthoderma, Xanthous; "Complexion" in this section).

Vision — Yellow Vision — (See Jaundice, Xantopsia).

YOGI BREATHING (See "Yogi" under Breath).

YOUNG—Immature—The Early Period of Life—

Dies Young — (See "Death" under Childhood, Children, Infancy; "Early Death" under Early; "Short Life" under Life; "Dies Before Middle Life" under Middle Life; Untimely; "Death In Youth" under Youth).

Females—Young Females At Puberty —(See "Females" under Puberty).

Young Men — Much Mortality Among —♂ in ♌ at the Vernal Equi., and lord of the year; Comets appearing in ♊. (See "Death of Men" under Men).

Young Mind — Youthful — (See Juvenility).

Young People — (See "Young" under Females, Women; "Young Men" in this section).

Young Women — (See "Young" under Women).

YOUTH—Youthful—Young People—The ☉ rules Youth, and when one is at the strongest. Also ♂ rules the flourishing time of youth. In the Kabala, youth was dedicated to ♂ and ♀. The period of youth from 14 to 28 years of age is said to be ruled by ♀, which is the mating time. In Hor'y Questions, youth, and a youthful person are indicated by ☿ as Sig. The following subjects have to do with youth, young men and women, and the period before middle life. See these subjects in the alphabetical arrangement when not considered here—

Boyishness — (See "Youthfulness" in this section).

Complexion—In Youth—♎ on the Asc. tends to a fair complexion in youth, and rather ruddy, with no excess of red or white, but tends to pimples and a high color toward old age.

Death In Youth — ♂ sole ruler at an eclipse tends to the death of many young people. The 9° ♓ on the Asc., many young people die thru dissipation and passional excesses. (See "Early Death" under Children, Early; Directions; "Death" under Females, Men, Women; "Dies Before Middle Life" under Middle Life; Untimely; "Early Youth" in this section).

Directions — The Effects of Primary Directions In Youth, and Over Youth — (See "Directions" under Childhood, Infancy, Parents).

Early Years — Not Strong or Robust In Early Years — Much Sickness In — Death During — (See "Early Death", "Early Years", under Early).

Early Youth — Death In — Not Apt to Live Until Adult Age — Rarely Lives to Maturity—The ☽ sepr. from ♄ and applying to ♂ if the ☽ be hyleg; ♅ in the M.C., elevated above, and affl. the ☉, ☽, or hyleg; ♄ in the 11th, and ♂ in the 5th, or □ the cusp of the 5th, not apt to live to adult age; the 5° ♒, or the 11° ♓ on the Asc. at B. (See "Death In Youth" in this section; "Young Men" under Young).

Excesses—Dies Young Thru Excesses —(See "Death In Youth" in this section; "Passional Excesses" under Passion).

Fevers In Youth — And Childhood — (See "Fevers" under Childhood).

Health—State of In Youth—♄ in the Asc., or ♑ upon the Asc., are bad for the health during the earlier years and in youth, and more so when the ☉, ☽, Asc. or hyleg are afflicted by malefics. Fiery signs upon the Asc., and with the ☉, ☽, Asc., and hyleg strong and well-asp. tend to good health in youth, strong vitality, and little sickness in life. (See Constitution, Vitality).

Hurts In — Injuries In — (See "Accidents" under Childhood, Children, Infancy; "Early Years of Life" under Early).

Juvenility — Young Looking — Well-Preserved—(See Juvenility, Well-Preserved; "Youthfulness" in this section).

Men — Young Men — Great Mortality Among — Much Sickness Among — Comets appearing in ♊. (See "Death" under Men; "Young Men" under Young; "Death" in this section).

Middle Life—(See "Dies Before Middle Life", and other paragraphs under Middle Life).

Passional Excesses—(See "Excesses" in this section).

Perpetual Youth — There is no such thing in the human body, and such is not intended by the Higher Powers for the masses of Humanity. The Adepts and great Masters, however, have learned the secrets of keeping the body young, or to take on, or throw off, a physical body at will, which matters are discussed in the Occult Books, and in the Rosicrucian and Theosophical Societies. After middle life, ♄ begins to get in his work, deposit wastes and excess minerals over the body, hardens the arteries, the muscles and tendons become less tense and more brittle, the functions of the body become lowered, and Man's time comes to pass out of the physical body. It is not so much how long we live in the physical body, but how we use it, how we occupy our time for the good and uplift of Humanity, and for our own growth, advancement, spiritual attainment, etc. Some physical bodies are not destined to endure very long, due to low vitality, and a very afflicting map of birth, while others are endowed with great vitality, and powers of endurance. (See "Youthfulness" in this section).

Planetary Periods—Of Childhood and Youth—(See Childhood, Periods).

Puberty; Robust—(See "Early Years" in this section; Robust).

Ruddy In Youth—(See Robust, Ruddy; "Good" under Vitality; "Complexion" in this section).

Scarlatina — Scarlet Fever — Smallpox — Many Young People Die of — (See "Mortality" under Children; Scarlatina, Smallpox).

Sickly During Youth—And Childhood —The 19° ♓ on the Asc. at B., but good health in old age. (See "Health" in this section; "Much Sickness" under Childhood; "Ill-Health" under Females; "Health Worse" under Men).

Slender In Youth—(See Slender).

Smallpox — (See "Scarlatina" in this section; Smallpox).

Strong In Youth — Not Strong — (See "Health" in this section).

Thin In Youth — ♑ infl.; ♑ on Asc. (See Slender).

Tomboyishness—Due to obscure positions of the ☉, ☽, ♆, ♅, ♃, ♂ and ♀, and with the positive signs prominent in a female nativity.

Vitality — Strong — Weak — (See "Health" in this section; Vitality).

Women—Chlorosis In—Ill-Health At Puberty—(See Chlorosis, Puberty).

Youthfulness — Youthful Looking — Boyishness—Given by the ♐ sign when this sign is strong, upon the Asc., well-aspected. Also given by the ♊ sign, the opposite and complementary sign to ♐, when well-placed and aspected. Venus tends to give prolonged youthfulness if dissipations and excesses are avoided. Saturn when strong and well-placed at B., and not severely afflicting the hyleg, tends to keep the native younger looking for some years in late life, and to give tenacity of life. (See Juvenility, Well-Preserved; "Pereptual Youth" in this section).

Z

ZEAL — Intemperate or Irrational Zeal —(See Ideals, Intemperate, Irrational, Reactionary; Reformers; "Fanatical" under Religion; Revolutionary).

ZENITH—(See Meridian, Tenth House).

ZEST — Given by planets in cardinal signs, and such signs on angles; planets rising and elevated in masculine signs. Aspects to the ☉ and ♂ are necessary to give zest, activity, and energy, and even bad asps. to the ☉ and ♂, or of ♂ to the ☉, are better than no aspects at all. (See Active, Energy, Exercise, Stamina, Tone).

ZINC—Ruled by ♅. A good Skin Remedy in Ointments. (See Actinium).

ZINZIBER — Zingiber — Ginger — Ruled by ♂. Is Tonic, Stimulant, and Counter-irritant.

ZODIAC—The Twelve Signs of the Zodiac constitute the Grand Man, and rule the different parts of the body from the head to the feet, ♈ ruling the head, ♉ the throat and neck, ♊ the lungs, shoulders, arms; ♋ the breasts; ♌ the heart; ♍ the bowels and abdomen; ♎ the kidneys; ♏ the sex organs and reproductive system; ♐ the hips, thighs; ♑ the knees; ♒ the calves and ankles; ♓ the feet. The planets in the signs tend to affect, for good or ill, the parts of the body, organs, or functions, ruled by such signs, and by knowing what signs were occupied by planets, and their nature, at the birth of a person, the diagnosis of the possible diseases of the native are made easier. (See Diagnosis, Prognosis, Subluxations, Vertebrae).

Aspects—Zodiacal Aspects—(See Aspects).

Azimene Degrees Of—(See Azimene).

Body—Zodiacal Rulership Over—This is three-fold, and is external, internal and structural. The external rulership relates to the external organs, the external parts and anatomy. The Internal rulership relates to the internal construction and internal organs. The structural rulership relates to the skeleton and bony structure. (See the various signs, as Aries, Taurus, etc., and also the various organs. Also see External, Internal, Structural).

Constellations—Many Fixed Stars in the Constellations are noted in Astrology as having influence in matters of health, disease, and the affairs of Humanity. (See Nebulous, Stars).

Critical Degrees — Of the Zodiac — (See "Sensitive" in this section).

Dark Degrees — Of the Zodiac — ♈ 3, 16; ♉ 3, 30; ♊ 7, 27; ♋ 14; ♌ 10; ♍ 5, 30; ♎ 10, 21; ♏ 3, 30; ♐ 12; ♑ 7, 22, 30; ♒ 13; ♓ 6, 18, 30. If the Asc., or its lord, be in any of these degrees at B., the native is more dark of complexion. (See "Dark" under Complexion"; Dark).

Degrees of the Zodiac—(See Azimene; "Zodiac" under Degrees; "Dark", "Sensitive", in this section).

Food—The Food Adapted to People Born under Each Sign of the Zodiac—(See "Signs of the Zodiac" under Food).

Monsters of the Zodiac—Many of the Signs of the Zodiac have Animals as Symbols, and the forces of the Zodiac which work over Humanity are intended to try, test, and examine into every trait of human character, and until Man is able to conquer these forces, and not allow his lower nature to dominate him, he is far from perfection. In the Writings of the Occult Masters, we are admonished to conquer these "Monsters of the Zodiac", rule and control them, otherwise they will rule us, and lead us astray for a time, and into many difficulties and trying situations. (See "Periods of Bad Health" under Health).

Negative Signs—Of the Zodiac—The Feminine Signs, as ♉, ♋, ♍, etc. (See "Signs" under Feminine; "Negative Signs" under Negative; "Negative" under Signs of the Zodiac).

Pitted Degrees—Of the Zodiac—(See Pitted; "Face" under Smallpox).

Polycrest Remedies—Of the Signs of the Zodiac — These Remedies correspond to the Twelve Signs of the Zodiac as follows—♈, Aconite Napellus; ♉, Belladonna; ♊, Bryonia Alba; ♋, Ipecac; ♌, Chamomilla; ♍, Nux Vomica; ♎, Rhus Toxicodendron; ♏, Pulsatilla; ♐, Mercurius; ♑, Sulphur; ♒, Arsenicum Album; ♓, Veratrum Album. There are also 12 Salts assigned to the 12 Signs of the Zodiac. (See "Salts" in this section).

Positive Signs—Of the Zodiac—(See Positive; "Electro-Positive" under Signs).

Remedies — Zodiac Remedies — (See "Polycrest", "Salts", in this section).

Salts—The Zodiac Salts—Cell Salts—Also known as the Schuessler Tissue Remedies — Each Sign of the Zodiac rules a different cell salt in the body, and these 12 salts make up the general chemical structure of the body, any one of which, when lacking, tends to disturb the chemical balance of the system. Dr. Schuessler, a Homeopathic Physician, prepared these 12 salts, finely triturated, in tablet form, so as to give the proper dosage, and in a form most easily assimilated. The Science of Biochemistry gives special attention to the use of these 12 Remedies, and to prescribe which are needed, and as indicated by the star map of birth. These Remedies are as follows, one for each Sign of the Zodiac — ♈, Potassium Phosphate; ♉, Sodium Sulphate; ♊, Chloride of Potassium; ♋, Fluoride of Lime (Calcium Fluoride); ♌, Phosphate of Magnesia; ♍, Potassium Sulphate; ♎, Sodium Phosphate; ♏, Sulphate of Lime (Calcium Sulphate); ♐, Silica (called the "Surgeon of the System"); ♑, Phosphate of Lime; ♒, Sodium Chloride; ♓, Phosphate of Iron (Ferrum Phosphate). (See these subjects).

Example—People born with the ☉ in the ♌ sign are apt to use up the Phosphate of Magnesia of the body faster, and in illness should receive this Salt to supply the need of the body, and the birthday, and the sign born under would indicate what salt is especially needed in an increased quantity, and more than has been taken in normally in the food. And so on with all the Signs, the Rising Signs at birth, the Signs containing the ☽ and malefics, and all the aspects, etc., should be considered in determining what Salts are needed. These Salts are Inorganic, and as Inorganic Salts in their raw forms are not as easily assimilated, or as beneficial for the system, but tend to be deposited as minerals in the body, these Salts should be taken in their vegetable forms, and taken from the food. All of these Salts are contained in vegetables, and food of various kinds, and the student, or patient, should make a study of the Diet question, of food values, and then take those special foods, meats, nuts, vegetables, or fruit juices, which predominate in the Salt needed. Mineral waters containing these Salts are not good for the system, as the minerals in water are inorganic. People should drink distilled water after middle life, and get their Salts and Minerals from their food, and not from their drink, or from Medicines. These are the views of the Occult Masters, and the best Authorities upon the subject. (See Chemistry; "Signs of the Zodiac" under Food; "Biochemistry" under Healers; Minerals; "Water" under Skin).

Sensitive Degrees — Of the Zodiac — Critical Degrees — The Sensitive, and more Critical Degrees of the Zodiac are the 13° and 26° of cardinal signs; the 9° and 21° of fixed signs; and the 4° and 17° of the common signs, and planets when in these degrees at birth tend to affect the native greatly, for good or ill, in health, or other matters, according to the nature of the planets, their power, and the aspects to them. (See Sensitive).

Signs—Signs of the Zodiac, their nature, qualities, rulership, etc. (See Aries, Taurus, etc.; Signs; the Introduction to this Article).

Vulnerable Spots—In the Zodiac—In the Horoscope—(See Vulnerable).

Zones—Zodiac Zones—(See Zones).

ZONES—Zone—

Zone Diseases — Zones of the Body Afflicted — Shown by the planets in Signs, as each Sign rules a certain Zone of the body. (See the Section on "Rules" under each of the Signs, as "Aries Rules" under Aries; "Taurus Rules" under Taurus, etc. Also see the Article, "Signs of the Zodiac").

Zones of the Spine—(See "Vertebrae" under Cervical, Dorsal, Lumbar; Spine, Subluxations, Vertebrae).

Zones of the Zodiac—Denoted by the Twelve Signs, as Aries, Taurus, Gemini, etc. (See each of the Signs in the alphabetical arrangement, as Aries, Taurus, etc.).

ZOSTER—Herpes Zoster—(See Herpes).

ZYMOSIS — Zymotic — The Process of Fermentation — To Ferment, Boil or Agitate—Yeast, etc.—Fermentation is the work of the ☽, and also ruled by the ♋ Sign. Heat and Moisture combined are positive, and tend to fermentation. Thru the different Processes of the body, the ☽ carries on the work of Cellular Zymosis, while the ☉ acts for Cellular Excitation. (See "Excitation" under Cells; Fermentation, Processes).

Bowels — Fermentation of Food In — (See "Putrid" under Bowels).

Break-Bone Fever—(See Dengue).

Dengue — Break-Bone Fever — A Zymotic Disease, with Fever, Pain in the Bones, Eruptions, etc. (See Dengue).

Diseases—Zymotic Diseases—Zymotic Fevers—Germ Diseases—Diseases with Fermentation — The Fermentative, or Nutritive Processes, are ruled by ♀, and ♀ afflicted, or an afflicted ☽, tend to zymotic disorders. Also an afflicted ♂ tends to zymotic skin disorders, such as Measles, and other forms of skin germ diseases, rashes, etc. (See Dengue, Germs, Measles, Moisture, Nutrition; "Fermentation" under Stomach).

Periodicity — Zymotic Periodicity— Fermentation—Ruled by the ☽. The general and physiological action of the ☽ Group of Herbs are zymotic in their influence, and also tend to Zymotic Periodicity. (See Microzymasis, Periodicity).

Stomach — Fermentation In—(See "Fermentation" under Stomach). See Assimilation, Diet, Digestion, Food, Indigestion, Nutrition.

Printed in the United States
86927LV00005B/2/A

9 780766 143661